# Foundations of ECONOMICS

## AP* Edition

Robin Bade

Michael Parkin

*University of Western Ontario*

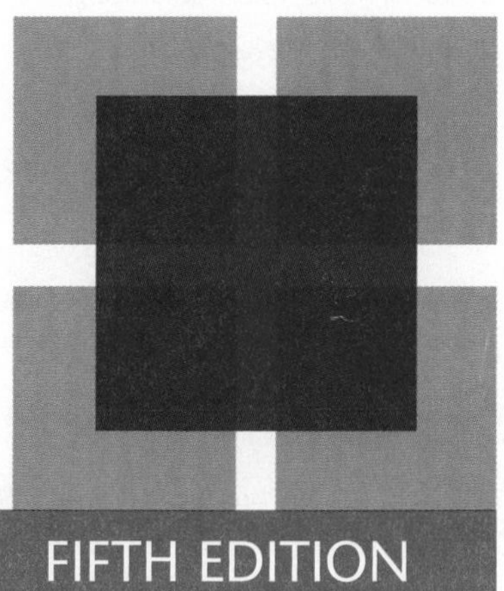

FIFTH EDITION

**Addison-Wesley**

Boston Columbus Indianapolis New York San Francisco Upper Saddle River
Amsterdam Cape Town Dubai London Madrid Milan Munich Paris Montreal Toronto
Delhi Mexico City Sao Paulo Sydney Hong Kong Seoul Singapore Taipei Tokyo

*Editor in Chief* Donna Battista
*Senior Acquisitions Editor* Adrienne D'Ambrosio
*Development Editor* Deepa Chungi
*Supplements Editor* Alison Eusden
*Director of Media* Susan Schoenberg
*Content Lead for MyEconLab* Noel Lotz
*Senior Media Producer* Melissa Honig
*Executive Marketing Manager* Lori DeShazo
*Marketing Assistant* Justin Jacob
*Managing Editor* Nancy Fenton
*Art Director, Cover* Linda Knowles
*Cover Designer* Anthony Saizon
*Copyeditor* Catherine Baum
*Technical Illustrator* Richard Parkin
*Senior Manufacturing Buyer* Carol Melville
*Project Management, Page Makeup, Design*
Elm Street Publishing Services

Cover photographs (clockwise from top left): © Shigeki Fujiwara/Sebun Photo/Getty Images; © Joel W. Rogers/Corbis; © Vector Images.com; © OJO Images/Getty Images

Text and photo credits appear on page C–1, which constitutes a continuation of the copyright page.



6 7 8 9 10—CKV—13

**Addison-Wesley**
is an imprint of

**www.PearsonSchool.com/Advanced**

AP* Edition, School Binding
ISBN 10: 0-13-237881-7
ISBN 13: 978-0-13-237881-9

To Erin, Tessa, Jack, Abby, and Sophie

# About the Authors

***Robin Bade*** was an undergraduate at the University of Queensland, Australia, where she earned degrees in mathematics and economics. After a spell teaching high school math and physics, she enrolled in the Ph.D. program at the Australian National University, from which she graduated in 1970. She has held faculty appointments at the University of Edinburgh in Scotland, at Bond University in Australia, and at the Universities of Manitoba, Toronto, and Western Ontario in Canada. Her research on international capital flows appears in the *International Economic Review* and the *Economic Record.*

Robin first taught the principles of economics course in 1970 and has taught it (alongside intermediate macroeconomics and international trade and finance) most years since then. She developed many of the ideas found in this text while conducting tutorials with her students at the University of Western Ontario.

***Michael Parkin*** studied economics in England and began his university teaching career immediately after graduating with a B.A. from the University of Leicester. He learned the subject on the job at the University of Essex, England's most exciting new university of the 1960s, and at the age of 30 became one of the youngest full professors. He is a past president of the Canadian Economics Association and has served on the editorial boards of the *American Economic Review* and the *Journal of Monetary Economics*. His research on macroeconomics, monetary economics, and international economics has resulted in more than 160 publications in journals and edited volumes, including the *American Economic Review*, the *Journal of Political Economy*, the *Review of Economic Studies*, the *Journal of Monetary Economics*, and the *Journal of Money, Credit, and Banking*. He is author of the best-selling textbook, *Economics* (Addison-Wesley), now in its Ninth Edition.

Robin and Michael are a wife-and-husband duo. Their most notable joint research created the Bade-Parkin Index of central bank independence and spawned a vast amount of research on that topic. They don't claim credit for the independence of the new European Central Bank, but its constitution and the movement toward greater independence of central banks around the world were aided by their pioneering work. Their joint textbooks include *Macroeconomics* (Prentice-Hall), *Modern Macroeconomics* (Pearson Education Canada), and *Economics: Canada in the Global Environment*, the Canadian adaptation of Parkin, *Economics* (Addison-Wesley). They are dedicated to the challenge of explaining economics ever more clearly to an ever-growing body of students.

Music, the theater, art, walking on the beach, and five fast-growing grandchildren provide their relaxation and fun.

# ECONOMICS Brief Contents

# Contents

## PART 1 INTRODUCTION

## PART 2 A CLOSER LOOK AT MARKETS

## PART 3 HOW GOVERNMENTS INFLUENCE THE ECONOMY

## PART 4 A CLOSER LOOK AT DECISION MAKERS

# PART 5 PRICES, PROFITS, AND INDUSTRY PERFORMANCE

# PART 6 INCOMES AND INEQUALITY

## PART 7 MONITORING THE MACROECONOMY

## CHAPTER 22 The CPI and the Cost of Living 563



# PART 8 THE REAL ECONOMY

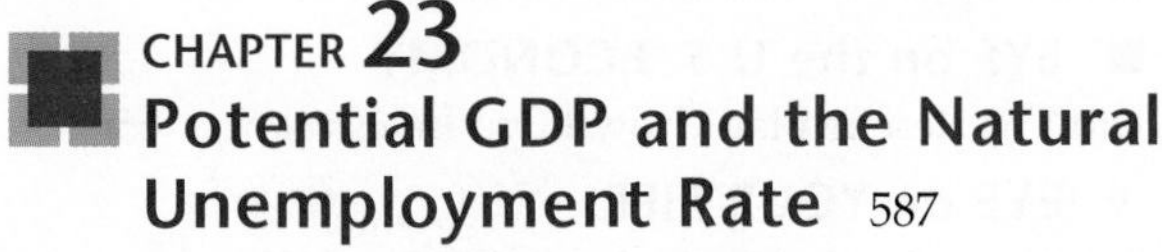

## CHAPTER 23 Potential GDP and the Natural Unemployment Rate 587

## CHAPTER 24 Economic Growth 611



## CHAPTER 25 Finance, Saving, and Investment 637

# PART 9 THE MONEY ECONOMY

## CHAPTER 26 The Monetary System 663



## CHAPTER 27 Money, Interest, and Inflation 693

# PART 10 ECONOMIC FLUCTUATIONS

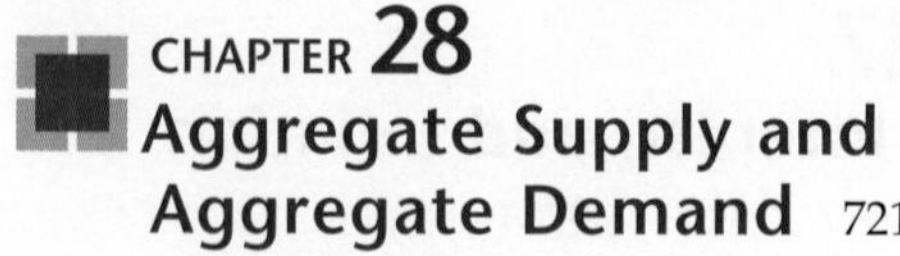

## CHAPTER 30 The Short-Run Policy Tradeoff 773



# PART 11 MACROECONOMIC POLICY

## CHAPTER 31 Fiscal Policy 795

## CHAPTER 32 Monetary Policy 821



## CHAPTER 33 International Finance 849

# Preface

Students know that throughout their lives they will make economic decisions and be influenced by economic forces. Students want to understand economic principles that help navigate these forces and guide their decisions. *Foundations of Economics*, AP* Edition is our solution to satisfy this need.

To achieve its goals, the principles course must do the following four things well.

- Motivate with compelling issues and questions
- Focus on core ideas
- Steer a path between an overload of detail and too much left unsaid
- Encourage and aid learning by doing

The Foundations icon with its four blocks (on the cover and throughout the book) symbolizes this four-point approach that has guided all our choices in writing this text and creating of its comprehensive teaching and learning components.

Economics is a core competency for the responsible citizen and is a foundation for every type of career. *Foundations of Economics*, AP* Edition, helps students understand the language of economics, integrate economic concepts into everyday life experiences, make more informed personal decisions, and better understand economic issues highlighted in the media.

## WHAT'S NEW IN THE FIFTH EDITION

The evolving U.S. and global economies provide a rich display of economic forces in action through which students can be motivated to discover the economic way of thinking. The global financial crisis and slump, ongoing tensions that result from globalization and international outsourcing, the continued spectacular expansion of China and India in the information-age economy, enhanced concern about the depletion of the world's rainforests and fish stocks, climate change, relentless pressure on the federal budget from the demands of an aging population and increased defense and homeland security expenditures, a falling dollar, and an ongoing U.S. international deficit and ever-growing national and international debt are just a few of these interest-arousing events. All of them feature at the appropriate points in our new edition, and the text and examples are all thoroughly updated to reflect the most recently available data and events.

Every chapter contains many small changes, all designed to enhance clarity and currency. We have also made some major changes that we now describe.

## FEATURE CHANGES

Each chapter opens with a photograph and a question about an issue that the chapter addresses. An *Eye On* box answers the question and an end-of-chapter problem (also in the instructor-assignable section of MyEconLab) makes the issues available for homework or quiz assignment. This feature enables students to get the point of the chapter quickly; it ties the chapter together; and it enables the teacher to focus on a core issue in class and for practice.

Checkpoint Practice Problems and end-of-chapter problems now include mini case studies from recent news stories. These problems feature in MyEconLab: some for student practice and some reserved for teacher homework and test assignments.

### ■ Major Content Changes in Introductory Chapters

Questions about the economic way of thinking (Did greed cause the global economic slump?); offshoring and outsourcing (Who makes the iPhone?); opportunity cost (Is wind power free?), and demand and supply (Why did home prices boom and bust?) are the motivating questions and features of *Eye On* boxes and end-of-chapter problems in the four introductory chapters.

We reorganized Chapter 2, but did not change its overall content. Chapter 4 has two new demand and supply application boxes on the markets for automobiles and wheat.

### ■ Major Content Changes in Micro Chapters

The micro policy chapters open with questions about elasticity, the efficiency of markets and other allocation mechanisms, market intervention, the gains from trade, health-care reform, and global warming. The consumer and producer chapters open with questions that focus the student on the value and cost of items in their lives ("How much would you pay for a song?" and "Which store has the lower costs: Wal-Mart or a 7–11?"). Chapters on market structure ask why GM failed, whether Microsoft's prices and profits are too high, and why there is so much variety in cell phones. And the factor markets chapter asks why a college football coach is worth 40 professors. These motivating questions that feature in the chapter opening photo and screamer are answered in *Eye On* boxes and tested in end-of-chapter problems.

The content of the fourth edition chapters, "Externalities", and "Public Goods and Common Resources" have been reorganized and repackaged. The first of the reorganized chapters, "Public Goods and Public Choices," covers the problems of underprovision of public goods (the free-rider problem) and underprovision of goods and services that have positive externalities. The principles are explained and illustrated in the markets for education and health care. In both cases, the focus is on the central resource allocation problem, not the minutiae of the public political debate. The second of the reorganized chapters, "Externalities and the Environment," examines the problems of overprovision in the face of external costs and the tragedy of the commons. Here, the principles are explained and illustrated with the problems of pollution and overfishing.

This repackaging of material makes for a more issues-oriented approach and one that better motivates an analysis of the potential solutions to these problems.

The fourth edition chapter "Uncertainty and Information" has been omitted and is available by request online.

## ■ Major Content Changes in Macro Chapters

The macroeconomic events and debates of 2008 and 2009 permeate the macro chapters, all of which have been radically updated and revised. Policy features at every possible opportunity throughout these chapters.

How do we track the booms and busts of the business cycle? How long does it take to find a job? How do we measure the changing value of money? Why do Americans earn and produce more than Europeans? Why are some nations rich and others poor? What created the global financial crisis? How does the Fed create money? What causes inflation? What causes the business cycle? Can we have low unemployment and low inflation? Did fiscal stimulus end the recession? Did the Fed save us from another Great Depression? Why is our dollar sinking? These are the motivating questions and features of *Eye On* boxes and end-of-chapter problems in the fourteen macro chapters.

The first macro chapter (20) now has a section that defines the business cycle and its phases and compares the NBER's method of dating the turning points with the message that real GDP gives for the onset of the 2008–2009 recession.

We reversed the order of the chapters on "Jobs and Unemployment" (21) and "The CPI and the Cost of Living" (22) to emphasize the importance of unemployment today. The unemployment chapter now explains the six alternative measures of unemployment and the idea of marginal labor force attachment. The chapter also has an improved explanation of the linkage between fluctuations in unemployment around the natural rate and the output gap. The CPI chapter now includes an explanation of the core inflation rate.

The chapter on "Finance, Saving, and Investment" (25) incorporates default risk as a factor influencing the supply of loanable funds and explains why lending dried up during the financial crisis. The chapter also examines the issue of crowding out in the face of a large fiscal deficit.

The two money chapters, "The Monetary System" (26) and "Money, Interest, and Inflation" (27), are revised to explain the extraordinary policy actions undertaken by the Fed following the collapse of Lehman Brothers. The chapters look at the enormous increase in the monetary base and corresponding increase in banks' desired reserves as they coped with enhanced default risk.

We also revised the two policy chapters, "Fiscal Policy" (31) and "Monetary Policy" (32), to include the major actions of 2008 and 2009. The fiscal policy chapter is restructured to begin with an account of the cracks in the consensus and the public debate on the merits of fiscal stimulus in recession. The chapter then examines discretionary and automatic fiscal stimulus and the challenges facing the conduct of discretionary policies. In 2009, the effect of automatic stimulus was vastly greater than the discretionary stimulus initiated by Congress. The monetary policy chapter contrasts the orderly near rule-based policies before 2008 with the radical and aggressive countercyclical actions since 2008.

## THE FOUNDATIONS VISION

### ■ Focus on Core Concepts

Each chapter of *Foundations of Economics*, AP* Edition concentrates on a manageable number of main ideas (most commonly three or four) and reinforces each idea several times throughout the chapter. This patient, confidence-building approach guides students through unfamiliar terrain and helps them to focus their efforts on the most important tools and concepts of our discipline.

### ■ Many Learning Tools for Many Learning Styles

*Foundations of Economics*, AP* Edition's integrated print and electronic package builds on the basic fact that students have a variety of learning styles. In MyEconLab, students have a powerful tool at their fingertips: They can complete all Checkpoint problems online, work interactive graphs, assess their skills by taking Practice Tests, receive a personalized Study Plan, and step through Guided Solutions.

### ■ Diagrams That Tell the Whole Story

We developed the style of our diagrams with extensive feedback from faculty focus group participants and student reviewers. All of our figures make consistent use of color to show the direction of shifts and contain detailed, numbered captions designed to direct students' attention step-by-step through the action. Because students of economics are often apprehensive about working with graphs, we have made a special effort to present material in as many as three ways—with graphs, words, and tables—in the same figure. In an innovation that seems necessary, but is to our knowledge unmatched, nearly all of the information supporting a figure appears on the same page as the figure itself. No more flipping pages back and forth!

### ■ Real-World Connections That Bring Theory to Life

Students learn best when they can see the purpose of what they are studying, apply it to illuminate the world around them, and use it in their lives.

*Eye On* boxes, and *Eye On* features offer fresh new examples to help students see that economics is everywhere. Current and recent events appear in *Eye On the U.S. Economy* boxes; we place current U.S. economic events in global and historical perspectives in our *Eye on the Global Economy* and *Eye on the Past* boxes; and we show how students can use economics in day-to-day decisions in *Eye On Your Life* boxes.

The new *Eye On* boxes that build off of the chapter-opening question help students see the economics behind key issues facing our world and highlight a major aspect of the chapter's story.

## ORGANIZATION/FLEXIBILITY

We have organized the sequence of material and chapters in what we think is the most natural order in which to cover the content. But we recognize that there are alternative views on the best order. We have kept this fact and the need for flexibility firmly in mind throughout the text. Many alternative sequences work, and the Flexibility Chart on pp. xxxviii—xli explains the alternatives that work well.

## MYECONLAB

MyEconLab is a powerful online assessment and tutorial system that works hand-in-hand with *Foundations of Economics*, AP* Edition. With comprehensive homework, quiz, test, and tutorial options, teachers can manage all assessment needs in one program.

- All of the Checkpoint and Chapter Checkpoint Problems and Applications are assignable and automatically graded in MyEconLab.
- Extra problems and applications, including algorithmic, draw-graph, and numerical exercises are available for student practice, or instructor assignment.
- Test Item File questions are available for assignment as homework.
- The Custom Exercise Builder allows instructors the flexibility of creating their own problems for assignment.
- The powerful Gradebook records each student's performance and time spent on the Tests and Study Plan and generates reports by student or by chapter.
- Economics in the News is a turn-key solution to bringing daily news into the classroom. Updated daily during the academic year, the authors upload two relevant articles (one micro, one macro) and provide discussion questions.
- A comprehensive suite of ABC news videos, which address current topics such as education, energy, Federal Reserve policy, and business cycles, is available for classroom use. Video-specific exercises are available for instructor assignment.

A more detailed walk-through of the student benefits and features of MyEconLab can be found on pp. xxviii–xxix. For more information, visit the online demonstration at www.myeconlab.com.

Upon textbook purchase, students and teachers are granted access to MyEconLab.

High school teachers can obtain student and teacher preview or adoption access for MyEconLab in the following way:

### Preview Access

- Ask your sales representative for a Preview Access Code Card (ISBN 0-13-111589-8).

### Adoption Access

- Register online at www.PearsonSchool.com/Access_Request, using Option 3 OR
- Ask your sales representative for an Adoption Access Code Card (ISBN 0-13-214300-3).

![myeconlab] www.myeconlab.com

## MyEconLab provides

### The Power of Practice

MyEconLab is the perfect tool for assigning homework, quizzes, and tests and for encouraging hands-on learning-by-doing.

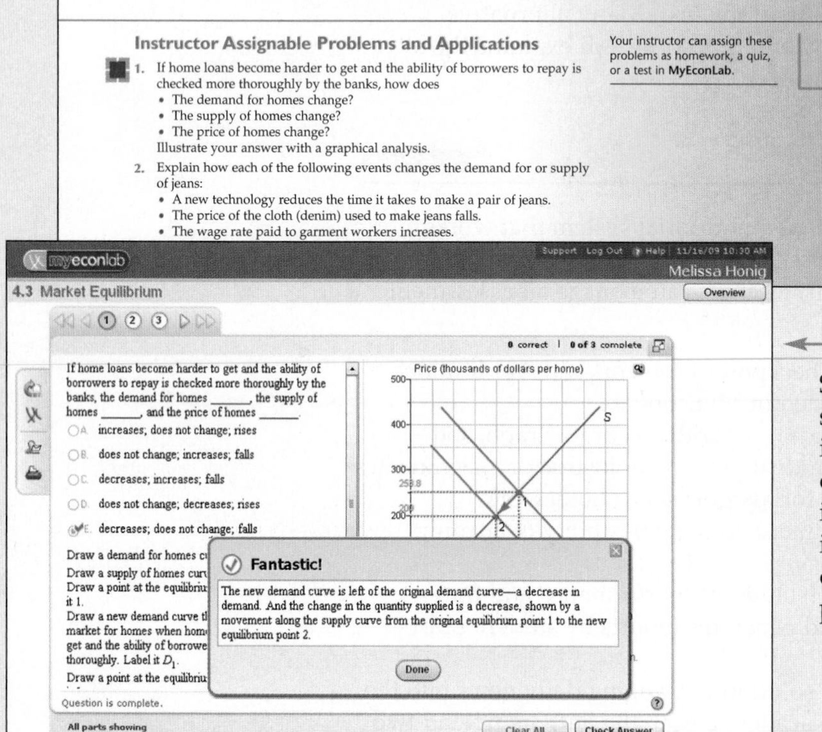


### Auto-graded Assignments

MyEconLab comes with preloaded assignments all of which are automatically graded and that include all the Instructor Assignable Problems and Applications in the textbook.

### Sample Tests and Quizzes

Sample tests and quizzes enable AP students to test their understanding and identify the areas in which they need to do further work. Sample Test questions include practice with graphs: interpreting them, manipulating them, and even drawing them. AP teachers can assign the pre-built tests or create their own tests.

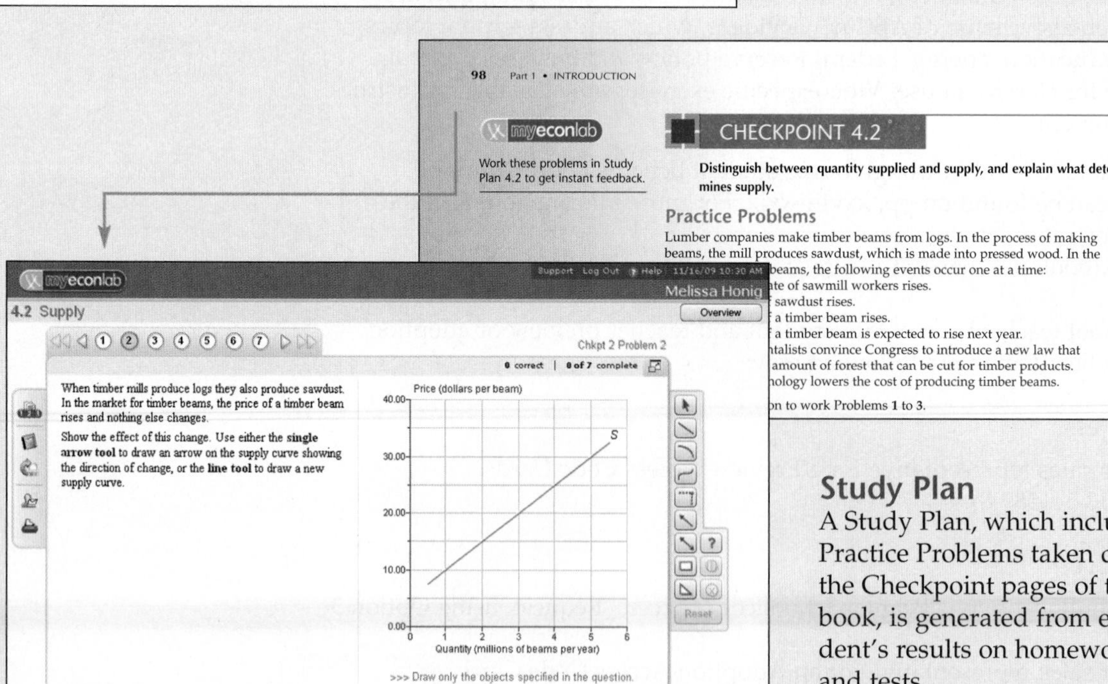


### Study Plan

A Study Plan, which includes Practice Problems taken directly from the Checkpoint pages of the textbook, is generated from each student's results on homework, quizzes, and tests.

## Unlimited Practice

Many Study Plan and Instructor Assignable exercises contain algorithms to ensure that students get as much practice as they need. As students work Study Plan or Homework exercises, instant feedback guides them toward understanding. When students work a Quiz or Test, feedback is provided only when the teacher chooses to make it available.

## Learning Resources

To further reinforce understanding, Study Plan and Homework problems link to four learning resources:

- A step-by-step Guided Solution [Helps students break down a problem much the same way as an instructor would do during office hours];
- The eText page on which the topic of the exercise is explained [Promotes reading the text when further explanation is needed];
- An animated graph with audio narration [Caters to a variety of learning styles];
- A graphing tool [Encourages students to draw and manipulate graphs and deepen their understanding by illustrating economic relationships and ideas].

## SUPPORT MATERIALS FOR TEACHERS AND STUDENTS

*Foundations of Economics*, AP* Edition is accompanied by the most comprehensive set of teaching and learning tools ever assembled. Each component of our package is organized by Checkpoint topic for a tight, seamless integration with both the textbook and the other components. In addition to authoring the MyEconLab and PowerPoint content, we have helped in the reviewing and revising of the Study Guide, Solutions Manual, Instructor's Manual, and Test Item Files to ensure that every element of the package achieves the consistency that students and teachers need.

### FOR THE TEACHER

Most of the teacher supplements and resources for this text are available electronically for download to qualified adopters on the Instructor Resource Center (IRC). Upon adoption or to preview, please go to www.PearsonSchool.com/Advanced and select "Online Teacher Supplements." You will be required to complete a onetime registration subject to verification before being emailed access information to download materials.

#### ■ Instructor's Resource CD-ROM

This CD-ROM contains the Instructor's Manual, Solutions Manual, and Test Item Files in Word and PDF formats. It also contains the Computerized Test Item Files (with a TestGen program installer) and PowerPoint® Resources. It is compatible with both Windows and Macintosh operating systems.

#### ■ Instructor's Manual

The Instructor's Manual, written by Luke Armstrong and edited by Mark Rush, contains chapter outlines and road maps, additional exercises with solutions, and a virtual encyclopedia of suggestions on how to enrich class presentation and use class time efficiently. The fifth edition is enhanced with a Chapter Lecture which incorporates lively Lecture Launchers to enrich your presentation, Landmines that point out potential stumbling blocks, and additional teaching tips, creating one comprehensive lecture resource. Both the micro and macro portions have been updated to reflect changes in the main text as well as infused with a fresh and intuitive approach to teaching this course. It is available for download in Word and PDF formats.

#### ■ Solutions Manual

The Solutions Manual, written by Mark Rush, contains the solutions to all the Checkpoint Practice Problems and Chapter Checkpoint Problems and Applications. It is available for download in Word and PDF formats.

#### ■ Three Test Item Files and TestGen

More than 12,000 multiple-choice, numerical, fill-in-the-blank, short answer, essay, and integrative questions make up the three Test Item Files that support *Foundations of Economics*, AP* Edition. While these questions continue to build on more than one Checkpoint or more than one chapter, this edition's Test Item

Files now feature a linear progression through the text, which will enable instructors to easily view, pick and choose questions for homework and exams. Mark Rush reviewed and edited questions from five dedicated principles instructors to form one of the most comprehensive testing systems on the market. Our microeconomics authors are Karen Gebhardt (Colorado State University); Dennis Debrecht (Carroll University); and Edward Creppy (Northern Virginia Community College). Our macroeconomics questions were written by Carol Dole (Jacksonville University) and Buffie Schmidt (Augusta State University). The entire set of questions is available for download in Word, PDF, and TestGen formats.

All three Test Item Files are available in test generator software (TestGen with QuizMaster). TestGen's graphical interface enables instructors to view, edit, and add questions; transfer questions to tests; and print different forms of tests. Instructors also have the option to reformat tests with varying fonts and styles, margins, and headers and footers, as in any word-processing document. Search and sort features let the instructor quickly locate questions and arrange them in a preferred order. QuizMaster, working with your school's computer network, automatically grades the exams, stores the results on disk, and allows the teacher to view and print a variety of reports.

### ■ PowerPoint Resources

We have created the PowerPoint resources based on our 15 years of experience using this tool in our own classrooms. Three types of PowerPoint presentations are available:

- Lecture notes with full-color, animated figures and tables from the textbook
- Figures and tables from the textbook. All of the textbook figures are animated for step-by-step walk-through.
- Clicker-enabled slides for your Personal Response System. The slides consist of 10 multiple choice questions from the Study Guide for each chapter. You can use these in class to encourage active learning.

### ■ MyEconLab

MyEconLab is an online homework and tutorial system that offers a suite of study and practice tools. Students can test themselves and based on the results, *MyEconLab* generates a personalized study plan with additional exercises and tutorials. *MyEconLab.*

Teachers can build assessments using a mix of MyEconLab-specific problems, Test Bank questions, and questions written by the teacher using the Econ Exercise Builder. Teachers are able to track student performance from online homework, quizzes, and tests within the online gradebook.

## FOR THE STUDENT

### ■ AP* Test Prep Workbook

Created specifically for *Foundations of Economics*, AP* Edition, this comprehensive guide is linked directly to the textbook to help students reinforce important connections between what they learn in class and the AP Exam. This workbook is available for purchase and includes:

- An overview of the AP program and the specific AP test covered by this guide, test taking tips, and strategies to prepare students for peak performance on the AP Exam.
- Correlation between key AP exam topics and the corresponding chapter and section of *Foundations of Economics*, AP* Edition.
- Hundreds of practice study questions written by experienced AP educators.

### MyEconLab

**MyEconLab** is an online homework and tutorial system that offers a suite of study and practice tools. Students can complete all Checkpoint problems online, work interactive graphs, assess their skills by taking Practice Tests, receive a personalized Study Plan, step though Guided Solutions, and much more. See page xxvii for complete description. Ask your teacher for access information and instructions.

## HOW TO SUCCEED IN YOUR AP ECONOMICS COURSE

Any AP course demands a significant commitment of time, and one of your biggest challenges will be to allocate your time efficiently. By applying some analysis to this challenge, you will already be thinking like an economist!

Here are some key strategies for success in this course.

***Keep up with the course material on a weekly basis.*** Skim the appropriate chapter in the textbook before it is covered in class to get a general understanding of the basic concepts and issues. After class, work through the problems in the appropriate chapter of The *AP* Test Prep Workbook*. The key to success is repeated practice with your new economic tools.

***Make the Checklist-Checkpoint structure work for you.*** To learn economics you have to do economics. The Checklist-Checkpoint system provides you with a structure for doing just that. To make it work for you, start by familiarizing yourself with the Checklist at the opening to each chapter: it tells you where you'll be heading. As you progress through the chapter, you'll see that each major section corresponds to one of the Checklist items. After studying each section, be sure to work the Checkpoint! That's the time to reinforce what you've just read—while it's still fresh in your mind. Don't jump to the next section until you feel you've mastered the Checkpoint of the section at hand. Then, when you reach the end of the chapter, review the Chapter Checklist. It corresponds seamlessly to the Checklist and the key points in the sections. This system is the glue that holds it all together. Used consistently and thoughtfully, it will help you attain success in mastering economics.

***Tailor your learning style to the many study tools available.*** Do you work best interactively in an online environment? Are you a visual learner? Do you like to break tasks down into smaller, bite-sized pieces? Whatever your learning style, there is something for you in this fully integrated learning system. If you like to be in charge of your own learning, you'll find that MyEconLab is a powerful tool; you'll be able to complete Checkpoints and exercises online, work graphs, take Practice Tests, receive a customized Study Plan, and step through guided solutions—all at your own pace. If you're a visual learner, the graphs will be key to your understanding—color is used consistently to convey specific actions, numbered captions walk you step by step through key figures, and accompanying data tables show you the main plotting points. If you like patient explanation of concepts, *The AP* Test Prep Workbook* will amplify the material in the text for you and allow you to work additional problems.

***Look for economics in the world around you.*** To give you some inspiration in this direction, read the "Eye On" features that will show you how the theory connects with the everyday world around you. Also, don't miss the Reality Check at the end of each chapter, which asks you to ponder how the economic concepts in a particular chapter actually have a real impact on your own life. You will finally have an answer to the perennial question, "What use is all this theory, anyway?"

The AP course description outline that follows on the subsequent pages provides the major topics included on the AP exam. Look closely at these topics and note how the textbook follows the sequence of ideas to be mastered.

## Understanding the AP Economics Examinations

The AP Economics Examinations make use of a variety of question types and graphical analysis to assess the skill level of AP students. The AP examinations reflect the types of assessment that occur at the college level.

The AP Economics Examinations take two hours and 10 minutes to complete. In both the multiple-choice and free-response sections of the exams, AP students can expect to work with graphs, charts, and tables. Each examination consists of a 70-minute, multiple-choice section and a 60-minute free-response section that may require graphical analysis. The free-response section begins with a mandatory 10-minute reading period that can be used to read each of the questions, sketch graphs, make notes, and plan answers in the green insert. AP students then have 50 minutes to write the answers in the booklet.

## Section I: Multiple-Choice Questions

The multiple-choice section of each exam contains 60 questions, with 70 minutes allotted for Section I. The multiple-choice section accounts for 2/3 of the AP student's examination grade. Each question has five choices and only one choice is judged correct. The questions are straightforward, and many require analysis and interpretation. Some will require analysis of a graph, chart, or table.

The AP Economics Examinations contain these distinct question types:

- Definition or identification questions
- Graph or table questions
- Analysis or cause and effect questions
- Multiple-choice questions

**Hints on Grading:** The multiple-choice section of each exam is worth 2/3 of the AP student's score. The questions are machine scored and determined by crediting one point for a correct answer and by deducting 1/4 of a point for an incorrect answer. No points are gained or lost for unanswered questions. If you have no idea what the correct answer is, leave the answer blank. But, if you can eliminate two or more of the five choices, you should make an educated guess.

### ■ Section II Free-Response Questions

The free-response section begins with a mandatory 10-minute reading period, during which AP students are encouraged to read the questions, sketch graphs, make notes, and plan answers in the green insert. AP students then have 50 minutes to write their answers in the booklet.

The free-response questions in Section II of each exam will require AP students to analyze a given economic situation and use economic principles to explain answers. Using explanatory diagrams that clarify the analysis and clearly explain the reasoning results in the greatest number of points. Sometimes a graph is given as part of the question and the AP student's task is to derive the answer from the graph data. Generally, the longer free-response questions require you to interrelate several content areas, while the two shorter free-response questions focus on a specific topic in a given content area.

**Hints on Grading:** This section of the exam is 1/3 of the score. The raw score for Section II is composed of the scores from the three questions and then apportioned according to value assigned to each (larger question—50% of score and two smaller questions each—25% of score).

## AP ECONOMICS CORRELATION CHARTS

This chart correlates the Advanced Placement Microeconomics topics as outlined by the College Board with the corresponding chapters and section numbers in *Foundations of Economics*, AP* Edition.

| AP Microeconomics Topics | Textbook Correlation |
|---|---|
| **I. Basic Economic Concepts** | **Chapters 1, 2, 3, 9** |
| A. Scarcity, choice, and opportunity cost | 1.1, 1.2, 3.2 |
| B. Production possibilities curve | 3.1 |
| C. Comparative advantage, absolute advantage, specialization, and trade | 3.4, 9.1, 9.2 |
| D. Economic systems | 2.3 |
| E. Property rights and the role of incentives | 1.2 |
| F. Marginal analysis | 1.2 |
| **II. The Nature and Functions of Product Markets** | **Chapters 4, 5, 6, 7, 8, 12, 13, 14, 15, 16, 17** |
| A. Supply and demand | Chapter 4 |
| 1. Market equilibrium | 4.3 |
| 2. Determinants of supply and demand | 4.1, 4.2 |
| 3. Price and quantity controls | Chapter 7 |
| 4. Elasticity | Chapter 5 |
| a. Price, income, and cross-price elasticities of demand | 5.1, 5.3 |
| b. Price elasticity of supply | 5.2 |
| 5. Consumer surplus, producer surplus, and market efficiency | 6.1, 6.2, 6.3, 6.4 |
| 6. Tax incidence and deadweight loss | 8.1, 8.2 |
| B. Theory of consumer choice | Chapter 12 |
| 1. Total utility and marginal utility | 12.2 |
| 2. Utility maximization: equalizing marginal utility per dollar | 12.2 |

| Topic | Chapter |
|---|---|
| 3. Individual and market demand curves | 4.1 |
| 4. Income and substitution effects | |
| C. Production and costs | Chapter 13 |
| 1. Production functions: short and long run | 13.1 |
| 2. Marginal product and diminshing returns | 13.2 |
| 3. Short-run costs | 13.3 |
| 4. Long-run costs and economies of scale | 13.4 |
| 5. Cost minimizing input combination | |
| D. Firm behavior and market structure | Chapters 13, 14, 15, 16, 17 |
| 1. Profit | Chapters 13, 14 |
| a. Accounting versus economic profits | 13.1 |
| b. Normal profit | 13.1, 14.2 |
| c. Profit maximization: MR = MC rule | 14.1, 15.2, 16.2 |
| 2. Perfect competition | Chapter 14 |
| a. Profit maximization | 14.1 |
| b. Short-run supply and shutdown decision | 14.1, 14.2 |
| c. Behavior of firms and markets in the short run and in the long run | 14.2, 14.3 |
| d. Efficiency and perfect competition | 14.3 |
| 3. Monopoly | Chapter 15 |
| a. Sources of market power | 15.1 |
| b. Profit maximization | 15.2 |
| c. Inefficiency of monopoly | 15.3 |
| d. Price discrimination | 15.4 |
| e. Natural monopoly | 15.1. 15.5 |
| 4. Oligopoly | Chapter 17 |
| a. Interdependence, collusion, and cartels | 17.1, 17.2 |
| b. Game theory and strategic behavior | 17.3 |
| 5. Monopolistic competition | Chapter 16 |
| a. Product differentiation and role of advertising | 16.1, 16.3 |
| b. Profit maximization | 16.2 |
| c. Short-run and long-run equilibrium | 16.2 |
| d. Excess capacity and inefficiency | 16.2 |
| **III. Factor Markets** | **Chapter 18, 19** |
| A. Derived factor demand | 18.1 |
| B. Marginal revenue product | 18.1 |
| C. Labor market and firms' hiring of labor | 18.2 |
| D. Market distribution of income | 19.1 |
| **IV. Market Failure and the Role of Government** | **Chapters 6, 10, 11, 15, 17, 19** |
| A. Externalities | Chapter 10, 11 |
| 1. Marginal social benefit and marginal social cost | 10.3, 11.1 |
| 2. Positive externalities | 10.1, 10.3 |
| 3. Negative externalities | 10.1, 11.1 |
| 4. Remedies | 10.3, 11.1 |
| B. Public goods | Chapter 10 |
| 1. Public versus private goods | 10.1 |
| 2. Provision of public goods | 10.2 |

| | |
|---|---|
| C. Public policy to promote competition | Chapters 15, 17 |
| 1. Antitrust policy | 17.4 |
| 2. Regulation | 15.5 |
| D. Income distribution | Chapter 19 |
| 1. Equity | 6.5, 19.3 |
| 2. Sources of income inequality | 19.1, 19.2 |

This chart correlates the Advanced Placement Macroeconomics topics as outlined by the College Board with the corresponding chapters and section numbers in *Foundations of Economics*, AP* Edition.

| **AP Macroeconomics Topics** | **Textbook Correlation** |
|---|---|
| **I. Basic Economic Concepts** | **Chapters 1, 3, 4, 20, 21, 22** |
| A. Scarcity, choice, and opportunity costs | 1.1, 1.2, 3.2 |
| B. Production possibilities curve | 3.1 |
| C. Comparative advantage, absolute advantage specialization, and exchange | 3.4, 9.2 |
| D. Demand, supply, and market equilibrium | 4.1, 4.2, 4.3 |
| E. Macroeconomic issues: business cycle, unemployment, inflation, growth | Chapters 20, 21, 22 |
| **II. Measurement of Economic Performance** | **Chapters 20, 21, 22, 27, 28** |
| A. National income accounts | Chapter 20 |
| 1. Circular flow | 2.3, 20.1 |
| 2. Gross domestic product | 20.1, 20.2 |
| 3. Components of gross domestic product | 20.1 |
| 4. Real versus nominal gross domestic product | 20.2 |
| B. Inflation measurement and adjustment | Chapters 22, 28 |
| 1. Price indices | 22.1, 22.2 |
| 2. Nominal and real values | 22.3 |
| 3. Costs of inflation | 27.3 |
| C. Unemployment | Chapter 21, 23 |
| 1. Definition and measurement | 21.1 |
| 2. Types of unemployment | 21.3 |
| 3. Natural rate of unemployment | 21.3, 23.2 |
| **III. National Income and Price Determination** | **Chapters 28, 29** |
| A. Aggregate demand | Chapter 28, 29 |
| 1. Determinants of aggregate demand | 28.2, 29.1, 29.2, 29.4 |
| 2. Multiplier and crowding-out effects | 29.3, 25.3 |
| B. Aggregate Supply | Chapter 28 |
| 1. Short-run and long-run analyses | 23.1, 28.3 |
| 2. Sticky versus flexible wages and prices | 28.1 |
| 3. Determinants of aggregate supply | 28.1 |
| C. Macroeconomic Equilibrium | Chapters 23, 28 |
| 1. Real output and price level | 28.3 |
| 2. Short and long run | 28.3 |
| 3. Actual versus full-employment output | 21.3, 28.3 |
| 4. Economic fluctuations | 28.3 |
| **IV. Financial Sector** | **Chapters 25, 26, 27** |
| A. Money, banking, and financial markets | Chapters 25, 26 |
| 1. Definition of financial assets: money, stocks, bonds | 25.1, 26.1 |

| | |
|---|---|
| 2. Time value of money (present and future value) | |
| 3. Measures of money supply | 26.1 |
| 4. Banks and creation of money | 26.2, 26.3, 26.4 |
| 5. Money demand | 27.1 |
| 6. Money market | 27.1, 27.2 |
| 7. Loanable funds market | 25.2 |
| B. Central bank and control of the money supply | Chapters 26, 27 |
| 1. Tools of central bank policy | 26.3 |
| 2. Quantity theory of money | 27.2 |
| 3. Real versus nominal interest rates | 22.3 |
| **V. Inflation, Unemployment, and Stabilization Policies** | **Chapters 30, 31** |
| A. Fiscal and monetary policies | Chapters 31, 32 |
| 1. Demand-side effects | 31.2, 32.2 |
| 2. Supply-side effects | 31.3 |
| 3. Policy mix | |
| 4. Government deficits and debt | 25.3, 31.1 |
| B. Inflation and unemployment | Chapter 30 |
| 1. Types of inflation | |
| a. Demand-pull inflation | |
| b. Cost-push inflation | |
| 2. The Phillips curve: short run versus long run | 30.1, 30.2 |
| 3. Role of expectations | 30.2, 30.3 |
| **VI. Economic Growth and Productivity** | **Chapters 24** |
| A. Investment in human capital | 24.2 |
| B. Investment in physical capital | 24.2 |
| C. Research and development, and technological progress | Chapter 24 |
| D. Growth policy | 24.4 |
| **VII. Open Economy: International Trade and Finance** | **Chapter 33** |
| A. Balance of payments accounts | Chapter 33 |
| 1. Balance of trade | 33.1 |
| 2. Current account | 33.1 |
| 3. Capital account | 33.1 |
| B. Foreign exchange market | Chapter 33 |
| 1. Demand for and supply of foreign exchange | 33.2 |
| 2. Exchange rate determination | 33.2 |
| 3. Currency appreciation and depreciation | 33.2 |
| C. Net exports and capital flows | 33.2 |
| D. Links to financial and goods markets | 33.2 |

Upon publication, this text was correlated to the College Board's Macroeconomics and Microeconomics Course Description dated May 2009, May 2010. We continually monitor the College Board's AP Course Description for updates to exam topics. For the most current AP Exam Topic correlation for this textbook, visit PearsonSchool.com/Advanced Correlations

# Foundations of Economics: Flexibility Chart

| | |
|---|---|
| **1. Getting Started**<br>*The questions and way of thinking that define economics.*<br>**1. Appendix: Making and Using Graphs**<br>*Good for students with a fear of graphs.*<br>**2. The U.S. and Global Economies**<br>*Describes 'what,' 'how,' and 'for whom' in the U.S. and global economies and introduces the circular flows that arise from interactions.* | We cover all the standard topics of the principles curriculum and we do so in the order that has increasingly found favor among teachers.<br>A powerful case can be made for teaching the subject in the order in which we present it here, but we recognize that there is a range of opinion about sequencing, and we have structured our text so that it works well if other sequences are preferred. This table provides a guide to the flexibility that we've built into our text. |
| **3. The Economic Problem**<br>*Carefully paced and complete first look at the fundamental economic problem. Includes the distinction between absolute advantage and an explanation of why comparative advantage is the source of the gains from trade.*<br>**4. Demand and Supply**<br>*Carefully paced and complete explanation of this core topic with painstaking emphasis on the distinction between a change demand (supply) and a change in the quantity demanded (supplied).*<br>**5. Elasticities of Demand and Supply**<br>*A gentle explanation of elasticity with the emphasis on understanding and interpreting elasticity.* | Deciding the order in which to teach the components of microeconomics involves a tradeoff between building foundations and getting to policy issues early in the course. There is little disagreement that the place to begin is with production possibilities and demand and supply. We provide a carefully paced and thoroughly modern treatment of these topics. |
| **6. Efficiency and Fairness of Markets**<br>*Describes the alternative methods of allocating resources and explains the efficiency and fairness of market outcomes. By introducing students to both efficiency and fairness (equity) issues early in the course we are able to engage in the discussion of topics such as price floors, price ceilings, production quotas, taxes, the benefits and costs of globalization of trade, externalities, public goods, and common resources, all of which we cover in Chapters 7 through 11.* | We introduce and explain the core ideas about efficiency and fairness early and then cover major policy issues in a series of chapters that use only the tools of demand and supply, marginal benefit and marginal cost, and consumer and producer surplus. More technical topics such as consumer choice and cost curves are covered later. |
| **7. Government Actions in Markets**<br>*Explains the effects of price ceilings, price floors, and price supports and their efficiency and fairness. Chapters 4, 5, and 6 are prerequisites.*<br>**8. Taxes**<br>*Explains the incidence of taxes and discusses efficiency and equity issues. Chapters 4, 5, and 6 are prerequisites.*<br>**9. Global Markets in Action**<br>*Explains how markets work when an economy trades with the world. Explains the gains and losses from exports and imports, the effects of tariffs and import quotas, and assesses arguments for protection. Chapters 4 and 6 are prerequisites.* | Teachers who prefer to cover policy issues later in the course can skip Chapters 6 through 11 and move straight from elasticity to consumer choice (Chapter 12) and then onto the economics of the firm. The policy-related chapters can be covered at any chosen point later in the course. |

**10. Public Goods and Public Choices**
*Describes and distinguishes among types of goods and sources of externalities. Explains the free-rider problem and the problem of underprovision of public goods and private goods with external benefits. Explains alternative solutions to these problems. Chapters 4 and 6 are prerequisites.*

**11. Externalities and the Environment**
*Explains why goods with negative externalities and common resources lead to overproduction. Explains the Coase theorem, and the use of taxes, subsidies, and market solutions to the problem of overproduction and the tragedy of the commons. Chapters 4 and 6 are prerequisites.*

---

**12. Consumer Choice and Demand**
*Explains both marginal utility theory and (in an appendix) indifference curve analysis.*

This optional chapter may be covered at any point after Chapter 3.

**13. Production and Cost**
*Explains a firm's product curves and cost curves and the sources of initially increasing marginal product (increased specialization) and eventually diminishing marginal product.*

Chapter 13, which may be covered at any point after Chapter 3, is prerequisite for Chapters 14 through 18.

---

**14. Perfect Competition**
*Explains decisions of firms in competitive markets and derives the firm's and market supply curves.*

**15. Monopoly**
*Explains how monopoly arises, how it maximizes profit, how price discrimination works, and why and how monopoly is regulated.*

**16. Monopolistic Competition**
*Explains product differentiation and its consequences of high advertising and marketing costs. Chapters 14 and 15 are prerequisites.*

**17. Oligopoly**
*Explains how oligopoly arises, the cartel dilemma, game theory, and antitrust regulation. Chapters 14 and 15 are prerequisites.*

---

**18. Markets for Factors of Production**
*Emphasis is on labor market but it covers all the factor markets and including nonrenewable factors. Chapters 4 and 13 are prerequisites.*

**19. Inequality and Poverty**
*Explains the sources of inequality and its trends, and evaluates alternative redistribution methods. Chapter 18 is a useful background for this chapter but not a prerequisite.*

**20. GDP: A Measure of Total Production of Income**
*Explains expenditure and income approaches to measuring real GDP and the uses and limitations of real GDP. An appendix explains the chained-dollar measure of real GDP.*

**21. Jobs and Unemployment**
*Describes labor market measures and trends and the link between unemployment and real GDP.*

**22. The CPI and the Cost of Living**
*Emphasizes the interpretation and use of the CPI and the measurement of real variables.*

The macro course divides naturally into five parts: (1) measurement, (2) the real economy in the long run, (3) the money economy in the long run, (4) fluctuations, and (5) policy issues.

These parts can be covered in sequence or in several alternative ways.

After Chapter 22, it is possible to jump either to Chapter 28 (Aggregate Supply and Aggregate Demand), or Chapter 29 (Aggregate Expenditure Multiplier), or Chapter 30 (The Short-Run Policy Tradeoff).

It is also possible to jump straight to the money chapters (Chapters 26 and 27).

Most of the content of Chapter 31 (Fiscal Policy) and Chapter 32 (Monetary Policy) can be covered after doing Chapters 26, 27, and 28.

**23. Potential GDP and the Natural Unemployment Rate**
*Explains how potential GDP and the natural unemployment rate are determined.*

**24. Economic Growth**
*Explains the sources of economic growth and the policies that might speed it.*

**25. Finance, Saving, and Investment**
*Describes the financial markets and institutions and explains how saving, investment, and the real interest rate are determined and influenced by the government budget deficit (or surplus).*

These chapters explain the real economy in the long run—classical macro. They may be studied after Chapters 28–30, but we think they work better at this point in the course.

At full employment, the real economy is influenced by only real variables, and the price level is proportional to the quantity of money. This idea has been incredibly productive in advancing our understanding of both the full-employment economy and the business cycle. By having a firm understanding of the forces that determine potential GDP, the student better appreciates the more complex interactions of real and monetary factors that bring economic fluctuations. The student also sees that the long-term trends in our economy play a larger role in determining our standard of living and cost of living than do the fluctuations around those trends.

Even if you defer Chapters 24 and 25, it is a good plan to cover Chapter 23.1 "Potential GDP" at this point.

**26. The Monetary System**
*Defines money and describes its functions. Describes the banking system and the Fed and explains how the Fed influences the quantity of money.*

**27. Money, Interest, and Inflation**
*Explains the demand for money and how the supply of and demand for money determine the nominal interest rate in the short run and the price level and inflation rate in the long run.*

These chapters explain the money economy in the long run and the short run. They may be studied after Chapters 28 and 29.

**28. Aggregate Supply and Aggregate Demand**
*A carefully paced but comprehensive account of the AS–AD model and its use in understanding the business cycle. This chapter may be studied before Chapter 23.*

**29. Aggregate Expenditure Multiplier**
*The Keynesian cross model. If you don't want to explain in detail how unplanned inventory changes set off a multiplier process, you may omit this chapter.*

**30. The Short-Run Policy Tradeoff**
*An explanation of the sources of the short-run tradeoff and the forces that keep shifting it.*

Chapters 28–30 explain economic fluctuations (interactions between the real and monetary sectors) using the ideas of aggregate supply and aggregate demand, and optionally the aggregate expenditure model and the Phillips curve.

**31. Fiscal Policy**
*Explains how fiscal policy is made, discusses the effectiveness of fiscal stabilization policy, and discusses the supply-side effects on potential GDP and economic growth. Chapter 28 is prerequisite for section 31.2 and Chapters 23 and 25 are prerequisites for section 32.2. Section 31.1 can be studied at any point.*

**32. Monetary Policy**
*Explains how monetary policy is made and its effects on inflation and real GDP. Includes a discussion of alternative approaches to monetary policy.*

*Chapters 26, 27, and 28 are prerequisites.*

**33. International Finance**
*The balance of payments section can be studied anytime after Chapter 20 and the exchange rate section can be studied anytime after Chapter 4.*

Policy runs through all the macro chapters. Macro *is* policy. These three chapters pull together all the policy issues and explain the decision-making institutions, the policy choices, and the debates surrounding them.

The final chapter extends the policy discussion to the open economy, the balance of payments, and the exchange rate. With a bit of care and imagination, parts of these chapters can be covered earlier in the course.

## Did greedy Wall Street bankers cause the global economic slump?

The banks incurred huge losses and their executives received fat bonuses and flew to Washington in private jets to ask for handouts from taxpayers. But did they *cause* the global financial crisis?

# Getting Started

**When you have completed your study of this chapter, you will be able to**

1 Define economics and explain the kinds of questions that economists try to answer.

2 Explain the core ideas that define the economic way of thinking.

## 1.1 DEFINITION AND QUESTIONS

Wall Street bankers might be greedy, but they are not alone. We all want more than we can get. We want good health and long lives. We want spacious and comfortable homes. We want running shoes and jet skis. We want the time to enjoy our favorite sports, video games, novels, music, and movies; to travel to exotic places; and just to hang out with friends. Human wants exceed the resources available to satisfy them, and this fact is the source of all economic questions and problems.

### ■ Scarcity

**Scarcity**
The condition that arises because wants exceed the ability of resources to satisfy them.

Our inability to satisfy all our wants is called **scarcity**. The ability of each of us to satisfy our wants is limited by the time we have, the incomes we earn, and the prices we pay for the things we buy. These limits mean that everyone has unsatisfied wants. The ability of all of us as a society to satisfy our wants is limited by the productive resources that exist. These resources include the gifts of nature, our labor and ingenuity, and the tools and equipment that we have made.

Everyone, poor and rich alike, faces scarcity. A student wants Beyonce's latest CD and a paperback but has only $10.00 in his pocket. He faces scarcity. Brad Pitt wants to spend a week in New Orleans discussing plans for his new eco-friendly housing and he also wants to spend the week promoting his new movie. He faces scarcity. The U.S. government wants to increase defense spending and cut taxes. It faces scarcity. An entire society wants improved health care, an Internet connection in every classroom, an ambitious space exploration program, clean lakes and rivers, and so on. Society faces scarcity.

Faced with scarcity, we must make choices. We must choose among the available alternatives. The student must choose the CD or the paperback. Brad Pitt must choose New Orleans or promoting his new movie. The government must choose defense or tax cuts. And society must choose among health care, computers, space exploration, the environment, and so on. Even parrots face scarcity!

Not only do I want a cracker—we all want a cracker!

## Economics Defined

**Economics** is the social science that studies the choices that individuals, businesses, governments, and entire societies make as they cope with *scarcity*, the *incentives* that influence those choices, and the arrangements that coordinate them.

**Economics**
The social science that studies the choices that individuals, businesses, governments, and entire societies make as they cope with *scarcity*, the *incentives* that influence those choices, and the arrangements that coordinate them.

The subject is extremely broad and touches all aspects of our lives. To get beyond this definition of economics, you need to understand the kinds of questions that economists try to answer and the way they think and go about seeking those answers.

We begin with some key economic questions. Although the scope of economics is broad and the range of questions that economists address is equally broad, two big questions provide a useful summary of the scope of economics:

- How do choices end up determining *what, how,* and *for whom* goods and services get produced?
- When do choices made in the pursuit of *self-interest* also promote the *social interest*?

## What, How, and For Whom?

**Goods and services** are the objects and actions that people value and produce to satisfy human wants. Goods are *objects* that satisfy wants. Running shoes and ketchup are examples. Services are *actions* that satisfy wants. Haircuts and rock concerts are examples. We produce a dazzling array of goods and services that range from necessities such as food, houses, and health care to leisure items such as DVD players and roller coaster rides.

**Goods and services**
The objects (goods) and the actions (services) that people value and produce to satisfy human wants.

### What?

*What* determines the quantities of corn we grow, homes we build, and health-care services we produce? Sixty years ago, 25 percent of Americans worked on a farm. That number has shrunk to less than 3 percent today. Over the same period, the number of people who produce goods—in mining, construction, and manufacturing—has also shrunk, from 30 percent to 20 percent. The decrease in farming and the production of goods is matched by an increase in the production of services. How will these quantities change in the future as ongoing changes in technology make an ever-wider array of goods and services available to us?

### How?

*How* are goods and services produced? In a vineyard in France, basket-carrying workers pick the annual grape crop by hand. In a vineyard in California, a huge machine and a few workers do the same job that a hundred grape pickers in France do. Look around you and you will see many examples of this phenomenon—the same job being done in different ways. In some stores, checkout clerks key in prices. In others, they use a laser scanner. One farmer keeps track of his livestock feeding schedules and inventories by using paper-and-pencil records, while another uses a personal computer. GM hires workers to weld auto bodies in some of its plants and uses robots to do the job in others.

Why do we use machines in some cases and people in others? Do mechanization and technological change destroy more jobs than they create? Do they make us better off or worse off?

*In a California vineyard a machine and a few workers do the same job as a hundred grape pickers in France.*

### For Whom?

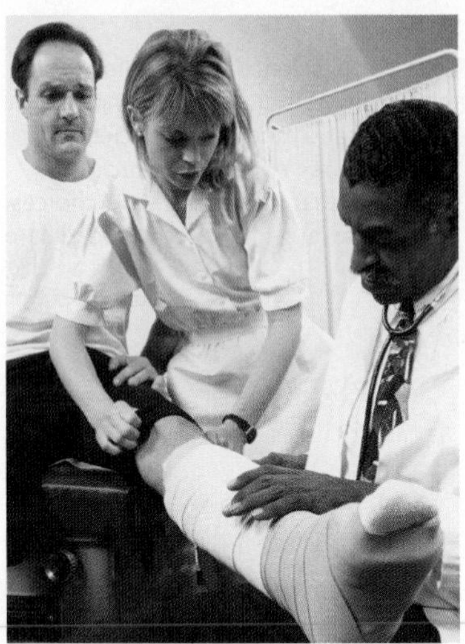

*A doctor gets more of the goods and services produced than a nurse or a medical assistant gets.*

*For whom* are goods and services produced? The answer to this question depends on the incomes that people earn and the prices they pay for the goods and services they buy. At given prices, a person who has a high income is able to buy more goods and services than a person who has a low income. Doctors earn much higher incomes than do nurses and medical assistants, so doctors get more of the goods and services produced than nurses and medical assistants get.

You probably know about many other persistent differences in incomes. Men, on the average, earn more than women. Whites, on the average, earn more than minorities. College graduates, on the average, earn more than high school graduates. Americans, on the average, earn more than Europeans, who in turn earn more, on the average, than Asians and Africans. But there are some significant exceptions. The people of Japan and Hong Kong now earn an average income similar to that of Americans. And there is a lot of income inequality throughout the world.

What determines the incomes we earn? Why do doctors earn larger incomes than nurses? Why do men earn more, on average, than women? Why do college graduates earn more, on average, than high school graduates? Why do Americans earn more, on average, than Africans?

Economics explains how the choices that individuals, businesses, and governments make and the interactions of those choices end up determining *what, how,* and *for whom* goods and services get produced. In answering these questions, we have a deeper agenda in mind. We're not interested in just knowing how many DVD players get produced, how they get produced, and who gets to enjoy them. We ultimately want to know the answer to the second big economic question that we'll now explore.

## ■ When Is the Pursuit of Self-Interest in the Social Interest?

Every day, you and 300 million other Americans, along with 6.8 billion people in the rest of the world, make economic choices that result in *"what," "how,"* and *"for whom"* goods and services are produced.

Are the goods and services produced, and the quantities in which they are produced, the right ones? Do the scarce resources get used in the best possible way? Do the goods and services that we produce go to the people who benefit most from them?

### Self-Interest and the Social Interest

**Self-interest**
The choices that are best for the individual who makes them.

**Social interest**
The choices that are best for society as a whole.

Choices that are the best for the individual who makes them are choices made in the pursuit of **self-interest**. Choices that are the best for society as a whole are said to be in the **social interest**. The social interest has two dimensions: *efficiency* and *equity*. We'll explore these concepts in later chapters. For now, think of efficiency as being achieved by baking the biggest possible pie, and think of equity as being achieved by sharing the pie in the fairest possible way.

You know that your own choices are the best ones for you—or at least you *think* they're the best at the time that you make them. You use your time and other resources in the way that makes most sense to you. But you don't think much about how your choices affect other people. You order a home delivery pizza because you're hungry and want to eat. You don't order it thinking that the delivery person or the cook needs an income. You make choices that are in your self-interest—choices that you think are best for you.

When you act on your economic decisions, you come into contact with thousands of other people who produce and deliver the goods and services that you decide to buy or who buy the things that you sell. These people have made their own decisions—what to produce and how to produce it, whom to hire or whom to work for, and so on.

Like you, everyone else makes choices that they think are best for them. When the pizza delivery person shows up at your home, he's not doing you a favor. He's earning his income and hoping for a good tip.

Could it be possible that when each one of us makes choices that are in our own best interest—our self-interest—it turns out that these choices are also the best for society as a whole—in the social interest?

Much of the rest of this book helps you to learn what economists know about this question and its answer. To help you start thinking about the question, we're going to illustrate it with seven topics that generate heated discussion in today's world. You're already at least a little bit familiar with each one of them. They are

- Financial crisis and global slump
- Globalization and international outsourcing
- The information-age economy
- Disappearing rainforests and fish stocks
- Water shortages
- Climate change
- A Social Security time bomb

### Financial Crisis and Global Slump

Most years, production increases and the standard of living rises. But sometimes production shrinks, jobs are lost, and incomes fall. In the United States, production has fallen, briefly, ten times since World War II, but in the world as a whole, it has fallen only once: in 2009. The global recession of 2009 is so widespread and severe that it is being called a global slump.

*The collapse of credit and falling home prices were at the epicenter of the global slump of 2009.*

Early warning signs became apparent to some farsighted observers in 2005 when U.S. home prices had increased to twice their 1999 level. This price explosion looked like a bubble that was about to burst. And burst it did in 2006. With falling home prices in 2007, people started to walk away from their mortgage debts and foreclosures increased. Banks that had been eager to lend were now in a bigger financial hole than the people to whom they had made loans. Bank lending dried up.

With credit hard to get, consumers and businesses cut back their spending, production slowed, and layoffs started to climb. The situation became so alarming that people began to compare 2009 with 1929, the year that saw the start of the *Great Depression,* what turned out to be a decade in which unemployment climbed to more than 20 percent of the labor force.

*During the 1930s, the longest lines were for jobs.*

Financial crisis and its consequences illustrate well the distinction and tension between self-interest and the social interest. The bankers that were eager to lend to home buyers between 2000 and 2006 were pursuing their self-interest (what has been called greed). Borrowers and homebuyers also acted in what they saw as their self-interest. When the home price bubble burst and a struggling homebuyer defaulted on loan repayments, that person, too, was acting in her or his self-interest. And when the bank foreclosed on a borrower, that too was done in the pursuit of self-interest. But when all these self-interested actions are combined, the consequences are an outcome that is clearly not in the social interest.

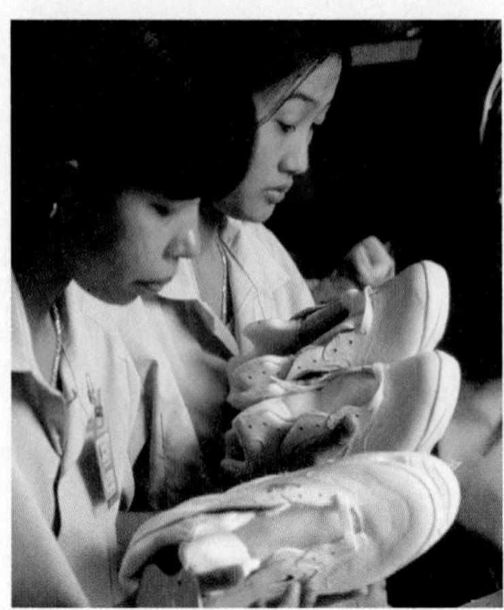

*Workers in Asia make our shoes.*

## Globalization and International Outsourcing

Globalization and international outsourcing—the expansion of international trade and the production of components and services by firms in other countries—has been going on for centuries. But during the 1990s, its pace accelerated as advances in microchips, satellites, and fiber-optic cables lowered the cost of communication. A phone call, a video-conference, or a face-to-face meeting involving people who live 10,000 miles apart has become an everyday and easily affordable event.

This explosion of communication has globalized production decisions. When Nike produces more sports shoes, people in China, Indonesia, or Malaysia get more work. When Steven Spielberg wants an animation sequence for a new movie, programmers in New Zealand write the code. And when China Airlines wants a new airplane, Americans who work for Boeing build it.

The number of jobs in manufacturing and routine services is shrinking in the United States and Europe and expanding in India, China, and other Asian economies. And production is growing more rapidly in Asia than in the United States and Europe. China is already the world's second largest economy, and if the current trends continue, it will become the largest economy during the 2020s.

But globalization is leaving some people behind. The nations of Africa and parts of South America are not sharing in the prosperity that globalization is bringing to other parts of the world.

Is globalization in the social interest, or does it benefit some at the expense of others? The owners of multinational firms clearly benefit from lower production costs. So do the consumers of low-cost imported goods and services. But don't displaced American workers lose? And doesn't even the worker in Malaysia, who sews your new running shoes for a few cents an hour, also lose?

## The Information-Age Economy

*The computer chip has transformed our lives.*

The 1980s and 1990s were years of extraordinary economic change that have been called the *Information Revolution*. This name suggests a parallel with the *Industrial Revolution* of the years around 1800 and the *Agricultural Revolution* of 12,000 years ago.

The changes that occurred during the last 25 years were based on one major technology: the microprocessor or computer chip. Gordon Moore of Intel predicted that the number of transistors that could be placed on one integrated chip would double every 18 months (Moore's law). This prediction turned out to be remarkably accurate.

The spin-offs from faster and cheaper computing have been widespread. Telecommunications became much faster and cheaper, music and movie recording became more realistic and cheaper, millions of routine tasks that previously required human decision and action were automated. You encounter these automated tasks every day when you check out at the supermarket, use an ATM, or call a government department or large business. All the new products and processes and the low-cost computing power that made them possible were produced by people who made choices in the pursuit of self-interest. They did not result from any grand design or government plan.

When Gordon Moore set up Intel and started making chips, he wasn't thinking how much easier it would be for you to turn in your essay on time if you had a faster PC. When Bill Gates quit Harvard to set up Microsoft, he wasn't trying to create the best operating system and improve people's computing experience. Moore and Gates and thousands of other entrepreneurs were in hot pursuit of the big payoffs that many of them achieved. Yet their actions did make many other people better off. They advanced the social interest.

But could more have been done? Were resources used in the best possible way during the information revolution? Did Intel make the best possible chips and sell them in the right quantities for the right prices? Or was the quality of the chips too low and the price too high? And what about Microsoft? Did Bill Gates have to be paid almost $50 billion to produce the successive generations of Windows and Word? Were these programs developed in the social interest?

### Disappearing Rainforests and Fish Stocks

Tropical rainforests in South America, Africa, and Asia support the lives of 30 million species of plants, animals, and insects—approaching 50 percent of all species on the planet. The Amazon rainforest alone converts about 1 trillion pounds of carbon dioxide into oxygen each year. These rainforests also provide us with the ingredients for many goods including soaps, mouthwashes, shampoos, food preservatives, rubber, nuts, and fruits.

Yet tropical rainforests cover less than two percent of the Earth's surface and are heading for extinction. Logging, cattle ranching, mining, oil extraction, hydroelectric dams, and subsistence farming are destroying the equivalent of two football fields every second, or an area larger than New York City every day. At the current rate of destruction, almost all the tropical rainforest ecosystems will be gone by 2030.

*Logging is destroying the world's rainforests ...*

A similar problem confronts the world's fish resources. Advances in fishing technology have lowered the cost of fishing and increased the daily catch. Every day, fishing boats scoop up 250,000 tons of fish. Almost 50 percent of the catch is wasted.

Of the 267 fish species used as food, 70 percent are overfished, which means that they are heading toward extinction. Some species such as Atlantic Cod and Blue Fin Tuna are near extinction. The stock of Atlantic Cod has fallen by 90 percent in the past 45 years. Fish can be farmed. But fish farming brings its own problems of waste management and pollution.

*... and overfishing is depleting the world's fish stocks.*

Each one of us makes economic choices that are in our self-interest to consume products, some of which are destroying our rainforests and others of which are killing our fish resources. But it seems that our self-interested choices are damaging the social interest. If they are, what can be done to change the incentives we face and change our behavior?

### Water Shortages

The world is awash with water—it is our most abundant resource. But 97 percent of it is seawater. Another 2 percent is frozen in glaciers and ice. The 1 percent of the Earth's water that is available for human consumption would be sufficient if only it were in the right places. Finland, Canada, and a few other places have more water than they can use, but Australia, Africa, and California (and many other places) could use much more water than they can get.

Some people pay less for water than others. California farmers, for example, pay less than California households. Some of the highest prices for water are faced by people in the poorest countries who must either buy from a water dealer's truck or carry water in buckets over many miles.

*Water is abundant but clean water is scarce.*

In the United States, water is provided by public enterprises. In the United Kingdom, private companies deliver the water.

In India and Bangladesh, plenty of rain falls, but it falls during a short wet season and the rest of the year is dry. Dams could help to reduce the shortage in the dry season but too few have been built in those countries.

Are we managing our water resources properly? Are the decisions that each of us makes in our self-interest to use, conserve, and transport water also in the social interest?

*Human activity is raising the Earth's temperature.*

## Climate Change

The Earth is getting hotter and the ice at the two poles is melting. Since the late nineteenth century, the Earth's surface temperature has increased about 1 degree Fahrenheit, and close to a half of that increase occurred over the past 25 years. While these changes are small, particularly when viewed against the temperature fluctuations associated with Ice Ages, they are large enough to have a lot of people worried.

Most climate scientists believe that the current warming has come at least in part from human economic activity—from self-interested choices—and that, if left unchecked, the warming will bring large future economic costs.

As part of an attempt to slow global warming, an international meeting in Japan in 1997 led to the Kyoto Protocol, an agreement that seeks legally binding emissions cuts for the industrialized nations. But the Protocol does not impose limits on the poorer developing nations. Almost the entire world signed onto Kyoto. But the United States and Australia refused to do so. They argue that the agreement does too little to address the global warming problem and that their own independent efforts will make a more effective contribution.

Are the choices that each of us makes to use energy damaging the social interest? What needs to be done to make our choices serve the social interest? Would the United States signing onto the Kyoto Protocol serve the social interest? What other measures must be introduced?

*A Social Security time bomb is ticking as benefits grow faster than contributions.*

## A Social Security Time Bomb

Every year since 2001, the U.S. government has run a budget deficit. On the average, the government has spent $1.6 billion a day more than it has received in taxes. The government's debt has increased each day by that amount. Over the nine years from 2001 through 2009, government debt has increased by $5.3 trillion. Your personal share of this debt is $18,000.

Also, since 2000, Americans bought goods and services from the rest of the world in excess of what foreigners bought from the United States to the tune of $4.8 trillion. To pay for these goods and services, Americans borrowed from the rest of the world.

These large deficits are just the beginning of an even bigger problem. From about 2019 onwards, the retirement and health-care benefits to which older Americans are entitled are going to cost increasingly more than the current Social Security taxes can cover. With no changes in taxes or benefit rates, the deficit and debt will swell ever higher.

Deficits and the debts they create cannot persist indefinitely, and debts must somehow be repaid. They will most likely be repaid by you, not by your parents. When we make our voter choices and our choices to buy from or sell to the rest of the world, we pursue our self-interest. Do our choices damage the social interest?

## CHECKPOINT 1.1

**Define economics and explain the kinds of questions that economists try to answer.**

myeconlab

Work these problems in Study Plan 1.1 to get instant feedback.

### Practice Problems

1. Economics studies choices that arise from one fact. What is that fact?
2. Provide three examples of wants in the United States today that are especially pressing but not satisfied.
3. Here are three news headlines. Find in these headlines examples of the *what*, *how*, and *for whom* questions: "With more research, we will cure cancer"; "A good education is the right of every child"; "The government must cut its budget deficit by raising taxes."
4. How does a new Starbucks in Beijing, China, influence self-interest and the social interest?
5. How does Facebook influence self-interest and the social interest?
6. **Job losses slow dramatically**

   In May, 2009, 345,000 U.S. jobs disappeared, fewer than the 504,000 jobs that disappeared in April. The jobs lost in May were spread across the economy: in manufacturing, construction, retail, and professional services. But 9.1 million part-time workers said that they are working part-time jobs because they could not find full-time work or their employers had shortened their hours.

   Source: CNN Money, June 5, 2009

   Describe the change in May 2009 in *What* and *For whom* goods and services were produced in the United States. Is the decision to work part-time a decision made in self-interest or the social interest? Is an employer's decision to shorten work hours a decision made in self-interest or the social interest?

### Guided Solutions to Practice Problems

1. The fact is scarcity—human wants exceed the resources available.
2. Security from international terrorism, cleaner air in our cities, better public schools. (You can perhaps think of some more.)
3. More research is a *how* question, and a cure for cancer is a *what* question. Good education is a *what* question, and every child is a *for whom* question. The government's raising taxes is a *for whom* question.
4. Decisions made by Starbucks are in Starbucks' self-interest but they serve the self-interest of its customers and so contribute to the social interest.
5. Facebook serves the self-interest of its investors, users, and advertisers. It also serves the social interest by enabling people to share information.
6. With job losses spread across the economy, the decrease in goods and services produced by most sectors slowed. So the change in What goods and services were produced was widespread. For whom goods and services were produced also changed. Job losers and new part-time workers earned lower incomes than in April, so they received fewer goods and services. A person's decision to work part-time is usually a self-interested decision—they want to earn an income. The employer's decision is in self-interest if the decision is to "save his or her own job," but if it is "to share" the job loss, the decision might be in the social interest.

## 1.2 THE ECONOMIC WAY OF THINKING

The definition of economics and the kinds of questions that economists try to answer give you a flavor of the scope of economics. But they don't tell you how economists *think* about these questions and how they go about seeking answers to them. You're now going to see how economists approach their work.

We'll break this task into three parts. First, we'll explain the core ideas that economists constantly and repeatedly use to frame their view of the world. These ideas will soon have you thinking like an economist. Second, we'll explain the distinction between the micro and macro views of the economic world. Finally, we'll look at economics both as a social science and as a policy tool that governments, businesses, and *you* can use.

### Core Economic Ideas

Five core ideas summarize the economic approach or economic way of thinking about the choices that must be made to cope with scarcity:

- People make *rational choices* by comparing costs and benefits.
- *Cost* is what you *must* give up to get something.
- *Benefit* is what you gain when you get something and is measured by what you *are willing to* give up to get it.
- A rational choice is made on the *margin.*
- Choices respond to *incentives.*

### Rational Choice

**Rational choice**
A choice that uses the available resources to best achieve the objective of the person making the choice.

The most basic idea of economics is that in making choices, people act rationally. A **rational choice** is one that uses the available resources to best achieve the objective of the person making the choice.

Only the wants and preferences of the person making a choice are relevant to determine its rationality. For example, you might like chocolate ice cream more than vanilla ice cream, but your friend prefers vanilla. So it is rational for you to choose chocolate and for your friend to choose vanilla.

A rational choice might turn out not to have been the best choice after the event. A farmer might decide to plant wheat rather than soybeans. Then, when the crop comes to market, the price of soybeans might be much higher than the price of wheat. The farmer's choice was rational when it was made, but subsequent events made it less profitable than the alternative choice.

The idea of rational choice provides an answer to the first economic question: What goods and services will get produced and in what quantities? The answer is: Those that people rationally choose to buy.

But how do people choose rationally? Why have most people chosen to buy Microsoft's Windows operating system rather than another? Why do more people today choose to drink bottled water and sports energy drinks than did in the past? Why has the U.S. government chosen to fund the building of an interstate highway system and not an interstate high-speed railroad system?

We make rational choices by comparing *costs* and *benefits.* But economists think about costs and benefits in a special and revealing way. Let's look at the economic concepts of cost and benefit.

## Cost: What You *Must* Give Up

The **opportunity cost** of something is the best thing that you must give up to get it. No matter what you choose to do, you make a choice among many alternatives. But only one of these alternatives is the *best alternative* that you gave up. And it is the best alternative—the highest-valued alternative forgone—that is the opportunity cost of the thing that you choose to do.

**Opportunity cost**
The opportunity cost of something is the best thing you *must* give up to get it.

We use the term *opportunity cost* to emphasize that when we make a choice in the face of scarcity, we give up an opportunity to do something else. You can quit school right now, or you can remain in school. Suppose that if you quit school, the best job you can get is at FedEx Kinko's, where you can earn $10,000 during the year. The opportunity cost of remaining in school includes the things that you could have bought with this $10,000. The opportunity cost also includes the value of the leisure time that you must forgo to study.

Opportunity cost of the thing you get is *only* the best alternative forgone. It does not include all the expenditures that you make. For example, your expenditure on tuition is part of the opportunity cost of being in school. But your meal plan and rent are not. Whether you're in school or working, you must eat and have somewhere to live. So the cost of your school meal plan and your rent are *not* part of the opportunity cost of being in school.

Also, past expenditures that cannot be reversed are not part of opportunity cost. Suppose you've paid your term's tuition and it is nonrefundable. If you now contemplate quitting school, the paid tuition is irrelevant. It is called a sunk cost. A **sunk cost** is a previously incurred and irreversible cost. Whether you remain in school or quit school, the tuition that you've paid is not part of the opportunity cost of remaining in school.

**Sunk cost**
A previously incurred and irreversible cost.

## Benefit: Gain Measured by What You *Are Willing to* Give Up

The **benefit** of something is the gain or pleasure that it brings. Benefit is how a person *feels* about something. For example, you might be anxious to get the latest game for Nintendo Wii. It will bring you a large benefit. And you might have almost no interest in a Yo Yo Ma CD of Vivaldi's cello concertos. It will bring you a small benefit.

**Benefit**
The benefit of something is the gain or pleasure that it brings.

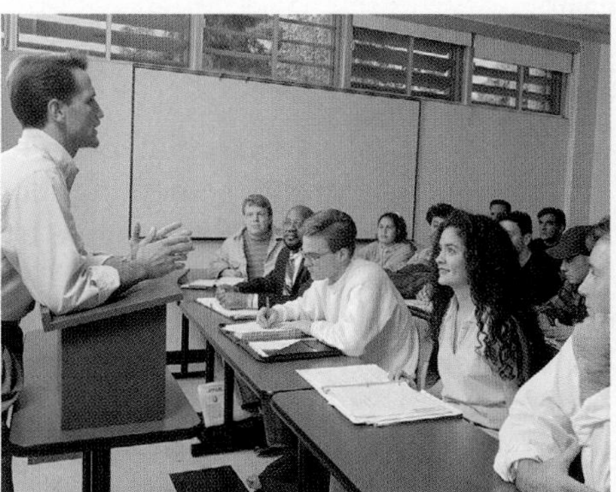

*For these students, the opportunity cost of being in school is worth bearing.*

*For the full-time fast-food worker, the opportunity cost of remaining in school is too high.*

Economists measure the benefit of something by what a person *is willing to* give up to get it. You can buy a DVD or magazines. The magazines that you are willing to give up to get a DVD measure the benefit that you get from a DVD.

## ■ On the Margin

**Margin**
A choice on the margin is a choice that is made by comparing *all* the relevant alternatives systematically and incrementally.

Margin means "border" or "edge." You can think of a choice on the margin as one that adjusts the borders or edges of a plan to determine the best course of action. Making a choice on the **margin** means comparing *all* the relevant alternatives systematically and incrementally.

For example, you must choose how to divide the next hour between studying and texting your friends. To make this choice, you must evaluate the costs and benefits of the alternative possible allocations of your next hour. You choose on the margin by considering whether you will be better off or worse off if you spend an extra few minutes studying or an extra few minutes texting.

The margin might involve a small change, as it does when you're deciding how to divide an hour between studying and texting friends. Or it might involve a large change, as it does, for example, when you're deciding whether to remain in school for another year. Attending school for part of the year is no better (and might be worse) than not attending at all. So you likely will want to commit the entire year to school or to something else. But you still choose on the margin. It is just that the marginal change is now a change for one year rather than a change for a few minutes.

### Marginal Cost

**Marginal cost**
The opportunity cost that arises from a one-unit increase in an activity. The marginal cost of something is what you *must* give up to get *one additional* unit of it.

The opportunity cost of a one-unit increase in an activity is called **marginal cost**. Marginal cost of something is what you *must* give up to get *one additional* unit of it. Think about your marginal cost of going to the movies for a third time in a week. Your marginal cost of seeing the movie is what you must give up to see that one additional movie. It is *not* what you give up to see all three movies. The reason is that you've already given up something for two movies, so you don't count this cost as resulting from the decision to see the third movie.

The marginal cost of any activity increases as you do more of it. You know that going to the movies decreases your study time and lowers your grade. Suppose that seeing a second movie in a week lowers your grade by five percentage points. Seeing a third movie will lower your grade by more than five percentage points. Your marginal cost of moviegoing is increasing.

### Marginal Benefit

**Marginal benefit**
The benefit that arises from a one-unit increase in an activity. The marginal benefit of something is *measured* by what you *are willing* to give up to get *one additional* unit of it.

The benefit of a one-unit increase in an activity is called **marginal benefit**. Marginal benefit is what you gain when you get *one more* unit of something. But the marginal benefit of something is *measured* by what you *are willing* to give up to get that *one additional* unit of it.

A fundamental feature of marginal benefit is that it diminishes. Think about your marginal benefit from movies. If you've been studying hard and haven't seen a movie this week, your marginal benefit from seeing your next movie is large. But if you've been on a movie binge this week, you now want a break and your marginal benefit from seeing your next movie is small.

Because the marginal benefit of a movie decreases as you see more movies, you are willing to give up less to see one more movie. For example, you know that going to the movies decreases your study time and lowers your grade. You pay for seeing a movie with a lower grade. You might be willing to give up ten percentage points to see your first movie in a week, but you won't be willing to take such a big hit on your grade to see a second movie in a week. Your willingness to pay to see a movie is decreasing.

### Making a Rational Choice

So, will you go to the movies for that third time in a week? If the marginal cost is less than the marginal benefit, your rational choice will be to see the third movie. If the marginal cost exceeds the marginal benefit, your rational choice will be to spend the evening studying. As long as the marginal benefit exceeds or equals the marginal cost, our choice is rational and our scarce resources are used to make us as well off as possible.

## Responding to Incentives

The choices we make depend on the incentives we face. An **incentive** is a reward or a penalty—a "carrot" or a "stick"—that encourages or discourages an action. We respond positively to "carrots" and negatively to "sticks." The carrots are marginal benefits; the sticks are marginal costs. A change in marginal benefit or a change in marginal cost changes the incentives that we face and leads us to change our actions.

**Incentive**
A reward or a penalty—a "carrot" or a "stick"—that encourages or discourages an action.

Most students believe that the payoff from studying just before a test is greater than the payoff from studying a month before a test. In other words, as a test date approaches, the marginal benefit of studying increases and the incentive to study becomes stronger. For this reason, we observe an increase in study time and a decrease in leisure pursuits during the last few days before a test. And the more important the test, the greater is this effect.

A change in marginal cost also changes incentives. For example, suppose that last week, you found your course work easy and you scored 100 percent on your practice quizzes. You figured that the marginal cost of taking an evening off to enjoy a movie was low and that your grade on the next test would not suffer, so you had a movie feast. But this week the going has gotten tough. You're just not getting it, and your practice test scores are low. If you take off even one evening, your grade on next week's test will suffer. The marginal cost of seeing a movie is now high so you decide to give the movies a miss.

A central idea of economics is that by observing *changes in incentives*, we can predict how *choices change*.

*Changes in marginal benefit and marginal cost change the incentive to study or to enjoy a movie.*

## EYE on WALL STREET

### Did Greedy Wall Street Bankers Cause the Global Slump?

The President has expressed outrage at the bonuses paid to the Wall Street bankers at the center of the economic slump. Isn't Wall Street greed the source of our economic problems?

Most economists would answer "No." Greed is an expression (an extreme one) of self-interest. We all act in our self-interest. Greed is persistent: It isn't something that comes and goes, and regulated greed can be a force for good.

The problem in recent years is that financial technology has outpaced financial regulation. A challenge for the President's economic team is to figure out and sell to Congress the regulations that will harness greed and restore financial strength and stability.

President Obama and his economic team:
Christina Romer Timothy Geithner Larry Summers

## The Micro and Macro Views of the World

Economics has two major parts: microeconomics (or micro) and macroeconomics (or macro).

### Microeconomics

**Microeconomics**
The study of the choices that individuals and businesses make and the way these choices interact and are influenced by governments.

**Microeconomics** is the study of the choices that individuals and businesses make and the way these choices interact and are influenced by governments. Some examples of microeconomic questions are: Will you buy a flat screen or traditional television? Will Nintendo sell more units of Wii if it cuts the price? Will a cut in the income tax rate encourage people to work longer hours? Will a hike in the gas tax lead to more hybrid or smaller automobiles? Are MP3 downloads killing CDs?

### Macroeconomics

**Macroeconomics**
The study of the aggregate (or total) effects on the national economy and the global economy of the choices that individuals, businesses, and governments make.

**Macroeconomics** is the study of the aggregate (or total) effects on the national economy and the global economy of the choices that individuals, businesses, and governments make. Some examples of macroeconomic questions are: Why did production and jobs expand so slowly in the United States in the early 2000s? Why are incomes growing much faster in China and India than in the United States? Why did production and incomes stagnate in Japan in the 1990s? Why are Americans borrowing more than $2 billion a day from the rest of the world?

## Economics as Social Science

As social scientists, economists seek to discover how the economic world works. In pursuit of this goal, like all scientists, they distinguish between two types of statements:

- Positive statements
- Normative statements

### Positive Statements

*Positive* statements are about what *is.* They say what is currently believed about the way the world operates. A positive statement might be right or wrong, but we can test a positive statement by checking it against the facts. "Our planet is warming because of the amount of coal that we're burning" is a positive statement. "A rise in the minimum wage will bring more teenage unemployment" is another positive statement. Each statement might be right or wrong, and it can be tested.

A central task of economists is to test positive statements about how the economic world works and to weed out those that are wrong. Economics first got off the ground in the late 1700s (see *Eye on the Past* on p. 17), so economics is a young subject compared with, for example, physics, and much remains to be discovered.

### Normative Statements

*Normative* statements are statements about what *ought to be.* These statements depend on values and cannot be tested. The statement "We ought to cut back on our use of coal" is a normative statement. "The minimum wage should not be increased" is another normative statement. You may agree or disagree with either of these statements, but you can't test them. They express an opinion, but they don't assert a fact that can be checked. They are not economics.

### Unscrambling Cause and Effect

Economists are especially interested in positive statements about cause and effect. Are computers getting cheaper because people are buying them in greater quantities? Or are people buying computers in greater quantities because they are getting cheaper? Or is some third factor causing both the price of a computer to fall and the quantity of computers bought to increase? These are examples of positive statements that economists want to test, but such testing can be difficult.

The central idea that economists (and all scientists) use to unscramble cause and effect is *ceteris paribus.* ***Ceteris paribus*** is a Latin term (often abbreviated as *cet. par.*) that means "other things being equal" or "if all other relevant things remain the same." Ensuring that other things are equal is crucial in many activities, including athletic events. All successful attempts to make scientific progress use this device. By changing one factor at a time and holding all the other relevant factors constant, we isolate the factor of interest and are able to investigate its effects in the clearest possible way.

***Ceteris paribus***
Other things remaining the same (often abbreviated as *cet. par.*).

*In track and field, other things are equal.*

In economics, we observe the outcomes of the simultaneous operation of many factors. Consequently, it is hard to sort out the effects of each individual factor and to compare the effects with what a model predicts. To cope with this problem, economists use natural experiments, statistical investigations, and economic experiments.

A natural experiment is a situation that arises in the ordinary course of economic life in which the one factor of interest is different and other things are equal (or similar). For example, Canada has higher unemployment benefits than the United States, but the people in the two nations are similar. So to study the effect of unemployment benefits on the unemployment rate, economists might compare the United States with Canada.

**Correlation**
The tendency for the values of two variables to move together in a predictable and related way.

A statistical investigation looks for a **correlation**—a tendency for the values of two variables to move together (either in the same direction or in opposite directions) in a predictable and related way. For example, cigarette smoking and lung cancer are correlated. Sometimes a correlation shows a causal influence of one variable on the other. For example, smoking causes lung cancer. But sometimes the direction of causation is hard to determine.

An economic experiment puts people in a decision-making situation and varies the influence of one factor at a time to discover how they respond.

## Economics as Policy Tool

Economics is useful, and you don't have to be an economist to think like one and to use the insights of economics as a policy tool. The subject provides a way of approaching problems in all aspects of our lives:

- Personal
- Business
- Government

### Personal Economic Policy

Should you take out a student loan? Should you get a weekend job? Should you buy a used car or a new one? Should you rent an apartment or take out a loan and buy a condominium? Should you pay off your credit card balance or make just the minimum payment? How should you allocate your time between study, working for a wage, caring for family members, and having fun? How should you allocate your time between studying economics and your other subjects? Should you leave school after getting a bachelor's degree or should you go for a masters or a professional qualification?

All these questions involve a marginal benefit and a marginal cost. Although some of the numbers might be hard to pin down, you will make more solid decisions if you approach these questions with the tools of economics.

### Business Economic Policy

Should Sony make only flat panel televisions and stop making conventional ones? Should Texaco get more oil and gas from the Gulf of Mexico or from Alaska? Should Palm outsource its online customer services to India or run the operation from California? Should Marvel Studios produce *Spider-Man 4*, a sequel to *Spider-Man 3*? Can Microsoft compete with Google in the search engine business? Can eBay compete with the surge of new Internet auction services? Is Alex Rodriguez really worth $33,000,000 to the New York Yankees?

Like personal economic questions, these business questions involve the evaluation of a marginal benefit and a marginal cost. Some of the questions require a broader investigation of the interactions of individuals and businesses. But again, by approaching these questions with the tools of economics and by hiring economists as advisers, businesses can make better decisions.

## EYE on the PAST

### Adam Smith and the Birth of Economics as a Social Science

Many people had written about economics before Adam Smith, but he made economics a social science.

Born in 1723 in Kirkcaldy, a small fishing town near Edinburgh, Scotland, Smith was the only child of the town's customs officer. Lured from his professorship (he was a full professor at 28) by a wealthy Scottish duke who gave him a pension of £300 a year—ten times the average income at that time—Smith devoted ten years to writing his masterpiece, *An Inquiry into the Nature and Causes of the Wealth of Nations,* published in 1776.

Why, Adam Smith asked in that book, are some nations wealthy while others are poor? He was pondering these questions at the height of the Industrial Revolution. During these years, new technologies were applied to the manufacture of textiles, iron, transportation, and agriculture.

Adam Smith answered his questions by emphasizing the role of the division of labor and free markets. To illustrate his argument, he used the example of a pin factory. He guessed that one person, using the hand tools available in the 1770s, might make 20 pins a day. Yet, he observed, by using those same hand tools but breaking the process into a number of individually small operations in which people specialize—by the division of labor—ten people could make a staggering 48,000 pins a day. One draws out the wire, another straightens it, a third cuts it, a fourth points it, a fifth grinds it. Three specialists make the head, and a fourth attaches it. Finally, the pin is polished and packaged.

But a large market is needed to support the division of labor: One factory employing ten workers would need to sell more than 15 million pins a year to stay in business!

### Government Economic Policy

How can California balance its budget? Should the federal government cut taxes or raise them? How can the tax system be simplified? Should people be permitted to invest their Social Security money in stocks that they pick themselves? Should Medicaid and Medicare be extended to the entire population? Should there be a special tax to penalize corporations that send jobs overseas? Should cheap foreign imports of furniture and textiles be limited? Should the farms that grow tomatoes and sugar beets receive a subsidy? Should water be transported from Washington and Oregon to California?

These government policy questions call for decisions that involve the evaluation of a marginal benefit and a marginal cost and an investigation of the interactions of individuals and businesses. Yet again, by approaching these questions with the tools of economics, governments can make better decisions.

Notice that all the policy questions we've just posed involve a blend of the positive and the normative. Economics can't help with the normative part—the objective. But for a given objective, economics provides a method of evaluating alternative solutions. That method is to evaluate the marginal benefits and marginal costs and to find the solution that brings the greatest available gain.

Work these problems in Study Plan 1.2 to get instant feedback.

**Explain the core ideas that define the economic way of thinking.**

## Practice Problems

Every week, Kate plays tennis for two hours, and her grade on each math test is 70 percent. Last week, after playing for two hours, Kate considered playing for another hour. She decided to play for another hour and cut her study time by one hour. But last week, her math grade fell to 60 percent. Use this information to work Problems **1** to **5**.

1. What was Kate's opportunity cost of the third hour of tennis?
2. Given that Kate played the third hour, what can you conclude about her marginal benefit and marginal cost of the second hour of tennis?
3. Was Kate's decision to play the third hour of tennis rational?
4. Did Kate make her decision on the margin?
5. Check the local media and find an example of a positive statement and an example of a normative statement.
6. Provide two examples of positive statements and two examples of normative statements.
7. Provide an example of economics as a personal policy tool.

## Guided Solutions to Practice Problems

1. Kate's opportunity cost of the third hour of tennis was the drop in her grade of ten-percentage points.
2. The marginal benefit from the second hour of tennis must have exceeded the marginal cost of the second hour because Kate chose to play the third hour.
3. If marginal benefit exceeded marginal cost, Kate's decision was rational.
4. Kate made her decision on the margin because she considered the benefit and cost of one additional hour.
5. "The Butterfly House must be kept near 80 degrees at all times, or butterflies won't fly" is a positive statement because it can be tested against the facts.

   "Flex-time, which allows employees to shift their work hours over a two-week period, will allow workers to better meet family needs" is a normative statement because it cannot be tested.
6. Positive statements are statements that can be tested by looking at the data. Examples are (1) On 7 June 2009, the price of gas is highest in Michigan and lowest in South Carolina. (2) College tuition in 2010 will be the same as in 2009.

   Normative statements are statements that cannot be tested: (1) Most cities don't have enough open green space and trees. (2) The workweek ought to be cut to 30 hours for all workers.
7. You are offered the chance to take a weekend cruise at a reduced price. Should you take it? What is the opportunity cost of the cruise? What is the best alternative you would forgo if you took the cruise? Perhaps you have a test next week. If you took the cruise, you'd forgo valuable study time and possibly receive a lower grade. What would be the marginal benefit from the cruise? Which is larger: Opportunity cost or marginal benefit?

# CHAPTER SUMMARY

## Key Points

**1 Define economics and explain the kinds of questions that economists try to answer.**

- Economics is the social science that studies the choices that we make as we cope with scarcity and the incentives that influence and reconcile our choices.
- The first big question of economics is: How do the choices that people make end up determining *what, how,* and *for whom* goods and services are produced?
- The second big question is: When do choices made in the pursuit of *self-interest* also promote the *social interest*?

**2 Explain the core ideas that define the economic way of thinking.**

- Five core ideas define the economic way of thinking:
  1. People make *rational* choices by comparing costs and benefits.
  2. Cost is what you *must* give up to get something.
  3. Benefit is what you gain when you get something and is measured by what you *are willing to* give up to get it.
  4. A rational choice is made on the *margin.*
  5. Choices respond to *incentives.*
- Microeconomics is the study of individual choices and interactions, and macroeconomics is the study of the national economy and global economy.
- Economists try to understand how the economic world works by testing positive statements using natural experiments, statistical investigations, and economic experiments.
- Economics is a tool for personal, business, and government decisions.

## Key Terms

Benefit, 11
*Ceteris paribus,* 15
Correlation, 16
Economics, 3
Goods and services, 3
Incentive, 13
Macroeconomics, 14
Margin, 12
Marginal benefit, 12
Marginal cost, 12
Microeconomics, 14
Opportunity cost, 11
Rational choice, 10
Scarcity, 2
Self-interest, 4
Social interest, 4
Sunk cost, 11

Work these problems in Chapter 1 Study Plan to get instant feedback.

# CHAPTER CHECKPOINT

## Study Plan Problems and Applications

1. Provide three examples of scarcity that illustrate why even the 691 billionaires in the world face scarcity.

Use the following information to work Problems 2 to 5.

*Spider-Man 3* was the most successful movie of 2007, with world-wide box office receipts of $891 million. The movie might have cost more to make than any film in Hollywood history. Sony put the budget at $260 million, with additional marketing costs of about $120 million. Creating a successful movie brings pleasure to millions, generates work for thousands, and makes a few rich.

2. What contribution does a movie like *Spider-Man 3* make to coping with scarcity? When you buy a ticket to see a movie in a theater, are you buying a good or a service?
3. Who decides whether a movie is going to be a blockbuster? How do you think the creation of a blockbuster movie influences what, how, and for whom goods and services are produced?
4. What are some of the marginal costs and marginal benefits that the producer of a movie faces?
5. Suppose that Tobey Maguire had been offered a bigger and better part in another movie and that to hire him for *Spider-Man 3,* the producer had to double Tobey's pay. What incentives would have changed? How might the changed incentives have changed the choices that people made?
6. Arnold Schwarzenegger chose politics over making movies such as a sequel to *Terminator 3.* In making his decision to run for governor of California, did he make his choice on the margin? Was his choice rational? Did he face an opportunity cost? If so, what might have been some of the components of his opportunity cost?
7. Pam, Pru, and Pat are deciding how they will celebrate the New Year. Pam prefers to take a cruise, is happy to go to Hawaii, but does not want to go skiing. Pru prefers to go skiing, is happy to go to Hawaii, but does not want to take a cruise. Pat prefers to go to Hawaii or to take a cruise but does not want to go skiing. Their decision is to go to Hawaii. Is this decision rational? What is the opportunity cost of the trip to Hawaii for each of them? What is the benefit that each gets?
8. Label each of the news items as a positive or a normative statement:
   - The Poor Pay Too Much for Housing
   - The Number of Farms Decreased over the Last 50 Years
   - Pets Killed for Food in Zimbabwe
   - Imports from China Swamping U.S. Department Stores
   - Rural Population Constant over the Past Decade
9. Explain the *ceteris paribus* assumption and why economists use it. Give an example of when you would use the *ceteris paribus* assumption.

## Instructor Assignable Problems and Applications

Your instructor can assign these problems as homework, a quiz, or a test in **MyEconLab**.

1. Suppose a person gets a loan from a bank to buy a new home.
   - Are the borrower and the bank pursuing self-interest, the social interest, or both?
   - If the borrower can't afford to keep up the payments and defaults, is the borrower pursuing self-interest, the social interest, or both?
   - If the bank forecloses on the delinquent borrower, is the bank pursuing self-interest, the social interest, or both?
2. On Friday May 14, 2009, the following headlines appeared in *The Wall Street Journal*. Classify each headline as a signal that the news article is about a microeconomic topic or a macroeconomic topic. Explain your answers.
   - US Set to Rethink Fed's Role
   - Wal-Mart Makes Electronics Push
   - VW, Porsche Take Break in Talks
   - Economists Foresee Protracted Recovery
3. Think about each of the following situations and explain how they affect incentives and might change the choices that people make:
   - A hurricane hits Central Florida.
   - The World Series begins tonight but a thunderstorm warning is in effect for the area in which the stadium is located.
   - The price of a personal computer falls to $50.
   - Political instability in the Middle East sends the price of gas to $5 a gallon.
4. Think about the following news items and label each as involving a *what, how,* or *for whom* question:
   - Today, most stores use computers to keep their inventory records, whereas 20 years ago most stores used paper records.
   - Health-care professionals and drug companies recommend that Medicaid drug rebates be made available to everyone in need.
   - A doubling of the gas tax might lead to a better public transit system.
5. Your school decides to increase the intake of new students next year. To make its decision, what economic concepts would it have considered? Would the school have used the "economic way of thinking" in reaching its decision? Would the school have made its decision on the margin?
6. Provide two examples of monetary and two examples of non-monetary incentives, a carrot and a stick of each, that government policies use to influence behavior.
7. Does the decision to make a blockbuster movie mean that some other more desirable activities get fewer resources than they deserve? Is your answer a positive or a normative? Explain your answer.
8. Provide two examples of economics being used as a tool by each of a student, a business, and a government. Classify your examples as dealing with microeconomic topics and macroeconomic topics.
9. Find in the media one example of economics being used as a tool by each of a person, a business, and a government to make a decision.

Use the following information to work Problems 10 to 16.

**Hundreds line up for 5 p.m. Eminem ticket giveaway**

Hundreds of Eminem fans lined up today for a chance to get a free ticket to the Detroit rapper's secret concert. Despite the fact that tickets would not be released before 5 p.m., people lined up all day.

Source: *Detroit Free Press*, May 18, 2009

Eminem announced on MySpace that he planned to release his new album *Relapse*— first album in 5 years—on the same day as his free concert in Detroit.

10. Eminem is giving away tickets to his show in a 1,500-seat theater in Detroit. What is free and what is scarce? Explain your answer.
11. What do you think Eminem's incentive is to give a free show?
12. Did Eminem make his decision to give a free concert in self-interest or in the social interest? Explain.
13. Because all the tickets were free, was the marginal benefit from the concert zero? Explain your answer.
14. For the people who scored tickets, is the concert really free? If not, explain why not?
15. Did the people who lined up but missed out on getting tickets incur any costs? What sort of a cost? Explain.
16. Was Eminem's decision to give a free concert a rational choice?

Use the following information to work Problems 17 to 21.

**Report: Obama will drive up miles-per-gallon requirements**

The Obama administration will announce sweeping revision of auto-emission and fuel-economy standards in the same package, which will require automakers to boost overall fuel economy to 35.5 miles per gallon by 2016, notching up 5% each year from 2012, to limit the amount of carbon dioxide cars can emit.

Source: *USA Today*, May 18, 2009

17. What are two benefits of the new miles-per-gallon requirements?
18. What are two benefits of the new auto-emission standards?
19. Are the benefits you listed in Problems 17 and 18 benefits in someone's self-interest or in the social interest?
20. What costs associated with the new miles-per-gallon requirements arise from decisions made in self-interest and in the social interest?
21. What costs associated with the new auto-emission standards arise from decisions made in self-interest and in the social interest?

# APPENDIX: MAKING AND USING GRAPHS

**When you have completed your study of this appendix, you will be able to**

1 Interpret a scatter diagram, a time-series graph, and a cross-section graph.

2 Interpret the graphs used in economic models.

3 Define and calculate slope.

4 Graph relationships among more than two variables.

## Basic Idea

A graph represents a quantity as a distance and enables us to visualize the relationship between two variables. To make a graph, we set two lines called *axes* perpendicular to each other, like those in Figure A1.1. The vertical line is called the $y$-axis, and the horizontal line is called the $x$-axis. The common zero point is called the *origin.* In Figure A1.1, the $x$-axis measures temperature in degrees Fahrenheit. A movement to the right shows an increase in temperature, and a movement to the left shows a decrease in temperature. The $y$-axis represents ice cream consumption, measured in gallons per day.

To make a graph, we need a value of the variable on the $x$-axis and a corresponding value of the variable on the $y$-axis. For example, if the temperature is 40°F, ice cream consumption is 5 gallons a day at point $A$ in Figure A1.1. If the temperature is 80°F, ice cream consumption is 20 gallons a day at point $B$ in Figure A1.1. Graphs like that in Figure A1.1 can be used to show any type of quantitative data on two variables.

**FIGURE A1.1**

Making a Graph

myeconlab Animation

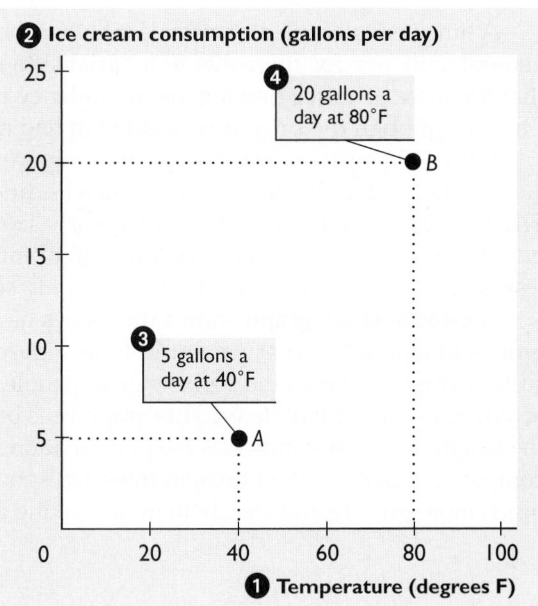


All graphs have axes that measure quantities as distances.

1. The horizontal axis ($x$-axis) measures temperature in degrees Fahrenheit. A movement to the right shows an increase in temperature.
2. The vertical axis ($y$-axis) measures ice cream consumption in gallons per day. A movement upward shows an increase in ice cream consumption.
3. Point $A$ shows that 5 gallons of ice cream are consumed on a day when the temperature is 40°F.
4. Point $B$ shows that 20 gallons of ice cream are consumed on a day when the temperature is 80°F.

## Interpreting Data Graphs

**Scatter diagram**
A graph of the value of one variable against the value of another variable.

A **scatter diagram** is a graph of the value of one variable against the value of another variable. It is used to reveal whether a relationship exists between two variables and to describe the relationship. Figure A1.2 shows two examples.

Figure A1.2(a) shows the relationship between expenditure and income. Each point shows expenditure per person and income per person in the United States in a given year from 1999 to 2009. The points are "scattered" within the graph. The label on each point shows its year. The point marked 04 shows that in 2004, income per person was $28,990 and expenditure per person was $27,400. This scatter diagram reveals that as income increases, expenditure also increases.

Figure A1.2(b) shows the relationship between the percentage of Americans who own a cell phone and the average monthly cell phone bill. This scatter diagram reveals that as the cost of using a cell phone falls, the number of cell phones increases.

**Time-series graph**
A graph that measures time on the $x$-axis and the variable or variables in which we are interested on the $y$-axis.

A **time-series graph** measures time (for example, months or years) on the $x$-axis and the variable or variables in which we are interested on the $y$-axis. Figure A1.2(c) shows an example. In this graph, time (on the $x$-axis) is measured in years, which run from 1979 to 2009. The variable that we are interested in is the price of coffee, and it is measured on the $y$-axis.

A time-series graph conveys an enormous amount of information quickly and easily, as this example illustrates. It shows when the value is

1. High or low. When the line is a long way from the $x$-axis, the price is high, as it was in 2008. When the line is close to the $x$-axis, the price is low, as it was in 1993.
2. Rising or falling. When the line slopes upward, as in 1994, the price is rising. When the line slopes downward, as in 1998, the price is falling.
3. Rising or falling quickly or slowly. If the line is steep, then the price is rising or falling quickly. If the line is not steep, the price is rising or falling slowly. For example, the price rose quickly in 1994 and slowly in 1984. The price fell quickly in 1998 and slowly in 2003.

**Trend**
A general tendency for the value of a variable to rise or fall over time.

A time-series graph also reveals whether the variable has a trend. A **trend** is a general tendency for the value of a variable to rise or fall over time. You can see that the price of coffee had a general tendency to rise from 1979 to the late 1990s. That is, although the price rose and fell, it had a general tendency to rise.

With a time-series graph, we can compare different periods quickly. Figure A1.2(c) shows that the period after 1990 was different from the period before 1990. The price of coffee jumped during the early 1990s and remained high for a number of years. This graph conveys a wealth of information, and it does so in much less space than we have used to describe only some of its features.

**Cross-section graph**
A graph that shows the values of an economic variable for different groups in a population at a point in time.

A **cross-section graph** shows the values of an economic variable for different groups in a population at a point in time. Figure A1.2(d) is an example of a cross-section graph. It shows the percentage of people who participate in selected sports activities in the United States. This graph uses bars rather than dots and lines, and the length of each bar indicates the participation rate. Figure A1.2(d) enables you to compare the participation rates in these ten sporting activities. And you can do so much more quickly and clearly than by looking at a list of numbers.

**FIGURE A1.2**

Data Graphs

myeconlab Animation

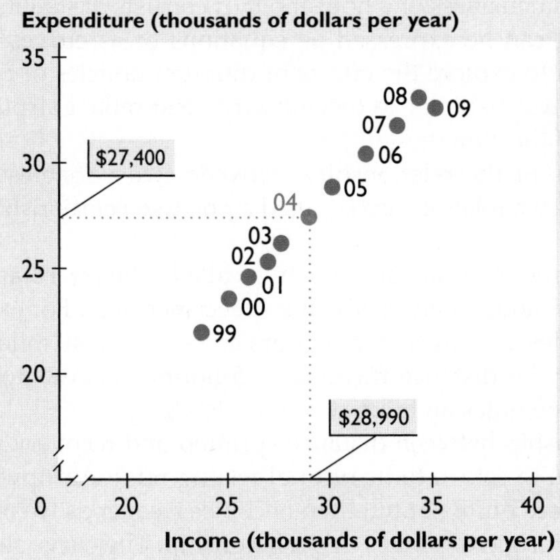


**(a) Scatter Diagram: Expenditure and income**

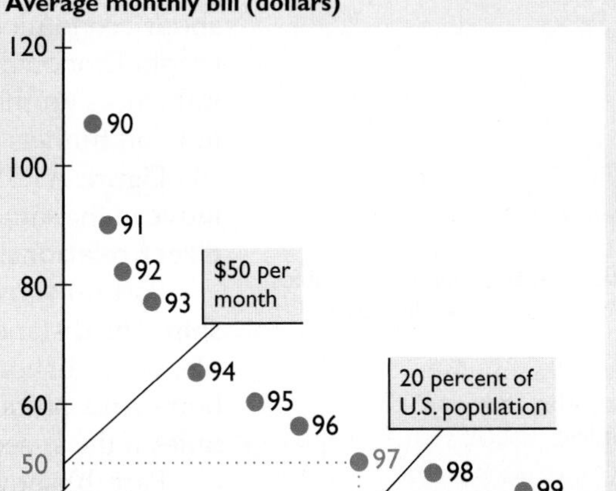


**(b) Scatter Diagram: Subscribers and cost**

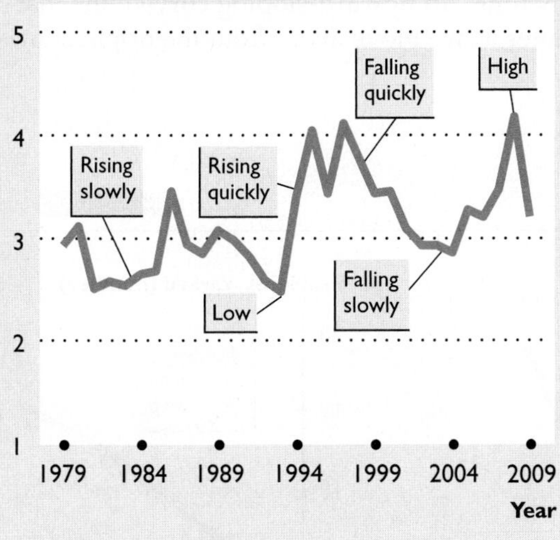


**(c) Time Series: The price of coffee**

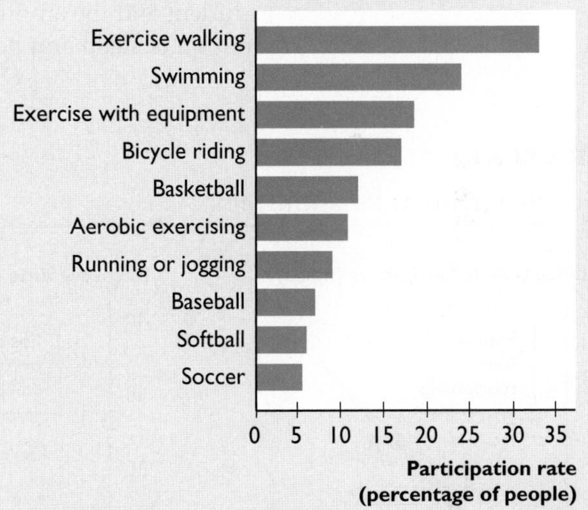


**(d) Cross Section: Participation in selected sports activities**

A scatter diagram reveals the relationship between two variables. In part (a), as income increases, expenditure almost always increases. In part (b), as the monthly cell phone bill falls, the percentage of people who own a cell phone increases.

A time-series graph plots the value of a variable on the *y*-axis against time on the *x*-axis. Part (c) plots the price of coffee each year from 1979 to 2009. The graph shows when the price of coffee was high and low, when it increased and decreased, and when it changed quickly and changed slowly.

A cross-section graph shows the value of a variable across the members of a population. Part (d) shows the participation rate in the United States in each of ten sporting activities.

## Interpreting Graphs Used in Economic Models

We use graphs to show the relationships among the variables in an economic model. An *economic model* is a simplified description of the economy or of a component of the economy such as a business or a household. It consists of statements about economic behavior that can be expressed as equations or as curves in a graph. Economists use models to explore the effects of different policies or other influences on the economy in ways similar to those used to test model airplanes in wind tunnels and models of the climate.

**Positive relationship or direct relationship**
A relationship between two variables that move in the same direction.

**Linear relationship**
A relationship that graphs as a straight line.

Figure A1.3 shows graphs of the relationships between two variables that move in the same direction. Such a relationship is called a **positive relationship** or **direct relationship**.

Part (a) shows a straight-line relationship, which is called a **linear relationship**. The distance traveled in 5 hours increases as the speed increases. For example, point *A* shows that 200 miles are traveled in 5 hours at a speed of 40 miles an hour. And point *B* shows that the distance traveled in 5 hours increases to 300 miles if the speed increases to 60 miles an hour.

Part (b) shows the relationship between distance sprinted and recovery time (the time it takes the heart rate to return to its normal resting rate). An upward-sloping curved line that starts out quite flat but then becomes steeper as we move along the curve away from the origin describes this relationship. The curve slopes upward and becomes steeper because the extra recovery time needed from sprinting another 100 yards increases. It takes 5 minutes to recover from sprinting 100 yards but 15 minutes to recover from sprinting 200 yards.

Part (c) shows the relationship between the number of problems worked by a student and the amount of study time. An upward-sloping curved line that starts out quite steep and becomes flatter as we move away from the origin shows this

**FIGURE A1.3**

Positive (Direct) Relationships

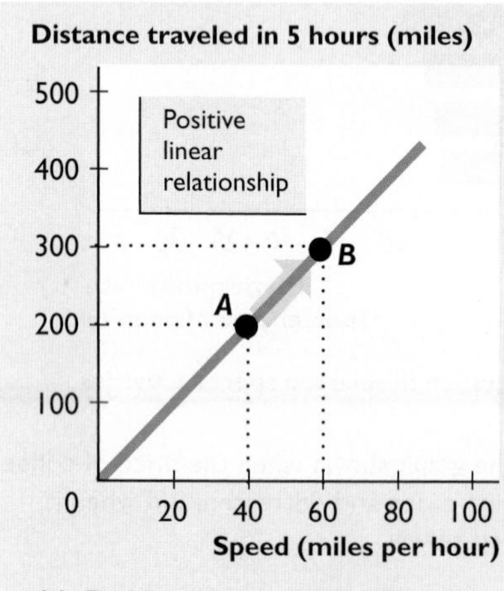


(a) Positive linear relationship

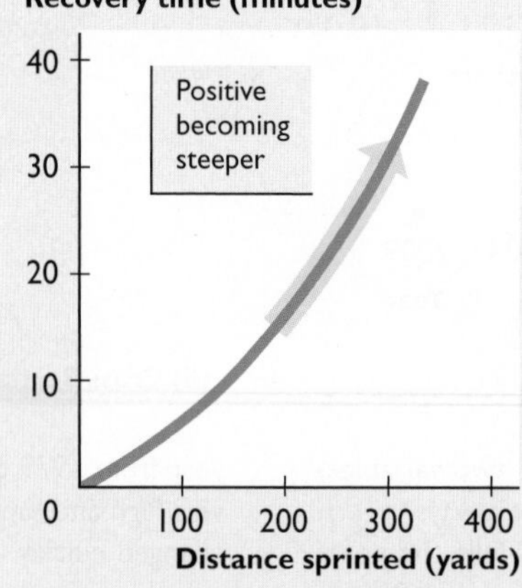


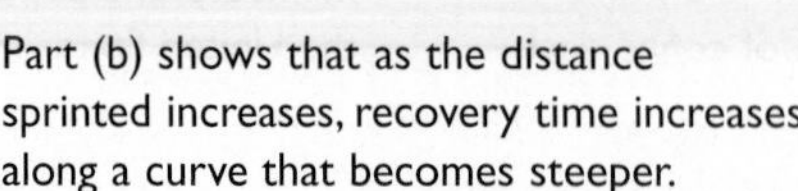

(b) Positive becoming steeper

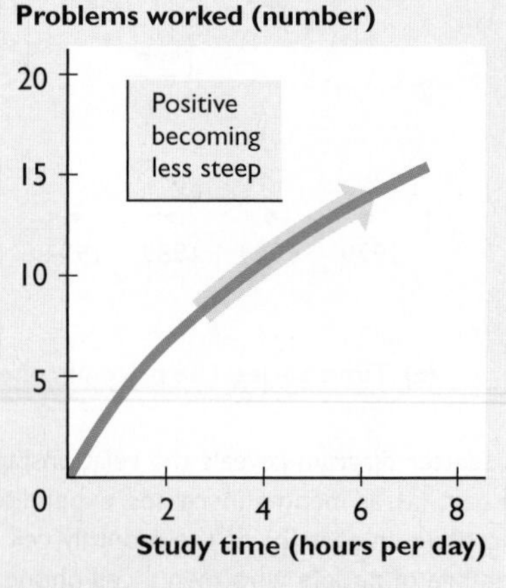


(c) Positive becoming less steep

Part (a) shows that as speed increases, the distance traveled in a given number of hours increases along a straight line.

Part (b) shows that as the distance sprinted increases, recovery time increases along a curve that becomes steeper.

Part (c) shows that as study time increases, the number of problems worked increases along a curve that becomes less steep.

relationship. Study time becomes less effective as you increase the hours worked and become more tired.

Figure A1.4 shows relationships between two variables that move in opposite directions. Such a relationship is called a **negative relationship** or **inverse relationship**.

**Negative relationship or inverse relationship**
A relationship between two variables that move in opposite directions.

Part (a) shows the relationship between the number of hours spent playing squash and the number of hours spent playing tennis when the total number of hours available is five. One extra hour spent playing tennis means one hour less playing squash and vice versa. This relationship is negative and linear.

Part (b) shows the relationship between the cost per mile traveled and the length of a journey. The longer the journey, the lower is the cost per mile. But as the journey length increases, the fall in the cost per mile becomes smaller. This feature of the relationship is shown by the fact that the curve slopes downward, starting out steep at a short journey length and then becoming flatter as the journey length increases. This relationship arises because some of the costs, such as auto insurance, are fixed, and as the journey length increases, the fixed costs are spread over more miles.

Part (c) shows the relationship between the amount of leisure time and the number of problems worked by a student. Increasing leisure time produces an increasingly large reduction in the number of problems worked. This relationship is a negative one that starts out with a gentle slope at a small number of leisure hours and becomes steeper as the number of leisure hours increases. This relationship is a different view of the idea shown in Figure A1.3(c).

Many relationships in economic models have a maximum or a minimum. For example, firms try to make the largest possible profit and to produce at the lowest possible cost. Figure A1.5 shows relationships that have a maximum or a minimum.

**FIGURE A1.4**

Negative (Inverse) Relationships

myeconlab Animation

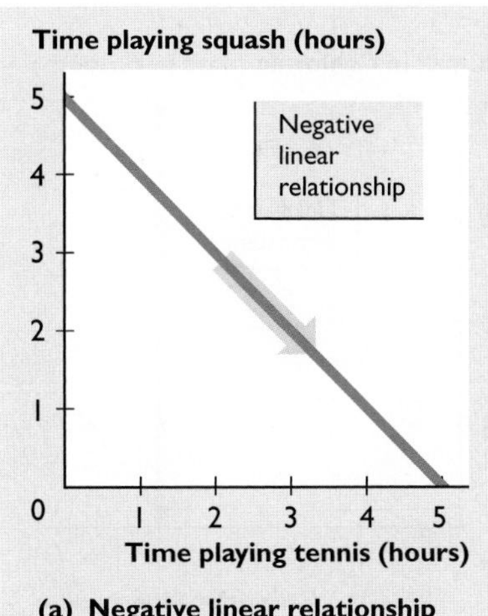


**(a) Negative linear relationship**

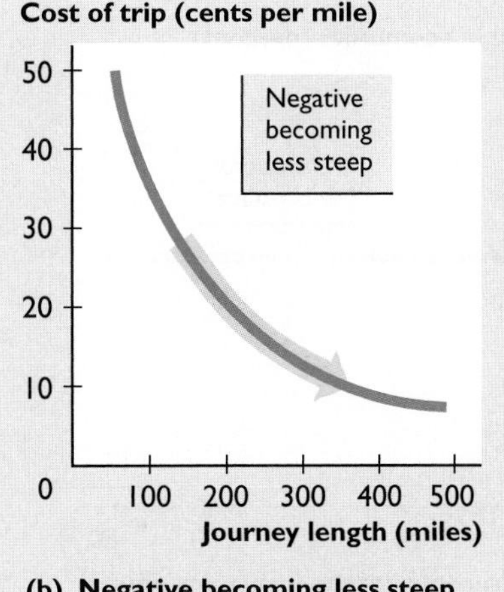


**(b) Negative becoming less steep**

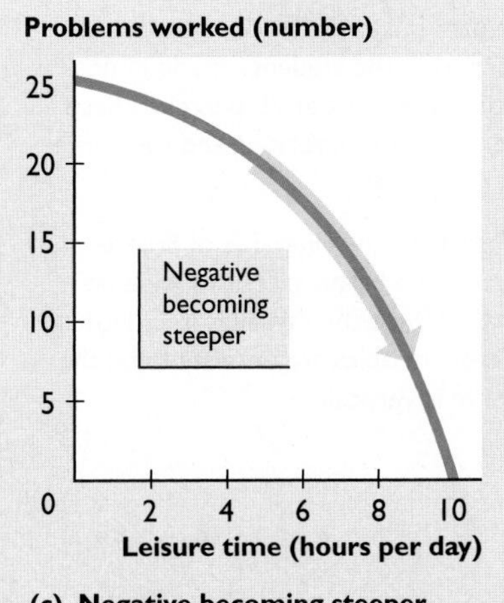


**(c) Negative becoming steeper**

Part (a) shows that as the time playing tennis increases, the time playing squash decreases along a straight line.

Part (b) shows that as the journey length increases, the cost of the trip falls along a curve that becomes less steep.

Part (c) shows that as leisure time increases, the number of problems worked decreases along a curve that becomes steeper.

## FIGURE A1.5

### Maximum and Minimum Points

myeconlab Animation

In part (a), as the rainfall increases, the curve ❶ slopes upward as the yield per acre rises, ❷ is flat at point *A*, the maximum yield, and then ❸ slopes downward as the yield per acre falls.

In part (b), as the speed increases, the curve ❶ slopes downward as the cost per mile falls, ❷ is flat at the minimum point *B*, and then ❸ slopes upward as the cost per mile rises.

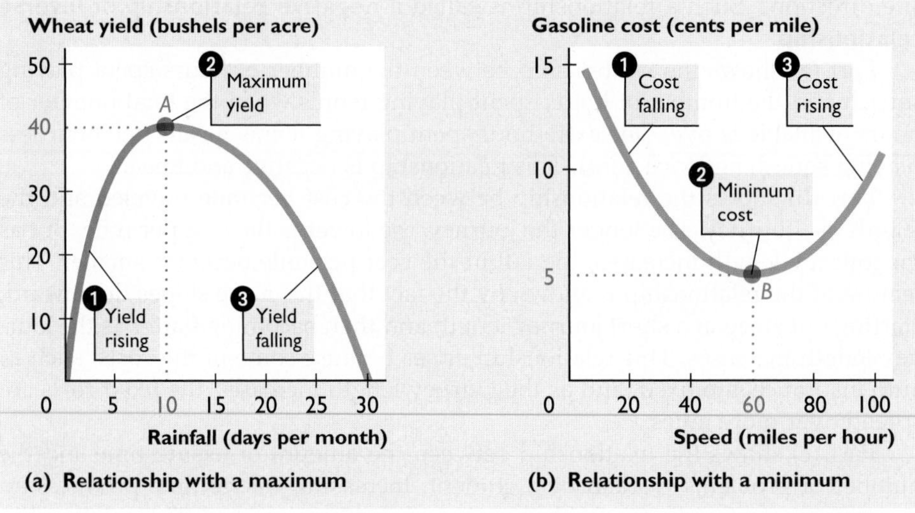


**(a) Relationship with a maximum**

**(b) Relationship with a minimum**

Part (a) shows a relationship that starts out sloping upward, reaches a maximum, and then slopes downward. Part (b) shows a relationship that begins sloping downward, falls to a minimum, and then slopes upward.

Finally, there are many situations in which, no matter what happens to the value of one variable, the other variable remains constant. Sometimes we want to show two variables that are unrelated in a graph. Figure A1.6 shows two graphs in which the variables are unrelated.

## FIGURE A1.6

### Variables That Are Unrelated

myeconlab Animation

In part (a), as the price of bananas increases, the student's grade in economics remains at 75 percent. These variables are unrelated, and the curve is horizontal.

In part (b), the vineyards of France produce 3 billion gallons of wine no matter what the rainfall is in California. These variables are unrelated, and the curve is vertical.

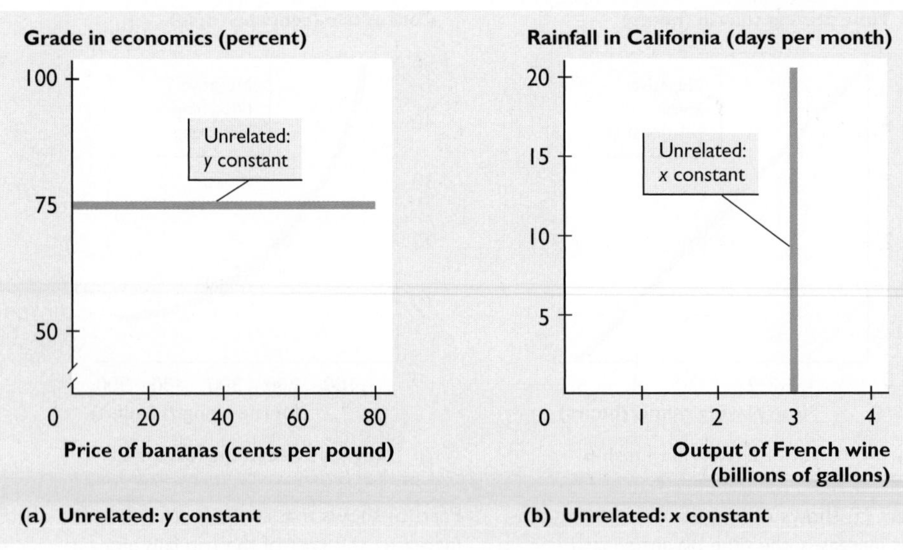


**(a) Unrelated: y constant**

**(b) Unrelated: x constant**

## The Slope of a Relationship

We can measure the influence of one variable on another by the slope of the relationship. The **slope** of a relationship is the change in the value of the variable measured on the $y$-axis divided by the change in the value of the variable measured on the $x$-axis. We use the Greek letter $\Delta$ (delta) to represent "change in." So $\Delta y$ means the change in the value of $y$, and $\Delta x$ means the change in the value of $x$. The slope of the relationship is

$$\Delta y \div \Delta x.$$

**Slope**
The change in the value of the variable measured on the $y$-axis divided by the change in the value of the variable measured on the $x$-axis.

If a large change in $y$ is associated with a small change in $x$, the slope is large and the curve is steep. If a small change in $y$ is associated with a large change in $x$, the slope is small and the curve is flat.

Figure A1.7 shows you how to calculate slope. The slope of a straight line is the same regardless of where on the line you calculate it—the slope is constant. In part (a), when $x$ increases from 2 to 6, $y$ increases from 3 to 6. The change in $x$ is 4—that is, $\Delta x$ is 4. The change in $y$ is 3—that is, $\Delta y$ is 3. The slope of that line is 3/4. In part (b), when $x$ increases from 2 to 6, *y decreases* from 6 to 3. The change in $y$ is *minus* 3—that is, $\Delta y$ is $-3$. The change in $x$ is plus 4—that is, $\Delta x$ is 4. The slope of the curve is $-3/4$.

In part (c), we calculate the slope at a point on a curve. To do so, place a ruler on the graph so that it touches point $A$ and no other point on the curve, then draw a straight line along the edge of the ruler. The slope of this straight line is the slope of the curve at point $A$. This slope is 3/4.

**FIGURE A1.7**

Calculating Slope

myeconlab Animation

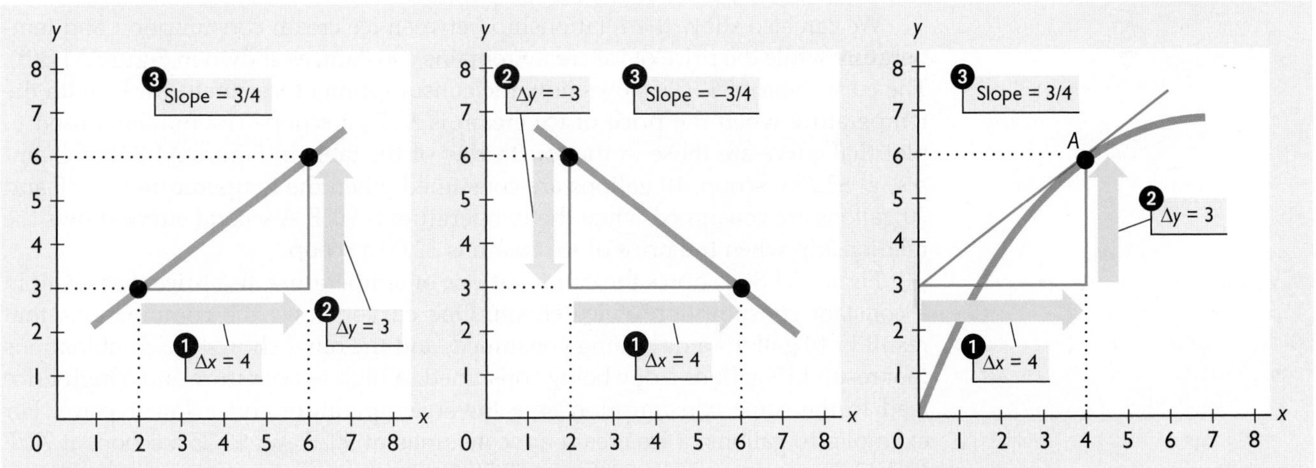

(a) Positive slope

(b) Negative slope

(c) Slope at a point

In part (a), ❶ when $\Delta x$ is 4, ❷ $\Delta y$ is 3, so ❸ the slope ($\Delta y \div \Delta x$) is 3/4.

In part (b), ❶ when $\Delta x$ is 4, ❷ $\Delta y$ is $-3$, so ❸ the slope ($\Delta y \div \Delta x$) is $-3/4$.

In part (c), the slope of the curve at point $A$ equals the slope of the red line. ❶ When $\Delta x$ is 4, ❷ $\Delta y$ is 3, so ❸ the slope ($\Delta y \div \Delta x$) is 3/4.

## Relationships Among More Than Two Variables

All the graphs that you have studied so far plot the relationship between two variables as a point formed by the $x$ and $y$ values. But most of the relationships in economics involve relationships among many variables, not just two. For example, the amount of ice cream consumed depends on the price of ice cream and the temperature. If ice cream is expensive and the temperature is low, people eat much less ice cream than when ice cream is inexpensive and the temperature is high. For any given price of ice cream, the quantity consumed varies with the temperature; and for any given temperature, the quantity of ice cream consumed varies with its price.

Figure A1.8 shows a relationship among three variables. The table shows the number of gallons of ice cream consumed per day at various temperatures and ice cream prices. How can we graph these numbers?

To graph a relationship that involves more than two variables, we use the *ceteris paribus* assumption.

### *Ceteris Paribus*

The Latin phrase *ceteris paribus* means "other things remaining the same." Every laboratory experiment is an attempt to create *ceteris paribus* and isolate the relationship of interest. We use the same method to make a graph.

Figure A1.8(a) shows an example. This graph shows what happens to the quantity of ice cream consumed when the price of ice cream varies while the temperature remains constant. The curve labeled 70°F shows the relationship between ice cream consumption and the price of ice cream if the temperature is 70°F. The numbers used to plot that curve are those in the first and fourth columns of the table in Figure A1.8. For example, if the temperature is 70°F, 10 gallons are consumed when the price is $2.75 a scoop and 18 gallons are consumed when the price is $2.25 a scoop. The curve labeled 90°F shows the relationship between consumption and the price when the temperature is 90°F.

We can also show the relationship between ice cream consumption and temperature while the price of ice cream remains constant, as shown in Figure A1.8(b). The curve labeled $2.75 shows how the consumption of ice cream varies with the temperature when the price of ice cream is $2.75 a scoop. The numbers used to plot that curve are those in the fourth row of the table in Figure A1.8. For example, at $2.75 a scoop, 10 gallons are consumed when the temperature is 70°F and 20 gallons are consumed when the temperature is 90°F. A second curve shows the relationship when the price of ice cream is $2.00 a scoop.

Figure A1.8(c) shows the combinations of temperature and price that result in a constant consumption of ice cream. One curve shows the combinations that result in 10 gallons a day being consumed, and the other shows the combinations that result in 7 gallons a day being consumed. A high temperature and a high price lead to the same consumption as a lower temperature and a lower price. For example, 10 gallons of ice cream are consumed at 90°F and $3.25 a scoop, at 70°F and $2.75 a scoop, and at 50°F and $2.50 a scoop.

With what you've learned about graphs in this Appendix, you can move forward with your study of economics. There are no graphs in this textbook that are more complicated than the ones you've studied here.

## FIGURE A1.8
Graphing a Relationship Among Three Variables

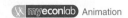

myeconlab Animation

| Price (dollars per scoop) | Ice cream consumption (gallons per day) | | | |
|---|---|---|---|---|
| | 30°F | 50°F | 70°F | 90°F |
| 2.00 | 12 | 18 | 25 | 50 |
| 2.25 | 10 | 12 | 18 | 37 |
| 2.50 | 7 | 10 | 13 | 27 |
| 2.75 | 5 | 7 | 10 | 20 |
| 3.00 | 3 | 5 | 7 | 14 |
| 3.25 | 2 | 3 | 5 | 10 |
| 3.50 | 1 | 2 | 3 | 6 |

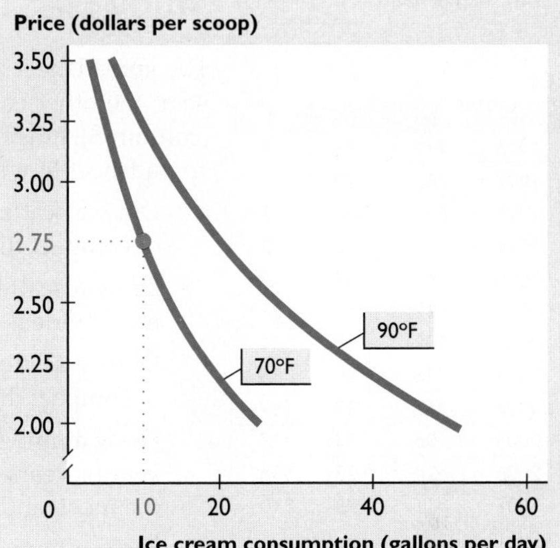

(a) Price and consumption at a given temperature

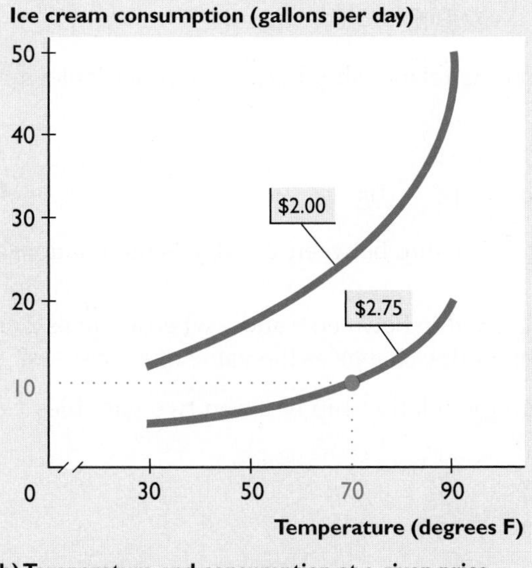

(b) Temperature and consumption at a given price

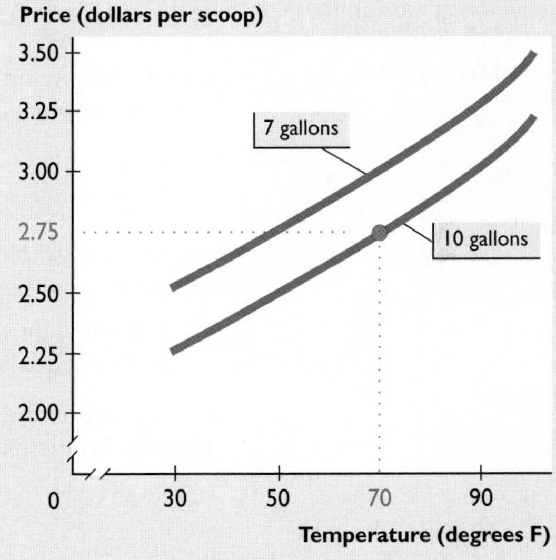

(c) Temperature and price at a given consumption

The table tells us how many gallons of ice cream are consumed at different prices and different temperatures. For example, if the price is $2.75 a scoop and the temperature is 70°F, 10 gallons of ice cream are consumed. This set of values is highlighted in the table and each part of the figure.

Part (a) shows the relationship between price and consumption when temperature is held constant. One curve holds temperature at 90°F, and the other at 70°F.

Part (b) shows the relationship between temperature and consumption when price is held constant. One curve holds the price at $2.75 a scoop, and the other at $2.00 a scoop.

Part (c) shows the relationship between temperature and price when consumption is held constant. One curve holds consumption at 10 gallons a day, and the other at 7 gallons a day.

Work these problems in Chapter 1 Study Plan to get instant feedback.

# APPENDIX CHECKPOINT

## Study Plan Problems

**TABLE 1**

| | A | B | C | D |
|---|---|---|---|---|
| 1 | 1996 | 779 | 17 | 3 |
| 2 | 1997 | 753 | 19 | 4 |
| 3 | 1998 | 847 | 27 | 7 |
| 4 | 1999 | 939 | 20 | 12 |
| 5 | 2000 | 943 | 18 | 19 |
| 6 | 2001 | 882 | 18 | 31 |
| 7 | 2002 | 803 | 15 | 51 |
| 8 | 2003 | 746 | 20 | 85 |
| 9 | 2004 | 767 | 33 | 139 |
| 10 | 2005 | 705 | 34 | 367 |
| 11 | 2006 | 620 | 23 | 586 |
| 12 | 2007 | 511 | 28 | 810 |

The spreadsheet in Table 1 provides data on the U.S. economy: Column A is the year; the other columns are quantities sold in millions per year of compact discs (column B), music videos (column C), and singles downloads (column D). Use this spreadsheet to work Problems 1 to 5.

1. Draw a scatter diagram to show the relationship between the quantities sold of compact discs and music videos. Describe the relationship.
2. Draw a scatter diagram to show the relationship between quantities sold of music videos and singles downloads. Describe the relationship.
3. Draw a scatter diagram to show the relationship between the quantities sold of compact discs and singles downloads. Describe the relationship.
4. Draw a time-series graph of quantity of compact discs sold. Say in which year or years the quantity sold (a) was highest, (b) was lowest, (c) increased the most, and (d) decreased the most. If the data show a trend, describe it.
5. Draw a time-series graph of the quantity of music videos sold. Say in which year or years the quantity sold (a) was highest, (b) was lowest, (c) decreased the most, and (d) decreased the least. If the data show a trend, describe it.

Your instructor can assign these problems as homework, a quiz, or a test in **MyEconLab**.

## Instructor Assignable Problems

Use the following information on the relationship between two variables $x$ and $y$ to work Problems 1 and 2.

| $x$ | 0 | 1 | 2 | 3 | 4 | 5 |
|---|---|---|---|---|---|---|
| $y$ | 0 | 1 | 4 | 9 | 16 | 25 |

1. Draw a graph to show the relationship between $x$ and $y$. Is the relationship positive or negative?
2. Calculate the slope of the relationship between $x$ and $y$ when $x$ equals 2 and when $x$ equals 4. How does the slope change as the value of $x$ increases?

Use the following information on the relationship between two variables $x$ and $z$ to work Problems 3 and 4.

| $x$ | 0 | 1 | 2 | 3 | 4 | 5 |
|---|---|---|---|---|---|---|
| $z$ | 32 | 31 | 28 | 23 | 16 | 7 |

3. Is the relationship between $x$ and $z$ positive or negative?
4. Calculate the slope of the relationship between $x$ and $z$ when $x$ equals 2 and when $x$ equals 4. How does the slope change as the value of $x$ increases?
5. Table 2 provides data on the price of a balloon ride, the temperature, and the number of rides a day. Draw graphs to show the relationship between
   - The price and the number of rides, when the temperature is constant.
   - The number of rides and the temperature, when the price is constant.
   - The temperature and the price, when the number of rides is constant.

**TABLE 2**

| Price (dollars per ride) | Balloon rides (number per day) 50°F | 70°F | 90°F |
|---|---|---|---|
| 5 | 32 | 50 | 40 |
| 10 | 27 | 40 | 32 |
| 15 | 18 | 32 | 27 |
| 20 | 10 | 27 | 18 |

## Who makes the iPhone?

Apple, right? Guess again!

The iPhone is an example of how, in the pursuit of self-interest, many people and businesses around the world end up determining what, how, and for whom goods and services are produced.

# The U.S. and Global Economies

CHAPTER CHECKLIST

**When you have completed your study of this chapter, you will be able to**

1 Describe what, how, and for whom goods and services are produced in the United States.

2 Describe what, how, and for whom goods and services are produced in the global economy.

3 Use the circular flow model to provide a picture of how households, firms, and governments interact in the U.S. economy and how the U.S. and other economies interact in the global economy.

## 2.1 WHAT, HOW, AND FOR WHOM?

Walk around a shopping mall and pay close attention to the range of goods and services that are being offered for sale. Go inside some of the shops and look at the labels to see where various items are manufactured. The next time you travel on an interstate highway, look at the large trucks and pay attention to the names and products printed on their sides and the places in which the trucks are registered. Open the Yellow Pages and flip through a few sections. Notice the huge range of goods and services that businesses are offering.

You've just done a sampling of *what* goods and services are produced and consumed in the United States today.

### What Do We Produce?

We divide the vast array of goods and services produced into four large groups:

- Consumption goods and services
- Capital goods
- Government goods and services
- Export goods and services

**Consumption goods and services**
Goods and services that are bought by individuals and used to provide personal enjoyment and contribute to a person's quality of life.

**Capital goods**
Goods that are bought by businesses to increase their productive resources.

**Government goods and services**
Goods and services that are bought by governments.

**Export goods and services**
Goods and services that are produced in one country and sold in other countries.

**Consumption goods and services** are items that are bought by individuals and used to provide personal enjoyment and contribute to a person's quality of life. They include items such as housing, SUVs, vitamin water and ramen noodles, chocolate bars and Po' Boy sandwiches, movies, downhill skiing lessons, and doctor and dental services.

**Capital goods** are goods that are bought by businesses to increase their productive resources. They include items such as auto assembly lines, shopping malls, airplanes, and oil tankers.

**Government goods and services** are items that are bought by governments. Governments purchase missiles and weapons systems, travel services, Internet services, police protection, roads, and paper and paper clips.

**Export goods and services** are items that are produced in one country and sold in other countries. U.S. export goods and services include the airplanes produced by Boeing that Singapore Airlines buys, the computers produced by Dell that Europeans buy, and licenses sold by U.S. film companies to show U.S. movies in European movie theaters.

Of the four groups of goods and services that we've just defined, consumption goods and services have the largest share and a share that doesn't fluctuate much. The volume of capital goods produced fluctuates as the economy cycles from boom to recession. Goods and services bought by governments are close to a fifth of total production and export goods around one tenth.

Breaking the goods and services down into smaller categories, health services is the largest category, with 13 percent of the value of total production. Real estate services come next at 12 percent. The main component of this item is the services of rental and owner-occupied housing. Education is the next largest service, followed by retail and wholesale trades and transportation and storage.

The categories of goods production are smaller than those of services. The largest category of goods—construction—accounts for less than 5 percent of the value of total production, and the next three—utilities, food, and chemicals—each accounts for 2 percent or less.

# EYE on the U.S. ECONOMY

## What We Produce

In 2009, consumption goods and services accounted for 62 percent of total production, both capital goods and export goods and services accounted for 10 percent, and government goods and services for 18 percent.

Health-care and real estate services, education, retail and wholesale trades, and transportation and storage are the six largest services produced. Construction, utilities, food, and chemicals are the largest categories of goods produced. Services production greatly exceeds goods production and is growing faster.

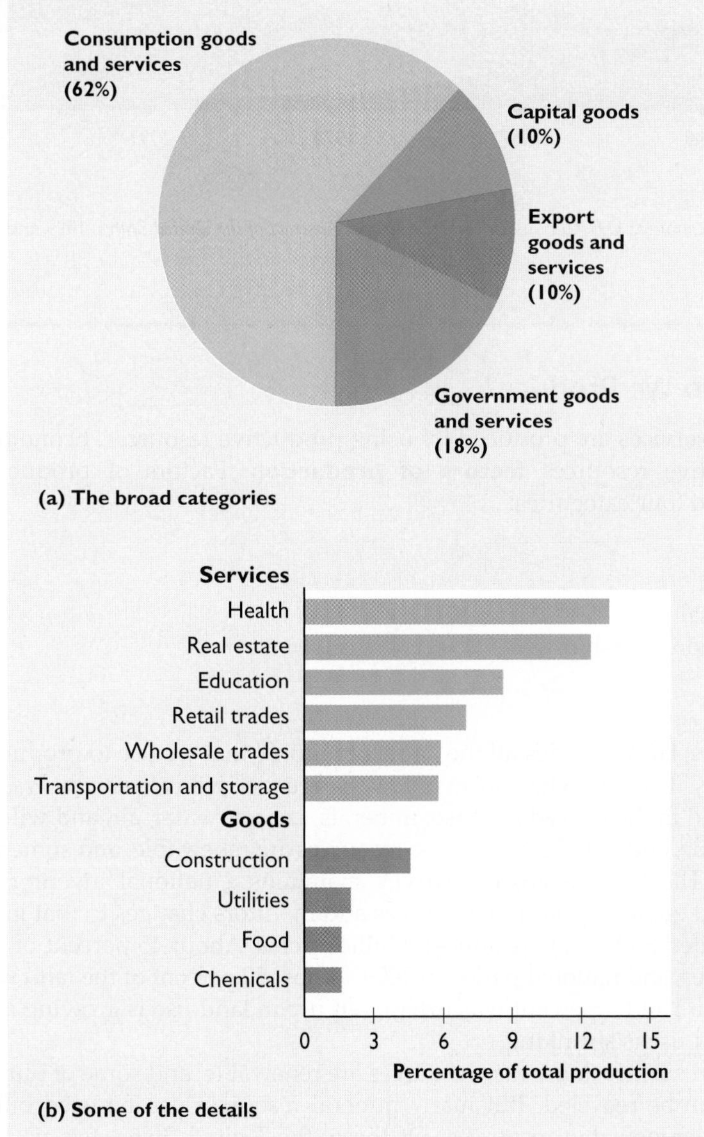

SOURCE OF DATA: Bureau of Economic Analysis.

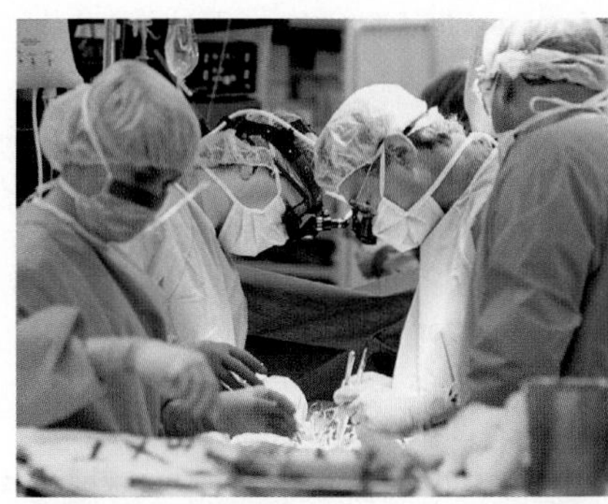

*Health-care services ...*

*education services ...*

*retail trades ...*

*and chemicals are among the largest categories of goods and services produced.*

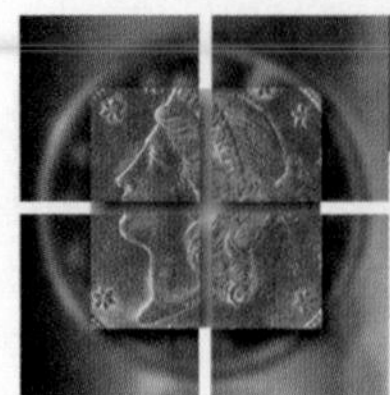

## EYE on the PAST

### Changes in What We Produce

Seventy years ago, one American in four worked on a farm. That number has shrunk to one in thirty-five. The number of people who produce goods—in mining, construction, and manufacturing—has also shrunk, from one in three to one in five. In contrast, the number of people who produce services has expanded from one in two to almost four in five. These changes in employment reflect changes in what we produce—services.

We hear a lot about globalization and American manufacturing jobs going overseas, but the expansion of service jobs and shrinking of manufacturing jobs is not new. It has been going on over the past 60 years and is likely to continue.

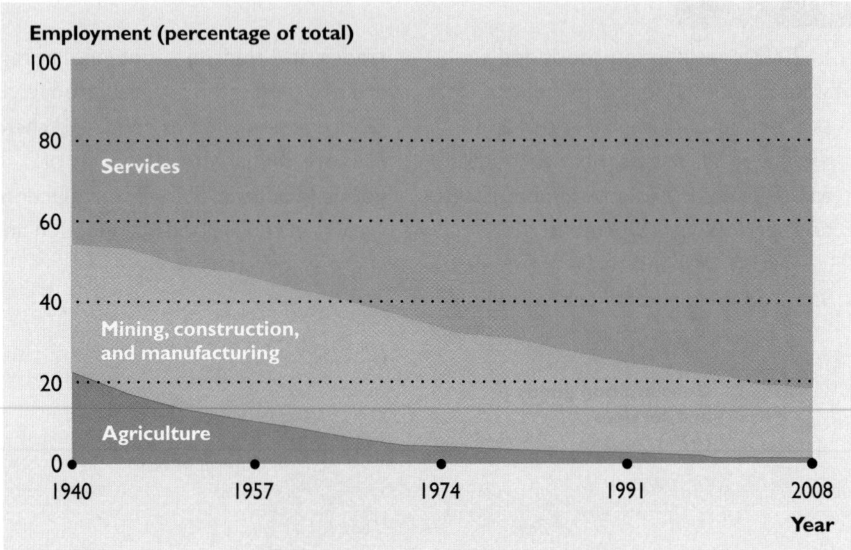


SOURCE OF DATA: U.S. Census Bureau, *Statistical Abstract of the United States,* 1999 and 2008.

## How Do We Produce?

**Factors of production**
The productive resources that are used to produce goods and services—land, labor, capital, and entrepreneurship.

Goods and services are produced by using productive resources. Economists call the productive resources **factors of production**. Factors of production are grouped into four categories:

- Land
- Labor
- Capital
- Entrepreneurship

### Land

**Land**
The "gifts of nature," or *natural resources,* that we use to produce goods and services.

In economics, **land** includes all the "gifts of nature" that we use to produce goods and services. Land is what, in everyday language, we call *natural resources.* It includes land in the everyday sense, minerals, energy, water, air, and wild plants, animals, birds, and fish. Some of these resources are renewable, and some are nonrenewable. The U.S. Geological Survey maintains a national inventory of the quantity and quality of natural resources and monitors changes to that inventory.

The United States covers almost 2 billion acres. About 45 percent of the land is forest, lakes, and national parks. In 2009, almost 50 percent of the land was used for agriculture and 5 percent was urban, but urban land use is growing and agricultural land use is shrinking.

Our land surface and water resources are renewable, and some of our mineral resources can be recycled. But many mineral resources can be used only once. They are nonrenewable resources. Of these, the United States has vast known reserves of coal but much smaller known reserves of oil and natural gas.

## Labor

**Labor** is the work time and work effort that people devote to producing goods and services. Labor includes the physical and mental efforts of all the people who work on farms and construction sites and in factories, shops, and offices. The Census Bureau and Bureau of Labor Statistics measure the quantity of labor at work every month.

**Labor**
The work time and work effort that people devote to producing goods and services.

In the United States in April 2009, 155 million people had jobs or were available for work. Some worked full time, some worked part time, and some were unemployed but looking for an acceptable vacant job. The total amount of time worked during 2009 was about 240 billion hours.

The quantity of labor increases as the adult population increases. The quantity of labor also increases if a larger percentage of the population takes jobs. During the past 50 years, a larger proportion of women have taken paid work and this trend has increased the quantity of labor. At the same time, a slightly smaller proportion of men have taken paid work and this trend has decreased the quantity of labor.

The *quality* of labor depends on how skilled people are. A laborer who can push a hand cart but can't drive a truck is much less productive than one who can drive. An office worker who can use a computer is much more productive than one who can't. Economists use a special name for human skill: human capital. **Human capital** is the knowledge and skill that people obtain from education, on-the-job training, and work experience.

**Human capital**
The knowledge and skill that people obtain from education, on-the-job training, and work experience.

You are building your own human capital right now as you work on your economics course and other subjects. Your human capital will continue to grow when you get a full-time job and become better at it. Human capital improves the *quality* of labor and increases the quantity of goods and services that labor can produce.

## Capital

**Capital** consists of the tools, instruments, machines, buildings, and other items that have been produced in the past and that businesses now use to produce goods and services. Capital includes hammers and screwdrivers, computers, auto assembly lines, office towers and warehouses, dams and power plants, airports and airplanes, shirt factories, and shopping malls.

**Capital**
Tools, instruments, machines, buildings, and other items that have been produced in the past and that businesses now use to produce goods and services.

Capital also includes inventories of unsold goods or of partly finished goods on a production line. And capital includes what is sometimes called *infrastructure capital,* such as highways and airports.

Capital, like human capital, makes labor more productive. A truck driver can produce vastly more transportation services than the pusher of a hand cart; the Interstate highway system enables us to produce vastly more transportation services than was possible on the old highway system that preceded it.

The Bureau of Economic Analysis in the U.S. Department of Commerce keeps track of the total value of capital in the United States and how it grows over time. Today, the value of capital in the U.S. economy is around $47 trillion.

### *Financial Capital Is Not Capital*

In everyday language, we talk about money, stocks, and bonds as being capital. These items are *financial capital,* and they are not productive resources. They enable people to provide businesses with financial resources, but they are *not* used to produce goods and services. They are not capital.

# EYE on the U.S. ECONOMY

## Changes in How We Produce in the Information Economy

The information economy consists of the jobs and businesses that produce and use computers and equipment powered by computer chips. This information economy is highly visible in your daily life.

The pairs of images here illustrate two examples. In each pair, a new technology enables capital to replace labor.

The top pair of pictures illustrate the replacement of bank tellers (labor) with ATMs (capital). Although the ATM was invented almost 40 years ago, when it made its first appearance, it was located only inside banks and was not able to update customers' accounts. It is only in the last decade that ATMs have spread to corner stores and enable us to get cash and check our bank balance from almost anywhere in the world.

The bottom pair of pictures illustrate a more recent replacement of labor with capital: self-check-in. Air passengers today issue their own boarding pass, often at their own computer before leaving home. For international flights, some of these machines now even check passport details.

The number of bank teller and airport check-in clerk jobs is shrinking, but these new technologies are creating a whole range of new jobs for people who make, program, install, and repair the vast number of machines.

## Entrepreneurship

**Entrepreneurship**
The human resource that organizes labor, land, and capital to produce goods and services.

**Entrepreneurship** is the human resource that organizes land, labor, and capital to produce goods and services. Entrepreneurs are creative and imaginative. They come up with new ideas about what and how to produce, make business decisions, and bear the risks that arise from these decisions. If their ideas work out, they earn a profit. If their ideas turn out to be wrong, they bear the loss.

The quantity of entrepreneurship is hard to describe or measure. During some periods, there appears to be a great deal of imaginative entrepreneurship around. People such as Sam Walton, who created Wal-Mart, one of the world's largest retailers; Bill Gates, who founded the Microsoft empire; and Mark Zuckerberg, who founded Facebook, are examples of extraordinary entrepreneurial talent. But these highly visible entrepreneurs are just the tip of an iceberg that consists of hundreds of thousands of people who run businesses, large and small.

## For Whom Do We Produce?

Who gets the goods and services depends on the incomes that people earn. A large income enables a person to buy large quantities of goods and services. A small income leaves a person with a small quantity of goods and services.

People earn their incomes by selling the services of the factors of production they own. **Rent** is paid for the use of land, **wages** are paid for the services of labor, **interest** is paid for the use of capital, and entrepreneurs receive a **profit** (or incur a **loss**) for running their businesses. What are the shares of these four factor incomes in the United States? Which factor receives the largest share?

Figure 2.1(a) answers these questions. It shows that wages were 65 percent of total income in 2008 and rent, interest, and profit and were 35 percent of total income. These percentages remain remarkably constant over time. We call the distribution of income among the factors of production the **functional distribution of income**.

Figure 2.1(b) shows the **personal distribution of income**—the distribution of income among households. Some households, like that of Tiger Woods, earn many million dollars a year. These households are in the richest 20 percent who earn 51 percent of total income. Households at the other end of the scale, like those of fast-food servers, are in the poorest 20 percent who earn only 3 percent of total income. The distribution of income has been changing and becoming more unequal. The rich have become richer. But it isn't the case, on the whole, that the poor have become poorer. They just haven't become richer as fast as the rich have.

**Rent**
Income paid for the use of land.

**Wages**
Income paid for the services of labor.

**Interest**
Income paid for the use of capital.

**Profit (or loss)**
Income earned by an entrepreneur for running a business.

**Functional distribution of income**
The distribution of income among the factors of production.

**Personal distribution of income**
The distribution of income among households.

**FIGURE 2.1**
For Whom?

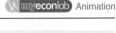

myeconlab Animation

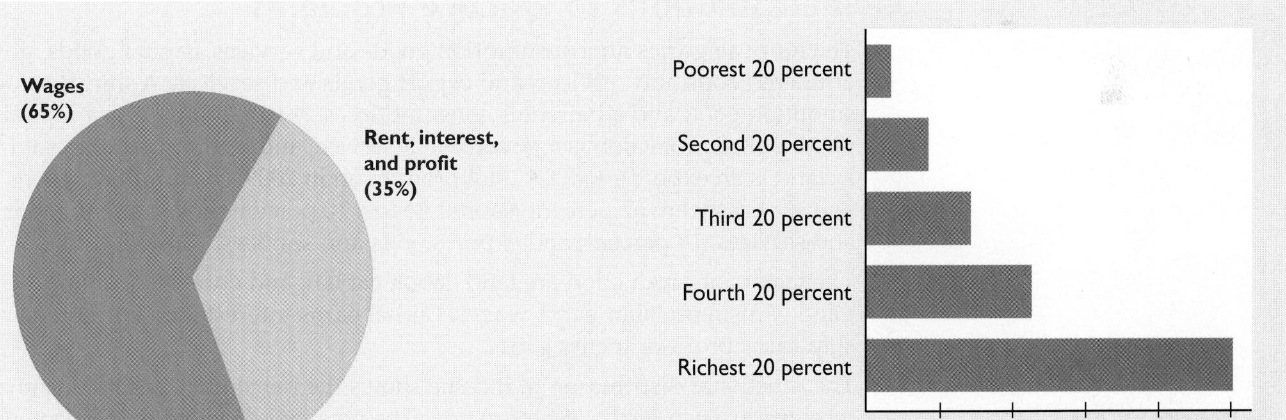


SOURCES OF DATA: Bureau of Economic Analysis, *National Income and Product Accounts*, Table 1.10 and U.S. Census Bureau, *Income, Poverty, and Health Insurance in the United States: 2008*, Current Population Reports P60-235, 2008.

In 2008, wages (the income from labor) were 65 percent of total income. Rent, interest, and profit (the income from the services of land, capital, and entrepreneurship) totaled the remaining 35 percent.

In 2008, the 20 percent of the population with the highest incomes received 51 percent of total income. The 20 percent with the lowest incomes received only 3 percent of total income.

Work these problems in Study Plan 2.1 to get instant feedback.

**Describe what, how, and for whom goods and services are produced in the United States.**

## Practice Problems

1. Name the four broad categories of goods and services that we use in economics. Provide an example of each (different from those in the chapter) and say what percentage of total production each accounted for in 2009.
2. Name the four factors of production and the incomes they earn.
3. Distinguish between the functional distribution of income and the personal distribution of income.
4. In the United States, which factor of production earned the largest share of income in 2008 and what percentage did it earn?
5. **What microloans miss**

   Muhammad Yunus (along with Grameen Bank) was awarded the Nobel Peace Prize in 2006. Yunus has said that "all people are entrepreneurs" and that microloans will pull poor people out of poverty. Only 14 percent of Americans are entrepreneurs while almost forty percent of Peruvians are.

   Source: James Surowiecki, *The New Yorker*, March 17, 2008

   With only 14 percent of Americans earning their income from entrepreneurship, from what factor of production do most Americans earn their income? What is that income called? Why do you think so many people in Peru are entrepreneurs?

## Guided Solutions to Practice Problems

1. The four categories are consumption goods and services, capital goods, government goods and services, and export goods and services. A shirt is a consumption good and a haircut is consumption service. An oil rig is a capital good, police protection is a government service, and a computer chip sold to Ireland is an export good. Of total production in 2009, consumption goods and services were 62 percent; capital goods, 10 percent; government goods and services, 18 percent; and export goods and services, 10 percent.
2. The factors of production are land, labor, capital, and entrepreneurship. Land earns rent; labor earns wages; capital earns interest; and entrepreneurship earns profit or incurs a loss.
3. The functional distribution of income shows the percentage of total income received by each factor of production. The personal distribution of income shows the percentage of total income received by households.
4. Labor is the factor of production that earns the largest share of income in the United States. In 2008, labor earned 65 percent of total income.
5. Most Americans earn their income from labor and the income they earn is called a wage. Peru is a poor country in which jobs are more limited than in the United States. So to earn an income, many people are self-employed and work as small entrepreneurs.

## 2.2 THE GLOBAL ECONOMY

We're now going to look at *what, how,* and *for whom* goods and services get produced in the global economy. We'll begin with a brief overview of the people and countries that form the global economy.

### The People

Visit the Web site of the U.S. Census Bureau and go to the population clocks to find out how many people there are today in both the United States and the entire world.

On the day these words were written, May 14, 2009, the U.S. clock recorded a population of 306,424,038. The world clock recorded a global population of 6,779,717,958. The U.S. clock ticks along showing a population increase of one person every 12 seconds. The world clock spins faster, adding 30 people in the same 12 seconds.

### The Countries

The world's 6.8 billion (and rising) population lives in 175 countries, which the International Monetary Fund classifies into two broad groups of economies:

- Advanced economies
- Emerging market and developing economies

#### Advanced Economies

Advanced economies are the richest 29 countries (or areas). The United States, Japan, Italy, Germany, France, the United Kingdom, and Canada belong to this group. So do four new industrial Asian economies: Hong Kong, South Korea, Singapore, and Taiwan. The other advanced economies include Australia, New Zealand, and most of the rest of Western Europe. Almost 1 billion people (15 percent of the world's population) live in the advanced economies.

#### Emerging Market and Developing Economies

Emerging market economies are the 28 countries in Central and Eastern Europe and Asia that were, until the early 1990s, part of the Soviet Union or one of its satellites. Russia is the largest of these economies. Others include the Czech Republic, Hungary, Poland, Ukraine, and Mongolia.

Almost 500 million people live in these countries—only about half of the number in the advanced economies. But these countries are important because they are emerging (hence the name) from a system of state-owned production, central economic planning, and heavily regulated markets to a system of free enterprise and unregulated markets.

Developing economies are the 118 countries in Africa, Asia, the Middle East, Europe, and Central and South America that have not yet achieved high average incomes for their people. Average incomes in these economies vary a great deal, but in all cases, these average incomes are much lower than those in the advanced economies, and in some cases, they are extremely low. More than 5 billion people—almost four out of every five people—live in developing economies.

## *What* in the Global Economy?

First, let's look at the big picture. Imagine that each year the global economy produces an enormous pie. In 2009, the pie was worth about $70 trillion! To give this number some meaning, if the pie were shared equally among the world's 6.8 billion people, each of us would get a slice worth a bit more than $10,300.

### Where Is the Global Pie Baked?

Figure 2.2 shows us where in the world the pie is baked. The advanced economies produce 56 percent—21 percent in the United States and 35 percent in the other advanced economies. Another 8 percent comes from the emerging market economies. These economies, which produce 64 percent of the world's goods and services (by value) are home to only 21 percent of the world's population.

Most of the rest of the global pie comes from Asia. China produces 11 percent of the total and the rest of the developing Asian economies produce 10 percent. The developing countries of Africa and the Middle East produce 7 percent, and the Western Hemisphere—Mexico and South America—produces the rest.

The sizes of the slices in the global production pie are gradually changing—the U.S. share is shrinking and China's share is expanding.

Unlike the slices of an apple pie, those of the global pie have different fillings. Some slices have more oil, some more food, some more clothing, some more housing services, some more autos, and so on. Let's look at some of these different fillings starting with energy.

**FIGURE 2.2**

*What* in the Global Economy in 2008

myeconlab Animation

If we show the value of production in the world economy as a pie, the United States produces a slice that is 21 percent of the total. The other advanced economies produce 35 percent of the total.

Most of the rest of the global pie comes from Asia. China produces a slice that is 11 percent of the total, and the rest of the developing Asian economies produce 10 percent. The developing countries of Africa, the Middle East, and the Western Hemisphere produce 16 percent, and the emerging market economies produce the rest.

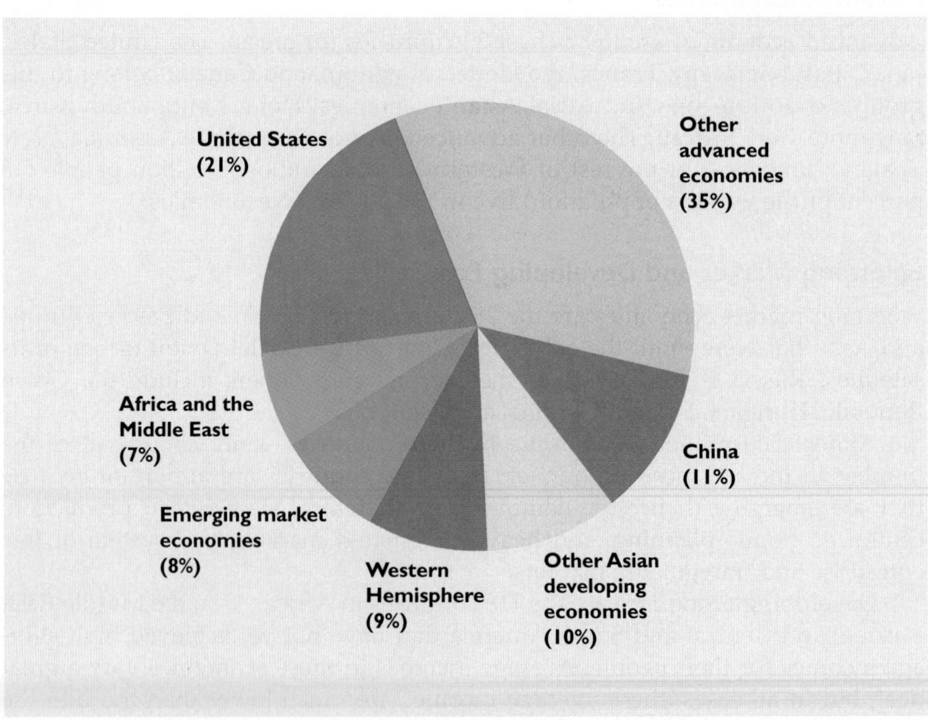


SOURCE OF DATA: International Monetary Fund, World Economic Outlook Database, April 2009.

## Energy

Oil, natural gas, and coal resources are distributed unevenly across the globe and Figure 2.3 shows where these energy sources are produced. All of these resources are non-renewable and will eventually run dry. At the current rate of use, proven reserves of the world's oil will last for about 40 years, gas for about 60 years, and coal will last for 200 years. As reserves of oil, natural gas, and coal run low and the cost of accessing them rises, we will make increasing use of wind and solar power. Already, these sources provide 2 percent of the world's electricity and that percentage is growing.

## Food

Food production is a small part of the U.S. and other advanced economies and a large part of the developing economies such as Brazil, China, and India. But the advanced economies produce about one third of the world's food. How come? Because *total* production is much larger in the advanced economies than in the developing economies, and a small percentage of a big number can be greater than a large percentage of a small number!

## Other Goods and Services

If you were to visit a shopping mall in Canada, England, Australia, Japan, or any of the other advanced economies, you would wonder whether you had left the United States. You would see Starbucks, Burger King, Pizza Hut, Domino's Pizza, KFC, Kmart, Wal-Mart, Target, the United Colors of Benetton, Gap, Tommy

**FIGURE 2.3**

Energy Sources in the World Economy

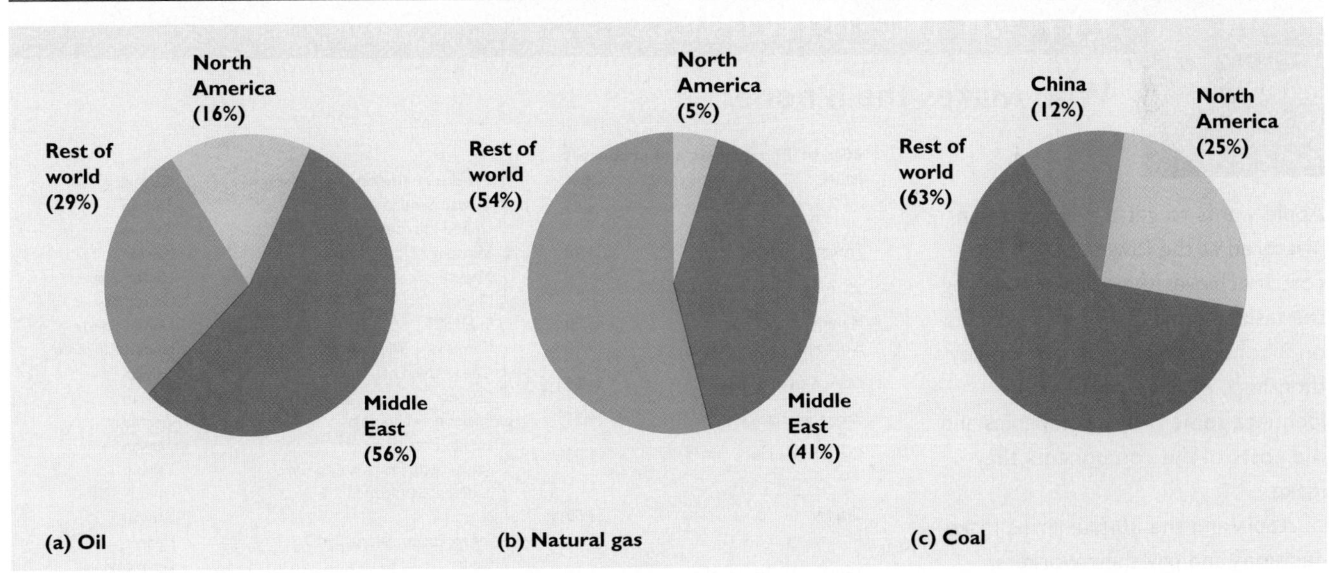


SOURCE OF DATA: Energy Information Administration.

Most of the world's proven oil reserves are in the Middle East (Saudi Arabia, Iraq, and Iran). North America has 16 percent of these reserves. The Middle East also has the largest share of natural gas reserves. North America has only 5 percent of these reserves. Coal is abundant in North America and in China.

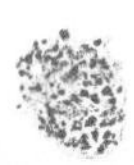

McDonald's in Shanghai.

Hilfiger, Tie Rack, the upscale Louis Vuitton and Burberry, and a host of other familiar names. And, of course, you would see McDonald's golden arches. You would see them in any of the 119 countries in which one or more of McDonald's 30,000 restaurants are located.

The similarities among the advanced economies go beyond the view from the shopping mall. The structure of *what* is produced is similar in these economies. As percentages of the total economy, agriculture and manufacturing are a small and shrinking: services are a large and expanding.

*What* is produced in the developing economies contrasts sharply with that of the advanced economies. Manufacturing is the big story. Developing economies have large and growing industries producing textiles, footwear, sports gear, toys, electronic goods, furniture, steel, and even automobiles.

## *How* in the Global Economy?

Each country or region has its own blend of land, labor, and capital. But there are some interesting common patterns and crucial differences between the advanced and developing economies that we'll now examine.

### Human Capital Differences

The proportion of the population with a degree or that has completed high school is small in developing economies. And in the poorest of the developing economies, many children even miss out on basic primary education. They just don't go to school at all. On-the-job training and experience are also much less extensive in the developing economies than in the advanced economies.

## EYE on the iPHONE

### Who Makes the iPhone?

Apple wants to get the iPhone manufactured at the lowest possible cost. It achieves this goal by assigning the task to more than 30 companies on 3 continents who in turn employ thousands of workers. The table identifies some of the companies and the costs of the components they make.

Apple and the 30-plus firms make decisions and pay their workers, investors, and raw material suppliers to play their parts in influencing *what*, *how*, and *for whom* goods and services are produced.

**4Gbyte iPhone costs and producers**

| Item | Cost | Producer (incomplete list) | Country |
|---|---|---|---|
| Processing chips | 31.40 | Taiwan Semiconductor | Taiwan |
| | | United Microelectronics Corp | Taiwan |
| | | Samsung | Korea |
| | | Marvell | United States |
| | | Micron | United States |
| Memory chips | 45.80 | Intel, SST | United States |
| Bluetooth | 19.10 | Cambridge Silicon Radio | United Kingdom |
| Printed circuit board | 36.05 | Cheng Uei, Entery | Taiwan |
| | | Cyntec | Taiwan |
| Phone interface | 19.25 | Infineon Technology | Germany |
| Camera module | 11.00 | Largan Precision | Taiwan |
| | | Altus-Tech, Primax, Lite On | Taiwan |
| Display | 33.50 | National Semiconductor | United States |
| | | Novatek | Taiwan |
| | | Sanyo Epson, Sharp, TMD | Japan |
| Touch screen controller | 1.15 | Balda | Germany |
| | | Broadcom | United States |
| Battery and power management | 8.60 | Delta Electronics | Taiwan |
| Case | 8.50 | Catcher, Foxconn Tech | Taiwan |
| Assembly | 15.50 | Foxconn? Quanta? | Taiwan |
| Royalties | 15.98 | | |
| **Total cost** | **245.83** | | |

### Physical Capital Differences

The major feature of an advanced economy that differentiates it from a developing economy is the amount of capital available for producing goods and services. The differences begin with the basic transportation system. In the advanced economies, a well-developed highway system connects all the major cities and points of production. You can see this difference most vividly by opening a road atlas of North America and contrasting the U.S. interstate highway system with the sparse highways of Mexico. You would see a similar contrast if you flipped through a road atlas of Western Europe and Africa.

But it isn't the case that the developing economies have no highways. In fact, some of them have the newest and the best. But the new and best are usually inside and around the major cities. The smaller centers and rural areas of developing economies often have some of the worst roads in the world.

The contrast in vehicles is perhaps even greater than that in highways. You're unlikely to run across a horse-drawn wagon in an advanced economy, but in a developing economy, animal power can still be found, and trucks are often old and unreliable.

The contrasts in the transportation system are matched by those on farms and in factories. In general, the more advanced the economy, the greater are the amount and sophistication of the capital equipment used in production. But again, the contrast is not all black and white. Some factories in India, China, and other parts of Asia use the very latest technologies. Furniture manufacture is an example. To make furniture of a quality that Americans are willing to buy, firms in Asia use machines like those in the furniture factories of North Carolina.

Again, it is the extensiveness of the use of modern capital-intensive technologies that distinguishes a developing economy from an advanced economy. All the factories in the advanced economies are capital intensive compared with only some in the developing economies.

The differences in human and physical capital between advanced and developing economies have a big effect on who gets the goods and services.

*Beijing has a highway system to match that of any advanced country. But away from the major cities, many of China's roads are unpaved and driving on them is slow and sometimes hazardous.*

## ■ *For Whom* in the Global Economy?

Who gets the world's goods and services depends on the incomes that people earn. So how are incomes distributed across the world?

### Personal Distribution of Income

You saw earlier (on p. 39) that in the United States, the lowest-paid 20 percent of the population receives 3 percent of total income and the highest-paid 20 percent receives 51 percent of total income. The personal distribution of income in the world economy is much more unequal. According to World Bank data, the lowest-paid 20 percent of the world's population receives 2 percent of world income, and the highest-paid 20 percent receives about 70 percent of world income.

### International Distribution

Much of the greater inequality at the global level arises from differences in average incomes among countries. Figure 2.4 shows some of these differences. It shows the dollar value of what people can afford each day on average. You can see that in the United States, that number is $128 a day—an average person in the United States can buy goods and services that cost $128. This amount is around five times the world average. Canada and the United Kingdom have average incomes of around 80 percent of that of the United States. Japan, Germany, France, Italy, and the other advanced economies have average incomes around 75 percent of U.S. average income. Income levels fall off quickly as we move farther down the graph, with Africa achieving an average income of only $7 a day.

As people have lost well-paid manufacturing jobs and found lower-paid service jobs, inequality has increased in the United States and in most other advanced economies. Inequality is also increasing in the developing economies. People with skills enjoy rapidly rising incomes but the incomes of the unskilled are falling.

## A Happy Paradox and a Huge Challenge

Despite the increase in inequality inside most countries, inequality across the entire world has decreased during the past 20 years. And most important, according to Xavier Sala-i-Martin, an economics professor at Columbia University, extreme poverty has declined. Professor Sala-i-Martin estimates that between 1976 and 1998, the number of people who earn $1 a day or less fell by 235 million and the number who earn $2 a day or less fell by 450 million. This happy situation arises because in China, the largest nation, incomes have increased rapidly and lifted millions from extreme poverty.

Lifting Africa from poverty is today's big challenge. In 1960, 11 percent of the world's poor lived in Africa, but in 1998, 66 percent did. Between 1976 and 1998, the number of people in Africa who earn $1 a day or less rose by 175 million, and the number who earn $2 a day or less rose by 227 million.

**FIGURE 2.4**

*For Whom* in the Global Economy in 2008

myeconlab Animation

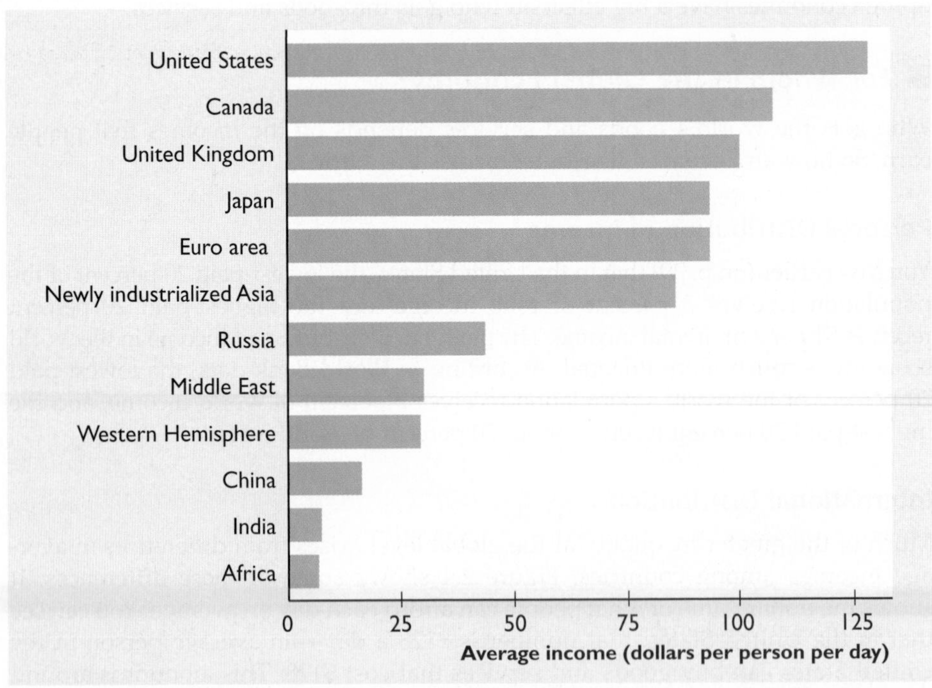


In 2008, the average income per day in the United States was $128. It was $107 in Canada and $100 in the United Kingdom. It was $93 in both Japan and the Euro area. The number falls off rapidly to $44 in Russia, $16 in China, $8 in India, and $7 in Africa.

SOURCE OF DATA: International Monetary Fund, World Economic Outlook Database, April 2009.

# EYE on YOUR LIFE

## The U.S. and Global Economies in Your Life

You've encountered a lot of facts and trends about what, how, and for whom goods and services are produced in the U.S. economy and the global economy. How can you use this information? You can use it in two ways:

1. To inform your choice of career
2. To inform your stand on the politics of protecting U.S. jobs

### Career Choices

As you think about your future career, you are now better informed about some of the key trends. You know that manufacturing is shrinking. The U.S. economy is what is sometimes called a *post-industrial economy*. Industries that provided the backbone of the economy in previous generations have fallen to barely a fifth of the economy today, and the trend continues. It is possible that by the middle of the current century, manufacturing will be as small a source of jobs as agriculture is today.

So, a job in a manufacturing business is likely to lead to some tough situations and possibly the need for several job changes over a working life.

As manufacturing shrinks, so services expand, and this expansion will continue. The provision of health care, education, communication, wholesale and retail trades, and entertainment are all likely to expand in the future and be sources of increasing employment and rising wages. A job in a service-oriented business is more likely to lead to steady advances in income.

### Political Stand on Job Protection

As you think about the stand you will take on the political question of protecting U.S. jobs, you are better informed about the basic facts and trends.

When you hear that manufacturing jobs are disappearing to China, you will be able to place that news in historical perspective. You might reasonably be concerned, especially if you or a member of your family has lost a job. But you know that trying to reverse or even halt this process is flying in the face of stubborn historical trends.

In later chapters, you will learn that there are good economic reasons to be skeptical about any form of protection and placing limits on competition.

# CHECKPOINT 2.2

**Describe what, how, and for whom goods and services are produced in the global economy.**

Work these problems in Study Plan 2.2 to get instant feedback.

## Practice Problems

1. Describe what, how, and for whom goods and services are produced in developing economies.
2. **Success story: Rwandan coffee farmers**
   The Clinton Foundation loaned $23,000 to Misozi to support improvements to coffee washing stations and provided technical support.
   Source: The Clinton Foundation
   What was the source of the success?

## Guided Solutions to Practice Problems

1. In developing countries, agriculture is the largest percentage, manufacturing is an increasing percentage, and services are important but a small percentage of total production. Most production does not use modern capital-intensive technologies, but some industries do. People who work in factories have rising income while those who work in rural industries are left behind.
2. Misozi growers improved their knowledge of coffee farming and increased their human capital and improved the operation of their washing stations.

## 2.3 THE CIRCULAR FLOWS

**Circular flow model**
A model of the economy that shows the circular flow of expenditures and incomes that result from decision makers' choices and the way those choices interact to determine what, how, and for whom goods and services are produced.

We can organize the data you've just studied using the **circular flow model**—a model of the economy that shows the circular flow of expenditures and incomes that result from decision makers' choices and the way those choices interact to determine what, how, and for whom goods and services are produced. Figure 2.5 shows the circular flow model.

### Households and Firms

**Households**
Individuals or groups of people living together.

**Households** are individuals or groups of people living together. The 112 million households in the United States own the factors of production—land, labor, capital, and entrepreneurship—and choose the quantities of these resources to provide to firms. Households also choose the quantities of goods and services to buy.

**Firms**
The institutions that organize the production of goods and services.

**Firms** are the institutions that organize the production of goods and services. The 20 million firms in the United States choose the quantities of the factors of production to hire and the quantities of goods and services to produce.

### Markets

Households choose the quantities of the factors of production to provide to firms, and firms choose the quantities of the services of the factors of production to hire. Firms choose the quantities of goods and services to produce, and households choose the quantities of goods and services to buy. How are these choices coordinated and made compatible? The answer is: by markets.

**Market**
Any arrangement that brings buyers and sellers together and enables them to get information and do business with each other.

A **market** is any arrangement that brings buyers and sellers together and enables them to get information and do business with each other. An example is the market in which oil is bought and sold—the world oil market. The world oil market is not a place. It is the network of oil producers, oil users, wholesalers, and brokers who buy and sell oil. In the world oil market, decision makers do not meet physically. They make deals by telephone, fax, and the Internet.

**Goods markets**
Markets in which goods and services are bought and sold.

**Factor markets**
Markets in which the services of factors of production are bought and sold.

Figure 2.5 identifies two types of markets: goods markets and factor markets. Goods and services are bought and sold in **goods markets**; and the services of factors of production are bought and sold in **factor markets**.

### Real Flows and Money Flows

When households choose the quantities of services of land, labor, capital, and entrepreneurship to offer in factor markets, they respond to the incomes they receive—rent for land, wages for labor, interest for capital, and profit for entrepreneurship. When firms choose the quantities of factor services to hire, they respond to the rent, wages, interest, and profits they must pay to households.

Similarly, when firms choose the quantities of goods and services to produce and offer for sale in goods markets, they respond to the amounts that they receive from the expenditures that households make. And when households choose the quantities of goods and services to buy, they respond to the amounts they must pay to firms.

Figure 2.5 shows the flows that result from these choices made by households and firms. The flows shown in orange are *real flows:* the flows of the factors of production that go from households through factor markets to firms and of the goods and services that go from firms through goods markets to households. The flows in the opposite direction are *money flows:* the flows of payments made in exchange for the services of factors of production (shown in blue) and of expenditures on goods and services (shown in red).

Lying behind these real flows and money flows are millions of individual choices about what to consume and what and how to produce. These choices result in buying plans by households and selling plans by firms in goods markets. And the choices result in selling plans by households and buying plans by firms in factor markets that interact to determine the prices that people pay and the incomes they earn, and so determine for whom goods and services are produced. You'll learn in Chapter 4 how markets coordinate the buying plans and selling plans of households and firms and make them compatible.

Firms produce most of the goods and services that we consume, but governments provide some of the services that we enjoy. Governments also play a big role in modifying for whom goods and services are produced by changing the personal distribution of income. We're now going to look at the role of governments in the U.S. economy and add them to the circular flow model.

**FIGURE 2.5**

The Circular Flow Model

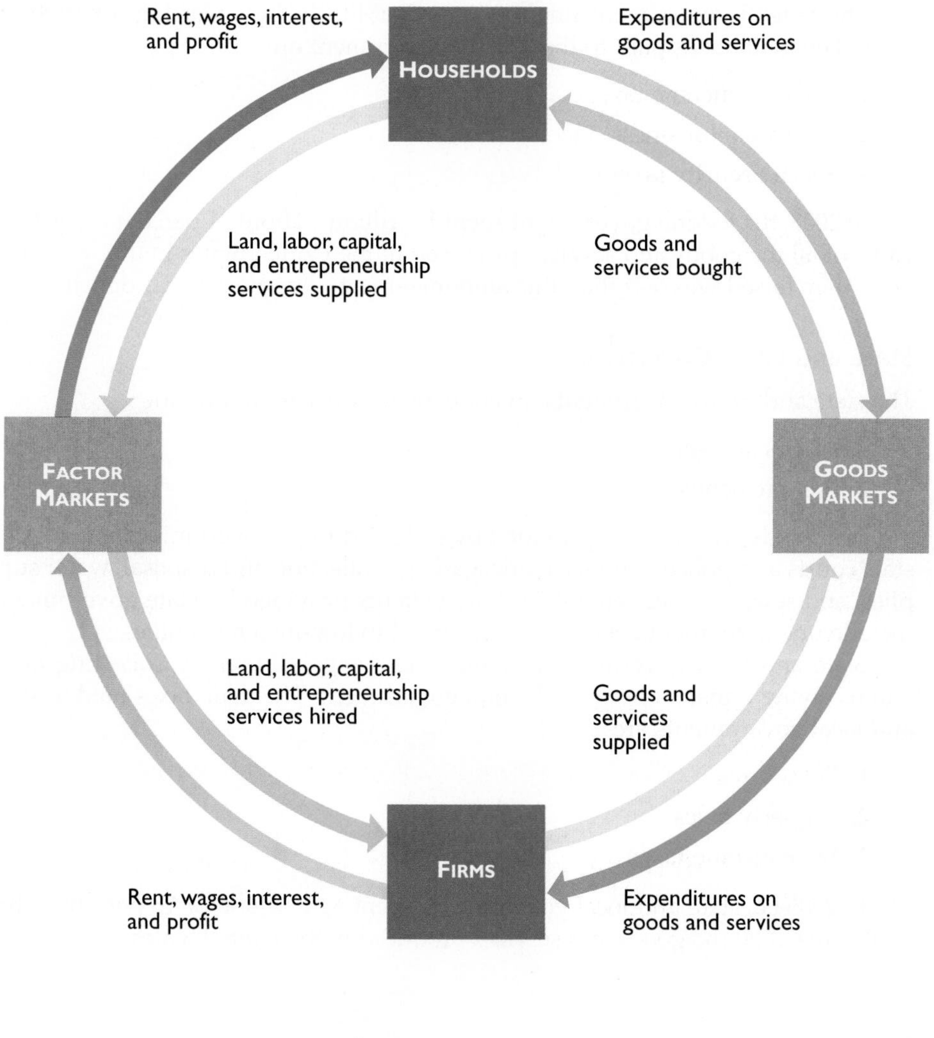

The orange flows are the services of factors of production that go from households through factor markets to firms and the goods and services that go from firms through goods markets to households. These flows are *real* flows.

The blue flow is the income earned by the factors of production, and the red flow is the expenditures on goods and services. These flows are *money* flows.

The choices that generate these real and money flows determine *what, how,* and *for whom* goods and services are produced.

## Governments

More than 86,000 organizations operate as governments in the United States. Some are tiny like the Yuma, Arizona, school district and some are enormous like the U.S. federal government. We divide governments into two levels:

- Federal government
- State and local government

### Federal Government

The federal government's major expenditures provide

1. Goods and services
2. Social Security and welfare payments
3. Transfers to state and local governments

The goods and services provided by the federal government include the legal system, which protects property and enforces contracts, and national defense. Social Security and welfare benefits, which include income for retired people and programs such as Medicare and Medicaid, are transfers from the federal government to households. Federal government transfers to state and local governments are payments designed to provide more equality across the states and regions.

The federal government finances its expenditures by collecting a variety of taxes. The main taxes paid to the federal government are

1. Personal income taxes
2. Corporate (business) income taxes
3. Social Security taxes

In 2008, the federal government spent $3 trillion—about 21 percent of the total value of all the goods and services produced in the United States in that year. The taxes they raised was less than this amount—the government had a deficit.

### State and Local Government

The state and local governments' major expenditures are to provide

1. Goods and services
2. Welfare benefits

The goods and services provided by state and local governments include the state courts and police, schools, roads, garbage collection and disposal, water supplies, and sewage management. Welfare benefits provided by state governments include unemployment benefits and other aid to low-income families.

State and local governments finance these expenditures by collecting taxes and receiving transfers from the federal government. The main taxes paid to state and local governments are

1. Sales taxes
2. Property taxes
3. State income taxes

In 2005-06, state and local governments spent $2.1 trillion or 16 percent of the total value of all the goods and services produced in the United States.

## Governments in the Circular Flow

Figure 2.6 adds governments to the circular flow model. As you study this figure, first notice that the outer circle is the same as in Figure 2.5. In addition to these flows, governments buy goods and services from firms. The red arrows that run from governments through the goods markets to firms show this expenditure.

Households and firms pay taxes to governments. The green arrows running directly from households and firms to governments show these flows. Also, governments make money payments to households and firms. The green arrows running directly from governments to households and firms show these flows. Taxes and transfers are direct transactions with governments and do not go through the goods markets and factor markets.

Not part of the circular flow and not visible in Figure 2.6, governments provide the legal framework within which all transactions occur. For example, governments operate the courts and legal system that enable contracts to be written and enforced.

**FIGURE 2.6**

Governments in the Circular Flow

myeconlab Animation

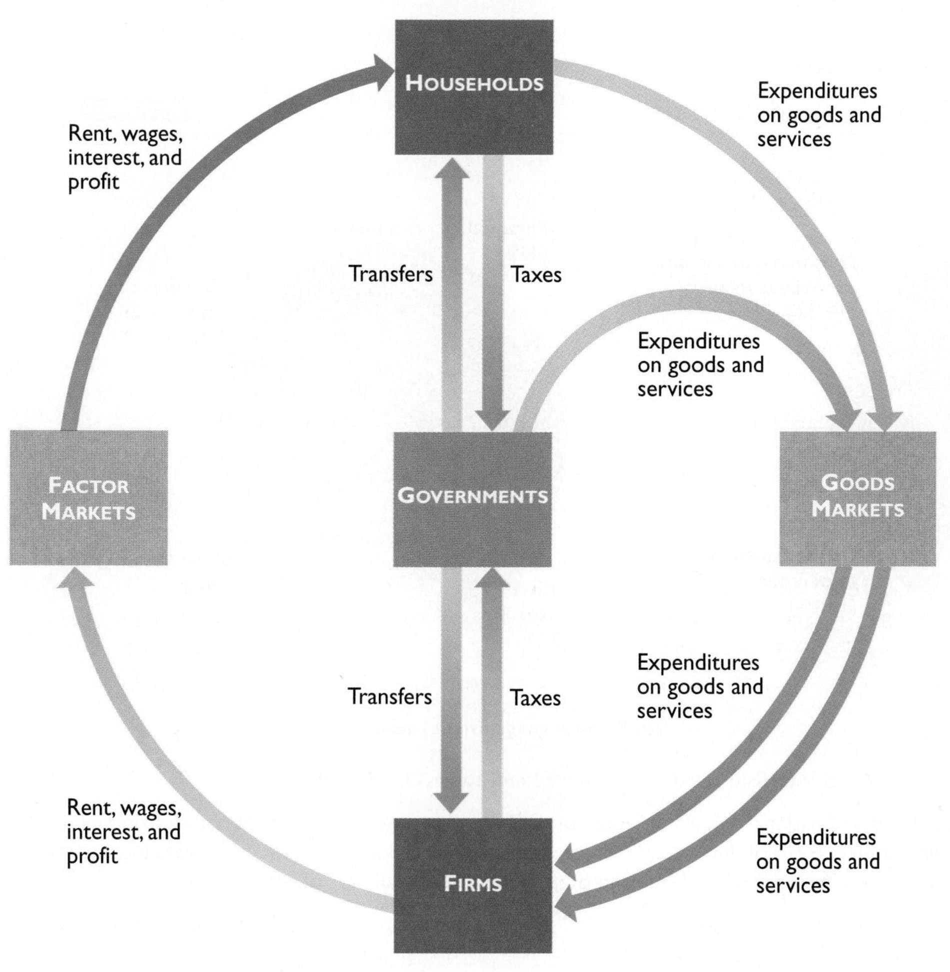


The green flows from households and firms to governments are taxes, and the green flows from governments to households and firms are money transfers.

The red flow from governments through goods markets to firms is the expenditures on goods and services by governments.

## Federal Government Expenditures and Revenue

What are the main items of expenditure by the federal government on goods and services and transfers? And what are its main sources of tax revenue? Figure 2.7 answers these questions.

Three items of expenditure are similar in magnitude—and large. They are Social Security benefits, Medicare and Medicaid, and national defense and homeland security. The combined total of these items is 60 percent of the government's expenditures. Other transfers to persons, which includes unemployment benefits, are also large. The "Others" category covers a wide range of items and includes transfers to state governments, NASA's space program, and the National Science Foundation's funding of research in the universities.

The interest payment on the national debt is another significant item. The **national debt** is the total amount that the federal government has borrowed to make expenditures that exceed tax revenue—to run a government budget deficit. The national debt is a bit like a large credit card balance, and paying the interest on the national debt is like paying the minimum required monthly payment.

**National debt**
The total amount that the federal government has borrowed to make expenditures that exceed tax revenue—to run a government budget deficit.

Most of the tax revenue of the federal government comes from personal income taxes and Social Security taxes. Corporate income taxes and other taxes are a small part of the federal government's revenue.

**FIGURE 2.7**
Federal Government Expenditures and Revenue

myeconlab Animation

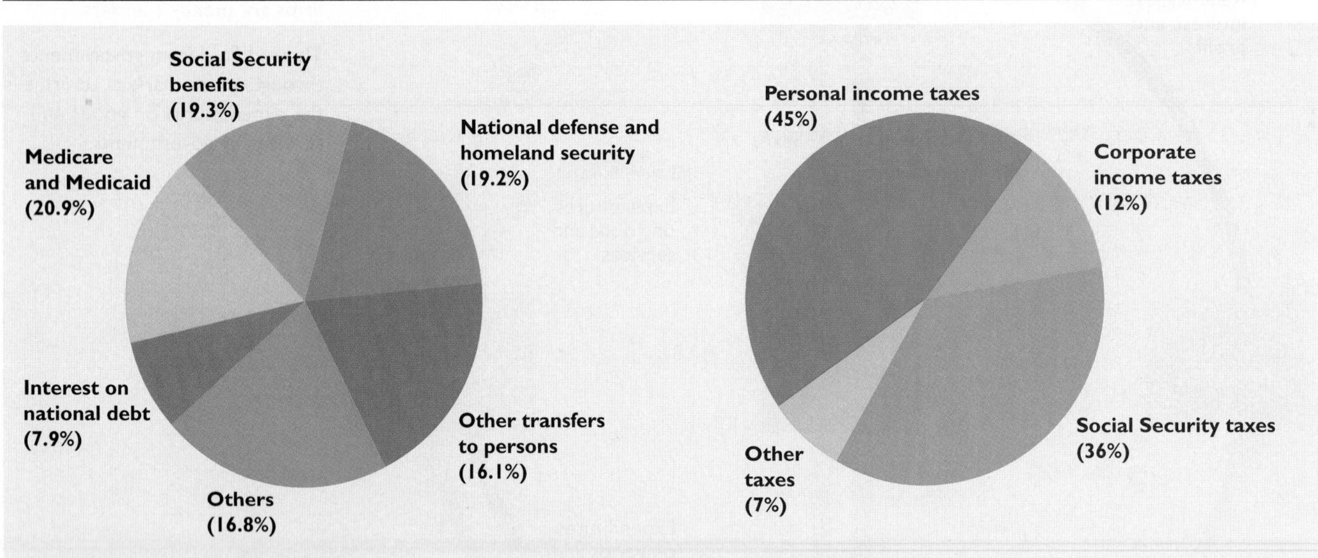


SOURCE OF DATA: Budget of the United States Government, Historical Tables, Table 2.1 and Table 3.1, 2008 data.

Social Security benefits, Medicare and Medicaid, and national defense and homeland security absorb almost 60 percent of the federal government's expenditures. Interest on the national debt is also a significant item.

Most of the federal government's revenue comes from personal income taxes and Social Security taxes. Corporate income taxes and other taxes are a small part of total revenue.

## State and Local Government Expenditures and Revenue

What are the main items of expenditure by the state and local governments on goods and services and transfers? And what are the main sources of state and local government revenue? Figure 2.8 answers these questions.

You can see that education is by far the largest part of the expenditures of state and local governments. This item covers the cost of public schools, colleges, and universities. It absorbs 34 percent of total expenditures—approximately $730 billion, or $2,400 per person.

Public welfare benefits are the second largest item and they take 18 percent of total expenditures. Highways are the next largest item, and they account for 6 percent of total expenditures. The remaining 42 percent is spent on other local public goods and services such as police services, garbage collection and disposal, sewage management, and water supplies.

Sales taxes and transfers from the federal government bring in similar amounts—about 19 percent and 21 percent of total revenue, respectively. Property taxes account for 16 percent of total revenue. Individual income taxes account for 12 percent, and corporate income taxes account for 2 percent. The remaining revenue comes from other taxes such as those on gasoline, cigarettes, and beer and wine.

**FIGURE 2.8**

State and Local Government Expenditures and Revenue

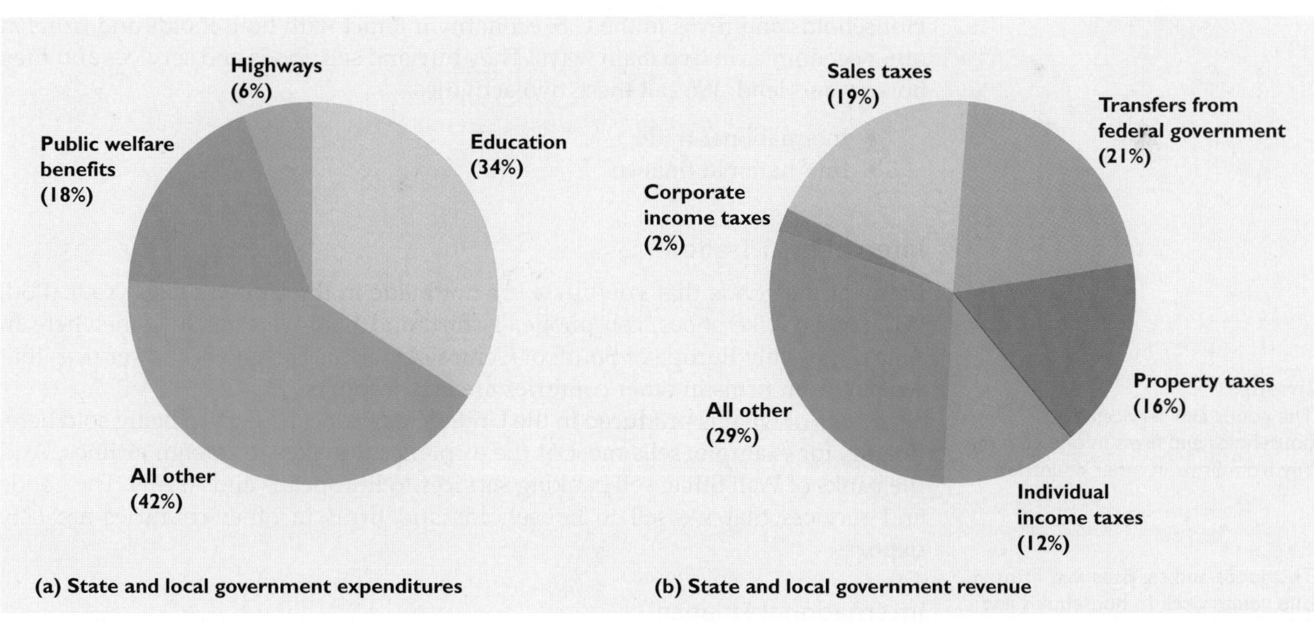


SOURCES OF DATA: *Economic Report of the President 2009*, Table B-86, 2005–2006 data..

Education, public welfare benefits, and highways are the largest slices of state and local government expenditures.

Most of the state and local government revenue comes from sales taxes, property taxes, and transfers from the federal government.

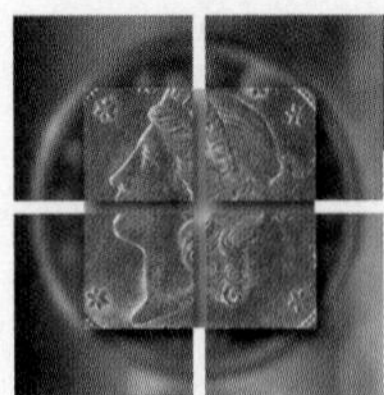

## EYE on the PAST

### Growing Government

One hundred years ago, the federal government spent 2 cents out of each dollar earned. Today, the federal government spends 20 cents. Government grew during the two world wars and during the 1960s and 1970s as social programs expanded.

Only during the 1980s and 1990s did big government begin to shrink in a process begun by Ronald Reagan and continued by Bill Clinton. But 9/11 saw the start of a new era of growing government.

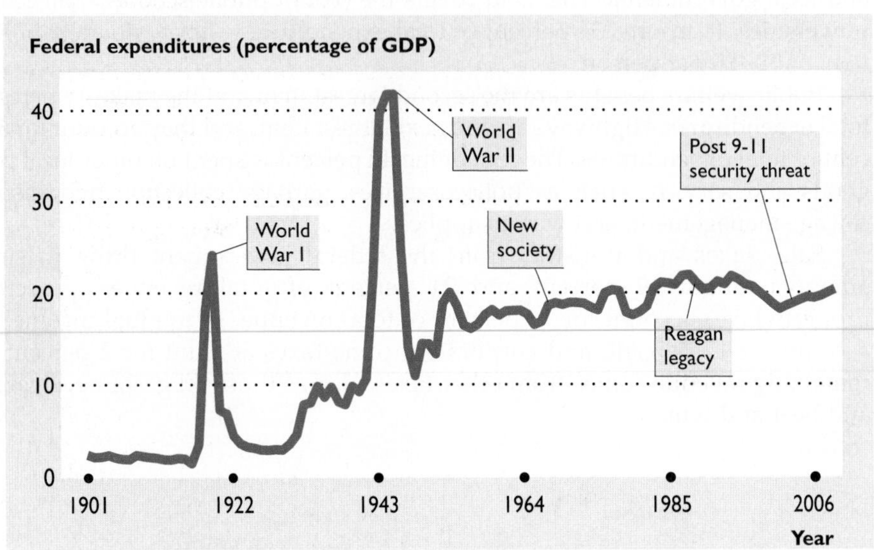


SOURCE OF DATA: Budget of the United States Government, Historical Tables, Table 1.1.

## Circular Flows in the Global Economy

Households and firms in the U.S. economy interact with households and firms in other economies in two main ways: They buy and sell goods and services and they borrow and lend. We call these two activities:

- International trade
- International finance

### International Trade

Many of the goods that you buy were not made in the United States. Your iPod, Wii games, Nike shoes, cell phone, T-shirt, and bike were made somewhere in Asia or possibly Europe or South or Central America. The goods and services that we buy from firms in other countries are U.S. **imports**.

**Imports**
The goods and services that households and firms in one country buy from firms in other countries.

Much of what is produced in the United States doesn't end up being sold here. Boeing, for example, sells most of the airplanes it makes to foreign airlines. And the banks of Wall Street sell banking services to Europeans and Asians. The goods and services that we sell to households and firms in other countries are U.S. **exports**.

**Exports**
The goods and services that firms in one country sell to households and firms in other countries.

### International Finance

When firms or governments want to borrow, they look for the lowest interest rate available. Sometimes, that is outside the United States. Also, when the value of our imports exceeds the value of our exports, we must borrow from the rest of the world.

Firms and governments in the rest of the world behave in the same way. They look for the lowest interest rate at which to borrow and the highest at which to lend. They might borrow from or lend to Americans.

Figure 2.9 shows the flows through goods markets and financial markets in the global economy. Households and firms in the U.S. economy interact with those in the rest of the world (other economies) in goods markets and financial markets.

The red flow shows the expenditure by Americans on imports of goods and services, and the blue flow shows the expenditure by the rest of the world on U.S. exports (other countries' imports). The green flow shows U.S. lending to the rest of the world, and the orange flow shows U.S. borrowing from the rest of the world.

It is these international trade and international finance flows that tie nations together in the global economy and through which global booms and slumps are transmitted.

**FIGURE 2.9**

Circular Flows in the Global Economy

myeconlab Animation

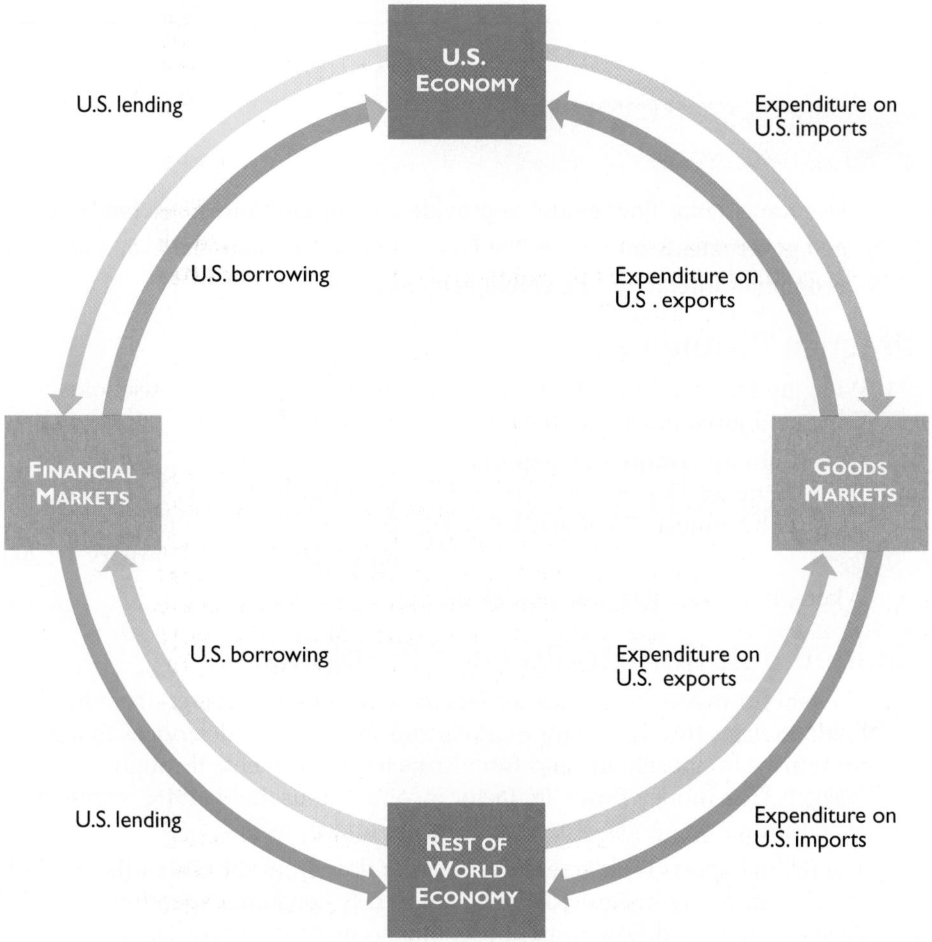

U.S. Economy
U.S. lending
Expenditure on U.S. imports
U.S. borrowing
Expenditure on U.S. exports
Financial Markets
Goods Markets
U.S. borrowing
Expenditure on U.S. exports
U.S. lending
Expenditure on U.S. imports
Rest of World Economy

Households and firms in the U.S. economy interact with those in the rest of the world (other economies) in goods markets and financial markets.

The red flow shows the expenditure by Americans on imports of goods and services, and the blue flow show the expenditure by the rest of the world on U.S. exports (other countries' imports).

The green flow shows U.S. lending to the rest of the world, and the orange flow shows U.S. borrowing from the rest of the world.

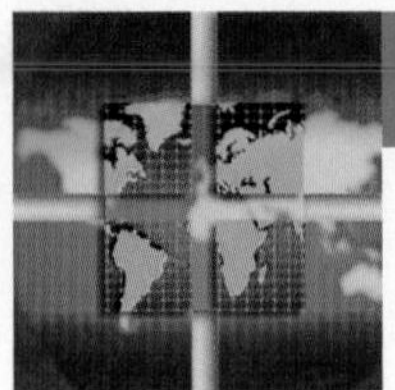

# EYE on the GLOBAL ECONOMY

## The 2009 Slump in International Trade

International trade has expanded rapidly during the past 25 years. At an average growth rate of close to 7 percent a year, world trade has doubled every decade.

In 2001, a mini-recession in the United States slowed world trade growth to a crawl.

But the 2001 slowdown looks mild compared to the collapse in world trade during the 2009 global economic slump. The International Monetary Fund projects world trade shrinking in 2009 by 11 percent and zero growth in 2010.

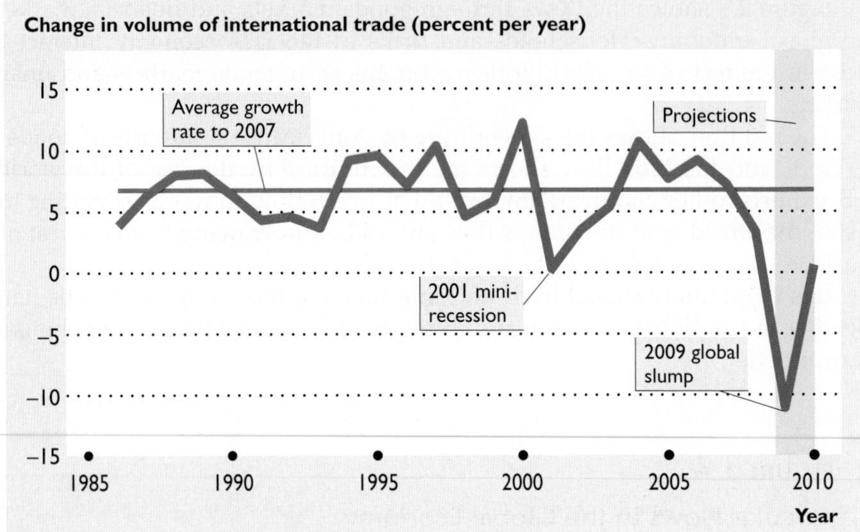


SOURCE OF DATA: International Monetary Fund, World Economic Outlook Database, April 2009.

Work these problems in Study Plan 2.3 to get instant feedback.

# CHECKPOINT 2.3

**Use the circular flow model to provide a picture of how households, firms, and governments interact in the U.S. economy and how the U.S. and other economies interact in the global economy.**

## Practice Problems

1. What are the real flows and money flows that run between households, firms, and governments in the circular flow model?
2. **Global slump crimps U.S. exports**

   The Commerce Department reports that export orders in the second half of 2008 fell by almost $35 billion while U.S. consumers slashed their spending.

   Source: *USA Today*, February 11, 2009

   Where, in the circular flow model, do these choices appear?

## Guided Solutions to Practice Problems

1. The real flows are the services of factors of production that go from households to firms through factor markets and the goods and services that go from firms to households and from firms to governments through goods markets. The money flows are factor incomes, household and government expenditures on goods and services, taxes, and transfers.
2. The fall in exports is a decrease in the blue flow from the rest of the world to the U.S. economy in Figure 2.9. The cut in U.S. consumer spending is a decrease in the red flow from households to firms in Figure 2.6.

# CHAPTER SUMMARY

## Key Points

1 **Describe what, how, and for whom goods and services are produced in the United States.**

- Consumption goods and services represent 62 percent of total production; capital goods represent 10 percent.
- Goods and services are produced by using the four factors of production: land, labor, capital, and entrepreneurship.
- The incomes people earn (rent for land, wages for labor, interest for capital, and profit for entrepreneurship) determine who gets the goods and services produced.

2 **Describe what, how, and for whom goods and services are produced in the global economy.**

- Sixty-four percent of the world's production (by value) comes from the advanced industrial countries and the emerging market economies.
- Production in the advanced economies uses more capital (both machines and human), but some developing economies use the latest capital and technologies.
- The global distribution of income is more unequal than the U.S. distribution. Poverty has fallen in Asia but has increased in Africa.

3 **Use the circular flow model to provide a picture of how households, firms, and governments interact in the U.S. economy and how the U.S. and other economies interact in the global economy.**

- The circular flow model of the U.S. economy shows the real flows of factors of production and goods and the corresponding money flows of incomes and expenditures.
- Governments in the circular flow receive taxes, make transfers, and buy goods and services.
- The circular flow model of the global economy shows the flows of U.S. exports and imports and the international financial flows that result from lending to and borrowing from other countries.

## Key Terms

Work these problems in Chapter 2 Study Plan to get instant feedback.

## CHAPTER CHECKPOINT

### Study Plan Problems and Applications

1. Explain which of the following items are not consumption goods and services:
   - A chocolate bar
   - A ski lift
   - A golf ball
2. Explain which of the following items are *not* capital goods:
   - An auto assembly line
   - A shopping mall
   - A golf ball
3. Explain which of the following items are *not* factors of production:
   - Vans used by a baker to deliver bread
   - 1,000 shares of Amazon.com stock
   - Undiscovered oil

Use the following information to work Problems 4 to 6.

**Why is income inequality in America so pronounced? Consider education**
Outsourcing, immigration, and the gains of the super-rich are the most common reasons for the income inequality in America. Tyler Cowen disagrees: The problem is largely the lack of education. To date, outsourcing is not yet common enough to have much effect. Immigration doesn't account for much of the change in the wages paid to unskilled workers since 1950. Advances in technology raises the incomes of highly skilled workers. Inequality will be reduced if more people undertake education.

Source: *The New York Times*, May 17, 2007

4. If outsourcing were to have a big effect on the personal distribution of income in Figure 2.1, how would the distribution have changed?
5. Immigrants to the United States include unskilled workers from Mexico and skilled workers from countries such as India and China. How would each of these types of immigrants influence the personal distribution of income?
6. Explain how more people undertaking education will change the personal distribution of income in the United States.
7. A Job Creation through Entrepreneurship Act, debated in the House of Representatives in 2009, would award grants to small business owners, some of which would be aimed at women, Native Americans, and veterans. The Act would provide $189 million in 2010 and $531 million between 2010 and 2014. Explain how you would expect this Act to influence *what*, *how*, and *for whom* goods and services are produced in the United States.
8. Indicate on a graph of the circular flow model, the real or money flow in which the following items belong:
   - You pay your tuition.
   - The University of Texas buys some Dell computers.
   - A student works at FedEx Kinko's.
   - Donald Trump rents a Manhattan building to a hotel.
   - You pay your income tax.

## Instructor Assignable Problems and Applications

Your instructor can assign these problems as homework, a quiz, or a test in **MyEconLab**.

1. Buzz surrounds Apple's iPhone. Can you explain:
   - Why doesn't Apple manufacture the iPhone at its own factory in the United States?
   - Why doesn't Apple offer a cheaper version of the iPhone without a camera?
   - In view of the cost of producing an iPhone (in the table on p. 44), why do you think the price of an iPhone is so high? What other costs must be incurred to bring the iPhone to market other than the cost of manufacturing it?
2. Explain which of the following items are *not* consumption goods and services:
   - An interstate highway
   - An airplane
   - A stealth bomber
3. Explain which of the following items are *not* capital goods:
   - An interstate highway
   - An oil tanker
   - A construction worker
4. Explain which of the following items are *not* factors of production:
   - A garbage truck
   - A pack of bubble gum
   - The President of the United States
5. Explain which of the following pairs does not match:
   - Labor and wages
   - Land and rent
   - Entrepreneurship and profit
   - Capital and profit
6. Compare the scale of agricultural production in the advanced and developing economies. In which is the percentage higher? In which is the total amount produced greater?
7. Think about the trends in what and how goods and services are produced in the U.S. and global economies. Which jobs will grow fastest in the future? What will happen to the quality of labor over the next decade?
8. **China's prosperity brings income gap**

   A study by the Asian Development Bank [ADB] reports that China has the largest gap between the rich and the poor in Asia. Ifzal Ali, the ADB's chief economist, claims it is not so much that the rich are getting richer and the poor are getting poorer, but that the rich are getting richer faster than the poor.

   Source: *Financial Times*, August 9, 2007

   Explain how the personal income distribution in China can be getting more unequal even though the poorest 20 percent are getting richer.
9. In the African nation of Senegal, to enroll in school a child needs a Birth Certificate that costs $25. This price is several week's income for many families. Explain how this requirement is likely to affect the growth of human

capital in Senegal. Predict the effects of this requirement on the human capital of girls and women and explain your prediction.

10. On a graph of the circular flow model, indicate in which real or money flow the following items belong:
    - General Motors pays its workers wages.
    - IBM pays a dividend to its stockholders.
    - You buy your groceries.
    - Chrysler buys robots.
    - Southwest rents some aircraft.
    - Nike pays Tiger Woods for promoting its golf ball.

Use the following information to work Problems 11 and 12.

**Poor India makes millionaires at fastest pace**

India, with the world's largest population of poor people living on less than a dollar a day, also paradoxically created millionaires at the fastest pace in the world in 2007. Millionaires increased by 22.7 per cent to 123,000 (measured in dollars). In contrast, the number of Indians living on less than a dollar a day is 350 million and those living on less than $2 a day is 700 million. In other words, there are 7,000 very poor Indians for every millionaire.

Source: *The Times of India*, June 25, 2008

11. How do you think the personal distribution of income in India is changing as the number of millionaires is growing at a "blistering pace"?
12. Why might incomes of a $1 a day and $2 a day underestimate the value of the goods and services that these households actually consume?

Use the following information to work Problems 13 to 15.

According to the International Telecommunications Union the global economy has three cell phone users for every fixed line user. Two in every three cell phone users lives in a developing nation and Africa has the fastest growth rate in cell phone users. In 2000, 1 African in 50 had a cell phone. In 2008, that number was 14 in 50.

13. Describe the changes in *what* telecommunication services the global economy produces.
14. Describe the changes in *how* telecommunication services are produced in the global economy.
15. Describe the changes in *for whom* telecommunication services are produced in the global economy.
16. The entire Arctic region is believed to be rich in oil and gas reserves and the cost of extracting these resources keeps falling. On August 5, 2007, a Russian submarine visited the seabed 2.5 miles beneath the North Pole and planted its nation's flag. Canada, the United States, Russia, Norway, Iceland, and Denmark all claim to "own" seabed in the Arctic Circle. Describe the changes in *what*, *how*, and *for whom* arctic oil and gas might be extracted in the future.

## Is wind power free?

South Dakota has enough wind to generate 55 percent of the nation's electricity. But what would be the cost—the opportunity cost—of that electricity?

# The Economic Problem

CHAPTER CHECKLIST

**When you have completed your study of this chapter, you will be able to**

1 Explain and illustrate the concepts of scarcity, production efficiency, and tradeoff using the production possibilities frontier.

2 Calculate opportunity cost.

3 Explain what makes production possibilities expand.

4 Explain how people gain from specialization and trade.

## 3.1 PRODUCTION POSSIBILITIES

Every working day in mines, factories, shops, and offices and on farms and construction sites across the United States, we produce a vast array of goods and services. In the United States in 2009, 240 billion hours of labor equipped with $47 trillion worth of capital produced $14 trillion worth of goods and services.

Although our production capability is enormous, it is limited by our available resources and by technology. At any given time, we have fixed quantities of the factors of production and a fixed state of technology. Because our wants exceed our resources, we must make choices. We must rank our wants and decide which to satisfy and which to leave unsatisfied. In using our scarce resources, we make rational choices. And to make a rational choice, we must determine the costs and benefits of the alternatives.

Your first task in this chapter is to learn about an economic model of scarcity, choice, and opportunity cost—a model called the production possibilities frontier.

### Production Possibilities Frontier

**Production possibilities frontier**
The boundary between the combinations of goods and services that can be produced and the combinations that cannot be produced, given the available factors of production and the state of technology.

The **production possibilities frontier** is the boundary between the combinations of goods and services that can be produced and the combinations that cannot be produced, given the available factors of production—land, labor, capital, and entrepreneurship—and the state of technology.

Although we produce millions of different goods and services, we can visualize the limits to production most easily if we imagine a simpler world that produces just two goods. Imagine an economy that produces only DVDs and cell phones. All the land, labor, capital, and entrepreneurship available gets used to produce these two goods.

Land can be used for movie studios and DVD factories or cell-phone factories. Labor can be trained to work as movie actors, camera and sound crews, movie producers and DVD makers or as cell-phone makers. Capital can be used for making movies, making and coating disks, and transferring images to disks, or for the equipment that makes cell phones. Entrepreneurs can put their creative talents to managing movie studios and running electronics businesses that make DVDs or to running cell-phone businesses. In every case, the more resources that are used to produce DVDs, the fewer are left to produce cell phones.

Suppose that if no factors of production are allocated to producing cell phones, the maximum number of DVDs that can be produced is 15 million a year. So one production possibility is no cell phones and 15 million DVDs. Another possibility is to allocate sufficient resources to produce 1 million cell phones a year. But these resources must be taken from DVD factories. Suppose that the economy can now produce only 14 million DVDs a year. As resources are moved from producing DVDs to producing cell phones, the economy produces more cell phones but fewer DVDs.

The table in Figure 3.1 illustrates these two combinations of cell phones and DVDs as possibilities *A* and *B*. Suppose that *C*, *D*, *E*, and *F* are other combinations of the quantities of these two goods that the economy can produce. Possibility *F* uses all the resources to produce 5 million cell phones a year and allocates no resources to producing DVDs. These six possibilities are alternative combinations of the quantities of the two goods that the economy can produce by using all of its resources, given the technology.

The graph in Figure 3.1 illustrates the production possibilities frontier, *PPF*, for cell phones and DVDs. It is a graph of the production possibilities in the table. The *x*-axis shows the production of cell phones, and the *y*-axis shows the production of DVDs. Each point on the graph labeled *A* through *F* represents the possibility in the table identified by the same letter. For example, point *B* represents the production of 1 million cell phones and 14 million DVDs. These quantities also appear in the table as possibility *B*.

The *PPF* is a valuable tool for illustrating the effects of scarcity and its consequences. The *PPF* puts three features of production possibilities in sharp focus. They are the distinctions between

- Attainable and unattainable combinations
- Efficient and inefficient production
- Tradeoffs and free lunches

**FIGURE 3.1**

The Production Possibilities Frontier

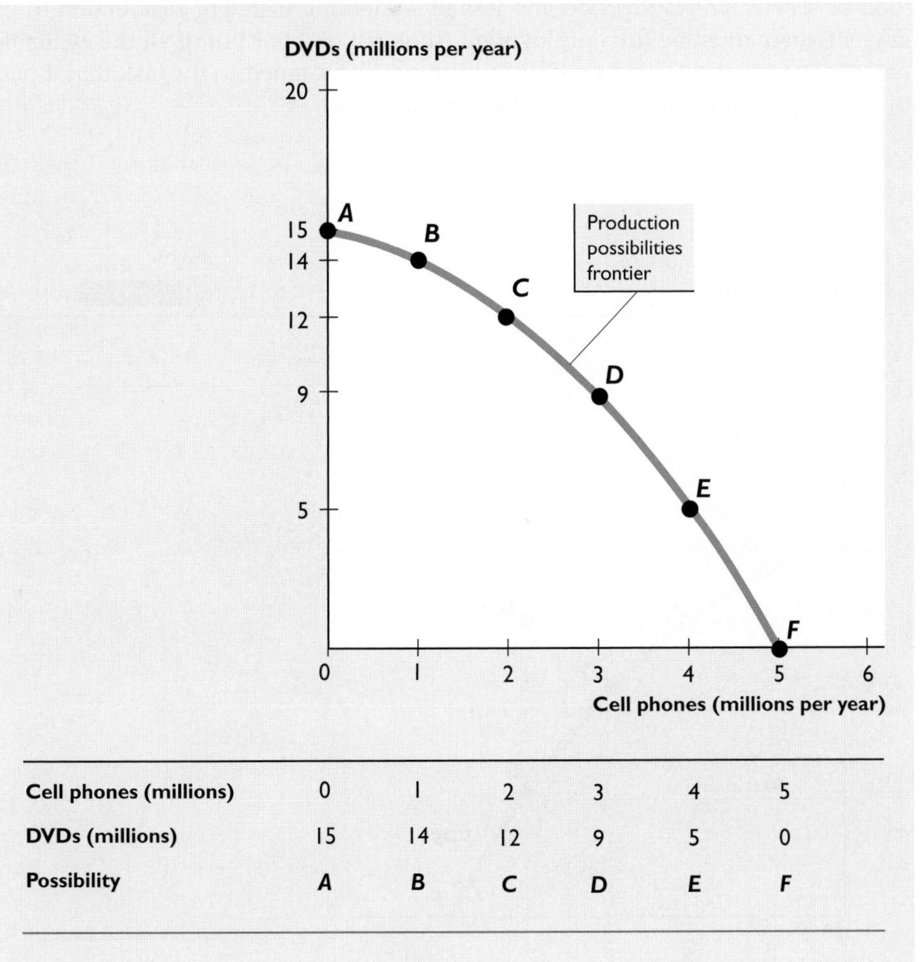


| Cell phones (millions) | 0 | 1 | 2 | 3 | 4 | 5 |
|---|---|---|---|---|---|---|
| DVDs (millions) | 15 | 14 | 12 | 9 | 5 | 0 |
| Possibility | *A* | *B* | *C* | *D* | *E* | *F* |

The table and the graph show the production possibilities frontier for cell phones and DVDs.

Point *A* tells us that if the economy produces no cell phones, the maximum quantity of DVDs it can produce is 15 million a year. Each point *A*, *B*, *C*, *D*, *E*, and *F* on the graph represents the possibility in the table identified by the same letter. The line passing through these points is the production possibilities frontier.

### Attainable and Unattainable Combinations

Because the *PPF* shows the *limits* to production, it separates attainable combinations from unattainable ones. The economy can produce combinations of cell phones and DVDs that are smaller than those on the *PPF*, and it can produce any of the combinations *on* the *PPF*. These combinations of cell phones and DVDs are attainable. But it is impossible to produce combinations that are larger than those on the *PPF*. These combinations are unattainable.

Figure 3.2 emphasizes the attainable and unattainable combinations. Only the points on the *PPF* and inside it (in the orange area) are attainable. The combinations of cell phones and DVDs beyond the *PPF* (in the white area), such as the combination at point *G*, are unattainable. These points illustrate combinations that cannot be produced with the current resources and technology. The *PPF* tells us that the economy can produce 4 million cell phones and 5 million DVDs at point *E or* 2 million cell phones and 12 million DVDs at point *C*. But the economy cannot produce 4 million cell phones and 12 million DVDs at point *G*.

### Efficient and Inefficient Production

**Production efficiency**
A situation in which the economy is getting all that it can from its resources and cannot produce more of one good or service without producing less of something else.

**Production efficiency** occurs when the economy is getting all that it can from its resources. When production is efficient it is not possible to produce more of one good or service without producing less of something else. For production to be efficient, there must be full employment—not just of labor but of all the available factors of production—and each resource must be assigned to the task that it performs comparatively better than other resources can.

**FIGURE 3.2**
Attainable and Unattainable Combinations

myeconlab Animation

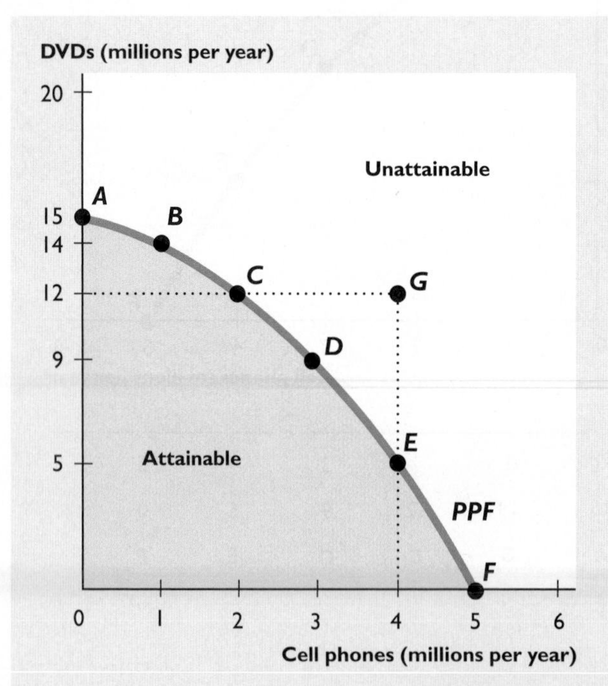


The production possibilities frontier, *PPF*, separates attainable combinations from unattainable ones. The economy can produce at any point *inside* the *PPF* (the orange area) or at any point *on* the frontier. Any point outside the production possibilities frontier, such as point *G*, is unattainable.

Figure 3.3 illustrates the distinction between efficient and inefficient production. With *inefficient* production, the economy might be producing 3 million cell phones and 5 million DVDs at point *H*. With an *efficient* use of the economy's resources, it is possible to produce at a point on the *PPF* such as point *D* or *E*. At point *D*, there are more DVDs and the same quantity of cell phones as at point *H*. And at point *E*, there are more cell phones and the same quantity of DVDs as at point *H*. At points *D* and *E*, production is efficient.

## Tradeoffs and Free Lunches

A **tradeoff** is an exchange—giving up one thing to get something else. You trade off income for a better grade when you decide to cut back on the hours you spend on your weekend job and allocate the time to extra study. The Ford Motor Company faces a tradeoff when it cuts the production of trucks and uses the resources saved to produce more hybrid SUVs. The federal government faces a tradeoff when it cuts NASA's space exploration program and allocates more resources to homeland security. As a society, we face a tradeoff when we decide to cut down a forest and destroy the habitat of the spotted owl.

**Tradeoff**
An exchange—giving up one thing to get something else.

The production possibilities frontier illustrates the idea of a tradeoff. The *PPF* in Figure 3.3 shows how. If the economy produces at point *E* and people want to produce more DVDs, they must forgo some cell phones. In the move from point *E* to point *D*, people trade off cell phones for DVDs.

Economists often express the central idea of economics—that choices involve tradeoff—with the saying "There is no such thing as a free lunch." A *free lunch* is a gift—getting something without giving up something else. What does the

**FIGURE 3.3**

Efficient and Inefficient Production, Tradeoffs, and Free Lunches

myeconlab Animation

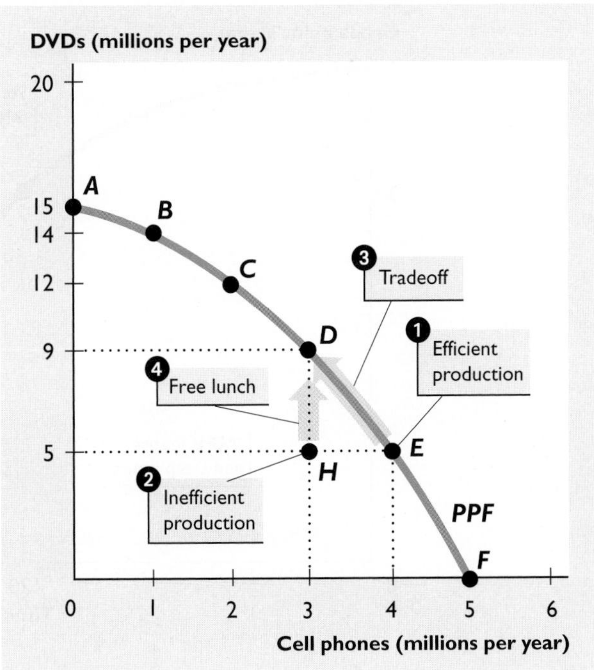


1. When production occurs at a point on the *PPF*, such as point *E*, resources are used efficiently.
2. When production occurs at a point inside the *PPF*, such as point *H*, resources are used inefficiently.
3. When production is efficient—on the *PPF*—the economy faces a tradeoff. To move from point *E* to point *D* requires that some cell phones be given up for more DVDs.
4. When production is inefficient—inside the *PPF*—there is a free lunch. To move from point *H* to point *D* does not involve a tradeoff.

famous saying mean? Suppose some resources are not being used or are not being used efficiently. Isn't it then possible to avoid a tradeoff and get a free lunch?

The answer is yes. You can see why in Figure 3.3. If production is taking place *inside* the *PPF* at point *H*, then it is possible to move to point *D* and increase the production of DVDs by using currently unused resources or by using resources in their most productive way. Nothing is forgone to increase production—there is a free lunch.

When production is efficient—at a point on the *PPF*—choosing to produce more of one good involves a tradeoff. But if production is inefficient—at a point inside the *PPF*—there is a free lunch. More of some goods and services can be produced without producing less of any others.

So "there is no such thing as a free lunch" means that when resources are used efficiently, every choice involves a tradeoff. Because economists view people as making rational choices, they expect that resources will be used efficiently. That is why they emphasize the tradeoff idea and deny the existence of free lunches. We might *sometimes* get a free lunch, but we *almost always* face a tradeoff.

## EYE on YOUR LIFE

### Your Production Possibilities Frontier

Two "goods" that concern you a great deal are your grade point average (GPA) and the amount of time you have available for leisure or earning an income. You face a tradeoff. To get a higher GPA you must give up leisure or income. Your forgone leisure or forgone income is the opportunity cost of a higher GPA. Similarly, to get more leisure or more income, you must accept a lower grade. A lower grade is the opportunity cost of increased leisure or increased income.

The figure illustrates a student's *PPF*. Any point on or beneath the *PPF* is attainable and any point above the *PPF* is unattainable. A student who wastes time or doesn't study efficiently ends up with a lower GPA than the highest attainable from the time spent studying. But a student who works efficiently achieves a point *on* the *PPF* and achieves production efficiency.

The student in the figure allocates the scarce 168 hours a week between studying (class and study hours) and other activities (work, leisure, and sleep hours). The student attends class and studies for 48 hours each week and works or has fun (and sleeps) for the other 120 hours. With this allocation of time, and studying efficiently, the student's GPA is 3.

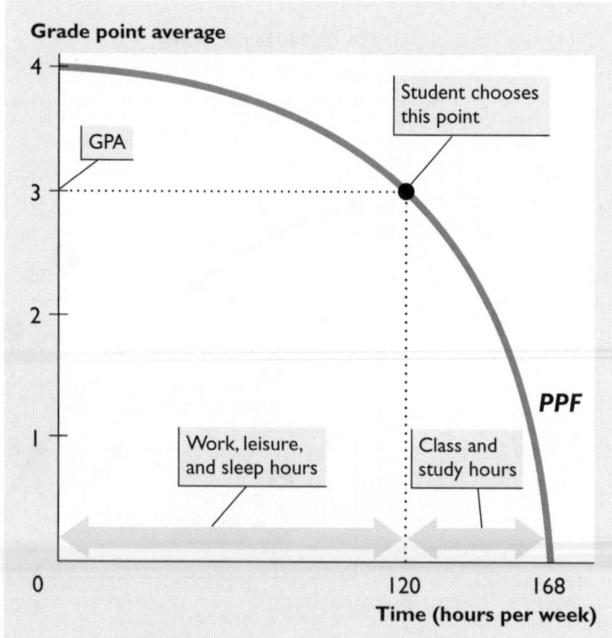

## CHECKPOINT 3.1

**Explain and illustrate the concepts of scarcity, production efficiency, and tradeoff using the production possibilities frontier.**

Work these problems in Study Plan 3.1 to get instant feedback.

### Practice Problems

1. Table 1 sets out the production possibilities of a small Pacific island economy. Draw the economy's *PPF*.

Figure 1 shows an economy's production possibilities frontier and identifies some production points. Use this figure to work Problems **2** to **4**.

2. Which points are attainable? Explain why.
3. Which points are efficient and which points are inefficient? Explain why.
4. Which points illustrate a tradeoff? Explain why.
5. **Loss of honeybees is less but still a threat**
During 2008, almost 29 percent of U.S. honeybee hives died off, less than expected, but the situation is still unsustainable. Honeybees are crucial for the pollination of many plants including almonds and pumpkins.
Source: *USA Today*, May 20, 2009
Farmers in the Central Valley of California grow 80 percent of the world's almonds along with other crops. In 2008, growers used 1.2 million bee hives to produce about 1 trillion pounds of almonds. Explain how a 30 percent drop in honeybees would affect the Central Valley *PPF* in 2009.

**TABLE 1**

| Possibility | Fish (pounds) | | Berries (pounds) |
|---|---|---|---|
| *A* | 0 | and | 20 |
| *B* | 1 | and | 18 |
| *C* | 2 | and | 15 |
| *D* | 3 | and | 11 |
| *E* | 4 | and | 6 |
| *F* | 5 | and | 0 |

**FIGURE 1**

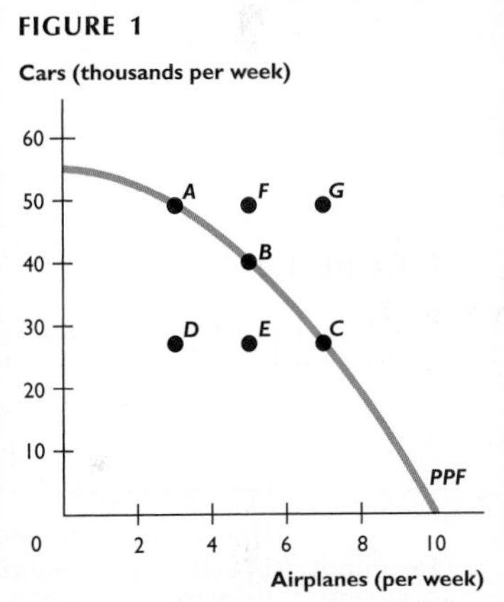


### Guided Solutions to Practice Problems

1. The *PPF* is the boundary between attainable and unattainable combinations of goods. Figure 2 shows the economy's *PPF*. The graph plots each row of the table as a point with the corresponding letter.
2. Attainable points: Any point on the *PPF* is attainable and any point below (inside) the *PPF* is attainable. Any point outside the *PPF* is unattainable. In Figure 1, only points *F* and *G* are outside the *PPF*, so they are unattainable. The other points (*A*, *B*, *C*, *D*, and *E*) are attainable.
3. Efficient points: Production is efficient when it is not possible to produce more of one good without producing less of another good. To be efficient, a point must be attainable, so points *F* and *G* can't be efficient. Points inside the *PPF* can't be efficient because more goods can be produced, so *D* and *E* are not efficient. The only efficient points are those *on* the *PPF*—*A*, *B*, and *C*.
Inefficient points: Inefficiency occurs when resources are misallocated or unemployed. Such points are *inside* the *PPF*. These points are *D* and *E*.
4. Tradeoff: Begin by recalling that a tradeoff is an exchange—giving up something to get something else. A tradeoff occurs when moving along the *PPF* from one point to another point. So moving from any point *on* the *PPF*, point *A*, *B*, or *C*, to another point *on* the *PPF* illustrates a tradeoff.
5. Honeybees are a resource used in the production of almonds. In 2008, Central Valley farmers were at a point on their *PPF*. A 30 percent drop in bees hives will reduce the quantity of almonds produced by about 30 percent. With no change in the quantity of other crops produced, the Central Valley *PPF* will shift inward.

**FIGURE 2**

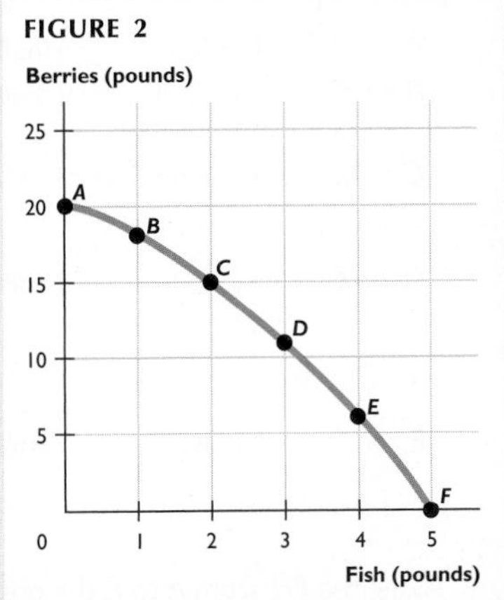

## 3.2 OPPORTUNITY COST

You've seen that moving from one point to another on the *PPF* involves a tradeoff. But what are the terms of the tradeoff? *How much* of one item must be forgone to obtain an additional unit of another item—a large amount or a small amount? The answer is given by opportunity cost—the best thing you must give up to get something (see p. 11). We can use the *PPF* to calculate opportunity cost.

### The Opportunity Cost of a Cell Phone

The opportunity cost of a cell phone is the number of DVDs forgone to get an additional cell phone. It is calculated as the number of DVDs forgone divided by the number of cell phones gained.

Figure 3.4 illustrates the calculation. At point *A*, the quantities produced are zero cell phones and 15 million DVDs; and at point *B*, the quantities produced are 1 million cell phones and 14 million DVDs. To gain 1 million cell phones by moving from point *A* to point *B*, 1 million DVDs are forgone, so the opportunity cost of 1 cell phone is 1 DVD.

At point *C*, the quantities produced are 2 million cell phones and 12 million DVDs. To gain 1 million cell phones by moving from point *B* to point *C*, 2 million DVDs are forgone. Now the opportunity cost of 1 cell phone is 2 DVDs.

If you repeat these calculations, moving from *C* to *D*, *D* to *E*, and *E* to *F*, you will obtain the opportunity costs shown in the table and the graph.

**FIGURE 3.4**

Calculating the Opportunity Cost of a Cell Phone

myeconlab Animation

| Movement along *PPF* | Decrease in quantity of DVDs | Increase in quantity of cell phones | Decrease in DVDs divided by increase in cell phones |
|---|---|---|---|
| **A** to **B** | 1 million | 1 million | 1 DVD per phone |
| **B** to **C** | 2 million | 1 million | 2 DVDs per phone |
| **C** to **D** | 3 million | 1 million | 3 DVDs per phone |
| **D** to **E** | 4 million | 1 million | 4 DVDs per phone |
| **E** to **F** | 5 million | 1 million | 5 DVDs per phone |



Along the *PPF* from *A* to *F*, the opportunity cost of a cell phone increases as the quantity of cell phones produced increases.

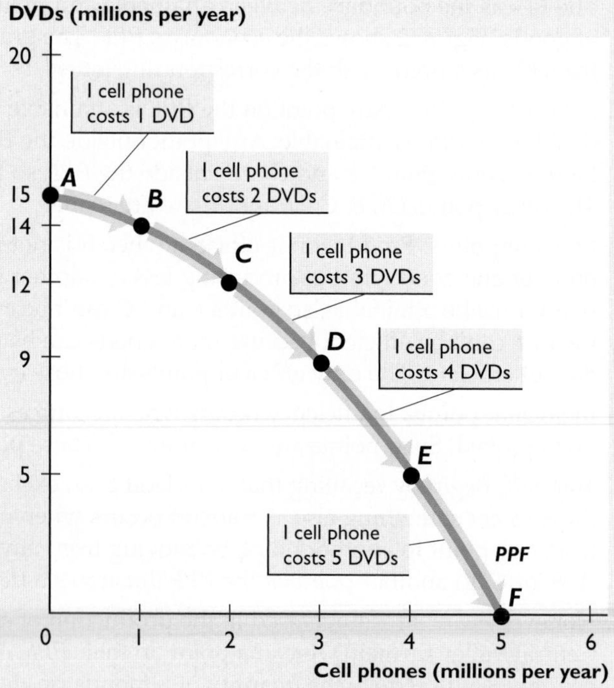

## Opportunity Cost and the Slope of the *PPF*

Look at the numbers that we've just calculated for the opportunity cost of a cell phone and notice that they follow a striking pattern. The opportunity cost of a cell phone increases as the quantity of cell phones produced increases.

The magnitude of the *slope* of the *PPF* measures the opportunity cost. Because the *PPF* in Figure 3.4 is bowed outward, its slope changes and gets steeper as the quantity of cell phones produced increases.

When a small quantity of cell phones is produced—between points *A* and *B*—the *PPF* has a gentle slope and the opportunity cost of a cell phone is low. A given increase in the quantity of cell phones costs a small decrease in the quantity of DVDs. When a large quantity of cell phones is produced—between *E* and *F*—the *PPF* is steep and the opportunity cost of a cell phone is high. A given increase in the quantity of cell phones costs a large decrease in the quantity of DVDs. Figure 3.5 shows the increasing opportunity cost of a cell phone.

## Opportunity Cost Is a Ratio

The opportunity cost of a cell phone is the *ratio* of DVDs forgone to cell phones gained. Similarly, the opportunity cost of a DVD is the *ratio* of cell phones forgone to DVDs gained. So the opportunity cost of a DVD is equal to the inverse of the opportunity cost of a cell phone. For example, moving along the *PPF* in Figure 3.4 from *C* to *D* the opportunity cost of a cell phone is 3 DVDs. Moving along the *PPF* in the opposite direction, from *D* to *C*, the opportunity cost of a DVD is 1/3 of a cell phone.

**FIGURE 3.5**

The Opportunity Cost of a Cell Phone

myeconlab Animation

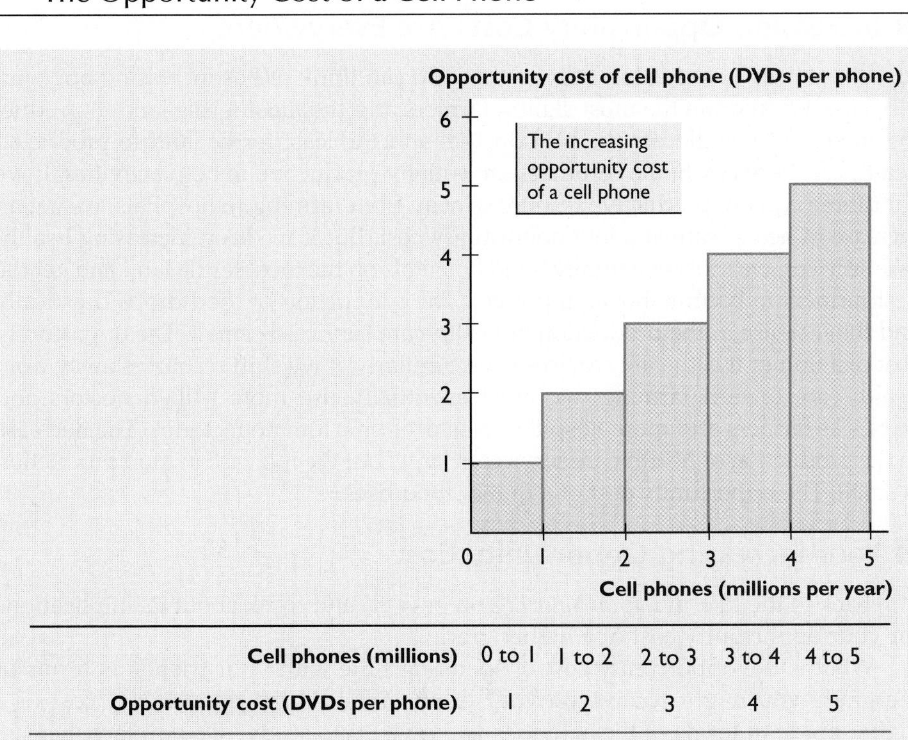


| Cell phones (millions) | 0 to 1 | 1 to 2 | 2 to 3 | 3 to 4 | 4 to 5 |
|---|---|---|---|---|---|
| Opportunity cost (DVDs per phone) | 1 | 2 | 3 | 4 | 5 |

Because the *PPF* in Figure 3.4 is bowed outward, the opportunity cost of a cell phone increases as the quantity of cell phones produced increases.

## EYE on the ENVIRONMENT

### Is Wind Power Free?

Wind power is not free. Its opportunity cost includes: (1) the cost of wind turbines, (2) the cost of transmission lines, and (3) power transmission loss.

Wind turbines can produce electricity only when there is wind, which turns out, at best, to be 40 percent of the time and, on average, about 25 percent of the time. Also some of the best wind farm locations are a long way from major population centers, so transmission lines would be long and power transmission losses large.

If we produced 55 percent of our electricity using South Dakota wind power, we would be operating inside the *PPF* at a point such as *Z*.

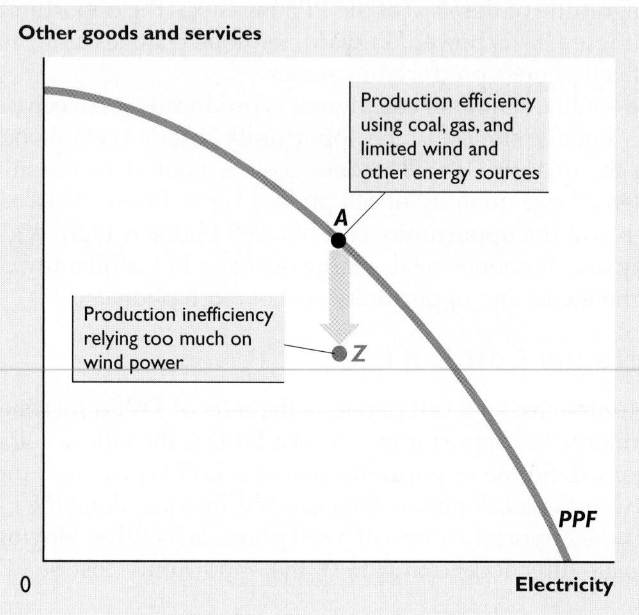


## Increasing Opportunity Costs Are Everywhere

Just about every production activity that you can think of has increasing opportunity cost. We allocate the most skillful farmers and the most fertile land to producing food, and we allocate the best doctors and the least fertile land to producing health-care services. Some resources are equally productive in both activities. If we shift these equally productive resources away from farming to hospitals, we get an increase in health care at a low opportunity cost. But if we keep increasing health-care services, we must eventually build hospitals on the most fertile land and get the best farmers to become hospital porters. The production of food drops drastically and the increase in the production of health-care services is small. The opportunity cost of a unit of health-care services rises. Similarly, if we shift resources away from health care toward farming, we must eventually use more skilled doctors and nurses as farmers and more hospitals as hydroponic tomato factories. The decrease in the production of health-care services is large, but the increase in food production is small. The opportunity cost of a unit of food rises.

## Your Increasing Opportunity Cost

Flip back to the *PPF* in *Eye on Your Life* on page 66 and think about its implications for your opportunity cost of a higher grade.

What is the opportunity cost of spending time with your friends in terms of the grade you might receive on your exam? What is the opportunity cost of a higher grade in terms of the activities you give up to study? Do you face increasing opportunity costs in these activities?

# EYE on the U.S. ECONOMY

## Guns Versus Butter

Guns versus butter is the classic economic tradeoff. "Guns" stand for defense goods and services and "butter" stands for food and more generally for all other goods and services. Recently, the U.S. economy has been producing more guns and less butter.

Figure 1 shows the fluctuations in the quantity of defense goods and services produced. (The quantity is measured by expenditure on defense using the prices in 2000 to remove the effects of price changes.) The quantity of defense goods and services produced increases in times of war and decreases in times of peace.

Figure 2 illustrates the recent changes in the production of defense goods and services using the *PPF*.

During the 1990s, the *PPF* was $PPF_0$. President Reagan raised the stakes in the Cold War between the United States and the (former) Soviet Union by a big expansion of military expenditure and we were at point *A*. By mid-decade, the Soviet Union had collapsed and we enjoyed a peace dividend by moving along $PPF_0$ to *B*.

During the next decade, production possibilities expanded from $PPF_0$ to $PPF_1$. Defense production and the production of other goods and services increased, and in 2001 we operated at point *C*. Then, in response to the attacks of September 11, 2001, defense spending increased again and by 2009 we had moved along $PPF_1$ to point *D*.

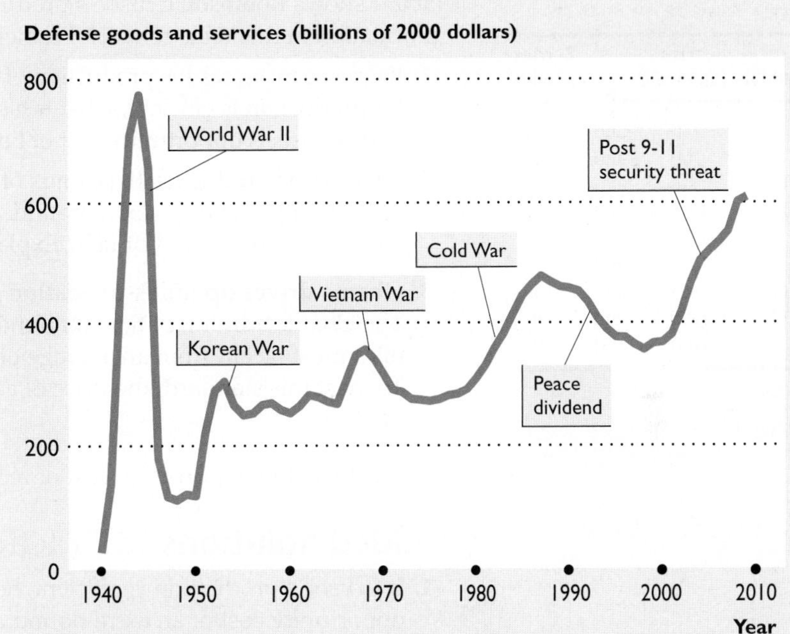


**Figure 1 The quantity of defense goods produced**

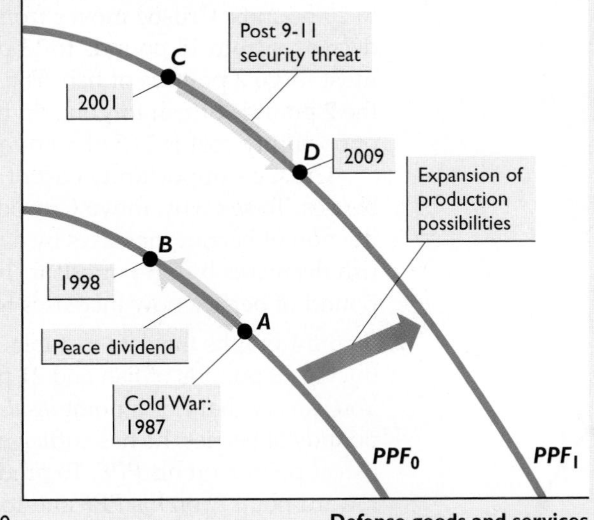


**Figure 2 The guns versus butter tradeoff**

Work these problems in Study Plan 3.2 to get instant feedback.

TABLE 1

| Possibility | Fish (pounds) | | Berries (pounds) |
|---|---|---|---|
| *A* | 0 | and | 36 |
| *B* | 4.0 | and | 35 |
| *C* | 7.5 | and | 33 |
| *D* | 10.5 | and | 30 |
| *E* | 13.0 | and | 26 |
| *F* | 15.0 | and | 21 |
| *G* | 16.5 | and | 15 |
| *H* | 17.5 | and | 8 |
| *I* | 18.0 | and | 0 |

## CHECKPOINT 3.2

**Calculate opportunity cost.**

### Practice Problems

Table 1 shows Robinson Crusoe's production possibilities in summer. Use the information in this table to work Problems **1** and **2**.

1. If Crusoe increases his production of berries from 21 pounds to 26 pounds and his production is efficient, what is his opportunity cost of a pound of berries? Does Crusoe's opportunity cost of berries increase as he produces more berries?
2. If Crusoe is producing 10 pounds of fish and 21 pounds of berries, what is his opportunity cost of an extra pound of berries? And what is his opportunity cost of an extra pound of fish? Explain your answers.
3. **Obama drives up miles-per-gallon requirements**
   The Obama administration announced that emission levels of new automobiles must be cut from an average of 354 grams in 2009 to 250 grams in 2016. To meet this standard, the price of a new vehicle will rise by $1,300.
   Source: *USA Today*, May 20, 2009
   Calculate the opportunity cost of reducing the emission level by 1 gram.

### Guided Solutions to Practice Problems

1. If Crusoe's production is efficient, he is producing at a point *on* his *PPF*. His opportunity cost of an extra pound of berries is the quantity of fish he must give up to get the berries and it is calculated as the decrease in the quantity of fish divided by the increase in the quantity of berries as he moves along his *PPF* in the direction of producing more berries.
   Table 1 tells you that to increase the quantity of berries from 21 pounds to 26 pounds, Crusoe moves from row *F* to row *E* and his production of fish decreases from 15 pounds to 13 pounds. To gain 5 pounds of berries, Crusoe must forgo 2 pounds of fish. The opportunity cost of 1 pound of berries is the 2 pounds of fish forgone divided by 5 pounds of berries gained. This opportunity cost is 2/5 of a pound of fish.
   Crusoe's opportunity cost of berries increases as he produces more berries. To see why, move Crusoe from row *E* to row *D* in Table 1. His production of berries increases by 4 pounds to 30 pounds and his production of fish decreases by 2.5 pounds to 10.5 pounds. His opportunity cost of 1 pound of berries now increases to 5/8 of a pound of fish.
2. Figure 1 graphs the data in Table 1 and shows Crusoe's *PPF*. If Crusoe is producing 10 pounds of fish and 21 pounds of berries, he is producing at point *Z*. You can see that *Z* is a point *inside* Crusoe's *PPF*. When Crusoe produces 21 pounds of berries, he has sufficient time available to produce 15 pounds of fish at point *F* on his *PPF*. To produce more berries, Crusoe can move from *Z* toward point *D* on his *PPF* and forgo no fish. His opportunity cost of a pound of berries is zero.
3. By spending $1,300 extra on a new car, you forgo $1,300 of other goods. With a new car, your emissions fall from 354 grams to 250 grams, a reduction of 104 grams. The opportunity cost of a 1-gram reduction in emissions is $1,300 of other goods divided by 104 grams, or $12.50 of other goods.

FIGURE 1

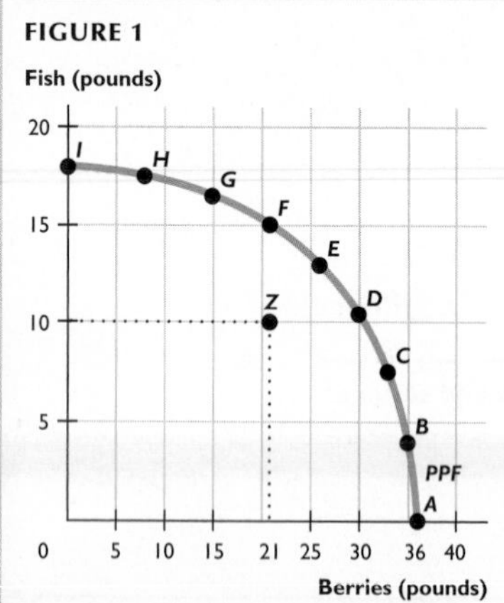

## 3.3 ECONOMIC GROWTH

**Economic growth** is the sustained expansion of production possibilities. Our economy grows when we develop better technologies for producing goods and services; improve the quality of labor by education, on-the-job training, and work experience; and acquire more machines to help us produce.

**Economic growth**
The sustained expansion of production possibilities.

To study economic growth, we must change the two goods and look at the production possibilities for a consumption good and a capital good. A cell phone is a consumption good and a cell-phone factory is a capital good. By using today's resources to produce cell-phone factories, the economy can expand its future production possibilities. The greater the production of new capital—number of new cell-phone factories—the faster is the expansion of production possibilities.

Figure 3.6 shows how the *PPF* can expand. If no new factories are produced (at point *L*), production possibilities do not expand and the *PPF* stays at its original position. By producing fewer cell phones and using resources to produce 2 new cell-phone factories (at point *K*), production possibilities expand and the *PPF* rotates outward to the new *PPF*.

But economic growth is *not* free. To make it happen, consumption must decrease. The move from *L* to *K* in Figure 3.6 means forgoing 2 million cell phones now. The opportunity cost of producing more cell-phone factories is producing fewer cell phones today.

Also, economic growth is no magic formula for abolishing scarcity. Economic growth shifts the *PPF* outward, but on the new *PPF* we continue to face opportunity costs. To keep producing capital, current consumption must be less than its maximum possible level.

**FIGURE 3.6**

Expanding Production Possibilities

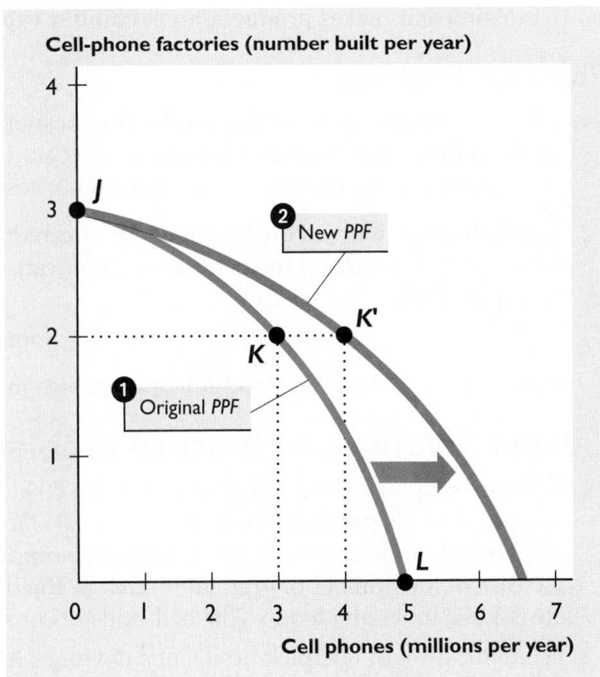


1. If firms allocate no resources to producing cell-phone factories and produce 5 million cell-phones a year at point *L*, the *PPF* doesn't change.
2. If firms decrease cell-phone production to 3 million a year and produce 2 cell-phone factories, at point *K*, production possibilities will expand. After a year, the *PPF* shifts outward to the new *PPF* and production can move to point *K'*.

# EYE on the GLOBAL ECONOMY

## Hong Kong's Rapid Economic Growth

Hong Kong's production possibilities per person were 25 percent of those of the United States in 1960. By 2009, they had grown to become 92 percent of U.S. production possibilities. Hong Kong grew faster than the United States because it allocated more of its resources to accumulating capital and less to consumption than did the United States.

In 1960, the United States and Hong Kong produced at point *A* on their respective *PPF*s. In 2009, Hong Kong was at point *B* and the United States was at point *C*.

If Hong Kong continues to produce at a point such as *B*, it will grow more rapidly than the United States and its *PPF* will eventually shift out beyond the *PPF* of the United States. But if Hong Kong produces at a point such as *D*, the pace of expansion of its *PPF* will slow.

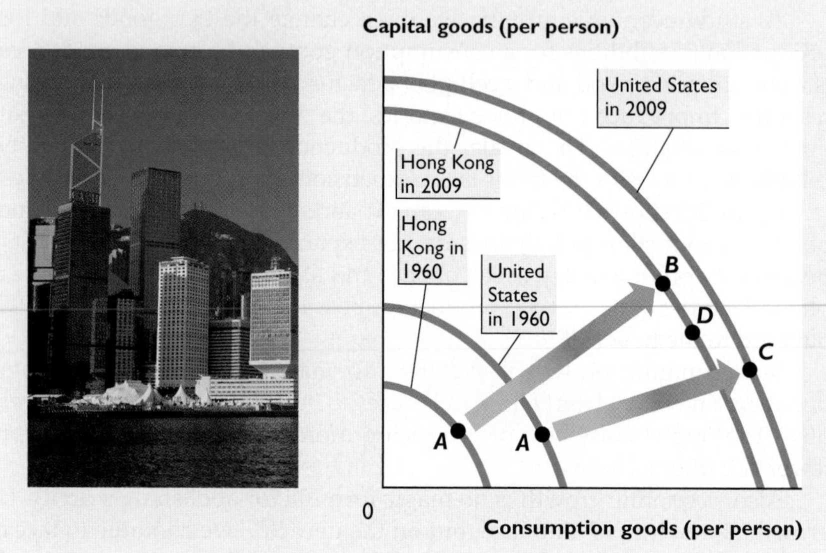

Work these problems in Study Plan 3.3 to get instant feedback.

**TABLE 1**

| Possibility | Education services (graduates) | Consumption goods (units) |
|---|---|---|
| *A* | 1,000 | 0 |
| *B* | 750 | 1,000 |
| *C* | 500 | 2,000 |
| *D* | 0 | 3,000 |

# CHECKPOINT 3.3

**Explain what makes production possibilities expand.**

## Practice Problems

1. Table 1 shows an economy that produces education services and consumption goods. If the economy currently produces 500 graduates a year and 2,000 units of consumption goods, what is the opportunity cost of one more graduate?
2. **Can Cuba cope with an onslaught of Americans?**
   Doing away with travel restrictions on Americans could unleash a flood of visitors to Cuba.

   Source: *USA Today*, April 14, 2009

   How can Cuba turn this flood into an increase in economic growth?

## Guided Solutions to Practice Problems

1. By increasing the number of graduates from 500 to 750, the quantity of consumption goods produced decreases from 2,000 to 1,000 units. The opportunity cost of a graduate is the decrease in consumption goods divided by the increase in the number of graduates. That is, the opportunity cost of a graduate is 1,000 units divided by 250, or 4 units of consumption goods.
2. Economic growth will pick up if Cuba develops its tourist hotels and facilities. This new capital will increase its resources and shift its *PPF* outward.

## 3.4 SPECIALIZATION AND TRADE

A person can produce several goods or can concentrate on producing one good and then trading some of that good for those produced by others. Concentrating on the production of only one good is called *specialization*. We are going to discover how people gain by specializing in the production of the good in which they have a *comparative advantage*.

### Comparative Advantage

A person has a **comparative advantage** in an activity if that person can perform the activity at a lower opportunity cost than anyone else. Let's explore the idea of comparative advantage by looking at two smoothie bars: one operated by Liz and the other operated by Joe.

**Comparative advantage**
The ability of a person to perform an activity or produce a good or service at a lower opportunity cost than anyone else.

#### Liz's Smoothie Bar

Liz produces smoothies and salads. In Liz's high-tech bar, she can turn out *either* a smoothie *or* a salad every 2 minutes. If she spends all her time making smoothies, she produces 30 an hour. If she spends all her time making salads, she also produces 30 an hour. If she splits her time equally between the two, she can produce 15 smoothies *and* 15 salads an hour. For each additional smoothie Liz produces, she must decrease her production of salads by one, and for each additional salad Liz produces, she must decrease her production of smoothies by one. So

**Liz's opportunity cost of producing 1 smoothie is 1 salad,**

and

**Liz's opportunity cost of producing 1 salad is 1 smoothie.**

Liz's customers buy smoothies and salads in equal quantities, so Liz splits her time equally between the items and produces 15 smoothies and 15 salads an hour.

**TABLE 3.1 LIZ'S PRODUCTION POSSIBILITIES**

| Item | Minutes to produce 1 | Quantity per hour |
|---|---|---|
| Smoothies | 2 | 30 |
| Salads | 2 | 30 |

#### Joe's Smoothie Bar

Joe also produces both smoothies and salads. Joe's bar is smaller than Liz's, and he has only one blender—a slow, old machine. Even if Joe uses all his resources to produce smoothies, he can produce only 6 an hour. But Joe is pretty good in the salad department, so if he uses all his resources to make salads, he can produce 30 an hour. Joe's ability to make smoothies and salads is the same regardless of how he splits an hour between the two tasks. He can make a salad in 2 minutes or a smoothie in 10 minutes. For each additional smoothie Joe produces, he must decrease his production of salads by 5. And for each additional salad Joe produces, he must decrease his production of smoothies by 1/5 of a smoothie. So

**Joe's opportunity cost of producing 1 smoothie is 5 salads,**

and

**Joe's opportunity cost of producing 1 salad is 1/5 of a smoothie.**

Joe's customers, like Liz's, buy smoothies and salads in equal quantities. Joe spends 50 minutes of each hour making smoothies and 10 minutes of each hour making salads. With this division of his time, Joe produces 5 smoothies and 5 salads an hour.

**TABLE 3.2 JOE'S PRODUCTION POSSIBILITIES**

| Item | Minutes to produce 1 | Quantity per hour |
|---|---|---|
| Smoothies | 10 | 6 |
| Salads | 2 | 30 |

### Liz's Absolute Advantage

**Absolute advantage**
When one person is more productive than another person in several or even all activities.

You can see from the numbers that describe the two smoothie bars that Liz is three times as productive as Joe—her 15 smoothies and 15 salads an hour are three times Joe's 5 smoothies and 5 salads. Liz has an **absolute advantage**—she is more productive than Joe in producing both smoothies and salads. But Liz has a comparative advantage in only one of the activities.

### Liz's Comparative Advantage

In which of the two activities does Liz have a *comparative* advantage? Recall that comparative advantage is a situation in which one person's opportunity cost of producing a good is lower than another person's opportunity cost of producing that same good. Liz has a comparative advantage in producing smoothies. Her opportunity cost of a smoothie is 1 salad, whereas Joe's opportunity cost of a smoothie is 5 salads.

### Joe's Comparative Advantage

If Liz has a comparative advantage in producing smoothies, Joe must have a comparative advantage in producing salads. His opportunity cost of a salad is 1/5 of a smoothie, while Liz's opportunity cost of a salad is 1 smoothie.

## Achieving Gains from Trade

Liz and Joe run into each other one evening in a singles bar. After a few minutes of getting acquainted, Liz tells Joe about her amazingly profitable smoothie business. Her only problem, she tells Joe, is that she wishes she could produce more because potential customers leave when her lines get too long.

Joe isn't sure whether to risk spoiling his chances by telling Liz about his own struggling business. But he takes the risk. When he explains to Liz that he spends 50 minutes of every hour making 5 smoothies and 10 minutes making 5 salads, Liz's eyes pop. "Have I got a deal for you!" she exclaims.

Here's the deal that Liz sketches on a paper napkin. Joe stops making smoothies and allocates all his time to producing salads. Liz stops making salads and allocates all her time to producing smoothies. That is, they both specialize in producing the good in which they have a comparative advantage—see Table 3.3(b). They then trade: Liz sells Joe 10 smoothies and Joe sells Liz 20 salads—the price of a smoothie is 2 salads—see Table 3.3(c).

After the trade, Joe has 10 salads (the 30 he produces minus the 20 he sells to Liz) and the 10 smoothies that he buys from Liz. So Joe doubles the quantities of smoothies and salads he can sell. Liz has 20 smoothies (the 30 she produces minus the 10 she sells to Joe) and the 20 salads she buys from Joe. See Table 3.3(d). From specialization and trade, each gains 5 smoothies and 5 salads—see Table 3.3(e).

Liz draws a figure (Figure 3.7) to illustrate her idea. The red *PPF* is Joe's and the blue *PPF* is Liz's. They are each producing at the points marked *A*. Liz's proposal is that they each produce at the points marked *B*. They then trade smoothies and salads at a price of 2 salads per smoothie, or 1/2 a smoothie per salad. Liz gets salads for 1/2 a smoothie each, which is less than the 1 smoothie that it costs her to produce them. Joe gets smoothies for 2 salads each, which is less than the 5 salads it costs him to produce them. Each moves to the point marked *C*, *outside* their respective *PPF*s. Because of the gains from trade, total production increases by 10 smoothies and 10 salads.

**TABLE 3.3 LIZ AND JOE GAIN FROM TRADE**

| (a) Before Trade | Liz | Joe |
|---|---|---|
| Smoothies | 15 | 5 |
| Salads | 15 | 5 |
| **(b) Specialization** | **Liz** | **Joe** |
| Smoothies | 30 | 0 |
| Salads | 0 | 30 |
| **(c) Trade** | | |
| Smoothies | sell 10 | buy 10 |
| Salads | buy 20 | sell 20 |
| **(d) After Trade** | | |
| Smoothies | 20 | 10 |
| Salads | 20 | 10 |
| **(e) Gains from Trade** | | |
| Smoothies | +5 | +5 |
| Salads | +5 | +5 |

**FIGURE 3.7**

The Gains from Specialization and Trade

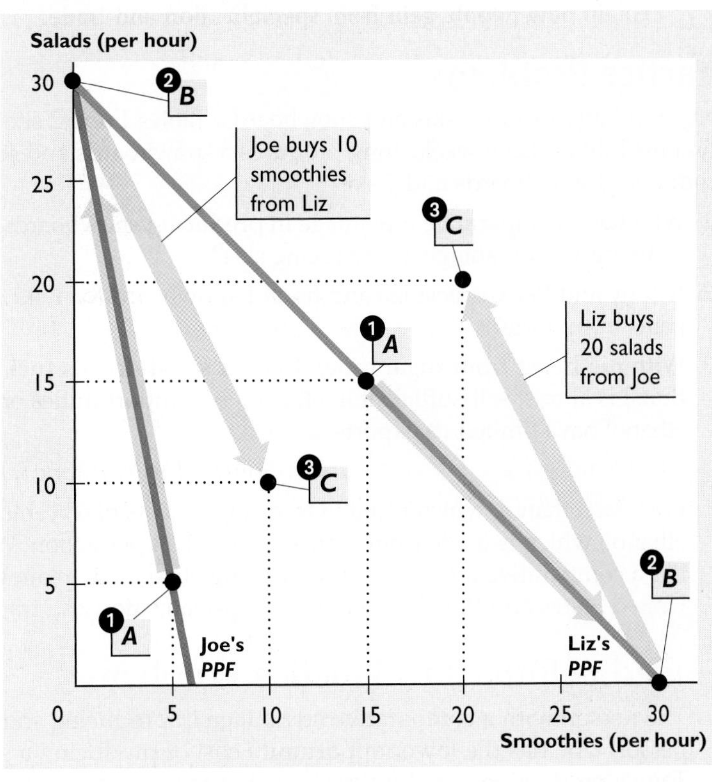


❶ Liz and Joe each produce at point *A* on their respective *PPFs*. Liz has a comparative advantage in producing smoothies, and Joe has a comparative advantage in producing salads.

❷ Joe specializes in salads and Liz specializes in smoothies, so they each produce at point *B* on their respective *PPFs*.

❸ They exchange smoothies for salads at a price of 2 salads per smoothie. Each goes to *C*—a point *outside* their individual *PPFs*. They each gain 5 salads and 5 smoothies.

## EYE on YOUR LIFE

### Your Comparative Advantage

What you have learned in this chapter has huge implications for the way you organize your life. It also has implications for the position that you take on the controversial issue of offshore outsourcing.

Just as an economy expands its production possibilities by accumulating capital, so also will you expand your production possibilities by accumulating human capital. That is what you're doing right now in school.

By discovering your comparative advantage, you will be able to focus on producing the items that make you as well off as possible. Think hard about what you enjoy doing and that you do comparatively better than others. That, most likely, is where your comparative advantage lies.

In today's world, it is a good idea to try to remain flexible so that you can switch jobs if you discover that your comparative advantage has changed.

Looking beyond your own self-interest, are you going to be a voice that supports or opposes offshore outsourcing?

You've learned in this chapter that regardless of whether outsourcing remains inside the United States, as it does with Liz and Joe at their smoothie bars, or is global like the outsourcing of jobs by U. S. producers to India, both parties gain from trade.

Americans pay less for goods and services and Indians earn higher incomes. But some Americans lose, at least in the short run.

Work these problems in Study Plan 3.4 to get instant feedback.

**TABLE 1 TONY'S PRODUCTION POSSIBILITIES**

| Snowboards (per week) | | Skis (per week) |
|---|---|---|
| 25 | and | 0 |
| 20 | and | 10 |
| 15 | and | 20 |
| 10 | and | 30 |
| 5 | and | 40 |
| 0 | and | 50 |

**TABLE 2 PATTY'S PRODUCTION POSSIBILITIES**

| Snowboards (per week) | | Skis (per week) |
|---|---|---|
| 20 | and | 0 |
| 10 | and | 5 |
| 0 | and | 10 |

## CHECKPOINT 3.4

**Explain how people gain from specialization and trade.**

## Practice Problems

Tony and Patty produce skis and snowboards. Tables 1 and 2 show their production possibilities. Each week, Tony produces 5 snowboards and 40 skis and Patty produces 10 snowboards and 5 skis.

1. Who has a comparative advantage in producing snowboards? Who has a comparative advantage in producing skis?
2. If Tony and Patty specialize and trade 1 snowboard for 1 ski, what are the gains from trade?
3. **With big boost from sugar cane, Brazil is satisfying its fuel needs**
   Brazil is almost self-sufficient in ethanol, but import duties on the Brazilian ethanol have limited its exports.

   Source: *The New York Times*, April 12, 2006

   Brazilian ethanol, which is made from sugar, costs of 83 cents per gallon. U.S. ethanol, which is made from corn, costs of $1.14 per gallon. Which country has a comparative advantage in producing ethanol? Explain why both the United States and Brazil can gain from specialization and trade.

## Guided Solutions to Practice Problems

1. The person with a comparative advantage in producing snowboards is the person who has the lower opportunity cost of producing a snowboard. Tony's production possibilities show that to produce 5 more snowboards he must produce 10 fewer skis. So Tony's opportunity cost of producing a snowboard is 2 skis.

   Patty's production possibilities show that to produce 10 more snowboards, she must produce 5 fewer skis. So Patty's opportunity cost of producing a snowboard is 1/2 a ski. Patty has a comparative advantage in producing snowboards because her opportunity cost of producing a snowboard is less than Tony's. Tony has a comparative advantage in producing skis. For each ski produced, Tony must give up making 1/2 a snowboard, whereas for each ski that Patty produces, she must give up making 2 snowboards. So Tony's opportunity cost of a ski is lower than Patty's.
2. Patty has a comparative advantage in producing snowboards, so she specializes in snowboards. Tony has a comparative advantage in producing skis, so he specializes in producing skis. Patty produces 20 snowboards and Tony produces 50 skis. Before specializing, they produced 15 snowboards (Patty's 10 plus Tony's 5) and 45 skis (Tony's 40 plus Patty's 5).

   By specializing, they increase their total output by 5 snowboards and 5 skis. They can share this gain by trading 1 ski for 1 snowboard. Patty can get skis from Tony for less than it costs her to produce them. Tony can buy snowboards from Patty for less than it costs him to produce them. Both Patty and Tony achieve gains from specialization and trade.
3. The cost of producing a gallon of ethanol is less in Brazil than in the United States, so Brazil has a comparative advantage in producing ethanol. If Brazil specialized in producing ethanol and the United States specialized in producing other goods (for example, movies or food) and engaged in free trade, each country would be able to get to a point outside its own *PPF*.

## Key Points

1 **Explain and illustrate the concepts of scarcity, production efficiency, and tradeoff using the production possibilities frontier.**

- The production possibilities frontier, *PPF,* describes the limits to what can be produced by using all the available resources efficiently.
- Points inside and on the *PPF* are attainable. Points outside the *PPF* are unattainable.
- Production at any point on the *PPF* achieves production efficiency. Production at a point inside the *PPF* is inefficient.
- When production is efficient—on the *PPF*—people face a tradeoff. If production is at a point inside the *PPF,* there is a free lunch.

2 **Calculate opportunity cost.**

- Along the *PPF,* the opportunity cost of *X* (the item on the *x*-axis) is the decrease in *Y* (the item on the *y*-axis) divided by the increase in *X.*
- The opportunity cost of *Y* is the inverse of the opportunity cost of *X.*
- The opportunity cost of producing a good increases as the quantity of the good produced increases.

3 **Explain what makes production possibilities expand.**

- Technological change and increases in capital and human capital expand production possibilities.
- The opportunity cost of economic growth is the decrease in current consumption.

4 **Explain how people gain from specialization and trade.**

- A person has a comparative advantage in an activity if he or she can perform that activity at a lower opportunity cost than someone else.
- People gain by increasing the production of the item in which they have a comparative advantage and trading.

## Key Terms

Work these problems in Chapter 3 Study Plan to get instant feedback.

# CHAPTER CHECKPOINT

## Study Plan Problems and Applications

**TABLE 1**

| Corn (bushels) | | Beef (pounds) |
|---|---|---|
| 250 | and | 0 |
| 200 | and | 300 |
| 100 | and | 500 |
| 0 | and | 550 |

1. Table 1 shows the quantities of corn and beef that a farm can produce in a year. Draw a graph of the farm's *PPF*. Mark on the graph:
   - An inefficient combination of corn and beef—label this point *A*.
   - An unattainable combination of corn and beef—label this point *B*.
   - An efficient combination of corn and beef—label this point *C*.

Use the following information to work Problems **2** and **3**.

The people of Leisure Island have 50 hours of labor a day that can be used to produce entertainment and good food. Table 2 shows the maximum quantity of *either* entertainment *or* good food that Leisure Island can produce with different quantities of labor.

**TABLE 2**

| Labor (hours) | Entertainment (units) | | Good food (units) |
|---|---|---|---|
| 0 | 0 | or | 0 |
| 10 | 20 | or | 30 |
| 20 | 40 | or | 50 |
| 30 | 60 | or | 60 |
| 40 | 80 | or | 65 |
| 50 | 100 | or | 67 |

2. Is an output of 50 units of entertainment and 50 units of good food attainable and efficient? With a production of 50 units of entertainment and 50 units of good food, do the people of Leisure Island face a tradeoff?
3. What is the opportunity cost of producing an additional unit of entertainment? Explain how the opportunity cost of producing a unit of entertainment changes as more entertainment is produced.

Use the following information to work Problems **4** and **5**.

**Malaria can be controlled**

The World Health Organization's malaria chief says that it is too costly to try to fully eradicate the disease. He says that by using nets, medicine, and DDT it is possible to eliminate 90 percent of malaria cases. But to eliminate 100 percent of cases would be extremely costly.

Source: *The New York Times*, March 4, 2008

4. Make a graph of the production possibilities frontier with malaria control on the *x*-axis and other goods and services on the *y*-axis.
5. Describe how the opportunity cost of controlling malaria changes as more resources are used to reduce the number of malaria cases.
6. Explain how the following events influence U.S. production possibilities:
   - Some retail workers are re-employed building dams and wind farms.
   - More people take early retirement.
   - Drought devastates California's economy.

**FIGURE 1**

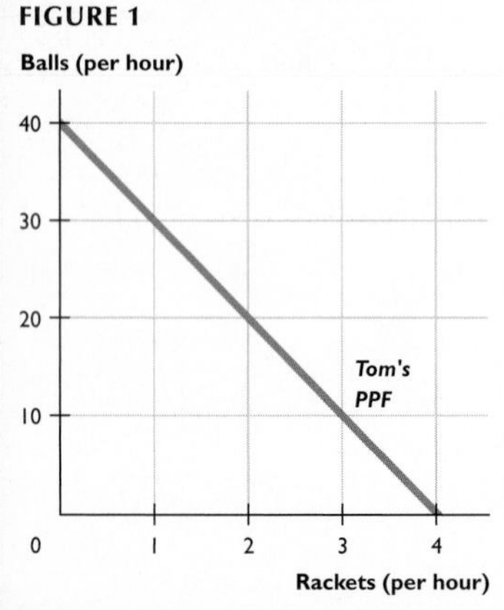


Use the following information to work Problems **7** and **8**.

Figure 1 shows Tom's production possibilities and Figure 2 shows Abby's production possibilities. Tom uses all his resources and produces 2 rackets and 20 balls an hour. Abby uses all her resources and produces 2 rackets and 40 balls an hour.

**FIGURE 2**

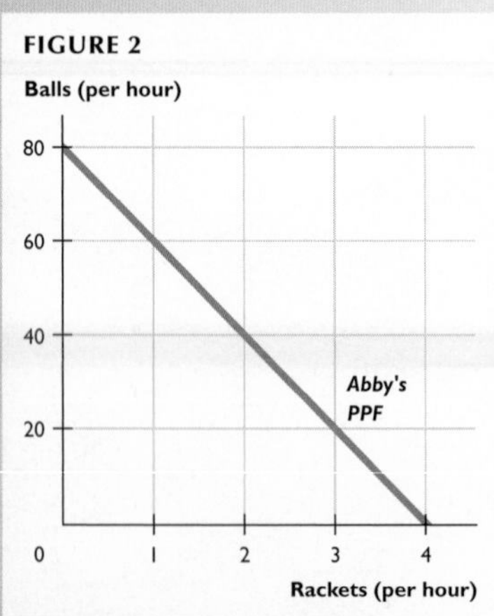


7. What is Tom's opportunity cost of producing a racket? What is Abby's opportunity cost of a racket? Who has a comparative advantage in producing rackets? Who has a comparative advantage in producing balls?
8. If Tom and Abby specialize and trade 15 balls for 1 racket, what are the gains from trade?

## Instructor Assignable Problems and Applications

Your instructor can assign these problems as homework, a quiz, or a test in **MyEconLab**.

Use the following information to work Problems **1** to **4**.

If the American Clean Energy and Security Act of 2009 becomes law, it will limit greenhouse gas emissions from electricity generation and require electricity producers to generate a minimum percentage of power using renewable fuels. Some of the rights to emit will be auctioned. The Congressional Budget Office estimates that the government will receive $846 billion from auctions and will spend $821 billion on incentive programs and compensation for higher energy prices. Electricity producers will spend $208 million a year to comply with the new rules. (Think of these dollar amounts as dollars' worth of other goods and services.)

1. Will the new law achieve production efficiency?
2. Is the $846 billion that electricity producers pay for the right to emit greenhouse gasses part of the opportunity cost of producing electricity?
3. Is the $821 billion that the government will spend on incentive programs and compensation for higher energy prices part of the opportunity cost of producing electricity?
4. Is the $208 million that electricity producers will spend to comply with the new rules part of the opportunity cost of producing electricity?
5. The people of Foodland have 40 hours of labor a day to bake pizza and bread. Table 1 shows the maximum quantity of *either* pizza *or* bread that Foodland can bake with different quantities of labor. Can Foodland produce 30 pizzas and 30 loaves of bread a day? If it can, is this output efficient, do the people of Foodland face a tradeoff, and what is the opportunity cost of producing an additional pizza?

**TABLE 1**

| Labor (hours) | Pizzas | | Bread (loaves) |
|---|---|---|---|
| 0 | 0 | or | 0 |
| 10 | 30 | or | 10 |
| 20 | 50 | or | 20 |
| 30 | 60 | or | 30 |
| 40 | 65 | or | 40 |

Use the following information to work Problems **6** to **8**.

**Cheap broadband's a winner**

Inexpensive broadband access has created a new generation of television producers and the Internet is their native medium.

Source: *The New York Times*, December 2, 2007

6. How has inexpensive broadband changed the production possibilities of video entertainment and other goods and services?
7. Sketch a *PPF* for video entertainment and other goods and services before broadband.
8. Show how the arrival of inexpensive broadband has changed the *PPF*.
9. Figure 1 illustrates the *PPF* in each of the economies: Atlantis, Bikini, and Cyber. Atlantis has no economic growth, Bikini is growing slowly, and Cyber is growing rapidly. Mark on the graph three points:
   - A point that shows the situation in Atlantis—label this point *A*.
   - A point that shows the situation in Bikini—label this point *B*.
   - A point that shows the situation in Cyber—label this point *C*.

   What is the cost of the economic growth in Bikini and Cyber?

**FIGURE 1**

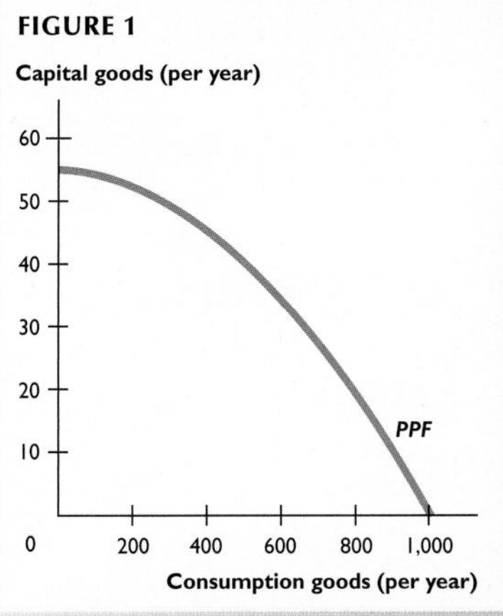

10. A farm grows wheat and fattens pigs. The opportunity cost of producing each of these goods increases as more of it is produced. If the farm adopts a new technology, which allows it to use fewer resources to fatten pigs, explain how the farm's production possibilities will change and the effect on the opportunity cost of producing a ton of wheat.

**TABLE 2**

| Corn (bushels per year) | | Beef (pounds per year) |
|---|---|---|
| 250 | and | 0 |
| 200 | and | 300 |
| 100 | and | 500 |
| 0 | and | 550 |

11. Table 2 shows a farm's production possibilities. If the farm uses its resources efficiently, what is the opportunity cost of an increase in beef production from 300 pounds to 500 pounds a year? Explain your answer.

Use the following information to work Problems 12 and 13.

**Viewpoint: Education and reform are vital for continued economic growth**

Manoj Singh says that many Indians lack the education to participate in the expansion of the country's high tech industries. To remedy this situation, he wants India to create more world-class universities. He also believes that India's labor laws are too restrictive and discourage the movement of people and human capital between regions and industries

Source: Manoj Singh, *Financial Times*, May 15, 2007

12. How would building more universities change India's current and future production possibilities? Illustrate your answer by drawing India's current and future *PPF*s.

13. How would greater movement of people and human capital change India's production possibilities?

14. **Robust corn and soybean crops**

Corn production in 2008 is forecast at 12.3 billion bushels, 6 percent less than the 2007 record harvest. Soybean production in 2008 is forecast at 2.97 billion bushels in 2008, an increase of 5 percent from last year.

Source: *USDA Crop Production*, August 12, 2008

Calculate the opportunity cost of a bushel of soybeans in terms of corn.

Use the following information to work Problems 15 and 16.

**Drought affected farmers face new battle**

Wheat farmers who had been struggling with a long drought now face a new battle. A South American weed called serrated tussock was spreading at a rapid rate across the bare earth of these drought-stricken wheat farms. And a major problem is that many wheat farmers cannot distinguish serrated tussock from a less harmful native tussock and are unaware of the large effect that serrated tussock can have on productivity and growing capacity.

Source: ABC News (Australia), May 18, 2009

15. Sketch Australia's production possibilities frontier with wheat on the $x$-axis and other goods and services on the $y$-axis. On your graph, show the effect of the South American weed on farmers' productivity and growing capacity.

16. Australia is a major exporter of wheat. If productivity does decrease, how will the fall in productivity influence Australia's opportunity cost of producing wheat and Australia's gains from international trade?

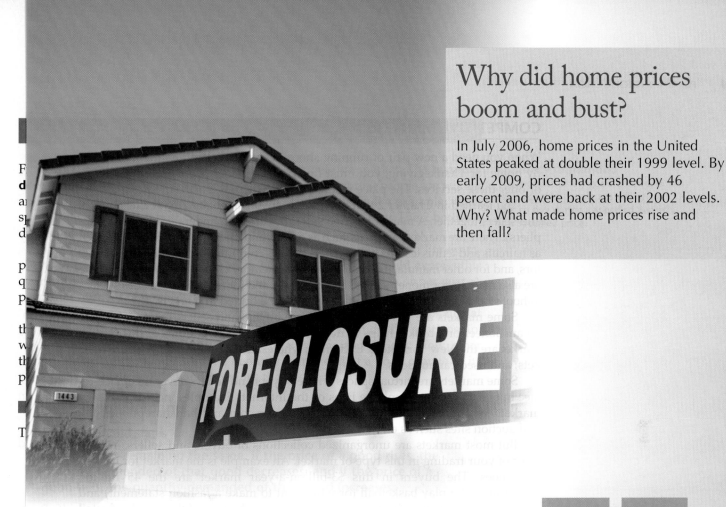

## Why did home prices boom and bust?

In July 2006, home prices in the United States peaked at double their 1999 level. By early 2009, prices had crashed by 46 percent and were back at their 2002 levels. Why? What made home prices rise and then fall?

# Demand and Supply

CHAPTER CHECKLIST

**When you have completed your study of this chapter, you will be able to**

1 Distinguish between quantity demanded and demand, and explain what determines demand.

2 Distinguish between quantity supplied and supply, and explain what determines supply.

3 Explain how demand and supply determine price and quantity in a market, and explain the effects of changes in demand and supply.

**Demand schedule**
A list of the quantities demanded at each different price when all the other influences on buying plans remain the same.

**Demand curve**
A graph of the relationship between the quantity demanded of a good and its price when all the other influences on buying plans remain the same.

A **demand schedule** is a list of the quantities demanded at each different price when *all the other influences on buying plans remain the same*. The table in Figure 4.1 is one person's (Tina's) demand schedule for bottled water. It tells us that if the price of water is $2.00 a bottle, Tina buys no water. Her quantity demanded is 0 bottles a day. If the price of water is $1.50 a bottle, her quantity demanded is 1 bottle a day. Tina's quantity demanded increases to 2 bottles a day at a price of $1.00 a bottle and to 3 bottles a day at a price of 50 cents a bottle.

A **demand curve** is a graph of the relationship between the quantity demanded of a good and its price when all the other influences on buying plans remain the same. The points on the demand curve labeled *A* through *D* represent the rows *A* through *D* of the demand schedule. For example, point *B* on the graph represents row *B* of the demand schedule and shows that the quantity demanded is 1 bottle a day when the price is $1.50 a bottle. Point *C* on the demand curve represents row *C* of the demand schedule and shows that the quantity demanded is 2 bottles a day when the price is $1.00 a bottle.

The downward slope of the demand curve illustrates the law of demand. Along the demand curve, when the price of the good *falls*, the quantity demanded *increases*. For example, in Figure 4.1, when the price of a bottle of water falls from $1.00 to 50 cents, the quantity demanded increases from 2 bottles a day to 3 bottles a day. Conversely, when the price *rises*, the quantity demanded *decreases*. For example, when the price rises from $1.00 to $1.50 a bottle, the quantity demanded decreases from 2 bottles a day to 1 bottle a day.

**FIGURE 4.1**

Demand Schedule and Demand Curve

myeconlab Animation

The table shows Tina's demand schedule that lists the quantity of water demanded at each price if all other influences on buying plans remain the same. At a price of $1.50 a bottle, the quantity demanded is 1 bottle a day.

The demand curve shows the relationship between the quantity demanded and price, other things remaining the same. The downward-sloping demand curve illustrates the law of demand. When the price falls, the quantity demanded increases; and when the price rises, the quantity demanded decreases.

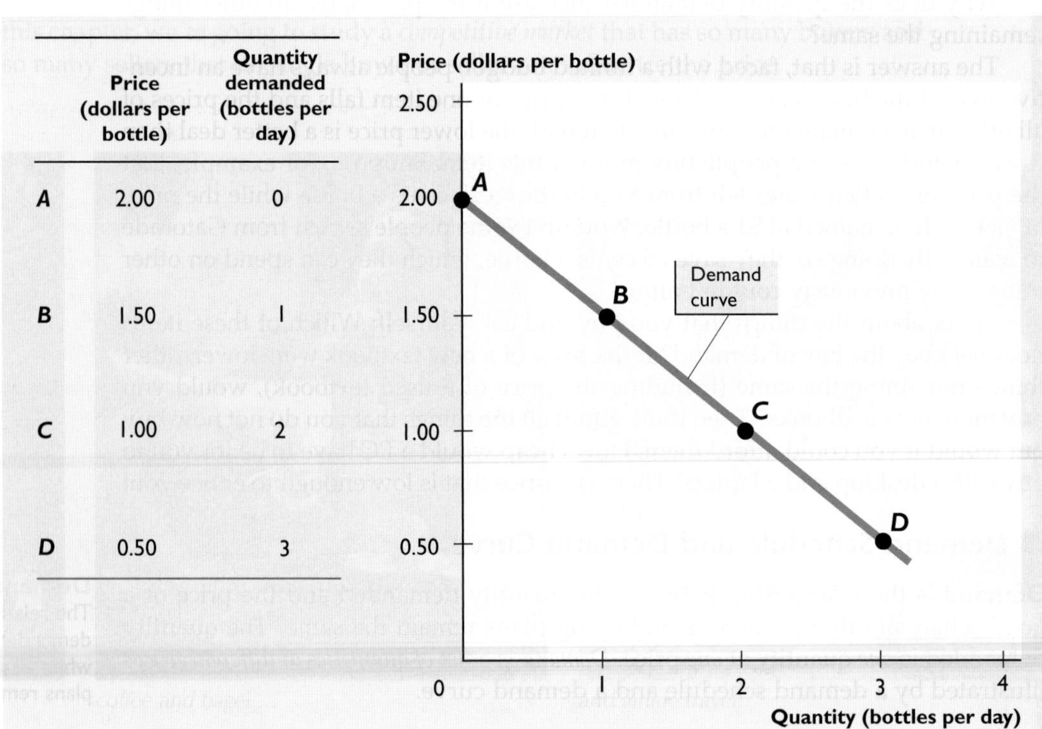

| | Price (dollars per bottle) | Quantity demanded (bottles per day) |
|---|---|---|
| *A* | 2.00 | 0 |
| *B* | 1.50 | 1 |
| *C* | 1.00 | 2 |
| *D* | 0.50 | 3 |

## Individual Demand and Market Demand

The demand schedule and the demand curve that you've just studied are for one person. To study a market, we must determine the market demand.

**Market demand** is the sum of the demands of all the buyers in a market. To find the market demand, imagine a market in which there are only two buyers: Tina and Tim. The table in Figure 4.2 shows three demand schedules: Tina's, Tim's, and the market demand schedule. Tina's demand schedule is the same as before. It shows the quantity of water demanded by Tina at each different price. Tim's demand schedule tells us the quantity of water demanded by Tim at each price. To find the quantity of water demanded in the market, we sum the quantities demanded by Tina and Tim. For example, at a price of $1.00 a bottle, the quantity demanded by Tina is 2 bottles a day, the quantity demanded by Tim is 1 bottle a day, and so the quantity demanded in the market is 3 bottles a day.

**Market demand**
The sum of the demands of all the buyers in the market.

Tina's demand curve in part (a) and Tim's demand curve in part (b) are graphs of the two individual demand schedules. The market demand curve in part (c) is a graph of the market demand schedule. At a given price, the quantity demanded on the market demand curve equals the horizontal sum of the quantities demanded on the individual demand curves.

**FIGURE 4.2**

Individual Demand and Market Demand

myeconlab Animation

| Price (dollars per bottle) | Quantity demanded (bottles per day) | | |
|---|---|---|---|
| | Tina | Tim | Market |
| 2.00 | 0 | 0 | 0 |
| 1.50 | 1 | 0 | 1 |
| 1.00 | 2 + | 1 = | 3 |
| 0.50 | 3 | 2 | 5 |

The market demand schedule is the sum of the individual demand schedules, and the market demand curve is the horizontal sum of the individual demand curves.

At a price of $1 a bottle, the quantity demanded by Tina is 2 bottles a day and the quantity demanded by Tim is 1 bottle a day, so the total quantity demanded in the market is 3 bottles a day.

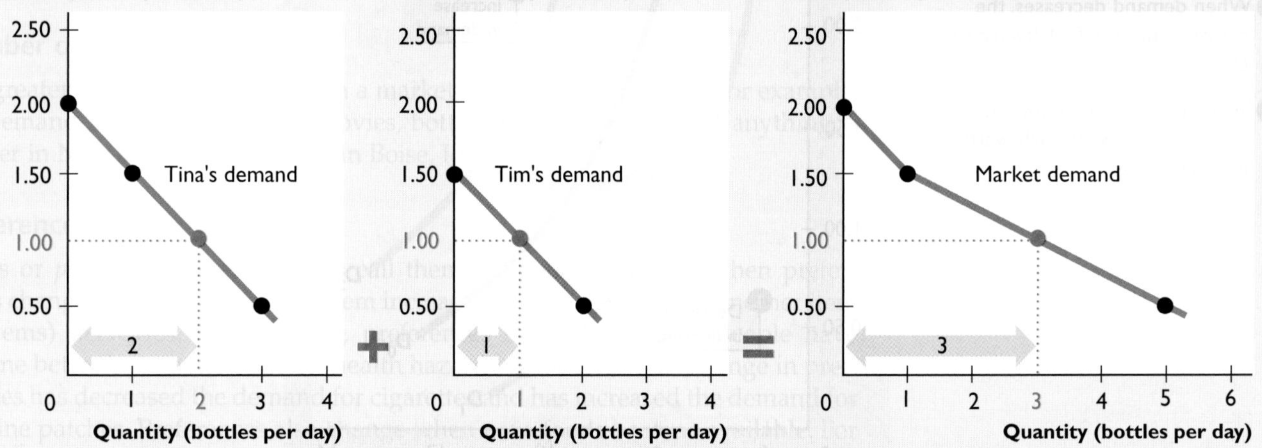

(a) Tina's demand

(b) Tim's demand

(c) Market demand

**FIGURE 4.10**

The Forces That Achieve Equilibrium

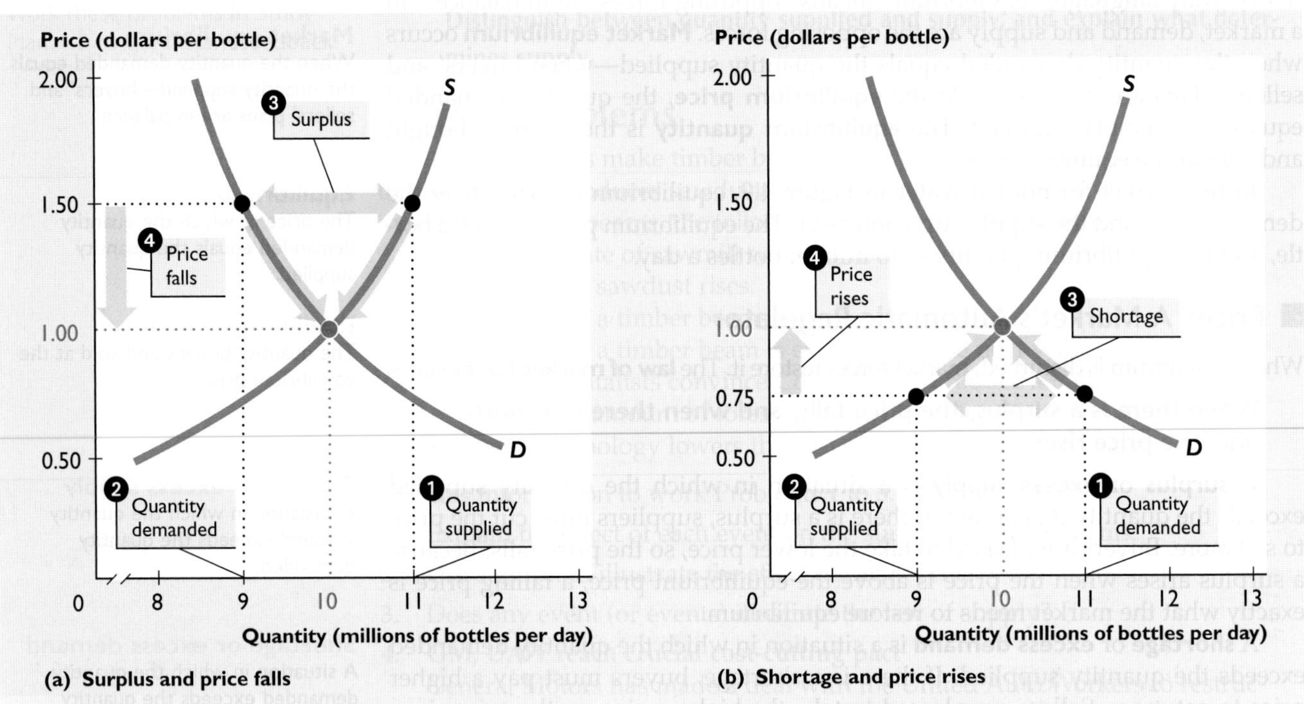


At $1.50 a bottle, ❶ the quantity supplied is 11 million bottles, ❷ the quantity demanded is 9 million bottles, ❸ the surplus is 2 million bottles, and ❹ the price falls.

At 75 cents a bottle, ❶ the quantity demanded is 11 million bottles, ❷ the quantity supplied is 9 million bottles, ❸ the shortage is 2 million bottles, and ❹ the price rises.

price is exactly what is needed to restore equilibrium.

In Figure 4.10(a), at $1.50 a bottle, there is a surplus: The price falls, the quantity demanded increases, the quantity supplied decreases, and the surplus is eliminated at $1.00 a bottle.

In Figure 4.10(b), at 75 cents a bottle, there is a shortage of water: The price rises, the quantity demanded decreases, the quantity supplied increases, and the shortage is eliminated at $1.00 a bottle.

## Predicting Price Changes: Three Questions

Because price adjustments eliminate shortages and surpluses, markets are normally in equilibrium. When an event disturbs an equilibrium, a new equilibrium soon emerges. To explain and predict changes in prices and quantities, we need to consider only changes in the *equilibrium* price and the *equilibrium* quantity. We can work out the effects of an event on a market by answering three questions:

1. Does the event influence demand or supply?
2. Does the event *increase* or *decrease* demand or supply—shift the demand curve or the supply curve *rightward* or *leftward*?
3. What are the new *equilibrium* price and *equilibrium* quantity and how have they changed?

## Effects of Changes in Demand

Let's practice answering the three questions by working out the effects of an event in the market for bottled water: A new study says that tap water is unsafe.

1. With tap water unsafe, the demand for bottled water changes.
2. The demand for bottled water *increases*, and the demand curve *shifts rightward*. Figure 4.11(a) shows the shift from $D_0$ to $D_1$.
3. There is now a *shortage* at $1.00 a bottle. The *price rises* to $1.50 a bottle, and the quantity increases to 11 million bottles.

Note that there is *no change in supply*; the rise in price brings an *increase in the quantity supplied*—a movement along the supply curve.

Let's work out what happens if the price of a zero-calorie sports drink falls.

1. The sports drink is a substitute for bottled water, so when its price changes, the demand for bottled water changes.
2. The demand for bottled water *decreases*, and the demand curve *shifts leftward*. Figure 4.11(b) shows the shift from $D_0$ to $D_2$.
3. There is now a *surplus* at $1.00 a bottle. The price *falls* to 75 cents a bottle, and the quantity decreases to 9 million bottles.

Note again that there is *no change in supply*; the fall in price brings a *decrease in the quantity supplied*—a movement along the supply curve.

**FIGURE 4.11**

The Effects of a Change in Demand

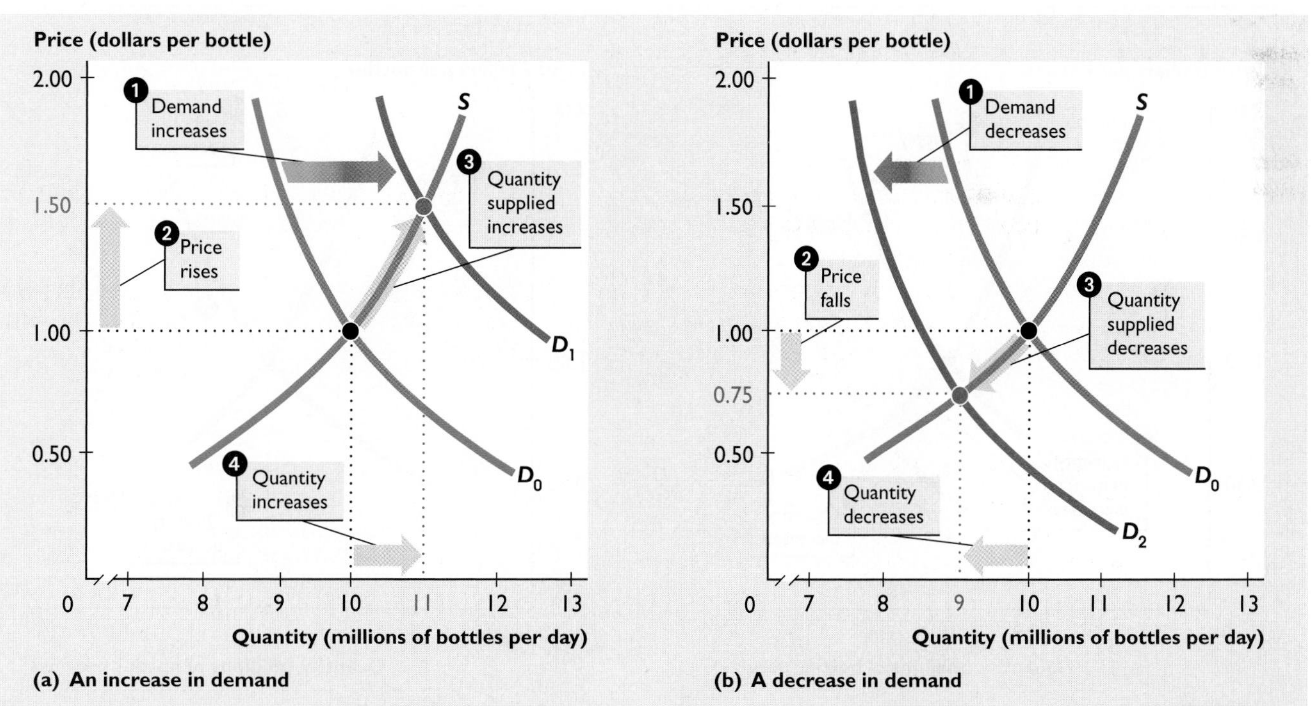


1 An increase in demand shifts the demand curve rightward to $D_1$ and creates a shortage. 2 The price rises, 3 the quantity supplied increases, and 4 the equilibrium quantity increases.

1 A decrease in demand shifts the demand curve leftward to $D_2$ and creates a surplus. 2 The price falls, 3 the quantity supplied decreases, and 4 the equilibrium quantity decreases.

## Effects of Changes in Supply

You can get more practice working out the effects of another event in the market for bottled water: European water bottlers buy springs and open new plants in the United States.

1. With more suppliers of bottled water, the supply changes.
2. The supply of bottled water *increases*, and the supply curve *shifts rightward*. Figure 4.12(a) shows the shift from $S_0$ to $S_1$.
3. There is now a *surplus* at $1.00 a bottle. The *price falls* to 75 cents a bottle, and the quantity increases to 11 million bottles.

Note that there is *no change in demand*; the fall in price brings an *increase in the quantity demanded*—a movement along the demand curve.

What happens if a drought dries up some springs?

1. The drought is a change in productivity, so the supply of water changes.
2. With fewer springs, the supply of bottled water *decreases*, and the supply curve *shifts leftward*. Figure 4.12(b) shows the shift from $S_0$ to $S_2$.
3. There is now a *shortage* at $1.00 a bottle. The *price rises* to $1.50 a bottle, and the quantity decreases to 9 million bottles.

Again, there is *no change in demand*; the rise in price brings a *decrease in the quantity demanded*—a movement along the demand curve.

**FIGURE 4.12**

The Effects of a Change in Supply

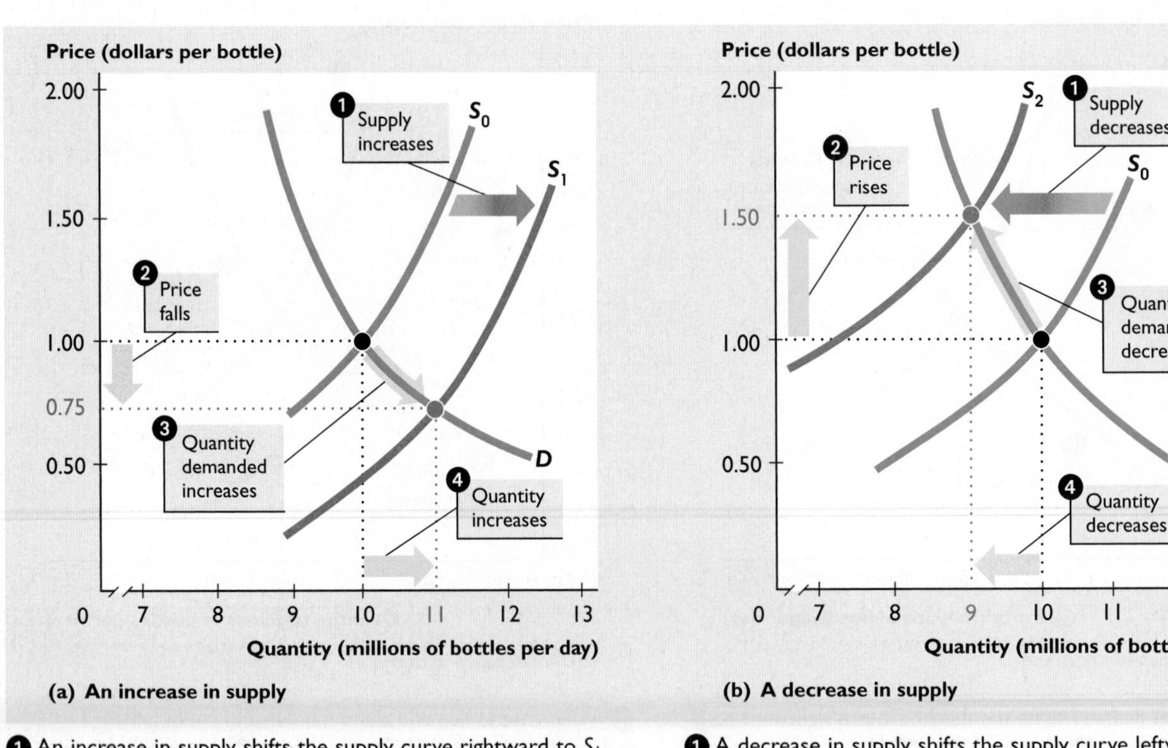


1 An increase in supply shifts the supply curve rightward to $S_1$ and creates a surplus. 2 The price falls, 3 the quantity demanded increases, and 4 the equilibrium quantity increases.

1 A decrease in supply shifts the supply curve leftward to $S_2$ and creates a shortage. 2 The price rises, 3 the quantity demanded decreases, and 4 the equilibrium quantity decreases.

# EYE on the U.S. ECONOMY

## The U.S. Market for Automobiles in 2008 and 2009

In 2008, the equilibrium price of an automobile was $20,000 and 16 million vehicles were bought and sold.

In 2009, millions of families decided to hold off buying a new car. Why? Layoffs had cut many people's incomes and many more feared being laid off in the near future. Also, as the value of people's homes tumbled, even those who still had a job felt poorer.

With lower incomes and lower expected future incomes, the demand for automobiles decreased from $D_{08}$ to $D_{09}$.

The equilibrium price fell to $19,000 per vehicle, and the equilibrium quantity decreased to 12 million vehicles—a decrease in the quantity supplied shown by a movement along the supply curve.

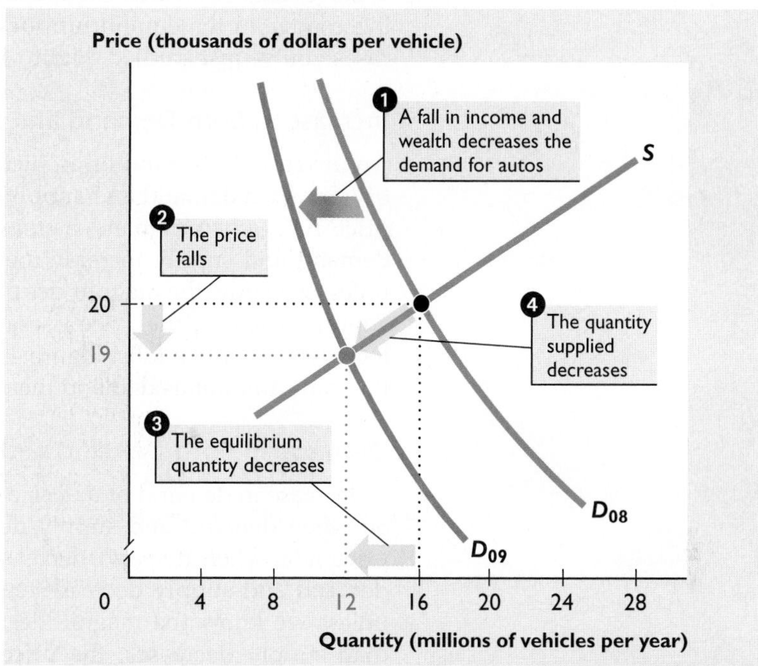


# EYE on the GLOBAL ECONOMY

## The Global Market for Wheat in 2008

In 2008, the price of wheat soared from $150 a ton to $240 a ton. Why? Because two events in the global wheat market decreased supply: widespread drought and a rise in the price of fertilizers.

Drought affected wheat growers in Argentina, Australia, China, Europe, and the United States, and wheat production fell.

Fertilizers—nitrogen, potassium, and potash—are used to grow wheat and the prices of fertilizers doubled.

Both of these large shocks to supply decreased the supply of wheat from $S_{07}$ to $S_{08}$. The price of wheat rose to its new equilibrium price of $240 per ton. As the price rose, the quantity of wheat demanded decreased and the equilibrium quantity decreased to 780 million tons.

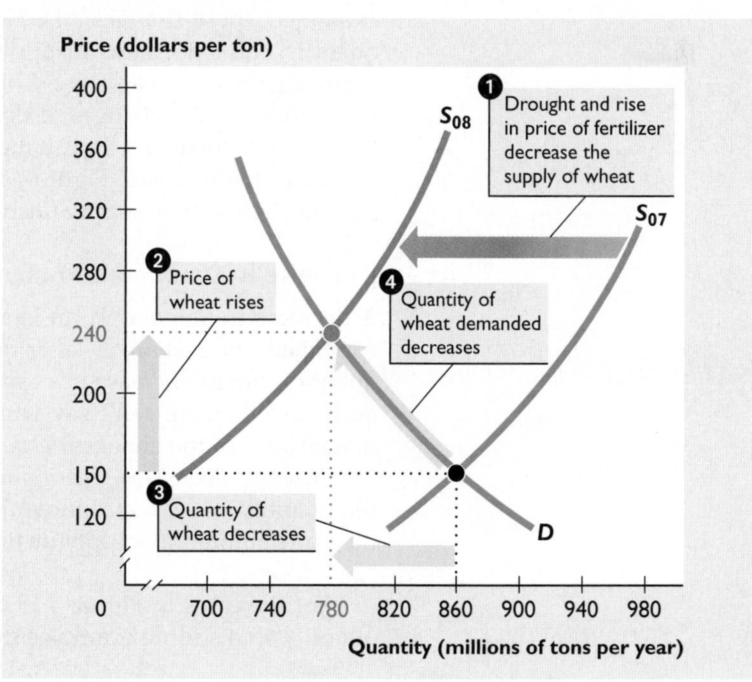

## Changes in Both Demand and Supply

When events occur that change *both* demand and supply, you can find the resulting change in the equilibrium price and equilibrium quantity by combining the cases you've just studied. Figure 4.13 summarizes all the possible cases.

### Increase in Both Demand and Supply

An increase in demand or an increase in supply increases the equilibrium quantity. So when demand and supply increase together, the *quantity increases*. But the price rises when demand increases and falls when supply increases. So when demand and supply increase together, we can't say what happens to the price unless we know the magnitudes of the changes. If demand increases by more than supply increases, the price rises. But if supply increases by more than demand increases, the price falls. Figure 4.13(e) shows the case when supply increases by the same amount as demand increases, so the price remains unchanged.

### Decrease in Both Demand and Supply

A decrease in demand or a decrease in supply decreases the equilibrium quantity. So when demand and supply decrease together, the *quantity decreases*. But the price falls when demand decreases and rises when supply decreases. So when demand and supply decrease together, we can't say what happens to the price unless we know the magnitudes of the changes. If demand decreases by more than supply decreases, the price falls. But if supply decreases by more than demand decreases, the price rises. Figure 4.13(i) shows the case when supply decreases by the same amount as demand decreases, so the price remains unchanged.

### Increase in Demand and Decrease in Supply

An increase in demand or a decrease in supply raises the equilibrium price, so combined, these changes *raise the price*. But an increase in demand increases the quantity, and a decrease in supply decreases the quantity. So when these changes occur together, we can't say what happens to the quantity unless we know the magnitudes of the changes. If demand increases by more than supply decreases, the quantity increases. But if supply decreases by more than demand increases, the quantity decreases. Figure 4.13(h) shows the case when demand increases by the same amount as supply decreases, so the quantity remains unchanged.

### Decrease in Demand and Increase in Supply

A decrease in demand or an increase in supply lowers the equilibrium price, so combined, these changes *lower the price*. But a decrease in demand decreases the quantity, and an increase in supply increases the quantity. So when these changes occur together, we can't say what happens to the quantity unless we know the magnitudes of the changes. If demand decreases by more than supply increases, the quantity decreases. But if supply increases by more than demand decreases, the quantity increases. Figure 4.13(f) shows the case when demand decreases by the same amount as supply increases, so the quantity remains unchanged.

For the cases in Figure 4.13 where you "can't say" what happens to price or quantity, make some examples that go in each direction.

# EYE on YOUR LIFE

## Using Demand and Supply

The demand and supply model is going to be a big part of the rest of your life!

First, you will use it again and again during your economics course. The demand and supply model is one of your major tools, so having a firm grasp of it will bring an immediate payoff.

But second, and much more important, by understanding the laws of demand and supply and being aware of how prices adjust to balance these two opposing forces, you will have a much better appreciation of how your economic world works.

Every time you hear someone complaining about a price hike and blaming it on someone's greed, think about the law of market forces and how demand and supply determine that price.

As you shop for your favorite clothing, music, and food items, try to describe how supply and demand influence the prices of these goods.

---

**FIGURE 4.13**

The Effects of All the Possible Changes in Demand and Supply

myeconlab Animation

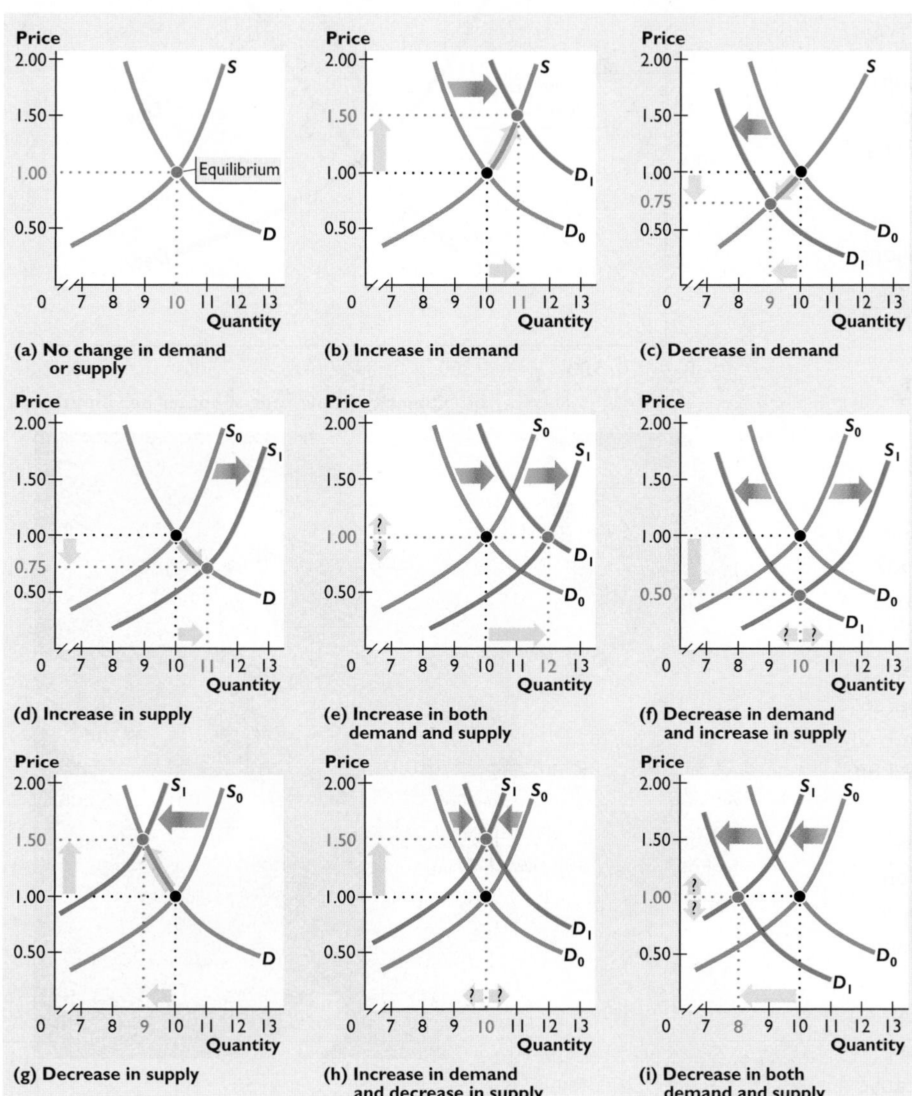


(a) No change in demand or supply

(b) Increase in demand

(c) Decrease in demand

(d) Increase in supply

(e) Increase in both demand and supply

(f) Decrease in demand and increase in supply

(g) Decrease in supply

(h) Increase in demand and decrease in supply

(i) Decrease in both demand and supply

This figure shows all the possible changes in demand or supply, or both demand and supply, and their effects on the equilibrium price and equilibrium quantity.

A green arrow shows an increase in the price or quantity. A red arrow shows a decrease in the price or quantity.

A double-headed green and red arrow shows that the price might rise or fall or the quantity might increase or decrease depending on the magnitudes of the changes in demand and supply.

# EYE on HOME PRICES

## Why Did Home Prices Boom and Bust?

In 1999, the price of an average home was $200,000, but home prices were rising by almost 10 percent per year. The pace of increase picked up and by 2004, home prices were rising by 15 percent per year. At the beginning of 2006, home prices stood at double their 1999 level. What caused this boom in home prices?

### The Boom

Home prices rose sharply because the demand for homes increased and the supply of homes offered for sale decreased. What caused these changes in the demand for and supply of homes?

Cheap and easy loans put the dream of owning a home within the reach of millions of Americans, many of whom had modest incomes. This flow of loans increased the demand for homes at a pace that outstripped the construction of new homes. With the increase in the demand for homes outpacing the increase in supply, home prices rose.

Once home prices started to rise, the expectation of continuing price rises took hold. Expected future price rises influence both demand and supply.

With a higher expected future price, even more people want to own a home, so the demand for homes increases faster. People with a home to sell want to hold off selling today to get tomorrow's higher price, so the supply of homes decreases.

The figure above shows the effects on price of the combination of an increase in demand and a decrease in supply. Demand increased from $D_{99}$ to $D_{06}$, supply decreased from $S_{99}$ to $S_{06}$, and the price increased, as expected. The expectation of a higher price becomes a reality because

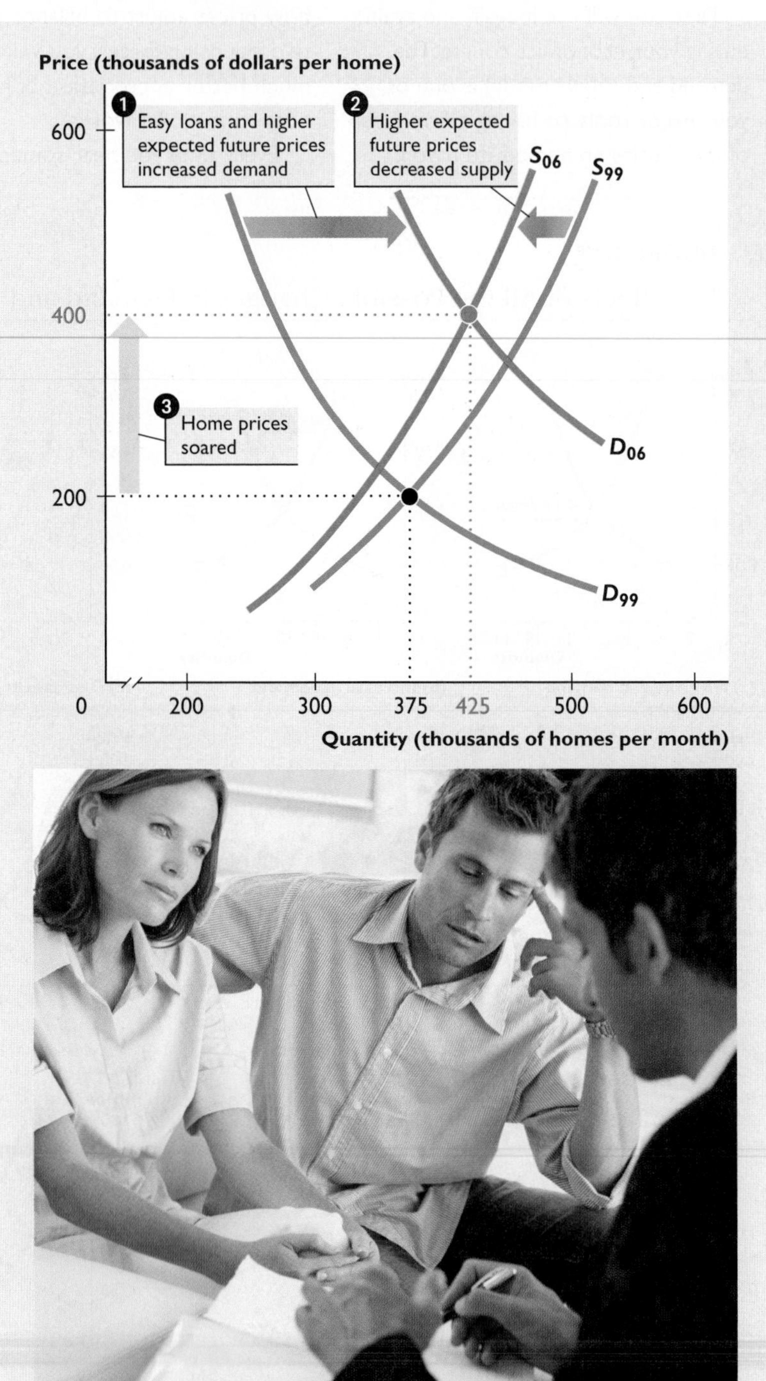

it increases demand, decreases supply, and creates what is called a *rational bubble*.

## The Bust

Home prices started to fall in 2006 and the pace of decrease accelerated, and by 2009, home prices had fallen to 54 percent of their 2006 peak. What caused the fall in home prices?

Home prices fell because the demand for homes decreased and the supply of homes offered for sale increased.

The cheap and easy loans that had enabled millions of Americans to own a home dried up. Demand decreased.

Banks had made loans to many people who could afford to make loan payments only at very low interest rates. In 2006, interest rates increased and the cost of carrying a home loan became too much for many household budgets. These households stopped paying the interest on their loans. When borrowers stop paying off their loans, the banks that made the loans are in trouble. (You'll learn about the details of the problems for banks when you study money and banking in your macroeconomics course.)

The banks increased the interest rate on home loans and made loans harder to get.

As a result, the demand for homes decreased. At the same time, foreclosures increased the supply of homes for sale. The decrease in demand and increase in supply brought a falling price.

As the price continued to fall, a falling price came to be expected. The demand for homes decreased faster and the supply of homes offered for sale increased faster.

The figure below shows the effects on price of the combination of a decrease in demand and an increase in supply. Demand decreased from $D_{06}$ to $D_{09}$, supply increased from $S_{06}$ to $S_{09}$, and the price fell, as expected.

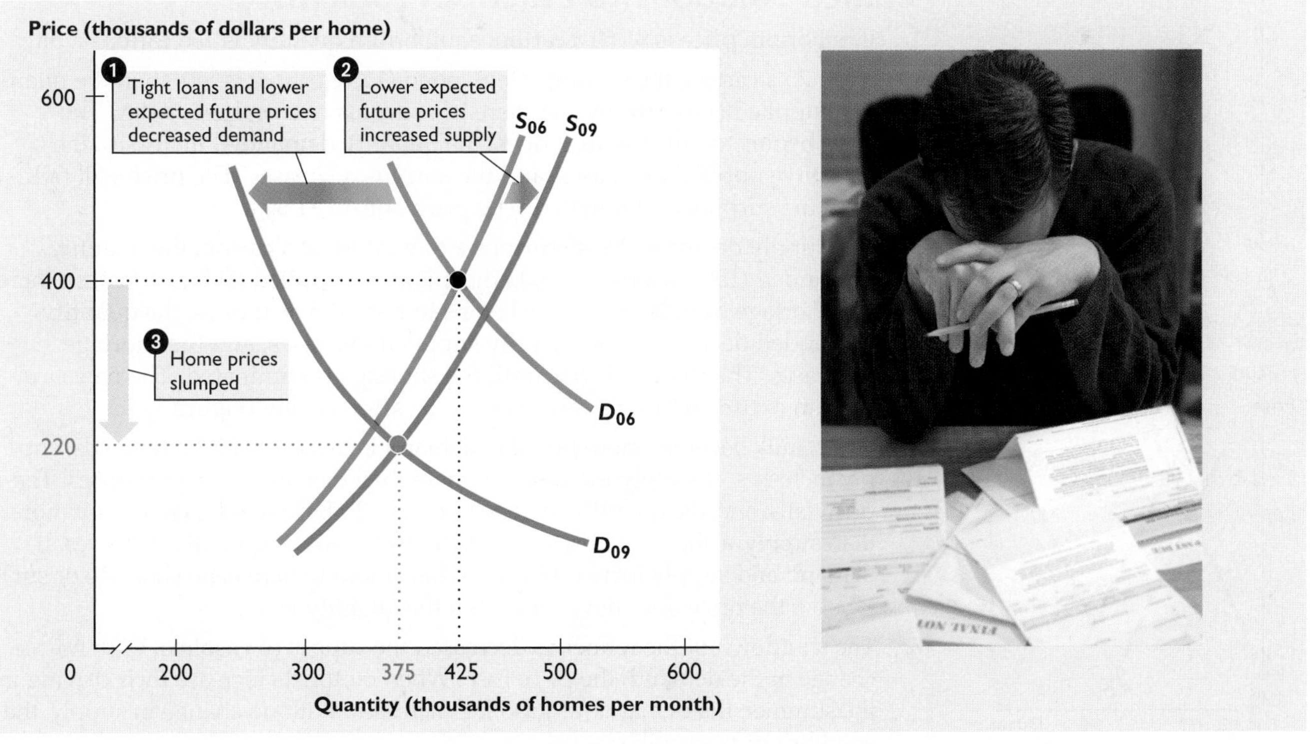

Work these problems in Study Plan 4.3 to get instant feedback.

# CHECKPOINT 4.3

**Explain how demand and supply determine price and quantity in a market, and explain the effects of changes in demand and supply.**

## Practice Problems

Use Table 1, which sets out the demand and supply schedules for milk, to work Problems **1** to **4**.

1. What is the equilibrium price and equilibrium quantity of milk?
2. Describe the situation in the milk market if the price were $1.75 a carton and explain how the market reaches its new equilibrium.
3. A drought decreases the quantity supplied by 45 cartons a day at each price. What is the new equilibrium and how does the market adjust to it?
4. Milk becomes more popular and better feeds increase milk production. How do these events influence demand and supply? Describe how the equilibrium price and equilibrium quantity change.
5. **Summer's here. So are higher gas prices**
   The price of gasoline increased 15 percent in the past three weeks, mainly because of refinery shutdowns in the United States. As motorists increase their driving in the coming months, the price is predicted to rise further.
   Source: CNN Money, May 21, 2009
   Explain why the price rose in the past 3 weeks and why it is expected to rise in the coming months.

**TABLE 1**

| Price (dollars per carton) | Quantity demanded (cartons per day) | Quantity supplied (cartons per day) |
|---|---|---|
| 1.00 | 200 | 110 |
| 1.25 | 175 | 130 |
| 1.50 | 150 | 150 |
| 1.75 | 125 | 170 |
| 2.00 | 100 | 190 |

**FIGURE 1**

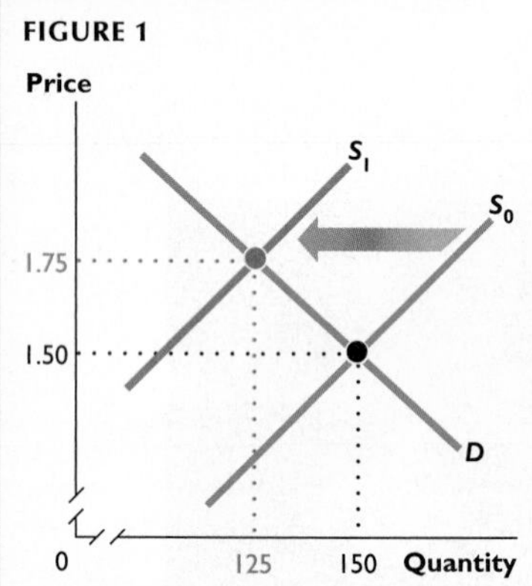


**FIGURE 2**

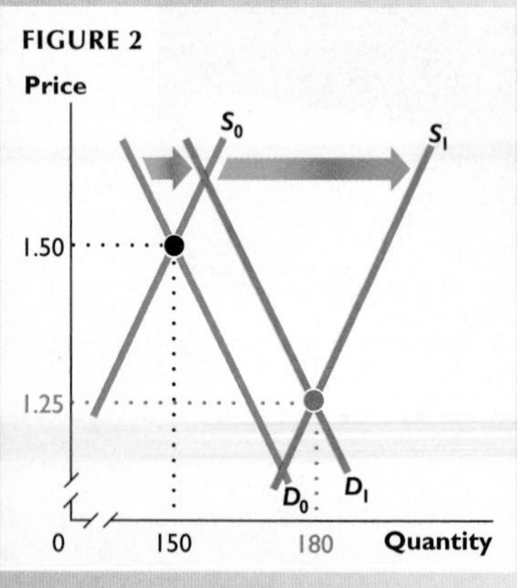


## Guided Solutions to Practice Problems

1. Equilibrium price is $1.50 a carton; equilibrium quantity is 150 cartons a day.
2. At $1.75 a carton, the quantity demanded (125 cartons) is less than the quantity supplied (170 cartons), so there is a surplus of 45 cartons a day. The price begins to fall, and as it does, the quantity demanded increases, the quantity supplied decreases, and the surplus decreases. The price will fall until the surplus is eliminated. The price falls to $1.50 a carton.
3. The supply decreases by 45 cartons a day. At $1.50 a carton, the quantity demanded (150 cartons) exceeds the quantity supplied (105 cartons), so there is a shortage of milk. The price begins to rise, and as it does, the quantity demanded decreases, the quantity supplied increases, and the shortage decreases. The price will rise until the shortage is eliminated. The new equilibrium occurs at $1.75 a carton and 125 cartons a day (Figure 1).
4. When milk becomes more popular, demand increases. With better feeds, supply increases. If supply increases by more than demand, a surplus arises. The price falls, and the quantity increases (Figure 2). If demand increases by more than supply, a shortage arises. The price rises, and the quantity increases. If demand and supply increase by the same amount, there is no shortage or surplus, so the price does not change, but the quantity increases.
5. The shutdown of the refineries decreased the supply of gasoline. With no change in the demand, the price rose. When motorists increase their driving in the summer, the demand for gasoline increases. With no change in supply, the equilibrium price will rise further.

# CHAPTER SUMMARY

## Key Points

1 **Distinguish between quantity demanded and demand, and explain what determines demand.**

- Other things remaining the same, the quantity demanded increases as the price falls and decreases as the price rises—the law of demand.
- The demand for a good is influenced by the prices of related goods, expected future prices, income, expected future income and credit, the number of buyers, and preferences. A change in any of these influences changes the demand for the good.

2 **Distinguish between quantity supplied and supply, and explain what determines supply.**

- Other things remaining the same, the quantity supplied increases as the price rises and decreases as the price falls—the law of supply.
- The supply of a good is influenced by the prices of related goods, prices of resources and other inputs, expectations about future prices, the number of sellers, and productivity. A change in any of these influences changes the supply of the good.

3 **Explain how demand and supply determine price and quantity in a market, and explain the effects of changes in demand and supply.**

- The law of market forces brings market equilibrium—the equilibrium price and equilibrium quantity at which buyers and sellers trade.
- The price adjusts to maintain market equilibrium—to keep the quantity demanded equal to the quantity supplied. A surplus brings a fall in the price to restore market equilibrium; a shortage brings a rise in the price to restore market equilibrium.
- Market equilibrium responds to changes in demand and supply. An increase in demand increases both the price and the quantity; a decrease in demand decreases both the price and the quantity. An increase in supply increases the quantity but decreases the price; and a decrease in supply decreases the quantity but increases the price.

## Key Terms

Work these problems in Chapter 4 Study Plan to get instant feedback.

# CHAPTER CHECKPOINT

## Study Plan Problems and Applications

1. Explain how each of the following events changes the demand for or supply of air travel.
   - Airfares tumble, while long-distance bus fares don't change.
   - The price of jet fuel rises.
   - Airlines reduce the number of flights each day.
   - People expect airfares to increase next summer.
   - The price of train travel falls.
   - The price of a pound of air cargo increases.

Use the laws of demand and supply to explain whether the statements in Problems 2 and 3 are true or false. In your explanation, distinguish between a change in demand and a change in the quantity demanded and between a change in supply and a change in the quantity supplied.

2. The United States does not allow oranges from Brazil (the world's largest producer of oranges) to enter the United States. If Brazilian oranges were sold in the United States, oranges and orange juice would be cheaper.
3. If the price of frozen yogurt falls, the quantity of ice cream consumed will decrease and the price of ice cream will rise.
4. Table 1 shows the demand and supply schedules for running shoes. What is the market equilibrium? If the price is $70 a pair, describe the situation in the market. Explain how market equilibrium is restored. If a rise in income increases the demand for running shoes by 100 pairs a day at each price, explain how the market adjusts to its new equilibrium.
5. "As more people buy fuel-efficient hybrid cars, the demand for gasoline will decrease and the price of gasoline will fall. The fall in the price of gasoline will decrease the supply of gasoline." Is this statement true? Explain.

**TABLE 1**

| Price (dollars per pair) | Quantity demanded | Quantity supplied |
|---|---|---|
| | (pairs per day) | |
| 60 | 1,000 | 400 |
| 70 | 900 | 500 |
| 80 | 800 | 600 |
| 90 | 700 | 700 |
| 100 | 600 | 800 |
| 110 | 500 | 900 |

Use the following information to work Problems 6 to 8.

**Consumers eating higher food costs**

The price of milk rose about 21% from July 2006 to July 2007, while the price of frozen orange juice increased 31%. At the same time, with higher gasoline prices, the demand for ethanol increased. Because ethanol is made from corn, the price of corn rose, which in turn increased the price of bread, chicken, cheese, and the fast-foods that use cheese. As people in China and India become richer, they are eating more beef and chicken and less rice and tofu—another source of higher food prices in the United States.

Source: *USA Today*, September 6, 2007

6. Explain why the demand for ethanol has influenced the price of corn.
7. Use graphs to show why the higher price of corn affects the price of milk and the price of cheese.
8. Explain why food prices in the United States will rise as people in India and China become richer and can afford to buy beef and chicken.

## Instructor Assignable Problems and Applications

Your instructor can assign these problems as homework, a quiz, or a test in **MyEconLab**.

1. If home loans become harder to get and the ability of borrowers to repay is checked more thoroughly by the banks, how does
   - The demand for homes change?
   - The supply of homes change?
   - The price of homes change?

   Illustrate your answer with a graphical analysis.
2. Explain how each of the following events changes the demand for or supply of jeans:
   - A new technology reduces the time it takes to make a pair of jeans.
   - The price of the cloth (denim) used to make jeans falls.
   - The wage rate paid to garment workers increases.
   - The price of a denim skirt doubles.
   - People's incomes increase.
3. What is the effect on the equilibrium price and equilibrium quantity of orange juice if the price of apple juice decreases and the wage rate paid to orange grove workers increases?
4. What is the effect on the equilibrium in the orange juice market if orange juice becomes more popular and a cheaper robot is used to pick oranges?

Table 1 shows the demand and supply schedules for boxes of chocolates in an average week. Use this information to work Problems **5** and **6**.

**TABLE 1**

| Price (dollars per box) | Quantity demanded | Quantity supplied |
|---|---|---|
| | (boxes per week) | |
| 13.00 | 1,600 | 1,200 |
| 14.00 | 1,500 | 1,300 |
| 15.00 | 1,400 | 1,400 |
| 16.00 | 1,300 | 1,500 |
| 17.00 | 1,200 | 1,600 |
| 18.00 | 1,100 | 1,700 |

5. If the price of chocolates is $17.00 a box, describe the situation in the market. Explain how market equilibrium is restored.
6. During Valentine's week, more people buy chocolates and chocolatiers offer their chocolates in special red boxes, which cost more to produce than the everyday box. Set out the three-step process of analysis and show on a graph the adjustment process to the new equilibrium. Describe the changes in the equilibrium price and the equilibrium quantity.
7. During 1994, Brazil experienced severe frosts, which wiped out many coffee plantations. New plantations in Brazil began to produce coffee beans in 1999. During the early 2000s, countries such as Vietnam started to produce coffee beans and Starbucks started to spring up across Europe. Use these events to explain why the price of coffee beans rose during the late 1990s, fell during the early 2000s, and rose again after 2003.
8. **Alabama food prices jump in May**

   Alabama Farmers Federation announced that food prices in May will increase. In previous unprofitable years, farmers reduced their herds with the result that in 2009 meat production will fall. Bacon is expected to rise by 32 cents a pound to $4.18 and steaks by 57 cents to $8.41 a pound.

   Source: *The Birmingham News*, May 21, 2009

   Explain why the reduction of herds will lead to a rise in meat prices today. Draw a graph to illustrate.
9. If the demand for a good decreases by 10 percent and the supply of the good decreases by 8 percent, will the price of the good rise or fall? Explain.

10. "As more people buy computers, the demand for Internet service increases and the price of Internet service decreases. The fall in the price of Internet service decreases the supply of Internet service." Is this statement true or false? Explain.

11. **Steel output set for historic drop**

    Steel producers expect to cut output by 10 percent in 2009 in response to cancelled orders from construction companies and car and household appliance producers.

    Source: *Financial Times*, December 28, 2008

    Does the cancellation of orders change the demand for steel, the quantity supplied, the supply of steel, or the quantity supplied? What happens to the equilibrium price of steel?

Use the following information to work Problems 12 to 14.

**Oil soars to new record over $135**

In the summer of 2008, the price of crude oil hit a record high above $135 a barrel. OPEC reported that there was no shortage of oil and that speculators had forced the price up.

Source: BBC News, May 22, 2008

12. Explain how the price of oil can rise even though there is no shortage of oil.
13. If a shortage of oil does occur, what does that imply about price adjustments and the role of price as a regulator in the market for oil?
14. If OPEC is correct, what factors might have changed demand and/or supply to cause the price to rise?
15. **Italians call for 1–day pasta strike**

    Italy's national dish is pasta. In 2007, as the world price of durum wheat rocketed, the price of durum flour rose by 20 percent. Seventy percent of pasta is durum flour. Italian consumer groups called for a one-day boycott of pasta in grocery stores, as a way of showing their unhappiness with the 20 percent increase. Be it fettuccine, linguine, or spaghetti, Italians will soon be paying up to 20 percent more for their pasta.

    Source: *The New York Times*, September 12, 2007

    Show on a graph the effect of the rise in the price of durum flour on the market price of pasta. Suppose that as a result of the one-day strike, grocery stores did not raise the price of pasta next month as predicted. Describe the situation in the market.

Use the following information to work Problems 16 and 17.

**Labels seek end to 99¢ per song music download**

The *Wall Street Journal* reported that five major recording companies think that music downloads at 99¢ per song are too cheap and they would like to see a price between $1.25 and $2.99 per song.

Source: *The Register*, April 9, 2004

16. What determines the price of a music download? What role does self-interest—of both the recording companies and the people who download songs—play in the market for music downloads?
17. What do you predict would happen in the market for music downloads if the major recording companies tried to hike the price to $2.99 a song?

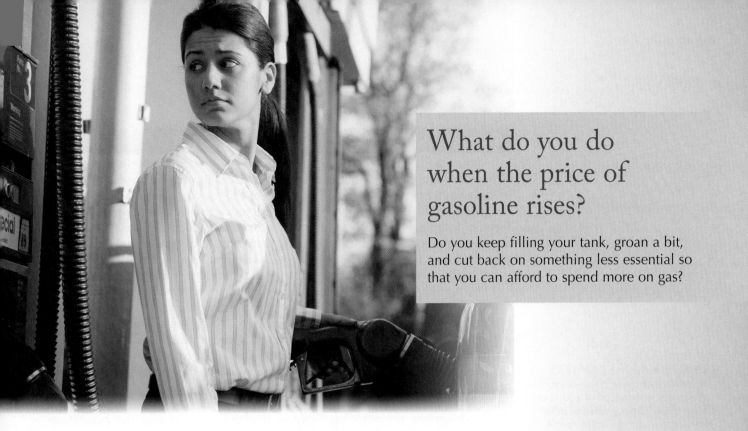

## What do you do when the price of gasoline rises?

Do you keep filling your tank, groan a bit, and cut back on something less essential so that you can afford to spend more on gas?

# Elasticities of Demand and Supply

**When you have completed your study of this chapter, you will be able to**

1. Define, explain the factors that influence, and calculate the price elasticity of demand.
2. Define, explain the factors that influence, and calculate the price elasticity of supply.
3. Define and explain the factors that influence the cross elasticity of demand and the income elasticity of demand.

## 5.1 THE PRICE ELASTICITY OF DEMAND

A decrease in supply of gasoline brings a large rise in its price and a small decrease in the quantity that people buy. The reason is that buying plans for gasoline are not very responsive to a change in price. But an increase in the supply of airline services brings a small decrease in its price and a large increase in the quantity of air travel. In the case of air travel, buying plans are highly sensitive to a change in price. By knowing how sensitive or responsive buying plans are to price changes, we can predict how a given change in supply will change price and quantity.

But we often want to go further and predict by how much a price will change when an event occurs. To make more precise predictions about the magnitudes of price and quantity changes, we need to know more about a demand curve than the fact that it slopes downward. We need to know how responsive the quantity demanded is to a price change. Elasticity provides this information.

**Price elasticity of demand**
A measure of the responsiveness of the quantity demanded of a good to a change in its price when all other influences on buyers' plans remain the same.

The **price elasticity of demand** is a measure of the responsiveness of the quantity demanded of a good* to a change in its price when all other influences on buyers' plans remain the same.

To determine the price elasticity of demand, we compare the percentage change in the quantity demanded with the percentage change in price. But we calculate percentage changes in a special way.

### Percentage Change in Price

Suppose that Starbucks raises the price of a latte from \$3 to \$5 a cup. What is the percentage change in price? The change in price is the new price minus the initial price. The percentage change is calculated as the change in price divided by the initial price, all multiplied by 100. The formula for the percentage change is

$$\text{Percentage change in price} = \left(\frac{\text{New price} - \text{Initial price}}{\text{Initial price}}\right) \times 100.$$

In this example, the initial price is \$3 and the new price is \$5, so

$$\text{Percentage change in price} = \left(\frac{\$5 - \$3}{\$3}\right) \times 100 = \left(\frac{\$2}{\$3}\right) \times 100 = 66.67 \text{ percent.}$$

Now suppose that Starbucks cuts the price of a latte from \$5 to \$3 a cup. Now what is the percentage change in price? The initial price is now \$5 and the new price is \$3, so the percentage change in price is calculated as

$$\text{Percentage change in price} = \left(\frac{\$3 - \$5}{\$5}\right) \times 100 = \left(\frac{-\$2}{\$5}\right) \times 100 = -40 \text{ percent.}$$

The same price change, \$2, over the same interval, \$3 to \$5, is a different percentage change (different absolute value or magnitude) depending on whether the price rises or falls.

Because elasticity compares the percentage change in the quantity demanded with the percentage change in price, we need a measure of percentage change that does not depend on the direction of the price change. The measure that economists use is called the *midpoint method.*

---

*What you learn in this chapter also applies to services and factors of production.

### The Midpoint Method

To calculate the percentage change in price using the midpoint method, we divide the change in the price by the *average price*—the *average* of the new price and the initial price—and then multiply by 100. The average price is at the midpoint between the initial and the new price, hence the name *midpoint method.*

The formula for the percentage change using the midpoint method is

$$\text{Percentage change in price} = \left(\frac{\text{New price} - \text{Initial price}}{(\text{New price} + \text{Initial price}) \div 2}\right) \times 100.$$

In this formula, the numerator, (New price − Initial price), is the same as before. The denominator, (New price + Initial price) ÷ 2, is the average of the new price and the initial price.

To calculate the percentage change in the price of a Starbucks latte using the midpoint method, put \$5 for new price and \$3 for initial price in the formula:

$$\begin{aligned}\text{Percentage change in price} &= \left(\frac{\$5 - \$3}{(\$5 + \$3) \div 2}\right) \times 100 = \left(\frac{\$2}{\$8 \div 2}\right) \times 100 \\ &= \left(\frac{\$2}{\$4}\right) \times 100 = 50 \text{ percent.}\end{aligned}$$

Because the average price is the same regardless of whether the price rises or falls, the percentage change in price calculated by the midpoint method is the same (absolute value or magnitude) for a price rise and a price fall. In this example, it is 50 percent.

## Percentage Change in Quantity Demanded

Suppose that when the price of a latte rises from \$3 to \$5 a cup, the quantity demanded decreases from 15 cups to 5 cups an hour. The percentage change in the quantity demanded using the midpoint method is

$$\begin{aligned}\text{Percentage change in quantity} &= \left(\frac{\text{New quantity} - \text{Initial quantity}}{(\text{New quantity} + \text{Initial quantity}) \div 2}\right) \times 100 \\ &= \left(\frac{5 - 15}{(5 + 15) \div 2}\right) \times 100 = \left(\frac{-10}{20 \div 2}\right) \times 100 \\ &= \left(\frac{-10}{10}\right) \times 100 = -100 \text{ percent.}\end{aligned}$$

When the price of a good *rises,* the quantity demanded of it *decreases*—a *positive* change in price brings a *negative* change in the quantity demanded. Similarly, when the price of a good *falls,* the quantity demanded of it *increases*—this time a *negative* change in price brings a *positive* change in the quantity demanded.

To compare the percentage change in the price and the percentage change in the quantity demanded, we use the absolute values or magnitudes of the percentage changes and we ignore the minus sign.

## Elastic and Inelastic Demand

To determine the responsiveness of the quantity of Starbucks latte demanded to its price, we need to compare the two percentage changes we've just calculated. The percentage change in quantity is 100 and the percentage change in price is 50, so the percentage change in quantity demanded is twice the percentage change in price. If we collected data on the prices and quantities of a number of goods and services (and we were careful to check that other things had remained the same), we could calculate lots of percentage changes. Our calculations would fall into three groups: The percentage change in the quantity demanded might exceed the percentage change in price, equal the percentage change in price, or be less than the percentage change in price. Which of these three possibilities arises depends on the elasticity of demand:

**Elastic demand**
When the percentage change in the quantity demanded exceeds the percentage change in price.

**Unit elastic demand**
When the percentage change in the quantity demanded equals the percentage change in price.

**Inelastic demand**
When the percentage change in the quantity demanded is less than the percentage change in price.

- When the percentage change in the quantity demanded exceeds the percentage change in price, demand is **elastic**.
- When the percentage change in the quantity demanded equals the percentage change in price, demand is **unit elastic**.
- When the percentage change in the quantity demanded is less than the percentage change in price, demand is **inelastic**.

**Perfectly elastic demand**
When the quantity demanded changes by a very large percentage in response to an almost zero percentage change in price.

**Perfectly inelastic demand**
When the percentage change in the quantity demanded is zero for any percentage change in the price.

Figure 5.1 shows the different types of demand curves that illustrate the range of possible price elasticities of demand. Part (a) shows an extreme case of an elastic demand called a **perfectly elastic demand**—an almost zero percentage change in the price brings a very large percentage change in the quantity demanded. Consumers are willing to buy any quantity of the good at a given price but none at a higher price. Part (b) shows an elastic demand—the percentage change in the quantity demanded exceeds the percentage change in price. Part (c) shows a unit elastic demand—the percentage change in the quantity demanded equals the percentage change in price. Part (d) shows an inelastic demand—the percentage change in the quantity demanded is less than the percentage change in price. Finally, part (e) shows an extreme case of an inelastic demand called a **perfectly inelastic demand**—the percentage change in the quantity demanded is zero for any percentage change in price.

## Influences on the Price Elasticity of Demand

What makes the demand for some things elastic and the demand for others inelastic? The influences on the price elasticity of demand fall into two groups:

- Availability of substitutes
- Proportion of income spent

### Availability of Substitutes

The demand for a good is elastic if a substitute for it is easy to find. Soft drink containers can be made of either aluminum or plastic and it doesn't matter which, so the demand for aluminum is elastic.

The demand for a good is inelastic if a substitute for it is hard to find. Oil has poor substitutes (imagine a coal-fueled car), so the demand for oil is inelastic.

Three main factors influence the ability to find a substitute for a good: whether the good is a luxury or a necessity, how narrowly it is defined, and the amount of time available to find a substitute for it.

**FIGURE 5.1**

The Range of Price Elasticities of Demand

myeconlab Animation

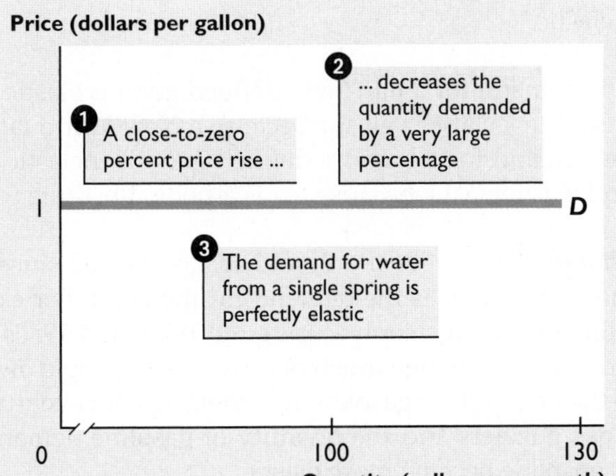


(a) Perfectly elastic demand

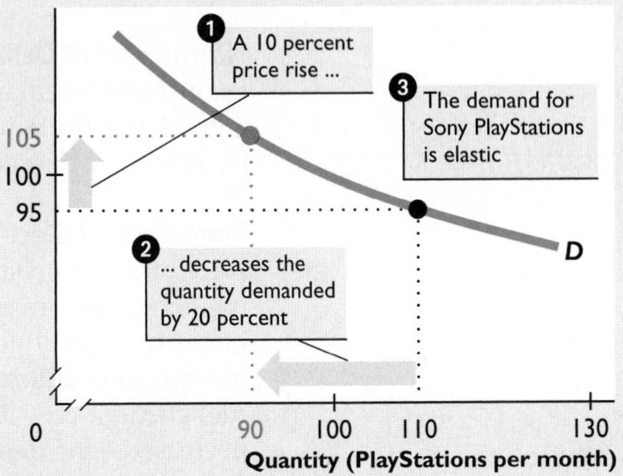


(b) Elastic demand

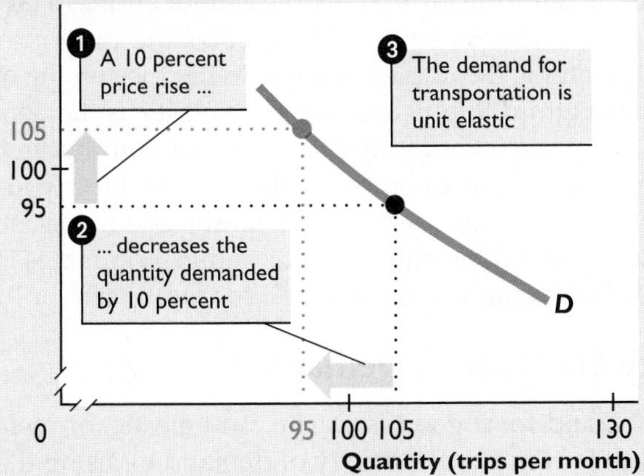


(c) Unit elastic demand

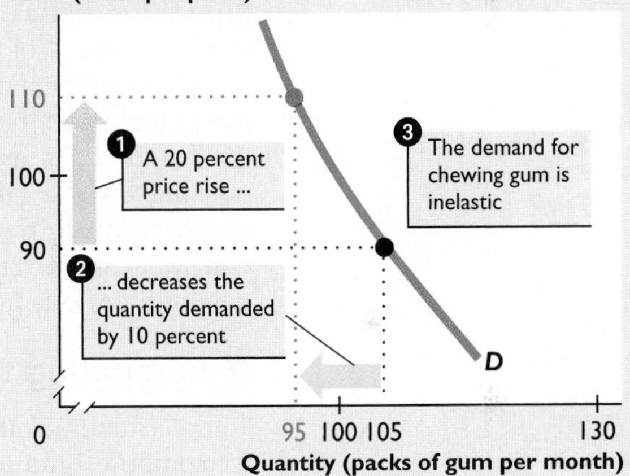


(d) Inelastic demand

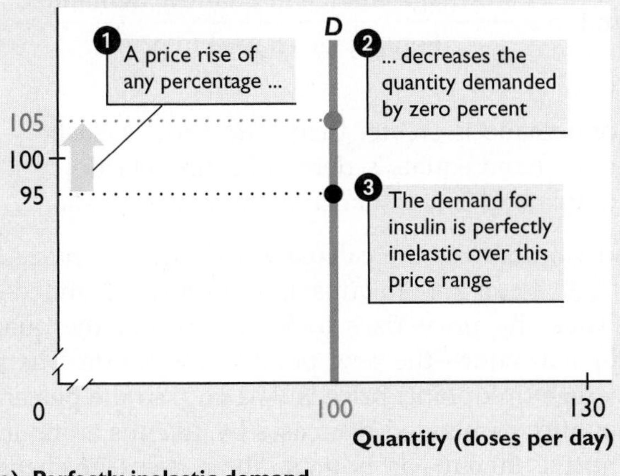


(e) Perfectly inelastic demand

❶ A price rise brings ❷ a decrease in the quantity demanded. The relationship between the percentage change in the quantity demanded and the percentage change in price determines ❸ the price elasticity of demand, which ranges from perfectly elastic (part a) to perfectly inelastic (part e).

***Luxury Versus Necessity*** We call goods such as food and housing *necessities* and goods such as exotic vacations *luxuries.* A necessity has poor substitutes—you must eat—so the demand for a necessity is inelastic. A luxury has many substitutes—you don't absolutely have to go to the Galapagos Islands this summer—so the demand for a luxury is elastic.

***Narrowness of Definition*** The demand for a narrowly defined good is elastic. For example, the demand for a Starbucks latte is elastic because a New World latte is a good substitute for it. The demand for a broadly defined good is inelastic. For example, the demand for coffee is inelastic because tea is a poor substitute for it.

***Time Elapsed Since Price Change*** The longer the time that has elapsed since the price of a good changed, the more elastic is the demand for the good. For example, when the price of gasoline increased steeply during the 1970s and 1980s, the quantity of gasoline demanded didn't change much because many people owned gas-guzzling automobiles—the demand for gasoline was inelastic. But eventually, fuel-efficient cars replaced gas guzzlers and the quantity of gasoline demanded decreased—the demand for gasoline became more elastic.

### Proportion of Income Spent

A price rise, like a decrease in income, means that people cannot afford to buy the same quantities of goods and services as before. The greater the proportion of income spent on a good, the greater is the impact of a rise in its price on the quantity of that good that people can afford to buy and the more elastic is the demand for the good. For example, toothpaste takes a tiny proportion of your budget and housing takes a large proportion. If the price of toothpaste doubles, you buy almost as much toothpaste as before. Your demand for toothpaste is inelastic. If your apartment rent doubles, you shriek and look for more roommates. Your demand for housing is more elastic than is your demand for toothpaste.

## Computing the Price Elasticity of Demand

To determine whether the demand for a good is elastic, unit elastic, or inelastic, we compute a numerical value for the price elasticity of demand by using the following formula:

$$\text{Price elasticity of demand} = \frac{\text{Percentage change in quantity demanded}}{\text{Percentage change in price}}.$$

- If the price elasticity of demand is greater than 1, demand is elastic.
- If the price elasticity of demand equals 1, demand is unit elastic.
- If the price elasticity of demand is less than 1, demand is inelastic.

Figure 5.2 illustrates and summarizes the calculation for the Starbucks latte example. Initially, the price is \$3 a cup and 15 cups an hour are demanded—the initial point in the figure. Then the price rises to \$5 a cup and the quantity demanded decreases to 5 cups an hour—the new point in the figure. The price rises by \$2 a cup and the average (midpoint) price is \$4 a cup, so the percentage change in price is 50. The quantity demanded decreases by 10 cups an hour and the average (midpoint) quantity is 10 cups an hour, so the percentage change in quantity demanded is 100.

**FIGURE 5.2**

Price Elasticity of Demand Calculation

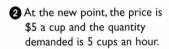

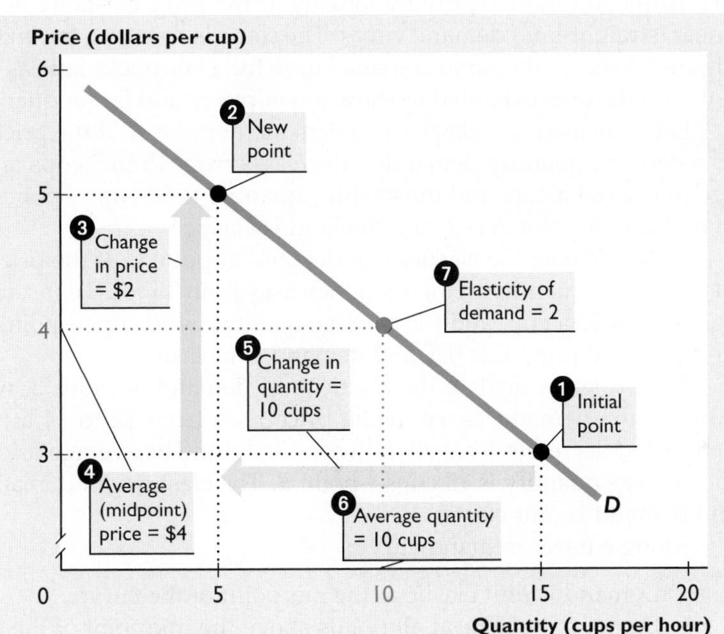


1. At the initial point, the price is $3 a cup and the quantity demanded is 15 cups an hour.

2. At the new point, the price is $5 a cup and the quantity demanded is 5 cups an hour.

3. The change in price is $2 and 4. the average price is $4, so the percentage change in price equals ($2 ÷ $4) × 100, which is 50 percent.

5. The change in the quantity demanded is 10 cups and 6. the average quantity demanded is 10 cups, so the percentage change in quantity demanded equals (10 cups ÷ 10 cups) × 100, which is 100 percent.

7. The price elasticity of demand equals 100 percent ÷ 50 percent, which is 2.

Using the above formula, you can see that the price elasticity of demand for a Starbucks latte is

$$\text{Price elasticity of demand} = \frac{100 \text{ percent}}{50 \text{ percent}} = 2.$$

The price elasticity of demand is 2 at the midpoint between the initial price and the new price on the demand curve. Over this price range, the demand for a Starbucks latte is elastic.

## Interpreting the Price Elasticity of Demand Number

The number we've just calculated for a Starbucks latte is only an example. We don't have real data on the price and quantity. But suppose we did have real data and we discovered that the price elasticity of demand for a Starbucks latte is 2. What does this number tell us?

It tells us three main things:

1. The demand for Starbucks latte is elastic. Being elastic, the good has plenty of convenient substitutes (such as other brands of latte) and takes only a small proportion of buyers' incomes.
2. Starbucks must be careful not to charge too high a price for its latte. Pushing the price up brings in more revenue per cup but wipes out a lot of potential business.
3. The flip side of the second point: Even a slightly lower price could create a lot of potential business and end up bringing in more revenue.

## Elasticity Along a Linear Demand Curve

Slope measures responsiveness. But elasticity is *not* the same as *slope*. You can see the distinction most clearly by looking at the price elasticity of demand along a linear (straight-line) demand curve. The slope is constant, but the elasticity varies. Figure 5.3 shows the same demand curve for a Starbucks latte as that in Figure 5.2 but with the axes extended to show lower prices and larger quantities demanded.

Let's calculate the elasticity of demand at point *A*. If the price rises from $3 to $5 a cup, the quantity demanded decreases from 15 to 5 cups an hour. The average price is $4 a cup, and the average quantity is 10 cups—point *A*. The elasticity of demand at point *A* is 2, and demand is elastic.

Let's calculate the elasticity of demand at point C. If the price falls from $3 to $1 a cup, the quantity demanded increases from 15 to 25 cups an hour. The average price is $2 a cup, and the average quantity is 20 cups—point C. The elasticity of demand at point C is 0.5, and demand is inelastic.

Finally, let's calculate the elasticity of demand at point *B*, which is the midpoint of the demand curve. If the price rises from $2 to $4 a cup, the quantity demanded decreases from 20 to 10 cups an hour. The average price is $3 a cup, and the average quantity is 15 cups—point *B*. The elasticity of demand at point *B* is 1, and demand is unit elastic.

Along a linear demand curve,

- Demand is unit elastic at the midpoint of the curve.
- Demand is elastic at all points above the midpoint of the curve.
- Demand is inelastic at all points below the midpoint of the curve.

**FIGURE 5.3**

Elasticity Along a Linear Demand Curve

myeconlab Animation

On a linear demand curve, the slope is constant but the elasticity decreases as the price falls and the quantity demanded increases.

1 At point *A*, demand is elastic.

2 At point *B*, which is the midpoint of the demand curve, demand is unit elastic.

3 At point *C*, demand is inelastic.

Demand is elastic at all points above the midpoint of the demand curve and inelastic at all points below the midpoint of the demand curve.

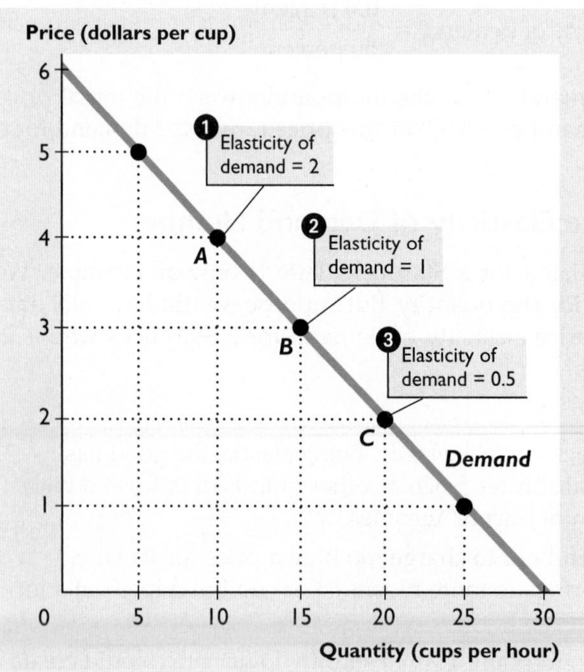

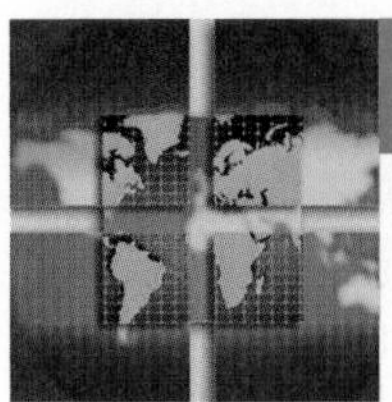

# EYE on the GLOBAL ECONOMY

## Price Elasticities of Demand

A rich American student is casual about her food. It costs only a few dollars a day, and she's going to have her burger, even at double the price. But a poor Tanzanian boy takes his food with deadly seriousness. He has a tough time getting, preparing, and even defending his food. A rise in the price of food means that he must cut back and eat even less.

The figure shows the percentage of income spent on food and the price elasticity of demand for food in ten countries. The larger the proportion of income spent on food, the larger is the price elasticity of demand for food.

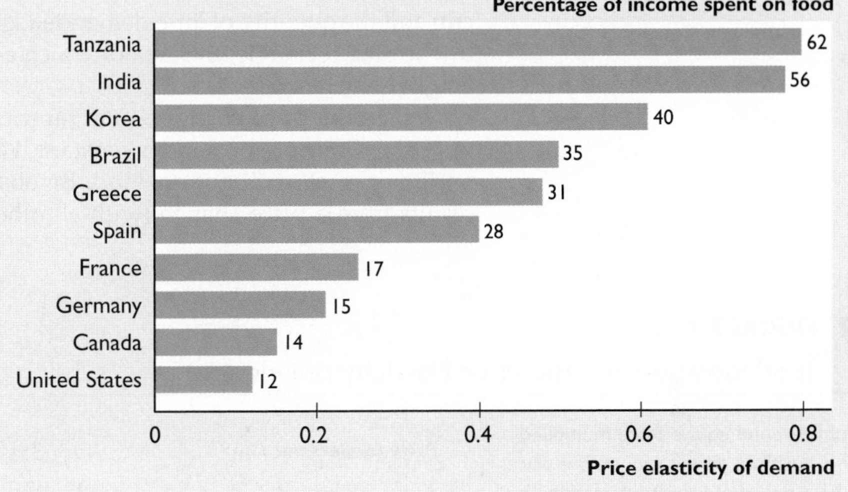


As the low-income countries become richer, the proportion of income they spend on food will decrease and their demand for food will become more inelastic. Consequently, the world's demand for food will become more inelastic.

Harvests fluctuate and bring fluctuations in the price of food. And as the world demand for food becomes more and more inelastic, the fluctuations in the prices of food items will become larger.

The table shows a few real-world price elasticities of demand. The numbers in the table range from 1.52 for metals to 0.12 for food. Metals have good substitutes, such as plastics, while food has virtually no substitutes. As we move down the list of items, they have fewer good substitutes and are more likely to be regarded as necessities.

**Some Price Elasticities of Demand**

| Good or Service | Elasticity |
|---|---|
| **Elastic Demand** | |
| Metals | 1.52 |
| Electrical engineering products | 1.39 |
| Mechanical engineering products | 1.30 |
| Furniture | 1.26 |
| Motor vehicles | 1.14 |
| Instrument engineering products | 1.10 |
| Professional services | 1.09 |
| Transportation services | 1.03 |
| **Inelastic Demand** | |
| Gas, electricity, and water | 0.92 |
| Oil | 0.91 |
| Chemicals | 0.89 |
| Beverages (all types) | 0.78 |
| Clothing | 0.64 |
| Tobacco | 0.61 |
| Banking and insurance services | 0.56 |
| Housing services | 0.55 |
| Agricultural and fish products | 0.42 |
| Books, magazines, and newspapers | 0.34 |
| Food | 0.12 |

SOURCES OF DATA: See page C1.

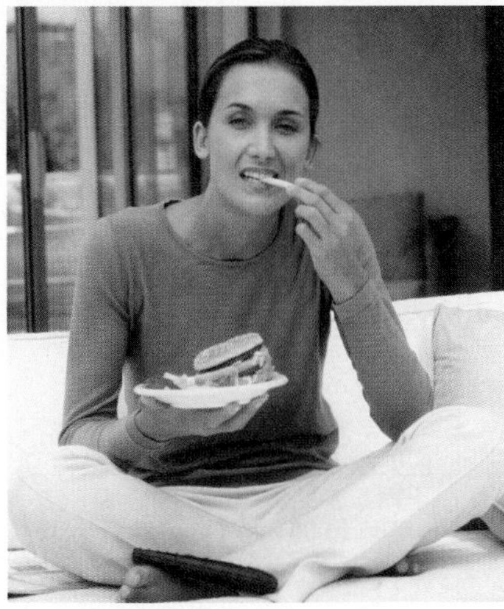

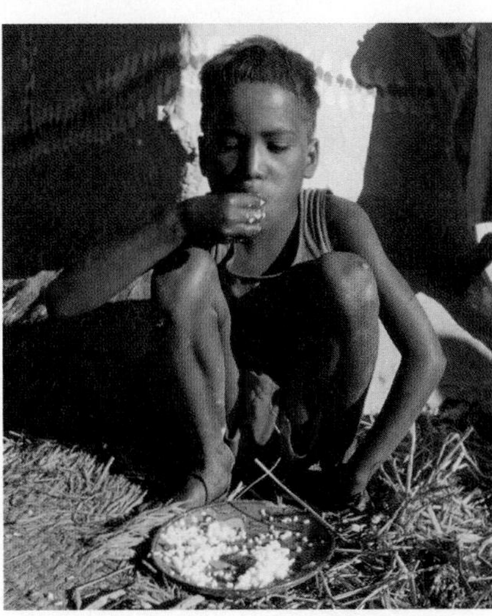

## Total Revenue and the Price Elasticity of Demand

**Total revenue**
The amount spent on a good and received by its seller and equals the price of the good multiplied by the quantity sold.

**Total revenue** is the amount spent on a good and received by its sellers and equals the price of the good multiplied by the quantity of the good sold. For example, suppose that the price of a Starbucks latte is $3 and that 15 cups an hour are sold. Then total revenue is $3 a cup multiplied by 15 cups an hour, which equals $45 an hour.

We can use the demand curve for Starbucks latte to illustrate total revenue. Figure 5.4(a) shows the total revenue from the sale of latte when the price is $3 a cup and the quantity of latte demanded is 15 cups an hour. Total revenue is shown by the blue rectangle, the area of which equals $3, its height, multiplied by 15, its length, which equals $45.

When the price changes, total revenue can change in the same direction, the opposite direction, or remain constant. Which of these outcomes occurs depends on the price elasticity of demand. By observing the change in total revenue that results from a price change (with all other influences on the quantity remaining

**FIGURE 5.4**

Total Revenue and the Price Elasticity of Demand

myeconlab Animation

Total revenue equals price multiplied by quantity. In part (a), when the price is $3 a cup, the quantity demanded is 15 cups an hour and total revenue equals $45 an hour. When the price rises to $5 a cup, the quantity demanded decreases to 5 cups an hour and total revenue decreases to $25 an hour. Demand is elastic.

In part (b), when the price is $50 a book, the quantity demanded is 5 million books a year and total revenue equals $250 million a year. When the price rises to $75 a book, the quantity demanded decreases to 4 million books a year and total revenue increases to $300 million a year. Demand is inelastic.

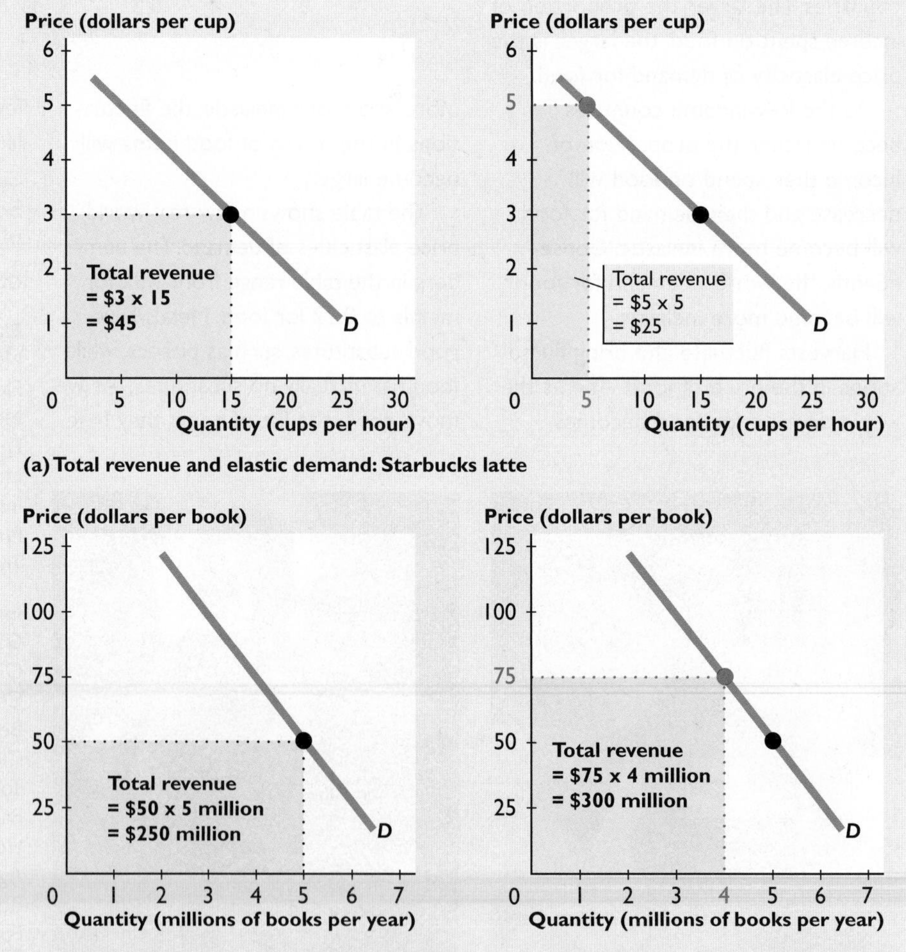


(a) Total revenue and elastic demand: Starbucks latte

(b) Total revenue and inelastic demand: textbooks

unchanged), we can estimate the price elasticity of demand. This method of estimating the price elasticity of demand is called the **total revenue test**.

**Total revenue test**
A method of estimating the price elasticity of demand by observing the change in total revenue that results from a price change (with all other influences on the quantity sold remaining unchanged).

If demand is elastic, a given percentage rise in price brings a larger percentage decrease in the quantity demanded, so total revenue—price multiplied by quantity—decreases. Figure 5.4(a) shows this outcome. When the price of a latte is \$3, the quantity demanded is 15 cups an hour and total revenue is \$45 (\$3 × 15). If the price of a latte rises to \$5, the quantity demanded decreases to 5 cups an hour and total revenue *decreases* to \$25 (\$5 × 5).

If demand is inelastic, a given percentage rise in price brings a smaller percentage decrease in the quantity demanded, so total revenue increases. Figure 5.4(b) shows this outcome. When the price of a textbook is \$50, the quantity demanded is 5 million textbooks a year and total revenue is \$250 million (\$50 × 5 million). If the price of a textbook rises to \$75, the quantity demanded decreases to 4 million textbooks a year and total revenue *increases* to \$300 million (\$75 × 4 million).

The relationship between the price elasticity of demand and total revenue is

- If price and total revenue change in opposite directions, demand is elastic.
- If a price change leaves total revenue unchanged, demand is unit elastic.
- If price and total revenue change in the same direction, demand is inelastic.

## EYE on the PRICE OF GAS

### What Do You Do When the Price of Gasoline Rises?

If you are like most people, you complain when the price of gasoline rises, but you don't cut back very much on your gas purchases.

University of London economists Phil Goodwin, Joyce Dargay, and Mark Hanly studied the effects of a hike in the price of gasoline on the quantity of gasoline demanded and on the volume of road traffic.

By using data for the United States and a large number of other countries, they estimated that a 10 percent rise in the price of gasoline decreases the quantity of gasoline used by 2.5 percent within one year and by 6 percent after five years.

#### Elasticity of Demand

We can translate these numbers into price elasticities of demand for gasoline.

The short-run (up to one year) price elasticity of demand is 2.5 percent divided by 10 percent, which equals 0.25. The long-run (after five years) price elasticity of demand is 6 percent divided by 10 percent, which equals 0.6. Because these price elasticities are less than one, the demand for gasoline is inelastic.

When the price of gasoline rises, the quantity of gasoline demanded decreases but the amount spent on gasoline increases.

The effect of a rise in the price of gasoline on the volume of traffic is smaller than on the quantity of gasoline used.

A 10-percent rise in the price of gasoline decreases the volume of traffic by only 1 percent within one year and by 3 percent after five years.

How can the volume of traffic fall by less than the quantity of gasoline used? The answer is by switching to smaller, more fuel-efficient vehicles.

The price elasticity of demand for gasoline is low—the demand for gasoline is inelastic—because gasoline has poor substitutes, but it does have a substitute—a smaller vehicle.

## Applications of the Price Elasticity of Demand

Does a frost in Florida bring a massive or a modest rise in the price of oranges? And does a smaller orange crop mean bad news or good news for orange growers? Knowledge of the price elasticity of demand for oranges enables us to answer these questions.

### Orange Prices and Total Revenue

*A Florida frost is bad news for buyers of orange juice and for growers who lose their crops, but good news for growers who escape the frost.*

Economists have estimated the price elasticity of demand for agricultural products to be about 0.4—an inelastic demand. If this number applies to the demand for oranges, then

$$\text{Price elasticity of demand} = 0.4 = \frac{\text{Percentage change in quantity demanded}}{\text{Percentage change in price}}.$$

If supply changes and demand doesn't, the percentage change in the quantity demanded equals the percentage change in the equilibrium quantity. So if a frost in Florida decreases the orange harvest and decreases the equilibrium quantity of oranges by 1 percent, the price of oranges will rise by 2.5 percent. The percentage change in the quantity demanded (1 percent) divided by the percentage change in price (2.5 percent) equals the price elasticity of demand (0.4).

So the answer to the first question is that when the frost strikes, the price of oranges will rise by a larger percentage than the percentage decrease in the quantity of oranges. But what happens to the total revenue of the orange growers?

The answer is again provided by knowledge of the price elasticity of demand. Because the price rises by a larger percentage than the percentage decrease in quantity, total revenue increases. A frost is bad news for consumers and those growers who lose their crops, but good news for growers who escape the frost.

### Addiction and Elasticity

*Cracking down on imports of illegal drugs limits supply, which leads to a large price increase. But it also increases the expenditure on drugs by addicts and increases the amount of crime that finances addiction.*

We can gain important insights that might help to design potentially effective policies for dealing with addiction to drugs, whether legal (such as tobacco and alcohol) or illegal (such as crack cocaine or heroin). Nonusers' demand for addictive substances is elastic. A moderately higher price leads to a substantially smaller number of people trying a drug and so exposing themselves to the possibility of becoming addicted to it. But the existing users' demand for addictive substances is inelastic. Even a substantial price rise brings only a modest decrease in the quantity demanded.

These facts about the price elasticity of demand mean that high taxes on cigarettes and alcohol limit the number of young people who become habitual users of these products, but high taxes have only a modest effect on the quantities consumed by established users.

Similarly, effective policing of imports of an illegal drug that limits its supply leads to a large price rise and a substantial decrease in the number of new users but only a small decrease in the quantity consumed by addicts. Expenditure on the drug by addicts increases. Further, because many drug addicts finance their purchases with crime, the amount of theft and burglary increases.

Because the price elasticity of demand for drugs is low for addicts, any successful policy to decrease drug use will be one that focuses on the demand for drugs and attempts to change preferences through rehabilitation programs.

## CHECKPOINT 5.1

myeconlab

Work these problems in Study Plan 5.1 to get instant feedback.

**Define, explain the factors that influence, and calculate the price elasticity of demand.**

### Practice Problems

When the price of a good increased by 10 percent, the quantity demanded of it decreased by 2 percent. Use this information to work Problems **1** to **3**.

1. Is the demand for this good elastic, unit elastic, or inelastic?
2. Are substitutes for this good easy to find or does it have poor substitutes? Is this good more likely to be a necessity or a luxury? Why? Is the good more likely to be narrowly or broadly defined? Why?
3. Calculate the price elasticity of demand for this good; explain how the total revenue from the sale of the good has changed; and explain which of the following goods this good is most likely to be: orange juice, bread, toothpaste, theater tickets, clothing, blue jeans, or Super Bowl tickets.
4. **Music giant chops price to combat downloads**
   In 2003, when music downloading first took off, Universal Music slashed the price of a CD from an average of \$21 to an average of \$15. The company said that it expected the price cut to boost the quantity of CDs sold by 30 percent, other things remaining the same.
   Source: *Globe and Mail*, September 4, 2003

   What was Universal Music's estimate of the price elasticity of demand for CDs and is the demand estimated to be elastic or inelastic?

### Guided Solutions to Practice Problems

1. The demand for a good is *inelastic* if the percentage decrease in the quantity demanded is less than the percentage increase in its price. In this example, a 10 percent price rise brings a 2 percent decrease in the quantity demanded, so demand is inelastic.
2. Because the good has an inelastic demand, it most likely has poor substitutes, is a necessity rather than a luxury, and is broadly defined.
3. Price elasticity of demand = Percentage change in the quantity demanded ÷ Percentage change in price. In this example, the elasticity of demand is 2 percent divided by 10 percent, or 0.2. An elasticity less than 1 means that demand is inelastic. When demand is inelastic, a price rise increases total revenue. This good is most likely a necessity (bread), or has poor substitutes (toothpaste), or is broadly defined (clothing).
4. Price elasticity of demand = Percentage change in the quantity demanded ÷ Percentage change in price.
   The percentage change in the price equals $[(\$21 - \$15)/(\$18)] \times 100$, which is 33.3 percent. The percentage change in the quantity is 30 percent. So Universal Music's estimate of the price elasticity of demand for CDs is 30 percent ÷ 33.3 percent, or 0.9. Because the percentage change in the quantity is less than the percentage change in the price, demand is estimated to be inelastic, which is what an elasticity of 0.9 means.

## 5.2 THE PRICE ELASTICITY OF SUPPLY

You know that when demand increases, the equilibrium price rises and the equilibrium quantity increases. But does the price rise by a large amount and the quantity increase by a little? Or does the price barely rise and the quantity increase by a large amount? To answer this question, we need to know the price elasticity of supply.

**Price elasticity of supply**
A measure of the responsiveness of the quantity supplied of a good to a change in its price when all other influences on sellers' plans remain the same.

The **price elasticity of supply** is a measure of the responsiveness of the quantity supplied of a good to a change in its price when all other influences on sellers' plans remain the same. We determine the price elasticity of supply by comparing the percentage change in the quantity supplied with the percentage change in price.

### Elastic and Inelastic Supply

The supply of a good might be

- Elastic
- Unit elastic
- Inelastic

**Perfectly elastic supply**
When the quantity supplied changes by a very large percentage in response to an almost zero percentage change in price.

**Elastic supply**
When the percentage change in the quantity supplied exceeds the percentage change in price.

**Unit elastic supply**
When the percentage change in the quantity supplied equals the percentage change in price.

**Inelastic supply**
When the percentage change in the quantity supplied is less than the percentage change in price.

**Perfectly inelastic supply**
When the percentage change in the quantity supplied is zero for any percentage change in the price.

Figure 5.5 illustrates the range of supply elasticities. Figure 5.5(a) shows the extreme case of a **perfectly elastic supply**—an almost zero percentage change in price brings a very large percentage change in the quantity supplied. Figure 5.5(b) shows an **elastic supply**—the percentage change in the quantity supplied exceeds the percentage change in price. Figure 5.5(c) shows a **unit elastic supply**—the percentage change in the quantity supplied equals the percentage change in price. Figure 5.5(d) shows an **inelastic supply**—the percentage change in the quantity supplied is less than the percentage change in price. And Figure 5.5(e) shows the extreme case of a **perfectly inelastic supply**—the percentage change in the quantity supplied is zero when the price changes.

### Influences on the Price Elasticity of Supply

What makes the supply of some things elastic and the supply of others inelastic? The two main influences on the price elasticity of supply are

- Production possibilities
- Storage possibilities

#### Production Possibilities

Some goods can be produced at a constant (or very gently rising) opportunity cost. These goods have an elastic supply. The silicon in your computer chips is an example of such a good. Silicon is extracted from sand at a tiny and almost constant opportunity cost, so the supply of silicon is perfectly elastic.

Some goods can be produced in only a fixed quantity. These goods have a perfectly inelastic supply. A beachfront home in Malibu can be built only on a unique beachfront lot, so the supply of these homes is perfectly inelastic.

Hotel rooms in New York City can't easily be used as office accommodation and office space cannot easily be converted into hotel rooms, so the supply of hotel rooms in New York City is inelastic. Paper and printing presses can be used to produce textbooks or magazines, and the supplies of these goods are elastic.

**FIGURE 5.5**
The Range of Price Elasticities of Supply

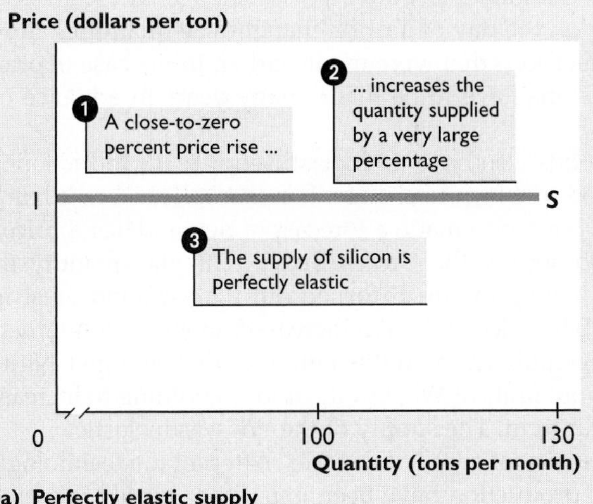


(a) Perfectly elastic supply

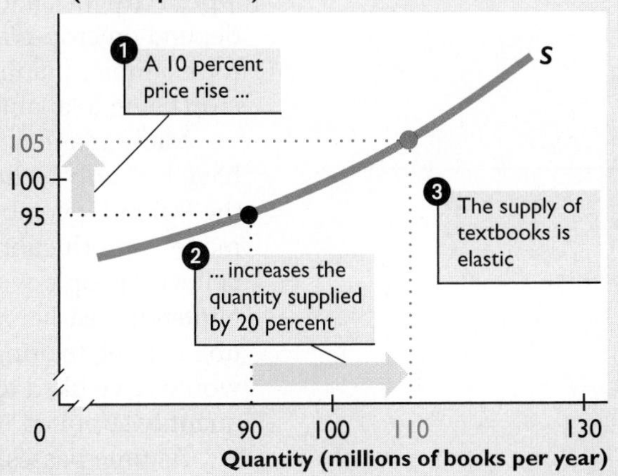


(b) Elastic supply

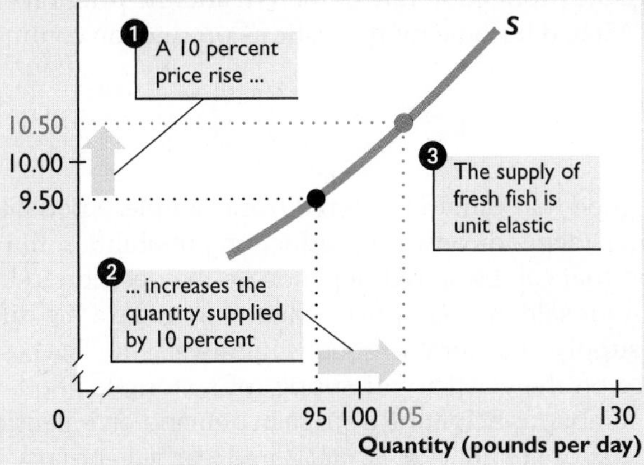


(c) Unit elastic supply

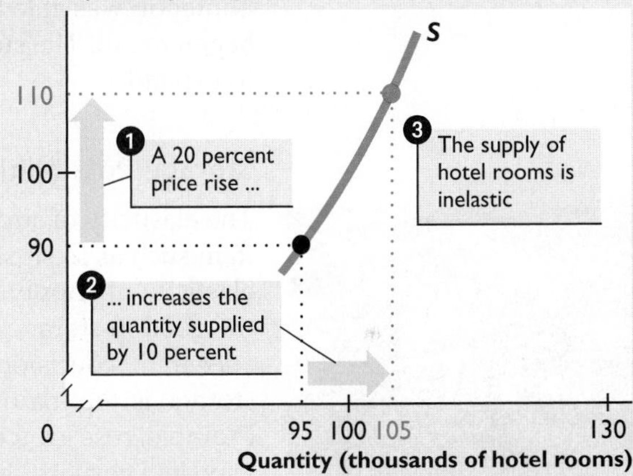


(d) Inelastic supply

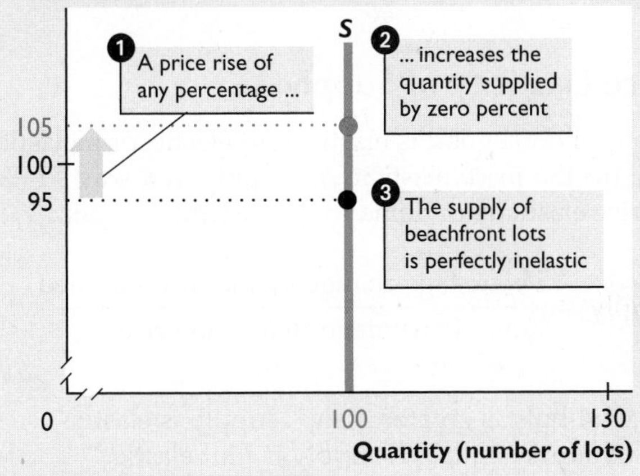


(e) Perfectly inelastic supply

❶ A price rise brings ❷ an increase in the quantity supplied. The relationship between the percentage change in the quantity supplied and the percentage change in price determines ❸ the price elasticity of supply, which ranges from perfectly elastic (part a) to perfectly inelastic (part e).

***Time Elapsed Since Price Change*** As time passes after a price change, it becomes easier to change production plans and supply becomes more elastic. For some items—fruits and vegetables are examples—it is difficult or perhaps impossible to change the quantity supplied immediately after a price change. These goods have a perfectly inelastic supply on the day of a price change. The quantities supplied depend on crop-planting decisions that were made earlier. In the case of oranges, for example, planting decisions have to be made many years in advance of the crop being available.

Many manufactured goods also have an inelastic supply if production plans have had only a short period in which to change. For example, before it launched the Wii in November 2006, Nintendo made a forecast of demand, set a price, and made a production plan to supply the United States with the quantity that it believed people would be willing to buy. It turned out that demand outstripped Nintendo's earlier forecast. The price of the Wii increased on eBay, an Internet auction market, to bring market equilibrium. At the high price that emerged, Nintendo would have liked to ship more units of Wii, but it could do nothing to increase the quantity supplied in the near term. The supply of the Wii was inelastic.

As time passes, the elasticity of supply increases. After all the technologically possible ways of adjusting production have been exploited, supply is extremely elastic—perhaps perfectly elastic—for most manufactured items. In 2007, Nintendo was able to step up the production rate of the Wii and the price on eBay began to fall. The supply of Wii had become more elastic as production continued to expand.

### Storage Possibilities

*Fresh strawberries must be sold before they deteriorate, so their supply is inelastic.*

The elasticity of supply of a good that cannot be stored (for example, a perishable item such as fresh strawberries) depends only on production possibilities. But the elasticity of supply of a good that can be stored depends on the decision to keep the good in storage or offer it for sale. A small price change can make a big difference to this decision, so the supply of a storable good is highly elastic. The cost of storage is the main influence on the elasticity of supply of a storable good. For example, rose growers in Colombia, anticipating a surge in demand on Valentine's Day in February, hold back supplies in late January and early February and increase their inventories of roses. They then release roses from inventory for Valentine's Day.

## Computing the Price Elasticity of Supply

To determine whether the supply of a good is elastic, unit elastic, or inelastic, we compute a numerical value for the price elasticity of supply in a way similar to that used to calculate the price elasticity of demand. We use the formula:

$$\text{Price elasticity of supply} = \frac{\text{Percentage change in quantity supplied}}{\text{Percentage change in price}}.$$

- If the price elasticity of supply is greater than 1, supply is elastic.
- If the price elasticity of supply equals 1, supply is unit elastic.
- If the price elasticity of supply is less than 1, supply is inelastic.

Let's calculate the price elasticity of supply of roses. Suppose that in a normal month, the price of roses is $40 a bouquet and 6 million bouquets are supplied, but in February, the price rises to $80 a bouquet and the quantity supplied increases to 24 million bouquets. Figure 5.6 illustrates the supply of roses and summarizes the calculation. The figure shows the initial point at $40 a bouquet and the new point at $80 a bouquet. The price increases by $40 a bouquet and the average, or midpoint, price is $60 a bouquet, so the percentage change in the price is 66.67 percent. The quantity supplied increases by 18 million bouquets and the average, or midpoint, quantity is 15 million bouquets, so the percentage change in the quantity supplied is 120 percent.

Using the above formula, you can see that the price elasticity of supply of roses is

$$\text{Price elasticity of supply} = \frac{120 \text{ percent}}{66.67 \text{ percent}} = 1.8.$$

The price elasticity of supply is 1.8 at the midpoint between the initial point and the new point on the supply curve. In this example, over this price range, the supply of roses is elastic.

**FIGURE 5.6**

Price Elasticity of Supply Calculation

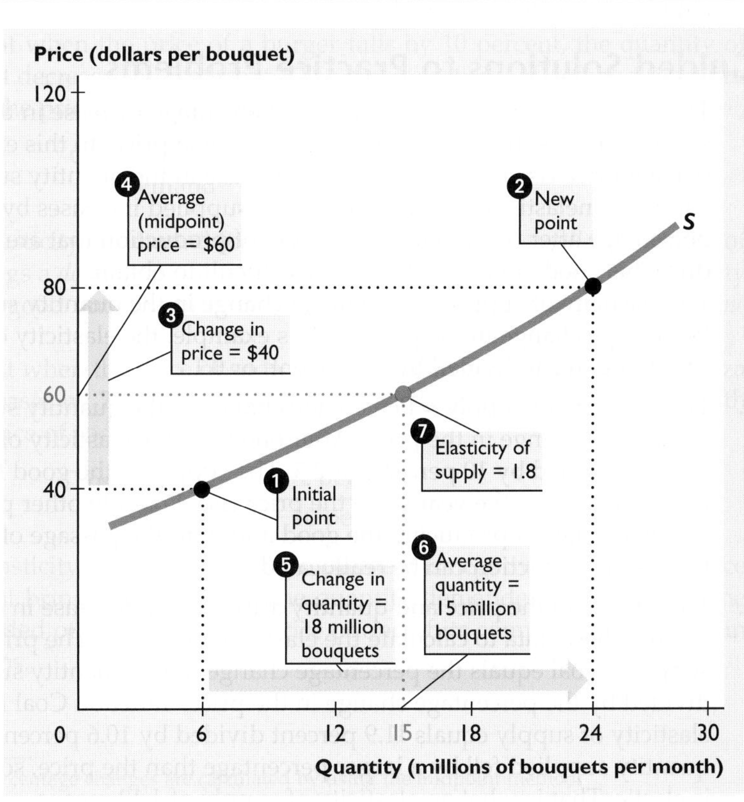


1. At the initial point, the price is $40 a bouquet and the quantity supplied is 6 million bouquets a month.
2. At the new point, the price is $80 a bouquet and the quantity supplied is 24 million bouquets a month.
3. The change in price is $40, and
4. the average price is $60, so the percentage change in price equals ($40 ÷ $60) × 100, which is 66.67 percent.
5. The change in the quantity supplied is 18 million bouquets and
6. the average quantity supplied is 15 million bouquets, so the percentage change in quantity supplied is (18 million ÷ 15 million) × 100, which is 120 percent.
7. The price elasticity of supply equals 120 percent ÷ 66.6 percent, which is 1.8.

Use the following information to work Problems 9 to 11.

**As gas costs soar, buyers are flocking to small cars**

Faced with high gas prices, Americans are substituting smaller cars for SUVs. In April 2008, Toyota Yaris sales increased 46 percent and Ford Focus sales increased 32 percent from a year earlier. Sales of SUVs decreased by more than 25 percent in 2008 and Chevrolet Tahoe sales fell 35 percent. Full-size pickup sales decreased more than 15 percent in 2008 and Ford F-Series pickup sales decreased by 27 percent in April 2008. The effect of a downsized vehicle fleet on fuel consumption is unknown. In California, gasoline bought decreased by 4 percent in January 2008 from a year earlier.

Source: *The New York Times*, May 2, 2009

In California the price of gasoline in January 2008 was about 30 percent higher from a year earlier.

9. Calculate the price elasticity of demand for gasoline in California.
10. Calculate the cross elasticity of demand for Toyota Yaris with respect to the price of gasoline and the cross elasticity of demand for Ford Focus with respect to the price of gasoline.
11. Calculate the cross elasticity of demand for Chevrolet Tahoe with respect to the price of gasoline and the cross elasticity of demand for a full-size pickup with respect to the price of gasoline.
12. "In a market in which demand is price inelastic, producers can gouge consumers and the government must set high standards of conduct for producers to ensure that consumers gets a fair deal." Do you agree or disagree with each part of this statement? Explain how you might go about testing the parts of the statement that are positive and lay bare the normative parts.
13. **Oil prices rise ahead of OPEC meeting**

    The Organization of the Petroleum Exporting Countries (OPEC) produces about 40 percent of the world's output of crude oil. With the global demand for oil falling, OPEC has cut production in an attempt to stop the price sliding further from its high of $147 a barrel. OPEC knows that to raise the world price of oil it has to cut the total production of its member countries.

    Source: AFP, May 2, 2009

    OPEC also knows that the demand for crude oil is inelastic. Explain why it is not possible to conclude from these facts that OPEC's total revenue would increase if it were to cut its production.

Use the following information to work Problems 14 and 15.

**Almonds galore!**

The quantity of almonds harvested in 2008–2009 is expected to increase by 22 percent, while total receipts of growers are expected to increase by 17 percent.

Source: Almond Board of California

14. Is the price of almonds expected to rise or fall? Did a change in the supply of or demand for almonds bring about this expected change in the price?
15. If the price of almonds changed as a result of a change in the supply of almonds, is the demand for almonds elastic or inelastic? Explain your answer.

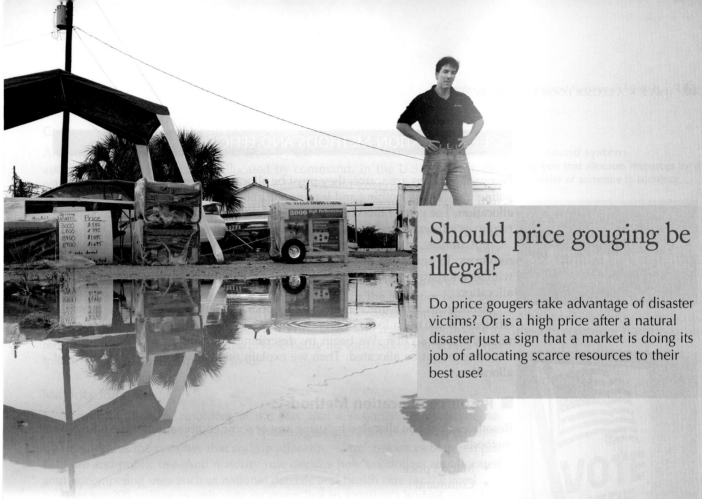

## Should price gouging be illegal?

Do price gougers take advantage of disaster victims? Or is a high price after a natural disaster just a sign that a market is doing its job of allocating scarce resources to their best use?

# Efficiency and Fairness of Markets

CHAPTER CHECKLIST

**When you have completed your study of this chapter, you will be able to**

1 Describe the alternative methods of allocating scarce resources and define and explain the features of an efficient allocation.

2 Distinguish between value and price and define consumer surplus.

3 Distinguish between cost and price and define producer surplus.

4 Evaluate the efficiency of the alternative methods of allocating scarce resources.

5 Explain the main ideas about fairness and evaluate the fairness of the alternative methods of allocating scarce resources.

## 6.2 VALUE, PRICE, AND CONSUMER SURPLUS

To investigate whether a market is efficient, we need to understand the connection between demand and marginal benefit and between supply and marginal cost.

### Demand and Marginal Benefit

In everyday life, when we talk about "getting value for money," we're distinguishing between *value* and *price.* Value is what we get, and price is what we pay. In economics, the everyday idea of value is *marginal benefit,* which we measure as the maximum price that people are willing to pay for another unit of the good or service. The demand curve tells us this price. In Figure 6.4(a), the demand curve shows the quantity demanded at a given price—when the price is $10 a pizza, the quantity demanded is 10,000 pizzas a day. In Figure 6.4(b), the demand curve shows the maximum price that people are willing to pay when there is a given quantity—when 10,000 pizzas a day are available, the most that people are willing to pay for the 10,000th pizza is $10. The marginal benefit from the 10,000th pizza is $10.

**A demand curve is a marginal benefit curve. The demand curve for pizza tells us the dollars' worth of other goods and services that people are willing to forgo to consume one more pizza.**

**FIGURE 6.4**

Demand, Willingness to Pay, and Marginal Benefit

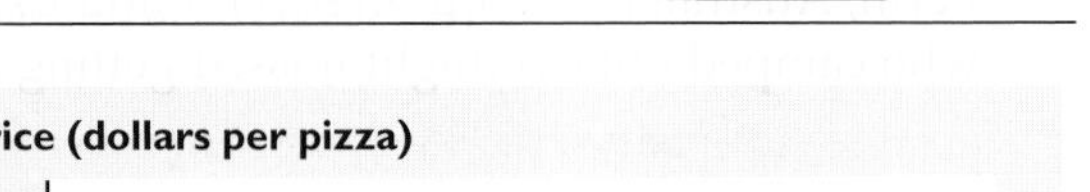


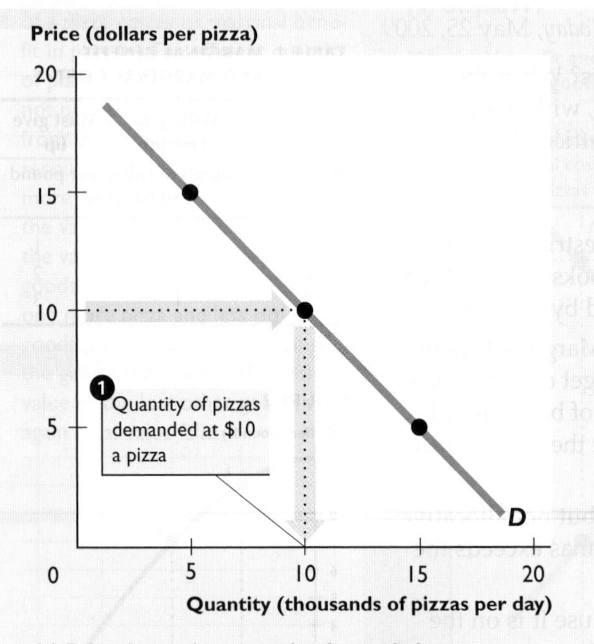


**(a) Price determines quantity demanded**

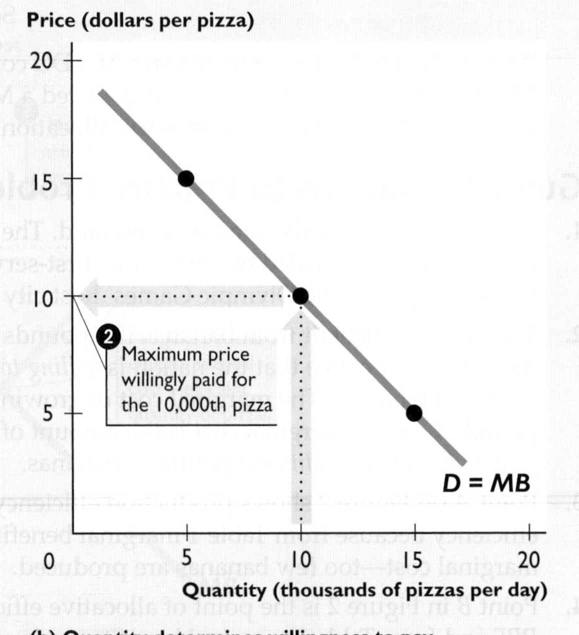


**(b) Quantity determines willingness to pay**

1 The demand curve for pizza, *D*, shows the quantity of pizza demanded at each price, other things remaining the same. At $10 a pizza, the quantity demanded is 10,000 pizzas a day.

2 The demand curve shows the maximum price willingly paid (marginal benefit) for a given quantity. If 10,000 pizzas are available, the maximum price willingly paid for the 10,000th pizza is $10. The demand curve is also the marginal benefit curve *MB*.

## Consumer Surplus

We don't always have to pay as much as we're willing to pay. When people buy something for less than it is worth to them, they receive a consumer surplus. **Consumer surplus** is the marginal benefit from a good minus the price paid for it, summed over the quantity consumed.

**Consumer surplus**
The marginal benefit from a good or service minus the price paid for it, summed over the quantity consumed.

Figure 6.5 illustrates consumer surplus. The demand curve for pizza tells us the quantity of pizza that people plan to buy at each price and the marginal benefit from pizza at each quantity. If the price of a pizza is $10, people buy 10,000 pizzas a day. Expenditure on pizza is $100,000, which is shown by the area of the blue rectangle.

To calculate consumer surplus, we must find the consumer surplus on each pizza and add these consumer surpluses together. For the 10,000th pizza, marginal benefit equals $10 and people pay $10, so the consumer surplus on this pizza is zero. For the 5,000th pizza (highlighted in the figure), marginal benefit is $15. So on this pizza, consumer surplus is $15 minus $10, which is $5. For the first pizza, marginal benefit is almost $20, so on this pizza, consumer surplus is almost $10.

Consumer surplus—the sum of the consumer surpluses on the 10,000 pizzas that people buy—is $50,000 a day, which is shown by the area of the green triangle. (The base of the triangle is 10,000 pizzas a day and its height is $10, so its area is $(10,000 \times \$10) \div 2 = \$50,000$.)

The total benefit is the amount paid, $100,000 (blue rectangle), plus consumer surplus, $50,000 (green triangle), and is $150,000. Consumer surplus is the total benefit minus the amount paid, or net benefit to consumers.

**FIGURE 6.5**
Demand and Consumer Surplus

myeconlab Animation

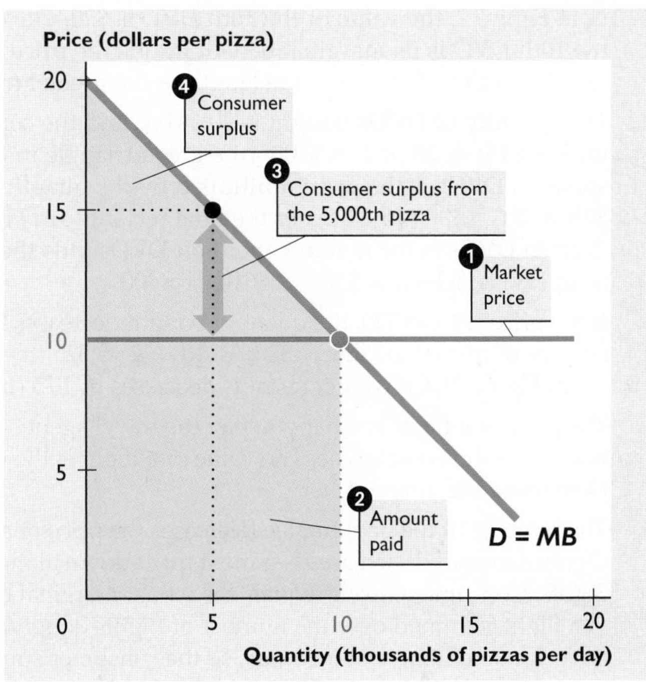


1. The market price of a pizza is $10.
2. At the market price, people buy 10,000 pizzas a day and spend $100,000 on pizza—the blue rectangle.
3. The demand curve tells us that people are willing to pay $15 for the 5,000th pizza, so consumer surplus on the 5,000th pizza is $5.
4. Consumer surplus from the 10,000 pizzas that people buy is $50,000—the area of the green triangle.

The total benefit from pizza is the $100,000 that people pay plus the $50,000 consumer surplus they receive, or $150,000.

Work these problems in Study Plan 6.2 to get instant feedback.

## CHECKPOINT 6.2

**Distinguish between value and price and define consumer surplus.**

### Practice Problems

Figure 1 shows the demand curve for DVDs and the market price of a DVD.

1. What is the willingness to pay for the 20th DVD? Calculate the value of the 10th DVD and the consumer surplus on the 10th DVD.
2. What is the quantity of DVDs bought? Calculate the consumer surplus, the amount spent on DVDs, and the total benefit from the DVDs bought.
3. If the price of a DVD rises to $20, what is the change in consumer surplus?

FIGURE 1

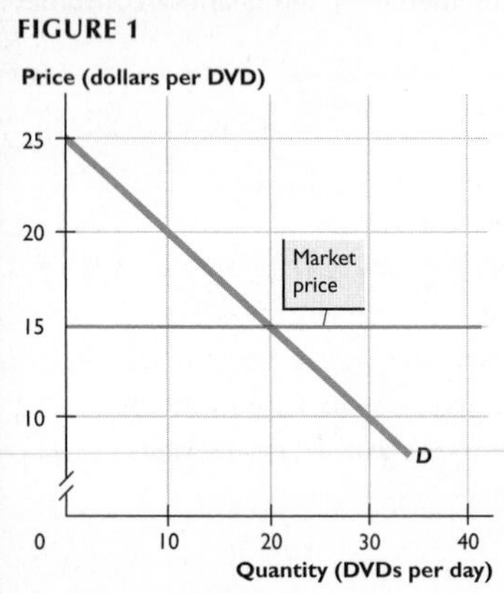


Use the following information to work Problems **4** and **5**.

**Online travel agencies drop ticket booking fees**

Online airline ticket agents have dropped the $7 booking fee and expedia.com and priceline.com have also dropped the $50 cancelation fee. Expedia.com reports that its ticket sales have increased by double-digits.

Source: *USA Today*, June 3, 2009

4. Distinguish between the price of a flight and the value of a flight before the fees were dropped.
5. With the removal of the booking fee, how have the price and the consumer surplus from flights changed?

### Guided Solutions to Practice Problems

1. The willingness to pay for the 20th DVD is the price on the demand curve at 20 DVDs, which is $15 (Figure 2). The value of the 10th DVD is its marginal benefit which also is the maximum price that someone is willing to pay for it. In Figure 2, the value of the 10th DVD is $20. The consumer surplus on the 10th DVD is its marginal benefit minus the price paid for the DVD, which is $20 − $15 = $5 (the length of the green arrow in Figure 2).
2. The quantity of DVDs bought is 20 a day, and the consumer surplus is ($25 − $15) × 20 ÷ 2 = $100 (the green triangle in Figure 2). The amount spent on DVDs is the price multiplied by the quantity bought, which is $15 × 20 = $300 (the area of the blue rectangle in Figure 2). The total benefit from DVDs is the amount spent on DVDs plus the consumer surplus from DVDs, which is $300 + $100 = $400.
3. If the price rises to $20, the quantity bought decreases to 10 a day. Consumer surplus decreases to ($25 − $20) × 10 ÷ 2 = $25 (the area of the green triangle in Figure 3). Consumer surplus decreases by $75 (from $100 to $25).
4. The price of a flight is what you pay the travel agent—the price of the airline ticket plus the booking fee. The value of a flight is the marginal benefit you get from using the airline ticket.
5. The removal of the booking fee decreases the price of a flight. The quantity of flights demanded increases —a movement down along the demand curve for flights. Consumer surplus equals the value (marginal benefit) minus the price of a flight, summed over the number of flights bought. Marginal benefit minus the price of a flight has increased, so the consumer surplus from any one flight has increased. With more flight bought, the consumer surplus has increased.

FIGURE 2

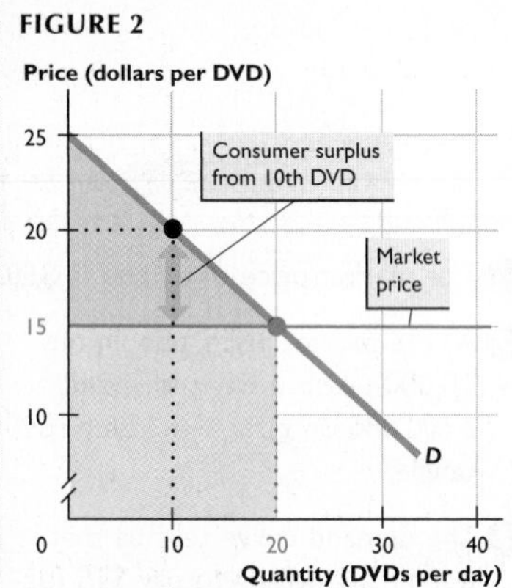


FIGURE 3

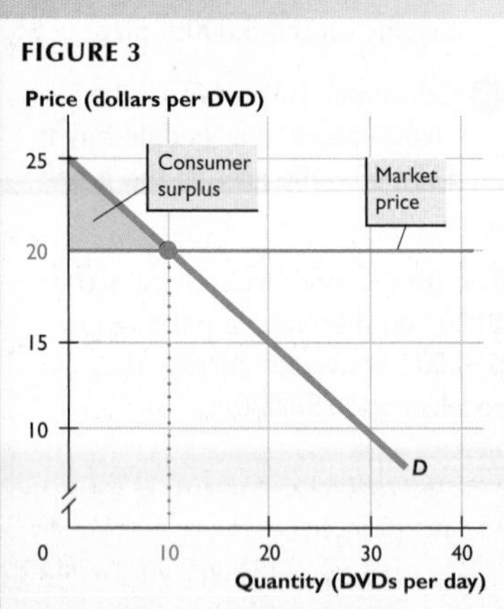

## 6.3 COST, PRICE, AND PRODUCER SURPLUS

You are now going to learn about cost, price, and producer surplus, which parallels what you've learned about value, price, and consumer surplus.

### Supply and Marginal Cost

Just as buyers distinguish between *value* and *price*, so sellers distinguish between *cost* and *price*. Cost is what a seller must give up to produce the good, and price is what a seller receives when the good is sold. The cost of producing one more unit of a good or service is its *marginal cost*. It is just worth producing one more unit of a good or service if the price for which it can be sold equals marginal cost. The supply curve tells us this price. In Figure 6.6(a), the supply curve shows the quantity supplied at a given price—when the price of a pizza is $10, the quantity supplied is 10,000 pizzas a day. In Figure 6.6(b), the supply curve shows the minimum price that producers must receive to supply a given quantity—to supply 10,000 pizzas a day, producers must be able to get at least $10 for the 10,000th pizza. The marginal cost of the 10,000th pizza is $10. So:

**A supply curve is a marginal cost curve. The supply curve of pizza tells us the dollars' worth of other goods and services that people must forgo if firms produce one more pizza.**

**FIGURE 6.6**

Supply, Minimum Supply Price, and Marginal Cost

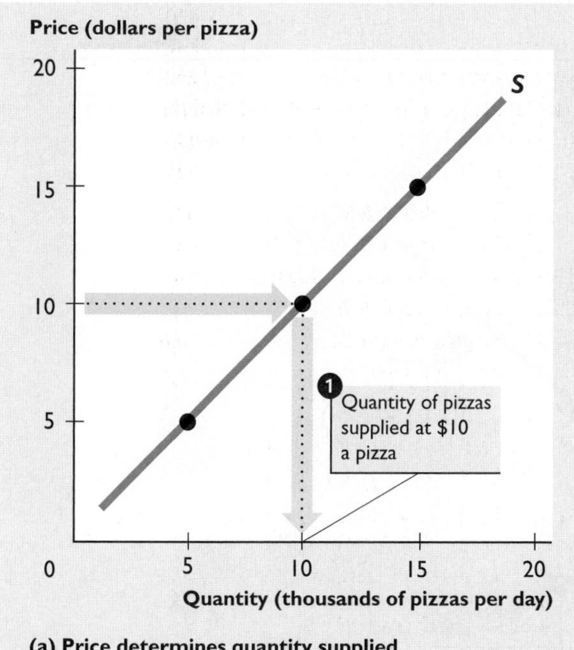


(a) Price determines quantity supplied

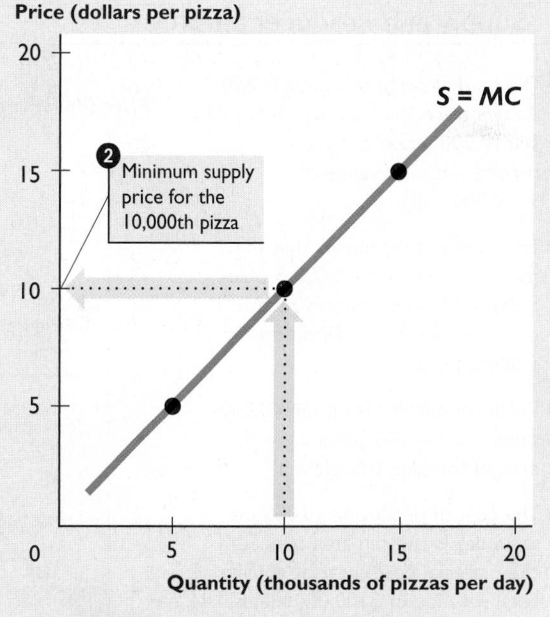


(b) Quantity determines minimum supply price

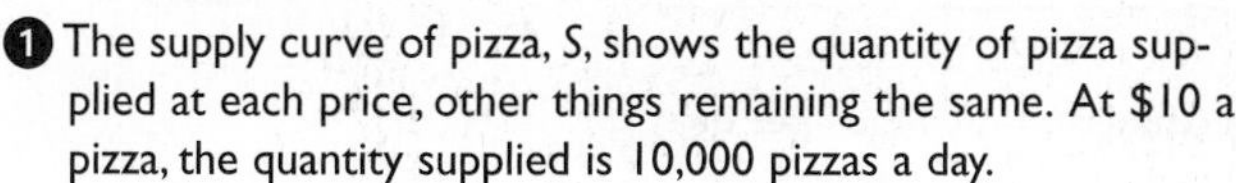

1 The supply curve of pizza, *S*, shows the quantity of pizza supplied at each price, other things remaining the same. At $10 a pizza, the quantity supplied is 10,000 pizzas a day.

2 The supply curve shows the minimum price that firms must be offered to supply a given quantity. The minimum supply price equals marginal cost, which for the 10,000th pizza is $10. The supply curve is also the marginal cost curve *MC*.

## Producer Surplus

**Producer surplus**
The price of a good minus the marginal cost of producing it, summed over the quantity produced.

When the price exceeds marginal cost, the firm obtains a producer surplus. **Producer surplus** is the price of a good minus the marginal cost of producing it, summed over the quantity produced.

Figure 6.7 illustrates the producer surplus for pizza producers. The supply curve of pizza tells us the quantity of pizza that producers plan to sell at each price. The supply curve also tells us the marginal cost of pizza at each quantity produced. If the price of a pizza is $10, producers plan to sell 10,000 pizzas a day. The total revenue from pizza is $100,000 per day.

To calculate producer surplus, we must find the producer surplus on each pizza and add these surpluses together. For the 10,000th pizza, marginal cost equals $10 and producers receive $10, so the producer surplus on this pizza is zero. For the 5,000th pizza (highlighted in the figure), marginal cost is $6. So on this pizza, producer surplus is $10 minus $6, which is $4. For the first pizza, marginal cost is $2, so on this pizza, producer surplus is $10 minus $2, which is $8.

Producer surplus—the sum of the producer surpluses on the 10,000 pizzas that firms produce—is $40,000 a day, which is shown by the area of the blue triangle. The base of the triangle is 10,000 pizzas a day and its height is $8, so its area is (10,000 × $8) ÷ 2 = $40,000.

The total cost of producing pizza is the amount received from selling it, $100,000, minus the producer surplus, $40,000 (blue triangle), and is $60,000 (the red area). Producer surplus is the total amount received minus the total cost, or net benefit to producers.

**FIGURE 6.7**

Supply and Producer Surplus

myeconlab Animation

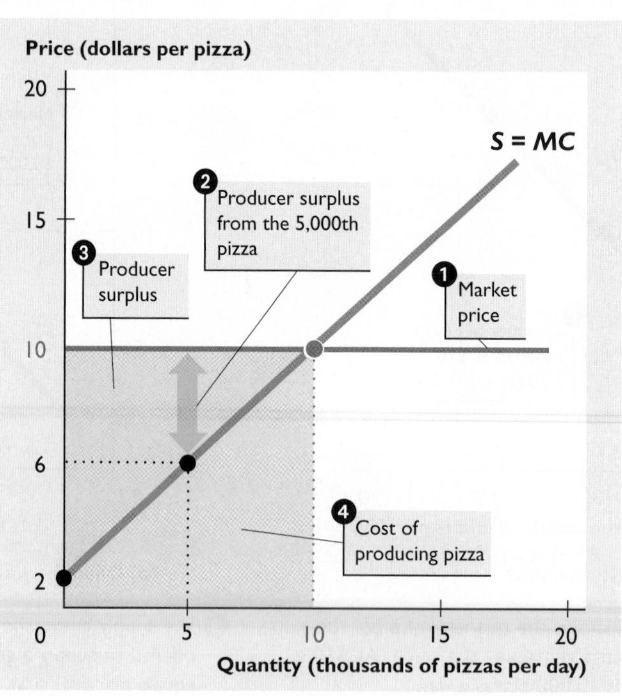


1. The market price of a pizza is $10. At this price, producers plan to sell 10,000 pizzas a day and receive a total revenue of $100,000 a day.
2. The supply curve shows that the marginal cost of the 5,000th pizza a day is $6, so producers receive a producer surplus of $4 on the 5,000th pizza.
3. Producer surplus from the 10,000 pizzas sold is $40,000 a day—the area of the blue triangle.
4. The cost of producing 10,000 pizzas a day is the red area beneath the marginal cost curve. It equals total revenue of $100,000 minus producer surplus of $40,000 and is $60,000 a day.

## CHECKPOINT 6.3

Work these problems in Study Plan 6.3 to get instant feedback.

**Distinguish between cost and price and define producer surplus.**

## Practice Problems

Figure 1 shows the supply curve of DVDs and the market price of a DVD.

1. What is the minimum supply price of the 20th DVD? Calculate the marginal cost of the 10th DVD and the producer surplus on the 10th DVD.
2. What is the quantity of DVDs sold? Calculate the producer surplus, the total revenue from the DVDs sold, and the cost of producing the DVDs sold.
3. If the price of a DVD falls to $10, what is the change in producer surplus?

Use the following information to work Problems **4** and **5**.

**Dealership has less than a week to sell all its cars**

Chrysler is shutting 800 dealerships and they must be closed by June 9, 2009. O'Bryhim, a dealer in Virginia, today sold a new Nitro at a discount of 40 percent—$17,510 instead of the regular price of $29,170. As June 9 approaches, O'Bryhim expects he will have to increase the discount and mark prices down further to sell all the cars on his lot.

Source: CNN.com, June 3, 2009

4. Distinguish between the price of a new car and the cost of the car.
5. If next week, O'Bryhim increases the discount to 50 percent, how will the producer surplus on a new Nitro change?

**FIGURE 1**

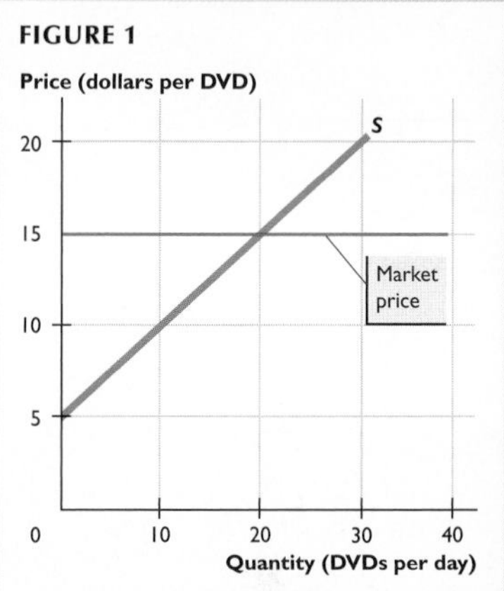


**FIGURE 2**

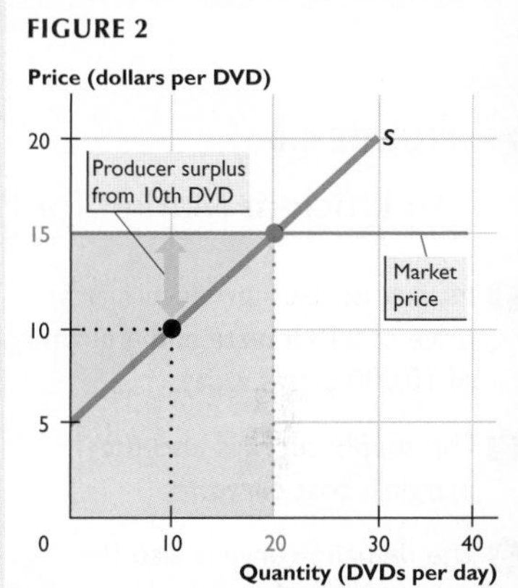


**FIGURE 3**

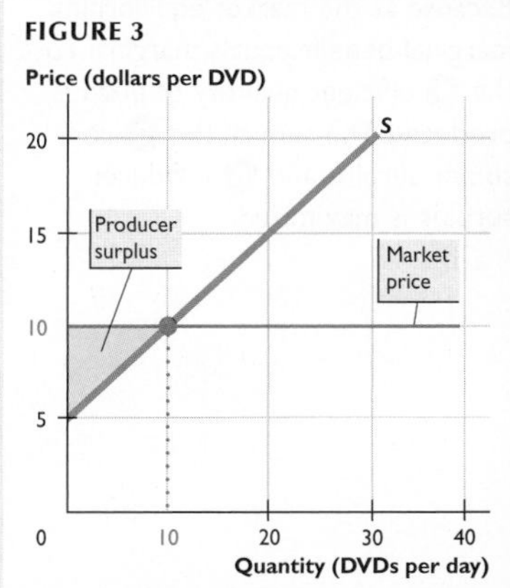


## Guided Solutions to Practice Problems

1. The minimum supply price of the 20th DVD is the marginal cost of the 20th DVD, which is $15 (Figure 2). The marginal cost of the 10th DVD is equal to the minimum supply price for the 10th DVD, which is $10. The producer surplus on the 10th DVD is its market price minus the marginal cost of producing it, which is $15 − $10 = $5 (the blue arrow in Figure 2).
2. The quantity sold is 20 a day. Producer surplus equals ($15 − $5) × 20 ÷ 2, which is $100 (the area of the blue triangle in Figure 2). The total revenue is price multiplied by quantity sold. Total revenue is $15 × 20 = $300. The cost of producing DVDs equals total revenue minus producer surplus, which is $300 − $100 = $200 (the red area in Figure 2).
3. The quantity sold decreases to 10 a day. The producer surplus decreases to ($10 − $5) × 10 ÷ 2 = $25 (the area of the blue triangle in Figure 3). The change in producer surplus is a decrease of $75 (from $100 down to $25).
4. The price of a new car is the amount received by the car dealership when it is sold—the regular price minus the discount. The dealer's cost of a new car (the marginal cost of a car) is what the dealer paid Chrysler (the manufacturer) for the car.
5. The producer surplus on a new Nitro is the price O'Bryhim receives for the Nitro when it is sold minus O'Bryhim's cost of the Nitro. As the discount increases, the price received falls and the producer surplus decreases.

## 6.4 ARE MARKETS EFFICIENT?

Figure 6.8 shows the market for pizza. The demand curve is *D*, the supply curve is *S*, the equilibrium price is \$10 a pizza, and the equilibrium quantity is 10,000 pizzas a day. The market forces that you studied in Chapter 4 (pp. 99–100) pull the pizza market to its equilibrium and coordinate the plans of buyers and sellers. But does this competitive equilibrium deliver the efficient quantity of pizza?

If the equilibrium is efficient, it does more than coordinate plans. It coordinates them in the best possible way. Resources are used to produce the quantity of pizza that people value most highly. It is not possible to produce more pizza without giving up some of another good or service that is valued more highly. And if a smaller quantity of pizza is produced, resources are used to produce some other good that is not valued as highly as the pizza that is forgone.

### Marginal Benefit Equals Marginal Cost

To check whether the equilibrium in Figure 6.8 is efficient, recall the interpretation of the demand curve as a marginal benefit curve and the supply curve as a marginal cost curve. The demand curve tells us the marginal benefit from pizza. The supply curve tells us the marginal cost of pizza. Where the demand curve and the supply curve intersect, marginal benefit equals marginal cost.

**FIGURE 6.8**

An Efficient Market for Pizza

myeconlab Animation

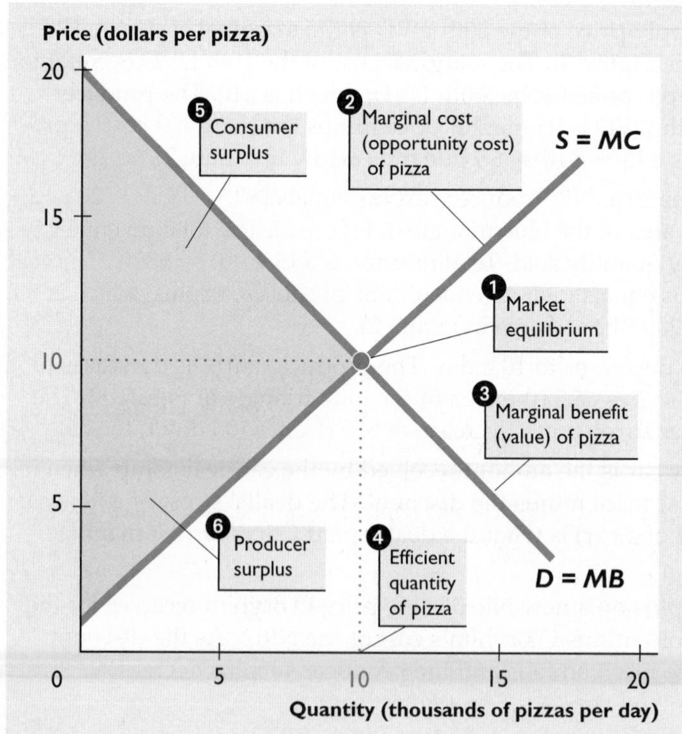


1 Market equilibrium occurs at a price of \$10 a pizza and a quantity of 10,000 pizzas a day.

2 The supply curve is also the marginal cost curve.

3 The demand curve is also the marginal benefit curve.

Because at the market equilibrium, marginal benefit equals marginal cost, the 4 efficient quantity of pizza is produced. The sum of the 5 consumer surplus and 6 producer surplus is maximized.

This condition—marginal benefit equals marginal cost—is the condition that delivers an efficient use of resources. Because a competitive equilibrium allocates resources to the activities that create the greatest possible value, it is efficient.

## Total Surplus Is Maximized

Another way of checking that the equilibrium is efficient is to look at the total surplus that it generates. **Total surplus** is the sum of producer surplus and consumer surplus. A price above the equilibrium might increase producer surplus, but it would decrease consumer surplus by more. And a price below the equilibrium price might increase consumer surplus, but it would decrease producer surplus by more. The competitive equilibrium price maximizes total surplus.

**Total surplus**
The sum of producer surplus and consumer surplus.

In Figure 6.8, if production is less than 10,000 pizzas a day, someone is willing to buy a pizza for more than it costs to produce. Buyers and sellers will gain if production increases. If production exceeds 10,000 pizzas a day, it costs more to produce a pizza than anyone is willing to pay for it. Buyers and sellers will gain if production decreases. Only when 10,000 pizzas a day are produced is there no unexploited gain from changing the quantity of pizza produced, and total surplus is maximized.

Buyers and sellers each attempt to do the best they can for themselves—they pursue their self-interest. No one plans for an efficient outcome for society as a whole. No one worries about the social interest. Buyers seek the lowest possible price, and sellers seek the highest possible price. But as buyers and sellers pursue their self-interest, this astonishing outcome occurs: The social interest is served.

## The Invisible Hand

Writing in his *Wealth of Nations* in 1776, Adam Smith was the first to suggest that competitive markets send resources to the uses in which they have the highest value. Smith believed that each participant in a competitive market is "led by an invisible hand to promote an end [the efficient use of resources] which was no part of his intention."

You can see the effects of the invisible hand at work every day. Your campus bookstore is stuffed with texts at the start of each term. It has the quantities that it predicts students will buy. The coffee shop has the variety and quantities of drinks and snacks that people plan to buy. Your local clothing store has the sweatpants and socks and other items that you plan to buy. Truckloads of textbooks, coffee and cookies, and sweatpants and socks roll along our highways and bring these items to where you and your friends want to buy them. Firms that don't know you anticipate your wants and work hard to help you satisfy them.

No government organizes all this production, and no government auditor monitors producers to ensure that they serve the social interest. The allocation of scarce resources is not planned. It happens because prices adjust to make buying plans and selling plans compatible, and it happens in a way that sends resources to the uses in which they have the highest value.

Adam Smith explained why all this amazing activity occurs. "It is not from the benevolence of the butcher, the brewer, or the baker that we expect our dinner," he wrote, "but from their regard to their own interest."

Publishing companies, coffee growers, garment manufacturers, and a host of other producers are led by their regard for *their* own interest to serve *your* interest.

# EYE on the U.S. ECONOMY

## The Invisible Hand and e-Commerce

You can see the influence of the invisible hand at work in the cartoon and in today's information economy.

The cold drinks vendor has both cold drinks and shade. He has an opportunity cost and a minimum supply price of each item. The park bench reader has a marginal benefit from a cold drink and from shade. The transaction that occurs tells us that for shade, the reader's marginal benefit exceeds the vendor's marginal cost but for a cold drink, the vendor's marginal cost exceeds the reader's marginal benefit. The transaction creates consumer surplus and producer surplus. The vendor obtains a producer surplus from selling the shade for more than its opportunity cost, and the reader obtains a consumer surplus from buying the shade for less than its marginal benefit. In the third frame of the cartoon, both the consumer and the producer are better off than they were in the first frame. The umbrella has moved to its highest-valued use.

The market economy relentlessly performs the activity illustrated in the cartoon to achieve an efficient allocation of resources. New technologies have cut the cost of using the Internet and during the past few years, hundreds of Web sites have been established that are dedicated to facilitating trade in all types of goods, services, and factors of production.

The electronic auction site eBay (http://www.ebay.com/), has brought a huge increase in consumer surplus and producer surplus, and helps to achieve ever greater allocative efficiency.

## Underproduction and Overproduction

Inefficiency can occur because either too little of an item is produced—underproduction—or too much is produced—overproduction.

### Underproduction

In Figure 6.9(a), the quantity of pizza produced is 5,000 a day. At this quantity, consumers are willing to pay $15 for a pizza that costs only $6 to produce. The quantity produced is inefficient—there is underproduction.

A **deadweight loss**, which is the decrease in total surplus that results from an inefficient underproduction or overproduction, measures the scale of the inefficiency. The area of the gray triangle in Figure 6.9(a) measures the deadweight loss.

**Deadweight loss**
The decrease in total surplus that results from an inefficient underproduction or overproduction.

### Overproduction

In Figure 6.9(b), the quantity of pizza produced is 15,000 a day. At this quantity, consumers are willing to pay only $5 for a pizza that costs $14 to produce. By producing the 15,000th pizza, $9 is lost. Again, the gray triangle shows the deadweight loss. The total surplus is smaller than its maximum by the amount of the deadweight loss. The deadweight loss is borne by the entire society. It is not a loss for the producer and a gain for the consumers. It is a *social* loss.

**FIGURE 6.9**

Underproduction and Overproduction

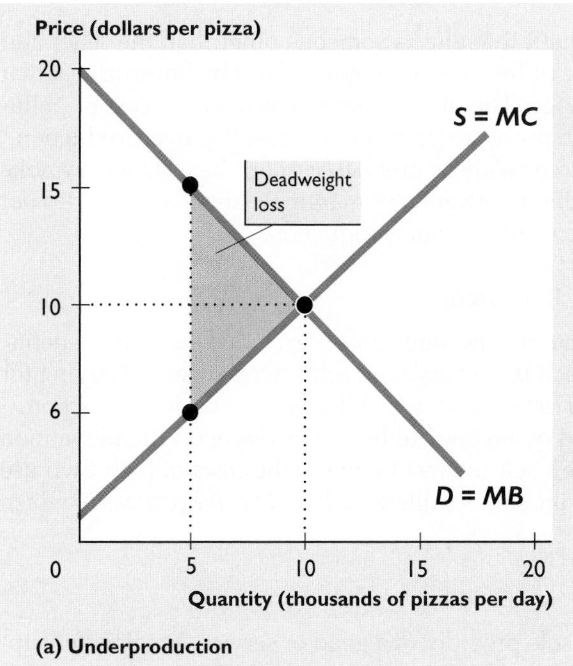


(a) Underproduction

If production is restricted to 5,000 pizzas a day, a deadweight loss (the gray triangle) arises. Total surplus is reduced by the area of the deadweight loss triangle. Underproduction is inefficient.

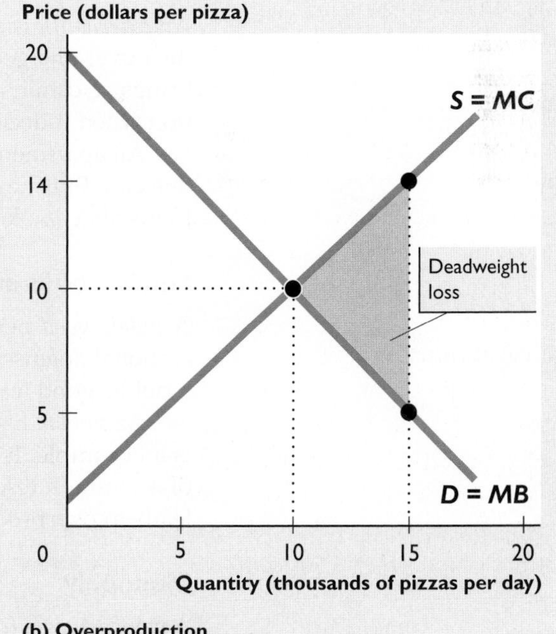


(b) Overproduction

If production increases to 15,000 pizzas, a deadweight loss arises. Total surplus is reduced by the area of the deadweight loss triangle. Overproduction is inefficient.

## Obstacles to Efficiency

The obstacles to efficiency that bring underproduction or overproduction are

- Price and quantity regulations
- Taxes and subsidies
- Externalities
- Public goods and common resources
- Monopoly
- High transactions costs

### Price and Quantity Regulations

*Price regulations* that put a cap on the rent a landlord is permitted to charge and laws that require employers to pay a minimum wage sometimes block the price adjustments that balance the quantity demanded and the quantity supplied and lead to underproduction. *Quantity regulations* that limit the amount that a farm is permitted to produce also lead to underproduction.

### Taxes and Subsidies

*Taxes* increase the prices paid by buyers and lower the prices received by sellers. So taxes decrease the quantity produced and lead to underproduction. *Subsidies,* which are payments by the government to producers, decrease the prices paid by buyers and increase the prices received by sellers. So subsidies increase the quantity produced and lead to overproduction.

### Externalities

An *externality* is a cost or a benefit that affects someone other than the seller and the buyer of a good. An electric utility creates an *external cost* by burning coal that brings acid rain and crop damage. The utility doesn't consider the cost of pollution when it decides how much power to produce. The result is overproduction.

An apartment owner would provide an *external benefit* if she installed a smoke detector. But she doesn't consider her neighbor's marginal benefit and decides not to install a smoke detector. The result is underproduction.

### Public Goods and Common Resources

A *public good* benefits everyone and no one can be excluded from its benefits. National defense is an example. It is in everyone's self-interest to avoid paying for a public good (called the *free-rider problem*), which leads to its underproduction.

A *common resource* is owned by no one but used by everyone. Atlantic salmon is an example. It is in everyone's self-interest to ignore the costs of their own use of a common resource that fall on others (called the *tragedy of the commons*), which leads to overproduction.

### Monopoly

A *monopoly* is a firm that is the sole provider of a good or service. Local water supply and cable television are supplied by firms that are monopolies.

The self-interest of a monopoly is to maximize its profit. Because the monopoly has no competitors, it can set the price to achieve its self-interested goal. To achieve its goal, a monopoly produces too little and charges too high a price, which leads to underproduction.

### High Transactions Costs

Stroll around a shopping mall and observe the retail markets in which you participate. You'll see that these markets employ enormous quantities of scarce labor and capital resources. It is costly to operate any market. Economists call the opportunity costs of making trades in a market **transactions costs**.

**Transactions costs**
The opportunity costs of making trades in a market.

To use market prices as the allocators of scarce resources, it must be worth bearing the opportunity cost of establishing a market. Some markets are just too costly to operate. For example, when you want to play tennis on your local "free" court, you don't pay a market price for your slot on the court. You hang around until the court becomes vacant, and you "pay" with your waiting time.

When transactions costs are high, the market might underproduce.

## Alternatives to the Market

When a market is inefficient, can one of the alternative non-market methods that we described at the beginning of this chapter do a better job? Sometimes it can.

Table 6.1 summarizes the sources of market inefficiency and the possible remedies. Often, majority rule might be used, but majority rule has its own shortcomings. A group that pursues the self-interest of its members can become the majority. For example, price and quantity regulations that create deadweight loss are almost always the result of a self-interested group becoming the majority and imposing costs on the minority. Also, with majority rule, votes must be translated into actions by bureaucrats who have their own agendas.

Managers in firms issue commands and avoid the transactions costs that they would incur if they went to a market every time they needed a job done. First-come, first-served saves a lot of hassle in waiting lines. These lines could have markets in which people trade their place in the line—but someone would have to enforce the agreements. Can you imagine the hassle at a busy Starbucks if you had to buy your spot at the head of the line?

There is no one mechanism for allocating resources efficiently. But markets bypassed inside firms by command systems and supplemented by majority rule and first-come, first-served do an amazingly good job.

**Table 6.1**
Market Inefficiencies and Some Possible Remedies

| Reason for market inefficiency | Possible remedy |
|---|---|
| **1.** Price and quantity regulations | Remove regulation by majority rule |
| **2.** Taxes and subsidies | Minimize deadweight loss by majority rule |
| **3.** Externalities | Minimize deadweight loss by majority rule |
| **4.** Public goods | Allocate by majority rule |
| **5.** Common resources | Allocate by majority rule |
| **6.** Monopoly | Regulate by majority rule |
| **7.** High transactions costs | Command or first-come, first-served |

Work these problems in Study Plan 6.4 to get instant feedback.

## CHECKPOINT 6.4

**Evaluate the efficiency of the alternative methods of allocating scarce resources.**

### Practice Problems

Figure 1 shows the market for paper. Use Figure 1 to work Problems **1** to **3**.

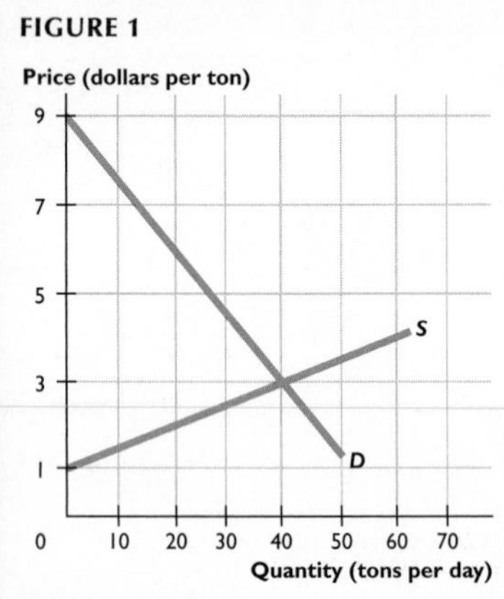


1. At the market equilibrium, what are consumer surplus, producer surplus, and total surplus? Is the market for paper efficient? Why or why not?
2. Lobbyists for a group of news magazines persuade the government to pass a law that requires producers to sell 50 tons of paper a day. Is the market for paper efficient? Why or why not? Shade the deadweight loss on the figure.
3. An environmental lobbying group persuades the government to pass a law that limits the quantity of paper that producers sell to 20 tons a day. Is the market for paper efficient? If not, what is the deadweight loss?

Use the following information to work Problems **4** and **5**.

**National parks to offer free-entry weekends**

Interior Secretary Ken Salazar has urged everyone to visit the national parks over the weekends of June 20-21, July 18-19, and August 15-16 when admission will be free. Kathy Kupper, spokeswoman for the National Parks Service, said that she couldn't remember the fee having been waived in more than 20 years.

Source: *Los Angeles Times*, June 3, 2009

4. How will waiving the admission charge influence consumer surplus?
5. Will the number of visitors be efficient on a weekend when the fee is waived?

### Guided Solutions to Practice Problems

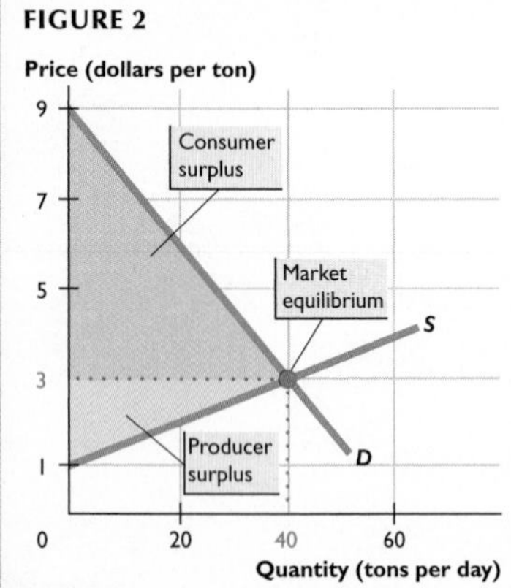


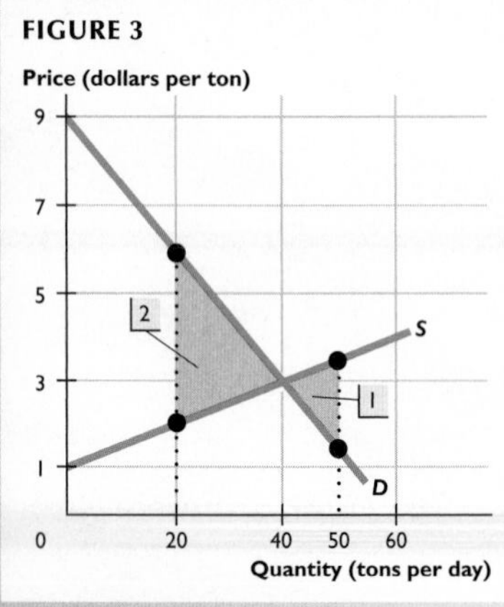


1. Market equilibrium is 40 tons a day at a price of \$3 a ton (Figure 2). Consumer surplus = (\$9 − \$3) × 40 ÷ 2 = \$120 (the area of the green triangle in Figure 2). Producer surplus is (\$3 − \$1) × 40 ÷ 2, which equals \$40 (the area of the blue triangle in Figure 2). Total surplus is the sum of consumer surplus and producer surplus, which is \$160.
   The market is efficient because marginal benefit (on the demand curve) equals marginal cost (on the supply curve) and total surplus (consumer surplus plus producer surplus) is maximized.
2. The market is inefficient because marginal cost exceeds marginal benefit. Deadweight loss is the gray triangle 1 in Figure 3.
3. This market is now inefficient because marginal benefit exceeds marginal cost. The deadweight loss is the gray triangle 2 in Figure 3.
4. Lowering the admission charge to zero will increase consumer surplus.
5. On a weekend when the fee is waived, the marginal benefit from a visit is zero. If a park does not become overcrowded and the marginal cost of a visit is also zero, then the number of visitors is efficient. But if overcrowding makes the marginal cost greater than zero, then the park will have too many visitors.

## 6.5 ARE MARKETS FAIR?

Following a severe winter storm or hurricane, the prices of many essential items jump. Is it fair that disaster victims should be hit with higher prices? Many low-skilled people work for a wage that is below what most would regard as a living wage. Is that fair? How do we decide whether something is fair or unfair?

Economists have a clear definition of efficiency but they do not have a similarly clear definition of fairness. Also, ideas about fairness are not exclusively economic ideas. They involve the study of ethics.

To study ideas about fairness, think of economic life as a game—a serious game—that has *rules* and a *result*. Two broad and generally conflicting approaches to fairness are

- It's not fair if the *rules* aren't fair.
- It's not fair if the *result* isn't fair.

### It's Not Fair If the *Rules* Aren't Fair

Harvard philosopher Robert Nozick argued for the fair rules view in a book entitled *Anarchy, State, and Utopia*, published in 1974. Nozick argued that fairness requires two rules:

- The state must establish and protect private property rights.
- Goods and services and the services of factors of production may be transferred from one person to another only by voluntary exchange with everyone free to engage in such exchange.

The first rule says that everything that is valuable—all scarce resources and goods—must be owned by individuals and that the state must protect private property rights. The second rule says that the only way a person can acquire something is to buy it in voluntary trade.

If these rules are followed, says Nozick, the outcome is fair. It doesn't matter how unequally the economic pie is shared provided that the people who bake it supply their services voluntarily in exchange for the share of the pie offered in compensation. Opportunity is equal but the result might be unequal. This fair rules approach is consistent with allocative efficiency.

### It's Not Fair If the *Result* Isn't Fair

Most people think that the fair rules approach leads to too much inequality—to an unfair result: For example, that it is unfair for a bank president to earn millions of dollars a year while a bank teller earns only thousands of dollars a year.

But what is "too unequal"? Is it fair for some people to receive twice as much as others but not ten times as much or a hundred times as much? Or is all that matters that the poorest people shouldn't be "too poor"?

There is no easy answer to these questions. Generally, greater equality is regarded as good but there is no measure of the most desirable shares.

The fair result approach conflicts with allocative efficiency and leads to what is called the **big tradeoff**—a tradeoff between efficiency and fairness that recognizes the cost of making income transfers.

**Big tradeoff**
A tradeoff between efficiency and fairness that recognizes the cost of making income transfers.

The big tradeoff is based on the fact that income can be transferred to people with low incomes only by taxing people with high incomes. But taxing people's

# EYE on PRICE GOUGING

## Should Price Gouging be Illegal?

**Price gouging** is the practice of selling an essential item for a much higher price than normal, and usually occurs following a natural disaster. In Florida and Texas, where hurricanes happen all too often, price gouging is illegal.

Whether price gouging *should* be illegal depends on the view of fairness employed and on the facts about whether the buyers or the sellers are the poorer group.

The standard economist view is that price gouging should *not* be illegal and that it is the expected and *efficient* response to a change in demand.

After a hurricane, the demand for items such as generators, pumps, lamps, gasoline, and camp stoves increases and the prices of these items rise in a natural response to the change in demand.

The figure illustrates the market for camp stoves. The supply of stoves is the curve *S*, and in normal times, the demand for stoves is $D_0$. The price is $20 per stove and the equilibrium quantity is 5 stoves per day.

Following a hurricane that results in a lengthy power failure, the demand for camp stoves increases to $D_1$. Provided there is no price gouging law, the equilibrium price of a stove jumps to $40 and the equilibrium quantity increases to 7 stoves per day.

This outcome is efficient because the marginal cost of a stove (on the supply curve) equals the marginal benefit from a stove (on the demand curve).

If a strict price gouging law requires the price after the hurricane to be the *same* as the price before the hurricane, the price of a stove is stuck at $20.

At this price, the quantity of stoves supplied remains at 5 per day and a deadweight loss shown by the gray triangle arises. The price gouging law is inefficient, and the price rise is efficient.

Whether a doubling of the price is *fair* depends on the idea of fairness used. On the *fair rules* view, the price rise is fair. Trade is voluntary and both the buyer and the seller are better off. On the *fair outcome* view, the price rise might be considered unfair if the buyers are poor and the sellers are rich. But if the buyers are rich and the sellers are poor, the price rise would be considered fair even on the fair result view.

After Hurricane Katrina, John Shepperson bought 19 generators, loaded them into a rented U-Haul vehicle, and drove the 600 miles from his home in Kentucky to a place in Mississippi that had no power. He offered his generators to eager buyers for twice the price he had paid for them. But before he could complete a sale, the Mississippi police swooped in on him. They confiscated his generators and put him in jail for four days. His crime: price gouging.

Was it efficient to stop Mr. Shepperson from selling his generators? Was it fair either to him or his deprived customers?

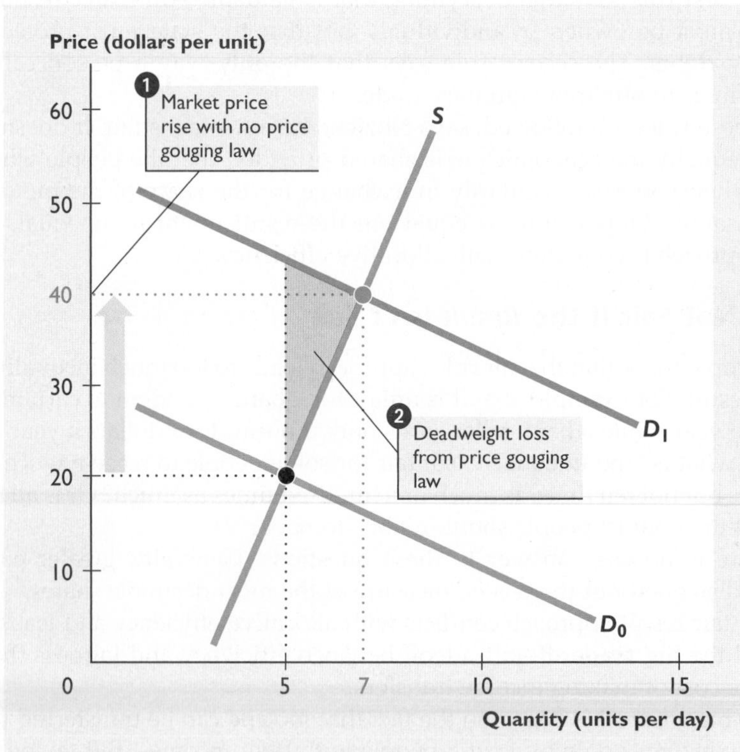

## EYE on YOUR LIFE

### Allocation Methods, Efficiency, and Fairness

You live in the national economy, your state economy, your regional economy, and your own household economy. The many decisions you must make affect efficiency and fairness at all these levels. Think about your household economy.

Make a spreadsheet and on it identify all the factors of production that your household owns. Count all the person-hours available and any capital. Show how these resources are allocated.

By what methods are your household's scarce resources allocated? Identify those allocated by market price; by command; by first-come, first-served; and by equal shares. Are any resources allocated by majority vote?

Now the tough part: Are these resources allocated efficiently—is the value of your household's resources maximized? Think about how you can check whether marginal benefit equals marginal cost for each of your household's activities.

And now an even tougher question: Are your household's resources allocated fairly? Think about the two ideas of fairness and how they apply in your household.

---

income from employment discourages work. It results in the quantity of labor being less than the efficient quantity. Taxing people's income from capital discourages saving. It results in the quantity of capital being less than the efficient quantity. With smaller quantities of both labor and capital, the quantity of goods and services produced is less than the efficient quantity. The economic pie shrinks.

Income redistribution creates a tradeoff between the size of the economic pie and the equality with which it is shared. The greater the scale of income redistribution through income taxes, the greater is the inefficiency—the smaller is the pie.

There is a second source of inefficiency: A dollar taken from a rich person does not end up as a dollar in the hands of a poorer person. Some of the dollar is spent on administration of the tax and transfer system, which includes the cost of accountants, auditors, and lawyers. These activities use skilled labor and capital resources that could otherwise be used to produce other goods and services that people value.

You can see that when all these costs are taken into account, transferring a dollar from a rich person does not give a dollar to a poor person. It is even possible that those with low incomes end up being worse off. For example, if a highly taxed entrepreneur decides to work less hard and shut down a business, low-income workers get fired and must seek other, perhaps even lower-paid, work.

## ■ Compromise

Most people, and probably most economists, have sympathy with the Nozick view but think it too extreme. They see a role for taxes and government income support schemes to transfer some income from the rich to the poor. Such transfers could be considered voluntary in the sense that they are decided by majority voting, and even those who vote against such transfers voluntarily participate in the political process.

Once we agree that using the tax system to make transfers from the rich to the poor is fair, we need to determine just what we mean by a fair tax. We'll look at this big question when we study the tax system in Chapter 8.

Work these problems in Study Plan 6.5 to get instant feedback.

## CHECKPOINT 6.5

**Explain the main ideas about fairness and evaluate the fairness of the alternative methods of allocating scarce resources.**

### Practice Problems

A winter storm cuts the power supply and isolates a small town in the mountains. The people rush to buy candles from the town store, which is the only source of candles. The store owner decides to ration the candles to one per family but to keep the price of a candle unchanged. Use this information to work Problems **1** and **2**.

1. Who gets to use the candles? Who receives the consumer surplus and who receives the producer surplus on candles?
2. Is the allocation efficient? Is the allocation fair?

Use the following information to work Problems **3** and **4**.

**National parks to offer free-entry weekends**

Interior Secretary Ken Salazar said he hoped American families would take the opportunity during these hard times to enjoy an affordable weekend vacation in our national parks. Most Americans live within an hour's drive of a national park.

Source: *Los Angeles Times*, June 3, 2009

3. Which American families will most likely visit the national parks on the free weekends?
4. Is the policy to waive the admission fair?

### Guided Solutions to Practice Problems

1. The people who buy candles from the town store are not necessarily the people who use the candles. A buyer from the town store can sell a candle and will do so if he or she can get a price that exceeds his or her marginal benefit. The people who value the candles most—who are willing to pay the most—will use the candles.
   Only the people who are willing to pay the most for candles receive the consumer surplus on candles, and the store owner receives the same producer surplus as normal. People who sell the candles they buy from the store receive additional producer surplus.
2. The allocation is efficient because the people who value the candles most use them. Two views of fairness: The rules view is that if the rule of one candle per family is followed and exchange is voluntary, then the outcome is fair. But the results view is that if the candles are allocated unequally, then the allocation is unfair.
3. Most of the visitors will be those who own a car and don't work on these weekends.
4. The idea of waiving the admission is to allow families to enjoy an affordable vacation in these hard times. If these families hit by the hard times are the ones that visit the national parks, then, in the fair result view, the policy is fair. But if families hit by the hard times are the ones who do not visit, then, in the fair result view, the policy is unfair. If the families who visit the national parks do so voluntarily, then, in the fair rules view, no matter which families visit, the policy is fair.

## CHAPTER SUMMARY

### Key Points

**1 Describe the alternative methods of allocating scarce resources and define and explain the features of an efficient allocation.**

- The methods of allocating scarce resources are market price; command; majority rule; contest; first-come, first-served; sharing equally; lottery; personal characteristics; and force.
- Allocative efficiency occurs when resources are used to create the greatest value, which means that marginal benefit equals marginal cost.

**2 Distinguish between value and price and define consumer surplus.**

- Marginal benefit is measured by the maximum price that consumers are willing to pay for another unit of a good or service.
- A demand curve is a marginal benefit curve.
- Value is what people are *willing to* pay; price is what they *must* pay.
- Consumer surplus equals marginal benefit minus price, summed over the quantity consumed.

**3 Distinguish between cost and price and define producer surplus.**

- Marginal cost is measured by the minimum price producers must be offered to increase production by one unit.
- A supply curve is a marginal cost curve.
- Opportunity cost is what producers *must* pay; price is what they *receive*.
- Producer surplus equals price minus marginal cost, summed over the quantity produced.

**4 Evaluate the efficiency of the alternative methods of allocating scarce resources.**

- In a competitive equilibrium, marginal benefit equals marginal cost and resource allocation is efficient.
- Price and quantity regulations, taxes, subsidies, externalities, public goods, common resources, monopoly, and high transactions costs lead to either underproduction or overproduction and create a deadweight loss.

**5 Explain the main ideas about fairness and evaluate the fairness of the alternative methods of allocating scarce resources.**

- Ideas about fairness divide into two groups: fair *results* and fair *rules*.
- Fair rules require private property rights and voluntary exchange, and fair results require income transfers from the rich to the poor.

### Key Terms

| | | |
|---|---|---|
| Allocative efficiency, 143 | Consumer surplus, 149 | Producer surplus, 152 |
| Big tradeoff, 161 | Deadweight loss, 157 | Total surplus, 155 |
| Command system, 141 | Price gouging, 162 | Transactions costs, 159 |

Work these problems in Chapter 6 Study Plan to get instant feedback.

## CHAPTER CHECKPOINT

### Study Plan Problems and Applications

At McDonald's, no reservations are accepted; at Puck's at St. Louis Art Museum, reservations are accepted; at the Bissell Mansion restaurant, reservations are essential. Use this information to answer Problems 1 to 3.

1. Describe the method of allocating table resources in these three restaurants.
2. Why do you think restaurants have different reservation policies, and why might each restaurant be using an efficient allocation method?
3. Why don't all restaurants use the market price to allocate their tables?

**TABLE 1**

| Price (dollars per sandwich) | Quantity demanded (sandwiches per hour) | Quantity supplied (sandwiches per hour) |
|---|---|---|
| 0 | 400 | 0 |
| 1 | 350 | 50 |
| 2 | 300 | 100 |
| 3 | 250 | 150 |
| 4 | 200 | 200 |
| 5 | 150 | 250 |
| 6 | 100 | 300 |
| 7 | 50 | 350 |
| 8 | 0 | 400 |

Table 1 shows the demand and supply schedules for sandwiches. Use Table 1 to work Problems 4 to 7.

4. Calculate the equilibrium price of a sandwich, the consumer surplus, and the producer surplus. What is the efficient quantity of sandwiches?
5. If the quantity demanded decreases by 100 sandwiches an hour at each price, what is the equilibrium price and what is the change in total surplus?
6. If the quantity supplied decreases by 100 sandwiches an hour at each price, what is the equilibrium price and what is the change in total surplus?
7. If Sandwiches To Go, Inc., buys all the sandwich producers and cuts production to 100 sandwiches an hour, what is the deadweight loss that is created? If Sandwiches To Go, Inc., rations sandwiches to two per person, by what view of fairness would the allocation be unfair?
8. **eBay saves billions for bidders**
On eBay, the bidder who places the highest bid wins the auction and pays only what the second highest bidder offered. Researchers Wolfgang Jank and Galit Shmueli reported that purchasers on eBay in 2003 paid $7 billion less than their winning bids. Because each bid shows the buyer's willingness to pay, winners receive a consumer surplus, estimated at an average of $4 or more.
Source: *InformationWeek*, January 28, 2008
    - What method is used to allocate goods on eBay? How does an eBay auction influence consumer surplus from the good?
    - Does the seller receive a producer surplus?
    - Are auctions on eBay efficient?
9. Table 2 shows the demand and supply schedules for sandbags before and during a major flood. During the flood, suppose that the government gave all families an equal quantity of sandbags.
    - How would total surplus and the price of a sandbag change?
    - Would the outcome be more efficient than if the government took no action? Explain.

**TABLE 2**

| Price (dollars per bag) | Quantity demanded before flood (thousands of bags) | Quantity demanded during flood (thousands of bags) | Quantity supplied (thousands of bags) |
|---|---|---|---|
| 0 | 40 | 70 | 0 |
| 1 | 35 | 65 | 5 |
| 2 | 30 | 60 | 10 |
| 3 | 25 | 55 | 15 |
| 4 | 20 | 50 | 20 |
| 5 | 15 | 45 | 25 |
| 6 | 10 | 40 | 30 |
| 7 | 5 | 35 | 35 |
| 8 | 0 | 30 | 40 |

## Instructor Assignable Problems and Applications

Your instructor can assign these problems as homework, a quiz, or a test in **MyEconLab**.

1. **Panic in paradise: Are high fares the new reality for Hawaii?**
   On March 31, 2008, Hawaii lost 15 percent of its air service as Aloha Airlines and the cheap-flight airline ATA suddenly shut down. Stranded travelers were offered flights to West coast cities at $1,000 one way. Within a month, the fare to west coast cities dropped to about $200 a round trip. Stranded travelers complained of price gouging.
   Source: *USA Today*, April 23, 2008
   Under what conditions would the $1,000 fare be considered "price gouging"? Under what conditions would the $1,000 fare be an example of the market price method of allocating scarce airline seats?

Table 1 shows the demand schedule for haircuts and the supply schedule of haircuts. Use Table 1 to work Problems 2 and 3.

**TABLE 1**

| Price (dollars per haircut) | Quantity demanded (haircuts per day) | Quantity supplied (haircuts per day) |
|---|---|---|
| 0 | 100 | 0 |
| 10 | 80 | 0 |
| 20 | 60 | 20 |
| 30 | 40 | 40 |
| 40 | 20 | 60 |
| 50 | 0 | 80 |

2. What is the quantity of haircuts bought, the value of a haircut, and the total surplus from haircuts?
3. Suppose that all salons agree to charge $40 a haircut. What is the change in consumer surplus, the change in producer surplus, and the deadweight loss created?
4. The winner of the men's or women's tennis singles at the U.S. Open is paid twice as much as the runner-up, but it takes two players to have a singles final. Is this compensation arrangement efficient? Is it fair? Explain why it might illustrate the big tradeoff.

Use the following information to work Problems 5 to 7.

**New Zealand's private forests**
In the early 1990s, the New Zealand government auctioned half the national forests, converting these forests from public ownership to private ownership. The government's decision was an incentive to get the owners to operate like farmers—that is, take care of the resource and to use it to make a profit.
Source: *Reuters*, September 7, 2007

5. When all forests in New Zealand were government owned, was the New Zealand timber industry efficient? Did logging companies operate in the social interest or self-interest?
6. Since the early 1990s, has the New Zealand timber industry been efficient? Have logging companies operated in the social interest or self-interest?
7. What incentive do private timber companies have to ensure that they take care of the resource?

In California, farmers pay a lower price for water than do city residents. Use this information to work Problems 8 to 10.

8. What is this method of allocation of water resources? Is this allocation of water efficient? Is this use of scarce water fair? Why or why not?
9. If farmers were charged the same price as city residents pay, how would the price of agricultural produce, the quantity of produce grown, consumer surplus, and producer surplus change?

10. If all water in California is sold for the market equilibrium price, would the allocation of water be more efficient? Why or why not?

Use the following information to work Problems 11 to 14.

**Scarce water and population boom leads California to "perfect drought"**

In Los Angeles, as the summer heats up, sprinklers spray a fine mist of water to cool the hot air. With only 3.2 inches of rain a year, southern California looks set for a perfect drought. Sprinklers and other items that make southern California habitable might be banned. Melanie Winter, of the LA-based River Project, reported that LA needs to conserve rain water rather than channeling it into the sea and make the city less dependent on water from the Colorado River.

Source: *The Guardian,* June 25, 2007

11. If sprinklers are banned, explain how consumer surplus and total surplus would change if the price of water remains unchanged.
12. In 2007, is water allocated in the social interest or self-interest? What allocation method would be more efficient than banning sprinklers? Explain.
13. Would channeling less water hundreds of miles from the Colorado River and conserving local rain water enable water use to be more efficient?
14. Would privatization of the urban water supply create an incentive to increase efficiency?

Use the following information to work Problems 15 to 17.

**The world's largest tulip and flower market**

Every day over 19 million tulips and flowers are auctioned at the Dutch market called "The Bloemenveiling." Each day 55,000 Dutch auctions take place, matching buyers and sellers.

Source: Tulip-Bulbs.com

A Dutch auction is one in which the auctioneer starts by announcing the highest price. If no one offers to buy the flowers, the auctioneer lowers the price until a buyer is found.

15. What method is used to allocate flowers at the Bloemenveiling?
16. How does a Dutch flower auction influence consumer surplus and producer surplus?
17. Are the flower auctions at the Bloemenveiling efficient?

Use the following information to work Problems 18 and 19.

**U.S. won't auction airport landing slots**

In October 2008, the Department of Transportation published the rules that would allow the auction of landing slots at LaGuardia airport. Today, the Department of Transportation announced that it proposed to rescind those auctions. Transportation Secretary Ray LaHood remarked that the department would work to resolve the congestion of New York's airspace.

Source: *New York Times,* May 13, 2009

18. What are the resource allocation problems at LaGuardia airport? Do those resource problems create a tradeoff between efficiency and fairness?
19. Would an auction of landing slots be efficient? Would it be fair? What effect would it have on the resource problems at LaGuardia airport?

## How powerful is the president's pen?

Can the President sign an order that caps executive pay and one that ensures every worker gets a decent wage?

# Government Actions in Markets

CHAPTER CHECKLIST

**When you have completed your study of this chapter, you will be able to**

1 Explain how a price ceiling works and show how a rent ceiling creates a housing shortage, inefficiency, and unfairness.

2 Explain how a price floor works and show how the minimum wage creates unemployment, inefficiency, and unfairness.

3 Explain how a price support in the market for an agricultural product creates a surplus, inefficiency, and unfairness.

## 7.1 PRICE CEILINGS

**Price ceiling or price cap**
A government regulation that places an *upper* limit on the price at which a particular good, service, or factor of production may be traded.

A **price ceiling** (also called a **price cap**) is a government regulation that places an *upper* limit on the price at which a particular good, service, or factor of production may be traded. Trading at a higher price is illegal.

A price ceiling has been used in several markets, but the one that looms largest in everyone's budget is the housing market. The price of housing is the rent that people pay for a house or apartment. Demand and supply in the housing market determine the rent and the quantity of housing available.

Figure 7.1 illustrates the apartment rental market in Biloxi, Mississippi. The rent is $550 a month, and 4,000 apartments are rented.

Suppose that Biloxi apartment rents have increased by $100 a month in the past two years and that a Citizens' Action Group asks the mayor to roll rents back.

### A Rent Ceiling

**Rent ceiling**
A regulation that makes it illegal to charge more than a specified rent for housing.

Responding to the demand, the mayor imposes a **rent ceiling**—a regulation that makes it illegal to charge more than a specified rent for housing.

The effect of a rent ceiling depends on whether it is imposed at a level above or below the equilibrium rent. In Figure 7.1, if the rent ceiling is set *above* $550 a month, nothing would change because people are already paying $550 a month.

But a rent ceiling that is set *below* the equilibrium rent has powerful effects on the market outcome. The reason is that the rent ceiling attempts to prevent the rent from rising high enough to regulate the quantities demanded and supplied. The law and the market are in conflict, and one (or both) of them must yield.

**FIGURE 7.1**
A Housing Market

myeconlab Animation

The figure shows the demand curve, *D*, and the supply curve, *S*, for rental housing.

1. The market is in equilibrium when the quantity demanded equals the quantity supplied.
2. The equilibrium price (rent) is $550 a month.
3. The equilibrium quantity is 4,000 units of housing.

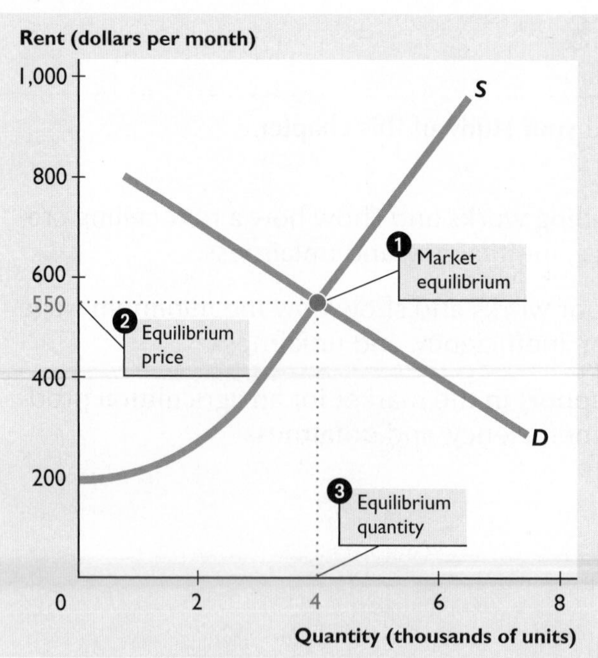

Figure 7.2 shows a rent ceiling that is set below the equilibrium rent at $400 a month. We've shaded the area *above* the rent ceiling because any rent in this region is illegal. The first effect of a rent ceiling is a housing shortage. At a rent of $400 a month, the quantity of housing supplied is 3,000 units and the quantity demanded is 6,000 units. So at $400 a month, there is a shortage of 3,000 units of housing.

But the story does not end here. The 3,000 units of housing that owners are willing to make available must somehow be allocated among people who are seeking 6,000 units. This allocation might be achieved in two ways:

- A black market
- Increased search activity

## A Black Market

A **black market** is an illegal market that operates alongside a government-regulated market. A rent ceiling sometimes creates a black market in housing as frustrated renters and landlords try to find ways of raising the rent above the legally imposed ceiling. Landlords want higher rents because they know that renters are willing to pay more for the existing quantity of housing. Renters are willing to pay more to jump to the front of the line.

**Black market**
An illegal market that operates alongside a government-regulated market.

Because raising the rent is illegal, landlords and renters use creative tricks to get around the law. One of these tricks is for a new tenant to pay a high price for worthless fittings—perhaps paying $2,000 for threadbare drapes. Another is for the tenant to pay a high price for new locks and keys—called "key money."

Figure 7.3 shows how high the black market rent might go in Biloxi. With strict enforcement of the rent ceiling, the quantity of housing available is 3,000

**FIGURE 7.2**

A Rent Ceiling Creates a Shortage

myeconlab Animation

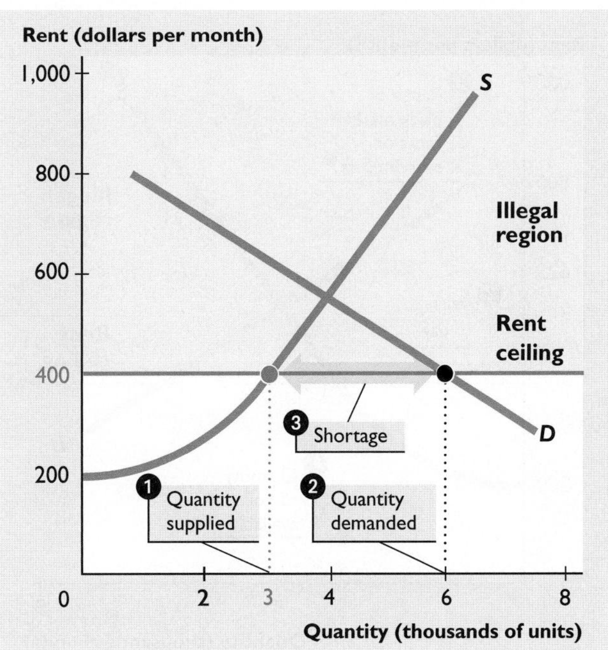


A rent ceiling is imposed below the equilibrium rent. In this example, the rent ceiling is $400 a month.

1. The quantity of housing supplied decreases to 3,000 units.
2. The quantity of housing demanded increases to 6,000 units.
3. A shortage of 3,000 units arises.

units. But at this quantity, renters are willing to offer as much as $625 a month—the amount determined on the demand curve.

So a small number of landlords illegally offer housing for rents up to $625 a month. The black market rent might be at any level between the rent ceiling of $400 and the maximum that a renter is willing to pay of $625.

### Increased Search Activity

**Search activity**
The time spent looking for someone with whom to do business.

The time spent looking for someone with whom to do business is called **search activity**. We spend some time in search activity almost every time we buy something, and especially when we buy a big item such as a car or a home. When a price ceiling creates a shortage of housing, search activity *increases.* In a rent-controlled housing market, frustrated would-be renters scan the newspapers. Keen apartment seekers race to be first on the scene when news of a possible apartment breaks.

The *opportunity cost* of a good is equal to its price *plus* the value of the search time spent finding the good. So the opportunity cost of housing is equal to the rent plus the value of the search time spent looking for an apartment. Search activity is costly. It uses time and other resources, such as telephones, automobiles, and gasoline that could have been used in other productive ways. In Figure 7.3, to find accommodation at $400 a month, someone who is willing to pay a rent of $625 a month would be willing to spend on search activity an amount that is equivalent to adding $225 a month to the rent ceiling.

A rent ceiling controls the rent portion of the cost of housing but not the search cost. So when the search cost is added to the rent, some people end up paying a higher opportunity cost for housing than they would if there were no rent ceiling.

**FIGURE 7.3**

A Rent Ceiling Creates a Black Market and Housing Search

myeconlab Animation

With a rent ceiling of $400 a month,

1. 3,000 units of housing are available.
2. Someone is willing to pay $625 a month for the 3,000th unit of housing.
3. Black market rent might be as high as $625 a month or search activity might be equivalent to adding $225 a month to the rent ceiling.

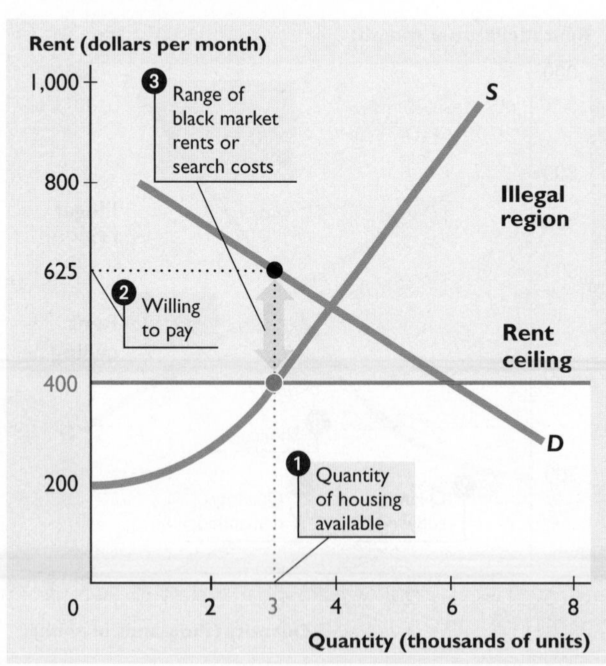

## Are Rent Ceilings Efficient?

In a housing market with no rent ceiling, market forces determine the equilibrium rent. The quantity of housing demanded equals the quantity of housing supplied. In this situation, scarce housing resources are allocated efficiently because the marginal cost of housing equals the marginal benefit. Figure 7.4(a) shows this efficient outcome in the Biloxi apartment rental market. In this efficient market, total surplus—the sum of *consumer surplus* (the green area) and *producer surplus* (the blue area)—is maximized at the equilibrium rent and quantity of housing (see Chapter 6, p. 155).

Figure 7.4(b) shows that with a rent ceiling, the outcome is inefficient. Marginal benefit exceeds marginal cost. Producer surplus and consumer surplus shrink, and a deadweight loss (the gray area) arises. This loss is borne by the people who can't find housing and by landlords who can't offer housing at the lower rent ceiling.

But the total loss exceeds the deadweight loss. Resources get used in costly search activity or in evading the law in the black market. The value of these resources might be as large as the red rectangle. There is yet a further loss: the cost of enforcing the rent ceiling law. This loss, which is borne by taxpayers, is not visible in the figure.

**FIGURE 7.4**

The Inefficiency of a Rent Ceiling

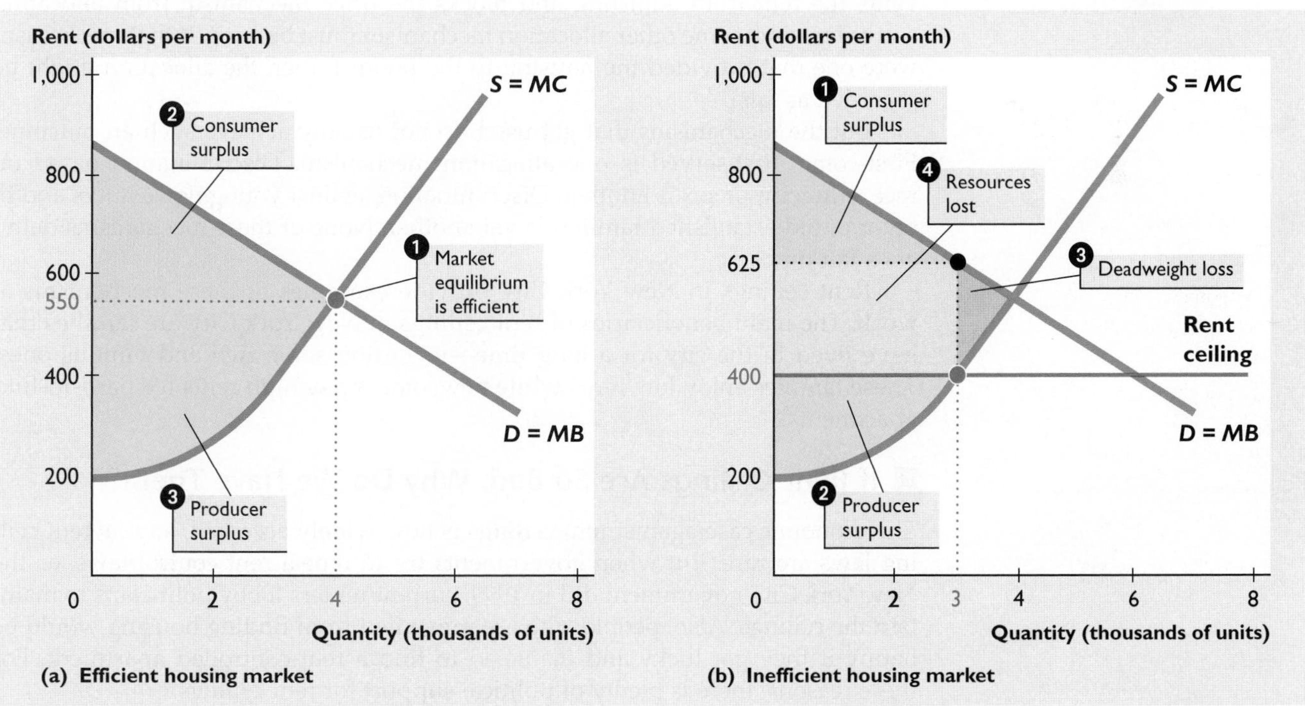


**1** The market equilibrium is efficient with marginal benefit equal to marginal cost. Total surplus, the sum of **2** consumer surplus (green area) and **3** producer surplus (blue area), is maximized.

A rent ceiling is inefficient. **1** Consumer surplus and **2** producer surplus shrink, a **3** deadweight loss arises, and **4** resources are lost in search activity and evading the rent ceiling law.

*With rent ceilings, landlords have no incentive to maintain buildings, and both the quality and quantity of housing supplied decrease.*

Although a rent ceiling creates inefficiency, not everyone loses. The people who pay the rent ceiling get an increase in consumer surplus, and landlords who charge a black market rent get an increase in producer surplus.

The costs of a rent ceiling that we've just considered are only the initial costs. With the rent below the market equilibrium rent, landlords have no incentive to maintain their buildings. So over time, both the quality and quantity of housing supplied *decrease* and the loss arising from a rent ceiling increases.

The size of the loss from a rent ceiling depends on the elasticities of supply and demand. If supply is inelastic, a rent ceiling brings a small decrease in the quantity of housing supplied. And if demand is inelastic, a rent ceiling brings a small increase in the quantity of housing demanded. So the more inelastic the supply or the demand, the smaller is the shortage of housing and the smaller is the deadweight loss.

## Are Rent Ceilings Fair?

We've seen that rent ceilings prevent scarce resources from being allocated efficiently—resources do not flow to their highest-valued use. But don't they ensure that scarce housing resources are allocated more fairly?

You learned in Chapter 6 (pp. 161–163) that fairness is a complex idea about which there are two broad views: fair *results* versus fair *rules.* Rent controls violate the fair rules view of fairness because they block voluntary exchange. But do they deliver a fair result? Do rent ceilings ensure that scarce housing goes to the poor people whose need is greatest?

Blocking rent adjustments that bring the quantity of housing demanded into equality with the quantity supplied doesn't end scarcity. So when the law prevents the rent from adjusting and blocks the price mechanism from allocating scarce housing, some other allocation mechanism must be used. If that mechanism were one that provided the housing to the poorest, then the allocation might be regarded as fair.

But the mechanisms that get used do not usually achieve such an outcome. First-come, first-served is one allocation mechanism. Discrimination based on race, ethnicity, or sex is another. Discrimination against young newcomers and in favor of old established families is yet another. None of these mechanisms delivers a fair outcome.

Rent ceilings in New York City provide examples of these mechanisms at work. The main beneficiaries of rent ceilings in New York City are families that have lived in the city for a long time—including some rich and famous ones. These families enjoy low rents while newcomers pay high rents for hard-to-find apartments.

## If Rent Ceilings Are So Bad, Why Do We Have Them?

The economic case against rent ceilings is now widely accepted, so *new* rent ceiling laws are rare. But when governments try to repeal rent control laws, as the New York City government did in 1999, current renters lobby politicians to maintain the ceilings. Also, people who are prevented from finding housing would be happy if they got lucky and managed to find a rent-controlled apartment. For these reasons, there is plenty of political support for rent ceilings.

Apartment owners who oppose rent ceilings are a minority, so their views are not a powerful influence on politicians. Because more people support rent ceilings than oppose them, politicians are sometimes willing to support them too.

# CHECKPOINT 7.1

Work these problems in Study Plan 7.1 to get instant feedback.

**Explain how a price ceiling works and show how a rent ceiling creates a housing shortage, inefficiency, and unfairness.**

## Practice Problems

Figure 1 shows the rental market for apartments in Corsicana, Texas. Use this figure to work Problems **1** to **3**.

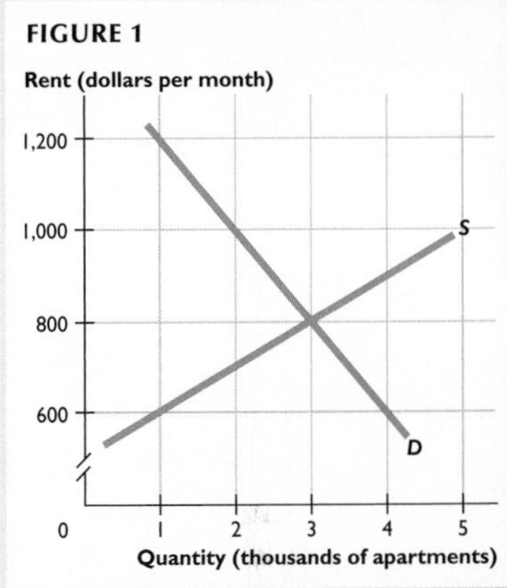


**FIGURE 1**

1. What is the rent in this city and how many apartments are rented? If the city government imposes a rent ceiling of $900 a month, what is the rent and how many apartments are rented?
2. If the city government imposes a rent ceiling of $600 a month, what is the rent and how many apartments are rented? If a black market develops, how high could the black market rent be? Explain.
3. With a strictly enforced rent ceiling of $600 a month, is the housing market efficient? What is the deadweight loss? Is the housing market fair? Explain.
4. **Oil price leaps to year's high**

   For the first time in years, analysts forecast that proven reserves have fallen. On this news, the price of oil rose above $71 a barrel. Oil will last for years, but some analysts predict that the price could go as high as $250 a barrel.

   Source: guardian.co.uk, June 10, 2009

   If the government puts a price cap on gasoline at today's average price of $2.60 a gallon, explain why a shortage will occur. Which allocation method is mostly likely to be used to distribute gasoline?

## Guided Solutions to Practice Problems

1. The equilibrium rent is $800 a month, and 3,000 apartments are rented. A rent ceiling of $900 a month is above the equilibrium rent, so the outcome is the market equilibrium rent of $800 a month with 3,000 apartments rented.
2. With the rent ceiling at $600 a month, the number of apartments rented is 1,000 and the rent is $600 a month (Figure 2). In a black market, some people are willing to rent an apartment for more than the rent ceiling. The highest rent that someone would offer is $1,200 a month. This rent equals someone's willingness to pay for the 1,000th apartment (Figure 2).
3. The housing market is not efficient. With 1,000 apartments rented, marginal benefit exceeds marginal cost and a deadweight loss arises (Figure 2). The deadweight loss equals the area of the gray triangle, which is $(1,200 - 600) \times (3,000 - 1,000) \div 2$. The deadweight loss is $600,000. The allocation of housing is less fair in both views of fairness: It blocks voluntary transactions, and it does not provide more housing to those in most need.
4. Gasoline is made from oil, so a rise in the price of oil increases the cost of making a gallon of gasoline and decreases the supply. The market price of gasoline will rise. A price cap at $2.60 a gallon will create a shortage because the price cap is below the market equilibrium price. Gasoline will be allocated by the first-come, first-served method unless the government rations gasoline, in which case it will be allocated by command.

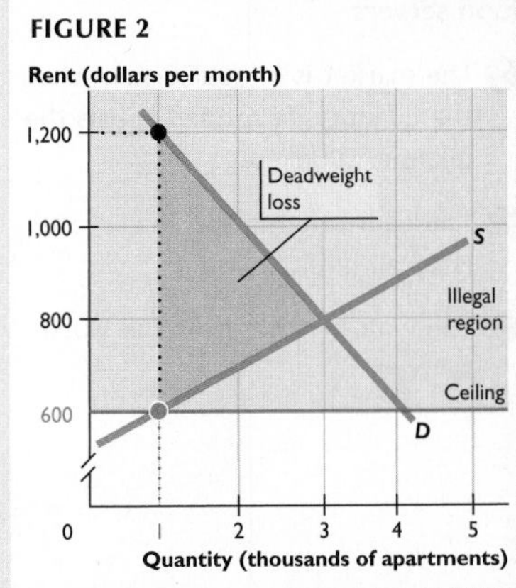


**FIGURE 2**

## 7.2 PRICE FLOORS

**Price floor**
A government regulation that places a *lower* limit on the price at which a particular good, service, or factor of production may be traded.

A **price floor** is a government regulation that places a *lower* limit on the price at which a particular good, service, or factor of production may be traded. Trading at a lower price is illegal.

Price floors are used in many markets, but the one that looms largest is the labor market. The price of labor is the wage rate that people earn. Demand and supply in the labor market determine the wage rate and the quantity of labor employed.

Figure 7.5 illustrates the market for fast-food servers in Yuma, Arizona. In this market, the demand for labor curve is *D*. On this demand curve, at a wage rate of $10 an hour, the quantity of fast-food servers demanded is zero. If A&W, Burger King, Taco Bell, McDonald's, Wendy's, and the other fast-food places had to pay servers $10 an hour, they wouldn't hire any. They would replace servers with vending machines! But at wage rates below $10 an hour, they would hire servers. At a wage rate of $5 an hour, firms would hire 5,000 servers.

On the supply side of the market, no one is willing to work for $2 an hour. To attract servers, firms must pay more than $2 an hour.

Equilibrium in this market occurs at a wage rate of $5 an hour with 5,000 people employed as servers.

Suppose that the government thinks that no one should have to work for a wage rate as low as $5 an hour and decides that it wants to increase the wage rate. Can the government improve conditions for these workers by passing a minimum wage law? Let's find out.

**FIGURE 7.5**

A Market for Fast-Food Servers

myeconlab Animation

The figure shows the demand curve, *D*, and the supply curve, *S*, for fast-food servers.

1. The market is in equilibrium when the quantity demanded equals the quantity supplied.
2. The equilibrium price (wage rate) is $5 an hour.
3. The equilibrium quantity is 5,000 servers.

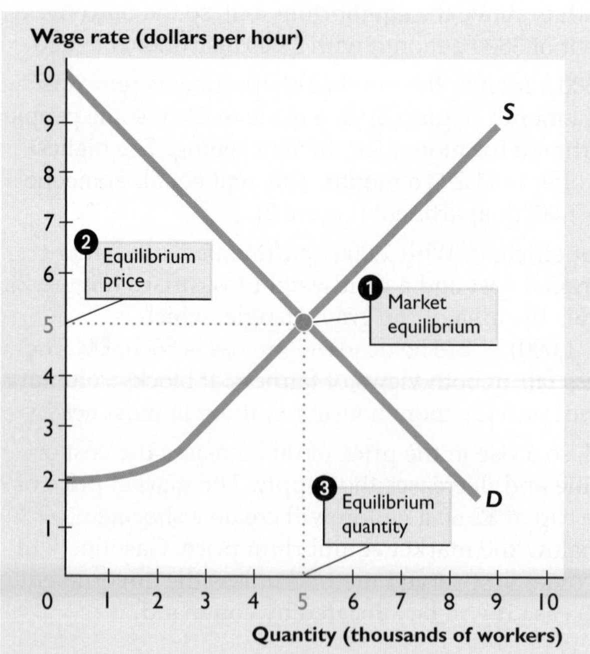

## The Minimum Wage

A **minimum wage law** is a government regulation that makes hiring labor services for less than a specified wage illegal. Firms are free to pay a wage rate that exceeds the minimum wage but may not pay less than the minimum. A minimum wage is an example of a price floor.

**Minimum wage law**
A government regulation that makes hiring labor services for less than a specified wage illegal.

The effect of a price floor depends on whether it is set below or above the equilibrium price. In Figure 7.5, the equilibrium wage rate is $5 an hour, and at this wage rate, firms hire 5,000 workers. If the government introduced a minimum wage below $5 an hour, nothing would change. The reason is that firms are already paying $5 an hour, and because this wage exceeds the minimum wage, the wage rate paid doesn't change. Firms continue to hire 5,000 workers.

But the aim of a minimum wage is to boost the incomes of low-wage earners. So in the markets for the lowest-paid workers, the minimum wage will exceed the equilibrium wage.

Suppose that the government introduces a minimum wage of $7 an hour. Figure 7.6 shows the effects of this law. Wage rates below $7 an hour are illegal, so we've shaded the illegal region *below* the minimum wage. Firms and workers are no longer permitted to operate at the equilibrium point in this market because it is in the illegal region. Market forces and political forces are in conflict.

The government can set a minimum wage, but it can't tell employers how many workers to hire. If firms must pay a wage rate of $7 an hour, they will hire only 3,000 workers. At the equilibrium wage rate of $5 an hour, firms hired 5,000 workers. So when the minimum wage is introduced, firms lay off 2,000 workers.

**FIGURE 7.6**

A Minimum Wage Creates Unemployment

myeconlab Animation

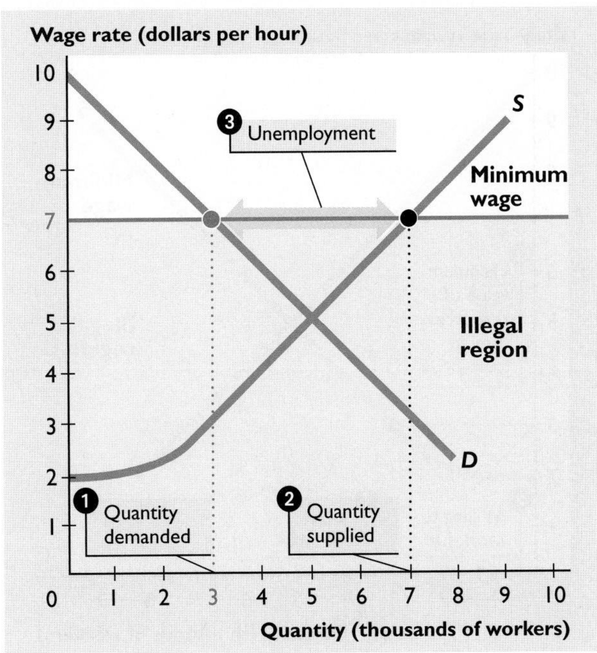


A minimum wage is introduced above the equilibrium wage rate. In this example, the minimum wage rate is $7 an hour.

1. The quantity of labor demanded decreases to 3,000 workers.
2. The quantity of labor supplied increases to 7,000 people.
3. 4,000 people are unemployed.

But at a wage rate of $7 an hour, 2,000 people who didn't want to work for $5 an hour will now try to find work as servers. So at $7 an hour, the quantity supplied is 7,000 people. With 2,000 workers fired and another 2,000 looking for work at the higher wage rate, 4,000 people who would like to work as servers are unemployed.

The 3,000 jobs available must somehow be allocated among the 7,000 people who are willing to work as servers. How is this allocation achieved? The answer is by increased job-search activity and illegal hiring.

## Increased Job-Search Activity

Finding a good job takes a great deal of time and other resources. With a minimum wage, more people are looking for jobs than the number of jobs available. Frustrated unemployed people spend time and other resources searching for hard-to-find jobs. In Figure 7.7, to find a job at $7 an hour, someone who is willing to work for $3 an hour would be willing to spend on job-search activity an amount that is equivalent to subtracting $4 an hour from the minimum wage rate. For a job that might last a year or more, this amount is large.

## Illegal Hiring

With more people looking for work than the number of jobs available, some firms and workers might agree to do business at an illegal wage rate below the minimum wage in a black market. An illegal wage rate might be at any level between the minimum wage rate of $7 an hour and the lowest wage rate at which someone is willing to work, $3 an hour.

**FIGURE 7.7**

A Minimum Wage Creates Job Search and Illegal Hiring

myeconlab Animation

The minimum wage rate is set at $7 an hour:

1. 3,000 jobs are available.
2. The lowest wage rate for which someone is willing to work is $3 an hour. In a black market, illegal wage rates might be as low as $3 an hour.
3. The maximum that might be spent on job search is an amount equivalent to subtracting $4 an hour—the $7 they would receive if they found a job minus the $3 they are willing to work for—from the wage rate.

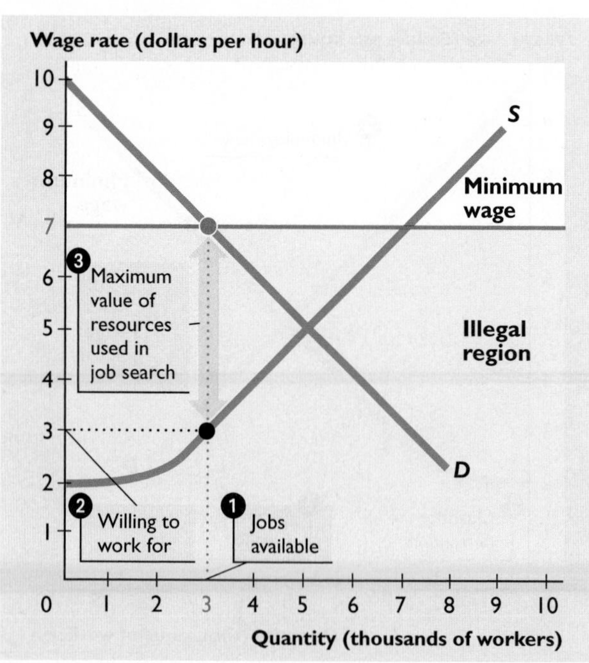

# EYE on the U.S. ECONOMY

## The Federal Minimum Wage

The *Fair Labor Standards Act* sets the federal minimum wage, but most states set their own minimum at a higher level than the federal minimum.

The figure shows the history of the minimum wage in terms of what it would buy at today's (2009) prices. At the end of World War II, the minimum wage was 40¢ per hour, enough to buy what $4.00 bought in 2009. At its peak in 1968, it stood at $10 in today's prices.

The minimum wage creates unemployment. But how much unemployment does it create? Until recently, most economists believed that a 10 percent increase in the minimum wage decreased teenage employment by between 1 and 3 percent.

David Card of the University of California at Berkeley and Alan Krueger of Princeton University have challenged this view. They claim that following a rise in the minimum wage in California, New Jersey, and Texas, the employment rate of low-income workers increased. They suggest three reasons why a rise in the wage rate might increase employment:

(1) Workers become more conscientious and productive.

(2) Workers are less likely to quit, so costly labor turnover is reduced.

(3) Managers make a firm's operations more efficient.

Most economists are skeptical about these ideas and say that if higher wages make workers more productive and reduce labor turnover, firms will freely pay workers a higher wage. They also argue that there are other explanations for the employment increase that Card and Krueger found.

Daniel Hamermesh of the University of Texas at Austin says that they got the timing wrong. Firms anticipated the minimum wage rise and so cut employment before it occurred. Looking at employment changes after the minimum wage increased missed its main effect. Finis Welch of Texas A&M University and Kevin Murphy of the University of Chicago say that the employment effects that Card and Krueger found are caused by regional differences in economic growth, not by changes in the minimum wage.

*Pizza delivery people gain from the minimum wage.*

Also, looking only at employment misses the supply-side effect of the minimum wage. It brings an increase in the number of people who drop out of high school to look for work.

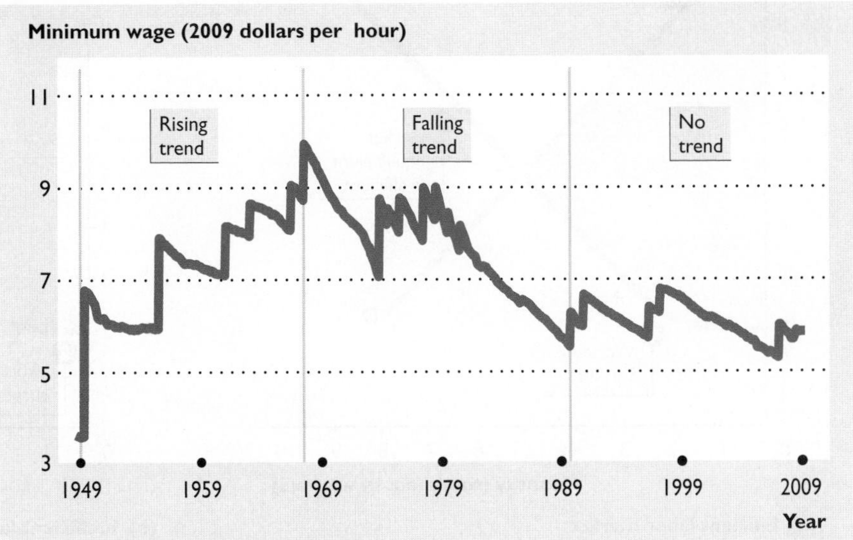


SOURCE OF DATA: Bureau of Labor Statistics.

## Is the Minimum Wage Efficient?

The efficient allocation of a factor of production is similar to that of a good or service, which you studied in Chapter 6. The demand for labor tells us about the marginal benefit of labor to the firms that hire it. Firms benefit because the labor they hire produces the goods or services that they sell. Firms are willing to pay a wage rate equal to the benefit they receive from an additional hour of labor. In Figure 7.8(a), the demand curve for labor tells us the marginal benefit that the firms in Yuma receive from hiring fast-food servers. The marginal benefit minus the wage rate is a surplus for the firms.

The supply of labor tells us about the marginal cost of working. To work, people must forgo leisure or working in the home, activities that they value. The wage rate received minus the marginal cost of working is a surplus for workers.

An efficient allocation of labor occurs when the marginal benefit to firms equals the marginal cost borne by workers. Such an allocation occurs in the labor market in Figure 7.8(a). Firms enjoy a surplus (the blue area), and workers enjoy a surplus (the green area). The sum of these surpluses is maximized.

Figure 7.8(b) shows the loss from a minimum wage. With a minimum wage of $7 an hour, 3,000 workers are hired. Marginal benefit exceeds marginal cost. The firms' surplus and workers' surplus shrink, and a deadweight loss (the gray area) arises. This loss falls on the firms that cut back employment and the people who can't find jobs at the higher wage rate.

**FIGURE 7.8**

The Inefficiency of the Minimum Wage

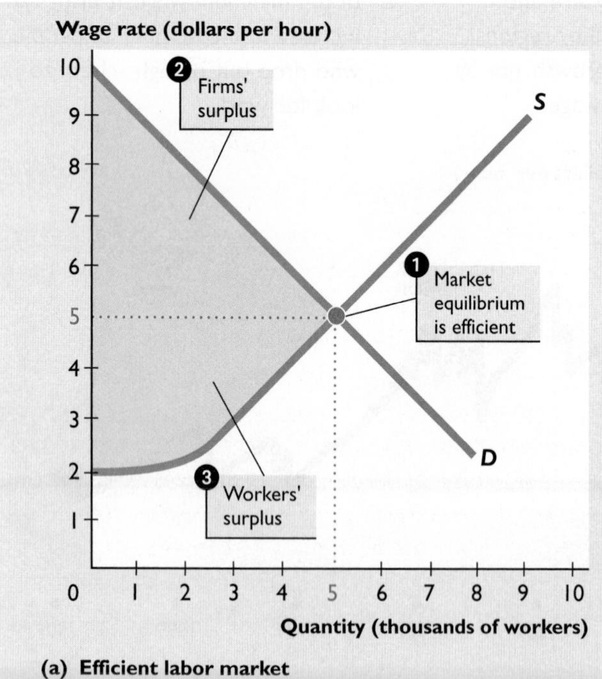


**(a) Efficient labor market**

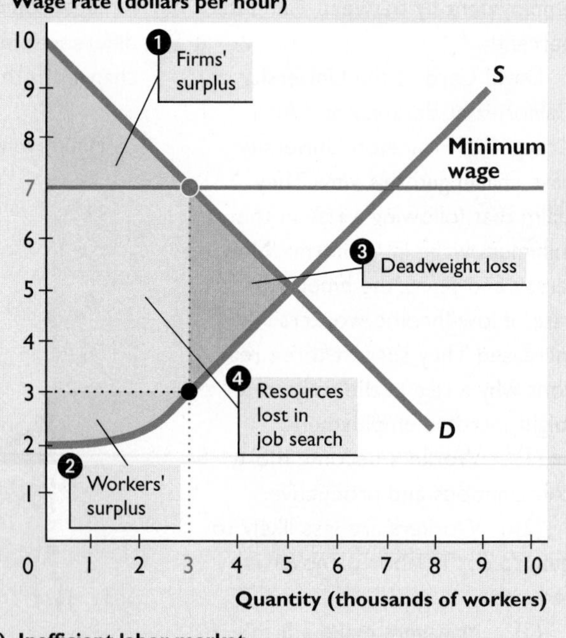


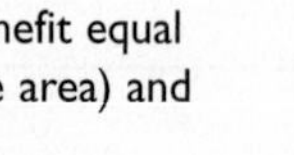

**(b) Inefficient labor market**

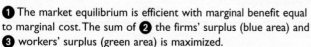

❶ The market equilibrium is efficient with marginal benefit equal to marginal cost. The sum of ❷ the firms' surplus (blue area) and ❸ workers' surplus (green area) is maximized.

A minimum wage is inefficient. ❶ The firms' surplus and ❷ workers' surplus shrink, a ❸ deadweight loss arises, and ❹ resources are lost in job search.

But the total loss exceeds the deadweight loss. Resources get used in costly job-search activity as each unemployed person keeps looking for a job—writing letters, making phone calls, going to interviews, and so on. The value of these resources might be as large as the red rectangle.

## Is the Minimum Wage Fair?

The minimum wage is unfair on both views of fairness: It delivers an unfair *result* and imposes unfair *rules*. The *result* is unfair because only those people who find jobs benefit. The unemployed end up worse off than they would be with no minimum wage. And those who get jobs were probably not the least well off. When the wage rate doesn't allocate jobs, discrimination, another source of unfairness, increases. The minimum wage imposes unfair *rules* because it blocks voluntary exchange. Firms are willing to hire more labor and people are willing to work more, but they are not permitted by the minimum wage law to do so.

## If the Minimum Wage Is So Bad, Why Do We Have It?

Although the minimum wage is inefficient, not everyone loses from it. The people who find jobs at the minimum wage rate are better off. Other supporters of the minimum wage believe that the elasticities of demand and supply in the labor market are low, so not much unemployment results. Labor unions support the minimum wage because it puts upward pressure on all wage rates, including those of union workers. Nonunion labor is a substitute for union labor, so when the minimum wage rises, the demand for union labor increases.

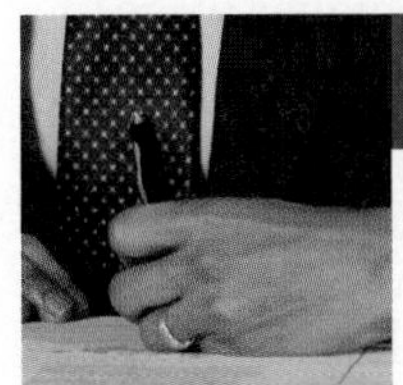

## EYE on PRICE REGULATION

### How Powerful Is the President's Pen?

The President has a powerful pen, but one that holds no magical powers. When the President signs a Bill or an Executive Order to bring in a new law or regulation, the outcome is not always exactly what was intended. A mismatch between intention and outcome is almost inevitable when a law or regulation seeks to block the laws of supply and demand.

You've seen the problems created by the federal minimum wage law, which leaves teenagers without jobs. There would also be problems at the other extreme of the labor market if the law tried to place a cap on executive pay.

In the spring of 2009, the "Cap Executive Officer Pay Act of 2009" was introduced in the Senate. The goal of the Act was to limit the compensation of executives and directors of firms receiving government handouts. The Act defined compensation broadly as all forms of cash receipts, property, and any perks. The cap envisaged was an annual compensation no greater than that of the President of the United States.

This Act never made it to the President's desk for his signature, but you can see some of the problems that would have risen if it had. Setting aside the difficult task of determining the President's compensation (does it include the use of the White House and Air Force One?), placing a cap on executive pay would work like putting a ceiling on home rents that you've studied in this chapter. The quantity of executive services supplied would decrease and the most talented executives would seek jobs with the unregulated employers. The firms in the most difficulty—those receiving government funding—would face the added challenge of recruiting and keeping competent executives and directors. The deadweight loss from this action would be large. It is fortunate that the idea didn't have legs!

Work these problems in Study Plan 7.2 to get instant feedback.

## CHECKPOINT 7.2

**Explain how a price floor works and show how the minimum wage creates unemployment, inefficiency, and unfairness.**

### Practice Problems

Figure 1 shows the market for tomato pickers in southern California. Use this figure to work Problems **1** to **3**.

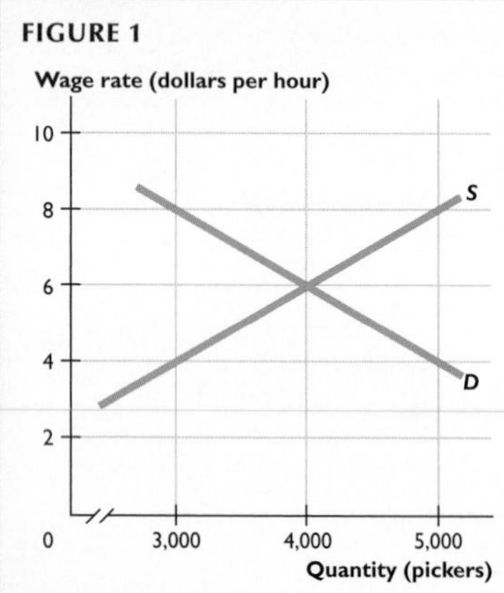


1. What is the equilibrium wage rate and what is the equilibrium quantity of tomato pickers employed? If California introduces a minimum wage of $4 an hour, how many tomato pickers are employed and how many are unemployed?
2. If California introduces a minimum wage of $8 an hour, how many tomato pickers are employed and how many are unemployed? What is the lowest wage that some workers might be able to earn if a black market develops?
3. Is the minimum wage of $8 an hour efficient? Who gains and who loses from the minimum wage of $8 an hour? Is it fair?
4. **India steps up pressure for minimum wage for its workers in the Gulf**
   India is pressuring the oil-rich countries in the [Persian] Gulf to pay minimum wages to the 5 million unskilled Indians working in the Gulf.
   Source: *International Herald Tribune*, March 27, 2008

   If the Persian Gulf countries paid Indian workers a minimum wage above the equilibrium wage paid to other unskilled workers, would migrant Indian workers be better off, worse off, or unaffected by the higher wage?

### Guided Solutions to Practice Problems

1. The equilibrium wage rate is $6 an hour, and 4,000 pickers are employed. The minimum wage of $4 an hour is below the equilibrium wage rate, so 4,000 tomato pickers are employed and no worker is unemployed.
2. The minimum wage of $8 an hour is above the equilibrium wage rate, so 3,000 pickers are employed (determined by the demand for tomato pickers) and 5,000 people would like to work as pickers for $8 an hour (determined by the supply), so 2,000 are unemployed (Figure 2). If a black market developed, the lowest wage that some workers might be able to earn would be $4 an hour (Figure 2).

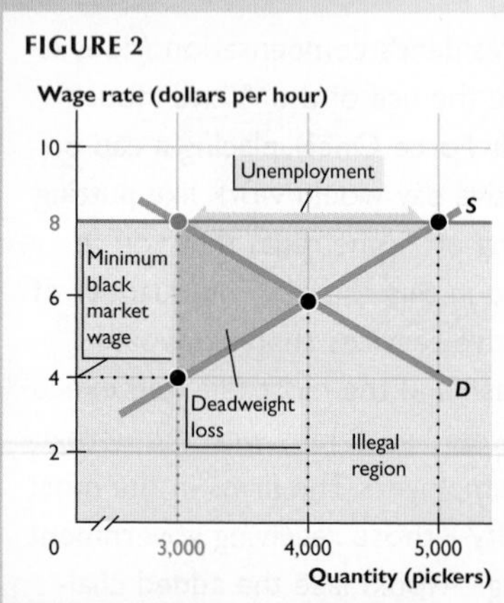


3. The minimum wage of $8 an hour is not efficient because it creates a deadweight loss—the marginal benefit to growers exceeds the marginal cost to workers. Tomato pickers who find work at $8 an hour gain. Tomato growers and unemployed pickers lose. The minimum wage is unfair on both the fair rules and fair results views of fairness.
4. The supply of immigrant workers in the Gulf is perfectly elastic, with workers coming from most South Asian countries. If the wage paid to Indian workers is above the equilibrium wage, the quantity of unskilled Indians employed would decrease. Most Indians would be unemployed and sent back to India. They would then compete to work in India and be worse off.

## 7.3 PRICE SUPPORTS IN AGRICULTURE

"The nation has got to eat," declared President George W. Bush when he asked Congress to spend $170 billion to support U.S. farmers. The United States is not alone among the advanced economies in spending billions of dollars each year on farm support. Governments in all the advanced economies do it, and none more than those of the European Union and Japan.

### How Governments Intervene in Markets for Farm Products

The methods that governments use to support farms vary, but they almost always involve three elements:

- Isolate the domestic market from global competition
- Introduce a price floor
- Pay farmers a subsidy

#### Isolate the Domestic Market

A government can't regulate a market price without first isolating the domestic market from global competition. If the cost of production in the rest of the world is lower than that in the domestic economy and if foreign producers are free to sell in the domestic market, the forces of demand and supply drive the price down and swamp any efforts by the government to influence the price.

To isolate the domestic market, the government restricts imports from the rest of the world.

#### Introduce a Price Floor

A price floor in an agricultural market is called a **price support**, because the floor is maintained by a government guarantee to buy any surplus output at that price. You saw that a price floor in the labor market—a minimum wage—creates a surplus of labor that shows up as unemployment. A price support in an agricultural market also generates a surplus. At the support price, the quantity supplied exceeds the quantity demanded. What happens to the surplus makes the effects of a price support different from those of a minimum wage. The government buys the surplus.

**Price support**
A price floor in an agricultural market maintained by a government guarantee to buy any surplus output at that price.

#### Pay Farmers a Subsidy

A **subsidy** is a payment by the government to a producer to cover part of the cost of production. When the government buys the surplus produced by farmers, it provides them with a subsidy. Without the subsidy, farmers could not cover their costs because they would not be able to sell the surplus.

Let's see how a price support works.

**Subsidy**
A payment by the government to a producer to cover part of the cost of production.

### Price Support: An Illustration

To see the effects of a price support, we'll look at the market for sugar beets. Both the United States and the European Union have price supports for sugar beets.

Figure 7.9 shows the market. This market is isolated from rest-of-world influences. The demand curve, *D*, tells us the quantities demanded at each price in the domestic economy only. And the supply curve, *S*, tells us the quantity supplied at each price by domestic farmers.

### Free Market Reference Point

With no price support, the equilibrium price is $25 a ton and the equilibrium quantity is 25 million tons a year. The market is efficient only if the price in the rest of the world is also $25 a ton. If the price in the rest of the world is less than $25 a ton, it is efficient for the domestic farmers to produce less and for some sugar beets to be imported at the lower price (lower opportunity cost) available in the rest of the world. But if the price in the rest of the world exceeds $25 a ton, it is efficient for domestic farmers to increase production and export some sugar beets.

### Price Support and Subsidy

Suppose the government introduces a price support at $35 a ton. To make the price support work, the government agrees to pay farmers $35 for every ton of sugar beets they produce and can't sell in the market.

The farmers produce the quantity shown by the market supply curve. At a price of $35 a ton, the quantity supplied is 30 million tons a year, so production increases to this amount.

Domestic users of sugar beets cut back their purchases. At $35 a ton, the quantity demanded is 20 million tons a year, and purchases decrease to this amount.

Because farmers produce a greater quantity than domestic users are willing to buy, something must be done with the surplus. If the farmers just dumped the surplus on the market, you can see what would happen. The price would fall to that at which consumers are willing to pay for the quantity produced.

To make the price support work, the government buys the surplus. In this example, the government buys 10 million tons for $35 a ton and provides a subsidy to the farmers of $350 million.

**FIGURE 7.9**

The Domestic Market for Sugar Beets

myeconlab Animation

The market for sugar beets is isolated from global competition.

1. With no intervention, the competitive equilibrium price is $25 a ton and the equilibrium quantity is 25 million tons a year.
2. The government intervenes in this market and sets a support price at $35 a ton.
3. The quantity produced increases to 30 million tons a year.
4. The quantity bought by domestic users decreases to 20 million tons a year.
5. The government buys the surplus of 10 million tons a year and pays the farmers a subsidy.
6. A deadweight loss arises.

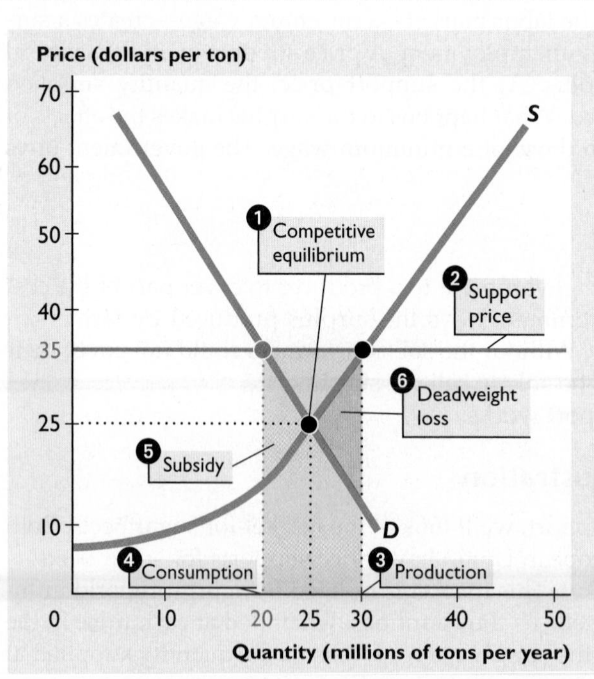

The price support increases farmers' total revenue. Without a subsidy, farmers would receive a total revenue of $625 million ($25 a ton multiplied by 25 million tons). With a subsidy, they receive a total revenue of $1,050 million ($35 a ton multiplied by 30 million tons).

The price support is inefficient because it creates a deadweight loss. Marginal cost exceeds marginal benefit. Farmers gain but buyers, who are also the taxpayers who end up paying the subsidy, lose. And buyers' losses exceed the farmers' gains by the amount of the deadweight loss.

### Effects on the Rest of the World

The rest of the world receives a double-whammy from price supports. First, import restrictions in advanced economies deny developing economies access to the food markets of the advanced economies. The result is lower prices and smaller farm production in the developing economies.

Second, the surplus produced in the advanced economies gets sold in the rest of the world. Both the price and the quantity produced in the rest of the world are depressed even further.

The subsidies received by U.S. farmers are paid not only by U.S. taxpayers and consumers but also by poor farmers in the developing economies.

We explore global markets in action in Chapter 9. There you will see other ways in which intervention in markets brings inefficiencies and redistributes the gains from trade.

## EYE on YOUR LIFE

### Price Ceilings and Price Floors

Price ceilings and price floors operate in many of the markets in which you trade, and they require you to take a stand as a citizen and voter.

Unless you live in New York City, you're not likely to live in a rent controlled house or apartment. Because economists have explained the unwanted effects of rent ceilings that you've learned about in this chapter, this type of market intervention is now rare.

But you run into a price ceiling almost every time you use a freeway. The zero price for using a freeway is a type of price ceiling. The next time you're stuck in traffic and moving at a crawl, think about how a free market in road use would cut the congestion and allow you to zip along.

In Singapore, a transponder on your dashboard would be clocking up the dollars and cents as you drive around the city. The price varies with the time of day, the traffic density, and where in the city you are. As a result, you would never be stuck in slow-moving traffic.

You encounter a price floor in the labor market. Have you wanted a job and been willing and available to work, but unable to get hired? Would you have taken a job for a slightly lower wage if one had been available?

You also encounter price floors (price supports) in markets for food. You pay more for tomatoes, sugar, oranges, and many other food items than the minimum cost of producing them.

Develop your own policy position on price floors and price ceilings.

Work these problems in Study Plan 7.3 to get instant feedback.

## CHECKPOINT 7.3

**Explain how a price support in the market for an agricultural product creates a surplus, inefficiency, and unfairness.**

### Practice Problems

Figure 1 shows the market for tomatoes. The government introduces a price support for tomatoes at $8 per pound. Use this figure to work Problems **1** to **3**.

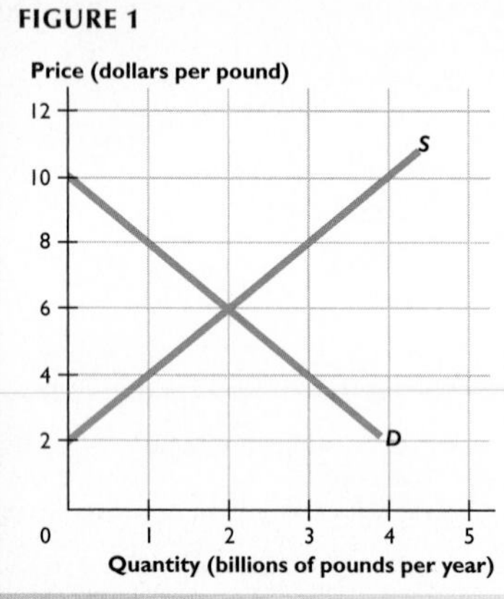


1. Before the price support is introduced, what are the equilibrium price and quantity of tomatoes? Is the market for tomatoes efficient?
2. After the government introduces a price support, what is the quantity of tomatoes produced, the quantity demanded, and the subsidy received by tomato farmers?
3. With the price support, is the market for tomatoes efficient? Who gains and who loses from the price support and what is the deadweight loss? Could the price support be regarded as being fair?
4. **French farmers man the blockades in Brussels**

   Farmers want the dairy industry to guarantee a minimum milk price of 300 euros a ton—against 210 euros a ton this month. Max Bottier, a dairy farmer in Normandy, said that he needs 300 euros a ton to break even.

   Source: *The Times*, May 26, 2009

   If a support price for milk is introduced and set at 300 euros a ton, how will such a support price change the quantity of milk produced, the quantity bought by consumers, and who buys the excess supply? Will the European milk market be more or less efficient than it is today?

### Guided Solutions to Practice Problems

1. The equilibrium price is $6 a pound, and the equilibrium quantity is 2 billion pounds a year. The market for tomatoes is efficient—marginal benefit equals marginal cost.
2. At a support price of $8 a pound, 3 billion pounds are produced and 1 billion pounds are demanded, so there is a surplus of 2 billion pounds (Figure 2). The subsidy is $8 per pound on 2 billion pounds, which is $16 billion.

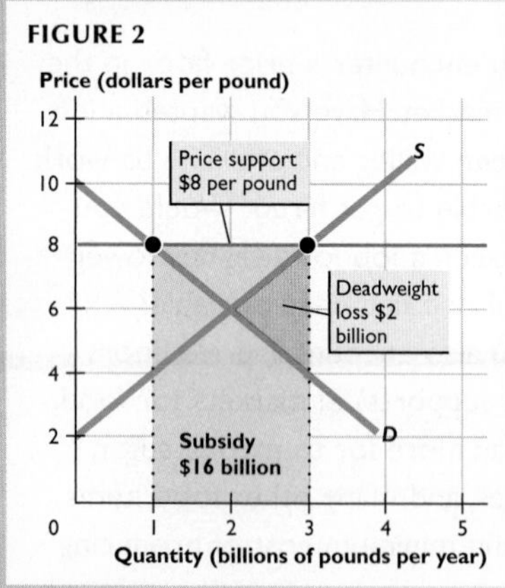


3. The market is not efficient because at the quantity produced, the marginal benefit (on the demand curve) is less than the marginal cost (on the supply curve). Farmers gain. They produce more and receive a higher price on what they sell in the market and the government subsidy. Consumers/taxpayers lose. They pay more for tomatoes and pay taxes to fund the subsidy. The deadweight loss is $2 billion (the area of the gray triangle). The outcome is unfair on both views of fairness unless farmers are poorer than the consumers, in which case it might be fair to boost farmers' incomes.
4. The market price today is 210 euros a ton. A support price of 300 euros a ton will increase the quantity of milk supplied and decrease the quantity of milk demanded. There will be a surplus of milk. To maintain the support price at 300 euros a ton, the government will have to buy the surplus of milk—that is, pay farmers a subsidy. The market will be less efficient because it creates a deadweight loss.

# CHAPTER SUMMARY

## Key Points

1 **Explain how a price ceiling works and show how a rent ceiling creates a housing shortage, inefficiency, and unfairness.**

- A price ceiling set above the equilibrium price has no effects.
- A price ceiling set below the equilibrium price creates a shortage and increased search activity or a black market.
- A price ceiling is inefficient and unfair.
- A rent ceiling is an example of a price ceiling.

2 **Explain how a price floor works and show how the minimum wage creates unemployment, inefficiency, and unfairness.**

- A price floor set below the equilibrium price has no effects.
- A price floor set above the equilibrium price creates a surplus and increased search activity or illegal trading.
- A price floor is inefficient and unfair.
- A minimum wage is an example of a price floor.

3 **Explain how a price support in the market for an agricultural product creates a surplus, inefficiency, and unfairness.**

- A price support increases the quantity produced, decreases the quantity consumed, and creates a surplus.
- To maintain the support price, the government buys the surplus and subsidizes the producer.
- A price support benefits the producer but costs the consumer/taxpayer more than the producer gains—it creates a deadweight loss.
- A price support is inefficient and is usually unfair.

## Key Terms

Black market, 171
Minimum wage law, 177
Price cap, 170
Price ceiling, 170
Price floor, 176
Price support, 183
Rent ceiling, 170
Search activity, 172
Subsidy, 183

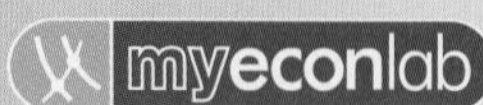

Work these problems in Chapter 7 Study Plan to get instant feedback.

# CHAPTER CHECKPOINT

## Study Plan Problems and Applications

**TABLE 1**

| Rent (dollars per month) | Quantity demanded (rooms) | Quantity supplied (rooms) |
|---|---|---|
| 500 | 2,500 | 2,000 |
| 550 | 2,250 | 2,000 |
| 600 | 2,000 | 2,000 |
| 650 | 1,750 | 2,000 |
| 700 | 1,500 | 2,000 |
| 750 | 1,250 | 2,000 |

Table 1 shows the demand and supply schedules for on-campus housing. Use Table 1 to work Problems **1** to **3**.

1. If the college puts a rent ceiling on rooms of $650 a month, what is the rent, how many rooms are rented, and is the on-campus housing market efficient?
2. If the college puts a strictly enforced rent ceiling on rooms of $550 a month, what is the rent, how many rooms are rented, and is the on-campus housing market efficient? Explain why or why not.
3. Suppose that with a strictly enforced rent ceiling on rooms of $550 a month, a black market develops. How high could the black market rent be and would the on-campus housing market be fair? Explain your answer.
4. Suppose the government introduced a ceiling on lawyers' fees. How would the amount of work done by lawyers, the consumer surplus of people who hire lawyers, and the producer surplus of law firms change? Would this fee ceiling result in an efficient use of resources? Why or why not?

**TABLE 2**

| Wage rate (dollars per hour) | Quantity demanded (student workers) | Quantity supplied (student workers) |
|---|---|---|
| 10.00 | 600 | 300 |
| 10.50 | 500 | 350 |
| 11.00 | 400 | 400 |
| 11.50 | 300 | 450 |
| 12.00 | 200 | 500 |
| 12.50 | 100 | 550 |

Use the following information to work Problems **5** to **7**.

Table 2 shows the demand and supply schedules for student workers at on-campus venues.

5. If the college introduces a minimum wage of $10.50 an hour, how many students are employed at on-campus venues and how many are unemployed?
6. If the college introduces a strictly enforced minimum wage of $11.50 an hour, how many students are employed, how many are unemployed, and what is the lowest wage at which some students would be willing to work?
7. If the college introduces a strictly enforced minimum wage of $11.50 an hour, who gains and who loses from the minimum wage, and is the campus labor market efficient or fair?

Use the following information to work Problems **8** and **9**.

**Coal shortage at China plants**

The government of China has set price controls on coal and gasoline in an attempt to shield poor urban families and farmers from rising world energy prices. Chinese power plants have run short of coal, sales of luxury, gas-guzzling cars have increased, and gasoline consumption has risen. Oil refiners are incurring losses and plan to cut production.

Source: CNN, May 20, 2008

8. Are China's price controls price floors or price ceilings? Draw a graph to illustrate the shortages created by the price controls in the markets for coal and gasoline.
9. Explain how China's price controls have changed consumer surplus, producer surplus, total surplus, and the deadweight loss in the markets for coal and gasoline. Draw a graph to illustrate your answer.

## Instructor Assignable Problems and Applications

Your instructor can assign these problems as homework, a quiz, or a test in **MyEconLab**.

1. Suppose that Congress caps executive pay at a level below the equilibrium.
   - Explain how the quantity of executives demanded, the quantity supplied, and executive pay will change, and explain why the outcome is inefficient.
   - Draw a graph of the market for corporate executives. On your graph, show the market equilibrium, the pay cap, the quantity of executives supplied and the quantity demanded at the pay cap, and the deadweight loss created. Also show the highest pay that an executive might be offered in a black market.

Use the following information to work Problems 2 and 4.

Concerned about the political fallout from rising gas prices, suppose that the U.S. government imposes a price ceiling of $3.00 a gallon on gasoline.

2. Explain how the market for gasoline would react to this price ceiling if the oil-producing nations increased production and drove the equilibrium price of gasoline to $2.50 a gallon. Would the U.S. gasoline market be efficient?
3. Explain how the market for gasoline would react to this price ceiling if a global shortage of oil sent the equilibrium price of gasoline to $3.50 a gallon. Would the U.S. gasoline market be efficient?
4. Under what conditions would the price ceiling create lines at the pumps?

Use the following information to work Problems 5 and 6.

**Australian unions lobbying for $21 wage rise for lowest paid**

Australia's Fair Trade Commission (FTC) sets the minimum wage for the year. In 2008, the minimum wage was set at $544 a week. In the current negotiations, unions are lobbying for $21 a week rise and businesses for $8 a week rise.

Source: Bloomberg, March 23, 2009

Suppose that in 2009 the equilibrium wage turns out to be $560 a week.

5. If the FTC raises the minimum wage by $8 a week, what wage per week will low-skilled workers be paid? Will the outcome be efficient?
6. If the FTC raises the minimum wage by $21 a week, what wage per week will low-skilled workers be paid? Will the outcome be efficient?
7. "Market prices might be fine in a rich country, but in a poor African nation where there are shortages of most items, without government control of prices everything would be too expensive." Do you agree or disagree with this statement? Use the concepts of efficiency and fairness to explain why.

Table 1 shows the demand and supply schedules for mushrooms. Use Table 1 to work Problems 8 and 9.

8. Suppose that the government introduces a price support for mushrooms of $4 per pound. What are the quantity of mushrooms produced, the surplus of mushrooms, and the deadweight loss created?
9. Suppose that the government introduces a price support for mushrooms of $6 per pound. Who gains and who loses? What are the quantity of mushrooms produced, the surplus of mushrooms, and the deadweight loss?

**TABLE 1**

| Price (dollars per pound) | Quantity demanded | Quantity supplied |
|---|---|---|
| | (pounds per week) | |
| 1.00 | 5,000 | 2,000 |
| 2.00 | 4,500 | 2,500 |
| 3.00 | 4,000 | 3,000 |
| 4.00 | 3,500 | 3,500 |
| 5.00 | 3,000 | 4,000 |
| 6.00 | 2,500 | 4,500 |

10. **Congress passes increase in the minimum wage**
    Congress voted to raise the minimum wage to $7.25 an hour from $5.15 in three stages over a two-year period. For about 4 percent of workers, or 5.6 million low-income workers, it was a major victory—the first increase in the federal minimum wage rate in a decade.

    Source: *The New York Times*, May 24, 2007

    Explain how the market for low-income workers will respond to the new minimum wage. Did Congress hand these workers a major victory?

Use the following information to work Problems 11 and 12.

**House passes farm bill**

The farm bill was hailed by Ms. Pelosi as "historic." The bill reduces subsidy payments, but supports growers of specialty crops: certain types of fruit and vegetable.

Source: *The New York Times*, July 28, 2007

11. Suppose that the subsidy and price support are switched from soybean farmers to growers of organic vegetables. How will the quantity of soybeans produced, the producer surplus from soybeans, and the deadweight loss from soybeans change?
12. Suppose that the subsidy and price support are switched from soybean farmers to growers of organic vegetables. How will the quantity of organic vegetables produced, the price of organic vegetables, and efficiency of the organic vegetable market change?

Use the following information to work Problems 13 to 16.

**Despite pleas for a freeze, stabilized rents to go up**

New York's Rent Guidelines Board ignored pleas from tenants and elected officials to freeze rents for the first time in its 40-year history and voted for increases of 3% on one-year leases and 6% on two-year leases. In 2008, the board approved its highest increases since 1989, 4.5% on one-year leases and 8.5% on two-year leases. Costs for rent-stabilized buildings increased 4% from April 2008 to April 2009, much lower than the 7.8% increase the year before.

Source: *The New York Times*, June 23, 2009

13. If rents for rent-stabilized apartments are frozen, how do you think the market for rental units in New York City will develop?
14. Are rent ceilings in New York City helpful to renters? Explain why or why not?
15. What effect will the increase in the rent ceiling have on the quantity of rent-stabilized apartments?
16. Why is rent stabilization a source of conflict between renters and owners of apartments?

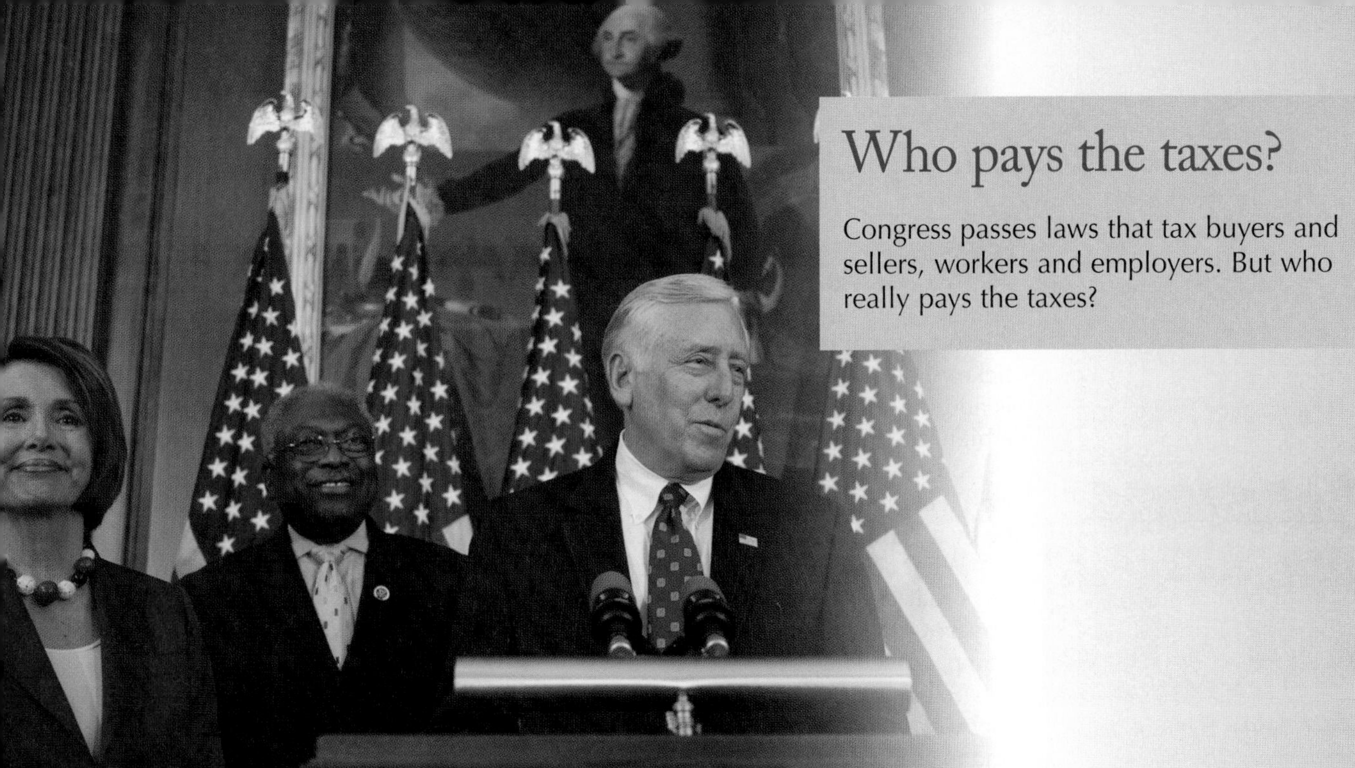

## Who pays the taxes?

Congress passes laws that tax buyers and sellers, workers and employers. But who really pays the taxes?

# Taxes

CHAPTER CHECKLIST

**When you have completed your study of this chapter, you will be able to**

1 Explain how taxes change prices and quantities, are shared by buyers and sellers, and create inefficiency.

2 Explain how income taxes and Social Security taxes change wage rates and employment, are shared by employers and workers, and create inefficiency.

3 Review ideas about the fairness of the tax system.

## 8.1 TAXES ON BUYERS AND SELLERS

Almost every time you buy something—a late-night order of chow mein, a plane ticket, a tank of gasoline—you pay a tax. On some items, you pay a sales tax that is added to the advertised price. On other items, you pay an excise tax—often at a high rate like the tax on gasoline—that is included in the advertised price.

Does "We Pay The Tax" really mean that the store pays the tax?

But do you really pay these taxes? When a tax is added to the advertised price, isn't it obvious that *you* pay the tax? Isn't the price higher than it otherwise would be by an amount equal to the tax?

What about a tax that is buried in the price, such as that on gasoline? Who pays that tax? Does the seller just pass on the full amount of the tax to you, the buyer? Or does the seller pay the tax by taking a lower price and leaving the price you pay unchanged?

To answer these questions, let's suppose that TIFS, the Tax Illegal File Sharing lobby, has persuaded the government to collect a $10 tax on every new MP3 player and to use the tax revenue to compensate artists. But an argument is raging between those who claim that the buyer benefits from using the MP3 player and should pay the tax and those who claim that the seller profits and should pay the tax.

### Tax Incidence

**Tax incidence**
The division of the burden of a tax between the buyer and the seller.

**Tax incidence** is the division of the burden of a tax between the buyer and the seller. We're going to find the incidence of a $10 tax on MP3 players with two different taxes: a tax on the buyer and a tax on the seller.

Figure 8.1 shows the market for MP3 players. With no tax, the equilibrium price is $100 and the equilibrium quantity is 5,000 players a week.

When a good is taxed, it has two prices: a price that excludes the tax and a price that includes the tax. Buyers respond only to the price that includes the tax, because that is the price they pay. Sellers respond only to the price that excludes the tax, because that is the price they receive. The tax is like a wedge between these two prices.

Figure 8.1(a) shows what happens if the government taxes the buyer. The tax doesn't change the buyer's willingness and ability to pay. The demand curve, *D*, tells us the *total* amount that buyers are willing and able to pay. Because buyers must pay $10 to the government on each item bought, the red curve *D* − *tax* tells us what the buyers are willing to pay to the sellers. The red curve, *D* − *tax*, lies $10 below the blue demand curve.

Market equilibrium occurs where the red *D* − *tax* curve intersects the supply curve, *S*. The buyer pays the equilibrium net-of-tax price $95 plus the $10 tax: $105. The seller receives the net-of-tax price $95. The government collects a tax revenue of $10 a player on 2,000 players, or $20,000 (shown by the purple rectangle).

Figure 8.1(b) shows what happens if the government taxes the seller. The tax acts like an increase in the suppliers' cost, so supply decreases and the supply curve shifts to the red curve labeled *S* + *tax*. This curve tells us what sellers are willing to accept, given that they must pay the government $10 on each item sold. The red curve, *S* + *tax*, lies $10 above the blue supply curve.

Market equilibrium occurs where the red *S* + *tax* curve intersects the demand curve, *D*. The buyer pays the equilibrium price $105. The seller receives the net-of-tax price $95. The government collects a tax revenue of $20,000.

In both cases, the buyer and the seller split the $10 tax and pay $5 each.

**FIGURE 8.1**

A Tax on MP3 Players

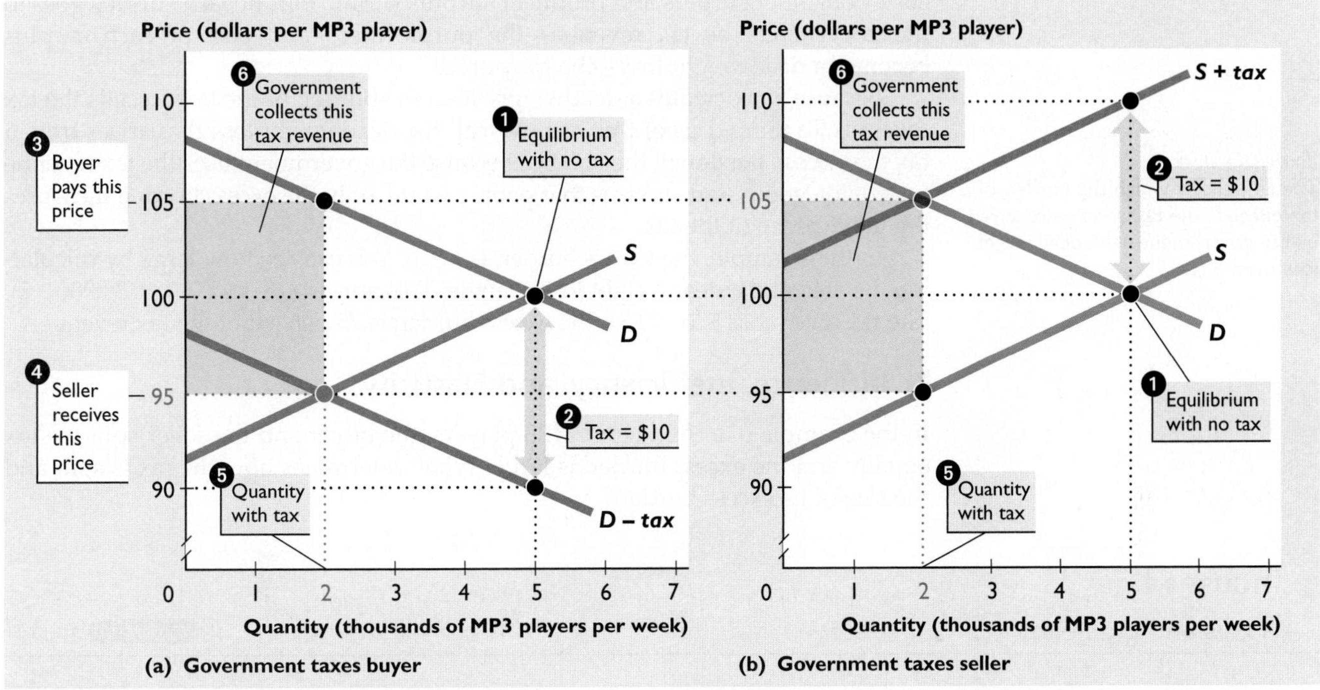


(a) Government taxes buyer

(b) Government taxes seller

1. In both part of the figure, with no tax, the price of an MP3 player is $100 and 5,000 players a week are bought.
2. In part (a), a $10 tax on buyers of MP3 players shifts the demand curve down to *D* − *tax*, and in part (b), a $10 tax on sellers of MP3 players shifts the supply curve up to *S* + *tax*.

In both parts of the figure:

3. The price paid by the buyer rises to $105—an increase of $5;
4. The price received by the seller falls to $95—a decrease of $5;
5. The quantity decreases to 2,000 players a week; and
6. The government collects tax revenue of $20,000 a week—the purple rectangle.

In both cases, the burden of the tax is split equally between the buyer and the seller—each pays $5 per player.

You can now see that the argument about making the buyer pay or the seller pay is futile. The buyer pays the same price, the seller receives the same price, and the government receives the same tax revenue on the same quantity regardless of whether the government taxes the buyer or the seller.

In this example, the buyer and the seller share the burden of the tax equally. But in most cases, the burden will be shared unequally and might even fall entirely on one side of the market. We'll explore what determines the incidence of a tax, but first, let's see how a tax creates inefficiency.

## Taxes and Efficiency

You've seen that resources are used efficiently when marginal benefit equals marginal cost. You've also seen that a tax places a wedge between the price the buyer pays and the price the seller receives. But the buyer's price equals marginal benefit and the seller's price equals marginal cost. So a tax puts a wedge between marginal benefit and marginal cost. The equilibrium quantity is less than the efficient quantity, and a deadweight loss arises.

Figure 8.2 shows the inefficiency of a tax. We'll assume that the government taxes the seller. In part (a), with no tax, marginal benefit equals marginal cost and the market is efficient. In part (b), with a tax, marginal benefit exceeds marginal cost. Consumer surplus and producer surplus shrink. Part of each surplus goes to the government as tax revenue—the purple area—and part of each surplus becomes a deadweight loss—the gray area.

Because a tax creates a deadweight loss, the burden of the tax exceeds the tax revenue. To remind us of this fact, we call the deadweight loss that arises from a tax the **excess burden** of the tax. But because the government uses the tax revenue to provide goods and services that people value, only the excess burden measures the inefficiency of the tax.

**Excess burden**
The amount by which the burden of a tax exceeds the tax revenue received by the government—the deadweight loss from a tax.

In this example, the excess burden is large. You can see how large by calculating the area of the deadweight loss triangle. This area is $15,000 ($10 × 3,000 ÷ 2). The tax revenue is $20,000, so the excess burden is 75 percent of the tax revenue.

## Incidence, Inefficiency, and Elasticity

In the example of a $10 tax on MP3 players, the buyer and the seller split the tax equally and the excess burden is large. What determines how the tax is split and the size of its excess burden?

**FIGURE 8.2**

Taxes and Efficiency

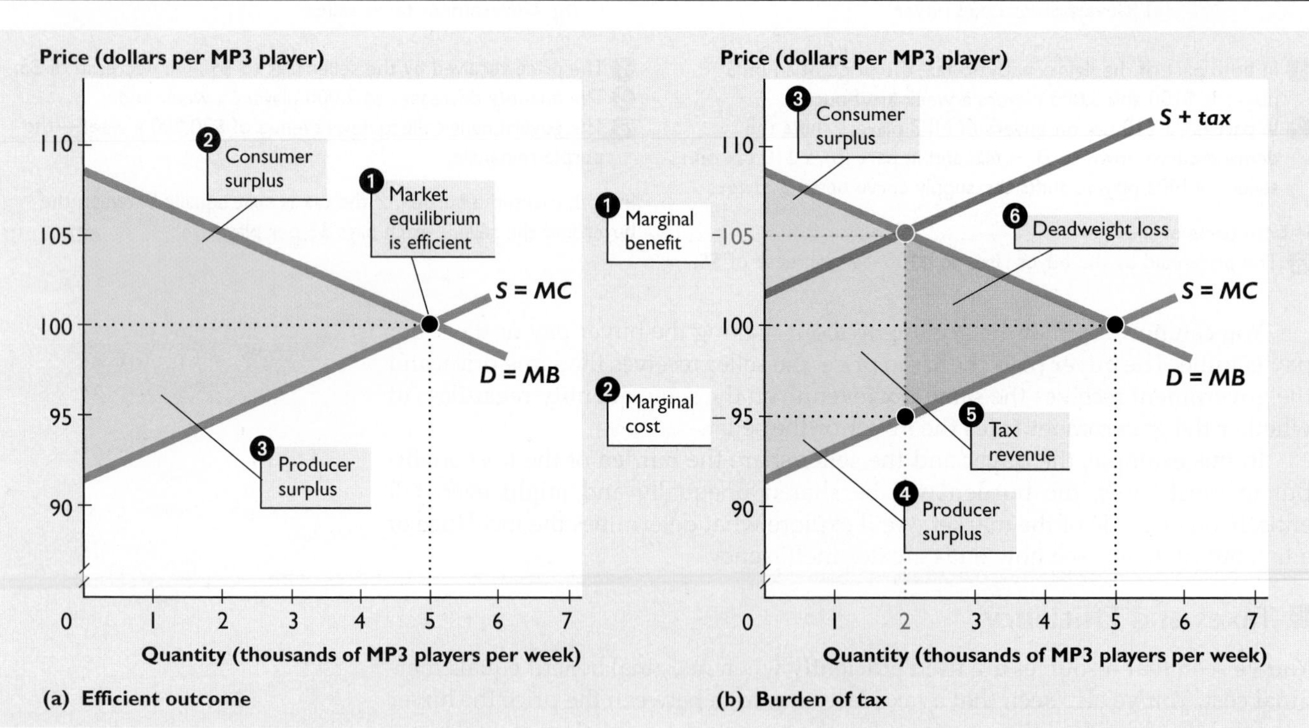


① The market is efficient with marginal benefit equal to marginal cost. Total surplus—the sum of ② consumer surplus (green area) and ③ producer surplus (blue area)—is at its maximum possible level.

A $10 tax drives a wedge between ① marginal benefit and ② marginal cost. ③ Consumer surplus and ④ producer surplus shrink by the amount of the ⑤ tax revenue plus the ⑥ deadweight loss. The deadweight loss is the excess burden of the tax.

The incidence of a tax and its excess burden depend on the elasticities of demand and supply in the following ways:

- For a given elasticity of supply, the more inelastic the demand for the good, the larger is the share of the tax paid by the buyer.
- For a given elasticity of demand, the more inelastic is the supply of the good, the larger is the share of the tax paid by the seller.
- The excess burden is smaller, the more inelastic is demand *or* supply.

## Incidence, Inefficiency, and the Elasticity of Demand

To see how the division of a tax between the buyer and the seller and the size of the excess burden depend on the elasticity of demand, we'll look at two extremes.

### Perfectly Inelastic Demand: Buyer Pays and Efficient

Figure 8.3(a) shows the market for insulin, a vital daily medication of diabetics. Demand is perfectly inelastic at 100,000 doses a week, as shown by the vertical demand curve. With no tax, the price is $2 a dose. A 20¢ a dose tax raises the price to $2.20, but the quantity does not change. The tax leaves the price received by the seller unchanged but raises the price paid by the buyer by the entire tax. The outcome is efficient (there is no deadweight loss) because marginal benefit equals marginal cost.

### Perfectly Elastic Demand: Seller Pays and Inefficient

Figure 8.3(b) shows the market for pink marker pens. Demand is perfectly elastic at $1 a pen, as shown by the horizontal demand curve. If pink pens are less expensive than other pens, everyone uses pink. If pink pens are more expensive than other pens, no one uses a pink pen. With no tax, the price of a pink pen is $1 and the quantity is 4,000 pens a week. A 10¢ a pen tax leaves the price at $1 a pen, but

**FIGURE 8.3**

Incidence, Inefficiency, and the Elasticity of Demand

myeconlab Animation

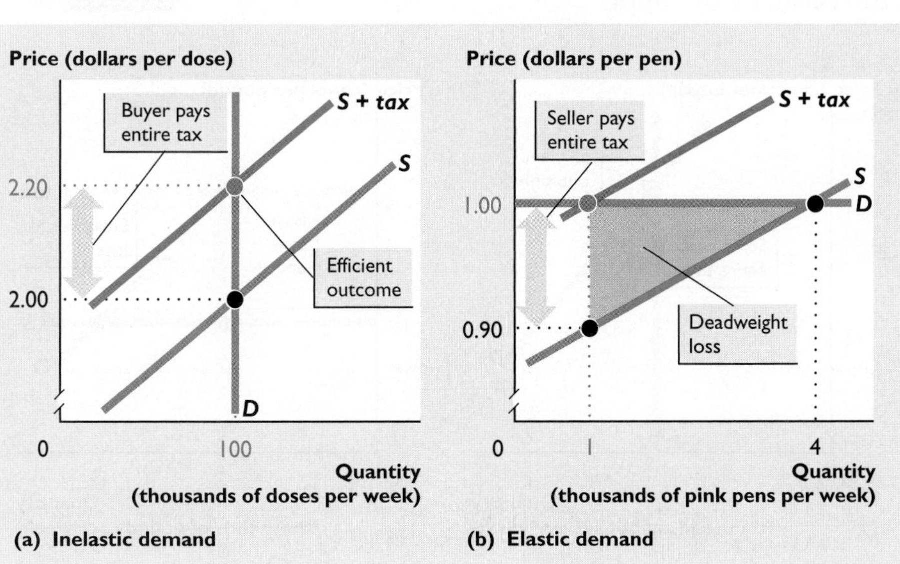


In part (a), the demand for insulin is perfectly inelastic. A tax of 20¢ a dose raises the price by 20¢, and the buyer pays all the tax. But marginal benefit still equals marginal cost, so the outcome is efficient.

In part (b), the demand for pink marker pens is perfectly elastic. A tax of 10¢ a pen lowers the price received by the seller by 10¢, and the seller pays all the tax. Marginal benefit exceeds marginal cost, so the outcome is inefficient. The deadweight loss is the excess burden of the tax and measures its inefficiency.

the quantity decreases to 1,000 a week. The price paid by the buyer is unchanged and the seller pays the entire tax. The outcome is inefficient because marginal benefit exceeds marginal cost and a deadweight loss arises.

## Incidence, Inefficiency, and the Elasticity of Supply

To see how the division of a tax between the buyer and the seller depends on the elasticity of supply, we'll again look at two extremes.

### Perfectly Inelastic Supply: Seller Pays and Efficient

Figure 8.4(a) shows the market for spring water that flows at a constant rate that can't be controlled. Supply is perfectly inelastic at 100,000 bottles a week, as shown by the vertical supply curve. With no tax, the price is 50¢ a bottle and the 100,000 bottles that flow from the spring are bought. A tax of 5¢ a bottle leaves the quantity unchanged at 100,000 bottles a week. Buyers are willing to buy 100,000 bottles a week only if the price is 50¢ a bottle. The price remains at 50¢ a bottle, but the tax lowers the price received by the seller by 5¢ a bottle. The seller pays the entire tax.

Because marginal benefit equals marginal cost, there is no deadweight loss and the outcome is efficient.

### Perfectly Elastic Supply: Buyer Pays and Inefficient

Figure 8.4(b) shows the market for sand from which computer-chip makers extract silicon. Supply of this sand is perfectly elastic at a price of 10¢ a pound as shown by the horizontal supply curve. With no tax, the price is 10¢ a pound and 5,000 pounds a week are bought. A 1¢ a pound sand tax raises the price to 11¢, and the quantity decreases to 3,000 pounds a week. The buyer pays the entire tax.

Because marginal benefit exceeds marginal cost, a deadweight loss arises and the outcome is inefficient.

**FIGURE 8.4**

Incidence, Inefficiency, and the Elasticity of Supply

myeconlab Animation

In part (a), the supply of bottled spring water is perfectly inelastic. A tax of 5¢ a bottle lowers the price received by the seller by 5¢ a bottle, and the seller pays all the tax. Marginal benefit equals marginal cost, so the outcome is efficient.

In part (b), the supply of sand is perfectly elastic. A tax of 1¢ a pound increases the price by 1¢ a pound, and the buyer pays all the tax. Marginal benefit exceeds marginal cost, so the outcome is inefficient. The deadweight loss is the excess burden of the tax and measures its inefficiency.

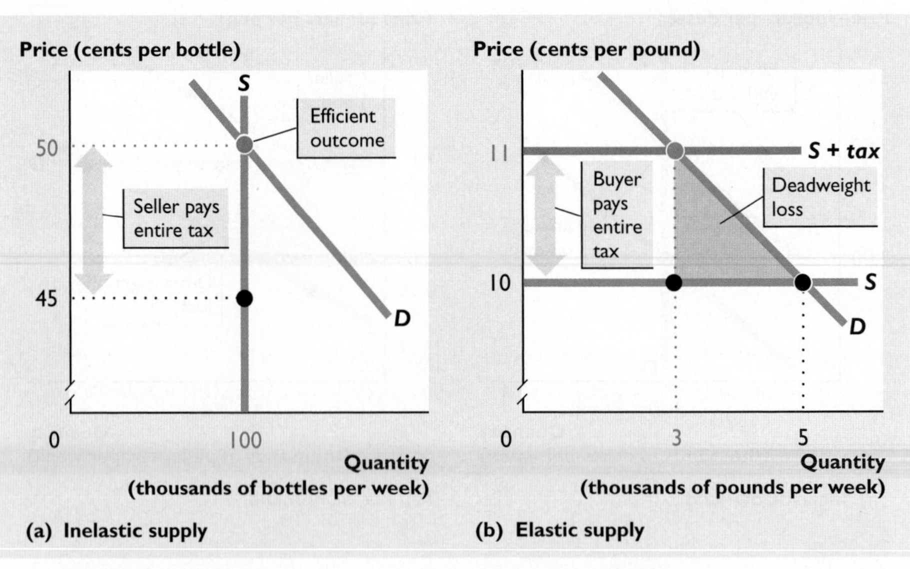

# CHECKPOINT 8.1

Work these problems in Study Plan 8.1 to get instant feedback.

**Explain how taxes change prices and quantities, are shared by buyers and sellers, and create inefficiency.**

## Practice Problems

Figure 1 shows the market for basketballs in which basketballs are not taxed. Now basketballs are taxed at $6 a ball. Use this information to work Problems **1** to **3**.

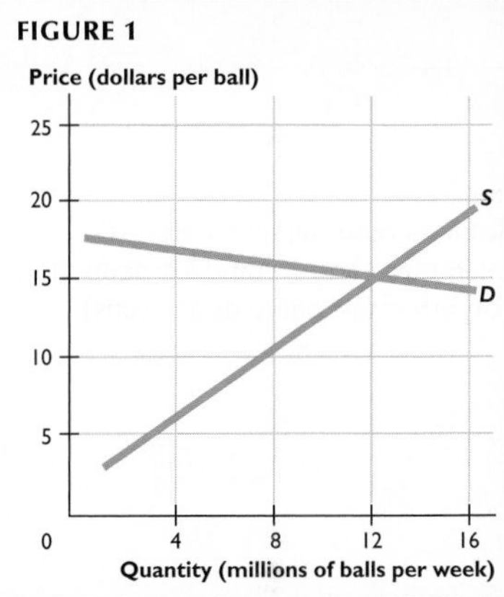

**FIGURE 1**

1. If buyers are taxed, what price does the buyer pay and how many basketballs are bought? What is the tax revenue from the sale of basketballs?
2. If sellers are taxed, what price does the seller receive and how many basketballs are sold? What is the tax revenue from the sale of basketballs?
3. What is the excess burden of the tax on basketballs? Which is more inelastic: the demand for basketballs or the supply of basketballs? Explain.
4. **Biggest U.S. tax hike on tobacco takes effect**
   The federal government has raised the tax on cigarettes from 39¢ to $1.01 a pack—an increase of 62¢. Before the tax hike, cigarettes were $5 a pack. Analysts say that in the past a price increase of 10 percent cut cigarette consumption by 4 percent. With this new tax, at least 1 million of the 45 million smokers are expected to quit.

   Source: *USA Today*, April 3, 2009

   Is the demand for cigarettes elastic or inelastic? Will the price rise to $5.62 a pack? Who pays most of the tax increase—smokers or tobacco companies?

## Guided Solutions to Practice Problems

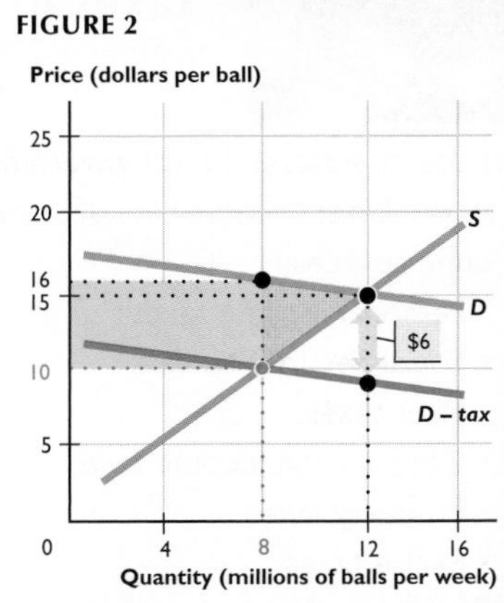

**FIGURE 2**

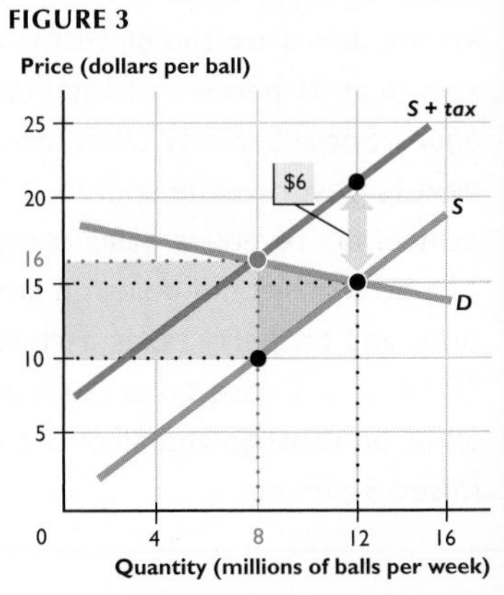

**FIGURE 3**

1. With a $6 tax on buyers, the demand curve shifts downward by $6 a ball as shown in Figure 2. The price that the buyer pays is $16 a basketball and 8 million basketballs a week are bought. The tax revenue is $6 × 8 million, which is $48 million a week (the purple rectangle in Figure 2).
2. With a $6 tax on sellers, the supply curve shifts upward by $6 a ball as shown in Figure 3. The price that the seller receives is $10 a basketball and 8 million basketballs a week are sold (Figure 3). The tax revenue is $6 × 8 million, which is $48 million a week (the purple rectangle in Figure 3).
3. The excess burden of the tax is $12 million. Excess burden equals the deadweight loss, the gray triangle in either Figure 2 or Figure 3, which is 4 million balls × $6 a ball ÷ 2. The $6 tax increases the price paid by buyers by $1 and lowers the price received by sellers by $5. Because the seller pays the larger share of the tax, the supply of basketballs is more inelastic than the demand for basketballs.
4. If a 10 percent price increase decreases consumption by 4 percent, the price elasticity of demand for cigarettes is 4/10, or 0.4. The demand for cigarettes is inelastic. With the demand for cigarettes inelastic, the 62¢ tax increase will not increase the price to $5.62. The price would rise to $5.62 only if the demand were perfectly inelastic. The tax will be shared between buyers and sellers. Because demand is inelastic, buyers (smokers) will pay more of the 62¢ tax than the sellers (tobacco companies).

## 8.2 INCOME TAX AND SOCIAL SECURITY TAX

Income taxes are paid on personal incomes and corporate profits. In 2009, personal income taxes raised $1.25 trillion for the federal government and another $300 billion for state and local governments. Corporation income taxes raised $300 billion for the federal government and $50 billion for the state governments. We'll look first at the effects of personal income taxes, then at corporation income taxes, and finally at Social Security taxes.

### The Personal Income Tax

**Taxable income**
Total income minus a personal exemption and a standard deduction (or other allowable deductions).

The amount of income tax that a person pays depends on her or his **taxable income**, which equals total income minus a *personal exemption* and a *standard deduction* (or other allowable deductions). For the federal income tax in 2009, the personal exemption was $3,650 and the standard deduction was $5,700 for a single person. So for a single person, taxable income equals total income minus $9,350.

The tax rate depends on the income level, and Figure 8.5 shows how the tax rate for a single person increases with income. The percentages in the table are

## EYE on the U.S. ECONOMY

### Taxes in the United States Today

Federal, state, and local governments in the United States have six main revenue sources:

- Personal income taxes
- Social Security taxes
- Sales taxes
- Corporation income taxes
- Property taxes
- Excise taxes

The figure shows the relative amounts raised by these taxes in 2008. Personal income taxes are the biggest tax source at 41 percent of total tax revenues. Social Security taxes are the next biggest revenue source at 25 percent of tax revenues. Sales taxes raised 11 percent; income taxes on corporations and property taxes each raised 10 percent. Excise taxes (such as the taxes on tobacco and alcoholic drinks) raised 3 percent.

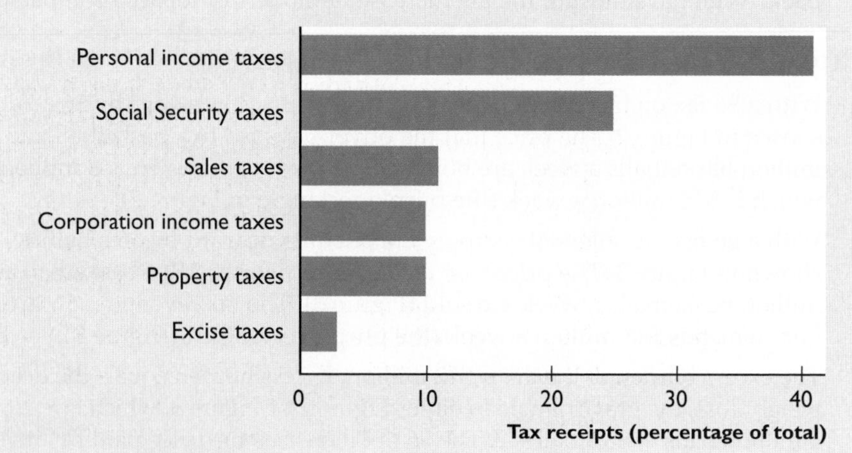


SOURCE OF DATA: *Economic Report of the President*, 2009.

Personal income taxes and Social Security taxes combine to create a high marginal tax rate on labor services that falls more on workers than on employers (see p. 200).

Taxes on corporate income mean that dividends on stocks get taxed twice, once as corporate income and once as personal income. These taxes fall mainly on firms rather than on the suppliers of capital and create a large deadweight loss (see p. 201).

## FIGURE 8.5

U.S. Marginal Tax Rates and Average Tax Rates in 2009

myeconlab Animation

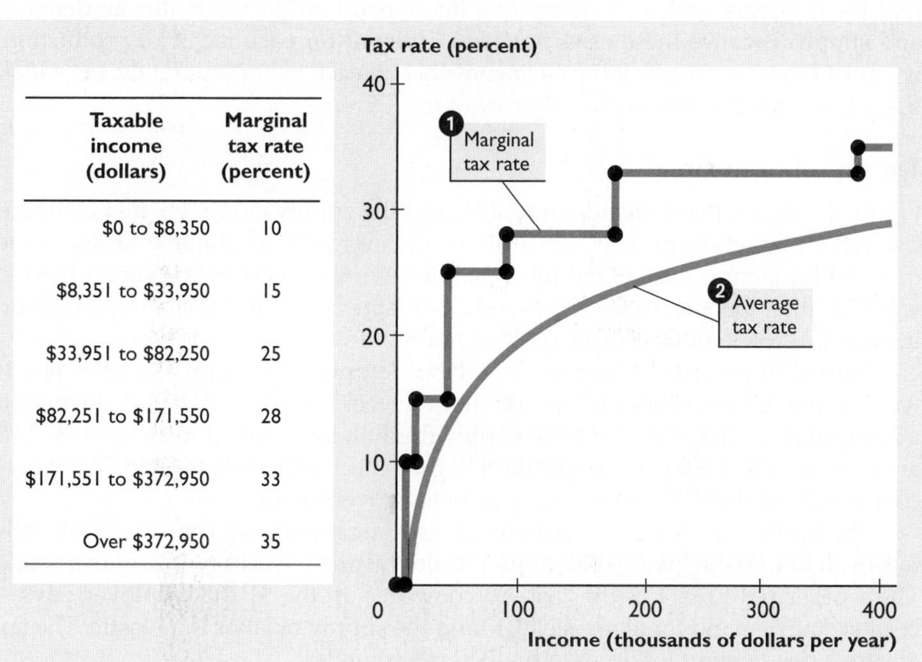


| Taxable income (dollars) | Marginal tax rate (percent) |
|---|---|
| $0 to $8,350 | 10 |
| $8,351 to $33,950 | 15 |
| $33,951 to $82,250 | 25 |
| $82,251 to $171,550 | 28 |
| $171,551 to $372,950 | 33 |
| Over $372,950 | 35 |

SOURCE OF DATA: Internal Revenue Service.

1 The marginal tax rate increases with income. The table provides the data for 2009.

2 The average tax rate increases with income, but the average rate is less than the marginal rate.

marginal tax rates. A **marginal tax rate** is the percentage of an additional dollar of income that is paid in tax. For example, if taxable income increases from $8,349 to $8,350, the tax paid on the additional dollar is 10¢ and the marginal tax rate is 10 percent. If taxable income increases from $372,950 to $372,951, the tax paid on the additional dollar is 35¢ and the marginal tax rate is 35 percent.

**Marginal tax rate**
The percentage of an additional dollar of income that is paid in tax.

The **average tax rate** is the percentage of income that is paid in tax. The average tax rate is less than the marginal tax rate. For example, suppose a single person earns $50,000 in a year. Tax paid is zero on the first $9,350 plus $835 (10 percent) on the next $8,350 plus $3,840 (15 percent) on the next $25,600 plus $1,675 (25 percent) on the remaining $6,700. Total taxes equal $6,350, which is 12.7 percent of $50,000. The average tax rate is 12.7 percent.

**Average tax rate**
The percentage of income that is paid in tax.

If the average tax rate increases as income increases, the tax is a **progressive tax**. The personal income tax is a progressive tax. To see this feature of the income tax, calculate another average tax rate for someone whose income is $100,000 a year. Tax paid is zero on the first $9,350 plus $835 (10 percent) on the next $8,350 plus $3,840 (15 percent) on the next $25,600 plus $12,075 (25 percent) on the next $48,300 plus $2,352 (28 percent) on the remaining $8,400. Total taxes equal $19,102, which is 19.1 percent of $100,000. The average tax rate is 19.1 percent.

**Progressive tax**
A tax whose average rate increases as income increases.

**Proportional tax**
A tax whose average rate is constant at all income levels.

A progressive tax contrasts with a **proportional tax**, which has the same average tax rate at all income levels, and a **regressive tax**, which has a decreasing average tax rate as income increases.

**Regressive tax**
A tax whose average rate decreases as income increases.

## The Effects of the Income Tax

Income tax is a tax on sellers of the services of labor, capital, and land. You know that the incidence and inefficiency of a tax depend on the elasticities of demand and supply. Because these elasticities are different for each factor of production, we must examine the effects of the income tax on each factor separately. Let's look first at the effects of the tax on labor income.

### Tax on Labor Income

Figure 8.6 shows the demand curve, *LD*, and the supply curve, *LS*, in a competitive labor market. Firms can substitute machines for labor in many tasks, so the demand for labor is elastic. But most people have few good options other than to work for their income, so the supply of labor is inelastic. In this example, with no income tax, workers would earn $19 an hour and work 40 hours a week.

With a 20 percent income tax, the labor supply curve shifts to *LS + tax*. If workers are willing to supply the 40th hour a week for $19 with no tax, then with a 20 percent tax, they are willing to supply the 40th hour only if the wage is $23.75 an hour. That is, they want to get the $19 they received before plus $4.75 (20 percent of $23.75) that they now must pay to the government.

The equilibrium wage rate rises to $20 an hour, but the after-tax wage rate falls to $16 an hour—the tax is $4 an hour. Employment decreases to 35 hours a week. The worker pays most of the tax—$3 compared to the $1 the employer pays—because the demand for labor is elastic and the supply of labor is inelastic. The tax creates a deadweight loss shown by the gray triangle.

**FIGURE 8.6**

A Tax on Labor Income

With no income tax, workers would earn $19 an hour and work 40 hours a week.

❶ Workers face a 20 percent marginal income tax rate. The income tax decreases the supply of labor, raises the wage rate, and lowers the after-tax wage rate. Because the demand for labor is elastic and the supply of labor is inelastic, the tax ❷ paid by the employer is less than that ❸ paid by the worker. The quantity of labor employed is less than the efficient quantity, so ❹ a deadweight loss arises.

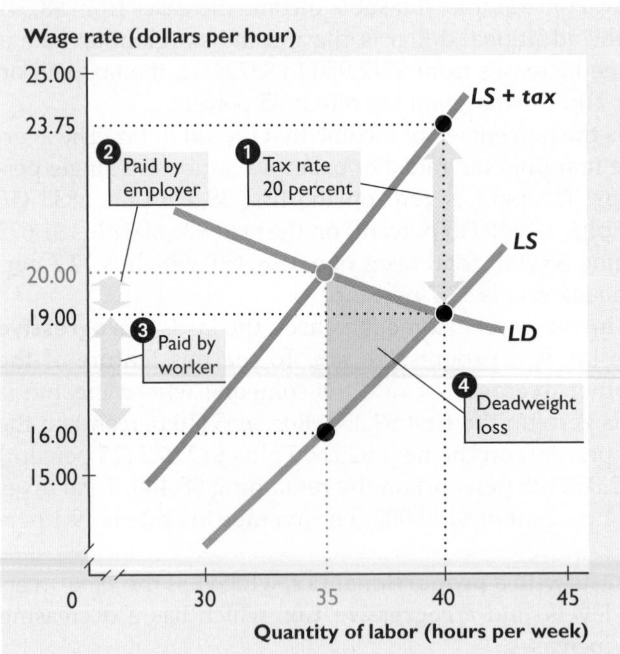

### Tax on Capital Income

Capital income in the form of interest on bonds and bank deposits is taxed at the normal income tax rate. But capital income in the form of dividends on stocks is taxed twice. It is taxed as a dividend at 15 percent and it is taxed as corporate profit at the corporation income tax rate. (From 2008 to 2010, low-income earners will pay no tax on dividends.)

Figure 8.7 shows the demand curve, *KD*, and the supply curve, *KS*, in a competitive capital market. Because many tasks can be done by machines or labor, the demand for capital is elastic. Capital is internationally mobile, and its supply is highly elastic. In this example, firms can obtain all the capital they wish at an interest rate of 6 percent a year, so the supply of capital is perfectly elastic. With no capital income tax, firms use $40 billion worth of capital.

With a 40 percent tax on capital income, the supply curve shifts to *KS + tax*. Lenders want to receive an additional 4 percent interest to pay their capital income tax and are not willing to lend for less than 10 percent a year.

With the capital income tax, the quantity of capital decreases to $20 billion and the interest rate rises to 10 percent a year. Firms pay the entire capital income tax, and lenders receive the same after-tax interest rate as they receive in the absence of a capital income tax. The tax creates a deadweight loss shown by the gray triangle.

### Tax on the Income from Land and Other Unique Resources

Each plot of land and reserve of mineral or other natural resource is unique, so its supply is perfectly inelastic. A fixed amount of the resource is supplied regardless of the rent offered for its use.

**FIGURE 8.7**

A Tax on Capital Income

myeconlab Animation

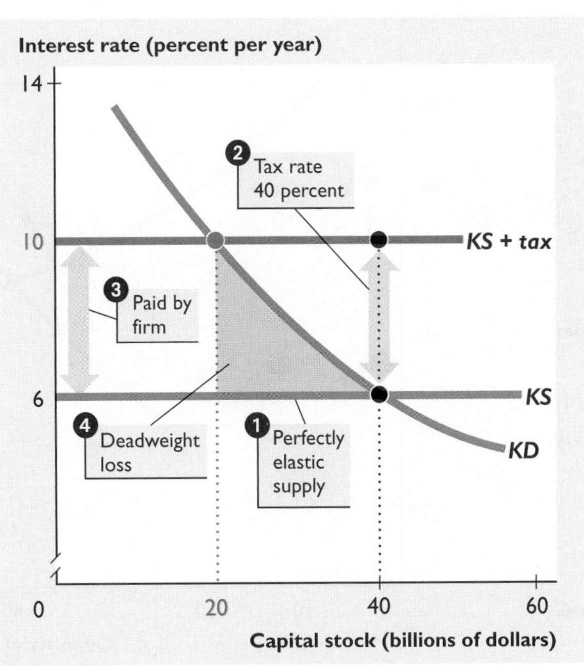


1 The supply of capital is highly elastic (here perfectly elastic). With no tax on capital income, the interest rate is 6 percent a year and firms use $40 billion of capital.

With a 2 40 percent tax on income from capital, the supply curve becomes *KS + tax*. The interest rate rises to 10 percent a year, and 3 firms pay the entire tax. The quantity of capital used is less than the efficient quantity, so 4 a deadweight loss arises.

## EYE on CONGRESS

### Who Pays the Taxes?

Congress says that employers and workers pay the same Social Security tax contributions (7.65 percent each in 2009), but because the elasticity of demand for labor is much greater than the elasticity of supply of labor, workers end up paying most of the Social Security tax (see pp. 204–205).

Similarly, because the elasticity of demand for labor is greater than the elasticity of supply, the tax on wage income is paid mainly by workers. In contrast, the tax on capital income falls mainly on borrowers because the supply of capital is highly elastic.

But there is one thing that Congress can do to influence who pays a tax. It can pass a tax law (or tax rebate law) that doesn't impact the margin on which decisions turn. Recently, Congress passed such a law.

On February 17, 2009, the President signed the American Recovery and Reinvestment Act. Among the Act's many provisions is a "Making Work Pay" tax credit of $400 for a single worker and $800 for a couple.

A tax credit is a fixed reduction in the amount paid in personal income tax (in the current case, $400). For most people, a tax credit has no effect on their supply of labor. A worker gets the $400 tax credit regardless of how many hours he or she works. The tax credit doesn't influence the work-hours choice.

What influences the work-hours choice is the after-tax hourly wage rate, and that depends on the *marginal* income tax rate.

The figure illustrates the effects of a tax credit. The figure is similar to Figure 8.6 on p. 200. A 20 percent income tax rate shifts the labor supply curve from *LS* to *LS* + *tax*. With the demand for labor curve *LD*, the 20 percent tax raises the pre-tax wage rate by $1 to $20 per hour, lowers the after-tax wage rate by $3 to $16 per hour, and lowers the average workweek from 40 hours to 35 hours. With no tax rebate, the worker pays 75 percent of the tax and the employer pays 25 percent.

Suppose that Congress now passes an Act that gives workers a tax rebate of $30 a week. This rebate has no effect on the supply of labor because it isn't a rebate per hour worked. It is a fixed amount independent of the hours worked. Workers now pay only 68 percent of the tax and employers pay 32 percent. Congress has worked around the elasticities!

*Director of the Office of Management and Budget, Peter Orszag*

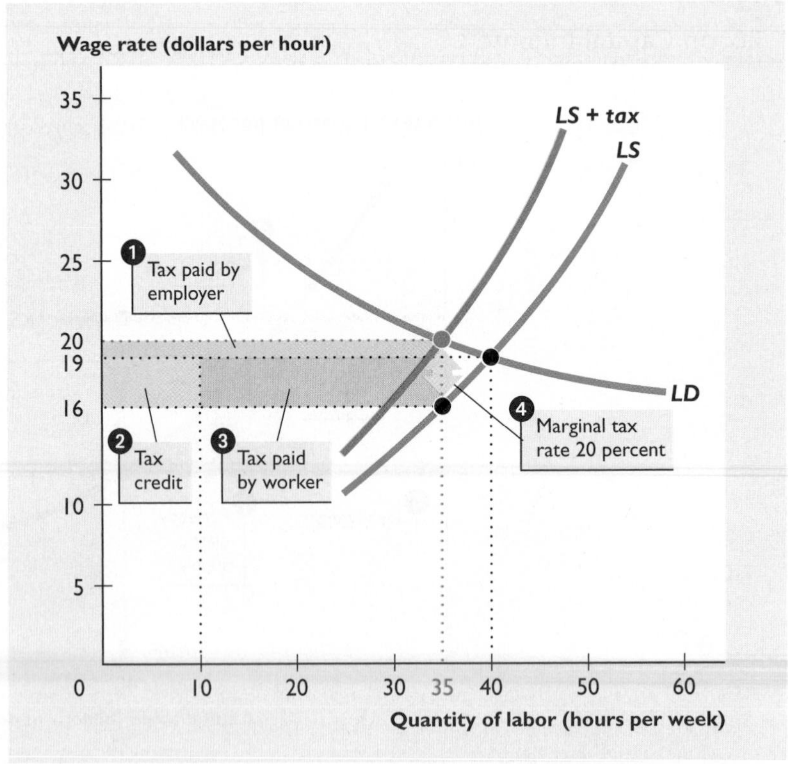

Figure 8.8(a) illustrates a tax on land income. In this example, a fixed 250 billion acres is supplied regardless of the rent. The equilibrium quantity of land is determined purely by supply and the equilibrium rent is determined by the demand for land. In this example, the equilibrium rent is $1,000 an acre.

When a 40 percent tax is imposed on rent income, landowners pay all of the tax. Their after-tax income falls to $600 an acre. This tax is efficient because the equilibrium quantity of land used is the same with the tax as without it. The tax generates no deadweight loss (excess burden) and is ideal from the perspective of efficiency.

The principle that applies to a tax on income from land also applies to the income from any unique resource that has a perfectly inelastic supply. Another example of such a resource is the talent of an outstanding movie star or television personality.

Figure 8.8(b) illustrates this case. Suppose that Oprah Winfrey is willing to work for 24 hours a week making and appearing on television shows. Her supply of services is perfectly inelastic at that quantity. The networks compete for her services, and the demand curve reflects their willingness to pay for them. The equilibrium price is $250,000 per hour. If Oprah pays a 40 percent tax on this income, she receives an after-tax income of $150,000 per hour. Oprah pays the entire tax. The price paid by the networks is unaffected by this tax, and Oprah makes the same number of hours of television shows with the tax as without it. This tax creates no deadweight loss (excess burden).

**FIGURE 8.8**

A Tax on Land and Other Unique Resource Income

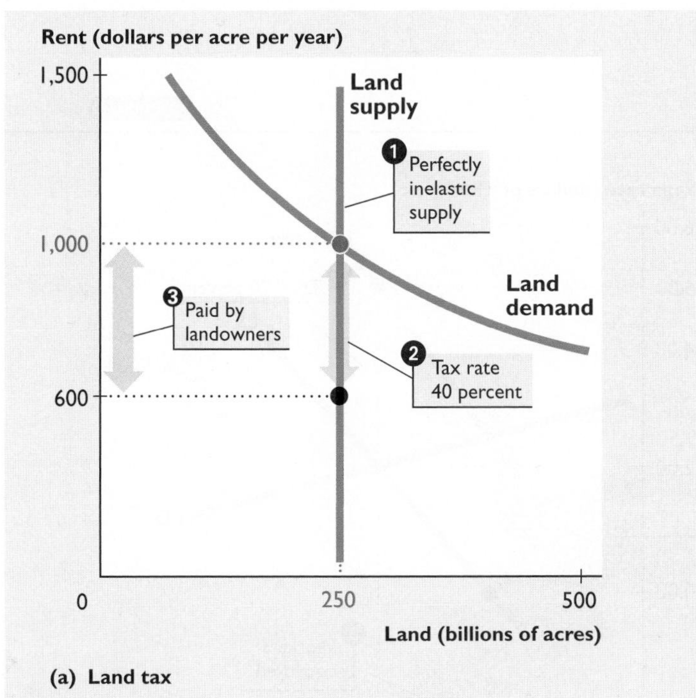


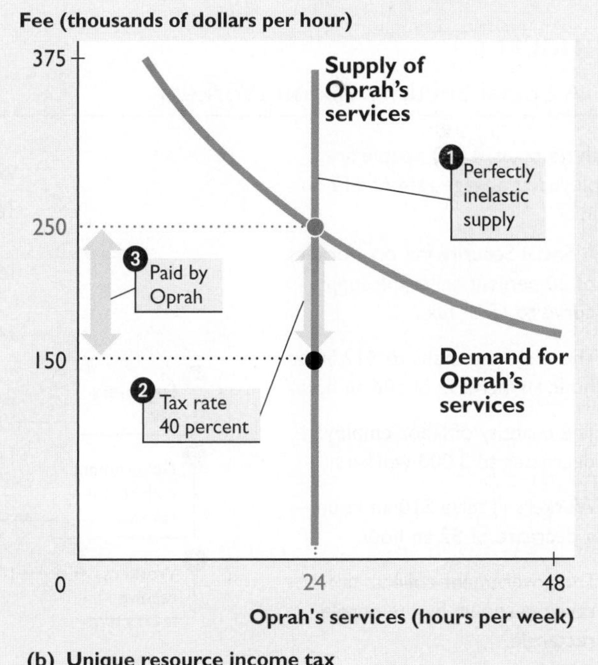

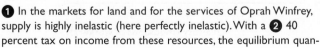

1 In the markets for land and for the services of Oprah Winfrey, supply is highly inelastic (here perfectly inelastic). With a 2 40 percent tax on income from these resources, the equilibrium quantity and the market price remain unchanged, and 3 landowners and Oprah pay the entire tax. Because the quantity of the resource used is unchanged, the tax is efficient.

## The Social Security Tax

Social Security is never far from the headlines. As the population gets older and more and more people begin to receive Social Security benefits, the cry to "fix Social Security" can only keep getting louder. The fundamental problem of ever-growing outlays must somehow be addressed.

One possible solution to the Social Security problem in the United States is to change the entitlements and cut the outlays. But this possibility is not popular and probably will not be the solution that is chosen. The other possibility is to increase the Social Security tax.

Currently, the law says that Social Security taxes fall equally on workers and employers. But does this outcome actually occur? If Congress decides to increase the Social Security tax, can Congress target employers and shield workers?

The Social Security tax is just like the other taxes you've studied in this chapter. Its incidence depends on the elasticities of demand and supply in the labor market and not on the wishes of Congress. Let's confirm this assertion by looking at two distinct arrangements: First, the tax is imposed only on workers, and second, the tax is imposed only on employers.

### A Social Security Tax on Workers

Figure 8.9 shows the effects of a Social Security tax when the law says that workers must pay the entire tax. Without any taxes, the wage rate is $12 an hour and 4,000 people are employed. Now suppose that the government introduces a 20 percent Social Security tax on workers. If 4,000 people were willing to work for $12 an hour, this quantity of labor will now be supplied only if people can earn

**FIGURE 8.9**

A Social Security Tax on Workers

myeconlab Animation

With no taxes, 4,000 people are employed at a wage rate of $12 an hour.

1. A Social Security tax on workers of 20 percent shifts the supply curve to *LS + tax*.
2. The wage rate rises to $12.50 an hour, an increase of 50¢ an hour.
3. The quantity of labor employed decreases to 3,000 workers.
4. Workers receive $10 an hour—a decrease of $2 an hour.
5. The government collects tax revenue shown by the purple rectangle.

Workers pay most of the tax because the supply of labor is more inelastic than the demand for labor.

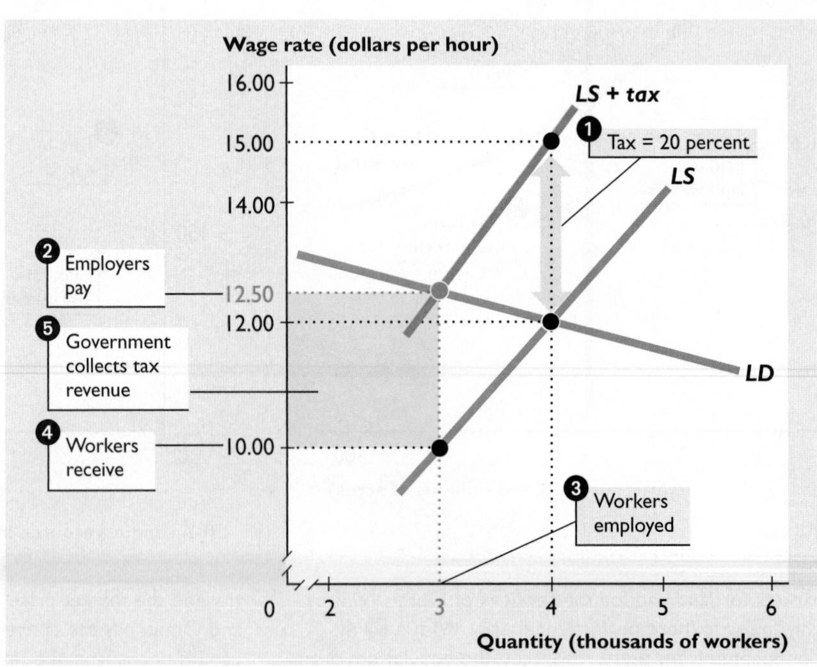

$12 an hour *after tax*. With a tax rate of 20 percent, the *pre-tax* wage rate will need to be $15 an hour to deliver an after-tax wage rate of $12 an hour. (Check that 20 percent of $15 is $3, so the wage rate *after* the tax is paid is $12.) The supply of labor curve shifts to the curve labeled *LS* + *tax*—a decrease in the supply of labor.

The wage rate rises to $12.50 an hour, and 3,000 workers are employed. Employees *receive* $12.50 an hour minus a 20 percent tax, which is $10 an hour. (Check that $2.50 equals 20 percent, or one fifth, of $12.50.)

So when the government puts a Social Security tax on workers, employers pay 50¢ an hour and workers pay $2 an hour. This division of the burden of the tax arises because the demand for labor is more elastic than the supply of labor.

## A Social Security Tax on Employers

Figure 8.10 shows the effects of a Social Security tax on employers. As before, with no taxes, the equilibrium wage rate is $12 an hour and 4,000 people are employed. With a $2.50 an hour tax, firms are no longer willing to hire 4,000 people at a $12 an hour wage rate. Because firms must pay $2.50 an hour to the government, they will hire 4,000 people at a wage rate of $12 minus $2.50, which is $9.50 an hour.

The demand for labor decreases, and the demand curve shifts to *LD* − *tax*. The wage rate falls to $10 an hour, and 3,000 workers are employed. The total cost of labor to the firm is $12.50 an hour—the $10 an hour wage plus the $2.50 an hour tax.

The tax on employers delivers the same outcome as the tax on workers. Workers receive the same take-home wage, and firms pay the same total wage. Congress cannot decide who pays the Social Security tax. When the laws of Congress come into conflict with the laws of economics, economics wins. Congress can't repeal the laws of supply and demand!

**FIGURE 8.10**

A Social Security Tax on Employers

myeconlab Animation

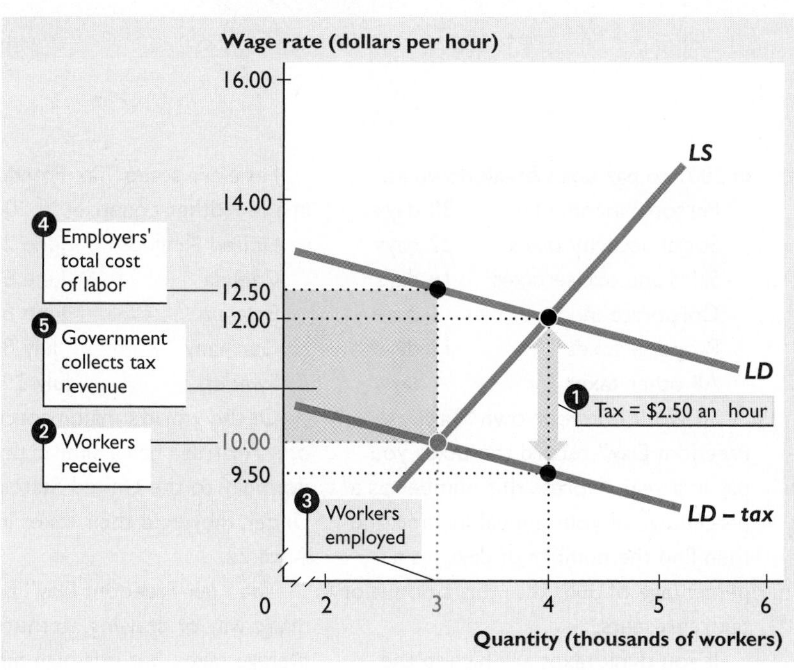


With no taxes, 4,000 people are employed at a wage rate of $12 an hour.

1. A tax on employers of $2.50 an hour shifts the demand curve leftward to *LD* − *tax*.
2. The wage rate falls to $10 an hour, a decrease of $2 an hour.
3. The quantity of labor employed decreases to 3,000 workers.
4. Employers' total cost of labor rises to $12.50 an hour—the wage rate of $10 an hour plus the $2.50 an hour tax.
5. The government collects tax revenue shown by the purple rectangle.

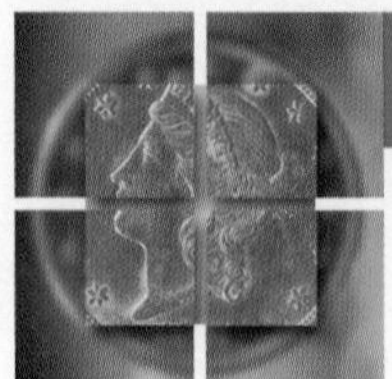

# EYE on the PAST

## The Origins and History of the U.S. Income Tax

**1861** First federal income tax—3 percent on all incomes above $800 a year.

**1872** Income tax was repealed. (Tariffs on imports provided government revenue.)

**1895** Income tax reestablished, but the Supreme Court ruled it unconstitutional.

**1913** The 16th Amendment to the Constitution made the federal income tax legal.

**1913–2009** Tax rates fluctuated. The top rate increased until 1920, decreased during the 1920s, and then increased until 1945 before decreasing in a number of steps to today's rate of 35 percent.

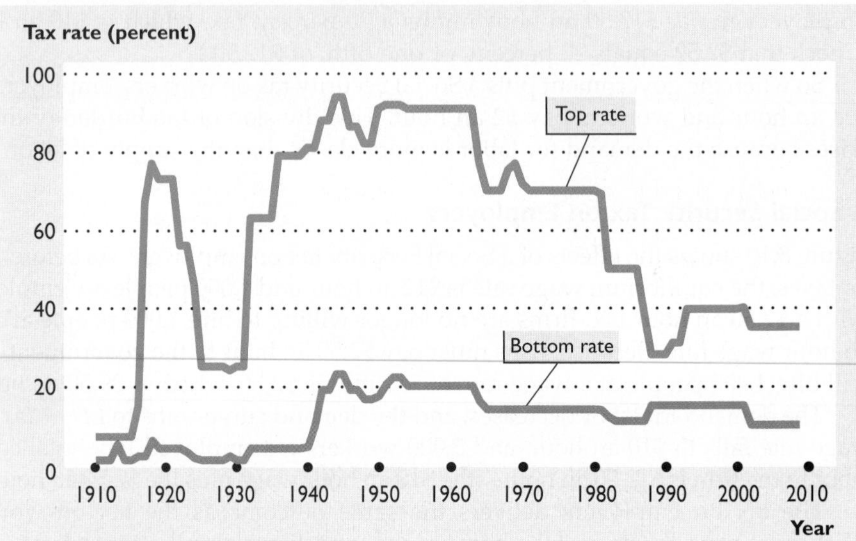


SOURCE OF DATA: Congressional Joint Committee on Taxation.

The bottom rate remained below 5 percent until the 1940s when it increased to 20 percent. In 1963 it decreased and since then, it has fluctuated between 10 percent and 15 percent.

# EYE on YOUR LIFE

## Tax Freedom Day

The Tax Foundation is an organization that seeks to promote a tax system that is as simple, transparent, and stable as possible, that minimizes excess burden, and that promotes trade and income growth.

Each year, to make the level of taxes as transparent as possible, the Tax Foundation calculates and publicizes "Tax Freedom Day"—the date by when an average U.S. citizen has worked long enough to pay the year's tax bill.

In 2009, "Tax Freedom Day" for Americans was April 13, the 103rd day of the year.

The 103 days Americans must work in 2009 to pay taxes break down as:

| | |
|---|---|
| Personal income taxes | 38 days |
| Social Security taxes | 27 days |
| Sales and excise taxes | 16 days |
| Corporate income taxes | 6 days |
| Property taxes | 12 days |
| All other taxes | 4 days. |

To work out your own "Tax Freedom Day," record the taxes you pay in a year. Express this number as a percentage of your annual income and then find the number of days (as a percentage of 365) that this amount of tax represents.

If you think taxes are high in the United States, think again.

Here are some "Tax Freedom Days" in a few other countries in 2008:

| | |
|---|---|
| United Kingdom | June 2 |
| Canada | June 6 |
| Belgium | June 8 |
| Germany | July 8 |
| Sweden | July 29 |

Of the world's major countries, only Australia has a similar tax freedom day to the United States. Down Under, they paid their taxes in 2008 by April 22.

The "Tax Freedom Day" is a dramatic way of drawing attention to high *average* taxes, but it is high *marginal* taxes that create inefficiency.

## CHECKPOINT 8.2

myeconlab

Work these problems in Study Plan 8.2 to get instant feedback.

**Explain how income taxes and Social Security taxes change wage rates and employment, are shared by employers and workers, and create inefficiency.**

## Practice Problems

1. Florida levies the following taxes: a 5.5 percent corporate income tax; a 6 percent sales tax; taxes of 4¢ a gallon on gasoline, 33.9¢ a pack on cigarettes, $0.48 a gallon on beer, and $2.25 a gallon on wine; and property taxes that vary across the counties and range from 1.4 percent to 2.0 percent of property values. Classify Florida's taxes into progressive, proportional, and regressive taxes.
2. Explain why Tiger Woods pays his own Social Security tax and the PGA (the Professional Golf Association) pays none of it.
3. Which tax is more inefficient: a tax on land rent or a tax on capital income? Explain.
4. **Illinois Governor proposes broad array of tax increases**

   Faced with a huge budget deficit, Illinois Governor Patrick Quinn has proposed the largest tax increase in 40 years, including a 50 percent increase in the personal income tax rate.

   Source: *The Wall Street Journal*, March 20, 2009

   Explain how an increase in the tax on labor income will change the quantity of labor employed, the wage rate paid by employers, the wage rate received by workers, and the deadweight loss. Will workers or employers pay most of the tax increase?

## Guided Solutions to Practice Problems

1. If counties with the higher rates are those with high property values, then Florida's property taxes are progressive. The corporate income tax does not vary with income, so this tax is a proportional tax. Because saving increases with income, expenditure as a fraction of income decreases as income increases. The taxes on expenditure (sales tax, gasoline tax, cigarette tax, beer tax, and wine tax) are regressive taxes.
2. Tiger Woods pays his Social Security tax and the PGA pays none of it because the supply of Tiger Woods' services is (most likely) perfectly inelastic. The elasticities of demand and supply determine who pays the tax.
3. A tax on capital income is more inefficient than a tax on land rent. A tax on capital income has the larger effect on the quantity of factors of production employed than does a tax on land rent because the supply of land is perfectly inelastic, whereas the supply of capital is highly elastic. The larger the decrease in the quantity, the larger the deadweight loss created by the tax (the excess burden of the tax) and the more inefficient is the tax.
4. A tax on labor income will not change the demand for labor, but it will decrease the quantity of labor employed. The wage rate paid by employers will rise, the wage rate received by workers will fall, and the deadweight loss will increase. Because the demand for labor is elastic and the supply of labor is inelastic, most of the increase in the tax will be paid by the worker.

## 8.3 FAIRNESS AND THE BIG TRADEOFF

We've examined the incidence and the efficiency of different types of taxes. These topics have occupied most of this chapter because they are the issues about taxes that economics can address. But when political leaders debate tax issues, it is fairness, not just incidence and efficiency, that gets the most attention. Democrats complain that Republican tax cuts are unfair because they give the benefits of lower taxes to the rich. Republicans counter that because the rich pay most of the taxes, it is fair that they get most of the tax cuts. No easy answers are available to the questions about the fairness of taxes. Economists have proposed two conflicting principles of fairness to apply to a tax system:

- The benefits principle
- The ability-to-pay principle

### The Benefits Principle

**Benefits principle**
The proposition that people should pay taxes equal to the benefits they receive from public goods and services.

The **benefits principle** is the proposition that people should pay taxes equal to the benefits they receive from public goods and services. This arrangement is fair because those who benefit most pay the most. The benefit principle makes tax payments and the consumption of government-provided services similar to private consumption expenditures. If taxes are based on the benefits principle, the people who enjoy the largest benefits pay the most for them.

To implement the benefits principle, it would be necessary to have an objective method of measuring each individual's marginal benefit from government-provided goods. In the absence of such a method, the principle can be used to justify a wide range of different taxes.

For example, the benefits principle can justify high fuel taxes to pay for public highways. Here, the argument would be that those who value the highways most are the people who use them most, and so they should pay most of the cost of providing them. Similarly, the benefits principle can justify high taxes on alcoholic beverages and tobacco products. Here, the argument would be that those who drink and smoke the most place the largest burden on public health-care services and so should pay the greater part of the cost of those services.

The benefits principle can also be used to justify a progressive income tax. Here, the argument would be that the rich receive a disproportionately large share of the benefit from law and order and from living in a secure environment, so they should pay the largest share of providing these services.

### The Ability-to-Pay Principle

**Ability-to-pay principle**
The proposition that people should pay taxes according to how easily they can bear the burden.

The **ability-to-pay principle** is the proposition that people should pay taxes according to how easily they can bear the burden. A rich person can more easily bear the burden of providing public goods than a poor person can, so the rich should pay higher taxes than the poor. The ability-to-pay principle involves comparing people along two dimensions: horizontally and vertically.

#### Horizontal Equity

**Horizontal equity**
The requirement that taxpayers with the same ability to pay should pay the same taxes.

If taxes are based on ability to pay, taxpayers with the same ability to pay should pay the same taxes, a situation called **horizontal equity**. While horizontal equity is easy to agree with in principle, it is difficult to implement in practice. If two people are identical in every respect, horizontal equity is easy to apply. But how do we compare people who are similar but not identical? The greatest difficulty arises in working out differences in ability to pay that arise from the state of a person's health and from a person's family responsibilities. The U.S. income tax has many special deductions and other rules that aim to achieve horizontal equity.

### Vertical Equity

If horizontal comparisons are difficult, vertical comparisons are impossible. **Vertical equity** is the requirement that taxpayers with a greater ability to pay bear a greater share of the taxes. This proposition easily translates into the requirement that people with higher incomes should pay higher taxes. But it provides no help in determining how steeply taxes should increase as income increases. Should taxes be proportional to income? Should they be regressive? Should they be progressive? All of these arrangements have higher-income people paying higher taxes, so they all satisfy the basic idea of vertical equity. But most people have strong views that include the extent to which the rich should pay more.

**Vertical equity**
The requirement that taxpayers with a greater ability to pay bear a greater share of the taxes.

You've seen that the U.S. tax code uses progressive income taxes—average tax rates that increase with income. Progressive taxes are justified as fair on the basis of the principle of vertical equity. But their use to achieve vertical equity produces a problem for the attainment of horizontal equity. The problem shows up most clearly in the U.S. tax code in its treatment of single people and married couples.

## The Marriage Tax Problem

Should a married couple (or two people living together) be treated as two individual taxpayers or as a single taxpayer? Until some changes were introduced in 2003, the U.S. tax code treated a married couple as a single taxpayer. This arrangement means that when a man and a woman get married, they stop paying income tax as two individuals and instead pay as one individual. To see the marriage tax problem, suppose the tax code (simpler than that in the United States) is as follows: no deductions or exemptions, incomes up to $20,000 a year bear no tax, and incomes in excess of $20,000 are taxed at 10 percent.

Now think about Al and Judy, two struggling young journalists, each of whom earns $20,000 a year and who get married. As single people, they paid no tax. Married, their income is $40,000, so they pay $2,000 a year in tax (10 percent of $20,000). Their marriage tax is $2,000 a year. (This example is *much* more severe than the marriage tax in the United States, but it serves to highlight the source of the problem.)

We could make a simple change to the tax law to overcome this problem for Al and Judy: Tax married couples as two single persons. That is what is done in most countries and what some economists say should be done in the United States. If we make this change in the tax law, Al and Judy pay no tax after their marriage just as before. We've solved the marriage tax problem.

*A married couple or two individuals?*

Before we conclude that this small change to the tax code would clean up a source of unfairness, let's think about its effect on Denise and Frank. Frank is a painter whose work just doesn't sell. He has no income. Denise is a successful artist whose work is in steady demand and earns her $40,000 a year. As two single artists, Frank pays no tax and Denise pays $2,000 a year (10 percent of $20,000). If they marry, under the arrangement that taxes a married couple as a single taxpayer, they still pay $2,000 in tax.

Now compare Frank and Denise with Al and Judy. If we tax married couples as a single taxpayer, both couples earn $40,000 a year and both pay income tax of $2,000 a year. But if we tax married couples as single persons, Frank and Denise pay $2,000 a year and Al and Judy pay nothing. So which is fair?

Horizontal equity requires Frank and Denise to be treated like Al and Judy. Taxing couples as a single taxpayer rather than taxing couples as single people achieves this outcome. But it taxes marriage, which seems unfair.

This problem arises from the progressive tax. It would not arise if taxes were proportional. Because horizontal equity conflicts with progressive taxes, some people say that only proportional taxes are fair.

## The Big Tradeoff

Questions about the fairness of taxes conflict with efficiency questions and create the *big tradeoff* that you met in Chapter 6. The taxes that generate the greatest deadweight loss are those on the income from capital. But most capital is owned by a relatively small number of people who have the greatest ability to pay taxes. So there is a conflict between efficiency and fairness. We want a tax system that is efficient, in the sense that it raises the revenue that the government needs to provide public goods and services, but we want a tax system that shares the burden of providing these goods and services fairly. Our tax system is an evolving compromise that juggles these two goals.

Work these problems in Study Plan 8.3 to get instant feedback.

## CHECKPOINT 8.3

**Review ideas about the fairness of the tax system.**

### Practice Problems

1. In Hong Kong, the marginal income tax rates range from 2 percent to 20 percent. Does Hong Kong place greater weight on the ability-to-pay principle than does the United States? Does Hong Kong place a greater weight on efficiency and a smaller weight on fairness than does the United States?
2. **Soda tax weighed to pay for health care**

   Senators are considering a new federal tax on soda and other sugary drinks. Sugar-sweetened drinks can lead to obesity and diabetes. The tax will encourage people to cut consumption, which will save medical costs.

   Source: *The Wall Street Journal*, May 12, 2009

   Which principle of fairness will the senators use to justify a tax on soda?

### Guided Solutions to Practice Problems

1. Income tax rates are lower in Hong Kong than in the United States, so Hong Kong places less weight on the ability-to-pay principle than does the United States. With income tax rates in Hong Kong lower than in the United States, Hong Kong places a greater weight on efficiency and a smaller weight on fairness than does the United States.
2. The two principles of fairness are the benefits principle and the ability-to-pay principle. Senators can justify the tax on the benefits principle if the tax revenue raised is used to pay for the health costs created by the soda.

## CHAPTER SUMMARY

### Key Points

1 **Explain how taxes change prices and quantities, are shared by buyers and sellers, and create inefficiency.**

- A tax on buyers has the same effect as a tax on sellers. It increases the price paid by the buyer and lowers the price received by the seller.
- A tax creates inefficiency by driving a wedge between marginal benefit and marginal cost and creating a deadweight loss.
- The less elastic the demand or the more elastic the supply, the greater is the price increase and the larger is the share of the tax paid by the buyer.
- If demand is perfectly elastic or supply is perfectly inelastic, the seller pays all the tax; if demand is perfectly inelastic or supply is perfectly elastic, the buyer pays all the tax.
- If demand or supply is perfectly inelastic, the tax creates no deadweight loss and is efficient.

2 **Explain how income taxes and Social Security taxes change wage rates and employment, are shared by employers and workers, and create inefficiency.**

- Taxes can be progressive (the average tax rate rises with income), proportional (the average tax rate is constant), or regressive (the average tax rate falls with income).
- The U.S. income tax is progressive.
- The shares of the income tax paid by firms and households depend on the elasticity of demand and the elasticity of supply of the factors of production.
- The elasticities of demand and supply, not Congress, determine who pays the income tax and who pays the Social Security tax.
- The more elastic is either the demand or supply of a factor of production, the greater is the excess burden of an income tax.

3 **Review ideas about the fairness of the tax system.**

- The two main principles of fairness of taxes—the benefits principle and the ability-to-pay principle—do not deliver universally accepted standards of fairness, and vertical equity and horizontal equity can come into conflict.

### Key Terms

Ability-to-pay principle, 208
Average tax rate, 199
Benefits principle, 208
Excess burden, 194
Horizontal equity, 208
Marginal tax rate, 199
Progressive tax, 199
Proportional tax, 199
Regressive tax, 199
Taxable income, 198
Tax incidence, 192
Vertical equity, 209

Work these problems in Chapter 8 Study Plan to get instant feedback.

# CHAPTER CHECKPOINT

## Study Plan Problems and Applications

1. In Florida, sunscreen and sunglasses are vital items. If the tax on sellers of these items is doubled from 5.5 percent to 11 percent, who will pay most of the tax increase: the buyer or the seller? Will the tax increase halve the quantity of sunscreen and sunglasses bought?

Table 1 illustrates the market for Internet service. Use the information in Table 1 and a demand-supply graph to work Problems **2** and **3**.

**TABLE 1**

| Price (dollars per month) | Quantity demanded (units per month) | Quantity supplied (units per month) |
|---|---|---|
| 0 | 30 | 0 |
| 10 | 25 | 10 |
| 20 | 20 | 20 |
| 30 | 15 | 30 |
| 40 | 10 | 40 |
| 50 | 5 | 50 |
| 60 | 0 | 60 |

2. What is the market price of Internet service? If the government taxes Internet service $15 a month, what price would the buyer of Internet service pay? What price would the seller of Internet service receive?
3. If the government taxes Internet service $15 a month, does the buyer or the seller pay more of the tax? What is the tax revenue? What is the excess burden of the tax? Is the tax proportional, progressive, or regressive?

Figure 1 illustrates the labor market in a country that does not tax labor income. Suppose that the government introduces a Social Security tax on workers of $2 per hour. Use this information to work Problems **4** and **5**.

**FIGURE 1**

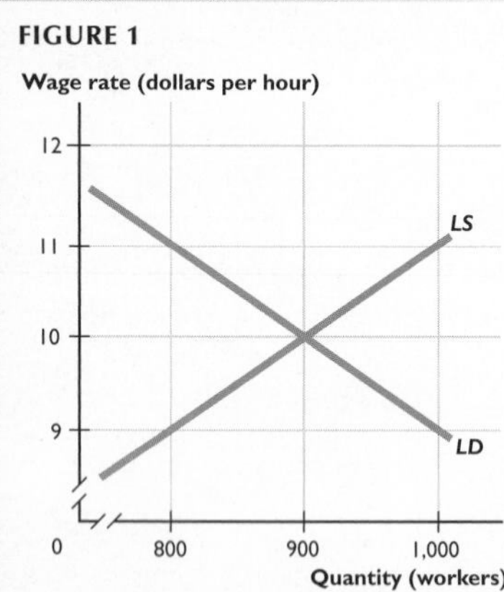


4. How many workers are employed? What is the wage rate paid by employers and what is the worker's after-tax wage rate? How many workers are no longer employed?
5. If the government splits the Social Security tax equally between workers and employers, how many workers are employed? What is the wage rate paid by employers and what is the worker's after-tax wage rate?
6. Suppose that the government imposes a $2 a cup tax on coffee. What determines by how much Starbucks will raise its price? How will the quantity of coffee bought in coffee shops change? Will this tax raise much revenue?

Concerned about the political fallout from rising gas prices, the government cuts the tax on gasoline. Use this information to work Problems **7** and **8**.

7. Explain the effect of this tax cut on the price of gasoline and the quantity bought if, at the same time, the oil-producing nations increase production.
8. Explain the effect of this tax cut on the price of gasoline and the quantity bought if, at the same time, a global shortage of oil sends the price up.
9. **The downside of lower gas taxes**

   The federal gas tax is 18.4¢ a gallon and state gas taxes range from 20¢ to 40¢ a gallon. As motorists switch to more efficient cars, the federal and state government gas tax revenue will fall. To raise revenue for infrastructure repairs, some states are considering dropping the gas tax and introducing a mileage tax, perhaps 2.3¢ per mile.

   Source: CNNMoney, June 9, 2009

   How would a mileage tax differ from the gas tax in its effects on an owner of a gas guzzler and an owner of a fuel-efficient hybrid? Which tax would be fairer: the mileage tax or the gas tax?

## Instructor Assignable Problems and Applications

Your instructor can assign these problems as homework, a quiz, or a test in **MyEconLab**.

Use the following information to work Problems **1** and **2**.

In 2002, New York State raised the cigarette tax by 39¢ to $1.50 a pack. Then New York City raised the tax from 8¢ to $1.50 a pack. The total tax increased to $3 a pack, and the price of cigarettes rose to $7.50 a pack—the highest in the nation. The average income of smokers is less than that of non-smokers.

1. Draw a graph to show the effects of the $3 tax on the buyer's price, the seller's price, the quantity of cigarettes bought, the tax revenue, the consumer surplus, the producer surplus, and the excess burden of the tax. Does the buyer or seller pay more of the tax? Why?
2. Is this tax on cigarettes a progressive, regressive, or proportional tax?

Use the following information to work Problems **3** and **4**.

The supply of luxury boats is perfectly elastic, the demand for luxury boats is unit elastic, and with no tax on luxury boats, the price is $1 million and 240 luxury boats a week are bought. Now luxury boats are taxed at 20 percent.

3. What is the price that buyers pay? How is the tax split between the buyer and the seller? What is the government's tax revenue?
4. On a graph, show the excess burden of this tax. Is this tax efficient? Is it fair?
5. Figure 1 shows the demand for and supply of chocolate bars. Suppose that the government levies a $1.50 tax on a chocolate bar. What is the change in the quantity of chocolate bars bought, who pays most of the tax, and what is the deadweight loss?

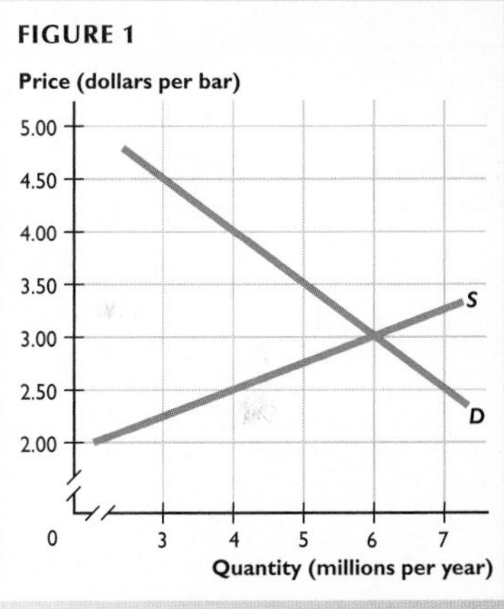


6. Larry earns $25,000 and pays $2,500 in tax, while Suzy earns $50,000 and pays $15,000 in tax. If Larry's income increases by $100, his tax increases by $12, but if Suzy's income increases by $100, her tax increases by $35. Calculate the average tax rate and marginal tax rate that Larry pays and that Suzy pays. Is this income tax fair? Explain.
7. In an hour, a baker earns $10, a gas pump attendant earns $6, and a copy shop worker earns $7. Suppose that the government introduces an income tax of $1 an hour. Calculate the marginal tax rates for bakers, gas pump attendants, and copy shop workers. Is this tax progressive or regressive?

Use the following information to work Problems **8** and **9**.

**Tax bites on travelers go deeper**

Travelers complain about delayed flights and poor service, but they don't seem to be too bothered by increased taxes on flights, car rentals, and hotel rooms. Taxes raise the average car rental bill 28 percent or more at airport locations. More municipalities are reported as taxing airport rental customers to fund local venues, such as sports stadiums and convention centers.

Source: *The New York Times*, April 10, 2007

8. Describe the effect of these municipal taxes on car rentals at airports. Who do you think pays more of the tax: the renter or the car company?
9. Why do you think municipalities tax things that travelers buy as a way of raising the revenue to build local venues?

Use the following information to work Problems **10** to **12**.

The government of the U.S. Virgin Islands seeks your help to evaluate two tax schemes. In scheme A, food is not taxed, luxury goods are taxed at 10 percent, and all other goods are taxed at 5 percent. In scheme B, there is a flat 3 percent tax on all goods and services.

**10.** The government asks you to explain what research must be undertaken and what features of the markets for food, luxury goods, and other goods will influence how the prices and quantities of food, luxury goods, and all other goods will differ under the two schemes.

**11.** Which tax scheme would be more efficient if both generated the same amount of tax revenue?

**12.** The government asks you to explain what research must be undertaken and what features of the markets for food, luxury goods, and other goods will influence the excess burden of the taxes under the two schemes.

Use the following information to work Problems **13** and **14**.

**Tax cuts offer most for very rich, study says**
A study of Bush tax cuts that Congress enacted in 2001 noted that while these tax cuts reduced rates for people at every income level, the top 1 percent of income earners will reap the biggest benefits.

Source: *The New York Times*, January 8, 2007

**13.** What assumptions about the elasticities of demand and supply for high-wage labor and capital might be consistent with this assessment? What other facts about demand and supply and market outcomes would you need to know to verify this claim?

**14.** If the assessment is correct, is such an outcome likely to be efficient? Is such an outcome fair on any of the standard principles of fairness?

**15.** A poll tax is a fixed amount per person. Mrs. Thatcher introduced a poll tax in the United Kingdom during the 1980s.

- Is a poll tax a progressive, regressive, or proportional tax?
- How do you think the effects of a poll tax differ from those of a sales tax?
- Do you think a poll tax is efficient? Is it fair? Explain why.

**16. Fair taxes for the 400 richest Americans?**
The IRS reported that the 400 richest taxpayers in 2006 paid just 17.2 percent of their taxable income in federal income taxes—less than 50 percent of the top income tax rate of 35 percent. The report also noted that about 65 percent of the taxable income of these 400 taxpayers consisted of capital gains and dividends, which are taxed at 15 percent.

Source: ataxingmatter, January 31, 2009

- Why are capital gains and dividends not taxed at 35 percent?
- What effect would a rise in the tax on capital gains and dividends have on the quantity of capital and the efficiency of the capital market?

## Who wins and who loses from globalization?

iPods, Wii games, and Nike shoes are just three of the many things you might buy that are not produced in the United States. Why don't we make these things here and by doing so, create more American jobs?

# Global Markets in Action

CHAPTER CHECKLIST

**When you have completed your study of this chapter, you will be able to**

1 Explain how markets work with international trade.

2 Identify the gains from international trade and its winners and losers.

3 Explain the effects of international trade barriers.

4 Explain and evaluate arguments used to justify restricting international trade.

## 9.1 HOW GLOBAL MARKETS WORK

Because we trade with people in other countries, the goods and services that we buy and consume are not limited by what we produce. The goods and services that we buy from people and firms in other countries are our **imports**; the goods and services that we sell to firms in other countries are our **exports**.

**Imports**
The goods and services that firms in one country buy from people and firms in other countries.

**Exports**
The goods and services that people and firms in one country sell to firms in other countries.

### International Trade Today

Global trade today is enormous. In 2009, global exports and imports (the two numbers are the same because what one country exports another imports) were about $15 trillion, which is 27 percent of the value of global production. The United States is the world's largest international trader and accounts for 10 percent of world exports and 15 percent of world imports. Germany and China, which rank 2 and 3 behind the United States, lag by a large margin.

In 2009, total U.S. exports were $1.5 trillion, which is about 11 percent of the value of U.S. production. Total U.S. imports were $1.9 trillion, which is about 13 percent of the value of total expenditure in the United States.

The United States trades both goods and services. In 2009, exports of services were $0.5 trillion (33 percent of total exports) and imports of services were $0.4 trillion (21 percent of total imports).

Our largest exports are services such as banking, insurance, business consulting, and other private services. Our largest exports of goods are airplanes. Our largest imports are crude oil and automobiles. *Eye on the U.S. Economy* (page 217) provides a bit more detail on our ten largest exports and imports.

### What Drives International Trade?

*Comparative advantage* is the fundamental force that drives international trade. We defined comparative advantage in Chapter 3 (page 75) as the ability of a person to perform an activity or produce a good or service at a lower opportunity cost than anyone else. This same idea applies to nations. We can define *national comparative advantage* as the ability of a *nation* to perform an activity or produce a good or service at a lower opportunity cost than *any other nation*.

The opportunity cost of producing a T-shirt is lower in China than in the United States, so China has a comparative advantage in producing T-shirts. The opportunity cost of producing an airplane is lower in the United States than in China, so the United States has a comparative advantage in producing airplanes.

You saw in Chapter 3 how Liz and Joe reaped gains from trade by specializing in the production of the good at which they have a comparative advantage and then trading. Both were better off. This same principle applies to trade among nations. Because China has a comparative advantage at producing T-shirts and the United States has a comparative advantage at producing airplanes, the people of both countries can gain from specialization and trade. China can buy airplanes from the United States at a lower opportunity cost than that at which it can produce them. And Americans can buy T-shirts from China for a lower opportunity cost than that at which U.S. firms can produce them. Also, through international trade, Chinese producers can get higher prices for their T-shirts and Boeing can sell airplanes for a higher price. Both countries gain from international trade.

Let's now illustrate the gains from trade that we've just described by studying demand and supply in the global markets for T-shirts and airplanes.

# EYE on the U.S. ECONOMY

## U.S. Exports and Imports

The blue bars in part (a) of the figure show the ten largest U.S. exports and the red bars in part (b) show the ten largest U.S. imports. The values are graphed as *net exports* and *net imports* because we both export and import items in most of the categories.

Six of our top ten exports are services—private services (such as the sale of advertising by Google to Adidas, a European sports-wear maker), royalties and license fees (such as fees received by Hollywood movie producers on films shown abroad), business services, financial services, travel (such as the expenditure on a Florida vacation by a visitor from England), and education services (foreign students in our colleges and universities).

Automobiles and the fuel that runs them are our largest imports. We also import large quantities of clothing, furniture, TV sets, DVD players, and computers. Insurance and freight services also feature in our ten largest imports.

Although we import a large quantity of computers, we export many of the semiconductors (computer chips) inside those computers. The Intel chip in a Lenovo laptop built in China and imported into the United States is an example. This chip was made in the United States and previously exported to China.

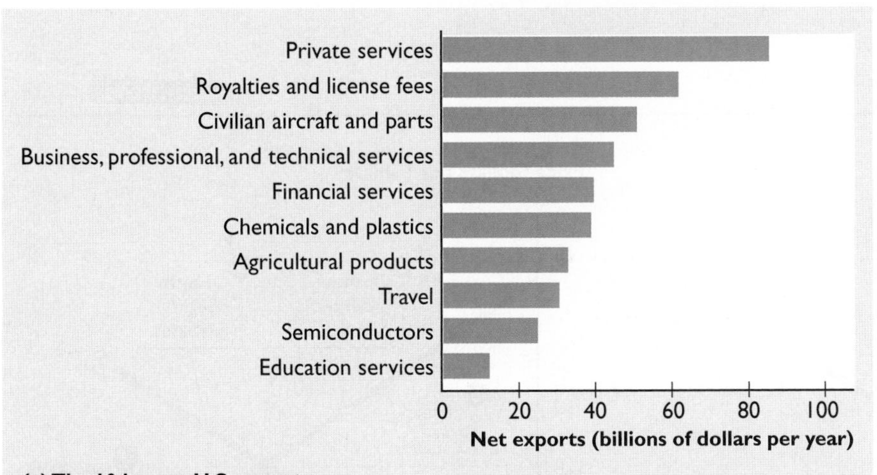


**(a) The 10 largest U.S. exports**

*The United States exports airplanes ...*

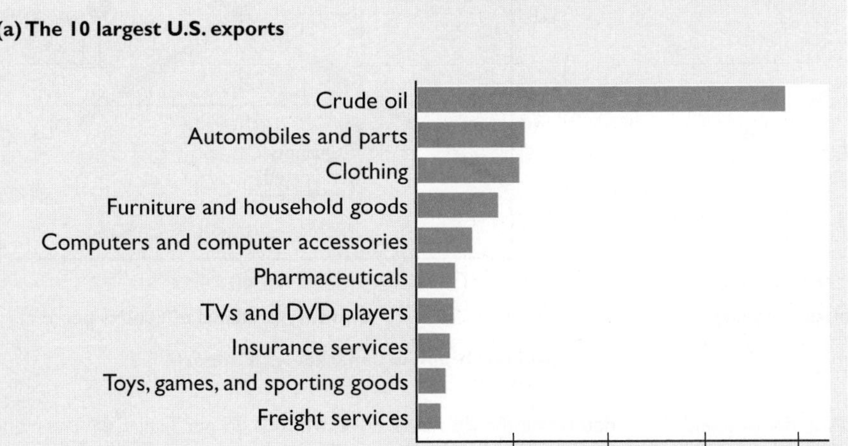


**(b) The 10 largest U.S. imports**

SOURCE OF DATA: Bureau of Economic Analysis.

*and imports crude oil.*

## Why the United States Imports T-Shirts

Figure 9.1 illustrates the effects of international trade in T-shirts. The demand curve $D_{US}$ and the supply curve $S_{US}$ show the demand and supply in the U.S. domestic market only. The demand curve tells us the quantity of T-shirts that Americans are willing to buy at various prices. The supply curve tells us the quantity of T-shirts that U.S. garment makers are willing to sell at various prices.

Figure 9.1(a) shows what the U.S. T-shirt market would be like with no international trade. The price of a T-shirt would be \$8 and 40 million T-shirts a year would be produced by U.S. garment makers and bought by U.S. consumers.

Figure 9.1(b) shows the market for T-shirts *with* international trade. Now the price of a T-shirt is determined in the world market, not the U.S. domestic market. The world price is *less than* \$8 a T-shirt, which means that the rest of the world has a comparative advantage in producing T-shirts. The world price line shows the world price as \$5 a T-shirt.

The U.S. demand curve, $D_{US}$, tells us that at \$5 a T-shirt, Americans buy 60 million T-shirts a year. The U.S. supply curve, $S_{US}$, tells us that at \$5 a T-shirt, U.S. garment makers produce 20 million T-shirts. To buy 60 million T-shirts when only 20 million are produced in the United States, we must import T-shirts from the rest of the world. The quantity of T-shirts imported is 40 million a year.

**FIGURE 9.1**

A Market With Imports

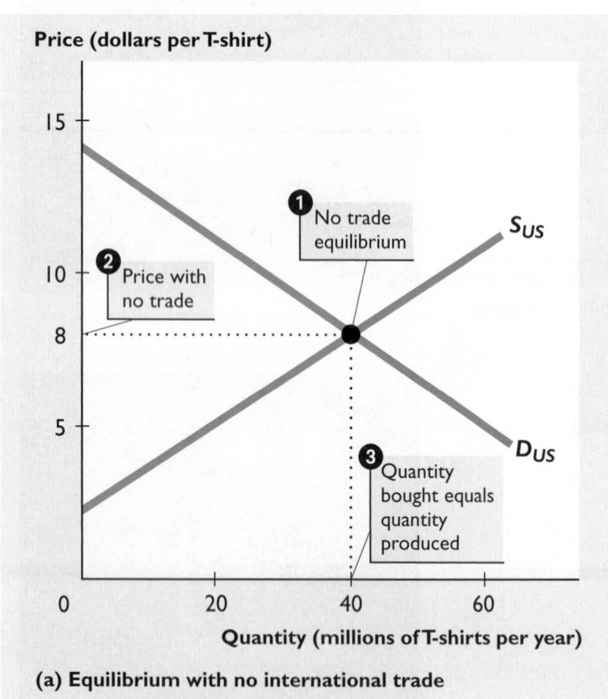


(a) Equilibrium with no international trade

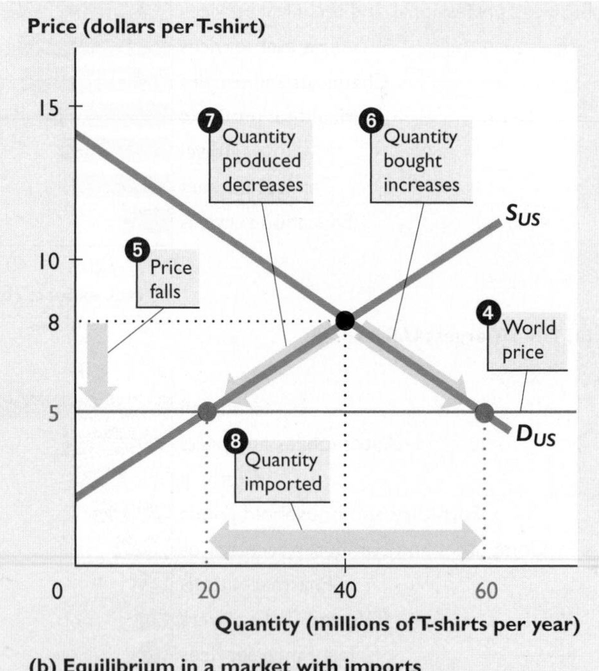


(b) Equilibrium in a market with imports

With no international trade, in part (a), ❶ domestic demand and domestic supply determine ❷ the equilibrium price at \$8 a T-shirt and ❸ the quantity at 40 million T-shirts a year.

With international trade, in part (b), world demand and world supply determine the ❹ world price, which is \$5 per T-shirt. ❺ The market price falls to \$5 a T-shirt. ❻ Domestic purchases increase to 60 million T-shirts a year, and ❼ domestic production decreases to 20 million T-shirts a year. ❽ 40 million T-shirts a year are imported.

## Why the United States Exports Airplanes

Figure 9.2 illustrates the effects of international trade in airplanes. The demand curve $D_{US}$ and the supply curve $S_{US}$ show the demand and supply in the U.S. domestic market only. The demand curve tells us the quantity of airplanes that U.S. airlines are willing to buy at various prices. The supply curve tells us the quantity of airplanes that U.S. aircraft makers are willing to sell at various prices.

Figure 9.2(a) shows what the U.S. airplane market would be like with no international trade. The price of an airplane would be $100 million and 400 airplanes a year would be produced by U.S. aircraft makers and bought by U.S. airlines.

Figure 9.2(b) shows the U.S. airplane market *with* international trade. Now the price of an airplane is determined in the world market, not the U.S. domestic market. The world price is *higher than* $100 million, which means that the United States has a comparative advantage in producing airplanes. The world price line shows the world price as $150 million.

The U.S. demand curve, $D_{US}$, tells us that at $150 million an airplane, U.S. airlines buy 200 airplanes a year. The U.S. supply curve, $S_{US}$, tells us that at $150 million an airplane, U.S. aircraft makers produce 700 airplanes a year. The quantity produced in the United States (700 a year) minus the quantity purchased by U.S. airlines (200 a year) is the quantity of U.S. exports, which is 500 airplanes a year.

**FIGURE 9.2**

A Market With Exports

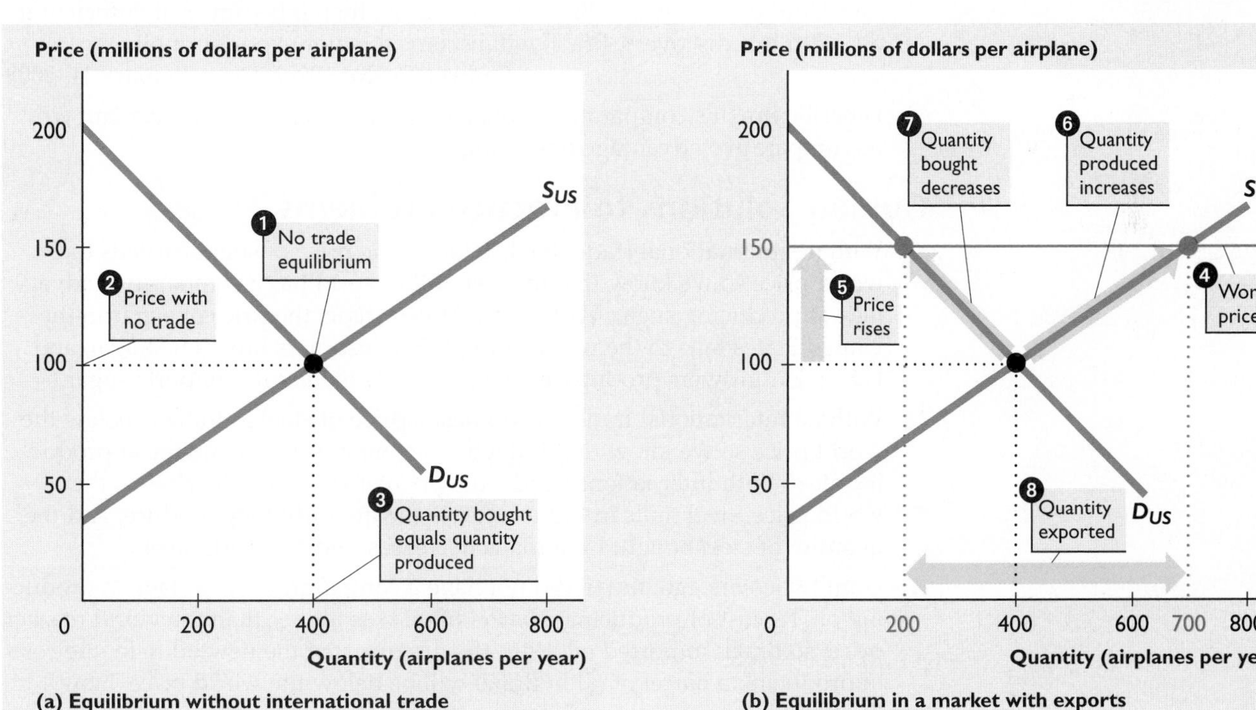


With no international trade, in part (a), ❶ domestic demand and domestic supply determine ❷ the equilibrium price at $100 million an airplane and ❸ the quantity at 400 airplanes a year.

With international trade, in part (b), world demand and world supply determine ❹ the world price, which is $150 million an airplane. ❺ The price rises. ❻ Domestic production increases to 700 airplanes a year, ❼ domestic purchases decrease to 200 airplanes a year, and ❽ 500 airplanes a year are exported.

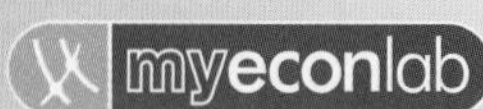

Work these problems in Study Plan 9.1 to get instant feedback.

## CHECKPOINT 9.1

**Explain how markets work with international trade.**

## Practice Problems

1. Suppose that the world price of sugar is 10 cents a pound, the United States does *not* trade internationally, and the equilibrium price of sugar in the United States is 20 cents a pound. The United States then begins to trade internationally.
   - How does the price of sugar in the United States change?
   - Do U.S. consumers buy more or less sugar?
   - Do U.S. sugar growers produce more or less sugar?
   - Does the United States export or import sugar?
2. Suppose that the world price of steel is $100 a ton, India does *not* trade internationally, and the equilibrium price of steel in India is $60 a ton. India then begins to trade internationally.
   - How does the price of steel in India change?
   - How does the quantity of steel produced in India change?
   - How does the quantity of steel bought by India change?
   - Does India export or import steel?
3. **Underwater oil discovery to transform Brazil into a major exporter**
   The discovery of a huge oil field could make Brazil a large exporter of gasoline. Until two years ago Brazil imported oil; then it became self-sufficient in oil. With this discovery, Brazil will become a major exporter of oil.
   Source: *The New York Times*, January 11, 2008
   
   Describe Brazil's comparative advantage in producing oil, and explain why its comparative advantage has changed.

## Guided Solutions to Practice Problems

1. With no international trade, the U.S. domestic price of sugar exceeds the world price so we know that the rest of the world has a comparative advantage at producing sugar. With international trade, the price of sugar in the United States falls to the world price, U.S. consumers buy more sugar, and U.S. sugar growers produce less sugar. The United States imports sugar.
2. With no international trade, the domestic price of steel in India is below the world price so we know that India has a comparative advantage at producing steel. With international trade, the price of steel in India rises to the world price, steel mills in India increase the quantity they produce, and the quantity of steel bought by Indians decreases. India exports steel.
3. Until two years ago, Brazil did not have a comparative advantage in producing oil. Its cost of producing a barrel of oil was higher than the world market price, so Brazil imported oil. With the discovery of the new oil field, the cost of producing a barrel of oil in Brazil will be below the world price. Now Brazil will have a comparative advantage in the production of oil. With this new comparative advantage, Brazil will become an exporter of oil.

## 9.2 WINNERS, LOSERS, AND NET GAINS FROM TRADE

You've seen how international trade lowers the price of an imported good and raises the price of an exported good. Buyers of imported goods benefit from lower prices, and sellers of exported goods benefit from higher prices. But some people complain about international competition: Not everyone gains. We're now going to see who wins and who loses from free international trade. You will then be able to understand who complains about international competition and why.

We'll also see why we never hear the consumers of imported goods complaining and why we never hear exporters complaining, except when they want greater access to foreign markets. And we'll see why we *do* hear complaints from producers about cheap foreign imports.

## EYE on GLOBALIZATION

### Who Wins and Who Loses from Globalization

Economists generally agree that the gains from globalization vastly outweigh the losses. But there are both winners and losers.

The U.S. consumer is a big winner. Globalization has brought iPods, Wii games, Nike shoes, and a wide range of other products to our shops at ever lower prices.

The Indian (and Chinese and other Asian) worker is another big winner. Globalization has brought a wider range of more interesting jobs and higher wages.

The U.S. (and European) textile workers and furniture makers are big losers. Their jobs have disappeared and many of them have struggled to find new jobs even when they've been willing to take a pay cut.

But one of the *biggest* losers is the African farmer. Blocked from global food markets by trade restrictions and subsidies in the United States and Europe, globalization is leaving much of Africa on the sidelines.

*The U.S. consumer ...*

*and the Indian worker gain from globalization.*

*But some U.S. workers ...*

*and African farmers lose.*

## Gains and Losses from Imports

We measure the gains and losses from imports by examining their effect on consumer surplus, producer surplus, and total surplus. The winners are those whose surplus increases and the losers are those whose surplus decreases.

Figure 9.3(a) shows what consumer surplus and producer surplus would be with no international trade. Domestic demand, $D_{US}$, and domestic supply, $S_{US}$, determine the price and quantity. The green area shows consumer surplus and the blue area shows producer surplus. Total surplus is the sum of consumer surplus and producer surplus.

Figure 9.3(b) shows how these surpluses change when the market opens to imports. The price falls to the world price. The quantity purchased increases to the quantity demanded at the world price, and consumer surplus expands to the larger green area $A + B + D$. The quantity produced decreases to the quantity supplied at the world price, and producer surplus shrinks to the smaller blue area $C$.

Part of the gain in consumer surplus, the area $B$, is a loss of producer surplus—a redistribution of total surplus. But the other part of the increase in consumer surplus, the area $D$, is a net gain. This increase in total surplus is the gain from imports and results from the lower price and increased purchases.

**FIGURE 9.3**

Gains and Losses in a Market with Imports

myeconlab Animation

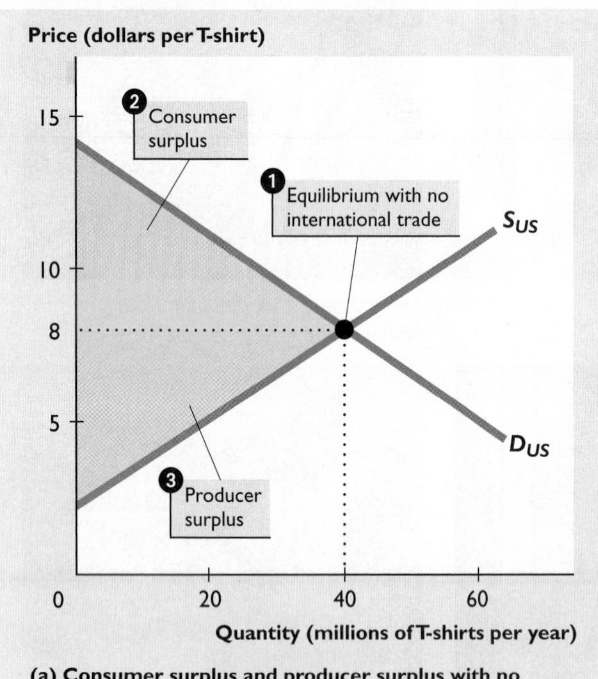


(a) Consumer surplus and producer surplus with no international trade

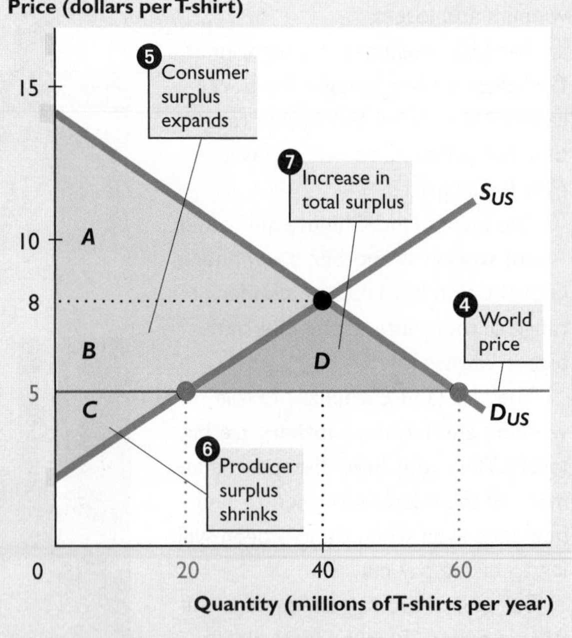


(b) Gains and losses from imports

With no international trade, 1 equilibrium at the intersection of the domestic demand and domestic supply curves determines the price and quantity. 2 The green area shows the consumer surplus and 3 the blue area shows the producer surplus.

With international trade, the price falls to 4 the world price. 5 Consumer surplus expands to the area $A + B + D$. Area $B$ is a transfer of surplus from producers to consumers, and 6 producer surplus shrinks to area $C$. 7 Area $D$ is an increase in total surplus.

## Gains and Losses from Exports

We measure the gains and losses from exports just like we measured those from imports, by examining their effect on consumer surplus, producer surplus, and total surplus.

Figure 9.4(a) shows what the consumer surplus and producer surplus would be with no international trade. Domestic demand, $D_{US}$, and domestic supply, $S_{US}$, determine the price and quantity. The green area shows consumer surplus and the blue area shows producer surplus. The two surpluses sum to total surplus.

Figure 9.4(b) shows how the consumer surplus and producer surplus change when the good is exported. The price rises to the world price. The quantity bought decreases to the quantity demanded at the world price, and the consumer surplus shrinks to the green area *A*. The quantity produced increases to the quantity supplied at the world price, and the producer surplus expands from the blue area *C* to the larger blue area *B* + *C* + *D*.

Part of the gain of producer surplus, the area *B*, is a loss in consumer surplus—a redistribution of the total surplus. But the other part of the increase in producer surplus, the area *D*, is a net gain. This increase in total surplus is the gain from exports and results from the higher price and increased production.

**FIGURE 9.4**

Gains and Losses in a Market with Exports

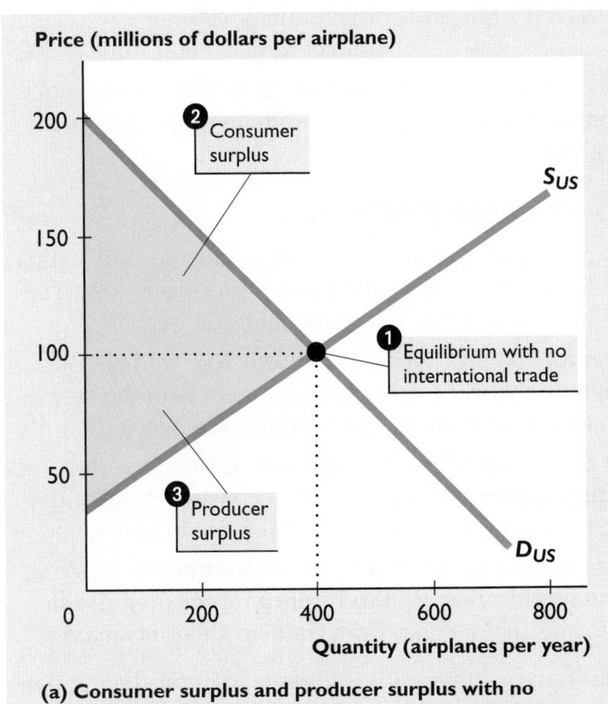


**(a) Consumer surplus and producer surplus with no international trade**

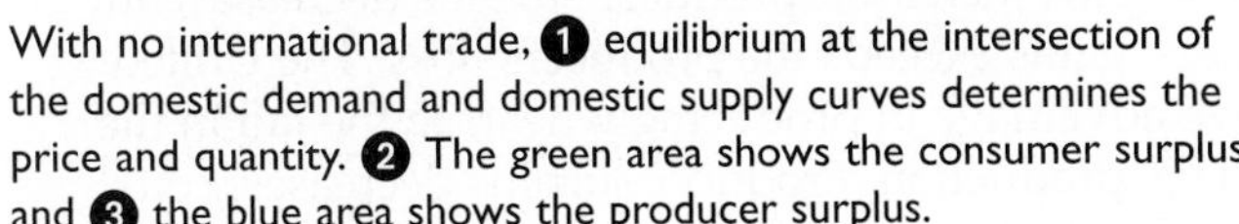

With no international trade, ❶ equilibrium at the intersection of the domestic demand and domestic supply curves determines the price and quantity. ❷ The green area shows the consumer surplus and ❸ the blue area shows the producer surplus.

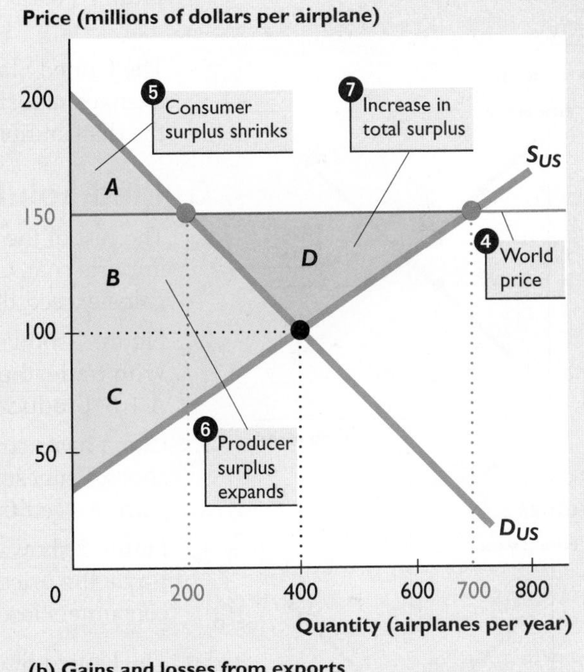


**(b) Gains and losses from exports**

With international trade, the price rises to ❹ the world price. ❺ Consumer surplus shrinks to the area *A*. ❻ Producer surplus expands to the area *B* + *C* + *D*. Area *B* is transferred from consumers to producers. ❼ Area *D* is an increase in total surplus.

Work these problems in Study Plan 9.2 to get instant feedback.

## CHECKPOINT 9.2

**Identify the gains from international trade and its winners and losers.**

### Practice Problems

Before the 1980s, China did not trade internationally: It was self-sufficient in coal and shoes. Then China began to trade internationally, the world price of coal was less than China's domestic price and the world price of shoes was higher than its domestic price. Use this information to work Problems **1** to **4**.

1. Does China import or export coal? Who, in China, gains and who loses from international trade in coal? Does China gain from this trade in coal?
2. Draw a graph to illustrate the market for coal in China before and after China trades coal internationally and show on your graph the gains, losses, and net gain or loss from international trade in coal.
3. Does China import or export shoes? Who, in China, gains and who loses from international trade in shoes? Does China gain from this trade in shoes?
4. On a graph of the market for shoes in China, show the gains, losses, and net gain or loss from international trade in shoes.
5. **Commodities post big drop**
   World commodity prices have fallen in the past six weeks. Natural gas plunged 8.6%, wheat prices fell 7.8%, and corn slumped 3.8%.
   Source: *National Post*, June 3, 2009
   The United States imports natural gas and exports wheat. How do the price changes reported here change the U.S. gains from trade in each good and the distribution of those gains?

**FIGURE 1**

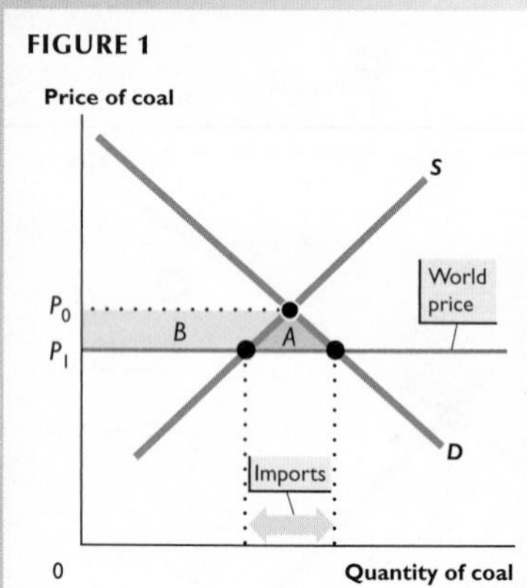


**FIGURE 2**

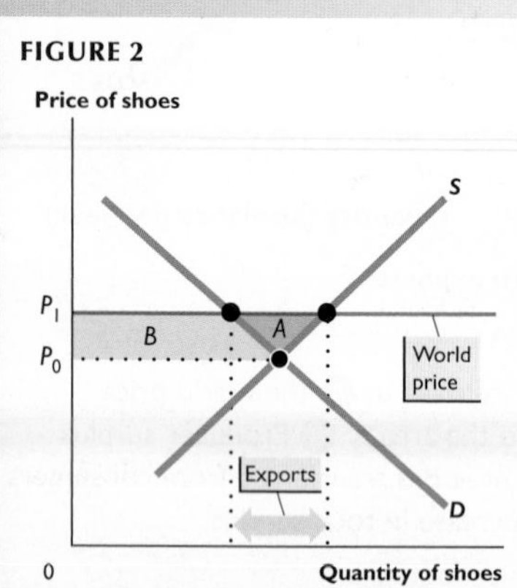


### Guided Solutions to Practice Problems

1. The rest of the world has a comparative advantage in producing coal. China imports coal, Chinese coal users gain, and Chinese coal producers lose. The gains exceed the losses: China gains from international trade in coal.
2. Figure 1 shows the market for coal in China. The price before trade is $P_0$. With trade, the price falls to the world price, $P_1$. Consumers gain the area $A + B$, producers lose the area $B$, and the net gain from trade in coal is $A$.
3. China has a comparative advantage in producing shoes. China exports shoes, Chinese shoe producers gain, and Chinese shoe consumers lose. The gains exceed the losses: China gains from international trade in shoes.
4. Figure 2 shows the shoe market in China. The price before trade is $P_0$. With trade, the price rises to the world price, $P_1$. Producers gain the area $A + B$, consumers lose the area $B$, and the net gain from trade in shoes is area $A$.
5. The United States does not have a comparative advantage in producing natural gas, so the fall in the world price increases imports and decreases U.S. production. Consumer surplus increases, producer surplus decreases, but the increase in consumers' gains exceeds the producers' loss. The United States has a comparative advantage in producing wheat, so the fall in the world price decreases U.S. production. Producer surplus decreases, consumer surplus increases, but the decrease in producer surplus exceeds the increase in consumer surplus.

## 9.3 INTERNATIONAL TRADE RESTRICTIONS

Governments use four sets of tools to influence international trade and protect domestic industries from foreign competition. They are

- Tariffs
- Import quotas
- Other import barriers
- Export subsidies

### Tariffs

A **tariff** is a tax that is imposed on a good when it is imported. For example, the government of India imposes a 100 percent tariff on wine imported from California. When an Indian firm imports a $10 bottle of Californian wine, it pays the Indian government a $10 import duty.

**Tariff**
A tax imposed on a good when it is imported.

The incentive for governments to impose tariffs is strong. First, they provide revenue to the government. Second, they enable the government to satisfy the self-interest of people who earn their incomes in import-competing industries. As you will see, tariffs and other restrictions on free international trade decrease the gains from trade and are not in the social interest. Let's see how.

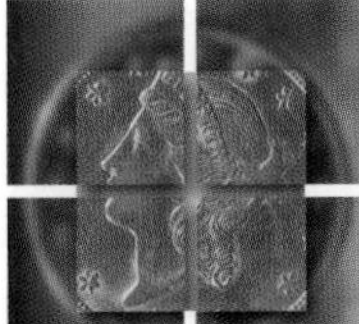

## EYE on the PAST

### The History of U.S. Tariffs

The figure shows the average tariff rate on U.S. imports since 1930. Tariffs peaked during the 1930s when Congress passed the Smoot-Hawley Act. With other nations, the United States signed the General Agreement on Tariffs and Trade (GATT) in 1947. In a series of rounds of negotiations, GATT achieved widespread tariff cuts for the United States and many other nations. Today, the World Trade Organization (WTO) continues the work of GATT and seeks to promote unrestricted trade among all nations.

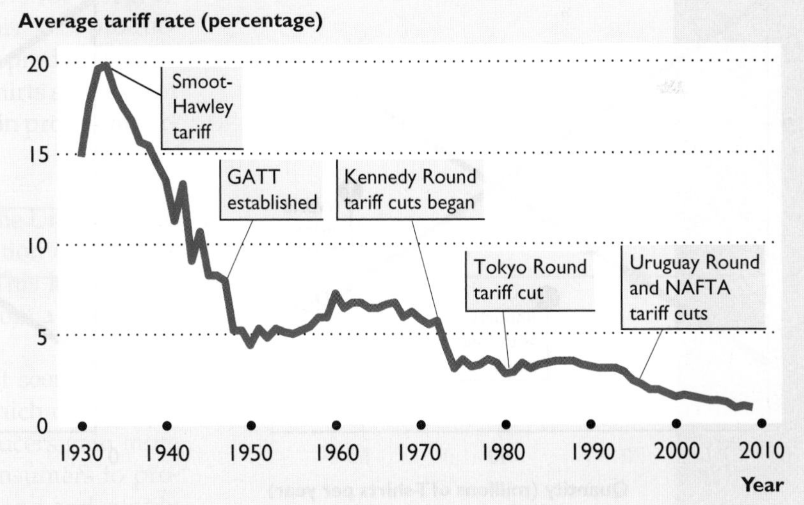


SOURCES OF DATA: The Budget for Fiscal Year 2006, Historical Tables, Table 2.5 and Bureau of Economic Analysis.

The United States is a party to many trade agreements with individual countries or regions. These include the North American Free Trade Agreement (NAFTA) and the Central American Free Trade Agreement (CAFTA). These agreements have eliminated tariffs on most goods traded between the United States and the countries of Central and North America.

**FIGURE 9.6**

## The Winners and Losers from a Tariff

Animation

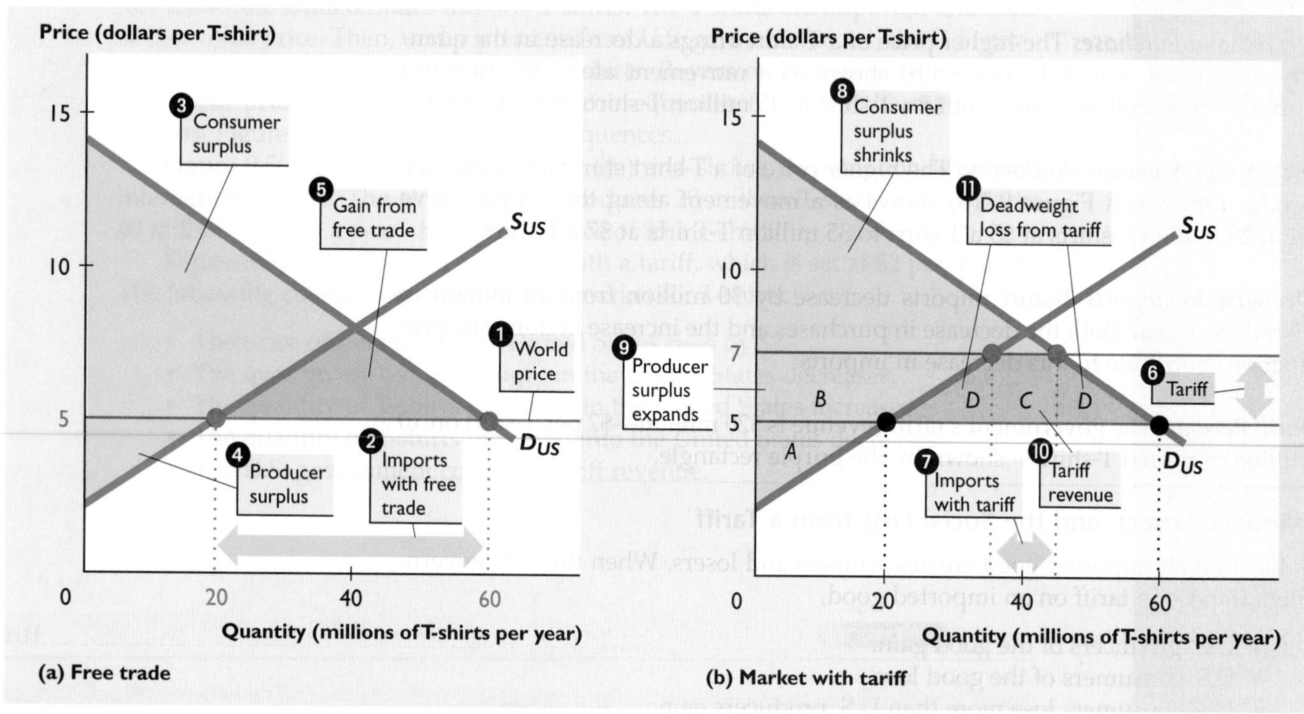


1 The world price of a T-shirt is \$5. With free trade, 2 the United States imports 40 million T-shirts. 3 Consumer surplus, 4 producer surplus, and 5 the gains from free international trade are as large as possible. 6 A tariff of \$2 per T-shirt raises the price of a T-shirt to \$7. 7 The quantity imported decreases. 8 Consumer surplus shrinks by the areas *B*, *C*, and *D*. 9 Producer surplus expands by area *B*. 10 The government's tariff revenue is area *C*, and 11 the tariff creates a deadweight loss equal to the areas *D*.

Figure 9.6(b) with Figure 9.6(a), you can see how a \$2 tariff on imported T-shirts changes the surpluses. Producer surplus—the blue area—increases by the area labeled *B*. The increase in producer surplus is the gain by U.S. producers from the tariff. Consumer surplus—the green area—shrinks.

The decrease in consumer surplus divides into three parts. First, some of the consumer surplus is transferred to producers. The blue area *B* represents this loss of consumer surplus (and gain of producer surplus). Second, part of the consumer surplus is transferred to the government. The purple area *C* represents this loss of consumer surplus (and gain of government revenue). When the tariff revenue is spent, both consumers and producers receive some benefit, but there is no expectation that the buyers of T-shirts will receive the benefits of the expenditure of this tariff revenue from T-shirts. The tariff revenue is a loss to buyers of T-shirts.

The third part of the loss of consumer surplus is a transfer to no one: it is a *deadweight loss*. Consumers buy a smaller quantity at a higher price. The two gray areas labeled *D* represent this loss of consumer surplus. Total surplus decreases by this amount, which is the social loss from the tariff.

Let's now look at the second tool for restricting trade: quotas.

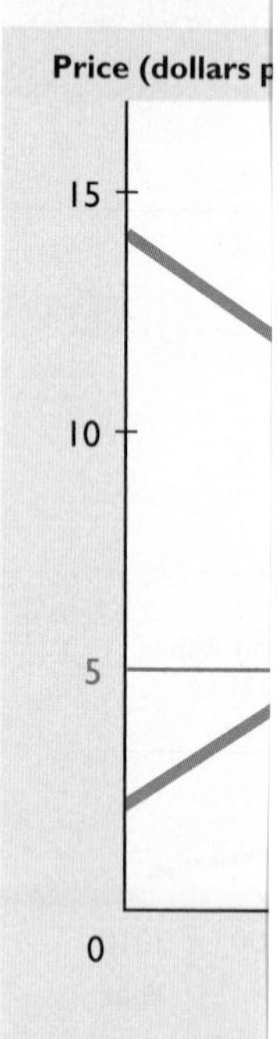

## Import Quotas

An **import quota** is a quantitative restriction on the import of a good that limits the maximum quantity of a good that may be imported in a given period. The United States imposes import quotas on many items, including sugar, bananas, and textiles.

**Import quota**
A quantitative restriction on the import of a good that limits the maximum quantity of a good that may be imported in a given period.

Quotas enable the government to satisfy the self-interest of people who earn their incomes in import-competing industries. You will see that like a tariff, a quota on imports decreases the gains from trade and is not in the social interest.

### The Effects of an Import Quota

The effects of an import quota are similar to those of a tariff. The price rises, the quantity bought decreases, and the quantity produced in the United States increases. Figure 9.7 illustrates the effects.

Figure 9.7(a) shows the situation with free international trade. Figure 9.7(b) shows what happens with a quota that limits imports to 10 million T-shirts a year. The U.S. supply curve of T-shirts becomes the domestic supply curve, $S_{US}$, plus the quantity that the quota permits to be imported. So the U.S. supply curve becomes the curve labeled $S_{US}$ + *quota*. The price of a T-shirt rises to $7, the

**FIGURE 9.7**

The Effects of an Import Quota

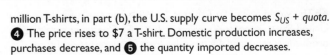

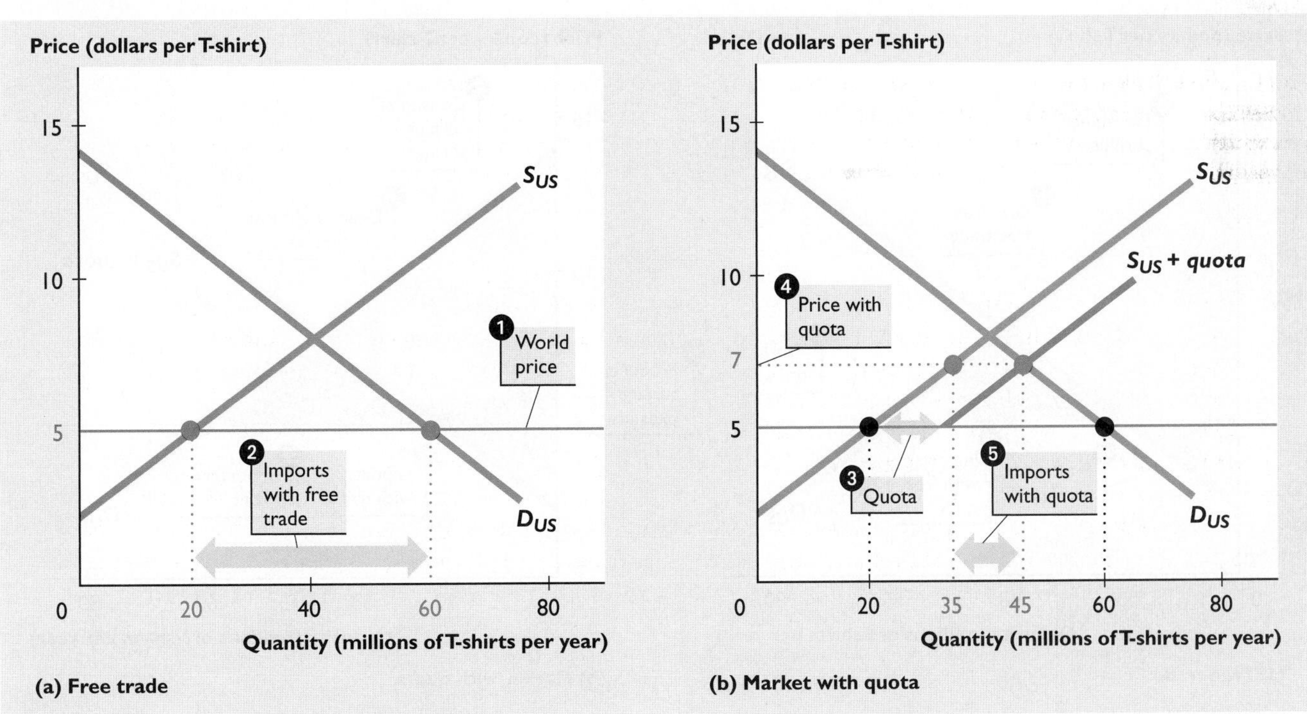


With free trade, in part (a), Americans buy 60 million T-shirts at ❶ the world price. The United States produces 20 million T-shirts and ❷ imports 40 million T-shirts. ❸ With an import quota of 10 million T-shirts, in part (b), the U.S. supply curve becomes $S_{US}$ + *quota*. ❹ The price rises to $7 a T-shirt. Domestic production increases, purchases decrease, and ❺ the quantity imported decreases.

quantity of T-shirts bought in the United States decreases to 45 million a year, the quantity of T-shirts produced in the United States increases to 35 million a year, and the quantity of T-shirts imported into the United States decreases to the quota quantity of 10 million a year. All these effects of a quota are identical to the effects of a $2 per T-shirt tariff, as you can check in Figure 9.6(b).

### Winners, Losers, and the Social Loss from an Import Quota

An import quota creates winners and losers that are similar to those of a tariff but with an interesting difference. When the government imposes an import quota,

- U.S. producers of the good gain.
- U.S. consumers of the good lose.
- Importers of the good gain.
- U.S. consumers lose more than U.S. producers and importers gain.

Figure 9.8 compares the gains from trade under free trade with those under a quota. Figure 9.8(a) shows the consumer surplus and producer surplus with free international trade in T-shirts. By comparing Figure 9.8(b) with Figure 9.8(a), you can see how an import quota of 10 million T-shirts changes the surpluses. Producer surplus—the blue area—increases by the area labeled *B*. The increase in

**FIGURE 9.8**

The Winners and Losers from an Import Quota

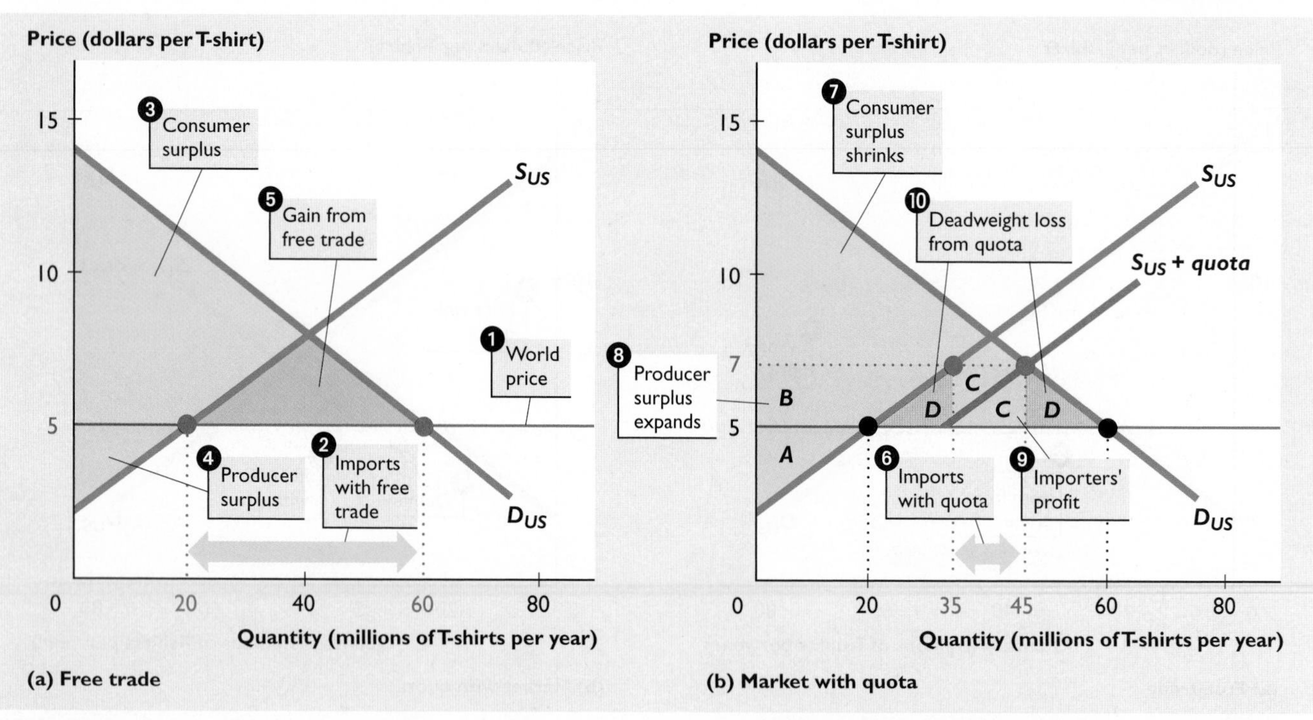


❶ The world price of a T-shirt is $5. With free trade, ❷ the United States imports 40 million T-shirts. ❸ Consumer surplus, ❹ producer surplus, and ❺ the gains from free international trade are as large as possible. An import quota raises the price of a T-shirt to $7. ❻ The quantity imported decreases. ❼ Consumer surplus shrinks by the areas *B*, *C*, and *D*. ❽ Producer surplus expands by area *B*. ❾ Importers' profit is areas *C*, and ❿ the quota creates a deadweight loss equal to the areas *D*.

producer surplus is the gain by U.S. producers from the import quota. Consumer surplus—the green area—shrinks. This decrease is the loss to consumers from the import quota.

The decrease in consumer surplus divides into three parts. First, some of the consumer surplus is transferred to producers. The blue area *B* represents this loss of consumer surplus (and gain of producer surplus). Second, part of the consumer surplus is transferred to importers who buy T-shirts for $5 (the world price) and sell them for $7 (the domestic price). The blue areas *C* represent this loss of consumer surplus and profit for importers.

The third part of the loss of consumer surplus is a transfer to no one: it is a *deadweight loss*. Consumers buy a smaller quantity at a higher price. The two gray areas labeled *D* represent this loss of consumer surplus. Total surplus decreases by this amount, which is the social loss from the import quota.

You can now see the one difference between an import quota and a tariff. A tariff brings in revenue for the government while an import quota brings a profit for the importer. All the other effects are the same, provided the quota is set at the same level of imports that results from the tariff.

## ■ Other Import Barriers

Two sets of policies that influence imports are

- Health, safety, and regulation barriers
- Voluntary export restraints

### Health, Safety, and Regulation Barriers

Thousands of detailed health, safety, and other regulations restrict international trade. For example, U.S. food imports are examined by the Food and Drug Administration to determine whether the food is "pure, wholesome, safe to eat, and produced under sanitary conditions." The discovery of BSE (mad cow disease) in just one U.S. cow in 2003 was enough to close down international trade in U.S. beef. The European Union bans imports of most genetically modified foods, such as U.S.-produced soybeans. Although regulations of the type we've just described are not designed to limit international trade, they have that effect.

### Voluntary Export Restraints

A *voluntary export restraint* is like a quota allocated to a foreign exporter of the good. A voluntary export restraint decreases imports just like an import quota does, but the foreign exporter gets the profit from the gap between the domestic price and the world price.

## ■ Export Subsidies

A **subsidy** is a payment by the government to a producer. An *export subsidy* is a payment by the government to the producer of an exported good. The U.S. and European Union governments subsidize farm products. These subsidies stimulate the production and export of farm products, but they make it harder for producers in other countries, notably in Africa and Central and South America, to compete in global markets. Export subsidies bring gains to domestic producers, but they result in overproduction in the domestic economy and underproduction in the rest of the world and so create a deadweight loss (see Chapter 6, p. 157).

**Subsidy**
A payment by the government to a producer.

Work these problems in Study Plan 9.3 to get instant feedback.

## CHECKPOINT 9.3

**Explain the effects of international trade barriers.**

### Practice Problems

Before 1995, the United States imposed tariffs on goods imported from Mexico and Mexico imposed tariffs on goods imported from the United States. In 1995, Mexico joined NAFTA. U.S. tariffs on imports from Mexico and Mexican tariffs on imports from the United States are gradually being removed. Use this information to work Problems **1** to **3**.

1. Explain how the price that U.S. consumers pay for goods imported from Mexico and the quantity of U.S. imports from Mexico have changed. Who, in the United States, are the winners and losers from this free trade?
2. Explain how the quantity of U.S. exports to Mexico and the U.S. government's tariff revenue from trade with Mexico have changed.
3. Suppose that in 2008, tomato growers in Florida lobby the U.S. government to impose an import quota on Mexican tomatoes. Explain who, in the United States, would gain and who would lose from such a quota.
4. **U.S. tariff angers French**
   Just days before Obama took office, the United States raised the tariff on imports of French sheep's-milk cheese to 300% from 100%—with the hope that the domestic price will be so high that imports of the cheese will cease.
   Source: *The Guardian*, January 17, 2009

   Explain how this tariff influences the price that U.S. consumers pay for sheep's-milk cheese, the quantity of sheep's-milk cheese produced in the United States, and the effect of the tariff on U.S. gains from trade with France. Who, in the United States, gains from the tariff and who loses?

### Guided Solutions to Practice Problems

1. The price that U.S. consumers pay for goods imported from Mexico has fallen and the quantity of U.S. imports from Mexico has increased. The winners are U.S. consumers of goods imported from Mexico and the losers are U.S. producers of goods imported from Mexico.
2. The quantity of U.S. exports to Mexico has increased and the U.S. government's tariff revenue from trade with Mexico has fallen.
3. With a quota, the price of tomatoes in the United States would rise and the quantity bought would decrease. Consumer surplus would decrease. Growers would receive a higher price, produce a larger quantity, and producer surplus would increase. The U.S. total surplus in the tomato market would be redistributed from consumers to producers, but it would decrease.
4. The tariff raises the price of sheep's-milk cheese in the United States to 400 percent of the world price (world price + 300 percent of the world price). U.S. imports decrease, U.S. production of sheep's-milk cheese increases, and the U.S. government collects a tariff revenue. With the higher U.S. domestic price, consumer surplus decreases—consumers lose. Producer surplus increases—producers gain. Some of the loss of consumer surplus goes to the government as tariff revenue and some becomes a deadweight loss.

## 9.4 THE CASE AGAINST PROTECTION

For as long as nations and international trade have existed, people have debated whether free international trade or protection from foreign competition is better for a country. The debate continues, but most economists believe that free trade promotes prosperity for all countries while protection reduces the potential gains from trade. We've seen the most powerful case for free trade: All countries benefit from their comparative advantage. But there is a broader range of issues in the free trade versus protection debate. Let's review these issues.

### Three Traditional Arguments for Protection

Three traditional arguments for protection and restricting international trade are

- The national security argument
- The infant-industry argument
- The dumping argument

Let's look at each in turn.

#### The National Security Argument

The national security argument is that a country must protect industries that produce defense equipment and armaments and those on which the defense industries rely for their raw materials and other intermediate inputs. This argument for protection can be taken too far.

First, it is an argument for international isolation, for in a time of war, there is no industry that does not contribute to national defense. Second, if the case is made for boosting the output of a strategic industry—say aerospace—it is more efficient to achieve this outcome with a subsidy financed out of taxes than with a tariff or import quota. A subsidy would keep the industry operating at the scale that is judged appropriate, and free international trade would keep the prices faced by consumers at their world market levels.

#### The Infant-Industry Argument

**Infant-industry argument**
The argument that it is necessary to protect a new industry to enable it to grow into a mature industry that can compete in world markets.

The **infant-industry argument** is that it is necessary to protect a new industry to enable it to grow into a mature industry that can compete in world markets. The argument is based on an idea called *learning-by-doing*. By working repeatedly at a task, workers become better at that task and can increase the amount they produce in a given period.

There is nothing wrong with the idea of learning-by-doing. It is a powerful engine of human capital accumulation and economic growth. Learning-by-doing can change comparative advantage. If on-the-job experience lowers the opportunity cost of producing a good, a country might develop a comparative advantage in producing that good. Learning-by-doing does not justify protection.

It is in the self-interest of firms and workers who benefit from learning-by-doing to produce the efficient quantities. If the government protected these firms to boost their production, there would be an inefficient overproduction (just like the overproduction in Chapter 6, p. 157).

The historical evidence is against the protection of infant industries. Countries in East Asia that have not given such protection have performed well. Countries that have protected infant industries, as India once did, have performed poorly.

## The Dumping Argument

**Dumping**
When a foreign firm sells its exports at a lower price than its cost of production.

**Dumping** occurs when a foreign firm sells its exports at a lower price than its cost of production. You might be wondering why a firm would ever want to sell any of its output at a price below the cost of production. Wouldn't such a firm be better off either selling nothing, or, if it could do so, raising its price to at least cover its costs? Two possible reasons why a firm might sell at a price below cost and therefore engage in dumping are

- Predatory pricing
- Subsidy

***Predatory Pricing*** A firm that engages in *predatory pricing* sets its price below cost in the hope that it can drive its competitors out of the market. If a firm in one country tries to drive out competitors in another country, it will be *dumping* its product in the foreign market. The foreign firm sells its output at a price below its cost to drive domestic firms out of business. When the domestic firms have gone, the foreign firm takes advantage of its monopoly position and charges a higher price for its product. The higher price will attract new competitors, which makes it unlikely that this strategy will be profitable. For this reason, economists are skeptical that this type of dumping occurs.

***Subsidy*** A *subsidy* is a payment by the government to a producer. A firm that receives a subsidy is able to sell profitably for a price below cost. Subsidies are very common in almost all countries. The United States and the European Union subsidize the production of many agricultural products and dump their surpluses on the world market. This action lowers the prices that farmers in developing nations receive and weakens the incentive to expand farming in poor countries. India and Europe have been suspected of dumping steel in the United States.

Whatever its source, dumping is illegal under the rules of the WTO, NAFTA, and CAFTA and is regarded as a justification for temporary tariffs. Consequently, anti-dumping tariffs have become important in today's world.

But there are powerful reasons to resist the dumping argument for protection. First, it is virtually impossible to detect dumping because it is hard to determine a firm's costs. As a result, the test for dumping is whether a firm's export price is below its domestic price. This test is a weak one because it can be rational for a firm to charge a lower price in markets in which the quantity demanded is highly sensitive to price and a higher price in a market in which demand is less price-sensitive.

Second, it is hard to think of a good that is produced by a single firm. Even if all the domestic firms were driven out of business in some industry, it would always be possible to find several and usually many alternative foreign sources of supply and to buy at prices determined in competitive markets.

Third, if a good or service were a truly global natural monopoly, the best way to deal with it would be by regulation—just as in the case of domestic monopolies. Such regulation would require international cooperation.

The three arguments for protection that we've just examined have an element of credibility. The counterarguments are in general stronger, so these arguments do not make the case for protection. They are not the only arguments that you might encounter. There are many others, four of which we'll now examine.

## Four Newer Arguments for Protection

Four newer and commonly made arguments for restricting international trade are that protection

- Saves jobs
- Allows us to compete with cheap foreign labor
- Brings diversity and stability
- Penalizes lax environmental standards

### Saves Jobs

When Americans buy imported goods such as shoes from Brazil, U.S. workers who produce shoes lose their jobs. With no earnings and poor prospects, these workers become a drain on welfare and spend less, which creates a ripple effect of further job losses. The proposed solution is to protect U.S. jobs by banning imports of cheap foreign goods. The proposal is flawed for the following reasons.

First, free trade does cost some jobs, but it also creates other jobs. It brings about a global rationalization of labor and allocates labor resources to their highest-valued activities. Because of international trade in textiles, tens of thousands of workers in the United States have lost jobs because textile mills and other factories have closed. Tens of thousands of workers in other countries now have jobs because textile mills have opened there. And tens of thousands of U.S. workers now have better-paying jobs than as textile workers because other export industries have expanded and created more jobs than have been destroyed.

Second, imports create jobs. They create jobs for retailers that sell imported goods and for firms that service those goods. They also create jobs by creating incomes in the rest of the world, some of which are spent on imports of U.S.-made goods and services.

Protection saves some particular jobs, but it does so at a high cost. For example, until 2005, textile jobs in the United States were protected by import quotas imposed under an international agreement called the Multifiber Arrangement (or MFA). The U.S. International Trade Commission (ITC) estimated that because of import quotas, 72,000 jobs existed in textiles that would otherwise disappear and annual clothing expenditure in the United States was $15.9 billion ($160 per family) higher than it would be with free trade. An implication of the ITC estimate is that each textile job saved cost consumers $221,000 a year. The end of the MFA led to the destruction of a large number of textile jobs in the United States and Europe in 2005.

### Allows Us to Compete with Cheap Foreign Labor

With the removal of protective tariffs in U.S. trade with Mexico, some people said that jobs would be sucked into Mexico and that the United States would not be able to compete with its southern neighbor. Let's see what's wrong with this view.

Labor costs depend on the wage rate and the quantity a worker produces. For example, if a U.S. auto worker earns $30 an hour and produces 15 units of output an hour, the average labor cost of a unit of output is $2. If a Mexican auto worker earns $3 an hour and produces 1 unit of output an hour, the average labor cost of a unit of output is $3. Other things remaining the same, the greater the output a worker produces, the higher is the worker's wage rate. High-wage workers produce a large output. Low-wage workers produce a small output.

Work these problems in Study Plan 9.4 to get instant feedback.

# CHECKPOINT 9.4

**Explain and evaluate arguments used to justify restricting international trade.**

## Practice Problems

1. Japan sets an import quota on rice. California rice growers would like to export more rice to Japan. What are Japan's arguments for restricting imports of Californian rice? Are these arguments correct? Who loses from this restriction in trade?
2. The United States has, from time to time, limited imports of steel from Europe. What argument has the United States used to justify this quota? Who wins from this restriction? Who loses?
3. The United States maintains an import quota on sugar. What is the argument for this import quota? Is this argument flawed? If so, explain why.
4. **U.S., China agree on free farm trade**

   Despite the failure of the Doha Round, the United States and China agree on the need to resist protectionist farm tariffs even in the face of the world economic crisis. In 2007, the United States exported $9.4 billion of farm and processed food products to China and imported $8 billion of farm products from China.

   Source: *USA Today*, December 6, 2008

   With the world in a global economic crisis, what arguments against free trade might U.S. producers of the farm products put forward? What would be wrong with the argument you suggest?

## Guided Solutions to Practice Problems

1. The main arguments are that Japanese rice is a better quality rice and that the quota limits competition faced by Japanese farmers. The arguments are not correct. If Japanese consumers do not like the quality of Californian rice, they will not buy it. The quota does limit competition and the quota allows Japanese farmers to use their land less efficiently. The big losers are the Japanese consumers who pay about three times the U.S. price for rice.
2. The U.S. argument is that European producers dump steel on the U.S. market. With an import quota, U.S. steel producers will face less competition and U.S. jobs will be saved. Workers in the steel industry and owners of steel companies will win at the expense of U.S. buyers of steel.
3. The argument is that the import quota protects the jobs of U.S. workers. The argument is flawed because the United States does not have a comparative advantage in producing sugar and so an import quota allows the U.S. sugar industry to be inefficient. With free international trade in sugar, the U.S. sugar industry would exist but it would be much smaller and more efficient.
4. With the United States in recession, a likely argument against free trade with China in farm products would be "impose restrictions to save U.S. jobs." By reducing imports of farm products, U.S. growers will receive a larger producer surplus, but U.S. total surplus will decrease.

# CHAPTER SUMMARY

## Key Points

1 **Explain how markets work with international trade.**

- Comparative advantage drives international trade.
- When the world price of a good is lower than the price that balances domestic demand and supply, a country gains by decreasing production and importing the good.
- When the world price of a good is higher than the price that balances domestic demand and supply, a country gains by increasing production and exporting the good.

2 **Identify the gains from international trade and its winners and losers.**

- Compared to a no-trade situation, in a market with imports, consumer surplus is larger, producer surplus is smaller, and total surplus is larger with free international trade.
- Compared to a no-trade situation, in a market with exports, consumer surplus is smaller, producer surplus is larger, and total surplus is larger with free international trade.

3 **Explain the effects of international trade barriers.**

- Countries restrict international trade by imposing tariffs, import quotas, and other import barriers, and export subsidies.
- Trade restrictions raise the domestic price of imported goods, lower the quantity imported, decrease consumer surplus, increase producer surplus, and create a deadweight loss.

4 **Explain and evaluate arguments used to justify restricting international trade.**

- The arguments that protection is necessary for national security, for infant industries, and to prevent dumping are weak.
- Arguments that protection saves jobs, allows us to compete with cheap foreign labor, makes the economy diversified and stable, and is needed to penalize lax environmental standards are flawed.
- Trade is restricted because protection brings small losses to a large number of people and large gains to a small number of people.

## Key Terms

Work these problems in Chapter 9 Study Plan to get instant feedback.

FIGURE 1 U.S. SHOE MARKET

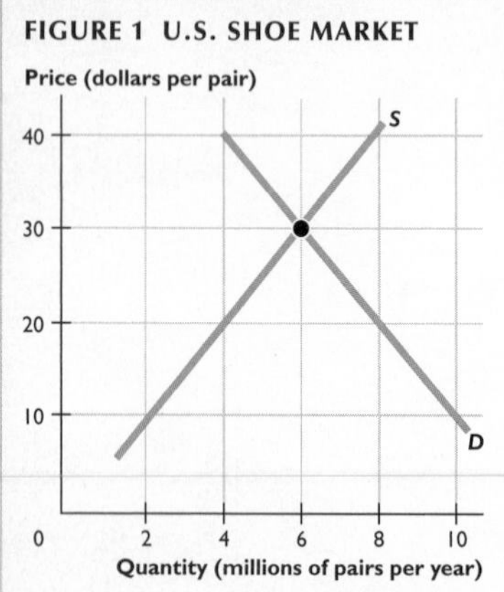


FIGURE 2 BRAZIL'S SHOE MARKET

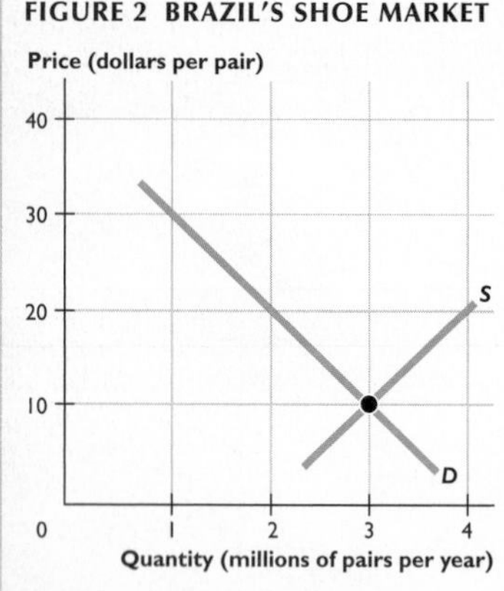


# CHAPTER CHECKPOINT

## Study Plan Problems and Applications

Use the information in Figures 1 and 2 to work Problems 1 to 4. Figure 1 shows the U.S. market for shoes and Figure 2 shows Brazil's market for shoes if there is no international trade in shoes between the United States and Brazil.

1. Which country has a comparative advantage in producing shoes? With international trade between Brazil and the United States, explain which country would export shoes and how the price of shoes in the importing country and the quantity produced by the importing country would change. Explain which country gains from this trade.
2. With international trade, the world price of a pair of shoes is $20. Explain how consumer surplus and producer surplus in the United States changes as a result of international trade. Show the change in U.S. consumer surplus (label it *A*) and the change in U.S. producer surplus (label it *B*).
3. The world price of a pair of shoes is $20. Explain how consumer surplus and producer surplus in Brazil changes as a result of international trade. Show the change in Brazil's consumer surplus (label it C) and the change in Brazil's producer surplus (label it *D*).
4. Who in the United States loses from free trade in shoes with Brazil? Explain why.

Use the following information to work Problems 5 to 7.

The supply of roses in the United States is made up of U.S. grown roses and imported roses. Draw a graph to illustrate the U.S. rose market with free international trade in roses. On your graph, mark the price of roses and the quantities of roses bought, produced, and imported into the United States.

5. Who in the United States loses from this trade in roses and would lobby for a restriction on the quantity of imported roses? If the U.S. government put a tariff on rose imports, show on your graph the U.S. consumer surplus that is redistributed to U.S. producers and also the government's tariff revenue.
6. Suppose that the U.S. government puts an import quota on roses. Show on your graph the consumer surplus that is redistributed to producers and importers and also the deadweight loss created by the import quota.
7. Suppose that the U.S. government bans rose imports. Show on your graph the loss of total surplus.
8. **Mexico to raise tariffs on 90 U.S. exports**

   Mexico plans to impose tariffs on 90 U.S. industrial and agricultural products imported into Mexico in retaliation for the cancellation earlier this year of a commercial trucking project that allowed small trucks to travel further inside each other's country.

   Source: CNNMoney.com, March 16, 2009

   Explain who in Mexico gains and who loses from these new tariffs on imported U.S. goods. Who in the United States gains and loses?

## Instructor Assignable Problems and Applications

Your instructor can assign these problems as homework, a quiz, or a test in **MyEconLab**.

Use the following information to work Problems **1** and **2**.

**The future of U.S.–India relations**

In May 2009, Secretary of State Hillary Clinton gave a major speech covering all the issues in U.S.–India relations. On economic and trade relations she noted that India maintains significant barriers to U.S. trade. The United States also maintains barriers against Indian imports such as textiles. Mrs. Clinton, President Obama, and Anand Sharma, the Indian Minister of Commerce and Industry, say they want to dismantle these trade barriers.

Source: www.state.gov

1. Explain who in the United States would gain and who might lose from dismantling trade barriers between the United States and India.
2. Draw a graph of the U.S. market for textiles and show how removing a tariff would change producer surplus, consumer surplus, and the deadweight loss from the tariff.
3. The United States exports wheat. Draw a graph to illustrate the U.S. wheat market if there is free international trade in wheat. On your graph, mark the price of wheat and the quantities bought, produced, and exported by the United States.

Use Figure 1 and the following information to work Problems **4** to **6**. Figure 1 shows the car market in Mexico when Mexico places no restriction on the quantity of cars imported. The world price of a car is $10,000.

4. If the government of Mexico introduces a $2,000 tariff on car imports, what will be the price of a car in Mexico, the quantity of cars produced in Mexico, the quantity imported into Mexico, and the government's tariff revenue?
5. If the government of Mexico introduces an import quota of 4 million cars a year, what will be the price of a car in Mexico, the quantity of cars produced in Mexico, and the quantity imported?
6. What argument might be used to encourage the government of Mexico to introduce a $2,000 tariff on car imports from the United States? Who will gain and who will lose as a result of Mexico's tariff?

**FIGURE 1**

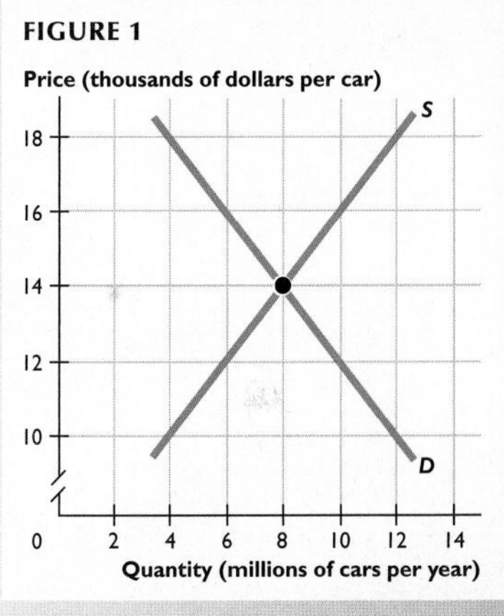


7. Suppose that the world price of sugar is 10 cents a pound, the United States does not trade internationally, and the equilibrium price of sugar in the United States is 20 cents a pound. The United States then begins to trade internationally.
   - How does the U.S. price of sugar change? Do U.S. consumers buy more or less sugar? Do U.S. sugar growers produce more or less sugar?
   - Does the United States export or import sugar and why?
8. In the 1950s, Ford and General Motors established a small car-producing industry in Australia and argued for a high tariff on car imports. The tariff has remained through the years. Until 2000, the tariff was 22.5 percent. What might have been Ford's and General Motors' argument for the high tariff? Is the tariff the best way to achieve the goals of the argument?
9. The United States exports services and imports coffee. Why does the United States gain from exporting services and importing coffee? How do economists measure the net gain from this international trade?

10. A semiconductor is a key component in your laptop, cell phone, and iPod. Table 1 provides information about the market for semiconductors in the United States. Producers of semiconductors can get $18 a unit on the world market. With no international trade, what would be the price of a semiconductor and how many semiconductors a year would be bought and sold in the United States? At $18 a unit, does the United States have a comparative advantage in producing semiconductors? If U.S. producers of semiconductors sell at the highest possible price, how many do they sell in the United States and how many do they export?

**TABLE 1**

| Price (dollars per unit) | Quantity demanded (billions of units per year) | Quantity supplied (billions of units per year) |
|---|---|---|
| 10 | 25 | 0 |
| 12 | 20 | 20 |
| 14 | 15 | 40 |
| 16 | 10 | 60 |
| 18 | 5 | 80 |
| 20 | 0 | 100 |

11. In 1845, French economist Frédéric Bastiat wrote a satirical "petition of the candlemakers" in which he argued that competition from the sun was unfair to the makers of artificial lighting. He suggested that to level the playing field, boost the production of artificial light, and create much employment and economic activity, the government should pass a law ordering the shutting up of all windows, openings, and chinks through which sunlight may enter buildings. Explain why the argument presented in Bastiat's petition is similar to that of people who argue for protection from foreign competition.

Use the following information to work Problems **12** to **14**.

**U.S. expands China paper anti-dumping tariff**

The U.S. Commerce Department has raised the tariff on imports of glossy paper from China up to 99.65 percent, as a result of complaints by NewPage Corp. of Dayton, Ohio. Imports from China increased 166 percent from 2005 to 2006. This glossy paper is used in art books, high-end magazines, and textbooks.

Source: *Reuters*, May 30, 2007

12. What is dumping? Who in the United States loses from China's dumping of glossy paper?
13. Explain what an anti-dumping tariff is. What argument might NewPage Corp. have used to persuade the U.S. Commerce Department to impose a 99.65 percent tariff?
14. Explain who, in the United States, will gain and who will lose from the tariff on glossy paper. How do you expect the prices of magazines and textbooks that you buy to change?
15. **Halved tariffs cut imported car prices by thousands**

    Prices of imported cars in Australia are set to plunge after a government review called for tariffs to be cut from 10 percent to 5 percent. The price of a small imported car will drop by $1,000 and the price of basic BMWs by more than $2,000. But the proposed tariff cut could be bad news for local car makers and a major union has demanded a "tariff freeze" to protect local industry and jobs.

    Source: *Courier Mail*, August 16, 2008

    Explain why the tariff cut is "bad news for local car makers." Why is the union demanding a tariff freeze? Who will gain from the tariff freeze?

## Does health care need fixing?

The United States has the world's most costly health care, but 47 million Americans have no health insurance. Does this situation matter? What might be done to fix it?

# Public Goods and Public Choices

CHAPTER CHECKLIST

**When you have completed your study of this chapter, you will be able to**

1. Distinguish among private goods, public goods, common resources, and externalities.
2. Explain how public provision might deliver an efficient quantity of public goods and overcome the free-rider problem.
3. Explain how public choices might deliver an efficient quantity of goods with external benefits such as education and health-care services.

## 10.1 CLASSIFYING GOODS AND RESOURCES

What's the difference between the services provided by a city police department and those provided by Brinks, a private security firm that loads ATMs for banks? What's the difference between fish in the Pacific Ocean and fish on East Point Seafood Company's Seattle fish farm? What's the difference between a live Taylor Swift concert and a concert on network television? What's the difference between health care and education and fast food? Each pair differs in many ways but key is the extent to which people can be *excluded* from consuming them and the extent to which one person's consumption *rivals* the consumption of others.

### Excludable

**Excludable**
A good, service, or resource is excludable if it is possible to prevent someone from enjoying its benefits.

**Nonexcludable**
A good, service, or resource is excludable if it is impossible (or extremely costly) to prevent someone from enjoying its benefits.

A good, service, or resource is **excludable** if it is possible to prevent someone from enjoying its benefits. Brinks's security services, East Point Seafood's fish, and Taylor Swift concerts are examples. You must pay to consume them.

A good, service, or resource is **nonexcludable** if it is impossible (or extremely costly) to prevent someone from benefiting from it. The services of the city police department, fish in the Pacific Ocean, and a concert on network television are examples. When a police cruiser slows the traffic on a highway to the speed limit, it lowers the risk of an accident to all the road users. It can't exclude some road users from the lower risk. Anyone with a boat can try to catch the fish in the ocean. Anyone with television can watch a network broadcast.

### Rival

**Rival**
A good, service, or resource is rival if its use by one person decreases the quantity available to someone else.

**Nonrival**
A good, service, or resource is nonrival if its use by one person does not decrease the quantity available to someone else.

A good, service, or resource is **rival** if its use by one person decreases the quantity available for someone else. Brinks might work for two banks, but one truck can't deliver cash to two banks at the same time. A fish, whether in the ocean or on a fish farm, can be consumed only once. One seat at a concert can hold only one person at a time. These items are rival.

A good, service, or resource is **nonrival** if its use by one person does not decrease the quantity available for someone else. The services of the city police department and a concert on network television are nonrival. The arrival of one more person in a neighborhood doesn't lower the level of police protection enjoyed by the community. When one additional person switches on the TV, no other viewer is affected.

### A Fourfold Classification

Figure 10.1 classifies goods, services, and resources into four types using the two criteria that we've just considered.

#### Private Goods

**Private good**
A good or service that can be consumed by only one person at a time and only by the person who has bought it or owns it.

A good or service that is both rival and excludable (top left of Figure 10.1) is a **private good**: It can be consumed by only one person at a time and only by the person who has bought it or owns it. The fish on East Point's farm are an example of a private good. One person's consumption of a fish rivals others, and everyone except the person who bought a fish is excluded from consuming it.

## Public Goods

A good or service that is both nonrival and nonexcludable (bottom right of Figure 10.1) is a **public good**: It can be consumed simultaneously by everyone, and no one can be excluded from enjoying its benefits. A flood-control levee is an example of a public good. Everyone who lives in a protected floodplain enjoys the benefits, and no one can be excluded from receiving those benefits. The system of law and order provided by the courts and the body of laws is another example.

**Public good**
A good or service that can be consumed simultaneously by everyone and from which no one can be excluded.

## Common Resources

A resource that is rival and nonexcludable (top right of Figure 10.1) is a **common resource**: A unit of it can be used only once, but no one can be prevented from using what is available. Ocean fish and the Earth's atmosphere are examples of common resources. Ocean fish are rival because a fish taken by one person is not available for anyone else, and they are nonexcludable because it is difficult to prevent people from catching them. The Earth's atmosphere is rival because oxygen used by one person is not available for anyone else, and it is nonexcludable because we can't prevent people from breathing!

**Common resource**
A resource that can be used only once, but no one can be prevented from using what is available.

## Natural Monopolies

A good that is nonrival but excludable (bottom left of Figure 10.1) is a good produced by a *natural monopoly*. We define natural monopoly in Chapter 15, p. 376. A natural monopoly is a firm that can produce at a lower cost than two or more firms can. Examples are the Internet, cable television, and a bridge or tunnel. One more user doesn't decrease the enjoyment of the other users, and people can be excluded with user codes, scramblers, and tollgates.

**FIGURE 10.1**
Fourfold Classification of Goods

| | Excludable | Nonexcludable |
|---|---|---|
| | **Private goods** | **Common resources** |
| **Rival** | Food and drink<br>Car<br>House | Fish in ocean<br>Atmosphere<br>National parks |
| | **Natural monopoly goods** | **Public goods** |
| **Nonrival** | Internet<br>Cable television<br>Bridge or tunnel | National defense<br>The law<br>Flood-control levees |

Source of data: Adapted from and inspired by E. S. Savas, *Privatizing the Public Sector*, Chatham House Publishers, Inc., Chatham, NJ, 1982, p. 34.

Goods that are rival and excludable are private goods (top left).

Goods that are nonrival and nonexcludable are public goods (bottom right).

Goods and resources that are rival but nonexcludable are common resources (top right).

Goods that are nonrival but excludable are goods produced by a natural monopoly (bottom left).

## Mixed Goods

**Mixed good**
A private good, the production or consumption of which creates an externality.

Some goods don't fit neatly into the fourfold classification of Figure 10.1. They are *mixed goods*. A **mixed good** is a private good, the production or consumption of which creates an *externality*. The two most important mixed goods are education and health care. Before we describe the features of these two mixed goods, we will define and provide examples of externalities.

### Externalities

**Externality**
A cost or a benefit that arises from production and that falls on someone other than the producer; or cost or a benefit that arises from consumption and that falls on someone other than the consumer.

An **externality** is a cost (external cost) or a benefit (external benefit) that arises from the production or consumption of a private good and that falls on someone other than its producer or consumer.

An externality can arise from either a production activity or a consumption activity and it can be either a *negative externality*, which imposes an external cost, or a *positive externality*, which provides an external benefit. So there are four types of externalities:

- Negative production externalities
- Positive production externalities
- Negative consumption externalities
- Positive consumption externalities

Negative production externality.

***Negative Production Externalities*** When the U.S. Open tennis tournament is being played at Flushing Meadows, players, spectators, and television viewers around the world share a negative production externality that many New Yorkers experience every day: the noise of airplanes taking off from LaGuardia Airport. Aircraft noise imposes a large cost on millions of people who live under the flight paths to airports in every major city.

Positive production externality.

***Positive Production Externalities*** Silicon Valley is home to the people and firms that design and develop computer chips, iPhones and iPods, video games, hot software applications, and a host of other high-tech products. This concentration of talent isn't an accident. By working in close proximity with others in the same field, a buzz is created in bars and restaurants and at ball games and parties that provides mutual external benefits—positive production externalities.

Negative consumption externality.

***Negative Consumption Externalities*** Negative consumption externalities are a source of irritation for most of us. Smoking tobacco in a confined space creates fumes that many people find unpleasant and that pose a health risk. So smoking in restaurants and public spaces generates a negative consumption externality.

Positive consumption externality.

***Positive Consumption Externalities*** When the owner of a historic building restores it, everyone who sees the building gets pleasure from it. Similarly, when someone erects a spectacular home—such as those built by Frank Lloyd Wright during the 1920s and 1930s—or other exciting building—such as the Chrysler and Empire State Buildings in New York or the Opera House in Sydney, Australia—an external consumption benefit flows to everyone who has an opportunity to view it.

Now that you know the different types of externalities and have seem examples of each, let's see how externalities affect some of the important goods and services that we consume.

### Mixed Goods with External Benefits

Some of the most important decisions you make involve mixed goods with external benefits: your health care and education. Think about a flu vaccination, which is a private good. A flu vaccination is *excludable* because it would be possible to sell vaccinations and exclude those not willing to pay from benefiting from them. A flu vaccination is *rival* because providing a flu vaccination to one person means that there is one fewer for everyone else.

If you decide to get a flu vaccination, you benefit from a lower risk of getting infected in the coming flu season. If *you* avoid the flu, your neighbor who didn't get vaccinated has a better chance of avoiding it too. A flu vaccination is a mixed good that brings a benefit to others—an external benefit. The external benefit of a flu vaccination is like a public good. It is nonexcludable because everyone with whom you come into contact benefits. You can't selectively benefit only your friends! And it is nonrival—protecting one person from the flu does not diminish the protection for others.

Your education is another example of a private good with external benefits. If all education were organized by private schools and universities, those not able or willing to pay would be excluded, and one person's spot in a class would rival another's spot. So education is a private good.

But your being educated brings benefits to others—external benefits. It brings benefits to your friends who enjoy your sharp, educated wit, and to the community in which you live. Well-educated people make good neighbors because they often have an enhanced sense of fellowship and responsibility toward others. These benefits are a public good. You can't selectively decide who benefits from your good neighborliness and one person's enjoyment of your good behavior doesn't rival someone else's.

### Mixed Goods with External Costs

Some mixed goods with external costs have become a huge political issue in recent years. Among these goods are electricity and road and air transportation services that are produced by burning coal and oil. Electricity and transportation are excludable—they are private goods—but when you use electricity or travel by car, bus, or airplane, you pour carbon dioxide and sulfur dioxide, and other chemicals into the atmosphere. Other private goods that generate external costs include logging, which destroys the habitat of wildlife and also influences the amount of carbon dioxide in the atmosphere, and smoking cigarettes in a confined space, which imposes a health risk on others.

Consuming these private goods imposes an external cost that is like a *public bad*. (A "bad" is the opposite of a good—a good is something that is valued so more is better and a bad is something that imposes costs so more is worse.) No one can be excluded from bearing the cost of the air pollution and one person's discomfort doesn't rival another's.

### Problems that Require Public Choices

Public goods and mixed goods with externalities, common resources, and natural monopoly goods all create inefficiency problems—overprovision and underprovision that create deadweight loss—and require public choices. You will study most of these problems and the public choice solutions to them in the rest of this chapter and the next one. (Monopoly is studied later in Chapter 15.) The rest of this chapter focuses on public goods and mixed goods with positive externalities.

Work these problems in Study Plan 10.1 to get instant feedback.

## CHECKPOINT 10.1

**Distinguish among private goods, public goods, common resources, and externalities.**

### Practice Problems

1. Classify the following services in 2009 for computer owners with an Internet connection as rival, nonrival, excludable, or nonexcludable:
   - eBay
   - A mouse
   - A Twitter page
   - MyEconLab Web site
2. Classify each of the following items as a public good, a private good, a mixed good, or a common resource:
   - Fire protection
   - The final match of the U.S. Open (tennis)
   - A well-stocked buffet that promises the most bang for your buck
   - The Mississippi River
3. Classify the externality created by the following events as a positive or negative externality and as a consumption externality or a production externality:
   - A huge noisy crowd gathers outside the lecture room
   - Your neighbor grows beautiful flowers on his apartment deck.
   - A fire alarm goes off in the middle of a lecture.
   - Your instructor offers a free tutorial after class.
4. **Wind farm off Cape Cod clears hurdle**

   The nation's first offshore wind farm with 130 turbines will be built 5 miles off the coast. Wind turbines are noisy, stand 440 feet tall, can be seen from the coast, and will produce power for 75 percent of nearby homes.

   Source: *The New York Times*, January 16, 2009

   List the externalities that this wind farm might create.

### Guided Solutions to Practice Problems

1. eBay is nonrival and nonexcludable. A mouse is rival and excludable. Twitter is nonrival and you can choose to make your page excludable or nonexcludable. MyEconLab is nonrival and excludable.
2. Fire protection is nonrival and nonexcludable, so it is a public good. The final match of the U.S. Open is rival and excludable (a private good) with an external benefit, so it is a mixed good. A well-stocked buffet is rival and excludable, so it is a private good. The Mississippi River is rival and nonexcludable, so it is a common resource.
3. The noise from a huge crowd creates a negative consumption externality. Your neighbor's beautiful flowers create a positive consumption externality. A fire alarm that goes off in the middle of a lecture creates a negative production externality. Your instructor's free tutorial is a positive production externality.
4. The wind farm will create negative externalities if the noise interferes with marine life, if tourists and Cape Cod residents find that the turbines spoil the scenery, and bird watchers find that sea birds fly into the turbines.

## 10.2 PUBLIC GOODS AND THE FREE-RIDER PROBLEM

Why does the U.S. government provide our national defense and district court system? Why do the state governments provide flood-control levees? Why do our city governments provide fire and police services? Why don't we buy our national defense from North Pole Protection, Inc., a private firm that competes for our dollars in the marketplace in the same way that McDonald's does? Why don't private engineering firms provide levees? Why don't we buy our policing and fire services from Brinks and other private firms? The answer is that all of these goods are public goods—goods that are nonexcludable and nonrival—and such goods create a free-rider problem.

### The Free-Rider Problem

A **free rider** is a person who enjoys the benefits of a good or service without paying for it. Because everyone consumes the same quantity of a public good and no one can be excluded from enjoying its benefits, no one has an incentive to pay for it. Everyone has an incentive to free ride. The free-rider problem is that the private market, left on its own, would provide too small a quantity of a public good. To produce the efficient quantity, government action is required.

**Free rider**
A person who enjoys the benefits of a good or service without paying for it.

To see how a private market would provide too little of a public good and how government might provide the efficient quantity, we need to consider the marginal benefit and the marginal cost of a public good. The marginal benefit of a public good is a bit different from that of a private good, so we'll begin on the benefit side of the calculation.

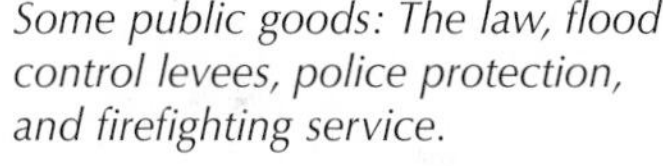

*Some public goods: The law, flood control levees, police protection, and firefighting service.*

## The Marginal Benefit of a Public Good

To learn about the marginal benefit of a public good, think about a concrete example. Lisa and Max share a common parking area that has no security lighting. Both of them would like some lights, but how many? What is the value or benefit of just one light, of adding a second, and perhaps of adding a third light? To answer this question, we must somehow combine the value of lights to both Lisa and Max and find the marginal benefit of different quantities of lights—the marginal benefit curve of lights.

For a private good, the marginal benefit curve is the market demand curve. Everyone pays the same market price for a private good, and each person chooses the quantity they wish to buy at that price. In contrast, for a public good, everyone must consume the same quantity, but each person puts a different private value on that quantity. So how are we to find the equivalent of the demand curve for a public good? Figure 10.2 answers this question and illustrates the calculation of marginal benefit and the marginal benefit curve.

Lisa and Max know their own marginal benefit from different levels of security lighting. The tables in parts (a) and (b) of Figure 10.2 show these marginal benefits. The curves $MB_L$ and $MB_M$ are Lisa's and Max's marginal benefit curves. Each person's marginal benefit from a public good diminishes as the quantity of the good increases—just as it does for a private good. For Lisa, the marginal benefit from the first light is $80, and from the second it is $60. By the time 5 lights are installed, Lisa's marginal benefit is zero. For Max, the marginal benefit from the first light is $50, and from the second it is $40. By the time 5 lights are installed, Max perceives only $10 worth of marginal benefit.

The table in part (c) of Figure 10.2 shows the marginal benefit for the entire economy. We obtain this curve by summing the individual marginal benefits at each quantity. For example, with 3 lights, the marginal benefit is $70 ($40 for Lisa plus $30 for Max) and with 4 lights, the marginal benefit is $40 ($20 for Lisa plus $20 for Max). The curve *MB* is the marginal benefit curve.

Because we find the marginal benefit of a public good by summing the marginal benefits of all individuals at each *quantity*, we find the marginal benefit curve by summing the individual marginal benefit curves *vertically*. In contrast, to obtain the *MB* curve for a private good—which is also the market demand curve—we sum the quantities demanded by all individuals at each *price*—we sum the individual demand curves *horizontally* (see Chapter 4, p. 87).

Notice that the marginal benefit curve for a public good is both a marginal private benefit curve and a marginal social benefit curve. A public good doesn't have external benefits (see p. 245). Because everyone can consume an equal quantity of a public good, everyone benefits from it. The marginal benefit curve includes all the benefits.

The principle that we've learned in this example of security lights for Lisa and Max applies to the marginal benefit of a public good such as national defense in our economy with its millions of people. The marginal benefit of national defense is the sum of the marginal benefits of all the people in the economy.

## The Marginal Cost of a Public Good

The marginal cost of a public good is determined in exactly the same way as that of a private good. The principle of *increasing marginal cost* that you learned in Chapter 6 applies to the marginal cost of a public good. So the marginal cost curve of a public good slopes upward.

## FIGURE 10.2

### Marginal Benefit of a Public Good

myeconlab Animation

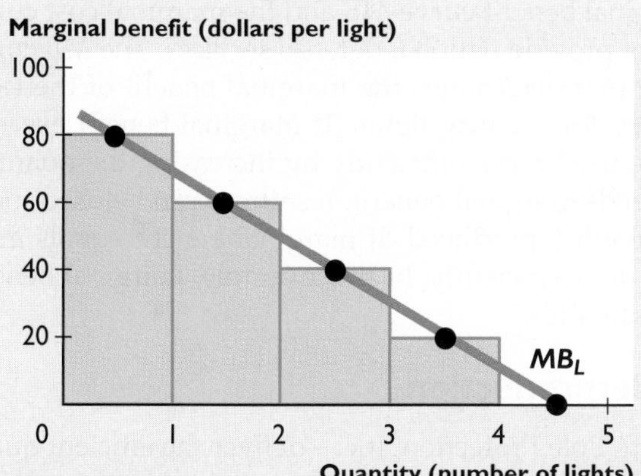


(a) Lisa's marginal benefit

The marginal benefit curves for a public good are $MB_L$ for Lisa and $MB_M$ for Max. The marginal benefit of the public good for the economy is the sum of the marginal benefits of all individuals at each quantity. The marginal benefit curve for the economy is *MB*.

| Quantity of lights | 0 | 1 | 2 | 3 | 4 | 5 |
|---|---|---|---|---|---|---|
| Lisa's *MB* (dollars per light) | 80 | 60 | 40 | 20 | 0 | |

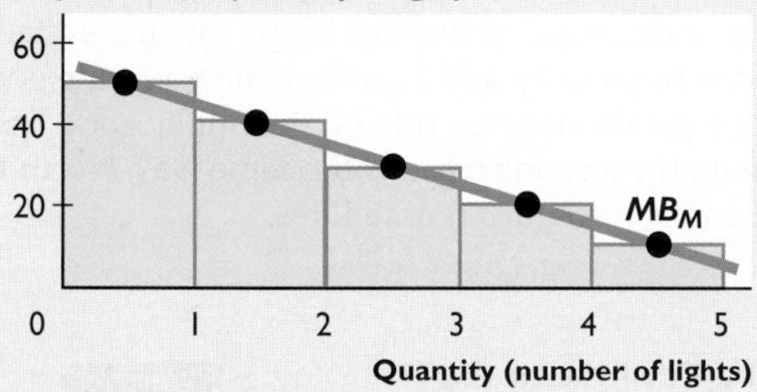


(b) Max's marginal benefit

| Quantity of lights | 0 | 1 | 2 | 3 | 4 | 5 |
|---|---|---|---|---|---|---|
| Max's *MB* (dollars per light) | 50 | 40 | 30 | 20 | 10 | |

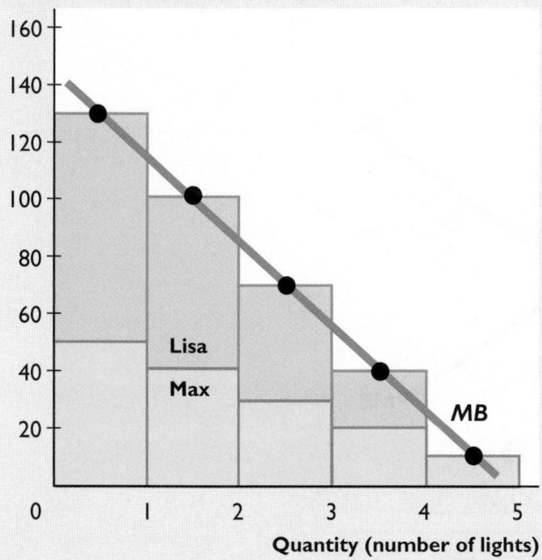


(c) Economy's marginal benefit

| Quantity of lights | 0 | 1 | 2 | 3 | 4 | 5 |
|---|---|---|---|---|---|---|
| Lisa's *MB* (dollars per light) | 80 | 60 | 40 | 20 | 0 | |
| Max's *MB* (dollars per light) | 50 | 40 | 30 | 20 | 10 | |
| Economy's *MB* (dollars per light) | 130 | 100 | 70 | 40 | 10 | |

## The Efficient Quantity of a Public Good

To determine the efficient quantity, we use the same principles that you learned in Chapter 6: We find the quantity at which marginal benefit equals marginal cost.

Figure 10.3 shows the marginal benefit curve *MB* and the marginal cost curve *MC* of surveillance satellites that provide national defense services. The *MB* curve is based on the same principle that determines the marginal benefit of the two-person (Lisa and Max) economy for security lights. If marginal benefit exceeds marginal cost, resources can be used more efficiently by increasing the quantity produced. If marginal cost exceeds marginal benefit, resources can be used more efficiently by decreasing the quantity produced. If marginal benefit equals marginal cost, resources are being used efficiently. In this example, marginal benefit equals marginal cost with 200 satellites.

## Private Provision: Underproduction

Could a private firm—say, North Pole Protection, Inc.—deliver the efficient quantity of satellites? Most likely, it couldn't because no one would have an incentive to buy his or her share of the satellite system. Everyone would reason as follows: "The number of satellites provided by North Pole Protection, Inc., is not affected by my decision to pay my share or not. My own private consumption will be greater if I free ride and do not pay my share of the cost of the satellite system. If I do not pay, I enjoy the same level of security and I can buy more private goods. I will spend my money on private goods and free ride on the public good." Such reasoning is the free-rider problem. If everyone reasons the same way, North Pole Protection, Inc., has no revenue and so provides no satellites.

**FIGURE 10.3**

The Efficient Quantity and Private Underproduction of a Public Good

myeconlab Animation

1. With fewer than 200 satellites, marginal benefit *MB* exceeds marginal cost *MC*. An increase in the quantity will make resource use more efficient.
2. With more than 200 satellites, marginal cost exceeds marginal benefit. A decrease in the quantity will make resource use more efficient.
3. With 200 satellites, marginal benefit *MB* equals marginal cost *MC*. Resource use is efficient.
4. The efficient quantity is 200 satellites.
5. Private provision leads to underproduction—in the extreme, to zero production.

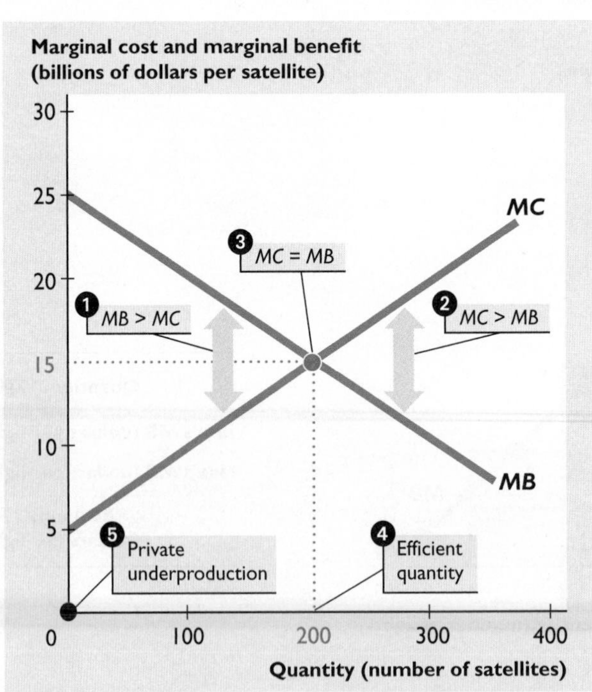

## Public Provision: Efficient Production

The political process might be efficient or inefficient. We look first at an efficient outcome. There are two political parties, the Hawks and the Doves, which agree on all issues except for the quantity of defense satellites. The Hawks want 300 satellites, and the Doves want 100 satellites. Both parties want to get elected, so they run a voter survey and discover the marginal benefit curve of Figure 10.4. They also consult with satellite producers to establish the marginal cost schedule. The parties then do a "what-if" analysis. If the Hawks propose 300 satellites and the Doves propose 100 satellites, the voters will be equally unhappy with both parties. Compared to the efficient quantity, the Doves want an underprovision of 100 satellites and the Hawks want an overprovision of 100 satellites. The deadweight losses are equal, and the election would be too close to call.

Contemplating this outcome, the Hawks realize that they are too hawkish to get elected. They figure that if they scale back to 250 satellites, they will win the election if the Doves propose 100 satellites. The Doves reason in a similar way and figure that if they increase the number of satellites to 150, they can win the election if the Hawks propose 300 satellites. Each party knows how the other is reasoning, and they realize that their party must provide 200 satellites, or it will lose the election. So both parties propose 200 satellites. The voters are indifferent between the parties, and each party receives 50 percent of the vote.

**FIGURE 10.4**

An Efficient Political Outcome

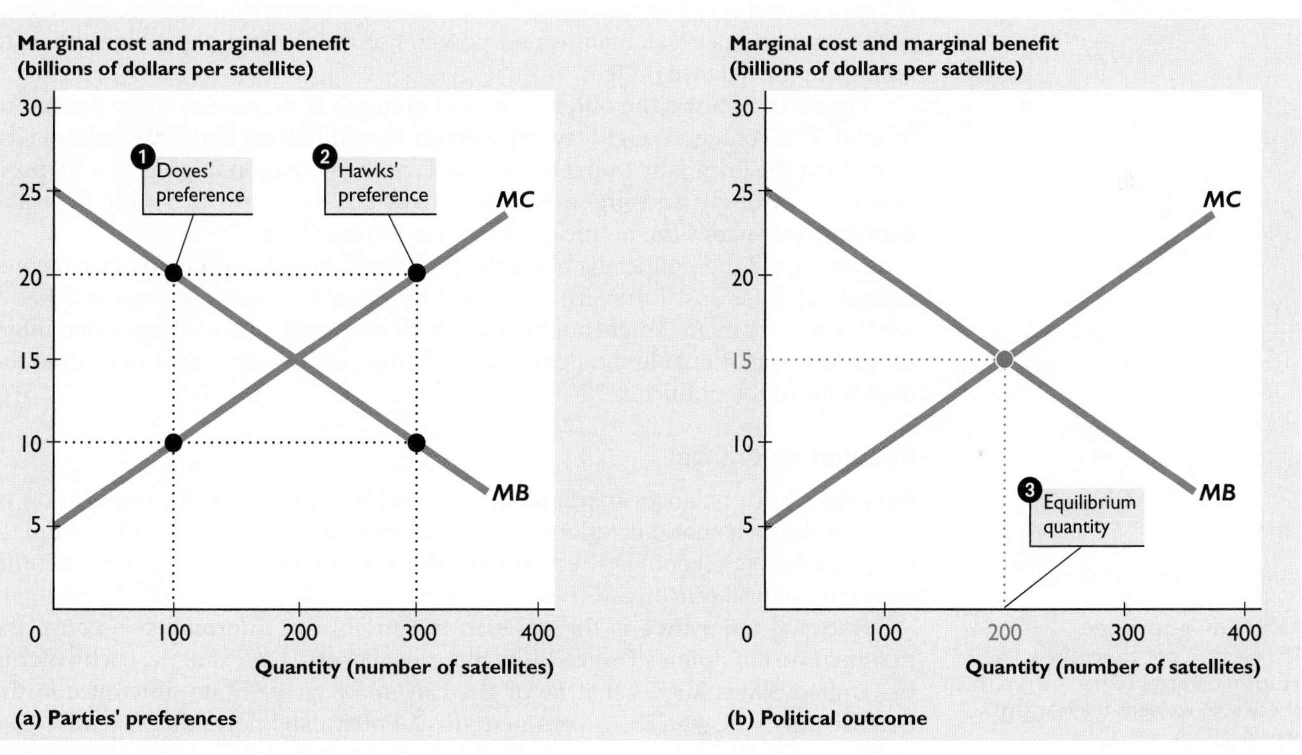


❶ The Doves would like to provide 100 satellites. ❷ The Hawks would like to provide 300 satellites.

❸ The political outcome is 200 satellites: Unless each party proposes 200 satellites, the other party can beat it in an election.

Regardless of which party wins the election, 200 satellites are provided, and this quantity is efficient. In this example, competition in the political marketplace results in the efficient provision of a public good.

For this outcome to occur, voters must be well informed, evaluate the alternatives, and vote in the election. Political parties must be well informed about voter preferences. As you will see, we can't expect to achieve this outcome.

### The Principle of Minimum Differentiation

**Principle of minimum differentiation**
The tendency for competitors to make themselves identical to appeal to the maximum number of clients or voters.

In the example that we've just studied, the two parties propose identical policies. This tendency toward identical policies is an example of the **principle of minimum differentiation**: To appeal to the maximum number of clients or voters, competitors tend to make themselves identical. This principle not only describes the behavior of political parties but also explains why fast-food restaurants cluster in the same block and even why new car models have similar features. If McDonald's opens a restaurant in a new location, it is more likely that Burger King will open next door to McDonald's rather than a mile down the road. If Chrysler designs a new van with a sliding door on the driver's side, most likely Ford will too.

## Public Provision: Overproduction

If competition between two political parties is to deliver the efficient quantity of satellites, the Defense Department—the Pentagon—must cooperate and help to achieve this outcome.

### Objective of Bureaucrats

A bureau head seeks to maximize her or his department's budget because a bigger budget brings greater status and power. For the Pentagon, the objective is to maximize the defense budget.

Figure 10.5 shows the outcome if the Pentagon is successful in the pursuit of its goal. The Pentagon might try to persuade the politicians that 200 satellites cost more than the originally budgeted amount; or the Pentagon might press its position more strongly and argue for more than 200 satellites. In Figure 10.5, the Pentagon persuades the politicians to go for 300 satellites.

Why don't the politicians block the Pentagon? Won't overpaying or overproducing satellites cost future votes? It will if voters are well informed and know what is best for them. Voters might not be well informed, and well-informed interest groups might enable the Pentagon to achieve its objective and overcome the objections of the politicians.

### Rational Ignorance

Rational choice balances marginal benefit and marginal cost. An implication of rational choice is that it is rational for a voter to be ignorant about an issue unless that issue has a perceptible effect on the voter's well-being and the voter can influence the political outcome.

**Rational ignorance**
The decision not to acquire information because the marginal cost of doing so exceeds the marginal benefit.

**Rational ignorance** is the decision not to acquire information because the marginal cost of doing so exceeds the marginal benefit. For example, each voter in the United States knows that he or she can make virtually no difference to the defense policy of the U.S. government. Each voter also knows that it would take an enormous amount of time and effort to become even moderately well informed about alternative defense technologies. So voters remain relatively uninformed

**FIGURE 10.5**

Inefficient Bureaucratic Overproduction

myeconlab Animation

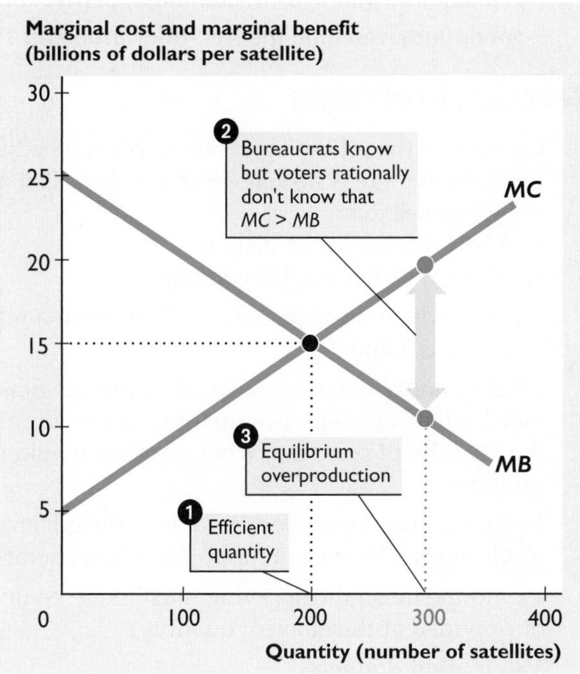


1 The efficient quantity is 200 satellites with marginal benefit *MB* equal to marginal cost *MC*.

2 Bureaucrats are well-informed and voters are rationally ignorant, so bureaucrats are able to increase production (and their budget) to a level at which marginal cost *MC* exceeds marginal benefit *MB*.

3 With 300 satellites, marginal cost exceeds marginal benefit and inefficient overproduction occurs.

about the technicalities of defense issues. (Although we are using defense policy as an example, the same principle applies to all aspects of government economic activity.)

All voters benefit from national defense, but not all voters produce national defense—only a small number work in the defense industry. Voters who own or work for firms that produce satellites have a direct personal interest in defense because it affects their incomes. These voters have an incentive to become well informed about defense issues and to lobby politicians to further their own interests. In collaboration with the defense bureaucracy, these voters exert a larger influence on public policy than do the relatively uninformed voters who only benefit from this public good.

## Why Government Is Large and Growing

Government is large and it grows faster than the rest of the economy to take an ever larger share of production. Why?

Voter preferences for public goods drive the growth of government. The demand for national and personal security and the demand for other public services are *income elastic*. As incomes increase, the demand for these services increase by a larger percentage than the increase in income.

Inefficient bureaucratic overprovision of public goods and services might make government too big and too costly. There is no easy fix for this problem. Our ever-growing demand for education and health-care services, which we study next, contribute to the large and growing scale of government.

Work these problems in Study Plan 10.2 to get instant feedback.

## CHECKPOINT 10.2

**Explain how public provision might deliver an efficient quantity of public goods and overcome the free-rider problem.**

### Practice Problems

1. For each of the following goods, explain whether there is a free-rider problem. If there is no such problem, how is it avoided?
   - Fire protection
   - A July 4th fireworks display
   - Interstate 80 in rural Wyoming

Use Table 1, which provides information about a mosquito control program, to work Problems **2** and **3**.

**TABLE 1**

| Quantity (square miles sprayed per day) | Marginal cost | Marginal benefit |
|---|---|---|
| | (dollars per day) | |
| 0 | 0 | 0 |
| 1 | 1,000 | 5,000 |
| 2 | 2,000 | 4,000 |
| 3 | 3,000 | 3,000 |
| 4 | 4,000 | 2,000 |
| 5 | 5,000 | 1,000 |

2. What quantity of spraying would a private mosquito control program provide? What is the efficient quantity of spraying? In a single-issue election on the quantity of spraying, what quantity would the winner of the election provide?
3. In the situation described in Table 1, the government sets up a Department of Mosquito Control and appoints a bureaucrat to run the department.

   Would the mosquito spraying most likely be underprovided, overprovided, or provided at the efficient quantity?
4. **Vaccination dodgers**

   Doctors struggle to eradicate polio worldwide, but one of their biggest problems is persuading parents to vaccinate their children. The discovery of the vaccine has eliminated polio from Europe and the law requires everyone to be vaccinated. People who refuse to be vaccinated are "free riders."

   Source: *USA Today*, March 12, 2008

   Explain why someone who has not opted out on medical or religious grounds and refuses to be vaccinated is a "free rider."

### Guided Solutions to Practice Problems

1. Fire protection is a public good; a July 4th fireworks display is a public good. In both cases, the free-rider problem is avoided by public provision and financing through taxes. Interstate 80 in rural Wyoming is a public good. The public good creates a free-rider problem that is avoided because governments collect various taxes via the tax on gas and the vehicle registration fee.
2. A private mosquito control program would provide zero spraying because the free-rider problem would prevail. The efficient quantity is 3 square miles a day—the quantity at which the marginal benefit equals the marginal cost. The winner will provide the efficient quantity: 3 square miles sprayed a day.
3. The Department of Mosquito Control would most likely overprovide because the bureau would try to maximize its budget.
4. Polio is a serious disease that causes much suffering. If everyone in a neighborhood except one person gets vaccinated, then the unvaccinated person benefits from all the neighbors' vaccinations. The unvaccinated person is a free rider.

## 10.3 EDUCATION AND HEALTH-CARE SERVICES

You are now going to study the efficient provision of education and health-care services. These are mixed goods with positive externalities. We'll use college education as the example. Then we'll apply the same ideas to health-care services. Your first task is to distinguish between private, external, and social benefit.

### Private Benefit, External Benefit, and Social Benefit

A *private benefit* is a benefit that the consumer of a good or service receives. The **marginal private benefit** (*MB*) is the benefit from an additional unit of a good or service that the consumer of that good or service receives.

An *external benefit* is a benefit from a good or service that someone other than the consumer receives. A **marginal external benefit** is the benefit from an additional unit of a good or service that people other than the consumer enjoy.

**Marginal social benefit** (*MSB*) is the marginal benefit enjoyed by society—by the consumers of a good or service (marginal private benefit) and by everyone else who benefits from it (the marginal external benefit). That is,

$$MSB = MB + \text{Marginal external benefit.}$$

Figure 10.6 shows an example of the relationship between marginal private benefit, marginal external benefit, and marginal social benefit of college education. The marginal benefit curve, *MB*, describes the marginal private benefit—such as expanded job opportunities and higher incomes—enjoyed by college graduates. Marginal private benefit decreases as the quantity of education increases.

**Marginal private benefit**
The benefit from an additional unit of a good or service that the consumer of that good or service receives.

**Marginal external benefit**
The benefit from an additional unit of a good or service that people other than the consumer of that good or service enjoy.

**Marginal social benefit**
The marginal benefit enjoyed by society—by the consumer of a good or service and by everyone else who benefits from it. It is the sum of marginal private benefit and marginal external benefit.

**FIGURE 10.6**
An External Benefit

myeconlab Animation

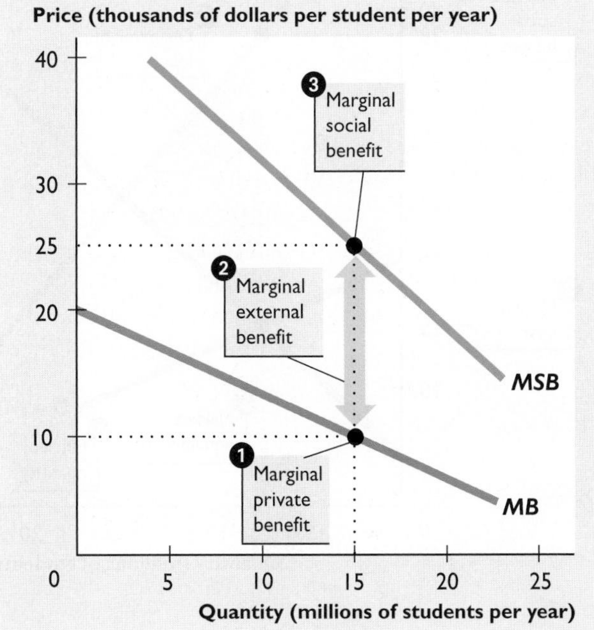


The *MB* curve shows the marginal private benefit enjoyed by the people who receive a college education. The *MSB* curve shows the sum of marginal private benefit and marginal external benefit.

When 15 million students attend college, ❶ marginal private benefit is $10,000 per student, ❷ marginal external benefit is $15,000 per student, and ❸ marginal social benefit is $25,000 per student.

But college graduates generate external benefits. On the average, college graduates communicate more effectively with others and tend to be better citizens. Their crime rates are lower, and they are more tolerant of the views of others. A society with a large number of college graduates can support activities such as high-quality music, theater, and other organized social activities.

In the example in Figure 10.6, the marginal external benefit is \$15,000 per student per year when 15 million students enroll in college. Marginal social benefit is the sum of marginal private benefit and marginal external benefit. For example, when 15 million students a year enroll in college, the marginal private benefit is \$10,000 per student and the marginal external benefit is \$15,000 per student, so the marginal social benefit is \$25,000 per student.

The marginal social benefit curve, *MSB*, is the sum of marginal private benefit and marginal external benefit. It is steeper than the *MB* curve because marginal external benefit diminishes for the same reasons that *MB* diminishes.

When people make decisions about how much schooling to undertake, they consider only its private benefits and if education were provided by private schools that charged full-cost tuition, there would be too few college graduates.

Figure 10.7 shows the underproduction that would occur if all college education were left to the private market. The supply curve is the marginal cost curve of the private schools, $S = MC$. The demand curve is the marginal private benefit curve, $D = MB$. Market equilibrium is at a tuition of \$15,000 per student per year and 7.5 million students per year. At this equilibrium, marginal social benefit is \$38,000 per student, which exceeds marginal cost by \$23,000. Too few students enroll in college. The efficient number is 15 million, where marginal social benefit equals marginal cost. The gray triangle shows the deadweight loss created by the underproduction.

**FIGURE 10.7**

## Underproduction with an External Benefit

myeconlab Animation

The market demand curve is the marginal private benefit curve, $D = MB$. The supply curve is the marginal cost curve, $S = MC$.

1. Market equilibrium is at a tuition of \$15,000 a year and 7.5 million students and is inefficient because 2 marginal social benefit exceeds 3 marginal cost.
4. The marginal social benefit curve is *MSB*, so the efficient number of students is 15 million a year.
5. The gray triangle shows the deadweight loss created because too few students enroll in college.

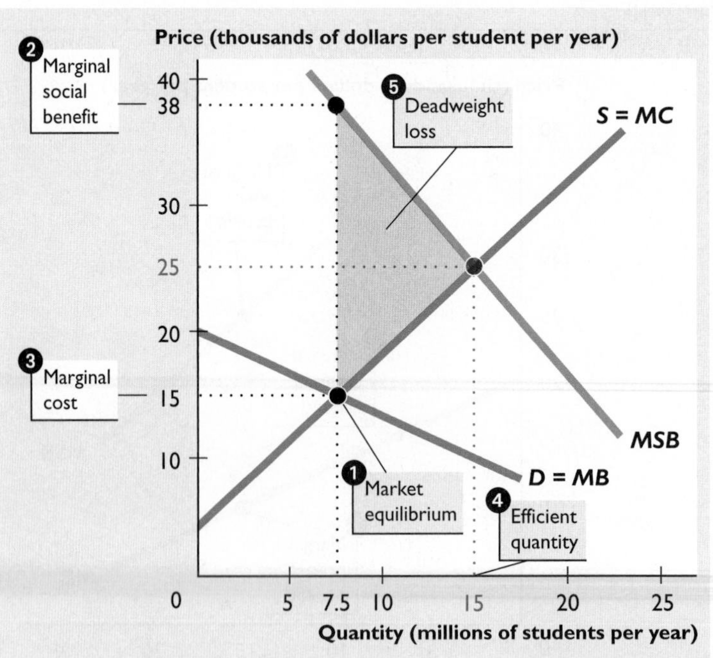

## Government Actions in the Face of External Benefits

To get closer to producing the efficient quantity of a good or service that generates an external benefit, we make public choices through governments and modify the market outcome. Three devices that governments can use to achieve a more efficient allocation of resources in the presence of external benefits, such as those that arise from education and health care, are

- Public provision
- Private subsidies
- Vouchers

### Public Provision

**Public provision** is the production of a good or service by a public authority that receives most of its revenue from the government. Education services produced by the public universities, colleges, and schools are examples of public provision.

**Public provision**
The production of a good or service by a public authority that receives most of its revenue from the government.

Figure 10.8 shows how public provision might overcome the underproduction that arises in Figure 10.7. Public provision cannot lower the cost of production, so marginal cost is the same as before. Marginal private benefit, marginal external benefit, and marginal social benefit are also the same as before.

The efficient quantity occurs where marginal social benefit equals marginal cost. In Figure 10.8, this quantity is 15 million students per year. Tuition is set to ensure that the efficient number of students enrolls. That is, tuition is set at the level that equals the marginal private benefit at the efficient quantity. In Figure 10.8, tuition is $10,000 a year. The rest of the cost of the public university is borne by the taxpayers and, in this example, is $15,000 per student per year.

**FIGURE 10.8**

Public Provision to Achieve an Efficient Outcome

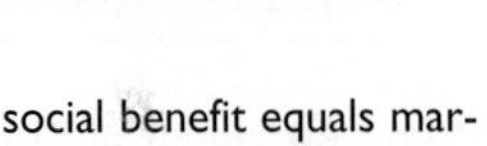


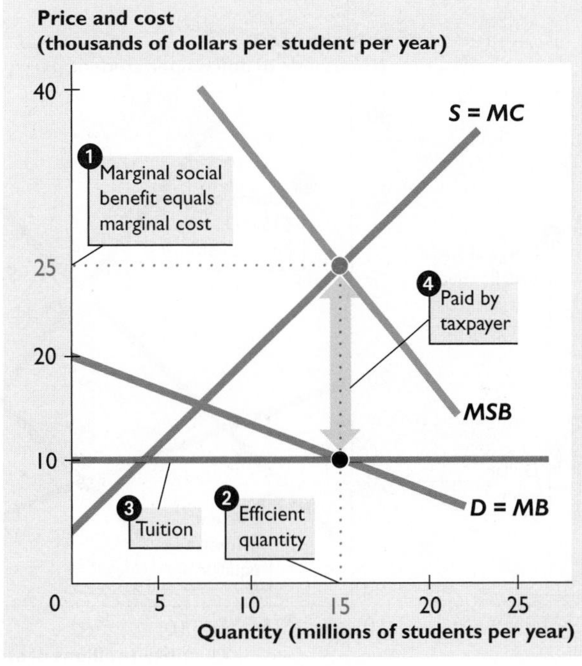


1 Marginal social benefit equals marginal cost with 15 million students enrolled in college, the 2 efficient quantity.

3 Tuition is set at $10,000 per year, and 4 the taxpayers cover the remaining $15,000 of marginal cost per student.

## Private Subsidies

**Subsidy**
A payment by the government to a producer to cover part of the costs of production.

A **subsidy** is a payment by the government to a producer to cover part of the costs of production. By giving producers a subsidy, the government can induce private decision makers to consider external benefits when they make their choices.

Figure 10.9 shows how a subsidy to private colleges works. In the absence of a subsidy, the marginal cost curve is the market supply curve of private college education, $S = MC$. The marginal benefit is the demand curve, $D = MB$. In this example, the government provides a subsidy to colleges of $15,000 per student per year. We must subtract the subsidy from the marginal cost of education to find the colleges' supply curve. That curve is $S = MC - \textit{subsidy}$ in the figure. The equilibrium tuition (market price) is $10,000 a year, and the equilibrium quantity is 15 million students. To educate 15 million students, colleges incur a marginal cost of $25,000 a year. The marginal social benefit is also $25,000 a year. So with marginal cost equal to marginal social benefit, the subsidy has achieved an efficient outcome. The tuition and the subsidy just cover the colleges' marginal cost.

***Public Provision Versus Private Subsidy*** In the examples in Figures 10.8 and 10.9, the outcome is efficient, the same number of students enroll and tuition is the same. So are these two methods of providing education services equally good? Whether a public school (public provision) or a subsidized private school (private subsidy) does a better job is a difficult question to resolve. Both methods run into the problem of bureaucratic cost padding and overprovision that you saw as a problem in achieving an efficient provision of public goods (see pp. 254–255), so neither might end up achieving the efficient outcome that we've just described.

**FIGURE 10.9**

Private Subsidy to Achieve an Efficient Outcome

myeconlab Animation

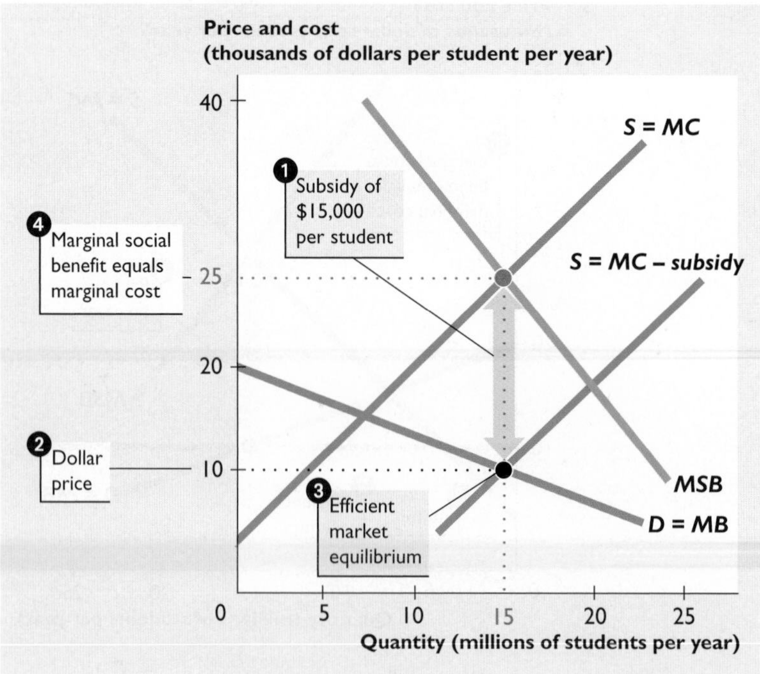


With a 1 subsidy of $15,000 per student, the supply curve is $S = MC - \textit{subsidy}$.

2 The equilibrium price is $10,000.

3 The market equilibrium is efficient with 15 million students enrolled in college because 4 marginal social benefit equals marginal cost.

## Vouchers

A **voucher** is a token that the government provides to households, which they can use to buy specified goods or services. Food stamps that the U.S. Department of Agriculture provides under a federal Food Stamp Program are examples of vouchers. Vouchers for college education could be provided to students. Let's see how they would work.

**Voucher**
A token that the government provides to households, which they can use to buy specified goods or services.

The government would issue each student with a voucher. Students would choose the school to attend and pay the tuition with dollars plus a voucher. Schools would exchange the vouchers they receive for dollars from the government. If the government set the value of a voucher equal to the marginal external benefit of a year of college at the efficient quantity, the outcome would be efficient.

Figure 10.10, illustrates an efficient voucher scheme in action. The government issues vouchers worth $15,000 a per student per year. Each student pays $10,000 tuition and the government pays $15,000 per voucher, so the school collects $25,000 per student. The voucher scheme results in 15 million students attending college, the marginal cost of a student equals the marginal social benefit, and the outcome is efficient.

***Do Vouchers Beat Public Provision and Subsidy?*** Vouchers provide public financial resources to the consumer rather than the producer. Economists generally believe that vouchers offer a more efficient outcome than public provision and subsidies because they combine the benefits of competition among private schools with the injection of the public funds needed to achieve an efficient level of output. Also, students and their parents can monitor school performance more effectively than the government can.

**FIGURE 10.10**

Vouchers Achieve an Efficient Outcome

myeconlab Animation

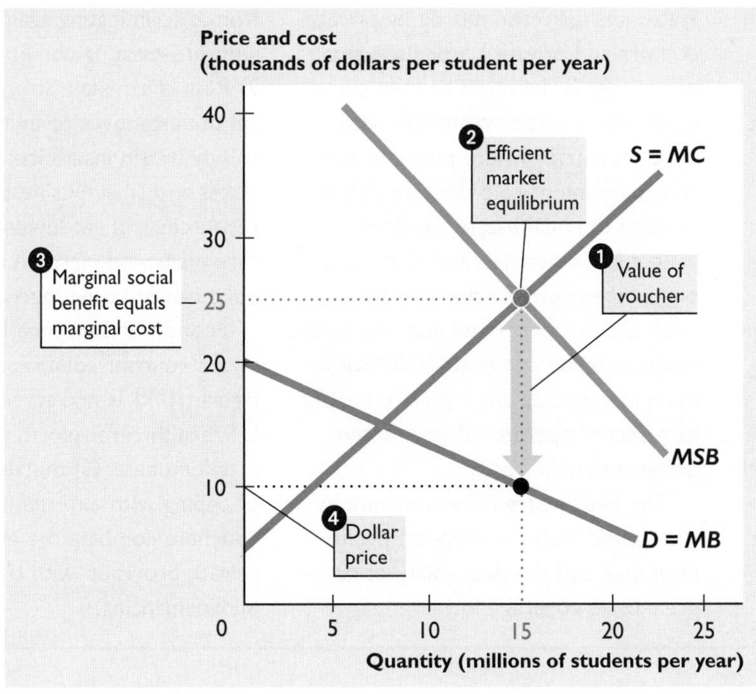


With vouchers, buyers are willing to pay *MB* plus the value of the voucher.

1. The government issues vouchers to each student valued at $15,000.
2. The market equilibrium is efficient. With 15 million students enrolled in college, 3 marginal social benefit equals marginal cost.
4. Each student pays tuition of $10,000 (the dollar price) and the school collects $15,000 (the value of the voucher) from the government.

## Underprovision of Health Care

Health care is a mixed good with positive externalities. The external benefits from include avoiding infectious diseases, living and working with healthy neighbors, and for many people, just knowing that poor, sick people have access to affordable health care. Because of external benefits, the marginal social benefit of health care exceeds the marginal private benefit and an unregulated market would provide too little health care.

Figure 10.11 illustrates a market for health-care services. A private market underprovides and creates a deadweight loss, so one or more of the methods we've studied in this chapter must be used to achieve efficiency. In practice, a mix of private subsidies and public provision is used and the outcome remains inefficient.

Laurence Kotlikoff, an economist at Boston University, has proposed issuing health-care vouchers that would work in a similar way to the education vouchers explained on p. 261. Vouchers enable the efficiencies of private provision to be combined with the benefits of public financing. The figure shows the effects of a voucher scheme that achieves an efficient outcome. Vouchers valued at the marginal external benefit enable and induce people to buy and provide the efficient quantity of health-care services.

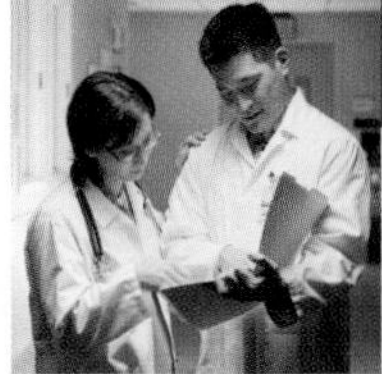

## EYE on HEALTH CARE

### Does Health Care Need Fixing?

Health care does need fixing. U.S. health-care spending is $2.5 trillion, which is 17 percent of total spending and $8,000 per person, more than double the average of other rich countries. This cost is projected to rise as the population ages with the retirement of the "baby boom" generation.

In all advanced economies except the United States, governments provide health insurance and everyone is covered.

In the United States, 47 million people have no health insurance and a further 25 million are insured on too small a scale. Of those who do have health insurance, nearly 40 million are covered by the government's Medicare and Medicaid programs. Medicare covers people age 65 or older and some people under age 65. Medicaid helps people with limited income. The rest of the population is covered by private health insurance, most of which is provided as an employment benefit.

Health-care services in the United States are delivered mostly by private doctors and private hospitals. A small percentage is delivered by public hospitals. This situation contrasts with other countries where public hospitals and government-paid doctors deliver most of the health-care services.

In a few countries, and Canada is one of them, private doctors and hospitals are not permitted and *only* public health-care service is available. But in most countries, a small private health-care sector operates alongside the dominant public sector.

The health-care reform debate in the United States centers on health insurance and the desirability of comprehensive coverage for all.

Alternatives under discussion are:

1) Obama plan: Create a public health insurer to compete with the private insurers and prohibit private insurers from discriminating against people with pre-existing conditions.

2) Republican plan: Strengthen individual tax incentives to encourage people to buy health insurance; encourage states and small businesses to pool resources and get lower-cost health-care plans; and increase incentives to build health savings accounts.

Economist Laurence Kotlikoff's proposed voucher solution illustrated in Figure 10.11 is not currently on the U.S. health-care reform agenda, which is unfortunate. Of the alternative ways of coping with external benefits, only vouchers combine the efficiencies of private provision with the benefits of public financing.

**FIGURE 10.11**

## Health-Care Vouchers Can Achieve an Efficient Outcome

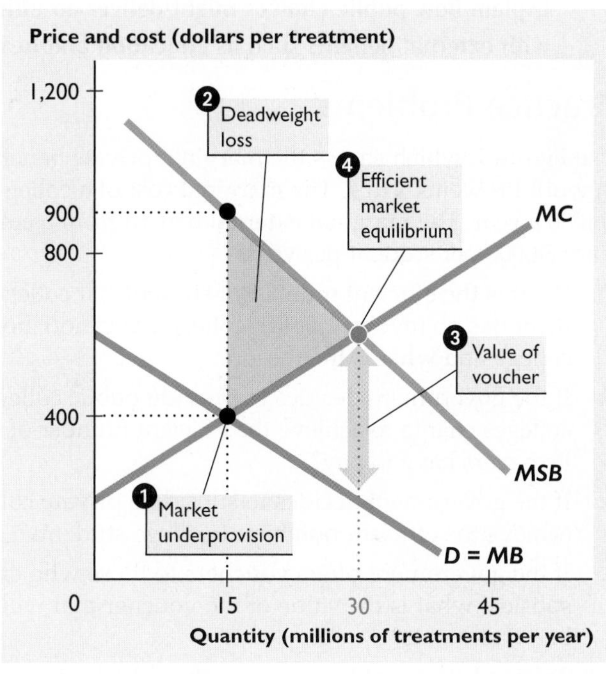


The demand and marginal private benefit curve for health-care services is *MB*, and the supply curve and marginal cost curve is *MC*.

1. A market equilibrium would produce too little health care.
2. A deadweight loss would arise.
3. Issuing people with health-insurance vouchers valued at the marginal external benefit would increase the demand for health-care services to *MSB*.
4. With demand equal to *MSB*, the market would move to an efficient equilibrium and the deadweight loss would be eliminated.

## EYE on YOUR LIFE

### A Student's Free-Rider Problem

MP3 files are nonrival because they can be duplicated at the click of a mouse. Files can be created at zero opportunity cost. An MP3 file is nonexcludable because it is costly to exclude anyone who wants to make an illegal copy of a file.

Because MP3 files are nonrival and effectively nonexcludable, they create a free-rider problem.

If everyone obtained their music by copying the files of their friends, you can see that it would not take long for the provision of songs to dry up. Only amateur performers who record for fun would be left in the business.

Should we try to solve this problem by having the government provide our pop, jazz, rock, and classical music? Can you imagine Hillary Clinton as Secretary of Songs appointing a committee to tell Alicia Keys what her next record will be? Not a good idea!

The way that we tackle this free-rider problem is by using the copyright laws that restrict the legal right to copy an MP3 file. The problem is that simply making something illegal isn't very effective if it is difficult to monitor, detect, and punish the illegal acts.

Another solution might be to put a tax on MP3 players and distribute the revenue to performers and recording companies, but this approach doesn't provide an incentive to limit illegal file sharing. Once the MP3 player tax has been paid, it has no effect on how the MP3 player is used.

The best solution currently available is for the government to uphold property rights so that recording companies can pursue illegal file sharers and hit them with large penalties. But the cost of enforcing these property rights is high.

Work these problems in Study Plan 10.3 to get instant feedback.

# CHECKPOINT 10.3

**Explain how public choices might deliver an efficient quantity of goods with external benefits such as education and health-care services.**

## Practice Problems

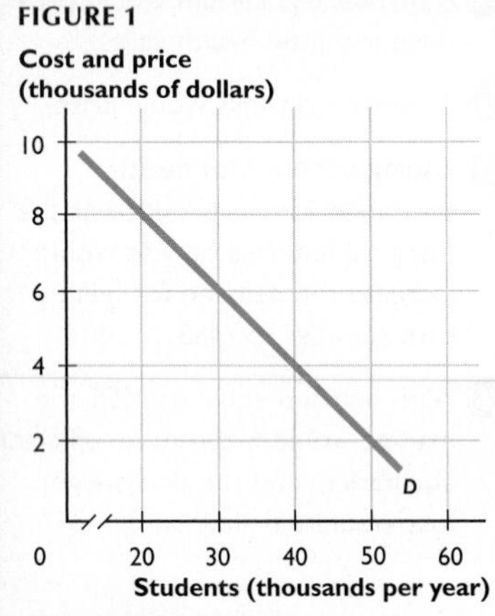


Use Figure 1, which shows the marginal private benefit from college education, to work Problems **1** to **4**. The marginal cost of a college education is a constant $6,000 a year. The marginal external benefit from a college education is a constant $4,000 per student per year.

1. What is the efficient number of students? If colleges are private and government has no involvement in college education, how many people enroll in college and what is the tuition?
2. If the government decides to provide public colleges, what tuition will these colleges charge to achieve the efficient number of students? How much will taxpayers have to pay?
3. If the government decides to subsidize private colleges, what subsidy will achieve the efficient number of college students?
4. If the government offers vouchers to those who enroll at a college and no subsidy, what is the value of the voucher that will achieve the efficient number of students?
5. **Tuition hikes, not loan access, should frighten students**
   Despite the credit crisis, families will not be deprived of access to federal student loans. A hundred banks are not issuing them but 2,000 are. The real danger is a hike in tuition. Often in past recessions, states have cut funding for colleges and tuition has skyrocketed. The Cato Institute says a better policy would be for the states to increase their deficits and maintain the subsidies to colleges.
   
   Source: Michael Dannenberg, *USA Today*, October 22, 2008
   
   If government cuts the subsidy to colleges, why will tuition rise and the number of students enrolled decrease? Why does the Cato Institute say that it's a better policy for government to maintain the subsidy?

## Guided Solutions to Practice Problems

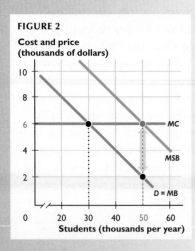

FIGURE 2

Cost and price (thousands of dollars)

10, 8, 6, 4, 2, 0; MC; MSB; D = MB; 20 30 40 50 60; Students (thousands per year)

1. Figure 2 illustrates: The efficient number of students is 50,000 a year—the intersection of the *MSB* and *MC* curves. Enrollment will be 30,000 students a year—the intersection of the *MB* and *MC* curves. Tuition is $6,000 a year.
2. To enroll the efficient 50,000 students, public colleges would charge $2,000 per student and taxpayers would pay $4,000 per student (Figure 2).
3. The subsidy would be $4,000 per student, which is equal to the marginal external benefit.
4. The value of the voucher will be $4,000. Enrollment will be 50,000 if the tuition is $2,000. The private college tuition is $6,000, so to get 50,000 students to enroll, the value of the voucher will have to be $4,000.
5. A cut in the subsidy will increase the college's marginal cost. Tuition will rise and the number of students will decrease—a movement up along the demand curve. Because fewer than the efficient number of students will be educated, the Cato Institute says maintaining the subsidy is a better policy.

# CHAPTER SUMMARY

## Key Points

1 **Distinguish among private goods, public goods, common resources, and externalities.**

- A private good is a good or service that is rival and excludable.
- A public good is a good or service that is nonrival and nonexcludable.
- A common resource is a resource that is rival but nonexcludable.
- A mixed good is a private good that has an externality.
- An externality is a cost or a benefit that falls on someone other than the producer or the consumer of a good or service.

2 **Explain how public provision might deliver an efficient quantity of public goods and overcome the free-rider problem.**

- A public good creates a free-rider problem—no one has a private incentive to pay her or his share of the cost of providing a public good.
- The efficient level of provision of a public good is that at which marginal benefit equals marginal cost.
- Competition between political parties, each of which tries to appeal to the maximum number of voters, can lead to the efficient scale of provision of a public good and to both parties proposing the same policies—the principle of minimum differentiation.
- Bureaucrats try to maximize their budgets, and if voters are rationally ignorant, they might vote to support taxes that provide public goods in quantities that exceed the efficient quantity.

3 **Explain how public choices might deliver an efficient quantity of goods with external benefits such as education and health-care services.**

- External benefits are benefits that are received by people other than the consumer of a good or service. Marginal social benefit equals marginal private benefit plus marginal external benefit.
- Public provision, subsidies, and vouchers can achieve a more efficient provision of a mixed good with positive externalities such as education and health care. Economists think that vouchers do the best job.

## Key Terms

Common resource, 245
Excludable, 244
Externality, 246
Free rider, 249
Marginal external benefit, 257
Marginal private benefit, 257
Marginal social benefit, 257
Mixed good, 246
Nonexcludable, 244
Nonrival, 244
Principle of minimum differentiation, 254
Private good, 244
Public good, 245
Public provision, 259
Rational ignorance, 254
Rival, 244
Subsidy, 260
Voucher, 261

## 11.1 NEGATIVE EXTERNALITIES: POLLUTION

We defined *externalities* in Chapter 10 (p. 246) and saw that pollution is an example of a *negative externality*. Both production and consumption activities create pollution. Here, we'll focus on pollution as a negative production externality. When a chemical factory dumps waste into a river, the people who live by the river and use it for fishing and boating bear the cost of the pollution. The chemical factory does not consider the cost of pollution when it decides the quantity of chemicals to produce. The factory's supply curve is based on its own costs, not on the costs that it inflicts on others. You're going to see that when external costs are present, we produce more output than the efficient quantity and we get more pollution than the efficient quantity.

Pollution and other environmental problems are not new. Preindustrial towns and cities in Europe had severe sewage disposal problems that created cholera epidemics and plagues that killed millions. Nor is the desire to find solutions to environmental problems new. The development in the fourteenth century of a pure water supply and the hygienic disposal of garbage and sewage are examples of early efforts to improve the quality of the environment.

Popular discussions about pollution focus on physical aspects of the environment, not on costs and benefits. A common assumption is that activities that damage the environment are wrong and must cease. An economic study of the environment emphasizes costs and benefits and economists talk about the efficient amount of pollution or environmental damage. This emphasis on costs and benefits does not mean that economists, as citizens, don't have the same goals as others and value a healthy environment. Nor does it mean that economists have the right answers and everyone else has the wrong ones. Rather, economics provides a set of tools and principles that help to clarify the issues.

The starting point for an economic analysis of the environment is the distinction between private costs and social costs.

### Private Costs and Social Costs

A *private cost* of production is a cost that is borne by the producer of a good or service. *Marginal cost* is the cost of producing an *additional unit* of a good or service. So **marginal private cost** (*MC*) is the cost of producing an additional unit of a good or service that is borne by the producer of that good or service.

**Marginal private cost**
The cost of producing an additional unit of a good or service that is borne by the producer of that good or service.

You've seen that an *external cost* is a cost of producing a good or service that is *not* borne by the producer but borne by other people. A **marginal external cost** is the cost of producing an additional unit of a good or service that falls on people other than the producer.

**Marginal external cost**
The cost of producing an additional unit of a good or service that falls on people other than the producer.

**Marginal social cost** (*MSC*) is the marginal cost incurred by the entire society—by the producer and by everyone else on whom the cost falls—and is the sum of marginal private cost and marginal external cost. That is,

**Marginal social cost**
The marginal cost incurred by the entire society—by the producer and by everyone else on whom the cost falls. It is the sum of marginal private cost and marginal external cost.

$$MSC = MC + \text{Marginal external cost.}$$

We express costs in dollars, but we must always remember that a cost is an opportunity cost—the best thing we give up to get something. A marginal external cost is what someone other than the producer of a good or service must give up when the producer makes one more unit of the item. Something real that people value, such as a clean river or clean air, is given up.

### Valuing an External Cost

Economists use market prices to put a dollar value on the cost of pollution. For example, suppose that there are two similar rivers, one polluted and the other clean. Five hundred identical homes are built along the side of each river. The homes on the clean river rent for $2,500 a month, and those on the polluted river rent for $1,500 a month. If the pollution is the only detectable difference between the two rivers and the two locations, the rent decrease of $1,000 per month is the cost of the pollution. For the 500 homes, the external cost is $500,000 a month.

### External Cost and Output

Figure 11.1 shows an example of the relationship between output and cost in a chemical industry that pollutes. The marginal cost curve, *MC,* describes the private marginal cost borne by the firms that produce the chemical. Marginal cost increases as the quantity of the chemical produced increases. If the firms dump waste into a river, they impose an external cost that increases with the amount of the chemical produced. The marginal social cost curve, *MSC,* is the sum of marginal private cost and marginal external cost. For example, when firms produce 4,000 tons of chemical a month, marginal private cost is $100 a ton, marginal external cost is $125 a ton, and marginal social cost is $225 a ton.

In Figure 11.1, as the quantity of the chemical produced increases, the amount of pollution increases and the external cost of pollution increases. The quantity of the chemical produced and the pollution created depend on how the market for the chemical operates. First, we'll see what happens when the industry is free to pollute.

**FIGURE 11.1**

An External Cost

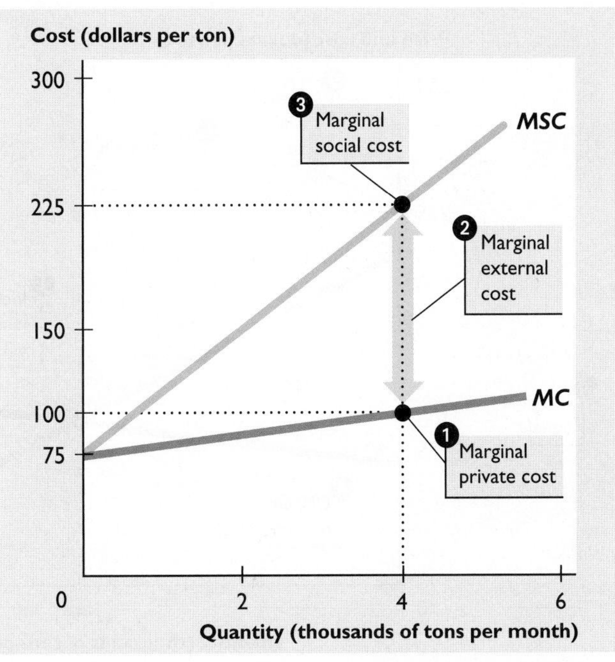


The *MC* curve shows the marginal private cost borne by the factories that produce a chemical. The *MSC* curve shows the sum of marginal private cost and marginal external cost.

When the quantity of chemical produced is 4,000 tons a month, 1 marginal private cost is $100 a ton, 2 marginal external cost is $125 a ton, and 3 marginal social cost is $225 a ton.

## Production and Pollution: How Much?

When an industry is unregulated, the amount of pollution it creates depends on the market equilibrium price and quantity of the good produced. Figure 11.2 illustrates the outcome in the market for a pollution-creating chemical.

The demand curve for the chemical is *D*. This curve also measures the marginal benefit, *MB*, to the buyers of the chemical (see Chapter 6, p. 148). The supply curve is *S*. This curve also measures the marginal private cost, *MC*, of the producers (see Chapter 6, p. 151). The supply curve is the marginal private cost curve because when firms make their production and supply decisions, they consider only the costs that they will bear. Market equilibrium occurs at a price of $100 a ton and a quantity of 4,000 tons of chemical a month.

This equilibrium is inefficient. You learned in Chapter 6 that the allocation of resources is efficient when marginal benefit equals marginal cost. But we must count all the costs—private and external—when we compare marginal benefit and marginal cost. With an external cost, the allocation is efficient when marginal benefit equals marginal *social* cost. This outcome occurs when the quantity of the chemical produced is 2,000 tons a month. The market equilibrium *overproduces* by 2,000 tons of chemical a month and creates a deadweight loss, the gray triangle.

Because the pollution creates a deadweight loss, reducing the amount of pollution and eliminating the deadweight loss brings potential gains for everyone. If some method can be found to achieve this outcome, everyone—the owners of the factories and the residents of the riverside homes—can gain. How can the people who live by the polluted river get the chemical factories to decrease their output of the chemical and create less pollution? Let's explore some solutions.

**FIGURE 11.2**

Inefficiency with an External Cost

myeconlab Animation

The market supply curve is the marginal private cost curve, *S* = *MC*. The demand curve is the marginal benefit curve, *D* = *MB*. The marginal social cost curve is *MSC*.

1 Market equilibrium at a price of $100 a ton and 4,000 tons of chemical a month is inefficient because 2 marginal social cost exceeds 3 marginal benefit.

4 The efficient quantity of chemical is 2,000 tons a month where marginal benefit equals marginal social cost.

5 The gray triangle shows the deadweight loss created by the pollution externality.

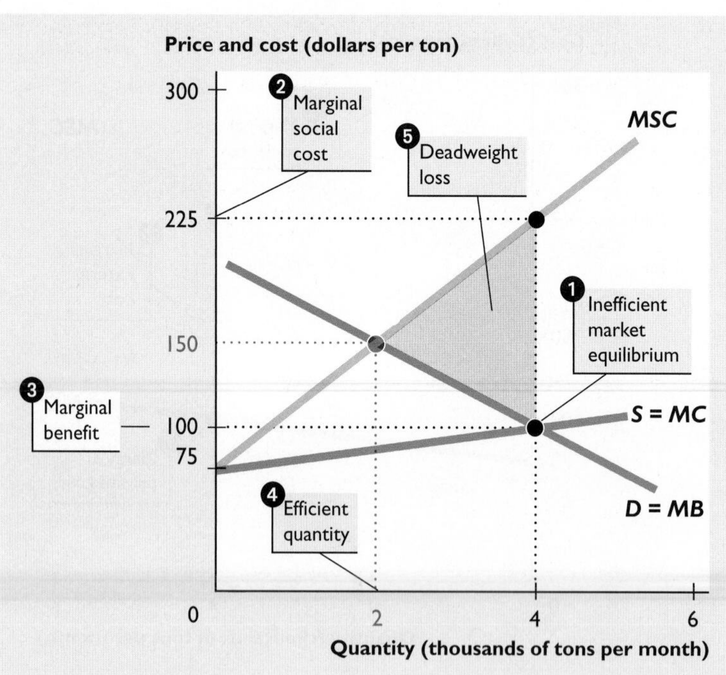

## Property Rights

Sometimes it is possible to reduce the inefficiency arising from an externality by establishing a property right where one does not currently exist. **Property rights** are legally established titles to the ownership, use, and disposal of factors of production and goods and services that are enforceable in the courts.

**Property rights**
Legally established titles to the ownership, use, and disposal of factors of production and goods and services that are enforceable in the courts.

Suppose that the chemical factories own the river and the 500 homes alongside it. The rent that people are willing to pay depends on the amount of pollution. Using the earlier example, suppose that people are willing to pay $2,500 a month to live alongside a pollution-free river but only $1,500 a month to live with the pollution created by 4,000 tons of chemical a month. If the factories produce this quantity of chemical, they forgo $1,000 a month for each home and a total of $500,000 a month.

Because they own the homes of the people who suffer from the pollution, the chemical factories are now confronted with the cost of their pollution decision. They might still decide to pollute, but if they do, they face the opportunity cost of their actions—forgone rent from the people who live by the river.

Figure 11.3 illustrates the outcome. With property rights in place, the marginal cost curve in Figure 11.2 no longer measures all the factories' costs of producing the chemical. It excludes the pollution cost that they must now bear. The former *MSC* curve now becomes the marginal private cost curve *MC*. The market supply curve is based on all the marginal costs and is the curve labeled *S* = *MC*.

Market equilibrium now occurs at a price of $150 a ton and a quantity of 2,000 tons a month. This outcome is efficient. The factories still produce some pollution, but it is the efficient quantity.

**FIGURE 11.3**

Property Rights Achieve an Efficient Outcome

myeconlab Animation

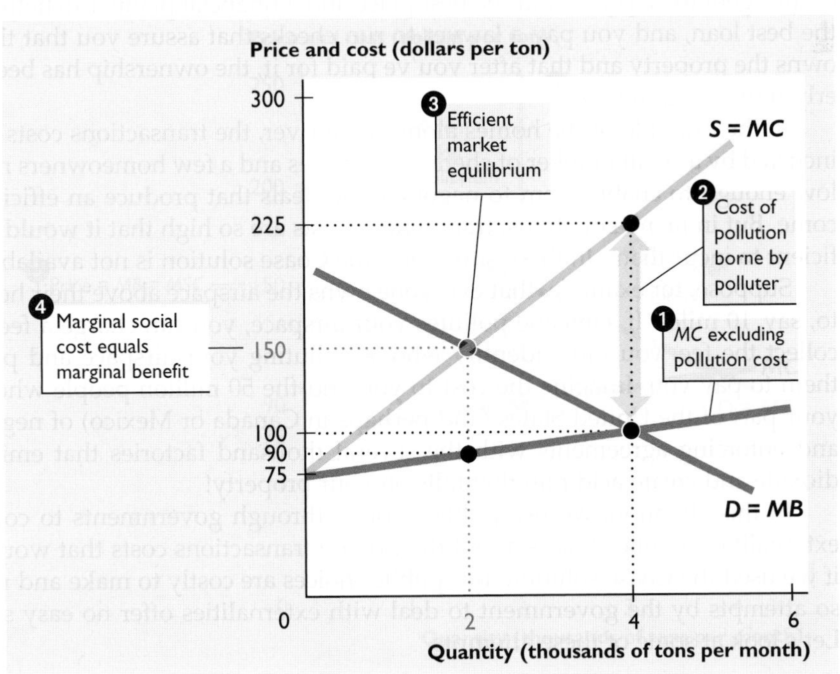


1 With property rights, the marginal cost curve that excludes the cost of pollution shows only part of the producers' marginal cost.

The marginal private cost curve includes 2 the cost of pollution, so the supply curve is *S* = *MC*.

3 Market equilibrium is at a price of $150 a ton and a quantity of 2,000 tons of chemical a month and is efficient because 4 marginal social cost equals marginal benefit.

Figure 11.5 illustrates the effects of a pollution charge or pollution tax. By charging or taxing the producer at a rate equal to marginal external cost, the marginal social cost curve becomes the market supply curve. The market moves to the efficient quantity and the government collects a tax or pollution charge revenue shown by the purple rectangle.

### Marketable Pollution Permits (Cap-and-Trade)

Marketable pollution permits (also called cap-and-trade), seek an efficient outcome by assigning or selling pollution rights to individual producers who are then free to trade permits with each other. The 1990 Clean Air Act and the 1994 Regional Clean Air Incentives Market (RECLAIM) in the Los Angeles basin successfully use this method of dealing with air pollution. This approach is also the centerpiece of a proposed American Clean Energy and Security Act of 2009 (see p. 277).

If marginal external cost is assessed correctly, an efficient outcome is achieved with any of the methods. But governments cannot make an accurate determination of external costs. Also, more importantly, some producers have a lower marginal cost of avoiding pollution than others.

In practice, pollution limits and pollution charges and taxes end up failing to achieve an efficient outcome because they confront all producers with the same incentives to avoid pollution. Cap-and-trade overcomes this problem and is the most effective of the three methods. Cap-and-trade requires an accurate determination of the overall quantity of pollution that brings efficiency but it provides the strongest available incentive to individual producers to find cost effective technologies that achieve the pollution targets.

**FIGURE 11.5**

A Pollution Charge or Pollution Tax

Animation

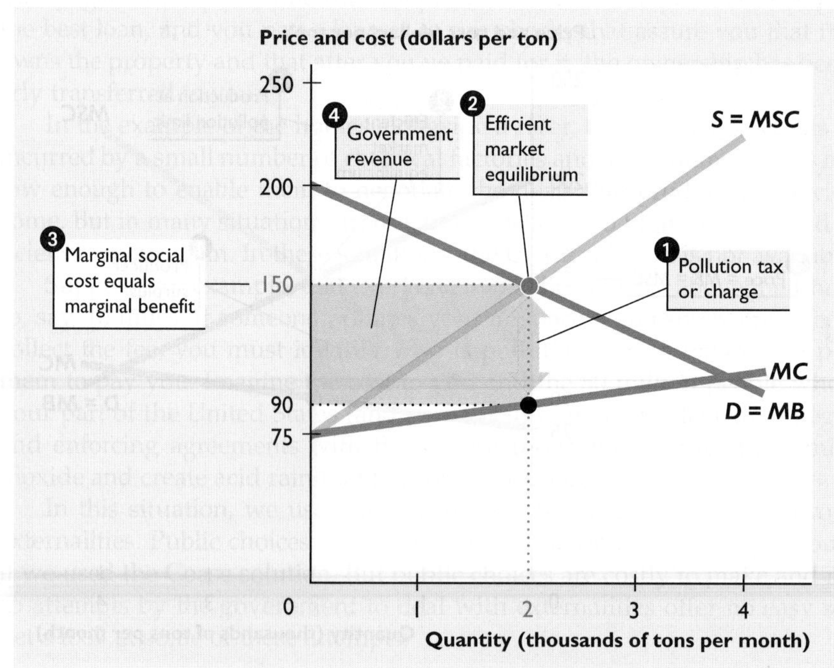

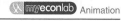

1. A pollution charge or tax is imposed that is equal to the marginal external cost of pollution.

   Because the pollution charge or tax equals the marginal external cost, the supply curve is the marginal social cost curve: $S = MSC$.

2. Market equilibrium is efficient because 3 marginal social cost equals marginal benefit.

4. The government collects tax revenue equal to the area of the purple rectangle.

# EYE on CLIMATE CHANGE

## How Can We Slow Global Warming?

The average temperature of the Earth is rising and so is the atmospheric concentration of carbon dioxide, $CO_2$. The top figure shows these upward trends.

Scientists debate the contribution of human economic activity to the trends, but most believe it to be the source. Economists debate the costs and benefits of alternative ways of slowing $CO_2$ and other greenhouse gas (GHG) emissions, but most favor action.

Economists agree that lowering GHG emissions requires *incentives* to change.

One idea is to cap emissions and issue tradeable emissions permits, a system called *cap-and-trade*. Carbon emission permits are already priced on a global carbon trading market.

The idea also has backers in Congress. On May 15, 2009, Representative Henry Waxman introduced the American Clean Energy and Security Act of 2009, which would use a cap-and-trade scheme. With 2005 levels as the base, GHG emissions would be capped at 97 percent by 2012, 83 percent by 2020, 58 percent by 2030, and 17 percent by 2050.

The Congressional Budget Office estimates that in 2020, a permit to emit one ton of GHG would cost $28 and the cost of the scheme would be about $175 per household per year.

Another incentive might be a hike in the tax on gasoline. Americans pay a much lower gas tax than Europeans pay. The bottom figure shows the stark difference between the United States and the United Kingdom.

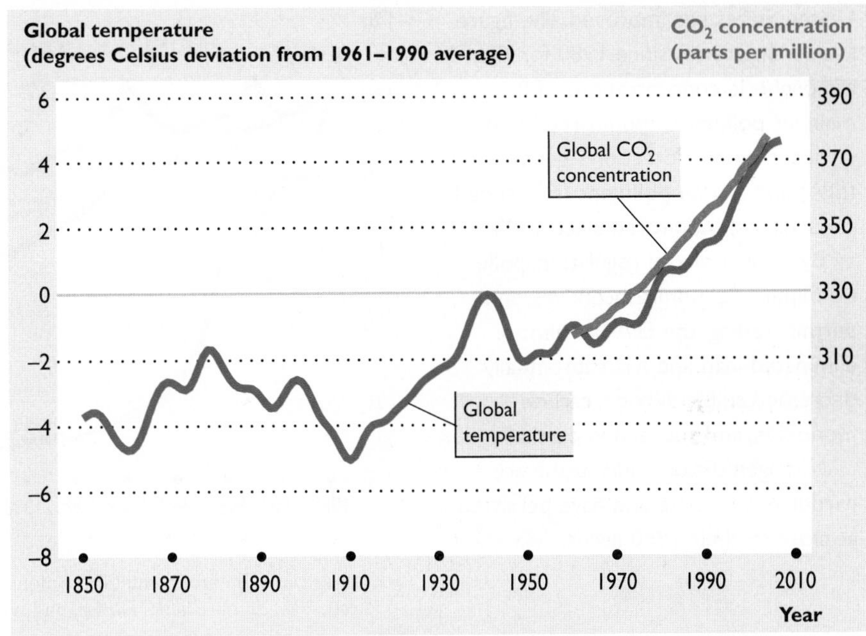


SOURCES OF DATA: Met Office Hadley Centre and Scripps Institution of Oceanography.

Why don't we have more aggressive caps and stronger incentives to encourage a larger reduction in GHG emissions? There are three reasons.

First, many people don't accept the scientific evidence that emissions produce global warming; second, the costs are certain and would be borne now, while the benefits would come many years in the future; and third, if current trends persist, by 2050, three quarters of carbon pollution will come not from the United States but from the developing economies.

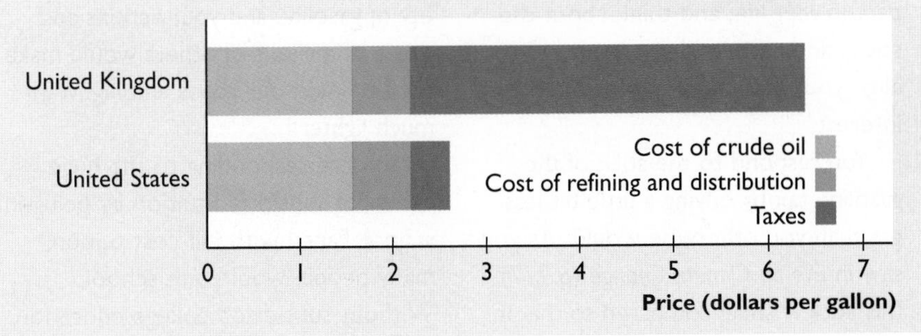


SOURCES OF DATA: Energy Information Administration, Automobile Association, and authors' assumptions.

## EYE on the U.S. ECONOMY

### U.S. Air Pollution Trends

Air quality in the United States has improved. The figure shows the trends since 1980 for the atmospheric concentrations of five main air pollutants monitored by the Environmental Protection Agency (EPA) and a sixth pollutant (suspended particulates) monitored since 1990.

By using a mix of regulation, pollution limits, economic incentives, and permit trading, the EPA has almost eliminated lead and has substantially decreased sulfur dioxide, carbon monoxide, and suspended particulates.

Nitrogen dioxide and ozone are harder to eliminate and have persisted at close to their 1980 levels.

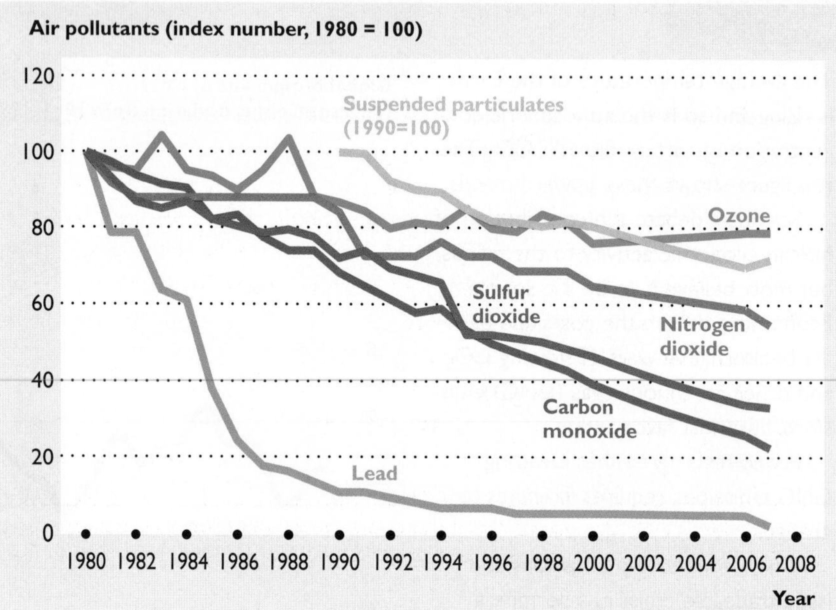


SOURCE OF DATA: Environmental Protection Agency, *National Air Quality and Emissions Trends Report, 2003 Special Studies Edition,* and www.epa.gov/air/airtrends/econ-emissions.html.

## EYE on YOUR LIFE

### Externalities in Your Life

Think about the externalities, both negative and positive, that play a huge part in *your* life; and think about the sticks and carrots that attempt to align your self-interest with the social interest.

You respond to the stick of the gasoline tax by buying a little bit less gas than you otherwise would. As you saw in *Eye on Climate Change* (p. 277), this stick is small compared to that in some other countries. With a bigger gas tax, such as that in the United Kingdom, for example, you would find ways of getting by with a smaller quantity of gasoline and your actions and those of millions of others would make the traffic on our roads and highways much lighter.

You are responding to the huge carrot of subsidized tuition by being in school. Faced with full-cost tuition, many people would quit school. Without subsidized college education (as you saw in Chapter 10), fewer people would attend college and university and with fewer college graduates, the benefits we all receive from living in a well-educated society would be smaller.

Think about your attitude as a citizen–voter to these two externalities.

Have our politicians set the right incentives? Should the gas tax be higher to discourage the use of the automobile? Should tuition be even lower to encourage even more people to enroll in school? Or have we got these incentives just right in the social interest?

## CHECKPOINT 11.1

**Explain why negative externalities lead to inefficient overproduction and how property rights and government actions can achieve a more efficient outcome.**

myeconlab

Work these problems in Study Plan 11.1 to get instant feedback.

## Practice Problems

Use the following information to answer Problems **1** to **4**.

Figure 1 illustrates the unregulated market for a pesticide. When factories produce pesticide, they also create waste, which they dump into a lake on the outskirts of the town. The marginal external cost of the dumped waste is equal to the marginal private cost of producing the pesticide (that is, the marginal social cost of producing the pesticide is double the marginal private cost).

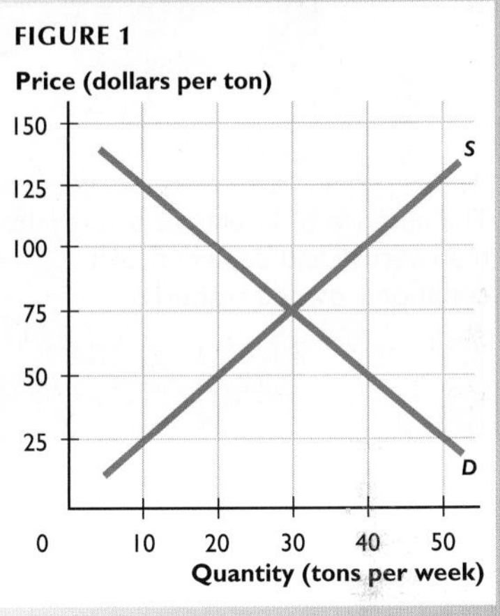


1. What is the quantity of pesticide produced if no one owns the lake and what is the efficient quantity of pesticide?
2. If the residents of the town own the lake, what is the quantity of pesticide produced and how much do residents of the town charge the factories to dump waste?
3. If the pesticide factories own the lake, how much pesticide is produced?
4. If no one owns the lake and the government levies a pollution tax, what is the tax per ton of pesticide that achieves the efficient outcome?
5. **Pollution rules squeeze strawberry crop**
   Last year, Ventura County farmers harvested nearly 12,000 acres of strawberries valued at more than $323 million (a quarter of the nation's crop). To comply with the federal Clean Air Act, growers must use 50 percent less pesticide. It is estimated that strawberry output will fall by 60 percent.
   Source: *USA Today*, February 29, 2008
   Explain how a limit on pesticide will change the efficiency of the strawberry industry. Would a cap-and-trade scheme be more efficient?

## Guided Solutions to Practice Problems

1. The quantity of pesticide produced is 30 tons a week and the efficient quantity of pesticide is 20 tons a week (Figure 2).
2. The quantity of pesticide produced is the efficient quantity, 20 tons a week, and the townspeople charge the factories $50 a ton of pesticide, which is the marginal external cost of the pollution produced by that quantity.
3. The factories produce the efficient quantity: 20 tons a week. The townspeople pay the factory $50 a ton for the benefits of an unpolluted lake.
4. The government can achieve an efficient outcome if it levies a pollution tax equal to the external cost because this tax confronts the factories with the social cost of pollution. A pollution tax of $50 a ton paid by the factories achieves the efficient quantity of pesticide.
5. If the limit on pesticide lowers the marginal external cost, then the strawberry industry will be more efficient. With a cap-and-trade scheme, the price of a cap will adjust until it equals the marginal external cost. With a cap-and-trade, the farmers' marginal cost equals the marginal social cost, so a cap-and-trade scheme would be efficient.

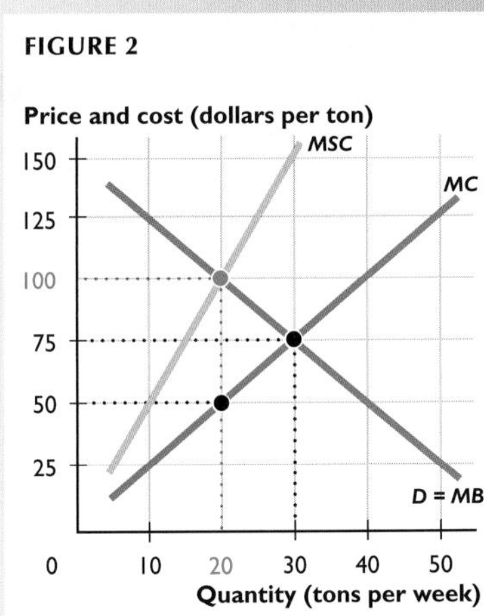

Work these problems in Chapter 11 Study Plan to get instant feedback.

# CHAPTER CHECKPOINT

## Study Plan Problems and Applications

Table 1 shows the demand schedule for electricity from a coal burning utility. Table 2 shows the utility's cost of producing electricity and the external cost of the pollution created. Use this information to work Problems 1 to 3.

1. With no pollution control, calculate the quantity of electricity produced, the price of electricity, and the marginal external cost of the pollution generated.
2. With no pollution control, calculate the quantity of electricity produced, the marginal social cost of the electricity generated, and the deadweight loss.
3. If the government levies a pollution tax such that the utility generates the efficient quantity of electricity, calculate the quantity of electricity generated, the price of electricity, the size of the pollution tax, and the tax revenue.

**TABLE 1 DEMAND FOR ELECTRICITY**

| Price (cents per kilowatt) | Quantity demanded (kilowatts per day) |
|---|---|
| 4 | 500 |
| 8 | 400 |
| 12 | 300 |
| 16 | 200 |
| 20 | 100 |
| 24 | 0 |

**TABLE 2 PRIVATE AND EXTERNAL COSTS**

| Quantity (kilowatts per day) | Marginal cost (cents per kilowatt) | Marginal external cost (cents per kilowatt) |
|---|---|---|
| 0 | 0 | 0 |
| 100 | 2 | 2 |
| 200 | 4 | 4 |
| 300 | 6 | 6 |
| 400 | 8 | 8 |
| 500 | 10 | 10 |

Use the following information to work Problems 4 and 5.

Tom and Larry must spend a day working together. Tom likes to smoke cigars and the price of a cigar is $2. Larry likes a smoke-free environment.

4. If Tom's marginal benefit from a cigar a day is $20 and Larry's marginal benefit from a smoke-free environment is $25 a day, what is the outcome if they meet at Tom's home? What is the outcome if they meet at Larry's home?
5. If Tom's marginal benefit from a cigar a day is $25 and Larry's marginal benefit from a smoke-free environment is $20 a day, what is the outcome if they meet at Tom's home? What is the outcome if they meet at Larry's home?

Use the following information to work Problems 6 to 9.

Table 3 shows the value of cod caught in the Atlantic Ocean by European and North American fishing boats. The marginal cost of operating a cod fishing boat is $50,000 a month.

**TABLE 3**

| Number of fishing boats | Value of cod caught (thousands of dollars per month) |
|---|---|
| 0 | 0 |
| 10 | 2,000 |
| 20 | 3,400 |
| 30 | 4,200 |
| 40 | 4,400 |
| 50 | 4,000 |
| 60 | 3,000 |
| 70 | 1,400 |

6. If the number of fishing boats increases from 20 to 30 to 40, what are the marginal private benefit and the marginal social benefit of a fishing boat?
7. With no regulation of cod fishing, what is the equilibrium number of boats and the value of the cod caught? Is there overfishing or not?
8. Draw a graph to show the efficient number of boats and the cod catch.
9. If the United States, Canada, and the European Union limit the number of fishing boats to 20, would the cod catch be sustainable and would it be efficient? Explain your answer.
10. The mayor of New York City, Michael Bloomberg, proposed a congestion charge of $4 a car and $21 a truck on vehicles in the city as a way of cutting congestion, reducing travel time, and improving public transportation.

    BBC News, New York, July 24, 2007

    With the congestion charge and better public transport, are New York City streets public goods or private goods? If the congestion charge reduces travel times, what benefits would the people who live or work in New York receive? Explain your answers.

## Instructor Assignable Problems and Applications

Your instructor can assign these problems as homework, a quiz, or a test in **MyEconLab**.

1. The price of gasoline in Europe is about three times that in the United States, mainly because the European gas tax is higher than the U.S. gas tax. In light of the principles you've learned in this chapter, what is the case for increasing the gas tax in the United States to the European level and what is the case against an increase in the gas tax to the European level?
2. **Polar ice cap shrinks further and thins**
   With the warming of the planet, the polar ice cap is shrinking and the Arctic Sea is expanding. As the ice cap shrinks further, more and more underwater mineral resources will become accessible. Many countries are staking out territorial claims to parts of the polar region.
   Source: *Wall Street Journal*, April 7, 2009

   Explain how ownership of these mineral resources will influence the amount of damage done to the Arctic Sea and its wildlife.
3. Table 1 shows the marginal benefit and marginal cost of driving a private car into central London. How many cars a day enter London? In 2009, the congestion charge was set at £10 per car per day. How many cars a day entered London after the congestion charge was levied? What was the reduction in congestion and how much revenue did the congestion charge create?

**TABLE 1**

| Number of cars per day | Marginal benefit (pounds per car) | Marginal cost (pounds per car) |
|---|---|---|
| 10,000 | 34 | 4 |
| 30,000 | 28 | 8 |
| 60,000 | 22 | 12 |
| 90,000 | 16 | 16 |
| 120,000 | 10 | 20 |

Use the following information to work Problems 4 to 6.

**Plans to curtail use of plastic bags, but not much action**
Plastic bags have been blamed for street litter, ocean pollution, and carbon emissions produced by manufacturing and shipping them. Last summer, Seattle approved a 20-cents charge on paper and plastic shopping bags, which was intended to reduce pollution by encouraging reusable bags. The plastic bag industry launched a petition drive to delay the plan and soon voters will make the decision.

Source: *The New York Times*, February 23, 2009

4. Explain how Seattle's 20-cent charge will change the use of plastic bags.
5. Draw a graph to show how Seattle's policy will change the deadweight loss created by plastic bags.
6. Explain why a complete ban on plastic bags would be inefficient.
7. **EPA pushes to have companies track greenhouse gases**
   "It's a very important step as we're moving forward to deal with climate change," says Dina Kruger, director of EPA's climate change division. Congress plans to make large polluters, such as oil refiners and automobile manufacturers, and makers of cement, aluminum, glass and paper, start tracking their emissions next year. A cap-and-trade scheme will be introduced for factories that emit 90 percent of U.S. greenhouse gases.
   Source: *USA Today*, March 11, 2009

   The monitoring cost of the scheme is expected to be about $127 million a year. Who will benefit from the scheme? Who will bear the burden of this scheme?

8. If hikers and others were required to pay a fee to use the Appalachian Trail, would the use of this common resource be more efficient? Would it be even more efficient if the most popular spots such as Annapolis Rock had more highly priced access? Why do you think we don't see more market solutions to the tragedy of the commons?

Use the following information to work Problems **9** to **11**.

Table 2 shows the value of bluefin tuna caught in the Southern Ocean by fishing boats from Australia, New Zealand, and Argentina. The marginal cost of operating a fishing boat is $60,000 a month.

**TABLE 2**

| Number of fishing boats | Value of bluefin tuna caught (thousands of dollars per month) |
|---|---|
| 0 | 0 |
| 10 | 1,200 |
| 20 | 2,000 |
| 30 | 2,400 |
| 40 | 2,400 |
| 50 | 2,000 |
| 60 | 1,200 |

9. With no regulation of bluefin tuna fishing, what is the equilibrium number of boats and the value of the tuna caught? Is there overfishing or not?
10. What is the efficient number of boats and value of the bluefin tuna catch?
11. If the governments agreed to issue ITQs to fishing boats to limit the bluefin tuna catch to the efficient quantity, what would be the price of an ITQ?

Use the following information to work Problems **12** to **15**.

A natural spring runs under plots of land owned by ten people. Each person has the right to sink a well on her or his land and take water from the spring. The amount of water taken depends on the number of wells sunk and is shown in Table 3. The marginal cost of sinking a well is the equivalent of 4 gallons of water a day.

**TABLE 3**

| Number of wells | Water output (gallons per day) |
|---|---|
| 0 | 0 |
| 2 | 12 |
| 4 | 22 |
| 6 | 30 |
| 8 | 36 |
| 10 | 40 |
| 12 | 42 |
| 14 | 42 |

12. What is the equilibrium number of wells and quantity of water taken? Draw a graph to illustrate your answer.
13. What is the efficient number of wells and quantity of water taken? Draw a graph to illustrate your answer.
14. If the government set a quota on the total amount of water such that the efficient number of wells would be sunk, what would that quota be?
15. How much would someone offer the ten owners to rent the rights to all the water in the common reserve? (Use gallons of water as the unit.)

## How much would you pay for a song?

You can download a song for 99¢, but how much would you be willing to pay for one?

# Consumer Choice and Demand

**When you have completed your study of this chapter, you will be able to**

1 Calculate and graph a budget line that shows the limits to a person's consumption possibilities.

2 Explain marginal utility theory and use it to derive a consumer's demand curve.

3 Use marginal utility theory to explain the paradox of value: why water is vital but cheap while diamonds are relatively useless but expensive.

## 12.1 CONSUMPTION POSSIBILITIES

We begin our study of consumption choices by learning about the limits to what a person can afford to buy. Consumption choices are limited by income and prices. We summarize these influences on buying plans in a budget line. We'll study the buying plans of a student like you whom we'll call Tina.

### The Budget Line

**Budget line**
A line that describes the limits to consumption possibilities and that depends on a consumer's budget and the prices of goods and services.

A **budget line** describes the limits to consumption possibilities. Tina has already committed most of her income to renting an apartment, buying textbooks, paying her campus meal plan, and saving a few dollars each month. Having made these decisions, Tina has a remaining budget of $4 a day, which she spends on two goods: bottled water and chewing gum. The price of water is $1 a bottle, and the price of gum is 50¢ a pack. If Tina spends all of her available budget, she reaches the limits of her consumption of bottled water and gum.

Figure 12.1 illustrates Tina's budget line. Rows *A* through *E* in the table show five possible ways of spending $4 on these two goods. If Tina spends all of her $4 on gum, she can buy 8 packs a day. In this case, she has nothing available to spend on bottled water. Row *A* shows this possibility. At the other extreme, if Tina spends her entire $4 on bottled water, she can buy 4 bottles a day and no gum. Row *E* shows this possibility. Rows *B*, *C*, and *D* show three other possible combinations that Tina can afford.

**FIGURE 12.1**

Consumption Possibilities

myeconlab Animation

Tina's budget line shows the boundary between what she can and cannot afford. The rows of the table list Tina's affordable combinations of bottled water and chewing gum when her budget is $4 a day, the price of water is $1 a bottle, and the price of chewing gum is 50¢ a pack. For example, row *A* tells us that Tina exhausts her $4 budget when she buys 8 packs of gum and no water.

The figure graphs Tina's budget line. Points *A* through *E* on the graph represent the rows of the table.

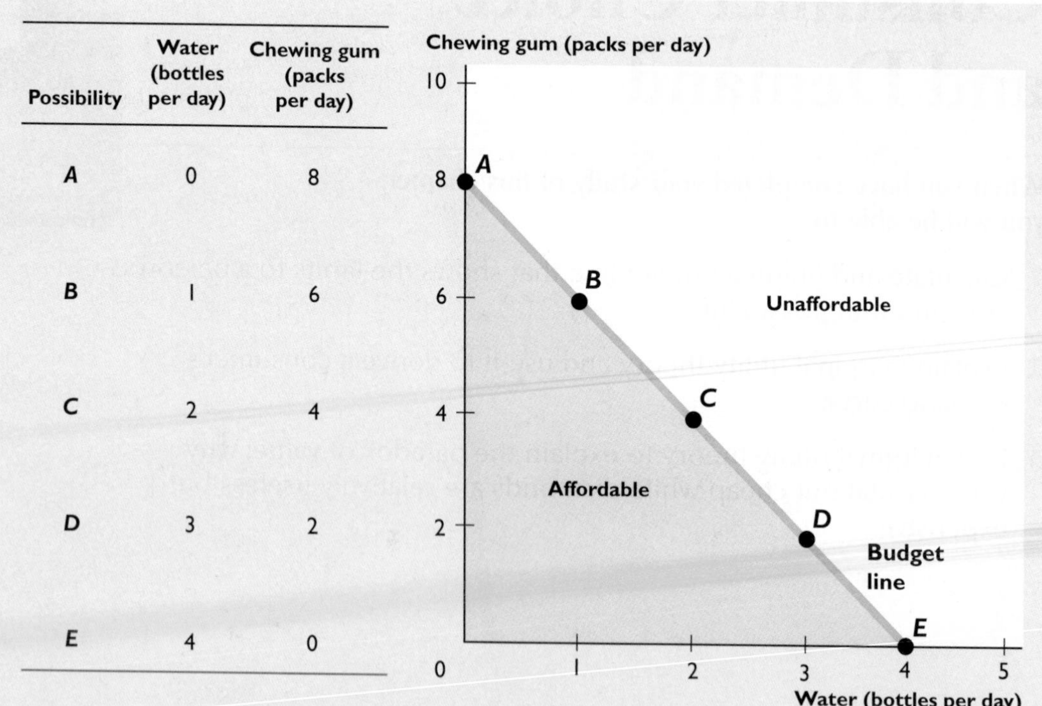

| Possibility | Water (bottles per day) | Chewing gum (packs per day) |
|---|---|---|
| *A* | 0 | 8 |
| *B* | 1 | 6 |
| *C* | 2 | 4 |
| *D* | 3 | 2 |
| *E* | 4 | 0 |

Points *A* through *E* in Figure 12.1 graph the possibilities in the table. The line passing through these points is Tina's budget line, which marks the boundary between what she can and cannot afford. She can afford any combination on the budget line and inside it (in the orange area). She cannot afford any combination outside the budget line (in the white area).

The budget line in Figure 12.1 is similar to the *production possibilities frontier*, or *PPF*, in Chapter 3 (pp. 62–63). Both curves show a limit to what is feasible. The *PPF* is a technological limit, so it changes only when technology changes. The budget line depends on the consumer's budget and on prices, so it changes when the budget or prices change.

## A Change in the Budget

Figure 12.2 shows the effect of a change in Tina's budget on her consumption possibilities. When Tina's budget increases, her consumption possibilities expand, and her budget line shifts outward. When her budget decreases, her consumption possibilities shrink and her budget line shifts inward.

On the initial budget line (the same as in Figure 12.1), Tina's budget is $4. On a day when Tina loses her wallet with $2 in it, she has only $2 to spend. Her new budget line in Figure 12.2 shows how much she can consume with a budget of $2. She can buy any of the combinations on the $2 budget line.

On a day when Tina sells an old CD for $2, she has $6 available and her budget line shifts rightward. She can now buy any of the combinations on the $6 budget line.

**FIGURE 12.2**

Changes in a Consumer's Budget

myeconlab Animation

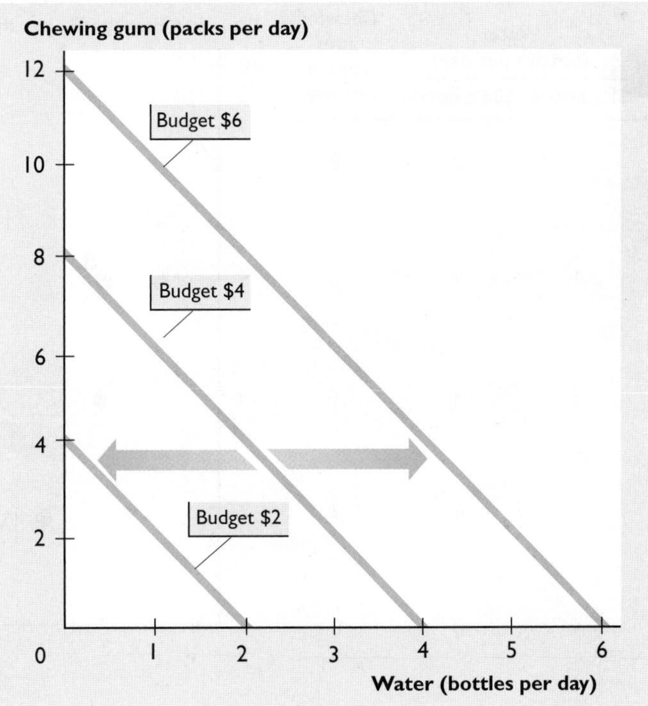


A decrease in the budget shifts the budget line leftward, and an increase in the budget shifts the budget line rightward.

*Lower prices in a sale expand consumption possibilities.*

## Changes in Prices

If the price of one good rises when the prices of other goods and the budget remain the same, consumption possibilities shrink. If the price of one good falls when the prices of other goods and the budget remain the same, consumption possibilities expand. To see these changes in consumption possibilities, let's see what happens to Tina's budget line when the price of a bottle of water changes.

### A Fall in the Price of Water

Figure 12.3 shows the effect on Tina's budget line of a fall in the price of a bottle of water from \$1 to 50¢ when the price of gum and her budget remain unchanged. If Tina spends all of her budget on bottled water, she can now afford 8 bottles a day. Her consumption possibilities have expanded. Because the price of gum is unchanged, if she spends all her budget on gum, she can still afford only 8 packs of gum a day. Her budget line has rotated outward.

### A Rise in the Price of Water

Figure 12.4 shows the effect on Tina's budget line of a rise in the price of a bottle of water from \$1 to \$2 when the price of gum and her budget remain unchanged. If Tina spends all of her budget on bottled water, she can now afford only 2 bottles a day. Tina's consumption possibilities have shrunk. Again, because the price of gum is unchanged, if Tina spends all her budget on gum, she can still afford only 8 packs of gum a day. Her budget line has rotated inward.

**FIGURE 12.3**

A Fall in the Price of Water

myeconlab Animation

When the price of water falls from \$1 a bottle to 50¢ a bottle, the budget line rotates outward and becomes less steep.

| Possibility | Water (bottles per day) \$1 a bottle | Water (bottles per day) 50¢ a bottle | Chewing gum (packs per day) |
|---|---|---|---|
| *A* | 0 | 0 | 8 |
| *B* | 1 | 2 | 6 |
| *C* | 2 | 4 | 4 |
| *D* | 3 | 6 | 2 |
| *E* | 4 | 8 | 0 |

## Prices and the Slope of the Budget Line

Notice that when the price of bottled water changes and the price of gum remains unchanged, the slope of the budget line changes. In Figure 12.3, when the price of bottled water falls, the budget line becomes less steep. In Figure 12.4, when the price of a bottle of water rises, the budget line becomes steeper.

Recall that "slope equals rise over run." The rise is an *increase* in the quantity of gum, and the run is a *decrease* in the quantity of bottled water. The slope of the budget line is negative, which means that there is a tradeoff between the two goods. Along the budget line, consuming more of one good implies consuming less of the other good. The slope of the budget line is an *opportunity cost*. It tells us what the consumer must give up to get one more unit of a good.

Let's calculate the slopes of the three budget lines in Figures 12.3 and 12.4:

- When the price of water is $1 a bottle, the slope of the budget line is 8 packs of gum divided by 4 bottles of water, which equals 2 packs of gum per bottle.
- When the price of water is 50¢ a bottle, the slope of the budget line is 8 packs of gum divided by 8 bottles of water, which equals 1 pack of gum per bottle.
- When the price of water is $2 a bottle, the slope of the budget line is 8 packs of gum divided by 2 bottles of water, which equals 4 packs of gum per bottle.

**FIGURE 12.4**

A Rise in the Price of Water

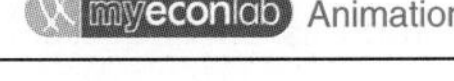

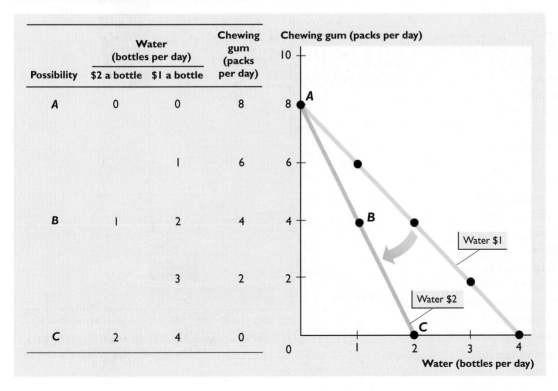


| Possibility | Water (bottles per day) $2 a bottle | Water (bottles per day) $1 a bottle | Chewing gum (packs per day) |
|---|---|---|---|
| A | 0 | 0 | 8 |
| | | 1 | 6 |
| B | 1 | 2 | 4 |
| | | 3 | 2 |
| C | 2 | 4 | 0 |

When the price of water rises from $1 a bottle to $2 a bottle, the budget line rotates inward and becomes steeper.

Think about what these slopes mean as opportunity costs. When the price of water is $1 a bottle and the price of gum is 50¢ a pack, it costs 2 packs of gum to buy a bottle of water. When the price of water is 50¢ a bottle and the price of gum is 50¢ a pack, it costs 1 pack of gum to buy a bottle of water. And when the price of water is $2 a bottle and the price of gum is 50¢ a pack, it costs 4 packs of gum to buy a bottle of water.

**Relative price**
The price of one good in terms of another good—an opportunity cost. It equals the price of one good divided by the price of another good.

Another name for an opportunity cost is a relative price. A **relative price** is the price of one good in terms of another good. If the price of gum is 50¢ a pack and the price of water is $1 a bottle, the relative price of water is 2 packs of gum per bottle. It is calculated as the price of water divided by the price of gum ($1 a bottle ÷ 50¢ a pack = 2 packs per bottle).

When the price of the good plotted on the *x*-axis falls, other things remaining the same, the budget line becomes less steep, and the opportunity cost and relative price of the good on the *x*-axis fall.

## EYE on the U.S. ECONOMY

### Relative Prices on the Move

Over a number of years, relative prices change a great deal. Some of the most dramatic changes have occurred in high-technology products such as computers. Many other relative prices have changed and many have fallen.

The figure shows the price changes between 1997 and 2007 of 16 items that feature in most student's budgets.

The largest relative price increases are those of gasoline and college textbooks. The relative prices of eggs, bread, beef, and electricity have also increased.

The largest relative price decrease is that of a personal computer, which has fallen by 90 percent. The relative prices of phone calls, oranges, and tomatoes have also fallen.

These changes in relative prices change people's consumption possibilities and change the choices they make.

Lower prices provide an incentive to buy greater quantities; higher prices provide an incentive to find substitutes and buy smaller quantities.

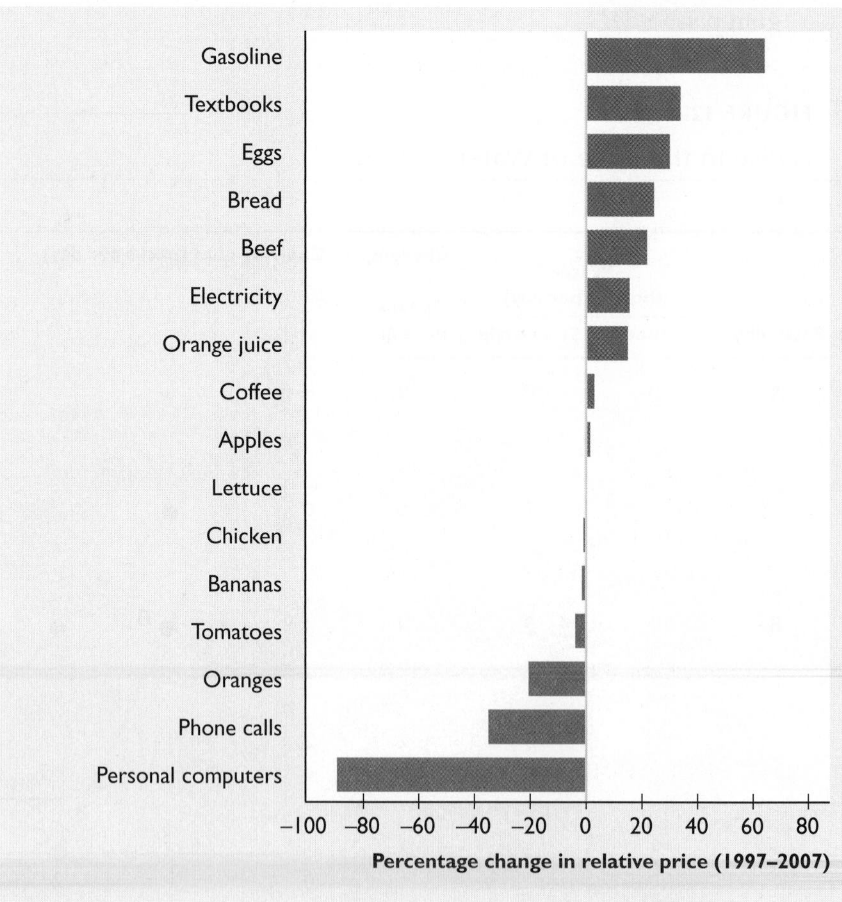


SOURCE OF DATA: Bureau of Labor Statistics.

# CHECKPOINT 12.1

**Calculate and graph a budget line that shows the limits to a person's consumption possibilities.**

myeconlab

Work these problems in Study Plan 12.1 to get instant feedback.

## Practice Problems

Jerry's burger and magazine budget is $12 a week. The price of a burger is $2, and the price of a magazine is $4.

1. List the combinations of burgers and magazines that Jerry can afford.
2. What is the relative price of a magazine? Explain your answer.
3. Draw a graph of Jerry's budget line with the quantity of magazines plotted on the *x*-axis. Describe how the budget line changes if, other things remaining the same, the following changes occur one at a time:
   - The price of a magazine falls.
   - Jerry's budget for burgers and magazines increases.
4. **Gas prices straining budgets**

   As gas prices hit $3.49 a gallon, many people cut back on eating out and shopping. Some people traded in their SUV or truck for a smaller car.

   Source: CNN, February 29, 2008

   Consider Mark who buys only two goods: gasoline and meals-to-go. As the gas price rises, describe the change in his consumption possibilities, the relative price of a meal-to-go, and Mark's real income in terms of meals-to-go.

## Guided Solutions to Practice Problems

1. Jerry can afford 3 magazines and no burgers; 2 magazines and 2 burgers; 1 magazine and 4 burgers; no magazines and 6 burgers.
2. The relative price of a magazine is the number of burgers that Jerry must forgo to get 1 magazine, which equals the price of a magazine divided by the price of a burger, or 2 burgers per magazine.
3. The budget line is a straight line from 6 burgers on the *y*-axis to 3 magazines on the *x*-axis (Figure 1).

   With a lower price of a magazine, Jerry can buy more magazines. His budget line rotates outward (Figure 2).

   With a bigger budget, Jerry can buy more of both goods. His budget line shifts outward (Figure 3).
4. As the price of gasoline rises, Mark's consumption possibilities shrink. His budget line rotates inward. The relative price of a meal-to-go is the price of a meal-to-go divided by the price of gasoline. As the gas price rises, the relative price of a meal-to-go will fall. Mark's real income in terms of meals-to-go is the number of meals-to-go that Mark can buy. A rise in the price of gasoline does not change his real income in terms of meals-to-go.

FIGURE 1

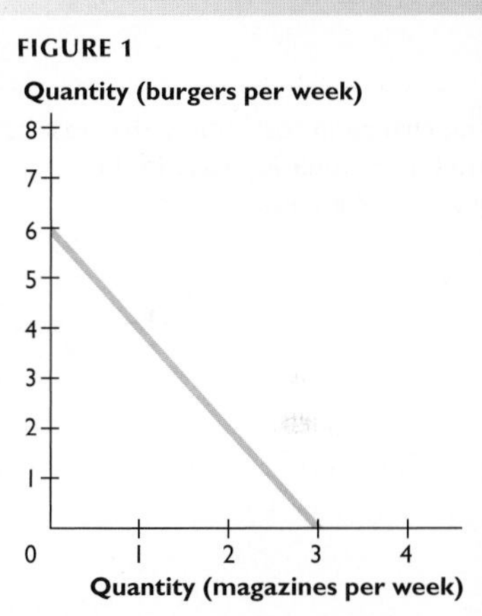


FIGURE 2

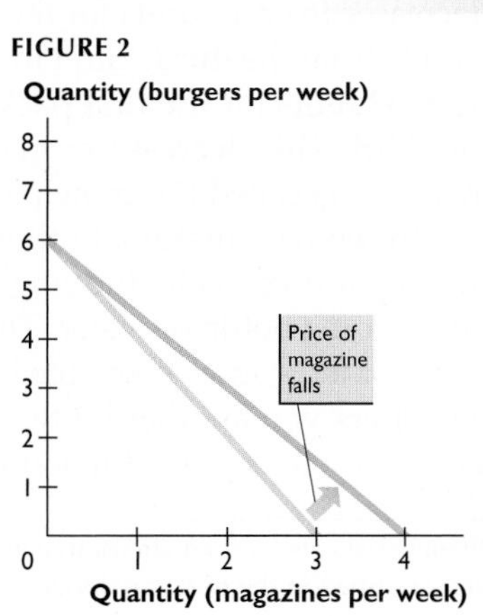


FIGURE 3

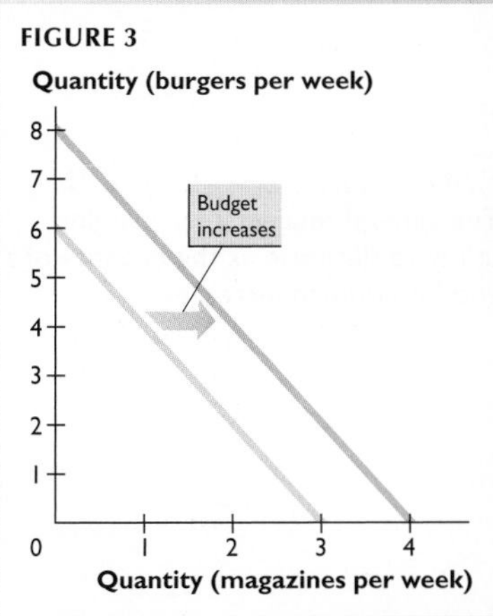

## 12.2 MARGINAL UTILITY THEORY

**Utility**
The benefit or satisfaction that a person gets from the consumption of a good or service.

The budget line tells us about consumption *possibilities*, but it doesn't tell us a person's consumption *choice*. Choices depend on *possibilities* and *preferences*. To describe preferences, economists use the concept of utility.* **Utility** is the benefit or satisfaction that a person gets from the consumption of a good or service. To understand how we use utility to explain people's choices, we distinguish between two concepts:

- Total utility
- Marginal utility

### Total Utility

**Total utility**
The total benefit that a person gets from the consumption of a good or service. Total utility generally increases as the quantity consumed of a good increases.

**Total utility** is the total benefit that a person gets from the consumption of a good or service. Total utility depends on the quantity of the good consumed *in a given period*—more consumption generally gives more total utility. Table 12.1 shows Tina's total utility from bottled water and chewing gum. If she consumes no bottled water and no gum, she gets no utility. If she consumes 1 bottle of water a day, she gets 15 units of utility. If she consumes 1 pack of gum a day, it provides her with 32 units of utility. As Tina increases the quantity of bottled water or the packs of gum she consumes, her total utility increases.

### Marginal Utility

**Marginal utility**
The change in total utility that results from a one-unit increase in the quantity of a good consumed.

**Marginal utility** is the change in total utility that results from a one-unit increase in the quantity of a good consumed. Table 12.1 shows the calculation of Tina's marginal utility from bottled water and chewing gum. Let's find Tina's marginal utility from a 3rd bottle of water a day (highlighted in the table). Her total utility from 3 bottles is 36 units, and her total utility from 2 bottles is 27 units. So for Tina, the marginal utility from drinking a 3rd bottle of water each day is

$$\text{Marginal utility of 3rd bottle} = 36 \text{ units} - 27 \text{ units} = 9 \text{ units.}$$

In the table, marginal utility appears midway between the quantities because the *change* in consumption produces the *marginal* utility. The table displays the marginal utility from each quantity of water and gum consumed.

Notice that Tina's marginal utility decreases as her daily consumption of water and gum increases. For example, her marginal utility from bottled water decreases from 15 units for the first bottle per day to 12 units from the second and 9 units from the third. Similarly, her marginal utility from chewing gum decreases from 32 units for the first pack per day to 16 units for the second and 8 units for the third. This decrease in marginal utility as the quantity of a good consumed increases is called the principle of **diminishing marginal utility**.

**Diminishing marginal utility**
The general tendency for marginal utility to decrease as the quantity of a good consumed increases.

To see why marginal utility diminishes, think about the following situations: In one, you've been studying all day and have had nothing to drink. Someone offers you a bottle of water. The marginal utility you get from that water is large. In the other, you've been drinking all day and you've drunk 7 bottles. Now someone offers you another bottle of water, and you say thanks very much and sip it slowly. You enjoy the 8th bottle of the day, but the marginal utility from it is tiny.

*Economists also use an alternative method of describing preferences called *indifference curves*, which are described in the optional appendix to this chapter.

**TABLE 12.1**

Tina's Total Utility and Marginal Utility

| Bottled water | | | Chewing gum | | |
|---|---|---|---|---|---|
| **Quantity** (bottles per day) | **Total utility** | **Marginal utility** | **Quantity** (packs per day) | **Total utility** | **Marginal utility** |
| 0 | 0 | | 0 | 0 | |
| | | 15 | | | 32 |
| 1 | 15 | | 1 | 32 | |
| | | 12 | | | 16 |
| 2 | 27 | | 2 | 48 | |
| | | 9 | | | 8 |
| 3 | 36 | | 3 | 56 | |
| | | 6 | | | 6 |
| 4 | 42 | | 4 | 62 | |
| | | 5 | | | 4 |
| 5 | 47 | | 5 | 66 | |
| | | 4 | | | 2 |
| 6 | 51 | | 6 | 68 | |
| | | 3 | | | 1 |
| 7 | 54 | | 7 | 69 | |
| | | 2 | | | 0 |
| 8 | 56 | | 8 | 69 | |

The table shows Tina's total utility and marginal utility from bottled water and chewing gum. Marginal utility is the change in total utility when the quantity consumed increases by one unit. When Tina's consumption of bottled water increases from 2 bottles a day to 3 bottles per day, her total utility from bottled water increases from 27 units to 36 units. So Tina's marginal utility of the 3rd bottle a day is 9 units. Total utility increases and marginal utility diminishes as the quantity consumed increases.

Similarly, suppose you've been unable to buy a pack of gum for more than a day. A friend offers you a pack. Relief! You chew and receive a lot of utility. On another day, you've chewed until your jaws ache and have gone through 7 packs. You're offered an 8th, and this time you say thanks very much but I'll pass on that one. The 8th pack of gum would bring you no marginal utility.

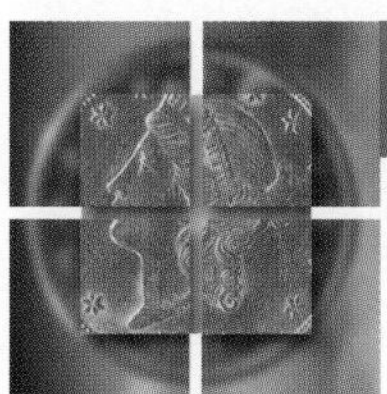

## EYE on the PAST

### Jeremy Bentham, William Stanley Jevons, and the Birth of Utility

The concept of utility was revolutionary when Jeremy Bentham (1748–1832) proposed it in the early 1800s. He used the idea to advance his then radical support for free education, free medical care, and social security. It was another fifty years before William Stanley Jevons (1835–1882) developed the concept of *marginal* utility and used it to predict people's consumption choices. For the first time, economists could distinguish between cost and value and a basic theory of demand was born.

*Jeremy Bentham*

*William Stanley Jevons*

## Graphing Tina's Utility Schedules

We illustrate a consumer's preferences with a total utility curve and a marginal utility curve like those in Figure 12.5. Part (a) shows that as Tina drinks more bottled water, her total utility from water increases. It also shows that total utility increases at a decreasing rate—diminishing marginal utility. Part (b) graphs Tina's marginal utility. The steps in part (a) are placed side by side in part (b). The curve that passes through the midpoints of the bars in part (b) is Tina's marginal utility curve.

The numbers in Table 12.1 and the graphs in Figure 12.5 describe Tina's preferences and, along with her budget line, enable us to predict the choices that she makes. That is our next task.

## Maximizing Total Utility

The consumer's goal is to allocate the available budget in the way that maximizes total utility. The consumer achieves this goal by choosing the affordable combination of goods at which the *sum* of the utilities obtained from all goods consumed is as large as possible.

**Utility-maximizing rule**
The rule that leads to the greatest total utility from all the goods and services consumed. The rule is
1. Allocate the entire available budget.
2. Make the marginal utility per dollar equal for all goods.

We can find a consumer's best budget allocation by using a two-step **utility-maximizing rule**:

1. Allocate the entire available budget.
2. Make the marginal utility per dollar equal for all goods.

### Allocate the Available Budget

If a consumer can buy more of one good without buying less of another good, utility can be increased. When utility is maximized, it isn't possible to buy more of one good without decreasing the quantity of another good. In this situation, the consumer has allocated the entire available budget.

With a budget of \$4, the price of water \$1 per bottle, and the price of gum 50¢ a pack, Tina allocates her budget to bottled water and gum at a point *on* her budget line in Figure 12.1 (p. 292). If she was at a point *inside* her budget line, she could buy more water or more gum without giving up any of the other good and she would not be maximizing utility.

### Equalize the Marginal Utility Per Dollar

**Marginal utility per dollar**
The marginal utility from a good relative to the price paid for the good.

The second step to maximizing utility is to find the affordable combination that makes the marginal utility per dollar equal for both goods. The **marginal utility per dollar** is the marginal utility from a good relative to the price of the good.

***Calculating the Marginal Utility per Dollar*** The marginal utility per dollar equals the marginal utility from a good divided by the price of the good. For example, if Tina buys 2 packs of gum, her marginal utility from gum is 16 units. At a price of 50¢ a pack, her marginal utility *per dollar* from gum is 16 units divided by 50¢, which equals 32 units of utility per dollar.

***Tina's Utility-Maximizing Choice*** If Tina spends \$1 more on water and \$1 less on gum, her total utility from water increases and her total utility from gum decreases. What happens to her total utility from both goods depends on the marginal utility per dollar for each good.

## FIGURE 12.5

Total Utility and Marginal Utility

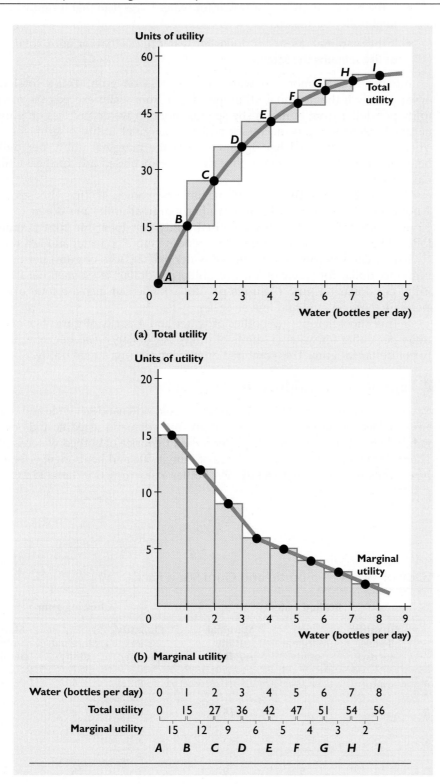

(a) Total utility



(b) Marginal utility

| Water (bottles per day) | 0 | 1 | 2 | 3 | 4 | 5 | 6 | 7 | 8 |
|---|---|---|---|---|---|---|---|---|---|
| Total utility | 0 | 15 | 27 | 36 | 42 | 47 | 51 | 54 | 56 |
| Marginal utility | 15 | 12 | 9 | 6 | 5 | 4 | 3 | 2 | |
| | A | B | C | D | E | F | G | H | I |

Part (a) graphs Tina's total utility from bottled water. It also shows the extra total utility she gains from each additional bottle of water—her marginal utility—as the steps along the total utility curve.

Part (b) shows how Tina's marginal utility from bottled water diminishes by placing the bars shown in part (a) side by side as a series of declining steps.

- If the marginal utility per dollar for water *exceeds* that for gum, total utility increases.
- If the marginal utility per dollar for water *is less than* that for gum, total utility decreases.
- If the marginal utility per dollar for water *equals* that for gum, total utility remains the same.

*Which one has the higher marginal utility per dollar?*

By spending \$1 more on water and \$1 less on gum, Tina's total utility increases only if the marginal utility per dollar from water exceeds the marginal utility per dollar from gum. As she spends more on water and less on gum, the marginal utility of water decreases and the marginal utility of gum increases. When Tina has allocated her dollars so that the marginal utility per dollar is the same for both goods, total utility cannot be increased any further: Utility is maximized.

Table 12.2 shows Tina's utility-maximizing choice. If Tina chooses row *B* (1 bottle of water and 6 packs of gum) her marginal utility per dollar for water (15 units per dollar) *exceeds* her marginal utility per dollar for gum (4 units per dollar). She can increase total utility by spending more on water and less on gum.

If Tina chooses row *D* (3 bottles of water and 2 packs of gum) her marginal utility per dollar for water (9 units of utility per dollar) *is less than* her marginal utility per dollar for gum (32 units per dollar). She can increase total utility by spending more on gum and less on water.

If Tina chooses row *C* (2 bottles of water and 4 packs of gum) her marginal utility per dollar for water (12 units of utility per dollar) *equals* her marginal utility per dollar for gum. This combination maximizes Tina's total utility.

## Finding an Individual Demand Curve

We can use marginal utility theory to find a person's demand schedule and demand curve. In fact, we've just found one entry in Tina's demand schedule and one point on her demand curve for bottled water: When the price of bottled water is \$1 and other things remain the same (the price of gum is 50¢ and her budget is \$4 a day), the quantity of water that Tina buys is 2 bottles a day (row *C* in Table 12.2).

**TABLE 12.2**

Tina's Marginal Utilities per Dollar: Water \$1 a Bottle and Gum 50¢ a Pack

The rows of the table show Tina's marginal utility per dollar from water and gum for the affordable combinations when the price of water is \$1 a bottle, the price of gum is 50¢ a pack, and her budget is \$4. By equalizing the marginal utilities per dollar from water and gum, Tina maximizes her total utility. Her utility-maximizing choice is to buy 2 bottles of water and 4 packs of gum.

| | Bottled water | | | Chewing gum | | |
|---|---|---|---|---|---|---|
| | Quantity (bottles per day) | Marginal utility | Marginal utility per dollar | Quantity (packs per day) | Marginal utility | Marginal utility per dollar |
| *A* | 0 | | | 8 | 0 | 0 |
| | | | | 7 | 1 | 2 |
| *B* | 1 | 15 | 15 | 6 | 2 | 4 |
| | | | | 5 | 4 | 8 |
| *C* | 2 | 12 | 12 | 4 | 6 | 12 |
| | | | | 3 | 8 | 16 |
| *D* | 3 | 9 | 9 | 2 | 16 | 32 |
| | | | | 1 | 32 | 64 |

**TABLE 12.3**

Tina's Marginal Utilities per Dollar: Water 50¢ a Bottle and Gum 50¢ a Pack

| | Bottled water | | | Chewing gum | | |
|---|---|---|---|---|---|---|
| | Quantity (bottles per day) | Marginal utility | Marginal utility per dollar | Quantity (packs per day) | Marginal utility | Marginal utility per dollar |
| *D* | 3 | 9 | 18 | 5 | 4 | 8 |
| *E* | 4 | 6 | 12 | 4 | 6 | 12 |
| *F* | 5 | 5 | 10 | 3 | 8 | 16 |

The rows of the table show Tina's marginal utility per dollar from water and gum for the affordable combinations when the price of water is 50¢ a bottle, the price of gum is 50¢ a pack, and her budget is $4. By equalizing the marginal utilities per dollar from water and gum, Tina maximizes her total utility. Her utility-maximizing choice is to buy 4 bottles of water and 4 packs of gum.

To find another point on Tina's demand curve for bottled water, let's see what Tina buys when the price of water falls to 50¢ a bottle. If Tina continued to buy 2 bottles of water and 4 packs of gum, her marginal utility per dollar for water would increase from 12 to 24 and be twice the marginal utility per dollar for gum (row C in Table 12.2). Also, Tina would spend only $3, so she would have another $1 available.

Row *E* of Table 12.3 shows Tina's new utility-maximizing choice, and this choice is a second point on her demand curve for bottled water: When the price of bottled water is 50¢ (other things remaining the same), Tina buys 4 bottles of water a day. Figure 12.6 shows Tina's demand curve that we've just derived.

**FIGURE 12.6**

Tina's Demand for Bottled Water

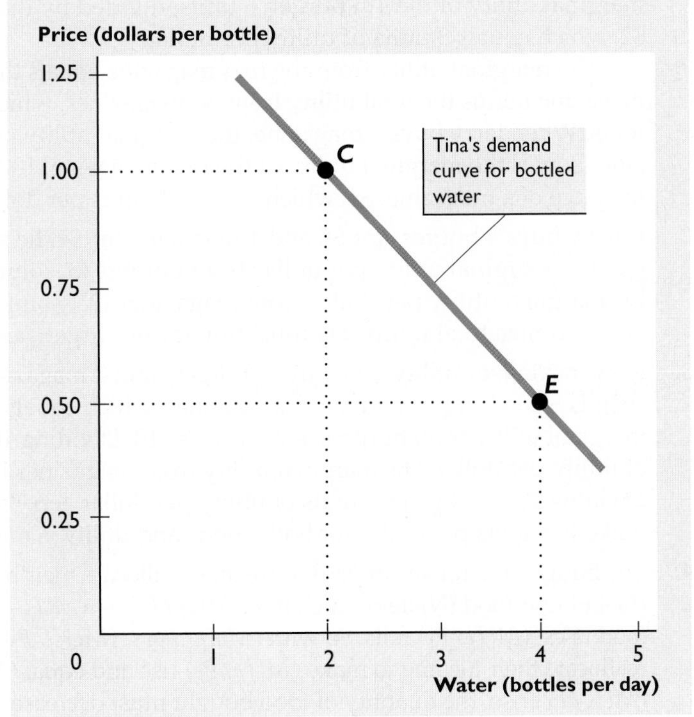


When the price of water is $1 a bottle (and her budget is $4 and the price of a pack of gum is 50¢), Tina buys 2 bottles of water and 4 packs of gum a day. She is at point *C* on her demand curve for water.

When the price of water falls to 50¢ a bottle and other things remain the same, Tina buys 4 bottles of water and 4 packs of gum a day and moves to point *E* on her demand curve for bottled water.

Work these problems in Study Plan 12.2 to get instant feedback.

# CHECKPOINT 12.2

**Explain marginal utility theory and use it to derive a consumer's demand curve.**

## Practice Problems

Table 1 shows Jerry's total utility from burgers and magazines. The price of a burger is $2, the price of a magazine is $4, and Jerry has $12 a week to spend. Use this information to work Problems **1** to **3**.

**TABLE 1**

| Burgers | | Magazines | |
|---|---|---|---|
| Quantity per week | Total utility | Quantity per week | Total utility |
| 0 | 0 | 0 | 0 |
| 1 | 14 | 1 | 100 |
| 2 | 24 | 2 | 120 |
| 3 | 32 | 3 | 134 |
| 4 | 38 | 4 | 144 |

1. Calculate Jerry's marginal utility and marginal utility per dollar from burgers when he buys 4 burgers a week. Calculate Jerry's marginal utility and marginal utility per dollar from magazines when he buys 1 magazine a week.
2. If Jerry buys 4 burgers and 1 magazine a week, does he maximize his total utility? To maximize total utility will he buy more or fewer burgers? Explain.
3. What quantities of burgers and magazines maximize Jerry's utility?
4. **When will food prices stop rising? No time soon**
   Food prices have risen almost 5 percent during the past year, the highest annual increase in almost 20 years.
   Source: *USA Today*, June 8, 2008
   How will the rise in the price of food change the budget line and the quantity of food that Americans buy?

## Guided Solutions to Practice Problems

1. The marginal utility from the 4th burger equals the total utility from 4 burgers minus the total utility from 3 burgers, which is 38 − 32 = 6 units. When Jerry buys 4 burgers, the marginal utility per dollar from burgers equals the marginal utility of the 4th burger, 6 units, divided by the price of a burger, $2, which equals 3 units of utility per dollar.
   The marginal utility from the first magazine equals the total utility from 1 magazine minus the total utility from no magazines, which is 100 − 0 = 100 units. When Jerry buys 1 magazine, the marginal utility per dollar from magazines equals the marginal utility of the first magazine, 100 units, divided by the price of a magazine, $4, which equals 25 units per dollar.
2. If Jerry buys 4 burgers for $8 and 1 magazine for $4, he spends his $12 budget. His marginal utility per dollar from burgers (3, solution **1**) is less than his marginal utility per dollar from magazines (25, solution **1**), so Jerry does *not* maximize total utility. He must buy fewer burgers and more magazines.
3. Jerry maximizes utility if he buys 2 burgers and 2 magazines a week. He spends $4 on burgers and $8 on magazines, which equals his $12 budget. His marginal utility from burgers is 24 − 14 = 10. Dividing 10 by $2 gives 5 units of utility per dollar. His marginal utility from magazines is 120 − 100 = 20. Dividing 20 by $4 gives 5 units of utility per dollar. Jerry's marginal utility per dollar is 5 units per dollar for both goods and utility is maximized.
4. The budget line rotates inward. Consumers allocate their budget between food (*F*) and non-food (*N*) items such that $(MU_F/P_F) = (MU_N/P_N)$. As the price of food rises, $(MU_F/P_F)$ falls. So with $(MU_F/P_F) < (MU_N/P_N)$, consumers will reallocate their income to make $(MU_F/P_F)$ rise and equal $(MU_N/P_N)$. To make $(MU_F/P_F)$ rise, the quantity of food bought must decrease.

## 12.3 EFFICIENCY, PRICE, AND VALUE

Marginal utility theory helps us to deepen our understanding of the concept of efficiency and to see more clearly the distinction between *value* and *price*. Let's see how.

### Consumer Efficiency

When Tina allocates her limited budget to maximize her total utility, she is using her resources efficiently. Any other allocation of her budget would leave her able to attain a higher level of total utility.

But when Tina has allocated her budget to maximize her total utility, she is *on* her demand curve for each good. A demand curve describes the quantity demanded at each price *when total utility is maximized*. When we studied efficiency in Chapter 6, we learned that a demand curve is also a willingness-to-pay curve. It tells us a consumer's *marginal benefit*—the benefit from consuming an additional unit of a good. You can now give the idea of marginal benefit a deeper meaning.

**Marginal benefit is the maximum price a consumer is willing to pay for an extra unit of a good or service when total utility is maximized.**

### The Paradox of Value

For centuries, philosophers were puzzled by the paradox of value. Water is more valuable than a diamond because water is essential to life itself. Yet water is much cheaper than a diamond. Why? Adam Smith tried to solve this paradox, but it was not until marginal utility theory had been developed that anyone could give a satisfactory answer.

You can solve this puzzle by distinguishing between *total* utility and *marginal* utility. Total utility tells us about relative value; marginal utility tells us about relative price. The total utility from water is enormous, but remember, the more we consume of something, the smaller is its marginal utility. We use so much water that its marginal utility—the benefit we get from one more glass of water—diminishes to a small value. Diamonds, on the other hand, have a small total utility relative to water, but because we buy few diamonds, they have a large marginal utility. When a household has maximized its total utility, it has allocated its budget so that the marginal utility per dollar is equal for all goods. Diamonds have a high price and a high marginal utility. Water has a low price and a low marginal utility. When the high marginal utility of diamonds is divided by the high price of a diamond, the result is a marginal utility per dollar that equals the low marginal utility of water divided by the low price of water. The marginal utility per dollar is the same for diamonds as for water.

#### Consumer Surplus

*Consumer surplus* measures value in excess of the amount paid. In Figure 12.7, the demand for and supply of water in part (a) determine the price of water $P_W$ and the quantity of water consumed $Q_W$. The demand for and supply of diamonds in part (b) determine the price of a diamond $P_D$ and the quantity of diamonds $Q_D$. Water is cheap but provides a large consumer surplus, while diamonds are expensive but provide a small consumer surplus.

**FIGURE 12.7**

The Paradox of Value

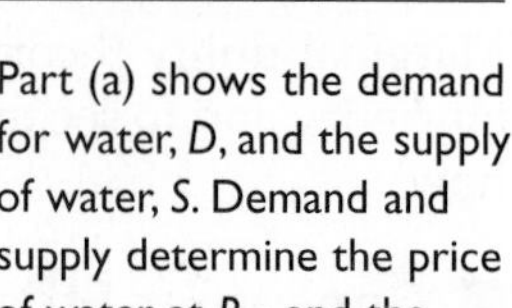


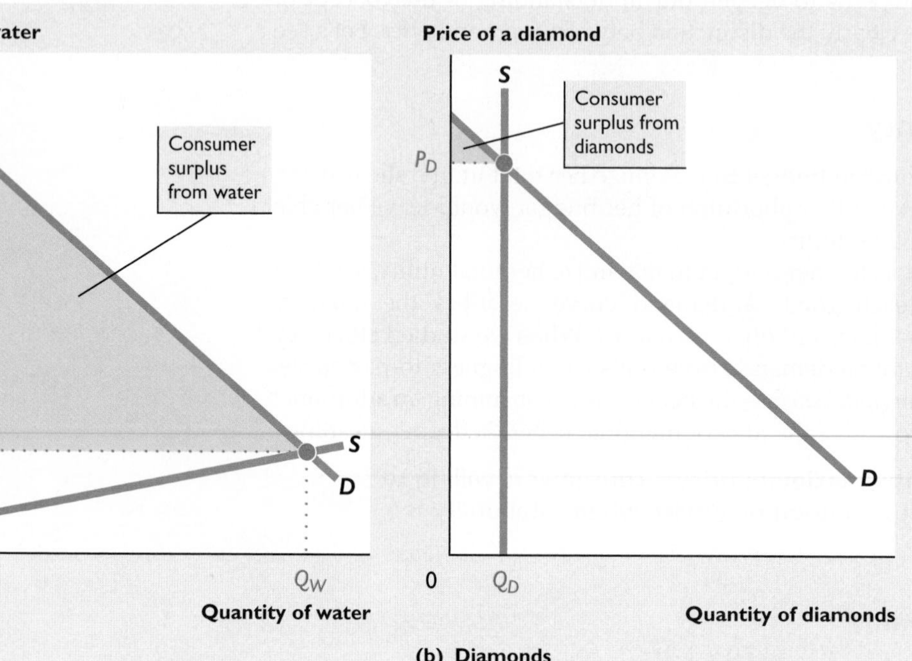


Part (a) shows the demand for water, *D*, and the supply of water, *S*. Demand and supply determine the price of water at $P_W$ and the quantity at $Q_W$. The consumer surplus from water is the large green triangle.

Part (b) shows the demand for diamonds, *D*, and the supply of diamonds, *S*. Demand and supply determine the price of a diamond at $P_D$ and the quantity at $Q_D$. The consumer surplus from diamonds is the small green triangle.

Water is valuable—has a large consumer surplus—but cheap. Diamonds are less valuable than water—have a smaller consumer surplus—but are expensive.

## EYE on SONG DOWNLOADS

### How Much Would You Pay for a Song?

You might say that you're willing to pay only 99¢ for a song, but that's not the answer of the average consumer. And it is probably not really your answer either. It is also not what the answer would have been just a few years ago.

We can work out what people are willing to pay for a song by finding the demand curve for songs and then finding the consumer surplus.

To find the demand curve, we need to look at the prices and quantities in the market for songs.

In 2007 (the most recent year for which we have the numbers) Americans spent $10 billion on all forms of recorded music, down from $14 billion in 2000. But the combined quantity of discs and downloads bought *increased* from 1 billion in 2000 to 1.8 billion in 2007 and the average price of a unit of recorded music fell from $14 to $5.50.

The average price fell because the mix of formats changed dramatically. In 2001, we bought 900 million CDs; in 2007, we bought only 500 million CDs and downloaded 1.2 billion music files. Figure 1 shows the longer history of the changing formats of recorded music.

The music that we buy isn't just one good—it is several different goods. We'll distinguish singles from albums and focus on the demand for singles.

In 2001, we bought 106 million singles and paid $4.95 on the average for each one. In 2007, we downloaded 802 million singles files and paid 99¢ for each one.

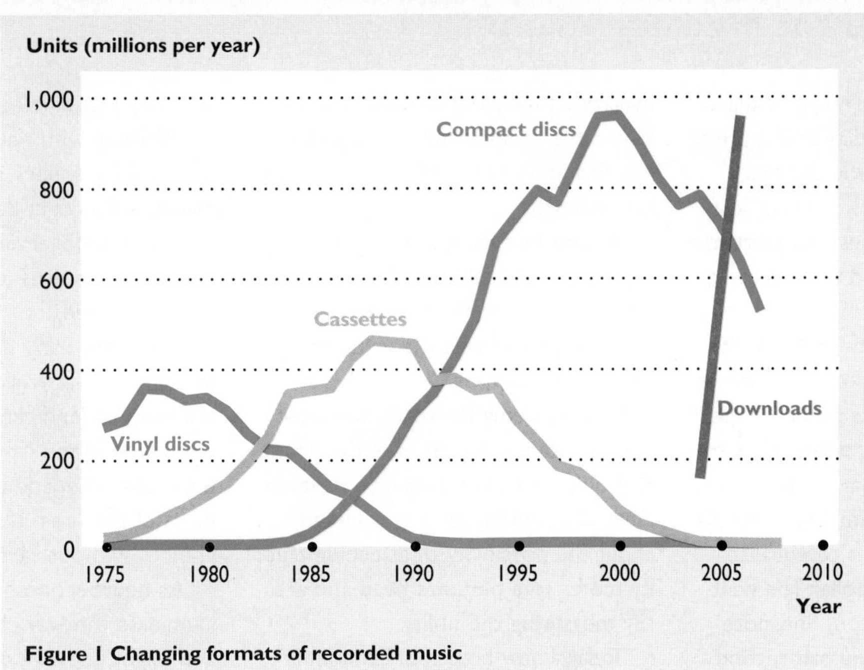


**Figure 1 Changing formats of recorded music**

The market for singles downloads has created a consumer surplus.

Figure 2 shows the demand curve in the market for singles. One point on the demand curve is the 2001 price and quantity—106 million singles were bought at an average price of $4.95. Another point on the demand curve is that for 2007—802 million singles downloaded at 99¢ each.

If the demand curve has not shifted and is linear (assumed here), we can calculate the change in consumer surplus generated by the fall in price and increase in quantity demanded. The green area is this change in consumer surplus. That increase in consumer surplus is $1.8 billion or $2.24 per single.

The $2.24 per song consumer surplus is an estimate of what the average buyer would be willing to pay for a song on average.

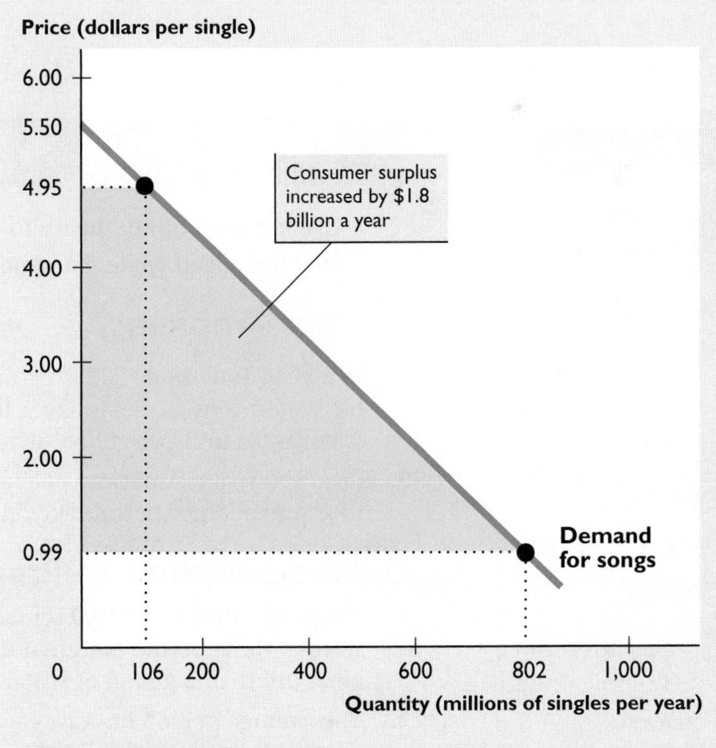


**Figure 2 The market for singles**

## EYE on YOUR LIFE

### Do You Maximize Your Utility?

You might be thinking that this marginal utility stuff is pretty unreal! You know that you don't go around the shops with a marginal utility calculator in hand. You just buy what you can afford and want, and that's all there is to it.

Well, marginal utility theory isn't about how people make their choices. It's about what choices people make. It's a tool that enables economists to explain the choices that people make.

You see lots of examples of people juggling their purchases to equalize marginal utilities per dollar. The next time you're in a checkout line, note the items that someone had second thoughts about and stuffed into the magazine rack alongside the tabloids. When the crunch came to pay, the marginal utility per dollar was just not high enough.

You might even find yourself actually using marginal utility to make your own decisions. It clarifies the options, and it helps to make the value of the alternatives explicit.

When Jeremy Bentham, and later William Stanley Jevons (see *Eye on the Past* on p. 299), first began to develop ideas about utility, they speculated about the possibility of attaching a utility meter to a person's head and actually measuring the utility.

Today, a new branch of economics called *neuroeconomics* is moving toward achieving that nineteenth-century dream.

Working with neuroscientists and using MRI scanners, economists are placing subjects in decision-making situations and observing how the brain behaves as choices are made and outcomes learned.

These are early days but results so far suggest that while some decisions are rational (and can be seen to be computed in the frontal cortex), other decisions are made using primitive parts of the brain that make snap choices without careful calculation.

As neuroeconomics advances, it will illuminate the way choices are made and might improve our ability to predict the choices that people make.

Work these problems in Study Plan 12.3 to get instant feedback.

## CHECKPOINT 12.3

**Use marginal utility theory to explain the paradox of value: why water is vital but cheap while diamonds are relatively useless but expensive.**

### Practice Problems

1. In a year, Tony rents 50 DVDs at \$3 each and pays \$50 for 10,000 gallons of tap water. Tony is maximizing total utility. If Tony's marginal utility from water is 0.5 unit per gallon, what is his marginal utility from a DVD rental?
2. Over the years, Americans have spent a smaller percentage of income on food and a larger percentage on cars. Explain the paradox of value.

### Guided Solutions to Practice Problems

1. Marginal utility of a DVD rental ÷ \$3 = Marginal utility of a gallon of water ÷ 0.5¢. So the marginal utility of a DVD rental is 600 times the marginal utility of a gallon of water: 600 × 0.5 or 300 units.
2. The average person has one car and the marginal utility from driving the car exceeds the marginal utility from food. While food is cheap and cars are expensive, consumers allocate their income to make the marginal utility per dollar equal for food and cars. There is no paradox of value.

# CHAPTER SUMMARY

## Key Points

**1 Calculate and graph a budget line that shows the limits to a person's consumption possibilities.**

- Consumption possibilities are constrained by the budget and prices. Some combinations of goods are affordable, and some are not affordable.
- The budget line is the boundary between what a person can and cannot afford with a given budget and given prices.
- The slope of the budget line determines the relative price of the good measured on the $x$-axis in terms of the good measured on the $y$-axis.
- A change in one price changes the slope of the budget line. A change in the budget shifts the budget line but does not change its slope.

**2 Explain marginal utility theory and use it to derive a consumer's demand curve.**

- Consumption possibilities and preferences determine consumption choices.
- Total utility is maximized when the entire budget is spent and marginal utility per dollar is equal for all goods.
- If the marginal utility per dollar from good $A$ exceeds that from good $B$, total utility increases if the quantity purchased of good $A$ increases and the quantity purchased of good $B$ decreases.
- Marginal utility theory implies the law of demand. That is, other things remaining the same, the higher the price of a good, the smaller is the quantity demanded of that good.

**3 Use marginal utility theory to explain the paradox of value: why water is vital but cheap while diamonds are relatively useless but expensive.**

- When consumers maximize total utility, they use resources efficiently.
- Marginal utility theory resolves the paradox of value.
- When we talk loosely about value, we are thinking of *total* utility or consumer surplus, but price is related to *marginal* utility.
- Water, which we consume in large amounts, has a high total utility and a large consumer surplus but a low price and low marginal utility.
- Diamonds, which we consume in small amounts, have a low total utility and a small consumer surplus but a high price and a high marginal utility.

## Key Terms

Budget line, 292
Diminishing marginal utility, 298
Marginal utility, 298
Marginal utility per dollar, 300
Relative price, 296
Total utility, 298
Utility, 298
Utility-maximizing rule, 300

Work these problems in Chapter 12 Study Plan to get instant feedback.

# CHAPTER CHECKPOINT

## Study Plan Problems and Applications

Amy has $12 a week to spend on coffee and soda. The price of coffee is $2 a cup, and soda is $1 a can. Use this information to work Problems **1** and **2**.

1. Draw a graph of Amy's budget line. Can Amy buy 7 cans of soda and 2 cups of coffee a week? Can she buy 7 cups of coffee and 2 cans of soda a week? What is the relative price of a cup of coffee?
2. Suppose that the price of soda remains at $1 a can but the price of coffee rises to $3 a cup. Draw Amy's new budget line. If she buys 6 cans of soda, what is the maximum number of cups of coffee she can buy in a week? Has the relative price of coffee changed?

Table 1 shows Ben's utility from orange juice. Use Table 1 to work Problems **3** and **4**.

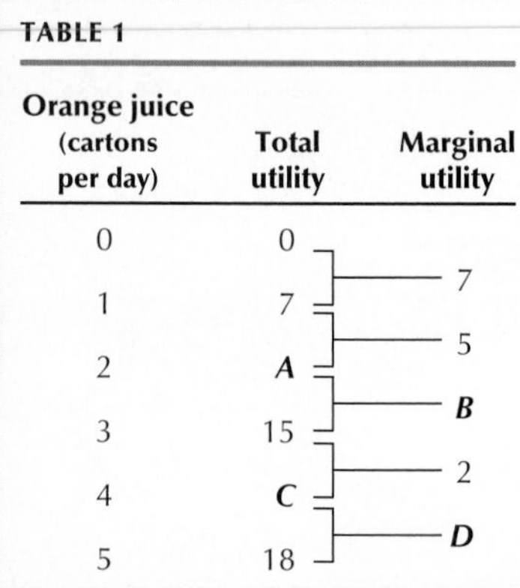

**TABLE 1**

| Orange juice (cartons per day) | Total utility | Marginal utility |
|---|---|---|
| 0 | 0 | |
| | | 7 |
| 1 | 7 | |
| | | 5 |
| 2 | *A* | |
| | | *B* |
| 3 | 15 | |
| | | 2 |
| 4 | *C* | |
| | | *D* |
| 5 | 18 | |

3. Calculate the values of *A*, *B*, *C*, and *D* in the table. Does the principle of diminishing marginal utility apply to Ben's consumption of orange juice? Why or why not?
4. Would Ben ever want to buy more than one carton of orange juice a day or no orange juice? Explain your answer.
5. Every day, Josie buys 2 cups of coffee and 1 sandwich for lunch. The price of coffee is $2 a cup and the price of a sandwich is $5. Josie's choice of lunch maximizes her total utility, and she spends only $9 on lunch. Compare Josie's marginal utility from coffee with her marginal utility from the sandwich.
6. Susie spends $28 a week on sundaes and magazines. The price of a sundae is $4 and the price of a magazine is $4. Table 2 shows Susie's marginal utility from sundaes and magazines. How many sundaes does she buy? If the price of a sundae doubles to $8 and other things remain the same, how many sundaes will she buy? What are two points on her demand curve for sundaes?

**TABLE 2**

| Sundaes | | Magazines | |
|---|---|---|---|
| Quantity per week | Marginal utility | Quantity per week | Marginal utility |
| 1 | 60 | 1 | 40 |
| 2 | 56 | 2 | 32 |
| 3 | 50 | 3 | 28 |
| 4 | 42 | 4 | 25 |
| 5 | 32 | 5 | 23 |
| 6 | 20 | 6 | 22 |

7. In a week, Erin buys 1 six-pack of soda and sees 2 movies when a movie ticket is $10, soda is $5 a six-pack, and she has $25 to spend. If her budget increases and she has $50 to spend on soda and movies, what is the change in the relative price of a movie ticket? How do the marginal utility per dollar from movies and the marginal utility from soda change?
8. **Gas prices send surge of travelers to mass transit**

   As the gas price shot up to $4 a gallon, more commuters switched from cars to trains and buses. In New York and Boston, public transit ridership is up 5 percent or more so far this year.

   Source: *The New York Times*, May 10, 2008

   Explain the effect of a rise in the price of gasoline on a commuter's budget line and the quantities of gasoline and public transit services purchased.

## Instructor Assignable Problems and Applications

Your instructor can assign these problems as homework, a quiz, or a test in **MyEconLab**.

1. In 2007, Americans downloaded 800 million singles at 99¢ each and 40 million albums at $10 each. They also bought 3 million singles on a disc at $4.75 each and 500 million albums on discs at $15. What does marginal utility theory tell you about the ratio of the marginal utility from singles on discs to the marginal utility from single downloads? What does it tell you about the ratio of the marginal utility from albums on discs to the marginal utility from album downloads?

Use the following information to work Problems 2 to 5.

**Compared to other liquids, gasoline is cheap**

In 2008, when gasoline hit $4 a gallon, motorists complained, but they didn't complain about $1.59 for a 20-oz Gatorade and $18 for 16 ml of HP ink.

Source: *The New York Times*, May 27, 2008

The prices per gallon are $10.17 for Gatorade and $4,294.58 for printer ink.

2. What does marginal utility theory predict about the marginal utility per dollar from gasoline, Gatorade, and printer ink?
3. What do the prices per gallon tell you about the marginal utility from a gallon of gasoline, Gatorade, and printer ink?
4. What do the prices per unit reported in this news clip tell you about the marginal utility from a gallon of gasoline, a 20-oz bottle of Gatorade, and a cartridge of printer ink?
5. How can the paradox of value be used to explain why the fluids listed in the news clip might be less valuable than gasoline, yet far more expensive?
6. Tim buys 2 pizzas and sees 1 movie a week when he has $16 to spend, a movie ticket is $8, and the price of a pizza is $4. What is the relative price of a movie ticket? If the price of a movie ticket falls to $4, how will Tim's consumption possibilities change? Explain.

Use Table 1, which shows Martha's total utility from cake and pasta, to work Problems 7 to 9.

**TABLE 1**

| Cake | | Pasta | |
|---|---|---|---|
| Quantity per week | Total utility | Dishes per week | Total utility |
| 0 | 0 | 0 | 0 |
| 1 | 10 | 1 | 20 |
| 2 | 18 | 2 | 36 |
| 3 | 25 | 3 | 48 |
| 4 | 31 | 4 | 56 |
| 5 | 36 | 5 | 60 |
| 6 | 40 | 6 | 60 |

7. When Martha buys 3 cakes and 2 dishes of pasta a week, what is her total utility and her marginal utility from the third cake? If the price of a cake is $4, what is her marginal utility per dollar from cake?
8. When the price of a cake is $4, the price of pasta is $8 a dish, and Martha has $24 a week to spend, she buys 2 cakes and 2 dishes of pasta. Does she maximize her total utility? Explain your answer.
9. When the price of a cake is $4, Martha has $24 to spend, and the price of pasta falls from $8 to $4 a dish, what quantities of cake and pasta does Martha buy? What are two points on Martha's demand curve for pasta?
10. Jim spends all his income on apartment rent, food, clothing, and vacations. He gets a pay raise from $3,000 a month to $4,000 a month. At the same time, airfares and other vacation-related expenses increase by 50 percent. How has Jim's real income in terms of airfares and other vacation-related expenses changed? Is Jim better off or worse off in his new situation?

Use the following information to work Problems 11 and 12.

**In the land of free flight**

As the time it takes to get through airports has increased, other means of travel have begun to look more attractive. Amtrak now competes comfortably with the airlines on its Boston–New York–Washington express rail service.

Source: *The Economist*, June 14, 2007

11. For a trip from Boston to Washington, compare the opportunity costs of taking Amtrak and United Airlines.
12. Compare the marginal utility per dollar from train travel and from air travel.

Use the following information to work Problems 13 and 14.

Table 2 shows the marginal utility that Ali gets from smoothies and movies. Ali has $30 a week to spend. The price of a movie ticket is $6, and the price of a smoothie is $3.

**TABLE 2**

| Quantity per week | Marginal utility from smoothies | movies |
|---|---|---|
| 1 | 7 | 30 |
| 2 | 6 | 24 |
| 3 | 5 | 18 |
| 4 | 4 | 12 |
| 5 | 3 | 6 |
| 6 | 2 | 0 |

13. If Ali buys 4 smoothies a week and sees 3 movies, does he spend all $30? What is his utility from smoothies and his utility from movies? Does he maximize his utility? If not, which good must he buy more of?
14. When Ali allocates his budget so as to maximize his utility, what does he buy and what is the marginal utility per dollar?

Use the following information to work Problems 15 and 16.

Adrienne loves riding and she pays $500 a month to the stable to care for her horse. She thinks she's getting a real bargain and would willingly pay twice the price for the service she gets. Adrienne rents an apartment for $1,000 a month. Unlike the stable, she doesn't think the deal she gets from her landlord is all that good, and she is on the verge of looking for something better for the same price.

15. Does Adrienne get greater total utility from her horse or her apartment?
16. Use Adrienne's horse-riding and apartment to explain the paradox of value.

Use the following information to work Problems 17 and 18.

**Starbucks coffee break March 15th**

On March 15th, 2007, Starbucks planned to give away free Tall cups of coffee.

Source: *Slashfoods.com*, March 5, 2007

17. At Second Cup, students can buy 1 cup of coffee and have a second one free. At the two coffee shops, the price of coffee is identical and students rate the coffee as equally good. Why would anyone go to Starbucks next door?
18. On "Starbucks coffee break"day, why would anyone go to the Second Cup?

Use the fact that some students buy a college meal plan and others pay as they go to work Problems 19 and 20.

19. Why would a student decide to buy a meal plan rather than pay for each meal as it is consumed? Explain using marginal utility theory.
20. What does marginal utility theory predict about the demand for lunches by the two groups?

# APPENDIX: INDIFFERENCE CURVES

You are going to discover a neat idea—that of drawing a map of a person's preferences. A preference map is based on the intuitively appealing assumption that people can sort all the possible combinations of goods into three groups: preferred, not preferred, and indifferent. To make this idea concrete, let's ask Tina to tell us how she ranks combinations of bottled water and chewing gum.

## An Indifference Curve

Figure A12.1(a) shows part of Tina's answer. She tells us that she currently consumes 2 bottles of water and 4 packs of gum a day at point C. She then lists all the combinations of bottled water and chewing gum that she says are as acceptable to her as her current consumption. When we plot these combinations of water and gum, we get the green curve. This curve is the key element in a map of preferences and is called an indifference curve.

An **indifference curve** is a line that shows combinations of goods among which a consumer is *indifferent*. The indifference curve in Figure A12.1(a) tells us that Tina is just as happy to consume 2 bottles of water and 4 packs of gum a day at point C as to consume the combination of water and gum at any other point along the indifference curve. Tina also says that she prefers all the combinations of bottled water and gum above the indifference curve—the yellow area—to those on the indifference curve. These combinations contain more water, more gum, or

**Indifference curve**
A line that shows combinations of goods among which a consumer is *indifferent*.

**FIGURE A12.1**

A Preference Map

myeconlab Animation

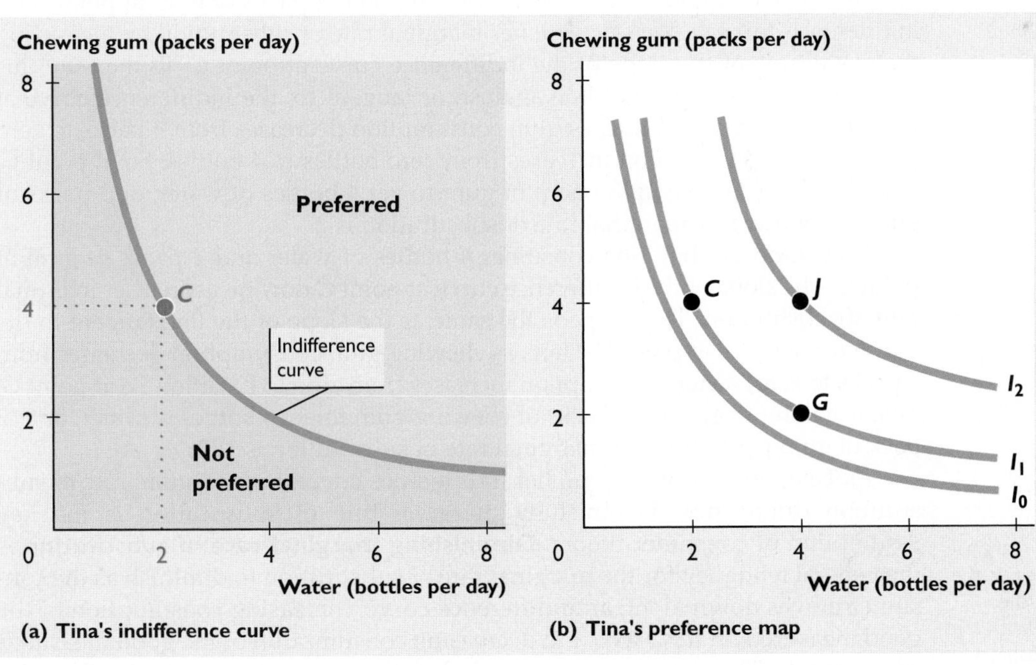


In part (a), Tina consumes 2 bottles of water and 4 packs of chewing gum a day at point C. She is indifferent between all the points on the green indifference curve. She prefers any point above the indifference curve (yellow area) to any point on it, and she prefers any point on the indifference curve to any point below it (gray area).

Part (b) shows three indifference curves of Tina's preference map. She prefers point J to point C or G, so she prefers any point on $I_2$ to any point on $I_1$.

more of both. She also prefers any combination on the indifference curve to any combination in the gray area below the indifference curve. These combinations contain less water, less gum, or less of both.

The indifference curve in Figure A12.1(a) is just one of a whole family of such curves. This indifference curve appears again in Figure A12.1(b) labeled $I_1$. The curves labeled $I_0$ and $I_2$ are two other indifference curves. Tina prefers any point on indifference curve $I_2$, such as point *J*, to any point on indifference curve $I_1$, such as points *C* or *G*. She prefers any point on $I_1$ to any point on $I_0$. We refer to $I_2$ as being a higher indifference curve than $I_1$ and to $I_1$ as being higher than $I_0$.

A preference map is a series of indifference curves that resemble the contour lines on a map. By looking at the shape of the contour lines on a map, we can draw conclusions about the terrain. Similarly, by looking at the shape of the indifference curves, we can draw conclusions about a person's preferences.

## Marginal Rate of Substitution

**Marginal rate of substitution**
The rate at which a person will give up good *y* (the good measured on the *y*-axis) to get more of good *x* (the good measured on the *x*-axis) and at the same time remain on the same indifference curve.

The concept of the marginal rate of substitution is the key to "reading" a preference map. The **marginal rate of substitution** (*MRS*) is the rate at which a person will give up good *y* (the good measured on the *y*-axis) to get more of good *x* (the good measured on the *x*-axis) and at the same time remain indifferent (remain on the same indifference curve). The marginal rate of substitution is measured by the magnitude of the slope of an indifference curve.

If the indifference curve is *steep*, the marginal rate of substitution is *high*. The person is willing to give up a large quantity of good *y* to get a small quantity of good *x* while remaining indifferent. If the indifference curve is *flat*, the marginal rate of substitution is *low*. The person is willing to give up only a small amount of good *y* to get a large amount of good *x* to remain indifferent.

Figure A12.2 shows you how to calculate the marginal rate of substitution. Suppose that Tina consumes 2 bottles of water and 4 packs of gum at point *C* on indifference curve $I_1$. We calculate her marginal rate of substitution by measuring the magnitude of the slope of the indifference curve at point C. To measure this magnitude, place a straight line against, or tangent to, the indifference curve at point C. Along that red line, as gum consumption decreases from 8 packs to zero packs, water consumption increases from zero bottles to 4 bottles. So at point *C*, Tina is willing to give up 8 packs of gum to get 4 bottles of water, or 2 packs of gum per bottle. Her marginal rate of substitution is 2.

Now suppose that Tina consumes 4 bottles of water and 2 packs of gum at point G. The slope of the indifference curve at point G now measures her marginal rate of substitution. That slope is the same as the slope of the line tangent to the indifference curve at point G. Here, as chewing gum consumption decreases from 4 packs to zero, water consumption increases from zero to 8 bottles. So at point G, Tina is willing to give up 4 packs of chewing gum to get 8 bottles of water, or 1/2 pack of gum per bottle. Her marginal rate of substitution is 1/2.

**Diminishing marginal rate of substitution**
The general tendency for the marginal rate of substitution to decrease as the consumer moves down along the indifference curve, increasing consumption of the good measured on the *x*-axis and decreasing consumption of the good measured on the *y*-axis.

As Tina moves down along her indifference curve, her marginal rate of substitution diminishes. Diminishing marginal rate of substitution is the key assumption of consumer theory. **Diminishing marginal rate of substitution** is the general tendency for the marginal rate of substitution to diminish as the consumer moves down along an indifference curve, increasing consumption of the good measured on the *x*-axis and decreasing consumption of the good measured on the *y*-axis. The shape of a person's indifference curves incorporates the principle of the diminishing marginal rate of substitution because the curves are bowed toward the origin.

**FIGURE A12.2**
The Marginal Rate of Substitution

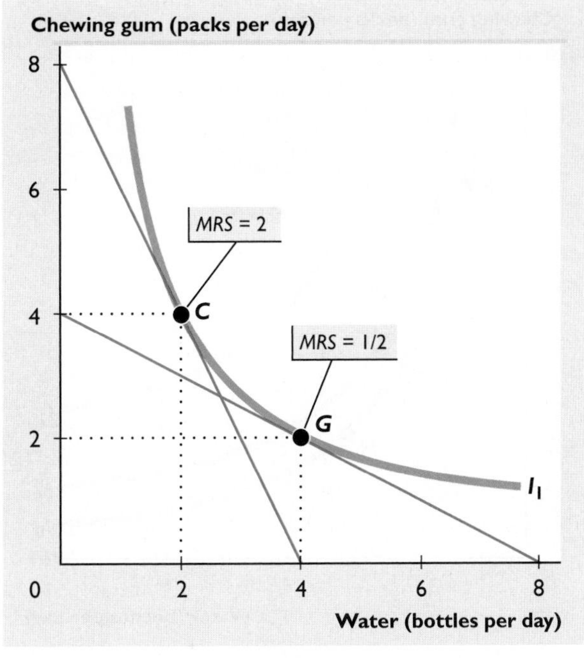


The magnitude of the slope of an indifference curve is called the marginal rate of substitution (*MRS*).

The red line at point *C* tells us that Tina is willing to give up 8 packs of gum to get 4 bottles of water. Her marginal rate of substitution at point *C* is 8 divided by 4, which equals 2.

The red line at point *G* tells us that Tina is willing to give up 4 packs of gum to get 8 bottles of water. Her marginal rate of substitution at point *G* is 4 divided by 8, which equals 1/2.

## Consumer Equilibrium

The consumer's goal is to buy the affordable quantities of goods that make her or him as well off as possible. The indifference curves describe the consumer's preferences, and they tell us that the higher the indifference curve, the better off is the consumer. So the consumer's goal can be restated as: to allocate his or her budget in such a way as to get onto the highest attainable indifference curve.

The consumer's budget and the prices of the goods limit the consumer's choices. The budget line illustrated in Figure 12.1 (p. 292) summarizes the limits on the consumer's choice. We combine the indifference curves of Figure A12.1(b) with the budget line of Figure 12.1 to work out the consumer's choice and find the consumer equilibrium.

Figure A12.3 shows Tina's budget line from Figure 12.1 and her indifference curves from Figure A12.1(b). Tina's best affordable point is 2 bottles of water and 4 packs of gum—at point *C*. Here, Tina

- Is on her budget line.
- Is on her highest attainable indifference curve.
- Has a marginal rate of substitution between water and gum equal to the relative price of water and gum.

For every point inside the budget line, such as point *L*, there are points *on* the budget line that Tina prefers. For example, she prefers any point on the budget line between *F* and *H* to point *L*. So she chooses a point on the budget line.

**FIGURE A12.3**

Consumer Equilibrium

myeconlab Animation

Tina's best affordable point is *C*. At that point, she is on her budget line and also on the highest attainable indifference curve.

At a point such as *H*, Tina is willing to give up more bottled water in exchange for chewing gum than she has to. She can move to point *L*, which is just as good as point *H*, and have some unspent budget. She can spend that budget and move to *C*, a point that she prefers to point *L*.

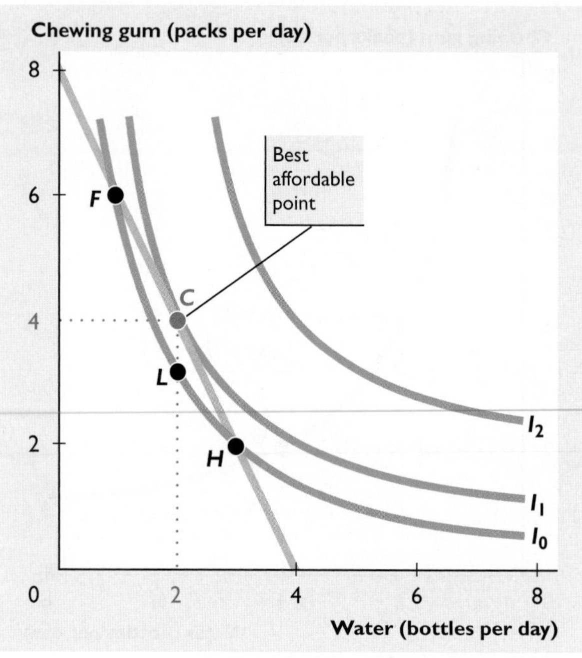

*Checked out at the best affordable point.*

Every point on the budget line lies on an indifference curve. For example, point *F* lies on the indifference curve $I_0$. At point *F*, Tina's marginal rate of substitution (the magnitude of the slope of the indifference curve $I_0$) is greater than the relative price (the magnitude of the slope of the budget line). Tina is willing to give up more chewing gum to get an additional bottle of water than the budget line says she must. So she moves along her budget line from *F* toward *C*. As she does so, she passes through a number of indifference curves (not shown in the figure) located between indifference curves $I_0$ and $I_1$. All of these indifference curves are higher than $I_0$, so Tina prefers any point on them to point *F*. When Tina gets to point *C*, she is on the highest attainable indifference curve. If she keeps moving along the budget line, she starts to encounter indifference curves that are lower than $I_1$. So Tina chooses point *C*—her best affordable point.

At the chosen point, the marginal rate of substitution (the magnitude of the slope of the indifference curve) equals the relative price (the magnitude of the slope of the budget line).

We can now use this model of consumer choice to predict the effect of a change in the price of water on the quantity of water demanded. That is, we can use this model to generate the demand curve for bottled water.

## Deriving the Demand Curve

To derive Tina's demand curve for bottled water, we change the price of water, shift the budget line, and work out the new best affordable point. Figure A12.4(a) shows the change in the budget line and the change in consumer equilibrium when the price of water falls from $1 a bottle to 50¢ a bottle.

Initially, when the price of water is $1 a bottle, Tina consumes at point *C* in part (a). When the price of a bottle of water falls from $1 to 50¢, her budget line rotates outward and she can now get onto a higher indifference curve. Her best affordable point is now point *K*. Tina increases the quantity of water she buys from 2 to 4 bottles a day. She continues to buy 4 packs of gum a day.

Figure A12.4(b) shows Tina's demand curve for bottled water. When the price of water is $1 a bottle, she buys 2 bottles a day, at point *A*. When the price of water falls to 50¢ a bottle, she buys 4 bottles a day, at point *B*. Tina's demand curve traces out her best affordable quantity of water as the price of a bottle of water varies.

**FIGURE A12.4**

## Deriving Tina's Demand Curve



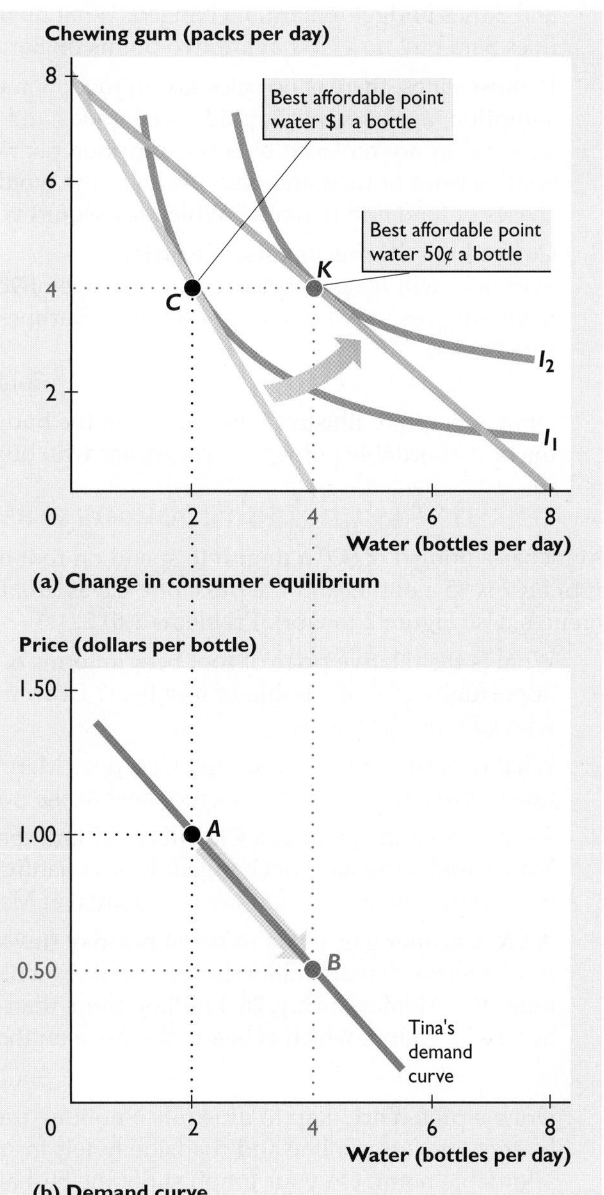


In part (a), when the price of water is $1 a bottle, Tina consumes at point *C*. When the price of water falls from $1 to 50¢ a bottle, she consumes at point *K*.

In part (b), when the price of water is $1 a bottle, Tina is at point *A*. When the price of water falls from $1 to 50¢ a bottle, Tina moves along her demand curve for bottled water from point *A* to point *B*.

Work these problems in Chapter 12 Study Plan to get instant feedback.

# APPENDIX CHECKPOINT

## Study Plan Problems and Applications

Each week Sara has $12 to spend on popcorn and cola. The price of popcorn is $3 a bag, and the price of cola is $3 a can. Figure 1 illustrates Sara's preferences. Use Figure 1 to work Problems 1 to 3.

FIGURE 1

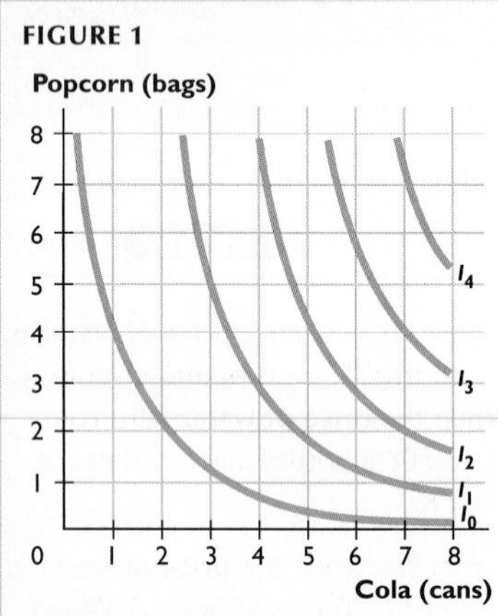


1. What is the relative price of cola and what is the opportunity cost of a can of cola? Draw a graph of Sara's budget line with cola on the $x$-axis.
2. What quantities of popcorn and cola does Sara buy and what is her marginal rate of substitution of popcorn for cola at her consumption point?
3. Suppose that the price of cola falls to $1.50 a can and the price of popcorn and Sara's budget remain unchanged. What quantities of popcorn and cola does Sara buy now? What are two points on Sara's demand curve for cola?
4. In most states, there is no sales tax on food. Some people say that a consumption tax, a tax that is paid on all goods and services, would be better. If all sales tax are replaced by a consumption tax, what would happen to the relative price of food and haircuts and how would you change your purchases of food and haircuts? Which tax would you prefer?
5. **Coffee king Starbucks raises its prices**

   Starbucks will raise its prices by an average of 9¢ per beverage to cover its increasing costs. Will rising prices cause Starbucks fans to cut back on their java habits?

   Source: *USA Today*, July 25, 2007

   Draw a graph to illustrate the change in the budget line and the change in the best affordable point for a consumer who buys fewer lattes a week.

Your instructor can assign these problems as homework, a quiz, or a test in **MyEconLab**.

## Instructor Assignable Problems and Applications

Marc has a budget of $20 a month to spend on root beer and CDs. The price of root beer is $5 a bottle, and the price of a CD is $10. Figure 2 illustrates his preferences. Use Figure 2 to work Problems 1 to 3.

FIGURE 2

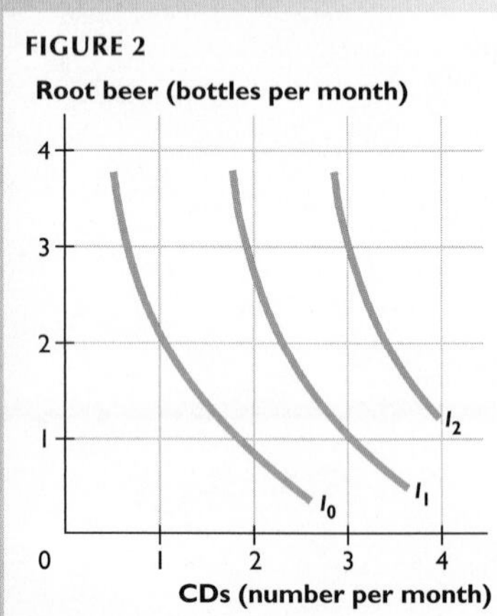


1. What is the relative price of root beer in terms of CDs and what is the opportunity cost of a bottle of root beer? Draw a graph of Marc's budget line with CDs on the $x$-axis.
2. What quantities of root beer and CDs does Marc buy? What is his marginal rate of substitution of CDs for root beer at the point at which he consumes?
3. Suppose that the price of a CD falls to $5 and the price of root beer and Marc's budget remain unchanged. What quantities of root beer and CDs does Marc now buy? What are two points on Marc's demand curve for CDs?
4. **AAA: Cheaper gas, deals to boost holiday travel**

   AAA reports that 27 million holiday makers will travel an average of 620 miles this Memorial Day, 26.3 million more than last year. The gas price will be $2.25 a gallon, which is below the price on the 2008 Memorial Day.

   Source: *USA Today*, May 13, 2009

   Draw a preference map to illustrate a holiday traveler's preferences. Draw a budget line for gasoline and roadside hotels in 2008 and identify the best affordable point. On your graph show the best affordable point in 2009 when the price of gasoline is lower.

## Which store has the lower costs, Wal-Mart or 7–11?

Wal-Mart's prices are lower, but are its operating costs per customer lower?

# Production and Cost

CHAPTER CHECKLIST

**When you have completed your study of this chapter, you will be able to**

1 Explain how economists measure a firm's cost of production and profit.

2 Explain the relationship between a firm's output and labor employed in the short run.

3 Explain the relationship between a firm's output and costs in the short run.

4 Derive and explain a firm's long-run average cost curve.

## 13.1 ECONOMIC COST AND PROFIT

The 20 million firms in the United States differ in size and in what they produce, but they all perform the same basic economic function: They hire factors of production and organize them to produce and sell goods and services. To understand the behavior of a firm, we need to know its goals.

### The Firm's Goal

If you asked a group of entrepreneurs what they are trying to achieve, you would get many different answers. Some would talk about making a high-quality product, others about business growth, others about market share, and others about job satisfaction of the work force. All of these goals might be pursued, but they are not the fundamental goal. They are a means to a deeper goal.

The firm's goal is to *maximize profit*. A firm that does not seek to maximize profit is either eliminated or bought by firms that *do* seek to achieve that goal. To calculate a firm's profit, we must determine its total revenue and total cost. Economists have a special way of defining and measuring cost and profit, which we'll explain and illustrate by looking at Sam's Smoothies, a firm that is owned and operated by Samantha.

### Accounting Cost and Profit

In 2009, Sam's Smoothies' total revenue from the sale of smoothies was $150,000. The firm paid $20,000 for fruit, yogurt, and honey; $22,000 in wages for the labor it hired; and $3,000 in interest to the bank. These expenses totaled $45,000.

Sam's accountant said that the depreciation of the firm's blenders, refrigerators, and shop during 2009 was $10,000. Depreciation is the fall in the value of the firm's capital, and accountants calculate it by using the Internal Revenue Service's rules, which are based on standards set by the Financial Accounting Standards Board. So the accountant reported Sam's Smoothies' total cost for 2009 as $55,000 and the firm's profit as $95,000—$150,000 of total revenue minus $55,000 of total costs.

Sam's accountant measures cost and profit to ensure that the firm pays the correct amount of income tax and to show the bank how Sam's has used its bank loan. Economists have a different purpose: to predict the decisions that a firm makes to maximize its profit. These decisions respond to *opportunity cost* and *economic profit*.

### Opportunity Cost

To produce its output, a firm employs factors of production: land, labor, capital, and entrepreneurship. Another firm could have used these same resources to produce other goods or services. In Chapter 3 (pp. 68–70), resources can be used to produce either cell phones or DVDs, so the opportunity cost of producing a cell phone is the number of DVDs forgone. Pilots who fly passengers for United Airlines can't at the same time fly freight for FedEx. Construction workers who are building an office high-rise can't simultaneously build apartments. A communications satellite operating at peak capacity can carry television signals or e-mail messages but not both at the same time. A journalist writing for the *New York Times* can't at the same time create Web news reports for CNN. And Samantha can't simultaneously run her smoothies business and a flower shop.

The highest-valued alternative forgone is the opportunity cost of a firm's production. From the viewpoint of the firm, this opportunity cost is the amount that the firm must pay the owners of the factors of production it employs to attract them from their best alternative use. So a firm's opportunity cost of production is the cost of the factors of production it employs.

To determine these costs, let's return to Sam's and look at the opportunity cost of producing smoothies.

### Explicit Costs and Implicit Costs

The amount that a firm pays to attract resources from their best alternative use is either an explicit cost or an implicit cost. A cost paid in money is an **explicit cost**. Because the amount spent could have been spent on something else, an explicit cost is an opportunity cost. The wages that Samantha pays labor, the interest she pays the bank, and her expenditure on fruit, yogurt, and honey are explicit costs.

**Explicit cost**
A cost paid in money.

A firm incurs an **implicit cost** when it uses a factor of production but does not make a direct money payment for its use. The two categories of implicit cost are economic depreciation and the cost of the resources of the firm's owner.

**Implicit cost**
An opportunity cost incurred by a firm when it uses a factor of production for which it does not make a direct money payment.

**Economic depreciation** is the opportunity cost of the firm using capital that it owns. It is measured as the change in the *market value* of capital—the market price of the capital at the beginning of the period minus its market price at the end of the period. Suppose that Samantha could have sold her blenders, refrigerators, and shop on December 31, 2008, for $250,000. If she can sell the same capital on December 31, 2009, for $246,000, her economic depreciation during 2009 is $4,000. This is the opportunity cost of using her capital during 2009, not the $10,000 depreciation calculated by Sam's accountant.

**Economic depreciation**
An opportunity cost of a firm using capital that it owns—measured as the change in the *market value* of capital over a given period.

Interest is another cost of capital. When the firm's owner provides the funds used to buy capital, the opportunity cost of those funds is the interest income forgone by not using them in the best alternative way. If Sam loaned her firm funds that could have earned her $1,000 in interest, this amount is an implicit cost of producing smoothies.

When a firm's owner supplies labor, the opportunity cost of the owner's time spent working for the firm is the wage income forgone by not working in the best alternative job. For example, instead of working at her next best job that pays $34,000 a year, Sam supplies labor to her smoothies business. This implicit cost of $34,000 is part of the opportunity cost of producing smoothies.

Finally, a firm's owner often supplies entrepreneurship, the factor of production that organizes the business and bears the risk of running it. The return to entrepreneurship is **normal profit**. Normal profit is part of a firm's opportunity cost because it is the cost of a forgone alternative—running another firm. Instead of running Sam's Smoothies, Sam could earn $16,000 a year running a flower shop. This amount is an implicit cost of production at Sam's Smoothies.

**Normal profit**
The return to entrepreneurship. Normal profit is part of a firm's opportunity cost because it is the cost of not running another firm.

## Economic Profit

A firm's **economic profit** equals total revenue minus total cost. Total revenue is the amount received from the sale of the product. It is the price of the output multiplied by the quantity sold. Total cost is the sum of the explicit costs and implicit costs and is the opportunity cost of production.

**Economic profit**
A firm's total revenue minus total cost.

**TABLE 13.1**

Economic Accounting

| Item | | |
|---|---|---|
| **Total Revenue** | | **$150,000** |
| ***Explicit Costs*** | | |
| **Cost of fruit, yogurt, and honey** | **$20,000** | |
| **Wages** | **$22,000** | |
| **Interest** | **$3,000** | |
| ***Implicit Costs*** | | |
| **Samantha's forgone wages** | **$34,000** | |
| **Samantha's forgone interest** | **$1,000** | |
| **Economic depreciation** | **$4,000** | |
| **Normal profit** | **$16,000** | |
| **Opportunity Cost** | | **$100,000** |
| **Economic Profit** | | **$50,000** |

Because one of the firm's implicit costs is *normal profit*, the return to the entrepreneur equals normal profit plus economic profit. If a firm incurs an economic loss, the entrepreneur receives less than normal profit.

Table 13.1 summarizes the economic cost concepts, and Figure 13.1 compares the economic view and the accounting view of cost and profit. Sam's total revenue (price multiplied by quantity sold) is $150,000; the opportunity cost of the resources that Sam uses is $100,000; and Sam's economic profit is $50,000.

**FIGURE 13.1**

Two Views of Cost and Profit

myeconlab Animation

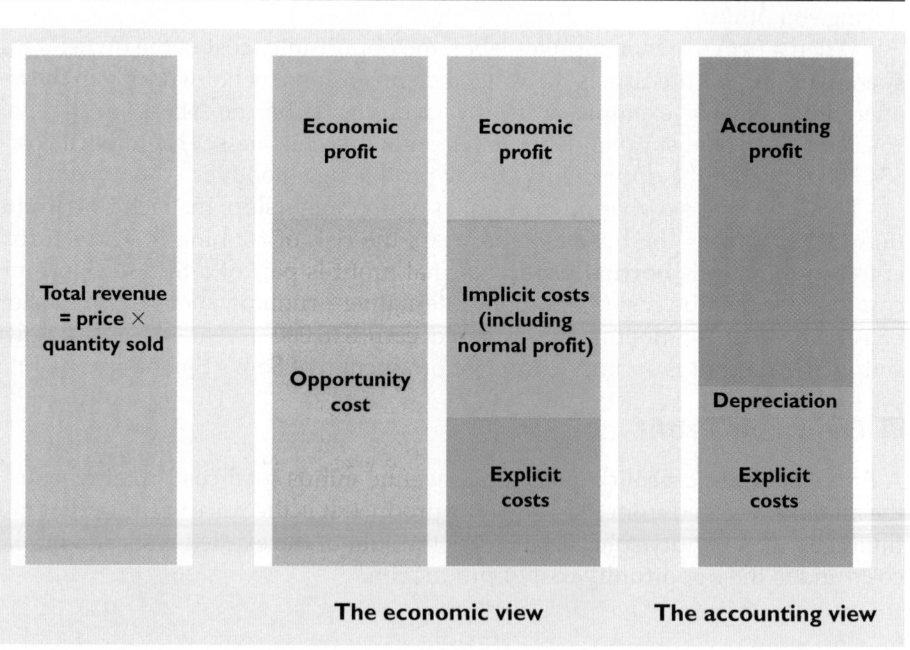


Both economists and accountants measure a firm's total revenue the same way. It equals the price multiplied by the quantity sold of each item. Economists measure economic profit as total revenue minus opportunity cost. Opportunity cost includes explicit costs and implicit costs. Normal profit is an implicit cost. Accountants measure profit as total revenue minus explicit costs—costs paid in money—and depreciation.

# CHECKPOINT 13.1

Work these problems in Study Plan 13.1 to get instant feedback.

**Explain how economists measure a firm's cost of production and profit.**

## Practice Problems

Lee is a computer programmer who earned $35,000 in 2008. But Lee loves water sports, and in 2009, he opened a body board manufacturing business. At the end of the first year of operation, he submitted the following information to his accountant. Use this information to work Problems **1** and **2**.

- He stopped renting out his cottage for $3,500 a year and used it as his factory. The market value of the cottage increased from $70,000 to $71,000.
- He spent $50,000 on materials, phone, utilities, etc.
- He leased machines for $10,000 a year.
- He paid $15,000 in wages.
- He used $10,000 from his savings account, which earns 5 percent a year interest.
- He borrowed $40,000 at 10 percent a year from the bank.
- He sold $160,000 worth of body boards.
- Normal profit is $25,000 a year.

1. Calculate Lee's explicit costs, implicit costs, and economic profit.
2. Lee's accountant recorded the depreciation on Lee's cottage during 2009 as $7,000. What did the accountant say Lee's profit or loss was?
3. **What does it cost to make 100 pairs of running shoes?**
   The Asian manufacturer of running shoes pays its workers $275 to make 100 pairs per hour. These workers use company-owned equipment that costs the company in forgone interest and economic depreciation $300 an hour. Materials cost $900.

   Source: washpost.com

   Which costs are explicit costs and which costs are implicit costs? If the total revenue from the sale of 100 pairs of shoes is $1,650, what is the manufacturer's economic profit?

## Guided Solutions to Practice Problems

1. Lee's explicit costs are costs paid with money: $50,000 on materials, phone, utilities, etc; $10,000 on leased machines; $15,000 in wages; and $4,000 in bank interest. These items total $79,000. Lee's implicit costs are $35,000 in forgone wages, $2,500 in forgone rent less the increase in the value of his cottage; $500 in forgone interest on his savings account; and $25,000 in normal profit. These items total $63,000. Lee's economic profit equals total revenue $160,000 minus total cost. Total cost is the sum of explicit costs plus implicit costs: $79,000 + $63,000, or $142,000. So Lee's economic profit is $160,000 − $142,000, or $18,000.

2. The accountant measures Lee's profit as total revenue minus explicit costs minus depreciation: $160,000 − $79,000 − $7,000, or $74,000.

3. Explicit costs are wages of $275 and materials of $900. Implicit costs are the forgone interest and economic depreciation of $300. Economic profit equals total revenue minus total cost. Total cost is $1,475. So economic profit equals $1,650 minus $1,475, which is $175.

## SHORT RUN AND LONG RUN

The main goal of this chapter is to explore the influences on a firm's costs. The key influence on cost is the quantity of output that the firm produces per period. The greater the output rate, the higher is the total cost of production. But the effect of a change in production on cost depends on how soon the firm wants to act. A firm that plans to change its output rate tomorrow has fewer options than a firm that plans ahead and intends to change its production six months from now.

To study the relationship between a firm's output decision and its costs, we distinguish between two decision time frames:

- The short run
- The long run

### The Short Run: Fixed Plant

**Short run**
The time frame in which the quantities of some resources are fixed. In the short run, a firm can usually change the quantity of labor it uses but not its technology and quantity of capital.

The **short run** is the time frame in which the quantities of some resources are fixed. For most firms, the fixed resources are the firm's technology and capital—its equipment and buildings. The management organization is also fixed in the short run. The fixed resources that a firm uses are its *fixed factors of production* and the resources that it can vary are its *variable factors of production*. The collection of fixed resources is the firm's *plant*. So in the short run, a firm's plant is fixed.

Sam's Smoothies' plant is its blenders, refrigerators, and shop. Sam's cannot change these inputs in the short run. An electric power utility can't change the number of generators it uses in the short run. An airport can't change the number of runways, terminal buildings, and traffic control facilities in the short run.

To increase output in the short run, a firm must increase the quantity of variable factors it uses. Labor is usually the variable factor of production. To produce more smoothies, Sam must hire more labor. Similarly, to increase the production of electricity, a utility must hire more engineers and run its generators for longer hours. To increase the volume of traffic it handles, an airport must hire more check-in clerks, cargo handlers, and air-traffic controllers.

Short-run decisions are easily reversed. A firm can increase or decrease output in the short run by increasing or decreasing the number of labor hours it hires.

### The Long Run: Variable Plant

**Long run**
The time frame in which the quantities of *all* resources can be varied.

The **long run** is the time frame in which the quantities of *all* resources can be varied. That is, the long run is a period in which the firm can change its *plant*.

To increase output in the long run, a firm can increase the size of its plant. Sam's Smoothies can install more blenders and refrigerators and increase the size of its shop. An electric power utility can install more generators. And an airport can build more runways, terminals, and traffic-control facilities.

Long-run decisions are *not* easily reversed. Once a firm buys a new plant, its resale value is usually much less than the amount the firm paid for it. The difference between the cost of the plant and its resale value is a *sunk cost*. A sunk cost is irrelevant to the firm's decisions (see Chapter 1, p. 11). The only costs that influence the firm's decisions are the short-run cost of changing its labor inputs and the long-run cost of changing its plant.

We're going to study costs in the short run and the long run. We begin with the short run and describe the limits to the firm's production possibilities.

## 13.2 SHORT-RUN PRODUCTION

To increase the output of a fixed plant, a firm must increase the quantity of labor it employs. We describe the relationship between output and the quantity of labor employed by using three related concepts:

- Total product
- Marginal product
- Average product

### Total Product

**Total product** (*TP*) is the total quantity of a good produced in a given period. Total product is an output *rate*—the number of units produced per unit of time (for example, per hour, day, or week). Total product increases as the quantity of labor employed increases, and we illustrate this relationship as a total product schedule and total product curve like those in Figure 13.2. The total product schedule (the table below the graph) lists the maximum quantities of smoothies per hour that Sam can produce with her existing plant at each quantity of labor. Points *A* through *H* on the *TP* curve correspond to the columns in the table.

**Total product**
The total quantity of a good produced in a given period.

**FIGURE 13.2**

Total Product Schedule and Total Product Curve

myeconlab Animation

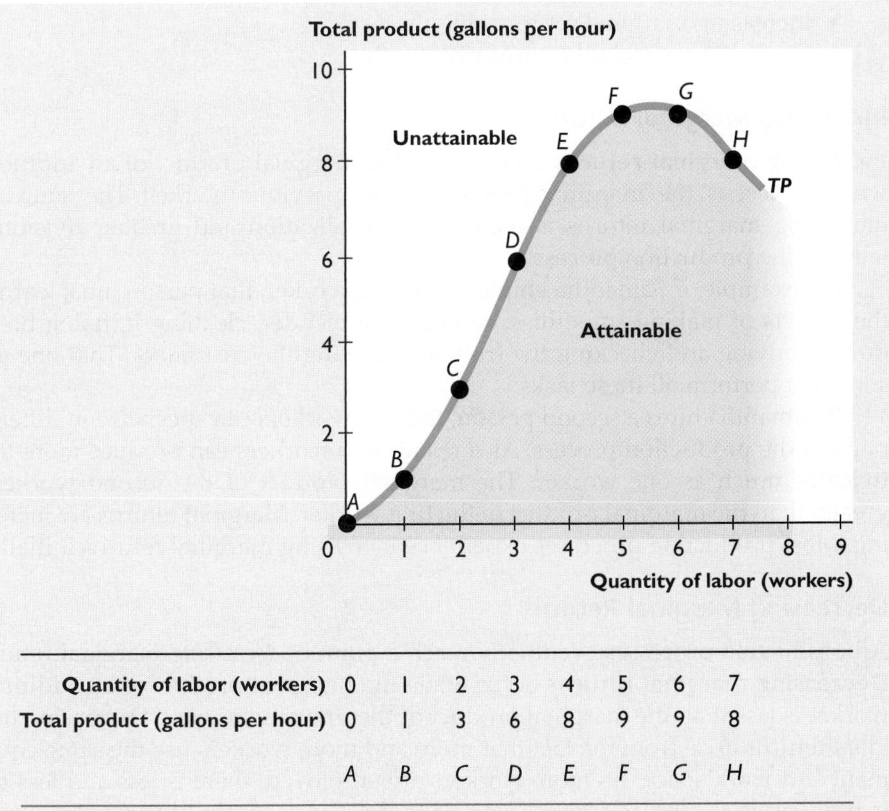


| Quantity of labor (workers) | 0 | 1 | 2 | 3 | 4 | 5 | 6 | 7 |
|---|---|---|---|---|---|---|---|---|
| Total product (gallons per hour) | 0 | 1 | 3 | 6 | 8 | 9 | 9 | 8 |
| | A | B | C | D | E | F | G | H |

The total product schedule shows how the quantity of smoothies that Sam's can produce changes as the quantity of labor employed changes. In column *C*, Sam's employs 2 workers and can produce 3 gallons of smoothies an hour.

The total product curve, *TP*, graphs the data in the table. Points *A* through *H* on the curve correspond to the columns of the table. The total product curve separates attainable outputs from unattainable outputs. Points below the *TP* curve are inefficient. Points on the *TP* curve are efficient.

Like the *production possibilities frontier* (see Chapter 3, p. 62), the total product curve separates attainable outputs from unattainable outputs. All the points that lie above the curve are unattainable. Points that lie below the curve, in the orange area, are attainable, but they are inefficient: They use more labor than is necessary to produce a given output. Only the points *on* the total product curve are efficient.

## Marginal Product

**Marginal product**
The change in total product that results from a one-unit increase in the quantity of labor employed.

**Marginal product** (*MP*) is the change in total product that results from a one-unit increase in the quantity of labor employed. It tells us the contribution to total product of adding one additional worker. When the quantity of labor increases by more than one worker, we calculate marginal product as

Marginal product = Change in total product ÷ Change in quantity of labor.

Figure 13.3 shows Sam's Smoothies' marginal product curve, *MP*, and its relationship with the total product curve. You can see that as the quantity of labor increases from 1 to 3 workers, marginal product increases. But as more than 3 workers are employed, marginal product decreases. When the seventh worker is employed, marginal product is negative.

Notice that the steeper the slope of the total product curve in part (a), the greater is marginal product in part (b). And when the total product curve turns downward in part (a), marginal product is negative in part (b).

The total product curve and marginal product curve in Figure 13.3 incorporate a feature that is shared by all production processes in firms as different as the Ford Motor Company, Jim's Barber Shop, and Sam's Smoothies:

- Increasing marginal returns initially
- Decreasing marginal returns eventually

### Increasing Marginal Returns

**Increasing marginal returns**
When the marginal product of an additional worker exceeds the marginal product of the previous worker.

**Increasing marginal returns** occur when the marginal product of an additional worker exceeds the marginal product of the previous worker. The source of increasing marginal returns is increased specialization and greater division of labor in the production process.

For example, if Samantha employs just one worker, that person must learn all the aspects of making smoothies: running the blender, cleaning it, fixing breakdowns, buying and checking the fruit, and serving the customers. That one person must perform all these tasks.

If Samantha hires a second person, the two workers can specialize in different parts of the production process. As a result, two workers can produce more than twice as much as one worker. The marginal product of the second worker is greater than the marginal product of the first worker. Marginal returns are increasing. Most production processes experience increasing marginal returns initially.

### Decreasing Marginal Returns

**Decreasing marginal returns**
When the marginal product of an additional worker is less than the marginal product of the previous worker.

All production processes eventually reach a point of *decreasing* marginal returns. **Decreasing marginal returns** occur when the marginal product of an additional worker is less than the marginal product of the previous worker. Decreasing marginal returns arise from the fact that more and more workers use the same equipment and work space. As more workers are employed, there is less and less that is productive for the additional worker to do. For example, if Samantha hires a

## FIGURE 13.3

Total Product and Marginal Product

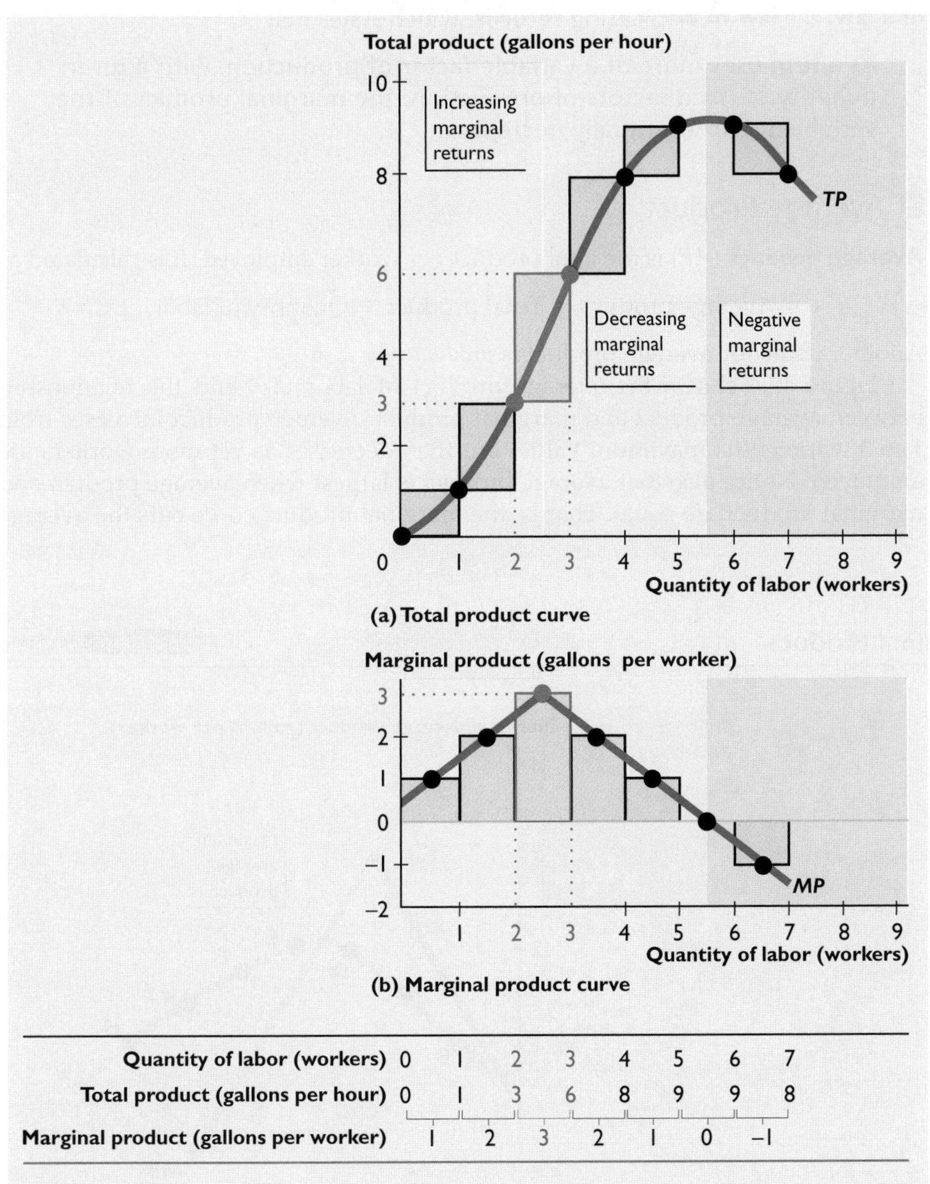


| Quantity of labor (workers) | 0 | | 1 | | 2 | | 3 | | 4 | | 5 | | 6 | | 7 |
|---|---|---|---|---|---|---|---|---|---|---|---|---|---|---|---|
| Total product (gallons per hour) | 0 | | 1 | | 3 | | 6 | | 8 | | 9 | | 9 | | 8 |
| Marginal product (gallons per worker) | | 1 | | 2 | | 3 | | 2 | | 1 | | 0 | | –1 | |

The table calculates marginal product, and the orange bars illustrate it. When labor increases from 2 to 3 workers, total product increases from 3 gallons to 6 gallons of smoothies an hour. So marginal product is the orange bar whose height is 3 gallons (in both parts of the figure).

In part (b), marginal product is graphed midway between the labor inputs to emphasize that it is the result of *changing* inputs. Marginal product increases to a maximum (when 3 workers are employed in this example) and then declines—diminishing marginal product.

fourth worker, output increases but not by as much as it did when she hired the third worker. In this case, three workers exhaust all the possible gains from specialization and the division of labor. By hiring a fourth worker, Sam's produces more smoothies per hour, but the equipment is being operated closer to its limits. Sometimes the fourth worker has nothing to do because the machines are running without the need for further attention.

Hiring yet more workers continues to increase output but by successively smaller amounts until Samantha hires the sixth worker, at which point total product stops rising. Add a seventh worker, and the workplace is so congested that the workers get in each other's way and total product falls.

Decreasing marginal returns are so pervasive that they qualify for the status of a law: the **law of decreasing returns**, which states that

> **As a firm uses more of a variable factor of production, with a given quantity of fixed factors of production, the marginal product of the variable factor eventually decreases.**

## Average Product

**Average product**
Total product divided by the quantity of a factor of production. The average product of labor is total product divided by the quantity of labor employed.

**Average product** (*AP*) is the total product per worker employed. It is calculated as

$$\text{Average product} = \text{Total product} \div \text{Quantity of labor}.$$

Another name for average product is *productivity*.

Figure 13.4 shows the average product of labor, *AP*, and the relationship between average product and marginal product. Average product increases from 1 to 3 workers (its maximum value) but then decreases as yet more workers are employed. Notice also that average product is largest when average product and marginal product are equal. That is, the marginal product curve cuts the average

**FIGURE 13.4**

Average Product and Marginal Product

myeconlab Animation

The table calculates average product. For example, when the quantity of labor is 3 workers, total product is 6 gallons an hour, so average product is 6 gallons ÷ 3 workers = 2 gallons a worker.

The average product curve is *AP*. When marginal product exceeds average product, average product is increasing. When marginal product is less than average product, average product is decreasing.

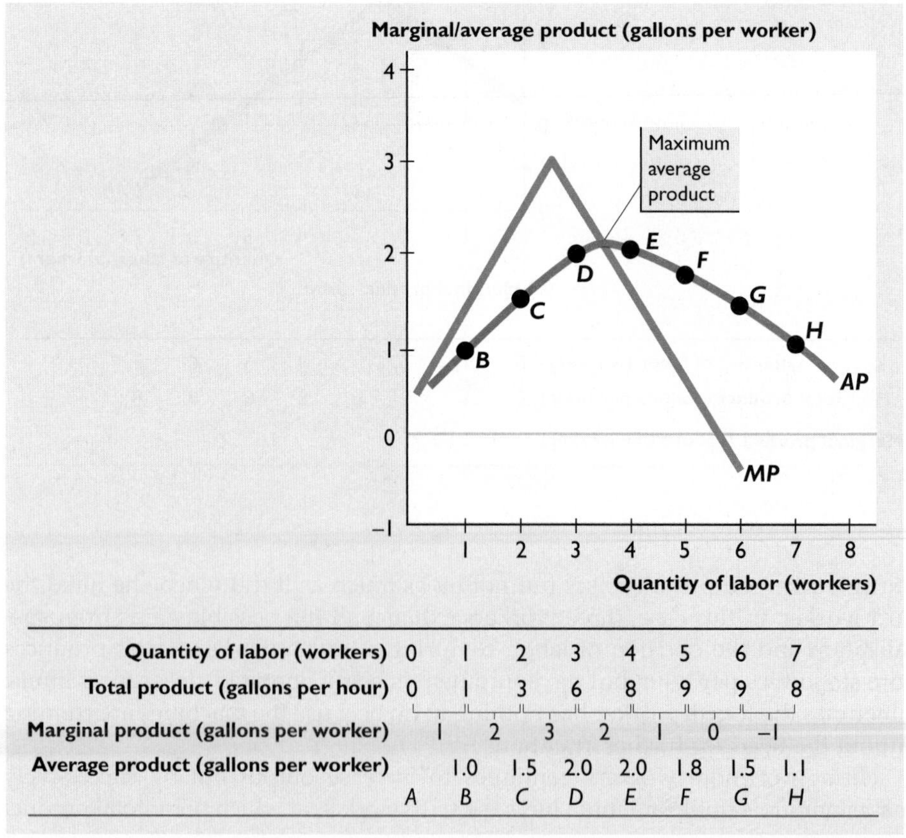


| Quantity of labor (workers) | 0 | 1 | 2 | 3 | 4 | 5 | 6 | 7 |
|---|---|---|---|---|---|---|---|---|
| Total product (gallons per hour) | 0 | 1 | 3 | 6 | 8 | 9 | 9 | 8 |
| Marginal product (gallons per worker) | | 1 | 2 | 3 | 2 | 1 | 0 | –1 |
| Average product (gallons per worker) | | 1.0 | 1.5 | 2.0 | 2.0 | 1.8 | 1.5 | 1.1 |
| | A | B | C | D | E | F | G | H |

product curve at the point of maximum average product. For employment levels at which marginal product exceeds average product, the average product curve slopes upward and average product increases as more labor is employed. For employment levels at which marginal product is less than average product, the average product curve slopes downward and average product decreases as more labor is employed.

The relationship between average product and marginal product is a general feature of the relationship between the average value and the marginal value of any variable. *Eye on Your Life* looks at a familiar example.

## EYE on YOUR LIFE

### Your Average and Marginal Grades

Jen, a part-time student, takes one course each semester over five semesters. In the first semester, she takes calculus and her grade is a C (2). This grade is her marginal grade. It is also her average grade—her GPA.

In the next semester, Jen takes French and gets a B (3)—her new marginal grade. When the marginal value exceeds the average value, the average rises. Because Jen's marginal grade exceeds her average grade, the marginal grade pulls her average up. Her GPA rises to 2.5.

In the third semester, Jen takes economics and gets an A (4). Again her marginal grade exceeds her average, so the marginal grade pulls her average up. Jen's GPA is now 3—the average of 2, 3, and 4.

In the fourth semester, she takes history and gets a B (3). Now her marginal grade equals her average. When the marginal value equals the average value, the average doesn't change. So Jen's average remains at 3.

In the fifth semester, Jen takes English and gets a C (2). When the marginal value is below the average value, the average falls. Because Jen's marginal grade, 2, is below her average of 3, the marginal grade pulls the average down. Her GPA falls.

This everyday relationship between average and marginal grades is similar to the relationship between average and marginal product.

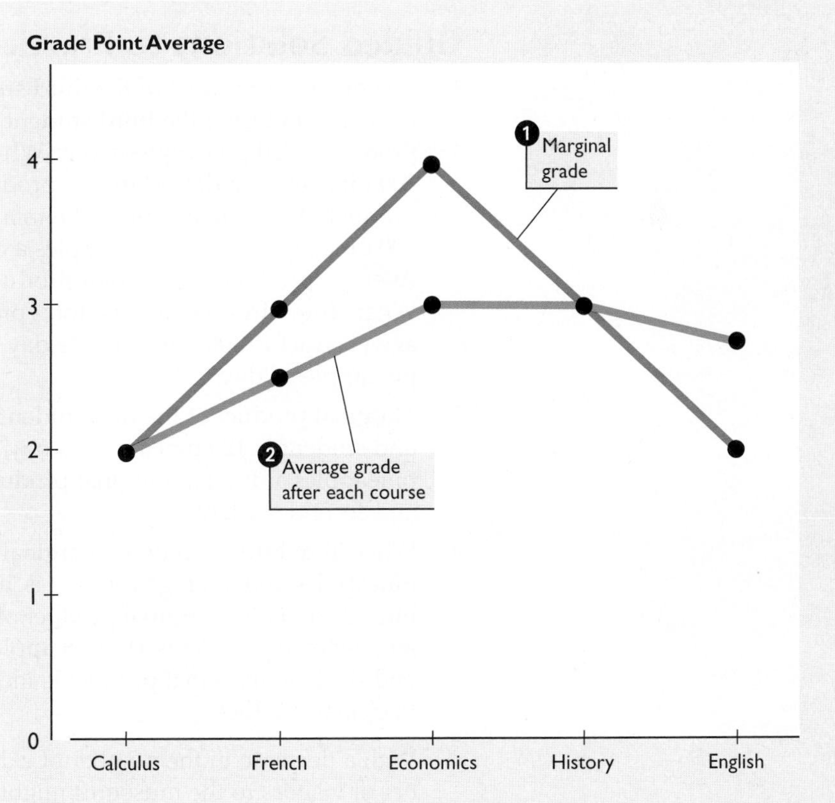

Work these problems in Study Plan 13.2 to get instant feedback.

## CHECKPOINT 13.2

**Explain the relationship between a firm's output and labor employed in the short run.**

## Practice Problems

Tom leases a farmer's field and grows pineapples. Tom hires students to pick and pack the pineapples. Table 1 sets out Tom's total product schedule. Use this information to work Problems **1** to **3**.

**TABLE 1**

| Labor (students) | Total product (pineapples per day) |
|---|---|
| 0 | 0 |
| 1 | 100 |
| 2 | 220 |
| 3 | 300 |
| 4 | 360 |
| 5 | 400 |
| 6 | 420 |
| 7 | 430 |

1. Calculate the marginal product of the third student and the average product of three students.
2. Over what range of numbers of students does marginal product increase?
3. When marginal product increases, is average product greater than, less than, or equal to marginal product?
4. **Budget cuts bring layoffs to museums**
The Detroit Institute of Arts cut its staff by 56 full-time and 7 part-time employees and canceled some of this year's planned exhibitions.
Source: *The New York Times*, February 25, 2009
As the number of museum workers decreased and some planned exhibitions were canceled, how do you think the marginal product and average product of a museum worker changed in the short run?

## Guided Solutions to Practice Problems

1. The marginal product of the third student is the change in total product that results from hiring the third student. When Tom hires 2 students, total product is 220 pineapples a day. When Tom hires 3 students, total product is 300 pineapples a day. Marginal product of the third student is the total product of 3 students minus the total product of 2 students, which is 300 pineapples − 220 pineapples a day, or 80 pineapples a day.
Average product equals total product divided by the number of students. When Tom hires 3 students, total product is 300 pineapples a day, so average product is 300 pineapples a day ÷ 3 students, which equals 100 pineapples a day.
2. Marginal product of the first student is 100 pineapples a day, that of the second student is 120 pineapples a day, and that of the third student is 80 pineapples a day. So marginal product increases when Tom hires the first and second students.
3. When Tom hires 1 student, marginal product of the first student is 100 pineapples and average product is 100 pineapples per student. When Tom hires 2 students, marginal product of the second student is 120 pineapples and average product is 110 pineapples per student. When Tom hires the second student, marginal product is increasing and average product is less than marginal product.
4. With a decrease in the number of exhibitions, output of the museum (number of visitors to the museum) might fall, but the percentage decrease in output is probably less than the percentage cut in labor services. Marginal product per worker will increase and the increase in marginal product will lead to an increase in the workers' average product.

## 13.3 SHORT-RUN COST

To produce more output (total product) in the short run, a firm must employ more labor, which means that it must increase its costs. We describe the relationship between output and cost using three cost concepts:

- Total cost
- Marginal cost
- Average cost

### Total Cost

A firm's **total cost** (*TC*) is the cost of all the factors of production used by the firm. Total cost divides into two parts: total fixed cost and total variable cost. **Total fixed cost** (*TFC*) is the cost of a firm's fixed factors of production: land, capital, and entrepreneurship. In the short run, the quantities of these inputs don't change as output changes, so total fixed cost doesn't change as output changes. **Total variable cost** (*TVC*) is the cost of a firm's variable factor of production—labor. To change its output in the short run, a firm must change the quantity of labor it employs, so total variable cost changes as output changes.

Total cost is the sum of total fixed cost and total variable cost. That is,

$$TC = TFC + TVC.$$

**Total cost**
The cost of all the factors of production used by a firm.

**Total fixed cost**
The cost of the firm's fixed factors of production—the cost of land, capital, and entrepreneurship.

**Total variable cost**
The cost of the firm's variable factor of production—the cost of labor.

Table 13.2 shows Sam's Smoothies' total costs. Sam's fixed costs are $10 an hour regardless of whether it operates or not—*TFC* is $10 an hour. To produce smoothies, Samantha hires labor, which costs $6 an hour. *TVC*, which increases as output increases, equals the number of workers per hour multiplied by $6. For example, to produce 6 gallons an hour, Samantha hires 3 workers, so *TVC* is $18 an hour. *TC* is the sum of *TFC* and *TVC*. So to produce 6 gallons an hour, *TC* is $28. Check the calculation in each row and note that to produce some quantities—2 gallons an hour, for example—Sam hires a worker for only part of the hour.

**TABLE 13.2**

Sam's Smoothies' Total Costs

| Labor (workers per hour) | Output (gallons per hour) | Total fixed cost (dollars per hour) | Total variable cost (dollars per hour) | Total cost (dollars per hour) |
|---|---|---|---|---|
| 0 | 0 | 10 | 0 | 10.00 |
| 1.00 | 1 | 10 | 6.00 | 16.00 |
| 1.60 | 2 | 10 | 9.60 | 19.60 |
| 2.00 | 3 | 10 | 12.00 | 22.00 |
| 2.35 | 4 | 10 | 14.10 | 24.10 |
| 2.65 | 5 | 10 | 15.90 | 25.90 |
| 3.00 | 6 | 10 | 18.00 | 28.00 |
| 3.40 | 7 | 10 | 20.40 | 30.40 |
| 4.00 | 8 | 10 | 24.00 | 34.00 |
| 5.00 | 9 | 10 | 30.00 | 40.00 |

Sam's fixed factors of production are land, capital, and entrepreneurship. Total fixed cost is constant regardless of the quantity produced. Sam's variable factor of production is labor. Total variable cost is the cost of labor. Total cost is the sum of total fixed cost and total variable cost.

The highlighted row shows that to produce 6 gallons of smoothies, Sam's hires 3 workers. Total fixed cost is $10 an hour. Total variable cost is the cost of the 3 workers. At $6 an hour, 3 workers cost $18. Sam's total cost of producing 6 gallons an hour is $10 plus $18, which equals $28.

Figure 13.5 illustrates Sam's total cost curves. The green total fixed cost curve (*TFC*) is horizontal because total fixed cost does not change when output changes. It is a constant at $10 an hour. The purple total variable cost curve (*TVC*) and the blue total cost curve (*TC*) both slope upward because variable cost increases as output increases. The arrows highlight total fixed cost as the vertical distance between the *TVC* and *TC* curve.

Let's now look at Sam's Smoothies' marginal cost.

## Marginal Cost

In Figure 13.5, total variable cost and total cost increase at a decreasing rate at small levels of output and then begin to increase at an increasing rate as output increases. To understand these patterns in the changes in total cost, we need to use the concept of *marginal cost*.

**Marginal cost**
The change in total cost that results from a one-unit increase in output.

A firm's **marginal cost** is the change in total cost that results from a one-unit increase in output. Table 13.3 calculates the marginal cost for Sam's Smoothies. When, for example, output increases from 5 gallons to 6 gallons an hour, total cost increases from $26.20 to $28. So the marginal cost of this gallon of smoothie is $1.80 ($28 − $26.20).

Marginal cost tells us how total cost changes as output changes. The final cost concept tells us what it costs, on the average, to produce a unit of output. Let's now look at Sam's average costs.

**FIGURE 13.5**

Total Cost Curves at Sam's Smoothies

myeconlab Animation

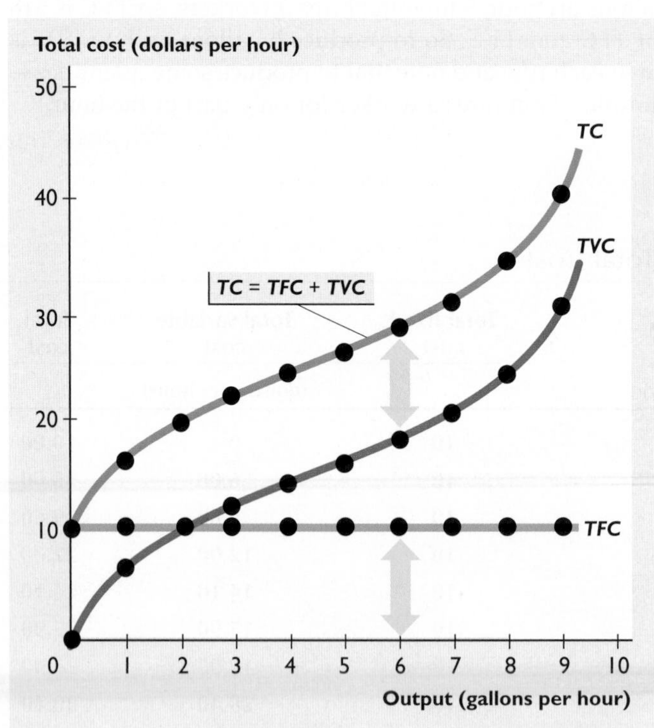


Total fixed cost (*TFC*) is constant—it graphs as a horizontal line—and total variable cost (*TVC*) increases as output increases. Total cost (*TC*) also increases as output increases. The vertical distance between the total cost curve and the total variable cost curve is total fixed cost, as illustrated by the two arrows.

## Average Cost

There are three average cost concepts:

- Average fixed cost
- Average variable cost
- Average total cost

**Average fixed cost** (*AFC*) is total fixed cost per unit of output. **Average variable cost** (*AVC*) is total variable cost per unit of output. **Average total cost** (*ATC*) is total cost per unit of output. The average cost concepts are calculated from the total cost concepts as follows:

$$TC = TFC + TVC.$$

Divide each total cost term by the quantity produced, $Q$, to give

$$\frac{TC}{Q} = \frac{TFC}{Q} + \frac{TVC}{Q}$$

or

$$ATC = AFC + AVC.$$

Table 13.3 shows these average costs. For example, when output is 6 gallons an hour, average fixed cost is ($10 ÷ 6), which equals $1.67; average variable cost is ($18 ÷ 6), which equals $3.00; and average total cost is ($28 ÷ 6), which equals $4.67. Note that average total cost ($4.67) equals average fixed cost ($1.67) plus average variable cost ($3.00).

**Average fixed cost**
Total fixed cost per unit of output.

**Average variable cost**
Total variable cost per unit of output.

**Average total cost**
Total cost per unit of output, which equals average fixed cost plus average variable cost.

**TABLE 13.3**

Sam's Smoothies' Marginal Cost and Average Cost

| Output (gallons per hour) | Total cost (dollars per hour) | Marginal cost (dollars per gallon) | Average fixed cost (dollars per gallon) | Average variable cost (dollars per gallon) | Average total cost (dollars per gallon) |
|---|---|---|---|---|---|
| 0 | 10.00 | | – | – | – |
| | | 6.00 | | | |
| 1 | 16.00 | | 10.00 | 6.00 | 16.00 |
| | | 3.60 | | | |
| 2 | 19.60 | | 5.00 | 4.80 | 9.80 |
| | | 2.40 | | | |
| 3 | 22.00 | | 3.33 | 4.00 | 7.33 |
| | | 2.10 | | | |
| 4 | 24.10 | | 2.50 | 3.53 | 6.03 |
| | | 1.80 | | | |
| 5 | 25.90 | | 2.00 | 3.18 | 5.18 |
| | | 2.10 | | | |
| 6 | 28.00 | | 1.67 | 3.00 | 4.67 |
| | | 2.40 | | | |
| 7 | 30.40 | | 1.43 | 2.91 | 4.34 |
| | | 3.60 | | | |
| 8 | 34.00 | | 1.25 | 3.00 | 4.25 |
| | | 6.00 | | | |
| 9 | 40.00 | | 1.11 | 3.33 | 4.44 |

To produce 6 gallons of smoothies an hour, Sam's total cost is $28. Table 13.2 shows that this total cost is the sum of total fixed cost ($10) and total variable cost ($18).

Marginal cost is the increase in total cost that results from a one-unit increase in output. When Sam's increases output from 5 gallons to 6 gallons an hour, total cost increases from $25.90 to $28.00, an increase of $2.10 a gallon. The marginal cost of the sixth gallon an hour is $2.10.

When Sam's produces 6 gallons an hour, average fixed cost ($10 ÷ 6 gallons) is $1.67 a gallon: average variable cost ($18 ÷ 6 gallons) is $3.00 a gallon: average total cost ($28 ÷ 6 gallons) is $4.67 a gallon.

Figure 13.6 graphs the marginal cost and average cost data in Table 13.3. The red marginal cost curve (*MC*) is U-shaped because of the way in which marginal product changes. Recall that when Samantha hires a second or a third worker, marginal product increases and output increases to 6 gallons an hour (Figure 13.3 on p. 327). Over this output range, marginal cost decreases as output increases. When Samantha hires a fourth or more workers, marginal product decreases but output increases up to 9 gallons an hour (Figure 13.3). Over this output range, marginal cost increases as output increases.

The green average fixed cost curve (*AFC*) slopes downward. As output increases, the same constant total fixed cost is spread over a larger output. The blue average total cost curve (*ATC*) and the purple average variable cost curve (*AVC*) are U-shaped. The vertical distance between the average total cost and average variable cost curves is equal to average fixed cost—as indicated by the two arrows. That distance shrinks as output increases because average fixed cost decreases with increasing output.

The marginal cost curve intersects the average variable cost curve and the average total cost curve at their minimum points. That is, when marginal cost is less than average cost, average cost is decreasing; and when marginal cost exceeds average cost, average cost is increasing. This relationship holds for both the *ATC* curve and the *AVC* curve and is another example of the relationship you saw in Figure 13.4 for average product and marginal product.

**FIGURE 13.6**

Average Cost Curves and Marginal Cost Curve at Sam's Smoothies

myeconlab Animation

Average fixed cost (*AFC*) decreases as output increases. The average total cost curve (*ATC*) and average variable cost curve (*AVC*) are U-shaped. The vertical distance between these two curves is equal to average fixed cost, as illustrated by the two arrows.

Marginal cost is the change in total cost when output increases by one unit. The marginal cost curve (*MC*) is U-shaped and intersects the average variable cost curve and the average total cost curve at their minimum points.

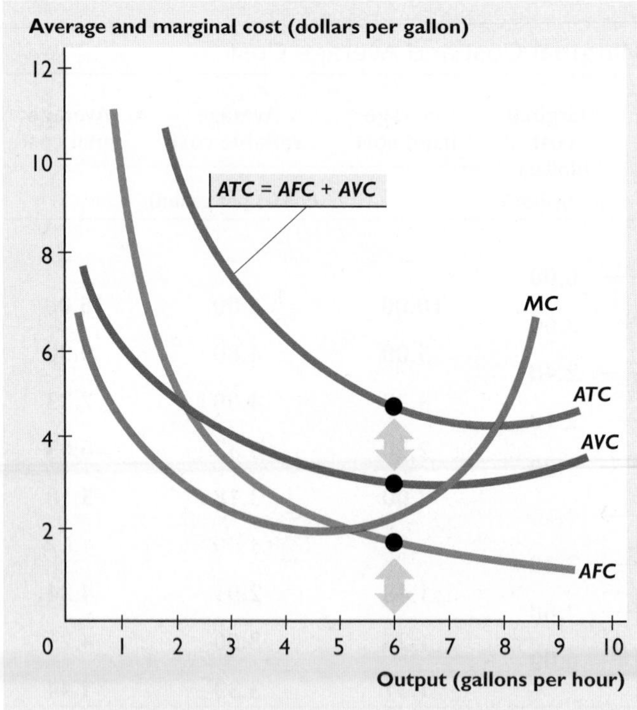

## Why the Average Total Cost Curve Is U-Shaped

Average total cost, *ATC*, is the sum of average fixed cost, *AFC*, and average variable cost, *AVC*. So the shape of the *ATC* curve combines the shapes of the *AFC* and *AVC* curves. The U-shape of the average total cost curve arises from the influence of two opposing forces:

- Spreading total fixed cost over a larger output
- Decreasing marginal returns

When output increases, the firm spreads its total fixed costs over a larger output and its average fixed cost decreases—its average fixed cost curve slopes downward.

Decreasing marginal returns means that as output increases, ever larger amounts of labor are needed to produce an additional unit of output. So average variable cost eventually increases, and the *AVC* curve eventually slopes upward.

The shape of the average total cost curve combines these two effects. Initially, as output increases, both average fixed cost and average variable cost decrease, so average total cost decreases and the *ATC* curve slopes downward. But as output increases further and decreasing marginal returns set in, average variable cost begins to increase. Eventually, average variable cost increases more quickly than average fixed cost decreases, so average total cost increases and the *ATC* curve slopes upward.

All the short-run cost concepts that you've met are summarized in Table 13.4.

**TABLE 13.4**

A Compact Glossary of Costs

| Term | Symbol | Definition | Equation |
|---|---|---|---|
| **Fixed cost** | | **The cost of a fixed factor of production that is independent of the quantity produced** | |
| **Variable cost** | | **The cost of a variable factor of production that varies with the quantity produced** | |
| **Total fixed cost** | *TFC* | **Cost of the fixed factors of production** | |
| **Total variable cost** | *TVC* | **Cost of the variable factor of production** | |
| **Total cost** | *TC* | **Cost of all factors of production** | $TC = TFC + TVC$ |
| **Marginal cost** | *MC* | **Change in total cost resulting from a one-unit increase in output (*Q*)** | $MC = \Delta TC \div \Delta Q$* |
| **Average fixed cost** | *AFC* | **Total fixed cost per unit of output** | $AFC = TFC \div Q$ |
| **Average variable cost** | *AVC* | **Total variable cost per unit of output** | $AVC = TVC \div Q$ |
| **Average total cost** | *ATC* | **Total cost per unit of output** | $ATC = AFC + AVC$ |

*In this equation, the Greek letter delta (Δ) stands for "change in."

## Cost Curves and Product Curves

A firm's cost curves and product curves are linked, and Figure 13.7 shows how. The upper graph shows the average product curve, *AP*, and the marginal product curve, *MP*. The lower graph shows the average variable cost curve, *AVC*, and the marginal cost curve, *MC*.

As labor increases up to 2.5 workers a day (upper graph), output increases to 4 units a day (lower graph). Marginal product and average product rise and marginal cost and average variable cost fall. At the point of maximum marginal product, marginal cost is at a minimum.

As labor increases to 3.5 workers a day, (upper graph) output increases to 7 units a day (lower graph). Marginal product falls and marginal cost rises, but average product continues to rise and average variable cost continues to fall. At the point of maximum average product, average variable cost is at a minimum. As labor increases further, output increases. Average product diminishes and average variable cost increases.

## Shifts in the Cost Curves

The position of a firm's short-run cost curves, in Figures 13.5 and 13.6, depends on two factors:

- Technology
- Prices of factors of production

### Technology

A technological change that increases productivity shifts the total product curve upward. It also shifts the marginal product curve and the average product curve upward. With a better technology, the same factors of production can produce more output, so an advance in technology lowers the average and marginal costs and shifts the short-run cost curves downward.

For example, advances in robotic technology have increased productivity in the automobile industry. As a result, the product curves of Chrysler, Ford, and GM have shifted upward, and their average and marginal cost curves have shifted downward. But the relationships between their product curves and cost curves have not changed. The curves are still linked, as in Figure 13.7.

Often a technological advance results in a firm using more capital, a fixed factor of production, and less labor, a variable factor of production. For example, today telephone companies use computers to connect long-distance calls instead of the human operators they used in the 1980s. When a telephone company makes this change, total variable cost decreases and total cost decreases, but total fixed cost increases. This change in the mix of fixed cost and variable cost means that at small output levels, average total cost might increase, but at large output levels, average total cost decreases.

### Prices of Factors of Production

An increase in the price of a factor of production increases costs and shifts the cost curves. But how the curves shift depends on which resource price changes. An increase in rent or some other component of *fixed* cost shifts the fixed cost curves (*TFC* and *AFC*) upward and shifts the total cost curve (*TC*) upward but leaves the variable cost curves (*AVC* and *TVC*) and the marginal cost curve (*MC*) unchanged.

**FIGURE 13.7**

Product Curves and Cost Curves

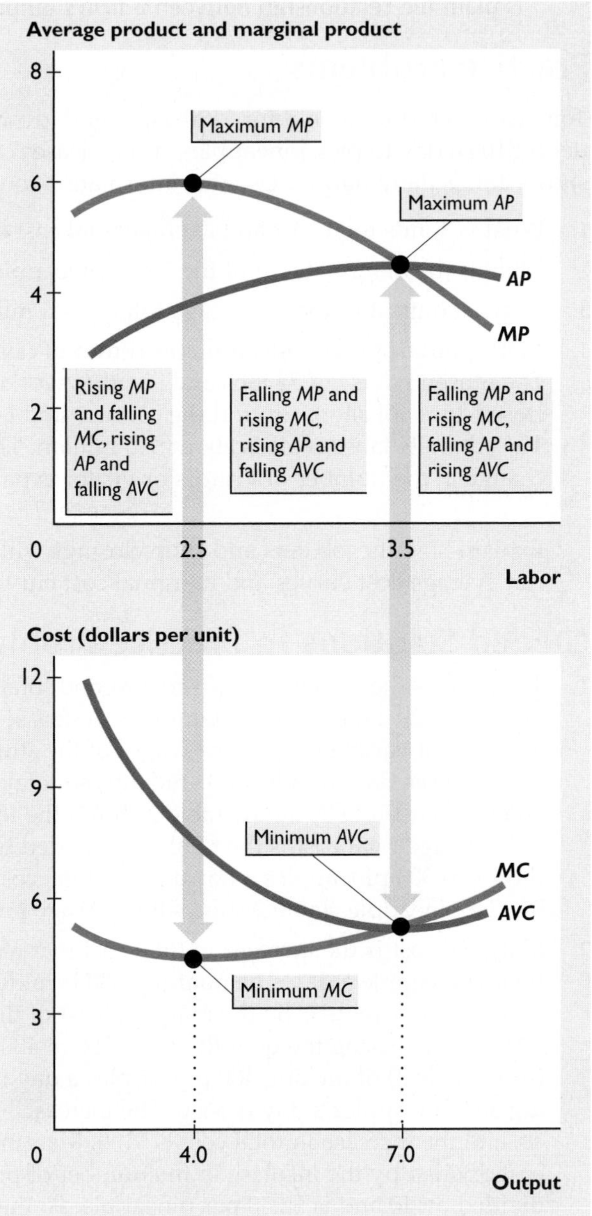


A firm's *MC* curve is linked to its *MP* curve. If, as the firm hires more labor up to 2.5 workers a day, the firm's marginal product rises, its marginal cost falls. If marginal product is at a maximum, marginal cost is at a minimum. If, as the firm hires more labor, its marginal product diminishes, its marginal cost rises.

A firm's *AVC* curve is linked to its *AP* curve. If, as the firm hires more labor up to 3.5 workers a day, its average product rises, its average variable cost falls. If average product is at a maximum, average variable cost is at a minimum. If as the firm hires more labor its average product diminishes, its average variable cost rises.

An increase in wage rates or some other component of *variable* cost shifts the variable cost curves (*TVC* and *AVC*) and the marginal cost curve (*MC*) upward but leaves the fixed cost curves (*AFC* and *TFC*) unchanged. So, for example, if the interest expense paid by a trucking company increases, the fixed cost of transportation services increases, but if the wage rate paid to truck drivers increases, the variable cost and marginal cost of transportation services increase.

Work these problems in Study Plan 13.3 to get instant feedback.

## CHECKPOINT 13.3

**Explain the relationship between a firm's output and costs in the short run.**

### Practice Problems

Tom leases a farmer's field for $120 a day and grows pineapples. He pays students $100 a day to pick pineapples and he leases capital at $80 a day. Table 1 shows Tom's daily output. Use this information to work Problems **1** to **3**.

**TABLE 1**

| Labor (students) | Output (pineapples per day) |
|---|---|
| 0 | 0 |
| 1 | 100 |
| 2 | 220 |
| 3 | 300 |
| 4 | 360 |
| 5 | 400 |
| 6 | 420 |
| 7 | 430 |

1. What is Tom's total cost and average total cost of 300 pineapples a day?
2. What is the marginal cost of the 380th pineapple?
3. At what output is Tom's average total cost a minimum?
4. **Metropolitan Museum completes round of layoffs**
   The museum has cut 74 jobs and 95 other workers retired. The museum also closed 15 retail shops around the country and laid off 127 other employees. The cut in its labor costs is about $10 million. The museum expects no change in the number of visitors or visitor experience.
   Source: *The New York Times*, June 22, 2009

   Explain how the job cuts and shop closings will change the museum's short-run average cost curves and marginal cost curve.

### Guided Solutions to Practice Problems

1. Total cost is the sum of total fixed cost and total variable cost. Tom leases the field for $120 a day and capital for $80 a day, so Tom's total fixed cost is $200 a day. Total variable cost is the wages of the students. To produce 300 pineapples a day, Tom hires 3 students, so total variable cost is $300 a day and total cost is $500 a day. Table 2 shows the total cost (*TC*) schedule.
   Average total cost is the total cost divided by total product. When Tom produces 300 pineapples a day and his total cost is $500, average total cost is $1.67 a pineapple. Table 2 shows the average total cost schedule.
2. Marginal cost is the increase in total cost that results from picking one additional pineapple a day. The quantity 380 is midway between 360 and 400 pineapples in Table 2. So the marginal cost of the 380th pineapple is calculated by increasing the quantity from 360 to 400 pineapples. The total cost (from Table 2) of picking 400 pineapples a day is $700. The total cost of picking 360 pineapples a day is $600. The increase in the number of pineapples is 40, and the increase in total cost is $100. Marginal cost is the increase in total cost divided by the increase in the number of pineapples, which equals $100 divided by 40 and is $2.50 per pineapple. So the marginal cost of the 380th pineapple is $2.50. The *MC* column of Table 2 shows the marginal cost schedule—marginal cost at each output.
3. At the minimum of average total cost, average total cost equals marginal cost. Minimum average total cost is $1.67 a pineapple at 330 pineapples a day—the midpoint between 300 and 360 pineapples.
4. A cut in labor but no change in output increases marginal product of labor and decreases marginal cost of producing the output. The *MC*, *AVC*, and *ATC* curves shift downward. The shop closures decrease total fixed cost and shift the *AFC* and *ATC* curves downward.

**TABLE 2**

| Labor | *TP* | *TC* | *MC* | *ATC* |
|---|---|---|---|---|
| 0 | 0 | 200 | | – |
| | | | 1.00 | |
| 1 | 100 | 300 | | 3.00 |
| | | | 0.83 | |
| 2 | 220 | 400 | | 1.82 |
| | | | 1.25 | |
| 3 | 300 | 500 | | 1.67 |
| | | | 1.67 | |
| 4 | 360 | 600 | | 1.67 |
| | | | 2.50 | |
| 5 | 400 | 700 | | 1.75 |
| | | | 5.00 | |
| 6 | 420 | 800 | | 1.90 |
| | | | 10.00 | |
| 7 | 430 | 900 | | 2.09 |

## 13.4 LONG-RUN COST

In the long run, a firm can vary both the quantity of labor and the quantity of capital. A small firm, such as Sam's Smoothies, can increase its plant size by moving into a larger building and installing more machines. A big firm such as General Motors can decrease its plant size by closing down some production lines.

We are now going to see how costs vary in the long run when a firm varies its plant—the quantity of capital it uses—along with the quantity of labor it uses.

The first thing that happens is that the distinction between fixed cost and variable cost disappears. All costs are variable in the long run.

### Plant Size and Cost

When a firm changes its plant size, its cost of producing a given output changes. In Table 13.3 on p. 333 and Figure 13.6 on p. 334, the lowest average total cost that Samantha can achieve is $4.25 a gallon, which occurs when she produces 8 gallons of smoothie an hour. Samantha wonders what would happen to her average total cost if she increased the size of her plant by renting a bigger building and installing a larger number of blenders and refrigerators. Will the average total cost of producing a gallon of smoothie fall, rise, or remain the same?

Each of these three outcomes is possible, and they arise because when a firm changes the size of its plant, it might experience

- Economies of scale
- Diseconomies of scale
- Constant returns to scale

#### Economies of Scale

If when a firm increases its plant size and labor employed by the same percentage, its output increases by a larger percentage, the firm's average total cost decreases. The firm experiences **economies of scale**. The main source of economies of scale is greater specialization of both labor and capital.

**Economies of scale**
A condition in which, when a firm increases its plant size and labor employed by the same percentage, its output increases by a larger percentage and its average total cost decreases.

***Specialization of Labor*** If Ford produced 100 cars a week, each production line worker would have to perform many different tasks. But if Ford produces 10,000 cars a week, each worker can specialize in a small number of tasks and become highly proficient at them. The result is that the average product of labor increases and the average total cost of producing a car falls.

Specialization also occurs off the production line. For example, a small firm usually does not have a specialist sales manager, personnel manager, and production manager. One person covers all these activities. But when a firm is large enough, specialists perform these activities. Average product increases, and the average total cost falls.

*Specialization of both labor and capital on an auto-assembly line.*

***Specialization of Capital*** At a small output rate, firms often must employ general-purpose machines and tools. For example, with an output of a few gallons an hour, Sam's Smoothies uses regular blenders like the one in your kitchen. But if Sam's produces hundreds of gallons an hour, it uses commercial blenders that fill, empty, and clean themselves. The result is that the output rate is larger and the average total cost of producing a gallon of smoothie is lower.

### Diseconomies of Scale

If when a firm increases its plant size and labor employed by the same percentage, output increases by a smaller percentage, the firm's average total cost increases. The firm experiences **diseconomies of scale**. Diseconomies of scale arise from the difficulty of coordinating and controlling a large enterprise. The larger the firm, the greater is the cost of communicating both up and down the management hierarchy and among managers. Eventually, management complexity brings rising average total cost. Diseconomies of scale occur in all production processes but in some perhaps only at a very large output rate.

**Diseconomies of scale**
A condition in which, when a firm increases its plant size and labor employed by the same percentage, its output increases by a smaller percentage and its average total cost increases.

### Constant Returns to Scale

If when a firm increases its plant size and labor employed by the same percentage, output increases by that same percentage, the firm's average total cost remains constant. The firm experiences **constant returns to scale**. Constant returns to scale occur when a firm is able to replicate its existing production facility including its management system. For example, Ford might double its production of Taurus by doubling its production facility for those cars. It can build an identical production line and hire an identical number of workers. With the two identical production lines, Ford produces exactly twice as many cars. The average total cost of producing a Taurus is identical in the two plants. Ford's average total cost remains constant as it increases production.

**Constant returns to scale**
A condition in which, when a firm increases its plant size and labor employed by the same percentage, its output increases by that same percentage and its average total cost remains constant.

## ■ The Long-Run Average Cost Curve

The **long-run average cost curve** shows the lowest average cost at which it is possible to produce each output when the firm has had sufficient time to change both its plant size and its labor force.

**Long-run average cost curve**
A curve that shows the lowest average cost at which it is possible to produce each output when the firm has had sufficient time to change both its plant size and labor employed.

Figure 13.8 shows Sam's Smoothies' long-run average cost curve *LRAC*. This long-run average cost curve is derived from the short-run average total cost curves for different possible plant sizes.

With its current small plant, Sam's Smoothies operates on the average total cost curve $ATC_1$ in Figure 13.8. The other three average total cost curves are for successively bigger plants. In this example, for outputs up to 5 gallons an hour, the existing plant with average total cost curve $ATC_1$ produces smoothies at the lowest attainable average cost. For outputs between 5 and 10 gallons an hour, average total cost is lowest on $ATC_2$. For outputs between 10 and 15 gallons an hour, average total cost is lowest on $ATC_3$. And for outputs in excess of 15 gallons an hour, average total cost is lowest on $ATC_4$.

The segment of each of the four average total cost curves for which that plant has the lowest average total cost is highlighted in dark blue in Figure 13.8. The scallop-shaped curve made up of these four segments is Sam's Smoothies' long-run average cost curve.

### Economies and Diseconomies of Scale

When economies of scale are present, the *LRAC* curve slopes downward. The *LRAC* curve in Figure 13.8 shows that Sam's Smoothies experiences economies of scale for output rates up to 9 gallons an hour. At output rates between 9 and 12 gallons an hour, the firm experiences constant returns to scale. And at output rates that exceed 12 gallons an hour, the firm experiences diseconomies of scale.

**FIGURE 13.8**

Long-Run Average Cost Curve

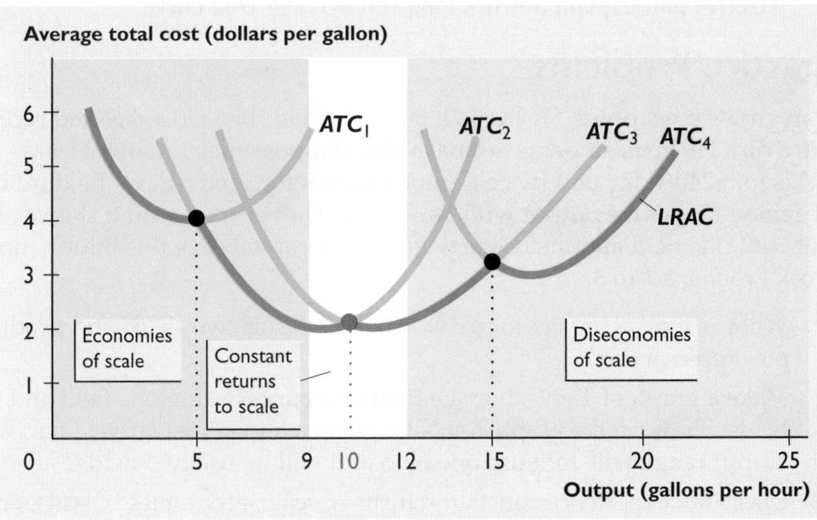


In the long run, Samantha can vary both the plant size and the quantity of labor she employs. The long-run average cost curve traces the lowest attainable average total cost of producing each output. The dark blue curve is the long-run average cost curve *LRAC*.

Sam's experiences economies of scale as output increases to 9 gallons an hour, constant returns to scale for outputs between 9 gallons and 12 gallons an hour, and diseconomies of scale for outputs that exceed 12 gallons an hour.

# EYE on RETAILERS' COSTS

## Which Store Has the Lower Costs: Wal-Mart or 7–11?

Wal-Mart's "small" supercenters measure 99,000 square feet and serve an average of 30,000 customers a week. The average 7–11 store, most of which today are attached to gas stations, measures 2,000 square feet and serves 5,000 customers a week.

Which retailing technology has the lower operating cost? The answer depends on the scale of operation.

At a small number of customers per week, it costs less per customer to operate a store of 2,000 square feet than one of 99,000 square feet.

In the figure, the average total cost curve of operating a 7–11 store of 2,000 square feet is $ATC_{7\text{–}11}$ and the average total cost curve of a store of 99,000 square feet is $ATC_{Wal\text{-}Mart}$. The dark blue curve is a retailer's long-run average cost curve *LRAC*.

If the number of customers is *Q* a week, the average total cost per transaction is the same for both stores. For a store that serves more than *Q* customers a week, the least-cost method is the big store. For fewer than *Q* customers a week, the least-cost method is the small store. The least-cost store is not always the biggest.

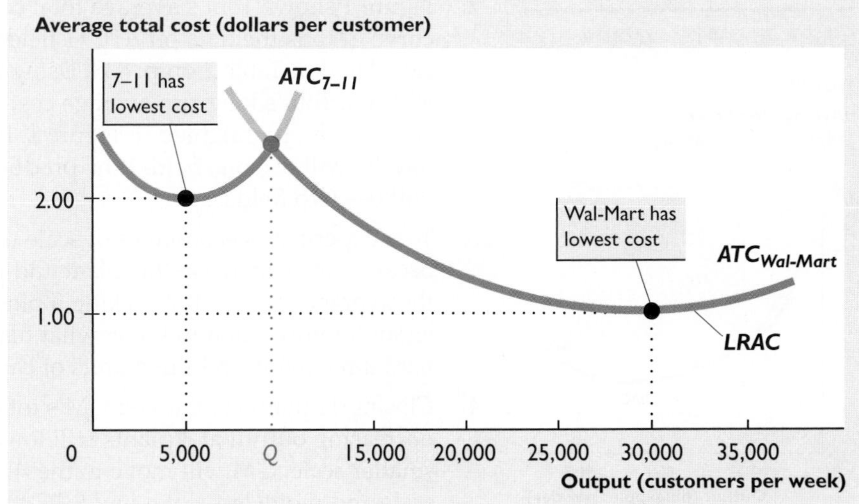

Work these problems in Study Plan 13.4 to get instant feedback.

## CHECKPOINT 13.4

**Derive and explain a firm's long-run average cost curve.**

### Practice Problems

Tom grows pineapples. He leases a farmer's field for $120 a day and capital for $80 a day. He hires students at $100 a day. Suppose that Tom now leases two fields for $240 a day and twice as much capital for $160 a day. The third column of Table 1 shows his output with two fields. The second column shows his output with one field and the original amount of capital. Use this information to work Problems **1** to **3**.

**TABLE 1**

| Labor (students per day) | Output 1 field (pineapples per day) | Output 2 fields (pineapples per day) |
|---|---|---|
| 0 | 0 | 0 |
| 1 | 100 | 220 |
| 2 | 220 | 460 |
| 3 | 300 | 620 |
| 4 | 360 | 740 |
| 5 | 400 | 820 |
| 6 | 420 | 860 |
| 7 | 430 | 880 |

1. What is Tom's average total cost when he farms two fields and produces 220 pineapples a day?
2. Make a graph of Tom's average total cost curves using one field and two fields. Show on the graph Tom's long-run average cost curve. Over what output range will Tom use one field and will he use two fields?
3. Does Tom experience constant returns to scale, economies of scale, or diseconomies of scale?
4. **GM restructuring plan released**
   The White House released details of its restructuring plan for GM: The firm will close 11 plants and reduce output at 3 others.
   Source: boston.com, May 31, 2009
   Explain the effects of the restructuring plan on GM's total fixed cost, total variable cost, short-run *ATC* curve, and *LRAC* curve.

**TABLE 2**

| *TP* (1 field) | *ATC* (1 field) | *TP* (2 fields) | *ATC* (2 fields) |
|---|---|---|---|
| 100 | 3.00 | 220 | 2.27 |
| 220 | 1.82 | 460 | 1.30 |
| 300 | 1.67 | 620 | 1.13 |
| 360 | 1.67 | 740 | 1.08 |
| 400 | 1.75 | 820 | 1.10 |
| 420 | 1.90 | 860 | 1.16 |
| 430 | 2.09 | 880 | 1.25 |

### Guided Solutions to Practice Problems

1. Total cost equals fixed cost ($400 a day) plus $100 a day for each student. Tom can produce 220 pineapples with two fields and 1 student, so total cost is $500 a day. Average total cost is the total cost divided by output, which at 220 pineapples a day is $500 divided by 220, or $2.27. The "*ATC* (2 fields)" column of Table 2 shows Tom's average total cost schedule for two fields.
2. Figure 1 shows Tom's average total cost curve using one field as $ATC_1$. This curve graphs the data on *ATC* (1 field) and *TP* (1 field) in Table 2, which was calculated in Table 2 on p. 338. Using two fields, the average total cost curve is $ATC_2$. Tom's long-run average cost curve is the lower segments of the two *ATC* curves, highlighted in Figure 1. If Tom produces up to 300 pineapples a day, he will use one field. If he produces more than 300 pineapples a day, he will use two fields.
3. Tom experiences economies of scale up to an output of 740 pineapples a day because as he increases his plant and produces up to 740 pineapples a day, the average total cost of picking a pineapple decreases. (We don't have enough information to know what happens to Tom's average total cost if he uses three fields and three units of capital.
4. Closing 11 plants will lower GM's total fixed cost; closing 11 plants and decreasing output at 3 plants will lower GM's total variable cost. With a smaller scale, GM will move to the *ATC* curve associated with that smaller scale and move left along its *LRAC* curve.

**FIGURE 1**

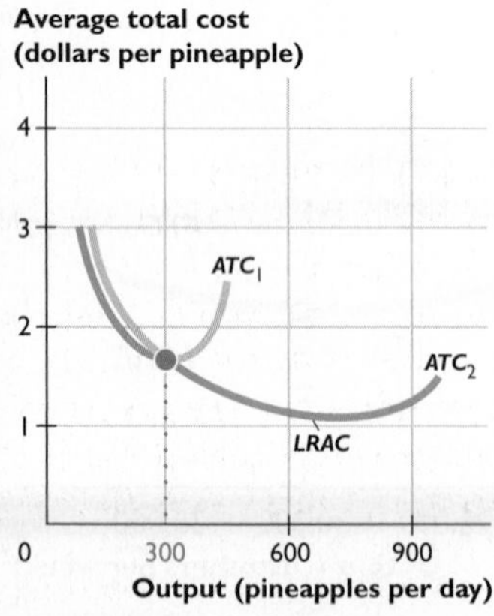

# CHAPTER SUMMARY

## Key Points

1 **Explain how economists measure a firm's cost of production and profit.**

- Firms seek to maximize economic profit, which is total revenue minus total cost.
- Total cost equals opportunity cost—the sum of explicit costs plus implicit costs and includes normal profit.

2 **Explain the relationship between a firm's output and labor employed in the short run.**

- In the short run, the firm can change the output it produces by changing only the quantity of labor it employs.
- A total product curve shows the limits to the output that the firm can produce with a given quantity of capital and different quantities of labor.
- As the quantity of labor increases, the marginal product of labor increases initially but eventually decreases—the law of decreasing returns.

3 **Explain the relationship between a firm's output and costs in the short run.**

- As total product increases, total fixed cost is constant, and total variable cost and total cost increase.
- As total product increases, average fixed cost decreases; average variable cost, average total cost, and marginal cost decrease at small outputs and increase at large outputs so their curves are U-shaped.

4 **Derive and explain a firm's long-run average cost curve.**

- In the long run, the firm can change the size of its plant.
- Long-run cost is the cost of production when all inputs have been adjusted to produce at the lowest attainable cost.
- The long-run average cost curve traces out the lowest attainable average total cost at each output when both the plant size and labor can be varied.
- The long-run average cost curve slopes downward with economies of scale and upward with diseconomies of scale.

## Key Terms

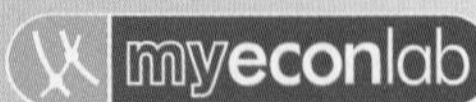


Work these problems in Chapter 13 Study Plan to get instant feedback.

## CHAPTER CHECKPOINT

### Study Plan Problems and Applications

1. Joe runs a shoeshine stand at the airport. With no skills and no job experience, Joe has no alternative employment. The other shoeshine stand operators that Joe knows earn $10,000 a year. Joe pays the airport $2,000 a year for the space he uses, and his total revenue from shining shoes is $15,000 a year. He spent $1,000 on a chair, polish, and brushes and paid for these items using his credit card. The interest on his credit card balance is 20 percent a year. At the end of the year, Joe was offered $500 for his business and all its equipment. Calculate Joe's explicit costs, implicit costs, and economic profit.

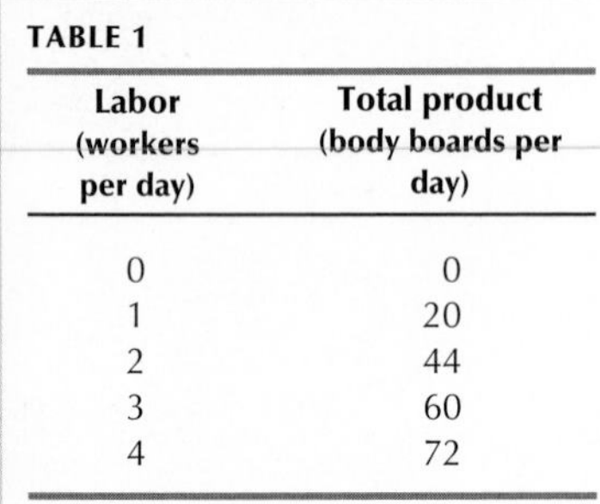

**TABLE 1**

| Labor (workers per day) | Total product (body boards per day) |
|---|---|
| 0 | 0 |
| 1 | 20 |
| 2 | 44 |
| 3 | 60 |
| 4 | 72 |

2. Len's body board factory rents equipment for shaping boards and hires students. Table 1 sets out Len's total product schedule. Construct Len's marginal product and average product schedules. Over what range of workers do marginal returns increase?

Use the following information to work Problems 3 to 6.

Len's body board factory pays $60 a day for equipment and $200 a day to each student it hires. Table 1 sets out Len's total product schedule.

3. Construct Len's total variable cost and total cost schedules. What does the difference between total cost and total variable cost at each output equal?
4. Construct the average fixed cost, average variable cost, and average total cost schedules and the marginal cost schedule.
5. At what output is Len's average total cost at a minimum? At what output is Len's average variable cost at a minimum?
6. Explain why the output at which average variable cost is at a minimum is smaller than the output at which average total cost is at a minimum.
7. Table 2 shows the costs incurred at Pete's peanut farm. Complete the table.

**TABLE 2**

| *L* | *TP* | *TVC* | *TC* | *AFC* | *AVC* | *ATC* | *MC* |
|---|---|---|---|---|---|---|---|
| 0 | 0 | 0 | 100 | | | | |
| 1 | 10 | 35 | | | | | |
| 2 | 24 | 70 | | | | | |
| 3 | 38 | 105 | | | | | |
| 4 | 44 | 140 | | | | | |

8. **Coffee king Starbucks raises its prices**

   Starbucks will raise its price because the wholesale price of milk has risen by nearly 70% in the past year. There's a lot of milk in those Starbucks lattes, noted John Glass, CIBC World Markets restaurant analyst.

   Source: *USA Today*, July 24, 2007

   Is the cost of milk a fixed cost or a variable cost? Describe how the increase in the price of milk changes Starbucks' short-run cost curves.

## Instructor Assignable Problems and Applications

Your instructor can assign these problems as homework, a quiz, or a test in **MyEconLab**.

1. If the *ATC* curves of a Wal-Mart store and a 7–11 are like those in *Eye on Retailers' Costs* on p. 341, and if each type of store operates at its minimum *ATC*, which store has the lower total cost? How can you be sure? Which has the lower marginal cost? How can you be sure? Sketch each firm's marginal cost curve.
2. Sonya used to earn $25,000 a year selling real estate, but she now sells greeting cards. Normal profit for the retailers of greeting cards is $14,000. Over the year, Sonya bought $10,000 worth of cards from manufacturers and sold them for $58,000. Sonya rents a shop for $5,000 a year and spends $1,000 on utilities and office expenses. Sonya owns a cash register, which she bought for $2,000 with funds from here savings account. Her bank pays 3 percent a year on savings accounts. At the end of the year, Sonya was offered $1,600 for her cash register. Calculate Sonya's explicit costs, implicit costs, and economic profit.

Use the following information to work Problems **3** to **5**.

Yolanda runs a bullfrog farm and when she employed one person, she produced 1,000 bullfrogs a week. When she hired a second worker, her total product doubled. Her total product doubled again when she hired a third worker. When she hired a fourth worker, her total product increased but by only 1,000 bullfrogs. Yolanda pays $1,000 a week for equipment and $500 a week to each worker she hires.

3. Construct Yolanda's marginal product and average product schedules. Over what range of workers do marginal returns increase?
4. Construct Yolanda's total variable cost and total cost schedules. What is Yolanda's total fixed cost?
5. At what output is Yolanda's average total cost at a minimum?
6. Table 1 shows some of the costs incurred at Bill's Bakery. Calculate the values of *A, B, C, D,* and *E*. Show your work.

**TABLE 1**

| *L* | *TP* | *TVC* | *TC* | *AFC* | *AVC* | *ATC* | *MC* |
|---|---|---|---|---|---|---|---|
| 1 | 100 | 350 | 850 | *C* | 3.50 | *D* | |
| | | | | | | | 2.50 |
| 2 | 240 | 700 | *B* | 2.08 | 2.92 | 5.00 | |
| | | | | | | | *E* |
| 3 | 380 | *A* | 1,550 | 1.32 | 2.76 | 4.08 | |
| | | | | | | | 5.83 |
| 4 | 440 | 1,400 | 1,900 | 1.14 | 3.18 | 4.32 | |
| | | | | | | | 11.67 |
| 5 | 470 | 1,750 | 2,250 | 1.06 | 3.72 | 4.79 | |

7. **Grain prices go the way of the oil price**

   Rising crop prices have started to impact the price of breakfast for millions of Americans—cereal prices are rising.

   Source: *The Economist*, July 21, 2007

   Explain how the rising price of grain affects the average total cost and marginal cost of producing breakfast cereals.

Use the following information to work Problems 8 and 9.

**Maryland farmers turn from tobacco to flowers**

Maryland tobacco farmers will be subsidized if they switch from growing tobacco to growing crops such as flowers and organic vegetables.

Source: *The New York Times*, February 25, 2001

8. How does offering farmers a payment to exit tobacco growing influence the opportunity cost of growing tobacco? What is the opportunity cost of using the equipment owned by a tobacco farmer?
9. How would a tobacco farmer decide whether to give up farming rather than grow another crop?

Use the following information to work Problems 10 to 15.

**Airlines seek new ways to save on fuel as costs soar**

Fuel is an airline's biggest single expense. In 2008, the cost of jet fuel rocketed. Airlines tried to switch to newer generation aircraft, which have more fuel-efficient engines.

Source: *The New York Times*, June 11, 2008

10. Is the price of fuel a fixed cost or a variable cost for an airline?
11. Explain how an increase in the price of fuel changes an airline's total costs, average costs, and marginal cost.
12. Explain how a technological advance that makes airplane engines more fuel efficient changes an airline's total product, marginal product, and average product.
13. Draw a graph to illustrate the effects of more fuel-efficient aircraft on an airline's *MP* and *AP* curves.
14. Explain how a technological advance that makes an airplane engine more fuel efficient changes an airline's average variable cost, marginal cost, and average total cost.
15. Draw a graph to illustrate how a technological advance that makes an airplane engine more fuel efficient changes an airline's *MC* and *ATC* curves.

Use the following information to work Problems 16 and 17.

**Gap will focus on smaller scale stores`**

Gap has too many stores of 12,500 square feet. The target store size is 6,000 square feet to 10,000 square feet, so Gap plans to combine previously separate concept stores. Some Gap Body, Gap Adult, Gap Maternity, babyGap and Gap Kids stores will be combined in one store.

Source: CNN, June 10, 2008

16. Thinking of a Gap store as a production plant, explain why Gap is making a decision to reduce the size of their stores. Is Gap's decision a long-run decision or a short-run decision?
17. How might combining Gap's concept stores into one store help better take advantage of economies of scale?

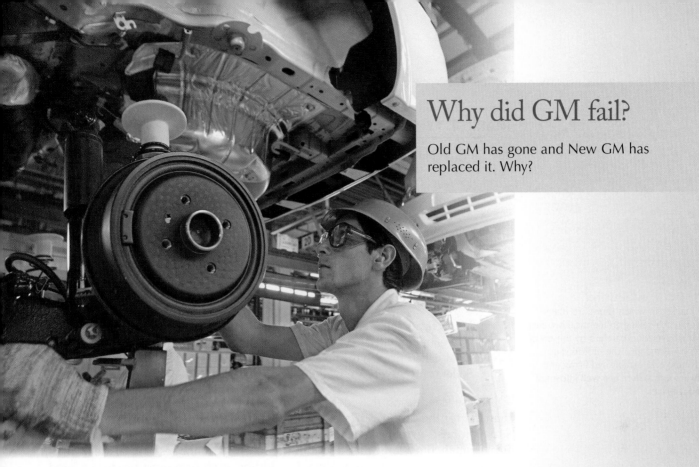

## Why did GM fail?

Old GM has gone and New GM has replaced it. Why?

# Perfect Competition

CHAPTER CHECKLIST

**When you have completed your study of this chapter, you will be able to**

1. Explain a perfectly competitive firm's profit-maximizing choices and derive its supply curve.
2. Explain how output, price, and profit are determined in the short run.
3. Explain how output, price, and profit are determined in the long run and explain why perfect competition is efficient.

## MARKET TYPES

The four market types are

- Perfect competition
- Monopoly
- Monopolistic competition
- Oligopoly

### Perfect Competition

**Perfect competition**
A market in which there are many firms, each selling an identical product; many buyers; no barriers to the entry of new firms into the industry; no advantage to established firms; and buyers and sellers are well informed about prices.

**Perfect competition** exists when

- Many firms sell an identical product to many buyers.
- There are no barriers to entry into (or exit from) the market.
- Established firms have no advantage over new firms.
- Sellers and buyers are well informed about prices.

These conditions that define perfect competition arise when the market demand for the product is large relative to the output of a single producer. This situation arises when economies of scale are absent so the efficient scale of each firm is small. But a large market and the absence of economies of scale are not sufficient to create perfect competition. In addition, each firm must produce a good or service that has no characteristics that are unique to that firm so that consumers don't care from which firm they buy. Firms in perfect competition all look the same to the buyer.

Wheat farming, fishing, wood pulping and paper milling, the manufacture of paper cups and plastic shopping bags, lawn service, dry cleaning, and the provision of laundry services are all examples of highly competitive industries.

### Other Market Types

**Monopoly**
A market in which one firm sells a good or service that has no close substitutes and a barrier blocks the entry of new firms.

**Monopolistic competition**
A market in which a large number of firms compete by making similar but slightly different products.

**Oligopoly**
A market in which a small number of interdependent firms compete.

**Monopoly** arises when one firm sells a good or service that has no close substitutes and a barrier blocks the entry of new firms. In some places, the phone, gas, electricity, and water suppliers are local monopolies—monopolies that are restricted to a given location. For many years, a global firm called DeBeers had a near international monopoly in diamonds. Microsoft has a near monopoly in producing the operating system for a personal computer.

**Monopolistic competition** arises when a large number of firms compete by making similar but slightly different products. Each firm is the sole producer of the particular version of the good in question. For example, in the market for running shoes, Nike, Reebok, Fila, Asics, New Balance, and many others make their own versions of the perfect shoe. The term "monopolistic competition" reminds us that each firm has a monopoly on a particular brand of shoe but the firms compete with each other.

**Oligopoly** arises when a small number of *interdependent* firms compete. Airplane manufacture is an example of oligopoly. Oligopolies might produce almost identical products, such as Duracell and Energizer batteries; or they might produce differentiated products, such as the colas produced by Coke and Pepsi.

We study perfect competition in this chapter, monopoly in Chapter 15, monopolistic competition in Chapter 16, and oligopoly in Chapter 17.

## 14.1 A FIRM'S PROFIT-MAXIMIZING CHOICES

A firm's objective is to maximize *economic profit,* which is equal to *total revenue* minus the *total cost* of production. *Normal profit,* the return that the firm's entrepreneur can obtain in the best alternative business, is part of the firm's cost.

In the short run, a firm achieves its objective by deciding the quantity to produce. This quantity influences the firm's total revenue, total cost, and economic profit. In the long run, a firm achieves its objective by deciding whether to enter or exit a market.

These are the key decisions that a firm in perfect competition makes. Such a firm does *not* choose the price at which to sell its output. The firm in perfect competition is a **price taker**—it cannot influence the price of its product.

**Price taker**
A firm that cannot influence the price of the good or service that it produces.

### Price Taker

To see why a firm in perfect competition is a price taker, imagine that you are a wheat farmer in Kansas. You have a thousand acres under cultivation—which sounds like a lot. But then you go on a drive through Colorado, Oklahoma, Texas, and back up to Nebraska and the Dakotas. You find unbroken stretches of wheat covering millions of acres. And you know that there are similar vistas in Canada, Argentina, Australia, and Ukraine. Your thousand acres are a drop in the ocean. Nothing makes your wheat any better than any other farmer's, and all the buyers of wheat know the price they must pay. If the going price of wheat is $4 a bushel, you are stuck with that price. You can't get a higher price than $4, and you have no incentive to offer it for less than $4 because you can sell your entire output at that price.

*Wheat farmers and maple syrup farmers are price takers.*

The producers of most agricultural products are price takers. We'll illustrate perfect competition with another agriculture example: the market for maple syrup. The next time you pour syrup on your pancakes, think about the competitive market that gets this product from the sap of the maple tree to your table!

Dave's Maple Syrup is one of the more than 11,000 similar firms in the maple syrup market of North America. Dave is a price taker. Like the Kansas wheat farmer, he can sell any quantity he chooses at the going price but none above that price. Dave faces a *perfectly elastic* demand. The demand for Dave's syrup is perfectly elastic because syrup from Don Harlow, Casper Sugar Shack, and all the other maple farms in North America are *perfect substitutes* for Dave's syrup.

We'll explore Dave's decisions and their implications for the way a competitive market works. We begin by defining some revenue concepts.

### Revenue Concepts

In perfect competition, market demand and market supply determine the price. A firm's *total revenue* equals this given price multiplied by the quantity sold. A firm's **marginal revenue** is the change in total revenue that results from a one-unit increase in the quantity sold.

**Marginal revenue**
The change in total revenue that results from a one-unit increase in the quantity sold.

**In perfect competition, marginal revenue equals price.**

The reason is that the firm can sell any quantity it chooses at the going market price. So if the firm sells one more unit, it sells it for the market price and total revenue increases by that amount. This increase in total revenue is marginal revenue.

The table in Figure 14.1 illustrates the equality of marginal revenue and price. The price of syrup is $8 a can. Total revenue is equal to the price multiplied by the quantity sold. So if Dave sells 10 cans, his total revenue is 10 × \$8 = \$80. If the quantity sold increases from 10 cans to 11 cans, total revenue increases from \$80 to \$88, so marginal revenue is \$8 a can, the same as the price.

Figure 14.1 illustrates price determination and revenue in the perfectly competitive market. Market demand and market supply in part (a) determine the market price. Dave is a price taker, so he sells his syrup for the market price. The demand curve for Dave's syrup is the horizontal line at the market price in part (b). Because price equals marginal revenue, the demand curve for Dave's syrup is Dave's marginal revenue curve (*MR*). The total revenue curve (*TR*), in part (c), shows the total revenue at each quantity sold. Because he sells each can for the market price, the total revenue curve is an upward-sloping straight line.

## Profit-Maximizing Output

As output increases, total revenue increases, but total cost also increases. Because of *decreasing marginal returns* (see pp. 326–328), total cost eventually increases faster than total revenue. There is one output level that maximizes economic profit, and a perfectly competitive firm chooses this output level.

**FIGURE 14.1**

Demand, Price, and Revenue in Perfect Competition

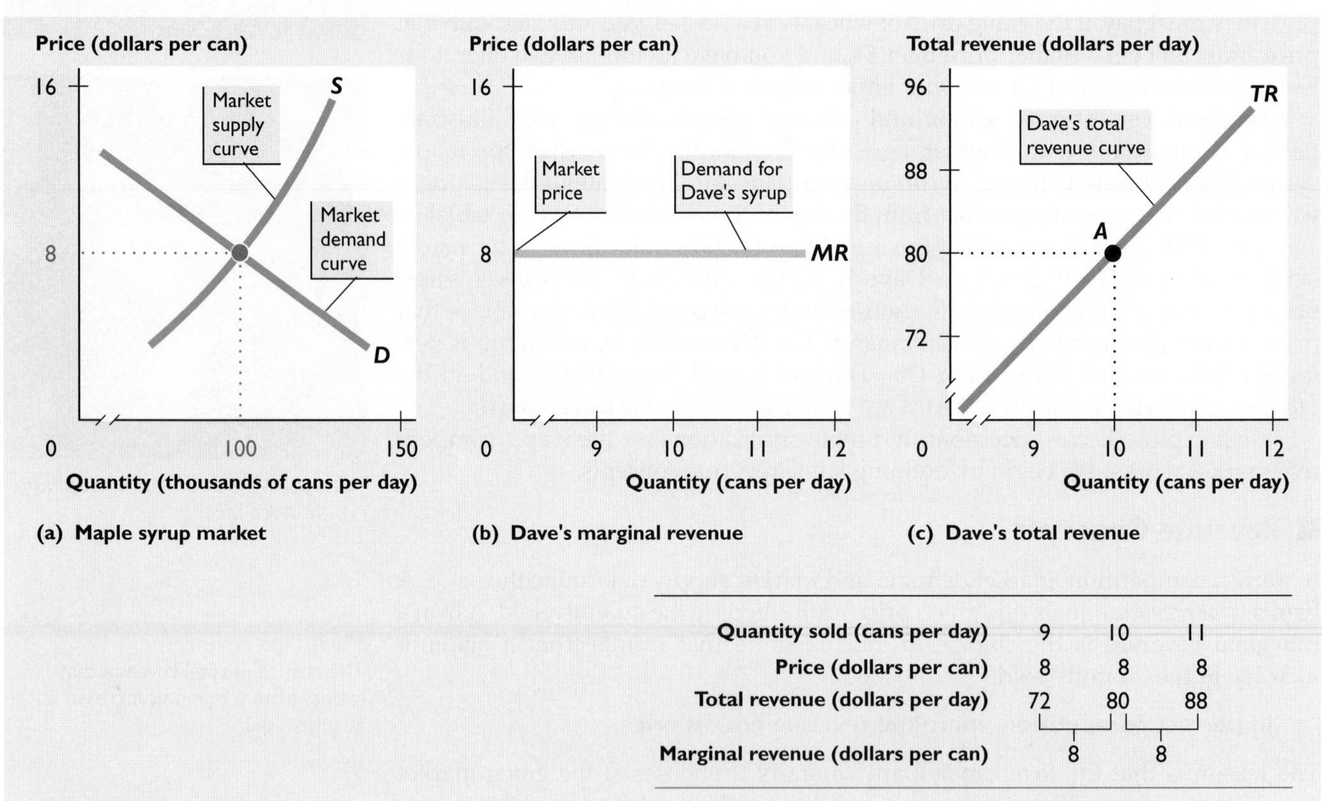


| Quantity sold (cans per day) | 9 | 10 | 11 |
|---|---|---|---|
| Price (dollars per can) | 8 | 8 | 8 |
| Total revenue (dollars per day) | 72 | 80 | 88 |
| Marginal revenue (dollars per can) | 8 | | 8 |

Part (a) shows the market for maple syrup. The market price is \$8 a can. The table calculates total revenue and marginal revenue.

Part (b) shows the demand curve for Dave's syrup, which is Dave's marginal revenue curve (*MR*).

Part (c) shows Dave's total revenue curve (*TR*). Point *A* corresponds to the second column of the table.

One way to find the profit-maximizing output is to use a firm's total revenue and total cost curves. Profit is maximized at the output level at which total revenue exceeds total cost by the largest amount. Figure 14.2 shows how to do this for Dave's Maple Syrup.

The table lists Dave's total revenue, total cost, and economic profit at different output levels. Figure 14.2(a) shows the total revenue and total cost curves. These curves are graphs of the numbers shown in the first three columns of the table. The total revenue curve (*TR*) is the same as that in Figure 14.1(c). The total cost curve (*TC*) is similar to the one that you met in Chapter 13 (p. 332). Figure 14.2(b) is an economic profit curve.

Dave makes an economic profit on outputs between 4 and 13 cans a day. At outputs of fewer than 4 cans a day and more than 13 cans a day, he incurs an economic loss. Outputs of 4 cans and 13 cans are *break-even points*—points at which total cost equals total revenue and economic profit is zero.

The profit curve is at its highest when the vertical distance between the *TR* and *TC* curves is greatest. In this example, profit maximization occurs at an output of 10 cans a day. At this output, Dave's economic profit is $29 a day.

**FIGURE 14.2**

Total Revenue, Total Cost, and Economic Profit

myeconlab Animation

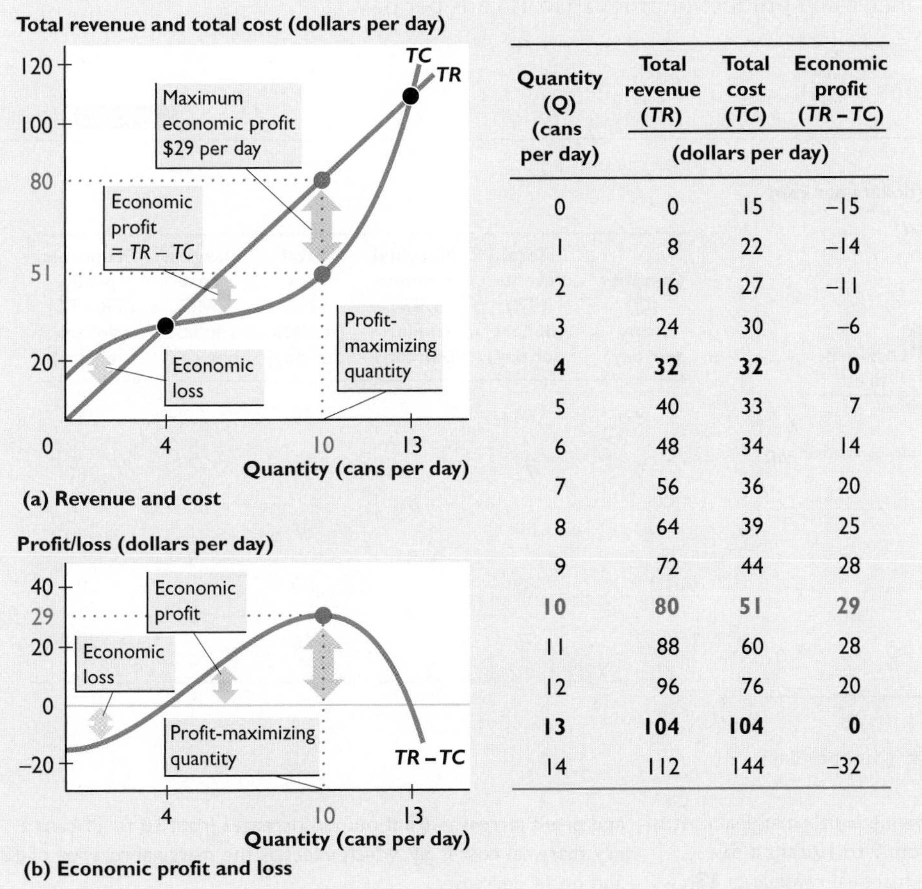


| Quantity (Q) (cans per day) | Total revenue (TR) | Total cost (TC) | Economic profit (TR – TC) |
|---|---|---|---|
| | (dollars per day) | | |
| 0 | 0 | 15 | –15 |
| 1 | 8 | 22 | –14 |
| 2 | 16 | 27 | –11 |
| 3 | 24 | 30 | -6 |
| **4** | **32** | **32** | **0** |
| 5 | 40 | 33 | 7 |
| 6 | 48 | 34 | 14 |
| 7 | 56 | 36 | 20 |
| 8 | 64 | 39 | 25 |
| 9 | 72 | 44 | 28 |
| **10** | **80** | **51** | **29** |
| 11 | 88 | 60 | 28 |
| 12 | 96 | 76 | 20 |
| **13** | **104** | **104** | **0** |
| 14 | 112 | 144 | –32 |

In part (a), economic profit is the vertical distance between the total cost and total revenue curves. Dave's maximum economic profit is $29 a day ($80 – $51) when output is 10 cans a day.

In part (b), economic profit is the height of the profit curve.

## Marginal Analysis and the Supply Decision

Another way to find the profit-maximizing output is to use *marginal analysis*, which compares marginal revenue, *MR*, with marginal cost, *MC*. As output increases, marginal revenue is constant but marginal cost eventually increases.

If marginal revenue exceeds marginal cost ($MR > MC$), then the revenue from selling one more unit exceeds the cost of producing that unit and an *increase* in output increases economic profit. If marginal revenue is less than marginal cost ($MR < MC$), then the revenue from selling one more unit is less than the cost of producing that unit and a *decrease* in output increases economic profit. If marginal revenue equals marginal cost ($MR = MC$), then the revenue from selling one more unit equals the cost incurred to produce that unit. Economic profit is maximized and either an increase or a decrease in output *decreases* economic profit. The rule $MR = MC$ is a prime example of marginal analysis.

Figure 14.3 illustrates these propositions. If Dave increases output from 9 cans to 10 cans a day, marginal revenue ($8) exceeds marginal cost ($7), so by producing the 10th can economic profit increases. The last column of the table shows that economic profit increases from $28 to $29. The blue area in the figure shows the increase in economic profit when production increases from 9 to 10 cans per day.

If Dave increases output from 10 cans to 11 cans a day, marginal revenue ($8) is less than marginal cost ($9), so by producing the 11th can, economic profit decreases. The last column of the table shows that economic profit decreases from $29 to $28. The red area in the figure shows the economic loss that arises from increasing production from 10 to 11 cans per day.

**FIGURE 14.3**

Profit-Maximizing Output

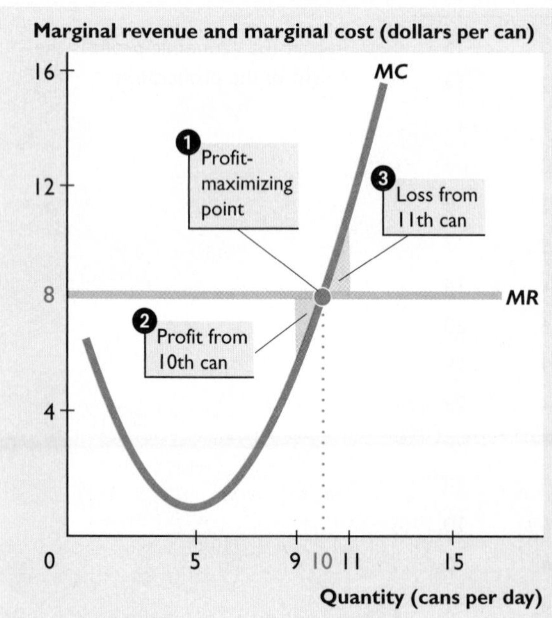


| Quantity (Q) (cans per day) | Total revenue (TR) (dollars per day) | Marginal revenue (MR) (dollars per can) | Total cost (TC) (dollars per day) | Marginal cost (MC) (dollars per can) | Economic profit (TR – TC) (dollars per day) |
|---|---|---|---|---|---|
| 8 | 64 | | 39 | | 25 |
| | | 8 | | 5 | |
| 9 | 72 | | 44 | | 28 |
| | | 8 | | 7 | |
| 10 | 80 | | 51 | | 29 |
| | | 8 | | 9 | |
| 11 | 88 | | 60 | | 28 |
| | | 8 | | 16 | |
| 12 | 96 | | 76 | | 20 |

❶ Profit is maximized when marginal revenue equals marginal cost at 10 cans a day. ❷ If output increases from 9 to 10 cans a day, marginal cost is $7, which is less than the marginal revenue of $8, and profit increases. ❸ If output increases from 10 to 11 cans a day, marginal cost is $9, which exceeds the marginal revenue of $8, and profit decreases.

Dave maximizes economic profit by producing 10 cans a day, the quantity at which marginal revenue equals marginal cost.

A firm's profit-maximizing output is its *quantity supplied*. Dave's *quantity supplied* at a price of $8 a can is 10 cans a day. If the price were higher than $8 a can, he would increase production. If the price were lower than $8 a can, he would decrease production. These profit-maximizing responses to different prices are the foundation of the law of supply:

**Other things remaining the same, the higher the price of a good, the greater is the quantity supplied of that good.**

## Temporary Shutdown Decision

Sometimes, the price falls so low that a firm cannot cover its costs. What does the firm do in such a situation? The answer depends on whether the firm expects the low price to be permanent or temporary.

If a firm incurs an economic loss that it believes is permanent and sees no prospect of ending, the firm exits the market. We'll study this action later in this chapter when we look at the firm's decisions in the long run (pp. 362–368).

If a firm incurs an economic loss that it believes is temporary, it remains in the market, but it might temporarily shut down. To decide whether to produce or to shut down, the firm compares the loss it would incur in the two situations.

### Loss When Shut Down

If the firm shuts down temporarily, it receives no revenue and incurs no variable costs. The firm still incurs fixed costs. So, if a firm shuts down, it incurs an economic loss equal to total fixed cost. This loss is the largest that a firm need incur.

### Loss When Producing

A firm that produces an output receives revenue and incurs both fixed costs and variable costs. The firm incurs an economic loss equal to total fixed cost *plus* total variable cost *minus* total revenue. If total revenue exceeds total variable cost, the firm's economic loss is less than total fixed cost. But if total revenue is less than total variable cost, the firm's economic loss will exceed total fixed cost.

### The Shutdown Point

If total revenue is less than total variable cost, a firm shuts down temporarily and limits its loss to an amount equal to total fixed cost. If total revenue just equals total variable cost, a firm is indifferent between producing and shutting down. This situation arises when price equals minimum average variable cost and the firm produces the quantity at which average variable cost is a minimum—called the **shutdown point.**

**Shutdown point**
The point at which price equals minimum average variable cost and the quantity produced is that at which average variable cost is at its minimum.

Figure 14.4 illustrates the firm's shutdown decision and the shutdown point that we've just described for Dave's maple syrup farm. Dave's average variable cost curve is *AVC* and his marginal cost curve is *MC*. Average variable cost has a minimum of $3 a can when output is 7 cans a day. The *MC* curve intersects the *AVC* curve at its minimum. (We explained this relationship between a marginal and average value in Chapter 13; see pp. 328–329 and pp. 332–334.) The figure shows the marginal revenue curve *MR* when the price is $3 a can, a *price equal to minimum average variable cost*.

**FIGURE 14.4**

The Shutdown Decision

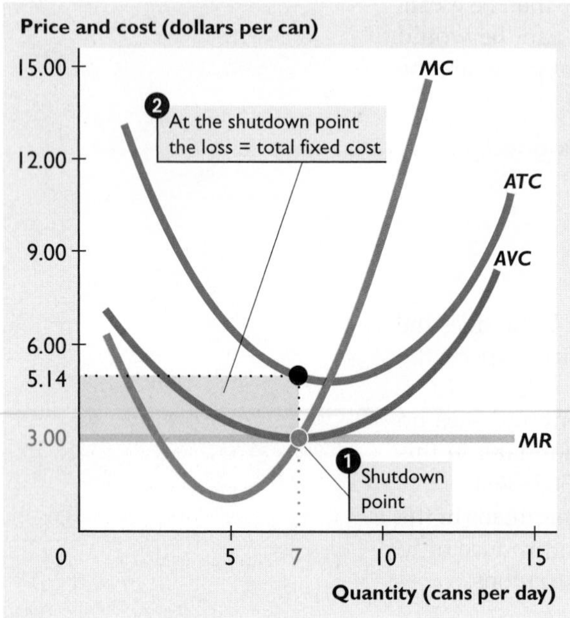


| Quantity (Q) (cans per day) | Total revenue (TR) | Total variable cost (TVC) | Total fixed cost (TFC) | Total cost (TC) | Economic profit (TR – TC) |
|---|---|---|---|---|---|
| | (dollars per day) | | | | |
| 6 | 18 | 19 | 15 | 34 | –16 |
| 7 | 21 | 21 | 15 | 36 | –15 |
| 8 | 24 | 25 | 15 | 40 | –16 |

❶ The shutdown point is at minimum average variable cost. At a price below minimum average variable cost, the firm shuts down and produces no output. At a price equal to minimum average variable cost, the firm is indifferent between shutting down and producing no output or producing the output at minimum average variable cost. Either way, ❷ the firm minimizes its economic loss and incurs a loss equal to total fixed cost.

If Dave produces at the shutdown point, he produces 7 cans a day and sells them for $3 a can. He incurs an economic loss equal to $2.14 a can and a total economic loss of $15 a day, which equals his total fixed cost. If Dave shuts down, he also incurs an economic loss equal to total fixed cost.

The table lists Dave's total revenue, total variable cost, total fixed cost, total cost, and economic profit at three output levels. The middle output, 7 cans a day, is that at which Dave's average variable cost is at its minimum—$3 a can. By examining the numbers in the table, you can see that when the price is $3 a can, Dave incurs a loss equal to total fixed cost by producing 7 cans a day.

## The Firm's Short-Run Supply Curve

A perfectly competitive firm's short-run supply curve shows how the firm's profit-maximizing output varies as the price varies, other things remaining the same. This supply curve is based on the marginal analysis and shutdown decision that we've just explored.

Figure 14.5 derives Dave's supply curve. Part (a) shows the marginal cost and average variable cost curves, and part (b) shows the supply curve. There is a direct link between the marginal cost and average variable cost curves and the firm's supply curve. Let's see what that link is.

In Figure 14.5(a), if the price is above minimum average variable cost, Dave maximizes profit by producing the output at which marginal cost equals marginal revenue, which also equals price. We determine the quantity produced at each price from the marginal cost curve. At a price of $8 a can, the marginal revenue curve is $MR_1$ and Dave maximizes profit by producing 10 cans a day. If the price rises to $12 a can, the marginal revenue curve is $MR_2$ and Dave increases production to 11 cans a day.

If price equals minimum average variable cost, Dave maximizes profit (minimizes loss) by either producing the quantity at the shutdown point or shutting down and producing no output. But if the price is below minimum average variable cost, Dave shuts down and produces no output.

Figure 14.5(b) shows Dave's short-run supply curve. At prices that exceed minimum average variable cost, the supply curve is the same as the marginal cost curve. At prices below minimum average variable cost, Dave shuts down and produces nothing. His supply curve runs along the vertical axis. At a price of $3 a can, Dave is indifferent between shutting down and producing 7 cans a day at the shutdown point ($T$). Either way, he incurs a loss equal to total fixed cost.

So far, we have studied one firm in isolation. We have seen that the firm's profit-maximizing actions depend on the price, which the firm takes as given. In the next section, you'll learn how market supply is determined.

**FIGURE 14.5**

A Perfectly Competitive Firm's Supply Curve

myeconlab Animation

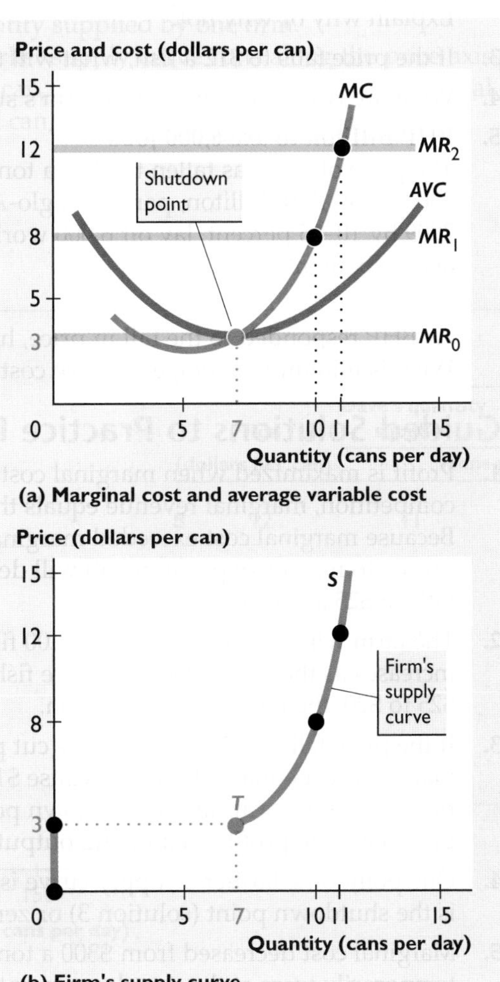


Part (a) shows that at $12 a can, Dave produces 11 cans a day; at $8 a can, he produces 10 cans a day; and at $3 a can, he produces either 7 cans a day or nothing. At any price below $3 a can, Dave produces nothing. The minimum average variable cost is the shutdown point.

Part (b) shows Dave's supply curve. At $3 a can, Dave is indifferent between producing the quantity at the shutdown point $T$ and not producing. At all prices above $3 a can, Dave's supply curve is made up of the marginal cost curve, in part (a), *above* minimum average variable cost. At all prices below $3 a can, Dave produces nothing and his supply curve runs along the vertical axis.

## Short-Run Equilibrium in Bad Times

Figure 14.9 shows the syrup market in a loss-incurring situation. The market demand curve is now $D_3$ The market still has 10,000 firms and their costs are the same as before, so the market supply curve, *S*, is also the same as before.

With the demand and supply curves shown in Figure 14.9(a), the equilibrium price of syrup is $3 a can and the equilibrium quantity is 70,000 cans a day.

Figure 14.9(b) shows the situation that Dave faces. The price is $3 a can, so Dave's marginal revenue is constant at $3 a can. Dave maximizes profit by producing 7 cans a day.

Figure 14.9(b) also shows Dave's average total cost curve (*ATC*), and you can see that when Dave produces 7 cans a day, his average total cost is $5.14 a can. Now the price of $3 a can is less than average total cost by $2.14 a can. This amount is Dave's economic loss per can. If we multiply the economic loss per can of $2.14 by the number of cans, 7 a day, we arrive at Dave's economic loss, which is shown by the red rectangle.

Figure 14.9(b) also shows Dave's average variable cost (*AVC*) curve. Notice that Dave is operating at the shutdown point. Dave might equally well produce no output. Either way, his economic loss would be equal to his total fixed cost. If the price were a bit higher than $3, Dave would still incur an economic loss, but a smaller one. And if the price were lower than $3, Dave would shut down and incur an economic loss equal to total fixed cost.

**FIGURE 14.9**

Economic Loss in the Short Run

myeconlab Animation

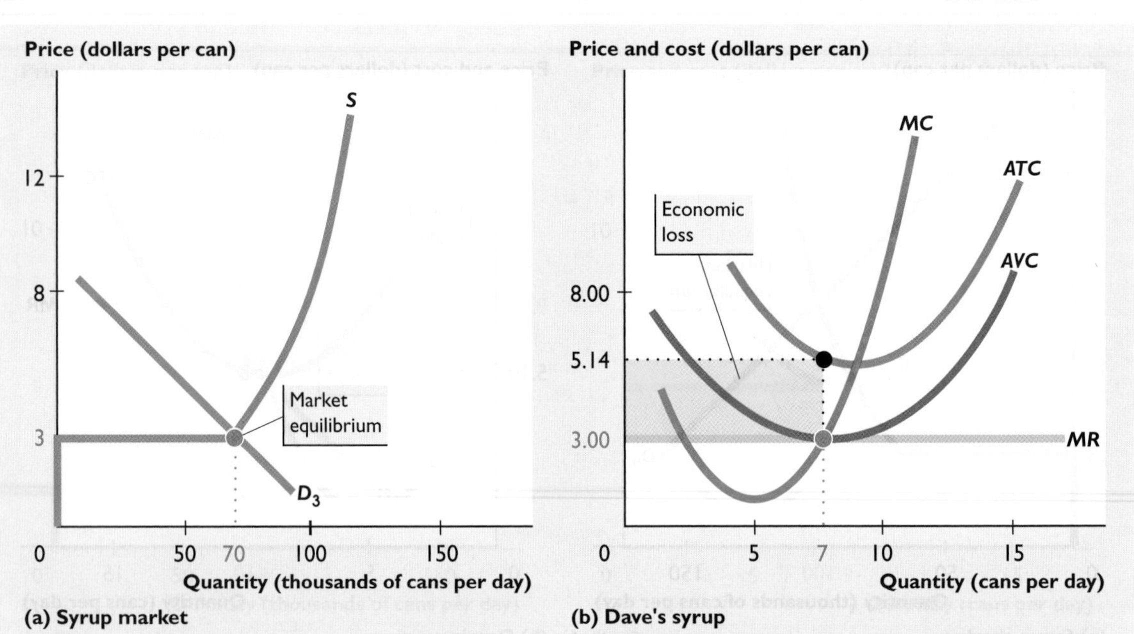


In part (a), with market demand curve $D_3$ and market supply curve S, the equilibrium market price is $3 a can.

In part (b), Dave's marginal revenue is $3 a can, so he produces 7 cans a day. At this quantity, price ($3) is less than average total cost ($5.14), so Dave incurs an economic loss shown by the red rectangle.

# CHECKPOINT 14.2

Work these problems in Study Plan 14.2 to get instant feedback.

**Explain how output, price, and profit are determined in the short run.**

## Practice Problems

Tulip growing is a perfectly competitive industry, and all growers have the same costs. The market price is $25 a bunch, and each grower maximizes profit by producing 2,000 bunches a week. The average total cost of producing tulips is $20 a bunch, and the average variable cost is $15 a bunch. Minimum average variable cost is $12 a bunch. Use this information to work Problems **1** to **3**.

1. What is the economic profit that each grower is making in the short run?
2. What is the price at the grower's shutdown point?
3. What is each grower's economic profit at the shutdown point?
4. **Corn hits record high price**
   Corn prices have surged 80 percent in the past year, driven up by a global rush for grains to feed people and livestock and to make biofuel.
   Source: *USA Today*, June 26, 2008

   Explain why the price of corn surged in the short run. Explain how the farmer's marginal revenue, marginal cost of producing corn, economic profit on a ton of corn, and the farmer's economic profit changed.

## Guided Solutions to Practice Problems

1. The market price ($25) exceeds the average total cost ($20), so growers are making an economic profit of $5 a bunch. Each grower produces 2,000 bunches a week, so each grower's economic profit is $10,000 a week. Figure 1 illustrates the situation. The grower's marginal revenue equals the market price ($25). The grower maximizes profit by producing 2,000 bunches, so at 2,000 bunches the marginal cost curve (*MC*) cuts the marginal revenue curve (*MR*). The average total cost of producing 2,000 bunches is $20, so the *ATC* curve passes through this point. Economic profit equals the area of the blue rectangle.
2. The price at which a grower will shut down temporarily is equal to minimum average variable cost—$12 a bunch (Figure 1).
3. At the shutdown point, the grower incurs an economic loss equal to total fixed cost. *ATC* = *AFC* + *AVC*. Figure 2 shows the data to calculate *TFC*. When 2,000 bunches a week are grown, *ATC* is $20 a bunch and *AVC* is $15 a bunch, so *AFC* is $5 a bunch. Total fixed cost equals $10,000 a week—$5 a bunch × 2,000 bunches a week. At the shutdown point, the grower incurs an economic loss of $10,000 a week.
4. An increase in the market demand for corn increased the market price. The market for corn is competitive, so the farmer's marginal revenue equals the market price. The marginal revenue increased. The farmer maximizes profit by producing the quantity at which marginal revenue equals marginal cost. Because marginal revenue has increased, the farmer increases the quantity produced and moves up along his *MC* curve. The economic profit on a ton of corn (the market price minus the marginal cost of producing it) increases. In the short run, economic profit increases.

**FIGURE 1**

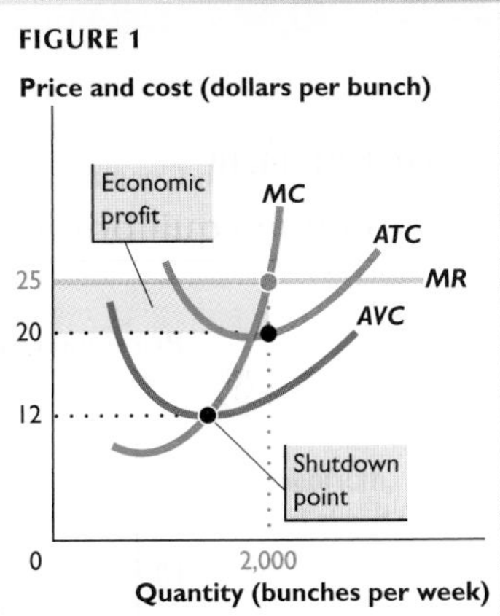


**FIGURE 2**

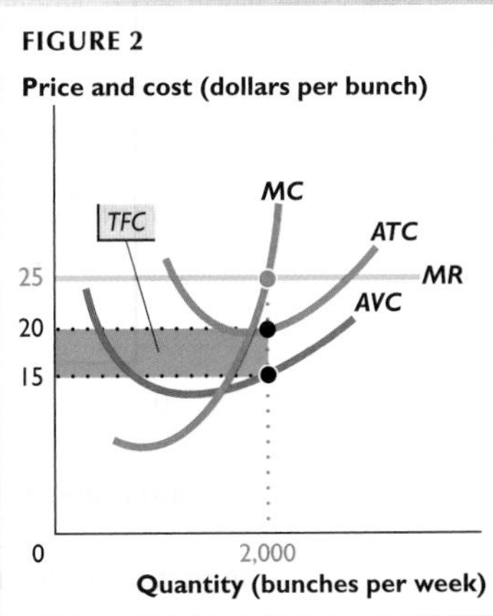

technology until they can no longer cover their average variable cost. Once average variable cost cannot be covered, a firm scraps even a relatively new plant (embodying an old technology) in favor of a plant with a new technology.

New technology lowers cost, so as firms adopt a new technology, their cost curves shift downward. With lower costs, firms are willing to supply a given quantity at a lower price, or, equivalently, they are willing to supply a larger quantity at a given price. In other words, market supply increases, and the market supply curve shifts rightward. With a given demand, the quantity produced increases and the price falls.

Firms that adopt the new technology make an economic profit, so new-technology firms enter. Firms that stick with the old technology incur economic losses, so they either exit or switch to the new technology. As new-technology firms enter and old-technology firms exit, the price falls and the quantity produced increases. Eventually, the market arrives at a long-run equilibrium in

## EYE on the AUTO INDUSTRY

### Why Did GM Fail?

On June 1, 2009, General Motors filed for bankruptcy protection.

#### Old GM

GM Chief Executive Officer Fritz Henderson blames GM's failure on the expansion of global competitors who produce at lower costs.

GM's operating costs are both fixed plant costs and variable labor costs. The firm also has "legacy" costs: fixed costs of honoring its pension obligations to its retirees and its debt obligations to its bond holders.

In 2008, (in round numbers) GM produced 8 million vehicles, received a total revenue of $144 billion, had a total cost of $176 billion, and incurred an economic loss of $32 billion. To remain in business, the firm obtained loans from the U.S. and Canadian governments.

The figure shows the situation that old GM faced in 2008. The average price at which it could sell a vehicle was $18,000. To maximize profit (minimize loss), GM sold 8 million vehicles. Average total cost at 8 million vehicles was $22,000, so the economic loss was $4,000 per vehicle. With no prospect of turning this loss around, old GM had no alternative but to exit the industry.

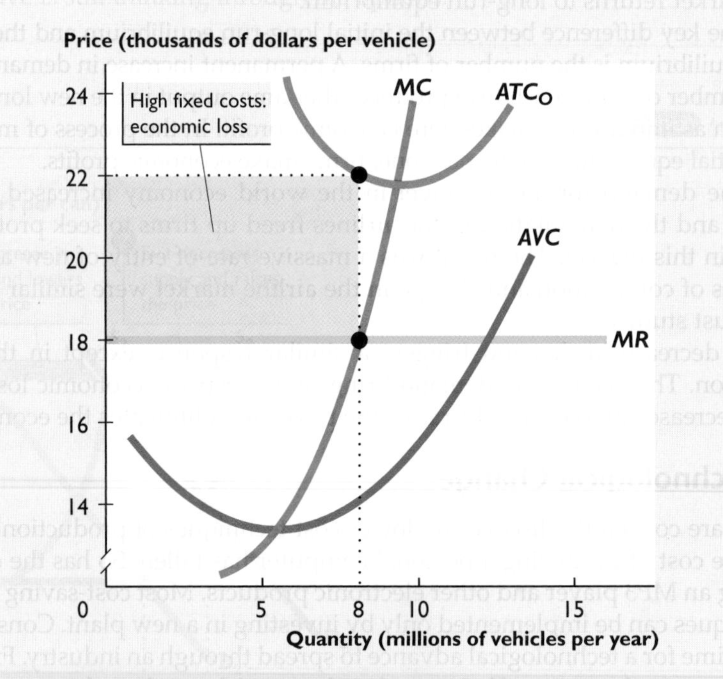


Old GM's Cost and Revenue Curves

which all the firms use the new technology and each firm makes zero economic profit.

Because competition eliminates economic profit in the long run, technological change brings only temporary gains to firms. But the lower prices and better products that technological advances bring are permanent gains for consumers.

The process that we've just described is one in which some firms experience economic profits and others experience economic losses—a period of dynamic change for a market. Some firms do well, and others do badly. Often, the process has a geographical dimension—the expanding new-technology firms bring prosperity to what was once the boondocks, and with old-technology firms going out of business, traditional industrial regions decline. Sometimes, the new-technology firms are in a foreign country, while the old-technology firms are in the domestic economy. The information revolution of the 1990s produced many examples of changes like these. Commercial banking (a competitive but less than perfectly

## New GM

On the day old GM filed for bankruptcy, its executives started to talk about the new GM. The firm's "restructuring" Web site reported plans for cost savings and investment in new green technology vehicles.

Creating a new profitable GM is a complex and detailed task that will require creative thinking and action by its management team. But one feature of the restructuring is crucial: cutting the fixed legacy costs.

Restructuring GM won't change the market price of vehicles—the global market determines that price. Nor is the restructuring likely to have much effect on the marginal cost of producing a vehicle—technology and factor prices determine marginal cost.

Cutting fixed cost is the only point at which the new GM can have a major impact on its profitability.

The figure (right) shows the minimum that the new GM must do: It must cut fixed cost to shift its *ATC* curve downward from $ATC_O$ to $ATC_N$.

GM can then maximize profit at the same quantity, 8 million vehicles a year, but operate with an average total cost equal to the price of a vehicle and so make zero economic profit.

A bigger cut in fixed cost would enable the new GM to make a positive economic profit. But in the long run as new firms enter the global market, economic profit will likely fall to zero.

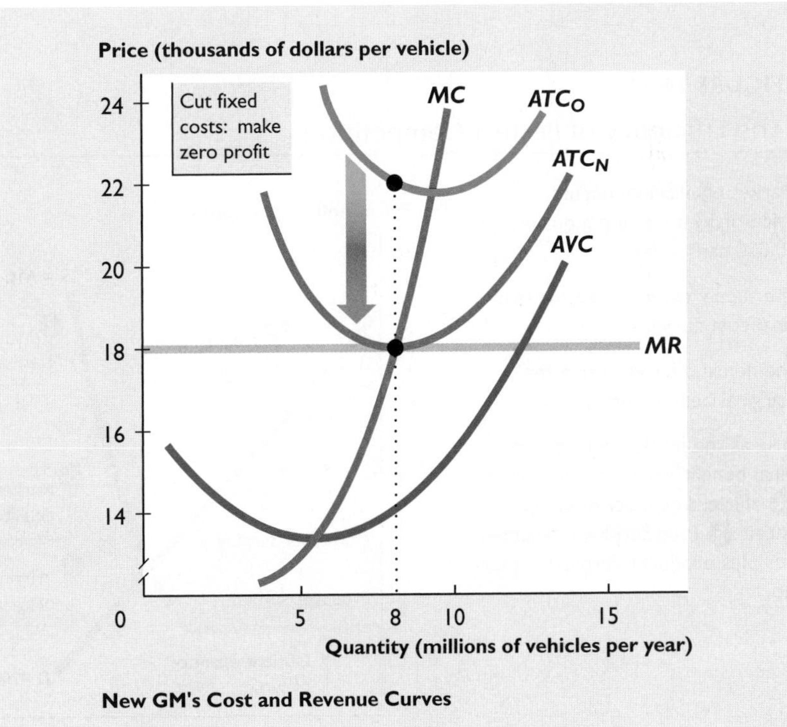


**New GM's Cost and Revenue Curves**

competitive industry), was traditionally concentrated in New York, San Francisco, and other large cities, but now flourishes in Charlotte, North Carolina, which has become the nation's number three commercial banking city. Television shows and movies, traditionally made in Los Angeles and New York, are now made in large numbers in Orlando and Toronto.

Technological advances are not confined to the information and entertainment market. Food production has seen major technological change, and today, genetic engineering is fueling that change.

## Is Perfect Competition Efficient?

Perfect competition is efficient. To see why, first recall the conditions for an efficient allocation of resources. Resources are used efficiently when it is not possible to get more of one good without giving up something that is valued more highly. To achieve this outcome, marginal benefit must equal marginal cost. That is the outcome that perfect competition achieves.

We derive a firm's supply curve in perfect competition from its marginal cost curve. The supply curve is the marginal cost curve at all points above the minimum of average variable cost (the shutdown price). Because the market supply curve is found by summing the quantities supplied by all the firms at each price, the market supply curve is the entire market's marginal cost curve.

The demand curve is the marginal benefit curve. Because the supply curve and demand curve intersect at the equilibrium price, that price equals both marginal cost and marginal benefit.

Figure 14.13 illustrates the efficiency of perfect competition. We've labeled the demand curve $D = MB$ and the supply curve $S = MC$ to remind you that these curves are also the marginal benefit ($MB$) and marginal cost ($MC$) curves.

**FIGURE 14.13**

The Efficiency of Perfect Competition

1 Market equilibrium occurs at a price of $5 a can and a quantity of 90,000 cans a day.

2 The supply curve is also the marginal cost curve.

3 The demand curve is also the marginal benefit curve.

Because at the market equilibrium, marginal benefit equals marginal cost, the 4 efficient quantity of syrup is produced. 5 Total surplus (consumer surplus plus producer surplus) is maximized.

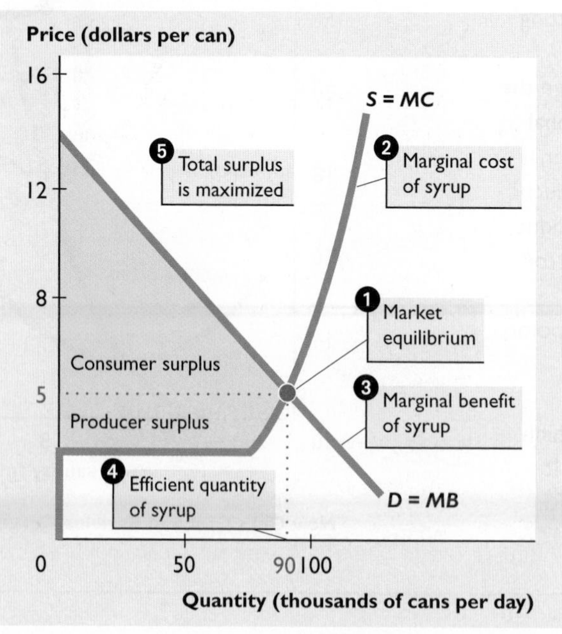

These curves intersect at the equilibrium price and quantity. The price equals marginal benefit and marginal cost, and the equilibrium quantity is efficient. The total surplus, which is the sum of consumer surplus and producer surplus, is maximized. Any departure from this outcome is inferior to it and brings an avoidable deadweight loss.

## ■ Is Perfect Competition Fair?

You studied the fairness of markets in Chapter 6 (pp. 161–163) and saw that there are two concepts of fairness: fair rules and fair outcomes. The rules are fair if property rights are enforced and people acquire resources, goods, and services through voluntary exchange. The outcome is fair if the poorest aren't too poor and the richest aren't too rich, but there is no unique criterion for determining what is too poor or too rich.

In the short run, if a temporary shortage occurs in a competitive market, perhaps caused by bad weather or natural disaster, the price shoots upward. In such situations, some people might make large windfall gains and others, possibly a majority, might be confronted with high prices for essential items. On the fair outcome view, such a situation might be considered unfair.

But perfect competition in the long run seems to be fair on both views of fairness. It places no restrictions on anyone's actions, all trade is voluntary, consumers pay the lowest possible prices, and entrepreneurs earn only normal profit.

## EYE on YOUR LIFE

### The Perfect Competition that You Encounter

Many of the markets that you encounter every day are highly competitive and almost perfectly competitive. And while you don't run into perfect competition on a daily basis, you do have dealings in some perfectly competitive markets. Two of those markets are the Internet auctions organized by eBay and one of its subsidiaries, StubHub.

If you have a ticket for a game between the Giants and the Braves but can't use it, you can sell it on StubHub for the going market price (minus a commission). And if you're desperate to see the game but missed out on getting a ticket, you can buy one for the going price (plus a commission) on the same Web site.

StubHub takes a commission and makes a profit. But competition between StubHub, TicketMaster, and other ticket brokers ensure that profits are competed away in the long run, with entrepreneurs earning normal profit.

Just about every good or service that you buy and take for granted, no matter where you buy it, is available because of the forces of competition. Your home, your food, your clothing, your books, your DVDs, your MP3 files, your computer, your bike, your car, . . . , the list is endless. No one organizes all the magic that enables you to buy this vast array of products. Competitive markets and entrepreneurs striving to make the largest possible profit make it happen.

When either demand or technology changes and makes the current allocation of resources the wrong one, the market swiftly and silently acts. It sends signals to entrepreneurs that bring entry and exit and a new and efficient use of scarce resources.

It is no exaggeration or hype to say that your entire life is influenced by and benefits immeasurably from the forces of competition. Adam Smith's invisible hand might be hidden from view, but it is enormously powerful.

## 15.4 PRICE DISCRIMINATION

*Why does a hairdresser charge seniors $2 less than other customers?*

Price discrimination—selling a good or service at a number of different prices—is widespread. You encounter it when you travel, go to the movies, get your hair cut, buy pizza, or visit an art museum. At first sight, it appears that price discrimination contradicts the assumption of profit maximization. Why would a movie operator allow children to see movies at half price? Why would a hairdresser charge students and senior citizens less? Aren't these firms losing profit by being nice to their customers?

Deeper investigation shows that far from lowering profit, price discriminators make a bigger profit than they would otherwise. So a monopoly has an incentive to find ways of discriminating and charging each buyer the highest possible price. Some people pay less with price discrimination, but others pay more.

Most price discriminators are *not* monopolies, but monopolies do price discriminate when they can. To be able to price discriminate, a firm must

- Identify and separate different types of buyers.
- Sell a product that cannot be resold.

Price discrimination is charging different prices for a single good or service because the willingness to pay varies across buyers. Not all price *differences* are price *discrimination.* Some goods that are similar but not identical have different prices because they have different production costs. For example, the cost of producing electricity depends on time of day. If an electric power company charges a higher price for consumption between 7:00 and 9:00 in the morning and between 4:00 and 7:00 in the evening than it does at other times of the day, the company is not price discriminating.

### Price Discrimination and Consumer Surplus

The key idea behind price discrimination is to convert consumer surplus into economic profit. To extract every dollar of consumer surplus from every buyer, the monopoly would have to offer each individual customer a separate price schedule based on that customer's own willingness to pay. Such price discrimination cannot be carried out in practice because a firm does not have enough information about each consumer's demand curve. But firms try to extract as much consumer surplus as possible, and to do so, they discriminate in two broad ways:

- Among groups of buyers
- Among units of a good

#### Discriminating Among Groups of Buyers

To price discriminate among groups of buyers, the firm offers different prices to different types of buyers, based on things such as age, employment status, or some other easily distinguished characteristic. This type of price discrimination works when each group has a different average willingness to pay for the good or service.

For example, a face-to-face sales meeting with a customer might bring a large and profitable order. For salespeople and other business travelers, the marginal benefit from an airplane trip is large and the price that such a traveler will pay for a trip is high. In contrast, for a vacation traveler, any of several different trips or even no vacation trip are options. So for vacation travelers, the marginal benefit of a trip is small and the price that such a traveler will pay for a trip is low. Because business travelers are willing to pay more than vacation travelers are, it is possible for an airline to profit by price discriminating between these two groups.

### Discriminating Among Units of a Good

To price discriminate among units of a good, the firm charges the same prices to all its customers but offers a lower price per unit for a larger number of units bought. When Pizza Hut charges $10 for one home-delivered pizza and $14 for two, it is using this type of price discrimination. In this example, the price of the second pizza is only $4.

Let's see how an airline exploits the differences in demand by business and vacation travelers and increases its profit by price discriminating.

## Profiting by Price Discriminating

Global Air has a monopoly on an exotic route. Figure 15.8 shows the demand curve (*D*) for travel on this route and Global Air's marginal revenue curve (*MR*). It also shows Global Air's marginal cost (*MC*) and average total cost (*ATC*) curves.

Initially, Global is a single-price monopoly and maximizes its profit by producing 8,000 trips a year (the quantity at which *MR* equals *MC*). The price is $1,200 a trip. The average total cost of a trip is $600, so economic profit is $600 a trip. On 8,000 trips, Global's economic profit is $4.8 million a year, shown by the blue rectangle. Global's customers enjoy a consumer surplus shown by the green triangle.

**FIGURE 15.8**

A Single Price of Air Travel



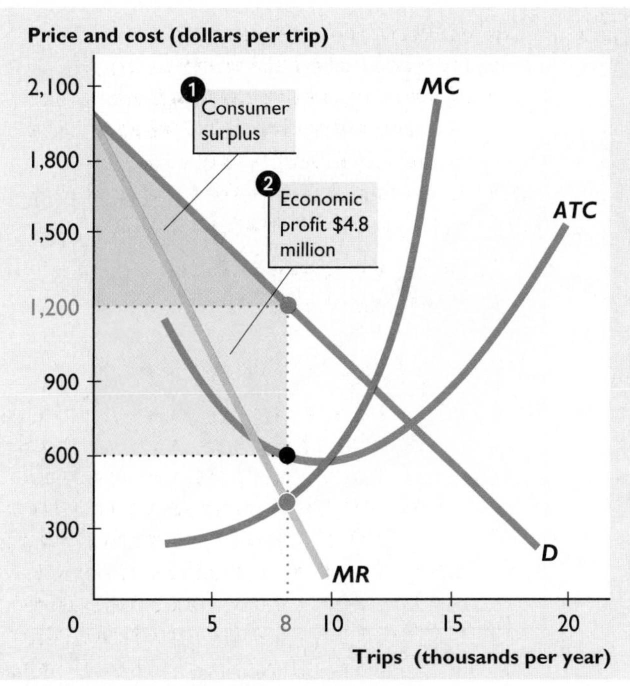


Global Air has a monopoly on an air route. The demand curve for travel on this route is *D*, and Global's marginal revenue curve is *MR*. Its marginal cost curve is *MC*, and its average total cost curve is *ATC*.

As a single-price monopoly, Global maximizes profit by selling 8,000 trips a year at $1,200 a trip. ❶ Global's customers enjoy a consumer surplus—the green triangle—and ❷ Global's economic profit is $4.8 million a year—the blue rectangle.

Global is struck by the fact that many of its customers are business travelers, and Global suspects that they are willing to pay more than $1,200 a trip. So Global does some market research, which tells Global that some business travelers are willing to pay as much as $1,800 a trip. Also, these customers almost always make their travel plans at the last moment. Another group of business travelers is willing to pay $1,600. These customers know a week ahead when they will travel, and they never want to stay over a weekend. Yet another group is willing to pay up to $1,400. These travelers know two weeks ahead when they will travel, and they don't want to stay away over a weekend.

So Global announces a new fare schedule. No restrictions, $1,800; 7-day advance purchase, non-refundable, $1,600; 14-day advance purchase, non-refundable, $1,400; 14-day advance purchase, must stay over weekend, $1,200.

Figure 15.9 shows the outcome with this new fare structure and also shows why Global is pleased with its new fares. It sells 2,000 trips at each of its four prices. Global's economic profit increases by the blue steps in the figure. Its economic profit is now its original $4.8 million a year plus an additional $2.4 million from its new higher fares. Consumer surplus has shrunk to the smaller green area.

## Perfect Price Discrimination

**Perfect price discrimination**
Price discrimination that extracts the entire consumer surplus by charging the highest price that consumers are willing to pay for each unit.

But Global thinks that it can do even better. It plans to achieve **perfect price discrimination**, which extracts the entire consumer surplus by charging the highest price that consumers are willing to pay for each unit. To do so, Global must get creative and come up with a host of additional business fares ranging between $2,000 and $1,200, each one of which appeals to a small segment of the business market.

**FIGURE 15.9**
Price Discrimination

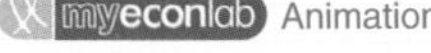


Global revises its fare structure. It now offers no restrictions at $1,800, 7-day advance purchase, non-refundable at $1,600, 14-day advance purchase, non-refundable at $1,400, and 14-day advance purchase, must stay over the weekend, at $1,200.

Global sells 2,000 units at each of its four new fares. Its economic profit increases by $2.4 million a year to $7.2 million a year, which is shown by the original blue rectangle plus the blue steps. Global's customers' consumer surplus shrinks to the sum of the green areas.

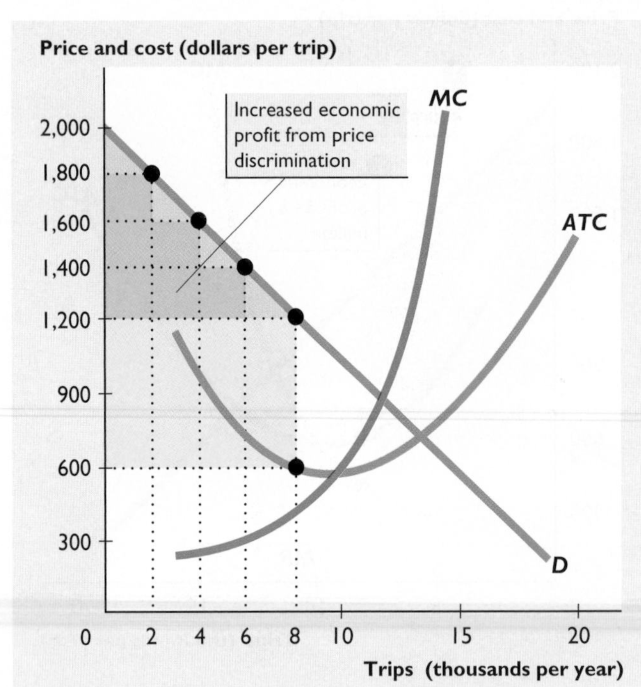

Once Global is discriminating finely between different customers and getting from each customer the maximum he or she is willing to pay, something special happens to marginal revenue. Recall that for the single-price monopoly, marginal revenue is less than price. The reason is that when the price is cut to sell a larger quantity, the price is lower on all units sold. But with perfect price discrimination, Global sells only the marginal seat at the lower price. All the other customers continue to buy for the highest price they are willing to pay. So for the perfect price discriminator, marginal revenue equals price and the demand curve becomes the marginal revenue curve.

With marginal revenue equal to price, Global can obtain yet greater profit by increasing output up to the point at which price (and marginal revenue) is equal to marginal cost.

So Global now seeks additional travelers who will not pay as much as $1,200 a trip but who will pay more than marginal cost. More creative pricing comes up with vacation specials and other fares that have combinations of advance reservation, minimum stay, and other restrictions that make these fares unattractive to Global's existing customers but attractive to a further group of travelers. With all these fares and specials, Global extracts the entire consumer surplus and maximizes economic profit.

Figure 15.10 shows the outcome with perfect price discrimination. The dozens of fares paid by the original travelers who are willing to pay between $1,200 and $2,000 have extracted the entire consumer surplus from this group and converted it into economic profit for Global. The new fares between $900 and $1,200 have attracted 3,000 additional travelers but have taken their entire consumer surplus also. Global is earning an economic profit of more than $9 million a year.

**FIGURE 15.10**

Perfect Price Discrimination

myeconlab Animation

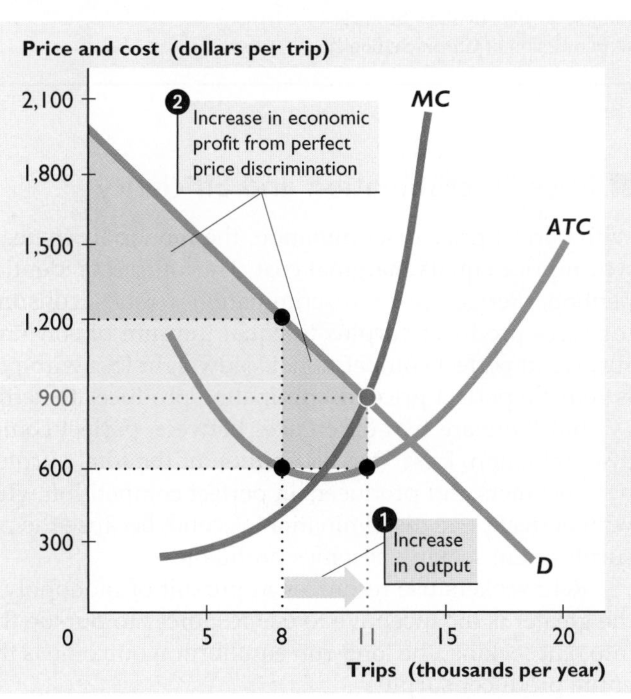


With perfect price discrimination, the demand curve becomes Global's marginal revenue curve. Economic profit is maximized when the lowest price equals marginal cost.

1 Output increases to 11,000 passengers a year, and 2 Global's economic profit increases to $9.35 million a year.

## EYE on the U.S. ECONOMY

### Airline Price Discrimination

The normal coach fare from San Francisco to Washington, D.C., is $670. Book 14 days in advance, and this fare is $290. On a typical flight, passengers might be paying as many as 20 different fares.

The airlines sort their customers according to their willingness to pay by offering a maze of advance-purchase and stayover restrictions that attract price-sensitive leisure travelers but don't get bought by business travelers.

Despite the sophistication of the airlines' pricing schemes, more than 20 percent of seats fly empty. The marginal cost of filling an empty seat is close to zero, so a ticket sold at a few dollars would be profitable.

Extremely low prices are now feasible, thanks to Expedia, Orbitz, and dozens of other online travel agents. Shopping around the airlines with bids from travelers, these online agents broker thousands of tickets a day and obtain the lowest possible fares for their customers.

Would it bother you to hear how little I paid for this flight?

From William Hamilton, "Voodoo Economics," © 1992 by the Chronicle Publishing Company, p. 3. Reprinted with permission of Chronicle Books.

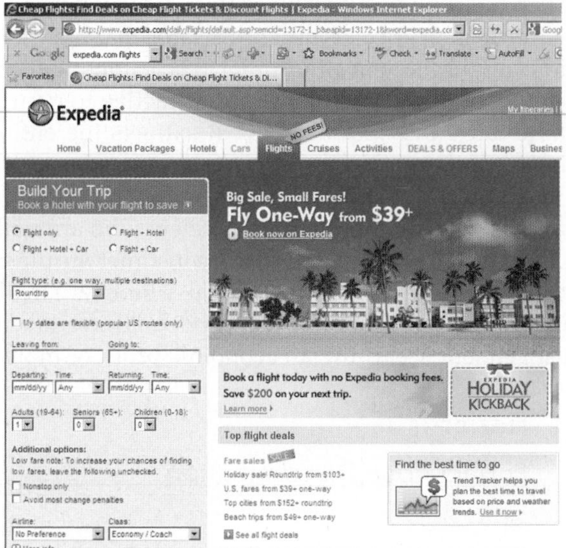


## ■ Price Discrimination and Efficiency

With perfect price discrimination, the monopoly increases output to the point at which price equals marginal cost. This output is identical to that of perfect competition. Perfect price discrimination pushes consumer surplus to zero but increases producer surplus to equal the sum of consumer surplus and producer surplus in perfect competition. Deadweight loss with perfect price discrimination is zero. So perfect price discrimination produces the efficient quantity.

But there are two differences between perfect competition and perfect price discrimination. First, the distribution of the total surplus is different. It is shared by consumers and producers in perfect competition while the producer gets it all with perfect price discrimination. Second, because the producer grabs all the total surplus, rent seeking becomes profitable.

Rent seekers use resources in pursuit of monopoly, and the bigger the rents, the greater is the incentive to use resources to pursue those rents. With free entry into rent seeking, the long-run equilibrium outcome is that rent seekers use up the entire producer surplus.

# CHECKPOINT 15.4

Work these problems in Study Plan 15.4 to get instant feedback.

**Explain how price discrimination increases profit.**

## Practice Problems

Village, a small isolated town, has one doctor. For a 30-minute consultation, the doctor charges a rich person twice as much as a poor person. Use this information to work Problems **1** and **2**.

1. Does the doctor practice price discrimination? Is the doctor using resources efficiently? Does the doctor's pricing scheme redistribute consumer surplus? If so, explain how.
2. If the doctor decided to charge everyone the maximum price that he or she would be willing to pay, what would be the consumer surplus? Would the market for medical service in Village be efficient?
3. **Can movie tickets move hotel rooms?**
   Marriott Hotels will give weekend vacationers (those who stay Thursday through Sunday) four free movie tickets. Tickets for two adults and two kids cost around $35 and even more in pricier cinema cities like New York.
   Source: *USA Today*, June 5, 2009

   Explain how Marriott is price discriminating. If this price discrimination encourages vacationers to stay an additional night, how will the vacationers' consumer surplus change and how will Marriott's producer surplus change?

## Guided Solutions to Practice Problems

1. The doctor practices price discrimination because rich people and poor people pay a different price for the same service: a 30-minute consultation.
   The doctor provides the profit-maximizing number of consultations and charges rich people more than poor people. As a monopoly, the total number of consultations is less than that at which marginal benefit equals the marginal cost of providing the medical service. Because marginal benefit does not equal marginal cost, the doctor is not using resources efficiently.
   With price discrimination, some consumer surplus is redistributed to the doctor as profit.
2. The doctor decides to practice perfect price discrimination. With perfect price discrimination, marginal revenue equals price. To maximize economic profit, the doctor increases the number of consultations to make the lowest price charged equal to the marginal cost of providing the service. The doctor takes the entire consumer surplus, so consumer surplus is zero.
   Marginal benefit equals price, so resources are being used efficiently.
3. Marriott's offer of free movie tickets price discriminates between vacationers who stay two nights and those who stay a third night. The price of the third night is equal to the price of a regular night minus the value of the movie tickets. If the free movie tickets increase the number of vacationers who stay an extra night, consumer surplus increases if the marginal benefit of the extra night exceeds the price (regular price minus value of tickets). But if the marginal benefit equals the price, consumer surplus doesn't change.
   Producer surplus increases if the marginal cost of an extra night is less than the regular price minus the cost to Marriott of the movie tickets. Marriott would not make this offer if it did not expect producer surplus (and economic profit) to increase.

## 15.5 MONOPOLY REGULATION

Natural monopoly presents a dilemma. With economies of scale, a natural monopoly produces at the lowest possible cost. But with market power, the monopoly has an incentive to raise the price above the competitive price and produce too little—to operate in the self-interest of the monopoly and not in the social interest.

**Regulation**
Rules administered by a government agency to influence prices, quantities, entry, and other aspects of economic activity in a firm or industry.

**Regulation**—rules administered by a government agency to influence prices, quantities, entry, and other aspects of economic activity in a firm or industry—is a possible solution to this dilemma.

To implement regulation, the government establishes agencies to oversee and enforce the rules. For example, the Surface Transportation Board regulates prices on interstate railroads and some trucking and bus lines, and water and oil pipelines. By the 1970s, almost a quarter of the nation's output was produced by regulated industries (far more than just natural monopolies) and a process of deregulation began.

**Deregulation**
The process of removing regulation of prices, quantities, entry, and other aspects of economic activity in a firm or industry.

**Deregulation** is the process of removing regulation of prices, quantities, entry, and other aspects of economic activity in a firm or industry. During the past 30 years, deregulation has occurred in domestic air transportation, telephone service, interstate trucking, and banking and financial services. Cable TV was deregulated in 1984, re-regulated in 1992, and deregulated again in 1996.

Regulation is a *possible* solution to the dilemma presented by natural monopoly but not a sure bet solution. There are two theories about how regulation actually works: the *social interest theory* and the *capture theory*.

**Social interest theory**
The theory that regulation achieves an efficient allocation of resources.

**Capture theory**
The theory that the regulation serves the self-interest of the producer and results in maximum profit, underproduction, and deadweight loss.

The **social interest theory** is that the political and regulatory process relentlessly seeks out inefficiency and introduces regulation that eliminates deadweight loss and allocates resources efficiently.

The **capture theory** is that the political and regulatory process gets captured by the regulated firm and ends up serving its self-interest, with maximum economic profit, underproduction, and deadweight loss. The regulator gets captured because the producer's gain is large and visible while each individual consumer's is small and invisible. No individual consumer has an incentive to oppose the regulation, but the producer has a big incentive to lobby for it.

Which theory of regulation best explains real-world regulations? Does regulation serve the social interest or the self-interest of monopoly producers?

### Efficient Regulation of a Natural Monopoly

A cable TV company is a *natural monopoly* (pp. 376–377)—it can supply the entire market at a lower price than two or more competing firms can. Cox Communications, based in Atlanta, supplies cable TV to households in 16 states. It has invested heavily in satellite receiving dishes, cables, and control equipment and so has large fixed costs. These fixed costs are part of the company's average total cost. Its average total cost decreases as the number of households served increases because the fixed cost is spread over a larger number of households. Unregulated, Cox Communications serves the number of households that maximizes profit. Like all single-price monopolies, the profit-maximizing quantity is less than the efficient quantity and underproduction results in a deadweight loss (see Figure 15.6, p. 386).

**Marginal cost pricing rule**
A rule that sets price equal to marginal cost to achieve an efficient output.

How can Cox be regulated to produce the efficient quantity of cable TV service? The answer is by being regulated to set its price equal to marginal cost, known as the **marginal cost pricing rule**. The quantity demanded at a price equal to marginal cost is the efficient quantity—the quantity at which marginal benefit equals marginal cost.

Figure 15.11 illustrates the marginal cost pricing rule. The demand curve for cable TV is *D*. Cox's marginal cost curve is *MC*. That marginal cost curve is (assumed to be) horizontal at $10 per household per month—that is, the cost of providing each additional household with a month of cable programming is $10. The efficient outcome occurs if the price is regulated at $10 per household per month with 8 million households served.

But there is a problem: Because average total cost exceeds marginal cost, a firm that follows the marginal cost pricing rule incurs an economic loss. So a cable TV company that is required to use a marginal cost pricing rule will not stay in business for long. How can the firm cover its costs and, at the same time, obey a marginal cost pricing rule?

One possibility is price discrimination (see pp. 390–394). Another possibility is to use a two-part price (called a *two-part tariff*). For example, local telephone companies charge consumers a monthly fee for being connected to the telephone system and then charge a price equal to marginal cost (zero) for each local call. A cable TV operator can charge a one-time connection fee that covers its fixed cost and then charge a monthly fee equal to marginal cost.

## Second-Best Regulation of a Natural Monopoly

A natural monopoly cannot always be regulated to achieve an efficient outcome. Two possible ways of enabling a regulated monopoly to avoid an economic loss are

- Average cost pricing
- Government subsidy

**FIGURE 15.11**

Natural Monopoly: Marginal Cost Pricing

The market demand curve for cable TV is *D*. A cable TV operator's marginal cost *MC* is a constant $10 per household per month. Its fixed cost is large, and the average total cost curve, which includes average fixed cost, is *ATC*.

❶ Price is set equal to marginal cost at $10 a month.

At this price, ❷ the efficient quantity (8 million households) is served.

❸ Consumer surplus is maximized as shown by the green triangle.

❹ The firm incurs a loss on each household served, shown by the red arrow.

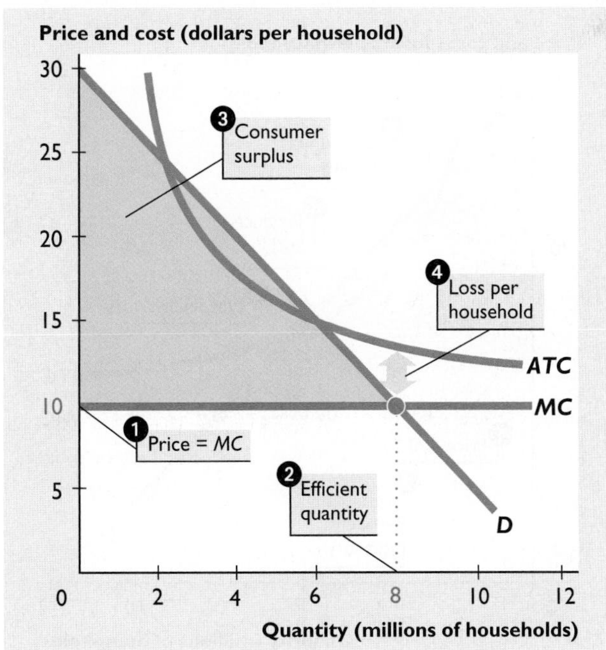

## Average Cost Pricing

**Average cost pricing rule**
A rule that sets price equal to average total cost to enable a regulated firm to avoid economic loss.

The **average cost pricing rule** sets price equal to average total cost. With this rule the firm produces the quantity at which the average total cost curve cuts the demand curve. This rule results in the firm making zero economic profit—breaking even. But because for a natural monopoly average total cost exceeds marginal cost, the quantity produced is less than the efficient quantity and a deadweight loss arises. Figure 15.12 illustrates the average cost pricing rule. The price is $15 a month and 6 million households get cable TV. The gray triangle shows the deadweight loss.

## Government Subsidy

A government subsidy is a direct payment to the firm equal to its economic loss. But to pay a subsidy, the government must raise the revenue by taxing some other activity. You saw in Chapter 8 that taxes themselves generate deadweight loss.

## And the Second-Best Is ...

Which is the better option, average cost pricing or marginal cost pricing with a government subsidy? The answer turns on the relative magnitudes of the two deadweight losses. Average cost pricing generates a deadweight loss in the market served by the natural monopoly. A subsidy generates deadweight losses in the markets for the items that are taxed to pay the subsidy. The smaller deadweight loss is the second-best solution to regulating a natural monopoly. Making this calculation in practice is too difficult and average cost pricing is generally preferred to a subsidy.

**FIGURE 15.12**

Natural Monopoly: Average Cost Pricing

myeconlab Animation

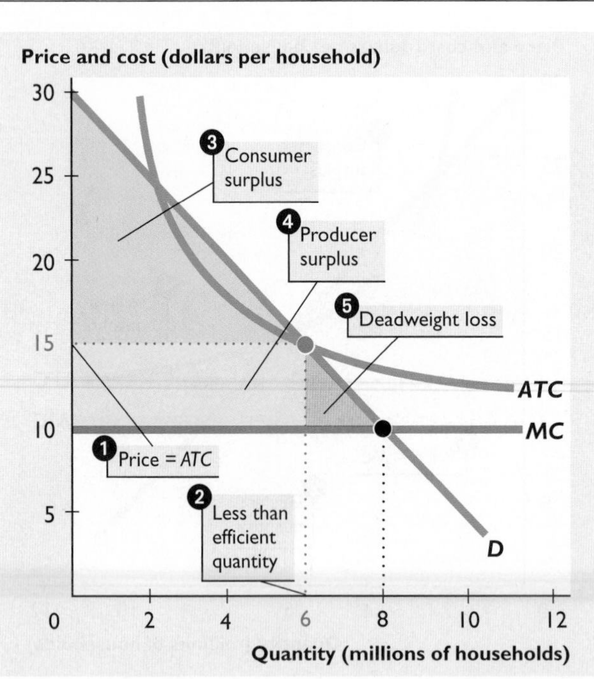


1 Price is set equal to average total cost at $15 a month.

At this price, 2 the quantity served (6 million households) is less than the efficient quantity (8 million households).

3 Consumer surplus shrinks to the smaller green triangle.

4 A producer surplus enables the firm to pay its total fixed cost and break even.

5 A deadweight loss, shown by the gray triangle, arises.

# EYE on MICROSOFT

## Are Microsoft's Prices Too High?

Microsoft's prices are too high in the sense that they exceed marginal cost and result in fewer copies of the Windows operating system and Office application than the efficient quantities.

### Profit Maximization

The figure illustrates how Microsoft prices its products to maximize profit. The demand for copies of the Windows Vista operating system is *D*. The marginal revenue curve is *MR*. The marginal cost of an additional copy of Vista is very small and we assume it to be zero, with marginal cost curve *MC*.

Profit is maximized by producing the quantity at which marginal revenue equals marginal cost. In the figure, that quantity is 4 million copies of Vista per month. The price is $300 per copy and Microsoft receives a producer surplus shown by the blue rectangle.

### Inefficiency

The efficient quantity is 8 million copies per month, where price and marginal benefit equal marginal cost. Because the actual quantity is smaller than the efficient quantity, a deadweight loss arises and the gray triangle shows its magnitude. The green triangle shows the consumer surplus.

### Fixed Cost

The marginal cost of a copy of Windows Vista might be close to zero but the fixed cost of developing the software is large. Microsoft must at least earn enough revenue to pay these fixed costs.

Earning enough to pay the firm's fixed costs does not inevitably lead to inefficiency. Some firms with zero marginal cost and the market power to charge a high price do choose to provide the efficient quantity of their services at a zero price.

### The Google Solution

Google is one such firm. The price of an Internet search on Google is zero. The quantity of searches is that at which the marginal benefit of a search equals the zero marginal cost, so the quantity of searches is the efficient quantity.

Google earns revenue, and a very large revenue, by selling advertising that more than pays its fixed operating costs.

Advertising on Google is more effective than a TV or poster advertisement because it is targeted at potential buyers of products based on the topics of their searches.

This solution is not entirely efficient. It gets the efficient quantity of the zero marginal cost activity. Whether it gets the efficient quantity of advertising is not clear. With no externalities, the profit-maximizing quantity of advertising is less than the efficient quantity. But advertising has a negative externality for many people, and the profit-maximizing quantity might be efficient.

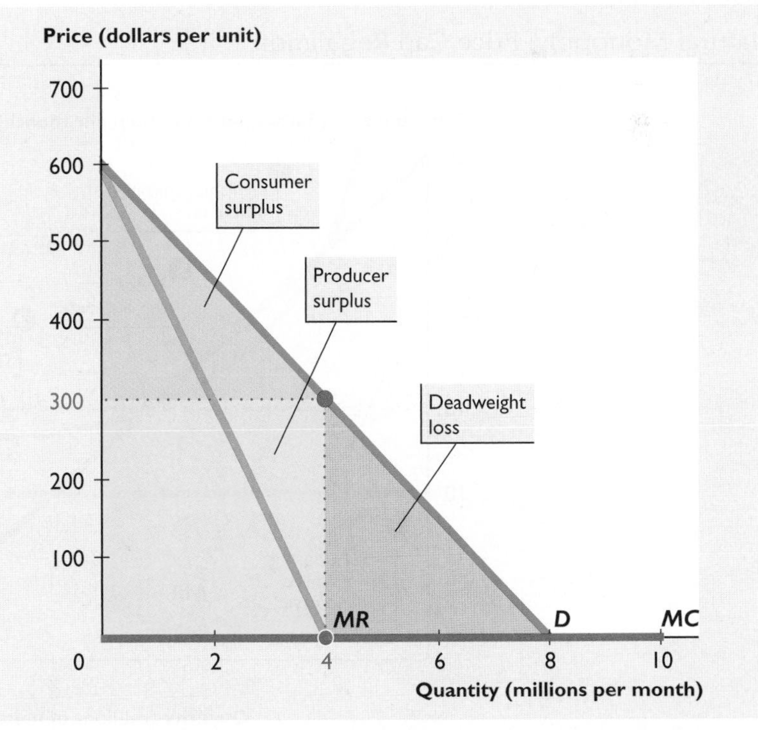

Implementing average cost pricing presents the regulator with a challenge because it is not possible to be sure of a firm's costs. So regulators use one of two practical rules:

- Rate of return regulation
- Price cap regulation

## Rate of Return Regulation

**Rate of return regulation**
A regulation that sets the price at a level that enables a firm to earn a specified target rate of return on its capital.

Under **rate of return regulation**, the price is set at a level that enables the firm to earn a specified target rate of return on its capital. This type of regulation can end up serving the self-interest of the firm rather than the social interest. The firm's managers have an incentive to inflate costs by spending on items such as private jets, free baseball tickets (disguised as public relations expenses), and lavish entertainment. Managers also have an incentive to use more capital than the efficient amount. The *rate* of return on capital is regulated but not the *total* return on capital, and the greater the amount of capital, the greater is the total return.

## Price Cap Regulation

**Price cap regulation**
A rule that specifies the highest price that a firm is permitted to set—a price ceiling.

For the reason that we've just examined, rate of return regulation is increasingly being replaced by price cap regulation. A **price cap regulation** is a price ceiling—a rule that specifies the highest price the firm is permitted to set. This type of regulation lowers the price and gives the firm an incentive to minimize its costs. But what happens to the quantity produced?

Recall that in a competitive market, a price ceiling set below the equilibrium price decreases output and creates a shortage (see Chapter 7, pp. 170–171). In con-

**FIGURE 15.13**
Natural Monopoly: Price Cap Regulation

myeconlab Animation

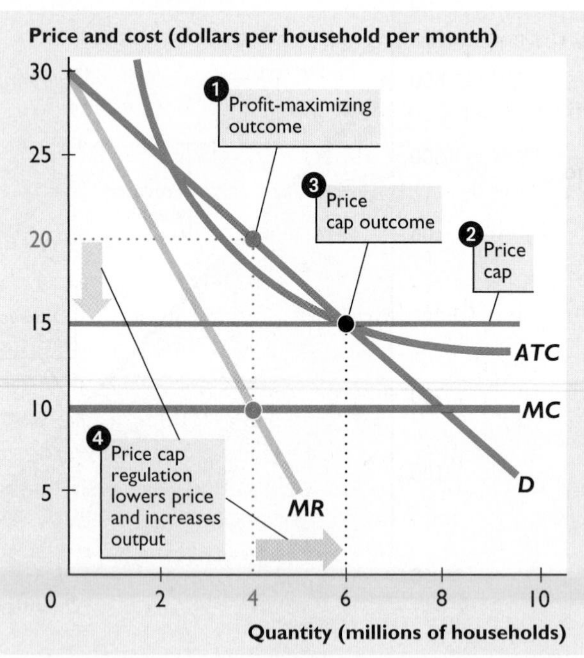


1 With no regulation, a cable TV operator serves 4 million households at a price of $20 a month.

2 A price cap regulation sets the maximum price at $15 a month.

3 Only when 6 million households are served can the firm break even. (When fewer than 6 million households are served or more than 6 million households are served, the firm incurs an economic loss.) The firm has an incentive to keep costs as low as possible and to produce the quantity demanded at the price cap.

4 The price cap regulation lowers the price and increases the quantity.

trast, in natural monopoly a price ceiling increases output. The reason is that at the regulated price, the firm can sell any quantity it chooses up to the quantity demanded. So each additional unit sold brings in the same additional revenue: marginal revenue equals price. The regulated price exceeds marginal cost, so the profit-maximizing quantity becomes the quantity demanded at the price ceiling.

Figure 15.13 illustrates this outcome. Unregulated, a cable TV operator maximizes profit by serving 4 million households at a price of $20 a month. With a price cap set at $15 a month, the firm is permitted to sell any quantity it chooses at that price or at a lower price. The profit-maximizing quantity now increases to 6 million households. Serving fewer than 6 million households, the firm incurs a loss—average total cost exceeds the price cap. Serving more than 6 million households is possible but only by lowering the price along the demand curve. Again, average total cost exceeds price and the firm incurs a loss.

In Figure 15.13, the price cap delivers average cost pricing. In practice, the regulator might set the cap too high. For this reason, price cap regulation is often combined with **earnings sharing regulation**—a regulation that requires firms to make refunds to customers when profits rise above a target level.

**Earnings sharing regulation**
A regulation that requires firms to make refunds to customers when profits rise above a target level.

## EYE on YOUR LIFE

### Monopoly in Your Everyday Life

When Bill Gates decided to quit Harvard in 1975, he realized that PCs would need an operating system and applications programs to interact with the computer's hardware. He also knew that whoever owned the copyright on these programs would have a license to print money. And he wanted to be that person.

In less than 30 years, Bill Gates became the world's richest person. Such is the power of the right monopoly.

You, along with millions of other PC users, have willingly paid the monopoly price for Windows and Microsoft Office. Sure, the marginal cost of a copy of these programs is close to zero, so the quantity sold is way too few. There is a big deadweight loss.

Compared with the alternative of no Windows, you're better off. But are you better off than you would be if there were many alternatives to Windows competing for your attention? To answer this question, think about the applications—spreadsheets, word processing, and so on—that you need to make your computer useful. With lots of operating systems, what would happen to the cost of developing applications? Would you have more or less choice?

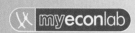

Work these problems in Study Plan 15.5 to get instant feedback.

## CHECKPOINT 15.5

**Explain why natural monopoly is regulated and the effects of regulation.**

### Practice Problems

An unregulated natural monopoly bottles Elixir, a unique health product that has no substitutes. The monopoly's total fixed cost is $150,000, and its marginal cost is 10¢ a bottle. Figure 1 illustrates the demand for Elixir. Use this information to work Problems **1** to **3**.

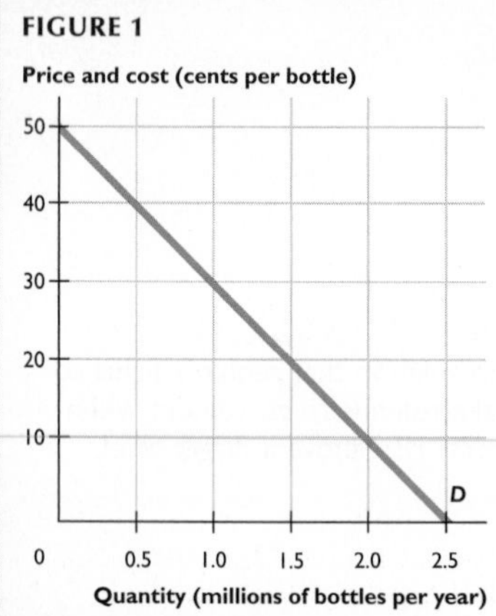


1. How many bottles of Elixir does the monopoly sell and what is the price of a bottle of Elixir? Is the monopoly's use of resources efficient?
2. Suppose that the government introduces a marginal cost pricing rule. What is the price of Elixir, the quantity sold, and the monopoly's economic profit?
3. Suppose that the government introduces an average cost pricing rule. What is the price of Elixir, the quantity sold, and the monopoly's economic profit?
4. **Mexicans protest the plan to end the state oil monopoly**
   Thousands of protesters have demonstrated to fight the plan to open Mexico's state oil monopoly to private investment. In Mexico, the government sets the price, currently $2.48 a gallon, while the U.S. average is $3.37 a gallon. The government taxes the state monopoly's profit 90 percent.
   Source: *USA Today*, April 13, 2008

   Describe how the Mexican government regulates the domestic oil market.

### Guided Solutions to Practice Problems

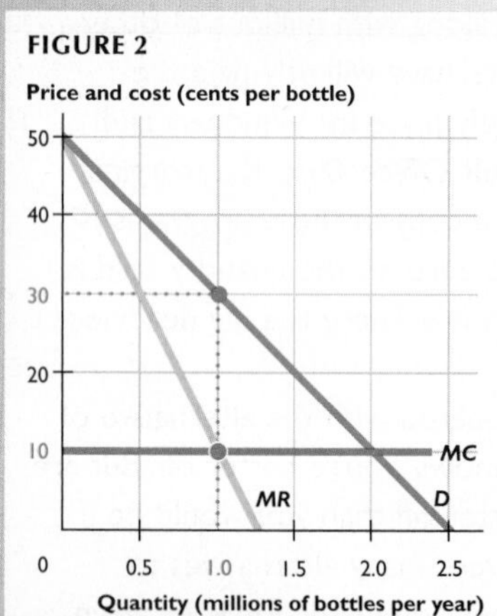


1. The monopoly will produce 1 million bottles a year—the quantity at which marginal revenue equals marginal cost. The price is 30¢ a bottle—the highest price at which the monopoly can sell the 1 million bottles a year (Figure 2). The monopoly's use of resources is inefficient. If resource use were efficient, the monopoly would produce the quantity at which marginal benefit (price) equals marginal cost: 2 million bottles a year.
2. With a marginal cost pricing rule, the price is 10¢ a bottle and the monopoly produces 2 million bottles a year. The monopoly makes an economic loss equal to its total fixed costs of $150,000 a year. The monopoly would need a subsidy from the government to keep it in business.
3. With an average cost pricing rule, the firm produces the quantity at which price equals average total cost. Average total cost equals average variable cost plus average fixed cost. Average variable cost equals marginal cost and is 10¢ a bottle. Average fixed cost is $150,000 divided by the quantity produced. For example, at 1 million bottles, average fixed cost is 15¢ and at 1.5 million bottles, average fixed cost is 10¢ a bottle. The average total cost of producing 1.5 million bottles is 20¢ a bottle and 1.5 million bottles can be sold for 20¢ a bottle. So the monopoly produces 1.5 million bottles a year and breaks even.
4. The price is not set equal to marginal cost (marginal cost pricing) because the oil company does not receive a subsidy. The price is not set equal to average total cost (average cost pricing) because the oil company does not break even. The government operates a price cap regulation and the company pays a profit tax of 90 percent.

# CHAPTER SUMMARY

## Key Points

**1 Explain how monopoly arises and distinguish between single-price monopoly and price-discriminating monopoly.**

- In monopoly, a single producer of a good or service that has no close substitutes operates behind natural, ownership, or legal barriers to entry.
- A monopoly can price discriminate when there is no resale possibility.
- Where resale is possible, a firm charges a single price.

**2 Explain how a single-price monopoly determines its output and price.**

- The demand for a monopoly's output is the market demand, and a single-price monopoly's marginal revenue is less than price.
- A monopoly maximizes profit by producing the quantity at which marginal revenue equals marginal cost and by charging the maximum price that consumers are willing to pay for that quantity.

**3 Compare the performance of a single-price monopoly with that of perfect competition.**

- A single-price monopoly charges a higher price and produces a smaller quantity than does a perfectly competitive market and creates a deadweight loss.
- Monopoly imposes a loss on society that equals its deadweight loss plus the cost of the resources devoted to rent seeking.

**4 Explain how price discrimination increases profit.**

- Perfect price discrimination captures the entire consumer surplus. Prices are the highest that each consumer is willing to pay for each unit.
- With perfect price discrimination, the monopoly is efficient but rent seeking uses some of the producer surplus.

**5 Explain why natural monopoly is regulated and the effects of regulation.**

- Regulation might achieve an efficient use of resources or help the monopoly to maximize economic profit.
- A natural monopoly is efficient if its price equals marginal cost, but a second-best outcome is for price to equal average total cost.
- A price cap supported by earnings sharing regulation is the most effective practical method of regulating a natural monopoly.

## Key Terms

Work these problems in Chapter 15 Study Plan to get instant feedback.

# CHAPTER CHECKPOINT

## Study Plan Problems and Applications

Use the following information to work Problems 1 to 3.

Elixir Spring produces a unique and highly prized mineral water. The firm's total fixed cost is $5,000 a day, and its marginal cost is zero. Table 1 shows the demand schedule for Elixir water.

**TABLE 1**

| Price (dollars per bottle) | Quantity (bottles per day) |
|---|---|
| 10 | 0 |
| 8 | 2,000 |
| 6 | 4,000 |
| 4 | 6,000 |
| 2 | 8,000 |
| 0 | 10,000 |

1. Make a graph of the demand for Elixir water and Elixir Spring's marginal revenue curve. What are Elixir's profit-maximizing price, output, and economic profit?
2. Compare Elixir's profit-maximizing price with the marginal cost of producing the profit-maximizing output. At the profit-maximizing price, is the demand for Elixir water inelastic or elastic?
3. Suppose that there are 1,000 springs, all able to produce this water at zero marginal cost and with zero fixed costs. Compare the equilibrium price and quantity produced with the price and quantity produced by Elixir water.
4. The Blue Rose Company is the only flower grower to have cracked the secret of making a blue rose. Figure 1 shows the demand for blue roses and the marginal cost of producing a blue rose. What is Blue Rose's profit-maximizing output? What price does it charge? Is the Blue Rose Company using its resources efficiently?

**FIGURE 1**

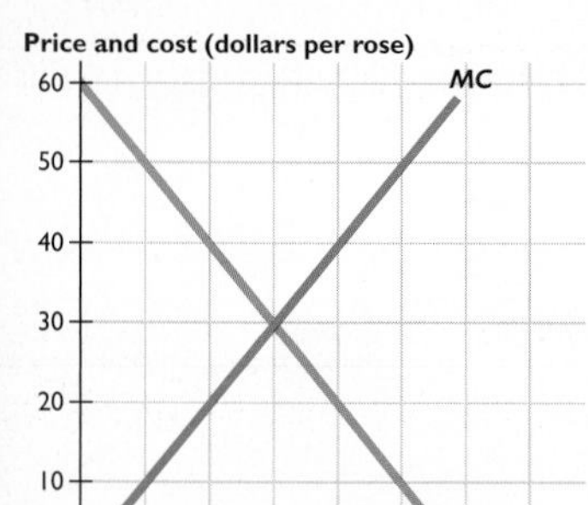


Hawaii Cable Television is a natural monopoly. Sketch a market demand curve, the firm's marginal revenue curve, an average total cost curve, and a marginal cost curve that illustrate Hawaii Cable's situation. Use your graph to work Problems 5 to 7.

5. If Hawaii Cable is unregulated and maximizes profit, show in your graph the price, quantity, economic profit, consumer surplus, and deadweight loss.
6. If Hawaii Cable is regulated in the social interest, show in your graph the price, quantity, economic profit, consumer surplus, and deadweight loss.
7. If Hawaii Cable is subject to a price cap regulation that enables it to break even, show in your graph the price, quantity, economic profit, consumer surplus, and deadweight loss.

Use the following information to work Problems 8 and 9.

**FCC planning rules to open cable market**

The Federal Communications Commission (FCC) will make it easier for independent programmers and rival video services to lease access to cable channels. The FCC will also limit the market share of a cable company to 30 percent.

Source: *The New York Times*, November 10, 2007

8. What barriers to entry exist in the cable television market? Are high cable prices evidence of monopoly power?
9. Draw a graph to illustrate the effects of the FCC's new regulations on the price, quantity, consumer surplus, producer surplus, and deadweight loss.

## Instructor Assignable Problems and Applications

Your instructor can assign these problems as homework, a quiz, or a test in **MyEconLab**.

Use the following information to work Problems 1 and 2.

**Microsoft: We're not gouging Europe on Windows 7 pricing**

Regulators in the European Union have charged Microsoft with illegally tying Internet Explorer (IE) to Windows and mandated that a version of Windows be offered stripped of IE. A news report suggested that when Microsoft launches Windows 7, it will charge a higher price for the IE-stripped version than the price for a full version that includes IE. Microsoft denied this report but announced that it would offer the full version for the upgrade price.

Source: computerworld.com

1. How does Microsoft set the price of Windows and would it be in the firm's self-interest to set a different price for a version stripped of IE?
2. Why might Microsoft offer the full version of Windows 7 to European customers at the upgrade price?

Use the following information to work Problems 3 and 4.

Bobbie's Hair Care is a natural monopoly. Table 1 shows the demand schedule (the first two columns) and Bobbie's marginal cost schedule (the middle and third columns). Bobbie has done a survey and discovered that she has four types of customers each hour: one woman who is willing to pay $18, one senior who is willing to pay $16, one student who is willing to pay $14, and one boy who is willing to pay $12. Suppose that Bobbie's fixed costs are $20 an hour and Bobbie's price discriminates.

3. What is the price each type of customer is charged and how many haircuts an hour does Bobbie's sell? What is the increase in Bobbie's economic profit that results from price discrimination?
4. Who benefits from Bobbie's price discrimination? Is the quantity of haircuts efficient?

**TABLE 1**

| Price (dollars per haircut) | Quantity (haircuts per hour) | Marginal cost (dollars per hour) |
|---|---|---|
| 20 | 0 | — |
| 18 | 1 | 1 |
| 16 | 2 | 4 |
| 14 | 3 | 8 |
| 12 | 4 | 12 |
| 10 | 5 | 18 |

Use the following information to work Problems 5 to 10.

Big Top is the only circus in the nation. Table 2 sets out the demand schedule for circus tickets and the cost schedule for producing the circus.

5. Calculate Big Top's profit-maximizing price, output, and economic profit if it charges a single price for all tickets.
6. When Big Top maximizes profit, what is the consumer surplus and producer surplus and is the circus efficient? Explain why or why not.
7. Big Top offers children a discount of 50 percent. How will this discount change the consumer surplus and producer surplus? Will Big Top be more efficient by offering the discount to children?
8. If Big Top is regulated to produce the efficient output, what is the quantity of tickets sold, what is the price of a ticket, and what would be the consumer surplus?
9. If Big Top is regulated to charge a price equal to average total cost, what is the quantity of tickets sold, the price of a ticket, and economic profit?

**TABLE 2**

| Price (dollars per ticket) | Quantity (tickets per show) | Total cost (dollars per show) |
|---|---|---|
| 20 | 0 | 1,000 |
| 18 | 100 | 1,600 |
| 16 | 200 | 2,200 |
| 14 | 300 | 2,800 |
| 12 | 400 | 3,400 |
| 10 | 500 | 4,000 |
| 8 | 600 | 4,600 |
| 6 | 700 | 5,200 |
| 4 | 800 | 5,800 |

**10.** Draw a graph to illustrate the circus market if regulators set a price cap that enables Big Top to break even. Show the deadweight loss in your graph.

Use the following information to work Problems **11** to **13**.

The National Collegiate Athletic Association (NCAA) controls the market for college athletes. It sets the amounts paid to these athletes below what they would be in a competitive market and ensures that colleges do not violate the rules that it lays down.

**11.** Is the NCAA a natural monopoly, a legal monopoly, or neither? Explain.

**12.** Who benefits and who loses from the NCAA's control of the market for college athletes?

**13.** Is the system operated by the NCAA efficient?

Use the following information to work Problems **14** to **16**.

Major League Baseball is exempt from laws designed to limit market power and it operates as a monopoly.

**14.** How might competition be introduced into the market for baseball?

**15.** If the baseball market became competitive, what do you predict would happen to the number of teams and the economic profit of a team?

**16.** If the baseball market became competitive, what do you predict would happen to the number of players and their average salaries?

Use the following information to work Problems **17** and **18**.

Before 1991, the eight Ivy League colleges (Brown, Columbia, Cornell, Dartmouth, Harvard, Princeton, the University of Pennsylvania, and Yale), along with MIT, shared information and agreed on rules for setting their prices of education (price equals tuition minus scholarship). Since 1991, these schools have set their prices in competition with each other.

**17.** Compare the market for an Ivy League education before and after 1991.

**18.** Predict what has happened to the efficiency of the market, to the distribution of producer surplus and consumer surplus, and to deadweight loss.

Use the following information to work Problems **19** and **20**.

**AT&T: A monopoly with iPhone?**

AT&T is the exclusive carrier for Apple's iPhone. Americans who buy an iPhone cannot unlock it and use another wireless carrier.

Source: *USA Today*, October 11, 2007

**19.** How does AT&T being the exclusive provider of wireless service for the iPhone influence the wireless telecommunication market?

**20.** Explain why the wireless market may "tend toward either a single firm or a small number of firms." Why might this justify allowing a regulated monopoly to exist in this market?

## Which cell phone?

In June 2009, you had a choice of 265 different cell phones. Why is there so much variety?

# Monopolistic Competition

CHAPTER CHECKLIST

**When you have completed your study of this chapter, you will be able to**

1. Describe and identify monopolistic competition.
2. Explain how a firm in monopolistic competition determines its output and price in the short run and the long run.
3. Explain why advertising costs are high and why firms use brand names in monopolistic competition.

## 16.1 WHAT IS MONOPOLISTIC COMPETITION?

Most real-world markets lie between the extremes of perfect competition in Chapter 14 and monopoly in Chapter 15. Most firms possess some power to set their prices as monopolies do, and they face competition from the entry of new firms as the firms in perfect competition do. We call the markets in which such firms operate *monopolistic competition*. (Another market that lies between perfect competition and monopoly is *oligopoly*, which we study in Chapter 17.)

*Monopolistic competition* is a market structure in which

- A large number of firms compete.
- Each firm produces a differentiated product.
- Firms compete on price, product quality, and marketing.
- Firms are free to enter and exit.

### Large Number of Firms

In monopolistic competition, as in perfect competition, the industry consists of a large number of firms. The presence of a large number of firms has three implications for the firms in the industry.

#### Small Market Share

Each firm supplies a small part of the market. Consequently, while each firm can influence the price of its own product, it has little power to influence the average market price.

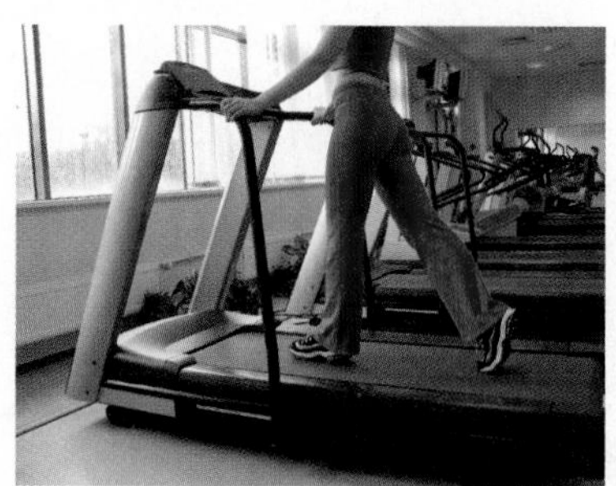

*About 20 firms, each with a small market share, produce a wide variety of treadmills.*

#### No Market Dominance

Each firm must be sensitive to the average market price of the product, but it does not pay attention to any one individual competitor. Because all the firms are relatively small, no single firm can dictate market conditions, so no one firm's actions directly affect the actions of the other firms.

#### Collusion Impossible

Firms sometimes try to profit from illegal agreements—collusion—with other firms to fix prices and not undercut each other. Collusion is impossible when the market has a large number of firms, as it does in monopolistic competition.

### Product Differentiation

**Product differentiation**
Making a product that is slightly different from the products of competing firms.

**Product differentiation** is making a product that is slightly different from the products of competing firms. A differentiated product has close substitutes but it does not have perfect substitutes. Some people will pay more for one variety of the product, so when its price rises, the quantity demanded decreases but it does not (necessarily) decrease to zero. For example, Adidas, Asics, Diadora, Etonic, Fila, New Balance, Nike, Puma, and Reebok all make differentiated running shoes. Other things remaining the same, if the price of Adidas running shoes rises and the prices of the other shoes remain constant, Adidas sells fewer shoes.

### Competing on Quality, Price, and Marketing

Product differentiation enables a firm to compete with other firms in three areas: quality, price, and marketing.

### Quality

The quality of a product is the physical attributes that make it different from the products of other firms. Quality includes design, reliability, the service provided to the buyer, and the buyer's ease of access to the product. Quality lies on a spectrum that runs from high to low. Go to the J.D. Power Consumer Center at jdpower.com, and you'll see the many dimensions on which this rating agency describes the quality of autos, boats, financial services, travel and accommodation services, telecommunication services, and new homes—all examples of products that have a large range of quality variety.

### Price

Because of product differentiation, a firm in monopolistic competition faces a downward-sloping demand curve. So, like a monopoly, the firm can set both its price and its output. But there is a tradeoff between the product's quality and price. A firm that makes a high-quality product can charge a higher price than a firm that makes a low-quality product.

### Marketing

Because of product differentiation, a firm in monopolistic competition must market its product. Marketing takes two main forms: advertising and packaging. A firm that produces a high-quality product wants to sell it for a suitably high price. To be able to do so, it must advertise and package its product in a way that convinces buyers that they are getting the higher quality for which they are paying. For example, drug companies advertise and package their brand-name drugs to persuade buyers that these items are superior to the lower-priced generic alternatives. Similarly, a low-quality producer uses advertising and packaging to persuade buyers that although the quality is low, the low price more than compensates for this fact.

## Entry and Exit

In monopolistic competition, there are no barriers to entry. Consequently, a firm cannot make an economic profit in the long run. When firms make economic profits, new firms enter the industry. This entry lowers prices and eventually eliminates economic profits. When economic losses are incurred, some firms leave the industry. This exit increases prices and profits of the remaining firms and eventually eliminates the economic losses. In long-run equilibrium, firms neither enter nor leave the industry and the firms in the industry make zero economic profit.

## Identifying Monopolistic Competition

Several factors must be considered to identify monopolistic competition and distinguish it from perfect competition on the one side and oligopoly and monopoly on the other side. One of these factors is the extent to which a market is dominated by a small number of firms. To measure this feature of markets, economists use two indexes called measures of concentration. These indexes are

- The four-firm concentration ratio
- The Herfindahl-Hirschman Index

## The Four-Firm Concentration Ratio

**Four-firm concentration ratio** The percentage of the total revenue in an industry accounted for by the four largest firms in the industry.

The **four-firm concentration ratio** is the percentage of the total revenue of the industry accounted for by the four largest firms in the industry. The range of the concentration ratio is from almost zero for perfect competition to 100 percent for monopoly. This ratio is the main measure used to assess market structure.

Table 16.1 shows two calculations of the four-firm concentration ratio: one for tire makers and one for printers. In this example, 14 firms produce tires. The four largest firms have 80 percent of the industry's total revenue, so the four-firm concentration ratio is 80 percent. In the printing industry, with 1,004 firms, the four largest firms have only 0.5 percent of the industry's total revenue, so the four-firm concentration ratio is 0.5 percent.

A low concentration ratio indicates a high degree of competition, and a high concentration ratio indicates an absence of competition. A monopoly has a concentration ratio of 100 percent—the largest (and only) firm has 100 percent of the total revenue. A four-firm concentration ratio that exceeds 60 percent is regarded as an indication of a market that is highly concentrated and dominated by a few firms in an oligopoly. A ratio of less than 40 percent is regarded as an indication of a competitive market—monopolistic competition.

**TABLE 16.1**

Concentration Ratio Calculations

**(a) Firms' total revenue**

| Tire makers | | Printers | |
|---|---|---|---|
| **Firm** | **(millions of dollars)** | **Firm** | **(millions of dollars)** |
| Top, Inc. | 200 | Fran's | 4 |
| ABC, Inc. | 250 | Ned's | 3 |
| Big, Inc. | 150 | Tom's | 2 |
| XYZ, Inc. | 100 | Jill's | 1 |
| 4 largest firms | 700 | 4 largest firms | 10 |
| Other 10 firms | 175 | Other 1,000 firms | 1,990 |
| Industry | 875 | Industry | 2,000 |

**(b) Four-firm concentration ratios**

| Tire makers | | Printers | |
|---|---|---|---|
| Total revenue of 4 largest firms | 700 | Total revenue of 4 largest firms | 10 |
| Industry's total revenue | 875 | Industry's total revenue | 2,000 |
| Four-firm concentration ratio | $\frac{700}{875} \times 100 = 80$ percent | Four-firm concentration ratio | $\frac{10}{2{,}000} \times 100 = 0.5$ percent |

## The Herfindahl-Hirschman Index

The **Herfindahl-Hirschman Index**—also called the HHI—is the square of the percentage market share of each firm summed over the 50 largest firms (or summed over all the firms if there are fewer than 50) in a market. For example, if there are four firms in a market and the market shares of the firms are 50 percent, 25 percent, 15 percent, and 10 percent, the Herfindahl-Hirschman Index is

$$\text{HHI} = 50^2 + 25^2 + 15^2 + 10^2 = 3{,}450.$$

**Herfindahl-Hirschman Index**
The square of the percentage market share of each firm summed over the 50 largest firms (or summed over all the firms if there are fewer than 50) in a market.

In perfect competition, the HHI is small. For example, if each of the 50 largest firms in an industry has a market share of 0.1 percent, the HHI is $0.1^2 \times 50 = 0.5$. In a monopoly, the HHI is 10,000—the firm has 100 percent of the market: $100^2 = 10{,}000$.

The HHI became a popular measure of the degree of competition during the 1980s, when the Justice Department used it to classify markets. A market in which the HHI is less than 1,000 is regarded as being competitive and an example of monopolistic competition. A market in which the HHI lies between 1,000 and 1,800 is regarded as being moderately competitive. It probably is an example of monopolistic competition. But a market in which the HHI exceeds 1,800 is regarded as being uncompetitive. The Justice Department scrutinizes any merger of firms in a market in which the HHI exceeds 1,000 and is likely to challenge a merger if the HHI exceeds 1,800.

Concentration measures are a useful indicator of the degree of competition in a market, but they must be supplemented by other information to determine a market's structure. Table 16.2 summarizes the range of other information, along with the measures of concentration that determine which market structure describes a particular real-world market.

**TABLE 16.2**

Market Structure

| Characteristics | Perfect competition | Monopolistic competition | Oligopoly | Monopoly |
|---|---|---|---|---|
| Number of firms in industry | Many | Many | Few | One |
| Product | Identical | Differentiated | Identical or differentiated | No close substitutes or regulated |
| Barriers to entry | None | None | Moderate | High |
| Firm's control over price | None | Some | Considerable | Considerable |
| Concentration ratio | 0 | Low | High | 100 |
| HHI | Close to 0 | Less than 1,800 | More than 1,800 | 10,000 |
| Examples | Wheat, corn | Food, clothing | Cereals | Local water supply |

### Limitations of Concentration Measures

The two main limitations of concentration measures alone as determinants of market structure are their failure to take proper account of

- The geographical scope of the market
- Barriers to entry and firm turnover

***Geographical Scope of the Market*** Concentration measures take a national view of the market. Many goods are sold in a *national* market, but some are sold in a *regional* market and some in a *global* one. The ready-mix concrete industry consists of local markets. The four-firm concentration ratio for ready-mix concrete is 6.2, and the HHI is 26. These numbers suggest a market that is close to perfect competition. But there is a high degree of concentration in the ready-mix concrete industry in most cities, so this industry is not competitive despite its low measured concentration. The four-firm concentration ratio for automobiles is 87, and the HHI is 2,725. These numbers suggest a highly concentrated market. But competition from imports gives the auto market many of the features of monopolistic competition.

***Barriers to Entry and Firm Turnover*** Concentration measures don't measure barriers to entry. Some industries are highly concentrated but have easy entry and an enormous amount of turnover of firms. For example, many small towns have few restaurants, but there are no restrictions on opening a restaurant and many firms attempt to do so.

A market with a high concentration ratio or HHI might nonetheless be competitive because low barriers to entry create *potential competition*. The few firms in a market face competition from many firms that can easily enter the market and will do so if economic profits are available.

## EYE on the U.S. ECONOMY

### Examples of Monopolistic Competition

These ten industries operate in monopolistic competition. They have a large number of firms, shown in parentheses after the industry's name. The red bars show the percentage of industry total revenue received by the 4 largest firms. The green bars show the percentage of industry total revenue received by the next 4 largest firms. The entire red, green, and blue bars show the percentage of industry total revenue received by the 20 largest firms. The Herfindahl-Hirschman Index is shown on the right.

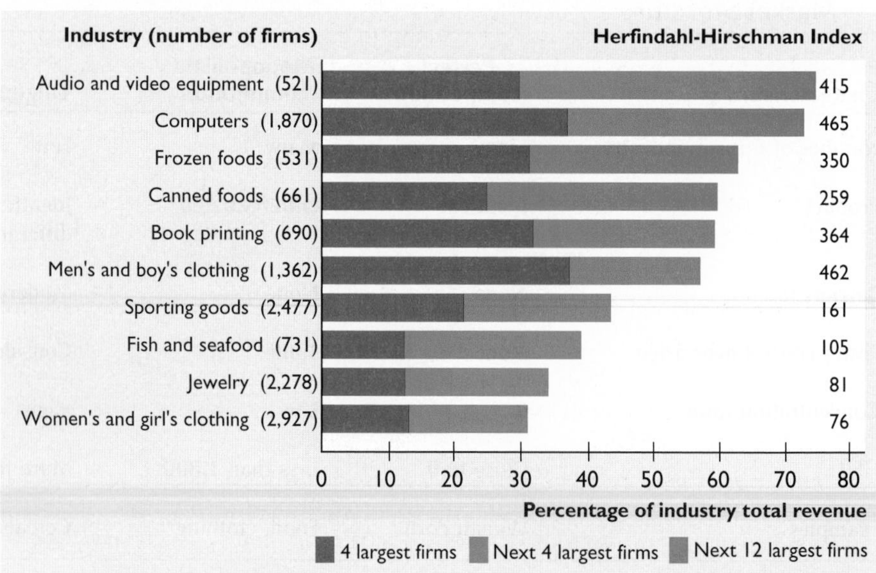

SOURCE OF DATA: U.S. Census Bureau.

## CHECKPOINT 16.1

Work these problems in Study Plan 16.1 to get instant feedback.

**Describe and identify monopolistic competition.**

### Practice Problems

Use Table 1, which shows the total revenue of the 50 firms in the tattoo industry, to work Problems **1** to **4**.

1. Calculate the four-firm concentration ratio and the HHI. What is the market structure of the tattoo industry?
2. What would the market structure of the tattoo industry be if each of the 50 firms operated in a different city and the cities were spread across the nation?
3. What additional information would you need about the tattoo industry to be sure that it is an example of monopolistic competition?
4. Suppose that a new tattoo technology makes it easier for anyone to enter the tattoo industry. How might the market structure of the tattoo industry change?
5. **Is a prepaid phone plan right for you?**
   Cell-phone providers are offering new no-contract plans. For example, T-Mobile has "flexpay" plans that allow users to buy monthly service; Boost Mobile's no-contract plan has unlimited talking, texting, and Web use; and Virgin Mobile's plan has unlimited calling for $49.99 a month. All providers of no-contract plans are actively marketing their plans.
   Source: *Wall Street Journal*, April 22, 2009
   In what type of market are cell-phone plans sold? Explain your answer.

**TABLE 1**

| Firm | Total revenue (dollars) |
|---|---|
| Bright Spots | 450 |
| Freckles | 325 |
| Love Galore | 250 |
| Native Birds | 200 |
| Next 16 firms (each) | 50 |
| Next 30 firms (each) | 20 |
| **Industry** | **2,625** |

### Guided Solutions to Practice Problems

1. The four-firm concentration ratio is 46.6. The market shares of the four largest firms are 17.1, 12.4, 9.5, and 7.6.
   The HHI is 671.14. The market shares from largest to smallest are 17.1, 12.4, 9.5, 7.6, 1.9, and 0.8 percent. Square these numbers to get $292.41 + 153.76 + 90.25 + 57.76 + (3.61 \times 16) + (0.64 \times 30) = 671.14$.
   The four-firm concentration ratio and the HHI suggest that the tattoo industry is an example of monopolistic competition unless there are other reasons that would make the concentration measures unreliable guides.
2. If the 50 firms in the tattoo industry operate in different cities spread across the nation, each firm is effectively without competition. The market might be a series of monopolies.
3. The additional information needed is information about product differentiation; competition on price, quality, and marketing; and evidence of low barriers to the entry of new firms.
4. This new tattoo technology would most likely lead to the entry of more firms, greater product differentiation, and more competition.
5. The market structure is monopolistic competition. The number of cell-phone providers is large, and they offer differentiated services. No firm dominates the market and the firms compete on quality, price, and marketing. New cell-phone providers can enter the market with their own plan.

## 16.2 OUTPUT AND PRICE DECISIONS

Think about the decisions that Tommy Hilfiger must make about Tommy jeans. First, the firm must decide on the design and quality of its jeans and on its marketing program. We'll suppose that Tommy Hilfiger has already made these decisions so that we can concentrate on the firm's output and pricing decision. But we'll study quality and marketing decisions in the next section.

Because Tommy Hilfiger has chosen the quality of its jeans and the amount of marketing activity, it faces given costs and market demand. How, with these costs and market demand for its jeans, does Tommy Hilfiger decide the *quantity* of jeans to produce and the *price* at which to sell them?

### The Firm's Profit-Maximizing Decision

A firm in monopolistic competition makes its output and price decision just as a monopoly firm does. Tommy Hilfiger maximizes profit by producing the quantity at which marginal revenue equals marginal cost and by charging the highest price that buyers are willing to pay for this quantity.

Figure 16.1 illustrates this decision for Tommy jeans. The demand curve for Tommy jeans is *D*. The *MR* curve shows the marginal revenue curve associated with this demand curve and is derived just like the marginal revenue curve of a single-price monopoly in Chapter 15. The *ATC* curve shows the average total cost of producing Tommy jeans, and *MC* is the marginal cost curve. Profit is maximized by producing 125 pairs of jeans a day and selling them at a price of $75 a pair. When Tommy Hilfiger produces 125 pairs of jeans a day, average total cost is $25 a pair and economic profit is $6,250 a day ($50 a pair multiplied by 125 pairs a day). The blue rectangle shows Tommy Hilfiger's economic profit.

**FIGURE 16.1**

Output and Price in Monopolistic Competition

myeconlab Animation

1. Profit is maximized where marginal revenue equals marginal cost.
2. The profit-maximizing quantity is 125 pairs of Tommy jeans a day.
3. The profit-maximizing price is $75 a pair, which exceeds the average total cost of $25 a pair, so the firm makes an economic profit of $50 a pair.
4. The blue rectangle illustrates economic profit and its area, which equals $6,250 a day ($50 a pair multiplied by 125 pairs) measures economic profit.

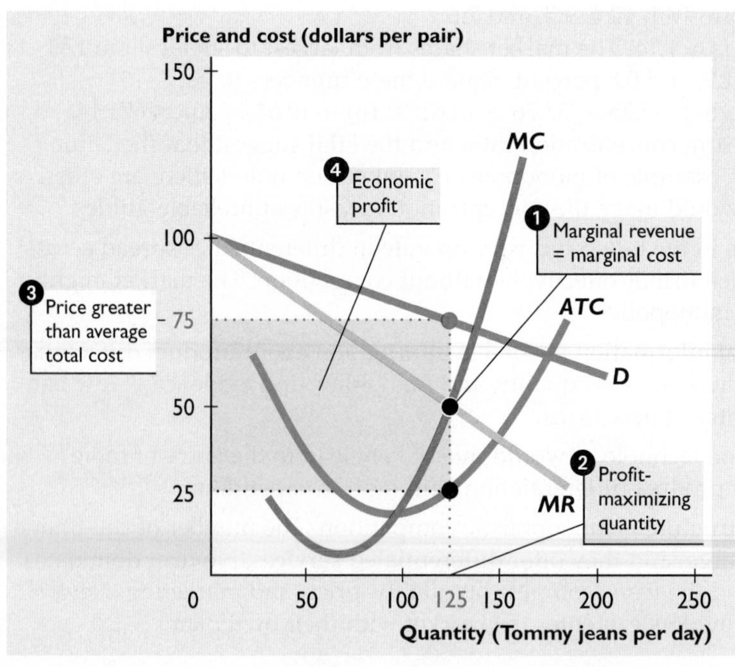

## Profit Maximizing Might Be Loss Minimizing

Tommy Hilfiger in Figure 16.1 is making a healthy economic profit, but such an outcome is not inevitable. The demand for a firm's product might be too low for it to make an economic profit. Excite@Home was such a firm. Offering high-speed Internet service over the same cable that provides television, Excite@Home hoped to capture a large share of the Internet portal market in competition with AOL, MSN, and a host of other providers.

Figure 16.2 illustrates the situation facing Excite@Home in 2001. The demand curve for its portal service is *D*, the marginal revenue curve is *MR*, the average total cost curve is *ATC*, and the marginal cost curve is *MC*. Excite@Home maximizes profit—equivalently, it minimizes its loss—by producing the output at which marginal revenue equals marginal cost. In Figure 16.2, this output is 40,000 customers. Excite@Home charges the price that buyers are willing to pay for this quantity, which is determined by the demand curve and which is $40 a month. With 40,000 customers, Excite@Home's average total cost is $50 a customer, so Excite@Home incurs an economic loss of $400,000 a month ($10 a customer multiplied by 40,000 customers). The red rectangle shows the firm's economic loss.

The largest loss that a firm will incur is equal to total fixed cost. The reason is that if the profit-maximizing (loss-minimizing) price is less than average variable cost, the firm will shut down temporarily and produce nothing (just like a firm in perfect competition—see pp. 353–354).

So far, the firm in monopolistic competition looks like a single-price monopoly. It produces the quantity at which marginal revenue equals marginal cost and then charges the highest price that buyers are willing to pay for that quantity. The difference between monopoly and monopolistic competition lies in what happens when firms either make an economic profit or incur an economic loss.

**FIGURE 16.2**

Economic Loss in the Short Run

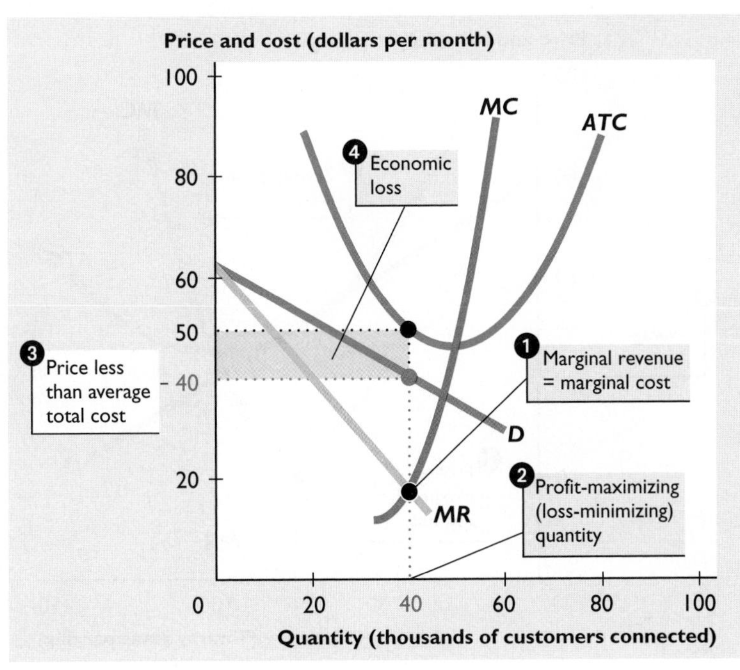


1. Profit is maximized and loss is minimized where marginal revenue equals marginal cost.
2. The loss-minimizing quantity is 40,000 customers connected.
3. The price of $40 a month is less than average total cost of $50 a month, so the firm incurs an economic loss of $10 a customer.
4. The red rectangle illustrates economic loss and its area, which equals $400,000 a month ($10 a customer multiplied by 40,000 customers) measures the economic loss.

## Long Run: Zero Economic Profit

A firm like Excite@Home is not going to incur an economic loss for long. Eventually, it exits the market. So in the long run, no firm in the market will be incurring an economic loss. Also, there is no restriction on entry in monopolistic competition, so if firms in an industry are making economic profits, other firms have an incentive to enter that industry and each firm's economic profit falls. So in the long run, firms will enter until all firms are making zero economic profit.

Tommy Hilfiger is making an economic profit, which is an incentive for the Gap and Calvin Klein to start to make jeans similar to Tommy jeans. As they enter the jeans market, the demand for Tommy jeans decreases. At each point in time, the firm maximizes its profit by producing the quantity at which marginal revenue equals marginal cost and by charging the highest price that buyers are willing to pay for this quantity. But as demand decreases, marginal revenue decreases and the profit-maximizing quantity and price fall.

Figure 16.3 shows the long-run equilibrium. The demand curve for Tommy jeans and the marginal revenue curve have shifted leftward. The firm produces 75 pairs of jeans a day and sells them for $50 each. At this output level, average total cost is also $50 a pair. So Tommy Hilfiger is making zero economic profit on its jeans. When all the firms in the industry are making zero economic profit, there is no incentive for new firms to enter.

If demand is so low relative to costs that firms incur economic losses, exit will occur. As firms leave an industry, the demand for the products of the remaining firms increases and their demand curves shift rightward. The exit process ends when all the firms in the industry are making zero economic profit.

**FIGURE 16.3**

Output and Price in the Long Run

myeconlab Animation

Economic profit encourages entry, which decreases the demand for each firm's product. Economic loss encourages exit, which increases the demand for each remaining firm's product.

When the demand curve touches the average total cost curve at the quantity at which marginal revenue equals marginal cost, the market is in long-run equilibrium.

1. The output that maximizes profit is 75 pairs of Tommy jeans a day.
2. The price, $50 a pair, equals average total cost.
3. Economic profit is zero.

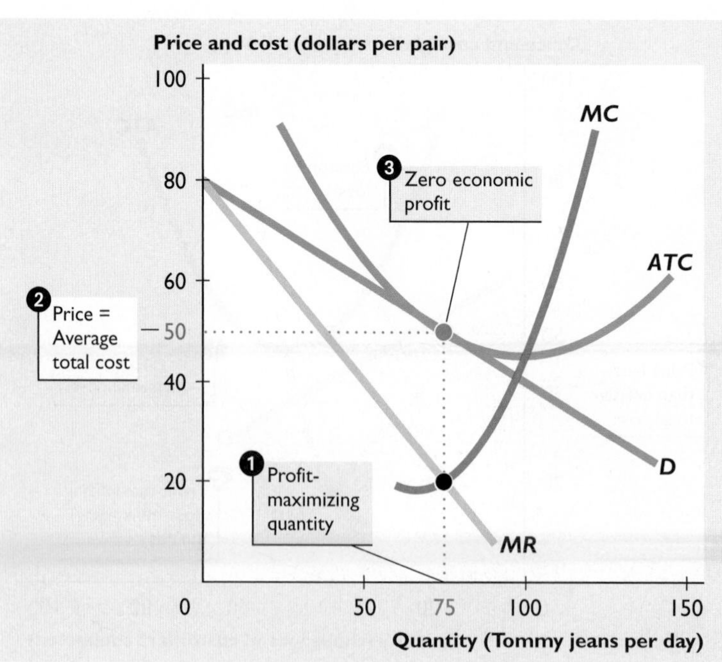

## Monopolistic Competition and Perfect Competition

Figure 16.4 compares monopolistic competition and perfect competition in the long run and highlights two key differences: excess capacity and markup.

### Excess Capacity

A firm **efficient scale** is the quantity at which average total cost is a minimum—the quantity at the bottom of the U-shaped *ATC* curve. A firm's **excess capacity** is the amount by which its efficient scale exceeds the quantity that it produces. Figure 16.4(a) shows that in the long run Tommy Hilfiger has *excess capacity*. Because the demand curve for Tommy jeans is downward sloping, zero economic profit occurs where the *ATC* curve is downward sloping. A firm in perfect competition in the long run, Figure 16.4(b), has no excess capacity. Because its demand curve is horizontal, zero economic profit occurs at minimum average total cost.

**Efficient scale**
The quantity at which average total cost is a minimum.

**Excess capacity**
The amount by which the efficient scale exceeds the quantity that the firm produces.

### Markup

A firm's **markup** is the amount by which its price exceeds its marginal cost. Figure 16.4(a) shows Tommy's markup. Figure 16.4(b) shows the zero markup of a firm in perfect competition. Buyers pay a higher price in monopolistic competition than in perfect competition and pay more than marginal cost.

**Markup**
The amount by which price exceeds marginal cost.

**FIGURE 16.4**

Excess Capacity and Markup in the Long Run

myeconlab Animation

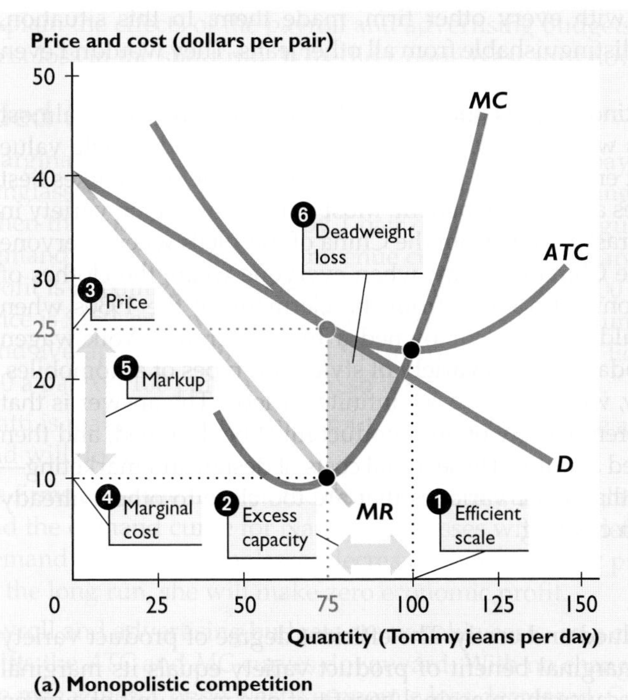


(a) Monopolistic competition

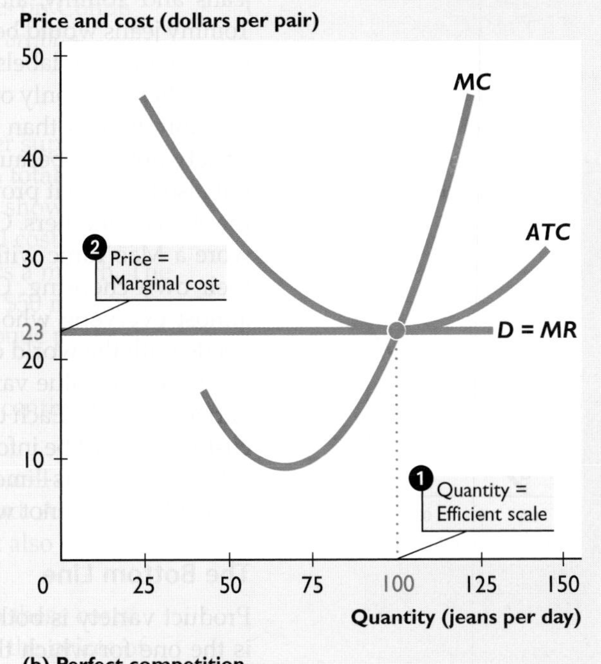


(b) Perfect competition

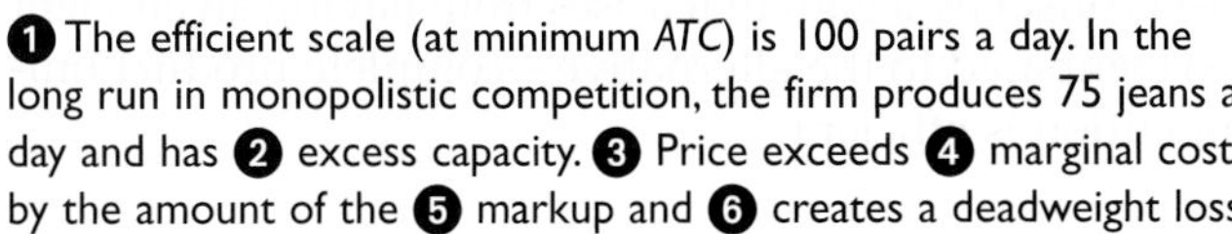

❶ The efficient scale (at minimum *ATC*) is 100 pairs a day. In the long run in monopolistic competition, the firm produces 75 jeans a day and has ❷ excess capacity. ❸ Price exceeds ❹ marginal cost by the amount of the ❺ markup and ❻ creates a deadweight loss.

In contrast, the firm in perfect competition has no excess capacity and no markup because the demand for the firm's output is perfectly elastic. ❶ The quantity produced equals the efficient scale and ❷ price equals marginal cost.

For the U.S. economy as a whole, there are some 20,000 advertising agencies, which employ more than 200,000 people and have total revenue of $45 billion. But these numbers are only part of the total cost of advertising because many firms have their own internal advertising departments, the costs of which we can only guess.

Advertising expenditures and other selling costs affect firms' profits in two ways: They increase costs and they change demand. Let's look at these effects.

### Selling Costs and Total Costs

Selling costs such as advertising expenditures increase the costs of a monopolistically competitive firm above those of a perfectly competitive firm or a monopoly. Advertising costs and other selling costs are fixed costs. They do not vary as total output varies. So, just like fixed production costs, advertising costs per unit of output decrease as production increases.

Figure 16.5 shows how selling costs and advertising expenditures change a firm's average total cost. The blue curve shows the average total cost of production. The red curve shows the firm's average total cost of production plus advertising. The height of the shaded area between the two curves shows the average fixed cost of advertising. The *total* cost of advertising is fixed. But the *average* cost of advertising decreases as output increases.

Figure 16.5 shows that if advertising increases the quantity sold by a large enough amount, it can lower average total cost. For example, if the quantity sold increases from 25 pairs of jeans a day with no advertising to 100 pairs of jeans a day with advertising, average total cost falls from $60 a pair to $40 a pair. The reason is that although the *total* fixed cost has increased, the greater fixed cost is spread over a greater output, so average total cost decreases.

**FIGURE 16.5**

Selling Costs and Total Costs

myeconlab Animation

Selling costs such as the cost of advertising are fixed costs.

1 When advertising costs are added to 2 the average total cost of production, 3 average total cost increases by more at small outputs than at large outputs.

4 If advertising enables the quantity sold to increase from 25 pairs of jeans a day to 100 pairs a day, it *lowers* average total cost from $60 a pair to $40 a pair.

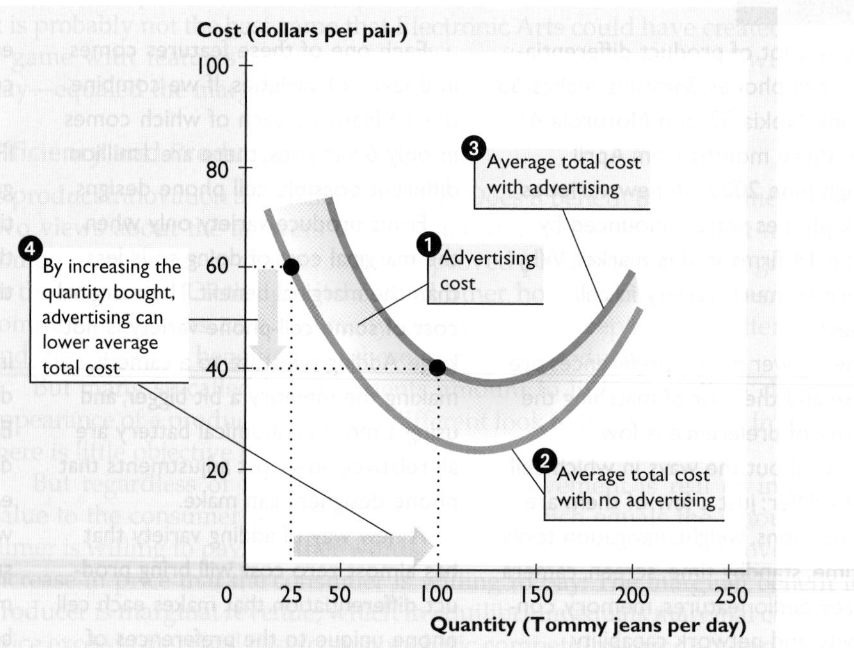

## Selling Costs and Demand

Advertising and other selling efforts change the demand for a firm's product. But how? Does demand increase or does it decrease? The most natural answer is that advertising increases demand. By informing people about the quality of its products or by persuading people to switch from the products of other firms, a firm might expect to increase the demand for its own products.

But all firms in monopolistic competition advertise. And all seek to persuade customers that they have the best deal. If advertising enables a firm to survive, it might increase the number of firms in the market. And to the extent that it increases the number of firms, it decreases the demand for any one firm's products. With all firms advertising, the demand for any one firm's product might become more elastic. So advertising can end up not only lowering average total cost but also lowering the price and decreasing the markup.

Figure 16.6 illustrates this possible effect of advertising. In part (a), with no advertising, the demand for Tommy jeans is not very elastic. Profit is maximized at 75 pairs of jeans a day, and the markup is large. In part (b), advertising, which is a fixed cost, increases average total cost and shifts the average total cost curve upward from $ATC_0$ to $ATC_1$ but leaves the marginal cost curve unchanged at $MC$. Demand becomes much more elastic, the profit-maximizing quantity increases, and the markup shrinks.

**FIGURE 16.6**

Advertising and the Markup

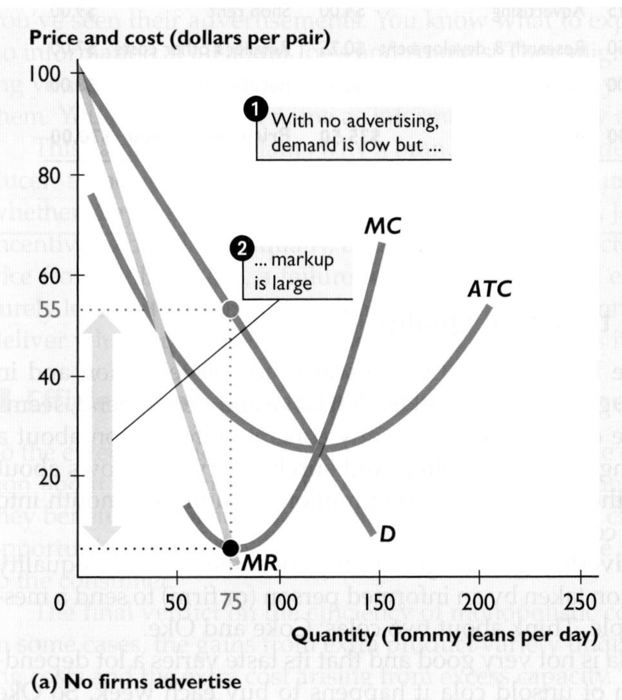


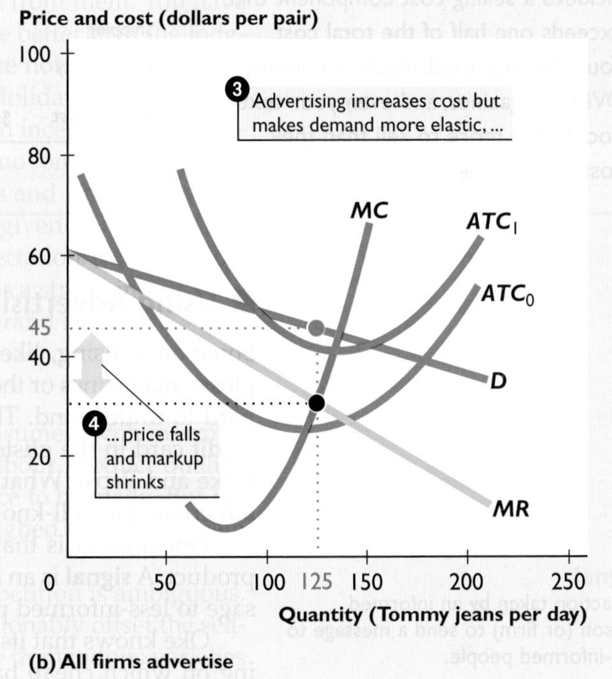


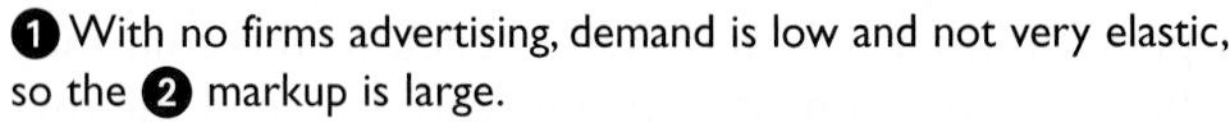

❶ With no firms advertising, demand is low and not very elastic, so the ❷ markup is large.

❸ Advertising shifts the average total cost curve upward from $ATC_0$ to $ATC_1$. If, with all firms advertising, demand becomes more elastic, ❹ the price falls and the markup shrinks.

## 17.2 THE OLIGOPOLISTS' DILEMMA

*Boeing and Airbus share the market for big passenger airplanes.*

Oligopoly might operate like monopoly, like perfect competition, or somewhere between these two extremes. To see these alternative possible outcomes, we'll study duopoly in the market for airplanes. Airbus and Boeing are the only makers of large commercial jet aircraft. Suppose that they have identical costs. To keep the numbers simple, assume that total fixed cost is zero and that regardless of the rate of production, the marginal cost of an airplane is $1 million.

Figure 17.2 shows the market demand curve for airplanes. Airbus and Boeing share this market. The total quantity sold and the quantities sold by each firm depend on the price of an airplane.

### Monopoly Outcome

If this industry had only one firm operating as a single-price monopoly, its marginal revenue curve would be the one shown in Figure 17.2. Marginal revenue equals marginal cost when 6 airplanes a week are produced and the price is $13 million an airplane. Total cost would be $6 million and total revenue would be $78 million, so economic profit would be $72 million a week.

**FIGURE 17.2**

A Market for Airplanes

myeconlab Animation

1. With market demand curve, *D*, marginal revenue curve, *MR*, and marginal cost curve, *MC*, a monopoly airplane maker maximizes profit by producing 6 airplanes a week and selling them at a price of $13 million an airplane.
2. With perfect competition among airplane makers, the market equilibrium quantity is 12 airplanes a week and the equilibrium price is $1 million an airplane.
3. A cartel might achieve the monopoly equilibrium, break down and result in the perfect competition equilibrium, or operate somewhere between these two extreme outcomes.

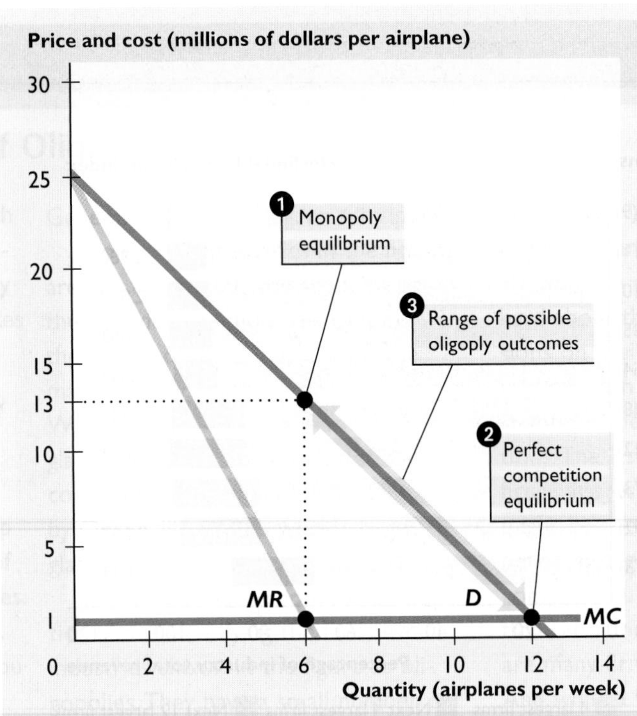

### Cartel to Achieve Monopoly Outcome

Can the two firms achieve the monopoly outcome that we've just found and maximize their joint profit? They can attempt to do so by forming a cartel.

Suppose that Airbus and Boeing agreed to limit the total production of airplanes to 6 a week. The market demand curve tells us that the price would be $13 million per airplane and economic profit would be $72 million a week. Suppose that the two firms also agree to split the market evenly and each produce 3 airplanes a week. They would each make an economic profit of $36 million a week—see Table 17.1.

Would it be in the self-interest of Airbus and Boeing to stick to their agreement and limit production to 3 aircraft a week each?

To begin answering this question, notice that with the price of an airplane exceeding marginal cost, if one firm increased production, it would increase its profit. But if both firms increased output whenever price exceeded marginal cost, the end of the process would be the same as perfect competition.

**TABLE 17.1 MONOPOLY OUTCOME**

| | Boeing | Airbus | Market total |
|---|---|---|---|
| Quantity (airplanes a week) | 3 | 3 | 6 |
| Price ($ million per airplane) | 13 | 13 | 13 |
| Total revenue ($ million) | 39 | 39 | 78 |
| Total cost ($ million) | 3 | 3 | 6 |
| Economic profit ($ million) | 36 | 36 | 72 |

## Perfect Competition Outcome

You can see the perfect competition outcome in Figure 17.2. The equilibrium is where the market supply curve, which is the marginal cost curve, intersects the market demand curve. The quantity is 12 airplanes a week, and the price is the same as marginal cost—$1 million per airplane.

## Other Possible Cartel Breakdowns

Because price exceeds marginal cost, a cartel is likely to break down. But a cartel might not unravel all the way to perfect competition. In *Eye on the Global Economy* on p. 439, you can see the brief history of a sometimes successful and sometimes unsuccessful cartel in the global market for oil. You can see why a cartel breaks down but not all the way to perfect competition by looking at some alternative outcomes in the airplane industry example.

### Boeing Increases Output to 4 Airplanes a Week

Suppose that starting from a cartel that achieves the monopoly outcome, Boeing increases output by 1 airplane a week. Table 17.2 keeps track of the data. With Boeing producing 4 airplanes a week and Airbus producing 3 airplanes a week, total output is 7 airplanes a week. To sell 7 airplanes a week, the price must fall. The market demand curve in Figure 17.2 tells us that the quantity demanded is 7 airplanes a week when the price is $11 million an airplane.

Market total revenue would now be $77 million, total cost would be $7 million, and economic profit would fall to $70 million. But the distribution of this economic profit is now unequal. Boeing would gain, and Airbus would lose.

Boeing would now receive $44 million a week in total revenue, have a total cost of $4 million, and make an economic profit of $40 million. Airbus would receive $33 million a week in total revenue, incur a total cost of $3 million, and make an economic profit of $30 million.

So by increasing its output by 1 airplane a week, Boeing can increase its economic profit by $4 million and cause the economic profit of Airbus to fall by $6 million.

Because the two firms in this example are identical, we could rerun the above story with Airbus increasing production by 1 airplane a week and Boeing holding

**TABLE 17.2 BOEING INCREASES OUTPUT TO 4 AIRPLANES A WEEK**

| | Boeing | Airbus | Market total |
|---|---|---|---|
| Quantity (airplanes a week) | 4 | 3 | 7 |
| Price ($ million per airplane) | 11 | 11 | 11 |
| Total revenue ($ million) | 44 | 33 | 77 |
| Total cost ($ million) | 4 | 3 | 7 |
| Economic profit ($ million) | 40 | 30 | 70 |

output at 3 a week. In this case, Airbus would make $40 million a week and Boeing would make $30 million a week.

Boeing is better off producing 4 airplanes a week if Airbus sticks with 3 a week. But is it in Airbus's interest to hold its output at 3 airplanes a week? To answer this question, we need to compare the economic profit Airbus makes if it maintains its output at 3 airplanes a week with the profit it makes if it produces 4 airplanes a week. How much economic profit does Airbus make if it produces 4 airplanes a week with Boeing also producing 4 airplanes a week?

### Airbus Increases Output to 4 Airplanes a Week

**TABLE 17.3 AIRBUS INCREASES OUTPUT TO 4 AIRPLANES A WEEK**

| | Boeing | Airbus | Market total |
|---|---|---|---|
| Quantity (airplanes a week) | 4 | 4 | 8 |
| Price ($ million per airplane) | 9 | 9 | 9 |
| Total revenue ($ million) | 36 | 36 | 72 |
| Total cost ($ million) | 4 | 4 | 8 |
| Economic profit ($ million) | 32 | 32 | 64 |

With both firms producing 4 airplanes a week, total output is 8 airplanes a week. To sell 8 airplanes a week, the price must fall further. The market demand curve in Figure 17.2 tells us that the quantity demanded is 8 airplanes a week when the price is $9 million an airplane.

Table 17.3 keeps track of the data. Market total revenue would now be $72 million, total cost would be $8 million, and economic profit would fall to $64 million. With both firms producing the same output, the distribution of this economic profit is now equal.

Both firms would now receive $36 million a week in total revenue, have a total cost of $4 million, and make an economic profit of $32 million. For Airbus, this outcome is an improvement on the previous one by $2 million a week. For Boeing, this outcome is worse than the previous one by $8 million.

This outcome is better for Airbus, but would Boeing go along with it? You know that Boeing would be worse off if it decreased its output to 3 airplanes a week because it would get the outcome that Airbus has in Table 17.2—an economic profit of only $30 million a week. But would Boeing be better off if it increased output to 5 airplanes a week?

### Boeing Increases Output to 5 Airplanes a Week

**TABLE 17.4 BOEING INCREASES OUTPUT TO 5 AIRPLANES A WEEK**

| | Boeing | Airbus | Market total |
|---|---|---|---|
| Quantity (airplanes a week) | 5 | 4 | 9 |
| Price ($ million per airplane) | 7 | 7 | 7 |
| Total revenue ($ million) | 35 | 28 | 63 |
| Total cost ($ million) | 5 | 4 | 9 |
| Economic profit ($ million) | 30 | 24 | 54 |

Suppose now that Airbus maintains its output at 4 airplanes a week and Boeing increases output to 5 a week. Table 17.4 keeps track of the data. Total output is now 9 airplanes a week. To sell this quantity, the price must fall to $7 million an airplane. Market total revenue is $63 million and total cost is $9 million, so economic profit for the two firms is $54 million. The distribution of this economic profit is again unequal. But now both firms would lose.

Boeing would now receive $35 million a week in total revenue, have a total cost of $5 million, and make an economic profit of $30 million—$2 million less than it would make if it maintained its output at 4 airplanes a week. Airbus would receive $28 million a week in total revenue, incur a total cost of $4 million, and make an economic profit of $24 million—$8 million less than before. So neither firm gains by increasing total output beyond 8 airplanes a week.

## The Oligopoly Cartel Dilemma

With a cartel, both firms make the maximum available economic profit. If both increase production, both see their profit fall. If only one firm increases production, that firm makes a larger economic profit while the other makes a lower economic profit. So what will the firms do? We can speculate about what they will do, but to work out the answer, we need some game theory.

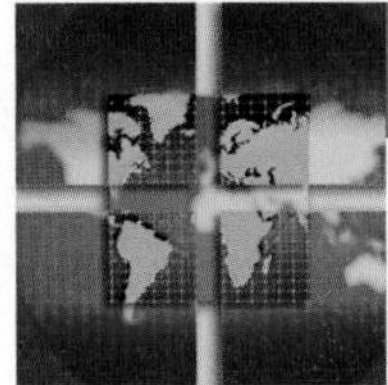

# EYE on the GLOBAL ECONOMY

## The OPEC Global Oil Cartel

The Organization of the Petroleum Exporting Countries (OPEC) is an international cartel of oil-producing nations. OPEC was created in Baghdad in 1960 by the governments of Iran, Iraq, Kuwait, Saudi Arabia, and Venezuela. Seven other nations, Qatar, Libya, United Arab Emirates, Algeria, Nigeria, Angola, and Ecuador are now members.

OPEC describes its objective as being "to co-ordinate and unify petroleum policies among member countries in order to secure fair and stable prices, . . . an efficient, economic, and regular supply of petroleum to consuming nations; and a fair return on capital to those investing in the industry." These words can be interpreted as being code for "restricting the production of oil to keep its price high."

During the 1960s, OPEC quietly built its organization and prepared the ground for its push to dominate the global oil market. Its first opportunity came in 1973 when, with an Arab-Israeli war raging, OPEC was able to organize an embargo on oil shipments to the United States and Europe and drive the price of oil to four times its previous level. OPEC's second opportunity came with a revolution in Iran in 1979 when the price of oil more than doubled.

The figure shows both these major price hikes. You can see that the price rose from about $8 a barrel in 1970 to more than $82 a barrel by 1980. (To compare prices over a number of years, we express them in terms of the value of the dollar in 2009.)

During the 1980s, many new sources of oil supply opened up and the OPEC cartel lost control of the global market. The cartel broke down, and the price of oil fell.

*OPEC ministers meeting at the organization's headquarters in Vienna*

The price of oil remained remarkably stable during the 1990s, and the power of OPEC was countered by a large supply of oil from other sources.

From 2003 to 2008, the demand for oil grew dramatically in China and other Asian economies and OPEC was again able to dominate the global market, restrict its own production, and push the world price to a new high in 2008. But OPEC lost power again in the global recession of 2009.

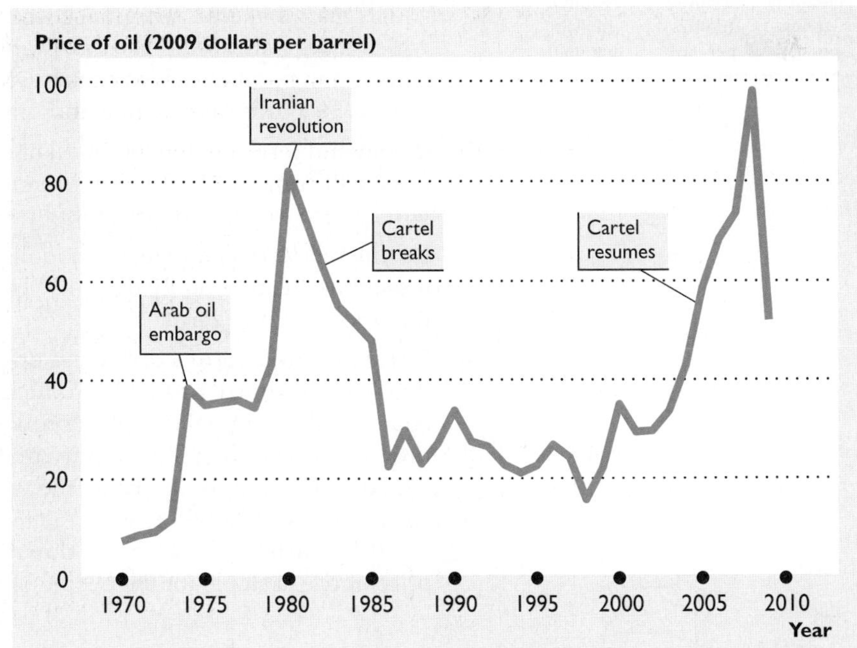


SOURCE OF DATA: OPEC and Bureau of Economic Analysis.

Work these problems in Study Plan 17.2 to get instant feedback.

## CHECKPOINT 17.2

**Explain the dilemma faced by firms in oligopoly.**

### Practice Problems

Isolated Island has two natural gas wells, one owned by Tom and the other owned by Jerry. Each well has a valve that controls the rate of flow of gas, and the marginal cost of producing gas is zero. Table 1 gives the demand schedule for gas on this island. Use this information to work Problems **1** to **3**.

1. If Tom and Jerry form a cartel and maximize their joint profit, what will be the price of gas and the quantity produced?
2. If Tom and Jerry are forced to sell at the perfectly competitive price, what will be the price of gas and the total quantity produced?
3. If Tom and Jerry compete as duopolists, what will be the price of gas?
4. **Asian rice exporters to discuss cartel**
   Thailand, the world's largest rice exporter, proposed that the Asian rice exporters (Thailand, Cambodia, Laos, and Myanmar) form a cartel. The Philippines said it was a bad idea.
   Source: CNN, May 6, 2008
   If the rice-exporting nations become a profit-maximizing cartel, explain how they would influence the global market for rice and the world price of rice. Is the Philippines correct?

**TABLE 1**

| Price (dollars per unit) | Quantity demanded (units per day) |
|---|---|
| 12 | 0 |
| 11 | 1 |
| 10 | 2 |
| 9 | 3 |
| 8 | 4 |
| 7 | 5 |
| 6 | 6 |
| 5 | 7 |
| 4 | 8 |
| 3 | 9 |
| 2 | 10 |
| 1 | 11 |
| 0 | 12 |

### Guided Solutions to Practice Problems

1. If Tom and Jerry form a cartel and maximize their joint profit, they will charge the monopoly price. This price is the highest price the market will bear when together they produce the quantity at which marginal revenue equals marginal cost. Marginal cost is zero, so we need to find the price at which marginal revenue is zero. Marginal revenue is zero when total revenue is a maximum, which occurs when output is 6 units a day (Table 2) and price is $6 a unit (see the demand schedule in Table 1).
2. If Tom and Jerry are forced to sell at the perfectly competitive price, the price will equal marginal cost. Marginal cost is zero, so in this case, the price will be zero and the total quantity produced will be 12 units a day.
3. If Tom and Jerry compete as duopolists, they will increase production to more than the monopoly quantity. The price will fall, but they will not drive the price down to zero.
4. If rice exporters form a cartel and operate as a profit-maximizing monopoly, they will maximize profit by producing the quantity at which marginal revenue equals marginal cost. The profit-maximizing quantity that a monopoly produces is less than the quantity that competitive rice growers currently produce. The supply of rice on the world market will decrease and the world price of rice will rise.

   If the cartel does not break down, then the Philippines is correct: The price of rice, a staple for the people of Asia, will rise.

**TABLE 2**

| Quantity (units per day) | Total revenue (dollars per day) | Marginal revenue (dollars per unit) |
|---|---|---|
| 0 | 0 | |
| | | 11 |
| 1 | 11 | |
| | | 9 |
| 2 | 20 | |
| | | 7 |
| 3 | 27 | |
| | | 5 |
| 4 | 32 | |
| | | 3 |
| 5 | 35 | |
| | | 1 |
| 6 | 36 | |
| | | −1 |
| 7 | 35 | |
| | | −3 |
| 8 | 32 | |
| | | −5 |
| 9 | 27 | |
| | | −7 |
| 10 | 20 | |
| | | −9 |
| 11 | 11 | |
| | | −11 |
| 12 | 0 | |

## 17.3 GAME THEORY

**Game theory** is the tool that economists use to analyze *strategic behavior*—behavior that recognizes mutual interdependence and takes account of the expected behavior of others. John von Neumann invented game theory in 1937, and today it is a major research field in economics.

Game theory helps us to understand oligopoly and many other forms of economic, political, social, and even biological rivalries. We will begin our study of game theory and its application to the behavior of firms by thinking about familiar games that we play for fun.

**Game theory**
The tool that economists use to analyze *strategic behavior*—behavior that recognizes mutual interdependence and takes account of the expected behavior of others.

### What Is a Game?

What is a game? At first thought, the question seems silly. After all, there are many different games. There are ball games and parlor games, games of chance and games of skill. But what is it about all these different activities that make them games? What do all these games have in common? All games share three features:

- Rules
- Strategies
- Payoffs

Let's see how these common features of games apply to a game called "the prisoners' dilemma." The **prisoners' dilemma** is a game between two prisoners that shows why it is hard to cooperate even when it would be beneficial to both players to do so. This game captures the essential feature of the duopolists' dilemma that we've just been studying. The prisoners' dilemma also provides a good illustration of how game theory works and how it generates predictions.

**Prisoners' dilemma**
A game between two prisoners that shows why it is hard to cooperate even when it would be beneficial to both players to do so.

### The Prisoners' Dilemma

Art and Bob have been caught red-handed, stealing a car. During the district attorney's interviews with the prisoners, he begins to suspect that he has stumbled on the two people who committed a multimillion-dollar bank robbery some months earlier. But this is just a suspicion. The district attorney has no evidence on which he can convict them of the greater crime unless he can get them to confess. He makes the prisoners play a game with the following rules.

#### Rules

Each prisoner (player) is placed in a separate room and cannot communicate with the other player. Each is told that he is suspected of having carried out the bank robbery and that

- If both of them confess to the larger crime, each will receive a reduced sentence of 3 years for both crimes.
- If he alone confesses and his accomplice does not, he will receive an even shorter sentence of 1 year, while his accomplice will receive a 10-year sentence.
- If neither of them confesses to the larger crime, each will receive a 2-year sentence for car theft.

## Strategies

**Strategies**
All the possible actions of each player in a game.

In game theory, **strategies** are all the possible actions of each player. Art and Bob each have two possible strategies:

- Confess to the bank robbery.
- Deny having committed the bank robbery.

## Payoffs

**Payoff matrix**
A table that shows the payoffs for each player for every possible combination of actions by the players.

Because there are two players, each with two strategies, there are four possible outcomes:

- Both confess.
- Both deny.
- Art confesses and Bob denies.
- Bob confesses and Art denies.

**TABLE 17.5 PRISONERS' DILEMMA PAYOFF MATRIX**

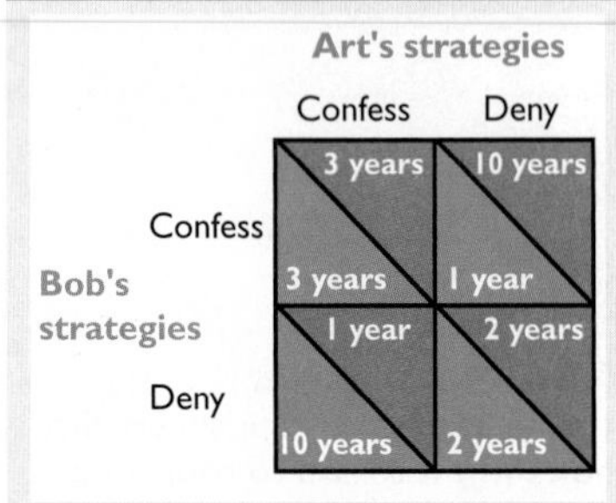

| | | Art's strategies | |
|---|---|---|---|
| | | Confess | Deny |
| Bob's strategies | Confess | 3 years / 3 years | 10 years / 1 year |
| | Deny | 1 year / 10 years | 2 years / 2 years |

Each square shows the payoffs for the two players, Art and Bob, for each possible pair of actions. In each square, the red triangle shows Art's payoff and the blue triangle shows Bob's. For example, if both confess, the payoffs are in the top left square.

Each prisoner can work out exactly what happens to him—his *payoff*—in each of these four situations. We can tabulate the four possible payoffs for each of the prisoners in what is called a payoff matrix for the game. A **payoff matrix** is a table that shows the payoffs for every possible action by each player given every possible action by the other player.

Table 17.5 shows a payoff matrix for Art and Bob. The squares show the payoffs for the two prisoners—the red triangle in each square shows Art's, and the blue triangle shows Bob's. If both prisoners confess (top left), each gets a prison term of 3 years. If Bob confesses but Art denies (top right), Art gets a 10-year sentence and Bob gets a 1-year sentence. If Art confesses and Bob denies (bottom left), Art gets a 1-year sentence and Bob gets a 10-year sentence. Finally, if both of them deny (bottom right), neither can be convicted of the bank robbery charge but both are sentenced for the car theft—a 2-year sentence.

## Equilibrium

**Nash equilibrium**
An equilibrium in which each player takes the best possible action given the action of the other player.

The equilibrium of a game occurs when each player takes the best possible action given the action of the other player. This equilibrium concept is called **Nash equilibrium**. It is so named because John Nash of Princeton University, who received the Nobel Prize for Economic Science in 1994, proposed it. (The same John Nash was portrayed by Russell Crowe in *A Beautiful Mind.*)

In the case of the prisoners' dilemma, equilibrium occurs when Art makes his best choice given Bob's choice and when Bob makes his best choice given Art's choice. Let's find the equilibrium.

First, look at the situation from Art's point of view. If Bob confesses, it pays Art to confess because in that case, he is sentenced to 3 years rather than 10 years. If Bob does not confess, it still pays Art to confess because in that case, he receives 1 year rather than 2 years. So no matter what Bob does, Art's best action is to confess.

Second, look at the situation from Bob's point of view. If Art confesses, it pays Bob to confess because in that case, he is sentenced to 3 years rather than 10 years. If Art does not confess, it still pays Bob to confess because in that case, he receives 1 year rather than 2 years. So no matter what Art does, Bob's best action is to confess.

Because each player's best action is to confess, each does confess, each gets a 3-year prison term, and the district attorney has solved the bank robbery. This is the equilibrium of the game.

### Not the Best Outcome

The equilibrium of the prisoners' dilemma game is not the best outcome for the prisoners. Isn't there some way in which they can cooperate and get the smaller 2-year prison term? There is not, because the players cannot communicate with each other. Each player can put himself in the other player's place and can figure out what the other will do. The prisoners are in a dilemma. Each knows that he can serve only 2 years if he can trust the other to deny. But each also knows that it is not in the best interest of the other to deny. So each prisoner knows that he must confess, thereby delivering a bad outcome for both.

Let's now see how we can use the ideas we've just developed to understand the behavior of firms in oligopoly. We'll start by returning to the duopolists' dilemma.

## ■ The Duopolists' Dilemma

The dilemma of Airbus and Boeing is similar to that of Art and Bob. Each firm has two strategies. It can produce airplanes at the rate of

- 3 a week
- 4 a week

Because each firm has two strategies, there are four possible combinations of actions for the two firms:

- Both firms produce 3 a week (monopoly outcome).
- Both firms produce 4 a week.
- Airbus produces 3 a week and Boeing produces 4 a week.
- Boeing produces 3 a week and Airbus produces 4 a week.

### The Payoff Matrix

Table 17.6 sets out the payoff matrix for this game. It is constructed in exactly the same way as the payoff matrix for the prisoners' dilemma in Table 17.5. The squares show the payoffs for Airbus and Boeing. In this case, the payoffs are economic profits. (In the case of the prisoners' dilemma, the payoffs were losses.)

The table shows that if both firms produce 4 a week (top left), each firm makes an economic profit of $32 million. If both firms produce 3 a week (bottom right), they make the monopoly profit, and each firm makes an economic profit of $36 million. The top right and bottom left squares show what happens if one firm produces 4 a week while the other produces 3 a week. The firm that increases production makes an economic profit of $40 million, and the one that keeps production at the monopoly quantity makes an economic profit of $30 million.

**TABLE 17.6 DUOPOLISTS' DILEMMA PAYOFF MATRIX**

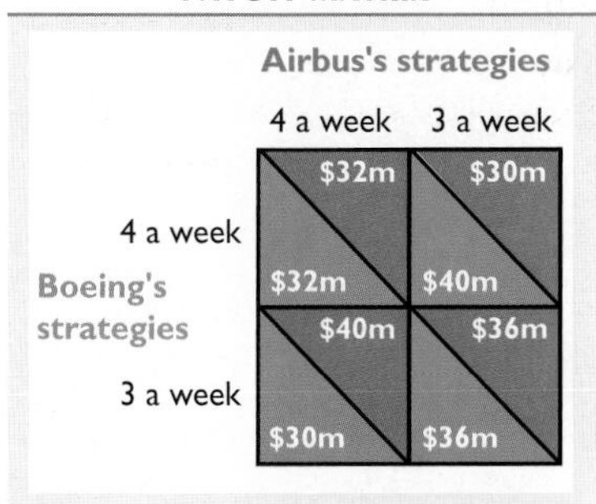


Each square shows the payoffs from a pair of actions. For example, if both firms produce 3 airplanes a week, the payoffs are recorded in the bottom right square. The red triangle shows Airbus's payoff, and the blue triangle shows Boeing's.

### Equilibrium of the Duopolists' Dilemma

What do the firms do? To answer this question, we must find the equilibrium of the duopoly game.

**TABLE 17.7 THE NASH EQUILIBRIUM**

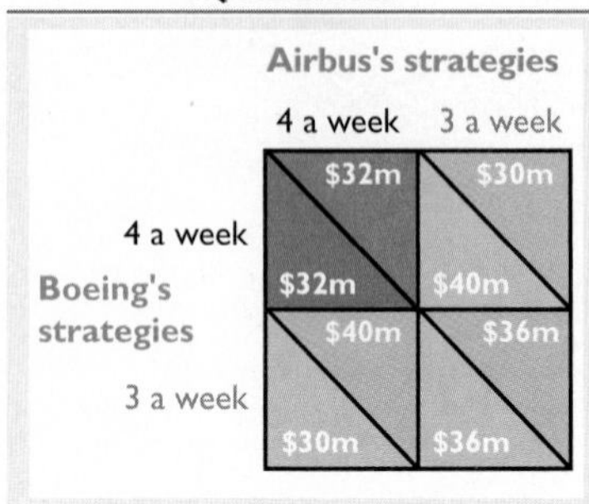


The Nash equilibrium is for each firm to produce 4 airplanes a week.

Using the information in Table 17.7, look at things from Airbus's point of view. Airbus reasons as follows: Suppose that Boeing produces 4 airplanes a week. If I, Airbus, produce 3 a week, I will make an economic profit of $30 million. If I also produce 4 a week, I will make an economic profit of $32 million. So I'm better off producing 4 airplanes a week. Airbus continues to reason: Now suppose Boeing produces 3 a week. If I produce 4 a week, I will make an economic profit of $40 million, and if I produce 3 a week, I will make an economic profit of $36 million. An economic profit of $40 million is better than an economic profit of $36 million, so I'm better off if I produce 4 airplanes a week. So regardless of whether Boeing produces 3 a week or 4 a week, it pays Airbus to produce 4 airplanes a week.

Because the two firms face identical situations, Boeing comes to the same conclusion as Airbus, so both firms produce 4 a week. The equilibrium of the duopoly game is that both firms produce 4 airplanes a week.

### Collusion Is Profitable but Difficult to Achieve

In the duopolists' dilemma that you've just studied, Airbus and Boeing end up in a situation that is similar to that of the prisoners in the prisoners' dilemma game. They don't achieve the best joint outcome. Because each produces 4 airplanes a week, each makes an economic profit of $32 million a week.

If firms were able to collude, they would agree to limit their production to 3 airplanes a week each and they would each make the monopoly profit of $36 million a week.

The outcome of the duopolists' dilemma shows why it is difficult for firms to collude. Even if collusion were a legal activity, firms in duopoly would find it difficult to implement an agreement to restrict output. Like the players of the prisoners' dilemma game, the duopolists would reach a Nash equilibrium in which they produce more than the joint profit-maximizing quantity.

If two firms have difficulty maintaining a collusive agreement, oligopolies with more than two firms have an even harder time. The operation of OPEC (see *Eye on the Global Economy* on p. 439) illustrates this difficulty. To raise the price of oil, OPEC must limit global oil production. The members of this cartel meet from time to time and set a production limit for each member nation. Almost always, within a few months of a decision to restrict production, some (usually smaller) members of the cartel break their quotas, production increases, and the price sags below the cartel's desired target. The OPEC cartel plays an oligopoly dilemma game similar to the prisoners' dilemma. Only in 1973, 1979–1980, and 2005–2007 did OPEC manage to keep its members' production under control and raise the price of oil.

## ■ Advertising and Research Games in Oligopoly

Every month, Coke and Pepsi, Nike and Adidas, Procter & Gamble and Kimberly-Clark, Nokia and Motorola, and hundreds of other pairs of big firms locked in fierce competition spend millions of dollars on advertising campaigns and on research and development (R&D). They make decisions about whether to increase or cut the advertising budget or whether to undertake a large R&D effort aimed at making the product more reliable (usually, the more reliable a product, the more expensive it is to produce, but the more people are willing to pay for it) or at lowering production costs. These choices can be analyzed as games. Let's look at some examples of these types of games.

## Advertising Game

A key to success in the soft drink industry is to run huge advertising campaigns. These campaigns affect market share but are costly to run. Table 17.8 shows some hypothetical numbers for the advertising game that Pepsi and Coke play. Each firm has two strategies: Advertise or don't advertise. If neither firm advertises, they each make $50 million (bottom right of the payoff matrix). If each firm advertises, each firm's profit is lower by the amount spent on advertising (top left square of the payoff matrix). If Pepsi advertises but Coke does not, Pepsi gains and Coke loses (top right square of the payoff matrix). Finally, if Coke advertises and Pepsi does not, Coke gains and Pepsi loses (bottom left square).

Pepsi reasons as follows: Regardless of whether Coke advertises, we're better off advertising. Coke reasons similarly: Regardless of whether Pepsi advertises, we're better off advertising. Because advertising is the best strategy for both players, it is the Nash equilibrium. The outcome of this game is that both firms advertise and make less profit than they would if they could collude to achieve the cooperative outcome of no advertising.

**TABLE 17.8 THE ADVERTISING GAME PAYOFF MATRIX**

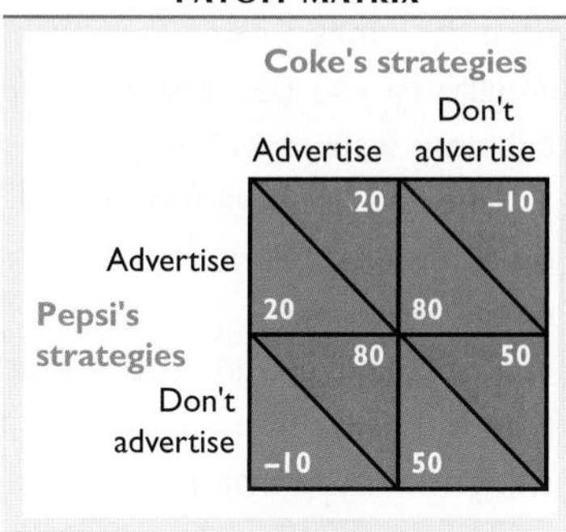


For each pair of strategies, the red triangle shows Coke's payoff, and the blue triangle shows Pepsi's. If both firms advertise, they make less than if neither firm advertises. But each firm is better off advertising if the other doesn't advertise. The Nash equilibrium for this prisoners' dilemma advertising game is for both firms to advertise.

## Research and Development Game

A key to success in the disposable diaper industry is to design a product that people value highly relative to the cost of producing it. The firm that develops the most highly valued product and also develops the least-cost technology for producing it gains a competitive edge, undercutting the rest of the market, increasing its market share, and increasing its profit. But the R&D that must be undertaken to achieve product improvements and cost reductions is costly. So the cost of R&D must be deducted from the profit resulting from the increased market share that lower costs achieve. If no firm does R&D, every firm can be better off, but if one firm initiates the R&D activity, all must follow.

Table 17.9 illustrates the dilemma (with hypothetical numbers) for the R&D game that Kimberly-Clark and Procter & Gamble play. Each firm has two strategies: Do R&D or do no R&D. If neither firm does R&D, Kimberly-Clark makes $30 million and Procter & Gamble makes $70 million (bottom right of the payoff matrix). If each firm does R&D, each firm's profit is lower by the amount spent on R&D (top left square of the payoff matrix). If Kimberly-Clark does R&D but Procter & Gamble does not, Kimberly-Clark gains and Procter & Gamble loses (top right square of the payoff matrix). Finally, if Procter & Gamble conducts R&D and Kimberly-Clark does not, Procter & Gamble gains and Kimberly-Clark loses (bottom left square).

Kimberly-Clark reasons as follows: Regardless of whether Procter & Gamble undertakes R&D, we're better off doing R&D. Procter & Gamble reasons similarly: Regardless of whether Kimberly-Clark does R&D, we're better off doing R&D.

Because R&D is the best strategy for both players, it is the Nash equilibrium. The outcome of this game is that both firms conduct R&D. They make less profit than they would if they could collude to achieve the cooperative outcome of no R&D.

The real-world situation has more players than Kimberly-Clark and Procter & Gamble. A large number of other firms strive to capture market share from Procter & Gamble and Kimberly-Clark. So the R&D effort by these two firms not only serves the purpose of maintaining shares in their own battle but also helps to keep barriers to entry high enough to preserve their joint market share.

**TABLE 17.9 THE R&D GAME PAYOFF MATRIX**

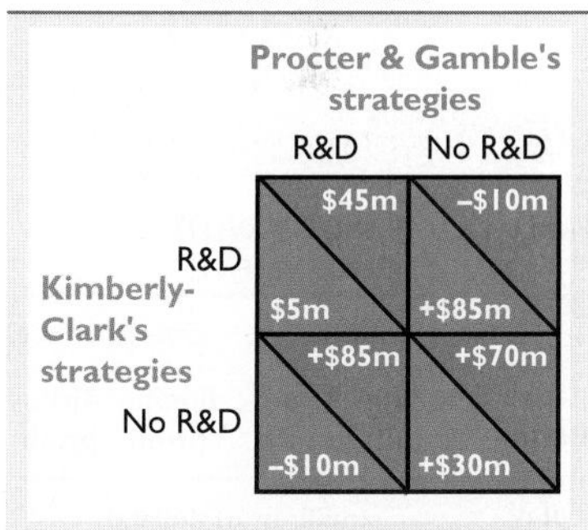


For each pair of strategies, the red triangle shows Procter & Gamble's payoff, and the blue triangle shows Kimberly-Clark's. If both firms do R&D, they make less than if neither firm undertakes R&D. But each firm is better off doing R&D if the other does no R&D. The Nash equilibrium for this prisoners' dilemma R&D game is for both firms to do R&D.

## EYE on YOUR LIFE

### A Game You Might Play

The payoff matrix here describes a game that might be familiar to you. But it isn't a prisoners' dilemma. It's a lovers' dilemma.

Jane and Jim have more fun if they do something together than if they do things alone.

But Jane likes the movies more than the ball game, and Jim likes the ball game more than the movies.

The payoff matrix describes how much they like the various outcomes (measured in units of utility).

What do they do?

By comparing the utility numbers for different strategies, you can figure out that Jim never goes to the movies alone and Jane never goes to the ball game alone.

You can also figure out that Jim doesn't go to the ball game alone and Jane doesn't go to the movies alone.

They always go out together. But do they go to the movies or the ball game?

The answer is that we can't tell. This game has no unique equilibrium. The payoffs tell you that Jane and Jim might go to either the game or the movies.

In a repeated game, they'll probably alternate between the two and might even toss a coin to decide which to go to on any given evening.

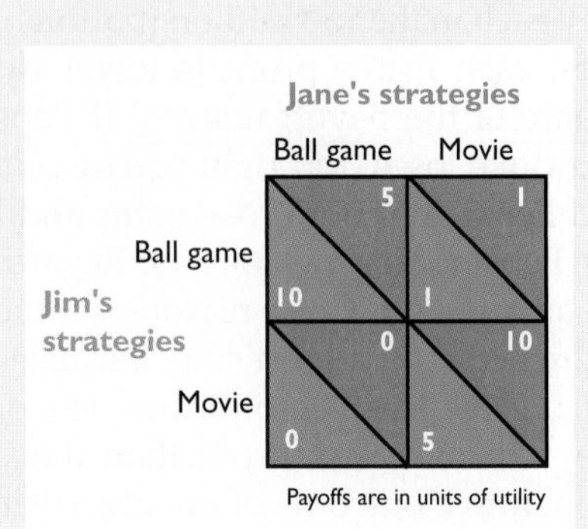


## Repeated Games

The games that we've studied are played just once. In contrast, most real-world games get played repeatedly. This fact suggests that real-world duopolists might find some way of learning to cooperate so that they can enjoy a monopoly profit. If a game is played repeatedly, one player has the opportunity to penalize the other player for previous "bad" behavior. If Airbus produces 4 airplanes this week, perhaps Boeing will produce 4 next week. Before Airbus produces 4 this week, won't it take account of the possibility of Boeing producing 4 next week? What is the equilibrium of this more complicated dilemma game when it is repeated indefinitely?

The monopoly equilibrium might occur if each firm knows that the other will punish overproduction with overproduction, "tit for tat." Let's see why.

**TABLE 17.10 PAYOFFS WITH PUNISHMENT**

| Period of play | Cooperate: Boeing profit | Cooperate: Airbus profit | Overproduce: Boeing profit | Overproduce: Airbus profit |
|---|---|---|---|---|
| | (millions of dollars) | | | |
| 1 | 36 | 36 | 40 | 30 |
| 2 | 36 | 36 | 30 | 40 |

Table 17.10 keeps track of the numbers. Suppose that Boeing contemplates producing 4 airplanes in week 1. This move will bring it an economic profit of \$40 million and will cut the economic profit of Airbus to \$30 million. In week 2, Airbus will punish Boeing and produce 4 airplanes. But Boeing must go back to 3 airplanes to induce Airbus to cooperate again in week 3. So in week 2, Airbus makes an economic profit of \$40 million, and Boeing makes an economic profit of \$30 million. Adding up the profits over these two weeks of play, Boeing would have made \$72 million by cooperating (2 × \$36 million) compared with \$70 million from producing 4 airplanes in week 1 and generating Airbus's tit-for-tat response.

What is true for Boeing is also true for Airbus. Because each firm makes a larger profit by sticking to the monopoly output, both firms do so and the monopoly price, quantity, and profit prevail.

In reality, whether a duopoly (or more generally an oligopoly) works like a one-play game or a repeated game depends primarily on the number of players and the ease of detecting and punishing overproduction. The larger the number of players, the harder it is to maintain the monopoly outcome.

## EYE on the CHIPS DUOPOLY

### Is Two Too Few?

The CPU in your computer or your game box—the brainpower of the machine—is made either by Intel Corporation or by Advanced Micro Devices, Inc. (AMD). Does competition between these duopolists achieve an efficient outcome—a win for the consumer—or just a win for one or both of the producers?

The answer is that Intel is the big winner. The pie chart shows that it dominates this market and the CPU prices graph shows that Intel's prices are generally higher than AMD's prices.

In the game that Intel and AMD play, the outcome is closer to monopoly than perfect competition. Producer surplus is maximized and consumer surplus is less than it would be in a competitive market. There is underproduction and a deadweight loss.

SOURCES OF DATA: Intel, AMD, and sharkyextreme.com.

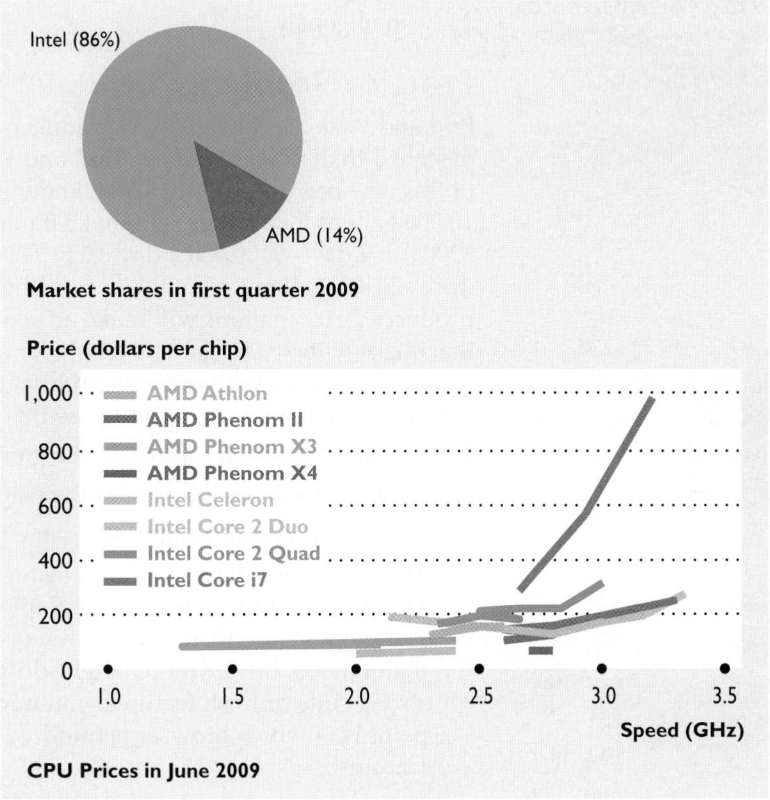


## Is Oligopoly Efficient?

The quantity produced of any good or service is the efficient quantity if the price (which measures marginal benefit) equals marginal cost. Does oligopoly produce efficient quantities of goods and services?

You've seen that if firms in oligopoly play a repeated prisoners' dilemma game, they can end up restricting output to the monopoly level and making the same economic profit as a monopoly would make. You've also seen that even when the firms don't cooperate, they don't necessarily drive the price down to marginal cost. So generally, oligopoly is not efficient. It suffers from the same source of inefficiency as monopoly.

Also, firms in oligopoly might end up operating at a higher average total cost than the lowest attainable cost because their advertising and research budgets are higher than the socially efficient level.

Because oligopoly creates inefficiency and has an incentive to try to behave like a monopoly, the United States has established antitrust laws that seek to reduce market power and move the outcome of oligopoly closer to the efficient outcome of competition. We study U.S. antitrust laws in the next section of this chapter.

Work these problems in Study Plan 17.3 to get instant feedback.

## CHECKPOINT 17.3

**Use game theory to explain how price and quantity are determined in oligopoly.**

### Practice Problems

Bud and Wise are the only two producers of aniseed beer, a New Age product designed to displace root beer. Bud and Wise are trying to figure out how much of this new beer to produce. They know that if they both limit production to 10,000 gallons a day, they will make the maximum attainable joint profit of \$200,000 a day—\$100,000 a day each. They also know that if either of them produces 20,000 gallons a day while the other produces 10,000 a day, the one that produces 20,000 gallons will make an economic profit of \$150,000 and the one that sticks with 10,000 gallons will incur an economic loss of \$50,000. Each also knows that if they both increase production to 20,000 gallons a day, they will both make zero economic profit. Use this information to work Problems **1** to **3**.

1. Construct a payoff matrix for the game that Bud and Wise must play.
2. Find the Nash equilibrium of the game that Bud and Wise play.
3. What is the equilibrium of the game if Bud and Wise play it repeatedly?
4. **Microsoft Internet Explorer is faster than Mozilla Firefox**
   Promotions of the new Internet Explorer IE8 say it is faster, more reliable, and more secure than rival browsers. One reviewer noted that IE8 is slower than Firefox, but if you're a light-duty user and attracted to the new IE's strong suite of fresh features, you might prefer it to Firefox. Another says the point isn't which browser is hundredths of a second faster, but other features.

   Source: *USA Today*, March 23, 2009

   What is the game that Microsoft and Mozilla have played in the past few years? How do you think the game will change in the coming years?

### Guided Solutions to Practice Problems

**TABLE 1**

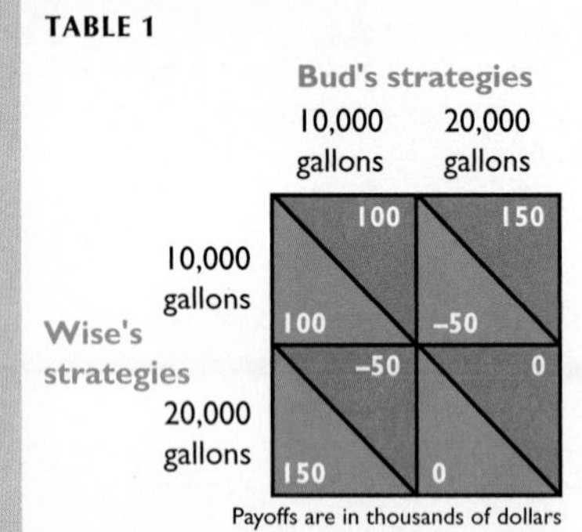

| | | Bud's strategies | |
|---|---|---|---|
| | | 10,000 gallons | 20,000 gallons |
| Wise's strategies | 10,000 gallons | 100 (Bud) / 100 (Wise) | 150 (Bud) / −50 (Wise) |
| | 20,000 gallons | −50 (Bud) / 150 (Wise) | 0 (Bud) / 0 (Wise) |

Payoffs are in thousands of dollars

1. Table 1 shows the payoff matrix for the game that Bud and Wise must play.
2. The Nash equilibrium is for both to produce 20,000 gallons a day. To see why, notice that regardless of the quantity that Bud produces, Wise makes more profit by producing 20,000 gallons a day. The same is true for Bud. So Bud and Wise each produce 20,000 gallons a day.
3. If Bud and Wise play this game repeatedly, each produces 10,000 gallons a day and makes maximum economic profit. They can achieve this outcome by playing a tit-for-tat strategy.
4. The game that Microsoft and Mozilla have played is product development: improving speed or adding features. The outcome has been that both have allocated development to increasing speed and as the reviewers imply their speeds are only hundredths of a second apart (basically the same). In the coming years, the development game will probably move away from speed and to additional features to maintain or expand market share.

## 17.4 ANTITRUST LAW

**Antitrust law** is the body of law that regulates oligopolies and prohibits them from becoming monopolies or behaving like monopolies.

**Antitrust law**
A law that regulates oligopolies and prohibits them from becoming monopolies or behaving like monopolies.

### The Antitrust Laws

Congress passed the first antitrust law, the Sherman Act, in 1890 in an atmosphere of outrage and disgust at the actions and practices of J. P. Morgan, John D. Rockefeller, and W. H. Vanderbilt—the so-called "robber barons."

A wave of mergers at the turn of the twentieth century produced stronger antitrust laws. The Clayton Act of 1914 supplemented the Sherman Act, and Congress created the Federal Trade Commission to enforce the antitrust laws.

Table 17.11 summarizes the two main provisions of the Sherman Act. Section 1 of the act is precise. Conspiring with others to restrict competition is illegal. But section 2 is general and imprecise. Just what is an "attempt to monopolize"? The Clayton Act and its two amendments, the Robinson-Patman Act of 1936 and Celler-Kefauver Act of 1950, which outlaw specific practices, answer this question. Table 17.11 describes these practices and summarizes the main provisions of these three acts.

### Three Antitrust Policy Debates

Price fixing is *always* a violation of the antitrust law. If the Justice Department can prove the existence of price fixing, a defendant can offer no acceptable excuse. But other practices are more controversial and generate debate among antitrust lawyers and economists. We'll examine three of these practices:

- Resale price maintenance
- Predatory pricing
- Tying arrangements

#### Resale Price Maintenance

Most manufacturers sell their products to the final consumer indirectly through a wholesale and retail distribution system. **Resale price maintenance** occurs when a manufacturer agrees with a distributor on the price at which the product will be resold.

**Resale price maintenance**
An agreement between a manufacturer and a distributor on the price at which a product will be resold.

Resale price maintenance (also called vertical price fixing) *agreements* are illegal under the Sherman Act. But it isn't illegal for a manufacturer to refuse to supply a retailer who doesn't accept the manufacturer's guidance on what the price should be.

Attorneys general in 41 states alleged that Universal, Sony, Warner, Bertelsmann, and EMI kept CD prices artificially high between 1995 and 2000 with a practice called "minimum-advertised pricing." The companies denied the allegation but made a large payment to settle the case.

Does resale price maintenance create an inefficient or efficient use of resources? Economists can be found on both sides of this question.

***Inefficient Resale Price Maintenance*** Resale price maintenance is inefficient if it enables dealers to charge the monopoly price. By setting and enforcing the resale price, the manufacturer might be able to achieve the monopoly price.

**TABLE 17.11**
The Antitrust Laws: A Summary

### The Sherman Act, 1890

**Section 1:**

Every contract, combination in the form of trust or otherwise, or conspiracy, in restraint of trade or commerce among the several States, or with foreign nations, is hereby declared to be illegal.

**Section 2:**

Every person who shall monopolize, or attempt to monopolize, or combine or conspire with any other person or persons, to monopolize any part of the trade or commerce among the several States, or with foreign nations, shall be deemed guilty of a felony.

### Clayton Act, 1914

### Robinson-Patman Act, 1936

### Celler-Kefauver Act, 1950

These acts prohibit the following practices only if they substantially lessen competition or create monopoly:

1. Price discrimination.
2. Contracts that require other goods to be bought from the same firm (called tying arrangements).
3. Contracts that require a firm to buy all its requirements of a particular item from a single firm (called requirements contracts).
4. Contracts that prevent a firm from selling competing items (called exclusive dealing).
5. Contracts that prevent a buyer from reselling a product outside a specified area (called territorial confinement).
6. Acquiring a competitor's shares or assets.
7. Becoming a director of a competing firm.

***Efficient Resale Price Maintenance*** Resale price maintenance might be efficient if it enables a manufacturer to induce dealers to provide the efficient standard of service. Suppose that SilkySkin wants shops to demonstrate the use of its new unbelievable moisturizing cream in an inviting space. With resale price maintenance, SilkySkin can offer all the retailers the same incentive and compensation. Without resale price maintenance, a discount drug store might offer SilkySkin products at a low price. Buyers would then have an incentive to visit a high-price shop and get the product demonstrated and then buy from the low-price shop. The low-price shop would be a free rider (like the consumer of a public good in Chapter 10, p. 249), and an inefficient level of service would be provided.

SilkySkin could pay a fee to retailers that provide good service and leave the resale price to be determined by the competitive forces of supply and demand. But it might be too costly for SilkySkin to monitor shops and ensure that they provided the desired level of service.

### Predatory Pricing

**Predatory pricing** is setting a low price to drive competitors out of business with the intention of setting a monopoly price when the competition has gone. John D. Rockefeller's Standard Oil Company was the first to be accused of this practice in the 1890s, and it has been claimed often in antitrust cases since then. Predatory pricing is an attempt to create a monopoly and as such it is illegal under Section 2 of the Sherman Act.

**Predatory pricing**
Setting a low price to drive competitors out of business with the intention of setting a monopoly price when the competition has gone.

It is easy to see that predatory pricing is an idea, not a reality. Economists are skeptical that predatory pricing occurs. They point out that a firm that cuts its price below the profit-maximizing level forgoes profit during the low-price period. Even if the firm succeeds in driving its competitors out of business, new competitors will enter when the firm raises its price above average total cost and makes an economic profit. So any potential gain from a monopoly position is temporary. A high and certain loss is a poor exchange for a temporary and uncertain gain. No case of predatory pricing has been definitively found.

### Tying Arrangements

A **tying arrangement** is an agreement to sell one product only if the buyer agrees to buy another, different product. With tying, the only way the buyer can get the one product is to buy the other product at the same time. Microsoft has been accused of tying Internet Explorer and Windows. Textbook publishers sometimes tie a Web site and a textbook and force students to buy both. (You can't buy the book you're now reading, new, without the Web site. But you can buy the Web site access without the book, so these products are not tied.)

**Tying arrangement**
An agreement to sell one product only if the buyer agrees to buy another, different product.

Could publishers of textbooks make more money by tying a book and access to a Web site? The answer is sometimes but not always. Think about what you are willing to pay for a book and access to a Web site. To keep the numbers simple, suppose that you and other students are willing to pay $40 for a book and $10 for access to a Web site. The publisher can sell these items separately for these prices or bundled for $50. There is no gain to the publisher from bundling.

But now suppose that you and only half of the students are willing to pay $40 for a book and $10 for a Web site. And suppose that the other half of the students are willing to pay $40 for a Web site and $10 for a book. Now if the two items are sold separately, the publisher can charge $40 for the book and $40 for the Web site. Half the students buy the book but not the Web site, and the other half buy the Web site but not the book. But if the book and Web site are bundled for $50, everyone buys the bundle and the publisher makes an extra $10 per student. In this case, bundling has enabled the publisher to price discriminate.

There is no simple, clear-cut test of whether a firm is engaging in tying or whether, by doing so, it has increased its market power and profit and created inefficiency.

## Recent Antitrust Showcase: The United States Versus Microsoft

In 1998, the U.S. Department of Justice, along with a number of states, charged Microsoft, the world's largest producer of software for personal computers, with violations of both sections of the Sherman Act. A 78-day trial followed that pitched two prominent MIT economics professors against each other (Franklin Fisher for the government and Richard Schmalensee for Microsoft).

### The Case Against Microsoft

The claims against Microsoft were that it

- Possessed monopoly power in the market for PC operating systems.
- Used *predatory pricing* and *tying arrangements* to achieve a monopoly in the market for Web browsers.
- Used other anticompetitive practices to strengthen its monopoly in these two markets.

It was claimed that with 80 percent of the market for PC operating systems, Microsoft had excessive monopoly power. This monopoly power arose from two barriers to entry: economies of scale and network economies. Microsoft's average total cost falls as production increases (economies of scale) because the fixed cost of developing an operating system like Windows is large while the marginal cost of producing one copy of Windows is small. Further, as the number of Windows users increases, the range of Windows applications expands (network economies), so a potential competitor would need to produce not only a competing operating system but also an entire range of supporting applications.

When Microsoft entered the Web browser market with its Internet Explorer (IE), it offered the browser for a zero price. This price was viewed as *predatory pricing.* Microsoft integrated IE with Windows so that anyone who uses this operating system would not need a separate browser such as Netscape Communicator. Microsoft's competitors claimed that this practice was an illegal *tying arrangement.*

### Microsoft's Response

Microsoft challenged all these claims. It said that although Windows was the dominant operating system, it was vulnerable to competition from other operating systems such as Linux and Apple's Mac OS and that there was a permanent threat of competition from new entrants.

Microsoft claimed that integrating Internet Explorer with Windows provided a single, unified product of greater consumer value. Instead of tying, Microsoft said, the browser and operating system constituted a single product. It was like a refrigerator with a chilled water dispenser or an automobile with a stereo player.

### The Outcome

The court agreed that Microsoft was in violation of the Sherman Act and ordered that it be broken into two firms: an operating systems producer and an applications producer. Microsoft successfully appealed this order. But in the final judgment, Microsoft was ordered to disclose details about how its operating system works to other software developers so that they could compete effectively against Microsoft. In the summer of 2002, Microsoft began to comply with this order.

## ■ Merger Rules

You've now seen how the antitrust laws can be used to prevent an oligopoly from becoming a monopoly or trying to behave like one. We end by examining another way of trying to gain monopoly power—two or more oligopoly firms merging to increase their ability to control the market price. Mergers are subject to rules that are designed to limit monopoly power from arising and we close our explanation of the antitrust laws by seeing how they are used to review and sometimes to block a merger.

The Federal Trade Commission (FTC) challenges proposed mergers that will substantially lessen competition and not bring lower costs. To determine the effects of a merger on competitiveness, the FTC uses guidelines based on the Herfindahl-Hirschman Index (HHI), which is explained in Chapter 16 (p. 411).

A market in which the HHI is less than 1,000 is regarded as competitive and a merger in such a market is not considered to be a problem.

An HHI between 1,000 and 1,800 indicates a moderately concentrated market, and a merger in this market would substantially lessen competition if the HHI increased by 100 points. An index above 1,800 indicates a concentrated market, and a merger in this market that would increase the index by 50 points is challenged.

*Eye on the U.S. Economy,* below, looks at a merger that was blocked by this rule.

## EYE on the U.S. ECONOMY

### No Soda Merger

The figure (part a) summarizes the Federal Trade Commission's (FTC) guidelines on mergers. In a market in which the Herfindahl-Hirschman Index (HHI) is less than 1,000, a proposed merger is not challenged. But if the HHI is above 1,000, the FTC considers a challenge. If the HHI is between 1,000 and 1,800, a merger is challenged if it would increase the HHI by 100 points. And if the HHI exceeds 1,800 the market is already so concentrated that a merger is challenged even if it increases the index by only 50 points.

In 1986, PepsiCo wanted to buy 7-Up and Coca-Cola wanted to buy Dr Pepper. But the market for soda is highly concentrated. Coca-Cola has a 39 percent share, PepsiCo has 28 percent, Dr Pepper is next with 7 percent, then comes 7-Up with 6 percent. One other producer, RJR, has a 5 percent market share. So the five largest firms in this market have an 85 percent market share. The Herfindahl-Hirschman index is more than 2,400.

With an HHI of this magnitude, a merger that increases the index by only 50 points is examined by the FTC.

Part (b) of the figure shows how the HHI would have changed with the mergers. A PepsiCo–7-Up merger would increase the index by more than 300 points, a Coca-Cola–Dr Pepper merger would increase it by more than 500 points, and both mergers together would increase the HHI by almost 800 points. The FTC decided to block these mergers.

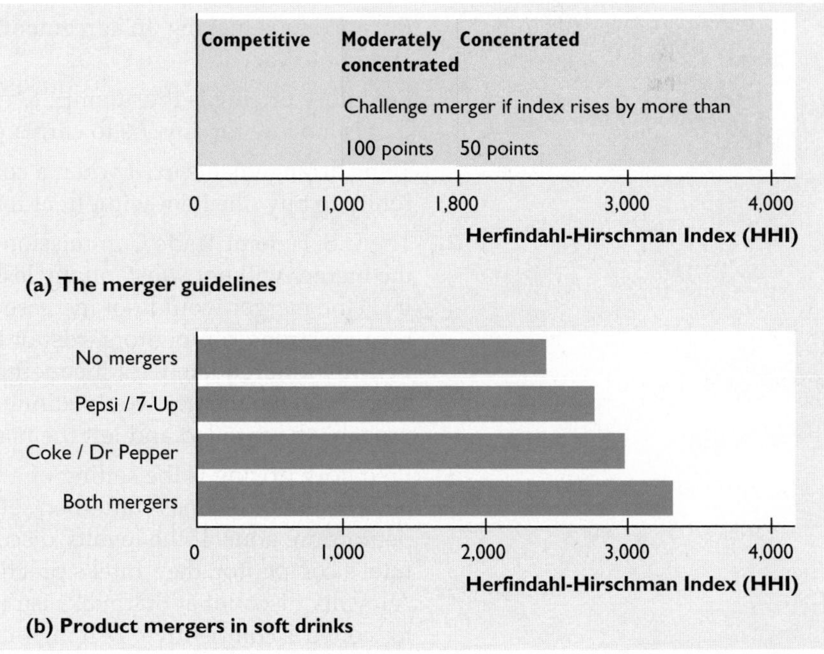


**(a) The merger guidelines**

**(b) Product mergers in soft drinks**

Work these problems in Study Plan 17.4 to get instant feedback.

## CHECKPOINT 17.4

**Describe the antitrust laws that regulate oligopoly.**

## Practice Problems

1. Explain each of the following terms:
   - Attempt to monopolize
   - Price fixing
   - Predatory pricing
   - Tying arrangements
2. Since 1987, hundreds of hospital mergers have taken place in the United States. Rarely has the U.S. Federal Trade Commission challenged a hospital merger. What can you infer about the structure of the market in hospital services?
3. **Intel will find refuge in the courts**

   The European Union recently fined Intel $1.45 billion because it gave "loyalty discounts" to repeat customers, presumably increasing Intel's dominance in the microprocessor business—called predatory pricing in the United States.

   Source: *Wall Street Journal*, June 2, 2009

   Did Intel practice predatory pricing? If every morning you pick up a coffee at Starbucks and it offers you a loyalty discount, is that predatory pricing?

## Guided Solutions to Practice Problems

1. An attempt to monopolize is an attempt by a company to drive out its competitors so that it can operate as a monopoly.

   Price fixing is making an agreement with competitors to set a specified price and not to vary it.

   Predatory pricing is the attempt to drive out competitors by charging a price that is too low for anyone to earn a profit.

   Tying arrangements exist when a company does not offer a buyer the opportunity to buy one item without at the same time buying another item.
2. The U.S. Federal Trade Commission will not challenge a hospital merger if the merger will not substantially lessen competition. Such a situation arises if (1) the merger would not increase the likelihood of market power either because strong competitors exist or because the merging hospitals were sufficiently differentiated; (2) the merger would allow the hospitals to reduce cost; or (3) the merger would eliminate a hospital that otherwise would probably have failed and left the market.
3. Predatory pricing is the setting of a low price with the aim of driving competitors out of business and then setting the monopoly price when the competitors are gone. If the loyalty discount was intended to drive out AMD, Intel's competitor, then Intel's practice was predatory pricing.

   A loyalty discount at Starbucks isn't predatory pricing because the market for coffee is competitive. Driving out one coffee outlet will not create monopoly.

## CHAPTER SUMMARY

### Key Points

1 **Describe and identify oligopoly and explain how it arises.**

- Oligopoly is a market type in which a small number of interdependent firms compete behind a barrier to entry.
- Both natural (economies of scale and market demand) and legal barriers to entry create oligopoly.

2 **Explain the dilemma faced by firms in oligopoly.**

- If firms in oligopoly act together to restrict output, they make the same economic profit as a monopoly, but each firm can make a larger profit by increasing production.
- The oligopoly dilemma is whether to restrict or expand output.

3 **Use game theory to explain how price and quantity are determined in oligopoly.**

- In the prisoners' dilemma game, two players acting in their own interests harm their joint interest. Oligopoly is a prisoners' dilemma game.
- If firms cooperated, they could earn the monopoly profit, but in a one-play game, they overproduce and drive the price and economic profit to the levels of perfect competition.
- Advertising and research and development create a prisoners' dilemma for firms in oligopoly.
- In a repeated game, a punishment strategy can lead to monopoly output, price, and economic profit.
- Oligopoly is usually inefficient because the price (marginal benefit) exceeds marginal cost and cost might not be the lowest attainable.

4 **Describe the antitrust laws that regulate oligopoly.**

- The Sherman Act (1890) and the Clayton Act (1914) make price-fixing agreements among firms illegal.
- Resale price maintenance might be efficient if it enables a producer to ensure the efficient level of service by distributors.
- Predatory pricing might bring temporary gains.
- Tying arrangements can facilitate price discrimination.
- The Federal Trade Commission examines and possibly blocks mergers if they would restrict competition too much.

### Key Terms

Antitrust law, 449
Cartel, 432
Duopoly, 432
Game theory, 441
Nash equilibrium, 442
Payoff matrix, 442
Predatory pricing, 451
Prisoners' dilemma, 441
Resale price maintenance, 449
Strategies, 442
Tying arrangement, 451

Work these problems in Chapter 17 Study Plan to get instant feedback.

# CHAPTER CHECKPOINT

## Study Plan Problems and Applications

Use the following information to work Problems 1 and 2.

When the first automobiles were built in 1901, they were manufactured by skilled workers using hand tools. Later, in 1913, Henry Ford introduced the moving assembly line, which lowered costs and speeded production. Over the years, the production line has become ever more mechanized, and today robots have replaced people in many operations.

1. Sketch the average total cost curve and the demand curve for automobiles in 1901 and in 2009.
2. Describe the changing barriers to entry in the automobile industry and explain how the combination of market demand and economies of scale has changed the structure of the industry over the past 100 years.

Use the following information to work Problems 3 to 5.

Isolated Island has two taxi companies, one owned by Ann and the other owned by Zack. Figure 1 shows the market demand curve for taxi rides, *D*, and the average total cost curve of one of the firms, *ATC*.

**FIGURE 1**

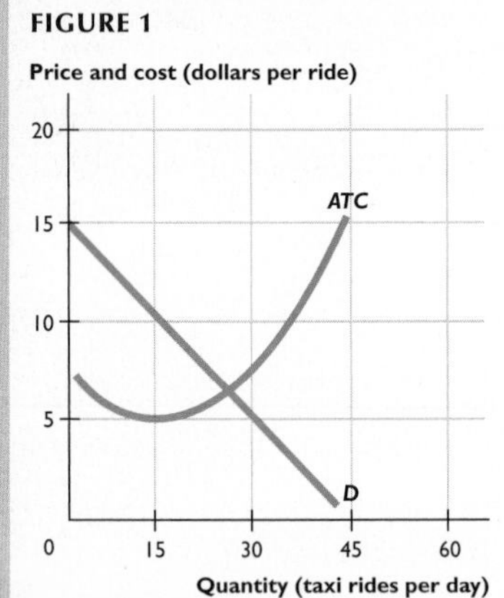


3. If Ann and Zack produce the same quantity of rides as would be produced in perfect competition, what are the quantity of rides, the price of a ride, and the economic profit of Ann and Zack? Would Ann and Zack have an incentive to collude and raise their price? Explain why or why not.
4. If Ann and Zack form a cartel and produce the same quantity of rides as would be produced in monopoly, what are the quantity of rides, the price of a ride, and the economic profit of Ann and Zack? Would Ann and Zack have an incentive to break the cartel agreement and cut their price? Explain why or why not.
5. Suppose that Ann and Zack have two strategies: collude, fix the monopoly price, and limit the number of rides or break the collusion, cut the price, and produce more rides. Create a payoff matrix for the game that Ann and Zack play, and find the Nash equilibrium for this game if it is played just once. Do the people of Isolated Island get the efficient quantity of taxi rides?

Use the following information to work Problems 6 and 7.

**Coke and Pepsi battle it out**

Until 2004, Pepsi was sold in the Gulf, but not Coca-Cola. Today, Pepsi is fighting to keep its dominant position in the Middle East. Coca-Cola and Pepsi have avoided a price war and have entered into a "display marketing" war. Each copies the other's promotions and tries to do even better. Coca-Cola and Pepsi are at each other's throats, and that's good news for everyone.

*AME Info*, April 8, 2004

6. Describe the game that Coca-Cola and PepsiCo play in the Middle East. Why is it "good news for everyone" in the Middle East?
7. Why would Coke and Pepsi steer clear of a price war even though they are "at each other's throats"?

## Instructor Assignable Problems and Applications

Your instructor can assign these problems as homework, a quiz, or a test in **MyEconLab**.

1. Intel and AMD have two pricing strategies: Set a high (monopoly) price or set a low (competitive) price. Suppose that if they both set a competitive price, economic profit for both is zero. If both set a monopoly price, Intel gets an economic profit of $860 million and AMD of $140 million. If Intel sets a low price and AMD sets a high price, Intel makes an economic profit of $100 million and AMD incurs an economic loss of $10 million; if Intel sets a high price and AMD sets a low price, Intel incurs an economic loss of $100 million and AMD makes an economic profit of $10 million.
   - Create the payoff matrix for this game.
   - What is the equilibrium of this game?
   - Is the equilibrium efficient?
   - Is this game a prisoner's dilemma?

Use the following information to work Problems 2 and 3.

The United States claims that Canada subsidizes the production of softwood lumber and that imports of Canadian lumber damage the interests of U.S. producers. The United States has imposed a tariff on Canadian imports to counter the subsidy. Canada is thinking of retaliating by refusing to export water to California. Table 1 shows a payoff matrix for the game that the United States and Canada are playing.

2. What is the United States' best strategy? What is Canada's best strategy? What is the outcome of this game? Explain.
3. Is this game like a prisoners' dilemma or different in some crucial way? Explain. Which country would benefit more from a free trade agreement?

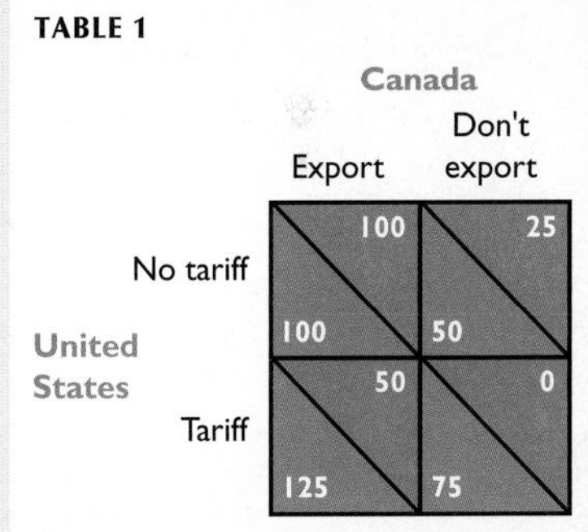


Use the following information to work Problems 4 and 5.

**Consumers drive bulk of BlackBerry growth**

Research in Motion (RIM) added 3.8 million new BlackBerry subscribers in the last quarter and increased its profit by 33 percent. Consumers made up 80 percent of the new subscribers as RIM introduced new features and lowered prices. But competition increased as Apple introduced its new iPhone and lowered the price of its older model. RIM said it "isn't worried about the competition."

Source: *Wall Street Journal*, June 19, 2009

4. Describe the game that RIM and Apple are playing in the market for smart phones.
5. Construct a payoff matrix for the game RIM and Apple are playing. What is the equilibrium of the game?.
6. Agile Airlines is making $10 million a year economic profit on a route on which it has a monopoly. Wanabe Airlines is considering entering the market and operating on this route. Agile warns Wanabe to stay out and threatens to cut the price to the point at which Wanabe will make no profit if it enters. Wanabe does some research and determines that the payoff matrix for the game in which it is engaged with Agile is that shown in Table 2. Does Wanabe believe Agile's assertion? Does Wanabe enter or not? Explain.

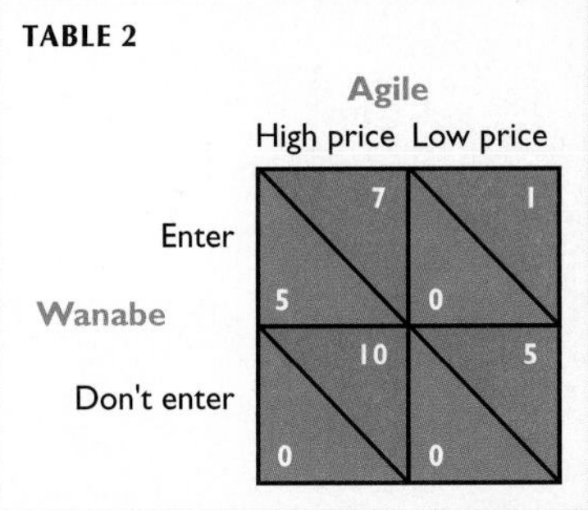

Use the following information to work Problems 7 and 8.

Coke and Pepsi know that they are spending millions of dollars on advertising just to counter each other's ads. The marketing managers of the two firms spend a weekend on the golf course plotting a collaboration that will cut each firm's costs by $100 million a year. Back at the office on Monday, they begin to sell their scheme to their chief financial officers (CFOs), who have studied some economics. The CFOs tell the marketing managers that their plan won't work.

7. Why are the CFOs so sure? Sketch a payoff matrix that describes the advertising game played by Coke and Pepsi that supports the CFOs. Find and describe the Nash equilibrium for the game.
8. Sketch a payoff matrix that describes an advertising game played by Coke and Pepsi that does not support the CFOs and that makes the sales managers' plan possible. Find and describe the Nash equilibrium for the game.

Use this information to work Problems 9 and 10.

**"I'm About to Lose You"**

The cell-phone industry ranks among the bottom five businesses in the American Customer Satisfaction Index. Critics say that the wireless industry has become a cozy cartel of a few dominant providers. They point to several unfair practices: high termination fees; costly to switch providers; handsets that only work with a single carrier; and limited access to Web sites. Now Washington is listening.

Source: *Newsweek*, August 6, 2007

9. If "the wireless industry has become a cozy cartel of a few dominant providers," explain how they set their prices and share the market.
10. If it were costless to switch providers, explain what changes would occur in the cell-phone market. Would there be a role for Washington?

Use this information to work Problems 11 and 12.

**Airlines pay $504M to settle price-fixing scam**

Four international airlines have agreed to pay $504 million in fines to settle charges that they set up a price-fixing scheme that raised cargo rates, fuel surcharges, and security costs between 2001 and 2006. The scheme cost consumers hundreds of millions of dollars. The Justice Department called the case one of the largest antitrust settlements in U.S. history.

Source: *USAToday*, June 26, 2008

11. Explain how the price-fixing scheme benefited the airlines and imposed costs on consumers.
12. Describe the price-fixing scheme as the equilibrium outcome of an oligopoly cartel game played by the four international airlines. Explain why the cartel survived and why a prisoners' dilemma didn't bring about a competitive equilibrium outcome
13. Adam Smith wrote in *The Wealth of Nations*, published in 1776, "People of the same trade seldom meet together, even for merriment and diversion, but the conversation ends in a conspiracy against the public, or in some contrivance to raise prices." What do you think this quotation implies about the predominant market structure in Adam Smith's world of the late 1700s? Why?

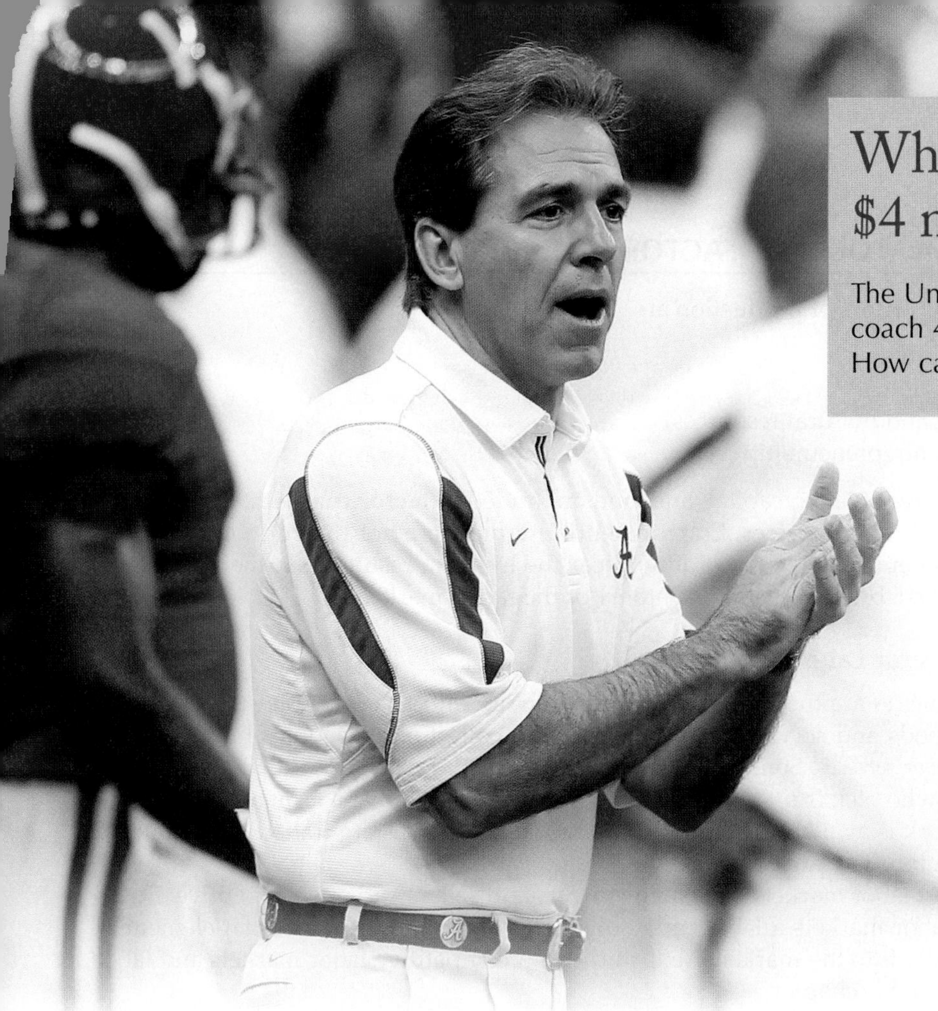

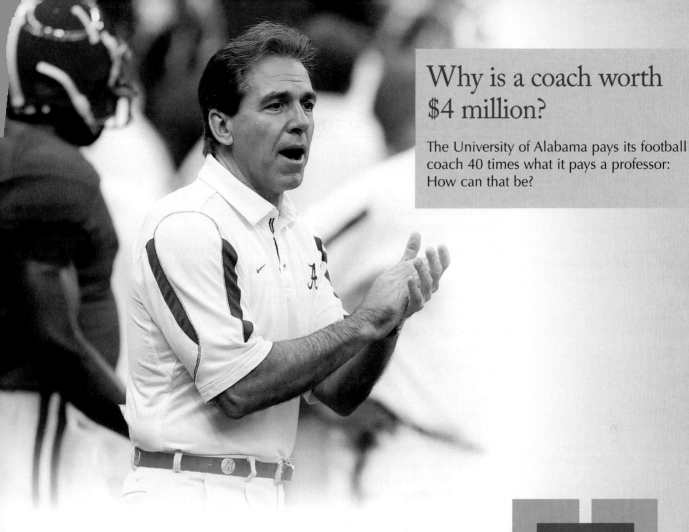

## Why is a coach worth $4 million?

The University of Alabama pays its football coach 40 times what it pays a professor: How can that be?

# Markets for Factors of Production

CHAPTER CHECKLIST

**When you have completed your study of this chapter, you will be able to**

1 Explain how the value of marginal product determines the demand for a factor of production.

2 Explain how wage rates and employment are determined and how labor unions influence labor markets.

3 Explain how capital and land rental rates and natural resource prices are determined.

## THE ANATOMY OF FACTOR MARKETS

The four factors of production are

- Labor
- Capital
- Land (natural resources)
- Entrepreneurship

**Factor markets**
The markets in which the services of the factors of production are traded.

**Factor prices**
The prices of the services of the factors of production.

The *services* of labor, capital, and land are traded in **factor markets**, which determine their **factor prices.** Entrepreneurial services are not traded in markets and entrepreneurs receive the profit or bear the loss that results from their decisions. Let's take a brief look at the anatomy of the factor markets.

### Markets for Labor Services

**Job**
A contract between a firm and a household to provide labor services.

*Labor services* are the physical and mental work effort that people supply to produce goods and services. A *labor market* is a collection of people and firms who trade *labor services*. Some labor services are traded day by day, called casual labor. People who pick fruit and vegetables often just show up at a farm and take whatever work is available that day. But most labor services are traded on a contract, called a **job**. The price of labor services is a wage rate.

Most labor markets have many buyers and sellers and are competitive. But in some labor markets a labor union organizes labor and introduces an element of monopoly into the market. We'll study both competitive labor markets and labor unions in this chapter.

### Markets for Capital Services

*Capital* consists of the tools, instruments, machines, buildings, and other constructions that have been produced in the past and that businesses now use to produce goods and services. These physical objects are themselves goods—*capital goods*—and are traded in goods markets, just as bottled water and toothpaste are.

A market for *capital services* is a *rental market*—a market in which the services of capital are hired. An example of a market for capital services is the vehicle rental market in which Avis, Budget, Hertz, U-Haul, and many other firms offer automobiles and trucks for hire. The price of capital services is a rental rate.

Most capital services are not traded in a market. Instead, a firm buys capital equipment and uses it itself. But the services of the capital that a firm owns and operates itself have an *implicit* price that arises from depreciation and interest costs (see Chapter 13, p. 321). You can think of the price as the *implicit rental rate* of capital.

### Markets for Land Services and Natural Resources

*Land* consists of all the gifts of nature—natural resources. The market for land as a factor of production is the market for the *services of land*—the *use* of land. The price of the services of land is a rental rate.

**Nonrenewable natural resources**
Natural resources that can be used only once and cannot be replaced once they have been used.

Most natural resources, such as farm land, can be used repeatedly. But a few natural resources are nonrenewable. **Nonrenewable natural resources** are resources that can be used only once and cannot be replaced once they have been used. Examples are oil, natural gas, and coal. The prices of natural resources are determined in global *commodity markets* and are called *commodity prices.*

## 18.1 THE DEMAND FOR A FACTOR OF PRODUCTION

We begin our study of factor markets by learning about the demand for factors of production, and we use labor as the example.The demand for a factor of production is a **derived demand**—it is derived from the demand for the goods and services that it is used to produce. You've seen, in Chapters 14 through 17, how a firm determines its profit-maximizing output. The quantities of factors of production demanded are a direct consequence of firms' output decisions. Firms hire the quantities of factors of production that maximize profit.

**Derived demand**
The demand for a factor of production, which is derived from the demand for the goods and services that it is used to produce.

To decide the quantity of a factor of production to hire, a firm compares the cost of hiring an additional unit of the factor with its value to the firm. The cost of hiring an additional unit of a factor of production is the factor price. The value to the firm of hiring one more unit of a factor of production is called the factor's **value of marginal product**, which equals the price of a unit of output multiplied by the marginal product of the factor of production. To study the demand for a factor of production, we'll examine the demand for labor.

**Value of marginal product**
The value to a firm of hiring one more unit of a factor of production, which equals the price of a unit of output multiplied by the marginal product of the factor of production.

### Value of Marginal Product

Table 18.1 shows you how to calculate the value of the marginal product of labor at Max's Wash 'n' Wax car wash service. The first two columns show Max's *total product* schedule—the number of car washes per hour that each quantity of labor can produce. The third column shows the *marginal product* of labor—the change in total product that results from a one-unit increase in the quantity of labor employed. (See Chapter 13, pp. 325–329, for a refresher on product schedules.) Max can sell car washes at the going market price of $3 a wash. Given this information, we can calculate the value of marginal product (fourth column). It equals price multiplied by marginal product. For example, the marginal product of hiring the second worker is 4 car washes an hour. Each wash brings in $3, so the value of the marginal product of the second worker is $12 (4 washes at $3 each).

**TABLE 18.1**

Calculating the Value of Marginal Product

| | Quantity of labor (workers) | Total product (car washes per hour) | Marginal product (washes per additional worker) | Value of marginal product (dollars per additional worker) |
|---|---|---|---|---|
| *A* | 0 | 0 | | |
| | | | 5 | 15 |
| *B* | 1 | 5 | | |
| | | | 4 | 12 |
| *C* | 2 | 9 | | |
| | | | 3 | 9 |
| *D* | 3 | 12 | | |
| | | | 2 | 6 |
| *E* | 4 | 14 | | |
| | | | 1 | 3 |
| *F* | 5 | 15 | | |

The price of a car wash is $3.The value of the marginal product of labor equals the price of the product multiplied by marginal product of labor (column 3).The marginal product of the second worker is 4 washes, so the value of the marginal product of the second worker (in column 4) is $3 a wash multiplied by 4 washes, which is $12.

### The Value of Marginal Product Curve

Figure 18.1 graphs the value of the marginal product of labor at Max's Wash 'n' Wax as the number of workers that Max hires changes. The blue bars that show the value of the marginal product of labor correspond to the numbers in Table 18.1. The curve labeled *VMP* is Max's value of marginal product curve.

## A Firm's Demand for Labor

The value of the marginal product of labor and the wage rate determine the quantity of labor demanded by a firm. The value of the marginal product of labor tells us the additional revenue the firm earns by hiring one more worker. The wage rate tells us the additional cost the firm incurs by hiring one more worker.

Because the value of marginal product decreases as the quantity of labor employed increases, there is a simple rule for maximizing profit: Hire labor up to the point at which the value of marginal product equals the wage rate. If the value of marginal product of labor exceeds the wage rate, a firm can increase its profit by employing one more worker. If the wage rate exceeds the value of marginal product of labor, a firm can increase its profit by employing one less worker. But if the wage rate equals the value of the marginal product of labor, the firm cannot increase its profit by changing the number of workers it employs. The firm is making the maximum possible profit.

So the quantity of labor demanded by a firm is the quantity at which the wage rate equals the value of the marginal product of labor.

**FIGURE 18.1**

The Value of the Marginal Product at Max's Wash 'n' Wax

myeconlab Animation

The blue bars show the value of the marginal product of the labor that Max hires based on the numbers in Table 18.1. The orange line is the firm's value of the marginal product of labor curve.

| | Quantity of labor (workers) | Value of marginal product (dollars per additional worker) |
|---|---|---|
| *A* | 1 | 15 |
| *B* | 2 | 12 |
| *C* | 3 | 9 |
| *D* | 4 | 6 |
| *E* | 5 | 3 |

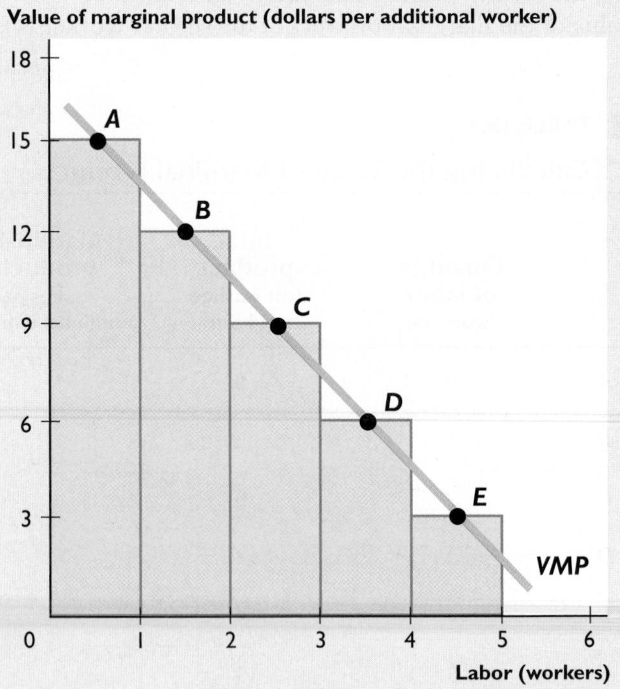

## A Firm's Demand for Labor Curve

A firm's demand for labor curve is also its value of marginal product curve. If the wage rate falls and other things remain the same, a firm hires more workers. Figure 18.2 shows Max's value of marginal product curve in part (a) and demand for labor curve in part (b). The $x$-axis measures the number of workers hired in both parts. The $y$-axis measures the value of marginal product in part (a) and the wage rate—dollars per hour—in part (b).

Suppose the wage rate is $10.50 an hour. You can see in part (a) that if Max hires 1 worker, the value of the marginal product of labor is $15 an hour. Because this 1 worker costs Max only $10.50 an hour, he makes a profit of $4.50 an hour. If Max hires 2 workers, the value of the marginal product of the second worker is $12 an hour. So on this second worker, Max makes a profit of $1.50 an hour. Max's total profit per hour on the first two workers is $6 an hour—$4.50 on the first worker plus $1.50 on the second worker.

If Max hired 3 workers, his profit would fall. The third worker generates a marginal product of only $9 an hour but costs $10.50 an hour, so Max does not hire

**FIGURE 18.2**

The Demand for Labor at Max's Wash 'n' Wax

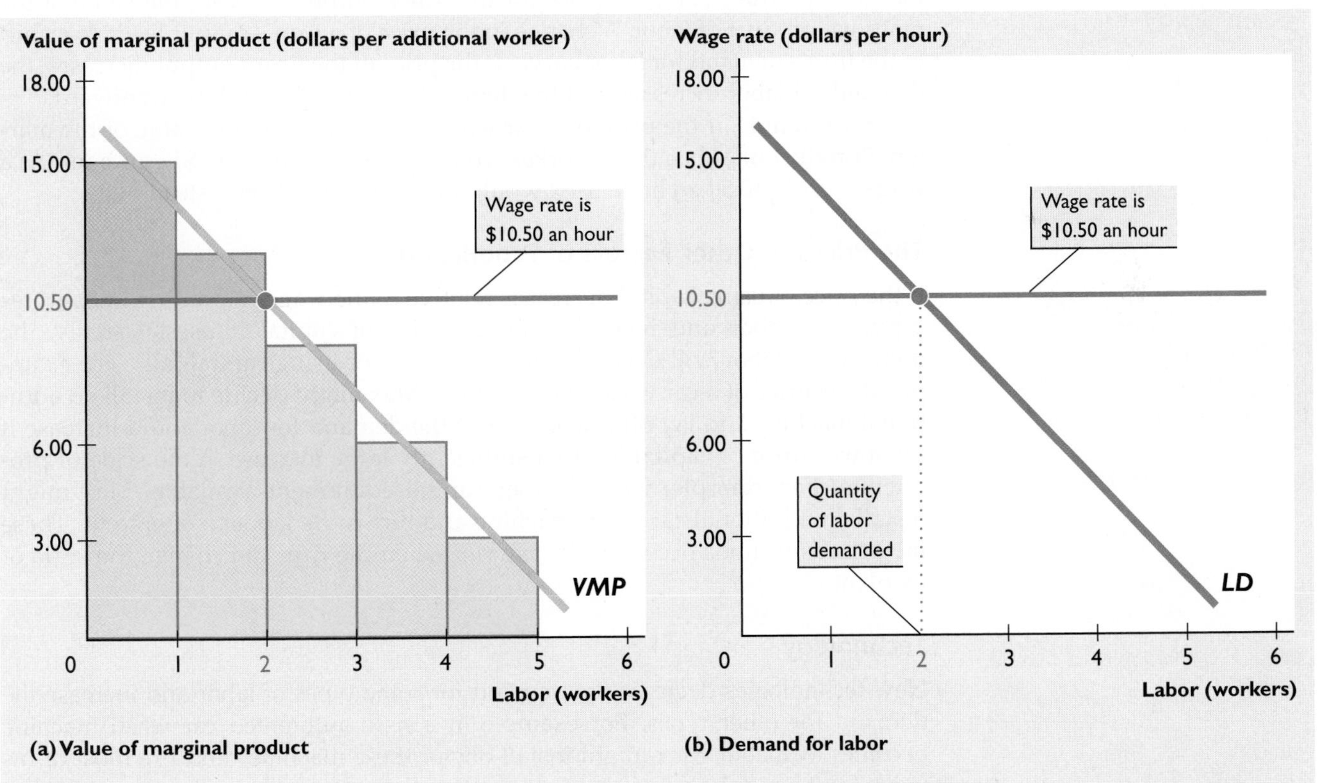


At a wage rate of $10.50 an hour, Max makes a profit on the first 2 workers but would incur a loss on the third worker in part (a), so the quantity of labor demanded is 2 workers in part (b). Max's demand for labor curve in part (b) is the same as the value of marginal product curve in part (a). The demand for labor curve slopes downward because the value of the marginal product of labor diminishes as the quantity of labor employed increases.

3 workers. The quantity of labor demanded by Max when the wage rate is $10.50 an hour is 2 workers, which is a point on Max's demand for labor curve, *LD*, in Figure 18.2(b).

If the wage rate increased to $12.50 an hour, Max would decrease the quantity of labor demanded to 1 worker. If the wage rate decreased to $7.50 an hour, Max would increase the quantity of labor demanded to 3 workers.

A change in the wage rate brings a change in the quantity of labor demanded and a movement along the demand for labor curve. A change in any other influence on the firm's labor-hiring plans changes the demand for labor and shifts the demand for labor curve.

## Changes in the Demand for Labor

The demand for labor depends on

- The price of the firm's output
- The prices of other factors of production
- Technology

### The Price of the Firm's Output

The higher the price of a firm's output, the greater is its demand for labor. The price of output affects the demand for labor through its influence on the value of marginal product. A higher price for the firm's output increases the value of the marginal product of labor. A change in the price of a firm's output leads to a shift in the firm's demand for labor curve. If the price of the firm's output increases, the demand for labor increases and the demand for labor curve shifts rightward.

For example, if the price of a car wash increased to $4, the value of the marginal product of Max's third worker would increase from $9 to $12 an hour. At a wage rate of $10.50 an hour, Max would now hire 3 workers instead of 2.

### The Prices of Other Factors of Production

If the price of using capital decreases relative to the wage rate, a firm substitutes capital for labor and increases the quantity of capital it uses. Usually, the demand for labor will decrease when the price of using capital falls. For example, if the price of a car wash machine falls, Max might decide to install an additional machine and lay off a worker. But the demand for labor could increase if the lower price of capital led to a sufficiently large increase in the scale of production. For example, with cheaper capital equipment available, Max might install an additional car wash machine and hire more labor to operate it. These factor substitutions occur in the *long run* when the firm can change the scale of its plant.

### Technology

New technologies decrease the demand for some types of labor and increase the demand for other types. For example, if a new automated car wash machine becomes available, Max might install one of these machines and fire most of his work force—a decrease in the demand for car wash workers. But the firms that manufacture and service automatic car wash machines hire more labor—an increase in the demand for these types of labor. During the 1980s and 1990s, electronic telephone exchanges decreased the demand for telephone operators and increased the demand for computer programmers and electronics engineers.

# CHECKPOINT 18.1

Work these problems in Study Plan 18.1 to get instant feedback.

**Explain how the value of marginal product determines the demand for a factor of production.**

## Practice Problems

Kaiser's produces smoothies. The market for smoothies is perfectly competitive, and the price is $4.00 a smoothie. The labor market is competitive, and the wage rate is $40 a day. Table 1 shows Kaiser's total product schedule. Use this information to work Problems **1** to **4**.

**TABLE 1**

| Workers | Smoothies per day |
|---|---|
| 1 | 7 |
| 2 | 21 |
| 3 | 33 |
| 4 | 43 |
| 5 | 51 |
| 6 | 55 |

1. Calculate the marginal product of hiring the fourth worker and the value of the marginal product of the fourth worker.
2. How many workers will Kaiser's hire to maximize its profit? How many smoothies a day will Kaiser's produce?
3. If the price rises to $5 a smoothie, how many workers will Kaiser's hire?
4. Kaiser's installs a machine that increases the productivity of workers by 50 percent. If the price remains at $4 a smoothie and the wage rises to $48 a day, how many workers does Kaiser's hire?
5. **What higher wages mean for small business**
   The Economic Policy Institute reports that retailers and fast-food restaurants will be required to raise the pay of millions of workers to at least $7.25 an hour. Many small businesses worry that such a requirement will force them to close.
   
   Source: *The Wall Street Journal*, July 27, 2009
   
   Explain the effect of the pay raise on the number of workers employed. Why would a small business close?

## Guided Solutions to Practice Problems

1. The marginal product of hiring the fourth worker equals the total product of 4 workers (43 smoothies) minus the total product of 3 workers (33 smoothies), which is 10 smoothies. The value of the marginal product (*VMP*) of the fourth worker equals the marginal product of the fourth worker (10 smoothies) multiplied by the price of a smoothie ($4), which is $40 a day.
2. Kaiser's maximizes profit by hiring the number of workers that makes *VMP* equal to the wage rate ($40 a day). Kaiser's hires 4 workers. When Kaiser's hires 4 workers, the marginal product of labor is 10 smoothies. The price of a smoothie is $4, so *VMP* is $40 a day. Kaiser's produces 43 smoothies a day.
3. Kaiser's maximizes profit by hiring 5 workers. When Kaiser's hires 5 workers, the *MP* of the 5th worker is 8 smoothies. The price of a smoothie is $5, so *VMP* is $40 a day—equal to the wage rate.
4. When Kaiser's hires 5 workers, the *MP* of the 5th worker is 12 smoothies. The price of a smoothie is $4, so *VMP* is $48 a day— equal to the wage rate.
5. A profit-maximizing firm pays the wage rate equal to the value of marginal product (*VMP*), which equals the marginal product multiplied by the price of the good produced. Marginal product diminishes as more workers are hired. A firm that pays $7.25 an hour will hire the number of workers that makes marginal product equal to $7.25 divided by the price of the good produced. A business will close if $7.25 an hour exceeds *VMP* of its workers.

## 19.1 ECONOMIC INEQUALITY IN THE UNITED STATES

**Market income**
A household's wages, interest, rent, and profit earned in factor markets before paying income taxes.

**Money income**
Market income plus cash payments to households by the government.

To measure economic inequality, we look at the distributions of income and wealth. A household's *income* is the amount that it *receives in a given period*. A household's **market income** equals the wages, interest, rent, and profit that the household earns in factor markets before paying income taxes. The Census Bureau defines another income concept, **money income**, which equals *market income* plus cash payments to households by the government.

A household's *wealth* is the value of the things it *owns at a point in time*. Wealth is measured as the market value of a household's home, the stocks and bonds that it owns, and the money in its bank accounts minus its debts such as outstanding credit card balances.

To describe the *distribution of income*, imagine the population of the United States lined up from the lowest to the highest income earner. Now divide the line into five equal-sized groups, each with 20 percent of the population. These groups are called *quintiles*.

Next share out total money income among these groups so that the shares represent the U.S. income distribution. Table 19.1(a) lists the percentages received by each group.

Share out the pie of total wealth in a similar way. Table 19.1(b) shows the percentages owned by each of seven groups. The richest quintile has been broken down into smaller groups to show the wealth distribution inside the highest quintile.

**TABLE 19.1**

The Distributions of Market Income and Wealth in the United States

In part (a), the 20 percent of households with the lowest incomes receive 0.9 percent of total market income, while the 20 percent of households with the highest incomes receive 53.3 percent of total income.

In part (b), the poorest 40 percent of households own 0.2 percent of total wealth, while the richest 1 percent own 34.4 percent.

**(a) Income distribution in 2007 (Median household income $49,240)**

| | Percentage of | | Cumulative percentage of | |
|---|---|---|---|---|
| | **Households** | **Income** | **Households** | **Income** |
| *A* | Lowest 20 | 0.9 | 20 | 0.9 |
| *B* | Second 20 | 7.1 | 40 | 8.0 |
| *C* | Third 20 | 14.3 | 60 | 22.3 |
| *D* | Fourth 20 | 24.4 | 80 | 46.7 |
| *E* | Highest 20 | 53.3 | 100 | 100.0 |

**(b) Wealth distribution in 2004 (Median household wealth $77,900)**

| | Percentage of | | Cumulative percentage of | |
|---|---|---|---|---|
| | **Households** | **Wealth** | **Households** | **Wealth** |
| *A'* | Lowest 40 | 0.2 | 40 | 0.2 |
| *B'* | Next 20 | 3.8 | 60 | 4.0 |
| *C'* | Next 20 | 11.3 | 80 | 15.3 |
| *D'* | Next 10 | 13.4 | 90 | 28.7 |
| *E'* | Next 5 | 12.3 | 95 | 41.0 |
| *F'* | Next 4 | 24.6 | 99 | 65.6 |
| *G'* | Highest 1 | 34.4 | 100 | 100.0 |

SOURCES OF DATA: Part (a) Current Population Survey 2008 Annual Social and Economic Supplement. Part (b) Edward N. Wolff, "Recent Trends in Household Wealth in the United States: Rising Debt and the Middle-Class Squeeze," www.levy.org/pubs/wp_502.pdf.

## Lorenz Curves

A **Lorenz curve** graphs the cumulative percentage of income (or wealth) on the $y$-axis against the cumulative percentage of households on the $x$-axis. Figure 19.1 shows the Lorenz curves for income and wealth in the United States. Graphing the cumulative percentage of income against the cumulative percentage of households makes the Lorenz curve for income and the points *A* to *D* on the graph correspond to the rows identified by those letters in the table. For example, row *B* and point *B* show that the 40 percent of households with the lowest incomes received 8.0 percent of total income—0.9 percent plus 7.1 percent from Table 19.1(a).

**Lorenz curve**
A curve that graphs the cumulative percentage of income (or wealth) against the cumulative percentage of households.

Graphing the cumulative percentage of wealth against the cumulative percentage of households makes the Lorenz curve for wealth and the points *A'* to *F'* on the graph correspond to the rows identified by those letters in the table of Figure 19.1. For example, row *C'* and point *C'* show that the poorest 80 percent of households owned 15.3 percent of total wealth—0.2 percent plus 3.8 percent plus 11.3 percent from Table 19.1(b).

If income (or wealth) were distributed equally, each 20 percent of households would receive 20 percent of total income (or own 20 percent of total wealth), and the Lorenz curve would be the straight line labeled "Line of equality." The Lorenz curves based on the actual distributions of income and wealth are always below the line of equality. The closer the Lorenz curve is to the line of equality, the more equal is the distribution. You can see that the Lorenz curve for wealth is much farther away from the line of equality than is the Lorenz curve for income. The distribution of wealth is much more unequal than the distribution of income.

**FIGURE 19.1**

Lorenz Curves for Income and Wealth in the United States

Animation

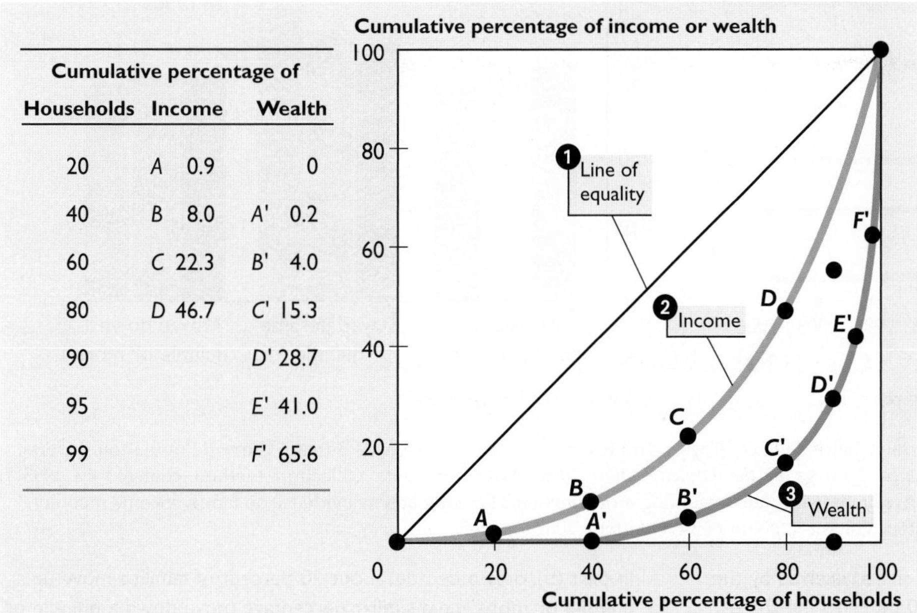

| Cumulative percentage of | | |
|---|---|---|
| **Households** | **Income** | **Wealth** |
| 20 | A 0.9 | 0 |
| 40 | B 8.0 | A' 0.2 |
| 60 | C 22.3 | B' 4.0 |
| 80 | D 46.7 | C' 15.3 |
| 90 | | D' 28.7 |
| 95 | | E' 41.0 |
| 99 | | F' 65.6 |



SOURCES OF DATA: See Table 19.1.

1. If income and wealth were distributed equally, the Lorenz curve would lie along the straight line labeled "Line of equality."
2. The income Lorenz curve shows the cumulative percentage of income graphed against the cumulative percentage of households. The 20 percent of households with the lowest incomes received 0.9 percent of total income, and the 80 percent of households with the lowest incomes received 46.7 percent.
3. The wealth Lorenz curve shows the cumulative percentage of wealth graphed against the cumulative percentage of households. The poorest 40 percent of households own 0.2 percent of total wealth, and 99 percent of households own 65.6 percent of total wealth. The richest 1 percent own 34.4 percent.

## Inequality over Time

U.S. income inequality has increased. The highest incomes have increased faster than the lower incomes and the gap between the rich and the poor has widened.

Figure 19.2(a) shows this widening gap by looking at the income share of each quintile between 1968 and 2008. The data are based on *money income*. The figure shows that the share received by the highest quintile increased from 43 percent during the late 1960s to 50 percent in the 2000s. The percentage of total income received by each of the other quintiles decreased. The poorest quintile share fell from 4 percent to 3 percent; the second poorest quintile share fell from 11 percent to 9 percent; and the third (middle) quintile fell from 17 percent to 15 percent.

## Economic Mobility

Economic mobility is the movement of a family up or down through the income distribution. If there were no economic mobility, a family would be stuck at a given point in the income distribution and be persistently poor, or rich, or somewhere in the middle. Also, in such a situation, the data on annual income distribution would be a good indicator of life-time inequality.

But if there is economic mobility, families move up or down through the income distribution and life-time inequality is not as severe as the inequality in the data for a single year. How much economic mobility is there?

**FIGURE 19.2**

Trends in the Distribution of Income and Economic Mobility

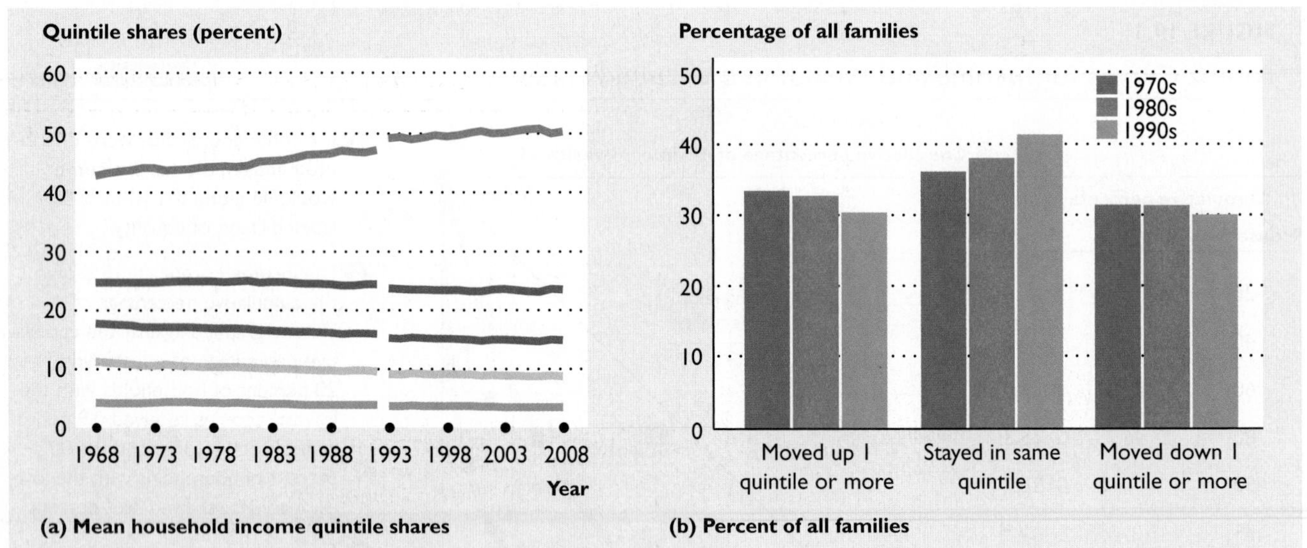


SOURCES OF DATA: Part (a) DeNavas-Walt, Carmen, Bernadette D. Proctor, and Jessica C. Smith, U.S. Census Bureau, Current Population Reports, P60-236 *Income, Poverty, and Health Insurance Coverage in the United States: 2008.* Note: The data collection method changed in 1993. Part (b) Katharine Bradbury and Jane Katz, "Are lifetime incomes becoming more unequal? Looking at new evidence on family income mobility," *Regional Review*, Federal Reserve Bank of Boston, Volume 12, Number 4, Quarter 4 2002, pp. 2–5.

In part (a), from 1968 to 2008 the income share received by the highest quintile rose from 43 percent to 50 percent. The shares received by the other quintiles fell. The lowest quintile share fell from 4 percent to 3 percent, the second lowest from 11 percent to 9 percent, and the middle from 17 percent to 15 percent.

In part (b), over a decade, about 30 percent of families move up a quintile or more and a similar percentage move down a quintile or more. Between 35 and 40 percent of families remain in the same quintile. Mobility through the quintiles has decreased over the 1980s and 1990s.

Katharine Bradbury and Jane Katz, economists at the Federal Reserve Bank of Boston, have provided an answer to this question and Figure 19.2(b) shows what they found. The figure shows the percentages of families that remained in the same quintile and that moved up or down by one quintile or more over a ten-year period.

About 30 percent of families move up by a quintile or more and a slightly smaller percentage move down by a quintile or more. Between 35 percent and 40 percent of families remain in the same quintile.

What is the source of economic mobility? Most of it arises from normal changes over a family's life cycle. Families experience income growth as their workers become more skilled and experienced. As a family continues to get older and its workers retire, its income falls. So if we look at three households that have identical *lifetime incomes*—that are *economically equal*—but one is young, one is middle-aged, and one is old, we will see a great deal of inequality. Inequality of annual incomes overstates the degree of lifetime inequality.

You've seen that income inequality is increasing, but is economic mobility also increasing? The data in Figure 19.2(b) answer this question, and they show a trend toward less economic mobility, not more. A decreasing percentage of families is moving either up or down a quintile or more and an increasing percentage of families is remaining in the same quintile. Why economic mobility has decreased remains a question for future research.

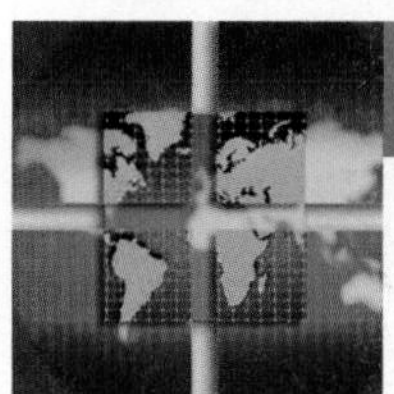

## EYE on the GLOBAL ECONOMY

### Global Inequality

There is much more income inequality in the global economy than in the United States. The Lorenz curves in this figure provide a comparative picture. You can see that the global Lorenz curve lies much farther from the line of equality than does the U.S. Lorenz curve.

Numbers that highlight the comparison are the percentages of families that get a half (50 percent) of the income. In the United States, the richest 20 percent of families get a half of the income and the remaining 80 percent share the other half. In the global economy the richest 10 percent of families get a half of the income and the remaining 90 percent share the other half.

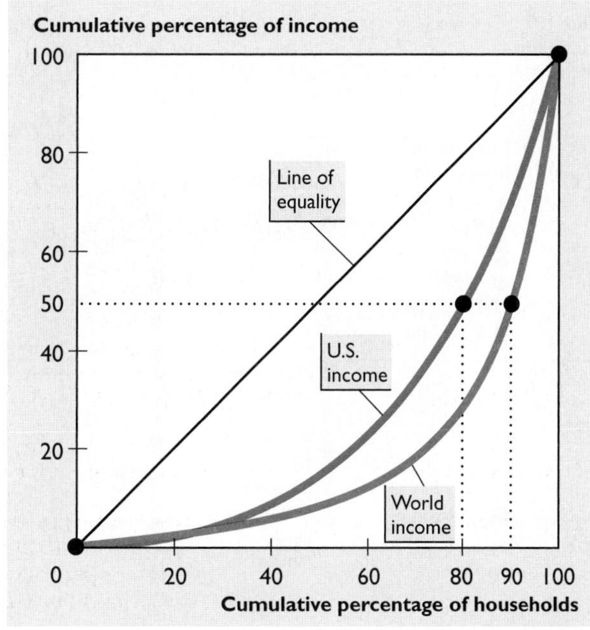


Sources of Data: U.S., see Figure 19.1. World, Branko Milanovic, "True World Income Distribution, 1988 and 1993: First Calculation Based on Household Surveys Alone," *Economic Journal*, 112, 2002.

Global incomes are rising and by some estimates, inequality is decreasing. But other estimates suggest that global inequality, like U.S. inequality, is increasing. Better data are needed to settle this issue.

# EYE on INEQUALITY

## Who Are the Rich and the Poor?

In the United States today (excluding the ultra rich sports and entertainment superstars and top corporate executives), the families with the highest incomes are likely to be college-educated Asian married couples between 45 and 54 years of age living together with two children somewhere in the West.

At the other extreme, the person with the lowest income is likely to be a black woman over 75 years of age who lives alone somewhere in the South and has fewer than nine years of elementary school education. Another low-income group are young women who have not completed high school, have a child (or children), and who live without a partner. These snapshot profiles are the extremes in the figure.

The figure illustrates the dominant importance of education in influencing income. Persons with a post-graduate professional degree (an MBA and a law degree are examples) or a doctorate degree earns, on average, five times the income of a person who has not completed high school.

Household size and type are the second largest influences on income. A married couple with two children have, on average, an income three times that of a single female household.

Age is almost as important as household size and type. People aged between 45 and 54 have incomes almost three times those of people aged 75 and over.

Race is another significant factor that influences income. Asian households earn, on average, double the income of Hispanic origin households.

Region of residence has a small influence on income, the West having the highest incomes at almost 20 percent higher than those in the South.

Within these categories, there is enormous individual variation.

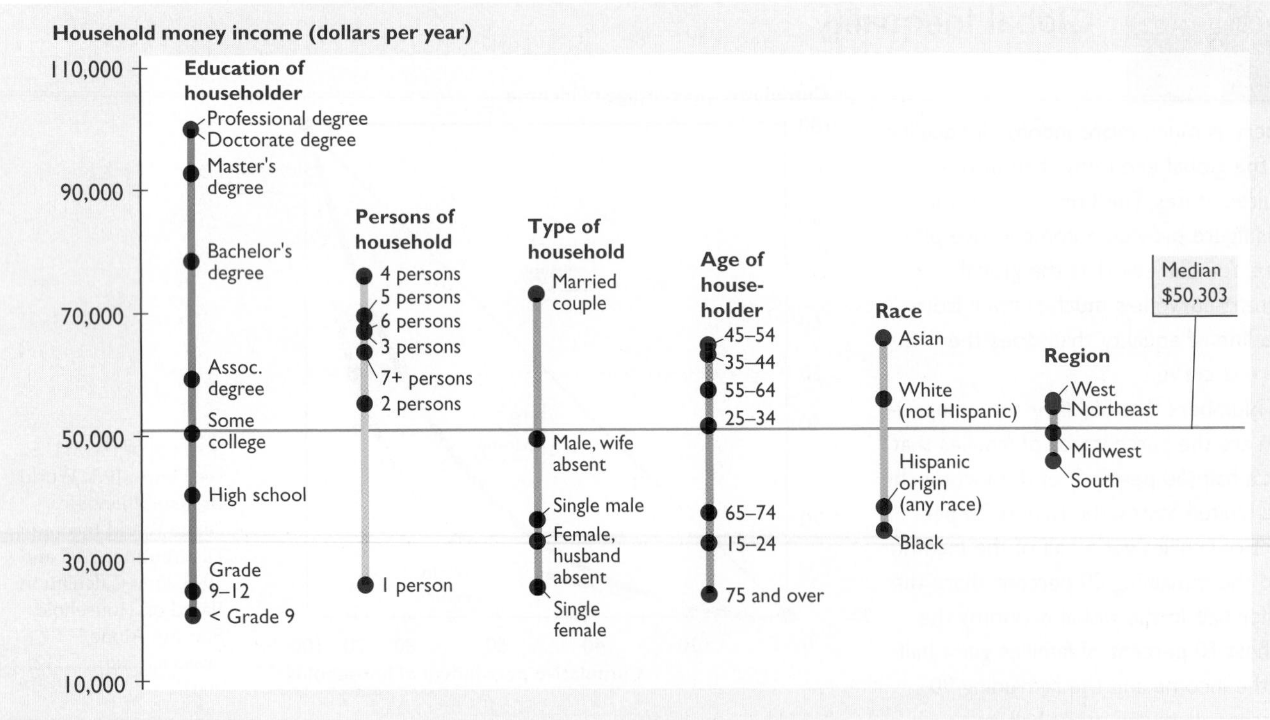


SOURCE OF DATA: Current Population Survey, HINC-01. Selected Characteristics of Households, by Total Money Income in 2008.

## Poverty

Households with very low incomes are considered to be living in poverty. What is poverty? How do we measure it, how much poverty is there, and is the amount of poverty decreasing or increasing?

### Poverty Defined and Measured

**Poverty** is a state in which a household's income is too low to be able to buy the quantities of food, shelter, and clothing that are deemed necessary.

**Poverty**
A state in which a household's income is too low to be able to buy the quantities of food, shelter, and clothing that are deemed necessary.

The Census Bureau considers a household to be living in poverty if its income is less than a defined level that varies with household size and is updated each year to reflect changes in the cost of living. In 2008, the poverty level for a household with 2 adults and 2 children was an income of $21,834.

In 2008, 39 million Americans had incomes below the poverty level. Figure 19.3(a) shows the distribution of poverty by race in 2008. Almost one half (44 percent) of families living in poverty are white.

### Poverty Incidence and Trends

To measure the *incidence* of poverty, we look at the poverty *rate*—the percentage of families living in poverty. In 2008, the poverty rate was 13.2 percent. Figure 19.3(b) shows the poverty rates and their trends for white, black, and Hispanic families from 1968 through 2008.

**FIGURE 19.3**
Poverty Rates in the United States

myeconlab Animation

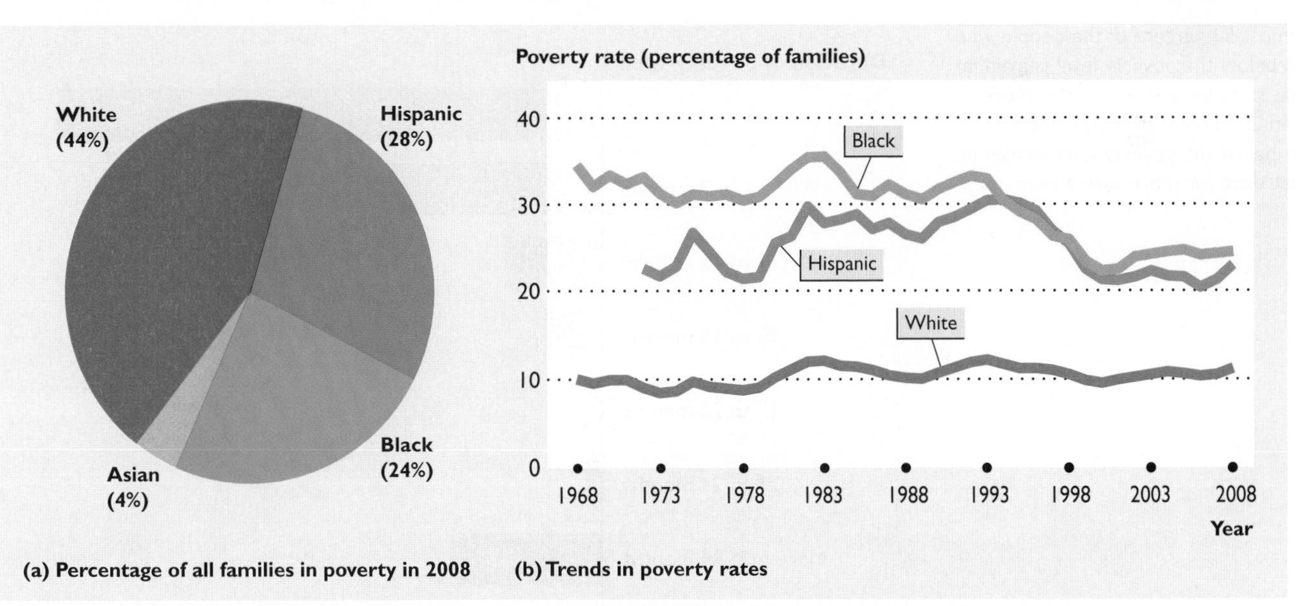


**(a) Percentage of all families in poverty in 2008** **(b) Trends in poverty rates**

SOURCE OF DATA: DeNavas-Walt, Carmen, Bernadette D. Proctor, and Jessica C. Smith, U.S. Census Bureau, Current Population Reports, P60–236, *Income, Poverty, and Health Insurance Coverage in the United States: 2008.*

White families account for 44 percent of the poor in part (a). But poverty *rates* for blacks and Hispanics are double those for whites in part (b). The poverty rate of black families fell during the 1960s and the 1990s. The poverty rate of Hispanics also fell during the 1990s, but it had previously increased. The poverty rate of whites has remained fairly steady.

For white families, the poverty rate has fluctuated around 10 percent. For black families, the poverty rate has fallen from almost 40 percent in 1968 to 24 percent in 2008. So between 1968 and 2008, the poverty rate for blacks almost halved. But it remained at more than twice the white poverty rate even after this large decrease. For Hispanic families, the poverty rate increased during the 1980s and then decreased during the 1990s. By 2008, the poverty rate for this group was similar to what it had been 30 years earlier.

## Poverty Duration

Another dimension of poverty is its duration. If a household is in poverty for a few months it faces serious hardship during those months, but it faces a less serious problem than it would if its poverty persisted for several months or, worse yet, for several years, or even generations.

Because the duration of poverty is an important additional indicator of the hardship that poverty brings, the Census Bureau provided measures of duration for the years 2001 to 2003. Figure 19.4 shows these data.

It turns out that almost 50 percent of poverty lasts for between 2 and 4 months. So for about a half of poor families, poverty is not persistent. But more than 20 percent of poverty lasts for more than a year, so a seriously large number of households experience chronic poverty.

In the next sections, we look at the sources of inequality and poverty and the policies that aim to redistribute income and lift the living standard of the poor.

**FIGURE 19.4**

The Duration of Poverty Spells in the United States

myeconlab Animation

Almost 50 percent of the people who fall below the poverty level remain in that state for 2 to 4 months. More than 20 percent of the people who fall below the poverty level remain in that state for more than a year.

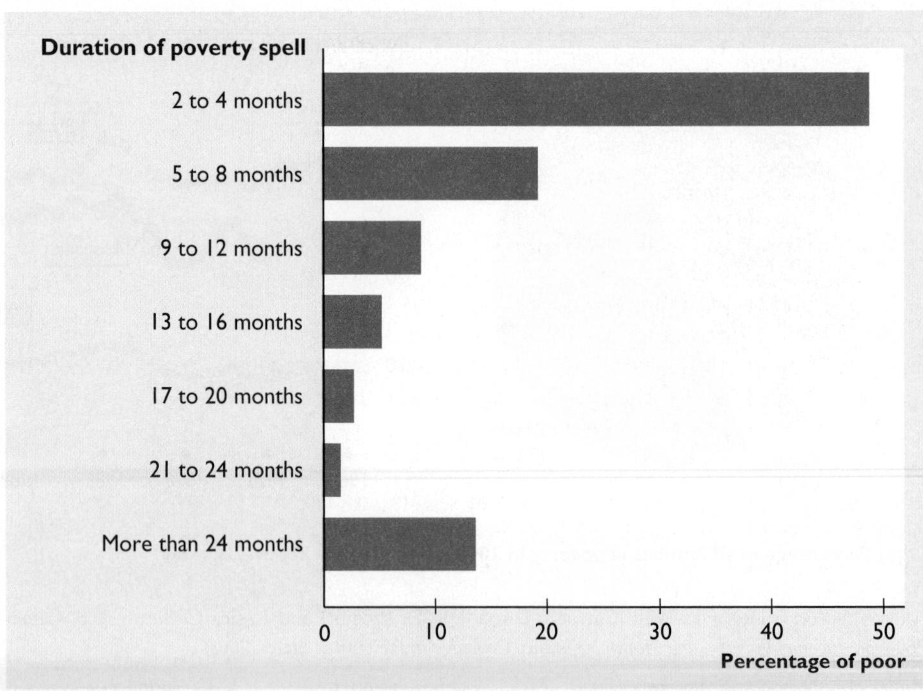


SOURCE OF DATA: U.S. Census Bureau, *Dynamics of Economic Well-Being: Poverty 2001–2003.*

## CHECKPOINT 19.1

**Describe the economic inequality and poverty in the United States.**

Work these problems in Study Plan 19.1 to get instant feedback.

## Practice Problems

Use Table 1, which shows the distribution of market income in Canada, and Table 19.1(a) on page 484, which shows the distribution of market income in the United States, to work Problems **1** and **2**.

**TABLE 1 CANADIAN DATA**

| Households | Market income (percentage) |
|---|---|
| Lowest 20 percent | 1.2 |
| Second 20 percent | 7.4 |
| Third 20 percent | 15.3 |
| Fourth 20 percent | 24.4 |
| Highest 20 percent | 51.7 |

1. Create a table that shows the cumulative percentages of households and income in Canada.
2. Draw the Lorenz curves for Canada and the United States. Compare the distribution of income in Canada with that in the United States. Which distribution is more unequal?
3. **Income gap closes in rural suburbs**
   Middle-income households are seeking affordable housing by fleeing the cities and moving into fast-growing suburbs on farmland near metropolitan areas.
   Source: *USA Today*, September 14, 2007
   Explain why fast-growing rural suburbs have greater income equality than metropolitan areas and why inequality is increasing in metropolitan areas.

## Guided Solutions to Practice Problems

1. Table 2 shows the cumulative percentages of households and income.

**TABLE 2**

| Households | Market income (percentage) | Cumulative percentage of Households | Cumulative percentage of Income |
|---|---|---|---|
| Lowest 20 percent | 1.2 | 20 | 1.2 |
| Second 20 percent | 7.4 | 40 | 8.6 |
| Third 20 percent | 15.3 | 60 | 23.9 |
| Fourth 20 percent | 24.4 | 80 | 48.3 |
| Highest 20 percent | 51.7 | 100 | 100.0 |

2. A Lorenz curve plots the cumulative percentage of income against the cumulative percentage of households. The blue curve in Figure 1 plots these data. The line of equality shows an equal distribution. The Canadian Lorenz curve lies closer to the line of equality than does the U.S. Lorenz curve, so the distribution of income in the United States is more unequal than that in Canada.
3. The middle-income households that are fleeing the cities and moving into rural suburbs are in the middle three income quintiles. The lowest and highest quintiles remain in the cities. Because there is a concentration of middle-income households in the rural suburbs, the range of incomes in these suburbs is narrow and inequality is low. The households that remain in metropolitan areas are the poor (lowest quintile) and rich (highest quintile) and inequality across these groups is large.

**FIGURE 1**

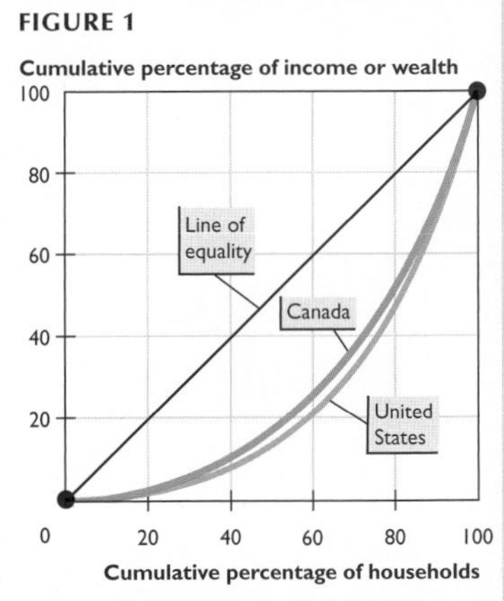

## 19.2 HOW INEQUALITY AND POVERTY ARISE

Economic inequality and poverty arise from a wide variety of factors. The five key ones that we'll examine here are

- Human capital
- Discrimination
- Financial and physical capital
- Entrepreneurial ability
- Personal and family characteristics

### Human Capital

*Human capital* is the accumulated skill and knowledge of human beings. To see how human capital differences affect economic inequality, we'll study an economy with two levels of human capital, which we'll call *high-skilled labor* and *low-skilled labor.* Low-skilled labor might be law clerks, hospital orderlies, or bank tellers, and high-skilled labor might be attorneys, surgeons, or bank CEOs.

#### The Demand for High-Skilled and Low-Skilled Labor

High-skilled workers can perform tasks that low-skilled workers would perform badly or couldn't even perform at all. Imagine an untrained person doing surgery or piloting an airplane. High-skilled workers have a higher value of marginal product (*VMP*) than low-skilled workers do. As we learned in Chapter 18, a firm's demand for labor curve is derived from and is the same as the firm's value of marginal product of labor curve.

Figure 19.5(a) shows the demand curves for high-skilled and low-skilled labor. At any given employment level, firms are willing to pay a higher wage rate to a high-skilled worker than to a low-skilled worker. The gap between the two wage rates measures the value of marginal product of skill—for example, at an employment level of 2,000 hours, firms are willing to pay a high-skilled worker $25 an hour and a low-skilled worker only $10 an hour, a difference of $15 an hour. Thus the value of marginal product of skill is $15 an hour.

#### The Supply of High-Skilled and Low-Skilled Labor

A skill is costly to acquire and its opportunity cost includes expenditures, such as tuition, and lower earnings while the skill is being acquired. When a person goes to school full time, that cost is the total earnings forgone. When a person acquires a skill through on-the-job training, he or she earns a lower wage rate than someone who is doing a comparable job but not undergoing training. In this case, the cost of acquiring the skill is equal to the wage paid to a person not being trained minus the wage paid to a person being trained.

Because skills are costly to acquire, a high-skilled person is not willing to work for the same wage that a low-skilled person is willing to accept. The position of the supply curve of high-skilled workers reflects the cost of acquiring the skill. Figure 19.5(b) shows two supply curves: one of high-skilled workers and the other of low-skilled workers. The supply curve of high-skilled workers is $S_H$, and that of low-skilled workers is $S_L$.

The high-skilled worker's supply curve lies above the low-skilled worker's supply curve. The vertical distance between the two supply curves is the com-

**FIGURE 19.5**

Skill Differentials

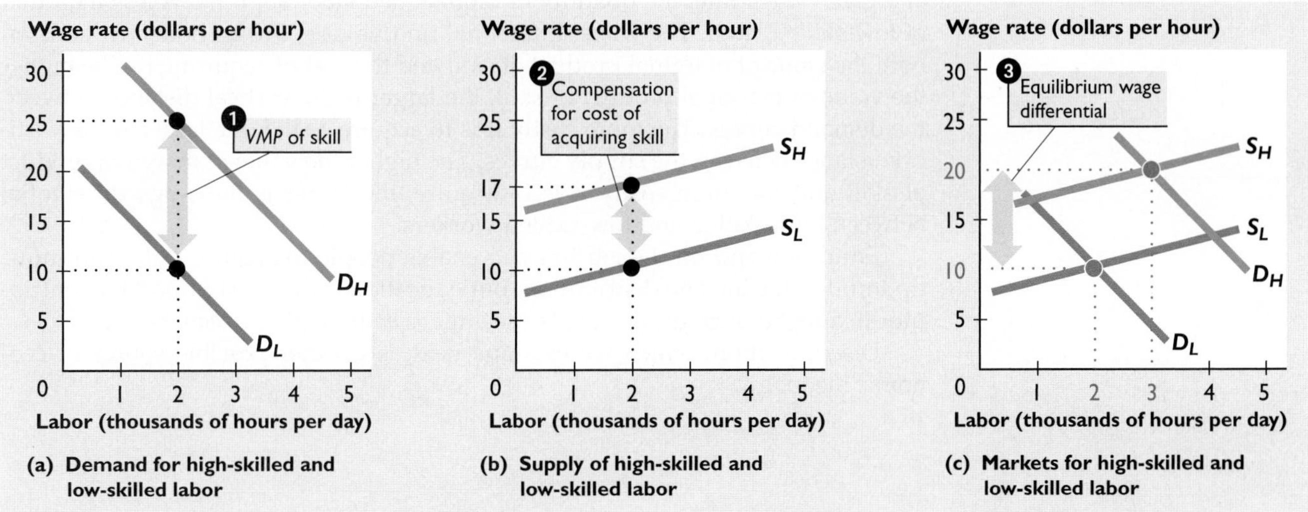


**(a) Demand for high-skilled and low-skilled labor**

**(b) Supply of high-skilled and low-skilled labor**

**(c) Markets for high-skilled and low-skilled labor**

In part (a), $D_L$ is the demand curve for low-skilled labor and $D_H$ is the demand curve for high-skilled labor. ❶ The vertical distance between these two curves is the value of marginal product of skill.

In part (b), $S_L$ is the supply curve of low-skilled workers and $S_H$ is the supply curve of high-skilled workers. ❷ The vertical distance between these two curves is the required compensation for the cost of acquiring a skill.

In part (c), in equilibrium, low-skilled workers earn a wage rate of $10 an hour and high-skilled workers earn a wage rate of $20 an hour. ❸ The $10 wage differential is the equilibrium effect of acquiring skill.

pensation that high-skilled workers require for the cost of acquiring the skill. For example, suppose that the quantity of low-skilled labor supplied is 2,000 hours at a wage rate of $10 an hour. This wage rate compensates the low-skilled workers mainly for their time on the job. Consider next the supply of high-skilled workers. To induce high-skilled labor to supply 2,000 hours, firms must pay a wage rate of $17 an hour. This wage rate for high-skilled labor is higher than that for low-skilled labor because high-skilled labor must be compensated not only for the time on the job but also for the time and other costs of acquiring the skill.

## Wage Rates of High-Skilled and Low-Skilled Labor

To work out the wage rates of high-skilled and low-skilled labor, we have to bring together the effects of skill on the demand for and supply of labor.

Figure 19.5(c) shows the demand curves and the supply curves for high-skilled and low-skilled labor. These curves are the same as those plotted in parts (a) and (b). Equilibrium occurs in the market for low-skilled labor where the supply and demand curves for low-skilled labor intersect. The equilibrium wage rate is $10 an hour, and the quantity of low-skilled labor employed is 2,000 hours. Equilibrium in the market for high-skilled workers occurs where the supply and demand curves for high-skilled workers intersect. The equilibrium wage rate is $20 an hour, and the quantity of high-skilled labor employed is 3,000 hours.

As you can see in Figure 19.5(c), the equilibrium wage rate of high-skilled labor is higher than that of low-skilled labor. There are two reasons why this occurs: First, high-skilled labor has a higher value of marginal product than does low-skilled labor, so at a given wage rate, the quantity of high-skilled labor demanded exceeds that of low-skilled labor. Second, skills are costly to acquire, so at a given wage rate, the quantity of high-skilled labor supplied is less than that of low-skilled labor. The wage differential (in this case, $10 an hour) depends on both the value of marginal product of skill and the cost of acquiring it. The higher the value of marginal product of skill, the larger is the vertical distance between the demand curves. The more costly it is to acquire a skill, the larger is the vertical distance between the supply curves. The higher the value of marginal product of skill and the more costly it is to acquire, the larger is the wage differential between high-skilled and low-skilled workers.

Education and on-the-job training enable people to acquire skills and move up through the income distribution. But education is the most important contributor to a higher income, as you can see in *Eye on the U.S. Economy* below.

Discrimination, which we examine next, is another possible source of economic inequality.

## EYE on the U.S. ECONOMY

### Does Education Pay?

The figure shows that there are large differences in earnings based on the degree of education.

Rates of return on high school and college education have been estimated to be in the range of 5 to 10 percent a year after allowing for inflation, which suggests that a college degree is a better investment than almost any other that a person can undertake.

Based on average income data, the gain from graduating from high school is $16,000 a year. But the gain from going to college or university and getting a bachelor's degree is greater and brings in an additional $47,000 a year.

Remaining at the university to complete a master's degree (usually one more year of study) brings in an extra $13,500 a year, and working for a professional degree increases income by another $50,000 a year.

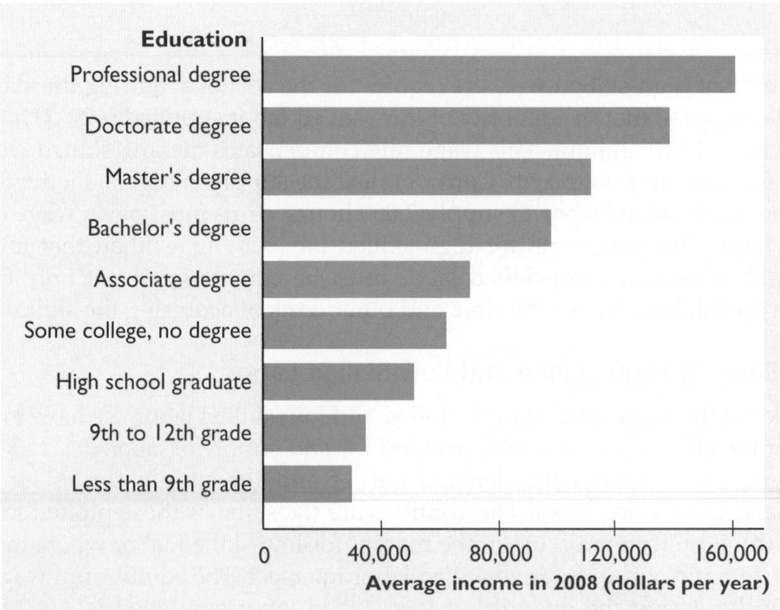


SOURCE OF DATA: Current Population Survey, HINC-01. Selected Characteristics of Households, by Total Money Income in 2008.

## Discrimination

Persistent earnings differences exist between women and men and among the races. You can see them in *Eye on the U.S. Economy* below. Does discrimination contribute to these differences? It might, but economists can't isolate and measure the effect of discrimination, so we can't say by how much, or even whether, earnings differences arise from this source.

To see the difficulty in isolating the effects of discrimination, consider the market for investment advisors. Suppose that black women and white men are equally good at providing investment advice. If there is no race and sex discrimination, average wage rates are the same for both groups.

But if some people are willing to pay more for investment advice from a white man than they are willing to pay for the same advice from a black woman, the market-determined value of marginal product of black women is lower than that of white men, and the demand for investment advice from black women is lower than that from white men. The result is a lower equilibrium wage rate (and fewer high-paying jobs) for black women than for white men.

For discrimination to work in this way and bring *persistent* wage differences, people must be *persistently* willing to pay more than necessary for investment advice. People will begin to notice that they can get a better deal if they buy investment advice from black women. Substitution away from high-cost white men toward lower-cost black women will shift demand and eventually eliminate the wage difference.

# EYE on the U.S. ECONOMY

## Sex and Race Earnings Differences

The figure shows the earnings of different race and sex groups expressed as a percentage of the earnings of white men.

In 2008, white women earned, on average, 80 percent of what white men earned. Black men earned 75 percent, and black women earned 67 percent. Men and women of Hispanic origin earned only 68 percent and 61 percent, respectively, of white men's wages.

These earnings differentials have persisted over many years, and only those of women have begun to narrow in a significant way.

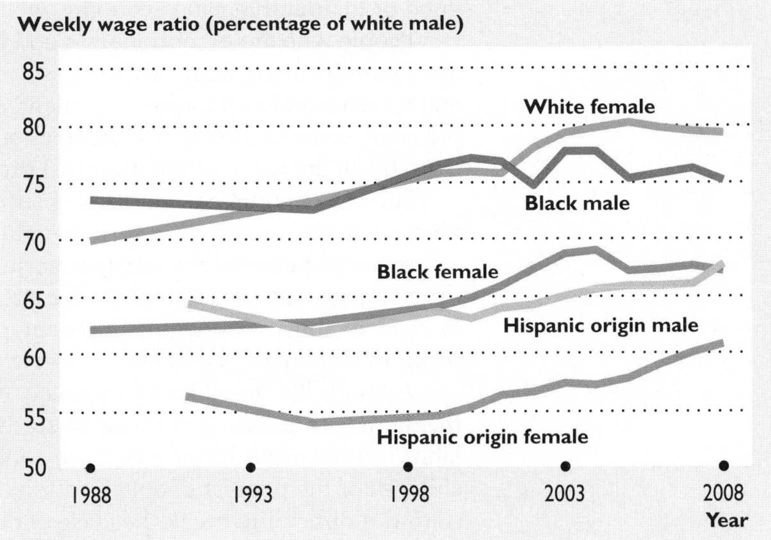


SOURCES OF DATA: Bureau of Labor Statistics and Current Population Reports.

## Financial and Physical Capital

The people with the highest incomes are usually those who own large amounts of financial capital and physical capital. These people receive incomes in the form of interest and dividend payments and from capital gains—increases in the stock market value.

Families with a large amount of capital tend to become even more wealthy across generations for two reasons. First, they bequeath wealth to their children and second, rich people marry rich partners (on the average).

Saving, and the wealth accumulation that it brings, is not inevitably a source of increased inequality and can even be a source of increased equality. When a household saves to redistribute an uneven income over the life cycle, it enjoys more equal consumption. Also, if a lucky generation that has a high income saves a large amount and makes a bequest to a generation that is unlucky, this act of saving also decreases the degree of inequality.

## Entrepreneurial Ability

Some of the most spectacularly rich people have benefited from unusual entrepreneurial talent. Household names such as Bill Gates (Microsoft), Michael Dell (Dell Computers), and Sam Walton (Wal-Mart) are examples of people who began life with modest amounts of wealth and modest incomes and through a combination of hard work, good luck, and outstanding entrepreneurship have become extremely rich.

But some very poor people, and some who fall below the poverty level, have also tried their hands at being entrepreneurs. We don't hear much about these people. They are not in the headlines. But they have put together a business plan, borrowed heavily, and through a combination of hard work, bad luck, and in some cases poor decisions have become extremely poor.

## Personal and Family Characteristics

Each individual's personal and family characteristics play a crucial role, for either good or ill, in influencing economic well-being.

People who are exceptionally good looking and talented with stable and creative families enjoy huge advantages over the average person. Many movie stars, entertainers, and extraordinarily talented athletes are in this category. These people enjoy some of the highest incomes because their personal or family characteristics make the value of the marginal product of their labor very large.

Success often breeds yet further success. A large income can generate a large amount of saving, which in turn generates yet more interest income.

Adverse personal circumstances, such as chronic physical or mental illness, drug abuse, or an unstable home life possibly arising from the absence of a parent or from an abusive or negligent parent, place a huge burden on many people and result in low incomes and even poverty.

A tough life, just like its opposite, can be self-reinforcing. Weak physical or mental health makes it difficult to study and obtain a skill and results in a low labor income or no income because a job is just too hard to hold down. And the children of the poorest people find it hard to get into college and university, and so find it difficult to break the cycle of poverty.

## CHECKPOINT 19.2

Work these problems in Study Plan 19.2 to get instant feedback.

**Explain how economic inequality and poverty arise.**

### Practice Problems

In the United States in 2000, 30 million people had full-time managerial and professional jobs that paid an average of $800 a week. At the same time, 10 million people had full-time sales positions that paid an average of $530 a week. Use this information to work Problems **1** to **3**.

1. Explain why managers and professionals are paid more than salespeople.
2. Explain why, despite the higher weekly wage, more people are employed as managers and professionals than as salespeople.
3. Shopping online has become popular and more and more firms offer their goods and services for sale online. If this trend continues, how do you think the market for salespeople will change in coming years?
4. **Trade schools boom with enrollees of all ages**
   Disappearing jobs have helped drive thousands of people to state-run trade schools, where they can receive training on anything from truck driving to medical billing. Patricia Parker, 58, said, "I'm tired of getting laid off at factories. I need to re-educate myself." She expects to have finished coursework in business system technology and get a job at a medical office. Some students are retraining as auto mechanics, a skill that won't be outsourced.
   Source: *USA Today*, July 19, 2009

   Why might people who previously worked in factories be going to trade school?

### Guided Solutions to Practice Problems

1. A typical manager or professional has incurred a higher cost of education and on-the-job training than has the typical salesperson. The supply curve of managers and professionals, $S_H$, lies above that of salespeople, $S_L$ (Figure 1). The better education and more on-the-job training result in managers and professionals having more human capital and a higher value of marginal product than that of a salesperson. The demand curve for managers and professionals, $D_H$, is greater than the demand for salespeople, $D_L$. Figure 1 shows that the combination of demand and supply leads to a higher wage rate for managers and professionals than for salespeople.
2. Figure 1 shows that the demand and supply for each type of labor leads to a greater employment for managers and professionals than for salespeople.
3. As shopping online continues to grow, firms will hire fewer salespeople. The demand for salespeople will decrease, and fewer people will work in sales. What will happen to their wage rate will depend on how the supply of salespeople changes.
4. Factory jobs are disappearing as factories (such as those making furniture and textiles) close or jobs are outsourced. Patricia Parker is acquiring a skill which she believes will not be outsourced and one that she might be able to use in many different jobs. Other students think that a mechanic's skill might serve them well in the future.

**FIGURE 1**

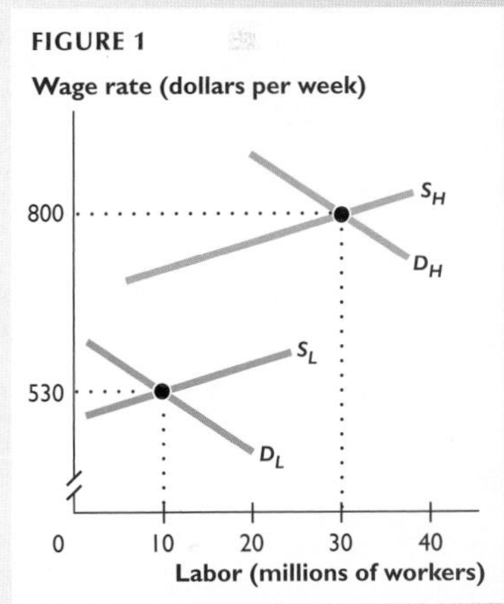

## 19.3 INCOME REDISTRIBUTION

We've described the distribution of income and wealth in the United States and examined the five main sources of economic inequality and poverty. Our task in this final section is to study the *redistribution* of income by government.

How do governments redistribute income? What is the scale of redistribution? Why do we vote for policies that redistribute income? What are the challenges in designing policies that achieve a fair and efficient distribution of income and reduction of poverty?

### How Governments Redistribute Income

The three main ways in which governments in the United States redistribute income are

- Income taxes
- Income maintenance programs
- Subsidized services

#### Income Taxes

Income taxes may be progressive, regressive, or proportional (see Chapter 8, p. 199). A *progressive income tax* is one that taxes income at an average rate that increases with the level of income. A *regressive income tax* is one that taxes income at an average rate that decreases with the level of income. A *proportional income tax* (also called a *flat-rate income tax*) is one that taxes income at a constant rate, regardless of the level of income.

The federal government, most state governments, and some city governments impose income taxes. The detailed tax arrangements vary across the individual states, but the income tax system overall is progressive. The poorest working households receive money from the government through an earned income tax credit. The federal income tax rate starts at 10 percent of each additional dollar earned on the lowest taxed incomes and rises through 15 percent, 25 percent, 28 percent, 33 percent, and 35 percent of each additional dollar earned on successively higher incomes.

#### Income Maintenance Programs

Three main types of programs redistribute income by making direct payments (in cash, services, or vouchers) to people in the lower part of the income distribution. They are

- Social Security programs
- Unemployment compensation
- Welfare programs

***Social Security Programs*** Social Security is a public insurance system paid for by compulsory payroll taxes on employers and employees. Social Security has two main components: Old Age, Survivors, Disability, and Health Insurance (OASDHI), which provides monthly cash payments to retired or disabled workers or their surviving spouses and children; and Medicare, which provides hospital and health insurance for the elderly and disabled. In 2008, Social Security supported 49 million people, who received average monthly checks of $1,000.

***Unemployment Compensation*** To provide an income to unemployed workers, every state has established an unemployment compensation program. Under these programs, a tax is paid that is based on the income of each covered worker and such a worker receives a benefit when he or she becomes unemployed. The details of the benefits vary from state to state.

***Welfare Programs*** The purpose of welfare programs is to provide incomes for people who do not qualify for Social Security or unemployment compensation. The programs are

1. Supplementary Security Income (SSI) program, which is designed to help the neediest elderly, disabled, and blind people
2. Temporary Assistance for Needy Families (TANF) program, which is designed to help families that have inadequate financial resources
3. Food Stamp program, which is designed to help the poorest households obtain a basic diet
4. Medicaid, which is designed to cover the costs of medical care for households that receive help under the SSI and TANF programs

### Subsidized Services

A great deal of redistribution takes place in the United States through the provision of subsidized services—services provided by the government at prices far below the cost of production. The taxpayers who consume these goods and services receive a transfer in kind from the taxpayers who do not consume them. The two most important areas in which this form of redistribution takes place are education—both kindergarten through grade 12 and college and university—and health care. But neither necessarily redistributes from the rich to the poor.

In 2009–2010, a student enrolled at the University of California, Berkeley, who is not a resident of California paid a tuition of $32,418. This amount is probably close to the cost of providing a year's education at Berkeley. But a California resident paid tuition of only $9,748. So California households with a member enrolled at Berkeley received a benefit from the government of close to $23,000 a year. Many of these households have above-average incomes.

Government provision of health-care services has grown to equal the scale of private provision. Medicaid provides high-quality and high-cost health care to millions of people who earn too little to buy such services themselves. Medicaid redistributes from the rich to the poor. Medicare, which is available to all over 65 years of age, is not targeted at the poor.

## ■ The Scale of Income Redistribution

A household's income in the absence of government redistribution is its *market income*. We can measure the scale of income redistribution by calculating the percentage of market income paid in taxes minus the percentage received in benefits at each income level. The available data include redistribution through taxes and cash and noncash benefits to welfare recipients. The data do not include the value of subsidized services such as a college education, which might decrease the total scale of redistribution from the rich to the poor.

Figure 19.6 shows how government actions changed the distribution of income in 2007. The figure shows two Lorenz curves and compares them with the

**Disposable income**
Market income plus cash benefits paid by the government minus taxes.

line of equality. The blue Lorenz curve describes the distribution of *market income*. The red Lorenz curve shows the distribution of **disposable income**, which is income after all taxes and benefits, including Medicaid and Medicare benefits. The Lorenz curve for *disposable income* is closer to the line of equality than that for *market income*, which tells us that the distribution of disposable income is more equal than the distribution of market income.

Figure 19.6(b) shows that redistribution increases the share received by the lowest three quintiles and decreases the share received by the highest two quintiles.

The sources of income at different income levels provide another measure of the scale of redistribution. The poorest quintile receives 80 percent of its income from the government. The second quintile receives 32 percent of its income from the government. In contrast, the richest quintile receives almost nothing from the government and receives a third of its income from capital—interest, dividends, and capital gains on financial assets.

## FIGURE 19.6
### The Scale of Income Redistribution

myeconlab Animation

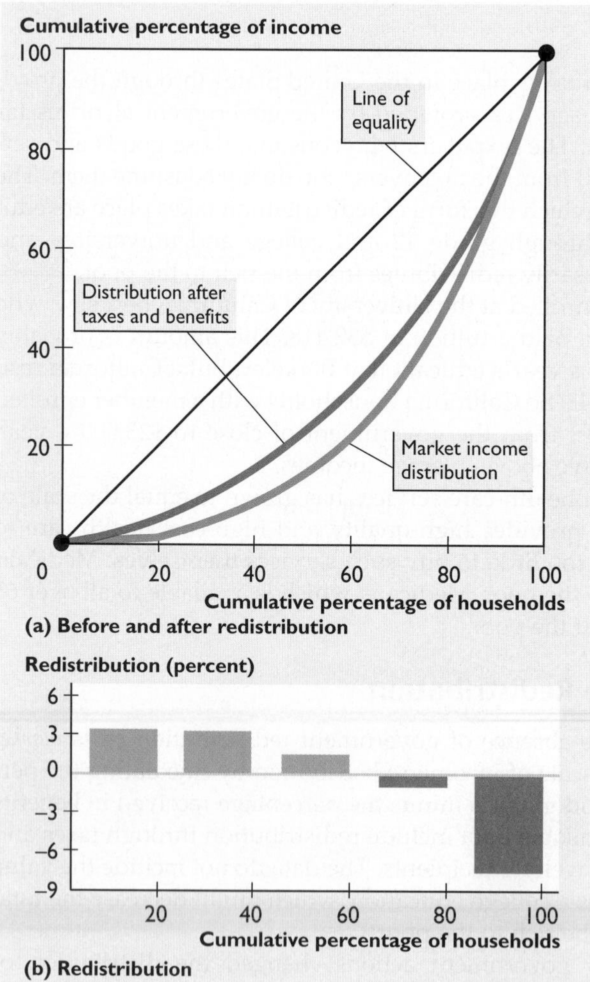


Taxes and income maintenance programs reduce the degree of inequality that the market generates. In part (a), the Lorenz curve moves closer to the line of equality.

Part (b) shows the redistribution in 2007. The quintile with the lowest incomes received net benefits that increased their share of total income by 3.5 percentage points. The quintile of total income with the highest incomes paid taxes that decreased their share of total income by 7.5 percentage points.

Source of data: U.S. Census Bureau, Current Population Survey Annual Social and Economic Supplement.

## Why We Redistribute Income

Why do we vote for government policies that redistribute income? Why don't we leave everyone to make voluntary contributions to charities that help the poor?

There are two ways of approaching these questions: normative and positive. The normative approach discusses why we *should* compel everyone to help the poor and looks for principles to guide the appropriate scale of redistribution. The positive approach seeks reasons why we *do* compel everyone to help the poor and tries to explain the actual scale of redistribution.

### Normative Theories of Income Redistribution

Philosophy and politics, not economics, are the subjects that consider the normative theories of redistribution. Not surprisingly, there are several different points of view on whether income should be redistributed and, if so, on what scale.

*Utilitarianism* points to the ideal distribution being one of equality. But efficiency is also desirable. And greater equality can be achieved only at the cost of greater inefficiency—the *big tradeoff* (defined in Chapter 6, p. 162). The redistribution of income creates the big tradeoff because it uses scarce resources and weakens incentives, which decreases the total size of the economic pie to be shared.

A dollar collected from a rich person does not translate into a dollar received by a poor person. Some of it gets used up in the process of redistribution. Tax-collecting agencies such as the Internal Revenue Service and welfare-administering agencies (as well as tax accountants and lawyers) use skilled labor, computers, and other scarce resources to do their work. The bigger the scale of redistribution, the greater is the opportunity cost of administering it.

But the cost of collecting taxes and making welfare payments is a small part of the total cost of redistribution. A bigger cost arises from the inefficiency—*excess burden*—of taxes and benefits (see Chapter 8, p. 194). Greater equality can be achieved only by taxing productive activities such as work and saving. Taxing people's income from their work and saving lowers the after-tax income they receive. This lower income makes them work and save less, which in turn results in smaller output and less consumption not only for the rich who pay the taxes but also for the poor who receive the benefits.

Benefit recipients as well as taxpayers face weaker incentives. In fact, under the welfare arrangements that prevailed before the 1996 reforms, the weakest incentives to work were those faced by households that benefited from welfare. When a welfare recipient got a job, benefits were withdrawn and eligibility for programs such as Medicaid ended, so the household in effect paid a tax of more than 100 percent on its earnings. This arrangement locked poor households in a welfare trap.

Recognizing the tension between equality and efficiency, philosopher John Rawls proposed the principle that income should be redistributed to the point at which it maximizes the size of the slice of the economic pie received by the person with the smallest slice.

Libertarian philosophers such as Robert Nozick (see Chapter 6, p. 161) say that any redistribution is wrong because it violates the sanctity of private property and voluntary exchange.

Modern political parties stand in the center of the extremes that we've just described. Some favor a bit more redistribution than others, but the major political parties are broadly happy with the prevailing scale of redistribution.

### Positive Theories of Income Redistribution

**Median voter theory**
The theory that governments pursue policies that make the median voter as well off as possible.

A good positive theory of income redistribution would explain why some countries have more redistribution than others and why redistribution has increased over the past 200 years. We don't have such a theory, but economists have proposed a promising idea called the median voter theory. The **median voter theory** is that the policies that governments pursue are those that make the median voter as well off as possible. If a proposal can be made that improves the well-being of the median voter, a political party that makes the proposal can improve its standing in an election.

The median voter theory arises from thinking about how a democratic political system such as that of the United States works. In this system, governments must propose policies that appeal to enough voters to get them elected. And in a majority voting system, the voter whose views carry the most weight is the one in the middle—the median voter.

The median voter wants income to be redistributed to the point at which her or his own after-tax income is as large as possible. Taxing the rich by too much would weaken their incentives to create businesses and jobs and lower the median voter's after-tax income. But taxing the rich by too little would leave some money on the table that could be transferred to the median voter.

The median voter might be concerned about the poor and want to reduce poverty. Unselfishly, the median voter might simply be concerned about the plight of the poor and want to help them. Self-interestedly, the median voter might believe that if there is too much poverty, there will be too much crime and some of it will touch her or his life.

If for either reason the median voter wants to help the poor, the political process will deliver a greater scale of redistribution to reflect this voter preference.

## ■ The Major Welfare Challenge

Among the poorest people in the United States (see p. 488) are young women who have not completed high school, have a child (or children), live without a partner, and are more likely to be black or Hispanic than white. These young women and their children present the major welfare challenge.

There are about 10 million single mothers, and a quarter of them receive no support from their children's fathers. The long-term solution to the problem of these women is education and job training—acquiring human capital. The short-term solution is welfare, but welfare must be designed in ways that strengthen the incentive to pursue the long-term solution. And a change in the U.S. welfare programs introduced during the 1990s pursues this approach.

### The Current Approach: TANF

Passed in 1996, the Personal Responsibility and Work Opportunities Reconciliation Act created the Temporary Assistance for Needy Families (TANF) program. TANF is a block grant that is paid to the states, which administer payments to individuals. It is not an open-ended entitlement program. An adult member of a household receiving assistance must either work or perform community service, and there is a five-year limit for assistance.

These measures go a long way toward removing one of the most serious poverty problems while being sensitive to the potential inefficiency of welfare. But some economists want to go further and introduce a negative income tax.

## Negative Income Tax

The negative income tax is not on the political agenda, but it is popular among economists, and it is the subject of several real-world experiments. A **negative income tax** provides every household with a guaranteed minimum annual income and taxes all earned income at a fixed rate. Suppose the guaranteed minimum annual income is $10,000 and the tax rate is 25 percent. A household with no earned income receives the $10,000 guaranteed minimum income from the government. This household "pays" income tax of *minus* $10,000, hence the name "negative income tax."

**Negative income tax**
A tax and redistribution scheme that provides every household with a guaranteed minimum annual income and taxes all earned income at a fixed rate.

A household that earns $40,000 a year pays $10,000—25 percent of its earned income—to the government. But this household also receives from the government the $10,000 guaranteed minimum income, so it pays no net income tax. It has the break-even income. Households that earn between zero and $40,000 a year receive more from the government than they pay to the government. They "pay" a negative income tax.

A household that earns $60,000 a year pays $15,000—25 percent of its earned income—to the government. But this household receives from the government the $10,000 guaranteed minimum income, so it pays a net income tax of $5,000. All households that earn more than $40,000 a year pay more to the government than they receive from it. They pay a positive amount of income tax.

A negative income tax doesn't eliminate the excess burden of taxation, but it does improve the incentives to work and save at all levels of income.

## EYE on YOUR LIFE

### What You Pay and Gain Through Redistribution

You are on both sides of the redistribution equation, but what's your bottom line? Are you a net receiver or a net payer? Try to figure out which.

#### Your Tax Payments

You might pay some income tax and you certainly pay sales taxes and taxes on gasoline and other items.

If you have a job, your payslip shows the amount of income tax you're paying.

You can calculate the sales taxes you pay by keeping track for a week every time you buy something.

You can work out how much gas and other taxes you pay by checking the scale of these taxes in your state at www.taxadmin.org.

#### Your Benefits

Now for the benefits. If you're receiving any direct cash payments such as unemployment benefits, these are easy to identify. But most likely, you don't receive any money from the government.

You do, though, receive the benefits of services provided by government. The biggest of these is most likely the cost of your education.

It costs much more than the tuition you're paying to provide your education. One estimate of the value of your education is the tuition paid by an out-of-state student minus the tuition paid by a state resident. Figure out that number.

Now think about all the other benefits you receive from government. Try to estimate what all the government-provided services are worth to you.

#### Your Bottom Line

Now work out your bottom line—the benefits you receive minus the taxes you pay. Most likely, you have a net benefit, but that situation will change when you graduate. As your income rises, you will move to the other side of the redistribution equation.

Work these problems in Study Plan 19.3 to get instant feedback.

# CHECKPOINT 19.3

**Explain how governments redistribute income and describe the effects of redistribution on economic inequality and poverty.**

## Practice Problems

Use Table 1, which shows the distribution of market income in an economy, and Table 2, which shows how the government redistributes income by collecting income taxes and paying benefits, to work Problems **1** and **2**.

1. Calculate the income shares of each quintile after tax and redistribution.
2. Draw this economy's Lorenz curve before and after taxes and benefits.
3. **The 0% tax rate solution**

   In 2006, the bottom 40 percent of income earners received net payments equal to 3.6% of total income tax revenues. The middle 20 percent of income earners pay 4.4% of total income tax revenues. That means the bottom 60 percent together pay less than 1% of income tax revenues.

   Source: *The Wall Street Journal*, July 14, 2009

   Would a policy that taxed the bottom 60 percent of income earners at a 0% tax rate and reduced redistribution by 1 percent of tax revenue have any merit?

**TABLE 1 MARKET INCOME**

| Households | Income (millions of dollars per year) |
|---|---|
| Lowest 20 percent | 5 |
| Second 20 percent | 10 |
| Third 20 percent | 18 |
| Fourth 20 percent | 28 |
| Highest 20 percent | 39 |

**TABLE 2 TAXES AND BENEFITS**

| Households | Income tax (percent) | Benefits (millions of dollars) |
|---|---|---|
| Lowest 20 percent | 0 | 10 |
| Second 20 percent | 10 | 8 |
| Third 20 percent | 18 | 3 |
| Fourth 20 percent | 28 | 0 |
| Highest 20 percent | 39 | 0 |

## Guided Solutions to Practice Problems

1. To find the distribution of income, multiply each quintile's market income by the tax rate, subtract the taxes paid, and add the benefits received to obtain the income after tax and benefits. Then calculate each quintile's income as a percentage of total income. Table 3 summarizes the calculations.

**TABLE 3**

| Households | Market income (millions of dollars) | Tax paid (millions of dollars) | Benefits received (millions of dollars) | Income after tax and benefits (millions of dollars) | Income after tax and benefits (percentage of total income) |
|---|---|---|---|---|---|
| Lowest 20 percent | 5 | 0.0 | 10 | 15.0 | 16.0 |
| Second 20 percent | 10 | 1.0 | 8 | 17.0 | 18.1 |
| Third 20 percent | 18 | 3.2 | 3 | 17.8 | 19.0 |
| Fourth 20 percent | 28 | 7.8 | 0 | 20.2 | 21.5 |
| Highest 20 percent | 39 | 15.2 | 0 | 23.8 | 25.4 |

2. To draw the Lorenz curves, calculate the cumulative shares. For example, before taxes and benefits, the lowest 20 percent have 5 percent of total income and the lowest 40 percent have 15 percent (5 + 10) of total income. After taxes and benefits, the lowest 20 percent have 16 percent of total income and the lowest 40 percent have 34.1 percent (16 + 18.1) of total income. Figure 1 plots the Lorenz curves.
3. The redistribution process uses resources. A dollar taken from a high income earner does not translate into a dollar for a low-income earner. Reducing the necessity of 60 percent of workers to file income tax will save resources. There would be a net social gain, which might be used to help the poor.

**FIGURE 1**

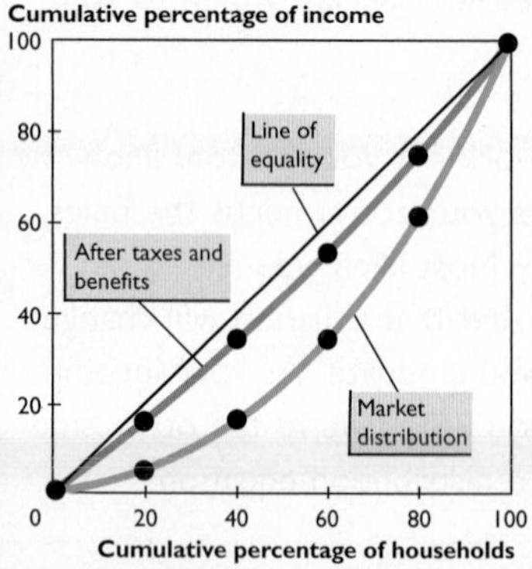

# CHAPTER SUMMARY

## Key Points

1 **Describe the economic inequality and poverty in the United States.**

- The distributions of income and wealth describe economic inequality.
- The 20 percent of households with the lowest incomes receive about 1 percent of total market income and the 1 percent of households with the highest wealth own about one third of total wealth.
- The distribution of income has become more unequal over the past few decades.
- During a decade, about 30 percent of families move up by a quintile or more and slightly fewer move down by a quintile or more.
- About 12 percent of Americans have incomes below the poverty level and for almost 20 percent, poverty lasts for more than one year.

2 **Explain how economic inequality and poverty arise.**

- Economic inequality arises from inequality of labor market outcomes, ownership of capital, entrepreneurial ability, and personal and family characteristics.
- In labor markets, skill differences result in earnings differences. Discrimination might also contribute to earnings differences.
- Inherited capital, unusual entrepreneurial talent, and personal or family good fortune or misfortune widen the gap between rich and poor.

3 **Explain how governments redistribute income and describe the effects of redistribution on economic inequality and poverty.**

- Governments redistribute income through progressive income taxes, income maintenance programs, and provision of subsidized services.
- Normative theories of redistribution recognize the tension between equality and efficiency—the big tradeoff—and seek principles to guide the political debate.
- The main positive theory of redistribution is the median voter theory.
- The negative income tax is a proposal for addressing the big tradeoff.

## Key Terms

Disposable income, 500
Lorenz curve, 485
Market income, 484
Median voter theory, 502
Money income, 484
Negative income tax, 503
Poverty, 489

Work these problems in Chapter 19 Study Plan to get instant feedback.

**TABLE 1**

| Households | Market income (percentage) |
|---|---|
| Lowest 20 percent | 1 |
| Second 20 percent | 3 |
| Third 20 percent | 15 |
| Fourth 20 percent | 26 |
| Highest 20 percent | 55 |

**FIGURE 1**

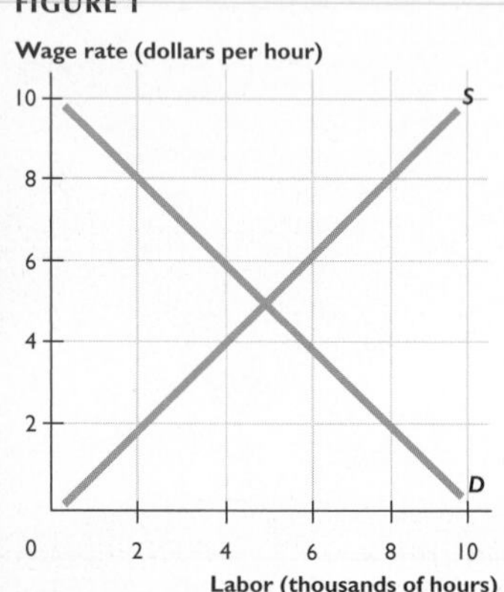


**TABLE 2**

| Households | Market income (percentage) |
|---|---|
| Lowest 20 percent | 5 |
| Second 20 percent | 9 |
| Third 20 percent | 20 |
| Fourth 20 percent | 30 |
| Highest 20 percent | 36 |

# CHAPTER CHECKPOINT

## Study Plan Problems and Applications

1. Table 1 shows the distribution of market income in Australia. Calculate the cumulative distribution of income for Australia and draw the Lorenz curve for Australian income. In which country is the income distribution more unequal: Australia or the United States?
2. Figure 1 shows the market for low-skilled workers. With on-the-job training, low-skilled workers can become high-skilled workers. The value of marginal product of high-skilled workers at each employment level is twice the value of marginal product of low-skilled workers, but the cost of acquiring skill adds $2 an hour to the wage rate that will attract high-skilled labor. What is the equilibrium wage rate of low-skilled labor and the number of low-skilled workers employed? What is the equilibrium wage rate of high-skilled labor and the number of high-skilled workers employed?
3. **Rich-poor gap worries Chinese planners**
   In 1985, urban Chinese earned 1.9 times as much as people in the countryside, which is home to 60 percent of the population. By 2007, they earned 3.3 times as much according to the United Nations.
   Source: *The New York Times*, November 22, 2008
   Explain how the Lorenz curve in China changed between 1985 and 2007.

Use Table 2, which shows the distribution of market income in an economy, to work Problems **4** to **6**. Suppose that the government redistributes income by taxing the 60 percent of households with the highest incomes 10 percent, then paying the tax collected as benefits distributed equally to the 40 percent with the lowest market income.

4. Calculate the distribution of income after taxes and benefits and draw the Lorenz curve before and after taxes and benefits.
5. If the cost of administering the redistribution scheme takes 50 percent of the taxes collected, calculate the new distribution of income.
6. If the people whose incomes are taxed cut their work hours and their incomes fall by 10 percent, what now is the distribution of income? (Ignore the cost of administering the redistribution scheme.)

Use the following information to work Problems **7** and **8**.

**A sobering census report: Americans' meager income gains**

The Census Bureau reported that median household income rose 0.7 percent in 2006 to $48,201, but it was still about $1,000 less than in 2000, before the start of the last recession. Households living in poverty fell to 12.3 percent from 12.6 percent in 2005. But in 2006, 36.5 million Americans were living in poverty—5 million more than in 2000, when the poverty rate was 11.3 percent.

Source: *The New York Times*, August 29, 2007

7. What does the data in the news clip tell us about the U.S. Lorenz curve?
8. Compare the numbers for 2000, 2005, and 2006. During these years, describe how the distribution of income changed.

## Instructor Assignable Problems and Applications

Your instructor can assign these problems as homework, a quiz, or a test in **MyEconLab**.

1. Education, household size, household type (marital status), age of householder, race, and region of residence all influence the degree of income inequality. Rank these influences in order of importance from most to least important.
2. Table 1 shows the distribution of prize money among the top 20 professional golfers. Calculate the cumulative distribution of income of these golfers and draw the prize money Lorenz curve of these golfers. Which distribution is more unequal: the distribution of income of these golfers or that of the United States as a whole?
3. Suppose the cost of acquiring a skill increases and the value of marginal product of skill increases. Draw demand-supply graphs of the labor markets for high-skilled and low-skilled labor to explain what happens to the equilibrium wage rate of low-skilled labor, the equilibrium wage rate of high-skilled labor, and the number of high-skilled workers employed.

**TABLE 1**

| Professional golfers | Income (percentage) |
|---|---|
| Lowest 20 percent | 15 |
| Second 20 percent | 16 |
| Third 20 percent | 18 |
| Fourth 20 percent | 20 |
| Highest 20 percent | 31 |

Use the following information to work Problems **4** and **5**.

In the United States in 2002, 130,000 aircraft mechanics and service technicians earned an average of $20 an hour whereas 30,000 elevator installers and repairers earned an average of $25 an hour. The skill and training for these two jobs are very similar.

4. Draw the demand and supply curves for these two types of labor. What feature of your graph accounts for the differences in the two wage rates and what feature accounts for the differences in the quantities employed of these two types of labor?
5. Suppose that a government law required both groups of workers to be paid $22.50 an hour. Draw a graph to illustrate what would happen to the quantities employed of the two types of labor.
6. Table 2 shows the income share for each household quintile and the cumulative shares. Provide the values for **A**, **B**, **C**, **D**, and **E**.

**TABLE 2**

| Households (quintile) | Income (%) | Income (cumulative %) |
|---|---|---|
| First | 7.4 | 7.4 |
| Second | 13.2 | **A** |
| Third | **B** | 38.7 |
| Fourth | 25.0 | **C** |
| Fifth | **D** | **E** |

Use the following information to work Problems **7** to **9**.

**Income gap in New York is called nation's highest**

New York continues to have the highest income gap of any state, according to a recent study. The average income ($130,431) of the highest quintile of families is 8.1 times that ($16,076) of the poorest quintile. Budget experts claim that the income gap arises from the large number of poor unskilled immigrants. Mobility of these workers arises from the lack of educational attainment and a barrier to education.

Source: nytimes.com, January 27, 2006

7. Explain the effect of a large increase in foreign immigrants who are largely poor, unskilled workers on the market for low-skilled labor.
8. Explain how better schools and more education would change the wage and employment of low-skilled labor.
9. Explain how lowering the "barrier to education" would reduce the income gap.

**TABLE 3**

| Households | Market income (percentage) |
|---|---|
| Lowest 20 percent | 1.1 |
| Second 20 percent | 7.1 |
| Third 20 percent | 13.9 |
| Fourth 20 percent | 22.8 |
| Highest 20 percent | 55.1 |

**TABLE 4**

| Households | Money income (percentage) |
|---|---|
| Lowest 20 percent | 3.4 |
| Second 20 percent | 8.6 |
| Third 20 percent | 14.6 |
| Fourth 20 percent | 23.0 |
| Highest 20 percent | 50.4 |

**10.** Table 3 shows the distribution of market income. Draw the economy's Lorenz curve.

Use Table 3, which shows the distribution of market income, and Table 4, which shows the distribution of money income, to work Problems **11** and **12.**

**11.** What is the percentage of total market income that is redistributed from the highest income group? What is the percentages of total market income that is redistributed to the lower income groups?

**12.** Describe the effects of increasing the amount of income redistribution to the point at which the lowest income group receives 15 percent of total income and the highest income group receives 30 percent of total income.

**13.** Why do economists think that discrimination in the labor market is an unlikely explanation for the persistent inequality in earnings between women and men and among the races?

**14.** Incomes in China and India are a small fraction of the incomes in the United States. But incomes in China and India are growing more quickly than those in the United States. Given this information what can you say about changes in inequality between the people in China and India and the people in the United States? How will the world Lorenz curve change?

**15.** Do you think the distributions of income and wealth in the United States today are too unequal, too equal, or about right? Provide a detailed justification for your opinion using the ideas of economic efficiency and fairness explained in Chapter 6, the concept of the big tradeoff, and the data presented in the tables in this chapter.

**16. Bernanke links education and equality**

Ben Bernanke, chairman of the Federal Reserve, said that expansion of education would help reduce the amount of inequality in the United States. Education would give workers better skills and higher life-time earnings.

Source: *International Herald Tribune*, June 5, 2008

Draw a graph to show how increased skill will raise incomes and reduce inequality.

**17. California progress**

In May, California voters rejected an increase in taxes to close a $26 billion budget gap. To generate more tax revenues, California will have to encourage new businesses and create jobs. With 50% of income tax revenues coming from the richest 1% of residents, the state needs lower rates. Income redistribution has gone too far.

Source: *Wall Street Journal*, July 22, 2009

Does the median voter theory explain voters' rejection? If California lowers the highest tax rate to below the current 10.5 percent and cuts some free benefits, how might California's Lorenz curve change?

**18.** "The distribution of income within a country is only a small part of the story of economic inequality. The truly disturbing inequality is that among nations. The rich countries must do much more to help the poor ones." Appraise this statement. Do you agree or disagree with it? Explain your opinion using the ideas of economic efficiency and fairness, the concept of the big tradeoff, and the data presented in the tables in this chapter.

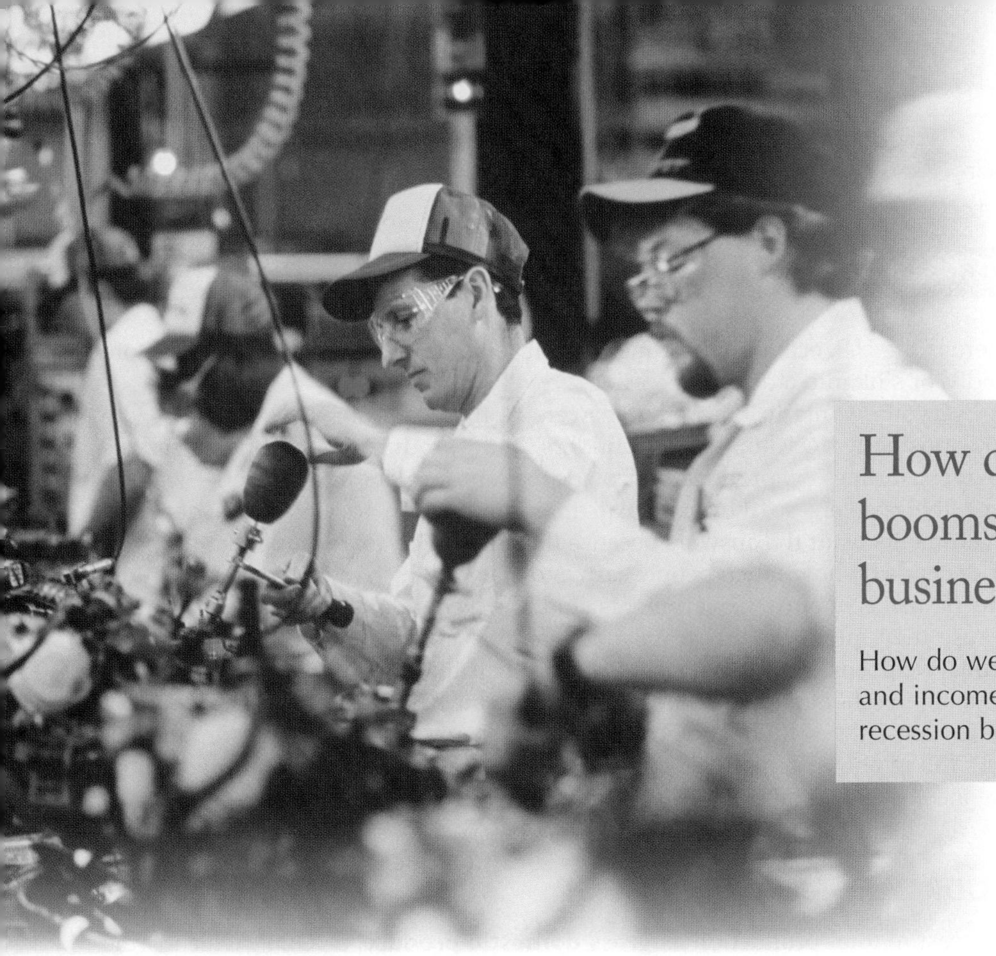

## How do we track the booms and busts of the business cycle?

How do we measure a nation's production and income and determine when a recession begins and ends?

# GDP: A Measure of Total Production and Income

CHAPTER CHECKLIST

**When you have completed your study of this chapter, you will be able to**

1 Define GDP and explain why the value of production, income, and expenditure are the same for an economy.

2 Describe how economic statisticians measure GDP and distinguish between nominal GDP and real GDP.

3 Describe the uses of real GDP and explain its limitations as a measure of the standard of living.

## 20.1 GDP, INCOME, AND EXPENDITURE

Where is the U.S. economy heading? Will it remain weak, begin to expand more rapidly, or sink into a deeper recession?

Everyone wants to know the answers to these questions. The people who make business decisions—homebuilders, auto-producers, cell-phone service providers, airlines, oil producers, airplane makers, farmers, and retailers—want to know the answers so they can plan their production to align with demand. Governments want the answers because the amount of tax revenue that they collect depends on how much people earn and spend, which in turn depends on the state of the economy. Governments and the Federal Reserve want to know because they might be able to take actions that avoid excessive bust or boom. Ordinary citizens want the answers to plan their big decisions such as how long to remain in school and whether to rent or buy a new home.

To assess the state of the economy we measure gross domestic product, or GDP. You're about to discover that GDP measures the value of total production, total income, and total expenditure.

### GDP Defined

**Gross domestic product (GDP)**
The market value of all the final goods and services produced within a country in a given time period.

We measure total production as **gross domestic product**, or **GDP**, which is the market value of all the final goods and services produced within a country in a given time period. This definition has four parts, which we'll examine in turn.

#### Value Produced

To measure total production, we must add together the production of apples and oranges, bats and balls. Just counting the items doesn't get us very far. Which is the greater total production: 100 apples and 50 oranges or 50 apples and 100 oranges?

GDP answers this question by valuing items at their *market value*—at the prices at which the items are traded in markets. If the price of an apple is 10 cents and the price of an orange is 20 cents, the market value of 100 apples plus 50 oranges is $20 and the market value of 50 apples and 100 oranges is $25. By using market prices to value production, we can add the apples and oranges together.

#### What Produced

**Final good or service**
A good or service that is produced for its final user and not as a component of another good or service.

**Intermediate good or service**
A good or service that is used as a component of a final good or service.

A **final good or service** is something that is produced for its final user and not as a component of another good or service. A final good or service contrasts with an **intermediate good or service**, which is used as a component of a final good or service. For example, a Ford car is a final good, but a Firestone tire that Ford buys and installs on the car is an intermediate good. But if you buy a replacement Firestone tire for your car, the tire is then a final good. The same good can be either final or intermediate depending on how it is used.

GDP does not count the value of everything that is produced. With one exception, it includes only those items that are traded in markets and does not include the value of goods and services that people produce for their own use. For example, if you buy a car wash, the value produced is included in GDP. But if you wash your own car, your production is not counted as part of GDP. The exception is the market value of homes that people own. GDP puts a rental value on these homes and pretends that the owners rent their homes to themselves.

### Where Produced

Only goods and services that are produced *within a country* count as part of that country's GDP. Nike Corporation, a U.S. firm, produces sneakers in Vietnam, and the market value of those shoes is part of Vietnam's GDP, not part of U.S. GDP. Toyota, a Japanese firm, produces automobiles in Georgetown, Kentucky, and the value of this production is part of U.S. GDP, not part of Japan's GDP.

### When Produced

GDP measures the value of production *during a given time period*. This time period is either a quarter of a year—called the quarterly GDP data—or a year—called the annual GDP data. The Federal Reserve and others use the quarterly GDP data to keep track of the short-term evolution of the economy, and economists use the annual GDP data to examine long-term trends.

GDP measures not only the value of total production but also total income and total expenditure. The circular flow model that you studied in Chapter 2 explains why.

## Circular Flows in the U.S. Economy

Four groups buy the final goods and services produced: households, firms, governments, and the rest of the world. Four types of expenditure correspond to these groups:

- Consumption expenditure
- Investment
- Government expenditure on goods and services
- Net exports of goods and services

### Consumption Expenditure

**Consumption expenditure** is the expenditure by households on consumption goods and services. It includes expenditures on *nondurable goods* such as orange juice and pizza, *durable goods* such as televisions and DVD players, and *services* such as rock concerts and haircuts. Consumption expenditure also includes house and apartment rents, including the rental value of owner-occupied housing.

**Consumption expenditure**
The expenditure by households on consumption goods and services.

### Investment

**Investment** is the purchase of new *capital goods* (tools, instruments, machines, and buildings) and additions to inventories. Capital goods are *durable goods* produced by one firm and bought by another. Examples are PCs produced by Dell and bought by Ford Motor Company, and airplanes produced by Boeing and bought by United Airlines. Investment also includes the purchase of new homes by households.

**Investment**
The purchase of new *capital goods* (tools, instruments, machines, buildings) and additions to inventories.

At the end of a year, some of a firm's output might remain unsold. For example, if Ford produces 4 million cars and sells 3.9 million of them, the other 0.1 million (100,000) cars remain unsold. In this case, Ford's inventory of cars increases by 100,000. When a firm adds unsold output to inventory, we count those items as part of investment.

It is important to note that investment does *not* include the purchase of stocks and bonds. In macroeconomics, we reserve the term "investment" for the purchase of new capital goods and the additions to inventories.

### Government Expenditure on Goods and Services

**Government expenditure on goods and services**
The expenditure by all levels of government on goods and services.

**Government expenditure on goods and services** is expenditure by all levels of government on goods and services. For example, the U.S. Defense Department buys missiles and other weapons systems, the State Department buys travel services, the White House buys Internet services, and state and local governments buy cruisers for law enforcement officers.

### Net Exports of Goods and Services

**Net exports of goods and services**
The value of exports of goods and services minus the value of imports of goods and services.

**Exports of goods and services**
Items that firms in the United States produce and sell to the rest of the world.

**Imports of goods and services**
Items that households, firms, and governments in the United States buy from the rest of the world.

**Net exports of goods and services** is the value of exports of goods and services minus the value of imports of goods and services. **Exports of goods and services** are items that firms in the United States produce and sell to the rest of the world. **Imports of goods and services** are items that households, firms, and governments in the United States buy from the rest of the world. Imports are produced in other countries, so expenditure on imports is not included in expenditure on U.S.-produced goods and services. If exports exceed imports, net exports are positive and expenditure on U.S.-produced goods and services increases. If imports exceed exports, net exports are negative and expenditure on U.S.-produced goods and services decreases.

### Total Expenditure

Total expenditure on goods and services produced in the United States is the sum of the four items that you've just examined. We call consumption expenditure $C$, investment $I$, government expenditure on goods and services $G$, and net exports of goods and services $NX$. So total expenditure, which is also the total amount received by the producers of final goods and services, is

$$\text{Total expenditure} = C + I + G + NX.$$

### Income

Labor earns wages, capital earns interest, land earns rent, and entrepreneurship earns profits. Households receive these incomes. Some part of total income, called *undistributed profit,* is a combination of interest and profit that firms retain and do not pay to households. But from an economic viewpoint, undistributed profit is income paid to households and then loaned to firms.

## Expenditure Equals Income

Figure 20.1 shows the circular flows of income and expenditure that we've just described. The figure is based on Figures 2.5 and 2.6 (on p. 49 and p. 51), but it includes some more details and additional flows.

**Net taxes**
Taxes paid minus cash benefits received from governments.

**Saving**
The amount of income that is not paid in net taxes or spent on consumption goods and services.

We call total income $Y$ and show it by the blue flow from firms to households. When households receive their incomes, they pay some in taxes and save some. Some households receive benefits from governments. **Net taxes** equal taxes paid minus cash benefits received and are the green flow from households to governments labeled $NT$. **Saving** is the amount of income that is not paid in net taxes or spent on consumption goods and services. Saving flows from households to financial markets and is the green flow labeled $S$. These two green flows are not expenditures on goods and services. They are just flows of money. Because households allocate all their incomes after paying net taxes to consumption and saving,

$$Y = C + S + NT.$$

The red flows show the four expenditure flows: consumption expenditure from households to firms, government expenditure from governments to firms, and net exports from the rest of the world to firms. Investment flows from the financial markets, where firms borrow, to the firms that produce capital goods.

Because firms pay out everything they receive as incomes to the factors of production, total expenditure equals total income. That is,

$$Y = C + I + G + NX.$$

From the viewpoint of firms, the value of production is the cost of production, which equals income. From the viewpoint of purchasers of goods and services, the value of production is the cost of buying it, which equals expenditure. So

**The value of production equals income equals expenditure.**

The circular flow and the equality of income and expenditure provide two approaches to measuring GDP that we'll study in the next section.

**FIGURE 20.1**

The Circular Flow of Income and Expenditure

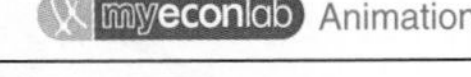

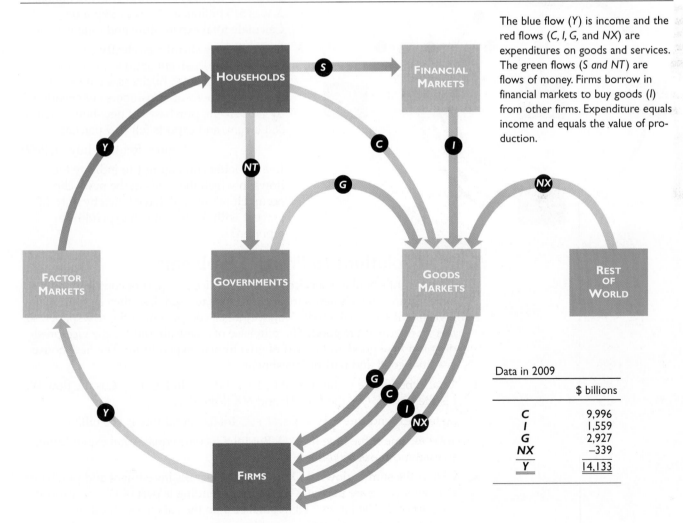


The blue flow (*Y*) is income and the red flows (*C*, *I*, *G*, and *NX*) are expenditures on goods and services. The green flows (*S and NT*) are flows of money. Firms borrow in financial markets to buy goods (*I*) from other firms. Expenditure equals income and equals the value of production.

Data in 2009

| | $ billions |
|---|---|
| **C** | 9,996 |
| **I** | 1,559 |
| **G** | 2,927 |
| **NX** | –339 |
| **Y** | 14,133 |

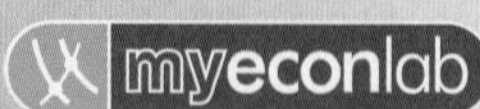

Work these problems in Study Plan 20.1 to get instant feedback.

## CHECKPOINT 20.1

**Define GDP and explain why the value of production, income, and expenditure are the same for an economy.**

## Practice Problems

1. Classify each of the following items as a final good or service or an intermediate good or service and identify which is a component of consumption expenditure, investment, or government expenditure on goods and services:
   - Banking services bought by a student.
   - New cars bought by Hertz, the car rental firm.
   - Newsprint bought by *USA Today* from International Paper.
   - The purchase of a new aircraft for the vice-president.
   - New house bought by the Al Gore family.

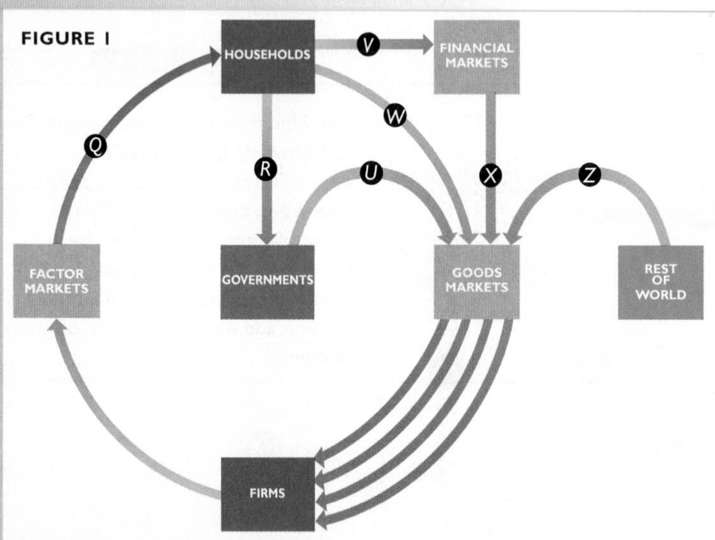


2. Figure 1 shows the flows of expenditure and income on Lotus Island. In 2008, *R* was \$10 billion; *W* was \$30 billion; *U* was \$12 billion; *X* was \$15 billion; and *Z* was \$3 billion. Calculate total expenditure and total income.
3. **U.S. economy shrinks modestly**

   GDP fell at a 1 percent annual rate in the second quarter of 2009. Businesses cut investment by 8.9 percent, consumers cut spending by 1.2 percent, purchases of new houses fell 38 percent, and exports fell 29.9 percent.

   Source: Reuters, July 31, 2009

   Use the letters on Figure 1 to indicate the flows in which the items in the news clip occur. How can GDP have fallen by only 1.0 percent with the big cuts in expenditure reported?

## Guided Solutions to Practice Problems

1. The student's banking service is a final service and part of consumption expenditure. Hertz's new cars are additions to capital, so they are part of investment and final goods. Newsprint is a component of the newspaper, so it is an intermediate good. The purchase of a new aircraft for the vice-president is a final good and is part of government expenditure. The new house is a final good and part of investment.
2. Total expenditure is the sum of *C*, *I*, *G*, and *NX*. In Figure 1, *C* is the flow *W*; *I* is the flow *X*; *G* is the flow *U*; and *NX* is the flow *Z*.

   So total expenditure = *W* + *X* + *U* + *Z*. Total expenditure is \$60 billion.

   Total income is the blue flow, *Q*. But total income equals total expenditure, so total income is \$60 billion.
3. GDP is the sum of flows *W*, *X*, *U*, and *Z*. Business investment and purchases of new housing are part of *X*, consumer spending is part of *W*, and exports are part of *Z*. The fall in GDP is smaller than the cuts in expenditures because either government expenditure increased or imports decreased.

## 20.2 MEASURING U.S. GDP

U.S. GDP is the market value of all the final goods and services produced within the United States during a year. In 2009, U.S. GDP was $14 trillion. The Bureau of Economic Analysis in the U.S. Department of Commerce measures GDP by using two approaches:

- Expenditure approach
- Income approach

### The Expenditure Approach

The expenditure approach measures GDP by using data on consumption expenditure, investment, government expenditure on goods and services, and net exports. This approach is like attaching a meter to the circular flow diagram on all the flows running through the goods markets to firms and measuring the magnitudes of those flows. Table 20.1 shows this approach. The first column gives the terms used in the U.S. National Income and Product Accounts. The next column gives the symbols we used in the previous section.

Using the expenditure approach, GDP is the sum of consumption expenditure on goods and services (*C*), investment (*I*), government expenditure on goods and services (*G*), and net exports of goods and services (*NX*). The third column gives the expenditures in 2009. GDP measured by the expenditure approach was $14,133 billion (the data are based on the second quarter of 2009).

Net exports were negative in 2009 because imports exceeded exports. Imports were $1,831 billion and exports were $1,492 billion, so net exports—exports minus imports—were –$339 billion as shown in the table.

The fourth column in Table 20.1 shows the relative magnitudes of the expenditures. Consumption expenditure is by far the largest component of total expenditure; government expenditure is the next largest. Investment and exports are a similar size; and net export is the smallest component. In 2009, consumption expenditure was 70.7 percent, investment was 11.0 percent, government expenditure was 20.7 percent, and net exports were a negative 2.4 percent of GDP.

**TABLE 20.1**

GDP: The Expenditure Approach

| Item | Symbol | Amount in 2009 (second quarter) (billions of dollars) | Percentage of GDP |
|---|---|---|---|
| **Consumption expenditure** | *C* | 9,996 | 70.7 |
| **Investment** | *I* | 1,559 | 11.0 |
| **Government expenditure** | *G* | 2,927 | 20.7 |
| **Net exports** | *NX* | –339 | –2.4 |
| **GDP** | *Y* | 14,133 | 100.0 |

SOURCE OF DATA: U.S. Department of Commerce, Bureau of Economic Analysis.

The expenditure approach measures GDP by adding together consumption expenditure (*C*), investment (*I*), government expenditure (*G*), and net exports (*NX*).

In 2009, GDP measured by the expenditure approach was $14,133 billion.

### Expenditures Not in GDP

Total expenditure (and GDP) does not include all the things that people and businesses buy. GDP is the value of *final goods and services,* so spending that is *not* on final goods and services is not part of GDP. Spending on intermediate goods and services is not part of GDP, although it is not always obvious whether an item is an intermediate good or a final good (see *Eye on the U.S. Economy* below). Also, we do not count as part of GDP spending on

- Used goods
- Financial assets

***Used Goods*** Expenditure on used goods is not part of GDP because these goods were part of GDP in the period in which they were produced and during which time they were new goods. For example, a 2008 automobile was part of GDP in 2008. If the car is traded on the used car market in 2010, the amount paid for the car is not part of GDP in 2010.

***Financial Assets*** When households buy financial assets such as bonds and stocks, they are making loans, not buying goods and services. The expenditure on newly produced capital goods is part of GDP, but the purchase of financial assets is not.

## EYE on the U.S. ECONOMY

### Is a Computer Program an Intermediate Good or a Final Good?

When American Airlines buys a new reservations software package, is that like General Motors buying tires? If it is, then software is an *intermediate good* and it is not counted as part of GDP. Airline ticket sales, like GM cars, are part of GDP, but the intermediate goods that are used to produce air transportation or cars are *not* part of GDP.

Or when American Airlines buys new software, is that like General Motors buying a new assembly-line robot? If it is, then the software is a capital good and its purchase is the purchase of a final good. In this case, the software purchase is an *investment* and it *is* counted as part of GDP.

Brent Moulton is a government economist who works in the Bureau of Economic Analysis (BEA). Moulton's job was to oversee periodic adjustments to the GDP estimates to incorporate new data and new ideas about the economy.

The biggest change made was in how the purchase of computer software by firms is classified. Before 1999, it was regarded as an *intermediate good.* But since 1999, it has been treated as an *investment.*

How big a deal is this? When the BEA recalculated the 1996 GDP, the change increased the estimate of the 1996 GDP by $115 billion. That is a lot of money. To put it in perspective, GDP in 1996 was $7,662 billion. So the adjustment was 1.5 percent of GDP.

This change is a good example of the ongoing effort by the BEA to keep the GDP measure as accurate as possible.

## The Income Approach

To measure GDP using the income approach, the Bureau of Economic Analysis uses income data collected by the Internal Revenue Service and other agencies. The BEA takes the incomes that firms pay households for the services of the factors of production they hire—wages for labor services, interest for the use of capital, rent for the use of land, and profits for entrepreneurship—and sums those incomes. This approach is like attaching a meter to the circular flow diagram on all the flows running through factor markets from firms to households and measuring the magnitudes of those flows. Let's see how the income approach works.

The U.S. National Income and Product Accounts divide incomes into two big categories:

- Wage income
- Interest, rent, and profit income

### Wage Income

Wage income, called *compensation of employees* in the national accounts, is the total payment for labor services. It includes net wages and salaries plus fringe benefits paid by employers such as health-care insurance, Social Security contributions, and pension fund contributions.

### Interest, Rent, and Profit Income

Interest, rent, and profit income, called *net operating surplus* in the national accounts, is the total income earned by capital, land, and entrepreneurship.

Interest income is the interest that households receive on the loans they make minus the interest households pay on their own borrowing.

Rent includes payments for the use of land and other rented factors of production. It includes payments for rented housing and imputed rent for owner-occupied housing. (Imputed rent is an estimate of what homeowners would pay to rent the housing they own and use themselves. By including this item in the national accounts, we measure the total value of housing services, whether they are owned or rented.)

Profit includes the profits of corporations and the incomes of proprietors who run their own businesses. These incomes are a mixture of interest and profit.

Table 20.2 shows these two components of incomes and their relative magnitudes. The sum of wages, interest, rent, and profit is **net domestic product at factor cost**.

**Net domestic product at factor cost**
The sum of the wages, interest, rent, and profit.

Net domestic product at factor cost is not GDP, and we must make two further adjustments to get to GDP: one from factor cost to market prices and another from net product to gross product.

### From Factor Cost to Market Price

The expenditure approach values goods and services at market prices, and the income approach values them at factor cost—the cost of the factors of production used to produce them. Indirect taxes (such as sales taxes) and subsidies (payments by government to firms) make these two values differ. Sales taxes make market prices exceed factor cost, and subsidies make factor cost exceed market prices. To convert the value at factor cost to the value at market prices, we must add indirect taxes and subtract subsidies.

**TABLE 20.2**

GDP: The Income Approach

The sum of all incomes equals net domestic product at factor cost. GDP equals net domestic product at factor cost plus indirect taxes less subsidies plus depreciation (capital consumption).

In 2009, GDP measured by the income approach was $13,919 billion. This amount is $214 billion less than GDP measured by the expenditure approach—a statistical discrepancy of $214 billion.

Wages are by far the largest part of total income.

| Item | Amount in 2009 (second quarter) (billions of dollars) | Percentage of GDP |
|---|---|---|
| Wages (compensation of employees) | 7,733 | 54.7 |
| Interest, rent, and profit (net operating surplus) | 3,358 | 23.8 |
| Net domestic product at factor cost | 11,091 | 78.5 |
| Indirect taxes less subsidies | 963 | 6.6 |
| Depreciation (capital consumption) | 1,865 | 13.2 |
| GDP (income approach) | 13,919 | 98.5 |
| Statistical discrepancy | 214 | 1.5 |
| GDP (expenditure approach) | 14,133 | 100.0 |

SOURCE OF DATA: U.S. Department of Commerce, Bureau of Economic Analysis.

## From Net to Gross

**Depreciation**
The decrease in the value of capital that results from its use and from obsolescence.

The income approach measures *net* product and the expenditure approach measures *gross* product. The difference is **depreciation**, which is the decrease in the value of capital that results from its use and from obsolescence. Firms' profits, which are included in the income approach, are net of depreciation, so the income approach gives a *net* measure. Investment, which is included in the expenditure approach, includes the purchase of capital to replace worn out or obsolete capital, so the expenditure approach gives a *gross* measure. To get *gross* domestic product from the income approach, we must *add* depreciation to total income.

Table 20.2 summarizes these adjustments and shows that the income approach gives almost the same estimate of GDP as the expenditure approach.

## Statistical Discrepancy

The expenditure approach and income approach do not deliver exactly the same estimate of GDP. If a taxi driver doesn't report all his tips, they get missed in the income approach. But they get caught by the expenditure approach when he spends his income. So the sum of expenditures might exceed the sum of incomes. But most income gets reported to the Internal Revenue Service on tax returns while many items of expenditure are not recorded and must be estimated. So the sum of incomes might exceed the sum of estimated expenditures.

**Statistical discrepancy**
The discrepancy between the expenditure approach and the income approach estimates of GDP, calculated as the GDP expenditure total minus the GDP income total.

The discrepancy between the expenditure approach and the income approach is called the **statistical discrepancy**, and it is calculated as the GDP expenditure total minus the GDP income total.

The two measures of GDP provide a check on the accuracy of the numbers. If the two are wildly different, we will want to know what mistakes we've made. Have we omitted some item? Have we counted something twice? The fact that the two estimates are close gives some confidence that they are reasonably accurate. But the expenditure total is regarded as the more reliable estimate of GDP, so the discrepancy is added to or subtracted from income to reconcile the two estimates.

## GDP and Related Measures of Production and Income

Although GDP is the main measure of total production, you will sometimes encounter another: gross *national* product or GNP.

### Gross National Product

A country's **gross national product**, or **GNP**, is the market value of all the final goods and services produced anywhere in the world in a given time period by the factors of production supplied by the residents of that country. For example, Nike's income from the capital that it supplies to its Vietnam shoe factory is part of U.S. GNP but not part of U.S. GDP. It is part of Vietnam's GDP. Similarly, Toyota's income on the capital it supplies to its Kentucky auto plant is part of U.S. GDP but not part of U.S. GNP. It is part of Japan's GNP.

**Gross national product (GNP)**
The market value of all the final goods and services produced anywhere in the world in a given time period by the factors of production supplied by the residents of the country.

GNP equals GDP plus net factor income received from or paid to other countries. The difference between U.S. GDP and GNP is small. But in an oil-rich Middle Eastern country such as Bahrain, where a large amount of capital is owned by foreigners, GNP is much smaller than GDP; and in a poor country such as Bangladesh, whose people work abroad and send income home, GNP is much larger than GDP.

### Disposable Personal Income

You've seen that consumption expenditure is the largest component of aggregate expenditure. The main influence on consumption expenditure is **disposable personal income**, which is the income received by households minus personal income taxes paid. Because disposable personal income plays an important role in influencing spending, the national accounts measure this item along with a number of intermediate totals that you can see in Figure 20.2. This figure shows how disposable personal income is calculated and how it relates to GDP and GNP.

**Disposable personal income**
Income received by households minus personal income taxes paid.

**FIGURE 20.2**

GDP and Related Product and Income Measures

myeconlab Animation

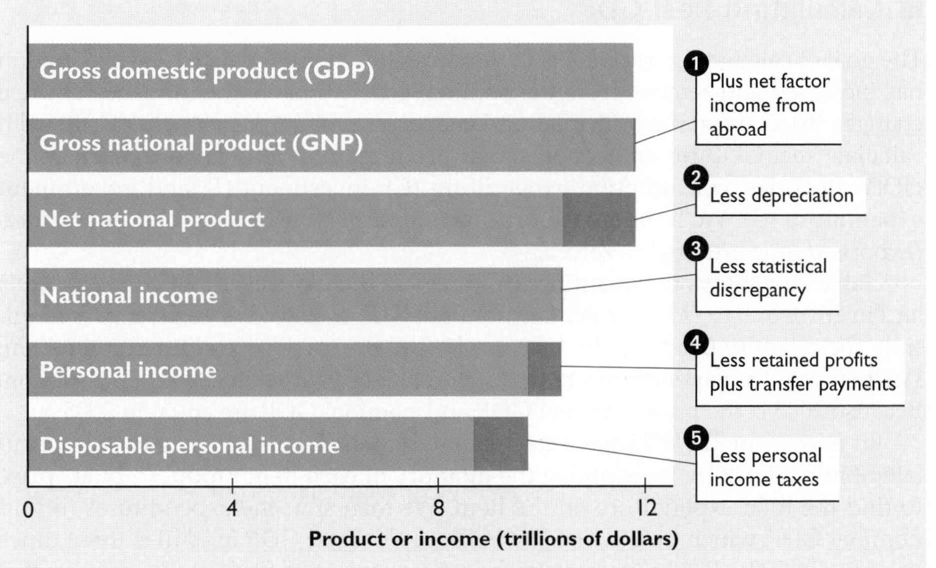


SOURCE OF DATA: U.S. Department of Commerce, Bureau of Economic Analysis.

The green bars show six related product and income measures and the relationship among them.

1. Add net factor income from abroad to GDP to get GNP.
2. Subtract depreciation from GNP to get net national product.
3. Subtract the statistical discrepancy between the expenditure and income measures (almost invisible in the figure because it is tiny) to get national income.
4. Subtract profits retained by firms and add transfer payments by governments to get personal income.
5. Finally, subtract personal income taxes to get disposable personal income.

## Real GDP and Nominal GDP

You've seen that GDP measures total expenditure on final goods and services in a given period. Suppose that we want to compare GDP in two periods, say 2005 and 2009. In 2005, GDP was $12,638 billion and by 2009, it was $14,133 billion—11.8 percent higher than in 2005. What does this 11.8 percent increase mean?

The answer is a combination of two things:

- We produced more goods and services.
- We paid higher prices for our goods and services.

Producing more goods and services contributes to an improvement in our standard of living. Paying higher prices means that our *cost of living* has increased but our standard of living has not. So it matters a great deal why GDP has increased. If the 11.8 percent increase is accounted for mainly by higher prices, our standard of living hasn't changed much. But if the 11.8 percent increase is accounted for mainly by the production of more goods and services, our standard of living might have increased a lot.

You're now going to see how economists at the Bureau of Economic Analysis isolate the effects on GDP of an increase in production. Their first step is to distinguish between two GDP concepts: real GDP and nominal GDP.

**Real GDP**
The value of the final goods and services produced in a given year expressed in terms of the prices in a *base year.*

**Nominal GDP**
The value of final goods and services produced in a given year expressed in terms of the prices of that same year.

**Real GDP** is the value of final goods and services produced in a given year expressed in terms of the prices in a *reference base year.* The *reference base year* is the year we choose against which to compare all other years. In the United States today, the *reference base year* is 2005.

Real GDP contrasts with **nominal GDP**, which is the value of the final goods and services produced in a given year expressed in terms of the prices of that same year. Nominal GDP is just a more precise name for GDP.

The method used to calculate real GDP has changed in recent years and is now a bit technical, but the essence of the calculation hasn't changed. Here, we describe the essence of the calculation. An appendix to this chapter describes the technical details of the method used by the Bureau of Economic Analysis.

## Calculating Real GDP

The goal of calculating *real GDP* is to measure the extent to which total production has increased and remove from the nominal GDP numbers the influence of price changes. To focus on the principles and keep the numbers easy to work with, we'll calculate real GDP for an economy that produces only one good in each of the GDP categories: consumption expenditure ($C$), investment ($I$), and government expenditure ($G$). We'll ignore exports and imports by assuming that net exports (exports minus imports) is zero.

Table 20.3 shows the quantities produced and the prices in 2005 (the *base year*) and in 2010. In part (a), we calculate nominal GDP in 2005. For each item, we multiply the quantity produced by its price to find the total expenditure on the item. We then sum the expenditures to find nominal GDP, which in 2005 is $100 million. Because 2005 is the base year, real GDP and nominal GDP are equal in 2005.

In part (b) of Table 20.3, we calculate nominal GDP in 2010. Again, we calculate nominal GDP by multiplying the quantity of each item produced by its price to find the total expenditure on the item. We then sum the expenditures to find nominal GDP, which in 2010 is $300 million. Nominal GDP in 2010 is three times its value in 2005. But by how much has the quantity of final goods and services produced increased? That's what real GDP will tell us.

**TABLE 20.3**

Calculating Nominal GDP and Real GDP in 2005 and 2010

| | Item | Quantity (millions of units) | Price (dollars per unit) | Expenditure (millions of dollars) |
|---|---|---|---|---|
| **(a) In 2005** | | | | |
| *C* | T-shirts | 10 | 5 | 50 |
| *I* | Computer chips | 3 | 10 | 30 |
| *G* | Security services | 1 | 20 | 20 |
| *Y* | Real GDP and Nominal GDP in 2005 | | | 100 |
| **(b) In 2010** | | | | |
| *C* | T-shirts | 4 | 5 | 20 |
| *I* | Computer chips | 2 | 20 | 40 |
| *G* | Security services | 6 | 40 | 240 |
| *Y* | Nominal GDP in 2010 | | | 300 |
| **(c) Quantities of 2010 valued at prices of 2005** | | | | |
| *C* | T-shirts | 4 | 5 | 20 |
| *I* | Computer chips | 2 | 10 | 20 |
| *G* | Security services | 6 | 20 | 120 |
| *Y* | Real GDP in 2010 | | | 160 |

The base year is 2005, so real GDP and nominal GDP are equal in that year.

Between 2005 and 2010, the production of security services (*G*) increased, but the production of T-shirts (*C*) and computer chips (*I*) decreased. In the same period, the price of a T-shirt remained constant, but the other two prices doubled.

Nominal GDP increased from $100 million in 2005 in part (a) to $300 million in 2010 in part (b).

Real GDP in part (c), which is calculated by using the quantities of 2010 in part (b) and the prices of 2005 in part (a), increased from $100 million in 2005 to $160 million in 2010, a 60 percent increase.

In part (c) of Table 20.3, we calculate real GDP in 2010. You can see that the quantity of each good and service produced in part (c) is the same as that in part (b). They are the quantities of 2010. You can also see that the prices in part (c) are the same as those in part (a). They are the prices of the base year—2005.

For each item, we now multiply the quantity produced in 2010 by its price in 2005 to find what the total expenditure would have been in 2010 if prices had remained the same as they were in 2005. We then sum these expenditures to find real GDP in 2010, which is $160 million.

Nominal GDP in 2010 is three times its value in 2005, but real GDP in 2010 is only 1.6 times its 2005 value—a 60 percent increase in *real* GDP.

## Using the Real GDP Numbers

In the example that we've just worked through, we found the value of real GDP in 2010 based on the prices of 2005. This number alone enables us to compare production in two years only. By repeating the calculation that we have done for 2010 using the data for each year between 2005 and 2010, we can calculate the *annual* percentage change of real GDP—the annual growth rate of real GDP. This is the most common use of the real GDP numbers. Also, by calculating real GDP every three months—known as *quarterly real GDP*—the Bureau of Economic Analysis is able to provide valuable information that is used to interpret the current state of the economy. This information is used to guide both government macroeconomic policy and business production and investment decisions.

Work these problems in Study Plan 20.2 to get instant feedback.

## CHECKPOINT 20.2

**Describe how economic statisticians measure GDP and distinguish between nominal GDP and real GDP.**

### Practice Problems

Table 1 shows some of the items in the U.S. National Income and Product Accounts in 2005. Use Table 1 to work Problems **1** to **3**.

**TABLE 1**

| Item | Amount (trillions of dollars) |
|---|---|
| Consumption expenditure | 8.7 |
| Government expenditure | 2.3 |
| Indirect taxes less subsidies | 0.8 |
| Depreciation | 1.5 |
| Net factor income from abroad | 0.1 |
| Investment | 2.0 |
| Net exports | –0.7 |
| Statistical discrepancy | 0 |

1. Use the expenditure approach to calculate U.S. GDP in 2005.
2. What was U.S. GDP as measured by the income approach in 2005? By how much did gross product and net product differ in 2005?
3. Calculate U.S. GNP and U.S. national income in 2005.
4. Table 2 shows some data for an economy. If the base year is 2006, calculate the economy's nominal GDP and real GDP in 2008.

**TABLE 2**

**(a) In 2006:**

| Item | Quantity | Price |
|---|---|---|
| Apples | 60 | $0.50 |
| Oranges | 80 | $0.25 |

**(b) In 2008:**

| Item | Quantity | Price |
|---|---|---|
| Apples | 160 | $1.00 |
| Oranges | 220 | $2.00 |

5. **As consumers reduce their spending, inventories are rising**
   The Commerce Department reported that sales of nondurable goods fell 0.6 percent, while sales of durable goods decreased 1.5 percent in August. Inventories of durable goods increased 1.4 percent.
   
   Source: Reuters, October 9, 2008
   
   Which component of GDP changed when (i) sales of nondurable goods fell, (ii) sales of durable goods decreased, and (iii) inventories of durable goods increased? Provide an example of each item of expenditure.

### Guided Solutions to Practice Problems

1. GDP was $12.3 trillion. The expenditure approach sums the expenditure on final goods and services. That is, GDP = $C + I + G + NX$.
   In 2005, U.S. GDP = ($8.7 + $2.0 + $2.3 − $0.7) trillion = $12.3 trillion.
2. GDP as measured by the income approach was $12.3 trillion.
   GDP (expenditure approach) = GDP (income approach) + Statistical discrepancy. The statistical discrepancy is zero, so GDP is $12.3 trillion.
   Gross product minus net product is depreciation, which was $1.5 trillion.
3. GNP = GDP + Net factor income from abroad.
   In 2005, GNP = $12.3 trillion + $0.1 trillion, which was $12.4 trillion.
   National income = GNP − Depreciation − Statistical discrepancy.
   The statistical discrepancy is zero, so in 2005,
   National income = $12.4 trillion − $1.5 trillion = $10.9 trillion.
4. Nominal GDP in 2008 equals (160 apples × $1) + (220 oranges × $2) = $600.
   Real GDP in 2008 at 2006 prices is equals (160 apples × $0.50 per apple) + (220 oranges × $0.25 per orange) = $135.
5. Sales of nondurable goods such as strawberries are bought by households and are part of consumption expenditure, *C*. Sales of durable goods such as iPhones that are bought by households are part of consumption expenditure, *C*, and sales of durable goods such as tower cranes bought by firms are part of investment, *I*. An inventory of durable goods, such as the auto parts at a Ford plant, is part of investment, *I*.

## 20.3 THE USES AND LIMITATIONS OF REAL GDP

We use estimates of real GDP for three main purposes:

- To compare the standard of living over time
- To track the course of the business cycle
- To compare the standard of living among countries

### The Standard of Living Over Time

A nation's **standard of living** is measured by the value of goods and services that its people enjoy, *on average*. Income per person determines what people can afford to buy and real GDP is a measure of real income. So **real GDP per person**—real GDP divided by the population—is a commonly used measure for comparing the standard of living over time.

**Standard of living**
The level of consumption of goods and services that people enjoy, *on average*.

**Real GDP per person**
Real GDP divided by the population.

Real GDP per person tells us the value of goods and services that the average person can enjoy. By using *real* GDP, we remove any influence that rising prices and a rising cost of living might have had on our comparison.

A handy way of comparing real GDP per person over time is to express it as a ratio of its value in some reference year. Table 20.4 provides the numbers for the United States that compare 2009 with 50 years earlier, 1959. In 1959, real GDP per person was $15,540 and in 2009 it was $42,106, or 2.7 times its 1959 level. To the extent that real GDP per person measures the standard of living, people were 2.7 times as well off in 2009 as their grandparents had been in 1959.

**TABLE 20.4 REAL GDP PER PERSON IN 1959 AND 2009**

| Year | 1959 | 2009 |
|---|---|---|
| Real GDP (billions) | $2,763 | $12,893 |
| Population (millions) | 177.8 | 306.2 |
| Real GDP per person | $15,540 | $42,106 |

Figure 20.3 shows the entire 50 years of real GDP per person from 1959 to 2009 and displays two features of our changing standard of living:

1. The growth of potential GDP per person
2. Fluctuations of real GDP per person around potential GDP

**Potential GDP** is the level of real GDP when all the economy's factors of production—labor, capital, land, and entrepreneurial ability—are fully employed. When some factors of production are *unemployed*, real GDP is *below* potential GDP. And when some factors of production are *over-employed* and working harder and for longer hours than can be maintained in the long run, real GDP *exceeds* potential GDP.

**Potential GDP**
The value of real GDP when all the economy's factors of production—labor, capital, land, and entrepreneurial ability—are fully employed.

You've seen that real GDP per person in 2009 was 2.7 times that of 1959. But in 2009, some labor and other factors of production were unemployed and the economy was producing less than potential GDP. To measure the trend in the standard of living, we must remove the influence of short-term fluctuations and focus on the path of potential GDP.

The growth rate of potential GDP fluctuates less than real GDP. During the 1960s, potential GDP per person grew at an average rate of 2.8 percent a year, but since 1970, its growth rate has slowed to 2 percent a year. This growth slowdown means that potential GDP is lower today (and lower by a large amount) than it would have been if the 1960s growth rate could have been maintained. If potential GDP had kept growing at the 1960s pace, potential GDP per person in 2009 would have been $20,000 more than it actually was. The cumulatively lost income from the growth slowdown of the 1970s is a staggering $284,500 per person. Understanding the reasons for the growth slowdown is one of the major tasks of macroeconomists.

**FIGURE 20.3**

Real GDP and Potential GDP Per Person in the United States: 1959–2009

myeconlab Animation

Real GDP grows and fluctuates around the growth path of potential GDP. Potential GDP per person grew at an annual rate of 2.8 percent during the 1960s and slowed to 2.0 percent after 1970.

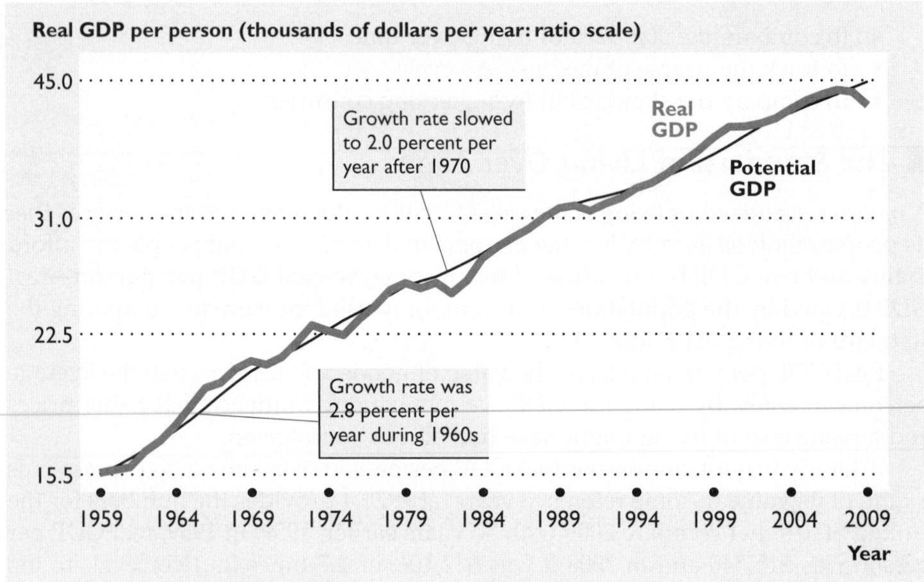


SOURCES OF DATA: Bureau of Economic Analysis and the Congressional Budget Office.

## Tracking the Course of the Business Cycle

**Business cycle**
A periodic but irregular up-and-down movement of total production and other measures of economic activity.

We call the fluctuations in the pace of economic activity the business cycle. A **business cycle** is a periodic but irregular up-and-down movement of total production and other measures of economic activity such as employment and income. The business cycle isn't a regular, predictable, and repeating cycle like the phases of the moon. The timing and the intensity of the business cycle vary a lot, but every cycle has two phases:

1. Expansion
2. Recession

and two turning points:

1. Peak
2. Trough

**Recession**
A period during which real GDP decreases for at least two successive quarters; or defined by the NBER as "a period of significant decline in total output, income, employment, and trade, usually lasting from six months to a year, and marked by contractions in many sectors of the economy."

Figure 20.4 shows these features of the most recent U.S. business cycle using real GDP as the measure of economic activity. An *expansion* is a period during which real GDP increases. In the early stage of an expansion, real GDP returns to potential GDP and as the expansion progresses, potential GDP grows and real GDP eventually exceeds potential GDP.

A common definition of **recession** is a period during which real GDP decreases—its growth rate is negative—for at least two successive quarters. The National Bureau of Economic Research (NBER), which dates the U.S. business cycle phases and turning points, defines a recession more broadly as "a period of significant decline in total output, income, employment, and trade, usually lasting from

**FIGURE 20.4**

The Most Recent U.S. Business Cycle

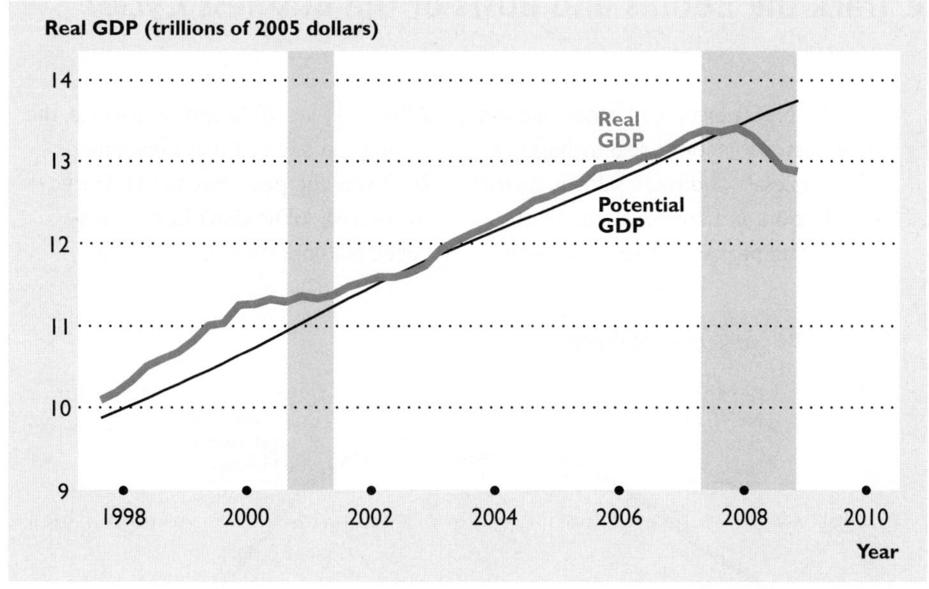


SOURCES OF DATA: Bureau of Economic Analysis the Congressional Budget Office, and the National Bureau of Economic Research.

The most recent business cycle peak was in December 2007 and the trough had not been reached by mid-2009. The most recent complete cycle had its peak in March 2001 and its trough in November 2001, but the recession was extremely shallow.

six months to a year, and marked by contractions in many sectors of the economy." This definition means that sometimes, the NBER declares a recession even though real GDP has not decreased for two successive quarters. The recession in 2001 was such a recession. An expansion ends and a recession begins at a business cycle peak. A peak is the highest level of real GDP that has been attained up to that time. A recession ends at a trough when real GDP reaches a temporary low point and from which the next expansion begins.

The shaded bars in Figure 20.4 highlight the 2001 and 2008–2009 recessions. The recession of 2001 was so mild that real GDP didn't fall. But the recession of 2008-2009 was so severe that it lowered real GDP per person back to its level at the end of 2005.

The period that began in 1991 following a severe recession and that ended with the global financial crisis of 2008 was so free from serious downturns in real GDP and other indicators of economic activity that it was called the *Great Moderation*, a name that contrasts it with the Great Depression. Some starry-eyed optimists even began to declare that the business cycle was dead. This long period of expansion also turned the attention of macroeconomists away from the business cycle and toward a focus on economic growth and the possibility of achieving faster growth.

But the 2008–2009 recession puts the business cycle back on the agenda. Economists were criticized for not predicting it, and old divisions among economists that many thought were healed erupted in the pages of *The Economist* and *The New York Times* and online on a host of blogs.

We'll be examining the causes of recession and the alternative views among economists in greater detail as you progress through the rest of your study of macroeconomics.

## EYE on the BUSINESS CYCLE

### How Do We Track the Booms and Busts of the Business Cycle?

The National Bureau of Economic Research (NBER) Business Cycle Dating Committee determines the dates of U.S. business cycle turning points.

To identify the date of a business cycle peak, the NBER committee looks at data on industrial production, total employment, real GDP, and wholesale and retail sales.

The NBER committee met in November 2008 to determine when the economy went into recession.

The committee reported that the two most reliable measures of aggregate domestic production are real GDP measured using the expenditure approach and the income approach.

Because of a statistical discrepancy, these two estimates of aggregate production differ and for a few quarters in 2007 and 2008 they told conflicting stories. As the committee noted: These estimates did "not speak clearly about the date of a peak in activity."

The NBER examined other data on real personal income, real manufacturing, wholesale and retail sales, industrial production, and employment. All of these data peaked between November 2007 and June 2008 and on balance, the committee decided that November 2007 was the peak. But as the figure shows, real GDP didn't begin a sustained fall until two quarters later.

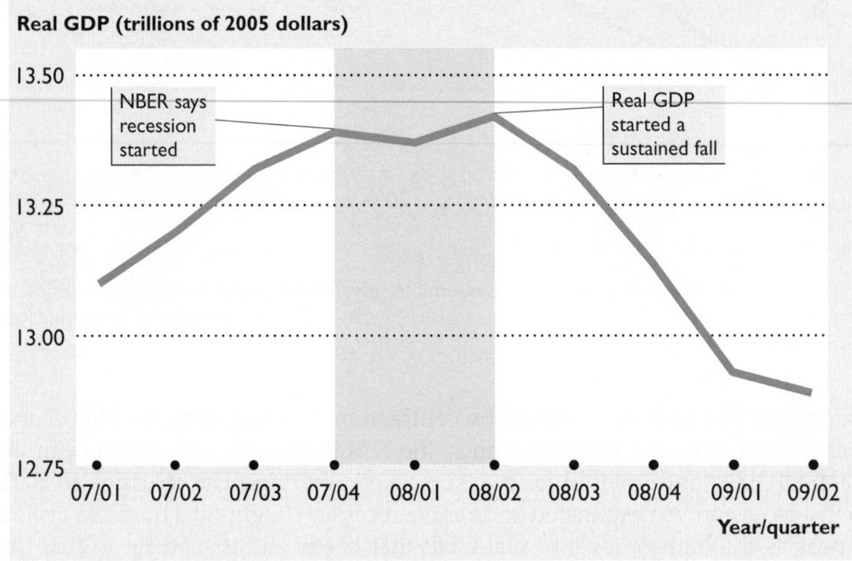


SOURCES OF DATA: Bureau of Economic Analysis and the National Bureau of Economic Research.

Let's now leave comparisons of the standard of living over time and business cycles and briefly see how we compare the standard of living among countries.

## The Standard of Living Among Countries

To use real GDP per person to compare the standard of living among countries, we must convert the numbers for other countries into U.S. dollars. To calculate real GDP, we must also use a common set of prices—called *purchasing power parity prices*—for all countries. The International Monetary Fund performs these calculations and if you turn back to Figure 2.4 on p. 46 you can see some comparisons based on these data. They tell, for example, that an average American has a standard of living almost 8 times that of an average person in China.

Real GDP provides an easy way of comparing living standards. But real GDP doesn't include *all* the goods and services produced. Also, real GDP has nothing to say about factors other than the goods and services that affect the standard of living. Let's explore these limitations of real GDP.

## Goods and Services Omitted from GDP

GDP measures the value of goods and services that are bought in markets. GDP excludes

- Household production
- Underground production
- Leisure time
- Environment quality

### Household Production

**Household production** is the production of goods and services (mainly services) in the home. Examples of this production are preparing meals, changing a light bulb, cutting grass, washing a car, and helping a student with homework. Because we don't buy these services in markets, they are not counted as part of GDP. The result is that GDP *underestimates* the value of the production.

**Household production**
The production of goods and services in the home.

Many items that were traditionally produced at home are now bought in the market. For example, more families now eat in fast-food restaurants—one of the fastest-growing industries in the United States—and use day-care services. These trends mean that food preparation and child-care services that were once part of household production are now measured as part of GDP. So real GDP grows more rapidly than does real GDP plus home production.

### Underground Production

**Underground production** is the production of goods and services hidden from the view of government because people want to avoid taxes and regulations or their actions are illegal. Because underground production is unreported, it is omitted from GDP.

**Underground production**
The production of goods and services hidden from the view of government.

Examples of underground production are the distribution of illegal drugs, farm work that uses illegal workers who are paid less than the minimum wage, and jobs that are done for cash to avoid paying income taxes. This last category might be quite large and includes tips earned by cab drivers, hairdressers, and hotel and restaurant workers.

Edgar L. Feige, an economist at the University of Wisconsin, estimates that U.S. underground production was about 16 percent of GDP during the early 1990s. Underground production in many countries is estimated to be larger than that in the United States and in most developing countries, much larger.

### Leisure Time

Leisure time is an economic good that is not valued as part of GDP. Yet the marginal hour of leisure time must be at least as valuable to us as the wage we earn for working. If it were not, we would work instead. Over the years, leisure time has steadily increased as the workweek gets shorter, more people take early retirement, and the number of vacation days increases. These improvements in our standard of living are not measured in real GDP.

### Environment Quality

Pollution is an economic *bad* (the opposite of a *good*). The more we pollute our environment, other things remaining the same, the lower is our standard of living. This lowering of our standard of living is not measured by real GDP.

## Other Influences on the Standard of Living

The quantity of goods and services consumed is a major influence on the standard of living. But other influences are

- Health and life expectancy
- Political freedom and social justice

### Health and Life Expectancy

Good health and a long life—the hopes of everyone—do not show up directly in real GDP. A higher real GDP enables us to spend more on medical research, health care, a good diet, and exercise equipment. As real GDP has increased, our life expectancy has lengthened. But we face new health and life expectancy problems every year. Diseases, such as AIDS, and drug abuse are taking young lives at a rate that causes serious concern. When we take these negative influences into account, real GDP growth might overstate the improvements in the standard of living.

### Political Freedom and Social Justice

A country might have a very large real GDP per person but have limited political freedom and social justice. For example, a small elite might enjoy political liberty and extreme wealth while the majority of people have limited freedom and live in poverty. Such an economy would generally be regarded as having a lower standard of living than one that had the same amount of real GDP but in which everyone enjoyed political freedom.

## EYE on YOUR LIFE

### Making GDP Personal

As you read a newspaper or business magazine, watch a TV news show, or browse a news Web site, you often come across reports about GDP.

What do these reports mean for you? Where in the National Income and Product Accounts do *your* transactions appear? How can you use information about GDP in your life?

#### Your Contribution to GDP

Your own economic transactions show up in the National Income and Product Accounts on both the expenditure side and the income side—as part of the expenditure approach and part of the income approach to measuring GDP.

Most of your expenditure is part of Consumption Expenditure. If you were to buy a new home, that item would appear as part of Investment. Because much of what you buy is produced in another country, expenditure on these goods shows up as part of Imports.

If you have a job, your income appears in Compensation of Employees.

Because the GDP measure of the value of production includes only market transactions, some of your own production of goods and services is most likely not counted in GDP.

What are the nonmarket goods and services that you produce? How would you go about valuing them?

#### Making Sense of the Numbers

To use the GDP numbers in a news report, you must first check whether the reporter is referring to *nominal* GDP or *real* GDP.

Using U.S. real GDP per person, check how your income compares with the average income in the United States. When you see GDP numbers for other countries, compare your income with that of a person in France, or Canada, or China.

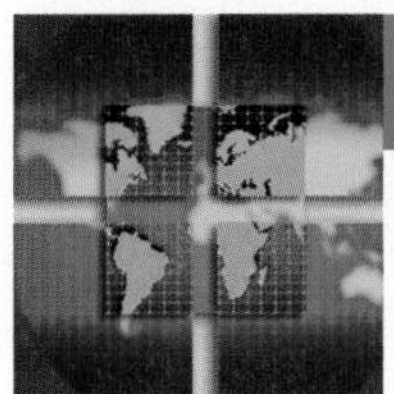

## EYE on the GLOBAL ECONOMY

### Which Country Has the Highest Standard of Living?

You've seen that as a measure of the standard of living, GDP has limitations. To compare the standard of living across countries, we must consider factors additional to GDP.

GDP measures only the market value of all the final goods and services produced and bought in markets. GDP omits some goods and services (those produced in the home and in the hidden economy). It omits the value of leisure time, of good health and long life expectancy, as well as of political freedom and social justice. It also omits the damage (negative value) that pollution does to the environment.

These limitations of GDP as a measure of the standard of living apply in every country. So to make international comparisons of the standard of living, we must look at real GDP and other indicators. Nonetheless, real GDP per person is a major component of international comparisons.

Many alternatives to GDP have been proposed. One, called Green GDP, subtracts from GDP an estimate of the cost of greenhouse gas emissions and other negative influences on the environment. Another measure, called the Happy Planet Index, or HPI, goes further and subtracts from GDP an estimate of the cost of depleting nonrenewable resources.

Neither the Green GDP nor the HPI are reliable measures because they rely on guesses about the costs of pollution and resource depletion that are subjective and unreliable.

Taking an approach that focuses on the quality of life factors, the United Nations (UN) has constructed a Human Development Index, or HDI, which combines real GDP, life expectancy and health, and education.

The figure shows the relationship between the HDI and GDP in 2007. (In the figure, each dot represents a country.) These two measures of the standard of living tell a similar but not identical story.

The United States has the highest GDP per person but only the 7th highest HDI. Why does the United States not have a higher HDI?

The UN says that the people who live in the 6 countries with higher HDIs live longer, have access to universal health care, and have better schools than do people in the United States. The HDI emphasized equality of access to these services.

The HDI doesn't include political freedoms and social justice. If it did, the United States would score highly on that component of the index.

The bottom line is that we don't know which country has the highest standard of living. We do know that GDP per person alone does not provide the complete answer.

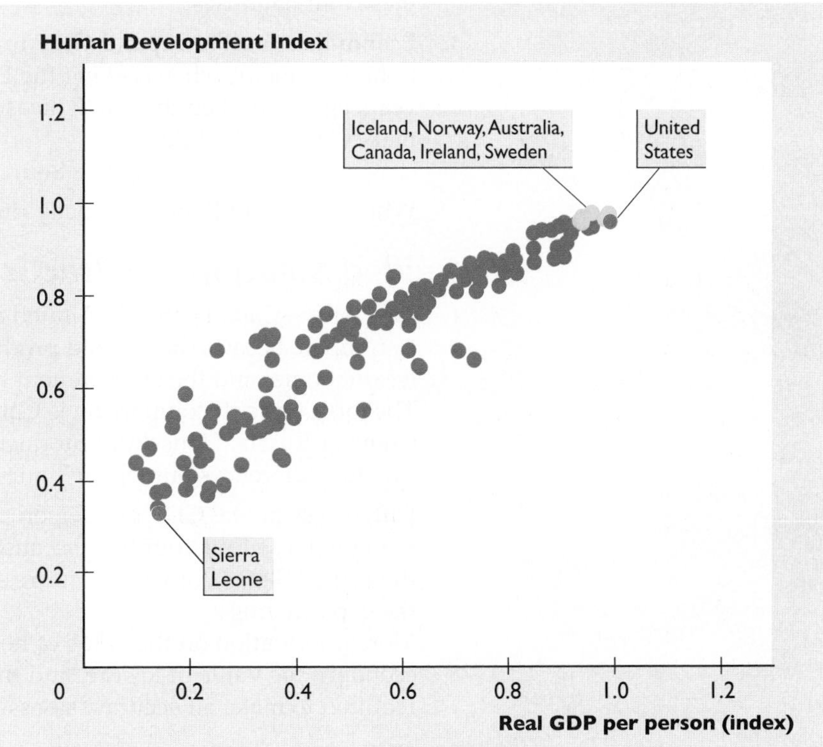


SOURCE OF DATA: *United Nations Human Development Report*, 2007, http://hdr.undp.org/.

Work these problems in Study Plan 20.3 to get instant feedback.

## CHECKPOINT 20.3

**Describe the uses of real GDP and explain its limitations as a measure of the standard of living.**

### Practice Problems

The United Nations Human Development Report gives the following data for real GDP per person in 2002: China, $4,580; Russia, $8,230; Canada, $29,480; United States, $35,750. Other information suggests that household production is similar in Canada and the United States and smaller in these two countries than in the other two. The underground economy is largest in Russia and China and a similar proportion of these economies. Canadians and Americans enjoy more leisure hours than do the Chinese and Russians. Canada and the United States spend significantly more to protect the environment, so air, water, and land pollution levels are lower in these countries than in China and Russia. Use this information and ignore any other influences to work Problems **1** and **2**.

1. In which pair (or pairs) of these four countries is it easiest to compare the standard of living? In which pair (or pairs) of these four countries is it most difficult to compare the standard of living? Why?
2. Do the differences in real GDP per person correctly rank the standard of living in these four countries? What additional information would we need to be able to make an accurate assessment of the relative standard of living in these four countries?
3. **Economists look to expand GDP to include the quality of life**
   Robert Kennedy, when seeking the Democratic presidential nomination 40 years ago, remarked that GDP measures everything except that which makes life worthwhile.

   Source: *The New York Times*, September 1, 2008

   Which items did Robert Kennedy probably think were missing?

### Guided Solutions to Practice Problems

1. Two pairs—Canada and the United States, and China and Russia—are easy to compare because household production, the underground economy, leisure hours, and the environment are similar in the countries in each pair. The most difficult comparison is Canada and the United States with either China or Russia. Household production and the underground economy narrow the differences but leisure hours and the environment widen them.
2. Differences in real GDP per person probably correctly rank the standard of living in these four countries because where the gap is small (Canada and the United States), other factors are similar, and where other factors differ, the gaps are huge.
   More information on the value of household production, the underground economy, the value of leisure, and the value of environmental differences is required to make an accurate assessment of relative living standards.
3. GDP measures production that is traded in markets. GDP does not include household production, leisure time, health and life expectancy, political freedom, and social justice. These items are probably the ones that Kennedy believed were missing from GDP as a measure of the quality of life.

# CHAPTER SUMMARY

## Key Points

1 **Define GDP and explain why the value of production, income, and expenditure are the same for an economy.**

- GDP is the market value of all final goods and services produced within a country in a given time period.
- We can value goods and services either by what they cost to produce (incomes) or by what people are willing to pay (expenditures).
- The value of production equals income equals expenditure.

2 **Describe how economic statisticians measure GDP and distinguish between nominal GDP and real GDP.**

- BEA measures GDP by summing expenditures and by summing incomes. With no errors of measurement the two totals are the same, but in practice, a small statistical discrepancy arises.
- A country's GNP is similar to its GDP, but GNP is the value of production by factors of production supplied by the residents of a country.
- Nominal GDP is the value of production using the prices of the current year and the quantities produced in the current year.
- Real GDP is the value of production using the prices of a base year and the quantities produced in the current year.

3 **Describe the uses of real GDP and explain its limitations as a measure of the standard of living.**

- We use real GDP per person to compare the standard of living over time.
- We use real GDP to determine when the economy has reached a business cycle peak or trough.
- We use real GDP per person expressed in purchasing power parity dollars to compare the standard of living among counties.
- Real GDP omits some goods and services and ignores some factors that influence the standard of living.
- The Human Development Index takes some other factors into account.

## Key Terms

Business cycle, 524
Consumption expenditure, 511
Depreciation, 518
Disposable personal income, 519
Exports of goods and services, 512
Final good or service, 510
Government expenditure on goods and services, 512
Gross domestic product (GDP), 510
Gross national product (GNP), 519
Household production, 527
Imports of goods and services, 512
Intermediate good or service, 510
Investment, 511
Net domestic product at factor cost, 517
Net exports of goods and services, 512
Net taxes, 512
Nominal GDP, 520
Potential GDP, 523
Real GDP, 520
Real GDP per person, 523
Recession, 524
Saving, 512
Standard of living, 523
Statistical discrepancy, 518
Underground production, 527

Work these problems in Chapter 20 Study Plan to get instant feedback.

# CHAPTER CHECKPOINT

## Study Plan Problems and Applications

1. Figure 1 shows the flows of income and expenditure in an economy. In 2009, *U* was $2 trillion, *V* was $1.5 trillion, *W* was $7 trillion, *X* was $1.5 trillion, and *Z* was zero. Calculate total income, net taxes, and GDP.

**FIGURE 1**

Use the following information to work Problems 2 and 3.

The national accounts of Parchment Paradise are kept on (you guessed it) parchment. A fire destroys the statistics office. The accounts are now incomplete but they contain the following data:

- GDP (income approach) $2,900
- Consumption expenditure $2,000
- Indirect taxes less subsidies $100
- Interest, rental, and profit $500
- Investment $800
- Government expenditure $400
- Wages $2,000
- Net factor income from abroad $50
- Net exports –$200

2. Calculate GDP (expenditure approach) and depreciation.
3. Calculate net domestic product at factor cost, the statistical discrepancy, and GNP.

Use the following information to work Problems 4 to 6.

An economy produces only fun and food. Table 1 shows the prices and the quantities of fun and food produced in 2009 and 2010. The base year is 2009.

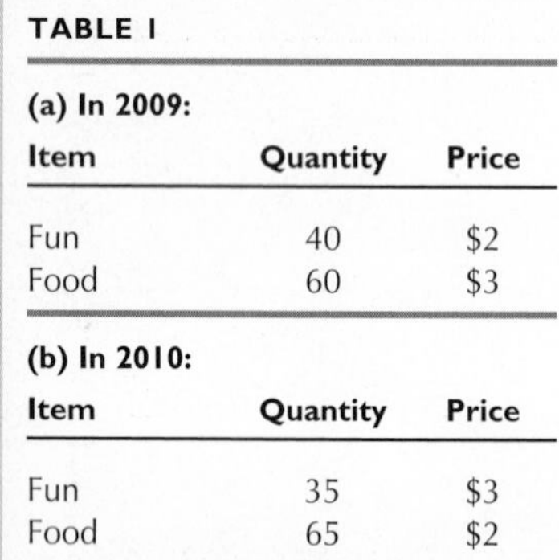

**TABLE 1**

(a) In 2009:

| Item | Quantity | Price |
|---|---|---|
| Fun | 40 | $2 |
| Food | 60 | $3 |

(b) In 2010:

| Item | Quantity | Price |
|---|---|---|
| Fun | 35 | $3 |
| Food | 65 | $2 |

4. Calculate nominal GDP in 2009 and 2010.
5. Calculate the percentage increase in production in 2010.
6. If potential GDP was $270 in 2009 and it grew by 1 percent in 2010, in which phase of the business cycle is the economy? Explain.

Use the following information to work Problems 6 to 8.

**Higher prices pushed up consumer spending for June**

The Commerce Department reported that retail sales increased 0.8 percent in June. But net exports were down 0.3 percent in the second quarter of 2009 and inventories held by business fell by 1.1 percent in June, while sales at all levels of production were up 0.9 percent.

Source: Commerce Department, August 13, 2009

7. Which component of GDP changed because retail sales increased? Which component of GDP changed because inventories held by businesses rose?
8. Explain the effect of the fall in net exports on GDP.
9. Does the statement that sales at all levels of production were up 0.9 percent mean that GDP increased by 0.9 percent? Explain your answer.

## Instructor Assignable Problems and Applications

Your instructor can assign these problems as homework, a quiz, or a test in **MyEconLab**.

1. In 2008, the population of China was 1.3 billion and real GDP (in purchasing power parity prices) was \$4.4 trillion. In the same year, the population of India was 1.2 billion and real GDP (in purchasing power parity prices) was \$1.2 trillion. In 2005, the most recent year for which we have the data, China's HDI was 0.777 and India's was 0.619.

   Based on this information, which country has the higher standard of living? What features of the information provided lead you to your conclusion?

2. Classify each of the following items as a final good or service or an intermediate good or service and identify which is a component of consumption expenditure, investment, or government expenditure on goods and services:
   - Banking services bought by Wal-Mart.
   - Security system bought by the White House.
   - Coffee beans bought by Starbucks.
   - New coffee grinders bought by Starbucks
   - Starbuck's grande mocha frappuccino bought by a student.
   - New battle ship bought by the U.S. navy.

Use the following data on the economy of Iberia to work Problems **3** and **4**.

- Net taxes \$18 billion
- Government expenditure on goods and services \$20 billion
- Household saving \$15 billion
- Consumption expenditure \$67 billion
- Investment \$21 billion
- Exports of goods and services \$30 billion

3. Calculate Iberia's GDP.
4. Calculate Iberia's imports of goods and services.

Use Table 1, which shows an economy's total production and the prices of the final goods it produced in 2009 and 2010, to work Problems **5** to **7**.

**TABLE 1**

**(a) In 2009:**

| Item | Quantity | Price |
|---|---|---|
| Fish | 100 | \$2 |
| Berries | 50 | \$6 |

**(b) In 2010:**

| Item | Quantity | Price |
|---|---|---|
| Fish | 75 | \$5 |
| Berries | 65 | \$10 |

5. Calculate nominal GDP in 2009 and 2010.
6. The base year is 2009. Calculate real GDP in 2009 and 2010 .
7. Calculate the percentage increase in production in 2010.

Use the following information to work Problems **8** and **9**.

**New-home sales jump as prices fall sharply**

Sales of new homes rose 11.0 percent in June, their largest monthly gain in nearly eight year, a sign that the housing market is bottoming as buyers take advantage of lower prices. Sales of previously owned homes also rose for another month.

Source: *The New York Times*, July 27, 2009

8. Where do new-home sales appear in the U.S. National Income and Product Accounts and the circular flow of expenditure and income ? How does a rise in new home sales affect real GDP? Explain your answer.
9. Where do sales of previously owned homes appear in the U.S. National Income and Product Accounts and the circular flow of expenditure and income? How does a rise in sales of previously owned homes affect real GDP? Explain your answer.

FIGURE 1

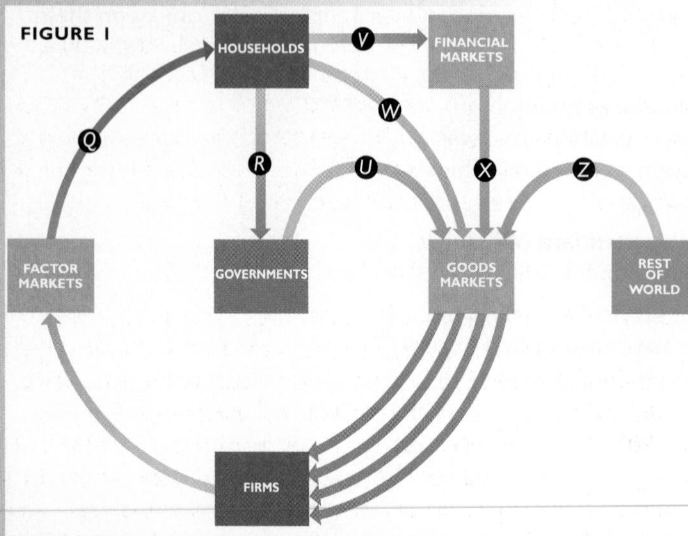


10. Figure 1 shows the flows of income and expenditure in an economy. In 2007, *Q* was $1,000 billion, *U* was $250 billion, *W* was $650 billion, *R* was $250 billion, and *Z* was $50 billion. Calculate investment and saving.
11. Figure 1 shows the flows of income and expenditure in an economy. In 2008, *X* was $2 trillion, *R* was $3 trillion, *Z* was –$1 trillion, *Q* was $10 trillion, and *U* was $4 trillion. Calculate saving and consumption expenditure.

Use the following information to work Problems 12 and 13.

Mitsubishi Heavy Industries makes the wings of the new Boeing 787 Dreamliner in Japan. Toyota assembles cars for the U.S. market in Kentucky.

12. Explain where these activities appear in the National Income and Product Accounts of the United States.
13. Explain where these activities appear in the National Income and Product Accounts of Japan.

TABLE 2

| Item | Amount (billions of dollars) |
|---|---|
| Consumption expenditure | 885 |
| Wages | 815 |
| Government expenditure | 350 |
| Interest, rent, and profit | 400 |
| Indirect taxes less subsidies | 165 |
| Depreciation | 200 |
| Investment | 300 |
| Net exports | 35 |

Use Table 2, which shows some of the items in Canada's National Income and Product Accounts in 2008, to work Problems 14 to 16.

14. Use the expenditure approach to calculate Canada's GDP in 2008.
15. Calculate Canada's net domestic product at factor cost in 2008.
16. What was Canada's GDP as measured by the income approach in 2008? Calculate the statistical discrepancy.
17. **A bit more bounce in the global economy**

    The global economy is in the early stages of an upturn that will deliver more GDP growth than is expected but less than is needed. The latest economic news points to sustained above-trend global growth.

    Source: J.P. Morgan Global Data Watch, September, 2009

    Does this news mean that the 2008–2009 recession had ended by September 2009? Does recession end only when real GDP returns to potential GDP?
18. The United Nation's HDI is based on GDP per person, life expectancy at birth, and indicators of the quality and quantity of education. Why does the United States not have the highest HDI? What items might be included in an expanded HDI to create a better standard of living index?
19. **Garage sales booming as recession grinds on**

    The Commerce Department report showed total retail sales across the country fell 0.1% in July, although garage sales springing up across the country are proving popular with buyers. Cathy, an unemployed nurse said that she uses the money she makes from her garage sales to pay bills.

    Source: Reuters, August 14, 2009

    Where do the items in the news clip appear in the U.S. National Income and Product Accounts and the circular flow of expenditure and income?

# APPENDIX: MEASURING REAL GDP

This appendix explains the principles used by the Bureau of Economic Analysis (BEA) to calculate real GDP using a measure called **chained-dollar real GDP**. We begin by explaining the problem that arises from using the prices of the base year (the method on pp. 520–521) and how the problem can be overcome.

**Chained-dollar real GDP**
The measure of real GDP calculated by the Bureau of Economic Analysis.

## The Problem With Base-Year Prices

When we calculated real GDP on pp. 520–521, we found that real GDP in 2010 was 60 percent greater than it was in 2005. But instead of using the prices of 2005 as the constant prices, we could have used the prices of 2010. In this case, we would have valued the quantities produced in 2005 at the prices of 2010. By comparing the values of real GDP in 2005 and 2010 at the constant prices of 2010, we get a different number for the percentage increase in production. If you use the numbers in Table 20.3 on p. 521 to value 2005 production at 2010 prices, you will get a real GDP in 2005 of $150 million (2010 dollars). Real GDP in 2010 at 2010 prices is $300 million. So by using the prices of 2010, production doubled—a 100 percent increase—from 2005 to 2010. Did production in fact increase by 60 percent or 100 percent?

The problem arises because to calculate real GDP, we weight the quantity of each item produced by its price. If all prices change by the same percentage, then the *relative* weight on each good or service doesn't change and the percentage change in real GDP from the first year to the second is the same regardless of which year's prices we use. But if prices change by different percentages, then the *relative* weight on each good or service *does* change and the percentage change in real GDP from the first year to the second depends on which prices we use. So which year's prices should we use: those of the first year or those of the second?

The answer given by the BEA method is to use the prices of both years. If we calculate the percentage change in real GDP twice, once using the prices of the first year and again using the prices of the second year, and then take the average of those two percentage changes, we get a unique measure of the change in real GDP and one that gives equal importance to the *relative* prices of both years.

To illustrate the calculation of the BEA measure of real GDP, we'll work through an example. The method has three steps:

- Value production in the prices of adjacent years.
- Find the average of two percentage changes.
- Link (chain) to the base year.

## Value Production in the Prices of Adjacent Years

The first step is to value production in *adjacent* years at the prices of both years. We'll make these calculations for 2010, and its preceding year, 2009.

Table A20.1 shows the quantities produced and prices in the two years. Part (a) shows the nominal GDP calculation for 2009—the quantities produced in 2009 valued at the prices of 2009. Nominal GDP in 2009 is $145 million. Part (b) shows the nominal GDP calculation for 2010—the quantities produced in 2010 valued at the prices of 2010. Nominal GDP in 2010 is $172 million. Part (c) shows the value of the quantities produced in 2010 at the prices of 2009. This total is $160 million. Finally, part (d) shows the value of the quantities produced in 2009 at the prices of 2010. This total is $158 million.

**TABLE A20.1**

Real GDP Calculation Step 1: Value Production in Adjacent Years at Prices of Both Years

Step I is to value the production of adjacent years at the prices of both years.

Here, we value the production of 2009 and 2010 at the prices of both 2009 and 2010.

The value of 2009 production at 2009 prices, in part (a), is nominal GDP in 2009.

The value of 2010 production at 2010 prices, in part (b), is nominal GDP in 2010.

Part (c) calculates the value of 2010 production at 2009 prices, and part (d) calculates the value of 2009 production at 2010 prices.

We use these numbers in Step 2.

| | Item | Quantity (millions of units) | Price (dollars per unit) | Expenditure (millions of dollars) |
|---|---|---|---|---|
| **(a) In 2009** | | | | |
| *C* | T-shirts | 3 | 5 | 15 |
| *I* | Computer chips | 3 | 10 | 30 |
| *G* | Security services | 5 | 20 | 100 |
| *Y* | Nominal GDP in 2009 | | | 145 |
| **(b) In 2010** | | | | |
| *C* | T-shirts | 4 | 4 | 16 |
| *I* | Computer chips | 2 | 12 | 24 |
| *G* | Security services | 6 | 22 | 132 |
| *Y* | Nominal GDP in 2010 | | | 172 |
| **(c) Quantities of 2010 valued at prices of 2009** | | | | |
| *C* | T-shirts | 4 | 5 | 20 |
| *I* | Computer chips | 2 | 10 | 20 |
| *G* | Security services | 6 | 20 | 120 |
| *Y* | 2010 production at 2009 prices | | | 160 |
| **(d) Quantities of 2009 valued at prices of 2010** | | | | |
| *C* | T-shirts | 3 | 4 | 12 |
| *I* | Computer chips | 3 | 12 | 36 |
| *G* | Security services | 5 | 22 | 110 |
| *Y* | 2009 production at 2010 prices | | | 158 |

## Find the Average of Two Percentage Changes

The second step is to find the percentage change in the value of production based on the prices in the two adjacent years. Table A20.2 summarizes these calculations.

Valued at the prices of 2009, production increased from $145 million in 2009 to $160 million in 2010, an increase of 10.3 percent. Valued at the prices of 2010, production increased from $158 million in 2009 to $172 million in 2010, an increase of 8.9 percent. The average of these two percentage changes in the value of production is 9.6. That is, $(10.3 + 8.9) \div 2 = 9.6$.

By applying this percentage change to real GDP, we can find the value of real GDP in 2010. Because real GDP in 2009 is in 2009 dollars, real GDP in 2010 is also in 2009 dollars. GDP in 2009 is $145 million, so a 9.6 percent increase is $14 million. Real GDP in 2010, expressed in 2009 dollars, is $145 million plus $14 million, which equals $159 million.

Although the real GDP of $159 million is expressed in 2009 dollars, the calculation uses the average of the *relative prices* of the final goods and services that make up GDP in 2009 and 2010.

**Table A20.2**

Real GDP Calculation Step 2: Find Average of Two Percentage Changes

| Value of Production in Adjacent Years | | Millions of dollars |
|---|---|---|
| 2009 production at 2009 prices | | 145 |
| 2010 production at 2009 prices | | 160 |
| **Percentage change in production at 2009 prices** | 10.3 | |
| 2009 production at 2010 prices | | 158 |
| 2010 production at 2010 prices | | 172 |
| **Percentage change in production at 2010 prices** | 8.9 | |
| **Average of two percentage changes in production** | 9.6 | |

Using the numbers calculated in Step 1, we find the percentage change in production from 2009 to 2010 valued at 2009 prices, which is 10.3 percent.

We also find the percentage change in production from 2009 to 2010 valued at 2010 prices, which is 8.9 percent.

We then find the average of these two percentage changes, which is 9.6 percent.

## Link (Chain) to the Base Year

The final step repeats the calculation that we've just described to obtain the real GDP growth rate each year. In the base year, which currently is 2005, real GDP equals nominal GDP. By applying the calculated growth rates to each successive year, we obtain *chained-dollar real GDP* in 2005 dollars.

Figure A20.1 shows an example. In the base year, 2005, real GDP equals nominal GDP, which is $66 million. The table shows the growth rates for each year between 2000 and 2010, the final one of which is the 9.6 percent that we calculated in Table A20.2 above.

Starting with real GDP in the base year, we apply the calculated percentage changes to find real GDP in other years. For example, in 2006, the growth rate was 8.2 percent, so real GDP in 2006 is 8.2 percent higher than $66 million and is $72 million. In 2005, the growth rate was 7.1 percent, so $66 million is 7.1 percent higher than real GDP in 2004, which is $62 million. Repeating the calculations, by 2009, real GDP was $83 million. In 2010, real GDP grew by 9.6 percent of $83 million, which is $8 million, so real GDP in 2010 was $91 million.

**FIGURE A20.1**

Real GDP Calculation Step 3: Link (Chain) to the Base Year

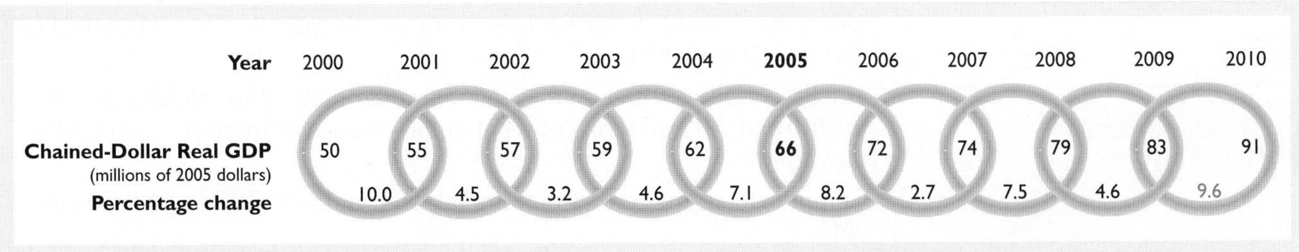

The percentage change in real GDP from one year to the next is calculated for every pair of years and then linked to the base year. Suppose that real GDP was $66 million in the base year, 2005. By applying the percentage change between each pair of years, we find chained-dollar real GDP for each year, expressed in terms of the value of the dollar in the base year. Here, the percentages for 2001 through to 2009 are assumed. By 2010, the chained-dollar real GDP has increased to $91 million in 2005 dollars.

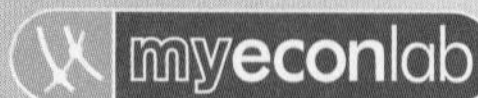

## APPENDIX CHECKPOINT

Work these problems in Chapter 20 Study Plan to get instant feedback.

**TABLE 1**

**(a) In 2010:**

| Item | Quantity | Price |
|---|---|---|
| Bananas | 100 | $10 |
| Coconuts | 50 | $12 |

**(b) In 2011:**

| Item | Quantity | Price |
|---|---|---|
| Bananas | 110 | $15 |
| Coconuts | 60 | $10 |

### Study Plan Problems

An island economy produces only bananas and coconuts. Table 1 gives the quantities produced and prices in 2010 and in 2011.

1. Calculate nominal GDP in 2010 and nominal GDP in 2011.
2. Calculate the value of 2011 production in 2010 prices and the percentage increase in production when valued at 2010 prices.
3. Calculate the value of 2010 production in 2011 prices and the percentage increase in production when valued at 2011 prices.
4. The base year is 2010. Use the chained-dollar method to calculate real GDP in 2010 and 2011. In terms of what dollars is each of these two real GDPs measured?
5. Using the chained-dollar method, compare the growth rates of nominal GDP and real GDP in 2011.
6. The base year is 2011. Use the chained-dollar method to calculate real GDP in 2010 and 2011. In terms of what dollars is each of these two real GDPs measured?
7. Compare the growth rates of nominal GDP and real GDP in 2011 dollars in 2011.

Your instructor can assign these problems as homework, a quiz, or a test in **MyEconLab**.

**TABLE 2**

**(a) In 2010:**

| Item | Quantity | Price |
|---|---|---|
| Food | 100 | $2 |
| Fun | 50 | $6 |

**(b) In 2011:**

| Item | Quantity | Price |
|---|---|---|
| Food | 75 | $5 |
| Fun | 65 | $10 |

### Instructor Assignable Problems

An economy produces only food and fun. Table 2 shows the quantities produced and prices in 2010 and 2011.

1. Calculate nominal GDP in 2010 and nominal GDP in 2011.
2. Calculate the value of 2011 production in 2010 prices and the percentage increase in production when valued at 2010 prices.
3. Calculate the value of 2010 production in 2011 prices and the percentage increase in production when valued at 2011 prices.
4. Using the chained-dollar method, calculate real GDP in 2010 and 2011 if the base year is 2011. In terms of what dollars is each of these two real GDPs measured?
5. Using the chained-dollar method, compare the growth rates of nominal GDP and real GDP in 2011.
6. The base year is 2010. Use the chained-dollar method to calculate real GDP in 2010 and 2011. In terms of what dollars is each of these two real GDPs measured?
7. Compare the growth rates of nominal GDP and real GDP in 2010 dollars in 2011.

## How long does it take to find a new job?

Does it take longer in a recession than at full employment? And who is most likely to be looking for a job?

# Jobs and Unemployment

**When you have completed your study of this chapter, you will be able to**

1 Define the unemployment rate and other labor market indicators.

2 Describe the trends and fluctuations in the indicators of labor market performance in the United States.

3 Describe the sources of unemployment, define full employment, and explain the link between unemployment and real GDP.

## 21.1 LABOR MARKET INDICATORS

Every month, 1,600 field interviewers and supervisors working on a joint project between the Bureau of Labor Statistics (or BLS) and the Bureau of the Census survey 60,000 households and ask a series of questions about the age and labor market status of its members. This survey is called the *Current Population Survey*. Let's look at the types of data collected by this survey.

### Current Population Survey

Figure 21.1 shows the categories into which the BLS divides the population. It also shows the relationships among the categories. The first category divides the population into two groups: the working-age population and others. The **working-age population** is the total number of people aged 16 years and over who are not in jail, hospital, or some other form of institutional care or in the U.S. Armed Forces. In June 2009, the estimated population of the United States was 306.8 million. In June 2009, the working-age population was 235.7 million; and 71.1 million people were under 16 years of age, in the military, or living in institutions.

**Working-age population**
The total number of people aged 16 years and over who are not in jail, hospital, or some other form of institutional care or in the U.S. Armed Forces.

The second category divides the working-age population into two groups: those in the labor force and those not in the labor force. The **labor force** is the number of people employed plus the number unemployed. In June 2009, the U.S. labor force was 154.9 million and 80.8 million people were not in the labor force. Most of those not in the labor force were in school full time or had retired from work.

**Labor force**
The number of people employed plus the number unemployed.

The third category divides the labor force into two groups: the employed and the unemployed. In June 2009 in the United States, 140.2 million people were employed and 14.7 million people were unemployed.

### Population Survey Criteria

The survey counts as *employed* all persons who, during the week before the survey, either

1. Worked at least 1 hour as paid employees or worked 15 hours or more as unpaid workers in their family business or
2. Were not working but had jobs or businesses from which they were temporarily absent.

The survey counts as *unemployed* all persons who, during the week before the survey,

1. Had no employment,
2. Were available for work,

and either

1. Had made specific efforts to find employment during the previous four weeks or
2. Were waiting to be recalled to a job from which they had been laid off.

People in the working-age population who by the above criteria are neither employed nor unemployed are classified as not in the labor force.

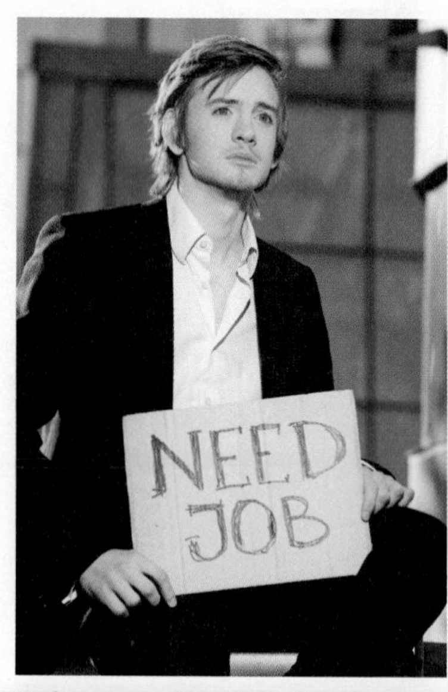

*To be counted as unemployed, a person must not only want a job but also have tried to find one.*

**FIGURE 21.1**

Population Labor Force Categories

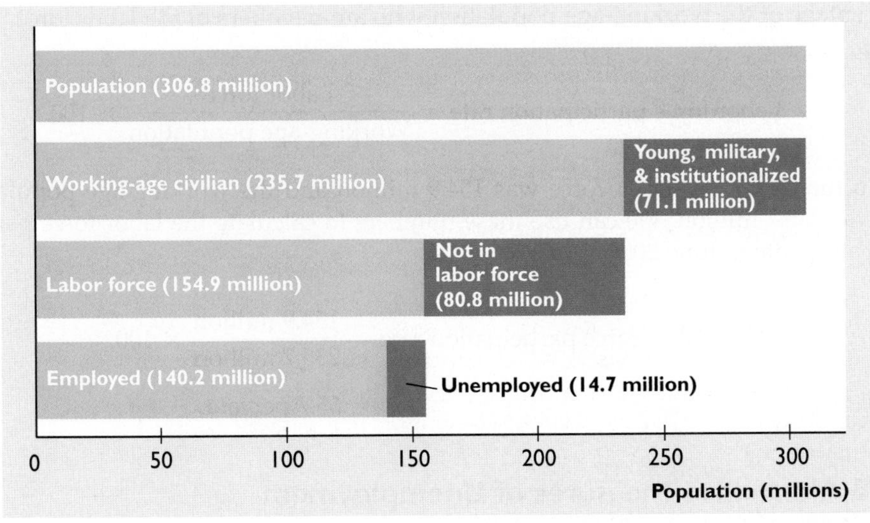


SOURCE OF DATA: Bureau of Labor Statistics.

The U.S. population is divided into the working-age population and the young, military, and institutionalized. The working-age population is divided into the labor force and those not in the labor force. The labor force is divided into the employed and the unemployed. The figure shows the data for June 2009.

## Two Main Labor Market Indicators

Using the numbers from the Current Population Survey, the BLS calculates several indicators of the state of the labor market. The two main labor market indicators are

- The unemployment rate
- The labor force participation rate

### The Unemployment Rate

The amount of unemployment is an indicator of the extent to which people who want jobs can't find them. It tells us the amount of slack in the labor market. The **unemployment rate** is the percentage of the people in the labor force who are unemployed. That is,

**Unemployment rate**
The percentage of the people in the labor force who are unemployed.

$$\text{Unemployment rate} = \frac{\text{Number of people unemployed}}{\text{Labor force}} \times 100.$$

In June 2009, the number of people unemployed was 14.7 million and the labor force was 154.9 million. We can use these numbers to calculate the unemployment rate in June 2009, which is

$$\text{Unemployment rate} = \frac{14.7 \text{ million}}{154.9 \text{ million}} \times 100$$
$$= 9.5 \text{ percent.}$$

### The Labor Force Participation Rate

**Labor force participation rate** The percentage of the working-age population who are members of the labor force.

The number of people in the labor force is an indicator of the willingness of people of working age to take jobs. The **labor force participation rate** is the percentage of the working-age population who are members of the labor force. That is,

$$\text{Labor force participation rate} = \frac{\text{Labor force}}{\text{Working-age population}} \times 100.$$

In June 2009, the labor force was 154.9 million and the working-age population was 235.7 million. We can use these numbers to calculate the labor force participation rate in June 2009, which is

$$\text{Labor force participation rate} = \frac{154.9 \text{ million}}{235.7 \text{ million}} \times 100$$
$$= 65.7 \text{ percent.}$$

## Alternative Measures of Unemployment

The unemployment rate based on the official definition of unemployment omits some types of underutilization of labor. The omissions are

- Marginally attached workers
- Part-time workers

### Marginally Attached Workers

**Marginally attached worker** A person who does not have a job, is available and willing to work, has not made specific efforts to find a job within the previous four weeks, but has looked for work sometime in the recent past.

**Discouraged worker** A marginally attached worker who has not made specific efforts to find a job within the past four weeks because previous unsuccessful attempts to find a job were discouraging.

Some people who think of themselves as being in the labor force and unemployed are not counted in the official labor force numbers. They are marginally attached workers. A **marginally attached worker** is a person who does not have a job, is available and willing to work, has not made specific efforts to find a job within the previous four weeks, but has looked for work sometime in the recent past. A **discouraged worker** is a marginally attached worker who has not made specific efforts to find a job within the previous four weeks because previous unsuccessful attempts were discouraging. Other marginally attached workers differ from discouraged workers only in their reasons for not having looked for a job during the previous four weeks. For example, Martin doesn't have a job and is available for work, but he hasn't looked for work in the past four weeks because he was busy cleaning up his home after a flood. He is a marginally attached worker but not a discouraged worker. Lena, Martin's wife, doesn't have a job and is available for work, but she hasn't looked for work in the past four weeks because she's been looking for six months and not managed to get a single job offer. She is a discouraged worker.

Neither the unemployment rate nor the labor force participation rate includes marginally attached workers. In June 2009, 860,000 people were discouraged workers. If we add them to both the number unemployed and the labor force, the unemployment rate becomes 10 percent—only slightly higher than the standard definition of the unemployment rate. Also in June 2009, 1,256,000 people were other marginally attached workers. If we add them and the discouraged workers to both the number unemployed and the labor force, the unemployment rate becomes 10.8 percent—1.3 percentage points to the standard definition.

## EYE on the U.S. ECONOMY

### The Current Population Survey

The Bureau of Labor Statistics and the Bureau of the Census go to great lengths to collect accurate labor force data. They constantly train and retrain around 1,600 field interviewers and supervisors. Each month, each field interviewer contacts 37 households and asks basic demographic questions about everyone living at the address and detailed labor force questions about those aged 16 or over.

Once a household has been selected for the survey, it is questioned for four consecutive months and then again for the same four months a year later. Each month, the addresses that have been in the panel eight times are removed and 6,250 new addresses are added. The rotation and overlap of households provide very reliable information about month-to-month and year-to-year changes in the labor market.

The first time that a household is in the panel, an interviewer, armed with a laptop computer, visits it. If the household has a telephone, most of the subsequent interviews are conducted by phone, many of them from one of the three telephone interviewing centers in Hagerstown, Maryland; Jeffersonville, Indiana; and Tucson, Arizona.

For more information about the Current Population Survey, visit http://www.bls.gov/cps/cps_faq.htm.

### Part-Time Workers

The Current Population Survey measures the number of full-time workers and part-time workers. **Full-time workers** are those who usually work 35 hours or more a week. **Part-time workers** are those who usually work less than 35 hours a week. Part-time workers are divided into two groups: part time for economic reasons and part time for noneconomic reasons.

**Full-time workers**
People who usually work 35 hours or more a week.

**Part-time workers**
People who usually work less than 35 hours a week.

**Part time for economic reasons**
People who work 1 to 34 hours per week but are looking for full-time work and cannot find it because of unfavorable business conditions.

People who work **part time for economic reasons** (also called *involuntary part-time workers)* are people who work 1 to 34 hours but are looking for full-time work. These people are unable to find full-time work because of unfavorable business conditions or seasonal decreases in the availability of full-time work.

People who work part time for noneconomic reasons do not want full-time work and are not available for such work. This group includes people with health problems, family or personal responsibilities, or education commitments that limit their availability for work.

The Bureau of Labor Statistics uses the data on full-time and part-time status to measure the slack in the labor market that results from people being underemployed—employed but not able to find as much employment as they would like.

In June 2009, when employment was 140.2 million, full-time employment was 112.9 million and part-time employment was 27.3 million. An estimated 10.7 million people worked part time for economic reasons. When this number along with marginally attached workers is added to both the number unemployed and the labor force, the unemployment rate becomes 16.5 percent.

Work these problems in Study Plan 21.1 to get instant feedback.

## CHECKPOINT 21.1

**Define the unemployment rate and other labor market indicators.**

## Practice Problems

The BLS reported that in July 2009, the labor force was 154.5 million, employment was 140.0 million, and the working-age population was 235.9 million. Use this information to work Problems **1** and **2**.

1. Calculate the unemployment rate and the labor force participation rate.
2. The BLS also reported that 24 percent of all employment in July 2009 was part time and that 9.1 million people worked part time for economic reasons. How many people worked part time for noneconomic reasons?
3. The Bureau of Labor Statistics reported that in July 2009, the labor force in Michigan was 4,864 thousand and employment was 4,134 thousand. Calculate the unemployment rate in Michigan in July 2009.
4. **Hawaiian Airlines hires 100 workers, plans to add 170 more**
   Hawaiian Airlines will hire more workers as it expands its fleet. The new hirings are a welcome sign for Hawaii's economy, which lost jobs during the year to May 2009 as the state's unemployment rate rose from 4% to 7%.
   Source: *USA Today*, August 18, 2009

   The labor force was 602,000 in May 2009 and 622,600 in May 2008. Calculate the change in the number unemployed between May 2008 and May 2009.

## Guided Solutions to Practice Problems

1. The unemployment rate is 9.4 percent. The labor force is the sum of the number employed plus the number unemployed. So the number unemployed equals the labor force minus the number employed, which equals 154.5 million minus 140.0 million, or 14.5 million. The unemployment rate is the number unemployed as a percentage of the labor force. The unemployment rate = (14.5 million ÷ 154.5 million) × 100, or 9.4 percent. The labor force participation rate is 65.5 percent. The labor force participation rate is the percentage of the working-age population who are in the labor force. Labor force participation rate = (154.5 ÷ 235.9) × 100, or 65.5 percent.
2. 24.5 million people worked part time for noneconomic reasons. Employment was 140 million. Part-time employment was 24 percent of 140 million, which equals 33.6 million. Given that 9.1 million worked part time for economic reasons, 33.6 million minus 9.1 million, or 24.5 million worked part time for noneconomic reasons.
3. The unemployment rate is 15 percent. The number unemployed equals the labor force minus the number employed. Unemployment equals 4,864 thousand minus 4,134 thousand, which equals 730 thousand. The unemployment rate = (730 thousand ÷ 4,864 thousand) × 100, or 15 percent.
4. The change in the number unemployed was 17,260.
   Unemployment rate = (Unemployment ÷ Labor force) × 100. Rearranging this equation gives: Unemployment = (unemployment rate × labor force) ÷ 100. In May 2008, unemployment was (4 × 622,600) ÷ 100, or 24,880. In May 2009, unemployment was (7 × 602,000) ÷ 100, or 42,140. The number unemployed increased by 42,140 minus 24,880, which equals 17,260.

## 21.2 LABOR MARKET TRENDS AND FLUCTUATIONS

What do we learn about the U.S. labor market from changes in the unemployment rate, the labor force participation rate, and the alternative measures of unemployment? Let's explore the trends and fluctuations in these indicators.

### Unemployment Rate

Figure 21.2 shows the U.S. unemployment rate over the 80 years from 1929 to 2009. Over these years, the average U.S. unemployment rate was 5.7 percent. The rate was below this long-term average during the 1940s through the 1960s and during the 2000s. It was above the long-term average during the 1970s to the mid 1990s.

During the 1960s, the unemployment rate gradually fell to 3.5 percent. These years saw a rapid rate of job creation, partly from the demands placed on the economy by the growth of defense production during the Vietnam War and partly from an expansion of consumer spending encouraged by an expansion of social programs. Another burst of rapid job creation driven by the "new economy"—the high-technology sector driven by the expansion of the Internet—lowered the unemployment rate from 1995 through most of the 2000s to below average.

The most striking event visible in Figure 21.2 is the **Great Depression,** a period of high unemployment, low incomes, and extreme economic hardship that lasted from 1929 to 1939. By 1933, the worst of the Great Depression years, real GDP had fallen by a huge 30 percent and as the figure shows, one in four of the people who wanted jobs couldn't find them. The horrors of the Great Depression led to the New Deal and shaped political attitudes that persist today.

**Great Depression**
A period of high unemployment, low incomes, and extreme economic hardship that lasted from 1929 to 1939.

**FIGURE 21.2**
The U.S. Unemployment Rate: 1929–2009

myeconlab Animation

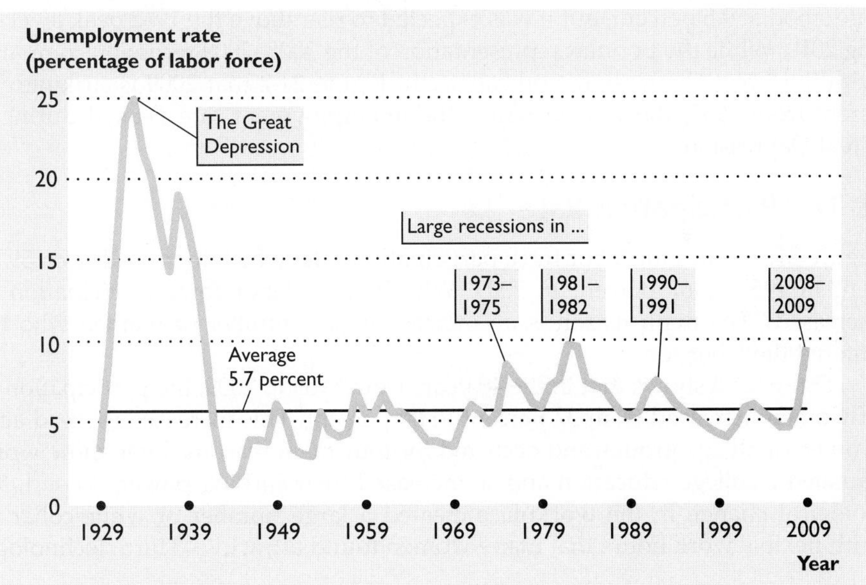


SOURCE OF DATA: Bureau of Labor Statistics.

The average unemployment rate from 1929 to 2009 was 5.7 percent. The unemployment rate increases in recessions and decreases in expansions. Unemployment was at its lowest during the expansions of the 1960s and the 1990s and at its highest during the Great Depression and the recessions of 1981–1982 and 2008–2009.

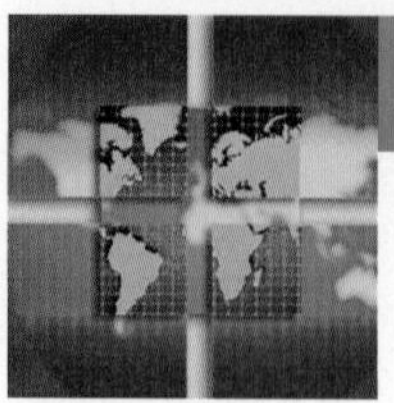

## EYE on the GLOBAL ECONOMY

### Unemployment Around the World

Before the 2008–2009 recession, the U.S. unemployment rate fell in the middle of the range experienced by other countries. The highest unemployment rates have been in Europe, Canada, and the United Kingdom and the lowest unemployment rates have been in Japan and the newly industrializing countries of Asia.

Differences in unemployment rates were much greater during the 1980s and 1990s than in the 2000s.

All of the countries with higher average unemployment rates than the United States also have higher unemployment benefits and more regulated labor markets.

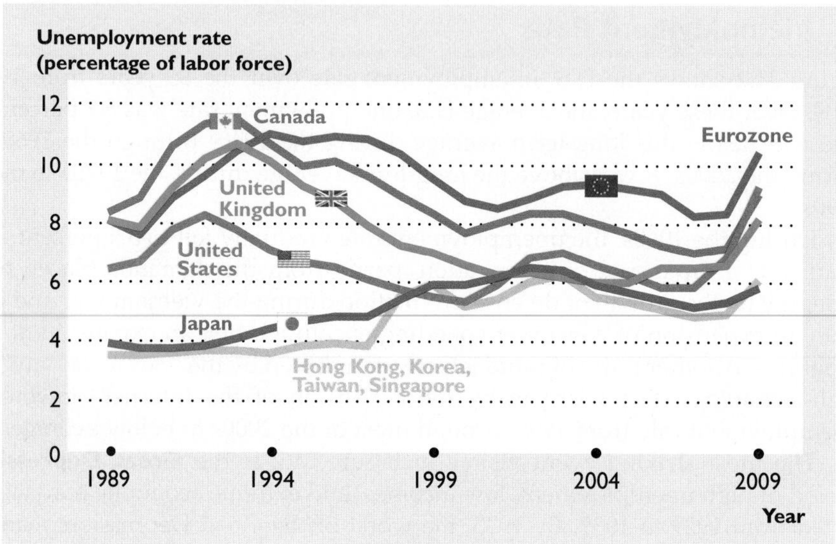


SOURCE OF DATA: International Monetary Fund, *World Economic Outlook*, April 2009.

During the recessions of 1973–1975, 1981–1982, 1990–1991, and 2008–2009, the unemployment rate increased. During the post-War years, the unemployment rate peaked in November–December 1982 when 10.8 percent of the labor force were unemployed. By mid-2009, with the economy still in recession, the unemployment rate stood at 9.5 percent, but it was expected to rise above the 1982 peak level during 2010. While the popular representation of the 2008–2009 recession compares it with the Great Depression, you can see in Figure 21.2 that 2009 is strikingly different from 1933, the year in which the unemployment rate peaked during the Great Depression.

## The Participation Rate

Figure 21.3 shows the labor force participation rate, which increased from 59 percent in 1959 to 67 percent in 2009. Why has the labor force participation rate increased? The main reason is an increase in the number of women who have entered the labor force.

Figure 21.3 shows that in the 40 years from 1959 to 2009, the participation rate of women increased from 37 percent to 60 percent. This increase is spread across women of all age groups and occurred for four main reasons. First, more women pursued a college education and so increased their earning power. Second, technological change in the workplace created a large number of white-collar jobs with flexible work hours that many women found attractive. Third, technological

**FIGURE 21.3**

The Changing Face of the Labor Market: 1959–2009

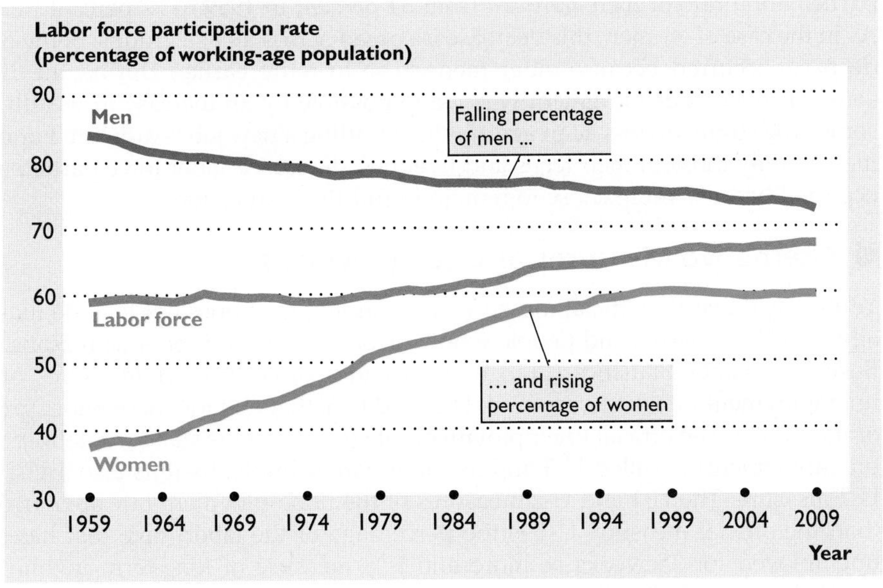


SOURCE OF DATA: Bureau of Labor Statistics.

During the past 50 years, the labor force participation rate has increased. The labor force participation rate of men has decreased, and that of women has increased.

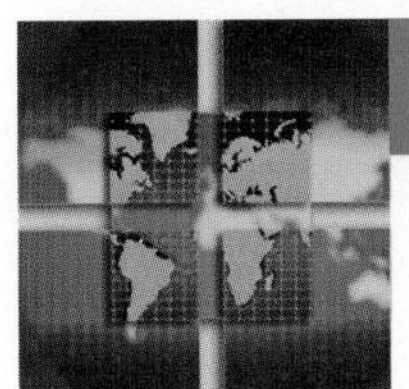

## EYE on the GLOBAL ECONOMY

### Women in the Labor Force

The labor force participation rate of women has increased in most advanced nations. But the participation rate of women in the labor force varies a great deal around the world. The figure compares seven other countries with the United States.

Cultural factors play a role in determining national differences in women's work choices. But economic factors such as the percentage of women with a college degree will ultimately dominate cultural influences and bring a convergence.

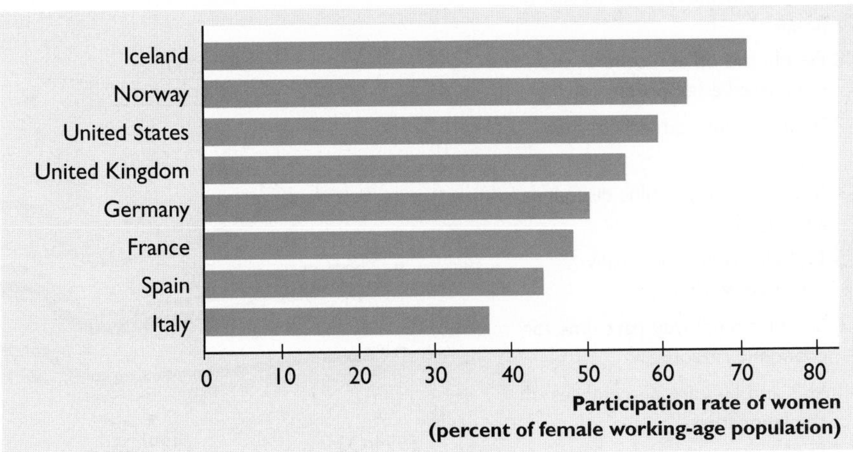


SOURCE OF DATA: OECD.

change in the home increased the time available for paid employment. And fourth, families looked increasingly to a second income to balance tight budgets.

Figure 21.3 also shows another remarkable trend in the U.S. labor force: The participation rate of men *decreased* from 84 percent in 1959 to 72 percent in 2009. As in the case of women, this decrease is spread across all age groups. Some of the decrease occurred because older men chose to retire earlier. During the 1990s, some of this earlier retirement was made possible by an increase in wealth. But some arose from job loss at an age at which finding a new job is difficult. For other men, mainly those in their teens and twenties, decreased labor force participation occurred because more chose to remain in full-time education.

## Alternative Measures of Unemployment

You've seen that the official measure of unemployment does not include marginally attached workers and people who work part time for economic reasons. The Bureau of Labor Statistics (BLS) now provides three broader measures of the unemployment rate, known as U-4, U-5, and U-6, that include these wider groups of the jobless. The official unemployment rate (based on the standard definition of unemployment) is called U-3 and as these names imply, there is also a U-1 and U-2 measure. The U-1 and U-2 measures of the unemployment rate are narrower than the official measure. U-1 is the percentage of the labor force that has been unemployed for 15 weeks or more and is a measure of long-term involuntary unemployment. U-2 is the percentage of the labor force who are laid off and is another measure of involuntary unemployment.

Figure 21.4 shows the history of these six measures of unemployment since 1994 (the year in which the BLS started to measure them). The relative magnitudes

**FIGURE 21.4**

Alternative Measures of Unemployment: 1994–2009

The alternative measures of unemployment are:

U-1 People unemployed 15 weeks or longer

U-2 People laid off and others who completed a temporary job

U-3 Total unemployed (official measure)

U-4 Total unemployed plus discouraged workers

U-5 U-4 plus other marginally attached workers

U-6 U-5 plus employed part time for economic reasons

U-1, U-2, and U-3 are percentages of the labor force.

U-4, U-5, and U-6 are percentages of the labor force plus the unemployed in the added category.

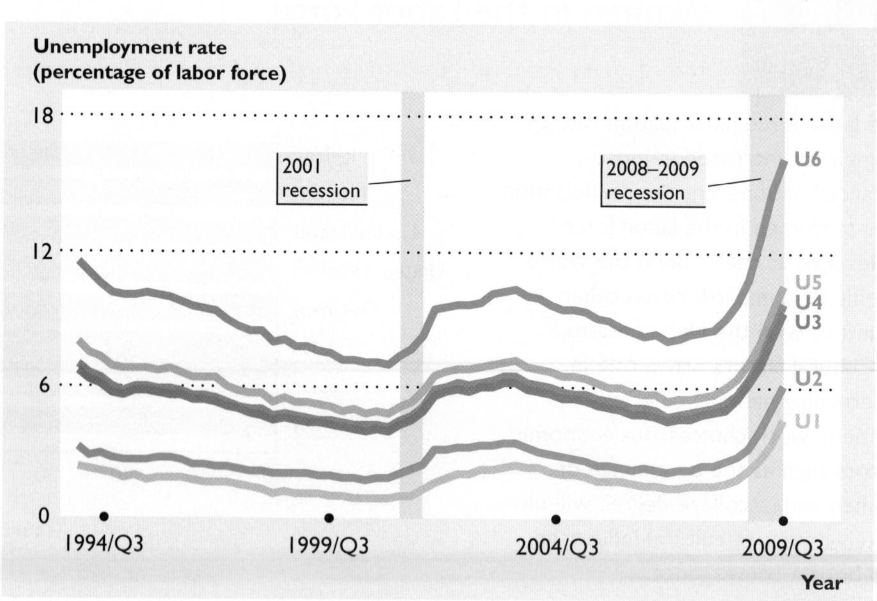


SOURCE OF DATA: Bureau of Labor Statistics.

of the six measures are explained by what they include—the broader the measure, the higher the average. The six measures follow similar but not identical tracks, rising during the recessions and falling in the expansions between the recessions. But during the 2001 recession, U-1 barely changed while during the 2008–2009 recession, it more than doubled in less than a year.

## A Closer Look at Part-Time Employment

The broadest measure of the unemployment rate, U-6, includes people who work part time for economic reasons. Let's take a closer look at part-time employment.

A part-time job is attractive to many workers because it enables them to balance family and other commitments with work. Part-time jobs are attractive to employers because they don't have to pay benefits to part-time workers and are less constrained by government regulations. People who choose part-time jobs are part time for noneconomic reasons. People who take a part-time job because they can't find a full-time job are part time for economic reasons. The BLS measures these two groups and Figure 21.5 shows the data since 1979 (but with a change in the definitions in 1994).

The number of people who work part time for noneconomic reasons is double the number who work part time for economic reasons. Also, the percentage of the labor force who are part time for noneconomic reasons is remarkably steady at an average of 13 percent (old definition) and 14 percent (new definition) of the labor force, and that percentage barely fluctuates with the business cycle.

The percentage of the labor force who work part-time for economic reasons experiences large swings. In the 1981–1982 recession, it climbed to 6.2 percent and in the 2008–2009 recession, it climbed to 6.4 percent.

**FIGURE 21.5**

Part-Time Workers: 1979–2009

myeconlab Animation

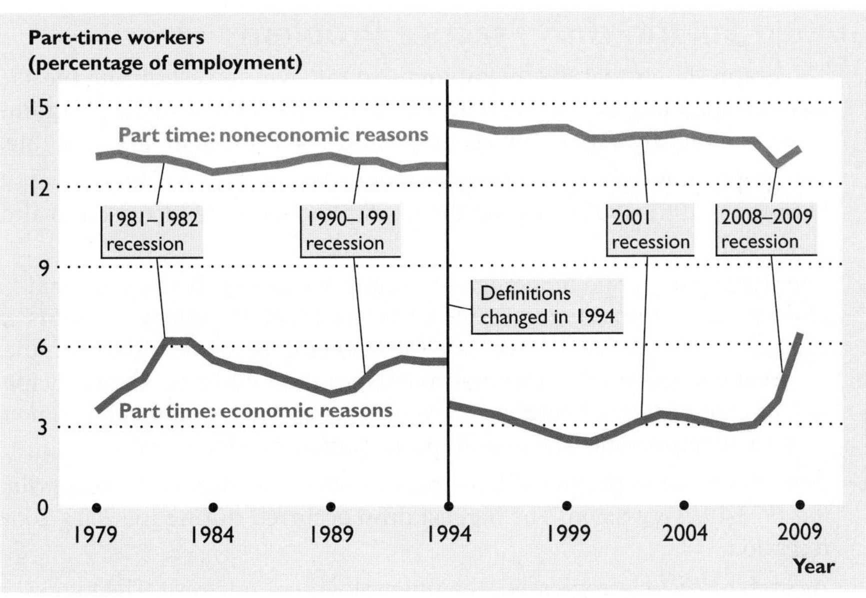


The annual average percentage of all employed workers who are part time for noneconomic reasons is a steady 13 percent (old definition) and 14 percent (new definition) and this percentage barely fluctuates with the business cycle.

But the percentage of all employed workers who are part time for economic reasons fluctuates with the business cycle. It increases in a recession and decreases in an expansion.

SOURCE OF DATA: Bureau of Labor Statistics.

Work these problems in Study Plan 21.2 to get instant feedback.

# CHECKPOINT 21.2

**Describe the trends and fluctuations in the indicators of labor market performance in the United States.**

## Practice Problems

**FIGURE 1**

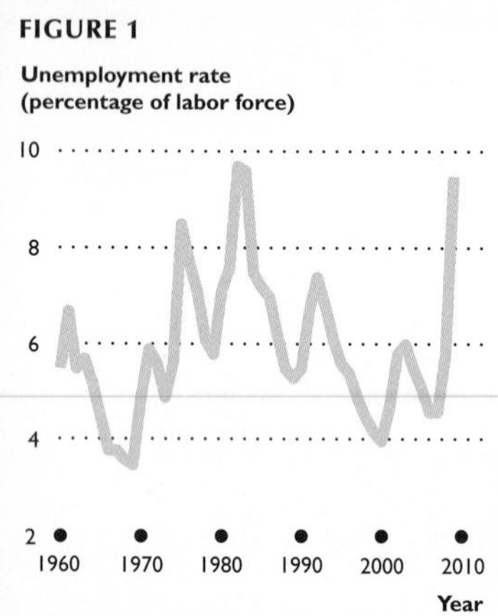


1. Figure 1 shows the unemployment rate in the United States from 1960 to 2010. In which decade—the 1960s, 1970s, 1980s, 1990s, or 2000s—was the average unemployment rate the lowest and what brought low unemployment in that decade? In which decade was the average unemployment rate the highest and what brought high unemployment in that decade?
2. Describe the trends in the participation rates of men and women and of all workers.

Use the following information to work Problems **3** and **4**.

**For young people, a jobless summer**

July, the peak for youth summer jobs, saw the youth unemployment rate hit 18.5% in July 2009, the highest level since the BLS started recording youth labor statistics in 1948. The participation rate of young people was 51.4%, another historic low for the month of July.

Source: *The Wall Street Journal*, August 27, 2009

In addition, Table 1 sets out data for the youth participation rate and unemployment rate during four major recent U.S. recessions.

**TABLE 1**

| Recession years | Participation rate (percent in July) | Unemployment rate (percent in July) |
|---|---|---|
| 1973 | 71.9 | 11.1 |
| 1974 | 73.2 | 12.4 |
| 1975 | 73.0 | 16.3 |
| 1981 | 75.3 | 16.2 |
| 1982 | 74.7 | 18.6 |
| 1990 | 75.1 | 10.9 |
| 1991 | 73.6 | 13.7 |
| 2008 | 65.1 | 14.0 |
| 2009 | 63.0 | 18.5 |

3. Compare the changes in the labor force participation rate during the recessions in Table 1. During which recession did the labor force participation rate drop the most?
4. Compare the changes in the unemployment rate during the recessions in Table 1. During which recession did the unemployment rate rise the most?

## Guided Solutions to Practice Problems

1. The graph shows that the unemployment rate was lowest during the 1960s. Defense spending on the Vietnam War and expansion of social programs brought a rapidly expanding economy and this low unemployment rate.

   The graph shows that the unemployment rate was highest during the 1980s. During the 1981–1982 recession the unemployment rate increased to almost 10 percent.
2. The participation rate of women increased because (1) better-educated women earn more, (2) more white-collar jobs with flexible work hours were created, (3) people have more time for paid employment, and (4) families increasingly needed two incomes to balance their budgets. The participation rate of men decreased because more men remained in school and some men took early retirement. The overall participation rate increased.
3. As each recession progressed, the participation rate dropped, except during the 1973-1975 recession. The biggest drop occurred during the 2008–2009 recession.
4. As each recession progressed, the unemployment rate rose. The biggest rise occurred during the 1973–1975 recession when youth unemployment in July rose from 11.1 percent to 16.3 percent—a 5.2 percentage point rise.

# 21.3 UNEMPLOYMENT AND FULL EMPLOYMENT

Why do people become unemployed, how long do they remain unemployed, and who is at greatest risk of becoming unemployed? What is full employment? How does the unemployment rate compare with real GDP as an indicator of the state of the economy? We begin to answer these questions by looking at the sources of unemployment.

## Sources of Unemployment

The labor market is constantly churning. New jobs are created, and old ones are destroyed; and some people move into the labor force, and some move out of it. Around 5 million people start a new job every month and a similar but normally slightly smaller number lose or leave their job every month. This churning creates unemployment. People become unemployed if they are

1. Job losers
2. Job leavers
3. Entrants or reentrants

### Job Losers

A *job loser* is someone who is gets a pink slip or is laid off from a job, either permanently or temporarily. People lose their jobs for many reasons. Some people are just not a good match for the job they're doing. Firms fail, or a new technology destroys some types of jobs. Offshore outsourcing also takes some jobs—but fewer than 2 million a year are lost for this reason (less than a half of a month's job turnover).

A job loser has two choices: Either look for another job or withdraw from the labor force. A job loser who decides to look for a new job remains in the labor force and becomes unemployed. A job loser who decides to withdraw from the labor force is classified as "not in the labor force." Most job losers decide to look for a new job, and some of them take a long time to find one.

*Some job losers take a long time to find a new job.*

### Job Leavers

A *job leaver* is someone who voluntarily quits a job. Most people who leave their jobs do so for one of two reasons: Either they've found a better job or they've decided to withdraw from the labor force. Neither of these types of job leavers becomes unemployed. But a few people quit their jobs because they want to spend time looking for a better one. These job leavers become unemployed.

### Entrants and Reentrants

An *entrant* is someone who has just left school and is looking for a job. Some entrants get a job right away and are never unemployed. But many entrants spend time searching for their first job, and during this period, they are unemployed.

A *reentrant* is someone who has previously had a job, has then quit and left the labor force, and has now decided to look for a job again. Some reentrants are people who have been out of the labor force rearing children, but most are discouraged workers—people who gave up searching for jobs because they were not able to find suitable ones and who have now decided to look again.

**FIGURE 21.6**

Unemployment by Reasons: 1979–2009

myeconlab Animation

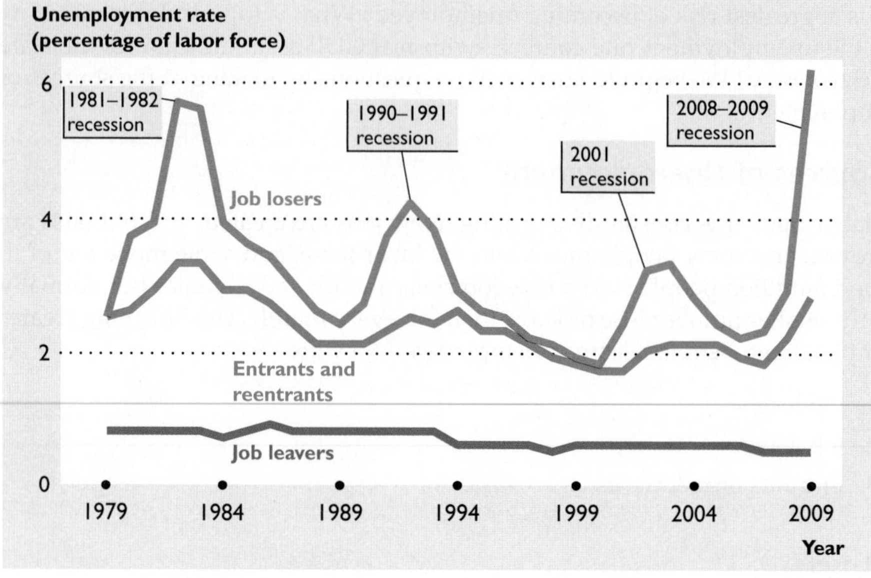


Everyone who is unemployed is a job loser, a job leaver, or an entrant or reentrant into the labor force.

Job losers are the biggest group, and their number fluctuates most.

Entrants and reentrants are the second biggest group. Their number also fluctuates.

Job leavers are the smallest group and their number fluctuates least.

SOURCE OF DATA: Bureau of Labor Statistics.

Figure 21.6 shows the magnitudes of the three sources of unemployment. Most unemployed people are job losers, and their number fluctuates most. The number of entrants and reentrants is also large and fluctuates. Job leavers are the smallest and most stable source of unemployment.

People who end a period of unemployment are either

1. Hires and recalls or
2. Withdrawals

### Hires and Recalls

A *hire* is someone who has been unemployed and has started a new job. A *recall* is someone who has been temporarily laid off and has started work again. Firms are constantly hiring and recalling workers, so there are always people moving from unemployment to employment.

### Withdrawals

A *withdrawal* is someone who has been unemployed and has decided to stop looking for a job. Most of these people are *marginally attached workers.* They will reenter the labor force later when job prospects improve.

## Types of Unemployment

Unemployment is classified into four types:

- Frictional
- Structural
- Seasonal
- Cyclical

## Frictional Unemployment

**Frictional unemployment** is the unemployment that arises from normal labor turnover—from people entering and leaving the labor force, from quitting jobs to find better ones, and from the ongoing creation and destruction of jobs. Frictional unemployment is a permanent and healthy phenomenon in a dynamic, growing economy.

**Frictional unemployment**
The unemployment that arises from normal labor turnover—from people entering and leaving the labor force, from quitting jobs to find better ones, and from the ongoing creation and destruction of jobs.

Businesses don't usually hire the first person who applies for a job, and unemployed people don't always take the first job that comes their way. Instead, both firms and workers spend time searching out what they believe will be the best attainable match. By this search process, people can match their own skills and interests with the available jobs and find a satisfying job and income. While these unemployed people are searching, they are frictionally unemployed.

*A new graduate interviews for a job.*

The amount of frictional unemployment changes slowly, and it depends on the rate at which people enter and reenter the labor force and on the rate at which jobs are created and destroyed. During the 1970s, the amount of frictional unemployment increased because of the postwar baby boom that began during the 1940s. By the late 1970s, the baby boom created a bulge in the number of people leaving school. As these people entered the labor force, the amount of frictional unemployment increased. Frictional unemployment remained high until the information-age expansion of the mid-1990s. Since 1994, frictional unemployment has decreased.

The amount of frictional unemployment is also influenced by unemployment compensation. The greater the number of unemployed people eligible for benefits and the more generous those benefits, the longer is the average time taken in job search and the greater is the amount of frictional unemployment. Unemployment benefits in Canada and Western Europe exceed those in the United States, and these economies have higher average unemployment rates.

## Structural Unemployment

**Structural unemployment** is the unemployment that arises when changes in technology or international competition change the skills needed to perform jobs or change the locations of jobs. Structural unemployment usually lasts longer than frictional unemployment because workers must retrain and possibly relocate to find a job. For example, when a telephone exchange in Gary, Indiana, is automated, some jobs in that city are destroyed. Meanwhile, new jobs for life-insurance salespeople and retail clerks are created in Chicago, Indianapolis, and other cities. The former telephone operators remain unemployed for several months until they move, retrain, and get one of these jobs. Structural unemployment is painful, especially for older workers for whom the best available option might be to retire early but with a lower income than they had expected.

**Structural unemployment**
The unemployment that arises when changes in technology or international competition change the skills needed to perform jobs or change the locations of jobs.

Sometimes, the amount of structural unemployment is small. At other times, it is large, and at such times, structural unemployment can become a serious long-term problem. It was especially large during the late 1970s and early 1980s. During those years, oil price hikes and an increasingly competitive international environment destroyed jobs in traditional U.S. industries, such as auto and steel making, and created jobs in new industries, such as information processing, electronics, and bioengineering. Structural unemployment was also present during the early 1990s as many businesses and governments downsized.

*A job lost to computer technology.*

## Seasonal Unemployment

**Seasonal unemployment**
The unemployment that arises because of seasonal patterns.

**Seasonal unemployment** is the unemployment that arises because of seasonal weather patterns. Seasonal unemployment increases during the winter months and decreases during the spring and summer. A fruit picker who is laid off after the fall harvest and who gets rehired the following summer experiences seasonal unemployment. A construction worker who gets laid off during the winter and who gets rehired in the spring also experiences seasonal unemployment.

## Cyclical Unemployment

**Cyclical unemployment**
The fluctuating unemployment over the business cycle that increases during a recession and decreases during an expansion.

**Cyclical unemployment** is the fluctuating unemployment over the business cycle. Cyclical unemployment increases during a recession and decreases during an expansion. An autoworker who is laid off because the economy is in a recession and who gets rehired some months later when the expansion begins has experienced cyclical unemployment.

The causes of cyclical unemployment are complex and are explained in Chapters 28 and 29.

You've seen that there is always *some* unemployment—someone looking for a job or laid off and waiting to be recalled. Yet one of the goals of economic policy is to achieve full employment. What do we mean by *full employment?*

## EYE on THE UNEMPLOYED

### How Long Does it Take to Find a New Job?

Some people are unemployed for a week or two and others for a year or more. Short unemployment spells are not a major problem, especially if they end by finding a job that is better than the previous one. But long spells of unemployment impose a large personal cost to the unemployed, lead to a loss of human capital, and lead to underproduction and waste.

The average duration of unemployment varies over the business cycle. In a recession, when the unemployment rate exceeds the natural rate, the average duration increases, and during an expansion, when the unemployment rate is below the natural rate, the average duration decreases.

The table opposite compares three years—2000, when the economy was expanding strongly and the unemployment rate was below the natural rate at 4 percent, 2006, when the economy was at full employment and the unemployment rate was 4.8 percent, and 2009, when the economy was in a deep recession and the unemployment rate was above the natural rate at almost 10 percent.

The average unemployment spell lasted for 6 weeks in the boom year 2000, 25 weeks in the recession year 2009, and for 17 weeks at full employment in 2006.

In 2000, 77 percent of the unemployed found jobs in 14 weeks or less and only 11 percent took 27 weeks or more. But in 2009, only 48 percent of the unemployed found jobs in 14 weeks or less and 29 percent took 27 weeks or more. And at full employment, 68 percent found jobs in 14 weeks or less and 18 percent took 27 weeks or longer.

These data tell us that not only does the number of people unemployed vary over the business cycle but also the severity with which it impacts the unemployed.

Unemployment does not affect all demographic groups in the same way and some of the differences are large. The figure opposite shows some averages for 2000–2009. During this ten-

## Full Employment

There can be a lot of unemployment at full employment, and the term "full employment" is an example of a technical economic term that does not correspond with everyday language. **Full employment** occurs when there is no cyclical unemployment or, equivalently, when all the unemployment is frictional, structural, or seasonal. The divergence of the unemployment rate from full employment is cyclical unemployment. The unemployment rate when the economy is at full employment is called the **natural unemployment rate**. The term "natural unemployment rate" is another example of a technical economic term that does not correspond with everyday language.

**Full employment**
When there is no cyclical unemployment or, equivalently, when *all* the unemployment is frictional, structural, or seasonal.

**Natural unemployment rate**
The unemployment rate when the economy is at full employment.

Why do economists call a situation with a lot of unemployment one of full employment? And why is the unemployment rate at full employment called the "natural" unemployment rate? The reason is that the natural state of the economy is one of change in its players, structure, and direction. For example, in 2007, around 3 million people retired and more than 3 million new workers entered the labor force. Thousands of businesses (including new startups) expanded and created jobs while thousands of others downsized or failed and destroyed jobs. This process of change creates frictions and dislocations that are unavoidable—that are natural. And they create unemployment.

year period, black teenagers had the highest unemployment rates, which averaged 30 percent. White people aged 20 years and over had the lowest unemployment rates, which averaged 4 percent. Women had slightly lower unemployment rates than men.

Why are teenage unemployment rates so high? There are two reasons.

First, young people are still discovering what they are good at and trying different lines of work, so they leave their jobs more frequently than older workers do.

Second, because teenagers have little job experience, firms often hire them on a short-term or trial basis, so the rate of job loss is higher for teenagers than for older workers.

**UNEMPLOYMENT DURATION**

| Duration | 2000 | 2006 | 2009 |
|---|---|---|---|
| Average duration (weeks) | 6 | 17 | 25 |
| Percentages unemployed for | | | |
| 14 weeks or less | 77 | 68 | 48 |
| 15 to 26 weeks | 12 | 14 | 23 |
| 27 weeks or more | 11 | 18 | 29 |

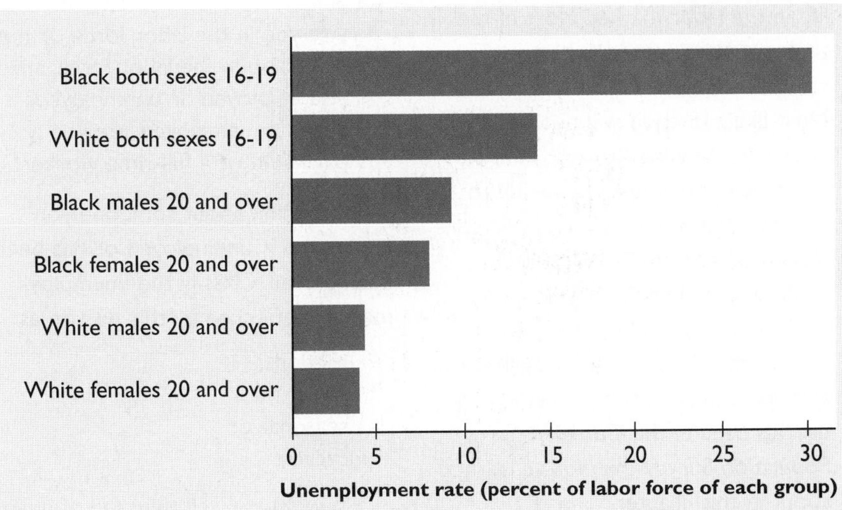


SOURCE OF DATA FOR TABLE AND FIGURE: Bureau of Labor Statistics.

## Unemployment and Real GDP

Cyclical unemployment is the fluctuating unemployment over the business cycle—unemployment that increases during a recession and decreases during an expansion. At full employment, there is *no* cyclical unemployment. At a business cycle trough, cyclical unemployment is *positive* and at a business cycle peak, cyclical unemployment is *negative.*

Figure 21.7(a) shows the unemployment rate in the United States between 1977 and 2009. It also shows the natural unemployment rate and cyclical unemployment. The natural unemployment rate in this figure was estimated by the Congressional Budget Office (CBO).

In Figure 21.7(a), you can see that during most of the 1980s, the early 1990s, early 2000s, and in 2008–2009, unemployment was above the natural unemployment rate, so cyclical unemployment was positive (shaded red). You can also see that during the late 1980s and from 1997 to 2001 unemployment was below the natural unemployment rate, so cyclical unemployment was negative (shaded blue).

**Potential GDP**
The value of real GDP when all the economy's factors of production—labor, capital, land, and entrepreneurial ability—are employed.

**Output gap**
Real GDP minus potential GDP expressed as a percentage of potential GDP.

As the unemployment rate fluctuates around the natural unemployment rate, real GDP fluctuates around potential GDP. **Potential GDP** is the value of real GDP when all the economy's factors of production—labor, capital, land, and entrepreneurial ability—are employed. Real GDP equals potential GDP when the economy is at full employment. Real GDP minus potential GDP expressed as a percentage of potential GDP is called the **output gap**.

Figure 21.7(b) shows the *U.S. output gap* from 1977 to 2009. You can see that as

## EYE on YOUR LIFE

### Your Labor Market Status and Activity

You are going to spend a lot of your life in the labor market. Most of the time, you'll be supplying labor services. But first, you must find a job. Most likely, one job will not last your entire working life. You will want to find a new job when you decide to quit or when changing economic conditions destroy your current job.

As you look for a job, get a job, quit a job or get laid off and look for a new job, you will pass through many and possibly all of the population categories used in the Current Population Survey that you've learned about in this chapter.

Think about your current labor market status while you are studying economics.

- Are you in the labor force or not?
- If you are in the labor force, are you employed or unemployed?
- If you are employed, are you a part-time or a full-time worker?

Now think about someone you know who is unemployed or has been unemployed. Classify the unemployment experienced by this person as

- frictional,
- structural,
- seasonal, or
- cyclical.

How can you tell the type of unemployment experienced by this person?

The labor market conditions that you face today or when you graduate and look for a job depend partly on general national economic conditions—on whether the economy is in recession or booming.

Labor market conditions also depend on where you live. Visit the Bureau of Labor Statistics' Web site at www.bls.gov/sae/sm_mrs.htm.

There you can find information on employment and unemployment for your state and metropolitan area or county. By comparing the labor market conditions in your own region with those in other areas, you can figure out where it might be easier to find work.

**FIGURE 21.7**

The Relationship Between Unemployment and the Output Gap

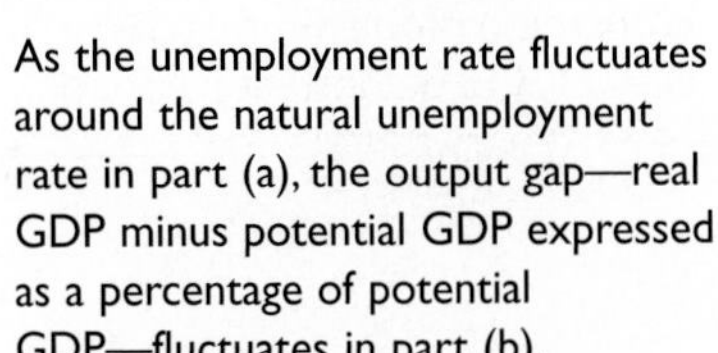


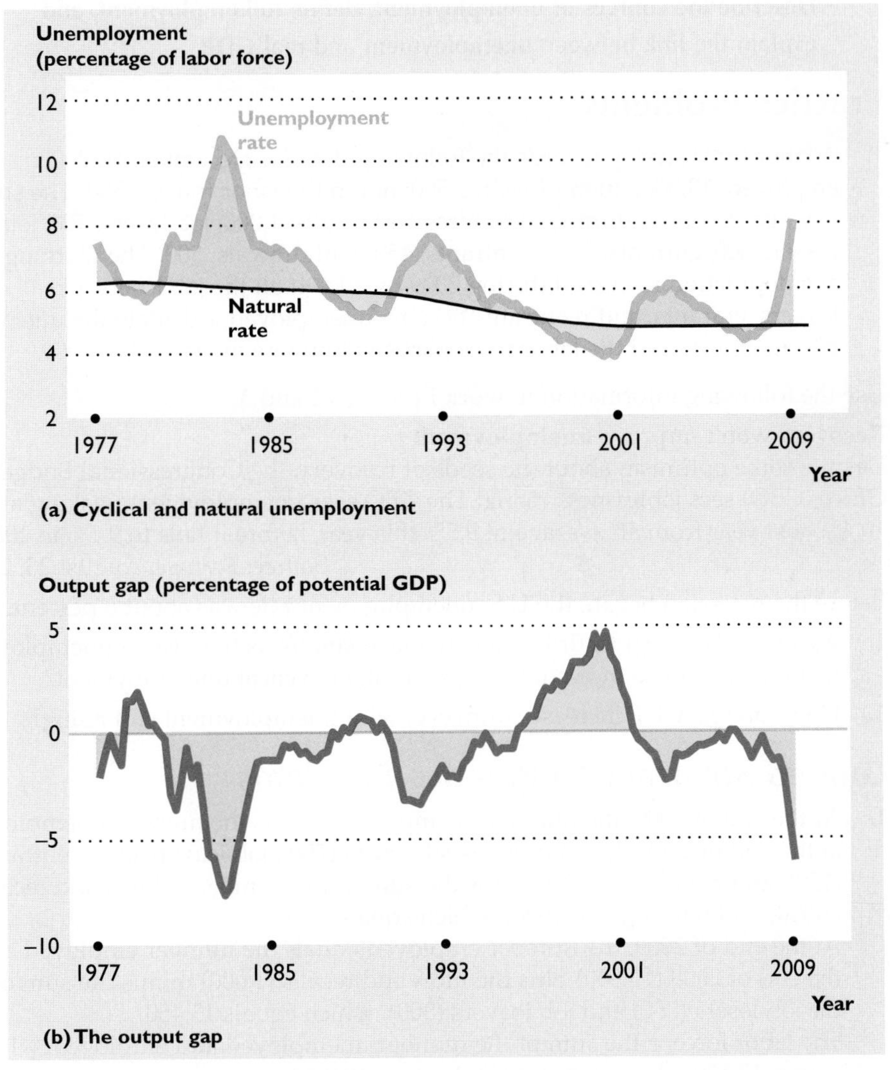


As the unemployment rate fluctuates around the natural unemployment rate in part (a), the output gap—real GDP minus potential GDP expressed as a percentage of potential GDP—fluctuates in part (b).

When the unemployment rate exceeds the natural unemployment rate, real GDP is below potential GDP and the output gap is negative (red shaded areas in both parts).

When the unemployment rate is below the natural unemployment rate, real GDP is above potential GDP and the output gap is positive (blue shaded areas in both parts).

SOURCES OF DATA: Bureau of Economic Analysis, Bureau of Labor Statistics, and Congressional Budget Office.

the unemployment rate fluctuates around the natural unemployment rate, the output gap also fluctuates. When the unemployment rate is above the natural unemployment rate, in part (a), the output gap is negative (real GDP is below potential GDP), in part (b); when the unemployment rate is below the natural unemployment rate, the output gap is positive (real GDP is above potential GDP); and when the unemployment rate equals the natural unemployment rate, the output gap is zero (real GDP equals potential GDP).

You can also see in Figure 21.7 that the unemployment rate is a lagging indicator of the business cycle. Long after a recession is over, the unemployment rate is still rising. You can expect the unemployment rate to rise through 2010.

You will learn what determines potential GDP in Chapter 23, and what brings the fluctuating output gap and cyclical unemployment in Chapters 28 and 29.

Work these problems in Study Plan 21.3 to get instant feedback.

**Describe the sources of unemployment, define full employment, and explain the link between unemployment and real GDP.**

## Practice Problems

1. A labor force survey records the following data for December 31, 2008: employed, 13,500; unemployed, 1,500; not in the labor force, 7,500. The survey also recorded during 2009: hires and recalls, 1,000; job losers, 750; job leavers 300; entrants, 150; reentrants, 450; withdrawals, 500. The working-age population increased during 2009 by 100. If all the job losers, job leavers, entrants, and reentrants became unemployed, calculate the unemployment rate and the labor force participation rate in December 2009.

Use the following information to work Problems **2** and **3**.

**Recovery won't improve unemployment**

Despite some optimism about the seeds of recovery, the Congressional Budget Office (CBO) sees joblessness rising. The CBO sees unemployment peaking at 10.4% next year from an average of 9.3% this year, before it falls to 9.1% in 2011.

Source: *Fortune*, August 25, 2009

Before the recession began, the U.S. unemployment rate was about 6 percent.

2. As a recession begins, firms quickly make layoffs. Is this rise in unemployment mostly a rise in frictional, structural, or cyclical unemployment?
3. How can real GDP increase (recovery) with unemployment still rising?

## Guided Solutions to Practice Problems

1. At the end of 2009, the number unemployed equals the number unemployed at the end of 2008 (1,500) plus the job losers (750), job leavers (300), entrants (150), and reentrants (450) minus the sum of the number of hires and recalls (1,000) and withdrawals (500), which equals 1,650.
   At the end of 2009, the number employed equals the number employed at the end of 2008 (13,500) plus the hires and recalls (1,000) minus the sum of the job losers (750) and job leavers (300), which equals 13,450.
   The labor force is the sum of the number unemployed and employed, which equals 15,100. The unemployment rate is 10.9 percent.
   The labor force participation rate is the percentage of the working-age population who are in the labor force. The working-age population at the end of 2008 is the sum of number employed (13,500), number unemployed (1,500), and the number not in the labor force (7,500), which equals 22,500. The working-age population increased during 2009 by 100, so at the end of 2009, the working-age population was 22,600. The labor force participation rate is $(15{,}100 \div 22{,}600) \times 100 = 66.8$ percent.
2. When a recession starts, firms are quick to layoff workers. Most of the rise in unemployment is cyclical—related to the state of the economy. The unemployment rate rises quickly as the number of layoffs increases.
3. The unemployment rate is a lagging indicator of the business cycle. When the recovery begins, firms start hiring. Unemployed workers get jobs, but reentry into the labor force increases as marginally attached workers start to look for jobs. In the early stages of a recovery, the number of entrants and reentrants exceeds the number of hires and the number unemployed increases.

# CHAPTER SUMMARY

## Key Points

1 **Define the unemployment rate and other labor market indicators.**

- The unemployment rate is the number of people unemployed as a percentage of the labor force, and the labor force is the sum of the number of people employed and the number unemployed.
- The labor force participation rate is the labor force as a percentage of the working-age population.

2 **Describe the trends and fluctuations in the indicators of labor market performance in the United States.**

- The unemployment rate fluctuates with the business cycle, increasing in recessions and decreasing in expansions.
- The labor force participation rate of women has increased, and the labor force participation rate of men has decreased.

3 **Describe the sources of unemployment, define full employment, and explain the link between unemployment and real GDP.**

- Unemployment arises from the process of job creation and job destruction and from the movement of people into and out of the labor force.
- Unemployment can be frictional, structural, seasonal, or cyclical.
- Full employment occurs when there is no cyclical unemployment and at full employment, the unemployment rate equals the natural unemployment rate.
- Potential GDP is the real GDP produced when the economy is at full employment.
- As the unemployment rate fluctuates around the natural unemployment rate, real GDP fluctuates around potential GDP and the output gap fluctuates between negative and positive values.

## Key Terms

Work these problems in Chapter 21 Study Plan to get instant feedback.

# CHAPTER CHECKPOINT

## Study Plan Problems and Applications

Use the following information gathered by a BLS labor market survey of four households to work Problems 1 and 2.

- Household 1: Candy worked 20 hours last week setting up her Internet shopping business. The rest of the week, she completed application forms and attended two job interviews. Husband Jerry worked 40 hours at his job at GM. Daughter Meg, a student, worked 10 hours at her weekend job at Starbucks.
- Household 2: Joey, a full-time bank clerk, was on vacation. Wife, Serena, who wants a full-time job, worked 10 hours as a part-time checkout clerk.
- Household 3: Ari had no work last week but was going to be recalled to his regular job in two weeks. Partner Kosta, after months of searching for a job and not being able to find one, has stopped looking and will go back to school.
- Household 4: Mimi and Henry are retired. Son Hank is a professional artist, who painted for 12 hours last week and sold one picture.

1. Classify each of the 10 people into the labor market category used by the BLS. Who are part-time workers and who are full-time workers? Of the part-time workers, who works part time for economic reasons?
2. Calculate the unemployment rate and the labor force participation rate, and compare these rates with those in the United States in 2009.
3. Give two examples of people who work part time for economic reasons and two examples of people who work part time for noneconomic reasons.
4. What are the labor market flows that create unemployment and that end a spell of unemployment? Of these flows, which fluctuate most and account for fluctuations in the unemployment rate?
5. Distinguish among the four types of unemployment: frictional, structural, seasonal and cyclical. Provide an example of each type of unemployment in the United States today.
6. Describe the relationship between the unemployment rate and the natural unemployment rate as the output gap fluctuates between being positive and being negative.

Use the following information to work Problems 7 and 8.

**July unemployment dips in 17 states, rises in 26**

The Labor Department said that the largest job gains occurred in New York, which added 62,100 jobs, while Minnesota added 10,300 jobs, its first gains in almost a year. Vermont added 900 jobs but its unemployment rate fell from 7.3% to 6.8%—the biggest drop of all states.

Source: The Associated Press, August 21, 2009

7. Explain how, other things remaining the same, the increase of 62,100 jobs in New York and of 10,300 in Minnesota changed the number of people employed, the labor force, and the unemployment rate.
8. Explain why when Vermont added only 900 jobs, its unemployment fell by more than any other state.

## Instructor Assignable Problems and Applications

Your instructor can assign these problems as homework, a quiz, or a test in **MyEconLab**.

1. In the United States,
   - Compare the duration of unemployment in 2009 with that in 2000 and explain whether the difference was most likely the result of frictions, structural change, or the business cycle.
   - Why are teenage unemployment rates much higher than those for older workers?
   - How do the unemployment rates of women compare with those of men? Suggest a reason for the difference using the concept of marginally attached workers.
2. The Bureau of Labor Statistics reported that in the second quarter of 2008 the working-age population was 233,410,000, the labor force was 154,294,000, and employment was 146,089,000. Calculate for that quarter the labor force participation rate and the unemployment rate.
3. In March 2007, the U.S. unemployment rate was 4.4 percent. In August 2008, the unemployment rate was 6.1 percent. Predict what happened between March 2007 and August 2008 to the numbers of (i) job losers and job leavers and (ii) entrants and reentrants into the labor force.
4. In July 2009, in the economy of Sandy Island, 10,000 people were employed and 1,000 were unemployed. During August 2009, 80 people lost their jobs and didn't look for new ones, 20 people quit their jobs and retired, 150 people were hired or recalled, 50 people withdrew from the labor force, and 40 people entered or reentered the labor force to look for work. Calculate the change in the unemployment rate from July 2009 to August 2009.
5. The BLS survey reported the following data in a community of 320 people: 200 worked at least 1 hour as paid employees; 20 did not work but were temporarily absent from their jobs; 40 had no employment; 10 were available for work and last week they had looked for work; and 6 were available for work and were waiting to be recalled to their previous job. Calculate the unemployment rate and the labor force participation rate.
6. Describe the trends and fluctuations in the unemployment rate in the United States from 1949 through 2009. In which periods was the unemployment rate above average and in which periods was it below average?
7. Describe the trends and fluctuations in the labor force participation rate in the United States from 1967 through 2009, and contrast and explain the different trends for women and men.

Use the following information to work Problems **8** and **9**.

**Nation's economic pain deepens**

The unemployment rate jumped to 5.5% in May 2008 from 5% in April 2008. This jump was the biggest one-month jump in unemployment since February 1986, and the 5.5% rate is the highest level seen since October 2004.

Source: CNN, June 6, 2008

8. Compare the unemployment rate in May 2008 with the unemployment rate during the past three recessions.
9. Why might the unemployment rate tend to actually underestimate the unemployment problem, especially during a recession?

10. The BLS survey reported the following data in a community of 100 people:
    - Total number of persons: 100
    - Worked at least 1 hour as paid employees or worked 15 hours or more as unpaid workers in their family business: 50
    - Were not working but had jobs or businesses from which they were temporarily absent: 20
    - Had no employment: 10
    - Were available for work and had made specific efforts to find employment some time during the previous 4 weeks: 15
    - Were available for work and were waiting to be recalled to a job from which they had been laid off: 5

    Calculate the unemployment rate and the labor force participation rate.
11. "Economics is supposed to be about scarcity. But if some labor is always unemployed, how can there be scarcity? All we need to do to produce more goods and services is employ the unemployed people." Do you agree or disagree with this statement? Why? Explain why scarcity and unemployment are not incompatible.

Use the following information to work Problems 12 and 13.

**Michigan unemployment tops 15%**

The U.S. Department of Labor reported that Michigan's unemployment rate in June 2009 rose to 15.2%, becoming the first state in 25 years to suffer an unemployment rate exceeding 15%. Michigan has been battered by the collapse of the auto industry and the housing crisis and has had the highest unemployment rate in the nation for the past 12 months.

Source: CNNMoney, July 17, 2009

12. Why is the reality of the unemployment problem in Michigan actually worse than the unemployment rate statistic of 15.2 percent?
13. Is this higher unemployment rate in Michigan frictional, structural, or cyclical? Explain.
14. Visit the Bureau of Labor Statistics Web site and find the following labor market data for the United States in the most recent month and for the same month one year ago: the labor force, the number employed, the number unemployed, and the working-age population. Calculate the unemployment rate and the labor force participation rate for the two months and describe the change in the labor market over the past year.

## How do we measure the changing value of money?

*Transformers: Revenge of the Fallen* earned $400 million at the box office. *Gone with the Wind* (made in 1939) earned $200 million. Which movie really had the larger box office revenues?

# The CPI and the Cost of Living

CHAPTER CHECKLIST

**When you have completed your study of this chapter, you will be able to**

1. Explain what the Consumer Price Index (CPI) is and how it is calculated.
2. Explain the limitations of the CPI and describe other measures of the price level.
3. Adjust money values for inflation and calculate real wage rates and real interest rates.

## 22.1 THE CONSUMER PRICE INDEX

**Consumer Price Index**
A measure of the average of the prices paid by urban consumers for a fixed market basket of consumption goods and services.

The **Consumer Price Index** (CPI) is a measure of the average of the prices paid by urban consumers for a fixed market basket of consumption goods and services. The Bureau of Labor Statistics (BLS) calculates the CPI every month, and we can use these numbers to compare what the fixed market basket costs this month with what it cost in some previous month or other period.

### Reading the CPI Numbers

**Reference base period**
A period for which the CPI is defined to equal 100. Currently, the reference base period is 1982–1984.

The CPI is defined to equal 100 for a period called the **reference base period**. Currently, the reference base period is 1982–1984. That is, the CPI equals 100 on the average over the 36 months from January 1982 through December 1984.

In June 2009, the CPI was 214.5. This number tells us that the average of the prices paid by urban consumers for a fixed market basket of consumption goods and services was 114.5 percent higher in June 2009 than it was on the average during 1982–1984.

In May 2009, the CPI was 212.9. Comparing the June CPI with the May CPI tells us that the average of the prices paid by urban consumers for a fixed market basket of consumption goods and services *increased* by 1.6 of a percentage point in June 2009.

### Constructing the CPI

Constructing the CPI is a huge operation that costs millions of dollars and involves three stages:

- Selecting the CPI market basket
- Conducting the monthly price survey
- Calculating the CPI

### The CPI Market Basket

The first stage in constructing the CPI is to determine the *CPI market basket*. This "basket" contains the goods and services represented in the index and the relative importance, or weight, attached to each of them. The idea is to make the weight of the items in the CPI basket the same as in the budget of an average urban household. For example, if the average household spends 2 percent of its income on public transportation, then the CPI places a weight of 2 percent on the prices of bus, subway, and other transit system rides.

Although the CPI is calculated every month, the CPI market basket isn't updated every month. The information used to determine the CPI market basket comes from a survey, called the *Consumer Expenditure Survey*, that discovers what people actually buy. This survey is an ongoing activity, and the CPI market basket in 2009 was based on a survey conducted during 2005 and 2006. More than 30,000 individuals and families contributed information. Some of them were interviewed every three months, and others kept detailed diaries for two weeks in which they listed absolutely everything they bought. (Before 1999, the Consumer Expenditure Survey was conducted much less frequently.)

The reference base period for the CPI has been fixed at 1982–1984 for more than 20 years and doesn't change when a new Consumer Expenditure Survey is used to update the market basket.

Figure 22.1 shows the CPI market basket at the end of 2008. The basket contains around 80,000 goods and services arranged in the eight large groups shown in the figure. The most important item in a household's budget is housing, which accounts for 43.4 percent of total expenditure. Food and beverage comes next at 15.8 percent. Third in relative importance is transportation at 15.3 percent. These three groups account for almost three quarters of the average household budget. Medical care, recreation, and education and communication take about 6 percent each, and apparel (clothing and footwear) takes 3.7 percent. Another 3.4 percent is spent on other goods and services.

The BLS breaks down each of these categories into smaller ones. For example, education and communication breaks down into textbooks and supplies, tuition, telephone services, and personal computer services.

As you look at these numbers, remember that they apply to the average household. Each individual household is spread around the average. Think about your own expenditure and compare it with the average.

## The Monthly Price Survey

Each month, BLS employees check the prices of the 80,000 goods and services in the CPI market basket in 30 metropolitan areas. Because the CPI aims to measure price changes, it is important that the prices recorded each month refer to exactly the same items. For example, suppose the price of a box of jelly beans has increased but a box now contains more beans. Has the price of a jelly bean increased? The BLS employee must record the details of changes in quality, size, weight, or packaging so that price changes can be isolated from other changes.

Once the raw price data are in hand, the next task is to calculate the CPI.

**FIGURE 22.1**

The CPI Market Basket

myeconlab Animation

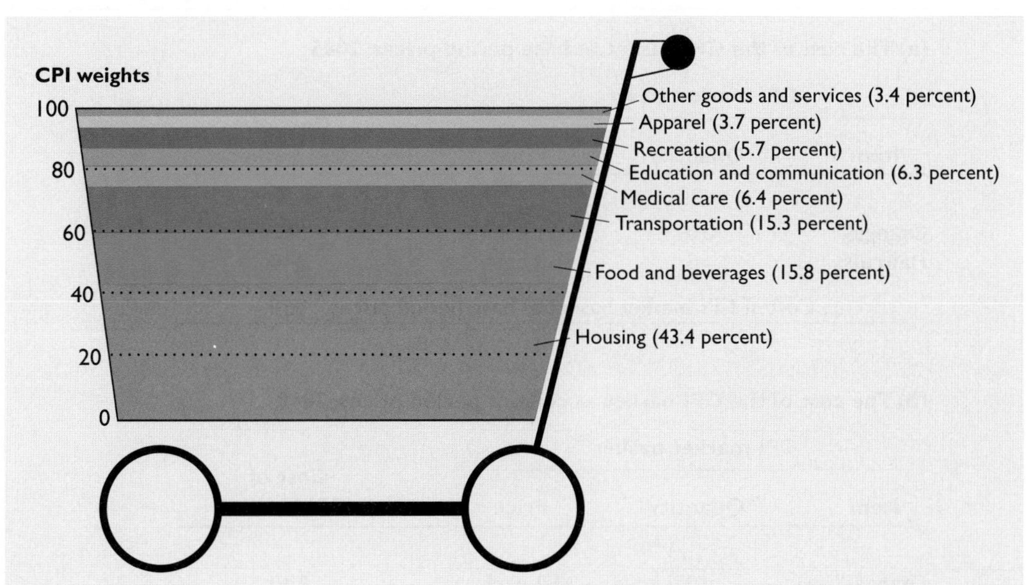


SOURCE OF DATA: Bureau of Labor Statistics.

This shopping cart is filled with the items that an average household buys. Housing (43.4 percent), food and beverages (15.8 percent), and transportation (15.3 percent) take almost 75 percent of household income.

## Calculating the CPI

The CPI calculation has three steps:

- Find the cost of the CPI market basket at base period prices.
- Find the cost of the CPI market basket at current period prices.
- Calculate the CPI for the base period and the current period.

We'll work through these three steps for a simple example. Suppose the CPI market basket contains only two goods and services: oranges and haircuts. We'll construct an annual CPI rather than a monthly CPI with the reference base period 2005 and the current period 2010.

Table 22.1 shows the quantities in the CPI market basket and the prices in the base period and the current period. Part (a) contains the data for the base period. In that period, consumers bought 10 oranges at $1 each and 5 haircuts at $8 each. To find the cost of the CPI market basket in the base period prices, multiply the quantities in the CPI market basket by the base period prices. The cost of oranges is $10 (10 at $1 each), and the cost of haircuts is $40 (5 at $8 each). So total expenditure in the base period on the CPI market basket is $50 ($10 + $40).

Part (b) contains the price data for the current period. The price of an orange increased from $1 to $2, which is a 100 percent increase ($1 ÷ $1 × 100 = 100 percent). The price of a haircut increased from $8 to $10, which is a 25 percent increase ($2 ÷ $8 × 100 = 25 percent).

The CPI provides a way of averaging these price increases by comparing the cost of the basket rather than the price of each item. To find the cost of the CPI market basket in the current period, 2010, multiply the quantities in the basket by their 2010 prices. The cost of oranges is $20 (10 at $2 each), and the cost of haircuts is $50 (5 at $10 each). So total expenditure on the fixed CPI market basket at current period prices is $70 ($20 + $50).

**TABLE 22.1**

The Consumer Price Index: A Simplified CPI Calculation

**(a) The cost of the CPI basket at base period prices: 2005**

| CPI market basket | | | |
|---|---|---|---|
| **Item** | **Quantity** | **Price** | **Cost of CPI basket** |
| Oranges | 10 | $1 each | $10 |
| Haircuts | 5 | $8 each | $40 |
| | | Cost of CPI market basket at base period prices | $50 |

**(b) The cost of the CPI basket at current period prices: 2010**

| CPI market basket | | | |
|---|---|---|---|
| **Item** | **Quantity** | **Price** | **Cost of CPI basket** |
| Oranges | 10 | $2 each | $20 |
| Haircuts | 5 | $10 each | $50 |
| | | Cost of CPI market basket at current period prices | $70 |

You've now taken the first two steps toward calculating the CPI. The third step uses the numbers you've just calculated to find the CPI for 2005 and 2010. The formula for the CPI is

$$\text{CPI} = \frac{\text{Cost of CPI basket at current period prices}}{\text{Cost of CPI basket at base period prices}} \times 100.$$

In Table 22.1, you established that in 2005, the cost of the CPI market basket was \$50 and in 2010, it was \$70. If we use these numbers in the CPI formula, we can find the CPI for 2005 and 2010. The base period is 2005, so

$$\text{CPI in 2005} = \frac{\$50}{\$50} \times 100 = 100.$$

$$\text{CPI in 2010} = \frac{\$70}{\$50} \times 100 = 140.$$

The principles that you've applied in this simplified CPI calculation apply to the more complex calculations performed every month by the BLS.

Figure 22.2(a) shows the CPI in the United States during the 30 years between 1979 and 2009. The CPI increased every year during this period until 2009 when it fell slightly. During the late 1970s and in 1980, the CPI was increasing rapidly, but since the early 1980s, the rate of increase has slowed.

## Measuring Inflation and Deflation

A major purpose of the CPI is to measure *changes* in the cost of living and in the value of money. To measure these changes, we calculate the **inflation rate**, which is the percentage change in the price level from one year to the next. To calculate the inflation rate, we use the formula

**Inflation rate**
The percentage change in the price level from one year to the next.

$$\text{Inflation rate} = \frac{(\text{CPI in current year} - \text{CPI in previous year})}{\text{CPI in previous year}} \times 100.$$

Suppose that the current year is 2010 and the CPI for 2010 is 140. And suppose that in the previous year, 2009, the CPI was 120. Then in 2010,

$$\text{Inflation rate} = \frac{(140 - 120)}{120} \times 100 = 16.7 \text{ percent}.$$

If the inflation rate is *negative*, the price level is *falling* and we have **deflation**. The United States has rarely experienced deflation but 2009 was one of those rare years. You can check the latest data by visiting the BLS Web site. In June 2009, the CPI was 214.5, and in June 2008, it was 217.0. So during the year to June 2009,

**Deflation**
A situation in which the price level is *falling* and the inflation rate is *negative*.

$$\text{Inflation rate} = \frac{(214.5 - 217.0)}{217.0} \times 100 = -1.2 \text{ percent}.$$

Figure 22.2(b) shows the inflation rate in the United States between 1979 and 2009. The change in the price level in part (a) and the inflation rate in part (b) are related. When the price *level* rises rapidly, the inflation rate is high; when the price level rises slowly, the inflation rate is low; and when the price level is falling, the inflation rate is negative.

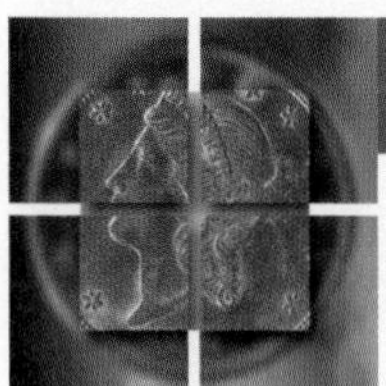

# EYE on the PAST

## 700 Years of Inflation and Deflation

These extraordinary data show that inflation became a persistent problem only after 1900. During the preceding 600 years, inflation was almost unknown. Inflation increased slightly during the sixteenth century after Europeans discovered gold in America. But this inflation barely reached 2 percent a year—less than we have today—and eventually subsided. The Industrial Revolution saw a temporary burst of inflation followed by a period of deflation.

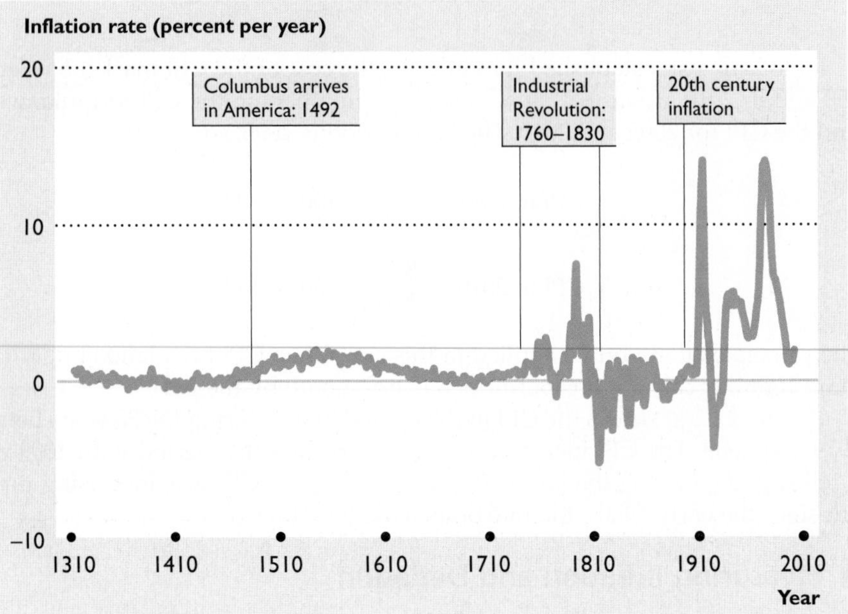


SOURCES OF DATA: E.H. Phelps Brown and Sheila V. Hopkins, *Economica,* 1955, and Robert Sahr, http://oregonstate.edu/dept/pol_sci/fac/sahr/sahr.htm.

**FIGURE 22.2**

The CPI and the Inflation Rate: 1979–2009

myeconlab Animation

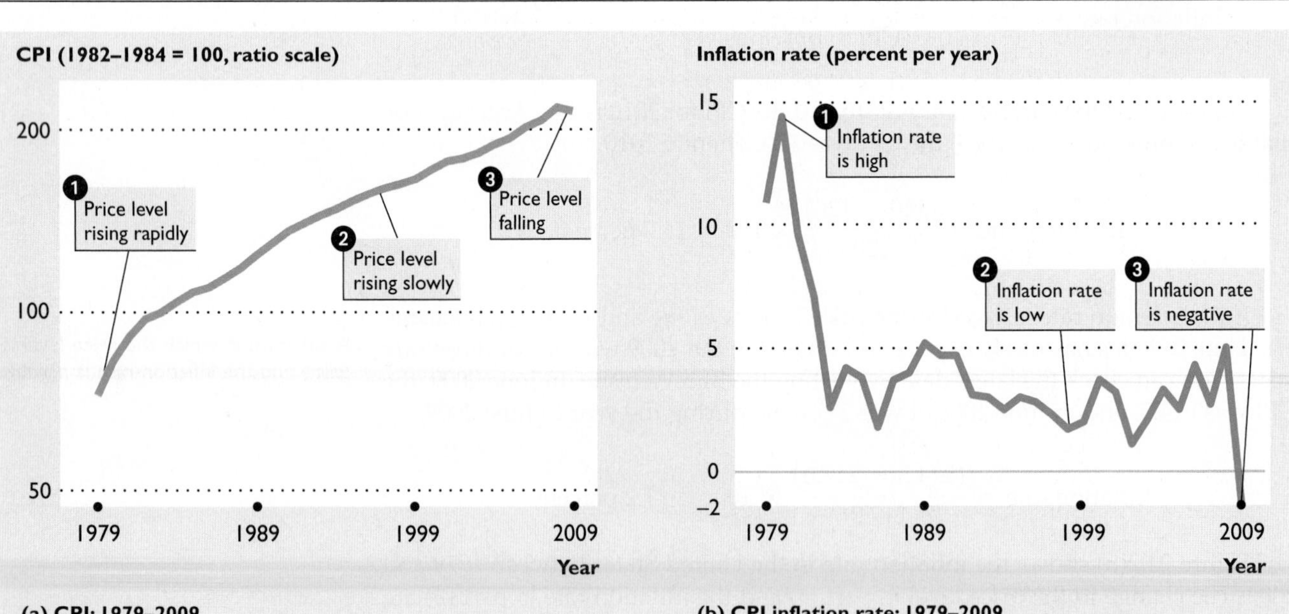


SOURCE OF DATA: Bureau of Labor Statistics.

❶ The price *level* (in part a) was rising rapidly in 1980 and the inflation rate (in part b) was high. ❷ The price level was rising slowly during the 1990s and 2000s and the inflation rate was low. ❸ In 2009, the price level fell and the inflation rate was negative.

## CHECKPOINT 22.1

Work these problems in Study Plan 22.1 to get instant feedback.

**Explain what the Consumer Price Index (CPI) is and how it is calculated.**

### Practice Problems

A Consumer Expenditure Survey in Sparta shows that people buy only juice and cloth. In 2008, the year of the Consumer Expenditure Survey and also the reference base year, the average household spent $40 on juice and $25 on cloth. Table 1 sets out the prices of juice and cloth in 2008 and 2010. Use this information to work Problems **1** and **2**.

**TABLE 1 PRICES**

| | 2008 | 2010 |
|---|---|---|
| Juice | $4 a bottle | $4 a bottle |
| Cloth | $5 a yard | $6 a yard |

1. Calculate the CPI market basket and the percentage of household budget spent on juice in the reference base year.
2. Calculate the CPI in 2010 and the inflation rate between 2008 and 2010.
3. Table 2 shows the CPI in Russia. Calculate the inflation rates in 2006 and 2007. Did the price level rise in 2007? Did the inflation rate increase in 2007?
4. **Consumer prices rise less than expected in May**
   The CPI in May 2009 was 212.9, 0.1% higher than the April CPI. The gasoline price rose 9.6% in May 2009, but gasoline was still cheaper than in May 2008 when it exceeded $4 a gallon. Because of the lower gas price, the CPI fell by 1.3% in the year to May 2009, the steepest drop since 1950.

   Source: *USA Today*, June 17, 2009

   Use the information in the news clip to distinguish between the price level and the inflation rate. Explain why the reason suggested for the fall in the CPI can't be entirely correct.

**TABLE 2**

| Year | CPI |
|---|---|
| 2005 | 200 |
| 2006 | 219 |
| 2007 | 237 |

### Guided Solutions to Practice Problems

1. The CPI market basket is the quantities bought during the Consumer Expenditure Survey year, 2008. Households spent $40 on juice at $4 a bottle, so the quantity of juice bought was 10 bottles. Households spent $25 on cloth at $5 a yard, so the quantity of cloth bought was 5 yards. The CPI market basket is made up of 10 bottles of juice and 5 yards of cloth.
   In the reference base year, the average household spent $40 on juice and $25 on cloth, so the household budget was $65. Expenditure on juice was 61.5 percent of the household budget: ($40 ÷ $65) × 100 = 61.5 percent.
2. To calculate the CPI in 2010, find the cost of the CPI market basket in 2008 and 2010. In 2008, the CPI basket costs $65 ($40 for juice + $25 for cloth). In 2010, the CPI market basket costs $70 (10 bottles of juice at $4 a bottle + 5 yards of cloth at $6 a yard). The CPI in 2010 is ($70 ÷ $65) × 100 = 107.7.

   The inflation rate is [(107.7 − 100) ÷ 100] × 100 = 7.7 percent.
3. The inflation rate in 2006 is [(219 − 200) ÷ 200] × 100 = 9.5 percent. The inflation rate in 2007 is [(237 − 219) ÷ 219] × 100 = 8.2 percent. In 2007, the price level increased, but the inflation rate decreased.
4. The CPI is the price level. The percentage change in the CPI is the inflation rate. Gasoline is one component of the transportation item in the CPI basket. The entire transportation item is only 15.3 percent of the CPI basket, so gasoline represents a small part of the CPI basket. For the CPI to have fallen in the year to May 2009, many other prices must also have fallen. The fall in gas prices is not the only or even the main reason why the CPI fell.

## 22.2 THE CPI AND OTHER PRICE LEVEL MEASURES

**Cost of living index**
A measure of the change in the amount of money that people need to spend to achieve a given standard of living.

The purpose of the CPI is to measure the cost of living or what amounts to the same thing, the *value of money*. The CPI is sometimes called a **cost of living index**—a measure of the change in the amount of money that people need to spend to achieve a given standard of living. The CPI is not a perfect measure of the cost of living (value of money) for two broad reasons.

First, the CPI does not try to measure all the changes in the cost of living. For example, the cost of living rises in a severe winter as people buy more natural gas and electricity to heat their homes. A rise in the prices of these items increases the CPI. The increased quantities of natural gas and electricity bought don't change the CPI because the CPI market basket is fixed. So part of this increase in spending—the increase in the cost of maintaining a given standard of living—doesn't show up as an increase in the CPI.

Second, even those components of the cost of living that are measured by the CPI are not always measured accurately. The result is that the CPI is possibly a biased measure of changes in the cost of living.

Let's look at some of the sources of bias in the CPI and the ways the BLS tries to overcome them.

### Sources of Bias in the CPI

The potential sources of bias in the CPI are

- New goods bias
- Quality change bias
- Commodity substitution bias
- Outlet substitution bias

#### New Goods Bias

*To measure the CPI, the BLS must compare the price of today's iPod with that of the 1970s Walkman and 1980s Discman.*

Every year, some new goods become available and some old goods disappear. Make a short list of items that you take for granted today that were not available 10 or 20 years ago. This list includes cell phones, iPods, laptop computers, and flat-panel, large-screen television sets. A list of items no longer available or rarely bought includes audiocassette players, vinyl records, photographic film, and typewriters.

When we want to compare the price level in 2009 with that in 1999, 1989, or 1979, we must do so by comparing the prices of different baskets of goods. We can't compare the same baskets because today's basket wasn't available 20 years ago and the basket of 20 years ago isn't available today.

To make comparisons, the BLS tries to measure the price of the service performed by yesterday's goods and today's goods. It tries to compare, for example, the price of listening to recorded music, regardless of the technology that delivers that service. But the comparison is hard to make. Today's iPod delivers an improved quality of sound and level of convenience compared to yesterday's Walkman and Discman.

How much of the new product represents an increase in consumption and how much represents a higher price? The BLS does its best to answer this question, but there is no sure way of making the necessary adjustment. It is believed that the arrival of new goods puts an upward bias into the CPI and its measure of the inflation rate.

### Quality Change Bias

To compare the price of today's cars with those of earlier years, the BLS must value the improvements in features and quality.

Cars, cell phones, laptops, and many other items get better every year. For example, central locking, airbags, and antilock braking systems all add to the quality of a car. But they also add to the cost. Is the improvement in quality greater than the increase in cost? Or do car prices rise by more than can be accounted for by quality improvements? To the extent that a price rise is a payment for improved quality, it is not inflation. Again, the BLS does the best job it can to estimate the effects of quality improvements on price changes. But the CPI probably counts too much of any price rise as inflation and so overstates inflation.

### Commodity Substitution Bias

When consumers substitute lower priced broccoli for higher priced carrots, the CPI overstates the rise in the price of vegetables.

Changes in relative prices lead consumers to change the items they buy. People cut back on items that become relatively more costly and increase their consumption of items that become relatively less costly. For example, suppose the price of carrots rises while the price of broccoli remains constant. Now that carrots are more costly relative to broccoli, you might decide to buy more broccoli and fewer carrots. Suppose that you switch from carrots to broccoli, spend the same amount on vegetables as before, and get the same enjoyment as before. Your cost of vegetables has not changed. The CPI says that the price of vegetables has increased because it ignores your substitution between goods in the CPI market basket.

### Outlet Substitution Bias

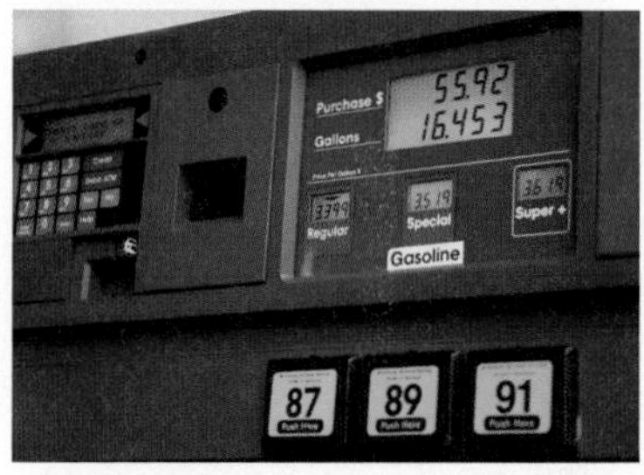

As consumers shop around for the lowest prices, outlet substitution occurs and the CPI overstates the rise in prices actually paid.

When confronted with higher prices, people use discount stores more frequently and convenience stores less frequently. This phenomenon is called *outlet substitution.* Suppose, for example, that gas prices rise by 10¢ a gallon. Instead of buying from your nearby gas station for $4.579 a gallon, you now drive farther to a gas station that charges $4.479 a gallon. Your cost of gas has increased because you must factor in the cost of your time and the gas that you use driving several blocks down the road. But your cost has not increased by as much as the 10¢ a gallon increase in the pump price. However, the CPI says that the price of gas has increased by 10¢ a gallon because the CPI does not measure outlet substitution.

The growth of online shopping in recent years has provided an alternative to discount stores that makes outlet substitution even easier and potentially makes this source of bias more serious.

## The Magnitude of the Bias

You have reviewed the sources of bias in the CPI. But how big is the bias? When this question was tackled in 1996 by a Congressional Advisory Commission chaired by Michael Boskin, an economics professor at Stanford University, the answer was that the CPI overstated inflation by 1.1 percentage points a year. That is, if the CPI reports that inflation is 3.1 percent a year, most likely inflation is actually 2 percent a year.

In the period since the Boskin Commission reported, the BLS has taken steps to reduce the CPI bias. The more frequent Consumer Expenditure Survey that we described earlier in this chapter is one of these steps. Beyond that, the BLS uses ever more sophisticated models and methods to try to eliminate the sources of bias and make the CPI as accurate as possible.

## Two Consequences of the CPI Bias

Avoiding bias in the CPI is important for two main reasons. Bias leads to

- Distortion of private contracts
- Increases in government outlays and decreases in taxes

### Distortion of Private Contracts

Many wage contracts contain a cost of living adjustment. For example, the United Auto Workers Union (UAW) and Ford Motor Company might agree on a wage rate of $30 an hour initially that increases over three years at the same rate as the cost of living increases. The idea is that both the union and the employer want a contract in "real" terms. As the cost of living rises, the firm wants to pay the workers the number of dollars per hour that buys a given market basket of goods and services. And the firm is happy to pay the higher wage because it can sell its output for a higher price.

Suppose that over the three years of a UAW and Ford contract, the CPI increases by 5 percent each year. The wage rate paid by Ford will increase to $31.50 in the second year and $33.08 in the third year.

But suppose that the CPI is biased and the true price increase is 3 percent a year. The workers' cost of living increases by this amount, so in the second year, $30.90 rather than $31.50 is the intended wage. In the third year, a wage rate of $31.83 and not $33.08 compensates for the higher cost of living. So in the second year, the workers gain 60¢ an hour, or $21 for a 35-hour workweek. And in the third year, they gain $1.25 an hour, or $43.75 for a 35-hour workweek.

The workers' gain is Ford's loss. With a work force of a few thousand, the loss amounts to several thousand dollars a week and a few million dollars over the life of a 3-year wage contract.

If the CPI bias was common knowledge and large, the CPI would not be used without some adjustment in contracts. Unions and employers would seek agreement on the extent of the bias and make an appropriate adjustment to their contract. But for a small bias, the cost of negotiating a more complicated agreement might be too large.

### Increases in Government Outlays and Decreases in Taxes

Because rising prices decrease the buying power of the dollar, the CPI is used to adjust the incomes of the 49 million Social Security beneficiaries, 27 million food stamp recipients, and 4 million retired former military personnel and federal civil servants (and their surviving spouses). The CPI is also used to adjust the budget for 3 million school lunches.

Close to a third of federal government outlays are linked directly to the CPI. If the CPI has a 1.1 percentage point bias, all of these expenditures increase by more than required to compensate for the fall in the buying power of the dollar and, although a bias of 1.1 percent a year seems small, accumulated over a decade, it adds up to almost a trillion dollars of additional government outlays.

The CPI is also used to adjust the income levels at which higher tax rates apply. The tax rates on large incomes are higher than those on small incomes so, as incomes rise, if these adjustments were not made, the burden of taxes would rise relentlessly. To the extent that the CPI is biased upward, the tax adjustments over-compensate for rising prices and decrease the amount paid in taxes.

## Alternative Measures of the Price Level and Inflation Rate

Several alternative measures of the price level and inflation rate are available. One based on wholesale prices and another based on producers' prices are similar to the CPI, both in the way they are constructed and their potential for bias. But three other price indexes that we'll briefly describe here are less biased. These indexes are the

- GDP price index
- Personal consumption expenditures (PCE) price index
- PCE price index excluding food and energy

### GDP Price Index

The **GDP price index** (also called the *GDP deflator*) is an average of the current prices of all the goods and services included in GDP expressed as a percentage of base-year prices. Two key differences between the GDP price index and the CPI result in different estimates of the price level and inflation rate.

**GDP price index**
An average of the current prices of all the goods and services included in GDP expressed as a percentage of base-year prices.

First, the GDP price index uses the prices of all the goods and services in GDP—consumption, investment, government purchases, and exports—while the CPI uses prices of consumption goods and services only. For example, the GDP price index includes the prices of paper mills bought by 3M to make Post-it® Notes, nuclear submarines bought by the Defense Department, and Boeing 747s bought by British Airways.

Second, the GDP price index weights each item using information about current quantities. In contrast, the CPI weights each item using information from a *past* Consumer Expenditure Survey. But because of the breadth of the items that the GDP price index includes, it is not an alternative to the CPI as a measure of the cost of living.

### Personal Consumption Expenditures (PCE) Price Index

The **Personal Consumption Expenditures price index** (or **PCE price index**) is an average of the current prices of the goods and services included in the consumption expenditure component of GDP expressed as a percentage of base-year prices. The PCE price index has the same advantages as the GDP price index—it uses current information on quantities and to some degree overcomes the sources of bias in the CPI. It also has an advantage shared by the CPI of focusing on consumption expenditure and therefore being a possible measure of the cost of living.

**PCE price index**
An average of the current prices of the goods and services included in the consumption expenditure component of GDP expressed as a percentage of base-year prices.

A weakness of the PCE price index is that it is based on data that become known after the lapse of several months. So the CPI provides more current information about the inflation rate than what the PCE price index provides.

### PCE Price Index Excluding Food and Energy

Food and energy prices fluctuate much more than other prices and their changes can obscure the underlying trends in prices. By excluding these highly variable items, the underlying price level and inflation trends can be seen more clearly. The percentage change in the PCE price index excluding food and energy is called the **core inflation rate**.

**Core inflation rate**
The annual percentage increase in the PCE price index excluding the prices of food and energy.

Figure 22.3(a) shows the three consumer price inflation rates measured by the CPI, the PCE price index, and PCE price index excluding food and energy. These measures move up and down in similar ways, but the CPI measure exceeds the

PCE price index measures. The average difference between the CPI and PCE measures is about a half a percentage point. The core inflation rate has exactly the same average as the PCE inflation rate but fluctuates less. You can see why this measure provides a better indication of the inflation trend than the index that includes food and energy prices.

Figure 22.3(b) shows the three price *levels*. The two measures based on the PCE price index are very similar but the CPI measure rises above the other two and the gap widens to 40 percentage points over the 30 years shown here.

This higher CPI is a reflection of its bias and a confirmation that the PCE price index, which is based on current period actual expenditures, avoids most of the sources of bias in the CPI.

**FIGURE 22.3**

Three Measures of Consumer Prices

myeconlab Animation

The three measures of the inflation rate in part (a) fluctuate together, but the CPI inflation rate is higher than the PCE price index inflation rate or the core inflation rate. The core inflation rate fluctuates less than the other two measures.

In part (b), the CPI rises above the two PCE measures of the price level reflecting the bias in the CPI.

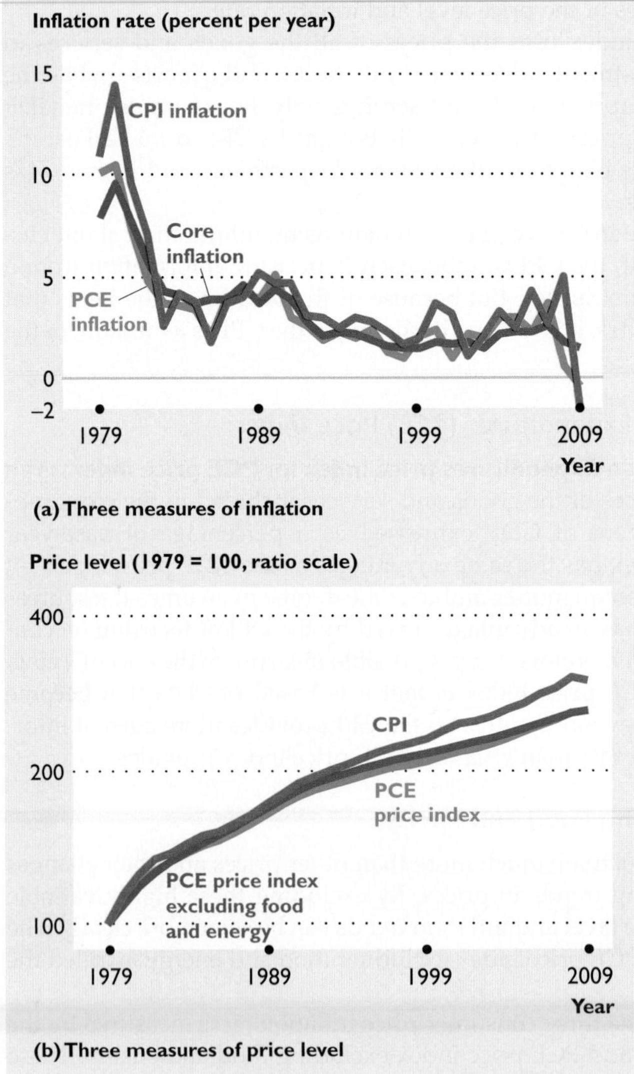


SOURCES OF DATA: Bureau of Labor Statistics and Bureau of Economic Analysis.

## CHECKPOINT 22.2

**Explain the limitations of the CPI and describe other measures of the price level.**

myeconlab

Work these problems in Study Plan 22.2 to get instant feedback.

### Practice Problems

Economists in the Statistics Bureau decide to check the CPI substitution bias. To do so, they conduct a Consumer Expenditure Survey in both 2008 and 2009. Table 1 shows the results of the survey. It shows the items that consumers buy and their prices. The Statistics Bureau fixes the reference base year as 2008. Use this information to work Problems **1** to **3**.

**TABLE 1**

| | 2008 | | 2009 | |
|---|---|---|---|---|
| **Item** | **Quantity** | **Price** | **Quantity** | **Price** |
| Broccoli | 10 | $3.00 | 15 | $3.00 |
| Carrots | 15 | $2.00 | 10 | $4.00 |

1. Calculate the CPI in 2009 if the CPI basket contains the 2008 quantities.
2. Calculate the CPI in 2009 if the CPI basket contains the 2009 quantities.
3. Is there any substitution bias in the CPI that uses the 2008 basket? Explain.
4. **News release**

   Personal consumption expenditures (PCE) increased from $9,978.2 billion in May to $10,019.6 billion in June, an increase of 0.4%. Real personal consumption expenditures decreased from $9,185.5 billion in May to $9,173.5 billion in June, a decrease of 0.1%.

   Source: Bureau of Economic Analysis, August 4, 2009

   Calculate the PCE price index in May 2009 and June 2009. How can real personal consumption expenditures decrease when personal consumption expenditures increases?

### Guided Solutions to Practice Problems

1. Table 2 shows the calculation of the CPI in 2009 when the CPI basket is made of the 2008 quantities. The cost of the 2008 basket at 2008 prices is $60, and the cost of the 2008 basket at 2009 prices is $90. So the CPI in 2009 using the 2008 basket is ($90 ÷ $60) × 100 = 150.

**TABLE 2**

| Item | 2008 basket at 2008 prices | 2008 basket at 2009 prices |
|---|---|---|
| Broccoli | $30 | $30 |
| Carrots | $30 | $60 |
| Total | $60 | $90 |

2. Table 3 shows the calculation of the CPI in 2009 when the CPI basket is made of the 2009 quantities. The cost of the 2009 basket at 2008 prices is $65, and the cost of the 2009 basket at 2009 prices is $85. So the CPI in 2009 using the 2009 basket is ($85 ÷ $65) × 100 = 131.

**TABLE 3**

| Item | 2009 basket at 2008 prices | 2009 basket at 2009 prices |
|---|---|---|
| Broccoli | $45 | $45 |
| Carrots | $20 | $40 |
| Total | $65 | $85 |

3. The CPI that uses the 2008 basket displays some bias. With the price of broccoli constant and the price of carrots rising, consumers buy fewer carrots and more broccoli and they spend $85 on vegetables. But they would have spent $90 if they had not substituted broccoli for some carrots. The cost of vegetables does not rise by 50 percent as shown by the CPI. Because of substitution, the cost of vegetables rises by only 42 percent ($85 is 42 percent greater than $60). Using the 2009 basket, the price of vegetables increases by only 31 percent ($85 compared with $65). The CPI is biased upward because it ignores the substitutions that people make when prices change.
4. The PCE price index = (Nominal PCE ÷ Real PCE) × 100. In May 2009, the PCE price index equaled (9,978.2 billion ÷ $9,185.5 billion) × 100, or 108.63. In June 2009, the PCE price index equaled ($10,019.6 billion ÷ $9,173.5 billion) × 100 or 109.22. The PCE price index rose by 0.55 percent, which exceeded the 0.4 percent increase in nominal PCE, so real PCE fell by 0.13 percent.

*Which postage stamp has the higher real price: the 2¢ stamp of 1909 or the 44¢ stamp of 2009?*

## 22.3 NOMINAL AND REAL VALUES

In 2009, it cost 44 cents to mail a first-class letter. One hundred years earlier, in 1909, that same letter would have cost 2 cents to mail. Does it *really* cost you 22 times the amount that it cost your great-great-grandmother to mail a letter?

You know that it does not. You know that a dollar today buys less than what a dollar bought in 1909, so the cost of a stamp has not really increased to 22 times its 1909 level. But has it increased at all? Did it really cost you any more to mail a letter in 2009 than it cost your great-great-grandmother in 1909?

The CPI can be used to answer questions like these. In fact, that is one of the main reasons for constructing a price index. Let's see how we can compare the price of a stamp in 1909 and the price of a stamp in 2009.

### Dollars and Cents at Different Dates

To compare dollar amounts at different dates, we need to know the CPI at those dates. Currently, the CPI has a base of 100 for 1982–1984. That is, the average of the CPI in 1982, 1983, and 1984 is 100. (The numbers for the three years are 96.4, 99.6, and 103.9, respectively. Calculate the average of these numbers and check that it is indeed 100.)

In 2009, the CPI was 214.5, and in 1909, it was 9.6. By using these two numbers, we can calculate the relative value of the dollar in 1909 and 2009. To do so, we divide the 2009 CPI by the 1909 CPI. That ratio is 214.5 ÷ 9.6 = 22.3. That is, prices on average were 22.3 times higher in 2009 than in 1909.

We can use this ratio to convert the price of a 2-cent stamp in 1909 into its 2009 equivalent. The formula for this calculation is

$$\text{Price of stamp in 2009 dollars} = \text{Price of stamp in 1909 dollars} \times \frac{\text{CPI in 2009}}{\text{CPI in 1909}}$$

$$= 2 \text{ cents} \times \frac{214.5}{9.6} = 44.69 \text{ cents.}$$

So your great-great-grandmother paid a bit more than you pay! It really cost her almost a cent more to mail that first-class letter as it cost you in 2009. She paid the equivalent of 44.69 cents in 2009 money, and you paid 44 cents.

We've just converted the 1909 price of a stamp to its 2009 equivalent. We can do a similar calculation the other way around—converting the 2009 price to its 1909 equivalent. The formula for this alternative calculation is

$$\text{Price of stamp in 1909 dollars} = \text{Price of stamp in 2009 dollars} \times \frac{\text{CPI in 1909}}{\text{CPI in 2009}}$$

$$= 44 \text{ cents} \times \frac{9.6}{214.5} = 1.97 \text{ cents.}$$

The interpretation of this number is that you pay the *equivalent* of 1.97 cents in 1909 dollars. Your *real* price of a stamp is 1.97 cents expressed in 1909 dollars.

The calculations that we've just done are examples of converting a *nominal* value into a *real* value. A nominal value is one that is expressed in current dollars. A real value is one that is expressed in the dollars of a given year. We're now going to see how we convert nominal macroeconomic variables into real variables using a similar method.

## Nominal and Real Values in Macroeconomics

Macroeconomics makes a big issue of the distinction between nominal and real values. Three nominal and real variables occupy a central position in macroeconomics. They are

- Nominal GDP and real GDP
- The nominal wage rate and the real wage rate
- The nominal interest rate and the real interest rate

We begin our examination of real and nominal variables in macroeconomics by reviewing what you've already learned about the distinction between nominal GDP and real GDP and interpreting that distinction in a new way.

## Nominal GDP and Real GDP

When we calculated the 1909 value of a 44 cent 2009 postage stamp, we multiplied the 2009 price by the ratio of the CPI in 1909 to the CPI in 2009. By this calculation, we found the "real" value of a 2009 stamp in 1909 dollars.

But when we calculated the real GDP of 2010 in 2005 dollars in Chapter 20 (pp. 520–521 and 535–537), we didn't multiply nominal GDP in 2010 by the ratio of a price index in the two years. Instead, we expressed the values of the goods and services produced in 2010 in terms of the prices that prevailed in 2005. We calculated real GDP directly.

But we can *interpret* real GDP in 2010 as nominal GDP in 2010 multiplied by the ratio of the GDP price index in 2005 to the GDP price index in 2010. The GDP price

# EYE on the U.S. ECONOMY

## Deflating the GDP Balloon

Nominal GDP increased every year between 1980 and 2008. Part of the increase reflects increased production, and part of it reflects rising prices.

You can think of GDP as a balloon that is blown up by growing production and rising prices. In the figure, the GDP price index or *GDP deflator* lets the inflation air—the contribution of rising prices—out of the nominal GDP balloon so that we can see what has happened to real GDP.

The small red balloon for 1980 shows real GDP in that year. The green balloon shows nominal GDP in 2008. The red balloon for 2008 shows real GDP for that year.

To see real GDP in 2008, we use the GDP price index to deflate nominal GDP. With the inflation air removed, we can see by how much real GDP grew from 1980 to 2008.

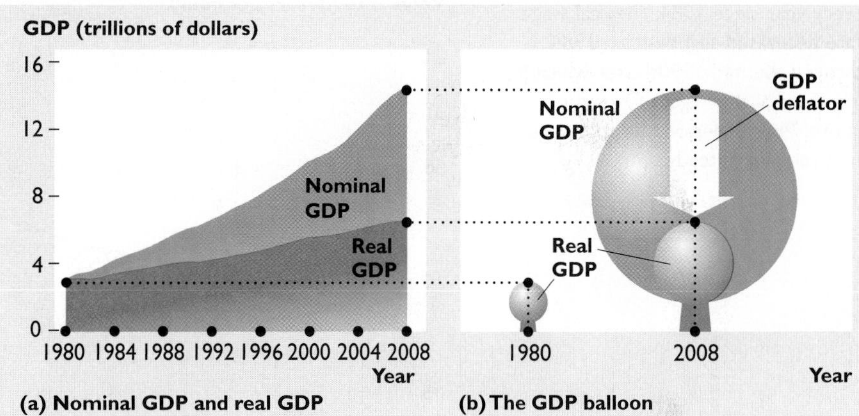


SOURCE OF DATA: Bureau of Economic Analysis.

index in 2005 (the base year) is defined to be 100, so we can interpret real GDP in any year as nominal GDP divided by the GDP price index in that year multiplied by 100. We don't calculate real GDP this way, but we can interpret it this way.

The GDP price index, or the CPI, or some other price index might be used to convert a nominal variable to a real variable.

## Nominal Wage Rate and Real Wage Rate

**Nominal wage rate**
The average hourly wage rate measured in *current* dollars.

**Real wage rate**
The average hourly wage rate measured in the dollars of a given reference base year.

The price of labor services is the wage rate—the income that an hour of labor earns. In macroeconomics, we are interested in economy-wide performance, so we focus on the *average* hourly wage rate. The **nominal wage rate** is the average hourly wage rate measured in *current* dollars. The **real wage rate** is the average hourly wage rate measured in the dollars of a given reference base year.

To calculate the real wage rate relevant to a consumer, we divide the nominal wage rate by the CPI and multiply by 100. That is,

$$\text{Real wage rate in 2008} = \frac{\text{Nominal wage rate in 2008}}{\text{CPI in 2008}} \times 100.$$

In 2008, the nominal wage rate (average hourly wage rate) of production workers was \$18.00 and the CPI was 215.3, so

$$\text{Real wage rate in 2008} = \frac{\$18.00}{215.3} \times 100 = \$8.36.$$

Because we measure the real wage rate in constant base-period dollars, a change in the real wage rate measures the change in the quantity of goods and ser-

**FIGURE 22.4**

Nominal and Real Wage Rates: 1984–2008

myeconlab Animation

The nominal wage rate has increased every year since 1984. The real wage rate decreased slightly from 1984 through the mid-1990s, after which it increased slightly again. Over the entire 24-year period, the real wage rate remained steady.

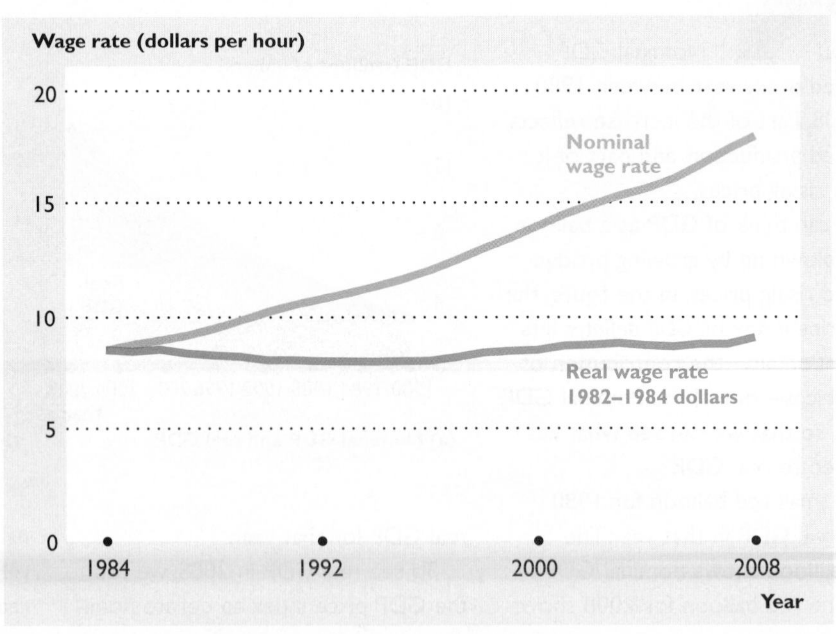


SOURCE OF DATA: *Economic Report of the President*, 2009.

vices that an hour's work can buy. In contrast, a change in the nominal wage rate measures a combination of a change in the quantity of goods and services that an hour's work can buy and a change in the price level. So the real wage rate removes the effects of inflation from the changes in the nominal wage rate.

The real wage rate is a significant economic variable because it measures the real reward for labor, which is a major determinant of the standard of living. The real wage rate is also significant because it measures the real cost of labor services, which influences the quantity of labor that firms are willing to hire.

Figure 22.4 shows what has happened to the nominal wage rate and the real wage rate in the United States between 1984 and 2008. The nominal wage rate is the average hourly earnings of production workers. This measure is just one of several different measures of average hourly earnings that we might have used.

The nominal wage rate increased from $8.48 an hour in 1984 to $18.00 an hour in 2008, but the real wage rate barely changed. In 1982–1984 dollars (the CPI base period dollars), the real wage rate in 2008 was only $8.36 an hour in 1982–1984 dollars.

The real wage rate barely changed as the nominal wage rate increased because the nominal wage rate grew at a rate almost equal to the inflation rate. When the effects of inflation are removed from the nominal wage rate, we can see what is happening to the buying power of the average wage rate.

You can also see that the real wage rate has fluctuated a little. It decreased slightly until the mid-1990s, after which it increased slightly.

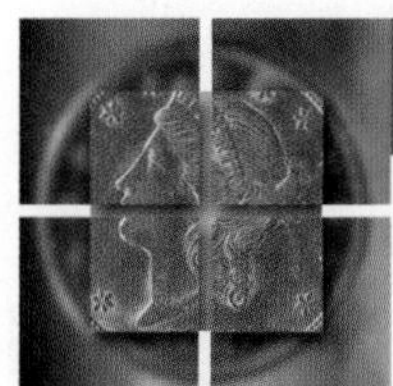

## EYE on the PAST

### The Nominal and Real Wage Rates of Presidents of the United States

Who earned more, Barack Obama in 2008, or George Washington in 1789? George Washington's pay was $25,000 (on the green line) but in 2005 dollars it was $521,000 (on the red line). Barack Obama was paid $400,000 in 2009.

But presidential accommodations are more comfortable today, and presidential travel arrangements are a breeze compared to earlier times. So adding in the perks of the job, Barack Obama doesn't get such a raw deal.

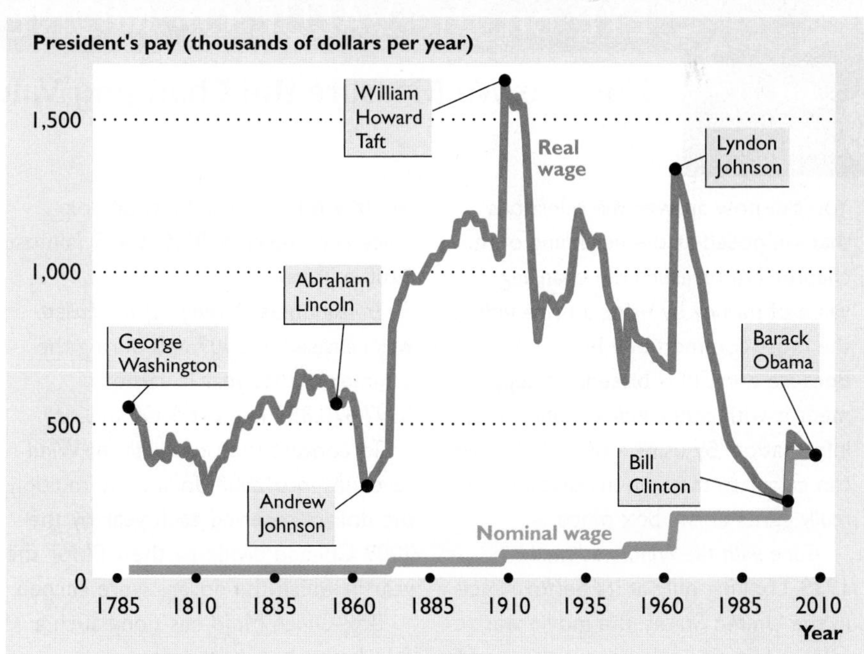


SOURCE OF DATA: Robert Sahr, Oregon State University, http://www.orst.edu/dept/pol_sci/sci/fac/sahr/sahr.htm.

## Nominal Interest Rate and Real Interest Rate

You've just seen that we can calculate real values from nominal values by deflating them using the CPI. And you've seen that to make this calculation, we *divide* the nominal value by a price index. Converting a nominal interest rate to a real interest rate is a bit different. To see why, we'll start with their definitions.

**Nominal interest rate**
The dollar amount of interest expressed as a percentage of the amount loaned.

**Real interest rate**
The goods and services forgone in interest expressed as a percentage of the amount loaned and calculated as the nominal interest rate minus the inflation rate.

A **nominal interest rate** is the dollar amount of interest expressed as a percentage of the amount loaned. For example, suppose that you have \$1,000 in a bank deposit—a loan by you to a bank—on which you receive interest of \$50 a year. The nominal interest rate is \$50 as a percentage of \$1,000, which is 5 percent a year.

A **real interest rate** is the goods and services forgone in interest expressed as a percentage of the amount loaned. Continuing with the above example, at the end of one year your bank deposit has increased to \$1,050—the original \$1,000 plus the \$50 interest. Suppose that prices have increased by 3 percent, so now you need \$1,030 to buy what \$1,000 would have bought a year earlier. How much interest have you *really* received? The answer is \$20, or a real interest rate of 2 percent a year.

To convert a nominal interest rate to a real interest rate, we *subtract* the *inflation rate*. That is,

$$\text{Real interest rate} = \text{Nominal interest rate} - \text{Inflation rate.}$$

Plug your numbers into this formula. Your nominal interest rate is 5 percent a year, and the inflation rate is 3 percent a year. Your real interest rate is 5 percent minus 3 percent, which equals 2 percent a year.

Figure 22.5 shows the nominal and the real interest rates in the United States between 1968 and 2008. When the inflation rate is high, the gap between the real interest rate and nominal interest rate is large. Sometimes, the real interest rate is negative (as it was in the mid-1970s) and the lender pays the borrower!

## EYE on the VALUE OF MONEY

### How Do We Measure the Changing Value of Money?

You can now answer the questions that we posed at the beginning of this chapter. We measure the changing value of money by using a price index, the most common one being the CPI. Because the CPI is biased, we supplement it with other indexes and other information. By using a price index, we can calculate the amount that a movie *really* earns at the box office.

*Gone with the Wind* was made in 1939. Looking only at its performance in the United States, the movie was re-released in nine subsequent years and by 2009 it had earned a total box office revenue of \$198,676,459 (almost \$200 million).

*Transformers: Revenge of the Fallen* was released in 2009 and during the summer of that year it earned \$397,470,858 (almost \$400 million).

To convert the *Gone with the Wind* revenues into 2009 dollars, we multiply the dollars received each year by the 2009 CPI and divide by the CPI for the year in which the dollars were earned.

Box-Office Mojo has done such a calculation, but rather than use the CPI, it uses the average prices of movie tickets (www.boxofficemojo.com).

According to Box-Office Mojo, valuing the tickets for *Gone with the Wind* at 2009 movie-ticket prices, it has earned \$1,450,680,400, or \$1,451 million, about 3.6 times *Transformers'* revenue.

Because Box-Office Mojo uses average ticket prices, the real variable that it compares is the number of tickets sold. The average ticket price in 2009 was \$7.18, so 202 million have seen *Gone with the Wind* and 55 million have seen *Transformers: Revenge of the Fallen.*

**FIGURE 22.5**

Nominal and Real Interest Rates: 1968–2008

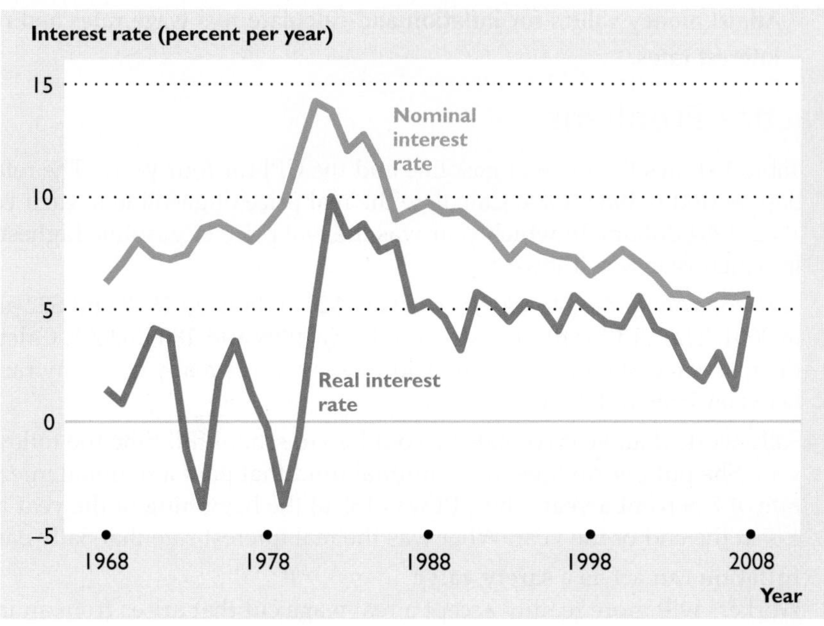


The real interest rate equals the nominal interest rate minus the inflation rate. The vertical gap between the nominal interest rate and the real interest rate is the inflation rate. The real interest rate is usually positive, but during the 1970s, it became negative.

SOURCE OF DATA: *Economic Report of the President,* 2009.

## EYE on YOUR LIFE

### A Student's CPI

The CPI measures the percentage change in the average prices paid for the basket of goods and services bought by a typical urban household.

A student is not a typical household. How have the prices of a student's basket of goods and services changed? The answer is by a lot more than those of an average household.

Suppose that a student spends 25 percent of her income on rent, 25 percent on tuition, 25 percent on books and study supplies, 10 percent on food, 10 percent on transportation, and 5 percent on clothing.

We can use these weights and the data collected by the BLS on individual price categories to find the student's CPI and the inflation rate that it implies.

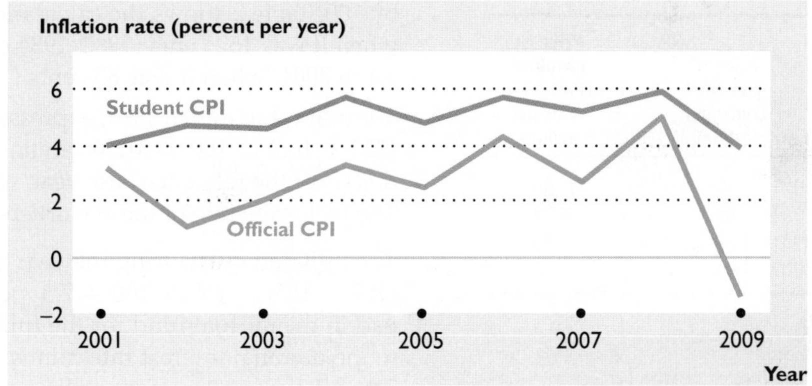


SOURCE OF DATA: Bureau of Labor Statistics.

The graph shows this student's inflation rate compared to that of the official CPI. Between 2001 and 2009, a student's CPI rose 23 percent above the official CPI. Rent, textbooks, and tuition are the main items whose prices rose faster than average.

Work these problems in Study Plan 22.3 to get instant feedback.

## CHECKPOINT 22.3

**Adjust money values for inflation and calculate real wage rates and real interest rates.**

### Practice Problems

**TABLE 1**

| Year | Price of gasoline (cents per gallon) | CPI |
|---|---|---|
| 1971 | 36 | 40.5 |
| 1981 | 138 | 90.9 |
| 1991 | 114 | 136.2 |
| 2001 | 146 | 176.6 |

1. Table 1 shows the price of gasoline and the CPI for four years. The reference base period is 1982–1984. Calculate the real price of gasoline in each year in 1982–1984 dollars. In which year was the real price of gasoline highest and in which year was it lowest?
2. Amazon.com agreed to pay its workers $20 an hour in 1999 and $22 an hour in 2001. The CPI for these years was 166 in 1999 and 180 in 2001. Calculate the real wage rate in each year. Did these workers really get a pay raise between 1999 and 2001?
3. Sally worked all year so that she could go to school full time the following year. She put her savings into a mutual fund that paid a nominal interest rate of 7 percent a year. The CPI was 165 at the beginning of the year and 177 at the end of the year. What was the real interest rate that Sally earned?
4. **Inflation can act as a safety valve**

   Workers will more readily accept a real wage cut that arises from an increase in the consumer prices than a cut in their nominal wage rate.

   Source: FT.com, May 28. 2009

   Explain why inflation influences a worker's real wage rate. Why might this observation be true?

### Guided Solutions to Practice Problems

**TABLE 2**

| Year | Price of gasoline (cents per gallon) | CPI | Price of gasoline (1982–1984 cents per gallon) |
|---|---|---|---|
| 1971 | 36 | 40.5 | 89 |
| 1981 | 138 | 90.9 | 152 |
| 1991 | 114 | 136.2 | 84 |
| 2001 | 146 | 176.6 | 83 |

1. To calculate the real price, divide the nominal price by the CPI and multiply by 100. Table 2 shows the calculations. The real price was highest in 1981, when it was 152 cents (1982–1984 cents) per gallon. The real price was lowest in 2001, when it was 83 cents (1982–1984 cents) per gallon.
2. The real wage rate in 1999, expressed in dollars of the reference base year, was ($20 ÷ 166) × 100 = $12.05 an hour. The real wage rate in 2001, expressed in dollars of the reference base year, was ($22 ÷ 180) × 100 = $12.22 an hour. The real wage rate of these workers increased between 1999 and 2001.
3. The inflation rate during the year that Sally worked was equal to $(177 - 165) \div 165 \times 100 = 7.3$ percent. On the savings that Sally had in the mutual fund for the full year, she earned a real interest rate equal to the nominal interest rate minus the inflation rate, which is $7.0 - 7.3 = -0.3$ percent. Sally's real interest rate was negative. (If Sally had just kept her savings in cash, her nominal interest rate would have been zero, and her real interest rate would have been −7.3 percent. She would have been worse off.)
4. The real wage rate in 2009 = (Nominal wage rate ÷ CPI in 2009) × 100. Inflation occurs when the CPI increases. If inflation during 2009 is 3 percent, then the CPI at the end of 2009 is 3 percent higher than at the start of 2009, and the real wage rate has fallen by 3 percent during 2009. Inflation gradually lowers the real wage rate over the year, while a cut in the nominal wage rate lowers the real wage rate at a point in time.

# CHAPTER SUMMARY

## Key Points

**1 Explain what the Consumer Price Index (CPI) is and how it is calculated.**

- The Consumer Price Index (CPI) is a measure of the average of the prices of the goods and services that an average urban household buys.
- The CPI is calculated by dividing the cost of the CPI market basket in the current period by its cost in the base period and then multiplying by 100.

**2 Explain the limitations of the CPI and describe other measures of the price level.**

- The CPI does not include all the items that contribute to the cost of living.
- The CPI cannot provide an accurate measure of price changes because of new goods, quality improvements, and substitutions that consumers make when relative prices change.
- Other measures of the price level include the GDP price index, the PCE price index, and the PCE price index excluding food and energy.
- Both the GDP price index and the PCE price index use current information on quantities and to some degree overcome the sources of bias in the CPI.
- The PCE price index excluding food and energy is used to calculate the core inflation rate, which shows the inflation trend.

**3 Adjust money values for inflation and calculate real wage rates and real interest rates.**

- To adjust a money value (also called a nominal value) for inflation, we express the value in terms of the dollars of a given year.
- To convert a dollar value of year *B* to the dollars of year *A*, multiply the value in year *B* by the price level in year *A* and divide by the price level in year *B*.
- The real wage rate equals the nominal wage rate divided by the CPI and multiplied by 100.
- The real interest rate equals the nominal interest rate minus the inflation rate.

## Key Terms

Consumer Price Index, 564
Core inflation rate, 573
Cost of living index, 570
Deflation, 567
GDP price index, 573
Inflation rate, 567
Nominal interest rate, 580
Nominal wage rate, 578
PCE price index, 573
Real interest rate, 580
Real wage rate, 578
Reference base period, 564

Work these problems in Chapter 22 Study Plan to get instant feedback.

# CHAPTER CHECKPOINT

## Study Plan Problems and Applications

1. Looking at some travel magazines, you read that the CPI in Turkey in 2008 was 434 and in Russia, it was 224. You do some further investigating and discover that the reference base period in Turkey is 2000 and in Russia it is 2001. The CPI in Russia in 2000 was 82. Calculate the percentage rise in the CPI in Turkey and in Russia from 2000 to 2008.
2. In Brazil, the reference base period for the CPI is 2000. By 2005, prices had risen by 51 percent since the base period. The inflation rate in Brazil in 2006 was 10 percent, and in 2007, the inflation rate was 9 percent. Calculate the CPI in Brazil in 2006 and 2007. Brazil's CPI in 2008 was 173. Did Brazil's inflation rate increase or decrease in 2008?
3. Tables 1 and 2 show the quantities of the goods that Suzie bought and the prices she paid during two consecutive weeks. Suzie's CPI market basket contains the goods she bought in Week 1. Calculate the cost of Suzie's CPI market basket in Week 1 and in Week 2. What percentage of the CPI market basket is gasoline? Calculate the value of Suzie's CPI in Week 2 and her inflation rate in Week 2.

**TABLE 1 DATA FOR WEEK 1**

| Item | Quantity | Price (per unit) |
|---|---|---|
| Coffee | 11 cups | \$3.25 |
| DVDs | 1 | \$25.00 |
| Gasoline | 15 gallons | \$2.50 |

**TABLE 2 DATA FOR WEEK 2**

| Item | Quantity | Price (per unit) |
|---|---|---|
| Coffee | 11 cups | \$3.25 |
| DVDs | 3 | \$12.50 |
| Gasoline | 5 gallons | \$3.00 |
| Concert | 1 ticket | \$95.00 |

Use the following information to work Problems 4 and 5.

The GDP price index in the United States in 2000 was about 90, and real GDP in 2000 was \$11 trillion (2005 dollars). The GDP price index in the United States in 2008 was about 108, and real GDP in 2008 was \$13.3 trillion (2005 dollars).

4. Calculate nominal GDP in 2000 and in 2008 and the percentage increase in nominal GDP between 2000 and 2008.
5. What was the percentage increase in production between 2000 and 2008, and by what percentage did the cost of living rise between 2000 and 2008?
6. Table 3 shows the prices that Terry paid for some of his expenditures in June and July 2009. Explain and discuss why these prices might have led to commodity substitution or outlet substitution.
7. In 2008, Annie, an 80-year-old, is telling her granddaughter Susie about the good old days. Annie says that in 1938, you could buy a nice house for \$15,000 and a jacket for \$5. Susie says that today such a house costs \$220,000 and such a jacket costs \$70. The CPI in 1938 was 14.1 and in 2008 it was 215.3. Which house and which jacket have the lower prices?

**TABLE 3**

| Item | Price in June | Price in July |
|---|---|---|
| | (dollars per unit) | |
| Steak | 4.11 | 4.01 |
| Bread | 3.25 | 3.12 |
| Bacon | 3.62 | 3.64 |
| Milk | 2.62 | 2.62 |
| Tomatoes | 1.60 | 1.62 |
| Apples | 1.18 | 1.19 |
| Bananas | 0.62 | 0.66 |
| Chicken | 1.28 | 1.26 |
| Lettuce | 1.64 | 1.68 |

Use the following information to work Problems 8 and 9.

**U.S. July CPI down 0.1%**

The CPI was down 0.1% in July in line with expectations. Housing prices fell 0.2%, while transportation prices rose 0.2% and apparel prices rose 0.6%.

Source: BLS, August 14, 2009

8. What percentage change in the CPI is accounted for by the changes in housing, transportation, and apparel in July 2009?
9. Given the changes in the prices of housing, transportation, and apparel, by what percentage did the prices of the other items in the CPI basket change?

## Instructor Assignable Problems and Applications

Your instructor can assign these problems as homework, a quiz, or a test in **MyEconLab**.

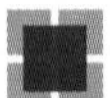

1. Made in 1982, *E.T.: The Extra-Terrestrial* earned $435 million at the box office. Made in 1997, *Titanic* earned $601 million. Using BLS data for the CPI in 1982 and 1997, determine which movie had the greater *real* box office revenues.
2. Pete is a student who spends 10 percent of his expenditure on books and supplies, 30 percent on tuition, 30 percent on rent, 10 percent on food and drink, 10 percent on transportation, and the rest on clothing. The price index for each item was 100 in 2000. Table 1 shows the prices in 2009. What is Pete's CPI in 2009? [Hint: The contribution of each item to the CPI is its price weighted by its share of total expenditure.] Did Pete experience a higher or lower inflation rate between 2000 and 2009 than the student whose CPI is shown on p. 581?
3. The people on Coral Island buy only juice and cloth. The CPI market basket contains the quantities bought in 2009. The average household spent $60 on juice and $30 on cloth in 2009 when the price of juice was $2 a bottle and the price of cloth was $5 a yard. In the current year, 2010, juice is $4 a bottle and cloth is $6 a yard. Calculate the CPI and the inflation rate in 2010.
4. Tables 2 and 3 show the quantities of the goods that Harry bought and the prices he paid during two consecutive weeks. Harry's CPI market basket contains the goods he bought in Week 1. Calculate Harry's CPI in Week 2. What was his inflation rate in Week 2?

**TABLE 1**

| Item | Price in 2009 |
|---|---|
| Books and supplies | 172.6 |
| Tuition | 169.0 |
| Rent | 159.0 |
| Food and drink | 129.8 |
| Transportation | 115.4 |
| Clothing | 92.9 |

**TABLE 2 DATA FOR WEEK 1**

| Item | Quantity | Price (per unit) |
|---|---|---|
| Coffee | 5 cups | $3.00 |
| iTunes songs | 5 | $1.00 |
| Gasoline | 10 gallons | $2.00 |

**TABLE 3 DATA FOR WEEK 2**

| Item | Quantity | Price (per unit) |
|---|---|---|
| Coffee | 4 cups | $3.25 |
| iTunes songs | 10 | $1.00 |
| Gasoline | 10 gallons | $3.00 |

Use the following information to work Problems 5 and 6.

The base year is 2005. Real GDP in 2005 was $10 trillion (2005 dollars). The GDP price index in 2009 was 112, and real GDP in 2009 was $11 trillion (2005 dollars).

5. Calculate nominal GDP in 2005 and in 2009 and the percentage increase in nominal GDP from 2005 to 2009.
6. What was the percentage increase in production from 2005 to 2009, and by what percentage did the cost of living rise from 2005 to 2009?

Use the following information to work Problems 7 and 8.

**Money market funds are yielding almost nothing**

Last month, the interest rate on a money fund averaged 0.08% a year and on 5-year CDs it was 2.6% a year. The inflation rate was 0.1% a year.

Source: *USA Today,* August 12, 2009

7. Calculate the real interest rates on each of these financial assets.
8. To maintain these real interest rates in the coming months, how will the nominal rates change if the inflation rate increases to 0.2 percent a year?
9. In Sahara, the CPI market basket contains 80 bottles of water, 20 units of food, and 10 units of housing. In Arctica, the CPI market basket contains 80 units of housing, 20 units of food, and no bottled water. The prices in these two countries are the same. In the base year, water is $1 a unit, food is $5 a unit, and housing is $10 a unit. In the current year, water is $2 a unit, food is $6 a unit, and housing is $11 a unit. In the current year, calculate the CPI and the inflation rate in each country. Which country's CPI is rising faster?

10. In 1988, the average wage rate was $9.45 an hour and in 2008 the average wage rate was $18.00 an hour. The CPI in 1988 was 118.3 and in 2008 it was 215.3. Which real wage rate is higher?

11. Table 3 sets out the CPI for the United States and for four regions of the United States in May 2008 and 2009. In which region was the price level highest in May 2009? In which regions did consumer prices fall by more than the U.S. average? In which region was the fall in consumer prices the smallest?

**TABLE 3 CPI IN MAY**

| Region | 2008 | 2009 |
|---|---|---|
| Midwest | 207 | 203 |
| Northeast | 230 | 228 |
| West | 221 | 218 |
| South | 210 | 207 |
| United States | 217 | 214 |

12. If the interest rate is 19 percent a year in Argentina and 0.01 percent a year in Japan, and the inflation rate is 39 percent a year in Argentina and −0.9 percent a year in Japan, which country has the higher real interest rate?

13. Table 4 shows the prices of the major components of the U.S. CPI market basket in August 2007 and August 2008. In August 2007, the CPI was 207.9 and in August 2008, it was 219.1. Compared to the CPI market basket, which components experienced a higher price increase and which experienced a lower price increase?

**TABLE 4 PRICES IN AUGUST**

| Item | 2007 | 2008 |
|---|---|---|
| Food | 203.9 | 216.4 |
| Apparel | 114.4 | 116.4 |
| Housing | 211.1 | 219.1 |
| Transport | 184.5 | 206.7 |
| Medical care | 353.0 | 364.5 |
| Education | 120.3 | 124.7 |
| Other goods | 333.3 | 347.0 |

14. In 1982–1984 dollars, the real average hourly wage rate in 2006 was $8.24 and in 2007, it was $8.32. In 2006, the CPI was 201.6 and in 2007, the CPI was 207.3. Calculate the nominal wage rates in 2006 and 2007.

Use the following information to work Problems 15 and 16.

Imagine that you are given $1,000 to spend and told that you must spend it all buying items from a Sears' catalog. But you do have a choice of catalog. You may select from the 1903 catalog or from Sears.com today. You will pay the prices quoted in the catalog that you choose.

15. Why might you lean toward choosing the 1903 catalog? Why might you lean toward choosing Sears.com?

16. Which catalog will you choose and why? Refer to any biases in the CPI that might be relevant to your choice.

17. Bureau of Economic Analysis data show that for the period 1929 through 2008 the average annual increase in the GDP price index is 3.0 percent. The Bureau of Labor Statistics data show that for the period 1929 through 2008, the average annual increase in the CPI is 3.2 percent. Although the difference of 0.2 percentage points is small, maintained over the 79 year period, the CPI rose by 17 percent more than the GDP price index. How would you explain the difference in these two inflation measures?

18. Bureau of Economic Analysis data show that with base year 2005 = 100, the GDP price index was 109.7 in the second quarter of 2009. In that same quarter, the PCE price index was 108.8. Given the further information that the prices of capital goods (investment) and foreign traded goods (exports and imports) increased at a slower pace than the prices of consumption goods and services, how would you explain the difference in the GDP price index and PCE price index measures of inflation?

## Why do Americans earn more and produce more than Europeans?

Compared to the average European, the average American works longer hours, produces more, earns more, and faces a labor market with less unemployment. Why?

# Potential GDP and the Natural Unemployment Rate

CHAPTER CHECKLIST

**When you have completed your study of this chapter, you will be able to**

1 Explain what determines potential GDP.

2 Explain what determines the natural unemployment rate.

## MACROECONOMIC APPROACHES AND PATHWAYS

In the three previous chapters, you learned how economists define and measure real GDP, employment and unemployment, the price level, and the inflation rate—the key variables that *describe* macroeconomic performance. Your task in this chapter and those that follow is to learn the *macroeconomic theory* that *explains* macroeconomic performance and provides the basis for *policies* that might improve it.

The macroeconomic theory that we present is today's consensus view on how the economy works. But it isn't the view of all macroeconomists. Today's consensus is a merger of three earlier schools of thought that have sharply contrasting views about the causes of recessions and the best policies for dealing with them. Some economists continue to identify with these schools of thought, and the severity of the 2008–2009 global recession intensified debate and gave economists of all shades of opinion a platform from which to present their views.

We begin with an overview of the three schools of thought from which today's consensus has emerged.

## The Three Main Schools of Thought

The three main schools of macroeconomic thought are:

- Classical macroeconomics
- Keynesian macroeconomics
- Monetarist macroeconomics

### Classical Macroeconomics

**Classical macroeconomics**
The view that the market economy works well, that aggregate fluctuations are a natural consequence of an expanding economy, and that government intervention cannot improve the efficiency of the market economy.

According to **classical macroeconomics**, markets work well and deliver the best available macroeconomic performance. Aggregate fluctuations are a natural consequence of an expanding economy with rising living standards, and government intervention can only hinder the ability of the market to allocate resources efficiently. The first classical macroeconomists included Adam Smith, David Ricardo, and John Stuart Mill, all of whom worked in the 18th and 19th centuries. Modern day classical economists include the 2004 Nobel Laureates Edward C. Prescott of the University of Arizona and Finn E. Kydland of Carnegie-Mellon University and the University of California at Santa Barbara.

Classical macroeconomics fell into disrepute during the Great Depression of the 1930s, a time when many people believed that *capitalism*, the political system of private ownership, free markets, and democratic political institutions, could not survive and began to advocate *socialism*, a political system based on state ownership of capital and central economic planning.

Classical macroeconomics predicted that the Great Depression would eventually end but offered no method for ending it more quickly.

### Keynesian Macroeconomics

**Keynesian macroeconomics**
The view that the market economy is inherently unstable and needs active government intervention to achieve full employment and sustained economic growth.

According to **Keynesian macroeconomics**, the market economy is inherently unstable and requires active government intervention to achieve full employment and sustained economic growth. One person, John Maynard Keynes, and his book *The General Theory of Employment, Interest, and Money*, published in 1936, began this school of thought. Keynes' theory was that depression and high unemployment occur when households don't spend enough on consumption goods and services and businesses don't spend enough investing in new capital. That is, too little *private* spending is the cause of depression (and recession). To counter the problem of too little private spending, *government* spending must rise.

This Keynesian view picked up many followers and by the 1950s it was the mainstream, but it lost popularity during the inflationary 1970s when it seemed ever more remote from the problems of that decade. The global recession of 2008–2009 and the fear of another great depression revived interest in Keynesian ideas and brought a new wave of attacks on classical macroeconomics with Nobel Laureate Paul Krugman leading the charge in the columns of the *New York Times*.

### Monetarist Macroeconomics

According to **monetarist macroeconomics**, the *classical* view of the world is broadly correct but in addition to fluctuations that arise from the normal functioning of an expanding economy, fluctuations in the quantity of money also bring the business cycle. A slowdown in the growth rate of money brings recession and a large decrease in the quantity of money brought the Great Depression.

**Monetarist macroeconomics**
The view that the market economy works well, that aggregate fluctuations are a natural consequence of an expanding economy, but that fluctuations in the quantity of money also bring the business cycle.

Milton Friedman, intellectual leader of the Chicago School of economists during the 1960s and 1970s, was the most prominent monetarist. The view that monetary contractions are the sole source of recessions and depressions is held by few economists today. But the view that the quantity of money plays a role in economic fluctuations is accepted by all economists and is part of today's consensus.

## ■ Today's Consensus

Each of the earlier schools provides insights and ingredients that survive in today's consensus. *Classical* macroeconomics provides the story of the economy at or close to full employment. But the classical approach doesn't explain how the economy performs in the face of a major slump in spending.

*Keynesian* macroeconomics takes up the story in a recession or depression. When spending is cut and the demand for most goods and services and the demand for labor all decrease, prices and wage rates don't fall but the quantity of goods and services sold and the quantity of labor employed do fall and the economy goes into recession. In a recession, an increase in spending by governments, or a tax cut that leaves people with more of their earnings to spend, can help to restore full employment.

*Monetarist* macroeconomics elaborates the Keynesian story by emphasizing that a contraction in the quantity of money brings higher interest rates and borrowing costs, which are a major source of cuts in spending that bring recession. Increasing the quantity of money and lowering the interest rate in a recession can help to restore full employment. And keeping the quantity of money growing steadily in line with the expansion of the economy's production possibilities can help to keep inflation in check and can also help to moderate the severity of a recession.

Another component of today's consensus is the view that the *long-term* problem of economic growth is more important than the *short-term* problem of recessions. Take a look at *Eye on the U.S. Economy,* on p. 590, and you will see why. Even a small slowdown in economic growth brings a huge cost in terms of a permanently lower level of income per person. This cost is much larger than that arising from the income lost during recessions. But the costs of recessions are serious because they are concentrated on those who are unemployed.

## The Road Ahead

This book bases your tour of macroeconomics on the new consensus. We begin in this chapter and the two that follow by explaining what determines potential GDP and the pace at which it grows. We then study money and explain what brings inflation. Finally, we explain how real and monetary forces interact to bring about the business cycle. We also explain the policy tools available to governments and central banks to improve macroeconomic performance.

## EYE on the U.S. ECONOMY

### The Lucas Wedge and the Okun Gap

During the 1960s, U.S. real GDP per person grew at a rate of 2.9 percent a year. The black line in part (a) shows the path that would have been followed if this growth rate had been maintained. After 1970, growth slowed to 2.0 percent per year and the red line shows the path that potential GDP followed. University of Chicago economist Robert E. Lucas, Jr. pointed out the large output loss that resulted from this growth slowdown. Part (a) shows this loss as the **Lucas wedge**, which is equivalent to a staggering $284,500 per person or more than 6 years' income.

Real GDP fluctuates around potential GDP and when the output gap is negative, output is lost. Brookings Institution economist Arthur B. Okun drew attention to this loss. Part (b) shows this loss as the **Okun gap**, which is equivalent to $12,850 per person or about 3 months' income.

Smoothing the business cycle and eliminating the Okun gap has a big payoff. But finding ways of restoring real GDP growth to its 1960s rate has a vastly bigger payoff.

Sources of Data: Bureau of Economic Analysis and the Congressional Budget Office.

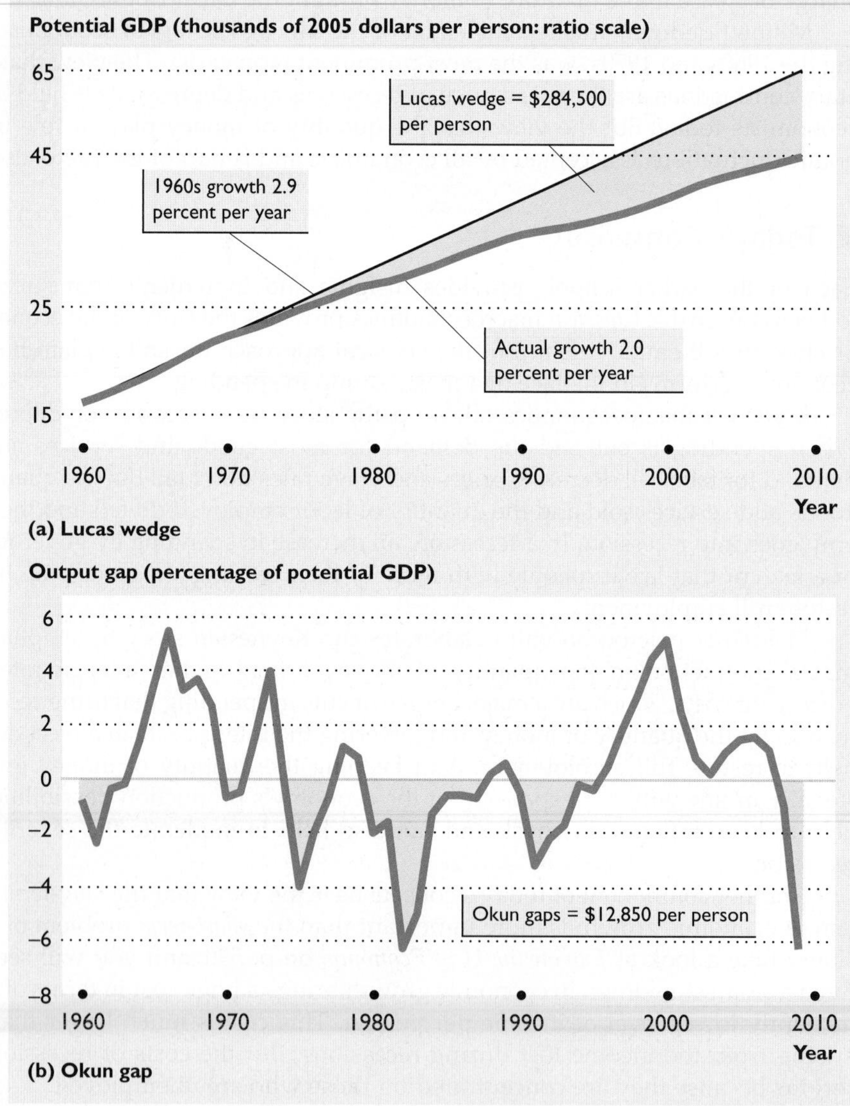


(a) Lucas wedge

(b) Okun gap

## 23.1 POTENTIAL GDP

**Potential GDP** is the value of real GDP when all the economy's factors of production—labor, capital, land, and entrepreneurial ability—are fully employed. It is vital to understand the forces that determine potential GDP for three reasons. First, when the economy is *at* full employment, real GDP equals potential GDP; so actual real GDP is determined by the same factors that determine potential GDP. Second, real GDP can exceed potential GDP only temporarily as it approaches and then recedes from a business cycle peak. So potential GDP is the *sustainable* upper limit of production. Third, real GDP fluctuates around potential GDP, which means that on the average over the business cycle, real GDP equals potential GDP.

**Potential GDP**
The value of real GDP when all the economy's factors of production—labor, capital, land, and entrepreneurial ability—are fully employed.

We produce the goods and services that make up real GDP by using the *factors of production:* labor and human capital, physical capital, land (and natural resources), and entrepreneurship. At any given time, the quantities of capital, land, and entrepreneurship and the state of technology are fixed. But the quantity of labor is not fixed. It depends on the choices that people make about the allocation of time between work and leisure. So with fixed quantities of capital, land, and entrepreneurship and fixed technology, real GDP depends on the quantity of labor employed. To describe this relationship between real GDP and the quantity of labor employed, we use a relationship that is similar to the production possibilities frontier, which is called the production function.

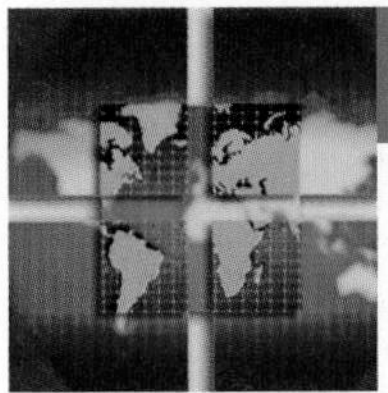

## EYE on the GLOBAL ECONOMY

### Potential GDP in the United States and European Union

In 2008, potential GDP per person in the United States was $44,000. In 11 major European economies, it was only $32,000—a gap of 38 percent. (Both numbers are measured in 2005 U.S. dollars.) Part (a) of the figure shows this large difference.

In the United States in 2008, the real wage rate was $34 an hour and in Europe, it was $29 an hour—a 17 percent gap.

How can the average American produce 38 percent more than the average European but earn in wages only 17 percent more?

The answer is that Americans work more than Europeans and in two ways.

First, 48 out of every 100 Americans have jobs compared with 46 out of every 100 Europeans.

Second, Europeans work shorter hours than Americans—30.5 hours a week compared to the 34 hours that an average American works—a 12 percent difference shown in part (c).

Europeans achieve their shorter work hours by taking longer vacations and having more sick days than Americans.

This chapter will enable you to understand the deeper sources of these differences in production and work.

Sources of data: Bureau of Economic Analysis, Bureau of Labor Statistics, and International Monetary Fund.

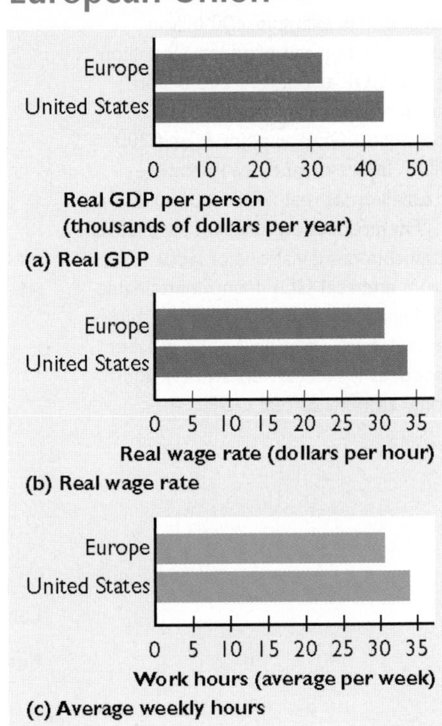

(a) Real GDP

(b) Real wage rate

(c) Average weekly hours

## The Production Function

**Production function**
A relationship that shows the maximum quantity of real GDP that can be produced as the quantity of labor employed changes and all other influences on production remain the same.

The **production function** is a relationship that shows the maximum quantity of real GDP that can be produced as the quantity of labor employed changes and all other influences on production remain the same. Figure 23.1 shows a production function, which is the curve labeled *PF*.

In Figure 23.1, 100 billion labor hours can produce a real GDP of $9 trillion (at point *A*); 200 billion hours can produce a real GDP of $13 trillion (at point *B*); and 300 billion hours can produce a real GDP of $16 trillion (at point *C*).

The production function shares a feature of the *production possibilities frontier* that you studied in Chapter 3 (p. 62). Like the *PPF*, the production function is a boundary between the attainable and the unattainable. It is possible to produce at any point along the production function and beneath it in the shaded area. But it is not possible to produce at points above the production function. Those points are unattainable.

**Diminishing returns**
The tendency for each additional hour of labor employed to produce a successively smaller additional amount of real GDP.

The production function displays **diminishing returns**—each additional hour of labor employed produces a successively smaller additional amount of real GDP. The first 100 billion hours of labor produces $9 trillion of real GDP. The second 100 billion hours of labor increases real GDP to $13 trillion and so produces only an

**FIGURE 23.1**

The Production Function

The production function shows the maximum quantity of real GDP that can be produced as the quantity of labor employed changes and all other influences on production remain the same. In this example, 100 billion hours of labor can produce $9 trillion of real GDP at point *A*, 200 billion hours of labor can produce $13 trillion of real GDP at point *B*, and 300 billion hours of labor can produce $16 trillion of real GDP at point *C*.

The production function separates attainable combinations of labor hours and real GDP from unattainable combinations and displays diminishing returns: Each additional hour of labor produces a successively smaller additional amount of real GDP.

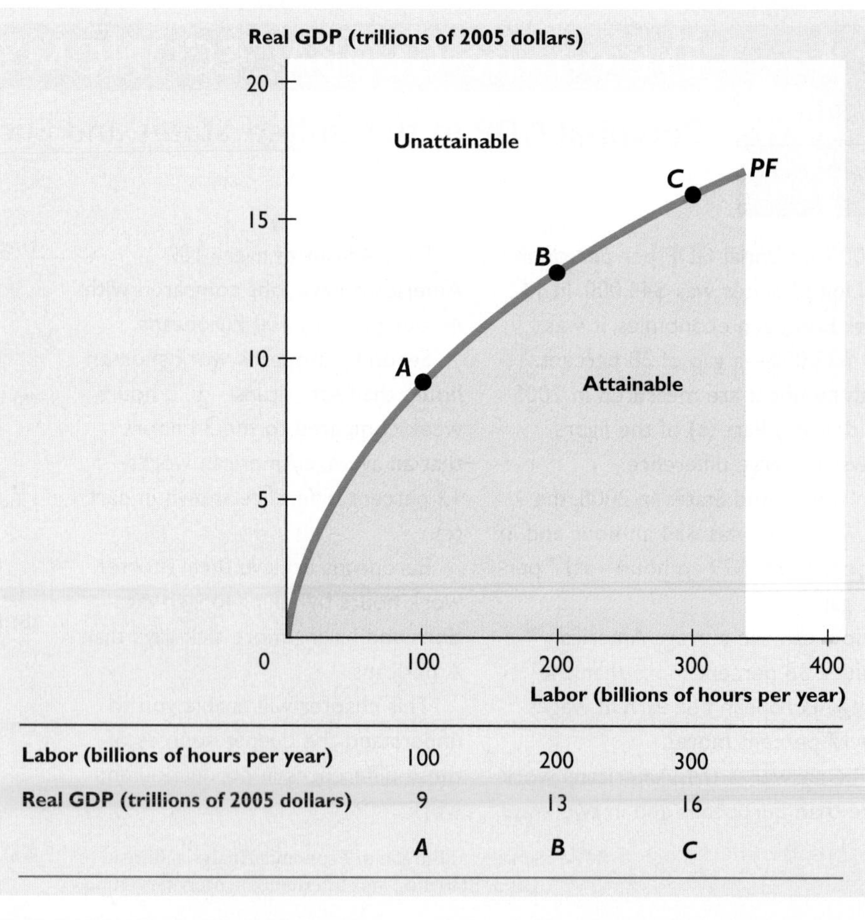


| Labor (billions of hours per year) | 100 | 200 | 300 |
|---|---|---|---|
| Real GDP (trillions of 2005 dollars) | 9 | 13 | 16 |
| | A | B | C |

additional $4 trillion of real GDP. The third 100 billion hours of labor increases real GDP to $16 trillion and so produces only an additional $3 trillion of real GDP.

Diminishing returns arise because the quantity of capital (and other factors of production) is fixed. As more labor is hired, the additional output produced decreases because the extra workers have less capital with which to work. For example, a forest service has three chain saws and an axe and hires three workers to clear roads and trails of fallen trees and debris during the spring thaw. Hiring a fourth worker will contribute less to the amount cleared than the amount that the third worker added, and hiring a fifth worker will add even less.

Because real GDP depends on the quantity of labor employed, potential GDP depends on the production function and the quantity of labor employed. To find potential GDP, we must understand what determines the quantity of labor employed.

## The Labor Market

You've already studied the tool that we use to determine the quantity of labor employed: demand and supply. In macroeconomics, we apply the concepts of demand, supply, and market equilibrium to the economy-wide labor market.

The quantity of labor employed depends on firms' decisions about how much labor to hire (the demand for labor). It also depends on households' decisions about how to allocate time between employment and other activities (the supply of labor). And it depends on how the labor market coordinates the decisions of firms and households (labor market equilibrium). So we will study

- The demand for labor
- The supply of labor
- Labor market equilibrium

### The Demand for Labor

The **quantity of labor demanded** is the total labor hours that all the firms in the economy plan to hire during a given time period at a given real wage rate. The **demand for labor** is the relationship between the quantity of labor demanded and the real wage rate when all other influences on firms' hiring plans remain the same. The lower the real wage rate, the greater is the quantity of labor demanded.

**Quantity of labor demanded**
The total labor hours that all the firms in the economy plan to hire during a given time period at a given real wage rate.

**Demand for labor**
The relationship between the quantity of labor demanded and the real wage rate when all other influences on firms' hiring plans remain the same.

The real wage rate is the *nominal wage rate* (the dollars per hour that people earn on average) divided by the price level (see Chapter 22, p. 578). We express the real wage rate in constant dollars—today in 2005 dollars. Think of the real wage rate as the quantity of real GDP that an hour of labor earns.

The lower the real wage rate, the greater is the quantity of labor that firms find it profitable to hire. The real wage rate influences the quantity of labor demanded because what matters to firms is not the number of dollars they pay for an hour of labor (the nominal wage rate) but how much output they must sell to earn those dollars. So firms compare the extra output that an hour of labor can produce with the real wage rate.

If an additional hour of labor produces at least as much additional output as the real wage rate, a firm hires that labor. At a small quantity of labor, an extra hour of labor produces more output than the real wage rate. But each additional hour of labor produces less additional output than the previous hour. As a firm hires more labor, eventually the extra output from an extra hour of labor equals the real wage rate. This equality determines the quantity of labor demanded at the real wage rate.

***The Demand for Labor in a Soda Factory*** You might understand the demand for labor better by thinking about a single firm rather than the economy as a whole. Suppose that the money wage rate is $15 an hour and that the price of a bottle of soda is $1.50. For the soda factory, the real wage rate is a number of bottles of soda. To find the soda factory's real wage rate, divide the money wage rate by the price of its output—$15 an hour ÷ $1.50 a bottle. The real wage rate is 10 bottles of soda an hour. It costs the soda factory 10 bottles of soda to hire an hour of labor. As long as the soda factory can hire labor that produces more than 10 additional bottles of soda an hour, it is profitable to hire more labor. Only when the extra output produced by an extra hour of labor falls to 10 bottles an hour has the factory reached the profit-maximizing quantity of labor.

***Labor Demand Schedule and Labor Demand Curve*** We can represent the demand for labor as either a demand schedule or a demand curve. The table in Figure 23.2 shows part of a demand for labor schedule. It tells us the quantity of labor demanded at three different real wage rates. For example, if the real wage rate is $40 an hour (row *B*), the quantity of labor demanded is 200 billion hours a year. If the real wage rate rises to $65 an hour (row *A*), the quantity of labor demanded decreases to 100 billion hours a year. And if the real wage rate falls to $20 an hour (row *C*), the quantity of labor demanded increases to 300 billion hours a year.

Figure 23.2 shows the demand for labor curve. Points *A*, *B*, and *C* on the demand curve correspond to rows *A*, *B*, and *C* of the demand schedule.

**FIGURE 23.2**

The Demand for Labor

myeconlab Animation

Firms are willing to hire labor only if the labor produces more than its real wage rate. So the lower the real wage rate, the more labor firms can profitably hire and the greater is the quantity of labor demanded.

At a real wage rate of $40 an hour, the quantity of labor demanded is 200 billion hours at point *B*.

1 If the real wage rate rises to $65 an hour, the quantity of labor demanded decreases to 100 billion hours at point *A*.

2 If the real wage rate falls to $20 an hour, the quantity of labor demanded increases to 300 billion hours at point *C*.

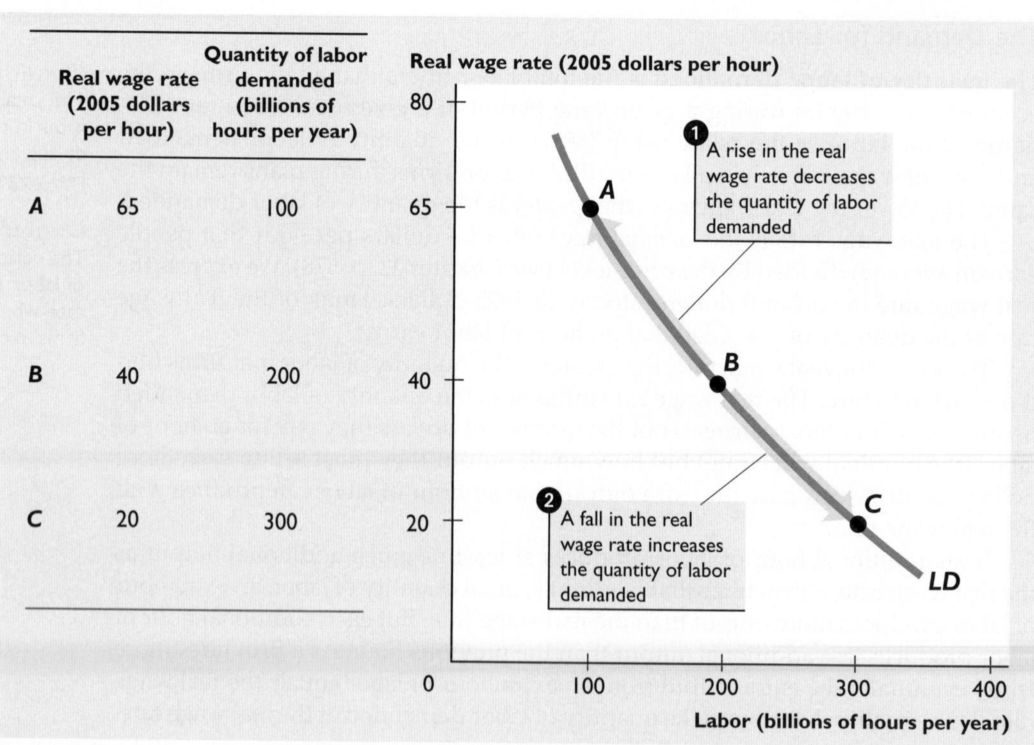

| | Real wage rate (2005 dollars per hour) | Quantity of labor demanded (billions of hours per year) |
|---|---|---|
| A | 65 | 100 |
| B | 40 | 200 |
| C | 20 | 300 |

## The Supply of Labor

The **quantity of labor supplied** is the number of labor hours that all the households in the economy plan to work during a given time period at a given real wage rate. The **supply of labor** is the relationship between the quantity of labor supplied and the real wage rate when all other influences on work plans remain the same.

We can represent the supply of labor as either a supply schedule or a supply curve. The table in Figure 23.3 shows a supply of labor schedule. It tells us the quantity of labor supplied at three different real wage rates. For example, if the real wage rate is $40 an hour (row *B*), the quantity of labor supplied is 200 billion hours a year. If the real wage rate falls to $20 an hour (row *A*), the quantity of labor supplied decreases to 100 billion hours a year. And if the real wage rate rises to $60 an hour (row *C*), the quantity of labor supplied increases to 300 billion hours a year.

Figure 23.3 shows the supply of labor curve. It corresponds to the supply schedule, and the points *A*, *B*, and *C* on the supply curve correspond to the rows *A*, *B*, and *C* of the supply schedule.

The real wage rate influences the quantity of labor supplied because what matters to people is not the number of dollars they earn but what those dollars will buy.

The quantity of labor supplied increases as the real wage rate increases for two reasons:

- Hours per person increase.
- Labor force participation increases.

**Quantity of labor supplied**
The number of labor hours that all the households in the economy plan to work during a given time period at a given real wage rate.

**Supply of labor**
The relationship between the quantity of labor supplied and the real wage rate when all other influences on work plans remain the same.

**FIGURE 23.3**

The Supply of Labor

myeconlab Animation

| | Real wage rate (2005 dollars per hour) | Quantity of labor supplied (billions of hours per year) |
|---|---|---|
| C | 60 | 300 |
| B | 40 | 200 |
| A | 20 | 100 |

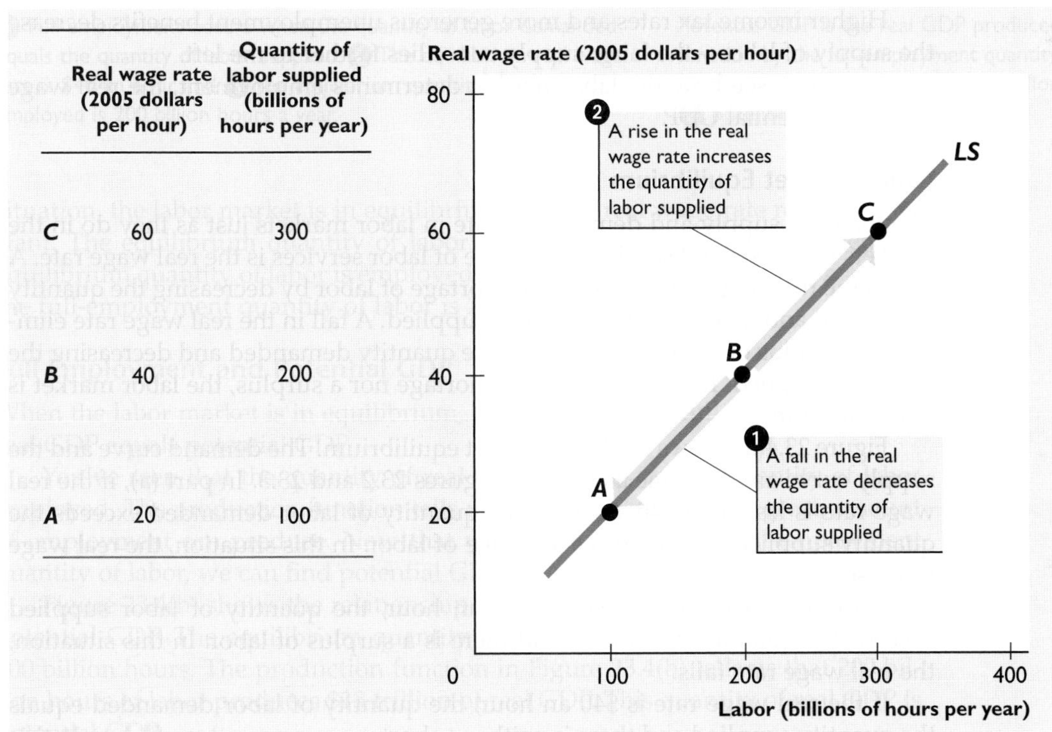


Households are willing to supply labor only if the real wage rate is high enough to attract them from other activities. The higher the real wage rate, the greater is the quantity of labor supplied.

At a real wage rate of $40 an hour, the quantity of labor supplied is 200 billion hours at point *B*.

1 If the real wage rate falls to $20 an hour, the quantity of labor supplied decreases to 100 billion hours at point *A*.

2 If the real wage rate rises to $60 an hour, the quantity of labor supplied increases to 300 billion hours at point *C*.

# EYE on U.S. POTENTIAL GDP

## Why Do Americans Earn More and Produce More Than Europeans?

The quantity of capital per worker is greater in the United States than in Europe, and U.S. technology, on the average, is more productive than European technology.

These differences between the United States and Europe mean that U.S. labor is more productive than European labor.

Because U.S. labor is more productive than European labor, U.S. employers are willing to pay more for a given quantity of labor than European employers are. So the demand for labor curve in the United States, $LD_{US}$, lies to the right of the European demand for labor curve, $LD_{EU}$, in part (a) of the figure.

This difference in the productivity of labor also means that the U.S. production function, $PF_{US}$, lies above the European production function, $PF_{EU}$, in part (b) of the figure.

Higher income taxes and unemployment benefits in Europe mean that to induce a person to take a job, a firm in Europe must offer a higher wage rate than a firm in the United States has to offer. So the European labor supply curve, $LS_{EU}$, lies to the left of the U.S. labor supply curve, $LS_{US}$.

Equilibrium employment is higher in the United States than in Europe—Americans work longer hours—and equilibrium real wage rate is higher in the United States than in Europe.

Potential GDP is higher in the United States than in Europe for two reasons: U.S. workers are more productive per hour of work and they work longer hours than Europeans.

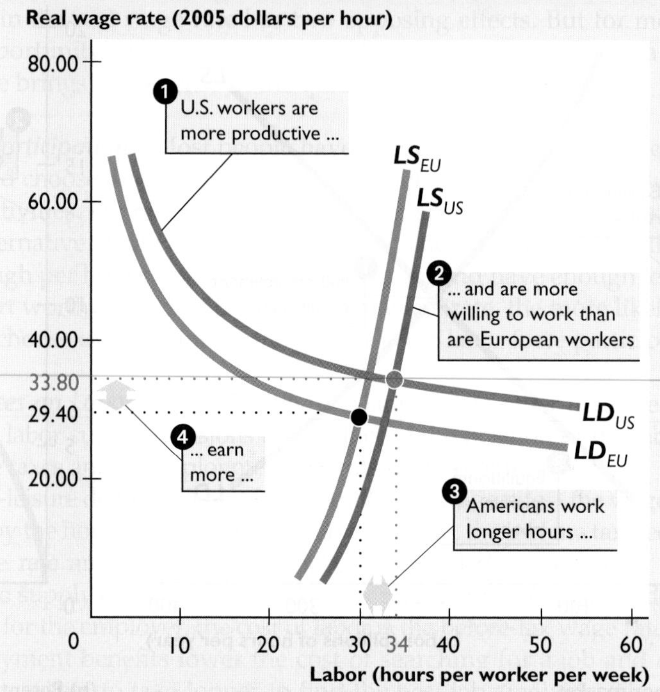


**(a) Labor market in Europe and the United States**

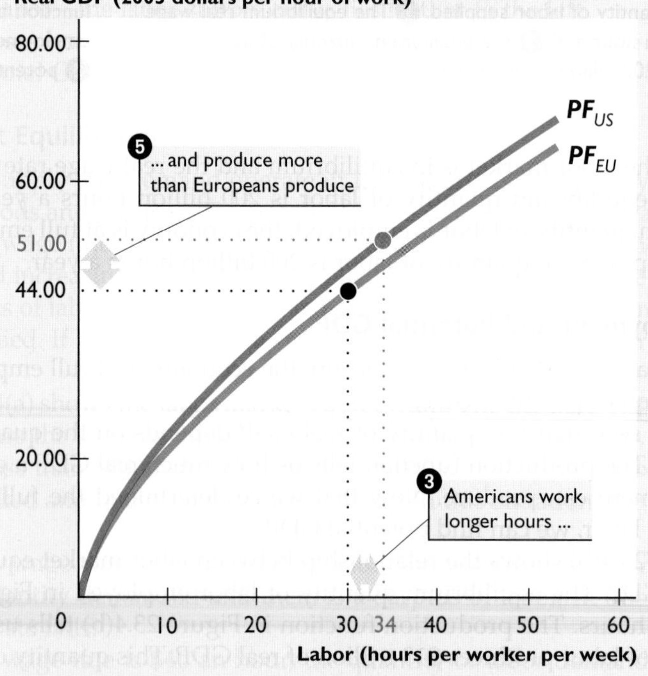


**(b) Production function in Europe and the United States**

# CHECKPOINT 23.1

Work these problems in Study Plan 23.1 to get instant feedback.

**Explain what determines potential GDP.**

## Practice Problems

1. Table 1 describes an economy's production function and demand for labor.

**TABLE 1**

| | | | | | |
|---|---|---|---|---|---|
| Quantity of labor demanded (billions of hours per year) | 0 | 1 | 2 | 3 | 4 |
| Real GDP (billions of 2005 dollars) | 0 | 40 | 70 | 90 | 100 |
| Real wage rate (2005 dollars per hour) | 50 | 40 | 30 | 20 | 10 |

Table 2 describes the supply of labor in this economy.

**TABLE 2**

| | | | | | |
|---|---|---|---|---|---|
| Quantity of labor supplied (billions of hours per year) | 0 | 1 | 2 | 3 | 4 |
| Real wage rate (2005 dollars per hour) | 10 | 20 | 30 | 40 | 50 |

Use the data in Tables 1 and 2 to make graphs of the labor market and production function. What are the equilibrium, real wage rate, and employment? What is potential GDP?

2. **Chevron signs $73b gas deal**

Gorgon, Chevron's huge liquefied natural gas project, is finally going forward. The company, along with Exxon Mobil and Shell will produce natural gas off the northwest coast of Australia. Gorgon and surrounding fields hold an estimated 40 trillion cubic feet of natural gas, the equivalent of 6.7 billion barrels of oil. Gorgon is located for easy shipment to growing markets in China and India and at its peak will employ 10,000 workers.

Source: Radio Australia, September 10, 2009

Explain how this huge project will influence Australia's potential GDP and U.S. potential GDP.

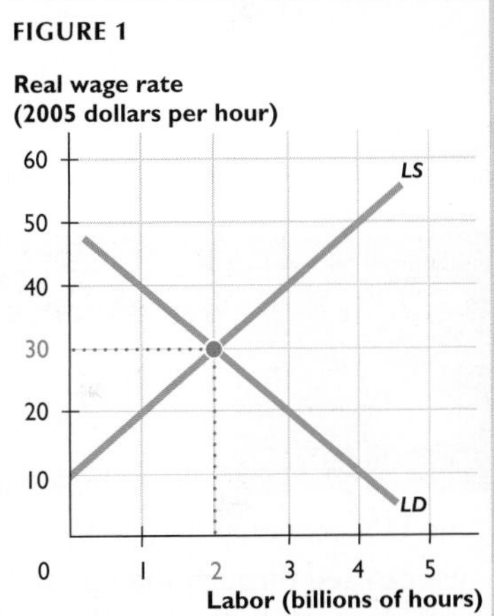


## Guided Solutions to Practice Problems

1. The demand for labor is a graph of the first and last row of Table 1 and the supply of labor is a graph of the data in Table 2 (Figure 1). The production function is a graph of the first two rows of Table 1 (Figure 2).

Labor market equilibrium occurs when the real wage rate is $30 an hour and 2 billion hours of labor are employed (Figure 1). Potential GDP is the real GDP produced by the equilibrium quantity of labor (2 billion hours in Figure 1). Potential GDP is $70 billion (Figure 2).

2. Australia's potential GDP will increase, but U.S. potential GDP will not change. Accessing these new resources will shift Australia's production function upward. With no change in employment, real GDP would increase. But the project will increase the demand for labor, increase the full-employment quantity of labor, and increase potential GDP. Even though this project is undertaken by U.S. firms, the production takes place in Australia. Neither the U.S. production function nor the U.S. demand for labor changes, so the project has no effect on U.S. potential GDP.

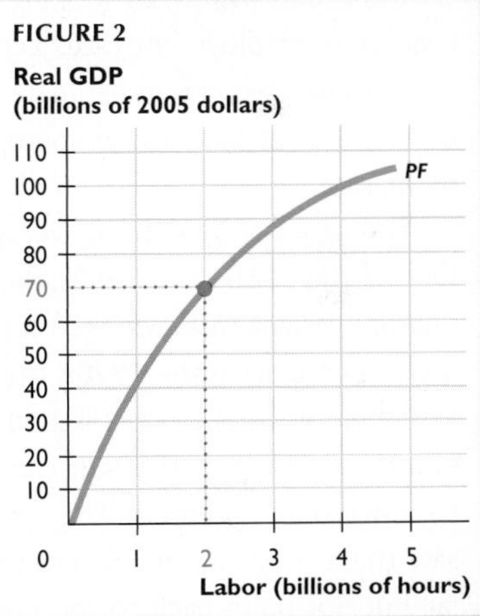

## 23.2 THE NATURAL UNEMPLOYMENT RATE

So far, we've focused on the forces that determine the real wage rate, the quantity of labor employed, and real GDP at full employment. We're now going to bring unemployment into the picture.

You learned in Chapter 21 how unemployment is measured. You also learned how people become unemployed by losing or leaving their jobs and by entering or reentering the labor force. And you learned how we classify unemployment as frictional, structural, seasonal, or cyclical. Finally, you learned that when the economy is at full employment, all the unemployment is frictional, structural, or seasonal, and the unemployment rate is called the *natural unemployment rate.*

Measuring, describing, and classifying unemployment tell us a lot about it. But these activities do not *explain* the amount of unemployment that exists or why its rate changes over time and varies across economies.

Many forces interact to determine the unemployment rate. Understanding these forces is a challenging task. Economists approach this task in two steps. The first step is to understand what determines the natural unemployment rate—the unemployment rate when the economy is at full employment. The second step is to understand what makes unemployment fluctuate around the natural unemployment rate. In this chapter, we take the first of these steps. We take the second step in Chapters 28–30 when we study economic fluctuations.

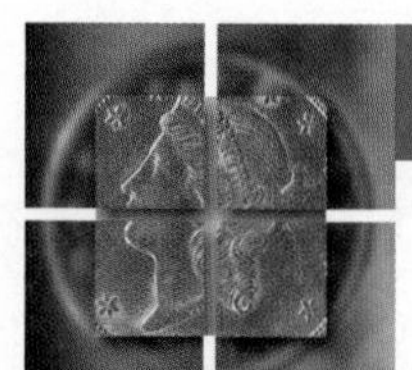

## EYE on the PAST

### Average Unemployment Rates over Six Decades

If we look back at the U.S. economy decade by decade, we can see through the ups and downs of the business cycle and focus on the broad trends. By looking at the average unemployment rates across the decades, we get an estimate of movements in the natural unemployment rate.

The figure shows these averages. During the 1950s and 1960s, the unemployment rate averaged less than 5 percent. During the 1970s, the average unemployment rate climbed to 6 percent, and in the 1980s, it climbed to more than 7 percent. The 1990s saw the average unemployment rate fall but not quite back to the rate of the 1950s and 1960s.

You will be a member of the labor force of the 2010s. The average unemployment rate of the second decade of the 2000s will have a big effect on your job market success.

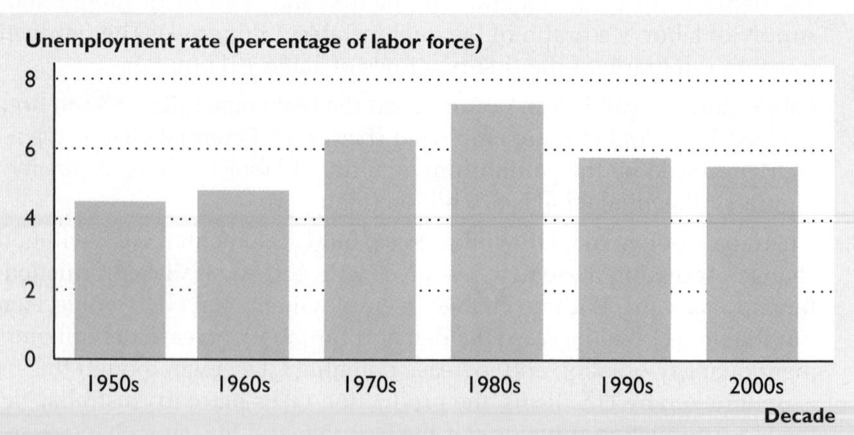


SOURCE OF DATA: Bureau of Labor Statistics.

To understand the amount of frictional and structural unemployment that exists at the natural unemployment rate, economists focus on two fundamental causes of unemployment that cut across the frictional-structural classification. These two fundamental causes of unemployment are

- Job search
- Job rationing

## Job Search

**Job search** is the activity of looking for an acceptable vacant job. Because the labor market is in a constant state of change, there are always some people who have not yet found suitable jobs and who are actively searching. The failure of businesses destroys jobs. The expansion of businesses and the startup of new businesses create jobs. As people pass through different stages of life, some enter or reenter the labor market, others leave their jobs to look for better ones, and others retire. This constant churning in the labor market means that there are always some people looking for jobs, and these people are part of the unemployed.

**Job search**
The activity of looking for an acceptable vacant job.

The amount of job search depends on a number of factors that change over time. The main ones are

- Demographic change
- Unemployment benefits
- Structural change

### Demographic Change

An increase in the proportion of the population that is of working age brings an increase in the entry rate into the labor force and an increase in the unemployment rate. This factor was important in the U.S. labor market during the 1970s. The bulge in the birth rate that occurred in the late 1940s and early 1950s increased the proportion of new entrants into the labor force during the 1970s and brought an increase in the unemployment rate.

As the birth rate declined, the bulge moved into higher age groups and the proportion of new entrants declined during the 1990s. During this period, the unemployment rate decreased.

Another source of demographic change has been an increase in the number of households with two incomes. When unemployment comes to one of these workers, it is possible, with income still flowing in, to take longer to find a new job. This factor might have increased frictional unemployment.

### Unemployment Benefits

The opportunity cost of job search influences the length of time that an unemployed person spends searching for a job. With no unemployment benefits, the opportunity cost of job search is high, and a person is likely to accept a job that is found quickly. With generous unemployment benefits, the opportunity cost of job search is low, and a person is likely to spend a considerable time searching for the ideal job.

Generous unemployment benefits are a large part of the story of high unemployment rates in Europe and some other countries such as Canada—see *Eye on the Global Economy* on p. 602.

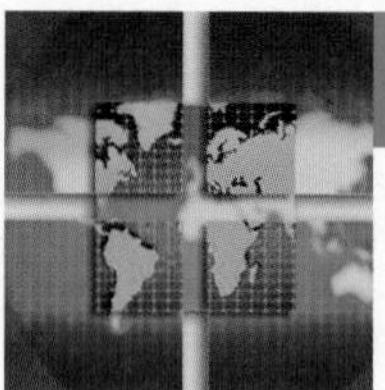

## EYE on the GLOBAL ECONOMY

### Unemployment Benefits and the Natural Unemployment Rate

Europe has higher unemployment benefits than the United States but are higher benefits the source of Europe's higher natural unemployment rate?

To isolate the effects of unemployment benefits, we need to keep other things the same. Canada provides an experiment in which other things are very similar to the United States.

The natural unemployment rate in Canada equalled that in the United States until 1980 but then it increased. Why? The key change in the 1980s was an increase in Canadian unemployment benefits. Close to 100 percent of Canada's unemployed receive generous benefits compared to 38 percent in the United States.

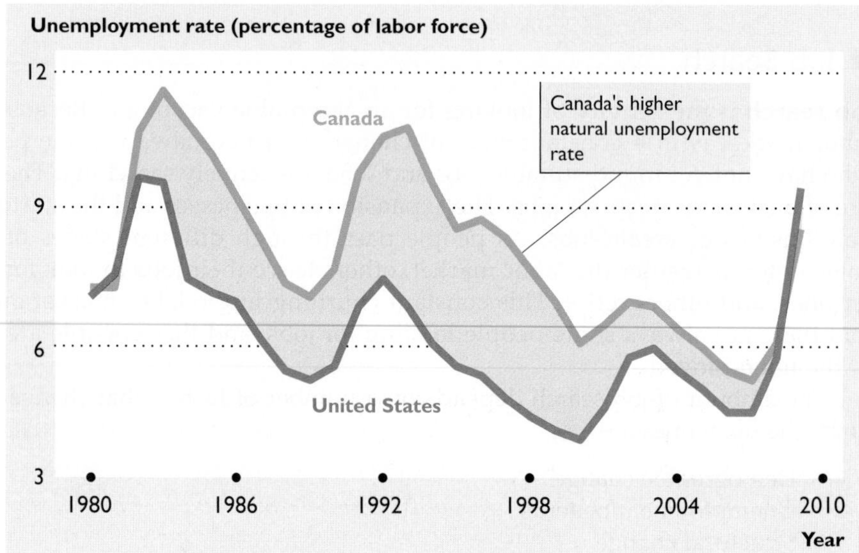


SOURCES OF DATA: Bureau of Labor Statistics and Statistics Canada.

Unemployment benefits appear to have a large effect on the natural unemployment rate. The gap narrowed after 2000 as cyclical unemployment rose less in Canada than in the United States during the last two recessions.

### Structural Change

Technological change influences unemployment. Sometimes it brings a structural slump, a condition in which some industries and even regions contract while other industries and regions flourish. When these events occur, labor turnover is high, job search increases, and the natural unemployment rate rises.

At other times, technological change brings a structural boom. It creates new jobs that are a good match for the people who are losing their jobs. When these events occur, labor turnover might be high, but job search decreases because new jobs are found quickly, and the natural unemployment rate falls. The Internet economy of the 1990s is an example of a structural boom. Lots of new jobs were created in every major population center, and these jobs were a good match for the skills available, so the natural unemployment rate decreased.

## ■ Job Rationing

**Job rationing**
A situation that arises when the real wage rate is above the full-employment equilibrium level.

**Job rationing** occurs when the real wage rate is above the full-employment equilibrium level. You have learned that markets allocate scarce resources by adjusting the market price to bring buying plans and selling plans into balance. You can think of the market as *rationing* scarce resources. In the labor market, the real wage rate rations employment and therefore rations jobs. Changes in the real wage rate keep the number of people seeking work and the number of jobs available in balance. But the real wage rate is not the only possible instrument for rationing jobs.

In some industries, the real wage rate is set above the full-employment equilibrium level, which brings a surplus of labor. In these labor markets, jobs are rationed by some other means.

The real wage rate might be set above the full-employment equilibrium level for three reasons:

- Efficiency wage
- Minimum wage
- Union wage

## Efficiency Wage

An **efficiency wage** is a real wage rate that is set above the full-employment equilibrium wage rate to induce a greater work effort. The idea is that if a firm pays only the going market average wage, employees have no incentive to work hard because they know that even if they are fired for slacking off, they can find a job with another firm at a similar wage rate. But if a firm pays *more* than the going market average wage, employees have an incentive to work hard because they know that if they are fired, they *cannot* expect to find a job with another firm at a similar wage rate.

**Efficiency wage**
A real wage rate that is set above the full-employment equilibrium wage rate to induce greater work effort.

Further, by paying an efficiency wage, a firm can attract the most productive workers. Also, its workers are less likely to quit their jobs, so the firm faces a lower rate of labor turnover and lower training costs. Finally, the firm's recruiting costs are lower because it always faces a steady stream of available new workers.

Paying an efficiency wage is costly, so only those firms that can't directly monitor the work effort of their employees use this device. For example, truck drivers and plant maintenance workers might receive efficiency wages. If enough firms pay an efficiency wage, the average real wage rate will exceed the full-employment equilibrium level.

## The Minimum Wage

A **minimum wage law** is a government regulation that makes hiring labor for less than a specified wage illegal. If the minimum wage is set below the equilibrium wage, the minimum wage has no effect. The minimum wage law and market forces are not in conflict. But if a minimum wage is set above the equilibrium wage, the minimum wage is in conflict with market forces and unemployment arises.

**Minimum wage law**
A government regulation that makes hiring labor for less than a specified wage illegal.

The current federal minimum wage is $7.25 an hour, and the minimum wage has a major effect in the markets for low-skilled labor. Because skill grows with work experience, teenage labor is particularly affected by the minimum wage.

## Union Wage

A **union wage** is a wage rate that results from collective bargaining between a labor union and a firm. Because a union represents a group of workers, it can usually achieve a wage rate that exceeds the level that would prevail in a competitive labor market.

**Union wage**
A wage rate that results from collective bargaining between a labor union and a firm.

For the United States, it is estimated that, on the average, union wage rates are 30 percent higher than nonunion wage rates. But this estimate probably overstates the true effects of labor unions on the wage rate. In some industries, union wages are higher than nonunion wages because union members do jobs that require greater skill than nonunion jobs. In these cases, even without a union, those workers would earn a higher wage.

One way to calculate the effects of unions is to examine the wages of union and nonunion workers who do nearly identical work. For workers with similar skill levels, the union-nonunion wage difference is between 10 and 25 percent. For example, pilots who are members of the Air Line Pilots Association earn about 25 percent more than nonunion pilots with the same level of skill.

Labor unions are much more influential in Europe than in the United States. In Europe, unions not only achieve wage rates above those of a competitive market but also have broad political influence on labor market conditions.

## Job Rationing and Unemployment

Whether because of efficiency wages, a minimum wage law, or the actions of labor unions, if the real wage rate is above the full-employment equilibrium level, the natural unemployment rate increases. The above-equilibrium real wage rate decreases the quantity of labor demanded and increases the quantity of labor supplied.

Figure 23.5 illustrates job rationing and the frictional and structural unemployment it creates. The full-employment equilibrium real wage rate is $40 an hour, and the equilibrium quantity of labor is 200 billion hours a year. The existence of efficiency wages, the minimum wage, and union wages raises the economy's average real wage rate to $50 an hour. At this wage rate, the quantity of labor demanded decreases to 150 billion hours and the quantity of labor supplied increases to 250 billion hours. Firms ration jobs and choose the workers to hire on the basis of criteria such as education and previous job experience. The labor market is like a game of musical chairs in which a large number of chairs have been removed. So the quantity of labor supplied persistently exceeds the quantity demanded, and additional unemployment arises from job rationing.

**FIGURE 23.5**

Job Rationing Increases the Natural Unemployment Rate

myeconlab Animation

The full-employment equilibrium real wage rate is $40 an hour. Efficiency wages, the minimum wage, and union wages put the average real wage rate above the full-employment equilibrium level—at $50 an hour.

1. The quantity of labor demanded decreases to 150 billion hours.
2. The quantity of labor supplied increases to 250 billion hours.
3. A surplus of labor arises and increases the natural unemployment rate.

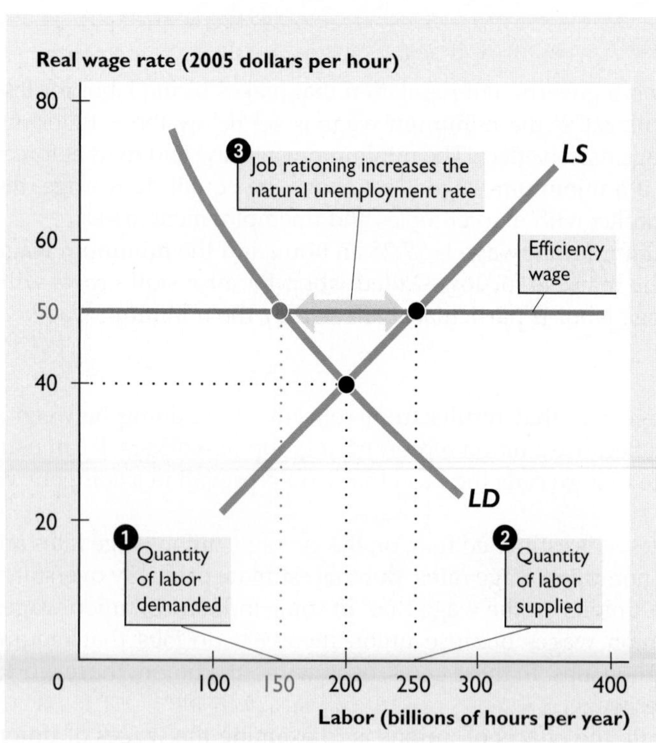

## EYE on the U.S. ECONOMY

### The Federal Minimum Wage

The Fair Labor Standards Act of 1938 set the federal minimum wage in the United States at 25¢ an hour. Over the years, the minimum wage has increased, and in 2009 it was $7.25 an hour. Although the minimum wage has increased, it hasn't kept up with the rising cost of living.

The figure shows the real minimum wage rate in 2005 dollars. You can see that during the late 1960s, the minimum wage in 2005 dollars was $7.50 an hour. It decreased during the 1970s and 1980s and has fluctuated around an average of about $6 an hour since the mid-1980s.

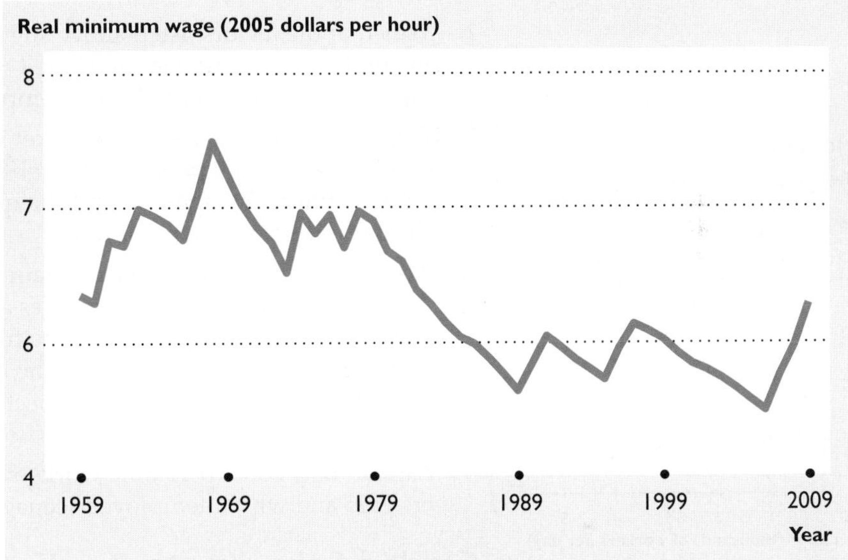


SOURCE OF DATA: Bureau of Labor Statistics.

## EYE on YOUR LIFE

### Natural Unemployment

You will encounter natural unemployment at many points in your life.

If you now have a job, you probably went through a spell of natural unemployment as you searched for it.

When you graduate and look for a full-time job, you will most likely spend some more time searching for the best match for your skills and location preferences.

In today's world of rapid technological change, most of us must retool and change our jobs at least once and for many of us, more than once.

You might know an older worker who has recently lost a job and is going through the agony of figuring out what to do next.

Although natural unemployment can be painful for people who experience it, from a social perspective, it is productive. It enables scarce labor resources to be *re*-allocated to their most valuable uses.

Work these problems in Study Plan 23.2 to get instant feedback.

## CHECKPOINT 23.2

**Explain what determines the natural unemployment rate.**

### Practice Problems

During the past 50 years, Singapore has seen huge changes: rapid population growth and the introduction of newer and newer technologies. Singapore has modest unemployment benefits, no minimum wage, and weak labor unions. Use this information to work Problems **1** and **2**.

1. Does Singapore's unemployment arise mainly from job search or job rationing?
2. Which of the factors listed above suggest that Singapore has a higher natural unemployment rate than the United States and which suggest that Singapore has a lower natural unemployment rate?
3. Figure 1 illustrates the labor market in an economy in which at full employment, 1,000 people a day job search. What is the full-employment equilibrium real wage rate and the quantity of labor employed? Calculate the natural unemployment rate.
4. **The minimum wage increases again**
   A minimum wage increase provides a silver lining for part-time workers, as employers choose to promote more from within the firm than from outside. Low-skilled and youth workers who are employed gain, but for unemployed teenage workers, job prospects look grim.
   Source: laborlawcenter.com
   Explain why some part-time workers, low-skilled workers, and youth workers gain and why unemployed teenagers find it hard to get jobs.

**FIGURE 1**

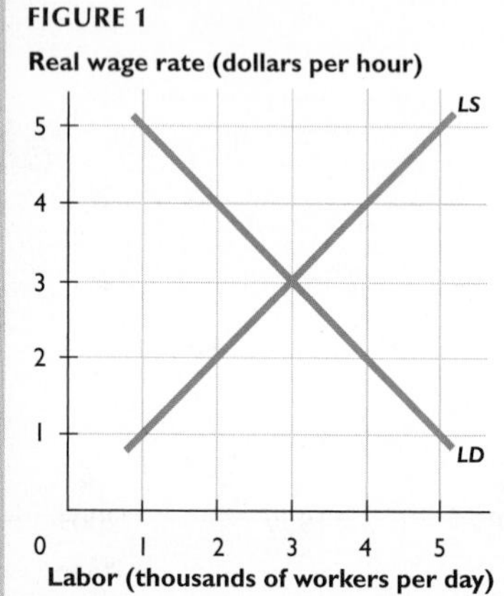


### Guided Solutions to Practice Problems

1. Singapore's unemployment arises mainly from job search. Of the sources of job rationing (efficiency wages, minimum wages, and union wages) only efficiency wages applies.
2. The factors that point toward a higher natural unemployment rate in Singapore are rapid population growth and the introduction of new technologies, both of which increase the amount of job search.

   The factors that point toward a lower natural unemployment rate in Singapore than in the United States are modest unemployment benefits, which limit the amount of job search, and the absence of a minimum wage and weak labor unions, which limit the amount of job rationing.
3. At full employment, the equilibrium real wage rate and the quantity of labor employed are determined by the demand for labor and the supply of labor. At full employment, the real wage rate is \$3 an hour and 3,000 workers are employed. Unemployment is 1,000, so the labor force is 4,000, and the natural unemployment rate equals $(1,000 \div 4,000) \times 100$, or 25 percent.
4. When the minimum wage rate is raised, firms retain those workers who produce at least as much output in an hour as the minimum wage rate. The job experience will help part-time and low-skilled employees retain their jobs, but teenagers with no experience will find it hard to get jobs.

# CHAPTER SUMMARY

## Key Points

**1 Explain what determines potential GDP.**

- Potential GDP is the quantity of real GDP that the full-employment quantity of labor produces.
- The production function describes the relationship between real GDP and the quantity of labor employed when all other influences on production remain the same. As the quantity of labor increases, real GDP increases.
- The quantity of labor demanded increases as the real wage rate falls, other things remaining the same.
- The quantity of labor supplied increases as the real wage rate rises, other things remaining the same.
- At full-employment equilibrium, the real wage rate makes the quantity of labor demanded equal the quantity of labor supplied.

**2 Explain what determines the natural unemployment rate.**

- The unemployment rate at full employment is the natural unemployment rate.
- Unemployment is always present because of job search and job rationing.
- Job search is influenced by demographic change, unemployment benefits, and structural change.
- Job rationing arises from an efficiency wage, the minimum wage, and a union wage.

## Key Terms

Classical macroeconomics, 588
Demand for labor, 593
Diminishing returns, 592
Efficiency wage, 603
Job rationing, 602
Job search, 601
Keynesian macroeconomics, 588
Minimum wage law, 603
Monetarist macroeconomics, 589
Potential GDP, 591
Production function, 592
Quantity of labor demanded, 593
Quantity of labor supplied, 595
Supply of labor, 595
Union wage, 603

Work these problems in Chapter 23 Study Plan to get instant feedback.

# CHAPTER CHECKPOINT

## Study Plan Problems and Applications

Use the following list of events that occur one at a time in the United States to work Problems 1 to 4.

- Dell introduces a new supercomputer that everyone can afford.
- A major hurricane hits Florida.
- More high school graduates go to college.
- The CPI rises.
- An economic slump in the rest of the world decreases U.S. exports.

1. Sort the items into four groups: those that change the production function, those that change the demand for labor, those that change the supply of labor, and those that do not change the production function, the demand for labor, or the supply of labor. Say in which direction any changes occur.
2. Which of the events increase the equilibrium quantity of labor and which decrease it?
3. Which of the events raise the real wage rate and which lower it?
4. Which of the events increase potential GDP and which decrease it?

Use the information set out in Table 1 and Table 2 about the economy of Athabasca to work Problems 5 and 6.

**TABLE 1 PRODUCTION FUNCTION**

| Labor hours (millions) | Real GDP (millions of 2005 dollars) |
|---|---|
| 0 | 0 |
| 1 | 10 |
| 2 | 19 |
| 3 | 27 |
| 4 | 34 |
| 5 | 40 |

**TABLE 2 LABOR MARKET**

| Real wage rate (dollars per hour) | Quantity of labor demanded (millions of hours per year) | Quantity of labor supplied (millions of hours per year) |
|---|---|---|
| 10 | 1 | 5 |
| 9 | 2 | 4 |
| 8 | 3 | 3 |
| 7 | 4 | 2 |
| 6 | 5 | 1 |

5. Calculate the quantity of labor employed, the real wage rate, and potential GDP.
6. If the labor force participation increases, explain how employment, the real wage rate, and potential GDP change.
7. Two island economies, Cocoa Island and Plantation Island, are identical in every respect except one. A survey tells us that at full employment, people on Cocoa Island spend 1,000 hours a day on job search, while the people on Plantation Island spend 2,000 hours a day on job search. Which economy has the greater level of potential GDP? Which has the higher real wage rate? And which has the higher natural unemployment rate?
8. If the United States cracks down on illegal immigrants and returns millions of workers to their home countries, explain what happens to U.S. employment, U.S. real wage rate, and U.S. potential GDP.

   In the countries to which the immigrants return, explain what happens to employment, the real wage rate, and potential GDP.
9. **Job openings and labor turnover: July 2009**

   Job openings were 2.4 million, down from 3.9 million in July 2008; hires were 4.1 million, down from 4.7 million in July 2008; and job losers were 4.3 million, down from 4.8 million in July 2008.

   Bureau of Labor Statistics, September 10, 2009

   Compare U.S. labor turnover (hires minus job losers) in July 2009 with that in July 2008. Is the U.S. labor market moving toward full employment? Is real GDP increasing or decreasing? Is U.S. potential GDP increasing or decreasing?

## Instructor Assignable Problems and Applications

Your instructor can assign these problems as homework, a quiz, or a test in **MyEconLab**.

Use the following information to work Problems **1** and **2**.

In Korea, real GDP per hour of labor is $22, the real wage rate is $15 per hour, and people work an average of 46 hours per week.

1. Draw a graph of the demand for and supply of labor in Korea and the United States. Mark a point at the equilibrium quantity of labor per person per week and the real wage rate in each economy. Explain the difference in the two labor markets.
2. Draw a graph of the production functions in Korea and the United States. Mark a point on each production function that shows potential GDP per hour of work in each economy. Explain the difference in the two production functions.

Use the following list of events that occur one at a time in the United States to work Problems **3** to **6**.

- An oil embargo in the Middle East cuts supplies of oil to the United States.
- The New York Yankees win the World Series.
- U.S. labor unions negotiate wage hikes that affect all workers.
- A huge scientific breakthrough doubles the output that an additional hour of U.S. labor can produce.
- Migration to the United States increases the working-age population.

3. Sort the items into four groups: those that change the production function, those that change the demand for labor, those that change the supply of labor, and those that do not change the production function, the demand for labor, or the supply of labor. Say in which direction each change occurs.
4. Which of the events increase the equilibrium quantity of labor and which decrease the equilibrium quantity of labor?
5. Which of the events raise the real wage rate and which of the events lower the real wage rate?
6. Which of the events increase potential GDP and which decrease potential GDP?

Use the following information to work Problems **7** and **8**.

**Obama vows to speed hurricane Katrina recovery effort**

On the fourth anniversary of Hurricane Katrina, President Obama pledged to speed up the recovery effort along the Gulf Coast. Over a thousand people lost their lives, more than a million people were displaced, and whole neighborhoods were left in ruins.

Source: *The New York Times*, September 10, 2009

7. Explain the effect of hurricane Katrina on employment along the Gulf Coast. Did the state of Louisiana move along its production function or did its production function shift? How did Louisiana's potential GDP change?
8. Explain how a speedup of the recovery effort will affect U.S. employment and potential GDP.

## 24.1 THE BASICS OF ECONOMIC GROWTH

Economic growth is a sustained expansion of production possibilities. Maintained over decades, rapid economic growth can transform a poor nation into a rich one. Such has been the experience of Hong Kong, South Korea, Taiwan, and some other Asian economies. Slow economic growth or the absence of growth can condemn a nation to devastating poverty. Such has been the fate of Sierra Leone, Somalia, Zambia, and much of the rest of Africa.

Economic growth is different from the rise in incomes that occurs during the recovery from a recession. Economic growth is a sustained trend, not a temporary cyclical expansion.

### Calculating Growth Rates

**Economic growth rate**
The annual percentage change of real GDP.

We express the **economic growth rate** as the annual percentage change of real GDP. To calculate this growth rate, we use the formula:

$$\text{Growth rate of real GDP} = \frac{\begin{matrix}\text{Real GDP} \\ \text{in current year}\end{matrix} - \begin{matrix}\text{Real GDP} \\ \text{in previous year}\end{matrix}}{\text{Real GDP in previous year}} \times 100.$$

For example, if real GDP in the current year is \$8.4 trillion and if real GDP in the previous year was \$8.0 trillion, then

$$\text{Growth rate of real GDP} = \frac{\$8.4 \text{ trillion} - \$8.0 \text{ trillion}}{\$8.0 \text{ trillion}} \times 100 = 5 \text{ percent}.$$

The growth rate of real GDP tells us how rapidly the total economy is expanding. This measure is useful for telling us about potential changes in the balance of economic power among nations, but it does not tell us about changes in the standard of living.

**Real GDP per person**
Real GDP divided by the population.

The standard of living depends on **real GDP per person** (also called *per capita real GDP*), which is real GDP divided by the population. So the contribution of real GDP growth to the change in the *standard of living* depends on the growth rate of real GDP per person. We use the above formula to calculate this growth rate, replacing real GDP with real GDP per person.

Suppose, for example, that in the current year, when real GDP is \$8.4 trillion, the population is 202 million. Then real GDP per person in the current year is \$8.4 trillion divided by 202 million, which equals \$41,584. And suppose that in the previous year, when real GDP was \$8.0 trillion, the population was 200 million. Then real GDP per person in that year was \$8.0 trillion divided by 200 million, which equals \$40,000.

Use these two values of real GDP per person with the growth formula to calculate the growth rate of real GDP per person. That is,

$$\text{Growth rate of real GDP per person} = \frac{\$41{,}584 - \$40{,}000}{\$40{,}000} \times 100 = 4 \text{ percent}.$$

We can also calculate the growth rate of real GDP per person by using the formula:

$$\text{Growth rate of real GDP per person} = \text{Growth rate of real GDP} - \text{Growth rate of population.}$$

In the example you've just worked through, the growth rate of real GDP is 5 percent. The population changes from 200 million to 202 million, so

$$\text{Growth rate of population} = \frac{202 \text{ million} - 200 \text{ million}}{200 \text{ million}} \times 100 = 1 \text{ percent}$$

and

$$\text{Growth rate of real GDP per person} = 5 \text{ percent} - 1 \text{ percent} = 4 \text{ percent.}$$

This formula makes it clear that real GDP per person grows only if real GDP grows faster than the population grows. If the growth rate of the population exceeds the growth of real GDP, then real GDP per person falls.

## The Magic of Sustained Growth

Sustained growth of real GDP per person can transform a poor society into a wealthy one. The reason is that economic growth is like compound interest. Suppose that you put $100 in the bank and earn 5 percent a year interest on it. After one year, you have $105. If you leave that money in the bank for another year, you earn 5 percent interest on the original $100 and on the $5 interest that you earned last year. You are now earning interest on interest! The next year, things get even better. Then you earn 5 percent on the original $100 and on the interest earned in the first year and the second year. Your money in the bank is *growing* at a rate of 5 percent a year. Before too many years have passed, you'll have $200 in the bank. But after *how many* years?

The answer is provided by a powerful and general formula known as the **Rule of 70,** which states that the number of years it takes for the level of any variable to double is approximately 70 divided by the annual percentage growth rate of the variable. Using the Rule of 70, you can now calculate how many years it takes your $100 to become $200. It is 70 divided by 5, which is 14 years.

**Rule of 70**
The number of years it takes for the level of any variable to double is approximately 70 divided by the annual percentage growth rate of the variable.

The Rule of 70 applies to any variable, so it applies to real GDP per person. Table 24.1 shows the doubling time for a selection of other growth rates. You can see that real GDP per person doubles in 70 years (70 divided by 1)—an average human life span—if the growth rate is 1 percent a year. It doubles in 35 years if the growth rate is 2 percent a year and in just 10 years if the growth rate is 7 percent a year.

We can use the Rule of 70 to answer other questions about economic growth. For example, in 2000, U.S. real GDP per person was approximately 8 times that of China. China's recent growth rate of real GDP per person was 7 percent a year. If this growth rate were maintained, how long would it take China's real GDP per person to reach that of the United States in 2000? The answer, provided by the Rule of 70, is 30 years. China's real GDP per person doubles in 10 (70 divided by 7) years. It doubles again to 4 times its current level in another 10 years, and it doubles yet again to 8 times its current level in another 10 years. So after 30 years of growth at 7 percent a year, China's real GDP per person is 8 times its current level and equals that of the United States in 2000.

**TABLE 24.1 GROWTH RATES**

| Growth rate (percent per year) | Years for level to double |
|---|---|
| 1 | 70 |
| 2 | 35 |
| 3 | 23 |
| 4 | 18 |
| 5 | 14 |
| 6 | 12 |
| 7 | 10 |
| 8 | 9 |
| 9 | 8 |
| 10 | 7 |

## 24.4 ACHIEVING FASTER GROWTH

Why did it take more than a million years of human life before economic growth began? Why are some countries even today still barely growing? Why don't all societies save and invest in new capital, expand human capital, and discover and apply new technologies on a scale that brings rapid economic growth? What actions can governments take to encourage growth?

### Preconditions for Economic Growth

The main reason economic growth is either absent or slow is that some societies lack the incentive system that encourages growth-producing activities. One of the fundamental preconditions for creating the incentives that lead to economic growth is economic freedom.

#### Economic Freedom

**Economic freedom**
A condition in which people are able to make personal choices, their private property is protected by the rule of law, and they are free to buy and sell in markets.

**Economic freedom** is present when people are able to make personal choices, their private property is protected by the rule of law, and they are free to buy and sell in markets. The rule of law, an efficient legal system, and the ability to enforce contracts are essential foundations for creating economic freedom. Impediments to economic freedom are corruption in the courts and government bureaucracy; barriers to trade, such as import bans; high tax rates; stringent regulations on business, such as health, safety, and environmental regulation; restrictions on banks; labor market regulations that limit a firm's ability to hire and lay off workers; and illegal markets, such as those that violate intellectual property rights.

No unique political system is necessary to deliver economic freedom. Democratic systems do a good job, but the rule of law, not democracy, is the key requirement for creating economic freedom. Nondemocratic political systems that respect the rule of law can also work well. Hong Kong is the best example of a place with little democracy but a lot of economic freedom—and a lot of economic growth. No country with a high level of economic freedom is economically poor, but many countries with low levels of economic freedom stagnate.

#### Property Rights

**Property rights**
The social arrangements that govern the protection of private property.

Economic freedom requires the protection of private property—the factors of production and goods that people own. The social arrangements that govern the protection of private property are called **property rights.** They include the rights to physical property (land, buildings, and capital equipment), to financial property (claims by one person against another), and to intellectual property (such as inventions). Clearly established and enforced property rights provide people with the incentive to work and save. If someone attempts to steal their property, a legal system will protect them. Such property rights also assure people that government itself will not confiscate their income or savings.

#### Markets

Economic freedom also requires free markets. Buyers and sellers get information and do business with each other in *markets.* Market prices send signals to buyers and sellers that create incentives to increase or decrease the quantities demanded and supplied. Markets enable people to trade and to save and invest. But markets cannot operate without property rights.

Property rights and markets create incentives for people to specialize and trade, to save and invest, to expand their human capital, and to discover and apply new technologies. Early human societies based on hunting and gathering did not experience economic growth because they lacked property rights and markets. Economic growth began when societies evolved the institutions that create incentives. But the presence of an incentive system and the institutions that create it do not guarantee that economic growth will occur. They permit economic growth but do not make it inevitable.

Growth begins when the appropriate incentive system exists because people can specialize in the activities at which they have a comparative advantage and trade with each other. You saw in Chapter 3 how everyone gains from such activity. By specializing and trading, everyone can acquire goods and services at the lowest possible cost. Consequently, people can obtain a greater volume of goods and services from their labor.

As an economy moves from one with little specialization to one that reaps the gains from specialization and trade, its production and consumption grow. Real GDP per person increases, and the standard of living rises.

But for growth to be persistent, people must face incentives that encourage them to pursue the three activities that generate *ongoing* economic growth: saving and investment, expansion of human capital, and the discovery and application of new technologies.

## Policies to Achieve Faster Growth

To achieve faster economic growth, we must increase the growth rate of capital per hour of labor, increase the growth rate of human capital, or increase the pace of technological advance. The main actions that governments can take to achieve these objectives are

- Create incentive mechanisms.
- Encourage saving.
- Encourage research and development.
- Encourage international trade.
- Improve the quality of education.

### Create Incentive Mechanisms

Economic growth occurs when the incentives to save, invest, and innovate are strong enough. These incentives require property rights enforced by a well-functioning legal system. Property rights and a legal system are the key ingredients that are missing in many societies. For example, they are absent throughout much of Africa. The first priority for growth policy is to establish these institutions so that incentives to save, invest, and innovate exist. Russia is a leading example of a country that is striving to take this step toward establishing the conditions in which economic growth can occur.

### Encourage Saving

Saving finances investment, which brings capital accumulation. So encouraging saving can increase the growth of capital and stimulate economic growth. The East Asian economies have the highest saving rates and the highest growth rates. Some African economies have the lowest saving rates and the lowest growth rates.

Tax incentives can increase saving. Individual Retirement Accounts (IRAs) are an example of a tax incentive to save. Economists claim that a tax on consumption rather than on income provides the best incentive to save.

### Encourage Research and Development

Everyone can use the fruits of basic research and development efforts. For example, all biotechnology firms can use advances in gene-splicing technology. Because basic inventions can be copied, the inventor's profit is limited and so the market allocates too few resources to this activity.

Governments can direct public funds toward financing basic research, but this solution is not foolproof. It requires a mechanism for allocating public funds to their highest-valued use. The National Science Foundation is one possibly efficient channel for allocating public funds to universities and public research facilities to finance and encourage basic research. Government programs such as national defense and space exploration also lead to innovations that have wide use. Laptop computers and nonstick coatings are two prominent examples of innovations that came from the U.S. space program.

### Encourage International Trade

Free international trade stimulates economic growth by extracting all the available gains from specialization and trade. The fastest-growing nations today are those with the fastest-growing exports and imports. The creation of the North American Free Trade Agreement and the integration of the economies of Europe through the formation of the European Union are examples of successful actions that governments have taken to stimulate economic growth through trade.

### Improve the Quality of Education

The free market would produce too little education because it brings social benefits beyond the benefits to the people who receive the education. By funding basic education and by ensuring high standards in skills such as language, mathematics, and science, governments can contribute enormously to a nation's growth potential. Education can also be expanded and improved by using tax incentives to encourage improved private provision. Singapore's Information Technology in Education program is one of the best examples of a successful attempt to stimulate growth through education.

## How Much Difference Can Policy Make?

It is easy to make a list of policy actions that could increase a nation's economic growth rate. It is hard to convert that list into acceptable actions that make a big difference.

Societies are the way they are because they balance the interests of one group against the interests of another group. Change brings gains for some and losses for others, so change is slow. And even when change occurs, if the economic growth rate can be increased by even as much as half a percentage point, it takes many years for the full benefits to accrue.

A well-intentioned government cannot dial up a big increase in the economic growth rate, but it can pursue policies that will nudge the economic growth rate upward. Over time, the benefits from these policies will be large.

# EYE on CONVERGENCE AND GAPS

## Why Are Some Nations Rich and Others Poor?

Political stability, property rights protected by the rule of law, limited government intervention in markets: These are key features of the economies that enjoy high incomes and they are the features missing in those that remain poor.

Most of the rich nations have experienced sustained economic growth over many decades. Europe's Big 4 economies (France, Germany, Italy, and the United Kingdom) have been enjoying economic growth for 200 years. The United States started to grow rapidly 150 years ago and overtook Europe in the early 20th century. In the past 50 years, the gaps between these countries haven't changed much. (See part (a) of the figure.)

In a transition from Communism to a market economy, Central Europe is growing faster than the United States.

Economic growth in Africa and Central and South America has been persistently slow and the gap between the United States and these regions has widened.

Real GDP per person in East Asian economies, in part (b), has converged toward that in the United States. These economies are like fast trains running on the same track at similar speeds with roughly constant gaps between them. Hong Kong and Singapore are the lead trains and run about 15 years in front of Taiwan, 20 years in front of South Korea, and almost 40 years in front of China.

Between 1960 and 2008, Hong Kong and Singapore transformed themselves from poor developing economies to take their places among the world's richest economies.

Real GDP per person (2005 dollars: ratio scale)
51,200
12,800
3,200
800
200
1960 1970 1980 1990 2000 2010
Year
United States
Europe's Big 4
Central Europe in transition
Central and South America
Africa

**(a) Persistent gaps**

Real GDP per person (2005 dollars: ratio scale)
51,200
12,800
3,200
800
200
1960 1970 1980 1990 2000 2010
Year
United States
Japan
Hong Kong
Singapore
Taiwan
Korea
China

**(b) Convergence**

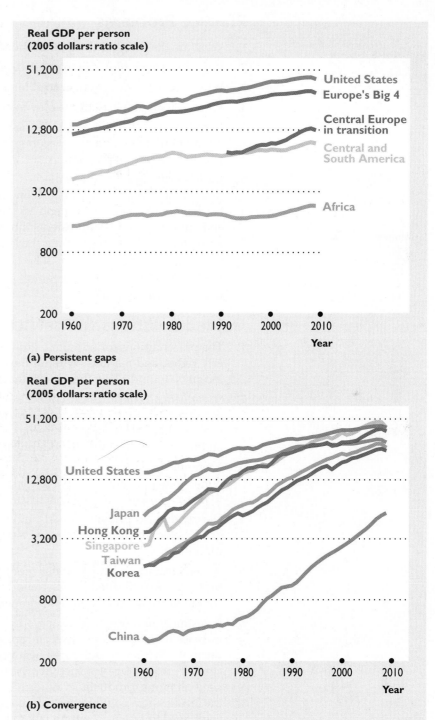

SOURCES OF DATA: Alan Heston, Robert Summers, and Bettina Aten, Penn World Table Version 6.2, Center for International Comparisons at the University of Pennsylvania, September 2006 and International Monetary Fund, *World Economic Outlook Database.*

Work these problems in Study Plan 24.4 to get instant feedback.

## CHECKPOINT 24.4

**Describe policies that might speed economic growth.**

### Practice Problems

1. What are the preconditions for economic growth?
2. Why does much of Africa experience slow economic growth?
3. Why is economic freedom crucial for achieving economic growth?
4. What role do property rights play in encouraging economic growth?
5. Explain why, other things remaining the same, a country with a well-educated population has a faster economic growth rate than a country that has a poorly educated population.
6. **India's economy hits the wall**

   Just six months ago, the Indian economy was growing rapidly; now growth has halted. India needs to spend $500 billion upgrading its infrastructure and education and health-care facilities. Agriculture remains unproductive; and reforms, like strengthening the legal system, have been ignored.

   Source: *BusinessWeek*, July 1, 2008

   Explain how the measures reported in the news clip could lead to faster economic growth in India.

### Guided Solutions to Practice Problems

1. The preconditions for economic growth are economic freedom, private property rights, and markets. Without these preconditions, people have little incentive to undertake the actions that lead to economic growth.
2. Some African countries experience slow economic growth because they lack economic freedom, private property rights are not enforced, and markets do not function well. People in these countries have little incentive to specialize and trade or to accumulate both physical and human capital.
3. Economic freedom is crucial for achieving economic growth because economic freedom allows people to make choices and gives them the incentives to pursue growth-producing activities.
4. Clearly defined private property rights and a legal system to enforce them give people the incentive to work, save, invest, and accumulate human capital.
5. A well-educated population has more skills and greater labor productivity than a poorly educated population. A well-educated population can contribute to the research and development that create new technology.
6. Investment in infrastructure and education and heath-care facilities would increase India's stock of physical capital, which would increase labor productivity. Better education and heath care would increase human capital and again increase labor productivity. With better technology and more capital used on farms, productivity of farm workers would increase. Strengthening the legal system could better enforce property rights. Each of these measures could lead to faster growth in labor productivity and faster growth in real GDP per person in India.

# CHAPTER SUMMARY

## Key Points

**1 Define and calculate the economic growth rate, and explain the implications of sustained growth.**

- Economic growth is the sustained expansion of production possibilities. The annual percentage change in real GDP measures the economic growth rate.
- Real GDP per person must grow if the standard of living is to rise.
- Sustained economic growth transforms poor nations into rich ones.
- The Rule of 70 tells us the number of years in which real GDP doubles—70 divided by the percentage growth rate of real GDP.

**2 Identify the main sources of economic growth.**

- Real GDP grows when aggregate hours and labor productivity grow.
- Real GDP per person grows when labor productivity grows.
- Saving, investment in physical capital, expansion of human capital, and technological advances bring labor productivity growth.

**3 Review the theories of economic growth that explain why growth rates vary over time and across countries.**

- Classical growth theory predicts that economic growth will end because a population explosion will lower real GDP per person to its subsistence level.
- Neoclassical theory predicts that economic growth will persist at a rate that is determined by the pace of technological change.
- New growth theory predicts that capital accumulation, human capital growth, and technological change respond to incentives and can bring persistent growth in labor productivity.

**4 Describe policies that might speed economic growth.**

- Economic growth requires an incentive system created by economic freedom, property rights, and markets.
- It might be possible to achieve faster growth by encouraging saving, subsidizing research and education, and encouraging international trade.

## Key Terms

Classical growth theory, 621
Economic freedom, 628
Economic growth rate, 612
Labor productivity, 616
Malthusian theory, 621
Neoclassical growth theory, 623
New growth theory, 623
Property rights, 628
Real GDP per person, 612
Rule of 70, 613

Work these problems in Chapter 24 Study Plan to get instant feedback.

# CHAPTER CHECKPOINT

## Study Plan Problems and Applications

1. Explain why sustained growth of real GDP per person can transform a poor country into a wealthy one.
2. In 2005 and 2006, India's real GDP grew by 9.2 percent a year and its population grew by 1.6 percent a year. If these growth rates are sustained, in what years would
   - Real GDP be twice what it was in 2006?
   - Real GDP per person be twice what it was in 2006?
3. Describe how U.S. real GDP per person has changed over the last 100 years.
4. Explain the link between labor hours, labor productivity, and real GDP.
5. Explain how saving and investment and advances in technology change labor productivity. Use a graph to illustrate your answer.

**TABLE 1 LABOR MARKET**

| Real wage rate (2005 dollars per hour) | Labor hours supplied | Labor hours demanded |
|---|---|---|
| 80 | 45 | 5 |
| 70 | 40 | 10 |
| 60 | 35 | 15 |
| 50 | 30 | 20 |
| 40 | 25 | 25 |
| 30 | 20 | 30 |
| 20 | 15 | 35 |
| 10 | 10 | 40 |

**TABLE 2 PRODUCTION FUNCTION**

| Labor (hours) | Real GDP (2005 dollars) |
|---|---|
| 5 | 425 |
| 10 | 800 |
| 15 | 1,125 |
| 20 | 1,400 |
| 25 | 1,625 |
| 30 | 1,800 |
| 35 | 1,925 |
| 40 | 2,000 |

Use Table 1 and Table 2 to work Problems 6 to 9. Table 1 describes an economy's labor market in 2009 and Table 2 describes its production function in 2009.

6. What are the equilibrium real wage rate, the quantity of labor employed in 2009, labor productivity, and potential GDP in 2009?
7. In 2010, the population increases and labor hours supplied increase by 10 at each real wage rate. What are the equilibrium real wage rate, labor productivity, and potential GDP in 2010?
8. In 2010, the population increases and labor hours supplied increase by 10 at each real wage rate. Does the standard of living in this economy increase in 2010? Explain why or why not.
9. If the subsistence real wage rate is $20 an hour, what will happen to the economy's population according to the classical growth theory?

Use the following information to work Problems 10 and 11.

**China's economy to grow 8% annually from 2006 to 2010**

The Chinese economy is expected to grow at a rate of 8 percent a year during the period of the 11th Five-Year Plan (2006–10). If China does maintain this growth rate, then China will achieve this goal of quadrupling its GDP from 2000 to 2020 ahead of schedule. Zhang Xiaoji, a senior researcher at the State Council Development Research Centre, reported that by the end of 2010, China's GDP will be equal to US $2.3 trillion or US $1,700 per person (2000 dollars) and by 2020, China's GDP will be equal to US $4.7 trillion, or US $3,200 per person.

Source: *China Daily*, March 21, 2005

10. If China continues to grow at 8 percent a year, how many years will it take for GDP to quadruple? In what year will China meet its goal?
11. What is the population growth rate assumed in the calculations of GDP per person from 2010 to 2020?

## Instructor Assignable Problems and Applications

Your instructor can assign these problems as homework, a quiz, or a test in **MyEconLab**.

1. Distinguish between a low and high income and a low and high economic growth rate. What are the key features of an economy that are present when incomes are high or fast growing and absent when incomes are low and stagnating or growing slowly? Provide an example of an economy with a low income and slow growth rate, a low income and rapid growth rate, and a high income with sustained growth over many decades.

Use the following information to work Problems 2 and 3. China's growth rate of real GDP in 2005 and 2006 was 10.5 percent a year and its population growth rate was 0.5 percent a year .

2. If these growth rates continue, in what year would real GDP be twice what it was in 2006?
3. If these growth rates continue, in what year would real GDP per person be twice what it was in 2006?
4. Explain how an increase in physical capital and an increase in human capital change labor productivity. Use a graph to illustrate your answer.

Use Table 1 and Table 2 to work Problems 5 to 7. Table 1 describes an economy's labor market in 2009, and Table 2 describes its production function in 2009.

5. What are the equilibrium real wage rate, employment, and real GDP in 2009?
6. What are labor productivity and potential GDP in 2009?
7. Suppose that labor productivity increases in 2010. What effect does the increased labor productivity have on the demand for labor, the supply of labor, potential GDP, and real GDP per person?

**TABLE 1 LABOR MARKET**

| Real wage rate (2005 dollars per hour) | Labor hours supplied | Labor hours demanded |
|---|---|---|
| 80 | 55 | 15 |
| 70 | 50 | 20 |
| 60 | 45 | 25 |
| 50 | 40 | 30 |
| 40 | 35 | 35 |
| 30 | 30 | 40 |
| 20 | 25 | 45 |
| 10 | 20 | 50 |

**TABLE 2 PRODUCTION FUNCTION**

| Labor (hours) | Real GDP (2005 dollars) |
|---|---|
| 15 | 1,425 |
| 20 | 1,800 |
| 25 | 2,125 |
| 30 | 2,400 |
| 35 | 2,625 |
| 40 | 2,800 |
| 45 | 2,925 |
| 50 | 3,000 |

Use the following information to work Problems 8 to 10.

**India's growth could be even better, says OECD**

India's already impressive economic growth could improve even more if it further opened its markets and relaxed government controls, according to the Organization for Economic Co-operation and Development (OECD).

The OECD said that while the current growth that has averaged 8.5 percent a year over the past four years was sustainable, a rate of 10 percent was possible if greater reforms were introduced. The OECD suggests that ongoing economic liberalization, which India began in 1991, could help the country double its real GDP per person in 10 years. The OECD said it would have taken India 55 years to double real GDP per person if it had stayed on the growth path experienced in the 30 years following independence in 1947.

Source: *The Independent*, October 10, 2007

8. What was the average growth rate achieved by India in the 30 years after 1947?
9. By raising the real GDP growth rate from 8.5 percent a year to 10 percent a year and maintaining a constant population growth rate, how many years earlier will real GDP per person be doubled?
10. Suggest some government controls that if removed might spur India's growth rate to a sustained 10 percent a year.

Use the following information to work Problems **11** to **13**.

**Make way for India—the next China**

China grows at around 9 percent a year, but its one-child policy will start to reduce the size of China's working-age population within the next 10 years. India, by contrast, will have an increasing working-age population for another generation at least.

Source: *The Independent*, March 1, 2006

**11.** Given the expected population changes, do you think China or India will have the greater economic growth rate? Why?

**12.** Would China's growth rate remain at 9 percent a year without the restriction on its population growth rate?

**13.** India's population growth rate is 1.6 percent a year while China's population growth rate is 0.6 percent a year. If India keeps its economic growth rate at 8 percent a year, and China keeps its economic growth rate at 9 percent a year, in what year will real GDP per person double in each country?

Use the following information to work Problems **14** and **15**.

**Optimistic about globalization**

Mark Carney, governor of the Bank of Canada, is optimistic that while the adjustment to the global financial crisis will be difficult, flexible labor markets will make it possible for workers to retrain and find more productive jobs.

Source: *Toronto Star*, February 24, 2008

**14.** Explain which growth theory most closely describes the arguments made in this news clip.

**15.** Explain the suggestions that can help an economy achieve faster economic growth.

**16.** What can governments in Africa do to encourage economic growth and raise their standard of living?

**17.** Why do you think the standard of living in Asian economies has increased in the last decade by so much more than the increase in the standard of living in the United States?

**18.** What are the ingredients of economic freedom and how does each ingredient make economic growth more likely? Provide examples of nations that do not enjoy political freedom and that have a low economic growth rate and examples of nations that do enjoy political freedom and have a high economic growth rate. Are there any notable examples that contradict the view that economic freedom and economic growth go together?

**19.** Why might high taxes hold back economic growth? Would you recommend any changes in the U.S. tax laws to encourage faster growth? How would the changes that you recommend work?

**20.** An increasing number of Chinese citizens who are educated in the United States are returning to China to work. How do you think this development might influence economic growth in China? Do you think the Chinese government would be wise to adopt policies that encourage more Chinese students to return to China when they have completed their studies?

## What created the global financial crisis?

Why did borrowing and lending almost disappear in the depth of the crisis?

# Finance, Saving, and Investment

CHAPTER CHECKLIST

**When you have completed your study of this chapter, you will be able to**

1 Describe the financial markets and the key financial institutions.

2 Explain how borrowing and lending decisions are made and how these decisions interact in the market for loanable funds.

3 Explain how a government budget surplus or deficit influences the real interest rate, investment, and saving.

## 25.1 FINANCIAL INSTITUTIONS AND MARKETS

Financial institutions and markets provide the channels through which saving flows to finance the investment in capital that makes our economy grow. The health of these institutions and markets spreads to affect the performance of every other market—of the labor market and the markets for goods and services.

When financial institutions are in good health and financial markets are working well, a high level of investment brings a rapidly growing economy and rising living standards. When financial institutions get sick and financial markets dry up, a low level of investment slows economic growth and sometimes puts the economy in recession with falling living standards.

### Some Finance Definitions

Finance, money, and capital are three terms that we use in our everyday lives almost interchangeably. Yet these terms have distinctly different meanings in the study of financial markets. Let's examine their differences.

#### Finance and Money

*Finance* is the lending and borrowing that moves funds from savers to spenders. *Money* is the object (or objects) that people use to make payments. You might say "I'm going to borrow some money to buy a car." Your borrowing and someone else's lending is a financial transaction—*finance*. You pay for the new car using *money*. By distinguishing between finance and money and studying them separately, we can better understand their roles and effects on the economy. For the rest of this chapter, we study finance and in Chapters 26 and 27, we study money.

#### Capital: Physical and Financial

**Capital or physical capital**
The tools, instruments, machines, buildings, and other items that have been produced in the past and that are used to produce goods and services.

**Capital**—also called **physical capital**—is the tools, instruments, machines, buildings, and other items that have been produced in the past and that are used to produce goods and services. Inventories of raw materials, semifinished goods, and components are part of physical capital. *Financial capital* is the funds used to buy physical capital. You're going to see how decisions about investment and saving, along with borrowing and lending, influence the quantity of physical capital.

#### Investment, Capital, Wealth, and Saving

**Gross investment**
The total amount spent on new capital goods.

**Net investment**
The change in the quantity of capital—equals gross investment minus depreciation.

**Wealth**
The value of all the things that people own.

*Investment* (Chapter 20, p. 511) increases the quantity of capital and *depreciation* (Chapter 20, p. 518) decreases it. The total amount spent on new capital is called **gross investment**. The change in the quantity of capital is called **net investment**. Net investment equals gross investment minus depreciation. Figure 25.1 illustrates these concepts. Tom's end-of-year capital of $40,000 equals his initial capital of $30,000 plus net investment of $10,000; and net investment equals gross investment of $30,000 minus depreciation of $20,000.

**Wealth** is the value of all the things that people own. What people own is related to what they earn, but it is not the same thing. People earn an income, which is the amount they receive during a given time period from supplying the services of the resources they own. *Saving* (Chapter 20, p. 512), the amount of income that is not paid in taxes or spent on consumption, adds to wealth. Wealth also increases when the market value of assets rises—called *capital gains*.

**FIGURE 25.1**

Capital and Investment

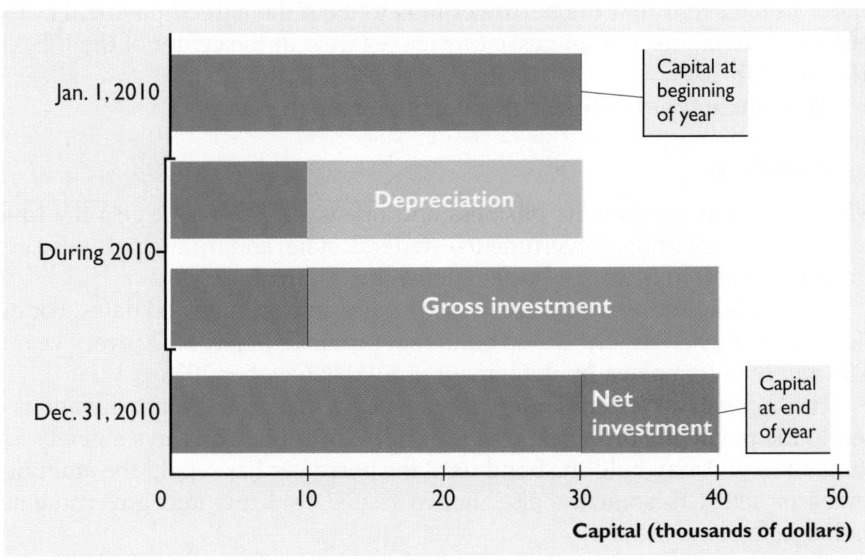


On January 1, 2010, Tom's DVD Burning, Inc. had DVD-recording machines valued at $30,000. During 2010, the value of Tom's machines fell by $20,000—depreciation—and he spent $30,000 on new machines—gross investment. Tom's net investment was $10,000, so at the end of 2010, Tom had capital valued at $40,000.

If at the end of the school year, you have $250 in the bank and textbooks worth $300 and that's all that you own, your wealth is $550. If during the summer, you earn $5,000 (after-tax income) and spend $1,000 on consumption, your bank account increases to $4,250 and your wealth becomes $4,550. Your wealth has increased by $4,000, which equals your saving—your income of $5,000 minus your consumption expenditure of $1,000.

National wealth and national saving work like this personal example. The wealth of a nation at the end of a year equals its wealth at the start of the year plus its saving during the year, which equals income minus consumption expenditure.

To make real GDP grow, saving and wealth must be transformed into investment and capital. This transformation takes place in the markets for financial capital and through the activities of financial institutions that we now describe.

## Markets for Financial Capital

Saving is the source of the funds that are used to finance investment, and these funds are supplied and demanded in three types of financial markets:

- Loan markets
- Bond markets
- Stock markets

### Loan Markets

Businesses often want short-term loans to buy inventories or to extend credit to their customers. Sometimes they get these funds in the form of a loan from a bank. Households often want funds to purchase big-ticket items, such as automobiles or household furnishings and appliances. They get these funds as bank loans, often in the form of outstanding credit card balances.

Households also get funds to buy new homes. (Expenditure on new homes is counted as part of investment.) These funds are usually obtained as a loan that is secured by a *mortgage*—a legal contract that gives ownership of a home to the lender in the event that the borrower fails to meet the agreed payment schedule (of loan repayments and interest). Mortgages were at the center of the U.S. credit crisis of 2007–2008.

All of these types of financing take place in loan markets.

## Bond Markets

When Wal-Mart expands its business and opens new stores, it gets the funds it needs by selling bonds. Governments—federal, state, and municipal—also get the funds they need to finance a budget deficit by issuing bonds.

**Bond**
A promise to pay specified sums of money on specified dates.

A **bond** is a promise to make specified payments on specified dates. For example, you can buy a Western Union bond that promises to pay $6.20 every year until 2035 and then to make a final payment of $100 in October 2036.

The buyer of a Western Union bond makes a loan to the company and is entitled to the payments promised by the bond. When a person buys a newly issued bond, he or she may hold the bond until the borrower has repaid the amount borrowed or sell it to someone else. Bonds issued by firms and governments are traded in the *bond market*.

The term of a bond might be long (decades) or short (just a month or two). Firms often issue very short-term bonds as a way of getting paid for their sales before the buyer is able to pay. For example, when GM sells $100 million of railway locomotives to Union Pacific, GM wants to be paid when the items are shipped. But Union Pacific doesn't want to pay until the locomotives are earning an income. In this situation, Union Pacific might promise to pay GM $101 million three months in the future. A bank would be willing to buy this promise for (say) $100 million. GM gets $100 million immediately and the bank gets $101 million in three months when Union Pacific honors its promise. The U.S. Treasury issues promises of this type, called *Treasury bills*.

Another type of bond is a *mortgage-backed security*, which entitles its holder to the income from a package of mortgages. Mortgage lenders create mortgage-backed securities. They make mortgage loans to home buyers and then create securities that they sell to obtain more funds to make more mortgage loans. The holder of a mortgage-backed security is entitled to receive payments that derive from the payments received by the mortgage lender from the homebuyer–borrower.

Mortgage-backed securities were at the center of the storm in the financial markets in 2007–2008.

## Stock Markets

When Boeing wants to raise funds to expand its airplane building business, it issues stock. A **stock** is a certificate of ownership and claim to a firm's profits. Boeing has issued about 900 million shares of its stock. If you owned 900 Boeing shares, you would own one millionth of Boeing and be entitled to receive one millionth of its profits.

**Stock**
A certificate of ownership and claim to the profits that a firm makes.

A *stock market* is a financial market in which shares in corporations' stocks are traded. The New York Stock Exchange, the London Stock Exchange (in England), the Frankfurt Stock Exchange (in Germany), and the Tokyo Stock Exchange are all examples of stock markets.

## Financial Institutions

Financial markets are highly competitive because of the role played by financial institutions in those markets. A **financial institution** is a firm that operates on both sides of the markets for financial capital: It borrows in one market and lends in another. The key financial institutions are

**Financial institution**
A firm that operates on both sides of the markets for financial capital: It borrows in one market and lends in another.

- Investment banks
- Commercial banks
- Government-sponsored mortgage lenders
- Pension funds
- Insurance companies

### Investment Banks

Investment banks are firms that help other financial institutions and governments raise funds by issuing and selling bonds and stocks, as well as providing advice on transactions such as mergers and acquisitions. Until the late 1980s, the United States maintained a sharp separation between investment banking and commercial banking—a separation that was imposed by the Glass-Steagall Act of 1933. Until 2008, four big Wall Street firms, Goldman Sachs, Lehman Brothers, Merrill Lynch, and Morgan Stanley provided investment banking services. But in the financial meltdown of 2008, Lehman disappeared and Merrill Lynch was taken over by the Bank of America, a commercial bank.

### Commercial Banks

The bank that you use for your own banking services and that issues your credit card is a commercial bank. We'll explain their role in Chapter 26 where we study the role of money in our economy.

### Government-Sponsored Mortgage Lenders

Two large financial institutions, the Federal National Mortgage Association, or Fannie Mae, and the Federal Home Loan Mortgage Corporation, or Freddie Mac, are government-sponsored enterprises that buy mortgages from banks, package them into *mortgage-backed securities*, and sell them. In September 2008, Fannie Mae and Freddie Mac owned or guaranteed $6 trillion worth of mortgages (half of the U.S. total of $12 trillion) and were taken over by the federal government.

### Pension Funds

Pension funds are financial institutions that use the pension contributions of firms and workers to buy bonds and stocks. The mortgage-backed securities of Fannie Mae and Freddie Mac are among the assets of pension funds. Some pension funds are very large and play an active role in the firms whose stock they hold.

### Insurance Companies

Insurance companies enter into agreements with households and firms to provide compensation in the event of accident, theft, fire, ill-health, and a host of other misfortunes. Some companies, for example, provide insurance that pays out if a firm fails and cannot meet its bond obligations; and some insure other insurers in a complex network of reinsurance.

Insurance companies receive premiums from their customers, make payments against claims, and use the funds they have received but not paid out as claims to buy bonds and stocks on which they earn interest.

In normal times, insurance companies have a steady flow of funds coming in from premiums and interest on the financial assets they hold and a steady, but smaller, flow of funds paying claims. Their profit is the gap between the two flows. But in unusual times, when large and widespread losses are being incurred, insurance companies can run into difficulty in meeting their obligations. Such a situation arose in 2008 for one of the biggest insurers, AIG, and the firm was taken into public ownership.

## Insolvency and Illiquidity

**Net worth**
The total market value of what a financial institution has lent minus the market value of what it has borrowed.

A financial institution's **net worth** is the total market value of what it has lent minus the market value of what it has borrowed. If net worth is positive, the institution is *solvent* and can remain in business. But if net worth is negative, the institution is *insolvent* and must stop trading. The owners of an insolvent financial institution—usually its stockholders—bear the loss when the assets are sold and debts paid.

A financial institution both borrows and lends, so it is exposed to the risk that its net worth might become negative. To limit that risk, institutions are regulated and a minimum amount of their lending must be backed by their net worth.

Sometimes, a financial institution is solvent but illiquid. A firm is *illiquid* if it has made long-term loans with borrowed funds and is faced with a sudden demand to repay more of what it has borrowed than its available cash. In normal times, a financial institution that is illiquid can borrow from another institution. But if all financial institutions are short of cash, the market for loans among financial institutions dries up.

Insolvency and illiquidity were at the core of the financial meltdown of 2007–2008.

## Interest Rates and Asset Prices

Stocks, bonds, short-term securities, and loans are collectively called *financial assets*. The *interest rate* on a financial asset is a percentage of the price of the asset.

Because the interest rate is a percentage of the price of an asset, if the asset price rises, other things remaining the same, the interest rate falls. And conversely, if the asset price falls, other things remaining the same, the interest rate rises.

To see this *inverse relationship* between an asset price and interest rate, look at the example of a Microsoft share. In September 2009, the price of a Microsoft share was \$25 and each share entitled its owner to 50 cents of Microsoft profit. The interest rate on a Microsoft share as a percentage was

$$\text{Interest rate} = (\$0.50 \div \$25) \times 100 = 2 \text{ percent.}$$

If the price of a Microsoft share increased to \$50 and each share still entitled its owner to 50 cents of Microsoft profit, the interest rate on a Microsoft share as a percentage would become

$$\text{Interest rate} = (\$0.50 \div \$50) \times 100 = 1 \text{ percent.}$$

This relationship means that an asset price and interest rate are determined simultaneously—one implies the other. In the next part of this chapter, we learn how asset prices and interest rates are determined in the financial markets.

# CHECKPOINT 25.1

Work these problems in Study Plan 25.1 to get instant feedback.

**Describe the financial markets and the key financial institutions.**

## Practice Problems

1. Michael is an Internet service provider. On December 31, 2009, he bought an existing business with servers and a building worth $400,000. During 2010, he bought new servers for $500,000. The market value of his older servers fell by $100,000. What was Michael's gross investment, depreciation, and net investment during 2010? What is Michael's capital at the end of 2010?
2. Lori is a student who teaches golf on the weekend and in a year earns $20,000 after paying her taxes. At the beginning of 2009, Lori owned $1,000 worth of books, DVDs, and golf clubs and she had $5,000 in a savings account at the bank. During 2009, the interest on her savings account was $300 and she spent a total of $15,300 on consumption goods and services. There was no change in the market value of her books, DVDs, and golf clubs. How much did Lori save in 2009? What was her wealth at the end of 2009?
3. **G-20 leaders look to shake off lingering economic troubles**

   The G-20 aims to take stock of the economic recovery. One achievement in Pittsburgh could be a deal to require that financial institutions hold more capital.

   Source: *USA Today*, September 24, 2009

   What are the financial institutions that the G-20 might require to hold more capital? What exactly is the "capital" referred to in the news clip? How might the requirement to hold more capital make financial institutions safer?

## Guided Solutions to Practice Problems

1. Michael's gross investment during 2010 was $500,000—the market value of the new servers he bought.

   Michael's depreciation during 2010 was $100,000—the fall in the market value of his older servers.

   Michael's net investment during 2010 was $400,000. Net investment equals gross investment minus depreciation, which is ($500,000 − $100,000).

   At the end of 2010, Michael's capital was $800,000. The capital grew during 2010 by the amount of net investment, so at the end of 2010 capital was $400,000 + $400,000, which equals $800,000.
2. Lori saved $5,000. Saving equals income (after tax) minus the amount spent. That is, Lori's saving equaled $20,300 minus $15,300, or $5,000.

   Lori's wealth at the end of 2009 was $11,000—the sum of her wealth at the start of 2009 ($6,000) plus her saving during 2009 ($5,000).
3. The institutions are banks and insurance companies. "Capital" in the news clip is the institutions' own funds. By using more of its own funds and less borrowed funds, a financial institution decreases its risk of insolvency.

## 25.2 THE MARKET FOR LOANABLE FUNDS

**Market for loanable funds**
The aggregate of all the individual financial markets.

In macroeconomics, we group all the individual financial markets into a single market for loanable funds. The **market for loanable funds** is the aggregate of the markets for loans, bonds, and stocks. In the market for loanable funds, there is just one average interest rate that we refer to as *the* interest rate.

Thinking about financial markets as a single market for loanable funds makes sense because the individual markets are highly interconnected with many common influences that move the interest rates on individual assets up and down together.

### Flows in the Market for Loanable Funds

The circular flow model (see Chapter 20, pp. 512–513) provides the accounting framework that describes the flows in the market for loanable funds.

Loanable funds are used for three purposes:

1. Business investment
2. Government budget deficit
3. International investment or lending

And loanable funds come from three sources:

1. Private saving
2. Government budget surplus
3. International borrowing

Firms often use *retained earnings*—profits not distributed to stockholders—to finance business investment. These earnings belong to the firm's stockholders and are borrowed from the stockholders rather than being paid to them as dividends. To keep the accounts in the clearest possible way, we think of these retained earnings as being both a use and a source of loanable funds. They are part of business investment on the uses side and part of private saving on the sources side.

We measure all the flows of loanable funds in real terms—in constant 2005 dollars.

You're now going to see how these real flows and the real interest rate are determined in the market for loanable funds by studying

- The demand for loanable funds
- The supply of loanable funds
- Equilibrium in the market for loanable funds

### The Demand for Loanable Funds

The *quantity of loanable funds demanded* is the total quantity of funds demanded to finance investment, the government budget deficit, and international investment or lending during a given period. Investment is the major item and the focus of our explanation of the forces that influence the demand side of the market for loanable funds. The other two items—the government budget deficit and international investment and lending—can be thought of as amounts to be added to investment. (We study the effects of the government budget later in this chapter on pp. 654–658 and international borrowing and lending in Chapter 33.)

What determines investment and the demand for loanable funds? How does Amazon.com decide how much to borrow to build some new warehouses? Many details influence such a decision, but we can summarize them in two factors:

1. The real interest rate
2. Expected profit

The real interest rate is the opportunity cost of the funds used to finance the purchase of capital, and firms compare the real interest rate with the rate of profit they expect to earn on their new capital. Firms invest only when they expect to earn a rate of profit that exceeds the real interest rate. Fewer projects are profitable at a high real interest rate than at a low real interest rate, so:

**Other things remaining the same, the higher the real interest rate, the smaller is the quantity of loanable funds demanded; and the lower the real interest rate, the greater is the quantity of loanable funds demanded.**

### Demand for Loanable Funds Curve

The **demand for loanable funds** is the relationship between the quantity of loanable funds demanded and the real interest rate when all other influences on borrowing plans remain the same. Figure 25.2 illustrates the demand for loanable funds as a schedule and as a curve.

**Demand for loanable funds**
The relationship between the quantity of loanable funds demanded and the real interest rate when all other influences on borrowing plans remain the same.

**FIGURE 25.2**

The Demand for Loanable Funds

myeconlab Animation

| | Real interest rate (percent per year) | Loanable funds demanded (trillions of 2005 dollars) |
|---|---|---|
| A | 10 | 1.0 |
| B | 8 | 1.5 |
| C | 6 | 2.0 |
| D | 4 | 2.5 |
| E | 2 | 3.0 |

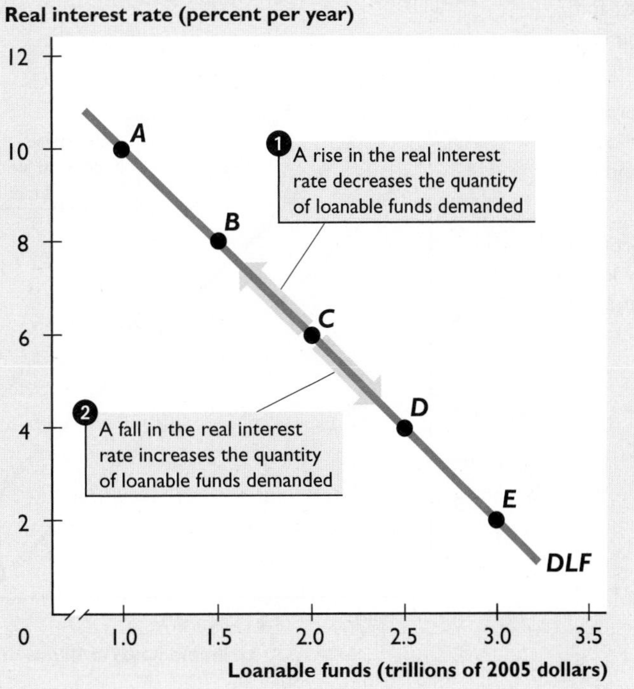

The table shows the quantity of loanable funds demanded at five real interest rates. The graph shows the demand for loanable funds curve, *DLF*. Points *A* through *E* correspond to the rows of the table.

1. If the real interest rate rises, the quantity of loanable funds demanded decreases.
2. If the real interest rate falls, the quantity of loanable funds demanded increases.

To understand the demand for loanable funds, think about Amazon.com's decision to borrow $100 million to build some new warehouses. Suppose that Amazon expects to get a return of $5 million a year from this investment before paying interest costs. If the interest rate is less than 5 percent a year, Amazon expects to make a profit, so it builds the warehouses. If the interest rate is more than 5 percent a year, Amazon expects to incur a loss, so it doesn't build the warehouses. The quantity of loanable funds demanded is greater, the lower is the interest rate.

### Changes in the Demand for Loanable Funds

When the expected profit changes, the demand for loanable funds changes. Other things remaining the same, the greater the expected profit from new capital, the greater is the amount of investment and the greater is the demand for loanable funds.

The expected profit rises during a business cycle expansion and falls during a recession; rises when technological change creates profitable new products; rises as a growing population brings increased demand; and fluctuates with contagious swings of optimism and pessimism, called "animal spirits" by Keynes and "irrational exuberance" by Alan Greenspan.

Figure 25.3 shows how the demand for loanable funds curve shifts when the expected profit changes. With average profit expectations, the demand for loanable funds is $DLF_0$. A rise in expected profit shifts the demand curve rightward to $DLF_1$ and a fall in expected profit shifts the demand curve leftward to $DLF_2$.

**FIGURE 25.3**

## Changes in the Demand for Loanable Funds

myeconlab Animation

A change in expected profit changes the demand for loanable funds and shifts the demand for loanable funds curve.

1. An increase in expected profit increases the demand for loanable funds and shifts the demand curve rightward to $DLF_1$.
2. A decrease in expected profit decreases the demand for loanable funds and shifts the demand curve leftward to $DLF_2$.

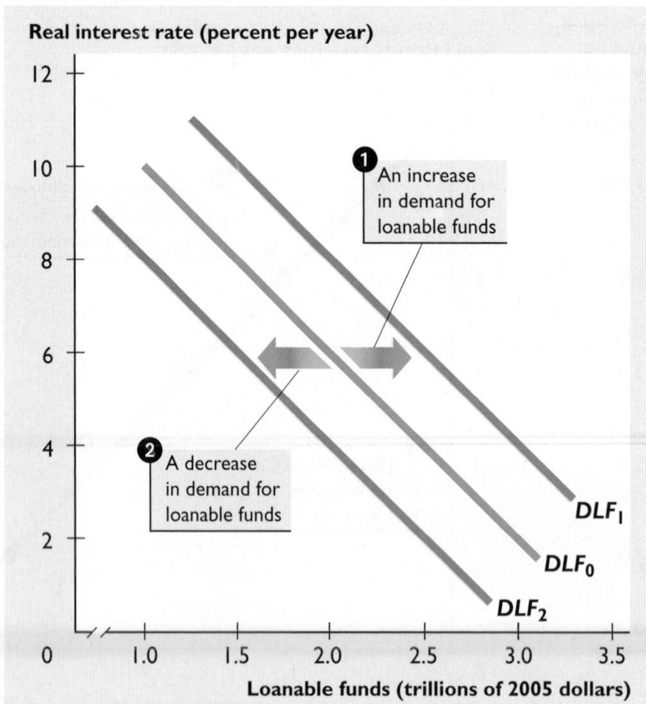

## The Supply of Loanable Funds

The *quantity of loanable funds supplied* is the total funds available from private saving, the government budget surplus, and international borrowing during a given period. Saving is the main source of supply of loanable funds. A government budget surplus and international borrowing are other sources.

Saving and the supply of loanable funds are determined by decisions by people like you. Suppose that you've graduated and landed a great job that pays you $50,000 a year. How do you decide how much of your income to spend on consumption goods and how much to save and supply in the market for loanable funds? Your decision will be influenced by many factors, but chief among them are

1. The real interest rate
2. Disposable income
3. Wealth
4. Expected future income
5. Default risk

We begin by focusing on the real interest rate.

**Other things remaining the same, the higher the real interest rate, the greater is the quantity of loanable funds supplied; and the lower the real interest rate, the smaller is the quantity of loanable funds supplied.**

### The Supply of Loanable Funds Curve

The **supply of loanable funds** is the relationship between the quantity of loanable funds supplied and the real interest rate when all other influences on lending plans remain the same. Figure 25.4 illustrates the supply of loanable funds.

**Supply of loanable funds**
The relationship between the quantity of loanable funds supplied and the real interest rate when all other influences on lending plans remain the same.

The key reason the supply of loanable funds curve slopes upward is that the real interest rate is the *opportunity cost* of consumption expenditure. A dollar spent is a dollar not saved, so the interest that could have been earned on that saving is forgone. Forgone interest is the opportunity cost of consumption regardless of whether a person is a lender or a borrower. For a lender, saving less means receiving less interest. For a borrower, saving less means paying less off a loan (or increasing a loan) and paying more interest.

By thinking about student loans, you can see why the real interest rate influences saving and the supply of loanable funds. If the real interest rate on student loans jumped to 20 percent a year, graduates would save more (buying cheaper food and finding lower-rent accommodations) to pay off their loans as quickly as possible and avoid, as much as possible, paying the higher interest cost of their loan. If the real interest rate on student loans fell to 1 percent a year, graduates would save less and take longer to pay off their loans because the interest burden was easier to bear.

### Changes in the Supply of Loanable Funds

A change in any influence on saving, other than the real interest rate, changes the supply of loanable funds. The other four factors listed above—disposable income, wealth, expected future income, and default risk—are the main things that change the supply of loanable funds.

**FIGURE 25.4**

The Supply of Loanable Funds

myeconlab Animation

The table shows the quantity of loanable funds supplied at five real interest rates. The graph shows the supply of loanable funds curve, *SLF*. Points *A* through *E* correspond to the rows of the table.

1. If the real interest rate rises, the quantity of loanable funds supplied increases.
2. If the real interest rate falls, the quantity of loanable funds supplied decreases.

| | Real interest rate (percent per year) | Loanable funds supplied (trillions of 2005 dollars) |
|---|---|---|
| *A* | 10 | 3.0 |
| *B* | 8 | 2.5 |
| *C* | 6 | 2.0 |
| *D* | 4 | 1.5 |
| *E* | 2 | 1.0 |

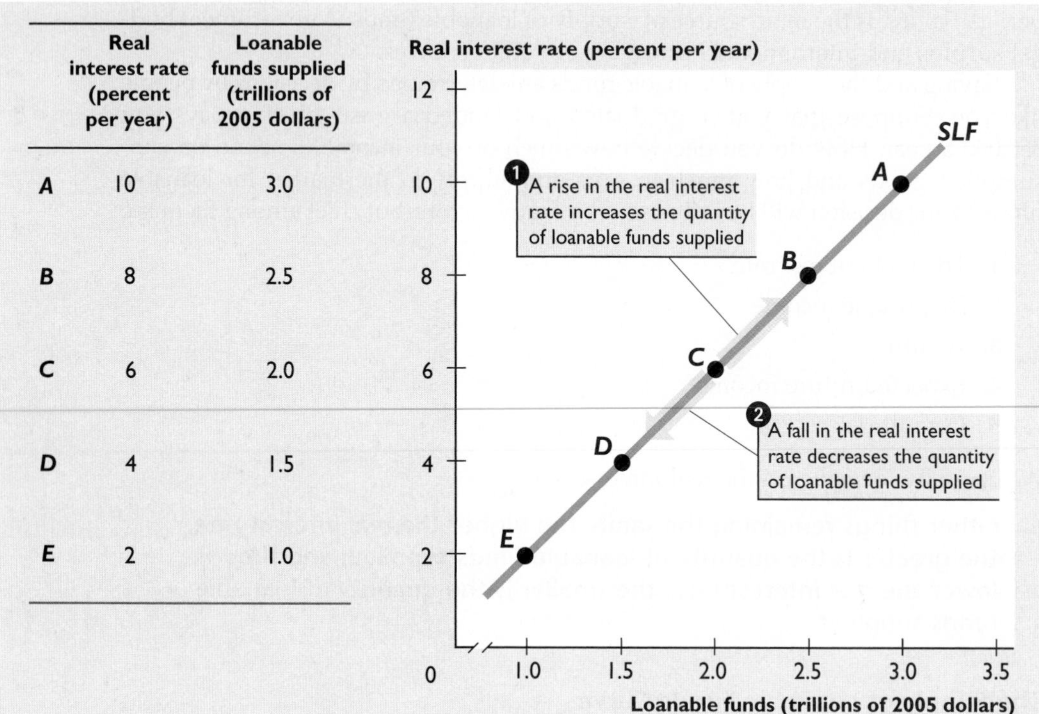


***Disposable Income*** A household's *disposable income* is the income earned minus net taxes. The greater a household's disposable income, other things remaining the same, the greater is its saving. For example, a student whose disposable income is $10,000 a year spends the entire $10,000 and saves nothing. An economics graduate whose disposable income is $50,000 a year spends $40,000 and saves $10,000.

***Wealth*** A household's wealth is what it owns. The greater a household's wealth, other things remaining the same, the less it will save.

Patty is a department store executive who has $15,000 in the bank and no debts: She decides to spend $5,000 on a vacation and save nothing this year. Tony, another department store executive, has nothing in the bank and owes $10,000 on his credit card: He decides to cut consumption and start saving.

***Expected Future Income*** The higher a household's expected future income, other things remaining the same, the smaller is its saving today: If two households have the same current disposable income, the household with the larger expected future disposable income will spend a larger portion of its current disposable income on consumption goods and services and so save less today.

Look at Patty and Tony again. Patty has just been promoted and will receive a $10,000 pay raise next year. Tony has just been told that he will be laid off at the end of the year. On receiving this news, Patty buys a new car—increases her consumption expenditure and cuts her saving—and Tony sells his car and takes the bus—decreases his consumption expenditure and increases his saving.

Most young households expect to have a higher future income for some years and then to have a lower income during retirement. Because of this pattern of income over the life cycle, young people save a small amount, middle-aged people save a lot, and retired people gradually spend their accumulated savings.

***Default Risk*** Default risk is the risk that a loan will not be repaid, or not repaid in full. The greater that risk, the higher is the interest rate needed to induce a person to lend and the smaller is the supply of loanable funds. In normal times, default risk is low but in times of financial crisis when asset prices tumble, default can become widespread as financial institutions become *illiquid* or *insolvent*.

## Shifts of the Supply of Loanable Funds Curve

When any of the four influences we've just described changes, the supply of loanable funds changes and the supply curve shifts. An increase in disposable income, or a decrease in wealth, expected future income, or default risk increases the supply of loanable funds.

Figure 25.5 shows how the supply of loanable funds curve shifts. Initially, the supply of loanable funds is $SLF_0$. Then disposable income increases or wealth, expected future income, or default risk decreases. The supply of loanable funds curve shifts rightward from $SLF_0$ to $SLF_1$. Changes in these factors in the opposite direction shift the supply curve leftward from $SLF_0$ to $SLF_2$.

**FIGURE 25.5**

Changes in the Supply of Loanable Funds

Animation

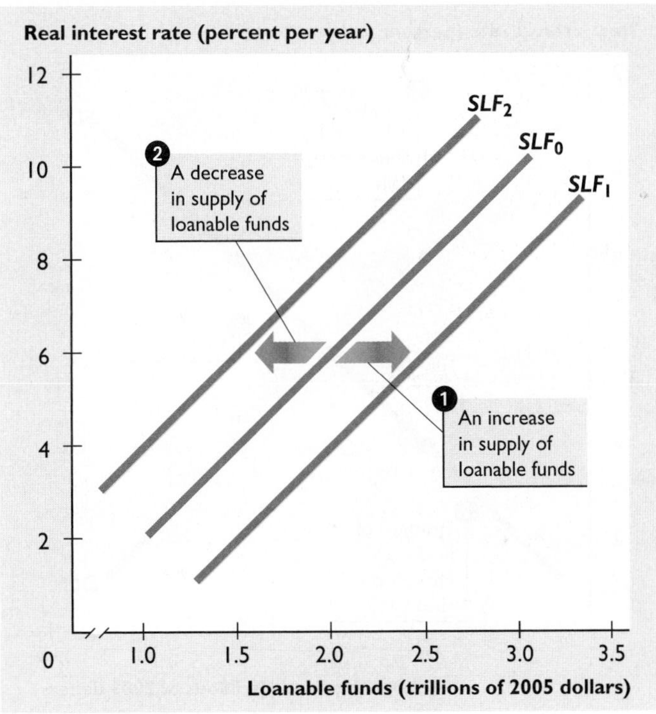


❶ An increase in disposable income or a decrease in wealth, expected future income, or default risk increases the supply of loanable funds and shifts the supply of loanable funds curve rightward from $SLF_0$ to $SLF_1$.

❷ A decrease in disposable income or an increase in wealth, expected future income, or default risk decreases the supply of loanable funds and shifts the supply of loanable funds curve leftward from $SLF_0$ to $SLF_2$.

## Equilibrium in the Market for Loanable Funds

You've seen that, other things remaining the same, the quantities of loanable funds demanded and supplied depend on the real interest rate. The higher the real interest rate, the greater is the amount of saving and the larger is the quantity of loanable funds supplied. But the higher the real interest rate, the smaller is the amount of investment and the smaller is the quantity of loanable funds demanded. There is one interest rate at which the quantities of loanable funds demanded and supplied are equal, and that interest rate is the equilibrium real interest rate.

Figure 25.6 shows how the demand for and supply of loanable funds determine the real interest rate. The *DLF* curve is the demand curve and the *SLF* curve is the supply curve. When the real interest rate exceeds 6 percent a year, the quantity of loanable funds supplied exceeds the quantity demanded. Borrowers have an easy time finding the funds they want, but lenders are unable to lend all the funds they have available. The real interest rate falls and continues to fall until the quantity of funds supplied equals the quantity of funds demanded.

Alternatively, when the interest rate is less than 6 percent a year, the quantity of loanable funds supplied is less than the quantity demanded. Borrowers can't find the funds they want, but lenders are able to lend all the funds they have available. So the real interest rate rises and continues to rise until the quantity of funds supplied equals the quantity demanded.

Regardless of whether there is a surplus or a shortage of loanable funds, the real interest rate changes and is pulled toward an equilibrium level. In Figure 25.6,

**FIGURE 25.6**

Equilibrium in the Market for Loanable Funds

myeconlab Animation

❶ If the real interest rate is 8 percent a year, the quantity of loanable funds demanded is less than the quantity supplied. There is a surplus of funds, and the real interest rate falls.

❷ If the real interest rate is 4 percent a year, the quantity of loanable funds demanded exceeds the quantity supplied. There is a shortage of funds, and the real interest rate rises.

❸ When the real interest rate is 6 percent a year, the quantity of loanable funds demanded equals the quantity supplied. There is neither a shortage nor a surplus of funds, and the real interest rate is at its equilibrium level.

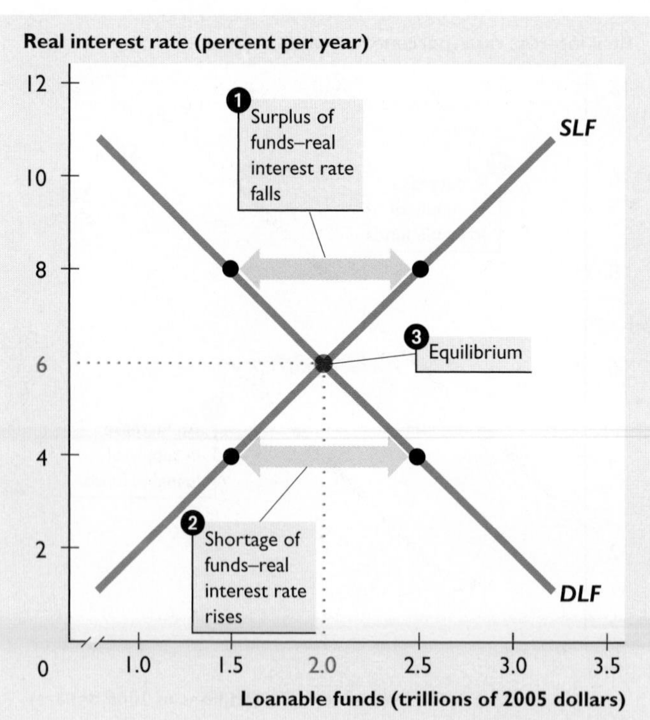

the equilibrium real interest rate is 6 percent a year. At this interest rate, there is neither a surplus nor a shortage of funds. Borrowers can get the funds they want, and lenders can lend all the funds they have available. The plans of borrowers (investors) and lenders (savers) are consistent with each other.

## Changes in Demand and Supply

Fluctuations in either the demand for loanable funds or the supply of loanable funds bring fluctuations in the real interest rate and in the equilibrium quantity of funds lent and borrowed. Here we'll illustrate the effects of an increase in each.

An increase in expected profit increases the demand for loanable funds. With no change in supply, there is a shortage of funds and the interest rate rises until the equilibrium is restored. In Figure 25.7(a), the increase in the demand for loanable funds shifts the demand for loanable funds curve rightward from $DLF_0$ to $DLF_1$. At a real interest rate of 6 percent a year, there is a shortage of funds. The real interest rate rises to 8 percent a year, and the equilibrium quantity of funds increases.

If one of the influences on saving plans changes and increases saving, the supply of loanable funds increases. With no change in demand, there is a surplus of funds and the interest rate falls until the equilibrium is restored. In Figure 25.7(b), the increase in the supply of loanable funds shifts the supply of loanable funds curve rightward from $SLF_0$ to $SLF_1$. At a real interest rate of 6 percent a year, there is a surplus of funds. The real interest rate falls to 4 percent a year, and the equilibrium quantity of funds increases.

Over time, both demand and supply in the market for loanable funds fluctuate and the real interest rate rises and falls. Both the supply of loanable funds and the demand for loanable funds tend to increase over time. On the average, they increase at a similar pace, so although demand and supply trend upward, the real interest rate has no trend. It fluctuates around a constant average level.

**FIGURE 25.7**

Changes in Demand and Supply in the Market for Loanable Funds

myeconlab Animation

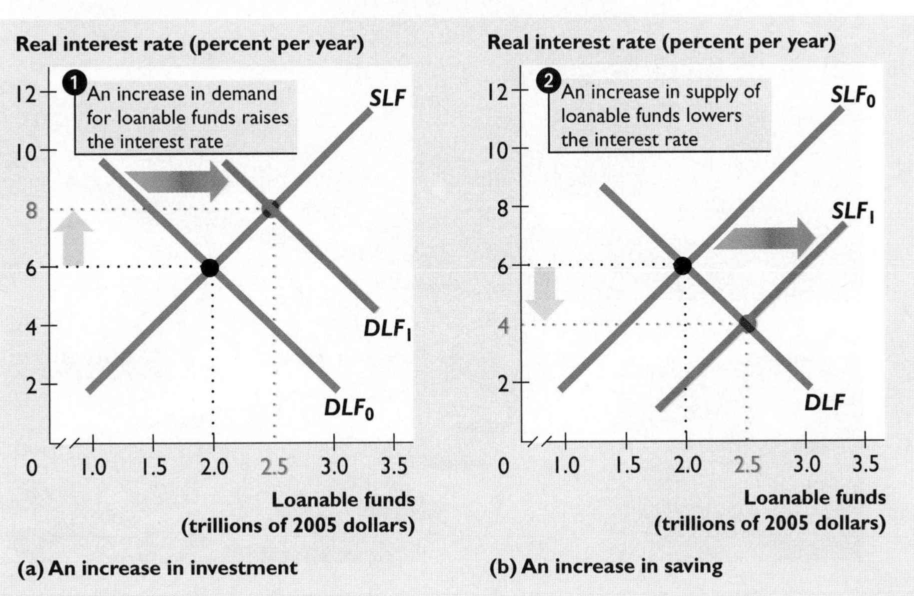


(a) An increase in investment

(b) An increase in saving

1 If the demand for loanable funds increases and the supply of loanable funds remains the same, the real interest rate rises and the equilibrium quantity of funds increases.

2 If the supply of loanable funds increases and the demand for loanable funds remains the same, the real interest rate falls and the equilibrium quantity of funds increases.

# EYE on FINANCIAL CRISIS

## What Created the Global Financial Crisis?

Events in the market for loanable funds, on both the supply side and demand side, created the global financial crisis.

An increase in default risk decreased supply; and the disappearance of some major Wall Street institutions and lowered profit expectations decreased demand.

Bear Stearns was absorbed by JP Morgan with help from the Federal Reserve; Lehman Brothers' assets were taken over by Barclays; Fannie Mae and Freddie Mac went into government oversight with U.S. taxpayer guarantees; Merrill Lynch became part of the Bank of America; AIG received an $85 billion lifeline from the Federal Reserve and sold off parcels of its business to financial institutions around the world; Wachovia was taken over by Wells Fargo and Washington Mutual by JP Morgan Chase.

But what caused the increase in default risk and the failure of so many financial institutions?

Between 2002 and 2005, interest rates were low. There were plenty of willing borrowers and plenty of willing lenders. Fuelled by easy loans, home prices rose rapidly. Lenders bundled their loans into mortgage-backed securities and sold them to eager buyers around the world.

Then, in 2006, interest rates began to rise and home prices began to fall. People defaulted on mortgages; banks took losses and some became insolvent. A downward spiral of lending was under way.

# CHECKPOINT 25.2

Work these problems in Study Plan 25.2 to get instant feedback.

**Explain how borrowing and lending decisions are made and how these decisions interact in the market for loanable funds.**

## Practice Problems

First Call, Inc. is a cellular phone company. It plans to build an assembly plant that costs \$10 million if the real interest rate is 6 percent a year. If the real interest rate is 5 percent a year, First Call will build a larger plant that costs \$12 million. And if the real interest rate is 7 percent a year, First Call will build a smaller plant that costs \$8 million. Use this information to work Problems **1** and **2**.

1. Draw a graph of First Call's demand for loanable funds curve.
2. First Call expects its profit from the sale of cellular phones to double next year. If other things remain the same, explain how this increase in expected profit influences First Call's demand for loanable funds.
3. Draw graphs that illustrate how an increase in the supply of loanable funds and a decrease in the demand for loanable funds can lower the real interest rate and leave the equilibrium quantity of loanable funds unchanged.
4. **Poof! How home loans transform**
   Banks make a profit by transforming home loans into mortgage-backed securities and trading them on financial loans markets. Banks then use this profit to issue more home loans. During the credit crisis, the market for mortgage-backed securities issued by banks almost stopped functioning.
   Source: *The New York Times*, September 18, 2009
   Explain why the market for mortgage-backed securities almost stopped functioning during the credit crisis of 2007–2008.

## Guided Solutions to Practice Problems

1. The demand for loanable funds curve is the downward-sloping curve $DLF_0$ and passes through the points highlighted in Figure 1.
2. An increase in the expected profit increases investment today, which increases the quantity of loanable funds demanded at each real interest rate. The demand for loanable funds curve shifts rightward to $DLF_1$ (Figure 1).
3. The increase in the supply of loanable funds shifts the supply curve rightward. The decrease in the demand for loanable funds shifts the demand curve leftward. The real interest rate falls. If the shifts are of the same magnitude, the equilibrium quantity of funds remains unchanged (Figure 2). If the shift of the supply curve is greater (less) than that of the demand curve, then the equilibrium quantity of funds increases (decreases).
4. The banks that create and sell mortgage-backed securities demand loanable funds and the banks that buy these securities supply loanable funds. When home prices started to fall and home owners defaulted, banks made fewer home loans and the demand for mortgage-backed securities decreased. These securities also became riskier, so the supply of loanable funds to buy them dried up.

FIGURE 1

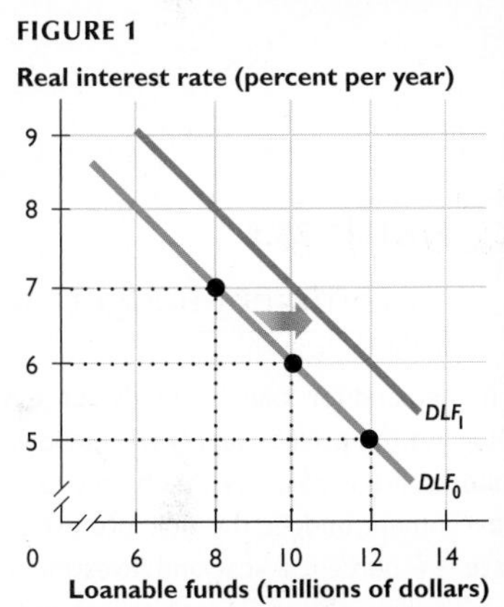


FIGURE 2

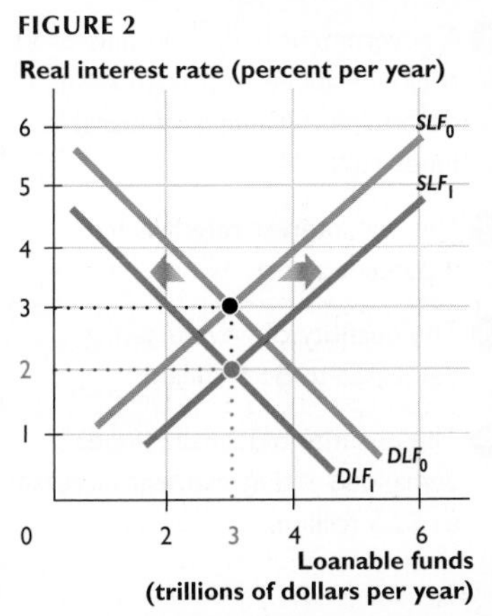

## 25.3 GOVERNMENT IN LOANABLE FUNDS MARKET

The government enters the market for loanable funds when it has a budget surplus or budget deficit. So actions that change the government's budget balance influence the market for loanable funds and the real interest rate. A change in the real interest rate influences both saving and investment. To complete our study of the forces that determine the quantity of investment and the real interest rate, we investigate the role played by the government's budget balance.

### A Government Budget Surplus

A government budget surplus increases the supply of loanable funds. The real interest rate falls, which decreases private saving and decreases the quantity of private funds supplied. The lower real interest rate increases the quantity of loanable funds demanded and increases investment.

Figure 25.8 shows these effects of a government budget surplus. The private supply of loanable funds curve is *PSLF*. The supply of loanable funds curve, *SLF*, shows the sum of the private supply and the government budget surplus. Here, the government budget surplus is $1 trillion, so at each real interest rate the *SLF* curve lies $1 trillion to the right of the *PSLF* curve. That is, the horizontal distance between the *PSLF* curve and the *SLF* curve is the government budget surplus.

**FIGURE 25.8**

Government Budget Surplus

myeconlab Animation

The demand for loanable funds curve is *DLF*, and the private supply of loanable funds curve is *PSLF*. With a balanced government budget, the real interest rate is 6 percent a year and investment is $2 trillion a year. Private saving and investment are $2 trillion a year.

1. A government budget surplus of $1 trillion is added to private saving to determine the supply of loanable funds curve *SLF*.
2. The real interest rate falls to 4 percent a year.
3. The quantity of private saving decreases to $1.5 trillion.
4. The quantity of loanable funds demanded and investment increase to $2.5 trillion.

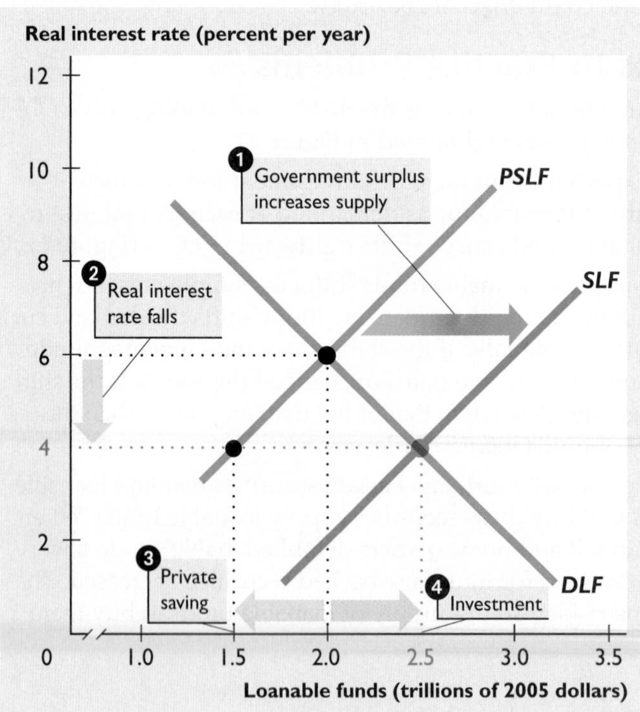

With no government budget surplus, the real interest rate is 6 percent a year, the quantity of loanable funds is $2 trillion a year and investment is $2 trillion a year. But with the government budget surplus of $1 trillion a year, the equilibrium real interest rate falls to 4 percent a year and the quantity of loanable funds increases to $2.5 trillion a year.

The fall in the real interest rate decreases private saving to $1.5 trillion, but investment increases to $2.5 trillion, which is financed by private saving and the government budget surplus (government saving).

## A Government Budget Deficit

A government budget deficit increases the demand for loanable funds. The real interest rate rises, which increases private saving and increases the quantity of private funds supplied. But the higher real interest rate decreases investment and the quantity of loanable funds demanded by firms to finance investment.

Figure 25.9 shows these effects of a government budget deficit. The private demand for loanable funds curve is *PDLF*. The demand for loanable funds curve, *DLF*, shows the sum of the private demand and the government budget deficit. Here, the government budget deficit is $1 trillion, so at each real interest rate the *DLF* curve lies $1 trillion to the right of the *PDLF* curve. That is, the horizontal distance between the *PDLF* curve and the *DLF* curve equals the government budget deficit.

With no government budget deficit, the real interest rate is 6 percent a year, the quantity of loanable funds is $2 trillion a year and investment is $2 trillion a

**FIGURE 25.9**

Government Budget Deficit

myeconlab Animation

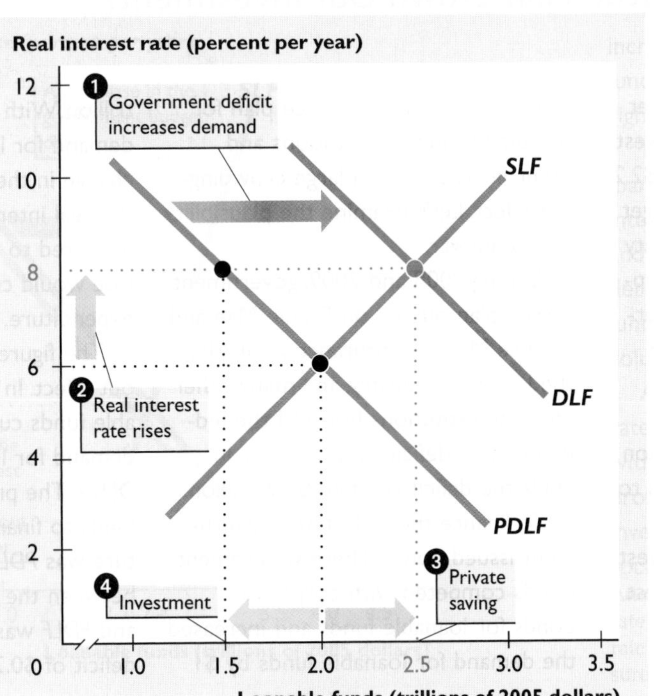


The supply of loanable funds curve is *SLF* and the private demand for loanable funds curve is *PDLF*. With a balanced government budget, the real interest rate is 6 percent a year and the quantity of loanable funds is $2 trillion a year. Private saving and investment are $2 trillion a year.

1. A government budget deficit of $1 trillion is added to the private demand for funds to determine the demand for loanable funds curve *DLF*.
2. The real interest rate rises to 8 percent a year.
3. The quantity of private fund supplied and the quantity of loanable funds increase to $2.5 trillion.
4. Investment decreases to $1.5 trillion. Investment is crowded out.

## Money Today

**Fiat money**
Objects that are money because the law decrees or orders them to be money.

Money in the world today is called **fiat money**. *Fiat* is a Latin word that means decree or order. Fiat money is money because the law decrees it to be so. The objects used as money have value only because of their legal status as money.

Today's fiat money consists of

- Currency
- Deposits at banks and other financial institutions

### Currency

**Currency**
Notes (dollar bills) and coins.

The notes (dollar bills) and coins that we use in the United States today are known as **currency**. The government declares notes to be money with the words printed on every dollar bill, "This note is legal tender for all debts, public and private."

### Deposits

Deposits at banks, credit unions, savings banks, and savings and loan associations are also money. Deposits are money because they can be used to make payments. You don't need to go to the bank to get currency to make a payment. You can write a check or use your debit card to tell your bank to move some money from your account to someone else's.

### Currency Inside the Banks Is Not Money

Although currency and bank deposits are money, currency *inside the banks* is *not money*. The reason is while currency is inside a bank, it isn't available as a means of payment. When you get some cash from the ATM, you convert your bank deposit into currency. You change the form of your money, but there is no change in the quantity of money that you own. Your bank deposit decreases, and your currency holding increases.

If we counted both bank deposits and currency inside the banks as money, when you get cash at the ATM, the quantity of money would appear to decrease—your currency would increase, but both bank deposits and currency inside the banks would decrease.

You can see that counting both bank deposits and currency inside the banks as money would be double counting.

## Official Measures of Money: M1 and M2

**M1**
Currency, traveler's checks, and checkable deposits owned by individuals and businesses.

**M2**
M1 plus savings deposits and small time deposits, money market funds, and other deposits.

Figure 26.1 shows the items that make up two official measures of money. **M1** consists of currency, traveler's checks, and checkable deposits owned by individuals and businesses. **M2** consists of M1 plus savings deposits and time deposits (less than $100,000), money market funds, and other deposits. Time deposits are deposits that can be withdrawn only after a fixed term. Money market funds are deposits that are invested in short-term securities.

### Are M1 and M2 Means of Payment?

The test of whether something is money is whether it is a generally accepted means of payment. Currency passes the test. Checkable deposits also pass the test because they can be transferred from one person to another by using a debit card or writing a check. So all the components of M1 serve as means of payment.

**FIGURE 26.1**

Two Measures of Money: September 2009

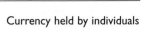

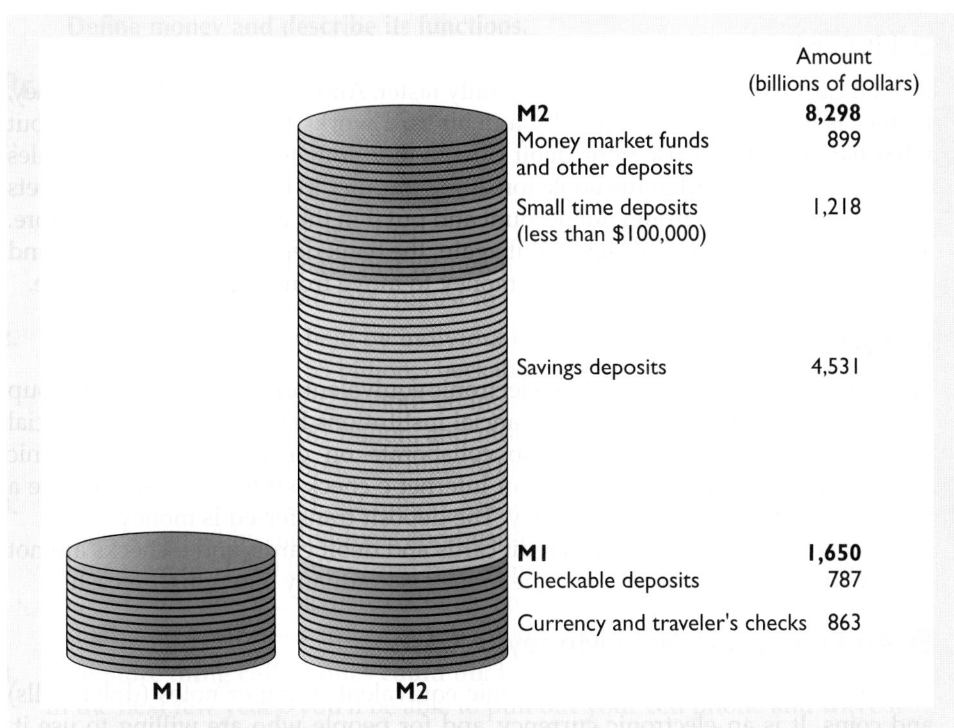


SOURCE OF DATA: Federal Reserve.

**M1** Currency held by individuals and businesses and traveler's checks plus checkable deposits owned by individuals and businesses.

**M2** M1 plus savings deposits plus small time deposits plus money market funds and other deposits.

Some of the savings deposits in M2 are also instantly convertible into a means of payment. You can use the ATM to get currency to pay for your groceries or gas. But other savings deposits, time deposits, and money market funds are not instantly convertible and are *not* a means of payment.

## Checks, Credit Cards, Debit Cards, and E-Checks

In defining money and describing the things that serve as money today, we have not included checks, credit cards and debit cards, or e-checks. Aren't these things that we use when we buy something also money?

### Checks

A check is not money. It is an instruction to a bank to make a payment. The easiest way to see why a check is not money is to think about how the quantity of money you own changes if you write a check. You don't suddenly have more money because you've written a check to pay a bill. Your money is your bank deposit, not the value of the checks you've written.

### Credit Cards

A credit card is not money. It is a special type of ID card that gets you an instant loan. Suppose that you use your credit card to buy a textbook. You sign or enter your PIN and leave the store with your book. The book may be in your possession,

### Liquid Assets

**Federal funds rate**
The interest rate on interbank loans (loans made in the federal funds market).

Banks' *liquid assets* are short-term Treasury Bills and overnight loans to other banks. The interest rates on liquid assets are low but these are low-risk assets. The interest rate on interbank loans, called the **federal funds rate**, is the central target of the Fed's monetary policy actions.

### Securities and Loans

*Securities* are bonds issued by the U.S. government and by other organizations. Some bonds have low interest rates and are safe. Some bonds have high interest rates and are risky. Mortgage-backed securities are examples of risky securities.

*Loans* are the provision of funds to businesses and individuals. Loans earn the bank a high interest rate, but they are risky and, even when not very risky, cannot be called in before the agreed date. Banks earn the highest interest rate on unpaid credit card balances, which are loans to credit card holders.

### Bank Deposits, Other Borrowing, and Assets: The Relative Magnitudes

Figure 26.3 shows the relative magnitudes of the banks' assets, deposits, and other borrowing in 2009. After performing their profit-versus-risk balancing acts, the banks kept 8 percent of total assets in reserves, placed 10 percent in liquid assets, 20 percent in securities, and 62 percent in loans. Checkable deposits (part of M1) were 6 percent of total assets. Another 43 percent of assets were savings deposits and small time deposits (part of M2).

In the financial crisis of 2008 and 2009, the percentage of total assets held in reserves was unusually large and the percentage in loans and securities was unusually small—see *Eye on the U.S. Economy* on the next page.

**FIGURE 26.3**

Commercial Banks' Assets, Deposits, Other Borrowing, and Net Worth

myeconlab Animation

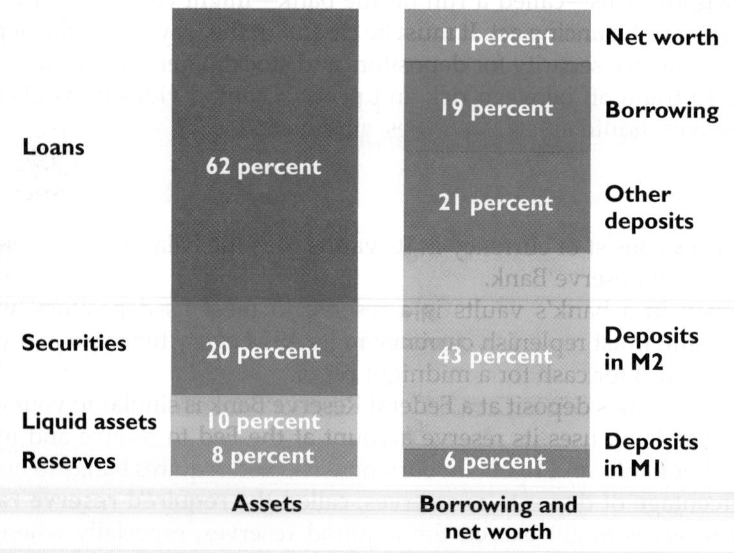

In 2009, commercial bank loans were 62 percent of total assets, securities were 20 percent, liquid assets were 10 percent, and reserves were 8 percent. Reserves were unusually large in 2009.

The banks obtained the funds allocated to these assets from checkable deposits in M1, which were 6 percent of total assets; savings deposits and small time deposits in M2 were 43 percent; other deposits were 21 percent; other borrowing was 19 percent; and bank stockholders' net worth was 11 percent.

SOURCE OF DATA: Federal Reserve.

# EYE on the U.S. ECONOMY

## Commercial Banks Under Stress in the Financial Crisis

In normal times, bank reserves are less than 1 percent of total assets and liquid assets are less than 4 percent. Loans are 68 percent and securities 28 percent. July 2007 was such a normal time (the orange bars).

During the financial crisis that started in 2007 and intensified in September 2008, the banks took big hits as the value of their securities and loans fell.

Faced with a riskier world, the banks increased their liquid assets and reserves. In September 2009 (the blue bars), liquid assets were almost 10 percent of total assets and reserves were 8 percent.

The balancing act tipped away from risk-taking and toward security.

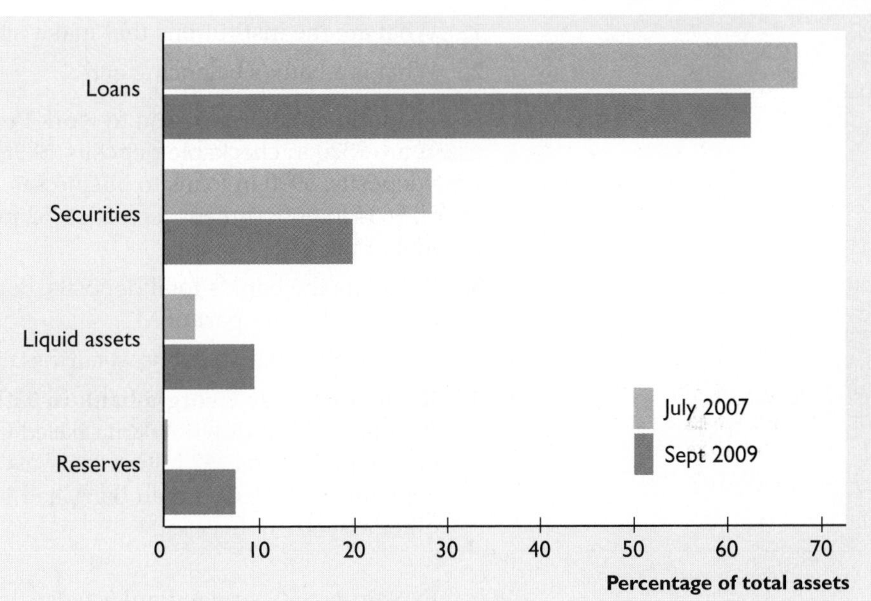


SOURCE OF DATA: Federal Reserve.

## Thrift Institutions

The three types of thrift institutions are savings and loan associations, savings banks, and credit unions. A *savings and loan association* (*S&L*) is a financial institution that accepts checkable deposits and savings deposits and that makes personal, commercial, and home-purchase loans. A *savings bank* is a financial institution that accepts savings deposits and makes mostly consumer and home-purchase loans. The depositors own some savings banks (called mutual savings banks). A *credit union* is a financial institution owned by a social or economic group, such as a firm's employees, that accepts savings deposits and makes mostly consumer loans.

Like commercial banks, the thrift institutions hold reserves and must meet minimum reserve ratios set by the Fed.

## Money Market Funds

A *money market fund* is a financial institution that obtains funds by selling shares and uses these funds to buy assets such as U.S. Treasury bills. Money market fund shares act like bank deposits. Shareholders can write checks on their money market fund accounts, but there are restrictions on most of these accounts. For example, the minimum deposit accepted might be $2,500 and the smallest check a depositor is permitted to write might be $500.

Work these problems in Study Plan 26.2 to get instant feedback.

## CHECKPOINT 26.2

**Describe the functions of banks.**

## Practice Problems

1. What are the institutions that make up the banking system?
2. What is a bank's balancing act?

Use the following information to work Problems **3** and **4**. A bank's deposits and assets are $320 in checkable deposits, $896 in savings deposits, $840 in small time deposits, $990 in loans to businesses, $400 in outstanding credit card balances, $634 in government securities, $2 in currency, and $30 in its reserve account at the Fed.

3. Calculate the bank's total deposits, deposits that are part of M1, and deposits that are part of M2.
4. Calculate the bank's loans, securities, and reserves.
5. **Regulators close Georgia bank in 95th failure for the year**
   Regulators shut down Atlanta-based Georgian Bank. On July 24, 2009, Georgian Bank has $2 billion in assets and $2 billion in deposits. By 29 September, 2009, Georgian Bank had lost about $2 billion in home loans and other assets.

   Source: *USA Today*, September 30, 2009

   Explain how Georgian Bank's balancing act failed.

## Guided Solutions to Practice Problems

1. The institutions that make up the banking system are the Fed, commercial banks, thrift institutions, and money market funds.
2. A bank makes a profit by borrowing from depositors at a low interest rate and lending at a higher interest rate. The bank must hold enough reserves to meet depositors' withdrawals. The bank's balancing act is to balance the risk of loans (profits for stockholders) against the security for depositors.
3. Total deposits are $320 + $896 + $840 = $2,056.
   Deposits that are part of M1 are checkable deposits, $320.
   Deposits that are part of M2 include all deposits, $2,056.
4. Loans are $990 + $400 = $1,390.
   Securities are $634.
   Reserves are $30 + $2 = $32.
5. In July, Georgian Bank's $2 billion of assets (home loans and securities) balanced its deposits of $2 billion. The bank expected to make a profit on its assets that exceeded the interest it paid to depositors. The financial crisis increased the risk on all financial assets. The bank was now holding assets that were more risky than it had planned to hold. As people defaulted on their home loans and the value of securities fell, the value of Georgian Bank's assets crashed to about minus $2 billion. With fewer assets than deposits, regulators had no choice other than close the bank and sell its assets and deposits. The bank failed to balance risk against profit.

## 26.3 THE FEDERAL RESERVE SYSTEM

The **Federal Reserve System (the Fed)** is the central bank of the United States. A **central bank** is a public authority that provides banking services to banks and governments and regulates financial institutions and markets. A central bank does not provide banking services to businesses and individual citizens. Its only customers are banks such as Bank of America and Citibank and the U.S. government. The Fed is organized into 12 Federal Reserve districts shown in Figure 26.4.

The Fed's main task is to regulate the interest rate and quantity of money to achieve low and predictable inflation and sustained economic expansion.

**Federal Reserve System (the Fed)**
The central bank of the United States.

**Central bank**
A public authority that provides banking services to banks and governments and regulates financial institutions and markets.

### The Structure of the Federal Reserve

The key elements in the structure of the Federal Reserve are

- The Chairman of the Board of Governors
- The Board of Governors
- The regional Federal Reserve Banks
- The Federal Open Market Committee

#### The Chairman of the Board of Governors

The Chairman of the Board of Governors is the Fed's chief executive, public face, and center of power and responsibility. When things go right, the Chairman gets the credit; when they go wrong, he gets the blame. Ben S. Bernanke, a former Princeton University economics professor, is the Fed's current Chairman.

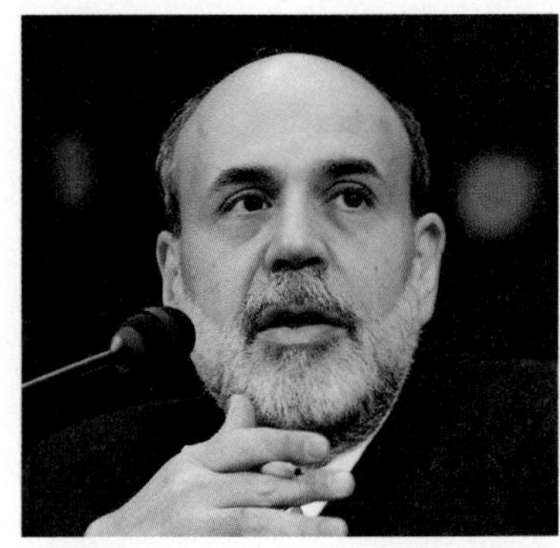

*Fed Chairman Ben S. Bernanke*

**FIGURE 26.4**
The Federal Reserve Districts

myeconlab Animation

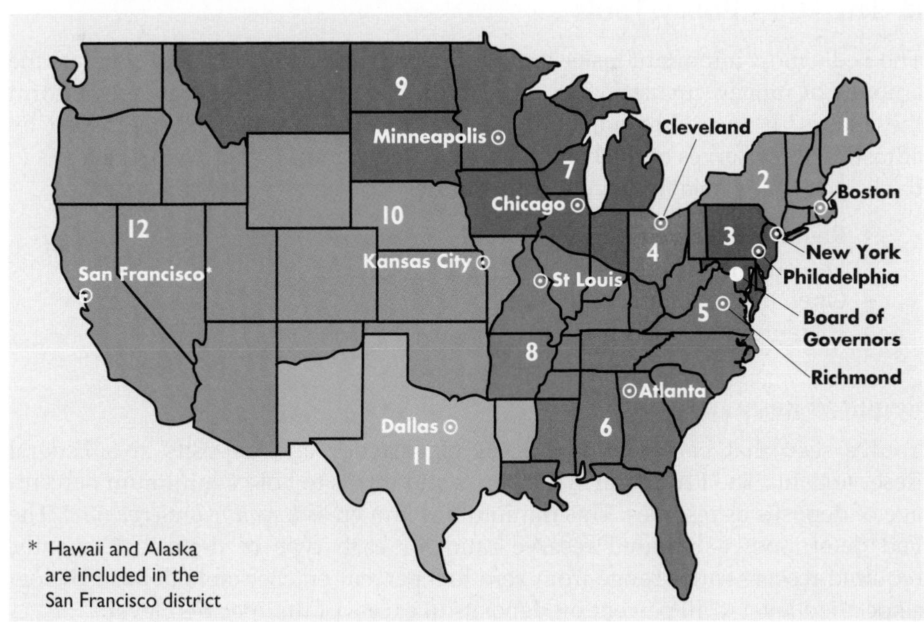


The nation is divided into 12 Federal Reserve districts, each having a Federal Reserve Bank. (Some of the larger districts also have branch banks.) The Board of Governors of the Federal Reserve System is located in Washington, D.C.

SOURCE: *Federal Reserve Bulletin.*

### The Board of Governors

The Board of Governors has seven members (including the Chairman), who are appointed by the President of the United States and confirmed by the Senate, each for a 14-year term. The terms are staggered so that one seat on the board becomes vacant every two years. The President appoints one of the board members as Chairman for a term of four years, which is renewable.

### The Regional Federal Reserve Banks

There are 12 regional Federal Reserve Banks, one for each of the 12 Federal Reserve districts shown in Figure 26.4. Each regional Federal Reserve Bank has nine directors, three of whom are appointed by the Board of Governors and six of whom are elected by the commercial banks in the Federal Reserve district. The directors of each regional Federal Reserve Bank appoint that Bank's president, and the Board of Governors approves this appointment.

The Federal Reserve Bank of New York (known as the New York Fed) occupies a special place because it implements some of the Fed's most important policy decisions.

### The Federal Open Market Committee

**Federal Open Market Committee**
The Fed's main policy-making committee.

The **Federal Open Market Committee** (FOMC) is the Fed's main policy-making committee. The FOMC consists of the following twelve members:

- The Chairman and the other six members of the Board of Governors
- The president of the Federal Reserve Bank of New York
- Four presidents of the other regional Federal Reserve Banks (on a yearly rotating basis)

The FOMC meets approximately every six weeks to review the state of the economy and to decide the actions to be carried out by the New York Fed.

## The Fed's Policy Tools

The Fed's most important tasks are to influence the interest rate and regulate the amount of money circulating in the United States. How does the Fed perform these tasks? It does so by adjusting the reserves of the banking system. Also, by adjusting the reserves of the banking system and standing ready to make loans to banks, the Fed is able to prevent bank failures. The Fed's policy tools are:

- Required reserve ratios
- Discount rate
- Open market operations
- Extraordinary crisis measures

### Required Reserve Ratios

You've seen that banks hold reserves of currency and deposits at a Federal Reserve Bank. The Fed requires the banks and thrifts to hold a minimum percentage of deposits as reserves. This minimum is known as a *required reserve ratio.* The Fed determines a required reserve ratio for each type of deposit. Currently, required reserve ratios range from zero to 3 percent on checkable deposits below a specified level to 10 percent on deposits in excess of the specified level.

### Discount Rate

The **discount rate** is the interest rate at which the Fed stands ready to lend reserves to commercial banks. A change in the discount rate begins with a proposal to the FOMC by at least one of the 12 Federal Reserve Banks. If the FOMC agrees that a change is required, it proposes the change to the Board of Governors for its approval.

**Discount rate**
The interest rate at which the Fed stands ready to lend reserves to commercial banks.

### Open Market Operations

An **open market operation** is the purchase or sale of government securities—U.S. Treasury bills and bonds—by the Federal Reserve in the open market. When the Fed conducts an open market operation, it makes a transaction with a bank or some other business but it does not transact with the federal government. The New York Fed conducts the Fed's open market operations.

**Open market operation**
The purchase or sale of government securities—U.S. Treasury bills and bonds—by the New York Fed in the open market.

### Extraordinary Crisis Measures

Before the financial crisis of 2008, the three tools that we've just described were regarded as sufficient for all situations. But following the collapse of Lehman Brothers, a major Wall Street investment bank, in September 2008, the Fed (working closely with the U.S. Treasury Department) took a number of major policy moves that created new policy tools. These new tools can be grouped under two broad headings:

- Quantitative easing
- Credit easing

***Quantitative Easing*** When the Fed creates bank reserves by conducting a large-scale open market purchase at a low or possibly zero federal funds rate, the action is called *quantitative easing*. This action differs from a normal open market purchase in its scale and purpose, and it might require the Fed to buy any of a number of private securities rather than government securities.

***Credit Easing*** When the Fed buys private securities or makes loans to financial institutions to stimulate their lending, the action is called *credit easing*.

## How the Fed's Policy Tools Work

The Fed's normal policy tools work by changing either the demand for or the supply of the monetary base, which in turn changes the interest rate. The **monetary base** is the sum of coins, Federal Reserve notes, and banks' reserves at the Fed.

**Monetary base**
The sum of coins, Federal Reserve notes, and banks' reserves at the Fed.

By increasing the required reserve ratio, the Fed can force the banks to hold a larger quantity of monetary base. By raising the discount rate, the Fed can make it more costly for the banks to borrow reserves—borrow monetary base. And by selling securities in the open market, the Fed can decrease the monetary base. All of these actions lead to a rise in the interest rate.

Similarly, by decreasing the required reserve ratio, the Fed can permit the banks to hold a smaller quantity of monetary base. By lowering the discount rate, the Fed can make it less costly for the banks to borrow monetary base. And by buying securities in the open market, the Fed can increase the monetary base. All of these actions lead to a decrease in the interest rate.

Open market operations are the Fed's main tool and in the next section you will learn in more detail how they work.

Work these problems in Study Plan 26.3 to get instant feedback.

## CHECKPOINT 26.3

**Describe the functions of the Federal Reserve System (the Fed).**

### Practice Problems

1. What is the Fed and what is the FOMC?
2. Who is the Fed's chief executive, and what are the Fed's main policy tools?
3. What is the monetary base?
4. Suppose that at the end of December 2009, the monetary base in the United States was $700 billion, Federal Reserve notes were $650 billion, and banks' reserves at the Fed were $20 billion. Calculate the quantity of coins.
5. **Risky assets: Counting to a trillion**

   Prior to the September 15, 2008, collapse of Lehman Brothers, which marked the start of the credit crisis, the Fed held less than $1 trillion in assets, most of which were in safe U.S. government securities. By mid-December, 2008, the Fed's balance sheet had more than doubled to over $2.3 trillion. Much of the increase was in mortgage-backed securities. The massive expansion began when the Fed rolled out its lending program—sending banks cash in exchange for risky assets.

   Source: CNNMoney, September 29, 2009

   What are the Fed's policy tools and which policy tool did the Fed use to increase its assets to $2.3 trillion in 2008?

### Guided Solutions to Practice Problems

1. The Federal Reserve (Fed) is the central bank in the United States. The central bank in the United States is a public authority that provides banking services to banks and the U.S. government and that regulates the quantity of money and the banking system. The FOMC is the Federal Open Market Committee. The FOMC is the Fed's main policy-making committee.
2. The Fed's chief executive is the Chairman of the Board of Governors, currently Ben Bernanke. The Fed's main policy tools are required reserve ratios, the discount rate, and open market operations.
3. The monetary base is the sum of coins, Federal Reserve notes (dollar bills), and banks' reserves at the Fed.
4. To calculate the quantity of coins, we use the definition of the monetary base: coins plus Federal Reserve notes plus banks' reserves at the Fed.

   Quantity of coins = Monetary base − Federal Reserve notes − Banks' reserves at the Fed.

   So at the end of December 2009,

   Quantity of coins = $700 billion − $650 billion − $20 billion
   = $30 billion.
5. The Fed's policy tools are the required reserve ratio, discount rate, open market operations, and extraordinary crisis measures. The Fed used an extraordinary crisis measure called credit easing—the Fed's lending program took banks' own risky assets to increase their reserve deposits at the Fed.

## 26.4 REGULATING THE QUANTITY OF MONEY

Banks create money, but this doesn't mean that they have smoke-filled back rooms in which counterfeiters are busily working. Remember, most money is deposits, not currency. What banks create is deposits, and they do so by making loans.

### Creating Deposits by Making Loans

The easiest way to see that banks create deposits is to think about what happens when Andy, who has a Visa card issued by Citibank, uses his card to buy a tank of gas from Chevron. When Andy signs the card sales slip, he takes a loan from Citibank and obligates himself to repay the loan at a later date. At the end of the business day, a Chevron clerk takes a pile of signed credit card sales slips, including Andy's, to Chevron's bank. For now, let's assume that Chevron also banks at Citibank. The bank immediately credits Chevron's account with the value of the slips (minus the bank's commission).

You can see that these transactions have created a bank deposit and a loan. Andy has increased the size of his loan (his credit card balance), and Chevron has increased the size of its bank deposit. And because deposits are money, Citibank has created money.

If, as we've just assumed, Andy and Chevron use the same bank, no further transactions take place. But the outcome is essentially the same when two banks are involved. If Chevron's bank is the Bank of America, then Citibank uses its reserves to pay the Bank of America. Citibank has an increase in loans and a decrease in reserves; the Bank of America has an increase in reserves and an increase in deposits. The banking system as a whole has an increase in loans, an increase in deposits, and no change in reserves.

## EYE on YOUR LIFE

### Money and Your Role in Its Creation

Imagine a world without money in which you must barter for everything you buy. What kinds of items would you have available for these trades? Would you keep some stocks of items that you know lots of people are willing to accept? Would you really be bartering, or would you be using a commodity as money? How much longer would it take you to conduct all the transactions of a normal day?

Now think about your own holdings of money today. How much money do you have in your pocket or wallet? How much do you have in the bank? How does the money you hold change over the course of a month?

Of the money you're holding, which items are part of M1 and which are part of M2? Are all the items in M2 means of payment?

Now think about the role that *you* play in creating money. Every time you charge something to your credit card, you help the bank that issued it to create money. The increase in your credit card balance is a loan from the bank to you. The bank pays the seller right away. So the seller's bank deposit and your outstanding balance increase together. Money is created.

You contribute to the currency drain that limits the ability of your bank to create money when you visit the ATM and get some cash to pay for your late-night pizza.

Of course, your transactions are a tiny part of the total. But together, you and a few million other students like you play a big role in the money creation process.

If Andy had swiped his card at an automatic payment pump, all these transactions would have occurred at the time he filled his tank, and the quantity of money would have increased by the amount of his purchase (minus the bank's commission for conducting the transactions).

Three factors limit the quantity of deposits that the banking system can create:

- The monetary base
- Desired reserves
- Desired currency holding

## The Monetary Base

You've seen that the monetary base is the sum of coins, Federal Reserve notes, and banks' deposits at the Fed. The size of the monetary base limits the total quantity of money that the banking system can create because banks have a desired level of reserves and households and firms have a desired level of currency holding and both of these desired holdings of the monetary base depend on the quantity of money.

## Desired Reserves

A bank's *desired* reserves are the reserves that the bank chooses to hold. The *desired reserve ratio* is the ratio of reserves to deposits that a bank wants to hold. This ratio exceeds the *required reserve ratio* by an amount that the banks determine to be prudent on the basis of their daily business requirements.

A bank's *actual reserve ratio* changes when its customers make a deposit or a withdrawal. If a bank's customer makes a deposit, reserves and deposits increase by the same amount, so the bank's reserve ratio increases. Similarly, if a bank's customer makes a withdrawal, reserves and deposits decrease by the same amount, so the bank's reserve ratio decreases.

**Excess reserves**
A bank's actual reserves minus its desired reserves.

A bank's **excess reserves** are its actual reserves minus its desired reserves. When the banking system as a whole has excess reserves, banks can create money by making new loans. When the banking system as a whole is short of reserves, banks must destroy money by decreasing the quantity of loans.

## Desired Currency Holding

We hold our money in the form of currency and bank deposits. The proportion of money held as currency isn't constant but at any given time, people have a definite view as to how much they want to hold in each form of money.

Because households and firms want to hold some proportion of their money in the form of currency, when the total quantity of bank deposits increases, so does the quantity of currency that they want to hold.

Because desired currency holding increases when deposits increase, currency leaves the banks when loans are made and deposits increase. We call the leakage of currency from the banking system the *currency drain*. And we call the ratio of currency to deposits the *currency drain ratio*.

The greater the currency drain ratio, the smaller is the quantity of deposits and money that the banking system can create from a given amount of monetary base. The reason is that as currency drains from the banks, they are left with a smaller level of reserves (and smaller excess reserves) so they make fewer loans.

## How Open Market Operations Change the Monetary Base

When the Fed buys securities in an open market operation, it pays for them with newly created bank reserves and money. With more reserves in the banking system, the supply of interbank loans increases, the demand for interbank loans decreases, and the federal funds rate—the interest rate in the interbank loans market—falls.

Similarly, when the Fed sells securities in an open market operation, buyers pay for the securities with bank reserves and money. With smaller reserves in the banking system, the supply of interbank loans decreases, the demand for interbank loans increases, and the federal funds rate rises. The Fed sets a target for the federal funds rate and conducts open market operations on the scale needed to hit its target.

A change in the federal funds rate is only the first stage in an adjustment process that follows an open market operation. If banks' reserves increase, the banks can increase their lending and create even more money. If banks' reserves decrease, the banks must decrease their lending, which decreases the quantity of money. We'll study the effects of open market operations in some detail, beginning with an open market purchase.

### The Fed Buys Securities

Suppose the Fed buys $100 million of U.S. government securities in the open market. There are two cases to consider, depending on who sells the securities. A bank might sell some of its securities, or a person or business that is not a commercial bank—the general public—might sell. The outcome is essentially the same in the two cases. To convince you of this fact, we'll study the two cases, starting with the simpler case in which a commercial bank sells securities. (The seller will be someone who thinks the Fed is offering a good price for securities and it is profitable to make the sale.)

*FOMC meeting.*

***A Commercial Bank Sells*** When the Fed buys $100 million of securities from the Manhattan Commercial Bank, two things happen:

1. The Manhattan Commercial Bank has $100 million less in securities, and the Fed has $100 million more in securities.
2. To pay for the securities, the Fed increases the Manhattan Commercial Bank's reserve account at the New York Fed by $100 million.

Figure 26.5 shows the effects of these actions on the balance sheets of the Fed and the Manhattan Commercial Bank. Ownership of the securities passes from the commercial bank to the Fed, so the bank's securities decrease by $100 million and the Fed's securities increase by $100 million, as shown by the red-to-blue arrow running from the Manhattan Commercial Bank to the Fed.

The Fed increases the Manhattan Commercial Bank's reserves by $100 million, as shown by the green arrow running from the Fed to the Manhattan Commercial Bank. This action increases the reserves of the banking system.

The commercial bank's total assets remain constant, but their composition changes. Its holdings of government securities decrease by $100 million, and its reserves increase by $100 million. The bank can use these additional reserves to make loans. When the bank makes loans, it creates deposits and the quantity of money increases.

We've just seen that when the Fed buys government securities from a bank, the bank's reserves increase. What happens if the Fed buys government securities from the public—say, from AIG, an insurance company?

**FIGURE 26.5**

The Fed Buys Securities from a Commercial Bank

**Federal Reserve Bank of New York**

| Assets | | Liabilities | |
|---|---|---|---|
| Securities | +$100 million | Reserves of Manhattan Commercial Bank | +$100 million |

The Fed buys securities from a commercial bank ...

... and pays for the securities by increasing the reserves of the commercial bank

**Manhattan Commercial Bank**

| Assets | | Liabilities |
|---|---|---|
| Securities | –$100 million | |
| Reserves | +$100 million | |

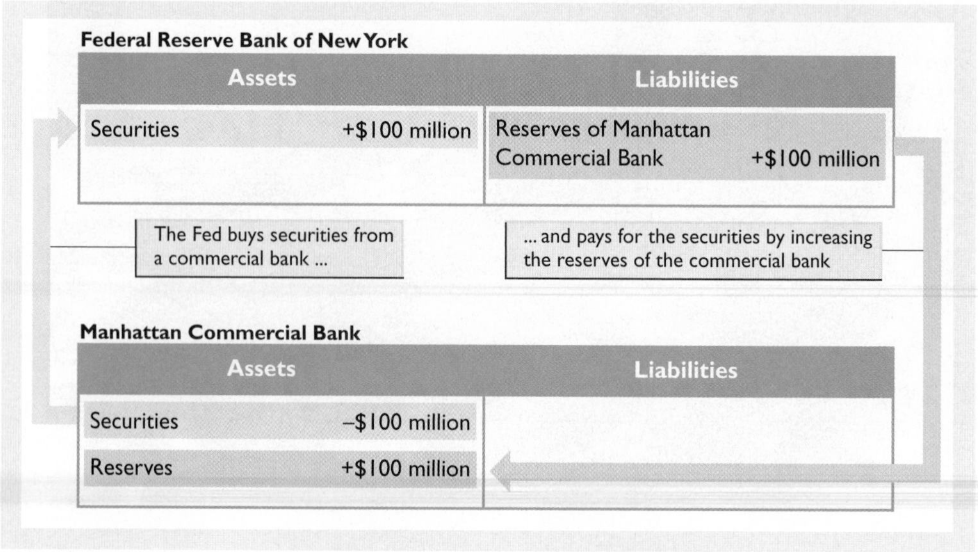

***The Nonbank Public Sells*** When the Fed buys $100 million of securities from AIG, three things happen:

1. AIG has $100 million less in securities, and the Fed has $100 million more in securities.
2. The Fed pays for the securities with a check for $100 million drawn on itself, which AIG deposits in its account at the Manhattan Commercial Bank.
3. The Manhattan Commercial Bank collects payment of this check from the Fed, and the Manhattan Commercial Bank's reserves increase by $100 million.

Figure 26.6 shows the effects of these actions on the balance sheets of the Fed, AIG, and the Manhattan Commercial Bank. Ownership of the securities passes from AIG to the Fed, so AIG's securities decrease by $100 million and the Fed's securities increase by $100 million (red-to-blue arrow). The Fed pays for the securities with a check payable to AIG, which AIG deposits in the Manhattan Commercial Bank. This payment increases Manhattan's reserves by $100 million (green arrow). It also increases AIG's deposit at the Manhattan Commercial Bank by $100 million (blue arrow). This action increases the reserves of the banking system.

**FIGURE 26.6**

The Fed Buys Securities from the Public

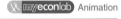

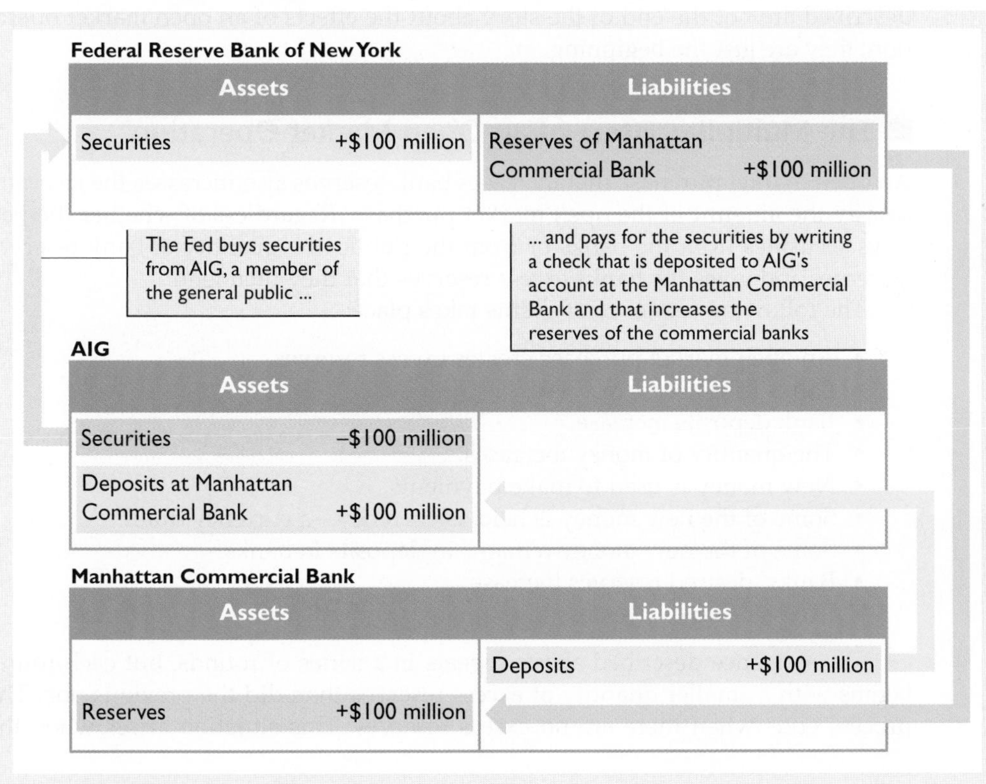

AIG has the same total assets as before, but their composition has changed. It now has more money and fewer securities. The Manhattan Commercial Bank's reserves increase, and so do its deposits—both by $100 million. Because bank reserves and deposits have increased by the same amount, the bank has excess reserves, which it can use to make loans. When it makes loans, the quantity of money increases.

We've worked through what happens when the Fed buys government securities from either a bank or the public. When the Fed sells securities, the transactions that we've just traced operate in reverse.

### The Fed Sells Securities

If the Fed sells $100 million of U.S. government securities in the open market, most likely a person or business other than a bank buys them. (A bank would buy them only if it had excess reserves and couldn't find a better use for its funds.)

When the Fed sells $100 million of securities to AIG, three things happen:

1. AIG has $100 million more in securities, and the Fed has $100 million less in securities.
2. AIG pays for the securities with a check for $100 million drawn on its deposit account at the Manhattan Commercial Bank.
3. The Fed collects payment of this check from the Manhattan Commercial Bank by decreasing its reserves by $100 million.

These actions decrease the reserves of the banking system. The Manhattan Commercial Bank is now short of reserves and must borrow in the federal funds market to meet its desired reserve ratio.

The changes in the balance sheets of the Fed and the banks that we've just described are not the end of the story about the effects of an open market operation; they are just the beginning.

## The Multiplier Effect of an Open Market Operation

An open market purchase that increases bank reserves also increases the *monetary base* by the amount of the open market purchase. Regardless of whether the Fed buys securities from the banks or from the public, the quantity of bank reserves increases and gives the banks excess reserves that they then lend.

The following sequence of events takes place:

- An open market purchase creates excess reserves.
- Banks lend excess reserves.
- Bank deposits increase.
- The quantity of money increases.
- New money is used to make payments.
- Some of the new money is held as currency—a currency drain.
- Some of the new money remains in deposits in banks.
- Banks' desired reserves increase.
- Excess reserves decrease but remain positive.

The sequence described above repeats in a series of rounds, but each round begins with a smaller quantity of excess reserves than did the previous one. The process ends when there are no excess reserves. This situation arises when the increase in the monetary base resulting from the open market operation is willingly held—when the increase in desired reserves plus the increase in desired currency holding equals the increase in the monetary base. Figure 26.7 illustrates and summarizes the sequence of events in one round of the multiplier process.

An open market *sale* works similarly to an open market *purchase*, but the sale *decreases* the monetary base and sets off a multiplier process similar to that described in Figure 26.7. At the end of the process the quantity of money has decreased by an amount that lowers desired reserves and desired currency holding by an amount equal to the decrease in the monetary base resulting from the open market sale. (Make your own version of Figure 26.7 to trace the multiplier process when the Fed *sells* and the banks or public *buys* securities.)

The magnitude of the change in the quantity of money brought about by an open market operation is determined by the money multiplier that we now explain.

## The Money Multiplier

The **money multiplier** is the number by which a change in the monetary base is multiplied to find the resulting change in the quantity of money. It is also the ratio of the change in the quantity of money to the change in the monetary base.

**Money multiplier**
The number by which a change in the monetary base is multiplied to find the resulting change in the quantity of money.

The magnitude of the money multiplier depends on the desired reserve ratio and the currency drain ratio. Call the desired reserve ratio $R$ and call the currency drain ratio (the ratio of currency to deposits) $C$.

**FIGURE 26.7**

A Round in the Multiplier Process Following an Open Market Operation

myeconlab Animation

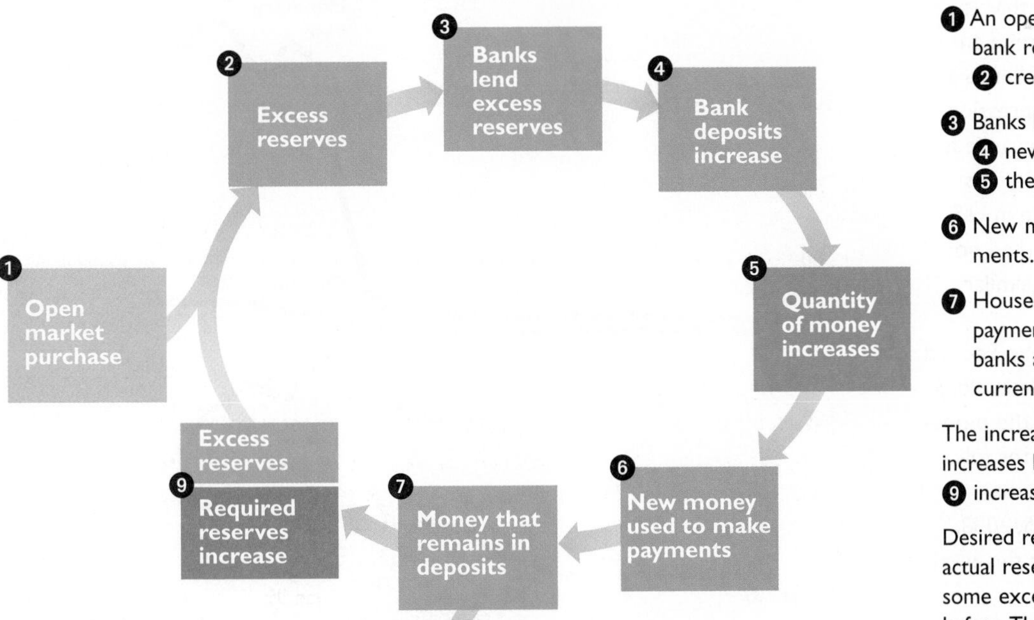


1 An open market purchase increases bank reserves and 2 creates excess reserves.

3 Banks lend the excess reserves, 4 new deposits are created, and 5 the quantity of money increases.

6 New money is used to make payments.

7 Households and firms receiving payments keep some on deposit in banks and 8 some in the form of currency—a currency drain.

The increase in bank deposits increases banks' reserves but also 9 increases banks' desired reserves.

Desired reserves increase by less than actual reserves, so the banks still have some excess reserves, but less than before. The process repeats until excess reserves have been eliminated.

To see how the desired reserve ratio and the currency drain ratio determine the size of the money multiplier, begin with the two facts that

$$\text{Desired reserves} = R \times \text{Deposits} \quad \text{and} \quad \text{Currency} = C \times \text{Deposits}.$$

The monetary base, *MB*, is the sum of reserves and currency, so

$$MB = (R + C) \times \text{Deposits}.$$

The quantity of money, *M*, is the sum of deposits and currency, so

$$M = \text{Deposits} + \text{Currency} = (1 + C) \times \text{Deposits}.$$

Now divide the quantity of money, *M*, by the monetary base, *MB*, using the fact that $M = (1 + C) \times \text{Deposits}$ and $MB = (R + C) \times \text{Deposits}$ to get

$$\frac{M}{MB} = \frac{(1 + C)}{(R + C)}.$$

## EYE on CREATING MONEY

### How Did the Fed Regulate the Quantity of Money in the 2008 Financial Crisis?

During the Great Depression, many banks failed, bank deposits were destroyed, and the quantity of money crashed by 25 percent. Most economists believe that it was these events that turned an ordinary recession in 1929 into a deep and decade-long depression.

Fed Chairman Ben Bernanke is one of the economists who has studied this tragic episode in U.S. economic history, and he had no intention of witnessing a similar event on his watch.

Figure 1 shows what the Fed did to pump reserves into the banking system. The Fed doubled the monetary base during the months following the collapse of Lehman Brothers in September 15, 2008, and reserves remained at this level into 2009.

This extraordinary increase in the monetary base did not bring a similar increase in the quantity of

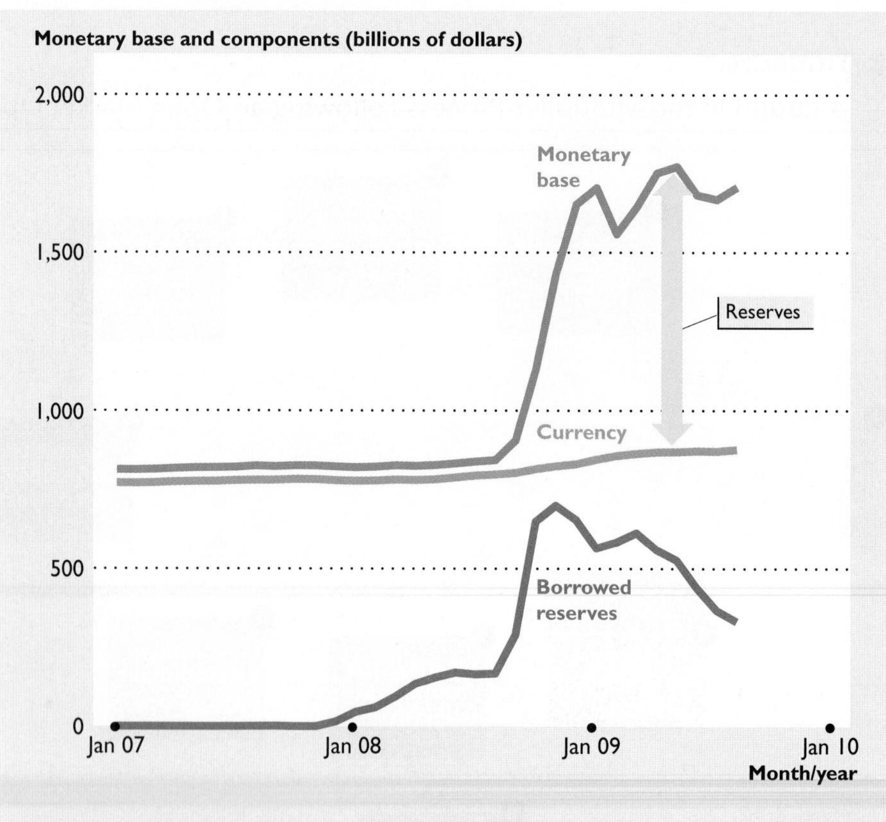


Figure 1 The Monetary Base

Now multiply both sides of the above equation by $MB$ to get

$$M = \frac{(1 + C)}{(R + C)} \times MB.$$

The quantity of money *changes* by the *change* in the monetary base multiplied by $(1 + C)/(R + C)$.

If the desired reserve ratio is 10 percent and the currency drain ratio is 50 percent, $R = 0.1$ and $C = 0.5$, so the money multiplier is $1.5/0.6 = 2.5$.

The larger the desired reserve ratio and the larger the currency drain ratio, the smaller is the money multiplier.

The desired reserve ratio and the currency drain ratio that determine the magnitude of the money multiplier are not constant, so neither is the money multiplier constant. You can see in *Eye on Money Creation* below that the desired reserve ratio and money multiplier changed dramatically in 2008.

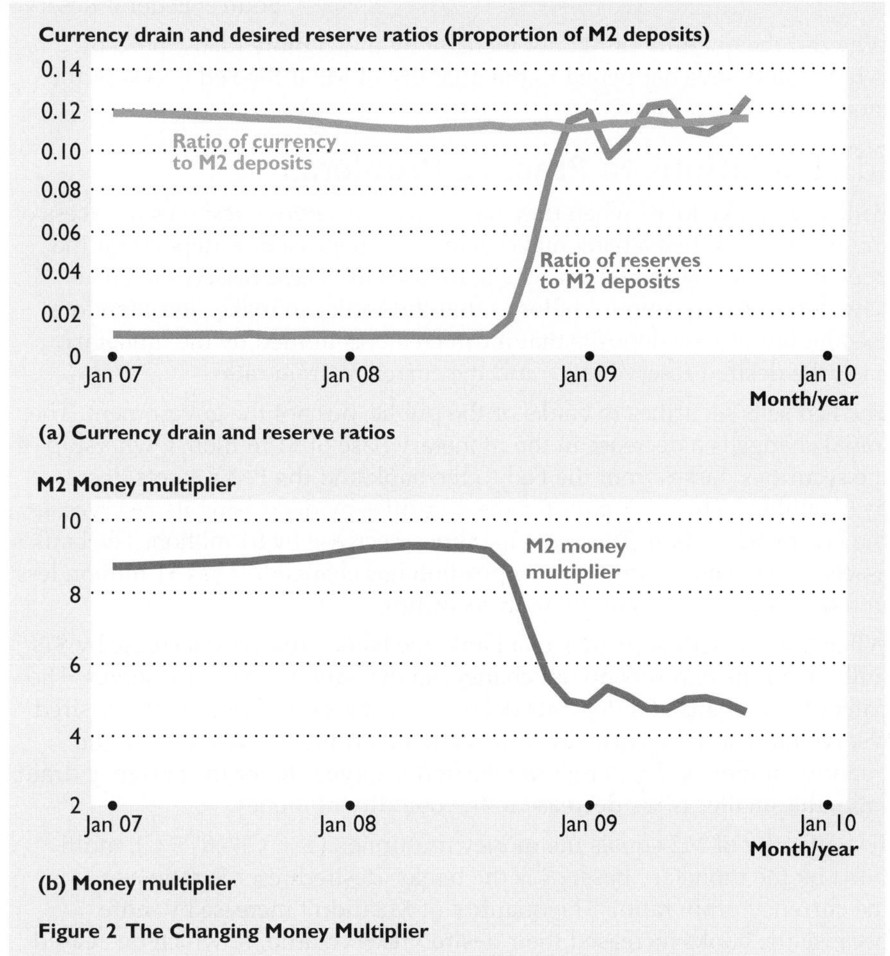


(a) Currency drain and reserve ratios

(b) Money multiplier

**Figure 2 The Changing Money Multiplier**

money. Figure 2 shows the reason.

In 2008, the banks' desired reserve ratio, in part (a), increased tenfold from its normal level of 0.012 (1.2 percent) to 0.12 (12 percent). This increase brought a crash in the money multiplier, in part (b), from its normal value of 9 to an unusually low value of 5.

The surge in the desired reserve ratio is the sole reason for the collapse in the money multiplier. You can see, in part (a), that the other influence on the multiplier, the currency drain ratio, barely changed.

The failure of Lehman Brothers signalled to the banks that they faced an unusually high level of risk and this was the main source of the increase in the desired reserve ratio. As the risk faced by banks returns to normal, the desired reserve ratio will fall, and when this happens the Fed will need to decrease the monetary base or face an explosion in the quantity of money.

SOURCES OF DATA: Federal Reserve and Bureau of Economic Analysis.

Work these problems in Study Plan 26.4 to get instant feedback.

## CHECKPOINT 26.4

**Explain how banks create money and how the Fed controls the quantity of money.**

## Practice Problems

1. How do banks create new deposits by making loans, and what factors limit the amount of deposits and loans that they can create?
2. If the Fed makes an open market sale of $1 million of securities, who can buy the securities from the Fed? What initial changes occur in the economy if the Fed sells to a bank?
3. If the Fed makes an open market sale of $1 million of securities, what is the process by which the quantity of money changes? What factors determine the change in the quantity of money?
4. **Fed doubles monetary base**
   During the fourth quarter of 2008, the Fed doubled the monetary base but the quantity of money (M2) increased by only 5 percent.

   Source: Federal Reserve

   Why did the quantity of M2 not increase by much more than 5 percent? What would have happened to the quantity of M2 if the Fed had kept the monetary base constant?

## Guided Solutions to Practice Problems

1. Banks can make loans when they have excess reserves—reserves in excess of those desired. When a bank makes a loan, it creates a new deposit for the person who receives the loan. The bank uses its excess reserves to create new deposits. The amount of loans that the bank can make, and therefore the amount of new deposits that it can create, is limited by the monetary base, the desired reserve ratio, and the currency drain ratio.
2. The Fed sells securities to banks or the public, but not the government. The initial change is a decrease in the monetary base of $1 million. Ownership of the securities passes from the Fed to the bank and the Fed's assets decrease by $1 million. The bank pays for the securities by decreasing its reserves at the Fed by $1 million. The Fed's liabilities decrease by $1 million. The bank's assets are the same, but their composition has changed. It has $1 million less in reserves and $1 million more in securities.
3. When the Fed sells securities to a bank, the bank's reserves decrease by $1 million, but its deposits do not change, so the bank is short of reserves. The bank calls in loans and deposits decrease by the same amount. The desired reserve ratio and the currency drain ratio determine the decrease in the quantity of money. The larger the desired reserve ratio or the currency drain ratio, the smaller is the decrease in the quantity of money.
4. The quantity of M2 equals the money multiplier, $(1 + C)/(R + C)$, multiplied by the monetary base. ($R$ is the banks' desired reserve ratio and $C$ is the currency drain ratio). The quantity of M2 didn't increase by more because the banks increased their desired reserve ratio, $R$, which decreased the money multiplier. If the Fed had not increased the monetary base, the quantity of M2 would have decreased because the money multiplier decreased.

# CHAPTER SUMMARY

## Key Points

**1 Define money and describe its functions.**

- Money is anything that serves as a generally accepted means of payment.
- Money functions as a medium of exchange, unit of account, and store of value.
- M1 consists of currency, travelers' checks, and checkable deposits. M2 consists of M1 plus savings deposits, small time deposits, and money market funds.

**2 Describe the functions of banks.**

- The deposits of commercial banks and thrift institutions are money.
- Banks borrow short term and lend long term and make a profit on the spread between the interest rates that they pay and receive.

**3 Describe the functions of the Federal Reserve System (the Fed).**

- The Federal Reserve is the central bank of the United States.
- The Fed influences the economy by setting the required reserve ratio for banks, by setting the discount rate, by open market operations, and by taking extraordinary quantitative easing and credit easing measures in a financial crisis.

**4 Explain how banks create money and how the Fed controls the quantity of money.**

- Banks create money by making loans.
- The maximum quantity of deposits the banks can create is limited by the monetary base, the banks' desired reserves, and desired currency holding.
- When the Fed buys securities in an open market operation, it creates bank reserves. When the Fed sells securities in an open market operation, it destroys bank reserves.
- An open market operation has a multiplier effect on the quantity of money.

## Key Terms

Banking system, 670
Barter, 665
Central bank, 675
Commercial bank, 670
Currency, 666
Discount rate, 677
Excess reserves, 680
Federal funds rate, 672
Federal Open Market Committee, 676
Federal Reserve System (the Fed), 675
Fiat money, 666
M1, 666
M2, 666
Means of payment, 664
Medium of exchange, 665
Monetary base, 677
Money, 664
Money multiplier, 685
Open market operation, 677
Required reserve ratio, 671
Reserves, 671
Store of value, 665
Unit of account, 665

Work these problems in Chapter 26 Study Plan to get instant feedback.

## CHAPTER CHECKPOINT

### Study Plan Problems and Applications

1. What is money? Would you classify any of the following items as money?
   - Store coupons for cat food
   - A $100 Amazon.com gift certificate
   - Frequent Flier Miles
   - Credit available on your Visa card
   - The dollar coins that a coin collector owns
2. What are the three functions that money performs? Which of the following items perform some but not all of these functions, and which perform all of these functions? Which of the items are money?
   - A checking account at the Bank of America
   - A dime
   - A debit card
3. Monica transfers $10,000 from her savings account at the Bank of Alaska to her money market fund. What is the immediate change in M1 and M2?
4. Terry takes $100 from his checking account and deposits the $100 in his savings account. What is the immediate change in M1 and M2?
5. Suppose that banks had deposits of $500 billion, a desired reserve ratio of 4 percent and no excess reserves. The banks had $15 billion in notes and coins. Calculate the banks' reserves at the central bank.
6. The Fed buys $2 million of securities from AIG. If the desired reserve ratio is 0.1 and there is no currency drain, calculate the bank's excess reserves as soon as the open market purchase is made, the maximum amount of loans that the banking system can make, and the maximum amount of new money that the banking system can create.

Use the following information to work Problems 7 and 8.

If the desired reserve ratio is 5 percent, the currency drain ratio is 20 percent of deposits, and the central bank makes an open market purchase of $1 million of securities, calculate the change in

7. The monetary base and the change in its components.
8. The quantity of money, and how much of the new money is currency and how much is bank deposits.

Use the following information to work Problems 9 and 10.

**South Korea: Bank reserves raised**

To rein in spending, the Bank of Korea raised the required reserve ratio to 7 percent from 5 percent—the first raise in almost 17 years. With higher required reserves, banks will have to cut the amount of loans they make.

Source: *The New York Times*, November 24, 2006

9. Explain why the higher required reserve ratio means that banks will have to cut the amount of loans they can make.
10. Assuming that the currency drain is zero and that the desired reserve ratio equals the required reserve ratio, calculate the change in the money multiplier that results from the increase in Korea's required reserve ratio.

## Instructor Assignable Problems and Applications

Your instructor can assign these problems as homework, a quiz, or a test in **MyEconLab**.

1. When the Fed increased the monetary base in 2008, which component of the monetary base increased most: banks' reserves or currency? What happened to the reserves that banks borrowed from the Fed?

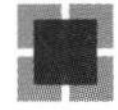

2. What happened to the money multiplier in 2008? What would the money multiplier have been if the currency drain ratio had not changed? What would the money multiplier have been if the banks' desired reserve ratio had not changed?
3. What are the three functions that money performs? Which of the following items perform some but not all of these functions and which of the items are money?
   - An antique clock
   - An S&L savings deposit
   - Your credit card
   - The coins in the Fed's museum
   - Government securities
4. Naomi buys $1,000 worth of American Express travelers' checks and charges the purchase to her American Express card. What is the immediate change in M1 and M2?
5. What can the Fed do to increase the quantity of money and keep the monetary base constant? Explain why the Fed would or would not
   - Change the currency drain ratio.
   - Change the required reserve ratio.
   - Change the discount rate.
   - Conduct an open market operation.

Use Table 1, which shows a bank's balance sheet, to work Problems 6 and 7. The desired reserve ratio on all deposits is 5 percent and there is no currency drain.

6. Calculate the bank's excess reserves. If the bank uses all of these excess reserves to make a loan, what is the quantity of the loan and the quantity of total deposits after the bank has made the loan?
7. If there is no currency drain, what is the quantity of loans and the quantity of total deposits when the bank has no excess reserves?

**TABLE 1**

| Assets | | Liabilities | |
|---|---|---|---|
| (millions of dollars) | | | |
| Reserves at the Fed | 25 | Checkable deposits | 90 |
| Cash in vault | 15 | Savings deposits | 110 |
| Securities | 60 | | |
| Loans | 100 | | |

Use the following information to work Problems 8 and 9.

**China tightens bank credit again**

For the second time in the month and fourth in a year, the People's Bank of China raised the required reserve ratio on big banks to 11 percent of deposits on May 15, 2007, up from 10.5 percent.

Source: *The New York Times*, April 30, 2007

8. Compare the required reserve ratio in China on May 15, 2007 and the required reserve ratio on checkable deposits in the United States today.
9. If the currency drain ratio in China and the United States is 1 percent of deposits, compare the money multipliers in the two countries.

Use the following information to work Problems **10** and **11**.

A bank has $500 million in checkable deposits, $600 million in savings deposits, $400 million in small time deposits, $950 million in loans to businesses, $500 million in government securities, $20 million in currency, and $30 million in its reserve account at the Fed.

**10.** Calculate the bank's total deposits, deposits that are part of M1, and deposits that are part of M2.

**11.** Calculate the bank's loans, securities, and reserves.

**12.** If the Fed wants to decrease the quantity of money, what type of open market operation might it undertake? Explain the process by which the quantity of money decreases.

Use the following information to work Problems **13** and **14**.

An early goldsmith banker earned a profit (sometimes a large profit) simply by writing notes to certify that a person had deposited a certain amount of gold in his vault. By writing more notes than the amount of gold held, the goldsmith could lend the notes and charge interest on them.

**13.** Did the goldsmith bankers make money out of thin air in a form of legal theft? Should the goldsmith bankers have been regulated to ensure that the amount of gold in their vaults equaled the value of the notes they created?

**14.** What were the main benefits from the activities of the goldsmith bankers?

**15.** If the central bank makes an open market purchase of $1 million of securities, what is the process by which the quantity of money changes? What factors determine the change in the quantity of money?

**16.** In an economy, the currency drain is 10 percent of deposits and the desired reserve ratio is 1 percent of deposits. If the central bank buys $100,000 of securities on the open market, calculate the money multiplier.

**TABLE 2**

| Assets | | Liabilities | |
|---|---|---|---|
| (millions of dollars) | | | |
| Reserves at the Fed | 20 | Checkable deposits | 80 |
| | | Savings deposits | 120 |
| Cash in vault | 5 | | |
| Securities | 75 | | |
| Loans | 100 | | |

Table 2 shows a bank's balance sheet. The bank has no excess reserves and there is no currency drain. Use the following information to work Problems **17** and **18**.

**17.** Calculate the bank's desired reserve ratio.

**18.** Calculate the new money that this bank can create if it sells $5 million of securities to the central bank in an open market operation.

**19. Fed starts buying government debt**

The Fed announced that it would buy up to $300 billion in Treasury securities over the next six months from big government "primary" securities dealers, such as Barclays Capital, Banc of America Securities, and Citigroup Global Markets.

Source: *USA Today*, March 24, 2009

What type of a transaction is the Fed's purchase of government securities from securities dealers? With no other actions, will these transactions change the quantity of money? If so, will they increase or decrease the quantity of money?

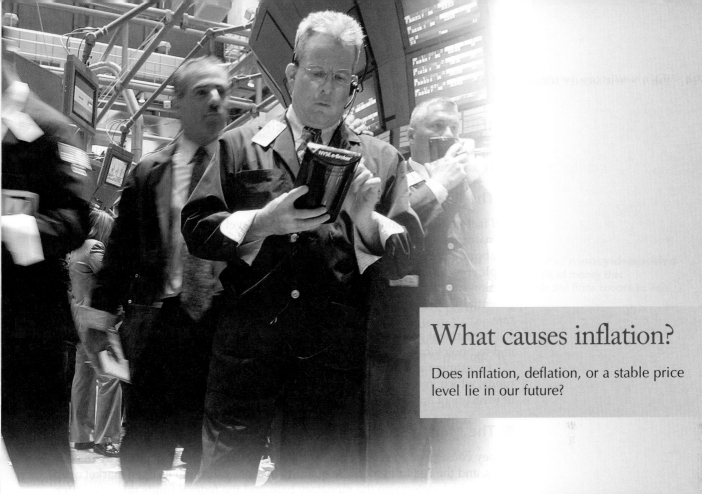

## What causes inflation?

Does inflation, deflation, or a stable price level lie in our future?

# Money, Interest, and Inflation

CHAPTER CHECKLIST

**When you have completed your study of this chapter, you will be able to**

1 Explain what determines the demand for money and how the demand for money and the supply of money determine the *nominal* interest rate.

2 Explain how in the long run, the quantity of money determines the price level and money growth brings inflation.

3 Identify the costs of inflation and the benefits of a stable value of money.

### Opportunity Cost: *Nominal* Interest Is a *Real* Cost

The opportunity cost of holding money is the nominal interest rate. In Chapter 22, (p. 580), you learned the distinction between the *nominal* interest rate and the *real* interest rate and that

Nominal interest rate = Real interest rate + Inflation rate.

We can use this equation to find the real interest rate for a given nominal interest rate and inflation rate. For example, if the nominal interest rate on a mutual fund account is 8 percent a year and the inflation rate is 2 percent a year, the real interest rate is 6 percent a year. Why isn't the real interest rate of 6 percent a year the opportunity cost of holding money? That is, why isn't the opportunity cost of holding $100 in money only $6 worth of goods and services forgone?

The answer is that if you hold $100 in money rather than in a mutual fund, your buying power decreases by $8, not by $6. With inflation running at 2 percent a year, on each $100 that you hold as money and that earns no interest, you lose $2 worth of buying power a year. On each $100 that you put into your mutual fund account, you gain $6 worth of buying power a year. So if you hold money rather than a mutual fund, you lose the buying power of $6 plus $2, or $8—equivalent to the nominal interest rate on the mutual fund, not the real interest rate.

Because the opportunity cost of holding money is the nominal interest rate on an alternative asset,

**Other things remaining the same, the higher the nominal interest rate, the smaller is the quantity of money demanded.**

This relationship describes the decision made by an individual or a firm about how much money to hold. It also describes money-holding decisions for the economy—the sum of the decisions of every individual and firm.

We summarize the influence of the nominal interest rate on money-holding decisions in a demand for money schedule and curve.

### The Demand for Money Schedule and Curve

**Demand for money**
The relationship between the quantity of money demanded and the nominal interest rate, when all other influences on the amount of money that people wish to hold remain the same.

The **demand for money** is the relationship between the quantity of money demanded and the nominal interest rate, when all other influences on the amount of money that people wish to hold remain the same. We illustrate the demand for money with a demand for money schedule and a demand for money curve, such as those in Figure 27.1. If the interest rate is 5 percent a year, the quantity of money demanded is $1 trillion. The quantity of money demanded decreases to $0.98 trillion if the interest rate rises to 6 percent a year and increases to $1.02 trillion if the interest rate falls to 4 percent a year.

The demand for money curve is *MD*. When the interest rate rises, everything else remaining the same, the opportunity cost of holding money rises and the quantity of money demanded decreases—there is a movement up along the demand for money curve. When the interest rate falls, the opportunity cost of holding money falls and the quantity of money demanded increases—there is a movement down along the demand for money curve.

**FIGURE 27.1**

The Demand for Money

| | Nominal interest rate (percent per year) | Quantity of money demanded (trillions of dollars) |
|---|---|---|
| *A* | 6 | 0.98 |
| *B* | 5 | 1.00 |
| *C* | 4 | 1.02 |

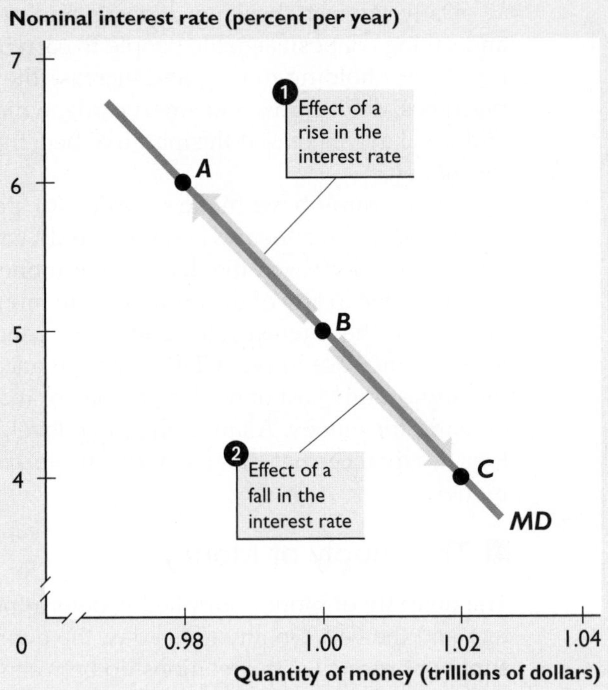

The demand for money schedule is graphed as the demand for money curve, *MD*. Rows *A*, *B*, and *C* in the table correspond to points *A*, *B*, and *C* on the curve. The nominal interest rate is the opportunity cost of holding money.

Other things remaining the same, (1) an increase in the nominal interest rate decreases the quantity of money demanded, and (2) a decrease in the nominal interest rate increases the quantity of money demanded.

## Changes in the Demand for Money

A change in the nominal interest rate brings a change in the quantity of money demanded and a movement along the demand for money curve. A change in any other influence on money holding changes the demand for money. The three main influences on the demand for money are

- The price level
- Real GDP
- Financial technology

### The Price Level

The demand for money is proportional to the price level—an $x$ percent rise in the price level brings an $x$ percent increase in the quantity of money demanded at each nominal interest rate. The reason is that we hold money to make payments: If the price level changes, the quantity of dollars that we need to make payments changes in the same proportion.

### Real GDP

The demand for money increases as real GDP increases. The reason is that when real GDP increases, expenditures and incomes increase. To make the increased expenditures and income payments, households and firms must hold larger average amounts of money.

### Financial Technology

Changes in financial technology change the demand for money. Most changes in financial technology come from advances in computing and record keeping. Some advances increase the quantity of money demanded, and some decrease it.

Daily interest checking deposits and automatic transfers between checking and savings deposits enable people to earn interest on money, lower the opportunity cost of holding money, and increase the demand for money. Automatic teller machines, debit cards, and smart cards, which have made money easier to obtain and use, have increased the marginal benefit of money and increased the demand for money.

Credit cards have made it easier for people to buy goods and services on credit and pay for them when their credit card account becomes due. This development has decreased the demand for money.

A change in any of the influences on money holdings that we've just reviewed other than the interest rate changes the demand for money. A rise in the price level, an increase in real GDP, or an advance in financial technology that lowers the opportunity cost of holding money or makes money more useful increases the demand for money. A fall in the price level, a decrease in real GDP, or a technological advance that creates a substitute for money decreases the demand for money.

## The Supply of Money

**Supply of money**
The relationship between the quantity of money supplied and the nominal interest rate.

The quantity of money supplied is determined by the actions of the banking system and the Fed. On any given day, the quantity of money supplied is fixed. The **supply of money** is the relationship between the quantity of money supplied and the nominal interest rate. In Figure 27.2, the quantity of money supplied is $1 trillion regardless of the nominal interest rate, so the supply of money curve is the vertical line *MS*.

## The Nominal Interest Rate

People hold some of their financial wealth as money and some in the form of other financial assets. You have seen that the amount of wealth that people hold as money depends on the nominal interest rate that they can earn on other financial assets. Demand and supply determine the nominal interest rate. We can study the forces of demand and supply in either the market for financial assets or the market for money. Because the Fed influences the quantity of money, we focus on the market for money.

On a given day, the price level, real GDP, and the state of financial technology are fixed. Because these influences on the demand for money are fixed, the demand for money curve is given.

The interest rate is the only influence on the quantity of money demanded that is free to fluctuate. Every day, the interest rate adjusts to make the quantity of money demanded equal the quantity of money supplied—to achieve money market equilibrium.

In Figure 27.2, the demand for money curve is *MD*. The equilibrium interest rate is 5 percent a year. At any interest rate above 5 percent a year, the quantity of money demanded is less than the quantity of money supplied. At any interest rate below 5 percent a year, the quantity of money demanded exceeds the quantity of money supplied.

**FIGURE 27.2**

Money Market Equilibrium

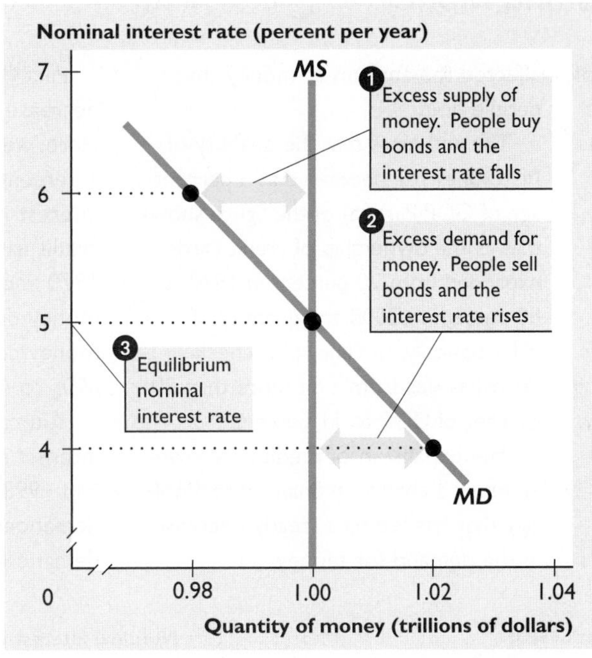


The supply of money curve is *MS*, and the demand for money curve is *MD*.

1. If the interest rate is 6 percent a year, the quantity of money held exceeds the quantity demanded. People buy bonds, the price of a bond rises, and the interest rate falls.
2. If the interest rate is 4 percent a year, the quantity of money held falls short of the quantity demanded. People sell bonds, the price of a bond falls, and the interest rate rises.
3. If the interest rate is 5 percent a year, the quantity of money held equals the quantity demanded. The money market is in equilibrium.

***The Interest Rate and Bond Price Move in Opposite Directions*** When the government issues a bond, it specifies the dollar amount of interest that it will pay each year on the bond. Suppose that the government issues a bond that pays $100 of interest a year. The interest *rate* that you receive on this bond depends on the price that you pay for it. If the price is $1,000, the interest rate is 10 percent a year—$100 is 10 percent of $1,000.

If the price of the bond *falls* to $500, the interest rate *rises* to 20 percent a year. The reason is that you still receive an interest payment of $100, but this amount is 20 percent of the $500 price of the bond. If the price of the bond *rises* to $2,000, the interest rate *falls* to 5 percent a year. Again, you still receive an interest payment of $100, but this amount is 5 percent of the $2,000 price of the bond.

***Interest Rate Adjustment*** If the interest rate is above its equilibrium level, people would like to hold less money than they are actually holding. They try to get rid of some money by buying other financial assets such as bonds. The demand for financial assets increases, the prices of these assets rise, and the interest rate falls. The interest rate keeps falling until the quantity of money that people want to hold increases to equal the quantity of money supplied.

Conversely, when the interest rate is below its equilibrium level, people are holding less money than they would like to hold. They try to get more money by selling other financial assets. The demand for these financial assets decreases, the prices of these assets fall, and the interest rate rises. The interest rate keeps rising until the quantity of money that people want to hold decreases to equal the quantity of money supplied.

## EYE on the U.S. ECONOMY

### Credit Cards and Money

Today, 80 percent of U.S. households own a credit card, and most of us use a credit card account as a substitute for money. When we buy goods or services, we use our credit card. When the monthly bill arrives, most of us pay off some of the outstanding balance but not all of it. In 2008, 57 percent of credit card holders had an outstanding balance after making their most recent payment, and the average card balance exceeded $5,000.

But back in 1970, only 20 percent of U.S. households had a credit card.

How has the spread of credit cards affected the amount of money that people hold?

The answer is that the quantity of M1 money has decreased as a percentage of GDP. Part (a) of the figure shows that as the ownership of credit cards expanded from 20 percent in 1970 to 80 percent in 2008, the quantity of M1—basically, currency plus checking deposits—fell from a bit more than 20 percent of GDP to 11 percent.

The expansion of credit card ownership is a change in financial technology that has led to a steady decrease in the demand for money.

Part (b) of the figure shows the decrease in the demand for money. Here, we graph the quantity of M1 as a percentage of GDP against the interest rate. You can see that as credit card use increased between 1970 and 2008, the demand for money decreased and the demand for money curve shifted leftward from $MD_0$ to $MD_1$ to $MD_2$.

You can also see that when the interest rate decreased between 1981 and 1993, the quantity of money demanded increased along the demand for money curve $MD_1$.

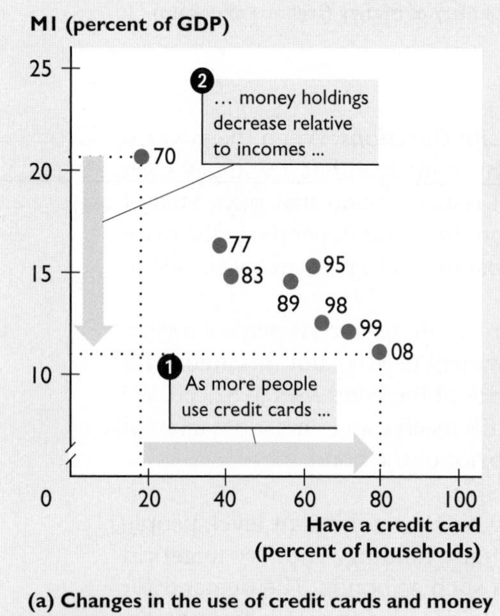


(a) Changes in the use of credit cards and money

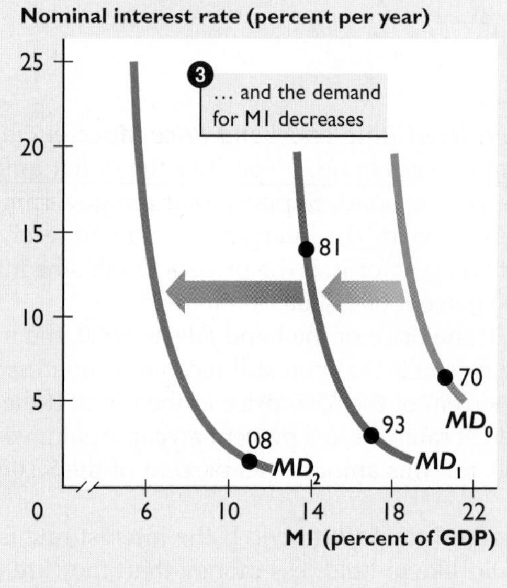


(b) Changes in the demand for M1

SOURCE OF DATA: Federal Reserve.

## ■ Changing the Interest Rate

To change the interest rate, the Fed changes the quantity of money. Figure 27.3 illustrates two changes. The demand for money curve is *MD*. If the Fed increases the quantity of money to $1.02 trillion, the supply of money curve shifts rightward from $MS_0$ to $MS_1$ and the interest rate falls to 4 percent a year. If the Fed decreases the quantity of money to $0.98 trillion, the supply of money curve shifts leftward from $MS_0$ to $MS_2$ and the interest rate rises to 6 percent a year.

**FIGURE 27.3**

Interest Rate Changes

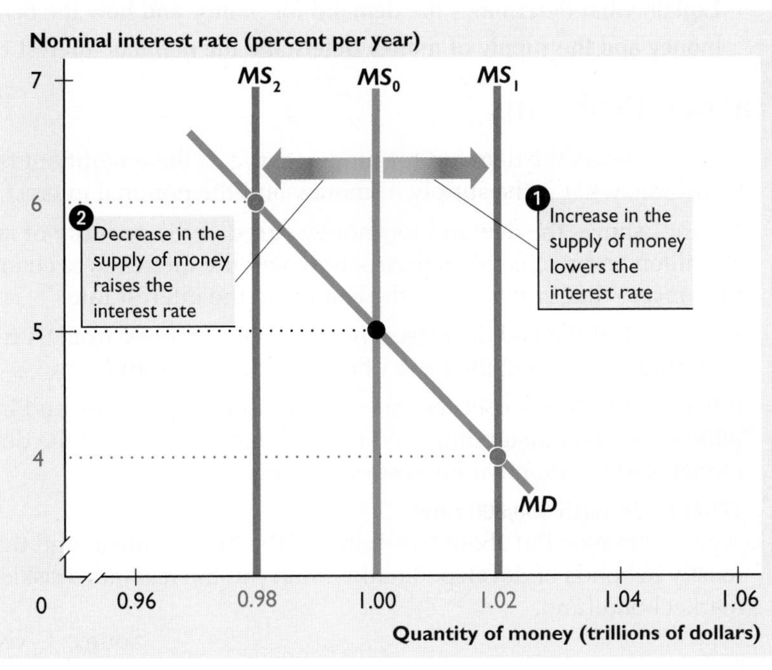


The demand for money is *MD*, and initially, the supply of money is $MS_0$. The interest rate is 5 percent a year.

1. If the Fed increases the quantity of money and the supply of money curve shifts rightward to $MS_1$, the interest rate falls to 4 percent a year.

2. If the Fed decreases the quantity of money and the supply of money curve shifts leftward to $MS_2$, the interest rate rises to 6 percent a year.

## EYE on YOUR LIFE

### Money Holding and Fed Watching

How much currency (cash) do you have in your wallet, on average? How much money do you keep in your bank account on average?

Why don't you hold a larger average bank balance by paying off a smaller part of your credit card balance than you can afford to pay?

Wouldn't it be better to keep a bit more money in the bank?

Almost certainly, that would not be a smart idea. Why? Because the opportunity cost of holding that money would be too high.

If you have an outstanding credit card balance, the interest rate on that balance is the opportunity cost of holding money.

By paying off as much of your credit card balance as you can afford, you avoid a high interest rate on the outstanding balance.

Your demand for money is sensitive to this opportunity cost.

Do you watch the Fed? Probably not, but you can learn to become an effective Fed watcher. In the process, you will become much better informed about the state of the U.S. economy and the state of the economy in your region.

To become a Fed watcher, try to get into the habit of visiting the Fed's Web site at www.federalreserve.gov.

Look specifically at the Beige Book, in which you can learn what is happening in your region. Also, keep an eye on the FOMC calendar for the dates of interest rate announcements. On these dates, check the media for opinions on what the Fed's interest rate decision will be. After the decision is made, check the Fed's explanation as to why it made its decision.

Work these problems in Study Plan 27.1 to get instant feedback.

## CHECKPOINT 27.1

**Explain what determines the demand for money and how the demand for money and the supply of money determine the *nominal* interest rate.**

### Practice Problems

1. Figure 1 shows the demand for money curve. If the quantity of money is \$4 trillion, what is the supply of money and the nominal interest rate?
2. Figure 1 shows the demand for money curve. If the quantity of money is \$4 trillion and real GDP increases, how will the interest rate change? Explain the process that brings about the change in the interest rate.
3. In Figure 1, if the Fed decreases the quantity of money from \$4 trillion to \$3.9 trillion, how will the price of a bond change? Why?
4. If banks introduce a user fee on every credit card purchase and increase the interest rate on outstanding credit card balances, how will the demand for money and the nominal interest rate change?
5. **What to do with \$50,000 now**

   A good strategy: Put about two-thirds of the money into a fund that invests mostly in bonds of developed nations and put the rest into a riskier emerging-market bond fund.

   Source: CNNMoney.com

   What is the opportunity cost of holding money? If lots of people followed this advice and put their money into bonds, explain what will happen to the demand for money, the price of bonds, and the interest rate on bonds.

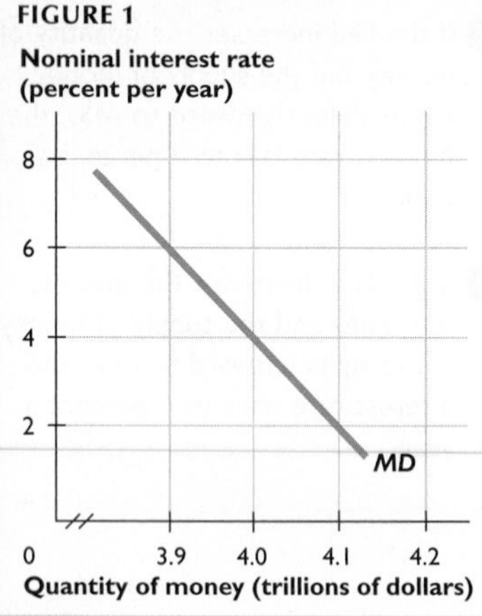


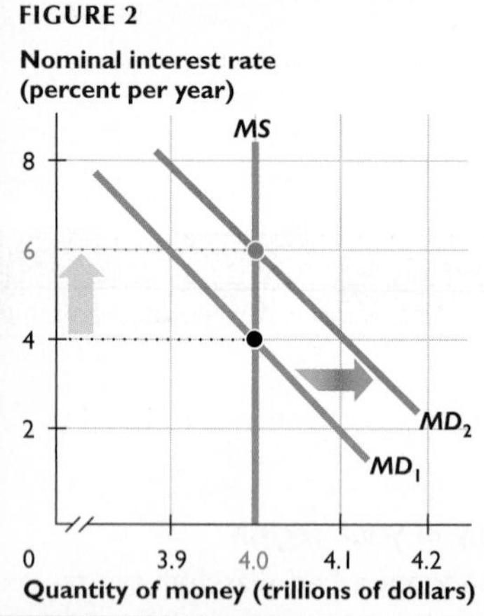


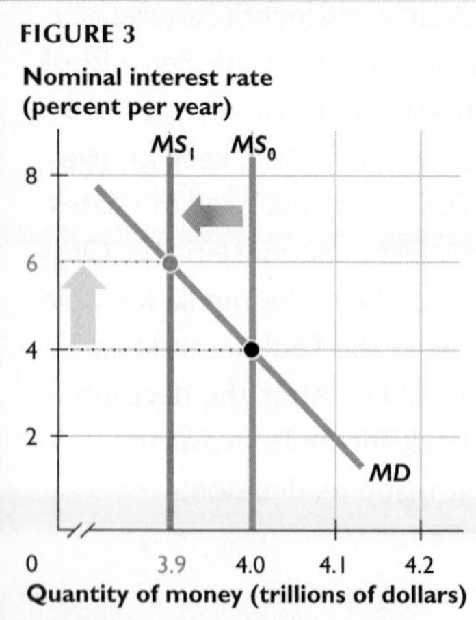


### Guided Solutions to Practice Problems

1. The supply of money is the curve *MS*. The interest rate is 4 percent a year, at the intersection of $MD_1$ and *MS* (Figure 2).
2. The demand for money increases, and the demand for money curve shifts from $MD_1$ to $MD_2$ (Figure 2). At an interest rate of 4 percent a year, people want to hold more money, so they sell bonds. The price of a bond falls, and the interest rate rises.
3. At an interest rate of 4 percent a year, people would like to hold \$4 trillion. With only \$3.9 trillion of money available, they sell bonds in an attempt to get more money. The price of a bond falls, and the interest rate rises. The price will continue to fall and the interest rate will continue to rise until the quantity of money that people want to hold equals the \$3.9 trillion available. The new equilibrium nominal interest rate is 6 percent a year (Figure 3).
4. With a fee on each transaction, people will use credit cards less frequently. With a higher interest rate on outstanding balances, the opportunity cost of holding money increases. The demand for money will increase and with no change in the supply of money, the nominal interest rate will rise.
5. The opportunity cost of cash is the highest interest rate forgone by not holding bonds of a similar risk. As lots of people decide to buy bonds, the demand for money decreases. The demand for bonds increases and with no change in the supply of bonds the price of a bond rises and the interest rate on bonds falls.

## 27.2 MONEY, THE PRICE LEVEL, AND INFLATION

A change in the nominal interest rate is the initial effect of a change in the quantity of money, but it is not the ultimate or long-run effect. When the interest rate changes, borrowing and lending and investment and consumption spending also change, which in turn change production and prices—change real GDP and the price level.

The details of this adjustment process are complex, and we explore them in the next two chapters. But the place where the process comes to rest—the *long-run* outcome—is easier to describe. It is crucial to understand the long-run outcome because that is where the economy is heading. We're now going to examine the long-run equilibrium in the money market.

### The Money Market in the Long Run

The *long run* refers to the economy at full employment when real GDP equals potential GDP (Chapter 23, p. 591). Over the business cycle, real GDP fluctuates around potential GDP. But averaging over an expansion and recession and a peak and trough, real GDP equals potential GDP. That is, real GDP equals potential GDP *on average*. So another way to think about the *long run* is as a description of the economy *on average* over the business cycle.

#### The Long-Run Demand for Money

In the long run, equilibrium in the market for loanable funds determines the real interest rate (Chapter 25, pp. 644–651). The nominal interest rate that influences money holding plans equals the real interest rate plus the inflation rate. For now, we'll consider an economy that has no inflation, so the real interest rate equals the nominal interest rate. (We'll consider inflation later in this chapter.)

With the interest rate determined by real forces in the long run, what is the variable that adjusts to make the quantity of money that people plan to hold equal the quantity of money supplied? The answer is the "price" of money. The law of demand applies to money just as it does to any other object. The lower the "price" of money, the greater is the quantity of money that people are willing to hold. What is the "price" of money? It is the *value* of money.

#### The Value of Money

The *value of money* is the quantity of goods and services that a unit of money will buy. It is the inverse of the *price level, P,* which equals the GDP price index divided by 100. That is,

$$\text{Value of money} = 1/P.$$

To see why, suppose that you have $100 in your wallet. If you spend that money, you can buy goods and services valued at $100. Now suppose that the price level rises by 10 percent. After the price rise, the quantity of goods and services that $100 can buy has fallen. Your $100 can now buy only $100 ÷ 1.1 or $91 of goods and services. Yesterday's $100 is worth $91 today. The price level has risen and the value of money has fallen and each percentage change is the same. The higher the value of money, the smaller is the quantity of money that people plan to hold. If it seems strange that a higher value of money makes people want to hold less money, think about how much money you would plan to hold if the price of a restaurant meal was 20 cents and the price of movie ticket was 10 cents. You would be happy to hold (say) $1 on average. But if the price of a meal is $20 and the price of a movie ticket is $10, you would want to hold $100 on average. The price level is lower and the value of money higher in the first case than in the second; and the amount of money you would plan to hold is lower in the first case than in the second.

### Money Market Equilibrium in the Long Run

In the long run, money market equilibrium determines the value of money. If the quantity of money supplied exceeds the long-run quantity demanded, people go out and spend their surplus money. The quantity of goods and services available is fixed equal to potential GDP, so the extra spending forces prices upward. As the price level rises, the value of money falls.

If the quantity of money supplied is less than the long-run quantity demanded, people lower their spending to build up the quantity of money they hold. The shortage of money translates into a surplus of goods and services, so the spending cut-back forces prices downward. The price level falls and the value of money rises. When the quantity of money supplied equals the long-run quantity demanded, the price level and the value of money are at their equilibrium levels.

Figure 27.4 illustrates long-run money market equilibrium. The long-run demand for money curve is *LRMD*. Its position depends on potential GDP and the equilibrium interest rate. The supply of money is *MS*. Equilibrium occurs when the value of money is 1.

**FIGURE 27.4**

Long-Run Money Market Equilibrium

myeconlab Animation

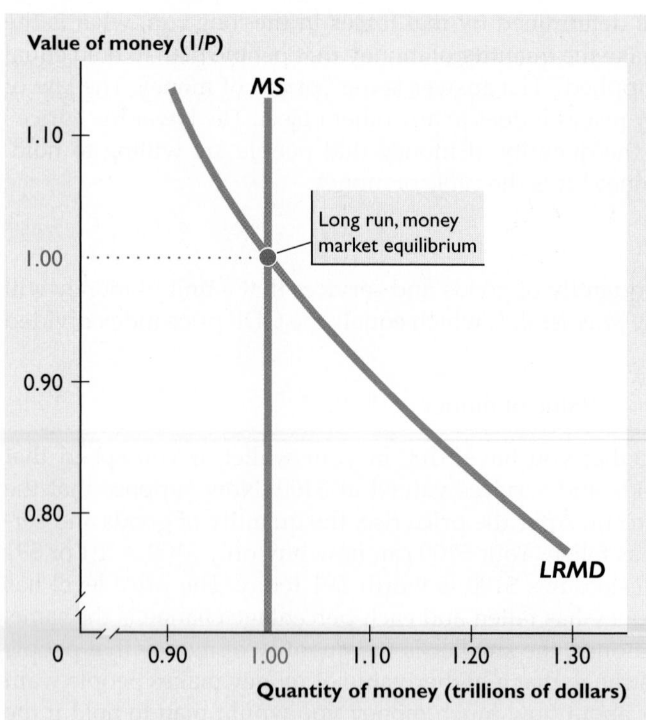


The long-run demand for money is determined by potential GDP and the equilibrium interest rate.

The *LRMD* curve shows how the quantity of money that households and firms plan to hold, in the long run, depends on the value of money (or 1/*P*, the inverse of the price level).

The *MS* curve shows the quantity of money supplied, which is $1 trillion.

The price level adjusts to make the value of money equal 1 and achieve long-run money market equilibrium.

## A Change in the Quantity of Money

Suppose that starting from a long-run equilibrium, the Fed increases the quantity of money by 10 percent. In the short run, the greater quantity of money lowers the nominal interest rate. With a lower interest rate, people and businesses borrow more and spend more. But with real GDP equal to potential GDP, there are no more goods and services to buy, so when people go out and spend, prices start to rise. Eventually, a new long-run equilibrium is reached at which the price level has increased in proportion to the increase in the quantity of money. Because the quantity of money increased by 10 percent, the price level has also risen by 10 percent from 1.0 to 1.1.

Figure 27.5 illustrates this outcome. Initially, the supply of money is $MS_0$ and the quantity of money is $1 trillion. The Fed increases the supply of money to $MS_1$ and the quantity of money is now $1.1 trillion—a 10 percent increase. There is now a surplus of money and people go out and spend it. The increased spending on the same unchanged quantity of goods and services raises the price level and lowers the value of money. Eventually, the price level has increased by 10 percent from 1.0 to 1.1 and the value of money has decreased by 10 percent from 1.00 to 0.91.

You've just seen a key proposition about the quantity of money and the price level.

**In the long run and other things remaining the same, a given percentage change in the quantity of money brings an equal percentage change in the price level.**

**FIGURE 27.5**

The Long-Run Effect of a Change in the Quantity of Money

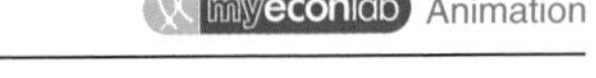


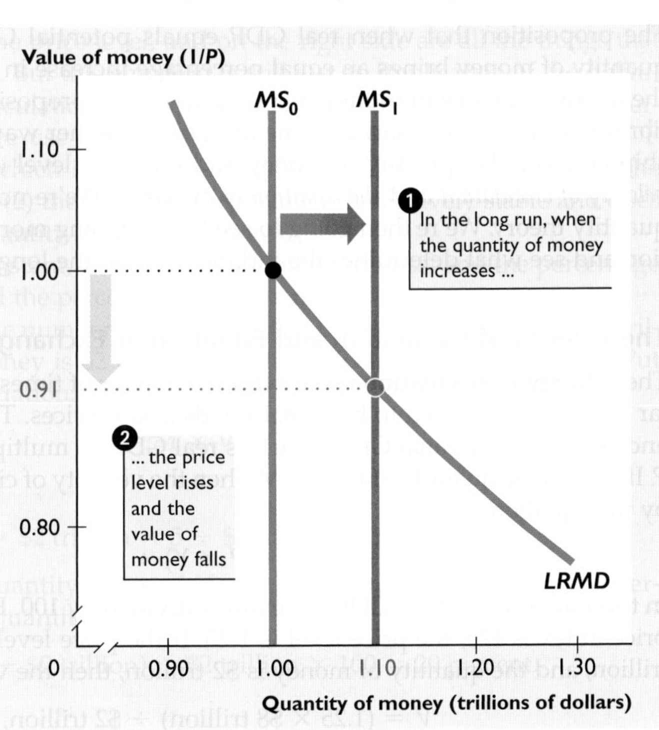


1 The Fed increases the supply of money from $MS_0$ to $MS_1$ and the quantity of money increases from $1 trillion to $1.1 trillion, a 10 percent increase.

2 The price level rises by 10 percent and the value of money falls by 10 percent to restore long-run money market equilibrium.

must sell 20 bottles of ketchup to buy one hour of labor. Now suppose the price of ketchup falls to 50 cents a bottle. The real wage rate of a bottling worker has increased to 40 bottles—the firm must now sell 40 bottles of ketchup to buy one hour of labor.

If the price of a bottle of ketchup increased, the real wage rate of a bottling worker would fall. For example, if the price increased to $2 a bottle, the real wage rate would be 10 bottles per worker—the firm needs to sell only 10 bottles of ketchup to buy one hour of labor.

Firms respond to a change in the real wage rate by changing the quantity of labor employed and the quantity produced. For the economy as a whole, employment and real GDP change. There are three ways in which these changes occur:

- Firms change their output rate.
- Firms shut down temporarily or restart production.
- Firms go out of business or start up in business.

### Change in Output Rate

To change its output rate, a firm must change the quantity of labor that it employs. It is profitable to hire more labor if the additional labor costs less than the revenue it generates. If the price level rises and the money wage rate doesn't change, an extra hour of labor that was previously unprofitable becomes profitable. So when the price level rises and the money wage rate doesn't change, the quantity of labor demanded and production increase. If the price level falls and the money wage rate doesn't change, an hour of labor that was previously profitable becomes unprofitable. So when the price level falls and the money wage rate doesn't change, the quantity of labor demanded and production decrease.

### Temporary Shutdowns and Restarts

A firm that is incurring a loss might foresee a profit in the future. Such a firm might decide to shut down temporarily and lay off its workers.

The price level relative to the money wage rate influences temporary shutdown decisions. If the price level rises relative to wages, fewer firms decide to shut down temporarily; so more firms operate and the quantity of real GDP supplied increases. If the price level falls relative to wages, a larger number of firms find that they cannot earn enough revenue to pay the wage bill and so temporarily shut down. The quantity of real GDP supplied decreases.

### Business Failure and Startup

People create businesses in the hope of earning a profit. When profits are squeezed or when losses arise, more firms fail, fewer new firms start up, and the number of firms decreases. When profits are generally high, fewer firms fail, more firms start up, and the number of firms increases.

The price level relative to the money wage rate influences the number of firms in business. If the price level rises relative to wages, profits increase, the number of firms in business increases, and the quantity of real GDP supplied increases. If the price level falls relative to wages, profits fall, the number of firms in business decreases, and the quantity of real GDP supplied decreases.

In a severe recession, business failure can be contagious. The failure of one firm puts pressure on both its suppliers and its customers and can bring a flood of failures and a large decrease in the quantity of real GDP supplied.

## Changes in Aggregate Supply

Aggregate supply changes when any influence on production plans other than the price level changes. In particular, aggregate supply changes when

- Potential GDP changes.
- The money wage rate changes.
- The money prices of other resources change.

### Change in Potential GDP

Anything that changes potential GDP changes aggregate supply and shifts the aggregate supply curve. Figure 28.2 illustrates such a shift. You can think of point *C* as an anchor point. The *AS* curve and potential GDP line are anchored at this point, and when potential GDP changes, aggregate supply changes along with it. When potential GDP increases from $13 trillion to $14 trillion, point *C* shifts to point *C*', and the *AS* curve and potential GDP line shift rightward together. The *AS* curve shifts from $AS_0$ to $AS_1$.

### Change in Money Wage Rate

A change in the money wage rate changes aggregate supply because it changes firms' costs. The higher the money wage rate, the higher are firms' costs and the smaller is the quantity that firms are willing to supply at each price level. So an increase in the money wage rate decreases aggregate supply.

**FIGURE 28.2**

An Increase in Potential GDP

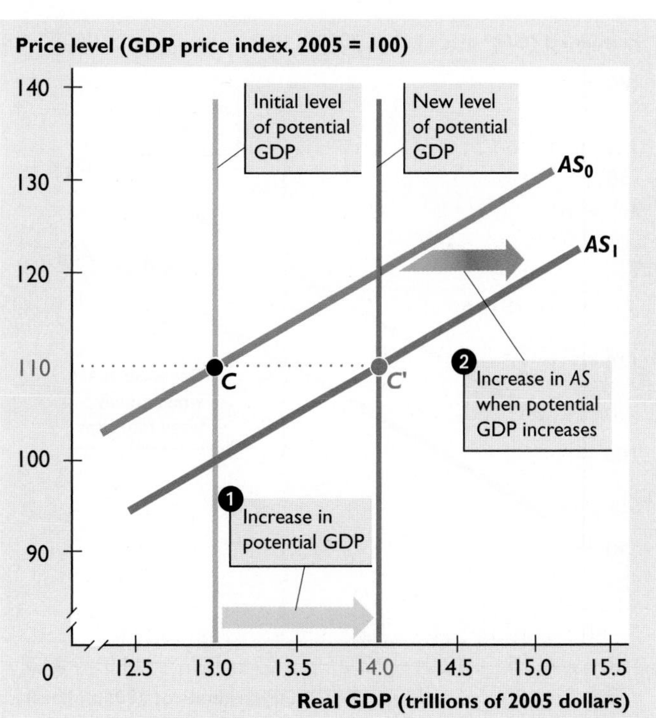


1 An increase in potential GDP increases aggregate supply.

2 When potential GDP increases from $13 trillion to $14 trillion, the aggregate supply curve shifts rightward from $AS_0$ to $AS_1$.

Suppose that the money wage rate is \$33 an hour and the price level is 110. Then the real wage rate is \$30 an hour (\$33 × 100 ÷ 110 = \$30)—see Chapter 22; page 578. If the full-employment equilibrium real wage rate is \$30 an hour, the economy is at full employment and real GDP equals potential GDP. In Figure 28.3, the economy is at point *C* on the aggregate supply curve $AS_0$. The money wage rate is \$33 an hour at all points on $AS_0$.

Now suppose the money wage rate rises to \$36 an hour but the full-employment equilibrium real wage rate remains at \$30 an hour. Real GDP now equals potential GDP when the price level is 120, at point *D* on the aggregate supply curve $AS_2$. (If the money wage rate is \$36 an hour and the price level is 120, the real wage rate is \$36 × 100 ÷ 120 = \$30 an hour.) The money wage rate is \$36 an hour at all points on $AS_2$. The rise in the money wage rate *decreases* aggregate supply and shifts the aggregate supply curve leftward from $AS_0$ to $AS_2$.

A change in the money wage rate does not change potential GDP. The reason is that potential GDP depends only on the economy's real ability to produce and on the full-employment quantity of labor, which occurs at the equilibrium *real* wage rate. The equilibrium real wage rate can occur at any money wage rate.

### Change in Money Prices of Other Resources

A change in the money prices of other resources has a similar effect on firms' production plans to a change in the money wage rate. It changes firms' costs. At each price level, firms' real costs change and the quantity that firms are willing to supply changes so aggregate supply changes.

**FIGURE 28.3**

A Change in the Money Wage Rate

myeconlab Animation

A rise in the money wage rate decreases aggregate supply. The aggregate supply curve shifts leftward from $AS_0$ to $AS_2$. A rise in the money wage rate does not change potential GDP.

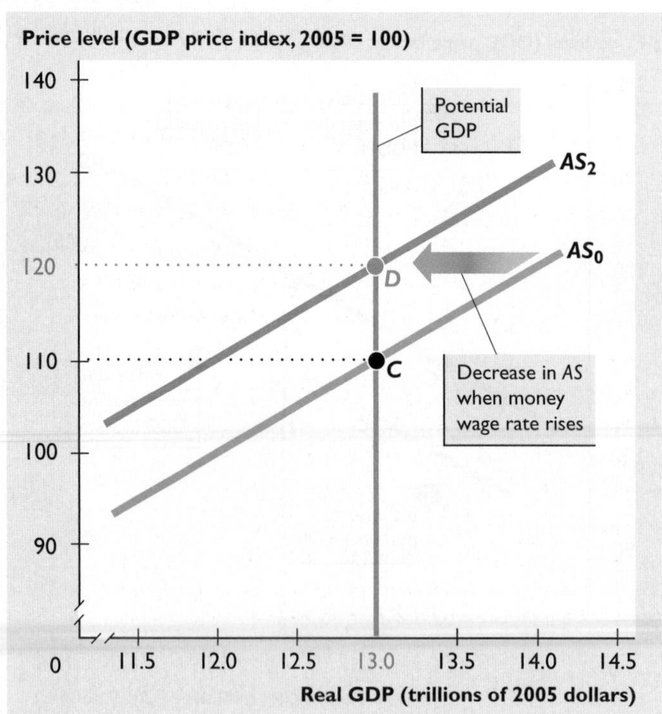

## CHECKPOINT 28.1

Work these problems in Study Plan 28.1 to get instant feedback.

**Define and explain the influences on aggregate supply.**

## Practice Problems

1. Explain the influence of each of the following events on the quantity of real GDP supplied and aggregate supply in India and use a graph to illustrate.
   - Fuel prices rise.
   - U.S. firms move their call handling, IT, and data functions to India.
   - Wal-Mart and Starbucks open in India.
   - Universities in India increase the number of engineering graduates.
   - The money wage rate in India rises.
   - The price level in India increases.
2. **Wages could hit steepest plunge in 18 years**

   A bad economy is starting to drag down wages for millions of workers. The average weekly wage of private-sector workers has fallen 1.4% this year through September. Colorado will become the first state to lower its minimum wage since the federal minimum wage law was passed in 1938, when the state cuts its rate by 4 cents an hour.

   Source: *USA Today*, October 16, 2009

   Explain how the fall in the average weekly wage and the minimum wage will influence aggregate supply.

## Guided Solutions to Practice Problems

1. As fuel prices rise, the quantity of real GDP supplied at the current price level decreases. The *AS* curve shifts leftward (Figure 1).

   As businesses move their call handling, IT, and data functions to India, real GDP supplied at the current price level increases. The *AS* curve shifts rightward (Figure 2).

   As Wal-Mart and Starbucks open, the quantity of real GDP supplied at the current price level increases. The *AS* curve shifts rightward (Figure 2).

   With more graduates, the number of skilled workers increases, and production increases at the current price level. The *AS* curve shifts rightward (Figure 2).

   As the money wage rate rises, firms' costs increase and the quantity of real GDP supplied at the current price level decreases. The *AS* curve shifts leftward (Figure 1).

   As the price level increases, other things remaining the same, businesses became more profitable and increase the quantity of real GDP supplied along the *AS* curve (Figure 3). The *AS* curve does not shift.
2. The cut in the money wage rate decreases the real wage rate and increases aggregate supply. If the cut in the minimum wage decreases the natural unemployment rate, potential GDP increases and aggregate supply increases further.

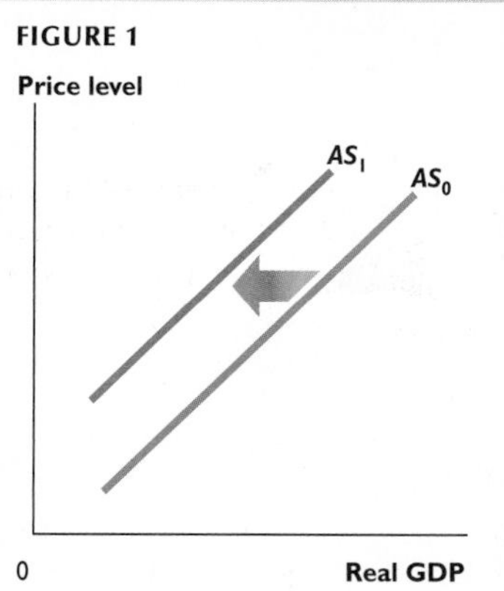

**FIGURE 1**

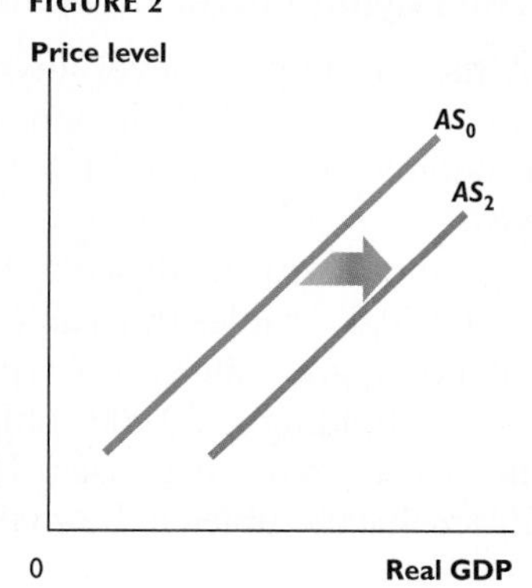

**FIGURE 2**

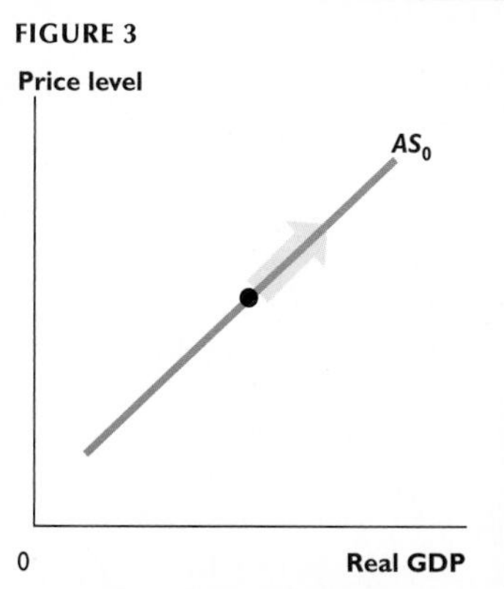

**FIGURE 3**

## 28.2 AGGREGATE DEMAND

The *quantity of real GDP demanded* (*Y*) is the total amount of final goods and services produced in the United States that people, businesses, governments, and foreigners plan to buy. This quantity is the sum of the real consumption expenditure (*C*), investment (*I*), government expenditure on goods and services (*G*), and exports (*X*) minus imports (*M*). That is,

$$Y = C + I + G + X - M$$

Many factors influence expenditure plans; to study aggregate demand, we divide them into two groups: the price level and everything else. We'll first consider the influence of the price level on expenditure plans and then consider the other influences.

### ■ Aggregate Demand Basics

**Aggregate demand**
The relationship between the quantity of real GDP demanded and the price level when all other influences on expenditure plans remain the same.

**Aggregate demand** is the relationship between the quantity of real GDP demanded and the price level when all other influences on expenditure plans remain the same. This relationship can be described as follows:

**Other things remaining the same, the higher the price level, the smaller is the quantity of real GDP demanded; and the lower the price level, the greater is the quantity of real GDP demanded.**

Figure 28.4 illustrates aggregate demand by using an aggregate demand schedule and aggregate demand curve. The aggregate demand schedule lists the quantities of real GDP demanded at each price level, and the downward-sloping *AD* curve graphs these points.

Along the aggregate demand curve, the only influence on expenditure plans that changes is the price level. A rise in the price level decreases the quantity of real GDP demanded and brings a movement up along the aggregate demand curve; a fall in the price level increases the quantity of real GDP demanded and brings a movement down along the aggregate demand curve.

The price level influences the quantity of real GDP demanded because a change in the price level brings a change in

- The buying power of money
- The real interest rate
- The real prices of exports and imports

#### The Buying Power of Money

A rise in the price level lowers the buying power of money and decreases the quantity of real GDP demanded. To see why, think about the buying plans in two economies—Russia and Japan—where the price level has changed a lot in recent years.

Anna lives in Moscow, Russia. She has worked hard all summer and has saved 20,000 rubles (the ruble is the currency of Russia), which she plans to spend attending graduate school when she has earned her economics degree. So Anna's money holding is 20,000 rubles. Anna has a part-time job, and her income from this job pays her expenses. The price level in Russia rises by 100 percent. Anna needs 40,000 rubles to buy what 20,000 rubles once bought. To make up some of

**FIGURE 28.4**

## Aggregate Demand Schedule and Aggregate Demand Curve

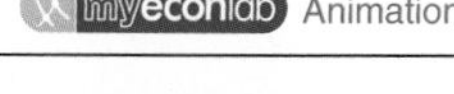


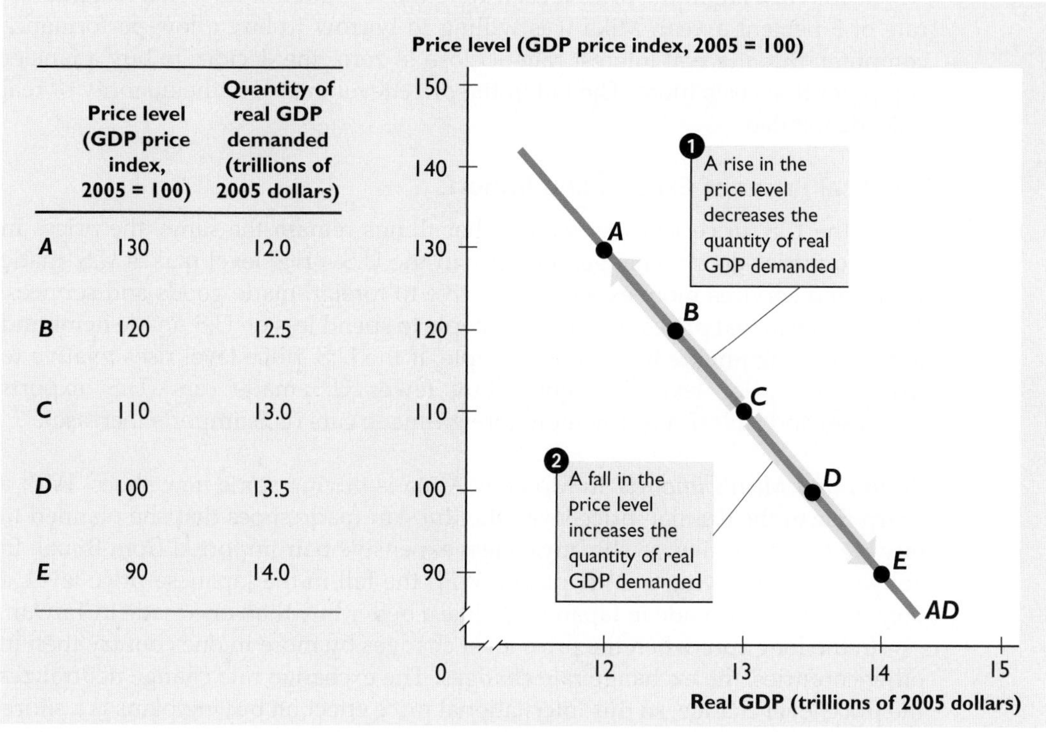

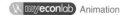

| | Price level (GDP price index, 2005 = 100) | Quantity of real GDP demanded (trillions of 2005 dollars) |
|---|---|---|
| **A** | 130 | 12.0 |
| **B** | 120 | 12.5 |
| **C** | 110 | 13.0 |
| **D** | 100 | 13.5 |
| **E** | 90 | 14.0 |



The aggregate demand schedule and aggregate demand curve, *AD*, show the relationship between the quantity of real GDP demanded and the price level when all other influences on expenditure plans remain the same. Each point *A* through *E* on the *AD* curve corresponds to the row identified by the same letter in the schedule.

The quantity of real GDP demanded

1. decreases when the price level rises and
2. increases when the price level falls.

the fall in the buying power of her money, Anna slashes her spending.

Similarly, a fall in the price level, other things remaining the same, brings an increase in the quantity of real GDP demanded. To see why, think about the buying plans of Mika, who lives in Tokyo, Japan. She too has worked hard all summer and has saved 200,000 yen (the yen is the currency of Japan), which she plans to spend attending school next year. The price level in Japan falls by 10 percent; now Mika needs only 180,000 yen to buy what 200,000 yen once bought. With a rise in what her money buys, Mika decides to buy a DVD player.

### The Real Interest Rate

When the price level rises, the real interest rate rises. You saw in Chapter 27 (page 697) that an increase in the price level increases the amount of money that people want to hold—increases the demand for money. When the demand for money increases, the nominal interest rate rises. In the short run, the inflation rate does not change, so a rise in the nominal interest rate brings a rise in the real interest rate. Faced with a higher real interest rate, businesses and people delay plans to buy new capital and consumer durable goods and they cut back on spending. As the price level rises, the quantity of real GDP demanded decreases.

***Anna and Mika Again*** Think about Anna and Mika again. Both of them want to buy a computer. In Moscow, a rise in the price level increases the demand for money and raises the real interest rate. At a real interest rate of 5 percent a year,

Anna was willing to borrow to buy the new computer. But at a real interest rate of 10 percent a year, she decides that the payments would be too high, so she delays buying it. The rise in the price level decreases the quantity of real GDP demanded.

In Tokyo, a fall in the price level lowers the real interest rate. At a real interest rate of 5 percent a year, Mika was willing to borrow to buy a low-performance computer. But at a real interest rate of close to zero, she decides to buy a fancier computer that costs more: The fall in the price level increases the quantity of real GDP demanded.

### The Real Prices of Exports and Imports

When the U.S. price level rises and other things remain the same, the prices in other countries do not change. So a rise in the U.S. price level makes U.S.-made goods and services more expensive relative to foreign-made goods and services. This change in real prices encourages people to spend less on U.S.-made items and more on foreign-made items. For example, if the U.S. price level rises relative to the foreign price level, foreigners buy fewer U.S.-made cars (U.S. exports decrease) and Americans buy more foreign-made cars (U.S. imports increase).

***Anna's and Mika's Imports*** In Moscow, Anna is buying some new shoes. With a sharp rise in the Russian price level, the Russian-made shoes that she planned to buy are too expensive, so she buys a less expensive pair imported from Brazil. In Tokyo, Mika is buying a DVD player. With the fall in the Japanese price level, a Sony DVD player made in Japan looks like a better buy than one made in Taiwan.

In the long run, when the price level changes by more in one country than in other countries, the exchange rate changes. The exchange rate change neutralizes the price level change, so this international price effect on buying plans is a short-run effect only. But in the short run, it is a powerful effect.

## Changes in Aggregate Demand

A change in any factor that influences expenditure plans other than the price level brings a change in aggregate demand. When aggregate demand increases, the aggregate demand curve shifts rightward, which Figure 28.5 illustrates as the rightward shift of the *AD* curve from $AD_0$ to $AD_1$. When aggregate demand decreases, the aggregate demand curve shifts leftward, which Figure 28.5 illustrates as the leftward shift of the *AD* curve from $AD_0$ to $AD_2$. The factors that change aggregate demand are

- Expectations about the future
- Fiscal policy and monetary policy
- The state of the world economy

### Expectations

An increase in expected future income increases the amount of consumption goods (especially big-ticket items such as cars) that people plan to buy now. Aggregate demand increases. An increase in expected future inflation increases aggregate demand because people decide to buy more goods and services now before their prices rise. An increase in expected future profit increases the investment that firms plan to undertake now. Aggregate demand increases.

A decrease in expected future income, future inflation, or future profit has the opposite effect and decreases aggregate demand.

**FIGURE 28.5**

Change in Aggregate Demand

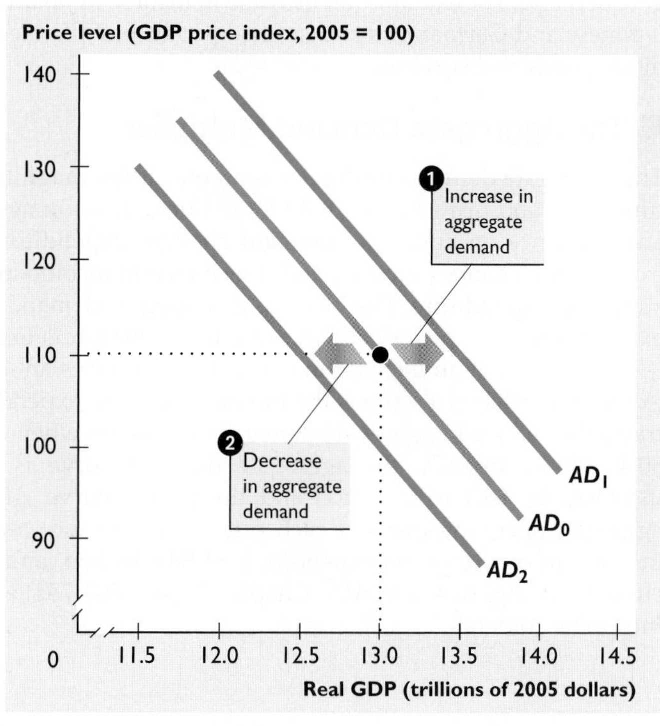


❶ Aggregate demand *increases if*

- Expected future income, inflation, or profits increase.
- The government or the Federal Reserve takes steps that increase planned expenditure.
- The exchange rate falls or the global economy expands.

❷ Aggregate demand *decreases if*

- Expected future income, inflation, or profits decrease.
- The government or the Federal Reserve takes steps that decrease planned expenditure.
- The exchange rate rises or the global economy contracts.

## Fiscal Policy and Monetary Policy

We study the effects of policy actions on aggregate demand in Chapters 31 and 32. Here, we'll just briefly note that the government can use **fiscal policy**—changing taxes, transfer payments, and government expenditure on goods and services—to influence aggregate demand. The Federal Reserve can use **monetary policy**—changing the quantity of money and the interest rate—to influence aggregate demand. A tax cut or an increase in either transfer payments or government expenditure on goods and services increases aggregate demand. A cut in the interest rate or an increase in the quantity of money increases aggregate demand.

**Fiscal policy**
Changing taxes, transfer payments, and government expenditure on goods and services.

**Monetary policy**
Changing the quantity of money and the interest rate.

## The World Economy

Two main influences that the world economy has on aggregate demand are the foreign exchange rate and foreign income. The foreign exchange rate is the amount of a foreign currency that you can buy with a U.S. dollar. Other things remaining the same, a rise in the foreign exchange rate decreases aggregate demand.

To see how the foreign exchange rate influences aggregate demand, suppose that $1 exchanges for 100 Japanese yen. A Fujitsu phone made in Japan costs 12,500 yen, and an equivalent Motorola phone made in the United States costs $110. In U.S. dollars, the Fujitsu phone costs $125, so people around the world buy the cheaper U.S. phone. Now suppose the exchange rate rises to 125 yen per dollar. At 125 yen per dollar, the Fujitsu phone costs $100 and is now cheaper than the Motorola phone. People will switch from the U.S. phone to the Japanese phone.

U.S. exports will decrease and U.S. imports will increase, so U.S. aggregate demand will decrease.

An increase in foreign income increases U.S. exports and increases U.S. aggregate demand. For example, an increase in income in Japan and Germany increases Japanese and German consumers' and producers' planned expenditures on U.S.-made goods and services.

## The Aggregate Demand Multiplier

The aggregate demand multiplier is an effect that magnifies changes in expenditure plans and brings potentially large fluctuations in aggregate demand. When any influence on aggregate demand changes expenditure plans, the change in expenditure changes income; and the change in income induces a change in consumption expenditure. The increase in aggregate demand is the initial increase in expenditure plus the induced increase in consumption expenditure.

Suppose that an increase in expenditure induces an increase in consumption expenditure that is 1.5 times the initial increase in expenditure. Figure 28.6 illustrates the change in aggregate demand that occurs when investment increases by \$0.4 trillion. Initially, the aggregate demand curve is $AD_0$. Investment then increases by \$0.4 trillion ($\Delta I$) and the purple curve $AD_0 + \Delta I$ now describes aggregate spending plans at each price level. An increase in income induces an increase in consumption expenditure of \$0.6 trillion, and the aggregate demand curve shifts rightward to $AD_1$. Chapter 29 (pp. 760–764) explains the expenditure multiplier in detail.

**FIGURE 28.6**

The Aggregate Demand Multiplier

myeconlab Animation

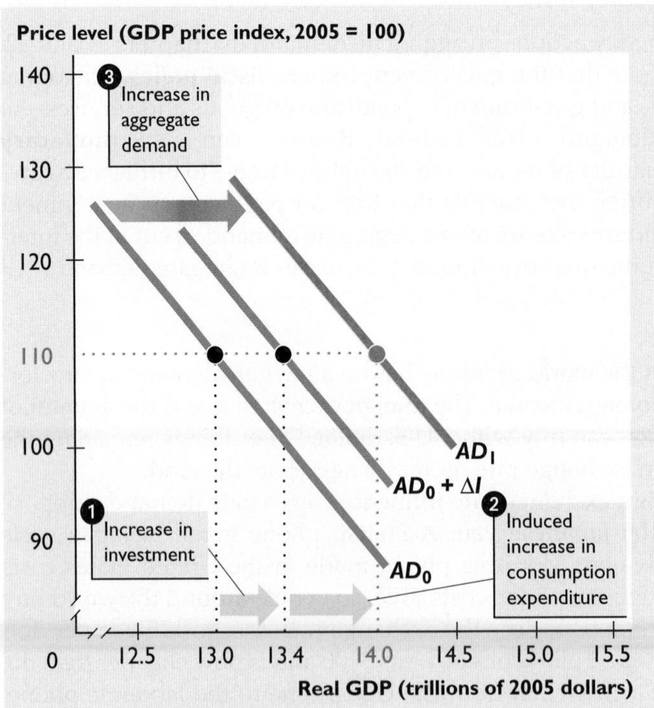


1. An increase in investment increases aggregate demand and increases income.
2. The increase in income induces an increase in consumption expenditure, so 3. aggregate demand increases by more than the initial increase in investment.

## CHECKPOINT 28.2

Work these problems in Study Plan 28.2 to get instant feedback.

**Define and explain the influences on aggregate demand.**

## Practice Problems

1. Mexico trades with the United States. Explain the effect of each of the following events on Mexico's aggregate demand.
   - The government of Mexico cuts income taxes.
   - The United States experiences strong economic growth.
   - Mexico sets new environmental standards that require factories to upgrade their production facilities.
2. Explain the effect of each of the following events on the quantity of real GDP demanded and aggregate demand in Mexico.
   - Europe trades with Mexico and goes into a recession.
   - The price level in Mexico rises.
   - Mexico increases the quantity of money.
3. **Durable goods orders surge in May, new-homes sales dip**

   The Commerce Department announced that demand for durable goods rose 1.8%, while new-home sales dropped 0.6% in May. U.S. companies suffered a sharp drop in exports as other countries struggle with recession.

   Source: *USA Today*, June 24, 2009

   Explain how the items in the news clip influence U.S. aggregate demand.

## Guided Solutions to Practice Problems

1. A tax cut increases disposable income, which increases Mexico's aggregate demand. Strong U.S. growth increases the demand for Mexican-produced goods, which increases Mexico's aggregate demand. As factories upgrade their facilities, investment increases. Aggregate demand increases. In each case, the *AD* curve shifts rightward (Figure 1).
2. A recession in Europe decreases the demand for Mexico's exports, so aggregate demand decreases. The *AD* curve shifts leftward (Figure 2).

   A rise in the price level decreases the quantity of real GDP demanded along the *AD* curve, but the *AD* curve does not shift (Figure 3).

   An increase in the quantity of money increases aggregate demand, and the *AD* curve shifts rightward (Figure 1).
3. The purchase of durable goods and new homes is investment. Investment increased, which increased aggregate demand. The drop in U.S. exports is a decrease in the demand for U.S.-produced goods and services, so the drop in U.S. exports decreased U.S. aggregate demand.

**FIGURE 1**

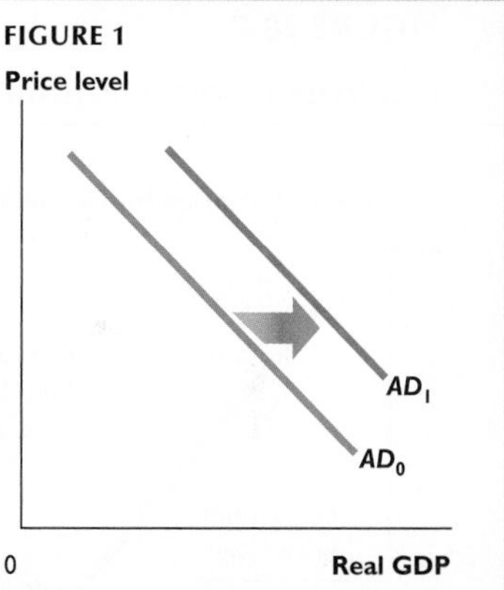


**FIGURE 2**

**FIGURE 3**

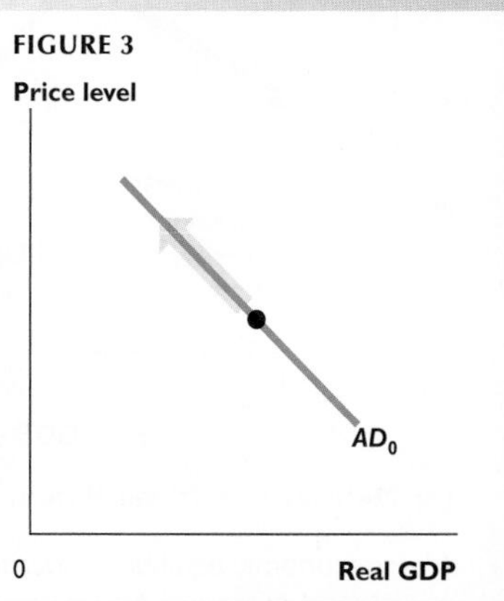

## 28.3 UNDERSTANDING THE BUSINESS CYCLE

**Macroeconomic equilibrium**
When the quantity of real GDP demanded equals the quantity of real GDP supplied at the point of intersection of the *AD* curve and the *AS* curve.

Aggregate supply and aggregate demand determine real GDP and the price level. **Macroeconomic equilibrium** occurs when the quantity of real GDP demanded equals the quantity of real GDP supplied at the point of intersection of the *AD* curve and the *AS* curve. Figure 28.7(a) shows such an equilibrium at a price level of 110 and real GDP of $13 trillion.

To see why this position is the equilibrium, think about what happens if the price level is something other than 110. Suppose that the price level is 120 and that real GDP is $14 trillion (point *E* on the *AS* curve). The quantity of real GDP demanded is less than $14 trillion, so firms are unable to sell all their output. Unwanted inventories pile up, and firms cut production and prices until they can sell all their output, which occurs only when real GDP is $13 trillion and the price level is 110.

Now suppose the price level is 100 and real GDP is $12 trillion (point *A* on the *AS* curve). The quantity of real GDP demanded exceeds $12 trillion, so firms are unable to meet the demand for their output. Inventories decrease, and customers clamor for goods and services. So firms increase production and raise prices until firms can meet demand, which occurs only when real GDP is $13 trillion and the price level is 110.

**FIGURE 28.7**

Macroeconomic Equilibrium

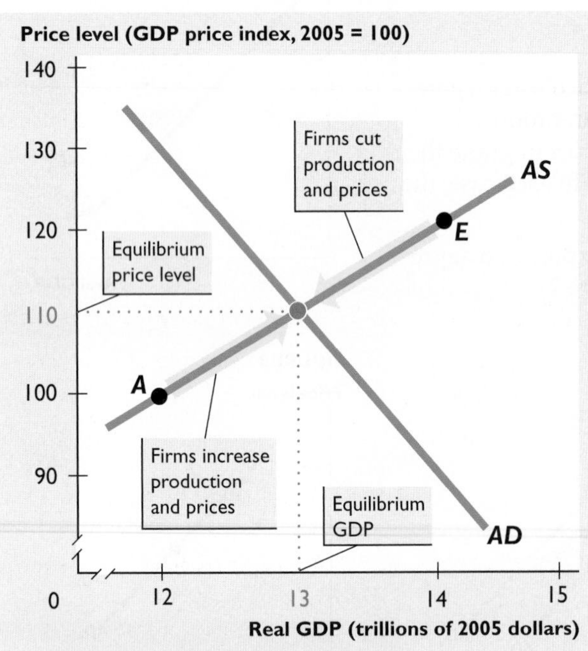


**(a) Macroeconomic equilibrium**

Macroeconomic equilibrium occurs at the intersection of the *AD* and *AS* curves. Macroeconomic equilibrium might be below full employment, at full employment, or above full employment.

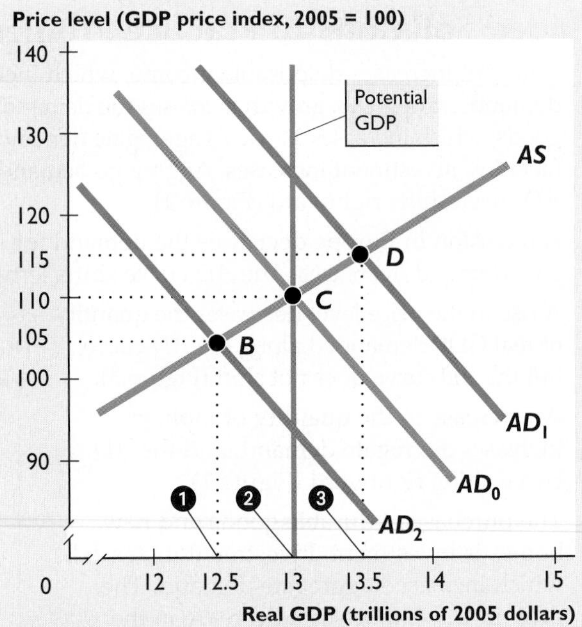


**(b) Three types of macroeconomic equilibrium**

1. Below full-employment equilibrium
2. Full-employment equilibrium
3. Above full-employment equilibrium

In macroeconomic equilibrium, the economy might be at full employment or above or below full employment. Figure 28.7(b) shows these three possibilities. **Full-employment equilibrium**—when equilibrium real GDP equals potential GDP—occurs where $AD_0$ intersects the aggregate supply curve *AS*. Fluctuations in aggregate demand bring fluctuations in real GDP around potential GDP. If aggregate demand increases to $AD_1$, firms increase production and raise prices until they can meet the higher demand. Real GDP increases to $13.5 trillion and exceeds potential GDP in an **above full-employment equilibrium**. If aggregate demand decreases to $AD_2$, firms decrease production and cut prices until they can sell all their output. Real GDP decreases to $12.5 trillion and is less than potential GDP in a **below full-employment equilibrium**.

**Full-employment equilibrium**
When equilibrium real GDP equals potential GDP.

**Above full-employment equilibrium**
When equilibrium real GDP exceeds potential GDP.

**Below full-employment equilibrium**
When potential GDP exceeds equilibrium real GDP.

## Aggregate Demand Fluctuations

Fluctuations in aggregate demand are one of the sources of the business cycle. To focus on the aggregate demand cycle, suppose that potential GDP and the full-employment price level remain constant. And suppose that aggregate demand fluctuates between $AD_1$ and $AD_2$ in Figure 28.7(b). The result of these fluctuations is the cycle in real GDP around potential GDP that Figure 28.8 shows.

In year 1, aggregate demand is $AD_0$ in Figure 28.7(b). The economy is at full employment with real GDP at $13 trillion. Then, in year 2, aggregate demand increases to $AD_1$. As aggregate demand increases, real GDP increases to $13.5 trillion at point *D* in Figure 28.7(b) and at a business cycle peak in Figure 28.8. In year 3, aggregate demand decreases to $AD_0$ in Figure 28.7(b). Real GDP now falls to $13 trillion, and the economy is back at full employment. Aggregate demand decreases further in year 4 to $AD_2$. Real GDP now decreases to $12.5 trillion at point *B* in Figure 28.7(b) and at a business-cycle trough in Figure 28.8. Finally, in year 5, aggregate demand increases to $AD_0$ and real GDP increases again to $13 trillion. The economy is again at full employment.

The sources of the fluctuations in aggregate demand could be any of the factors that we reviewed: Changes in expectations about the future, changes in fiscal policy and monetary policy, and changes in the world economy.

**FIGURE 28.8**

An Aggregate Demand Cycle

myeconlab Animation

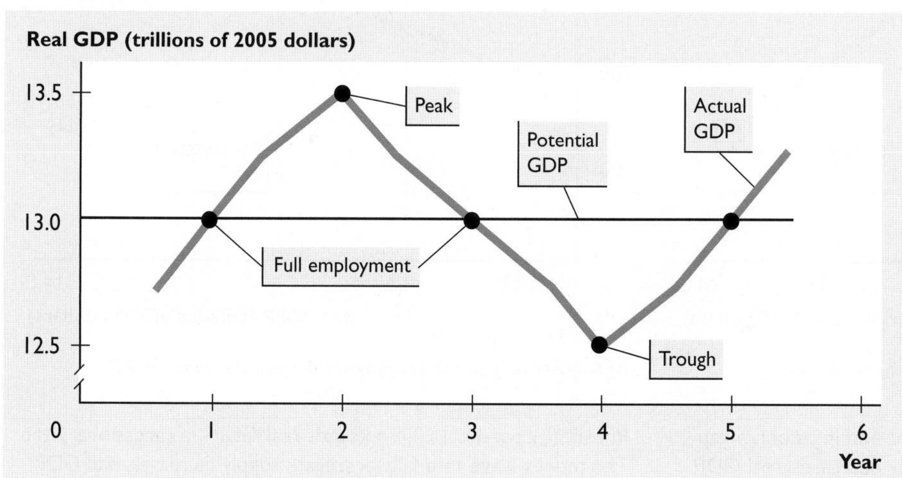


Fluctuations in aggregate demand bring fluctuations in real GDP around potential GDP.

In year 1, real GDP equals potential GDP. The economy is at full employment, such as at point *C* in Figure 28.7(b). In year 2, at a business cycle peak, real GDP exceeds potential GDP. The economy is operating above full employment, such as at point *D* in Figure 28.7(b). In year 3, there is full employment again. In year 4, at a business cycle trough, real GDP is below potential GDP. The economy is operating below full employment, such as at point *B* in Figure 28.7(b).

## Adjustment Toward Full Employment

The cycle in real GDP that we've just described is modified by forces that begin to operate when the economy is away from full employment and that move real GDP toward potential GDP. Let's examine these forces.

**Inflationary gap**
A gap that exists when real GDP exceeds potential GDP and that brings a rising price level.

In Figure 28.9(a), aggregate supply is $AS_0$ and aggregate demand increases from $AD_0$ to $AD_1$. Real GDP is above full employment. There is now an **inflationary gap**—a gap that brings a rising price level. Workers have experienced a fall in the buying power of their wages, and firms' profits have increased. Workers demand higher wages, and firms, anxious to maintain employment and output levels in the face of a labor shortage, meet those demands. As the money wage rate rises, aggregate supply decreases and the aggregate supply curve shifts leftward. Eventually, it reaches $AS_1$, where real GDP is back at potential GDP.

**Recessionary gap**
A gap that exists when potential GDP exceeds real GDP and that brings a falling price level.

In Figure 28.9(b), aggregate supply is $AS_1$ and aggregate demand decreases from $AD_1$ to $AD_2$. Real GDP is below full employment. There is a **recessionary gap**—a gap that brings a falling price level. The people who are lucky enough to have jobs see the buying power of their wages rise and firms' profits shrink. In these circumstances, and with a labor surplus, the money wage rate gradually falls and the aggregate supply curve gradually shifts rightward. Eventually, it reaches $AD_2$, where real GDP is back at potential GDP.

**FIGURE 28.9**
Adjustment Toward Full Employment

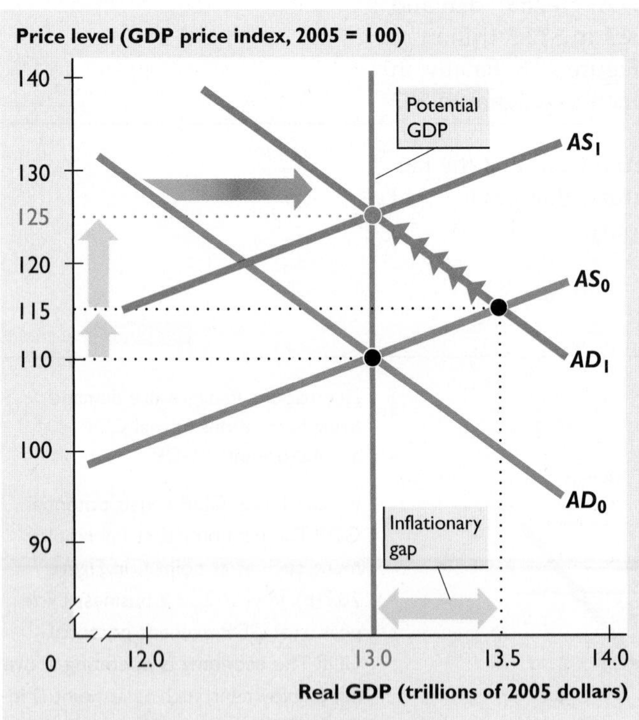


(a) Adjustment to full employment from increase in AD

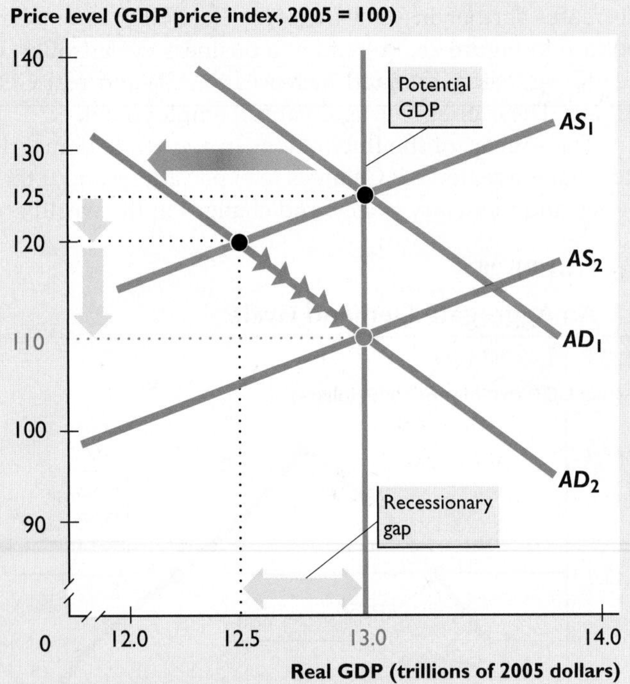


(b) Adjustment to full employment from decrease in AD

In part (a), real GDP exceeds potential GDP—an inflationary gap. The money wage rate rises, aggregate supply decreases, real GDP decreases to $13 trillion and the price level rises to 125.

In part (b), potential GDP exceeds real GDP—a recessionary gap. The money wage rate falls, aggregate supply increases, real GDP increases to $13 trillion and the price level falls to 110.

## Aggregate Supply Fluctuations

Aggregate supply can fluctuate for two types of reasons. First, potential GDP grows at an uneven pace. During a period of rapid technological change and capital accumulation, potential GDP grows rapidly and above its long-term trend. The second half of the 1990s experienced this type of expansion.

Second, the money price of a major resource, such as crude oil, might change. Oil is used so widely throughout the economy that a large change in its price affects almost every firm and impacts the aggregate economy.

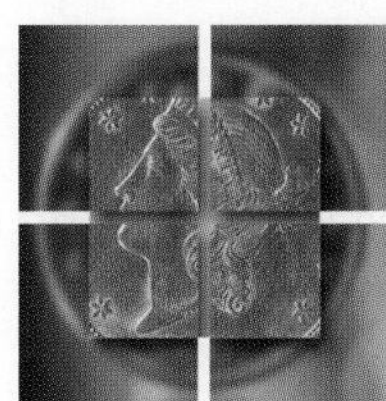

## EYE on the PAST

### Oil Price Cycles in the U.S. and Global Economies

In 1970, a barrel of crude oil cost around $3.50—about $14 in 2005 dollars (see the figure). Most of the world's crude oil came from a handful of nations and the large producer nations were (and still are) members of an international cartel known as OPEC—the Organization of Petroleum Exporting Countries. (A cartel, illegal in the United States, is an organization that controls supply and manipulates the price of a commodity.)

In September 1973, OPEC cut the production of crude oil and raised its price to $10 a barrel—about $31 in 2005 dollars. This near tripling of the price of crude oil decreased aggregate supply and sent the United States, Europe, Japan, and the developing nations into recession.

In 1980, OPEC delivered a second jolt to the global economy by again cutting production and then raising the price to $37 a barrel—almost $80 in 2005 dollars. Aggregate supply decreased again and brought another recession. This recession was much more severe than that of the mid-1970s because the oil price shock was accompanied by a large decrease in aggregate demand that resulted from the Fed's monetary policy.

Faced with a high price of oil, the United States intensified exploration and increased domestic oil production. As additional supplies came onstream, the price of oil tumbled and through the rest of the 1980s and the 1990s, the U.S. and global economies entered a period of sustained expansion.

During the 2000s, rapid economic growth in Asia brought an increase in the demand for oil and its price began to rise again. By late 2007, the price of oil had surged to a new record high of more than $90 a barrel. This high price again decreased aggregate supply and was one of several influences that played a role in intensifying the 2008–2009 recession.

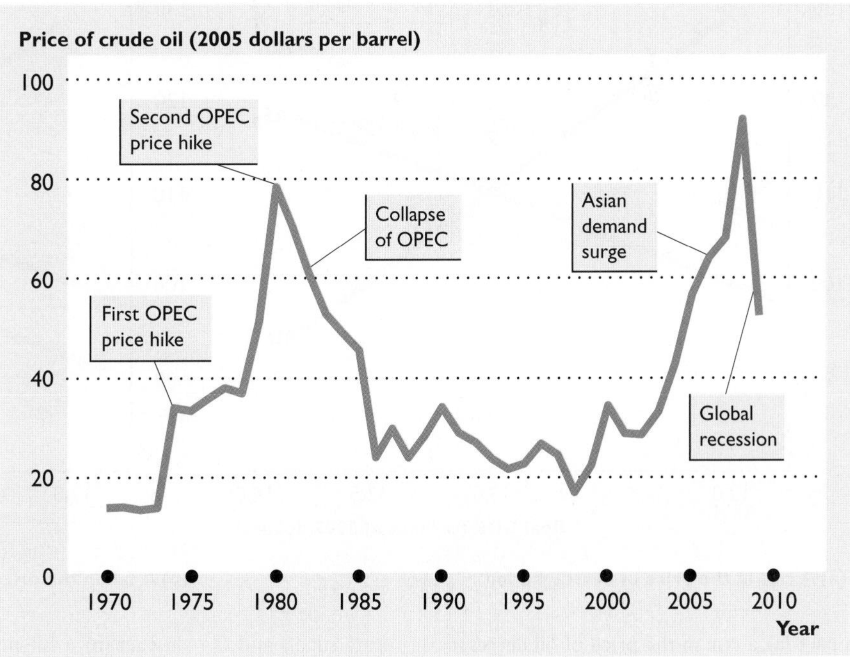


Sources of data: Energy Information Administration and Bureau of Economic Analysis.

*Eye on the Past* on the previous page looks at the recent history of the price of crude oil, and Figure 28.10 illustrates how a rise in the price of oil brings recession and how a fall in the price of oil brings expansion.

In Figure 28.10(a), starting at full employment on aggregate demand curve $AD$ and aggregate supply curve $AS_0$, the price of oil rises. Faced with higher energy costs, firms decrease production. Aggregate supply decreases, and the aggregate supply curve shifts leftward to $AS_1$. The price level rises and real GDP decreases. Because real GDP decreases, the economy experiences recession. Because the price level increases, the economy experiences inflation. A combination of recession and inflation, called **stagflation**, actually occurred in the United States and the global economy in the mid-1970s.

**Stagflation**
A combination of recession (falling real GDP) and inflation (rising price level).

In Figure 28.10(b), starting from the same full-employment equilibrium as before, the price of oil falls. With lower energy costs, firms increase production and the aggregate supply curve shifts rightward to $AS_2$. The price level falls and real GDP increases. The economy experiences expansion and moves above full employment. Similar events to these occurred in the United States and global economies during the mid-1980s, bringing strong economic expansion with a slowdown in the inflation rate.

**FIGURE 28.10**
An Oil Price Cycle

myeconlab Animation

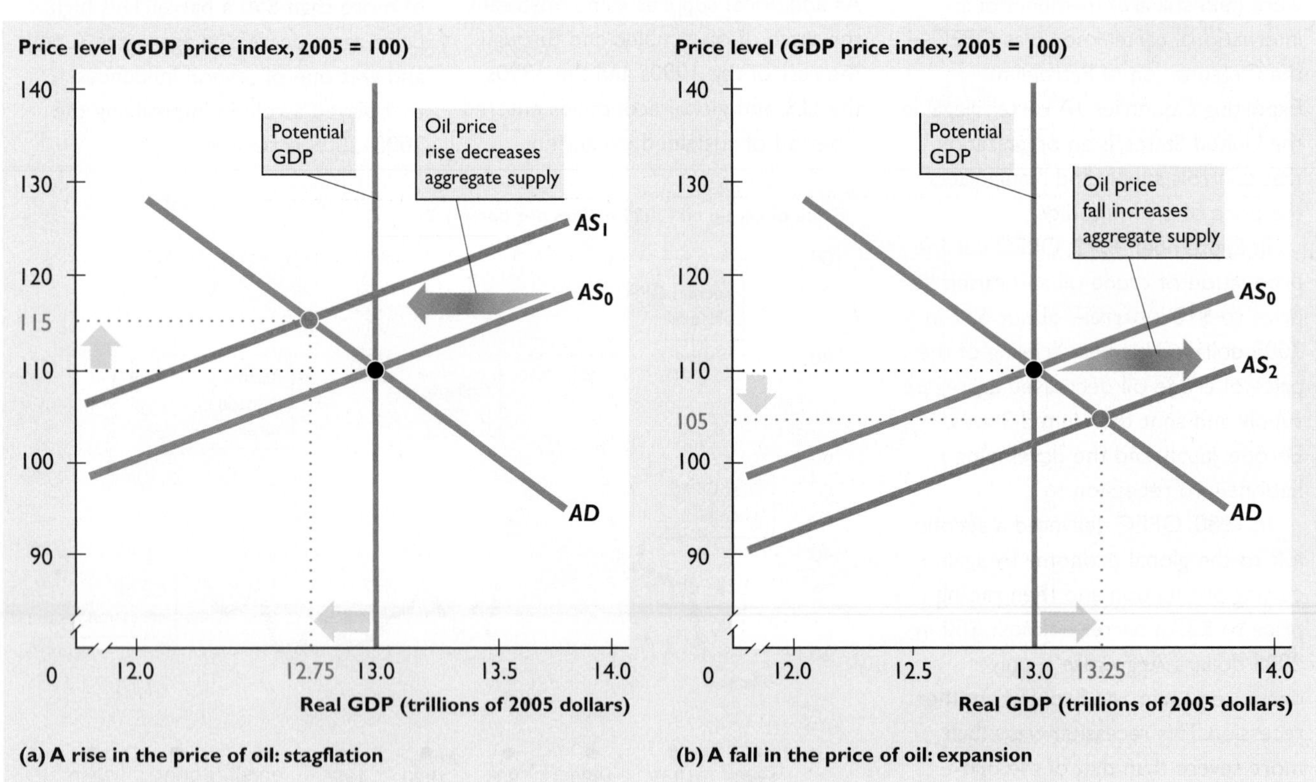


**(a) A rise in the price of oil: stagflation**

**(b) A fall in the price of oil: expansion**

In part (a), a rise in the price of oil decreases aggregate supply and shifts the *AS* curve leftward to $AS_1$. Real GDP decreases to $12.75 trillion, and the price level rises to 115.

In part (b), a fall in the price of oil increases aggregate supply and shifts the *AS* curve rightward to $AS_2$. Real GDP increases to $13.25 trillion, and the price level falls to 105.

# EYE on the BUSINESS CYCLE

## What Causes the Business Cycle?

What causes the business cycle and what in particular caused the 2008–2009 recession?

### Business Cycle Theory

The mainstream business cycle theory is that potential GDP grows at a steady rate while aggregate demand grows at a fluctuating rate.

Because the money wage rate is slow to change, if aggregate demand grows more quickly than potential GDP, real GDP moves above potential GDP and an inflationary gap emerges. The inflation rate rises and real GDP is pulled back toward potential GDP.

If aggregate demand grows more slowly than potential GDP, real GDP moves below potential GDP and a recessionary gap emerges. The inflation rate slows, but the money wage rate responds very slowly to the recessionary gap and real GDP does not return to potential GDP until another increase in aggregate demand occurs.

Fluctuations in investment are the main source of aggregate demand fluctuations. Consumption expenditure responds to changes in income.

A recession can also occur if aggregate supply decreases to bring stagflation. Also, a recession might occur because both aggregate demand and aggregate supply decrease.

### The 2008–2009 Recession

The 2008–2009 recession is an example of a recession caused by a decrease in both aggregate demand and aggregate supply. The figure illustrates these two contributing forces.

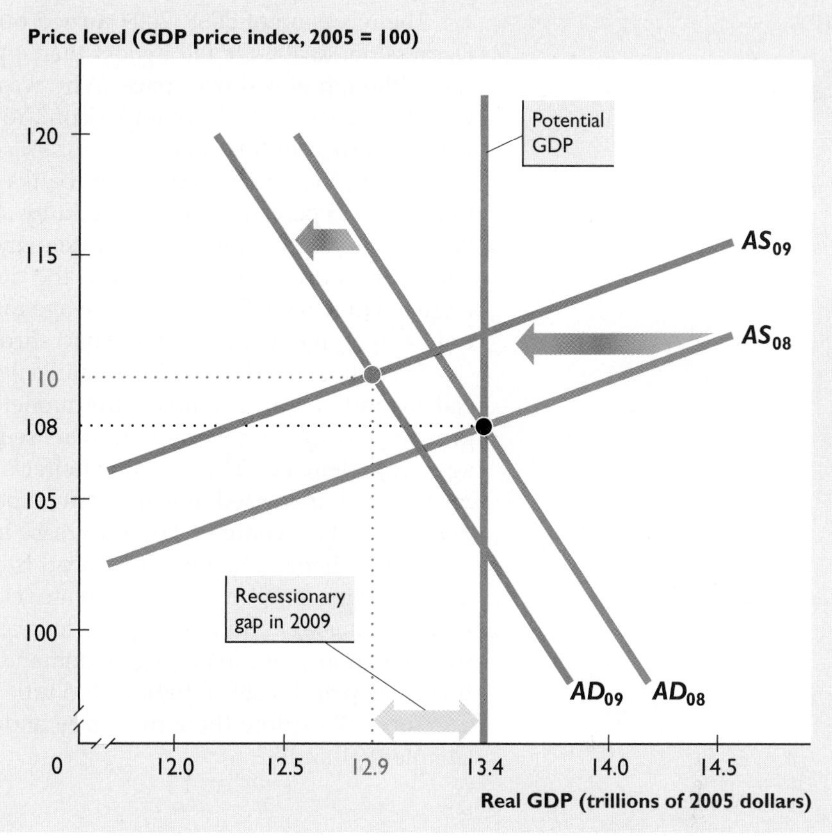


SOURCES OF DATA: Bureau of Economic Analysis and Congressional Budget Office.

At the peak in 2008, real GDP was $13.4 trillion and the price level was 108. In the second quarter of 2009, real GDP had fallen to $12.9 trillion and the price level had risen to 110.

The financial crisis that began in 2007 and intensified in 2008 decreased the supply of loanable funds and lowered investment expenditure. In particular, construction investment collapsed.

Recession in the global economy lowered the demand for U.S. exports so this component of aggregate demand also decreased.

The decrease in aggregate demand was moderated by a large injection of spending by the U.S. government, but this move was not enough to stop aggregate demand from decreasing.

We cannot account for the combination of a rise in the price level and a fall in real GDP with a decrease in aggregate demand alone. Aggregate supply must also have decreased. The rise in oil prices in 2007 and a rise in the money wage rate were the two factors that brought about the decrease in aggregate supply.

## Deflation and the Great Depression

When a financial crisis hit the United States in October 2008, many people feared a repeat of the dreadful events of the 1930s. From 1929 through 1933, the United States and most of the world experienced deflation and depression—the *Great Depression*. The price level fell by 22 percent and real GDP fell by 31 percent.

The recession of 2008–2009 turned out to be much less severe than the Great Depression. Real GDP fell by less than 4 percent and the price level continued to rise, although at a slower pace. Why was the Great Depression so bad and why was 2008–2009 so mild in comparison? You can answer these questions with what you've learned in this chapter.

During the Great Depression, banks failed and the quantity of money contracted by 25 percent. The Fed stood by and took no action to counteract the collapse of buying power so aggregate demand also collapsed. Because the money wage rate didn't fall immediately, the decrease in aggregate demand brought a large fall in real GDP. The money wage rate and price level fell eventually, but not until employment and real GDP had shrunk to 75 percent of their 1929 levels.

In contrast, during the 2008 financial crisis, the Fed bailed out troubled financial institutions and doubled the monetary base. The quantity of money kept growing. Also, the government increased its own expenditures, which added to aggregate demand. The combined effects of continued growth in the quantity of money and increased government expenditure limited the fall in aggregate demand and prevented a large decrease in real GDP.

The challenge that now lies ahead is to unwind the monetary and fiscal stimulus as the components of private expenditure—consumption expenditure, investment, and exports—begin to increase and return to more normal levels and so bring an increase in aggregate demand. Too much stimulus will bring an inflationary gap and faster inflation. Too little stimulus will leave a recessionary gap.

You will explore these monetary and fiscal policy actions and their effects in Chapters 31 and 32.

## EYE on YOUR LIFE

### Using the *AS-AD* Model

Using all the knowledge that you have accumulated over the term, and by watching or reading the current news, try to figure out where the U.S. economy is in its business cycle right now.

First, can you determine if real GDP is currently above, below, or at potential GDP? Second, can you determine if real GDP is expanding or contracting in a recession?

Next, try to form a view about where the U.S. economy is heading. What do you see as the main pressures on aggregate supply and aggregate demand, and in which directions are they pushing or pulling the economy?

Do you think that real GDP will expand more quickly or more slowly over the coming months? Do you think the gap between real GDP and potential GDP will widen or narrow?

How do you expect the labor market to be affected by the changes in aggregate supply and aggregate demand that you are expecting? Do you expect the unemployment rate to rise, fall, or remain constant?

Talk to your friends in class about where they see the U.S. economy right now and where it is heading. Is there a consensus or is there a wide range of opinion?

# EYE on the U.S. ECONOMY

## Real GDP Growth, Inflation, and the Business Cycle

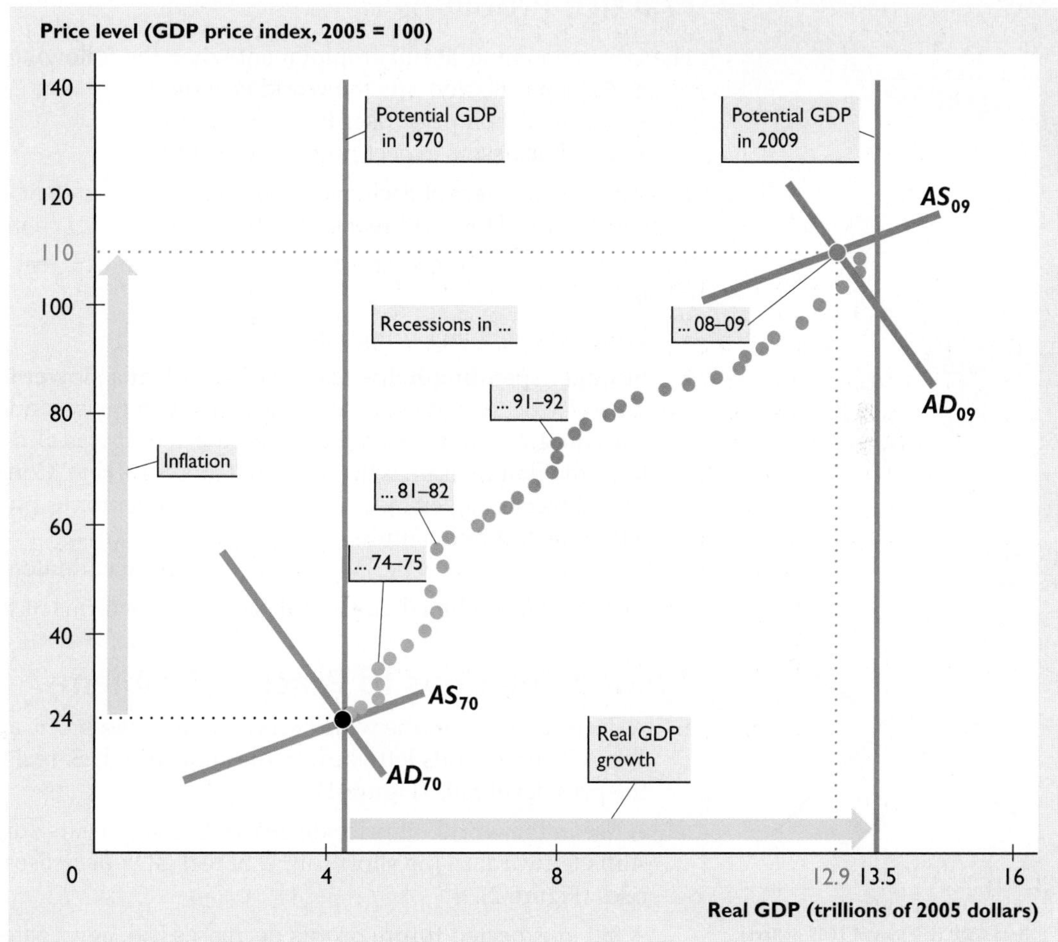


SOURCES OF DATA: Bureau of Labor Statistics, Bureau of Economic Analysis, and Congressional Budget Office.

Each dot in the figure represents the value of real GDP and the price level in a year from 1970 through 2009.

The figure interprets these data points as being generated by aggregate demand and aggregate supply.

The rightward movement in the dots shows increasing real GDP or economic growth, and a leftward movement shows recession.

The upward movement of the dots shows a rising price level or inflation.

When the path that the dots follow is steep, as it was during the 1970s, inflation is rapid and economic growth is slow.

When the dots follow a path that is gently rising, as it was during the 1990s, the inflation rate is low and real GDP growth is more rapid.

Notice that the dots move rightward and upward in waves and occasionally move leftward. These patterns show the business cycle expansions and recessions.

By comparing the dots with potential GDP, we can see that the economy was at full employment in 1970, and that the recessionary gap during the recession of 2008–2009 was large.

Work these problems in Study Plan 28.3 to get instant feedback.

**Explain how fluctuations in aggregate demand and aggregate supply create the business cycle.**

## Practice Problems

The U.S. economy is at full employment when the following events occur:

- A deep recession hits the world economy.
- The world oil price rises by a large amount.
- U.S. businesses expect future profits to fall.

1. Explain the effect of each event separately on aggregate demand and aggregate supply. How will real GDP and the price level change in the short run?
2. Explain the combined effect of these events on U.S. real GDP and the price level.
3. Which event, if any, brings stagflation?
4. **Stronger spending helps real GDP shrink at a slower 0.7%**
   The 0.7% decline in U.S. economic activity in the second quarter was better than the 1.2% contraction that was expected. It was also an improvement from the first quarter, when GDP fell at a 6.4% rate. Consumer spending fell 0.9%, business investment fell by 9.6% as inventories plunged, and exports fell in the last two months.

   Source: Reuters, September 30, 2009

   Explain the combined effect of these events in terms of the *AS-AD* model.

**FIGURE 1**

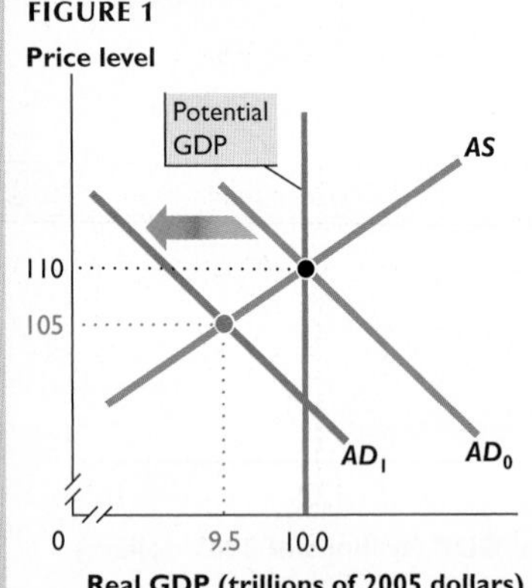


**FIGURE 2**

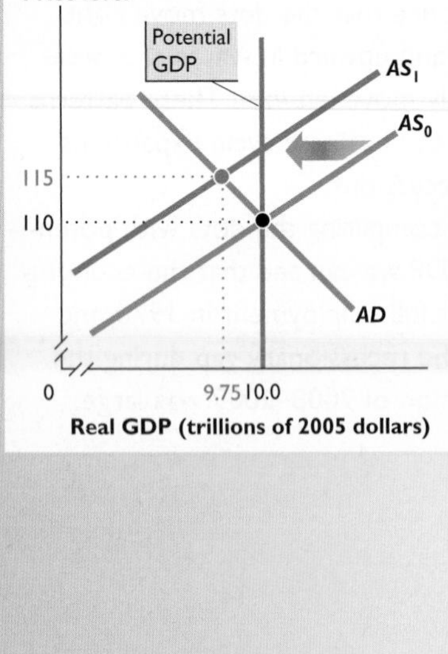

Price level

Potential GDP

$AS_1$

$AS_0$

115

110

AD

0

9.75 10.0

Real GDP (trillions of 2005 dollars)

## Guided Solutions to Practice Problems

1. A deep recession in the world economy decreases U.S. aggregate demand. The *AD* curve shifts leftward. In the short run, U.S. real GDP decreases and the price level falls (Figure 1).

   A rise in the world oil price decreases U.S. aggregate supply. The *AS* curve shifts leftward. In the short run, U.S. real GDP decreases and the price level rises (Figure 2).

   A fall in expected future profits decreases U.S. aggregate demand. The *AD* curve shifts leftward. In the short run, U.S. real GDP decreases and the price level falls (Figure 1).
2. All three events decrease U.S. real GDP (Figures 1 and 2). The deep world recession and the fall in expected future profits decrease the price level (Figure 1). The rise in the world oil price increases the price level (Figure 2). So the combined effect on the price level is ambiguous.
3. The rise in the world oil price brings stagflation because it decreases aggregate supply, decreases real GDP, and raises the price level (Figure 2). Stagflation occurs when the price level rises and real GDP decreases at the same time.
4. The news clip gives no information about aggregate supply. Consumer spending, business investment, and exports influence aggregate demand, so the news clip pins all the change in real GDP as arising from a slowing of the decrease in aggregate demand and a movement along the *AS* curve.

# CHAPTER SUMMARY

## Key Points

**1 Define and explain the influences on aggregate supply.**

- Aggregate supply is the relationship between the quantity of real GDP supplied and the price level when all other influences on production plans remain the same.
- The *AS* curve slopes upward because with a given money wage rate, a rise in the price level lowers the real wage rate, increases the quantity of labor demanded, and increases the quantity of real GDP supplied.
- A change in potential GDP, a change in the money wage rate, or a change in the money price of other resources changes aggregate supply.

**2 Define and explain the influences on aggregate demand.**

- Aggregate demand is the relationship between the quantity of real GDP demanded and the price level when all other influences on expenditure plans remain the same.
- The *AD* curve slopes downward because a rise in the price level decreases the buying power of money, raises the real interest rate, raises the real price of domestic goods compared with foreign goods, and decreases the quantity of real GDP demanded.
- A change in expected future income, inflation, and profits; a change in fiscal policy and monetary policy; and a change in the foreign exchange rate and foreign real GDP all change aggregate demand—the aggregate demand curve shifts.

**3 Explain how fluctuations in aggregate demand and aggregate supply create the business cycle.**

- Aggregate demand and aggregate supply determine real GDP and the price level.
- Business cycles occur because aggregate demand and aggregate supply fluctuate.
- Away from full employment, gradual adjustment of the money wage rate moves real GDP toward potential GDP.

## Key Terms

Above full-employment equilibrium, 735
Aggregate demand, 728
Aggregate supply, 722
Below full-employment equilibrium, 735
Fiscal policy, 731
Full-employment equilibrium, 735
Inflationary gap, 736
Macroeconomic equilibrium, 734
Monetary policy, 731
Recessionary gap, 736
Stagflation, 738

Work these problems in Chapter 28 Study Plan to get instant feedback.

## CHAPTER CHECKPOINT

### Study Plan Problems and Applications

1. As more people in India have access to higher education, explain how potential GDP and aggregate supply will change in the long run.
2. Explain the effect of each of the following events on the quantity of U.S. real GDP demanded and the demand for U.S. real GDP:
   - The world economy goes into a strong expansion.
   - The U.S. price level rises.
   - Congress raises income taxes.
3. Table 1 sets out an economy's aggregate demand and aggregate supply schedules. What is the macroeconomic equilibrium? If potential GDP is \$600 billion, what is the type of macroeconomic equilibrium? Explain how real GDP and the price level will adjust in the long run.

**TABLE 1**

| Price level (GDP price index) | Real GDP demanded | Real GDP supplied |
|---|---|---|
| | (billions of 2005 dollars) | |
| 90 | 900 | 600 |
| 100 | 850 | 700 |
| 110 | 800 | 800 |
| 120 | 750 | 900 |
| 130 | 700 | 1,000` |

4. The United States is at full employment when the Fed cuts the quantity of money, and all other things remain the same. Explain the effect of the cut in the quantity of money on aggregate demand in the short run.
5. Suppose that the United States is at a below full-employment equilibrium when the world economy goes into an expansion. Explain the effect of the expansion on U.S. real GDP and unemployment in the short run.
6. Suppose that the Fed increases the quantity of money. On an *AS-AD* graph show the effect of the increased quantity of money on the macroeconomic equilibrium in the short run. Explain the adjustment process that restores the economy to full employment.

**FIGURE 1**

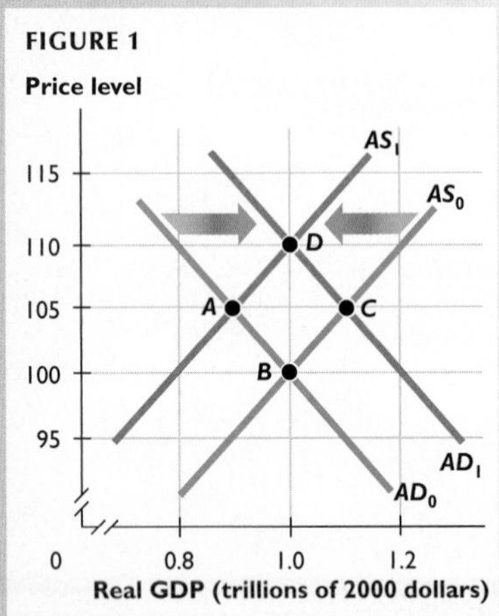


Use Figure 1 and the following information to work Problems 7 to 9.

Initially, the aggregate supply is $AS_0$ and aggregate demand is $AD_0$.

7. Some events changed aggregate demand from $AD_0$ to $AD_1$. Describe two events that could have created this change in aggregate demand. What is the equilibrium after aggregate demand changed? If potential GDP is \$1 trillion, the economy is at what the type of macroeconomic equilibrium?
8. Some events changed aggregate supply from $AS_0$ to $AS_1$. Describe two events that could have created this change in aggregate supply. What is the equilibrium after aggregate supply changed? If potential GDP is \$1 trillion, does the economy have an inflationary gap, a recessionary gap, or no output gap?
9. Some events changed aggregate demand from $AD_0$ to $AD_1$ and aggregate supply from $AS_0$ to $AS_1$. What is the new macroeconomic equilibrium?
10. **Japan in a tail-spin?**
    Not long ago, Japan was "the economic miracle," but today unemployment is at a record high of 5.7 percent, and both prices and wages are falling fast. In the first quarter of 2009, Japan's economy shrank at an annualized rate of 11.7 percent, before recovering to a modest 2.3 percent annual rate of growth in the second quarter.

    Source: *The New York Times*, October 1, 2009

    On an *AS-AD* graph show the macroeconomic equilibrium in Japan at the start of 2009. Show why "prices and wages are falling fast."

## Instructor Assignable Problems and Applications

Your instructor can assign these problems as homework, a quiz, or a test in **MyEconLab**.

1. What, according to the mainstream theory of the business cycle, is the most common source of recession: a decrease in aggregate demand, a decrease in aggregate supply, or both? Which is the most likely component of aggregate demand to start a recession? How does the aggregate demand multiplier influence a recession?
2. Suppose that the United States is at full employment. Explain the effect of each of the following events on aggregate supply:
   - Union wage settlements push the money wage rate up by 10 percent.
   - The price level increases.
   - Potential GDP increases.
3. Suppose that the United States is at full employment. Then the federal government cuts taxes, and all other influences on aggregate demand remain the same. Explain the effect of the tax cut on aggregate demand in the short run.

In 2009, the Japanese economy was at a below full-employment equilibrium. Use this information to work Problems 4 and 5.

4. Compare the amount of unemployment in Japan with Japan's natural unemployment and compare Japan's real GDP with its potential GDP.
5. What policies could Japan adopt to restore full employment? Would any of these policies create inflation? Explain.
6. Suppose that the world price of oil rises. On an *AS-AD* graph, show the effect of the world oil price rise on the macroeconomic equilibrium in the short run. Explain the adjustment process that restores the economy to full employment.
7. Explain the effects of a global recession on the U.S. macroeconomic equilibrium in the short run. Explain the adjustment process that restores the economy to full employment.

Use the following information to work Problems 8 and 9.

**Recession puts wind power projects on hold**

The wind-power industry will fall short of earlier growth projections for 2009 as many companies put projects on hold in 2008. The federal government provided about $950 million to the wind sector since August, helping bring some of the projects back. A slowdown in announcements of new facilities to manufacture the equipment to generate wind power has also occurred.

Source: *USA Today*, October 21, 2009

8. Explain the effect of the government's allocation of $950 million to the wind-power industry on U.S. aggregate demand and aggregate supply in 2009.
9. Use the *AS-AD* model to explain the effect on the U.S. economy as new facilities to manufacture the equipment to generate wind power and the planned wind-industry projects become completed.

**TABLE 1**

| Price level (GDP price index) | Real GDP demanded | Real GDP supplied |
|---|---|---|
| | (trillions of 2000 yen) | |
| 75 | 600 | 400 |
| 85 | 550 | 450 |
| 95 | 500 | 500 |
| 105 | 450 | 550 |
| 115 | 400 | 600 |
| 125 | 350 | 650 |
| 135 | 300 | 700 |

Table 1 sets out the aggregate demand and aggregate supply schedules in Japan. Potential GDP is 600 trillion yen. Use this information to work Problems 10 and 11.

10. What is the short-run macroeconomic equilibrium?
11. Does Japan have an inflationary gap or a recessionary gap and what is its magnitude?

Use the following information to work Problems 12 to 14.

Because fluctuations in the world oil price make the U.S. short-run macroeconomic equilibrium fluctuate, someone suggests that the government should vary the tax rate on oil, lowering the tax when the world oil price rises and increasing the tax when the world oil price falls, to stabilize the oil price in the U.S. market.

12. How do you think such an action would influence aggregate demand?
13. How do you think such an action would influence aggregate supply?
14. What are the arguments for and against such a policy?

Use the following information to work Problems 15 to 17.

**Shoppers stimulate discount stores**

As the economy remains weak, shoppers flock to discount stores for low prices. In June, Wal-mart's sales were up 5.8 percent and Costco Wholesale's sales were up 9 percent. Analysts attributed the increase in sales to the government's tax credits, which increased consumers' disposable incomes and consumers sought the biggest bang for their economic stimulus bucks.

Source: *CNN*, July 10, 2008

15. Explain and draw a graph to illustrate the effect of the government's tax credits on real GDP and the price level in the short run.
16. At what type of macroeconomic equilibrium would the government want to use such a policy?
17. If the government used this policy when the economy was at full employment, explain what would happen in the long run.

Use the following information to work Problems 18 and 19.

**Still on the job, but at half the pay**

In past recessions, firms have cut their labor costs by laying off workers. During this recession, many firms and state governments have trimmed labor costs by cutting pay or shortening the workweek, rather than laying off workers.

Source: *The New York Times*, October 13, 2009

18. Draw an *AS-AD* graph to illustrate an economy with a recessionary gap. Now as the recession continues, firms and governments trim their labor costs. In the graph, show the change in real GDP and the price level in the short run.
19. What effect might the strategy of cutting pay or the workweek rather than laying off workers have on the depth of the recession and the unemployment rate?

## What is the expenditure multiplier?

How much income does a dollar of government expenditure generate?

# Aggregate Expenditure Multiplier

CHAPTER CHECKLIST

**When you have completed your study of this chapter, you will be able to**

1 Distinguish between autonomous expenditure and induced expenditure and explain how real GDP influences expenditure plans.

2 Explain how real GDP adjusts to achieve equilibrium expenditure.

3 Explain the expenditure multiplier.

4 Derive the *AD* curve from equilibrium expenditure.

## 29.1 EXPENDITURE PLANS AND REAL GDP

When the government spends $1 million on a highway construction project, does that expenditure stimulate consumption expenditure in a multiplier effect? This question lies at the core of this chapter.

To answer the question, we use the *aggregate expenditure model,* a model that explains what determines the quantity of real GDP demanded and changes in that quantity *at a given price level.*

The aggregate expenditure model—also known as the *Keynesian model*—was originally designed to explain what happens in an economy in deep recession when firms can't cut their prices any further but can increase production without raising their prices, so the price level is actually fixed. The severity of the global recession of 2008–2009 gave the model a rebirth and the question of the size of the government expenditure multiplier became a hot issue.

You learned in Chapter 20 (pp. 511–513) that aggregate expenditure equals the sum of consumption expenditure, *C*, investment, *I*, government expenditure on goods and services, *G*, and net exports, *NX*. **Aggregate planned expenditure** is the sum of the spending plans of households, firms, and governments. We divide expenditure plans into autonomous expenditure and induced expenditure. *Autonomous expenditure* does not respond to changes in real GDP and *induced expenditure* does respond to changes in real GDP. We start by looking at induced expenditure and its main component, consumption expenditure.

**Aggregate planned expenditure**
Planned consumption expenditure plus planned investment, plus planned government expenditure, plus planned exports minus planned imports.

### The Consumption Function

The **consumption function** is the relationship between consumption expenditure and disposable income, other things remaining the same. *Disposable income* is aggregate income—GDP—minus net taxes. (Net taxes are taxes paid to the government minus transfer payments received from the government.)

**Consumption function**
The relationship between consumption expenditure and disposable income, other things remaining the same.

Households must either spend their disposable income on consumption or save it. A decision to spend a dollar on consumption is a decision not to save a dollar. The consumption decision and the saving decision is one decision.

#### Consumption Plans

For households and the economy as a whole, as disposable income increases, planned consumption expenditure increases. But the increase in planned consumption is less than the increase in disposable income. The table in Figure 29.1 shows a consumption schedule. It lists the consumption expenditure that people plan to undertake at each level of disposable income.

Figure 29.1 shows a consumption function based on the consumption schedule. Along the consumption function, the points labeled *A* through *E* correspond to the columns of the table. For example, when disposable income is $9 trillion at point *D*, consumption expenditure is $8 trillion. Along the consumption function, as disposable income increases, consumption expenditure increases.

At point *A* on the consumption function, consumption expenditure is $2 trillion even though disposable income is zero. This consumption expenditure is called *autonomous consumption,* and it is the amount of consumption expenditure that would take place in the short run, even if people had no current income. This consumption expenditure would be financed either by spending past savings or by borrowing.

## FIGURE 29.1

The Consumption Function

myeconlab Animation

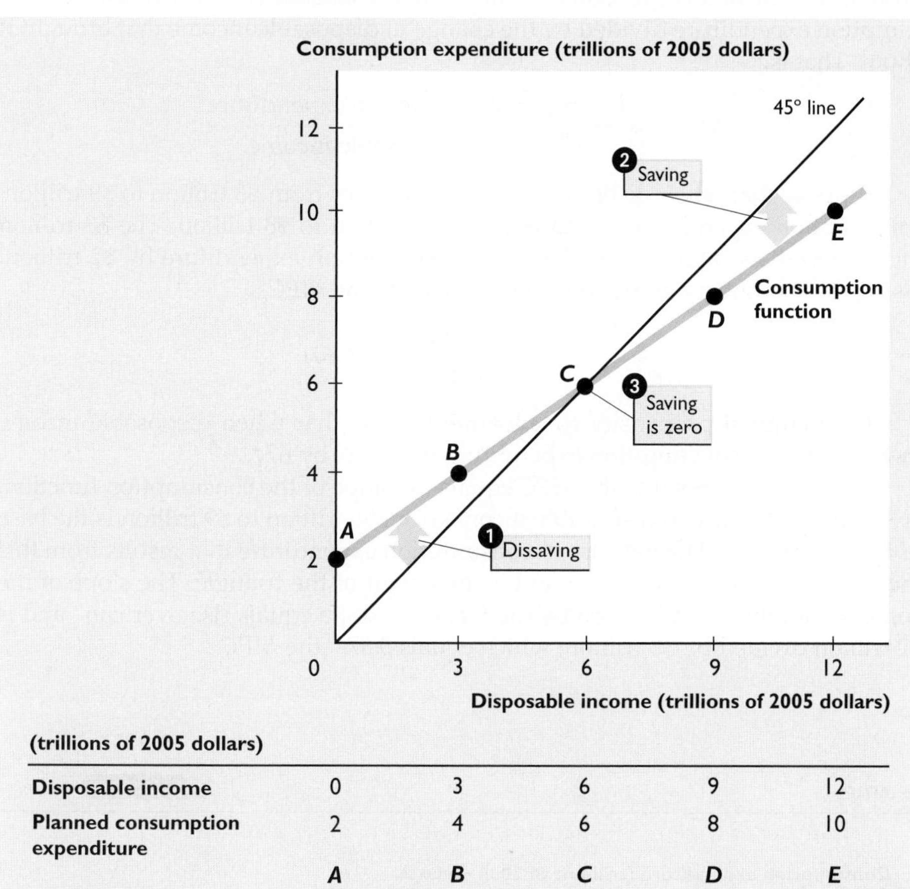


| (trillions of 2005 dollars) | | | | | |
|---|---|---|---|---|---|
| **Disposable income** | 0 | 3 | 6 | 9 | 12 |
| **Planned consumption expenditure** | 2 | 4 | 6 | 8 | 10 |
| | *A* | *B* | *C* | *D* | *E* |

The table shows consumption expenditure (and saving) plans at various levels of disposable income. The figure graphs these data as the consumption function. The figure also shows a 45° line along which consumption expenditure equals disposable income.

1. When the consumption function is above the 45° line, saving is negative (dissaving occurs).
2. When the consumption function is below the 45° line, saving is positive.
3. At the point where the consumption function intersects the 45° line, all disposable income is consumed and saving is zero.

Figure 29.1 also shows a 45° line. Because the scale on the $x$-axis measures disposable income and the scale on the $y$-axis measures consumption expenditure, and because the two scales are equal, along the 45° line consumption expenditure equals disposable income. So the 45° line serves as a reference line for comparing consumption expenditure and disposable income. Between *A* and *C*, consumption expenditure exceeds disposable income; between *C* and *E*, disposable income exceeds consumption expenditure; and at point *C*, consumption expenditure equals disposable income.

You can see saving in Figure 29.1. When consumption expenditure exceeds disposable income (and the consumption function is above the 45° line), saving is negative—called *dissaving*. When consumption expenditure is less than disposable income (the consumption function is below the 45° line), saving is positive. And when consumption expenditure equals disposable income (the consumption function intersects the 45° line), saving is zero.

When consumption expenditure exceeds disposable income, past savings are used to pay for current consumption. Such a situation cannot last forever, but it can and does occur if disposable income falls temporarily.

## Marginal Propensity to Consume

**Marginal propensity to consume**
The fraction of a change in disposable income that is spent on consumption—the change in consumption expenditure divided by the change in disposable income that brought it about.

The **marginal propensity to consume** (*MPC*) is the fraction of a change in disposable income that is spent on consumption. It is calculated as the change in consumption expenditure divided by the change in disposable income that brought it about. That is,

$$MPC = \frac{\text{Change in consumption expenditure}}{\text{Change in disposable income}}.$$

Suppose that when disposable income increases from $6 trillion to $9 trillion, consumption expenditure increases from $6 trillion to $8 trillion. The $3 trillion increase in disposable income increases consumption expenditure by $2 trillion. Using these numbers in the formula to calculate the *MPC*,

$$MPC = \frac{\$2 \text{ trillion}}{\$3 \text{ trillion}} = \$0.67.$$

The marginal propensity to consume tells us that when disposable income increases by $1, consumption expenditure increases by 67¢.

Figure 29.2 shows that the *MPC* equals the slope of the consumption function. A $3 trillion increase in disposable income from $6 trillion to $9 trillion is the base of the red triangle. The increase in consumption expenditure that results from this increase in income is $2 trillion and is the height of the triangle. The slope of the consumption function is given by the formula "slope equals rise over run" and is $2 trillion divided by $3 trillion, which equals 0.67—the *MPC*.

**FIGURE 29.2**

Marginal Propensity to Consume

myeconlab Animation

The marginal propensity to consume, *MPC*, is equal to the change in consumption expenditure divided by the change in disposable income, other things remaining the same.

The slope of the consumption function measures the *MPC*.

In the figure:

1. A $3 trillion change in disposable income brings
2. A $2 trillion change in consumption expenditure, so
3. The *MPC* equals $2 trillion ÷ $3 trillion = 0.67.

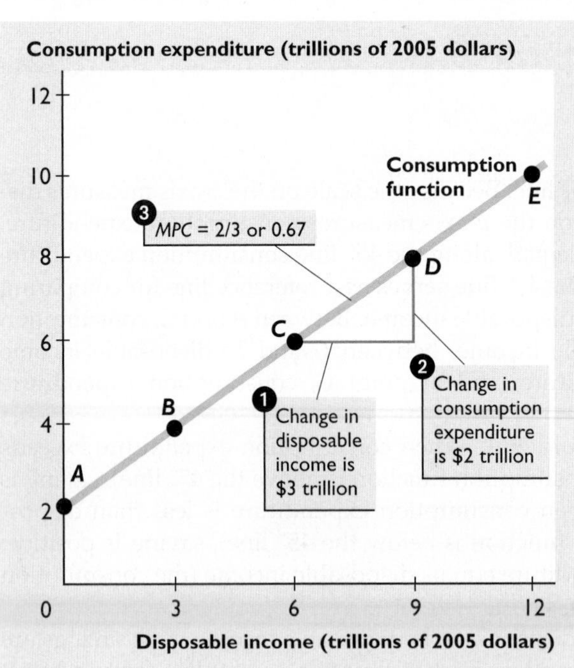

### Other Influences on Consumption Expenditure

Consumption plans are influenced by many factors other than disposable income. The more important influences are:

- Real interest rate
- Wealth
- Expected future income

***Real Interest Rate*** When the real interest rate falls, consumption expenditure increases (and saving decreases) and when the real interest rate rises, consumption expenditure decreases (and saving increases).

***Wealth and Expected Future Income*** When either wealth or expected future income decreases, consumption expenditure also decreases and when wealth or expected future income increases, consumption expenditure also increases.

Figure 29.3 shows the effects of these influences on the consumption function. When the real interest rate falls or when wealth or expected future income increases, the consumption function shifts upward from $CF_0$ to $CF_1$. Such a shift occurs during the expansion phase of the business cycle if a stock market boom increases wealth and expected future income increases.

When the real interest rate rises, or when wealth or expected future income decreases, the consumption function shifts downward from $CF_0$ to $CF_2$. Such a shift occurs during a recession if a stock market crash decreases wealth and expected future income decreases.

**FIGURE 29.3**

Shifts in the Consumption Function

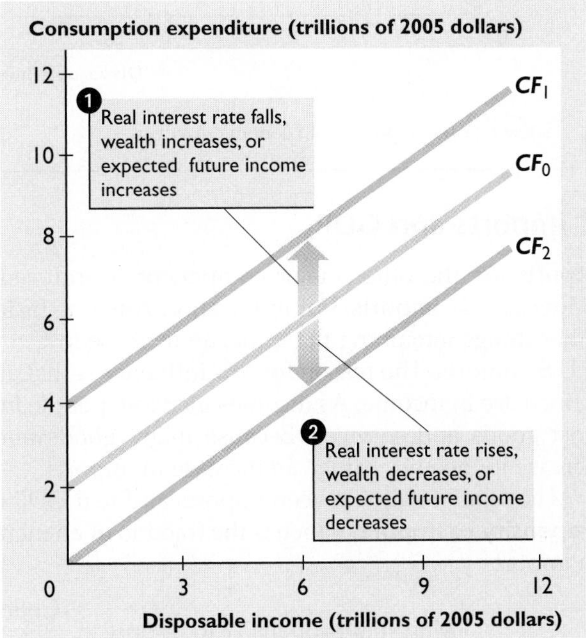


1. A fall in the real interest rate or an increase in either wealth or expected future income increases consumption expenditure and shifts the consumption function upward from $CF_0$ to $CF_1$.

2. A rise in the real interest rate or a decrease in either wealth or expected future income decreases consumption expenditure and shifts the consumption function downward from $CF_0$ to $CF_2$.

# EYE on the U.S. ECONOMY

## The U.S. Consumption Function

Each blue dot in the figure represents consumption expenditure and disposable income in the United States for a year between 1960 and 2009 (some labeled).

The lines labeled $CF_0$, $CF_1$, and $CF_2$ are estimates of the U.S. consumption function in 1960, 2008, and 2009, respectively.

The slope of these consumption functions—the marginal propensity to consume—is 0.87, which means that a $1 increase in disposable income brings an 87¢ increase in consumption expenditure.

The consumption function shifted upward from the 1960s to 2008 because economic growth brought higher expected future income and higher wealth.

The consumption function shifted downward in 2009 as the fall in home prices and stock prices lowered wealth and recession lowered expected future income.

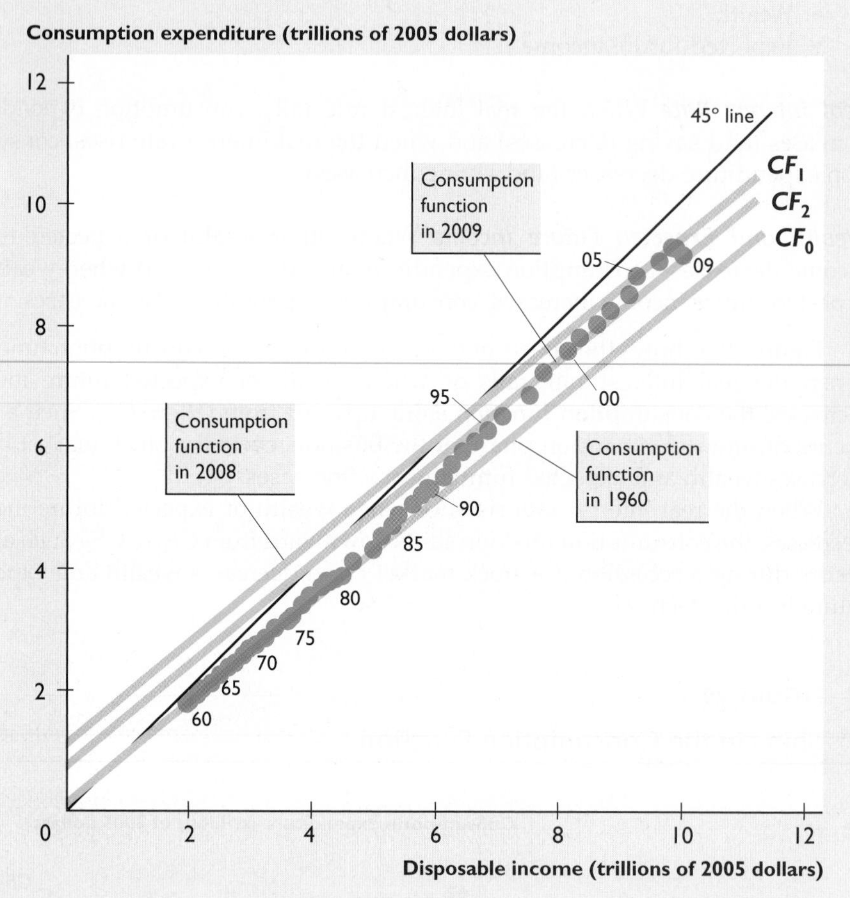


SOURCE OF DATA: Bureau of Economic Analysis.

## Imports and GDP

Imports are the other major component of induced expenditure. Many factors influence U.S. imports, but in the short run, one factor dominates: U.S. real GDP. Other things remaining the same, an increase in U.S. real GDP brings an increase in U.S. imports. The reason for this influence is that an increase in real GDP is also an increase in income. As incomes increase, people increase their expenditures on most goods and services. Because many goods and services are imported, an increase in incomes brings an increase in imports.

**Marginal propensity to import**
The fraction of an increase in real GDP that is spent on imports—the change in imports divided by the change in real GDP.

The relationship between imports and real GDP is described by the **marginal propensity to import**, which is the fraction of an increase in real GDP that is spent on imports.

$$\text{Marginal propensity to import} = \frac{\text{Change in imports}}{\text{Change in real GDP}}.$$

For example, if, with other things remaining the same, a $1 trillion increase in real GDP increases imports by $0.2 trillion, then the marginal propensity to import is 0.2.

## CHECKPOINT 29.1

myeconlab

Work these problems in Study Plan 29.1 to get instant feedback.

**Distinguish between autonomous expenditure and induced expenditure and explain how real GDP influences expenditure plans.**

## Practice Problems

1. If the marginal propensity to consume is 0.8 and disposable income increases by $0.5 trillion, by how much will consumption expenditure change?
2. Explain how each of the following events influences the U.S. consumption function:
   - The marginal propensity to consume decreases.
   - U.S. autonomous consumption decreases.
   - Americans expect an increase in future income.
3. Figure 1 shows the consumption function. What is the marginal propensity to consume, and what is autonomous consumption?
4. **Americans cut back sharply on spending**
   In December 2007, consumer spending grew at the slowest rate in seven years. Despite the fact that average wages and salaries did not fall, consumer confidence, a barometer of economic health, plunged. Spending across the country dropped, but it was worse in states like Florida and California where home prices have fallen the most.
   Source: *The New York Times*, January 14, 2008
   Explain why consumers cut their spending when consumer confidence drops and house prices fall. Does the drop in consumer spending arise from a movement along the consumption function or a shift of the consumption function? Explain your answer.

FIGURE 1

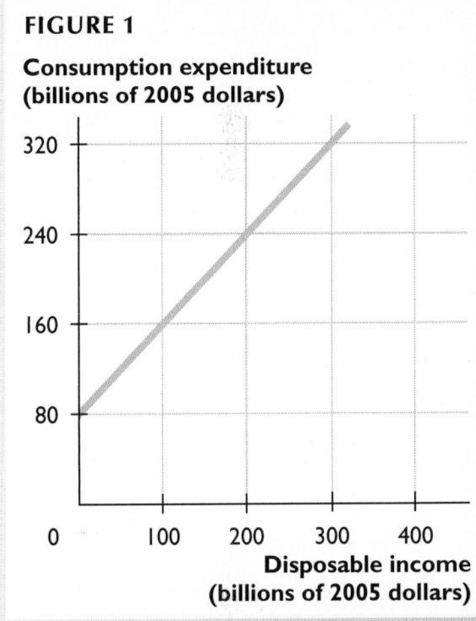


## Guided Solutions to Practice Problems

1. Consumption expenditure will increase by $0.4 trillion, which is 0.8 multiplied by the change in disposable income of $0.5 trillion.
2. The marginal propensity to consume equals the slope of the consumption function. So when the marginal propensity to consume decreases, the consumption function becomes flatter.
   Autonomous consumption is the *y*-axis intercept of the consumption function. So when autonomous expenditure decreases, the consumption function shifts downward.
   When expected future income increases, current consumption expenditure increases and the consumption function shifts upward.
3. When disposable income increases by $100 billion, consumption expenditure increases by $80 billion. The *MPC* is $80 billion ÷ $100 billion = 0.8. Autonomous consumption (consumption expenditure that is independent of disposable income) equals the *y*-axis intercept and is $80 billion (Figure 2).
4. Consumer confidence drops when people become less certain about their future income. A fall in house prices decreases consumers' wealth. Both the fall in expected future income and the decrease in wealth shift the consumption function downward.

FIGURE 2

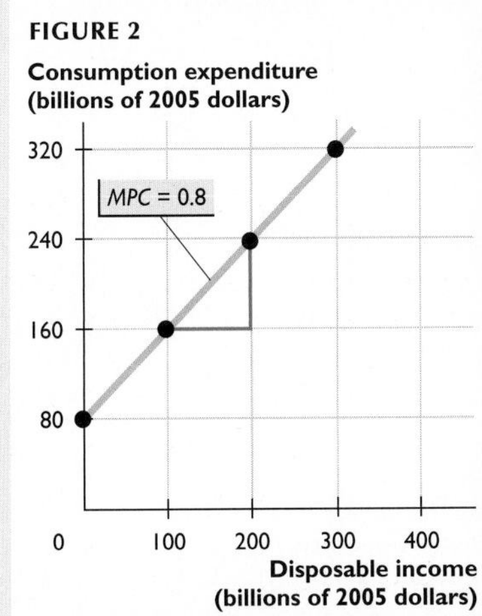

## 29.2 EQUILIBRIUM EXPENDITURE

You are now going to discover how, with a fixed price level, aggregate expenditure plans interact to determine real GDP. First we will study the relationship between aggregate planned expenditure and real GDP. Then we'll study the forces that make aggregate planned expenditure and actual expenditure equal.

An aggregate expenditure schedule and an aggregate expenditure curve describe the relationship between aggregate planned expenditure and real GDP.

### Aggregate Planned Expenditure and Real GDP

You've seen that consumption expenditure increases when disposable income increases. Disposable income equals aggregate income—real GDP—minus net taxes, so disposable income and consumption expenditure increase when real GDP increases. We use this link between consumption expenditure and real GDP to determine equilibrium expenditure.

The table in Figure 29.4 sets out an aggregate expenditure schedule together with the components of aggregate planned expenditure. All the variables are measured in real (constant dollar) values. To calculate aggregate planned expenditure at a given real GDP, we add the various components together.

The first column of the table shows real GDP, and the second column shows the consumption expenditure generated by each level of real GDP. In this example, a \$6 trillion increase in real GDP generates a \$4.5 trillion increase in consumption expenditure—the *MPC* is 0.75. The next three columns show investment, government expenditure on goods and services, and exports. These items do not depend on real GDP. They are *autonomous expenditure*. Investment is \$1.25 trillion, government expenditure is \$1.0 trillion, and exports are \$2.25 trillion.

The next column shows imports, which increase as real GDP increases. A \$6 trillion increase in real GDP generates a \$1.5 trillion increase in imports. The marginal propensity to import is 0.25.

The final column shows aggregate planned expenditure—the sum of planned consumption expenditure, investment, government expenditure on goods and services, and exports minus imports.

Figure 29.4 plots an aggregate expenditure curve. Real GDP is shown on the $x$-axis, and aggregate planned expenditure is shown on the $y$-axis. The aggregate expenditure curve is the red line *AE*. Points *A* through *F* on that curve correspond to the rows of the table. The *AE* curve is a graph of aggregate planned expenditure (the last column) plotted against real GDP (the first column).

Figure 29.4 also shows the components of aggregate expenditure. The horizontal lines show the components of autonomous expenditure—investment ($I$), government expenditure ($G$), and exports ($X$). The line labeled $C + I + G + X$ adds consumption expenditure to the autonomous expenditure.

Finally, to construct the *AE* curve, subtract imports ($M$) from the $C + I + G + X$ line. Aggregate expenditure is expenditure on U.S.-made goods and services. But $C + I + G + X$ includes expenditure on imports. For example, if a student buys a Honda motorbike made in Japan, the student's expenditure is part of $C$, but it is not an expenditure on a U.S.-produced good. To find the expenditure on U.S.-produced goods, we subtract the value of the imported motorbike.

Figure 29.4 shows that aggregate planned expenditure increases as real GDP increases. But notice that for each \$1 increase in real GDP, aggregate planned

## FIGURE 29.4
Aggregate Expenditure

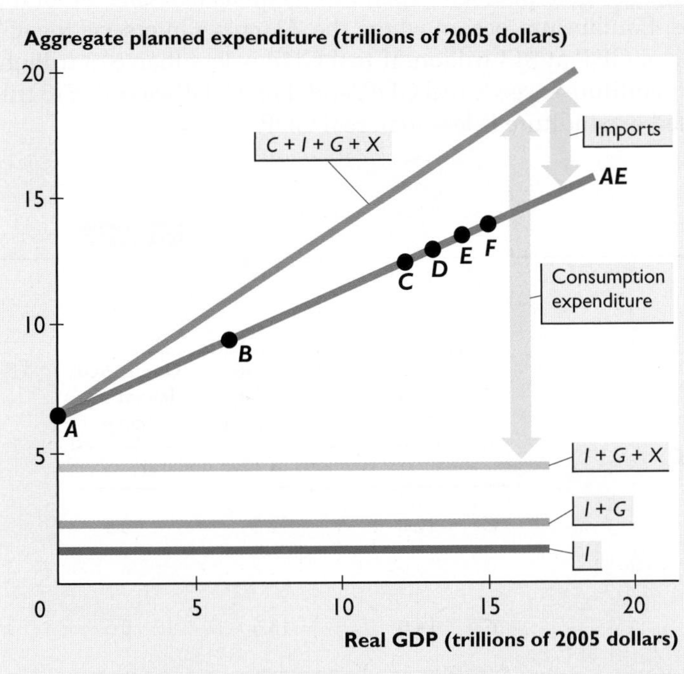


The aggregate expenditure schedule shows the relationship between aggregate planned expenditure and real GDP. For example, in row *B* of the table, when real GDP is \$6 trillion, aggregate planned expenditure is \$9.50 trillion (\$6.50 + \$1.25 + \$1.00 + \$2.25 – \$1.50). As real GDP increases, aggregate planned expenditure increases.

This relationship is graphed as the aggregate expenditure curve *AE*. The components of aggregate expenditure that increase with real GDP are consumption expenditure and imports. The other components—investment, government expenditure, and exports—do not vary with real GDP.

| | Real GDP (*Y*) | Consumption expenditure (*C*) | Investment (*I*) | Government expenditure (*G*) | Exports (*X*) | Imports (*M*) | Aggregate planned expenditure (*AE* = *C* + *I* + *G* + *X* – *M*) |
|---|---|---|---|---|---|---|---|
| | | Planned expenditure (trillions of 2005 dollars) | | | | | |
| **A** | 0.00 | 2.00 | 1.25 | 1.00 | 2.25 | 0.00 | 6.50 |
| **B** | **6.00** | **6.50** | **1.25** | **1.00** | **2.25** | **1.50** | **9.50** |
| **C** | 12.00 | 11.00 | 1.25 | 1.00 | 2.25 | 3.00 | 12.50 |
| **D** | 13.00 | 11.75 | 1.25 | 1.00 | 2.25 | 3.25 | 13.00 |
| **E** | 14.00 | 12.50 | 1.25 | 1.00 | 2.25 | 3.50 | 13.50 |
| **F** | 15.00 | 13.25 | 1.25 | 1.00 | 2.25 | 3.75 | 14.00 |

expenditure increases by less than \$1. For example, when real GDP increases from \$12 trillion to \$13 trillion (row *C* to row *D* of the table), aggregate planned expenditure increases from \$12.5 trillion to \$13 trillion. A \$1 trillion increase in real GDP brings a \$0.5 trillion increase in aggregate planned expenditure. This feature of the *AE* curve is important and plays a big role in determining equilibrium expenditure and the effect of a change in autonomous expenditure.

The *AE* curve summarizes the relationship between aggregate planned expenditure and real GDP. But what determines the point on the *AE* curve at which the economy operates? What determines actual aggregate expenditure?

## Equilibrium Expenditure

**Equilibrium expenditure**
The level of aggregate expenditure that occurs when aggregate *planned* expenditure equals real GDP.

**Equilibrium expenditure** occurs when aggregate *planned* expenditure equals real GDP. In Figure 29.5(a) aggregate planned expenditure equals real GDP at all the points on the 45° line. Equilibrium occurs where the *AE* curve intersects the 45° line at point *D* with real GDP at $13 trillion. If real GDP is less than $13 trillion, aggregate planned expenditure exceeds real GDP; and if real GDP exceeds $13 trillion, aggregate planned expenditure is less than real GDP.

**FIGURE 29.5**

Equilibrium Expenditure

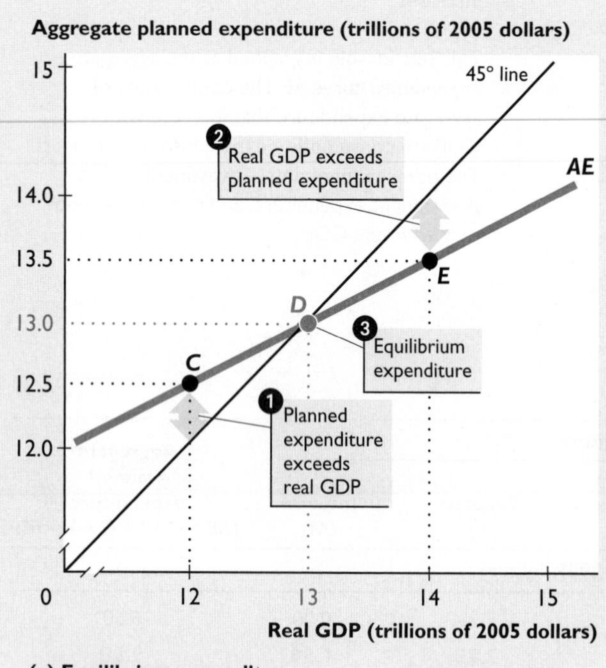


(a) Equilibrium expenditure

| | Real GDP | Aggregate planned expenditure | Unplanned inventory change |
|---|---|---|---|
| | (trillions of 2005 dollars) | | |
| C | 12.0 | 12.5 | –0.5 |
| D | 13.0 | 13.0 | 0.0 |
| E | 14.0 | 13.5 | 0.5 |

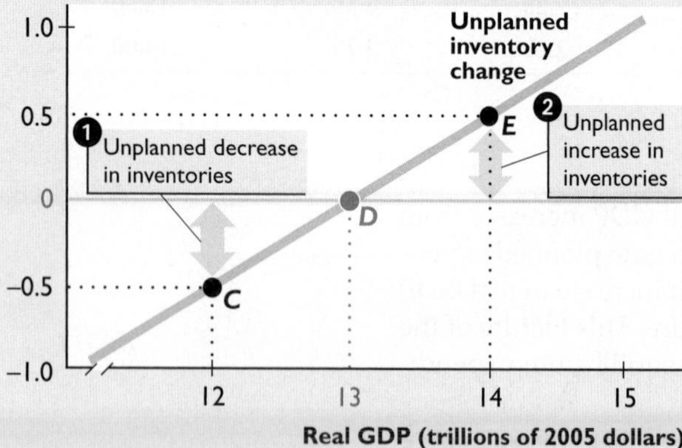


(b) Unplanned inventory change

The table shows expenditure plans and unplanned changes in inventories at different levels of real GDP. Part (a) illustrates equilibrium expenditure, and part (b) shows the unplanned inventory changes that bring changes in real GDP.

1. When aggregate planned expenditure exceeds real GDP, an unplanned decrease in inventories occurs. Firms increase production, and real GDP increases.

2. When real GDP exceeds aggregate planned expenditure, an unplanned increase in inventories occurs. Firms decrease production, and real GDP decreases.

3. When aggregate planned expenditure equals real GDP, there are no unplanned inventory changes and real GDP remains at its equilibrium level.

## Convergence to Equilibrium

At equilibrium expenditure, production plans and spending plans agree, and there is no reason for production or spending to change. But when aggregate planned expenditure and actual aggregate expenditure are unequal, production plans and spending plans are misaligned, and a process of convergence toward equilibrium expenditure occurs. Throughout this convergence process, real GDP adjusts.

What are the forces that move aggregate expenditure toward equilibrium? To answer this question, we look at a situation in which aggregate expenditure is away from equilibrium.

### Convergence from Below Equilibrium

Suppose that in Figure 29.5, real GDP is $12 trillion. At this level of real GDP, actual aggregate expenditure is also $12 trillion, but aggregate planned expenditure is $12.5 trillion—point *C* in Figure 29.5(a). Aggregate planned expenditure exceeds actual expenditure. When people spend $12.5 trillion and firms produce goods and services worth $12 trillion, firms' inventories decrease by $0.5 trillion—point *C* in Figure 29.5(b). This change in inventories is *unplanned*. Because the change in inventories is part of investment, the decrease in inventories decreases actual investment. So actual investment is $0.5 trillion less than planned investment.

Real GDP doesn't remain at $12 trillion for long. Firms have inventory targets based on their sales, and when inventories fall below target, firms increase production. Firms keep increasing production as long as unplanned decreases in inventories occur.

Eventually firms will have increased production by $1 trillion, so real GDP will have increased to $13 trillion. At this real GDP, aggregate planned expenditure rises to $13 trillion—point *D* in Figure 29.5(a). With aggregate planned expenditure equal to actual expenditure, the unplanned change in inventories is zero and firms hold production constant. The economy has converged on equilibrium expenditure.

### Convergence from Above Equilibrium

Now suppose that in Figure 29.5, real GDP is $14 trillion. Actual aggregate expenditure is also $14 trillion, but aggregate planned expenditure is $13.5 trillion—point *E* in Figure 29.5(a). Actual expenditure exceeds planned expenditure and firms' inventories pile up by an unwanted $0.5 trillion—point *E* in Figure 29.5(b).

Real GDP doesn't remain at $14 trillion. Firms now want to lower their inventories, so they decrease production.

Eventually, firms will have decreased production by $1 trillion, so real GDP will have decreased to $13 trillion. At this real GDP, aggregate planned expenditure falls to $13 trillion—point *D* in Figure 29.5(a). With aggregate planned expenditure equal to actual expenditure, the unplanned change in inventories is zero and firms hold production constant. The economy has converged on equilibrium expenditure.

Starting from below equilibrium, unplanned decreases in inventories induce firms to increase production; starting from above equilibrium, unplanned increases in inventories induce firms to decrease production. In both cases, production is pulled toward the equilibrium level at which there are no unplanned inventory changes.

and rearrange the equation:

$$\Delta Y = \frac{1}{(1 - MPC)}\Delta I.$$

Finally, divide both sides of the equation by $\Delta I$ to give

$$\text{Multiplier} = \frac{\Delta Y}{\Delta I} = \frac{1}{(1 - MPC)}.$$

In Figure 29.6, the *MPC* is 0.75. So if we use this value of *MPC*,

$$\text{Multiplier} = \frac{\Delta Y}{\Delta I} = \frac{1}{(1 - 0.75)} = \frac{1}{0.25} = 4.$$

The greater the marginal propensity to consume, the larger is the multiplier. For example, with a marginal propensity to consume of 0.9, the multiplier would be 10. Let's now look at the influence of imports and income taxes.

## The Multiplier, Imports, and Income Taxes

The size of the multiplier depends on imports and income taxes, both of which make the multiplier smaller.

When an increase in investment increases consumption and real GDP, part of the increase in expenditure is on imports, not U.S.-produced goods and services. Only expenditure on U.S.-produced goods and services increases U.S. real GDP. The larger the marginal propensity to import, the smaller is the multiplier.

When an increase in investment increases real GDP, income tax payments increase so disposable income increases by less than the increase in real GDP, which means that consumption expenditure increases by less than it would if income tax payments had not changed. The marginal tax rate determines the extent to which income tax payments change when real GDP changes. The **marginal tax rate** is the fraction of a change in real GDP that is paid in income taxes. The larger the marginal tax rate, the smaller are the changes in disposable income and real GDP that result from a given change in autonomous expenditure.

**Marginal tax rate**
The fraction of a change in real GDP that is paid in income taxes—the change in tax payments divided by the change in real GDP.

The marginal propensity to import and the marginal tax rate together with the marginal propensity to consume determine the multiplier, and their combined influence determines the slope of the *AE* curve. The general formula for the multiplier is

$$\text{Multiplier} = \frac{\Delta Y}{\Delta I} = \frac{1}{(1 - \text{Slope of } AE \text{ curve})}.$$

Figure 29.7 compares two situations. In Figure 29.7(a), there are no imports and no income taxes. The slope of the *AE* curve equals *MPC*, which is 0.75, so the multiplier is 4 (as we calculated above). In Figure 29.7(b), imports and income taxes decrease the slope of the *AE* curve to 0.5. In this case,

$$\text{Multiplier} = \frac{\Delta Y}{\Delta I} = \frac{1}{(1 - 0.5)} = 2.$$

Over time, the value of the multiplier changes as the marginal tax rate, the marginal propensity to consume, and the marginal propensity to import change. These ongoing changes make the multiplier hard to predict.

## FIGURE 29.7

The Multiplier and the Slope of the *AE* Curve

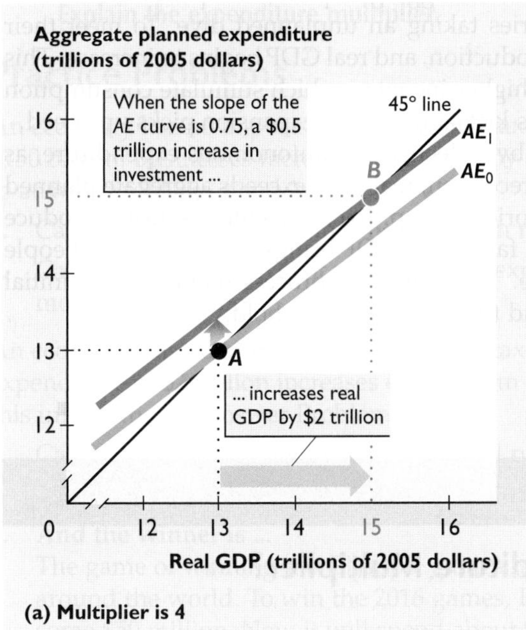


(a) Multiplier is 4

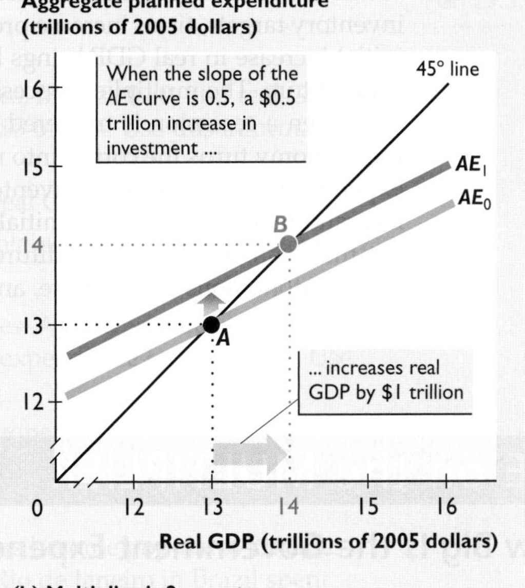


(b) Multiplier is 2

In part (a), with no imports and no income taxes, the slope of the *AE* curve equals the marginal propensity to consume, which in this example is 0.75. The multiplier is 4.

In part (b), with imports and income taxes, the slope of the *AE* curve is less than the marginal propensity to consume. In this example, the slope of the *AE* curve is 0.5 and the multiplier is 2.

## EYE on YOUR LIFE

### Looking for Multipliers

You can see multipliers in your daily life if you look in the right places and in the right way.

Look for an event in your home city or state that brings new economic activity. It might be a major construction project that is going on near your home or school. It might be a major sporting event that occurs infrequently and brings a large number of people to a city. Or it might be a major new business that moves into an area or expands its activity level.

What supplies do you see being delivered to the site, event, or new business? How many people do you estimate have jobs at this new activity? Where do the supplies and the workers come from?

This new economic activity sets off a multiplier process. What are the first round multiplier effects? Whose incomes are higher because of the purchase of these supplies and expenditure of the workers hired by the project?

Where do the workers buy their coffee and lunch? Do their purchases create new jobs for students and others in local coffee shops and fast-food outlets?

Where do the workers and suppliers spend the rest of their incomes?

Now think about the second round and subsequent round effects. Where do the students hired by coffee shops spend their incomes and what additional jobs do those expenditures create?

The process goes on and on.

## 29.4 THE *AD* CURVE AND EQUILIBRIUM EXPENDITURE

In this chapter, we've studied the aggregate expenditure model, in which firms change production when sales and inventories change but they don't change their prices. The aggregate expenditure model determines equilibrium expenditure and real GDP at a given price level. In Chapter 28, we studied the simultaneous determination of real GDP and the price level using the *AS–AD* model. The aggregate demand curve and equilibrium expenditure are related, and this section shows you how.

### Deriving the *AD* Curve from Equilibrium Expenditure

The *AE* curve is the relationship between aggregate planned expenditure and real GDP when all other influences on expenditure plans remain the same. A movement along the *AE* curve arises from a change in real GDP.

The *AD* curve is the relationship between the quantity of real GDP demanded and the price level when all other influences on expenditure plans remain the same. A movement along the *AD* curve arises from a change in the price level.

Equilibrium expenditure depends on the price level. When the price level rises, other things remaining the same, aggregate planned expenditure decreases and equilibrium expenditure decreases. And when the price level falls, other things remaining the same, aggregate planned expenditure increases and equilibrium expenditure increases. The reason is that a change in the price level changes the buying power of money, the real interest rate, and the real prices of exports and imports (see Chapter 28, pp. 728–730).

When the price level rises, each of these effects decreases aggregate planned expenditure at each level of real GDP. So the *AE* curve shifts downward. A fall in the price level has the opposite effect. When the price level falls, the *AE* curve shifts upward.

Figure 29.8(a) shows the effects of a change in the price level on the *AE* curve and equilibrium expenditure. When the price level is 110, the *AE* curve is $AE_0$, and it intersects the 45° line at point *B*. Equilibrium expenditure is $14 trillion. If the price level rises to 130, aggregate planned expenditure decreases and the *AE* curve shifts downward to $AE_1$. Equilibrium expenditure decreases to $13 trillion at point *A*. If the price level falls to 90, aggregate planned expenditure increases and the *AE* curve shifts upward to $AE_2$. Equilibrium expenditure increases to $15 trillion at point *C*.

The price level changes that shift the *AE* curve and change equilibrium expenditure bring movements along the *AD* curve. Figure 29.8(b) shows these movements. At a price level of 110, the quantity of real GDP demanded is $14 trillion—point *B* on the *AD* curve. If the price level rises to 130, the quantity of real GDP demanded decreases along the *AD* curve to $13 trillion at point *A*. If the price level falls to 90, the quantity of real GDP demanded increases along the *AD* curve to $15 trillion at point *C*.

The two parts of Figure 29.8 are connected and illustrate the relationship between the *AE* curve and the *AD* curve. Each point of equilibrium expenditure corresponds to a point on the *AD* curve. The equilibrium expenditure points *A*, *B*, and *C* (part a) correspond to the points *A*, *B*, and *C* on the *AD* curve (part b).

## FIGURE 29.8

## Equilibrium Expenditure and Aggregate Demand

Aggregate planned expenditure (trillions of 2005 dollars)

AE curve when price level is ...

45° line

$AE_2$

$AE_0$

$AE_1$

❸ ... 90

❶ ... 110

❷ ... 130

C

B

A

16
15
14
13
12
0

12 13 14 15 16

Real GDP (trillions of 2005 dollars)

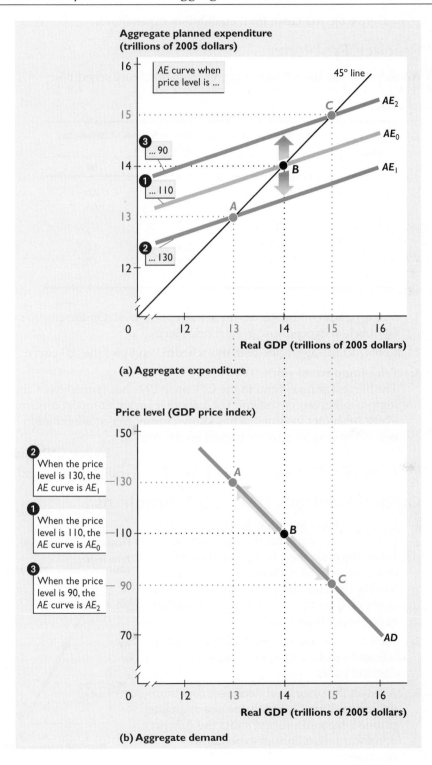

(a) Aggregate expenditure

Price level (GDP price index)

❷ When the price level is 130, the *AE* curve is $AE_1$

❶ When the price level is 110, the *AE* curve is $AE_0$

❸ When the price level is 90, the *AE* curve is $AE_2$

A

B

C

AD

150
130
110
90
70
0

12 13 14 15 16

Real GDP (trillions of 2005 dollars)

(b) Aggregate demand

A change in the price level shifts the *AE* curve and results in a movement along the *AD* curve.

❶ When the price level is 110, equilibrium expenditure is $14 trillion at point *B* on the *AE* curve $AE_0$ and the quantity of real GDP demanded is $14 trillion at point *B* on the *AD* curve.

❷ When the price level rises to 130, the *AE* curve shifts downward to $AE_1$ and equilibrium expenditure decreases to $13 trillion at point *A*. The quantity of real GDP demanded decreases along the *AD* curve to point *A*.

❸ When the price level falls to 90, the *AE* curve shifts upward to $AE_2$ and equilibrium expenditure increases to $15 trillion at point *C*. The quantity of real GDP demanded increases along the *AD* curve to point *C*.

Points *A*, *B*, and *C* on the *AD* curve in part (b) correspond to the equilibrium expenditure points *A*, *B*, and *C* in part (a).

Work these problems in Study Plan 29.4 to get instant feedback.

## CHECKPOINT 29.4

**Derive the *AD* curve from equilibrium expenditure.**

### Practice Problems

An economy has the following aggregate expenditure schedules:

**TABLE 1**

| Real GDP (trillions of 2005 dollars) | Aggregate planned expenditure in trillions of 2005 dollars when the price level is | | |
|---|---|---|---|
| | 110 | 100 | 90 |
| 0 | 1.0 | 1.5 | 2.0 |
| 1.0 | 1.5 | 2.0 | 2.5 |
| 2.0 | 2.0 | 2.5 | 3.0 |
| 3.0 | 2.5 | 3.0 | 3.5 |
| 4.0 | 3.0 | 3.5 | 4.0 |
| 5.0 | 3.5 | 4.0 | 4.5 |
| 6.0 | 4.0 | 4.5 | 5.0 |

1. Make a graph of the *AE* curves at each price level. On the graph, mark the equilibrium expenditure at each price level.
2. Construct the aggregate demand schedule and plot the *AD* curve.
3. **Price jump worst since '91**
The biggest annual jump in the CPI since 1991 has fanned fears about growing pressures on consumers. The Labor Department report confirms what every consumer in America has known for months now: Inflation is soaring and it's having an adverse impact on the economy.
Source: CNN, July 16, 2008
Explain the effect of a rise in the price level on equilibrium expenditure.

**FIGURE 1**

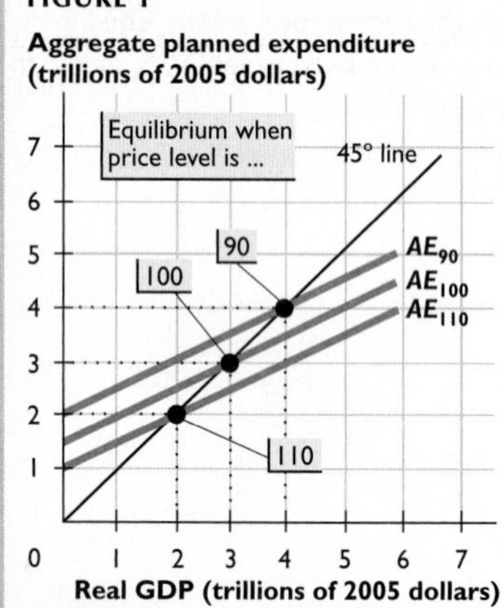


**TABLE 2**

| Price level | Real GDP demanded (trillions of 2005 dollars) |
|---|---|
| 90 | 4 |
| 100 | 3 |
| 110 | 2 |

### Guided Solutions to Practice Problems

1. Figure 1 shows the three *AE* curves and the three levels of equilibrium expenditure. When the price level is 90, equilibrium expenditure is $4 trillion. When the price level is 100, equilibrium expenditure is $3 trillion. When the price level is 110, equilibrium expenditure is $2 trillion.
2. Table 2 shows the aggregate demand schedule, and Figure 2 shows the aggregate demand curve.
3. A rise in the price level decreases consumption expenditure, which decreases aggregate planned expenditure and shifts the *AE* curve downward. Equilibrium expenditure decreases.

**FIGURE 2**

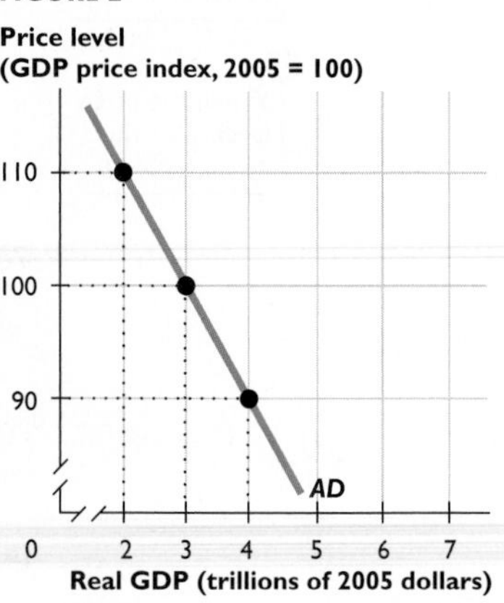

# CHAPTER SUMMARY

## Key Points

**1 Distinguish between autonomous expenditure and induced expenditure and explain how real GDP influences expenditure plans.**

- Autonomous expenditure is the sum of the components of aggregate expenditure that real GDP does not influence directly.
- Induced expenditure is the sum of the components of aggregate expenditure that real GDP influences.
- Consumption expenditure varies with disposable income and real GDP and depends on the marginal propensity to consume.
- Imports vary with real GDP and depend on the marginal propensity to import.

**2 Explain how real GDP adjusts to achieve equilibrium expenditure.**

- Actual aggregate expenditure equals real GDP, but when aggregate planned expenditure differs from real GDP, firms have unplanned inventory changes.
- If aggregate planned expenditure exceeds real GDP, firms increase production and real GDP increases. If real GDP exceeds aggregate planned expenditure, firms decrease production and real GDP decreases.
- Real GDP changes until aggregate planned expenditure equals real GDP.

**3 Explain the expenditure multiplier.**

- When autonomous expenditure changes, equilibrium expenditure changes by a larger amount: There is a multiplier.
- The multiplier is greater than 1 because a change in autonomous expenditure changes induced expenditure.
- The larger the marginal propensity to consume, the larger is the multiplier.
- Income taxes and imports make the multiplier smaller.

**4 Derive the *AD* curve from equilibrium expenditure.**

- The *AD* curve is the relationship between the quantity of real GDP demanded and the price level when all other influences on expenditure plans remain the same.
- The quantity of real GDP demanded on the *AD* curve is the equilibrium real GDP when aggregate planned expenditure equals real GDP.

## Key Terms

Aggregate planned expenditure, 748
Consumption function, 748
Equilibrium expenditure, 756
Marginal propensity to consume, 750
Marginal propensity to import, 752
Marginal tax rate, 762
Multiplier, 760

## CHAPTER CHECKPOINT

Work these problems in Chapter 29 Study Plan to get instant feedback.

### Study Plan Problems and Applications

**TABLE 1**

| Disposable income | Saving |
|---|---|
| (trillions of dollars) | |
| 0 | −5 |
| 10 | −3 |
| 20 | −1 |
| 30 | 1 |
| 40 | 3 |
| 50 | 5 |

Table 1 shows disposable income and saving in an economy. Use Table 1 to answer Problems **1** and **2**.

1. Calculate consumption expenditure at each level of disposable income. Over what range of disposable income is there dissaving? Estimate the level of disposable income at which saving is zero.
2. Calculate the marginal propensity to consume. If wealth increases by $10 trillion, in which direction will the consumption function change?

Table 2 shows real GDP, *Y*, consumption expenditure, *C*, investment, *I*, government expenditure on goods and services, *G*, exports, *X*, imports, *M*, and aggregate planned expenditure, *AE*, in millions of dollars. Taxes are constant. Use Table 2 to work Problems **3**, **4**, and **5**.

**TABLE 2**

| | Planned expenditure | | | | | |
|---|---|---|---|---|---|---|
| *Y* | *C* | *I* | *G* | *X* | *M* | *AE* |
| 0 | 2.0 | 1.75 | 1.0 | 1.25 | 0 | 6.0 |
| 2 | **Q** | 1.75 | 1.0 | 1.25 | 0.4 | 6.8 |
| 4 | 4.4 | **R** | 1.0 | 1.25 | 0.8 | 7.6 |
| 6 | 5.6 | 1.75 | **S** | 1.25 | 1.2 | 8.4 |
| 8 | 6.8 | 1.75 | 1.0 | **T** | 1.6 | 9.2 |
| 10 | 8.0 | 1.75 | 1.0 | 1.25 | **U** | 10.0 |
| 12 | 9.2 | 1.75 | 1.0 | 1.25 | 2.4 | **V** |

3. Find the value of Q, R, S, T, U, and V.
4. Calculate the marginal propensity to consume and the marginal propensity to import. What is equilibrium expenditure?
5. If investment crashes to $0.55 million but nothing else changes, what is equilibrium expenditure and what is the multiplier?
6. Figure 1 shows aggregate planned expenditure when the price level is 100. When the price level increases to 110, aggregate planned expenditure changes by $0.5 trillion. What is the quantity of real GDP demanded when the price level is 100 and 110?

**FIGURE 1**

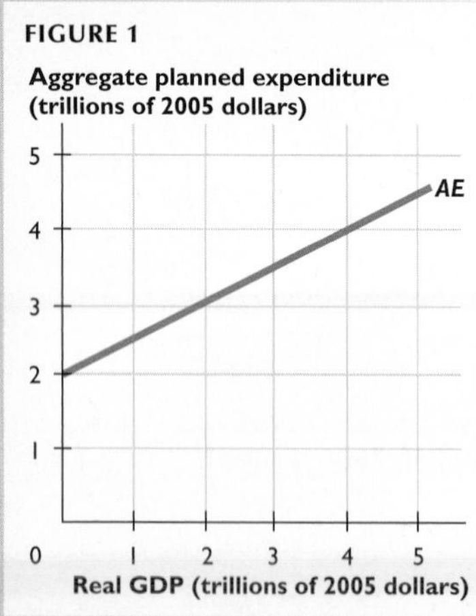


**Business spending looks up**

Producers of equipment such as the bulldozer maker Caterpillar Inc. and hydraulic-parts maker Parker Hannifin Corp. say that there is an upturn in spending by businesses with companies raising their investment plans.

Source: *Wall Street Journal*, October 21, 2009

Use this information to work Problems **7** and **8**.

7. Explain how the increase in planned investment at a constant price level changes equilibrium expenditure.
8. What determines the increase in aggregate demand resulting from an increase in business investment?

## Instructor Assignable Problems and Applications

Your instructor can assign these problems as homework, a quiz, or a test in **MyEconLab**.

1. The output gap in the second quarter of 2009 was $0.8 trillion. How much fiscal stimulus would be required to close the output gap if the multiplier was as large as the Obama team believes? How much fiscal stimulus would be required if the multiplier was as large as Robert Barro believes?

Table 1 shows disposable income and consumption expenditure in an economy. Use Table 1 to work Problems 2 and 3.

2. Calculate saving at each level of disposable income. Over what range of disposable income does consumption expenditure exceed disposable income? Calculate autonomous consumption expenditure.
3. Calculate the marginal propensity to consume. At what level of disposable income will saving be zero? If expected future income increases, in which direction will the consumption function change?

**TABLE 1**

| Disposable income | Consumption expenditure |
|---|---|
| (billions of dollars) | |
| 200 | 350 |
| 400 | 500 |
| 600 | 650 |
| 800 | 800 |
| 1,000 | 950 |

Use the following information to work Problems 4 to 6.

In an economy with no exports and no imports, autonomous consumption is $1 trillion, the marginal propensity to consume is 0.8, investment is $5 trillion, and government expenditure on goods and services is $4 trillion. Taxes are $4 trillion and do not vary with real GDP.

4. If real GDP is $30 trillion, calculate disposable income, consumption expenditure, and aggregate planned expenditure. What is equilibrium expenditure?
5. If real GDP is $30 trillion, explain the process that takes the economy to equilibrium expenditure. If real GDP is $40 trillion, explain the process that takes the economy to equilibrium expenditure.
6. If investment increases by $0.5 trillion, calculate the change in equilibrium expenditure and the multiplier.

Use the following information to work Problems 7 and 8.

Figure 1 shows the aggregate demand curve in an economy. Suppose that aggregate planned expenditure increases by $0.75 trillion for each $1 trillion increase in real GDP.

7. If investment increases by $1 trillion, calculate the change in the quantity of real GDP demanded if the price level is 100.
8. Compare the shift of the *AD* curve with the $1 trillion increase in investment. Explain the magnitude of the shift of the *AD* curve.
9. **Federal deficit hits record $1.42 trillion**

   The 2009 federal budget deficit of $1.42 trillion is more than three times as large as the deficit in any other single year. In September, the government spent $46.6 billion more than it collected in tax revenue. The 2008 budget deficit was $459 billion.

   Source: *USA Today*, October 16, 2009

   By how much did real GDP increase as a result of the government's additional $46.6 billion of expenditure if the multiplier is what the Obama team believed it to be?

**FIGURE 1**

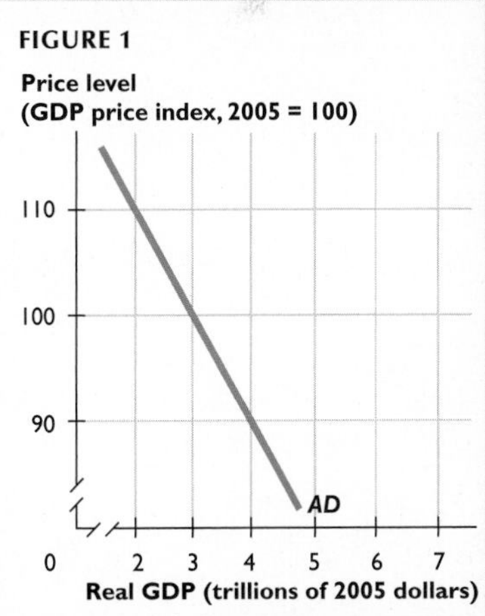

10. It is 2000 and the Japanese economy is in a recession. Economists suggested that the Japanese government increase its expenditure on goods and services but not change taxes. Explain how such a policy change would influence equilibrium expenditure. Would such a policy change help to turn the economy from recession to expansion?

Table 2 shows real GDP, *Y*, consumption expenditure, *C*, investment, *I*, government expenditure on goods and services, *G*, exports, *X*, imports, *M*, and aggregate planned expenditure, *AE*, in trillions of dollars. Taxes are constant. Use Table 2 to work Problems **11** to **14**.

**TABLE 2**

| | Planned expenditure | | | | | |
|---|---|---|---|---|---|---|
| *Y* | *C* | *I* | *G* | *X* | *M* | *AE* |
| 0 | 0.4 | 1.4 | 0.4 | 1.0 | 0 | 3.2 |
| 2 | 2.0 | 1.4 | 0.4 | 1.0 | 0.4 | **T** |
| 4 | 3.6 | 1.4 | 0.4 | 1.0 | 0.8 | 5.6 |
| 6 | 5.2 | 1.4 | 0.4 | 1.0 | **S** | 6.8 |
| 8 | 6.8 | **R** | 0.4 | 1.0 | 1.6 | 8.0 |
| 10 | **Q** | 1.4 | 0.4 | 1.0 | 2.0 | 9.2 |
| 12 | 10.0 | 1.4 | 0.4 | 1.0 | 2.4 | 10.4 |

11. Find the value of Q, R, S, and T.
12. Calculate autonomous expenditure and induced expenditure when real GDP is $4 trillion.
13. Calculate the marginal propensity to consume, the marginal propensity to import, and equilibrium expenditure.
14. If government expenditure increases to $1.2 trillion but other things remain the same, what is equilibrium expenditure and what is the multiplier?

Use the following information to work Problems **15** and **16**.

It is 2012, and real GDP in the U.S. economy is in an expansion phase of the business cycle. Consumption expenditure and other components of aggregate expenditure are increasing.

15. Explain how these events will influence the U.S. consumption function, the U.S. saving function, and the U.S. aggregate expenditure curve.
16. Explain how these events will influence equilibrium expenditure and the quantity of real GDP demanded in the United States.
17. Zimbabwe is in a deep recession. Use the aggregate expenditure model to illustrate the state of the economy. Then Zimbabwe's new platinum mine starts production and its exports increase. Explain how the increase in exports will influence Zimbabwe's aggregate expenditure and equilibrium expenditure.
18. In an economy in which the marginal propensity to consume is 0.7, real GDP increased by $11.2 trillion in 2009 while inventories fell by $13.4 billion, less than the fall of $16.6 billion in 2008. Describe the process that is going on in this economy: As real GDP grows, inventories continue to fall but at a slower pace.

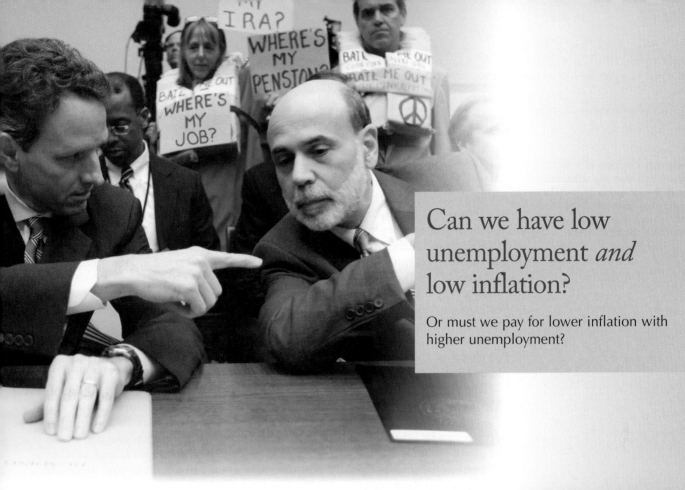

# Can we have low unemployment *and* low inflation?

Or must we pay for lower inflation with higher unemployment?

# The Short-Run Policy Tradeoff

## CHAPTER CHECKLIST

**When you have completed your study of this chapter, you will be able to**

1. Describe the short-run tradeoff between inflation and unemployment.
2. Distinguish between the short-run and the long-run Phillips curves and describe the shifting tradeoff between inflation and unemployment.
3. Explain how the Fed can influence the expected inflation rate and how expected inflation influences the short-run tradeoff.

## 30.1 THE SHORT-RUN PHILLIPS CURVE

**Short-run Phillips curve**
A curve that shows the relationship between the inflation rate and the unemployment rate when the natural unemployment rate and the expected inflation rate remain constant.

The **short-run Phillips curve** is a curve that shows the relationship between the inflation rate and the unemployment rate when the natural unemployment rate and the expected inflation rate remain constant.

Figure 30.1 illustrates the short-run Phillips curve. Here, the natural unemployment rate is 6 percent and the expected inflation rate is 3 percent a year. At full employment, the unemployment rate equals the natural unemployment rate and the inflation rate equals the expected inflation rate at point *B*. This point is the anchor point for the short-run Phillips curve.

In an expansion, the unemployment rate decreases and the inflation rate rises. For example, the economy might move to a point such as *A*, where the unemployment rate is 5 percent and the inflation rate is 4 percent a year.

In a recession, the unemployment rate increases and the inflation rate falls. For example, the economy might move to a point such as *C*, where the unemployment rate is 7 percent and the inflation rate is 2 percent a year.

The short-run Phillips curve presents a *tradeoff* between inflation and unemployment. Along a given short-run Phillips curve, a lower unemployment rate can be achieved only by paying the cost of a higher inflation rate, and a lower inflation rate can be achieved only by paying the cost of a higher unemployment rate. For example, in Figure 30.1, a decrease in the unemployment rate from 6 percent to 5 percent costs a 1-percentage point increase in the inflation rate from 3 percent a year to 4 percent a year.

**FIGURE 30.1**

A Short-Run Phillips Curve

myeconlab Animation

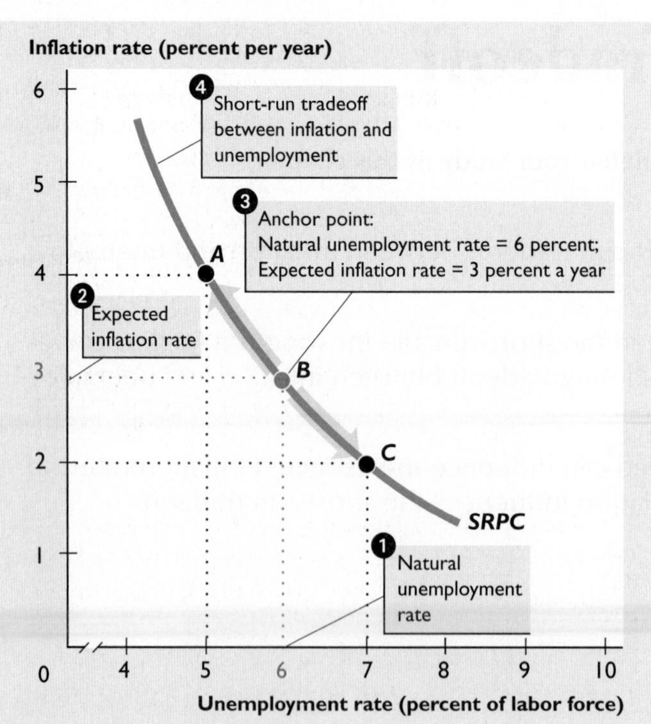


1 If the natural unemployment rate is 6 percent, and 2 the expected inflation rate is 3 percent a year, then 3 point *B* is at full employment on a short-run Phillips curve.

4 The short-run Phillips curve (*SRPC*) shows the tradeoff between inflation and unemployment at the given natural unemployment rate and expected inflation rate.

A higher unemployment rate brings a lower inflation rate, and a lower unemployment rate brings a higher inflation rate.

## Aggregate Supply and the Short-Run Phillips Curve

The short-run Phillips curve is another way of looking at the upward-sloping aggregate supply curve that you learned about in Chapter 28—see pp. 722–725.

Both the short-run Phillips curve and the aggregate supply curve arise because the money wage rate is fixed in the short run.

Along an aggregate supply curve, the money wage rate is fixed. So when the price level rises, the *real wage rate* falls, and a fall in the real wage rate increases the quantity of labor employed and increases the quantity of real GDP supplied.

The events that we've just described also play out along a short-run Phillips curve. The rise in the price level means that the inflation rate has (perhaps temporarily) increased. The increase in the quantity of labor employed means a decrease in the number unemployed and a fall in the unemployment rate.

So a movement along an aggregate supply curve is equivalent to a movement along a short-run Phillips curve. Let's explore these connections between the aggregate supply curve and the short-run Phillips curve a bit more closely.

### Unemployment and Real GDP

In a given period, with a fixed amount of capital and a given state of technology, real GDP depends on the quantity of labor employed. At full employment, the quantity of real GDP is *potential GDP* and the unemployment rate is the natural unemployment rate. If real GDP exceeds potential GDP, employment exceeds its full-employment level and the unemployment rate falls below the natural unemployment rate. Similarly, if real GDP is less than potential GDP, employment is less than its full-employment level and the unemployment rate rises above the natural unemployment rate.

The quantitative relationship between the unemployment rate and real GDP was first estimated by economist Arthur M. Okun and is called **Okun's Law**. Okun's Law states that for each percentage point that the unemployment rate is above the natural unemployment rate, real GDP is 2 percentage points below potential GDP. For example, if the natural unemployment rate is 6 percent and potential GDP is $10 trillion, then when the actual unemployment rate is 7 percent, real GDP is $9.8 trillion—98 percent of potential GDP, or 2 percentage points below potential GDP. And when the actual unemployment rate is 5 percent, real GDP is $10.2 trillion—102 percent of potential GDP, or 2 percentage points above potential GDP. Table 30.1 summarizes this relationship.

**Okun's Law**
For each percentage point that the unemployment rate is above the natural unemployment rate, real GDP is 2 percentage points below potential GDP.

**TABLE 30.1**

| | Unemployment rate (percent) | Real GDP (trillions of 2005 dollars) |
|---|---|---|
| *A* | 5 | 10.2 |
| *B* | 6 | 10.0 |
| *C* | 7 | 9.8 |

### Inflation and the Price Level

The inflation rate is the percentage change in the price level. So starting from last period's price level, the higher the inflation rate, the higher is the current period's price level. Suppose that last year, the price level was 100. If the inflation rate is 2 percent, the price level rises to 102; if the inflation rate is 3 percent, the price level rises to 103; and if the inflation rate is 4 percent, the price level rises to 104.

With these relationships between the unemployment rate and real GDP (in Table 30.1) and between the inflation rate and the price level, we can establish the connection between the short-run Phillips curve and the aggregate supply curve. Figure 30.2 shows this connection.

First suppose that in the current year, real GDP equals potential GDP and the unemployment rate equals the natural unemployment rate. In Figure 30.2, real

GDP is $10 trillion and the unemployment rate is 6 percent. The economy is at point *B* on the short-run Phillips curve in part (a) and point *B* on the aggregate supply curve in part (b). The inflation rate is 3 percent a year (its expected rate) in part (a), and the price level is 103 (also its expected level) in part (b).

Next suppose that instead of being at full employment, the economy is above full employment with real GDP of $10.2 trillion at point *A* on the aggregate supply curve in Figure 30.2(b). In this case, the unemployment rate is 5 percent in Table 30.1 and the economy is at point *A* on the short-run Phillips curve in Figure 30.2(a). The inflation rate is 4 percent a year (higher than expected) in part (a), and the price level is 104 (also higher than expected) in part (b).

Finally, suppose that the economy is below full employment with real GDP of $9.8 trillion at point *C* on the aggregate supply curve in Figure 30.2(b). In this case, the unemployment rate is 7 percent in Table 30.1 and the economy is at point *C* on the short-run Phillips curve in Figure 30.2(a). The inflation rate is 2 percent a year (lower than expected) in part (a), and the price level is 102 (also lower than expected) in part (b).

**FIGURE 30.2**

The Short-Run Phillips Curve and the Aggregate Supply Curve

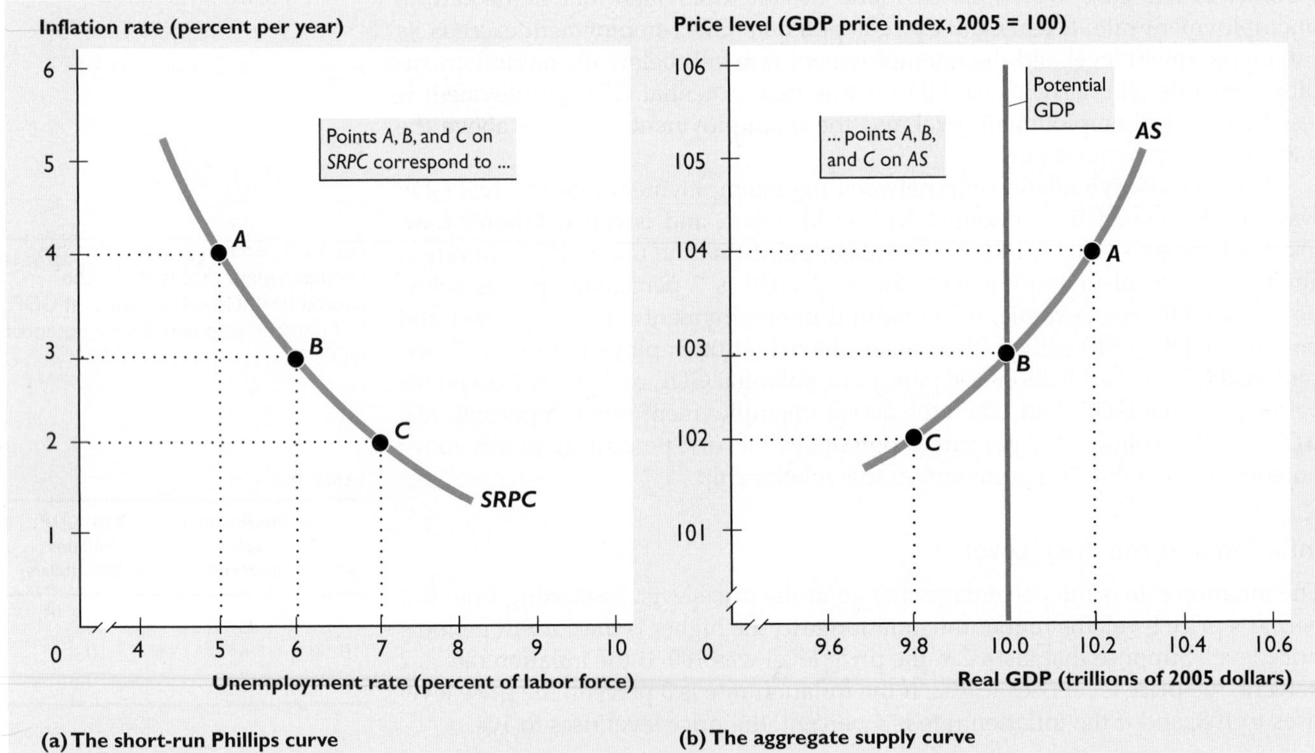


Point *A* on the Phillips curve corresponds to point *A* on the aggregate supply curve: The unemployment rate is 5 percent and the inflation rate is 4 percent a year in part (a), and real GDP is $10.2 trillion and the price level is 104 in part (b).

Point *B* on the Phillips curve corresponds to point *B* on the aggregate supply curve: The unemployment rate is 6 percent and the inflation rate is 3 percent a year in part (a), and real GDP is $10 trillion and the price level is 103 in part (b).

Point *C* on the Phillips curve corresponds to point *C* on the aggregate supply curve: The unemployment rate is 7 percent and the inflation rate is 2 percent a year in part (a), and real GDP is $9.8 trillion and the price level is 102 in part (b).

### Aggregate Demand Fluctuations

A decrease in aggregate demand that brings a movement down along the aggregate supply curve from point *B* to point *C* lowers the price level and decreases real GDP. That same decrease in aggregate demand brings a movement down along the Phillips curve from point *B* to point *C*.

Similarly, an increase in aggregate demand that brings a movement up along the aggregate supply curve from point *B* to point *A* raises the price level and increases real GDP relative to what they would have been. That same increase in aggregate demand brings a movement up along the Phillips curve from point *B* to point *A*.

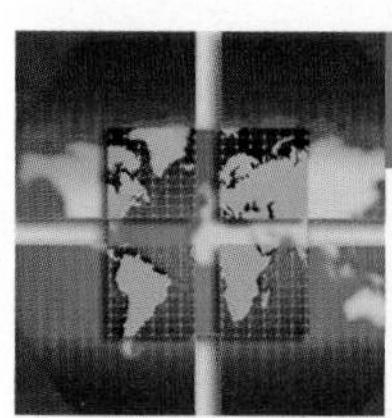

## EYE on the GLOBAL ECONOMY

### Inflation and Unemployment

The Phillips curve is so named because New Zealand economist A. W. (Bill) Phillips discovered the relationship in about 100 years of unemployment and wage inflation data for the United Kingdom.

The figure shows data on inflation and unemployment in the United Kingdom over most of the twentieth century—1900 to 1997. The data reveal no neat, tight tradeoff. The short-run tradeoff shifts around a great deal.

The highest inflation rate did not occur at the lowest unemployment rate, and the lowest inflation rate did not occur at the highest unemployment rate. But the lowest unemployment rate in 1917 did bring a high inflation rate. And the highest unemployment rate during the Great Depression of the 1930s brought a gently falling price level.

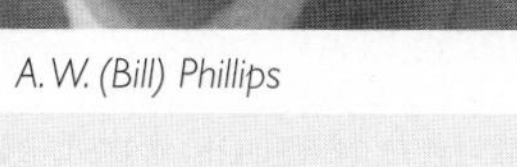

A. W. (Bill) Phillips

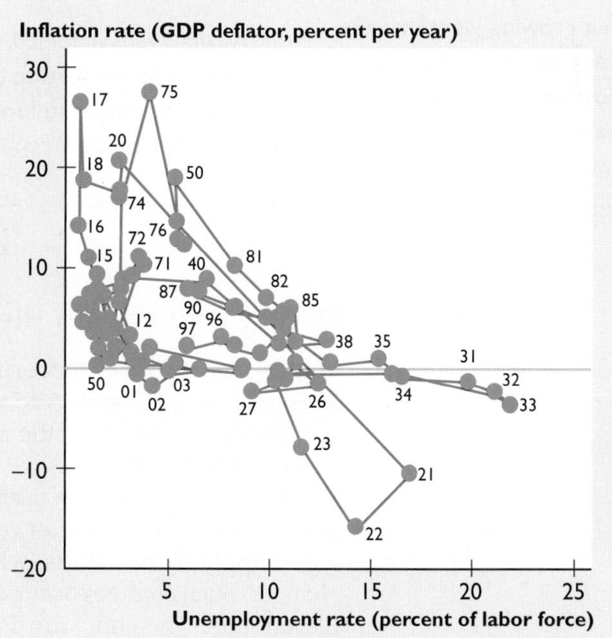


SOURCE: Michael Parkin, "Unemployment, Inflation, and Monetary Policy," *Canadian Journal of Economics*, November 1998.

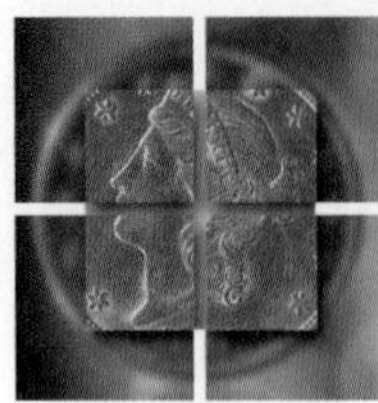

# EYE on the PAST

## The U.S. Phillips Curve

Phillips made his discovery in 1958, two years before the election of John F. Kennedy as President of the United States. Very soon thereafter, two young American economists, Paul A. Samuelson and Robert M. Solow, both at MIT and eager to help the new Kennedy administration to pursue a low-unemployment strategy, looked for a Phillips curve in the U.S. data. The figure shows what they found: The red line joining the blue dots shows no recognizable relationship between inflation and unemployment for the 20 or so years that they studied.

Giving more weight to the 1950s experience, Samuelson and Solow proposed the Phillips curve shown in the figure. They believed that the U.S. Phillips curve provided support for the then growing view that the new Kennedy administration could pursue a low unemployment policy with only a moderate rise in the inflation rate.

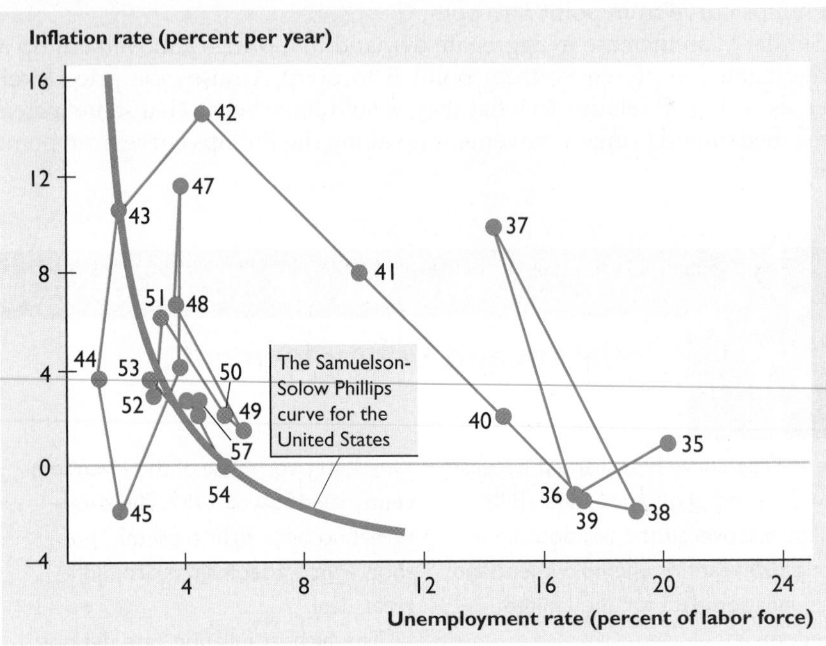


SOURCE OF DATA: Paul A. Samuelson and Robert M. Solow, "Problem of Achieving and Maintaining a Stable Price Level, Analytical Aspects of Anti-Inflation Policy." *American Economic Review*, 50(2), May 1960.

As the 1960s unfolded, the Samuelson-Solow version of the Phillips curve began to look like a permanent tradeoff between inflation and unemployment. But in the late 1960s and early 1970s, the relationship disappeared in the face of rising inflation expectations.

## Why Bother with the Phillips Curve?

You've seen that the short-run Phillips curve is another way of looking at the aggregate supply curve. And you might be wondering, why bother with the short-run Phillips curve? Isn't the aggregate supply curve adequate for describing the short-run tradeoff?

The Phillips curve is useful for two reasons. First, it focuses directly on two policy targets: the inflation rate and the unemployment rate. Second, the aggregate supply curve shifts whenever the money wage rate or potential GDP changes. Such changes occur every day, so the aggregate supply curve is not a stable tradeoff. The short-run Phillips curve isn't a stable tradeoff either, but it is more stable than the aggregate supply curve. The short-run Phillips curve shifts only when the natural unemployment rate changes or when the expected inflation rate changes.

# CHECKPOINT 30.1

**Describe the short-run tradeoff between inflation and unemployment.**

Work these problems in Study Plan 30.1 to get instant feedback.

## Practice Problems

Table 1 describes five possible outcomes for 2010, depending on the level of aggregate demand in that year. Potential GDP is $10 trillion, and the natural unemployment rate is 5 percent. Use Table 1 to work Problems **1** to **5**.

1. Calculate the inflation rate for each possible outcome.
2. Use Okun's Law to find real GDP at each unemployment rate in Table 1.
3. What are the expected price level and the expected inflation rate in 2010?
4. Plot the short-run Phillips curve for 2010. Mark the points *A*, *B*, *C*, *D*, and *E* that correspond to the data in Table 1 and that you have calculated.
5. Plot the aggregate supply curve for 2010. Mark the points *A*, *B*, *C*, *D*, and *E* that correspond to the data in Table 1.
6. **Inflation at lowest rate in 5 years**
   In September, inflation in the United Kingdom fell to 1.1% a year, its lowest in 5 years. Analysts expected an inflation rate of 1.3% a year.
   Source: *The New York Times*, October 13, 2009
   With the unemployment rate at 8 percent and the natural unemployment rate at 6 percent, sketch the short-run Phillips curve and mark on your graph the point which shows the situation in September. Label the point *A*.

**TABLE 1**

| | Price level (2009 = 100) | Unemployment rate (percentage) |
|---|---|---|
| *A* | 102.5 | 9 |
| *B* | 105.0 | 6 |
| *C* | 106.0 | 5 |
| *D* | 107.5 | 4 |
| *E* | 110.0 | 3 |

## Guided Solutions to Practice Problems

1. The inflation rate equals the price level minus 100. So for *A*, the inflation rate is $102.5 - 100 = 2.5$. Calculate the other inflation rates in the same way.
2. Okun's law is that the output gap $= -2 \times (U - U^*)$ percent, where $U$ is the unemployment rate and $U^*$ is the natural unemployment rate. So for *A*, the output gap $= -2 \times (9 - 5) = -8$, which means that real GDP is 8 percent below potential GDP and equals $9.2 trillion. Calculate the other levels of real GDP in the same way.
3. The expected price level is 106 and the expected inflation rate is 6 percent—row *C* at full employment.
4. Plot the inflation rate (Problem 1) against the unemployment rate (Table 1) to get the short-run Phillips curve (Figure 1).
5. Plot the price level (Table 1) against real GDP (Problem 2) to get the aggregate supply curve (Figure 2).
6. With the natural unemployment rate of 6 percent and expected inflation of 1.3 percent the Phillips curve passes through point *B* on Figure 3. Point *A* lies on the Phillips curve at the unemployment rate of 8 percent and actual inflation rate of 1.1 percent a year.

**FIGURE 1**

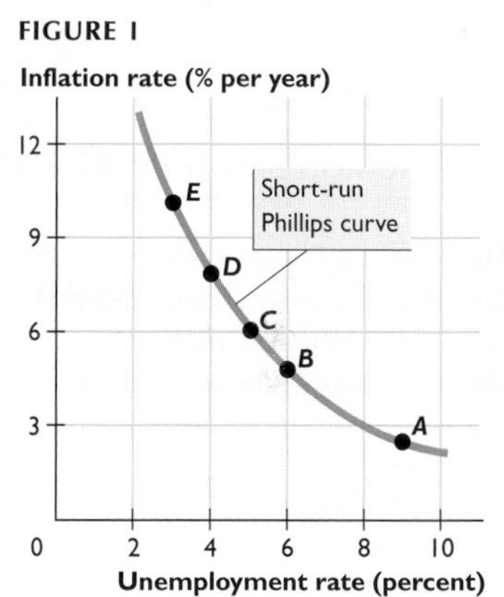


**FIGURE 2**

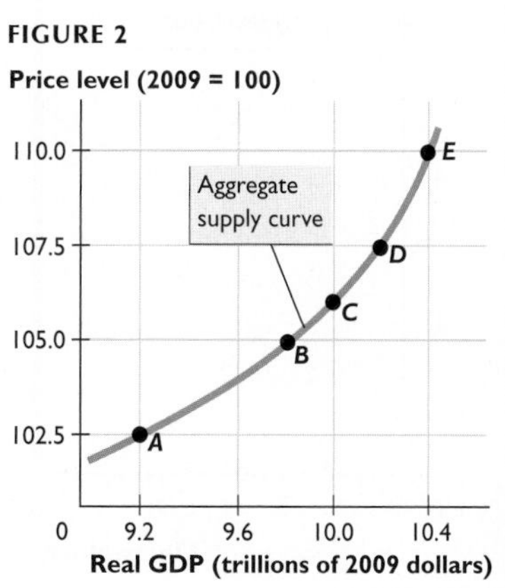


**FIGURE 3**

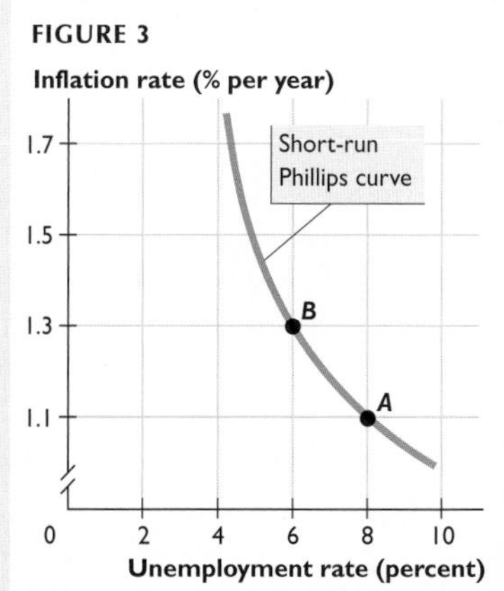

## 30.2 SHORT-RUN AND LONG-RUN PHILLIPS CURVES

The short-run Phillips curve shows the *tradeoff* between inflation and unemployment when the natural unemployment rate and expected inflation rate remain the same. Changes in the natural unemployment rate and the expected inflation rate change the short-run tradeoff and changes in the expected inflation rate give rise to a *long-run* Phillips curve that we'll now examine.

### The Long-Run Phillips Curve

**Long-run Phillips curve**
The vertical line that shows the relationship between inflation and unemployment when the economy is at full employment.

The **long-run Phillips curve** shows the relationship between inflation and unemployment when the economy is at full employment. At full employment, the unemployment rate is the *natural unemployment rate,* so on the long-run Phillips curve, there is only one possible unemployment rate: the natural unemployment rate.

In contrast, the inflation rate can take on any value at full employment. You learned in Chapter 27 (pp. 706–709) that at full employment, for a given real GDP growth rate, the greater the money growth rate, the greater is the inflation rate.

This description of the economy at full employment tells us the properties of the long-run Phillips curve: It is a vertical line located at the natural unemployment rate. In Figure 30.3, the long-run Phillips curve is *LRPC* along which the unemployment rate equals the natural unemployment rate and any inflation rate is possible.

**FIGURE 30.3**

The Long-Run Phillips Curve

myeconlab Animation

The long-run Phillips curve is a vertical line at the natural unemployment rate. In the long run, there is no unemployment–inflation tradeoff.

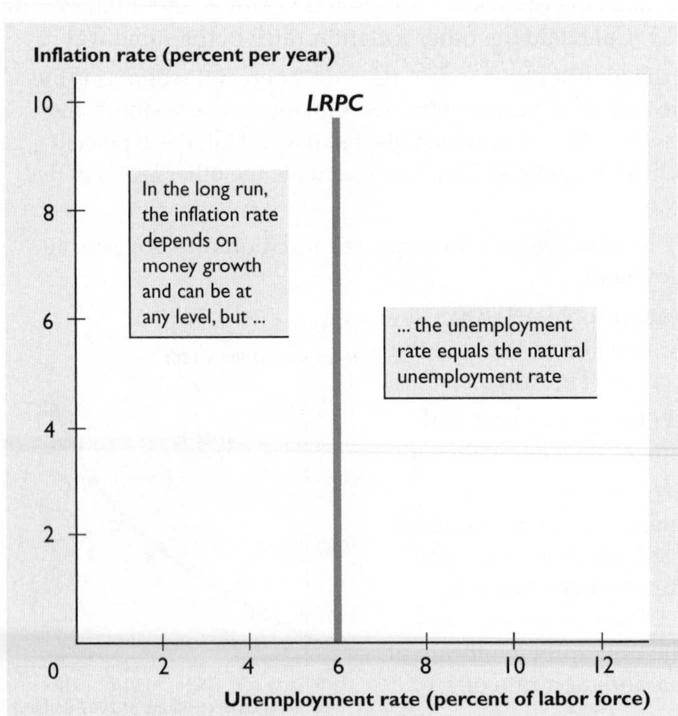

## Expected Inflation

The **expected inflation rate** is the inflation rate that people forecast and use to set the money wage rate and other money prices. Suppose there is full employment and McDonald's servers earn $7 an hour. With no inflation, a money wage rate of $7 an hour keeps the market for servers in equilibrium. But with 10 percent inflation, a constant money wage rate means a falling real wage rate and a shortage of servers. Now, a 10 percent rise in the money wage rate to $7.70 is needed to keep the market for servers in equilibrium. If McDonald's and everyone else expect 10 percent inflation, the money wage rate will rise by 10 percent to prevent a labor shortage from arising.

**Expected inflation rate**
The inflation rate that people forecast and use to set the money wage rate and other money prices.

If expectations about the inflation rate turn out to be correct, the price level rises by the 10 percent expected and the real wage rate remains constant at its full-employment equilibrium level and unemployment remains at the natural unemployment rate.

Because the actual inflation rate equals the expected inflation rate at full employment, we can interpret the long-run Phillips curve as the relationship between inflation and unemployment when the inflation rate equals the expected inflation rate.

Figure 30.4 shows short-run Phillips curves for two expected inflation rates. A short-run Phillips curve shows the tradeoff between inflation and unemployment at *a particular expected inflation rate.* When the expected inflation rate changes, the short-run Phillips curve shifts to intersect the long-run Phillips curve at the new expected inflation rate.

**FIGURE 30.4**

Short-Run and Long-Run Phillips Curves

myeconlab Animation

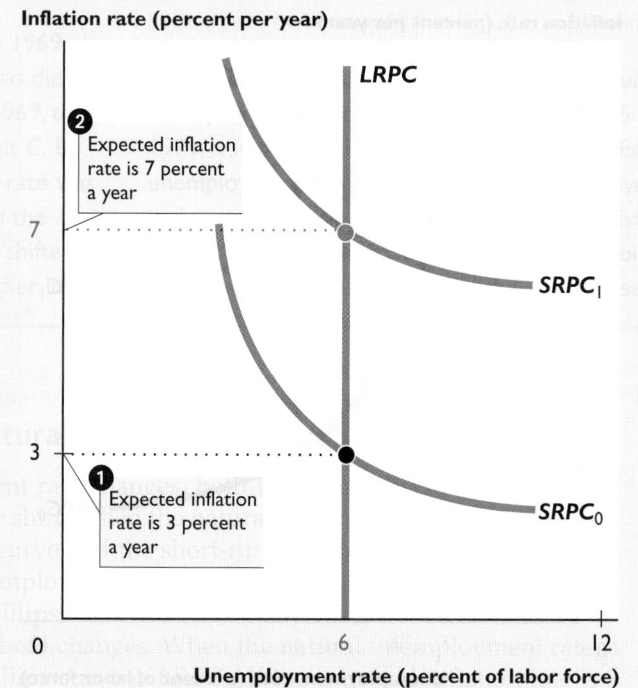


If the natural unemployment rate is 6 percent, the long-run Phillips curve is *LRPC*.

1. If the expected inflation rate is 3 percent a year, the short-run Phillips curve is $SRPC_0$.
2. If the expected inflation rate is 7 percent a year, the short-run Phillips curve is $SRPC_1$.

Work these problems in Study Plan 30.2 to get instant feedback.

## CHECKPOINT 30.2

**Distinguish between the short-run and the long-run Phillips curves and describe the shifting tradeoff between inflation and unemployment.**

### Practice Problems

Use Figure 1, which shows a short-run Phillips curve and a long-run Phillips curve, to work Problems **1** to **4**.

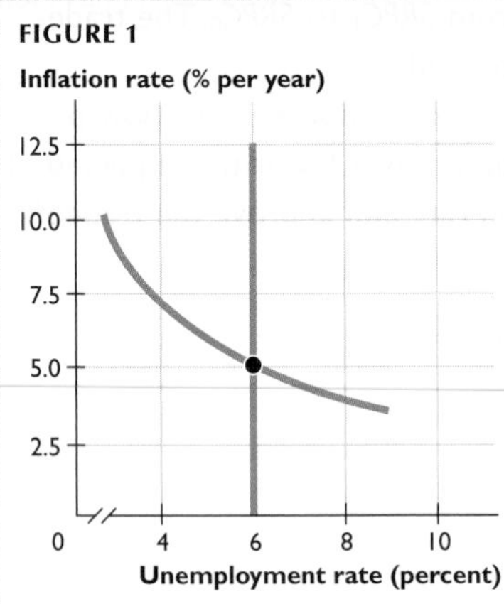


1. Identify the curves and label them. What is the expected inflation rate and what is the natural unemployment rate?
2. If the expected inflation rate increases to 7.5 percent a year, show the new short-run and long-run Phillips curves.
3. If the natural unemployment rate increases to 8 percent, show the new short-run and long-run Phillips curves.
4. If aggregate demand starts to grow more rapidly and the inflation rate eventually hits 10 percent a year, how do unemployment and inflation change?
5. **From the Fed's minutes**

   The Fed expects the unemployment rate will drop from 9.8 percent today to 9.25 percent by the end of 2010 and to 8 percent by the end of 2011. Private economists predict that the unemployment rate won't drop to a more normal 5 or 6 percent until 2013 or 2014. Inflation should stay subdued, but the Fed needs to keep its eye on inflation expectations.

   Source: *The New York Times*, October 14, 2009

   Is the Fed predicting that the U.S. economy will move rightward or leftward along a short-run Phillips curve or that the short-run Phillips curve will shift up or down through 2011?

### Guided Solutions to Practice Problems

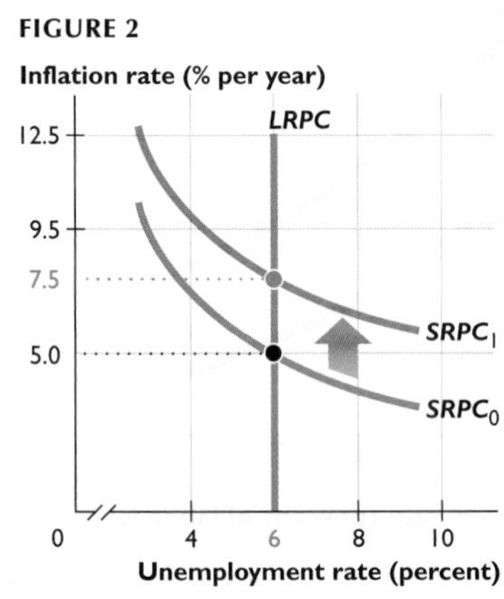


1. The long-run Phillips curve is the vertical curve, *LRPC*, and the short-run Phillips curve is the downward-sloping curve, $SRPC_0$ (Figure 2). The expected inflation rate is the inflation rate at which *LRPC* and $SRPC_0$ intersect, which is 5 percent a year. The natural unemployment rate is 6 percent. The *LRPC* is vertical at the natural unemployment rate.
2. The short-run Phillips curve shifts upward, but the long-run Phillips curve does not change (Figure 2).
3. Both the short-run and long-run Phillips curves shift rightward (Figure 3).
4. Figure 4 shows that as expectations change, the inflation rate rises to 10 percent a year and unemployment falls and then gradually returns to its natural rate.
5. If inflation remains subdued and inflation expectations do not change, the economy is on a short-run Phillips curve to the right of the *LRPC* and is predicted to move leftward up along the *SRPC* toward the *LRPC*.

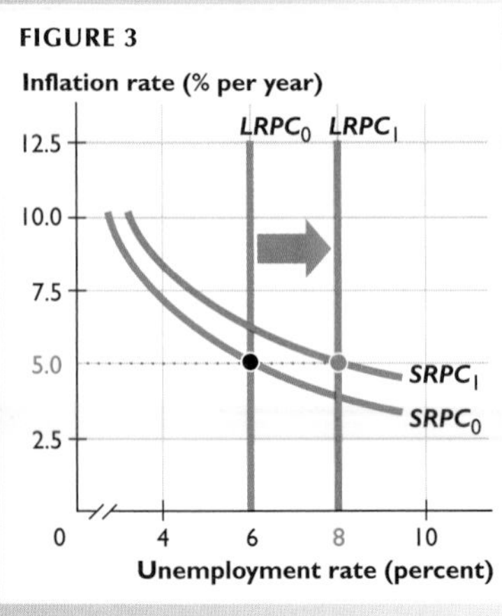


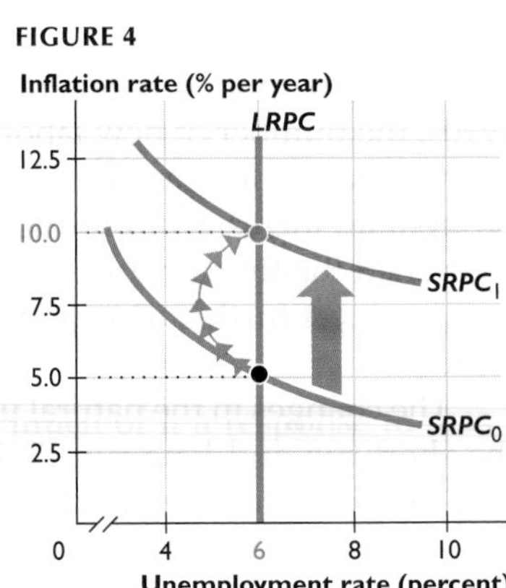

## 30.3 EXPECTED INFLATION

You've seen that expected inflation plays a big role in determining the position of the short-run tradeoff. When the expected inflation rate is low, as it was in 2000, the tradeoff is more favorable than when the expected inflation rate is high, as it was in 1980. The effect of expected inflation on the short-run tradeoff raises two questions:

- What determines the expected inflation rate?
- What can policy do to lower expected inflation?

### What Determines the Expected Inflation Rate?

The *expected inflation rate* is the inflation rate that people forecast and use to set the money wage rate and other money prices. To forecast the inflation rate, people use the same basic method that they use to forecast other variables that affect their lives.

Data make up the first ingredient in forecasting—data about the past behavior of the phenomenon that we want to forecast. When people laid heavy bets that Tiger Woods would win the British Open in 2005, they based their forecast on the performance of Tiger and the other golfers in the months leading up to that event.

Science is the second ingredient in forecasting—the specific science that seeks to understand the phenomenon that we wish to forecast. If we want to know whether it is likely to rain tomorrow, we turn to the science of meteorology. Science is not a substitute for data. It is knowledge that tells people how to interpret data.

So to forecast inflation, people use data about past inflation and other relevant variables and the science of economics, which seeks to understand the forces that cause inflation.

You already know the relevant economics: the *AS-AD* model. You know that the money growth rate determines the growth of aggregate demand in the long run. And you know that the trend growth rate of real GDP is the growth rate of aggregate supply in the long run. So the trend money growth rate minus the trend real GDP growth rate determines the trend inflation rate.

The inflation rate fluctuates around its trend as the state of the economy changes over the business cycle. In an expansion, the inflation rate rises above trend, and in a recession, the inflation rate falls below trend as aggregate demand fluctuates to bring movements along the aggregate supply curve. And you know that the money growth rate is one of the influences on these aggregate demand fluctuations.

The Fed determines the money growth rate, so the major ingredient in a forecast of inflation is a forecast of the Fed's actions. Professional Fed watchers and economic forecasters use these ideas along with a lot of data and elaborate statistical models of the economy to forecast the inflation rate.

When all the relevant data and economic science are used to forecast inflation, the resulting forecast is called a **rational expectation**. The rational expectation of the inflation rate is a forecast based on the Fed's forecasted monetary policy along with forecasts of the other forces that influence aggregate demand and aggregate supply. But the dominant factor is the Fed's monetary policy.

**Rational expectation**
The forecast that results from the use of all the relevant data and economic science.

Work these problems in Chapter 30 Study Plan to get instant feedback.

**TABLE 1 DATA 2011**

| | Price level (2010 = 100) | Real GDP (trillions of 2010 dollars) | Unemployment rate (percent) |
|---|---|---|---|
| *A* | 102 | 11.0 | 9 |
| *B* | 104 | 11.1 | 7 |
| *C* | 106 | 11.2 | 5 |
| *D* | 110 | 11.4 | 3 |

**TABLE 2 DATA 2012**

| | Price level (2010 = 100) | Real GDP (trillions of 2010 dollars) | Unemployment rate (percent) |
|---|---|---|---|
| *A* | 108 | 11.1 | 9 |
| *B* | 110 | 11.2 | 7 |
| *C* | 112 | 11.3 | 5 |
| *D* | 116 | 11.5 | 3 |

# CHAPTER CHECKPOINT

## Study Plan Problems and Applications

Table 1 describes four situations that might arise in 2011, depending on the level of aggregate demand. Table 2 describes four situations that might arise in 2012. Use Tables 1 and 2 to work Problems **1** to **4**.

1. Plot the short-run Phillips curve and aggregate supply curve for 2011 and mark the points *A*, *B*, *C*, and *D* on each curve that correspond to the data in Table 1.
2. In 2011, the outcome turned out to be row *C* of Table 1. Plot the short-run Phillips curve for 2012 and mark the points *A*, *B*, *C*, and *D* that correspond to the data in Table 2.
3. Compare the short-run Phillips curve of 2012 with that of 2011.
4. What is Okun's Law? If the natural unemployment rate is 6 percent, does this economy behave in accordance with Okun's Law?
5. Suppose that the natural unemployment rate is 5 percent in 2010 and it increases to 6 percent in 2011 with no change in expected inflation. Explain how the short-run and long-run tradeoffs change.
6. Suppose that the natural unemployment rate is 5 percent and the expected inflation rate is 4 percent a year in 2010. If the inflation rate is expected to fall to 3 percent a year in 2011, explain how the short-run and the long-run Phillips curves will change.
7. The inflation rate is 2 percent a year, and the quantity of money is growing at a pace that will maintain that inflation rate. The natural unemployment rate is 5.5 percent, and the current unemployment rate is 9 percent. In what direction will the unemployment rate change? How will the short-run Phillips curve and the long-run Phillips curve shift?
8. Inflation in Brazil and Uruguay have repeatedly risen to levels unheard of in the United States. Explain how a history of rapid inflation might influence the short-run and long-run Phillips curves in these countries.

Use the following information to work Problems **9** to **11**.

**Changing course, Australia raises interest rate**

The Reserve Bank of Australia (the central bank) raised its overnight rate (equivalent to the U.S. federal funds rate) by a quarter of a percentage point, to 3.25 percent a year, amid concerns about rising inflation. The interest rate rise came earlier than many economists had expected.

Source: *New York Times*, October 6, 2009

9. Sketch the Phillips curves if expected inflation is 2 percent a year and the natural unemployment rate is 5 percent.
10. If with the Reserve bank's "concerns about rising inflation," people increase the expected inflation rate, explain how the short-run tradeoff will change.
11. If actual inflation had risen prior to the Reserve Bank raising the overnight rate, explain how the short-run tradeoff would change.

## Instructor Assignable Problems and Applications

Your instructor can assign these problems as homework, a quiz, or a test in **MyEconLab**.

1. Suppose that as the U.S. economy recovers from the global financial crisis and recession the natural unemployment rate rises to its 1970s level and the expected inflation rate falls to zero. How would the short-run and long-run Phillips curves change? Would the tradeoff be more favorable or less favorable than that of 2009? Draw a graph to illustrate your answer.
2. In an economy, the natural unemployment rate is 4 percent and the expected inflation rate is 3 percent a year. Draw a graph of the short-run and long-run Phillips curves that display this information. Label each curve.

Table 1 describes four possible situations that might arise in 2011, depending on the level of aggregate demand in 2011. Table 2 describes four possible situations that might arise in 2012. Use Tables 1 and 2 to work Problems 3 and 4.

**TABLE 1 DATA 2011**

| | Price level (2010 = 100) | Real GDP (trillions of 2010 dollars) | Unemployment rate (percent) |
|---|---|---|---|
| *A* | 102 | 10.0 | 8 |
| *B* | 104 | 10.1 | 6 |
| *C* | 106 | 10.2 | 4 |
| *D* | 110 | 10.4 | 2 |

**TABLE 2 DATA 2012**

| | Price level (2010 = 100) | Real GDP (trillions of 2010 dollars) | Unemployment rate (percent) |
|---|---|---|---|
| *A* | 108 | 10.3 | 8 |
| *B* | 110 | 10.4 | 6 |
| *C* | 112 | 10.5 | 4 |
| *D* | 116 | 10.7 | 2 |

3. Plot the short-run Phillips curve and aggregate supply curve for 2011 and mark the points *A, B, C,* and *D* on each curve that correspond to the data in Table 1.
4. In 2011, the outcome turned out to be row *D* of Table 1. Plot the short-run Phillips curve for 2012 and mark the points *A, B, C,* and *D* that correspond to the data in Table 2.
5. Explain the relationship between the long-run Phillips curve and potential GDP and the short-run Phillips curve and the aggregate supply curve.
6. The inflation rate is 3 percent a year, and the quantity of money is growing at a pace that will maintain the inflation rate at 3 percent a year. The natural unemployment rate is 4 percent, and the current unemployment rate is 3 percent. In what direction will the unemployment rate change? How will the short-run Phillips curve and the long-run Phillips curve shift?
7. The inflation rate is 6 percent a year, the unemployment rate is 4 percent, and the economy is at full employment. The Fed announces that it intends to slow the money growth rate to keep the inflation rate at 3 percent a year for the foreseeable future. People believe the Fed. Explain how unemployment and inflation change in the short run and in the long run.

Use the following information to work Problems 8 and 9.

**U.S. consumer confidence hits a 9-month high**

The Reuters/University of Michigan Surveys of Consumers reported a rise in June of consumer confidence that exceeded economists' expectations and a rise in expected inflation to 3.1 percent a year. Such a rise should be a concern to the Federal Reserve, which has been pumping money into the economy in an attempt to contain the recession and spur a recovery.

Source: *The New York Times*, June 12, 2009

8. Show on a graph the effect of an increase in the expected inflation rate on the Phillips curves if there is no change in the natural unemployment rate.
9. If the Fed is concerned about inflation and unexpectedly slows money growth, explain how unemployment will change in the short run and in the long run.

10. The inflation rate is 1.5 percent a year, the unemployment rate is 4 percent, and the economy is at full employment. Unexpectedly, the Fed increases the money growth rate to raise the inflation rate to 3 percent a year. Explain how unemployment and inflation change in the short run.
11. In light of the fact that whenever the inflation rate is lowered, the unemployment rate increases, is lowering inflation ever a good policy? Would it be better to simply live with the inflation rate we've currently got?
12. In light of the fact that whenever the inflation rate is lowered, the unemployment rate increases, do you think we should ever permit the inflation rate to rise to an unacceptable level? Would it be better to nip an increase in inflation in the bud even if it meant a small and brief recession?
13. Looking at the data on inflation and unemployment, it is very difficult to see any sign of a short-run tradeoff. Explain why it is difficult to see the short-run tradeoff. Does the fact that the short-run tradeoff is hard to see in the data mean that we can ignore it? Why or why not?
14. Explain why the Phillips curve is a useful model and describe how it relates to and supplements the *AS-AD* model.

Use the following information to work Problems **15** and **16**.

Because the Fed doubled the monetary base in 2008 and because the government has spent billions of dollars bailing out troubled banks, insurance companies, and auto producers, some people are concerned that a serious upturn in the inflation rate will occur, not immediately but in a few years' time. At the same time, massive changes in the global economy might bring the need for structural change in the United States.

15. Explain how the Fed's doubling of the monetary base and government bailouts might influence the short-run and long-run unemployment–inflation tradeoffs. Will the influence come from changes in the expected inflation rate, the natural unemployment rate, or both?
16. Explain how large-scale structural change might influence the short-run and long-run unemployment–inflation tradeoffs. Will the influence come from changes in the expected inflation rate, the natural unemployment rate, or both?
17. Describe the changes in inflation and unemployment in the United States between 1935 and 1957 and explain how these changes might have resulted from shifts of the short-run and long-run Phillips curves and from movements along the short-run Phillips curve.
18. Describe the changes in inflation and unemployment in the United States since 2000 and explain how these changes have resulted from shifts of the short-run and long-run Phillips curves and from movements along the short-run Phillips curve.
19. How would you expect an increase in unemployment benefits and a rise in the minimum wage to influence the short-run and long-run Phillips curves?

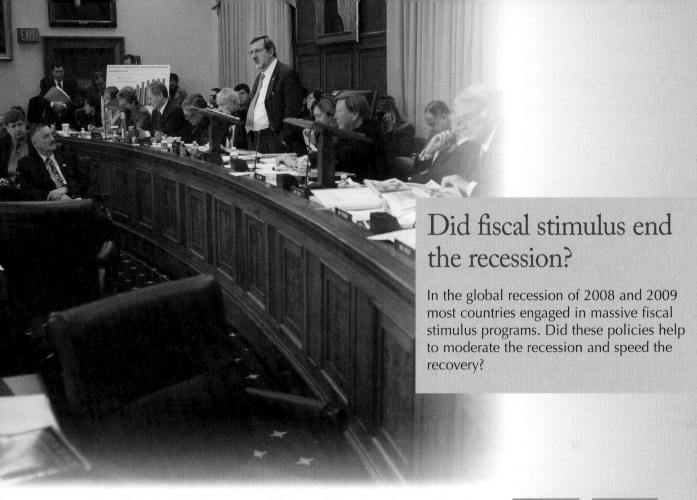

## Did fiscal stimulus end the recession?

In the global recession of 2008 and 2009 most countries engaged in massive fiscal stimulus programs. Did these policies help to moderate the recession and speed the recovery?

# Fiscal Policy

CHAPTER CHECKLIST

**When you have completed your study of this chapter, you will be able to**

1. Describe the federal budget process and the recent history of revenues, outlays, deficits, and debts.
2. Explain the demand-side effects of fiscal policy on employment and real GDP.
3. Explain the supply-side effects of fiscal policy on employment, potential GDP, and the economic growth rate.

## 31.1 THE FEDERAL BUDGET

**Federal budget**
An annual statement of the revenues, outlays, and surplus or deficit of the government of the United States.

The **federal budget** is an annual statement of the revenues, outlays, and surplus or deficit of the government of the United States, together with the laws and regulations that authorize these revenues and outlays.

The federal budget has two purposes:

1. To finance the activities of the federal government
2. To achieve macroeconomic objectives

The first purpose of the federal budget was its only purpose before the Great Depression years of the 1930s. The second purpose evolved as a response to the Great Depression and was initially based on the ideas of *Keynesian macroeconomics* (described in Chapter 23, pp. 588–589).

**Fiscal policy**
The use of the federal budget to achieve the macroeconomic objectives of high and sustained economic growth and full employment.

The use of the federal budget to achieve macroeconomic objectives is **fiscal policy**. During the 1960s, in the heyday of Keynesian macroeconomics, full employment was the main macroeconomic objective of fiscal policy. But as economics has advanced and ideas have changed, productivity and economic growth have assumed an increasingly prominent place in the objectives of fiscal policy. So today, fiscal policy is concerned with achieving *both* full employment and high and sustained economic growth.

### The Institutions and Laws

**Fiscal year**
A year that begins on October 1 and ends on September 30. Fiscal 2011 *begins* on October 1, 2010.

The President and Congress make the budget and develop fiscal policy on a fixed annual time line and fiscal year. The U.S. **fiscal year** runs from October 1 to September 30 in the next calendar year. Fiscal 2011 is the fiscal year that begins on October 1, 2010.

#### The Roles of the President and Congress

The President *proposes* a budget to Congress each February. After Congress has passed the budget acts in September, the President either signs those acts into law or vetoes the entire budget bill. The President does not have the veto power to eliminate specific items in a budget bill and approve others—known as a line-item veto. Many state governors have long had line-item veto authority, and Congress attempted to grant these powers to the President of the United States in 1996. But a 1998 Supreme Court ruling declared the line-item veto for the President to be unconstitutional. Although the President proposes and ultimately approves the budget, the task of making the tough decisions on spending and taxes rests with Congress.

Congress begins its work on the budget with the President's proposal. The House of Representatives and the Senate develop their own budget ideas in their respective House and Senate Budget Committees. Formal conferences between the two houses eventually resolve differences of view, and a series of spending acts and an overall budget act are usually passed by both houses before the start of the fiscal year.

During a fiscal year, Congress often passes supplementary budget laws, and the budget outcome is influenced by the evolving state of the economy. For example, if a recession begins, tax revenues fall and welfare payments increase.

Figure 31.1 summarizes the budget time line and the roles of the President and Congress in the budget process.

**FIGURE 31.1**

The Federal Budget Time Line for Fiscal 2011

| | |
|---|---|
| Jan. 1, 2010 | |
| Feb. 2, 2010 | The President submits a budget proposal to Congress. |
| Oct. 1, 2010 | Congress debates, amends, and enacts the budget. The President signs the budget act into law. |
| | Fiscal 2011 begins. Supplementary budget laws may be passed. |
| | State of the economy influences outlays, tax revenues, and the budget balance. |
| Sept. 30, 2011 | Fiscal 2011 ends. |
| | Accounts for Fiscal 2011 are prepared. Outlays, tax revenues, and the budget balance are reported. |

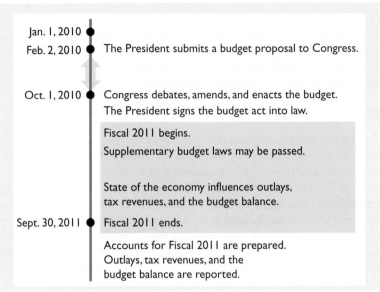

The federal budget process begins with the President's proposals in February. Congress debates and amends these proposals and enacts a budget before the start of the fiscal year on October 1. The President signs the budget act into law. Throughout the fiscal year, Congress might pass supplementary budget laws. The budget outcome is calculated after the end of the fiscal year.

## Budget Surplus, Deficit

You've seen that the federal budget is the annual statement of the outlays and tax revenues of the government of the United States. The government's budget balance is equal to tax revenues minus outlays. That is,

$$\text{Budget balance} = \text{Tax revenues} - \text{Outlays}.$$

If tax revenues equal outlays, the government has a **balanced budget**. The government has a **budget surplus** if tax revenues exceed outlays. The government has a **budget deficit** if outlays exceed tax revenues.

The budget projections for the 2010 fiscal year were tax revenues of $2,703 billion, outlays of $3,973 billion, and a budget deficit of $1,270 billion. You can see that $2,703 billion − $3,973 billion = −$1,270 billion.

**Balanced budget**
The budget balance when tax revenues equal outlays.

**Budget surplus**
The positive budget balance when tax revenues exceed outlays.

**Budget deficit**
The negative budget balance when outlays exceed tax revenues.

## Surplus, Deficit, and Debt

The government budget balance is equal to government saving, which might be zero (balanced budget), positive (budget surplus), or negative (budget deficit). When the government has a budget deficit, it incurs debt. That is, the government borrows to finance a budget deficit. When the government has a budget surplus, it repays some of its debt. The amount of government debt outstanding—debt that has arisen from past budget deficits—is called **national debt**.

The national debt at the end of a fiscal year equals the national debt at the end of the previous fiscal year plus the budget deficit or minus the budget surplus. For example,

$$\text{Debt at end of 2010} = \text{Debt at end of 2009} + \text{Budget deficit in 2010}.$$

**National debt**
The amount of government debt outstanding–debt that has arisen from past budget deficits.

At the end of the 2009 fiscal year, national debt was $8,531 billion. With a deficit of $1,270 billion in 2010, national debt at the end of the 2010 fiscal year becomes $9,801 billion. That is, $8,531 billion + $1,270 billion = $9,801 billion.

### A Personal Analogy

The government's budget and debt are like your budget and debt, only bigger. If you take a student loan each year to go to school, you have a budget deficit and a growing debt. After graduating, if you have a job and repay some of your loan each year, you have a budget surplus each year and a shrinking debt.

## The Federal Budget in 2010

You've just seen some numbers that describe the scale of the federal budget in the 2010 fiscal year. Table 31.1 provides a bit more detail and enables you to see the relative magnitudes of the main items in the federal budget.

On the tax revenues side of the budget, the largest item is personal income taxes. These are the taxes that people pay on wages and salaries and on interest income. The second largest item is Social Security taxes. These are the taxes paid by workers and employers to fund Social Security benefits. Corporate income taxes, which are the taxes paid by corporations on their profits, are the next item but they are much smaller than the two largest ones. Indirect taxes are the smallest revenue source. These are sales taxes and customs and excise taxes.

**Transfer payments**
Social Security benefits, Medicare and Medicaid benefits, unemployment benefits, and other cash benefits.

On the outlays side of the budget, **transfer payments**—Social Security benefits, Medicare and Medicaid benefits, unemployment benefits, and other cash benefits paid to individuals and firms—take the largest share of the government's financial resources. Expenditure on goods and services includes the government's defense and homeland security budgets. Debt interest is the interest on the national debt.

We've described the budget process and are now ready to study the effects on the economy. We begin in the next section with the demand-side effects.

**TABLE 31.1**

The Federal Budget in Fiscal 2010

The federal budget for 2010 was expected to be in a large deficit. Tax revenues of $2,703 billion were expected to be $1,270 billion less than outlays of $3,973 billion.

Personal income taxes are the largest revenue source and transfer payments are the largest outlay.

| Item | Projections (billions of dollars) | |
|---|---|---|
| **Tax Revenues** | **2,703** | |
| Personal income taxes | | 1,068 |
| Social Security taxes | | 1,026 |
| Corporate income taxes | | 233 |
| Indirect taxes | | 376 |
| **Outlays** | **3,973** | |
| Transfer payments | | 2,322 |
| Expenditure on goods and services | | 1,244 |
| Debt interest | | 407 |
| **Balance** | **–1,270** | |

SOURCE OF DATA: *Budget of the United States Government, Fiscal Year 2010*, Table 14.1.

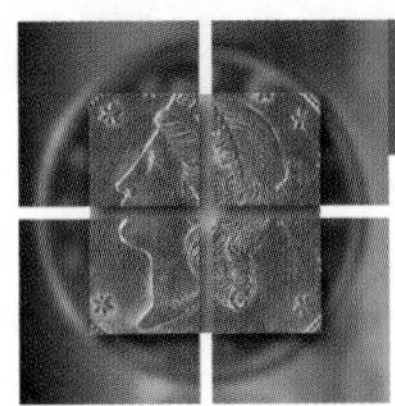

# EYE on the PAST

## Federal Revenues, Outlays, Deficits, and Debt

In 1940, in the first year of World War II, for every dollar earned, the federal government collected 6.5 cents in taxes and spent 9.3 cents. By 1943, at the depth of the most terrible war in history, the government was spending 40 cents of every dollar earned and collecting 12 cents in taxes. The government deficit in 1943 and 1944 was almost 30 percent of GDP.

The result of these enormous deficits was a mushrooming government debt. By 1946, when the debt-to-GDP ratio (debt as a percentage of GDP) peaked, the government owed more than a year's GDP.

During the 1950s and 1960s, the government's debt-to-GDP ratio tumbled as balanced budgets combined with rapid real GDP growth. By 1974, the debt-to-GDP ratio had fallen to a low of 23 percent.

Budget deficits returned during the 1980s as the defense budget swelled and some tax rates were cut. The result was a growing debt-to-GDP ratio that climbed to almost 50 percent by 1995.

Expenditure restraint combined with sustained real GDP growth lowered the debt-to-GDP ratio during the 1990s, but a surge in expenditures on defense and homeland security, further tax cuts, and a spending surge in 2009 and 2010 to fight global financial crisis and recession, all combined to swell the debt-to-GDP ratio again.

Source of data: *Budget of the U.S. Government, Fiscal Year 2010*, Historical Tables, Tables 7.1 and 14.1.



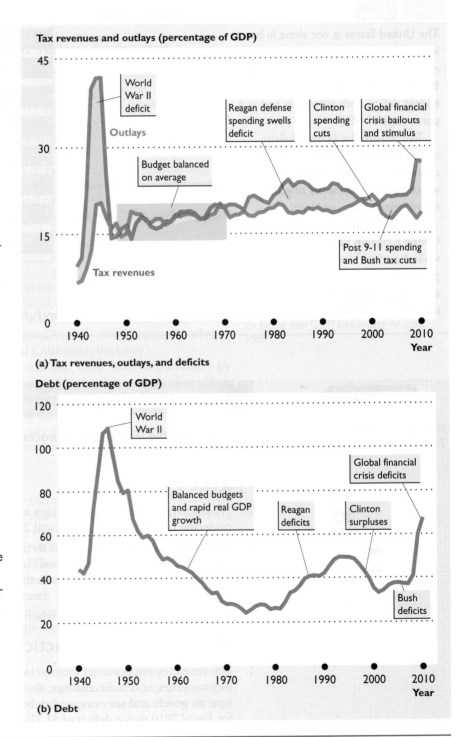

**(a) Tax revenues, outlays, and deficits**



**(b) Debt**

## A Successful Contractionary Fiscal Policy

**Contractionary fiscal policy**
A decrease in government expenditure on goods and services, a decrease in transfer payments, or an increase in taxes designed to decrease aggregate demand.

If real GDP is above potential GDP, the government might pursue a **contractionary fiscal policy**—decrease its expenditure on goods and services, decrease transfer payments, raise taxes, or do some combination of all three. Figure 31.3 shows us how these actions decrease aggregate demand.

In Figure 31.3(a), potential GDP is $13 trillion but real GDP is $14 trillion. The economy is at point *A* and there is an *inflationary gap* (see Chapter 28, p. 736).

To eliminate the inflationary gap and restore full employment, the government takes a contractionary fiscal policy action. A decrease in government expenditure or a rise in taxes decreases aggregate expenditure by $\Delta E$. If this were the only change in spending plans, the *AD* curve would become $AD_0 - \Delta E$. But the initial decrease in aggregate expenditure sets off a multiplier process, which decreases consumption expenditure. As the multiplier process plays out, aggregate demand decreases and the *AD* curve shifts leftward to $AD_1$.

With no change in the price level, the economy would move from the initial point *A* to point *B* on $AD_1$. But the decrease in aggregate demand combined with the upward-sloping *AS* curve brings a fall in the price level, and the economy moves to a new equilibrium at point *C*. The price level falls to 110, real GDP decreases to $13 trillion, and the inflationary gap is eliminated.

**FIGURE 31.3**

Contractionary Fiscal Policy

myeconlab Animation

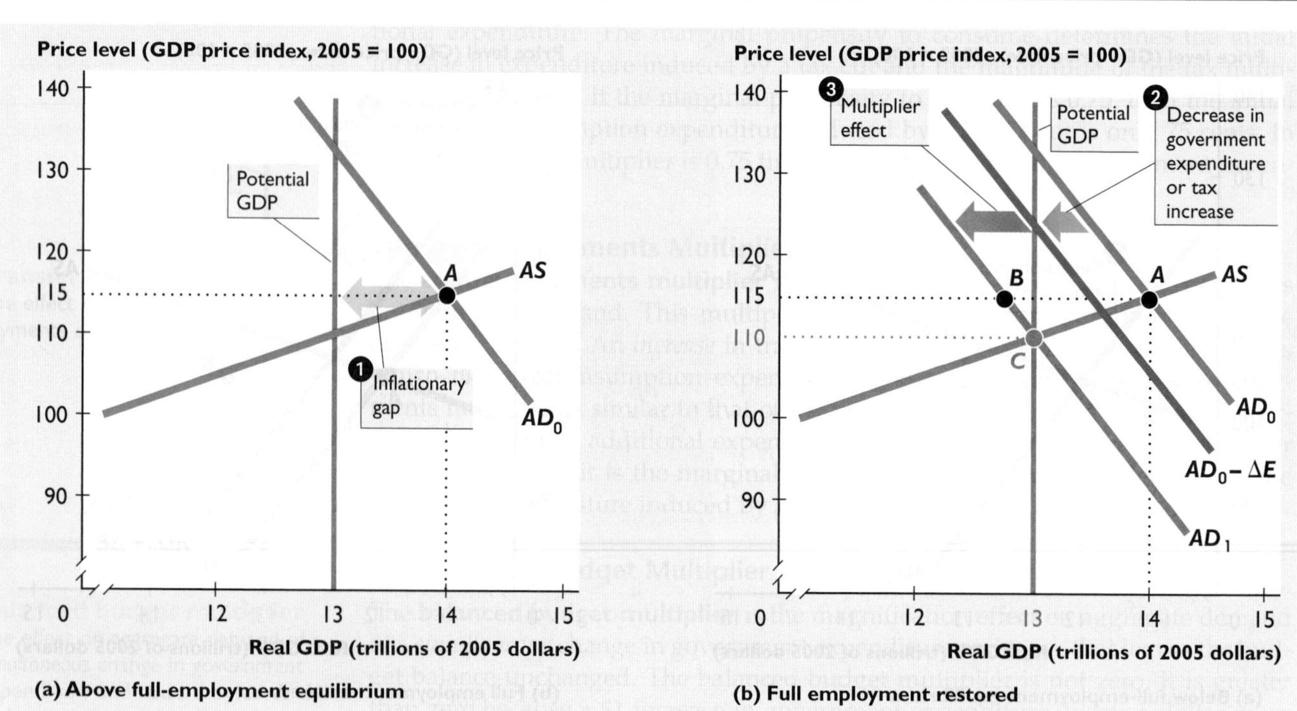


Potential GDP is $13 trillion, real GDP is $14 trillion, and ❶ there is a $1 trillion inflationary gap. ❷ A decrease in government expenditure or a tax increase decreases expenditure by $\Delta E$.

❸ The multiplier decreases induced expenditure. The *AD* curve shifts leftward to $AD_1$, the price level falls to 110, real GDP decreases to $13 trillion, and the inflationary gap is eliminated.

## Automatic and Discretionary Fiscal Stimulus

Fiscal policy actions that are aimed at stimulating aggregate demand can be automatic or discretionary.

### Automatic Fiscal Policy

A fiscal policy action that is triggered by the state of the economy is called an **automatic fiscal policy**. For example, an increase in unemployment induces an increase in transfer payments, and a fall in incomes induces a decrease in tax revenues.

**Automatic fiscal policy**
A fiscal policy action that is triggered by the state of the economy.

### Discretionary Fiscal Policy

A fiscal policy action that is initiated by an act of Congress is called a **discretionary fiscal policy**. A discretionary fiscal policy action requires a change in a spending program or in a tax law. Increases in defense spending or cuts in the income tax rate are examples of discretionary fiscal policy.

**Discretionary fiscal policy**
A fiscal policy action that is initiated by an act of Congress.

## Automatic Fiscal Policy

Automatic fiscal policy is a consequence of tax revenues and outlays that fluctuate with real GDP. These features of fiscal policy are called **automatic stabilizers** because they work to stabilize real GDP without explicit action by the government.

**Automatic stabilizers**
Features of fiscal policy that stabilize real GDP without explicit action by the government.

### Induced Taxes

On the revenue side of the budget, tax laws define tax *rates*, not tax *dollars*. Tax dollars paid depend on tax rates and incomes. But incomes vary with real GDP, so tax revenues depend on real GDP. Taxes that vary with real GDP are called **induced taxes**. When real GDP increases in an expansion, wages and profits rise, so the taxes on these incomes—induced taxes—rise. When real GDP decreases in a recession, wages and profits fall, so the induced taxes on these incomes fall.

**Induced taxes**
Taxes that vary with real GDP.

### Needs-Tested Spending

On the expenditure side of the budget, the government creates programs that entitle suitably qualified people and businesses to receive benefits. The spending on such programs is called **needs-tested spending**, and it results in transfer payments that depend on the economic state of individual citizens and businesses. When the economy is in a recession, the number of people experiencing unemployment and economic hardship increases, but needs-tested spending on unemployment benefits and food stamps increases. When the economy expands, the number of people experiencing unemployment and economic hardship decreases, and needs-tested spending decreases.

**Needs-tested spending**
Spending on programs that entitle suitably qualified people and businesses to receive transfer payments that vary with need and with the state of the economy.

Induced taxes and needs-tested spending decrease the multiplier effects of changes in investment or exports, so they moderate both expansions and recessions and make real GDP more stable. They achieve this outcome by weakening the link between real GDP and disposable income and so reduce the effect of a change in real GDP on consumption expenditure. When real GDP increases, induced taxes increase and needs-tested spending decreases, so disposable income does not increase by as much as the increase in real GDP. As a result, consumption expenditure does not increase by as much as it otherwise would have done and the multiplier effect is reduced.

11. If the deficit-reduction plan includes an increase in the tax rate on interest income and a decrease in the tax rate on wage income, how will this policy influence the labor market and the equilibrium amount of loanable funds? Also explain how this policy will influence potential GDP.

Use the following information to work Problems 12 and 13.

Suppose that in an economy, investment is $160 billion, saving is $140 billion, government expenditure on goods and services is $150 billion, exports are $200 billion, and imports are $250 billion.

12. Calculate the tax revenue and the budget balance.
13. What fiscal policy action might increase investment and speed economic growth? Explain how the policy would work.
14. Suppose that the output gap in an economy becomes a large recessionary gap. Describe the automatic fiscal policy actions that might occur. Explain how they would work.
15. Suppose that an economy is in a boom and the inflationary gap is large. Describe the discretionary fiscal policy that the government might introduce. Explain how it would work.

Use the following information to work Problems 16 and 17.

Suppose that the tax on interest income is levied on the nominal interest rate, the tax rate is 20 percent, and the real interest rate is 3 percent a year.

16. If there is no inflation, calculate the after-tax real interest rate and the true tax rate on interest income.
17. If there is 5 percent inflation, calculate the after-tax real interest rate and the true tax rate on interest income.
18. **Australian GDP to grow faster than expected**

    The Australian economy will grow faster than previously forecast. Growth was driven by a surge in consumer spending after the government distributed more than $20 billion in cash to households and the government has begun spending $22 billion on roads, railways, and schools. The current deficit is $57 billion.

    Source: Bloomberg.com, November 3, 2009

    The economy is no longer in recession. Explain why the faster than expected growth might have pushed the economy into an inflationary gap.

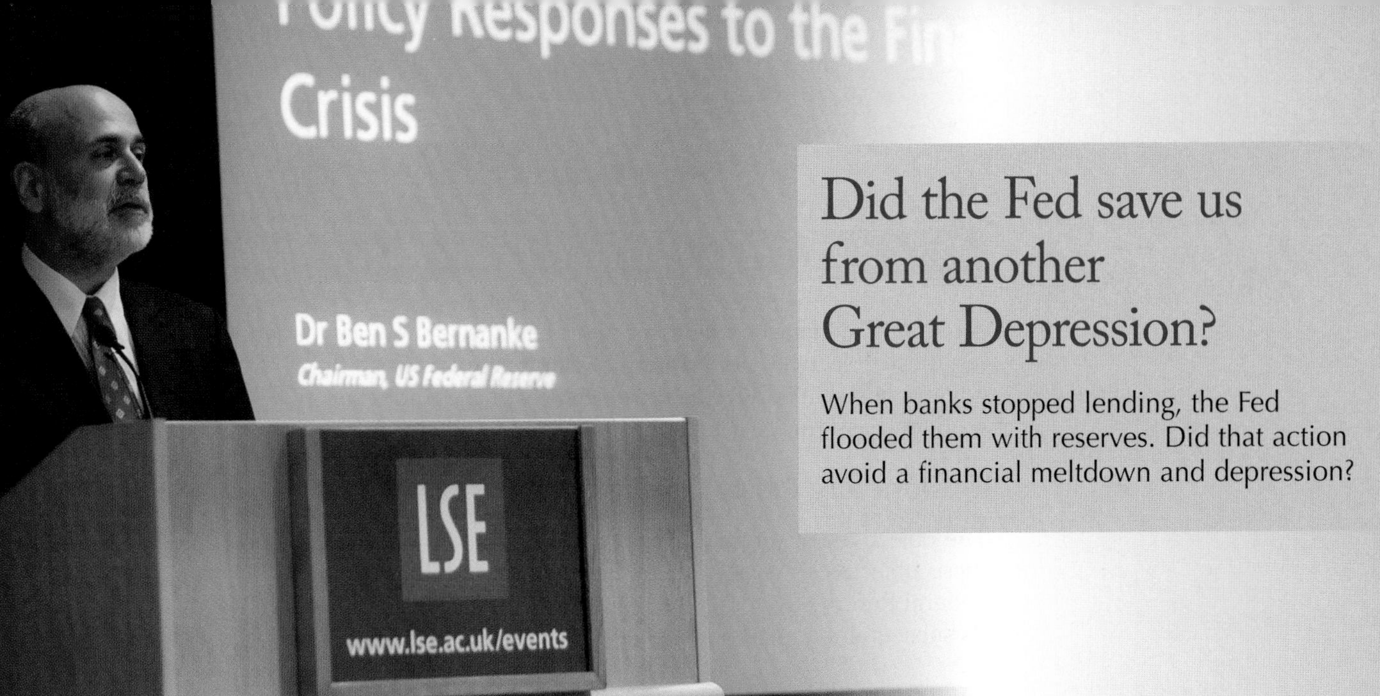


## Did the Fed save us from another Great Depression?

When banks stopped lending, the Fed flooded them with reserves. Did that action avoid a financial meltdown and depression?

# Monetary Policy

CHAPTER CHECKLIST

**When you have completed your study of this chapter, you will be able to**

1. Describe the objectives of U.S. monetary policy, the framework for achieving those objectives, and the Fed's monetary policy actions.
2. Explain the transmission channels through which the Fed influences real GDP and the inflation rate.
3. Explain and compare alternative monetary policy strategies.

## 32.1 HOW THE FED CONDUCTS MONETARY POLICY

A nation's monetary policy objectives and the framework for setting and achieving those objectives stem from the relationship between the central bank and the government. We'll describe the objectives of U.S. monetary policy and the framework and assignment of responsibility for achieving those objectives.

### Monetary Policy Objectives

The objectives of monetary policy are ultimately political. In the United States, these objectives are set out in the mandate of the Board of Governors of the Federal Reserve System, which is defined by the Federal Reserve Act of 1913 and its subsequent amendments.

#### Federal Reserve Act

The Fed's mandate was most recently clarified in an amendment to the Federal Reserve Act passed by Congress in 2000, which states that

> The Board of Governors of the Federal Reserve System and the Federal Open Market Committee shall maintain long-run growth of the monetary and credit aggregates commensurate with the economy's long-run potential to increase production, so as to promote effectively the goals of maximum employment, stable prices, and moderate long-term interest rates.

#### Goals and Means

This description of the Fed's monetary policy objectives has two distinct parts: a statement of goals and a prescription of the means by which to pursue the goals.

#### Goals of Monetary Policy

The Fed's goals are "maximum employment, stable prices, and moderate long-term interest rates." In the *long run*, these goals are in harmony and reinforce each other.

The goal of "maximum employment" means attaining the maximum sustainable growth rate of potential GDP, keeping real GDP close to potential GDP, and keeping the unemployment rate close to the natural unemployment rate. The goal of "stable prices" means keeping the inflation rate low. Achieving the goal of "moderate long-term interest rates" means keeping long-term *nominal* interest rates close to the long-term *real* interest rate.

Price stability is the key goal. It provides the best available environment for households and firms to make the saving and investment decisions that bring economic growth. So price stability encourages the maximum sustainable growth rate of potential GDP.

Price stability delivers moderate long-term interest rates because the nominal interest rate equals the real interest rate plus the inflation rate. With stable prices, the nominal interest rate is close to the real interest rate, and most of the time, this rate is likely to be moderate.

While the Fed's goals are in harmony in the long run, in the short run, the Fed faces a tradeoff. You saw in Chapter 30 that taking an action that is designed to lower the inflation rate and achieve stable prices lowers employment and real GDP and increases the unemployment rate in the short run.

### Means for Achieving the Goals

The 2000 law instructs the Fed to pursue its goals by "maintain[ing] long-run growth of the monetary and credit aggregates commensurate with the economy's long-run potential to increase production." You can perhaps recognize this statement as being consistent with the quantity theory of money that you studied in Chapter 27 (see pp. 706–709). The "economy's long-run potential to increase production" is the growth rate of potential GDP. The "monetary and credit aggregates" are the quantities of money and loans. By keeping the growth rate of the quantity of money in line with the growth rate of potential GDP, the Fed is expected to be able to maintain full employment and keep the price level stable.

### Prerequisite for Achieving the Goals

The financial crisis that started in the summer of 2007 and intensified in the fall of 2008 brought the problem of financial instability to the top of the Fed's agenda. The focus of policy became the single-minded pursuit of **financial stability**—of enabling financial markets and institutions to resume their normal functions of allocating capital resources and risk.

**Financial stability**
A situation in which financial markets and institutions function normally to allocate capital resources and risk.

The pursuit of financial stability by the Fed is not an abandonment of the mandated goals of maximum employment and stable prices. Rather, it is a prerequisite for attaining those goals. Financial instability has the potential to bring severe recession and deflation—falling prices—and undermine the attainment of the mandated goals.

To pursue its mandated monetary policy goals, the Fed must make the general concepts of maximum employment and stable prices precise and operational.

## Operational "Maximum Employment" Goal

The Fed pays close attention to the business cycle and tries to steer a steady course between inflation and recession. To gauge the state of output and employment relative to full employment, the Fed looks at a large number of indicators that include the labor force participation rate, the unemployment rate, measures of capacity utilization, activity in the housing market, the stock market, and regional information gathered by the regional Federal Reserve Banks. All these data are summarized in the Fed's *Beige Book*.

The *output gap*—the percentage deviation of real GDP from potential GDP—summarizes the state of aggregate demand relative to potential GDP. A positive output gap—an *inflationary gap*—brings rising inflation. A negative output gap—a *recessionary gap*—results in lost output and unemployment above the natural unemployment rate. The Fed tries to minimize the output gap.

## Operational "Stable Prices" Goal

The Fed believes that core inflation provides the best indication of whether price stability is being achieved. The *core inflation rate* is the annual percentage change in the Personal Consumption Expenditure deflator (PCE deflator) *excluding* the prices of food and fuel (see Chapter 22, pp. 573–574).

The Fed has not defined price stability but many economists regard it as meaning a core inflation rate of between 1 and 2 percent a year. Former Fed Chairman Alan Greenspan said that "price stability is best thought of as an environment in which inflation is so low and stable over time that it does not materially enter into the decisions of households and firms."

## Responsibility for Monetary Policy

Who is responsible for monetary policy in the United States? What are the roles of the Fed, Congress, and the President?

### The Role of the Fed

The Federal Reserve Act makes the Board of Governors of the Federal Reserve System and the Federal Open Market Committee (FOMC) responsible for the conduct of monetary policy. We described the composition of the FOMC in Chapter 26 (see p. 676). The FOMC makes a monetary policy decision at eight scheduled meetings a year and publishes its minutes three weeks after each meeting.

### The Role of Congress

Congress plays no role in making monetary policy decisions, but the Federal Reserve Act requires the Board of Governors to report on monetary policy to Congress. The Fed makes two reports each year, one in February and another in July. These reports, along with the Fed Chairman's testimony before Congress and the minutes of the FOMC, communicate the Fed's thinking on monetary policy to lawmakers and the public.

### The Role of the President

The formal role of the President of the United States is limited to appointing the members and the Chairman of the Board of Governors. But some Presidents—Richard Nixon was one—have tried to influence Fed decisions.

You now know the objectives of monetary policy and can describe the framework and assignment of responsibility for achieving those objectives. Your next task is to see how the Fed conducts its monetary policy.

## Choosing a Policy Instrument

**Monetary policy instrument**
A variable that the Fed can directly control or closely target and that influences the economy in desirable ways.

**Federal funds rate**
The interest rate at which banks can borrow and lend reserves in the federal funds market.

To conduct its monetary policy, the Fed must select a **monetary policy instrument**, a variable that the Fed can directly control or closely target and that influences the economy in desirable ways.

As the sole issuer of the *monetary base*, the Fed is a monopoly. A monopoly can fix the quantity of its product and leave the market to determine the price; or it can fix the price of its product and leave the market to choose the quantity. The "price" of monetary base is the **federal funds rate**, the interest rate at which banks can borrow and lend reserves in the federal funds market. The Fed can target the monetary base or the federal funds rate, but not both. If the Fed wants to decrease the monetary base, the federal funds rate must rise; and if the Fed wants to raise the federal funds rate, the monetary base must decrease.

## The Federal Funds Rate

The Fed's choice of monetary policy instrument is the federal funds rate. Given this choice, the Fed permits the monetary base and the quantity of money to find their own equilibrium values and has no preset targets for them.

Figure 32.1 shows the federal funds rate since 2000. You can see that the federal funds rate was 5.5 percent at the beginning of 2000 and during 2000 and 2001, the Fed increased the rate to 6.5 percent. The Fed raised the interest rate to this high level to lower the inflation rate.

**FIGURE 32.1**

The Fed's Key Monetary Policy Instrument: The Federal Funds Rate

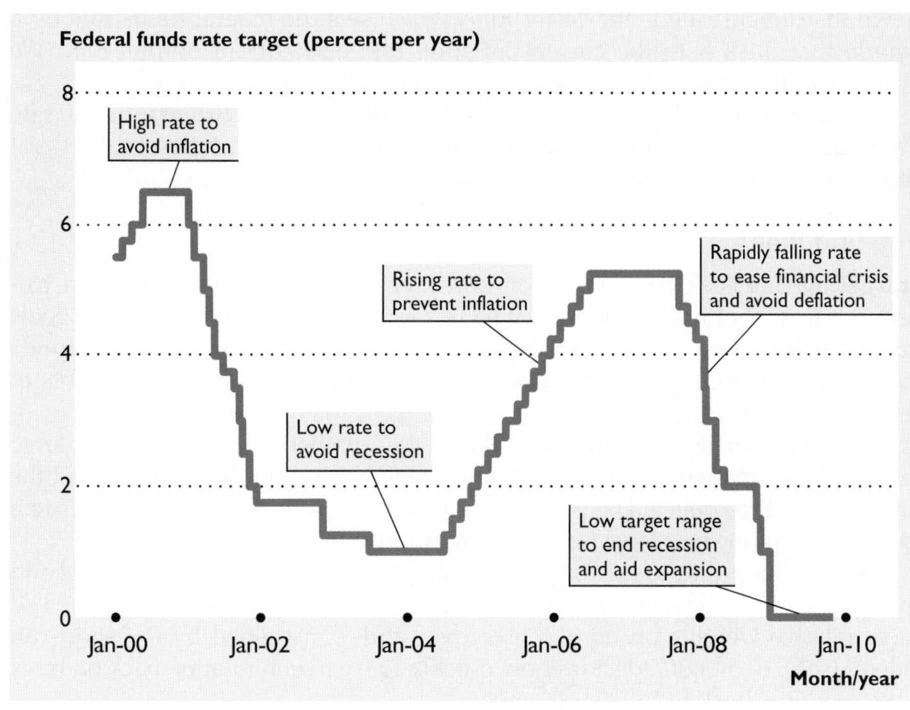


The Fed sets a target for the federal funds rate and then takes actions to keep the rate close to target.

When the Fed wants to slow inflation, it raises the federal funds rate target.

When the inflation rate is below target and the Fed wants to avoid recession, it lowers the federal funds rate target.

When the Fed focussed on restoring financial stability, it cut the federal funds rate target aggressively to almost zero.

SOURCE OF DATA: Board of Governors of the Federal Reserve System.

Between 2002 and 2004, the federal funds rate was set at historically low levels. The reason is that with inflation well anchored at close to 2 percent a year, the Fed was less concerned about inflation than it was about recession so it wanted to lean in the direction of avoiding recession.

From mid-2004 through early 2006, the Fed was increasingly concerned about the build-up of inflation pressures and it raised the federal funds rate target on 17 occasions to take it to 5.25 percent, a level that was held until September 2007.

When the global financial crisis began, the Fed acted cautiously in cutting the federal funds rate target. But as the crisis intensified, rate cuts became more frequent and larger, ending in December 2008 with an interest rate close to zero. The normal changes of a quarter of a percentage point (also called 25 *basis points*) were abandoned as the Fed slashed the rate, first by an unusual 50 basis points and finally, in December 2008, by an unprecedented 100 basis points.

How does the Fed decide the appropriate level for the federal funds rate? And how, having made that decision, does the Fed move the federal funds rate to its target level?

## The Fed's Decision-Making Strategy

Two alternative decision-making strategies might be used by a central bank and they are summarized as two alternative *rules*:

- Instrument rule
- Targeting rule

### Instrument Rule

**Instrument rule**
A decision rule for monetary policy that sets the policy instrument by a formula based on the current state of the economy.

An **instrument rule** is a decision rule for monetary policy that sets the policy instrument by a formula based on the current state of the economy. The best-known instrument rule is the *Taylor Rule*, which sets the federal funds rate by a formula that links it to the current inflation rate and current output gap. (We describe the Taylor Rule in *Eye on the U.S. Economy* on the opposite page.)

To implement the Taylor rule, the FOMC would plug the current inflation rate and output gap into the formula and calculate the level at which to set the federal funds rate. A computer would make the interest rate decision.

### Targeting Rule

**Targeting rule**
A decision rule for monetary policy that sets the policy instrument at a level that makes the central bank's forecast of the ultimate policy goals equal to their targets.

A **targeting rule** is a decision rule for monetary policy that sets the policy instrument at a level that makes the central bank's forecast of the ultimate policy goals equal to their targets. The Fed employs such a rule. The Fed sets the federal funds rate that gets its forecasts of inflation and the output gap as close as possible to their target levels.

To implement its targeting rule, the FOMC gathers and processes a large amount of information about the economy, the way it responds to shocks, and the way it responds to policy. The FOMC then processes all these data and comes to a judgment about the best level for the federal funds rate.

The Fed does not pursue formal published targets: It has implicit targets and when the economy deviates from these targets, as it does most of the time, the Fed places relative weights on its two objectives and, constrained by the short-run tradeoff (see Chapter 30), decides how quickly to try to get inflation back on track or the economy back to full employment.

We've now described the Fed's monetary policy instrument and the FOMC's strategy for setting it. We next see what the Fed does to make the federal funds rate hit its target.

## ■ Hitting the Federal Funds Rate Target

The federal funds rate is the interest rate that banks earn (or pay) when they lend (or borrow) reserves. The federal funds rate is also the opportunity cost of holding reserves. Holding a larger quantity of reserves is the alternative to lending reserves to another bank, and holding a smaller quantity of reserves is the alternative to borrowing reserves from another bank. So the quantity of reserves that banks are willing to hold varies with the federal funds rate: The higher the federal funds rate, the smaller is the quantity of reserves that the banks plan to hold.

The Fed controls the quantity of reserves supplied, and the Fed can change this quantity by conducting an open market operation. You learned in Chapter 26 (pp. 681–684) how an open market purchase increases reserves and an open market sale decreases reserves. To hit the federal funds rate target, the New York Fed conducts open market operations until the supply of reserves is at just the right quantity to hit the target federal funds rate.

Figure 32.2 illustrates this outcome in the market for bank reserves. The $x$-axis measures the quantity of bank reserves on deposit at the Fed, and the $y$-axis measures the federal funds rate. The demand for reserves—the willingness of the banks to hold reserves—is the curve labeled *RD*.

The Fed's open market operations determine the supply of reserves, which is the supply curve *RS*. To decrease reserves, the Fed conducts an open market sale.

**FIGURE 32.2**
Equilibrium in the Market for Bank Reserves

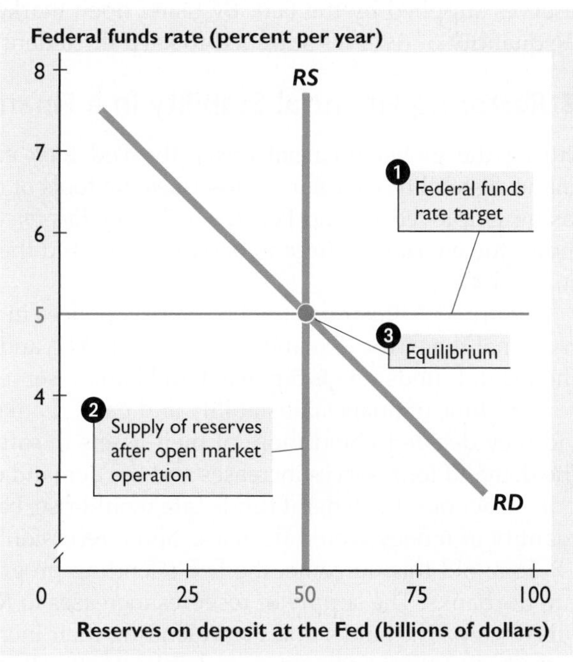


The federal funds rate (on the *y*-axis) is the opportunity cost of holding reserves: The higher the federal funds rate, the smaller is the quantity of reserves that banks want to hold. The demand curve for bank reserves is *RD*.

1. The FOMC sets the federal funds rate target at 5 percent a year.
2. The New York Fed conducts open market operations to make the quantity of reserves supplied equal to $50 billion and the supply of reserves curve is *RS*.
3. Equilibrium in the market for bank reserves occurs at the target federal funds rate.

## EYE on the U.S. ECONOMY

### The Fed's Interest Rate Decisions and the Taylor Rule

John B. Taylor (Stanford University) has proposed a formula for setting the federal funds rate—the *Taylor Rule*.

If the inflation rate is 2 percent a year and there is no output gap, the Taylor rule sets the federal funds rate to neutral at 4 percent a year.

A 1 percent deviation of the inflation rate from target and a 1 percent deviation of real GDP from potential GDP moves the federal funds rate up or down by 0.5 percent.

The Taylor Rule was derived by crunching a large amount of U.S. macroeconomic data to construct a statistical model of the economy.

The figure shows the Fed's decision and the Taylor rule since 2000. Taylor thinks the Fed moved the interest rate too low and kept it too low for too long and then raised the interest rate too fast and by too much. He believes the Fed's deviation from his rule contributed to the global financial crisis.

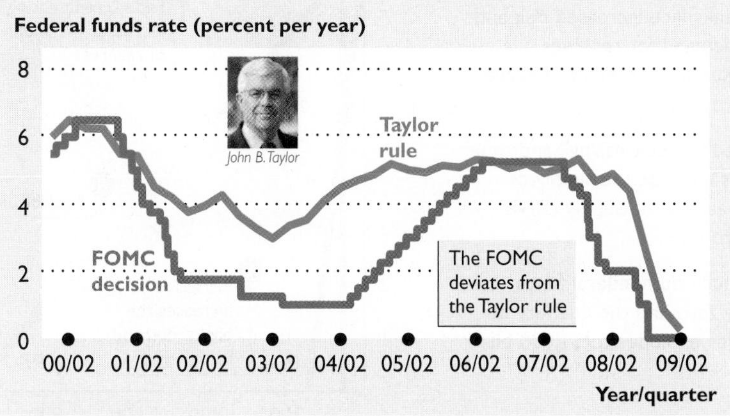


SOURCES OF DATA: Federal Reserve Board and Federal Reserve Bank of St Louis.

To increase reserves, the Fed conducts an open market purchase.

Equilibrium in the market for bank reserves determines the federal funds rate where the quantity of reserves demanded by the banks equals the quantity of reserves supplied by the Fed. By using open market operations, the Fed adjusts the quantity of reserves supplied to keep the federal funds rate on target.

## Restoring Financial Stability in a Financial Crisis

During the global financial crisis, the Fed took extraordinary steps to restore financial stability. Chapter 26 describes the tools of quantitative easing and credit easing employed by the Fed (p. 677) and *Eye on Creating Money* (pp. 686–687) shows the enormous surge in bank reserves and the monetary base that occurred during 2008.

Figure 32.3 illustrates the Fed's crisis polices in the market for bank reserves. In normal times, the demand for reserves is $RD_0$ and the supply of reserves is $RS_0$. The federal funds rate is 5 percent and bank reserves are $50 billion.

At a time of financial instability and panic, banks' assessments of risk increase and they decide to hold more of their assets in safe, reserve deposits at the Fed. The demand for reserves increases and the demand curve becomes $RD_1$. If the Fed took no actions, the federal funds rate would rise, bank lending would shrink, the quantity of money would decrease, and a recession would intensify.

To avoid this outcome, the Fed's lending programs pump billions of dollars into the banks. The supply of reserves increases to $RS_1$, and the federal funds rate falls to zero. The banks don't start lending their increased reserves. They hang on to them. But flush with reserves, banks don't call in loans and deepen the recession. The Fed's action averted a worsening credit crisis and worsening recession.

**FIGURE 32.3**

The Market for Bank Reserves in a Financial Crisis

myeconlab Animation

In a normal time, the demand for bank reserves is $RD_0$ and the supply of reserves is $RS_0$. The federal funds rate is 5 percent per year.

In a financial crisis:

1. The banks face increased risk and their demand for reserves increases and the demand curve shifts to $RD_1$.
2. The Fed's "credit easing" and other actions increase the supply of reserves and the supply curve shifts to $RS_1$.
3. The equilibrium federal funds rate falls to zero and the quantity of reserves explodes to $1,000 billion.

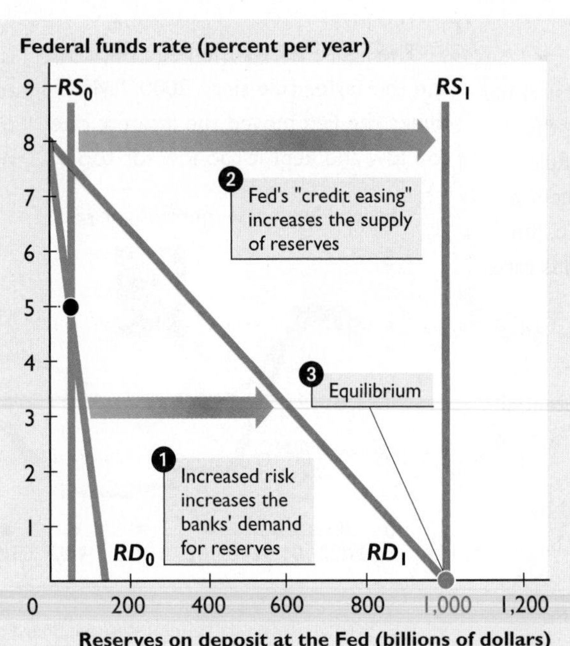

## CHECKPOINT 32.1

myeconlab

Work these problems in Study Plan 32.1 to get instant feedback.

**Describe the objectives of U.S. monetary policy, the framework for achieving those objectives, and the Fed's monetary policy actions.**

### Practice Problems

1. What are the objectives of U.S. monetary policy?
2. What is core inflation and how does it differ from total PCE inflation?
3. What is the Fed's monetary policy instrument and what influences the level at which the Fed sets it?
4. Figure 1 shows the demand curve for bank reserves, *RD*. The current quantity of reserves supplied is $20 billion. The Fed wants to set the federal funds rate at 4 percent a year. Illustrate the target on the graph and show the supply of reserves that will achieve the target. Does the Fed conduct an open market operation and if so, does it buy or sell securities?
5. **Money on autopilot**
   In the third quarter of 2009, GDP grew at 3.5% a year. With no risk of inflation, the FOMC is mainly focused on the output gap.
   Source: *The Wall Street Journal*, November 5, 2009
   Explain whether this description of the Fed's focus in the third quarter of 2009 is consistent with its monetary policy objectives.

**FIGURE 1**

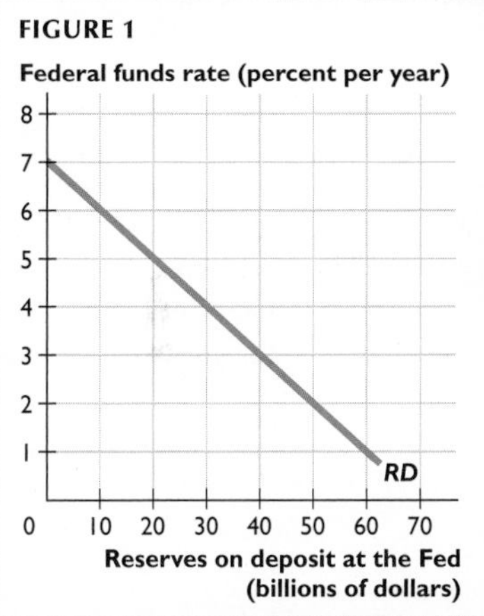


### Guided Solutions to Practice Problems

1. The objectives of U.S. monetary policy are to achieve stable prices (interpreted at a core inflation rate of about 2 percent per year) and maximum employment (interpreted as full employment).
2. Core inflation excludes the changes in the prices of food and fuel. The total PCE inflation rate includes the changes in all consumer prices. The core inflation rate fluctuates less than the total PCE inflation rate.
3. The federal funds rate is the Fed's monetary policy instrument and the inflation rate and output gap are two of the influences on the level at which the Fed sets the federal funds rate.
4. Figure 2 shows the market for bank reserves. If the initial quantity of reserves supplied was $20 billion, the federal funds rate must have been 5 percent a year at point *A*. To set the federal funds rate at 4 percent a year, the Fed must conduct an open market purchase of securities to increase the supply of reserves to *RS*. With supply *RS*, the equilibrium federal funds rate equals the 4 percent target rate.
5. The objectives of monetary policy are maximum employment and stable prices. The maximum-employment goal means keeping the economy as close as possible to potential GDP. The stable-prices goal means keeping the inflation rate low. In 2009, the inflation rate was low but the unemployment rate and the output gap were high. By focusing on the output gap, the Fed was seeking to re-establish "maximum employment." The Fed believed that inflation would remain low, so its focus was consistent with its monetary policy objectives.

**FIGURE 2**

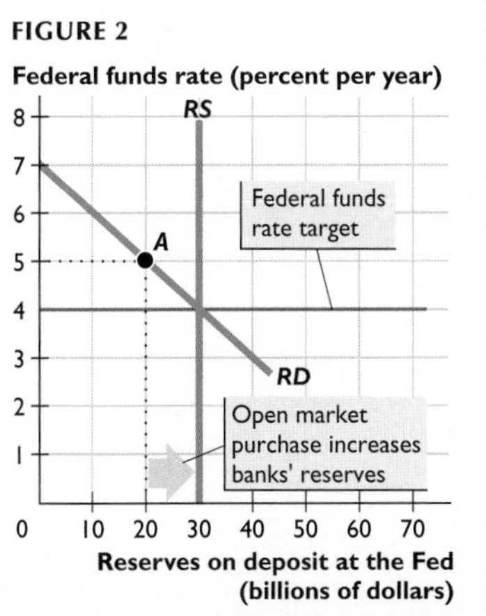

## 32.2 MONETARY POLICY TRANSMISSION

You've seen that the Fed's goal is to keep the inflation rate around 2 percent a year and to keep the output gap close to zero. You've also seen how the Fed uses its market power to set the federal funds rate at the level that is designed to achieve these objectives. We're now going to trace the events that follow a change in the federal funds rate and see how those events lead to the ultimate policy goals. We'll begin with a quick overview of the transmission process and then look a bit more closely at each step.

### Quick Overview

When the Fed lowers the federal funds rate, other short-term interest rates and the exchange rate also fall. The quantity of money and the supply of loanable funds increase. The long-term real interest rate falls. The lower real interest rate increases consumption expenditure and investment. The lower exchange rate makes U.S. exports cheaper and imports more costly, so net exports increase. Easier bank loans reinforce the effect of lower interest rates on aggregate expenditure. Aggregate demand increases, which increases real GDP and the price level relative to what they would have been. Real GDP growth and inflation speed up.

When the Fed raises the federal funds rate, as the sequence of events that we've just reviewed plays out, the effects are in the opposite directions.

Figure 32.4 provides a schematic summary of these ripple effects for both a cut and a rise in the federal funds rate. These ripple effects stretch out over a period of between one and two years. The interest rate and exchange rate effects are immediate. The effects on money and bank loans follow in a few weeks and run for a few months. Real long-term interest rates change quickly and often in anticipation of the short-term rate changes. Spending plans change and real GDP growth changes after about one year. The inflation rate changes between one year and two years after the change in the federal funds rate. But these time lags are not entirely predictable and can be longer or shorter. We're going to look at each stage in the transmission process, starting with the interest rate effects.

### Interest Rate Changes

The first effect of a monetary policy decision by the FOMC is a change in the federal funds rate. Other interest rates then change. These interest rate effects occur quickly and relatively predictably.

The interest rates on U.S. government 3-month Treasury bills is immediately affected by a change in the federal funds rate. A powerful substitution effect keeps these two rates close to each other. Banks have a choice about how to hold their short-term liquid assets and a loan to another bank is a close substitute for holding Treasury bills. If the interest rate on Treasury bills is higher than the federal funds rate, the banks increase the quantity of Treasury bills held and decrease loans to other banks. The price of a Treasury bill rises and the interest rate falls. Similarly, if the interest rate on Treasury bills is lower than the federal funds rate, the banks decrease the quantity of Treasury bills held and increase loans to other banks. The price of a Treasury bill falls, and the interest rate rises. When the interest rate on Treasury bills is close to the federal funds rate, there is no incentive for a bank to switch between making loans to other banks and holding Treasury bills. Both the Treasury bill market and the federal funds market are in equilibrium.

## FIGURE 32.4
Ripple Effects of the Fed's Actions

| | (a) The Fed tightens | (b) The Fed eases |
|---|---|---|
| FOMC meeting | ❶ The Fed raises the federal funds rate | ❶ The Fed lowers the federal funds rate |
| Same day/ next day | ❷ Other short-term interest rates rise and the exchange rate rises | ❷ Other short-term interest rates fall and the exchange rate falls |
| A few weeks through a few months later | ❸ The quantity of money and supply of loanable funds decrease | ❸ The quantity of money and supply of loanable funds increase |
| A few weeks through a few months later | ❹ The long-term real interest rate rises | ❹ The long-term real interest rate falls |
| Up to a year later | ❺ Consumption expenditure, investment, and net exports decrease | ❺ Consumption expenditure, investment, and net exports increase |
| Up to a year later | ❻ Aggregate demand decreases | ❻ Aggregate demand increases |
| About a year later | ❼ Real GDP growth rate decreases | ❼ Real GDP growth rate increases |
| About two years later | ❽ Inflation rate decreases | ❽ Inflation rate increases |

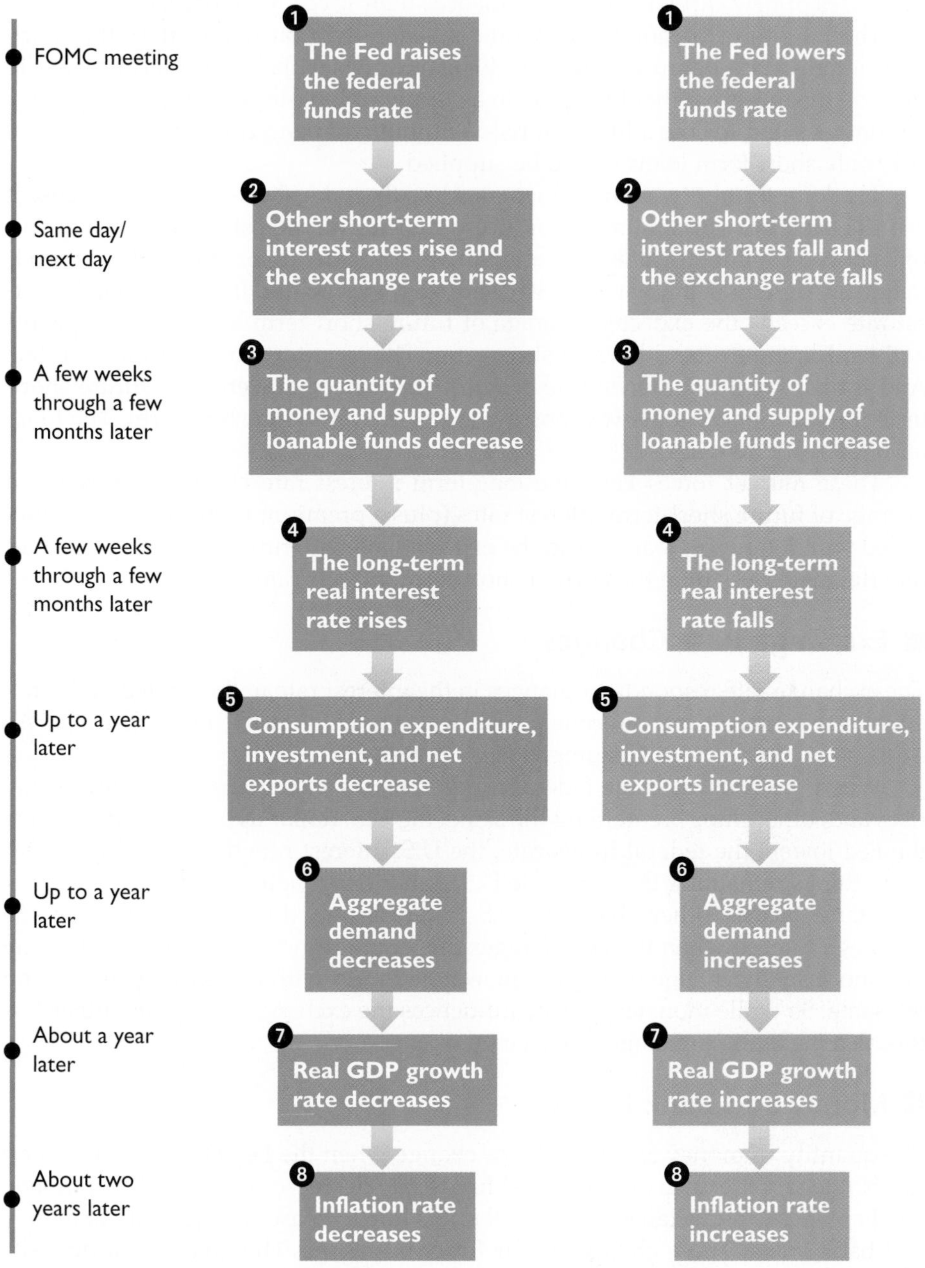

**(a) The Fed tightens** **(b) The Fed eases**

The Fed changes its interest rate target and conducts open market operations to ❶ change the federal funds rate. The same day ❷ other short-term interest rates change and so does the exchange rate. A few weeks through a few months after the FOMC meeting, ❸ the quantity of money and supply of loanable funds changes, which ❹ changes the long-term real interest rate.

Up to a year after the FOMC meeting, ❺ consumption, investment, and net exports change, so ❻ aggregate demand changes. Eventually, the change in the federal funds rate has ripple effects that ❼ change real GDP and about two years after the FOMC meeting, ❽ the inflation rate changes.

Long-term interest rates also change, but not by as much as short-term rates. The long-term corporate bond rate, the interest rate paid on bonds issued by large corporations, is the most significant interest rate to be influenced by the federal funds rate. It is this interest rate that businesses pay on the loans that finance their purchases of new capital and that influences their investment decisions.

The long-term corporate bond rate is generally a bit higher than the short-term interest rate because long-term loans are riskier than short-term loans. To provide the incentive that brings forth a supply of long-term loans, lenders must be compensated for the additional risk. Without compensation for the additional risk, only short-term loans would be supplied.

The long-term interest rate fluctuates less than the short-term rate because it is influenced by expectations about future short-term interest rates as well as current short-term interest rates. The alternative to borrowing or lending long term is to borrow or lend using a sequence of short-term securities. If the long-term interest rate exceeds the expected average of future short-term interest rates, people will lend long term and borrow short term. The long-term interest rate will fall. And if the long-term interest rate is below the expected average of future short-term interest rates, people will borrow long term and lend short term. The long-term interest rate will rise.

These market forces keep the long-term interest rate close to the expected average of future short-term interest rates (plus a premium for the extra risk associated with long-term loans). And the expected average future short-term interest rate fluctuates less than the current short-term interest rate.

## Exchange Rate Changes

The exchange rate responds to changes in the interest rate in the United States relative to the interest rates in other countries—the *U.S. interest rate differential*. We explain this influence in Chapter 33 (see pp. 860, 863, 865).

When the Fed raises the federal funds rate, the U.S. interest rate differential rises and, other things remaining the same, the U.S. dollar appreciates. And when the Fed lowers the federal funds rate, the U.S. interest rate differential falls and, other things remaining the same, the U.S. dollar depreciates.

Many factors other than the U.S. interest rate differential influence the exchange rate, so when the Fed changes the federal funds rate, the exchange rate does not usually change in exactly the way it would with other things remaining the same. So while monetary policy influences the exchange rate, many other factors also make the exchange rate change.

## Money and Bank Loans

The quantity of money and bank loans change when the Fed changes the federal funds rate target. A rise in the federal funds rate decreases the quantity of money and bank loans; and a fall in the federal funds rate increases the quantity of money and bank loans. These changes occur for two reasons: The quantity of deposits and loans created by the banking system changes and the quantity of money demanded changes.

You've seen that to change the federal funds rate, the Fed must change the quantity of bank reserves. A change in the quantity of bank reserves changes the monetary base, which in turn changes the quantity of deposits and loans that the banking system can create. A rise in the federal funds rate decreases reserves and decreases the quantity of deposits and bank loans created; and a fall in the federal funds rate increases reserves and increases the quantity of deposits and bank loans created.

The quantity of money created by the banking system must be held by households and firms. The change in the interest rate changes the quantity of money demanded. A fall in the interest rate increases the quantity of money demanded and a rise in the interest rate decreases the quantity of money demanded.

A change in the quantity of money and the supply of bank loans directly affects consumption and investment plans. With more money and easier access to loans, consumers and firms spend more. With less money and loans harder to get, consumers and firms spend less.

## The Long-Term Real Interest Rate

Demand and supply in the market for loanable funds determine the long-term real interest rate, which equals the long-term nominal interest rate minus the expected inflation rate. The long-term real interest rate influences expenditure decisions.

In the long run, demand and supply in the loanable funds market depend only on real forces—on saving and investment decisions. But in the short run, when the price level is not fully flexible, the supply of loanable funds is influenced by the supply of bank loans. Changes in the federal funds rate change the supply of bank loans, which changes the supply of loanable funds and changes the real interest rate in the loanable funds market.

A fall in the federal funds rate that increases the supply of bank loans increases the supply of loanable funds and lowers the equilibrium real interest rate. A rise in the federal funds rate that decreases the supply of bank loans decreases the supply of loanable funds and raises the equilibrium real interest rate.

These changes in the real interest rate, along with the other factors we've just described, change expenditure plans.

## Expenditure Plans

The ripple effects that follow a change in the federal funds rate change three components of aggregate expenditure:

- Consumption expenditure
- Investment
- Net exports

Other things remaining the same, the lower the real interest rate, the greater is the amount of consumption expenditure and the smaller is the amount of saving.

Again, other things remaining the same, the lower the real interest rate, the greater is the amount of investment.

Finally, and again other things remaining the same, the lower the interest rate, the lower is the exchange rate and the greater are exports and the smaller are imports.

A cut in the federal funds rate increases all the components of aggregate expenditure; a rise in the federal funds rate decreases all the components of aggregate expenditure. These changes in aggregate expenditure plans change aggregate demand, which in turn changes real GDP and the inflation rate.

## The Fed Fights Recession

We're now going to pull all the steps in the transmission story together. We'll start with inflation below target and real GDP below potential GDP. The Fed takes actions that are designed to restore full employment. Figure 32.5 shows the effects of the Fed's actions, starting in the market for bank reserves and ending in the market for real GDP.

In Figure 32.5(a), which shows the market for bank reserves, the FOMC lowers the target federal funds rate from 5 percent to 4 percent a year. To achieve the new target, the New York Fed buys securities and increases the supply of reserves in the banking system from $RS_0$ to $RS_1$.

With increased reserves, the banks create deposits by making loans and the supply of money increases. The short-term interest rate falls and the quantity of money demanded increases. In Figure 32.5(b), the supply of money increases from $MS_0$ to $MS_1$, the interest rate falls from 5 percent to 4 percent a year, and the quantity of money increases from $3 trillion to $3.1 trillion. The interest rate in the money market and the federal funds rate are kept close to each other by the powerful substitution effect described on page 830.

**FIGURE 32.5**

The Fed Fights Recession

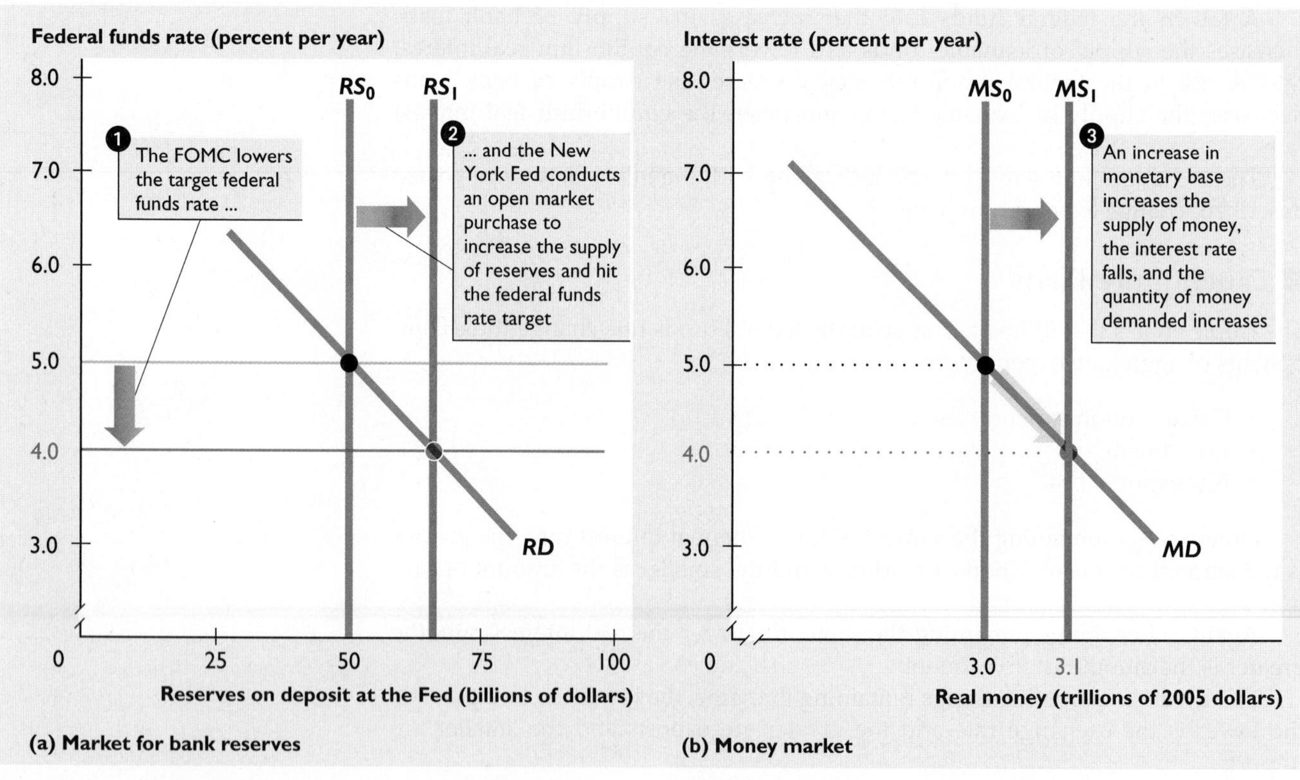


(a) Market for bank reserves

(b) Money market

❶ The FOMC lowers the federal funds rate target from 5 percent to 4 percent a year. ❷ The New York Fed buys securities in an open market operation and increases reserves from $RS_0$ to $RS_1$ to hit the new federal funds rate target.

❸ The supply of money increases from $MS_0$ to $MS_1$, the short-term interest rate falls, and the quantity of money demanded increases. The short-term interest rate and the federal funds rate change by similar amounts.

Banks create money by making loans. In the long run, an increase in the supply of bank loans is matched by a rise in the price level and the quantity of real loans is unchanged. But in the short run, with a sticky price level, an increase in the supply of bank loans increases the supply of (real) loanable funds. In Figure 32.5(c), the supply of loanable funds curve shifts rightward from $SLF_0$ to $SLF_1$. With the demand for loanable funds at *DLF*, the real interest rate falls from 6 percent to 5.5 percent a year.

Figure 32.5(d) shows aggregate demand and aggregate supply and the recessionary gap that triggered the Fed's action. The increase in money and loans and the decrease in the real interest rate increase aggregate planned expenditure. (Not shown in the figure, a fall in the interest rate lowers the exchange rate, which increases net exports and aggregate planned expenditure.) The increase in aggregate expenditure, $\Delta E$, increases aggregate demand and shifts the aggregate demand curve rightward to $AD_0 + \Delta E$. A multiplier process begins. The increase in expenditure increases income, which induces an increase in consumption expenditure. Aggregate demand increases further, and the aggregate demand curve eventually shifts rightward to $AD_1$. The new equilibrium is at full employment but with a higher price level (and faster inflation).



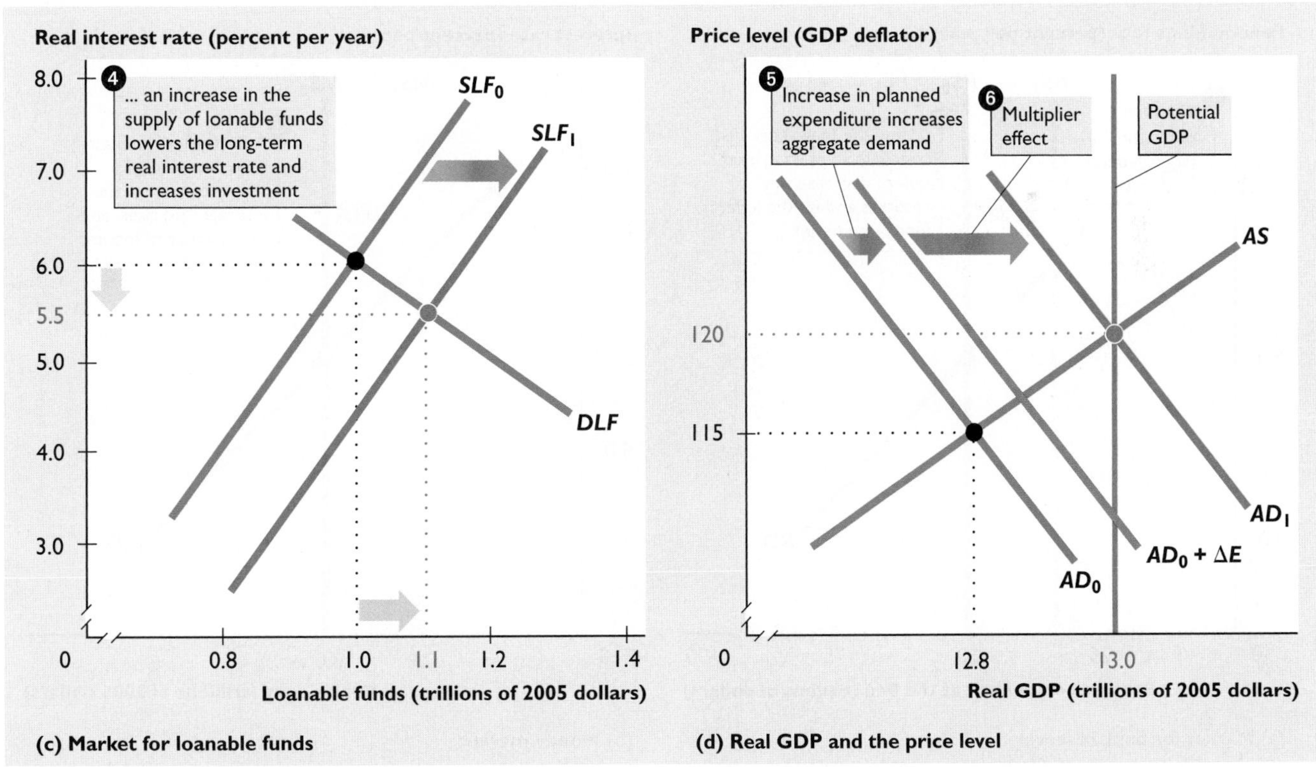


(c) Market for loanable funds

(d) Real GDP and the price level

❹ An increase in the supply of bank loans increases the supply of loanable funds from $SLF_0$ to $SLF_1$ and the real interest rate falls. Investment increases.

❺ Aggregate planned expenditure increases and the aggregate demand curve shifts to $AD_0 + \Delta E$. ❻ A multiplier effect increases aggregate demand to $AD_1$. Real GDP increases and the price level rises (inflation speeds up).

## The Fed Fights Inflation

If the inflation rate is too high and real GDP is above potential GDP, the Fed takes actions that are designed to lower the inflation rate and restore price stability. Figure 32.6 shows the effects of the Fed's actions starting in the market for reserves and ending in the market for real GDP.

In Figure 32.6(a), which shows the market for bank reserves, the FOMC raises the target federal funds rate from 5 percent to 6 percent a year. To achieve the new target, the New York Fed sells securities and decreases the supply of reserves in the banking system from $RS_0$ to $RS_1$.

With decreased reserves, the banks shrink deposits by decreasing loans and the supply of money decreases. The short-term interest rate rises and the quantity of money demanded decreases. In Figure 32.6(b), the supply of money decreases from $MS_0$ to $MS_1$, the interest rate rises from 5 percent to 6 percent a year, and the quantity of money decreases from \$3 trillion to \$2.9 trillion.

With a decrease in reserves, banks must decrease the supply of loans. The supply of (real) loanable funds decreases, and the supply of loanable funds curve shifts leftward in Figure 32.6(c) from $SLF_0$ to $SLF_1$. With the demand for loanable

**FIGURE 32.6**

The Fed Fights Inflation

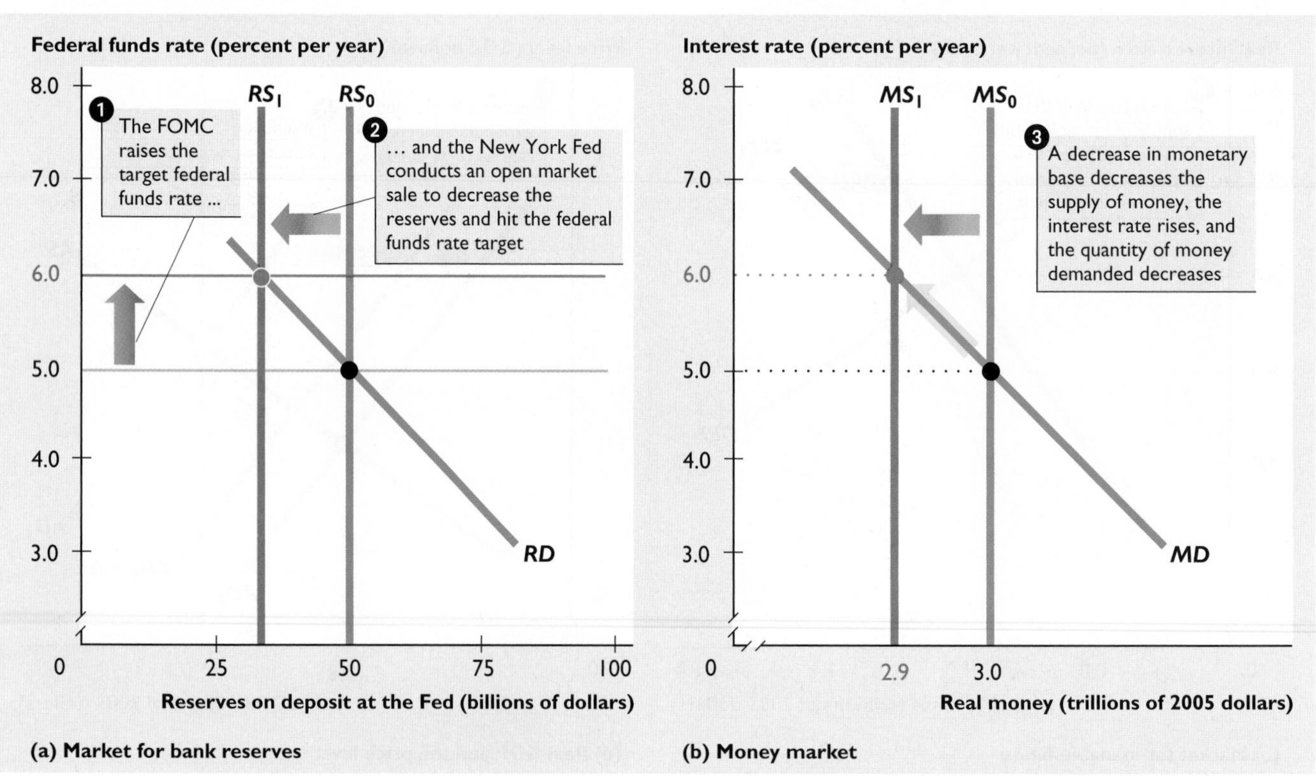


(a) Market for bank reserves

(b) Money market

❶ The FOMC raises the federal funds rate target from 5 percent to 6 percent a year. ❷ The New York Fed sells securities in an open market operation and decreases reserves from $RS_0$ to $RS_1$ to hit the new federal funds rate target.

❸ The supply of money decreases from $MS_0$ to $MS_1$, the short-term interest rate rises, and the quantity of money demanded decreases. The short-term interest rate and the federal funds rate change by similar amounts.

funds at *DLF*, the real interest rate rises from 6 percent to 6.5 percent a year.

Figure 32.6(d) shows aggregate demand and aggregate supply in the market for real GDP and the inflationary gap to which the Fed is reacting. The decrease in the quantity of money and loans and the rise in the real interest rate decrease aggregate planned expenditure. The decrease in aggregate expenditure, $\Delta E$, decreases aggregate demand and shifts the aggregate demand curve leftward to $AD_0 - \Delta E$. A multiplier process begins. The decrease in expenditure decreases income, which induces a decrease in consumption expenditure. Aggregate demand decreases further, and the aggregate demand curve eventually shifts leftward to $AD_1$. The economy returns to full employment. Real GDP is equal to potential GDP. The price level falls (the inflation rate slows).

In both of the examples, we have given the Fed a perfect hit at achieving full employment and keeping the price level stable. If the Fed changed aggregate demand by too little and too late, or by too much and too early, the economy would not have returned to full employment. Too little action would leave a recessionary or an inflationary gap. Too much action would overshoot the objective. If the Fed hits the brakes too hard, it pushes the economy from inflation to recession. If it stimulates too much, it turns recession into inflation.

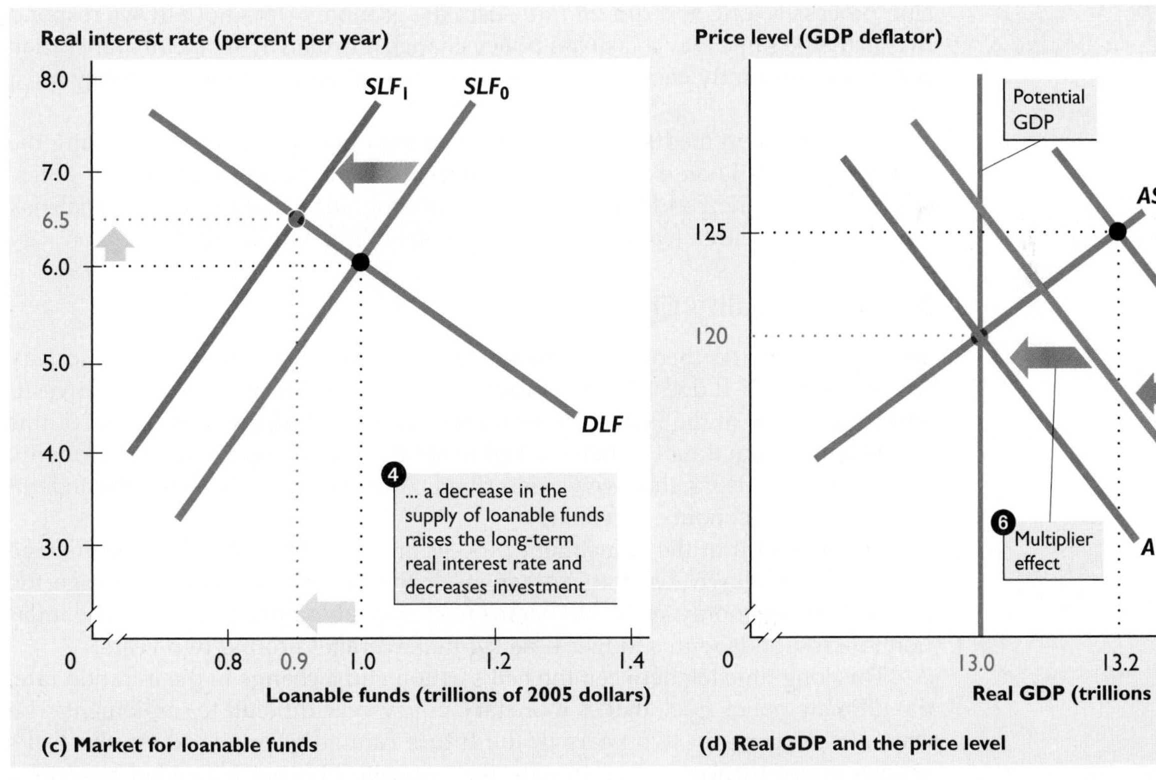


**(c) Market for loanable funds**

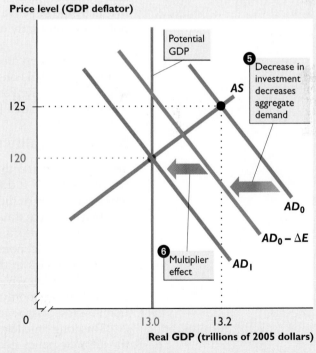

**(d) Real GDP and the price level**

❹ A decrease in the supply of bank loans decreases the supply of loanable funds from $SLF_0$ to $SLF_1$ and the real interest rate rises. Investment decreases.

❺ Aggregate planned expenditure decreases and the aggregate demand curve shifts to $AD_0 - \Delta E$. ❻ A multiplier decreases aggregate demand to $AD_1$. Real GDP decreases and the price level falls (inflation slows down).

## Loose Links and Long and Variable Lags

The ripple effects of monetary policy that we've just analyzed with the precision of an economic model are, in reality, very hard to predict and anticipate.

To achieve its goals of price stability and full employment, the Fed needs a combination of good judgment and good luck. Too large an interest rate cut in an underemployed economy can bring inflation, as it did during the 1970s. And too large an interest rate rise in an inflationary economy can create unemployment, as it did in 1981 and 1991.

Loose links in the chain that runs from the federal funds rate to the ultimate policy goals make unwanted policy outcomes inevitable. And time lags that are both long and variable add to the Fed's challenges.

### Loose Links from Federal Funds Rate to Spending

The long-term real interest rate that influences spending plans is linked only loosely to the federal funds rate. Also, the response of the long-term real interest rate to a change in the nominal rate depends on how inflation expectations change. The response of expenditure plans to changes in the real interest rate depends on many factors that make the response hard to predict.

### Time Lags in the Adjustment Process

The Fed is especially handicapped by the fact that the monetary policy transmission process is long and drawn out. Also, the economy does not always respond in exactly the same way to a given policy change. Further, many factors other than policy are constantly changing and bringing new situations to which policy must respond.

The turmoil in credit markets and home loan markets that began during the summer of 2007 is an example of unexpected events to which monetary policy must respond. The Fed found itself facing an ongoing inflation risk but that risk was combined with a fear that a collapse of spending would bring recession.

## A Final Reality Check

You've studied the theory of monetary policy. Does it really work in the way we've described? It does. An enormous amount of statistical research has investigated the effects of the Fed's actions on the economy and the conclusions of this research are not in doubt. When the Fed raises the federal funds rate, the economy slows for the reasons that we've described. And when the Fed cuts the federal funds rate, the economy speeds up.

The time lags in the adjustment process are not predictable, but the average time lags are known. On the average, after the Fed takes action to change the course of the economy, real GDP begins to change about one year later. The inflation rate responds with a longer time lag that averages around two years.

This long time lag between the Fed's action and a change in the inflation rate, the ultimate policy goal, makes monetary policy very difficult to implement. The state of the economy two years in the future cannot be predicted, so the Fed's actions might turn out to be exactly the opposite of what is needed to steer a steady course between recession and inflation.

You've now seen how the Fed operates and studied the effects of its actions. We close this chapter by looking at alternative approaches to monetary policy.

## CHECKPOINT 32.2

Work these problems in Study Plan 32.2 to get instant feedback.

**Explain the transmission channels through which the Fed influences real GDP and the inflation rate.**

## Practice Problems

1. List the sequence of events in the transmission from a rise in the federal funds rate to a change in the inflation rate.

The economy has slipped into recession and the Fed takes actions to lessen its severity. Use this information to work Problems **2** and **3**.

2. What action does the Fed take? Illustrate the effects of the Fed's actions in the money market and the loanable funds market.
3. Explain how the Fed's actions change aggregate demand and real GDP.
4. **The Fed's tricky balancing act**
   The FOMC was a bit more optimistic about the economy recovering, but said that policy tightening was not going to happen any time soon.
   Source: *Business Week*, June 6, 2009
   What are the ripple effects and time lags that the Fed must consider in deciding when to start raising the federal funds rate?

## Guided Solutions to Practice Problems

1. When the Fed raises the federal funds rate, other short-term interest rates rise and the exchange rate rises; the quantity of money and supply of loanable funds decrease and the long-term real interest rate rises; consumption, investment, and net exports decrease; aggregate demand decreases; and eventually the real GDP growth rate and the inflation rate decrease.
2. The Fed lowers the federal funds rate, which lowers other short-term interest rates, and increases the supply of money (Figure 1). The lower federal funds rate increases the supply of bank loans, which increases the supply of loanable funds. The real interest rate falls (Figure 2).
3. A lower real interest rate (and lower exchange rate) and greater quantity of money and loans increase aggregate expenditure. Aggregate demand increases and the *AD* curve shifts to $AD_0 + \Delta E$. A multiplier effect increases aggregate demand and the *AD* curve shifts rightward to $AD_1$. Real GDP increases and recession is avoided (Figure 3).
4. Figure 32.4 (p. 831) describes the ripple effects and the time lags. The Fed can influence interest rates quickly but several months pass before the quantity of money and loans respond, up to a year before expenditure plans respond, and up to two years before the inflation rate responds to the Fed's interest rate actions.

**FIGURE 1**

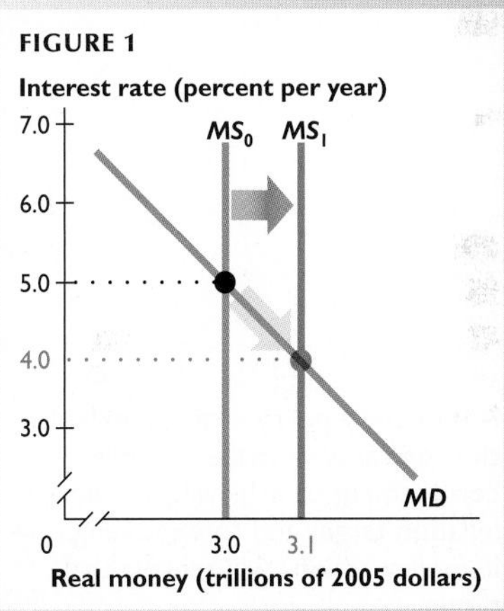


**FIGURE 2**

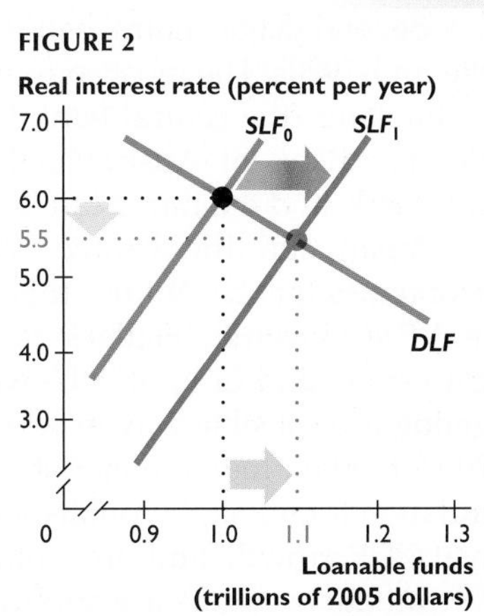


**FIGURE 3**

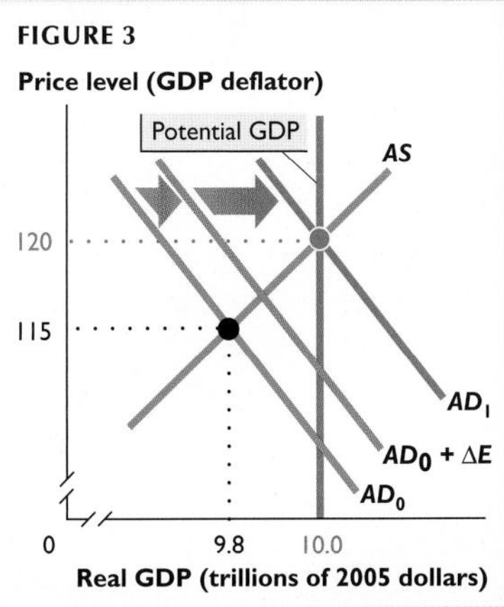

## 32.3 ALTERNATIVE MONETARY POLICY STRATEGIES

So far in this chapter, we've described and analyzed the Fed's method of conducting monetary policy. But the Fed does have choices among alternative monetary policy strategies. We're going to end our discussion of monetary policy by examining the alternatives and explaining why the Fed has rejected them in favor of the interest rate strategy that we've described.

You've seen that we can summarize monetary policy strategies in two broad categories: *instrument rules* and *targeting rules*.

### Why Rules?

**Discretionary monetary policy**
A monetary policy that is based on an expert assessment of the current economic situation.

You might be wondering why all monetary policy strategies involve *rules*. Why doesn't the Fed pursue a **discretionary monetary policy** and just do what seems best every day, month, and year, based on its expert assessment of the current economic situation? The answer is that monetary policy must keep inflation expectations anchored close to the target inflation rate. In both financial markets and labor markets, people must make long-term commitments. These markets work best when plans are based on correctly anticipated inflation outcomes. A well-understood monetary policy rule helps to create an environment in which inflation is easier to forecast and manage.

Although rules beat discretion, there are three alternative rules that the Fed might have chosen. They are

- An inflation targeting rule
- A money targeting rule
- A gold price targeting rule (gold standard)

### Inflation Targeting Rule

**Inflation targeting**
A monetary policy strategy in which the central bank makes a public commitment to achieving an explicit inflation target and to explaining how its policy actions will achieve that target.

**Inflation targeting** is a monetary policy strategy in which the central bank makes a public commitment to achieving an explicit inflation target and to explaining how its policy actions will achieve that target.

Of the alternatives to the Fed's current strategy, inflation targeting is the most likely to be considered. In fact, some economists see it as a small step from what the Fed currently does.

Several major central banks practice inflation targeting and have done so since the mid-1990s. The most committed inflation-targeting central banks are the Bank of England (the central bank of the United Kingdom), the Bank of Canada, the Reserve Bank of Australia, the Reserve Bank of New Zealand, the Swedish Riksbank, and the European Central Bank (the central bank of the euro countries).

Japan and the United States are the most prominent major industrial economies that do not use this monetary policy strategy. But when Ben Bernanke and Fed Governor Frederic S. Mishkin were economics professors (at Princeton University and Columbia University, respectively) they argued that inflation targeting is a sensible way in which to conduct monetary policy. And in November 2007, the Fed took a major step toward greater transparency, a central feature of inflation targeting, by publishing FOMC members' detailed forecasts of inflation, real GDP growth, and unemployment through 2010.

Inflation targets are specified in terms of a range for the CPI inflation rate. This range is typically between 1 percent and 3 percent a year, with an aim to

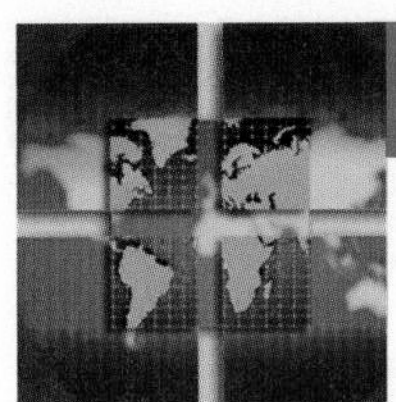

## EYE on the GLOBAL ECONOMY

### Inflation Targeting Around the World

Five advanced economies and the Eurozone have inflation targets (shown by the green bars) designed to anchor inflation expectations.

Most inflation targets have been achieved (orange lines), which makes it easier for the central bank to stabilize both the inflation rate and real GDP.

High-quality central bank inflation reports encourage an enhanced level of public discussion about inflation and awareness of each central bank's views.

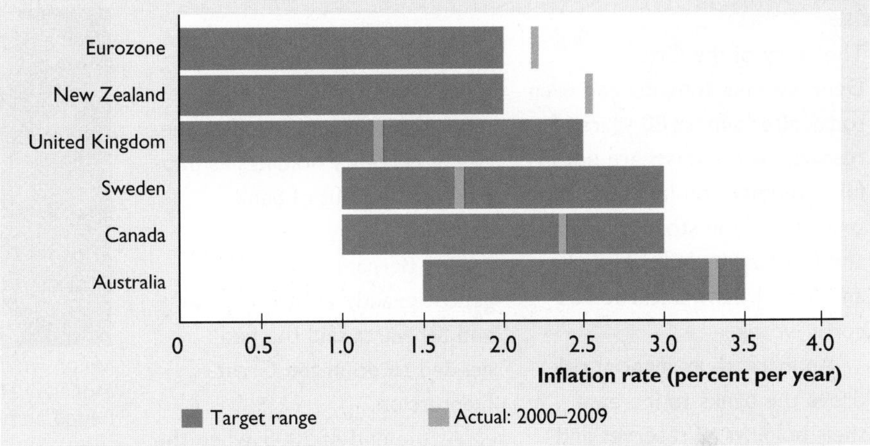


SOURCES OF DATA: National central banks and World Economic Outlook database, April 2009.

achieve an average inflation rate of 2 percent a year. Because the lags in the operation of monetary policy are long, if the inflation rate falls outside the target range, the expectation is that the central bank will move the inflation rate back on target over the next two years.

The idea of inflation targeting is to state clearly and publicly the goals of monetary policy, to establish a framework of accountability, and to keep the inflation rate low and stable while maintaining a high and stable level of employment.

There is wide agreement that inflation targeting achieves its first two goals. It's also clear that the inflation reports of inflation targeters have raised the level of discussion and understanding of the monetary policy process.

It is less clear whether inflation targeting does better than the implicit targeting that the Fed currently pursues in achieving low and stable inflation. The Fed's own record, without a formal inflation target, had been impressive until the global financial crisis called into question its neglect of a potential bubble and bust.

## Money Targeting Rule

As long ago as 1948, Nobel Laureate Milton Friedman proposed a targeting rule for the quantity of money. Friedman's ***k*-percent rule** makes the quantity of money grow at a rate of *k* percent a year, where *k* equals the growth rate of potential GDP. Friedman's *k*-percent rule relies on a stable demand for money, which translates to a stable velocity of circulation. Friedman had examined data on money and nominal GDP and argued that the velocity of circulation of money was one of the most stable macroeconomic variables and that it could be exploited to deliver a stable price level and small business cycle fluctuations.

***k*-percent rule**
A monetary policy rule that makes the quantity of money grow at *k* percent per year, where *k* equals the growth rate of potential GDP.

Friedman's idea remained just that until the 1970s, when inflation increased to more than 10 percent a year in the United States and to much higher rates in some other major countries.

# EYE on THE FED in a CRISIS

## Did the Fed Save Us From Another Great Depression?

The story of the Great Depression is complex and even today, after almost 80 years of research, economists are not in full agreement on its causes. But one part of the story is clear and it is told by Milton Friedman and Anna J. Schwartz: The Fed got it wrong.

An increase in financial risk drove the banks to increase their holdings of reserves and everyone else to lower their bank deposits and hold more currency.

Between 1929 and 1933, (Figure 1) the banks' desired reserve ratio increased from 8 percent to 12 percent and the currency drain ratio increased from 9 percent to 19 percent.

The money multiplier (Figure 2) fell from 6.5 to 3.8.

The quantity of money (Figure 3) crashed by 35 percent.

This massive contraction in the quantity of money was accompanied by a similar contraction of bank loans and by the failure of a large number of banks.

Friedman and Schwartz say that this contraction of money and bank loans and failure of banks could (and should) have been avoided by a more alert and wise Fed.

The Fed could have injected reserves into the banks to accommodate their desire for greater security by holding more reserves and to offset the rise in currency holdings as people switched out of bank deposits.

Ben Bernanke's Fed did almost exactly what Friedman and Schwartz said the Fed needed to do in the Great Depression.

At the end of 2008, when the banks faced increased financial risk, the Fed flooded them with the reserves that they wanted to hold (Figure 1).

The money multiplier fell from 9.1 in 2008 to 4.6 in 2009 (Figure 2)—much more than it had fallen between 1929 and 1933—but there was no contraction of the quantity of money (Figure 3). Rather, the quantity of M2 increased by 8 percent in the year to August 2009.

We can't be sure that the Fed averted a Great Depression in 2009, but we can be confident that the Fed's actions helped to limit the depth and duration of the 2008–2009 recession.

The Fed's next challenge will be to reverse the monetary policy stimulus when the economy begins to build momentum, and investment and exports begin to increase more quickly.

*Milton Friedman and Anna J. Schwartz, authors of* A Monetary History of the United States, *who say the Fed turned an ordinary recession into the Great Depression.*

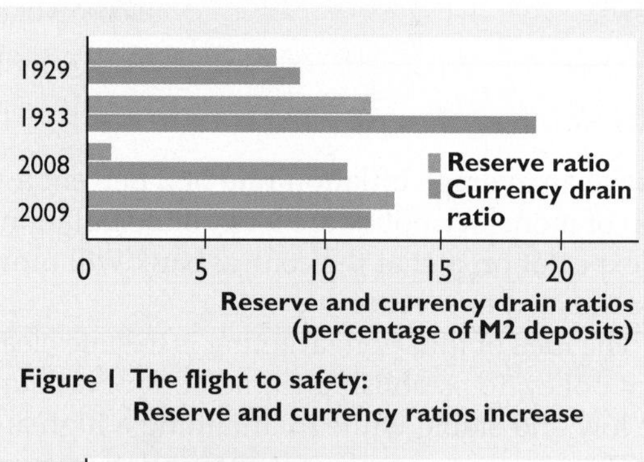


**Figure 1 The flight to safety: Reserve and currency ratios increase**

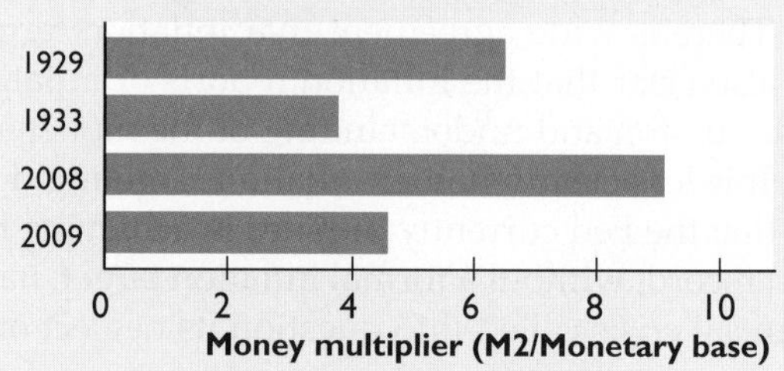


**Figure 2 The collapsing money multiplier**

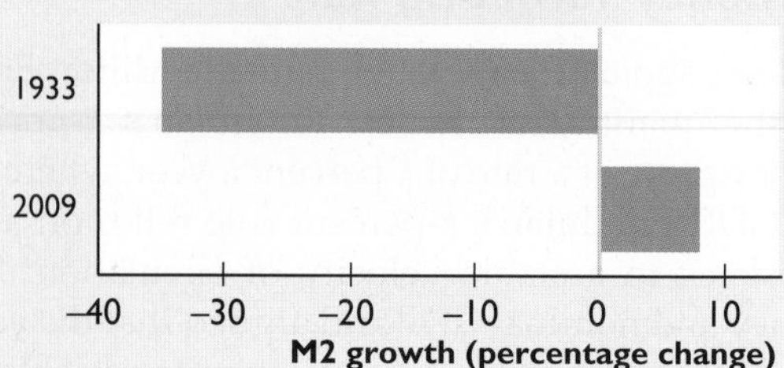


**Figure 3 Money contraction versus growth**

SOURCE OF DATA: Federal Reserve Board.

During the mid-1970s, in a bid to end the inflation, the central banks of most major countries adopted the *k*-percent rule for the growth rate of the quantity of money. The Fed, too, began to pay close attention to the growth rates of money aggregates, including M1 and M2.

Inflation rates fell during the early 1980s in the countries that had adopted a *k*-percent rule. But one by one, these countries abandoned the *k*-percent rule.

Money targeting works when the demand for money curve is stable and predictable—when the velocity of circulation is stable. But in the world of the 1980s, and possibly in the world of today, technological change in the banking system leads to large and unpredictable shifts in the demand for money curve, which make the use of monetary targeting unreliable.

With monetary targeting, aggregate demand fluctuates because the demand for money fluctuates. With interest rate targeting, aggregate demand is insulated from fluctuations in the demand for money (and the velocity of circulation).

## Gold Price Targeting Rule

The Fed could intervene in the market for gold and keep the dollar price of gold at a specified level. This monetary policy regime is called a **gold standard** and it was operated for much of the nineteenth and early twentieth centuries. At that time, this monetary regime was regarded as the only one that could be trusted to deliver price stability. Also, it had the virtue of providing one monetary standard for the world, for it was an *international* gold standard.

**Gold standard**
A monetary policy rule that fixes the dollar price of gold.

Under the gold standard, a country has no direct control over its inflation rate. And the inflation that occurs is determined by changes in the prices of consumption goods and services relative to the (fixed) price of gold. Historically, under the gold standard, prices were stable on the average but swung between periods of inflation (when new gold was discovered) and deflation (when economic growth outpaced the discovery of gold).

Today, most economists regard the gold standard as an outmoded system, but advocates continue to regret its passing.

## EYE on YOUR LIFE

### Your Views on Monetary Policy and How Monetary Policy Affects You

Using the knowledge that you have accumulated during your course and by reading or watching the current news, try to determine the monetary policy issues that face the U.S. economy today.

What is the greater monetary policy risk: inflation or recession? If the risk is inflation, what action do you expect the Fed to take? If the risk is recession, what do you expect the Fed to do?

Which of these problems, inflation or recession, do you care most about? Do you want the Fed to be more cautious about inflation and keep the interest rate high, or more cautious about recession and keep the interest rate low?

When Ben Bernanke was an economics professor at Princeton, he studied inflation targeting and found that it works well.

Do you think the United States should join the ranks of inflation targeters? Should the Fed announce an inflation target?

Watch the media for commentary on the Fed's interest rate decisions and evolving monetary policy strategy.

Work these problems in Study Plan 32.3 to get instant feedback.

## CHECKPOINT 32.3

**Explain and compare alternative monetary policy strategies.**

## Practice Problems

1. What are the three alternative monetary policy strategies that the Fed could have adopted and why is discretionary monetary policy not one of them?
2. Why does the Fed not target the quantity of money?
3. Which countries practice inflation targeting? How does this monetary policy strategy work and does it achieve a lower inflation rate?
4. **One tool, one target**
   The one-tool, one-target rule by which central banks operated has gone. Monetary policy is now a messier business.
   Source: *The Economist*, April 25, 2009
   What is the tool and the target that the news clip says is gone and what is the problem with "messy" monetary policy?

## Guided Solutions to Practice Problems

1. The Fed could have adopted three alternative monetary policy strategies: an inflation targeting rule, a *k*-percent money targeting rule, and a gold price targeting rule (gold standard). A rule-based monetary policy beats discretionary monetary policy because it provides a more secure anchor for inflation expectations, which in turn makes long-term contracts in labor and capital markets more efficient.
2. The Fed does not target the quantity of money because it believes that the demand for money is too unstable and fluctuations in demand would bring unwanted fluctuations in interest rates, aggregate demand, real GDP, and the inflation rate.
3. The countries that practice inflation targeting are the United Kingdom, Canada, Australia, New Zealand, Sweden, and the European countries that use the euro. Inflation targeting works by announcing a target inflation rate, setting the overnight interest rate (equivalent to the federal funds rate) to achieve the target, and publishing reports that explain how and why the central bank believes that its current policy actions will achieve its ultimate policy goals. Eurozone and New Zealand have missed their inflation targets, but the other inflation targeters have achieved their goals.
4. The tool is the overnight interest rate (the federal funds rate in the United States). There never has been one target. The Fed targets the inflation rate and the output gap and even the central banks that have formal inflation targets also pay attention to the output gap. The problem with "messy" monetary policy is that it might fail to anchor inflation expectations and lead to a worsening of the short-run policy tradeoff.

# CHAPTER SUMMARY

## Key Points

**1 Describe the objectives of U.S. monetary policy, the framework for achieving those objectives, and the Fed's monetary policy actions.**

- The Federal Reserve Act requires the Fed to use monetary policy to achieve maximum employment, stable prices, and moderate long-term interest rates.
- The Fed's goals can come into conflict in the short run.
- The Fed translates the goal of stable prices as a core inflation rate of between 1 and 2 percent a year.
- The Fed's monetary policy instrument is the federal funds rate.
- The Fed sets the federal funds rate at the level that makes its forecast of inflation and other goals equal to their targets.
- The Fed hits its federal funds rate target by using open market operations and in times of financial crisis by quantitative easing and credit easing.

**2 Explain the transmission channels through which the Fed influences real GDP and the inflation rate.**

- A change in the federal funds rate changes other interest rates, the exchange rate, the quantity of money and loans, aggregate demand, and eventually real GDP and the inflation rate.
- Changes in the federal funds rate change real GDP about one year later and change the inflation rate with an even longer time lag.

**3 Explain and compare alternative monetary policy strategies.**

- The main alternatives to setting the federal funds rate are an inflation targeting rule, a money targeting rule, or a gold standard.
- Rules dominate discretion in monetary policy because they better enable the central bank to manage inflation expectations.

## Key Terms

Discretionary monetary policy, 840
Federal funds rate, 824
Financial stability, 823
Gold standard, 843
Inflation targeting, 840
Instrument rule, 826
*k*-percent rule, 841
Monetary policy instrument, 824
Targeting rule, 826

Work these problems in Chapter 32 Study Plan to get instant feedback.

# CHAPTER CHECKPOINT

## Study Plan Problems and Applications

1. **Bernanke raises alarm on spending**
   Federal Reserve Chairman Ben Bernanke warned that government spending and budget deficits threaten financial stability and might be setting the scene for the next crisis.
   Source: *The Globe and Mail*, June 4, 2009
   How might a large increase in government spending and the government's budget deficit threaten financial stability and make the Fed's job harder?

Use the following information to work Problems 2 to 4.

The U.S. economy is at full employment when strong economic growth in Asia increases the demand for U.S.-produced goods and services.

2. Explain how the U.S. price level and real GDP will change in the short run.
3. Explain how the U.S. price level and real GDP will change in the long run if the Fed takes monetary policy actions that are consistent with its objectives as set out in the Federal Reserve Act of 2000.
4. Explain whether the Fed faces a tradeoff in the short run.

Use the following information to work Problems 5 to 7.

**FIGURE 1**

Price level (GDP deflator): 140, 130, 120, 110, 100; curves *AS* and *AD*; Real GDP (billions of 2005 dollars): 0, 100, 200, 300, 400, 500

Figure 1 shows the aggregate demand curve, *AD*, and the short-run aggregate supply curve, *AS*, in the economy of Artica. Potential GDP is $300 billion.

5. What are the price level and real GDP? Does Artica have an unemployment problem or an inflation problem? Why?
6. What do you predict will happen if the central bank takes no monetary policy actions? What monetary policy action would you advise the central bank to take and what do you predict will be the effect of that action?
7. Suppose that a drought decreases potential GDP in Artica to $250 billion. Explain what happens if the central bank lowers the federal funds rate. Do you recommend that the central bank lower the interest rate? Why?

Use the following information to work Problems 8 and 9.

**Fed sees no need to raise interest rates soon**
The Fed has consistently said that it will not raise the federal funds rate any time soon. The Fed's challenge will be how to get monetary policy back to normal over the next several years. The Fed has to make a judgment about timing—tightening too early could send the economy back into recession, as happened during the late 1930s; waiting too long would set the stage for inflation.
Source: *The New York Times*, November 5, 2009

8. If the recovery continues and inflation starts to rise, what effect will the Fed's decision to not change the federal funds rate have on the U.S. economy?
9. If the economic recovery slows and the economy slips back into recession, what effect will the Fed's no-change decision have on the economy?

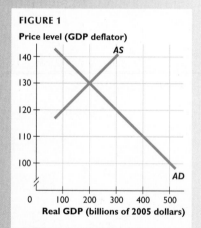

## Instructor Assignable Problems and Applications

Your instructor can assign these problems as homework, a quiz, or a test in **MyEconLab**.

1. In which episode, the Great Depression or the 2008–2009 recession, did the banks' desired reserve ratio and the currency drain ratio increase by the larger amount and the money multiplier fall by the larger amount?
2. Compare and contrast the Fed's monetary policy response to the surge in desired reserves and currency holdings in the Great Depression and the 2008–2009 recession.

Use the following information to work Problems 3 to 5.

The U.S. economy is at full employment when the world price of oil begins to rise sharply. Short-run aggregate supply decreases.

3. Explain how the U.S. price level and real GDP will change in the short run.
4. Explain how the U.S. price level and real GDP will change in the long run if the Fed takes monetary policy actions that are consistent with its objectives as set out in the Federal Reserve Act of 2000.
5. Does the Fed face a tradeoff in the short run? Explain why or why not.

Use the following information to work Problems 6 to 9.

Figure 1 shows the aggregate demand curve, *AD*, and the short-run aggregate supply curve, *AS*, in the economy of Freezone. Potential GDP is $300 billion.

**FIGURE 1**

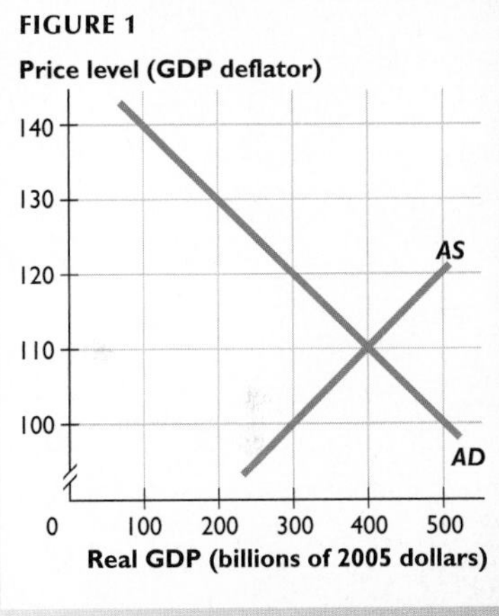


6. What are the price level and real GDP? Does Freezone have an unemployment problem or an inflation problem? Why?
7. What do you predict will happen in Freezone if the central bank takes no monetary policy actions? What monetary policy action would you advise the central bank to take and what do you predict will be the effect of that action?
8. What happens in Freezone if the central bank lowers the federal funds rate? Do you recommend that the central bank lower the interest rate? Why?
9. What happens in Freezone if the central bank conducts an open market sale of securities? How will the interest rate change? Do you recommend that the central bank conduct an open market sale of securities? Why?

Use the following information to work Problems 10 and 11.

**Many ways to blow up an economy**

Excessive stimulus could bring inflation in the United States in the long term, but for now, inflation is falling. Bond interest rates reflect inflation expectations that are within the Fed's long-term target levels.

Source: *Australian Financial Review*, May 9, 2009

10. Explain why inflation was falling in 2009 and how excessive stimulus could bring inflation in the long term.
11. What does it mean to say that inflation expectations are within the Fed's target levels?

Use the following information to work Problems 12 and 13.

**Fed Is Split Over Timing of Rate Rise**

In October 2009, the Fed was forecasting that unemployment will average 9.8 percent in 2010 and said the federal funds rate will remain "exceptionally low" for "an extended period." But some officials were beginning to worry about unwinding the $2 trillion in special credits that have boosted the monetary base and to wonder if the interest rate might need to start rising soon.

Source: *The New York Times,* October 9, 2009

12. Describe the time lags in the operation of monetary policy and explain why they pose a challenge for the Fed in deciding when to start raising the federal funds rate target in a recession.
13. Explain why unwinding the $2 trillion in special credits that have boosted the monetary base and the federal funds rate target are linked.
14. **Bernanke warns against meddling with Fed**

    Testifying on Capitol Hill, Fed chairman Bernanke warned that if Congress limits the Fed's independence, financial markets will send interest rates higher.

    Source: *The Independent*, July 22, 2009

    How might limiting the Fed's independence make interest rates rise?
15. In the summer of 2007, the Fed conducted aggressive open market operations to increase the monetary base but didn't change the federal funds rate target. Then, a few weeks later, the Fed cut the federal funds rate by 50 basis points. Why did the Fed need to increase the monetary base if it didn't want to change the interest rate?
16. Inflation is rising toward 5 percent a year, and the Fed, Congress, and the White House are discussing ways of containing inflation without damaging employment and output. The President wants to cut aggregate demand but to do so in a way that will give the best chance of keeping investment high to encourage long-term economic growth. Explain which of the following actions would best meet the President's objectives and which would present the greatest obstacles to those objectives.
    - A rise in the federal funds rate.
    - A fall in the federal funds rate.
    - No change in the federal funds rate and some fiscal policy action.
17. In a deep recession, the Fed, Congress, and the White House are discussing ways of restoring full employment. The President wants to stimulate aggregate demand but to do so in a way that will give the best chance of boosting investment and long-term economic growth. Explain which of the following actions would best meet the President's objectives and which would present the greatest obstacles to those objectives.
    - A rise in the federal funds rate.
    - A fall in the federal funds rate.
    - No change in the federal funds rate and some fiscal policy action.

## Why has our dollar been sinking?

One U.S. dollar was worth 1.17 euros in 2001 but only 68 euro cents in 2009. Why?

# International Finance

**When you have completed your study of this chapter, you will be able to**

1 Describe a country's balance of payments accounts and explain what determines the amount of international borrowing and lending.

2 Explain how the exchange rate is determined and why it fluctuates.

## 33.1 FINANCING INTERNATIONAL TRADE

When Apple Computer, Inc. imports iPods that it manufactures in Taiwan, it pays for them using Taiwanese dollars. When a French construction company buys an earthmover from Caterpillar, Inc., it uses U.S. dollars. Whenever we buy things from another country, we pay in the currency of that country. It doesn't make any difference what the item being traded is; it might be a consumption good or a service or a capital good, a building, or even a firm.

We're going to study the markets in which different types of currency are bought and sold. But first we're going to look at the scale of international trading and borrowing and lending and at the way in which we keep our records of these transactions. These records are called the balance of payments accounts.

### Balance of Payments Accounts

**Balance of payments accounts**
The accounts in which a nation records its international trading, borrowing, and lending.

A country's **balance of payments accounts** record its international trading, borrowing, and lending. There are in fact three balance of payments accounts:

- Current account
- Capital account
- Official settlements account

**Current account**
Record of receipts from the sale of goods and services to other countries (exports), minus payments for goods and services bought from other countries (imports), plus the net amount of interest and transfers received from and paid to other countries.

**Capital account**
Record of foreign investment in the United States minus U.S. investment abroad.

**Official settlements account**
Record of the change in U.S. official reserves.

**U.S. official reserves**
The government's holdings of foreign currency.

The **current account** records receipts from the sale of goods and services to other countries (exports), minus payments for goods and services bought from other countries (imports), plus the net amount of interest and transfers (such as foreign aid payments) received from and paid to other countries. The **capital account** records foreign investment in the United States minus U.S. investment abroad. The **official settlements account** records the change in U.S. official reserves. **U.S. official reserves** are the government's holdings of foreign currency. If U.S. official reserves increase, the official settlements account balance is negative. The reason is that holding foreign money is like investing abroad and U.S. investment abroad is a minus item in the capital account. (By the same reasoning, if official reserves decrease, the official settlements account balance is positive.)

The sum of the balances on the three accounts always equals zero. That is, to pay for our current account deficit, we must either borrow more from abroad than we lend abroad or use our official reserves to cover the shortfall.

Table 33.1 shows the U.S. balance of payments accounts in 2008. Items in the current account and capital account that provide foreign currency to the United States have a plus sign; items that cost the United States foreign currency have a minus sign. The table shows that in 2008, U.S. imports exceeded U.S. exports and the current account deficit was $706 billion. We paid for imports that exceeded the value of our exports by borrowing from the rest of the world. The capital account tells us by how much. We borrowed $534 billion (foreign investment in the United States) and, net, made no loans to the rest of the world (no U.S. investment abroad). Other net foreign borrowing of –$29 billion and a statistical discrepancy of $206 billion made our capital account balance $711 billion. Our official reserves increased by $5 billion and are shown in Table 33.1 as a negative $5 billion, a convention that makes the three accounts sum to zero.

You might better understand the balance of payments accounts and the way in which they are linked if you think about the income and expenditure, borrowing and lending, and bank account of an individual.

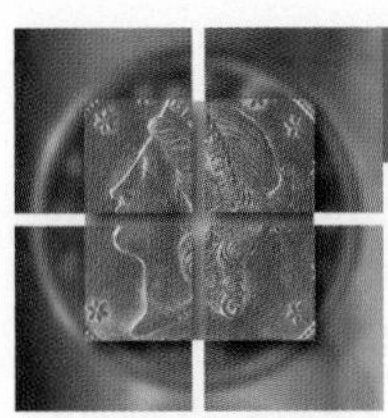

# EYE on the PAST

## The U.S. Balance of Payments

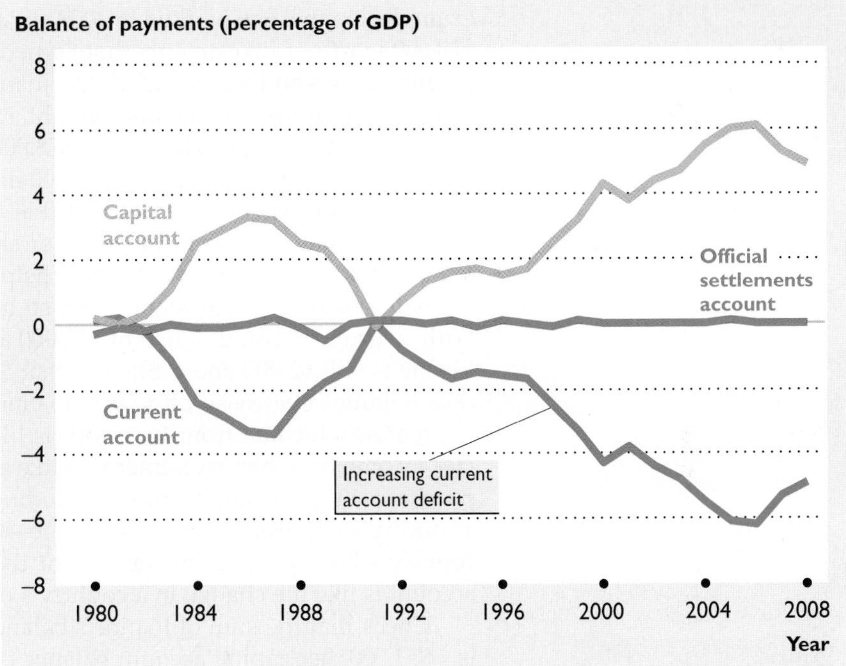


SOURCE OF DATA: Bureau of Economic Analysis.

The numbers in Table 33.1 provide a snapshot of the U.S. balance of payments in 2008. The figure puts this snapshot into perspective by showing how the balance of payments evolved from 1980 to 2008.

A current account deficit emerged during the 1980s but briefly disappeared with a near-zero balance in the recession of the early 1990s.

As the economy resumed its expansion during the 1990s the current account deficit increased. It continued to increase through the 2000s.

The current account deficit has decreased only in recessions and increased again once a recovery gets going.

The capital account balance is almost a mirror image of the current account balance and the reason is that the official settlements balance—the change in gold and foreign exchange reserves—is very small in comparison with the balances on the other two accounts.

**TABLE 33.1**

The U.S. Balance of Payments Accounts in 2008

| **Current account** | **(billions of dollars)** |
|---|---|
| Exports of goods and services | +1,827 |
| Imports of goods and services | –2,524 |
| Net interest | +119 |
| Net transfers | –128 |
| **Current account balance** | **–706** |
| **Capital account** | |
| Foreign investment in the United States | +534 |
| U.S. investment abroad | 0 |
| Other net foreign investment in the United States | –29 |
| Statistical discrepancy | 206 |
| **Capital account balance** | **+711** |
| **Official settlements account** | |
| **Official settlements account balance** | **–5** |

SOURCE OF DATA: Bureau of Economic Analysis.

### Personal Analogy

You have a set of personal balance of payments accounts that parallel those of a nation. You have a current account, a capital account, and a settlements account.

Your current account records your income from supplying the services of factors of production and your expenditure on goods and services. Consider, for example, Joanne. She worked in 2009 and earned an income of $25,000. Joanne has $10,000 worth of investments that earned her interest of $1,000. Joanne's current account shows an income of $26,000. Joanne spent $18,000 buying goods and services for consumption. She also bought a new apartment, which cost her $60,000. So Joanne's total expenditure was $78,000. The difference between her expenditure and her income is $52,000 ($78,000 minus $26,000).

To pay for expenditure of $52,000 in excess of her income, Joanne has to use the money that she has in the bank or she has to take out a loan. Suppose that Joanne took a mortgage of $50,000 to help buy her apartment. This mortgage was the only borrowing that Joanne did, so her capital account surplus was $50,000. With a current account deficit of $52,000 and a capital account surplus of $50,000, Joanne is still $2,000 short. She got that $2,000 from her own bank account. Her cash holdings decreased by $2,000. Joanne's settlements balance was $2,000.

Joanne's income from her work is like a country's income from its exports. Her income from her investments is like a country's interest from foreigners. Her purchases of goods and services, including her purchase of an apartment, are like a country's imports. Joanne's mortgage—borrowing from someone else—is like a country's borrowing from the rest of the world. The change in Joanne's bank account is like the change in a country's official reserves.

Check that the sum of Joanne's balances is zero. Her current account balance is −$52,000, her capital account balance is +$50,000, and her settlements account balance is +$2,000, so the sum of the three balances is zero.

## Borrowers and Lenders, Debtors and Creditors

**Net borrower**
A country that is borrowing more from the rest of the world than it is lending to the rest of the world.

**Net lender**
A country that is lending more to the rest of the world than it is borrowing from the rest of the world.

A country that is borrowing more from the rest of the world than it is lending to the rest of the world is called a **net borrower**. Similarly, a **net lender** is a country that is lending more to the rest of the world than it is borrowing from it.

The United States is a net borrower, but it is a relative newcomer to the ranks of net borrower nations. Throughout the 1960s and most of the 1970s, the United States was a net lender. It had a surplus on its current account and a deficit on its capital account. It was not until 1983 that the United States became a significant net borrower. Between 1983 and 1987, U.S. borrowing increased each year. Then it decreased and was briefly zero in 1991. After 1991, U.S. borrowing started to increase again. The average net foreign borrowing by the United States between 1983 and 2009 was $286 billion a year.

Most countries are net borrowers like the United States. But a small number of countries, including Japan and oil-rich Saudi Arabia, are net lenders.

**Debtor nation**
A country that during its entire history has borrowed more from the rest of the world than it has lent to the rest of the world.

**Creditor nation**
A country that during its entire history has invested more in the rest of the world than other countries have invested in it.

A net borrower might be reducing its net assets held in the rest of the world, or it might be going deeper into debt. A nation's total stock of foreign investment determines whether the nation is a debtor or creditor. A **debtor nation** is a country that during its entire history has borrowed more from the rest of the world than it has lent to the rest of the world. It has a stock of outstanding debt to the rest of the world that exceeds the stock of its own claims on the rest of the world. A **creditor nation** is a country that during its entire history has invested more in the rest of the world than other countries have invested in it.

### Flows and Stocks

At the heart of the distinction between a net borrower and a net lender on the one hand and between a debtor nation and a creditor nation on the other hand is the distinction between flows and stocks, which you have encountered many times in your study of macroeconomics. Borrowing and lending are flows—amounts borrowed or lent per unit of time. Debts are stocks—amounts owed at a point in time. The flow of borrowing and lending changes the stock of debt.

The United States was a debtor nation through the nineteenth century as we borrowed from Europe to finance our westward expansion, railroads, and industrialization. The United States paid off its debt and became a creditor nation for most of the twentieth century. But following a string of current account deficits, the United States became a debtor nation again in 1989.

Since 1989, the total stock of U.S. borrowing from the rest of the world has exceeded U.S. lending to the rest of the world. The largest debtor nations are the capital-hungry developing countries (as the United States was during the nineteenth century). The international debt of these countries grew from less than a third to more than a half of their gross domestic product during the 1980s and created what is called the "Third World debt crisis."

Should we be concerned that the United States is a net borrower? The answer to this question depends mainly on what the net borrower is doing with the borrowed money. If the borrowed money is financing investment that in turn is generating economic growth and higher income, then the borrowing is not a problem. If the borrowed money is being used to finance consumption, then higher interest payments are being incurred, and consequently, consumption will eventually have to be reduced. In this case, the more the borrowing and the longer it goes on, the greater is the reduction in consumption that will eventually be necessary. We'll see below whether the United States is borrowing for investment or consumption.

## Current Account Balance

What determines a country's current account balance and net foreign borrowing? You've seen in Table 33.1 that exports of goods and services ($X$) and imports of goods and services ($M$) are the largest items in the current account. We call exports minus imports net exports ($NX$). So net exports is the main component of the current account. We can define the current account balance ($CAB$) as

$$CAB = NX + \text{Net interest and transfers from abroad.}$$

Fluctuations in net exports are the main source of fluctuations in the current account balance. Net interest and transfers from abroad are small and have trends, but they do not fluctuate much. So we can study the current account balance by looking at what determines net exports.

## Net Exports

The government budget and private saving and investment determine net exports. To see how they determine net exports, we need to recall some of the things that we learned about the national income accounts in Chapter 20. Table 33.2 will refresh your memory and summarize some calculations.

**TABLE 33.2**

Net Exports, the Government Budget, Saving, and Investment

| | Symbols and equations | United States in 2008 (billions of dollars) |
|---|---|---|
| **(a) Variables** | | |
| Exports | $X$ | 1,831 |
| Imports | $M$ | 2,539 |
| Investment | $I$ | 2,136 |
| Saving | $S$ | 2,362 |
| Government expenditure on goods and services | $G$ | 2,883 |
| Net taxes | $NT$ | 1,940 |
| **(b) Balances** | | |
| Net exports | $X - M$ | 1,831 – 2,539 = –708 |
| Private sector balance | $S - I$ | 2,362 – 2,136 = 226 |
| Government sector balance | $NT - G$ | 1,950 – 2,883 = –934 |
| **(c) Relation among balances** | | |
| National accounts | $Y = C + I + G + X - M = C + S + NT$ | |
| Rearranging: | $X - M = S - I + NT - G$ | |
| Net exports | $X - M$ | –708 |
| Equals: | | |
| Private sector balance | $S - I$ | 226 |
| Plus: | | |
| Government sector balance | $NT - G$ | –934 |

SOURCE OF DATA: Bureau of Economic Analysis, 2009. (The National Income and Product Accounts measures of exports and imports are slightly different from the Balance of Payments Accounts measures in Table 33.1 on p. 851. The government sector includes state and local governments.)

Part (a) of Table 33.2 lists the national income variables with their symbols. Part (b) defines three balances. *Net exports* are exports of goods and services minus imports of goods and services.

**Private sector balance**
Saving minus investment.

The **private sector balance** is saving minus investment. If saving exceeds investment, a private sector surplus is lent to other sectors. If investment exceeds saving, borrowing from other sectors finances a private sector deficit.

**Government sector balance**
Net taxes minus government expenditure on goods and services.

The **government sector balance** is equal to net taxes minus government expenditure on goods and services. If that number is positive, a government sector surplus is lent to other sectors; if that number is negative, borrowing from other sectors must finance a government deficit. The government sector is the sum of the federal, state, and local governments.

Part (b) also shows the values of these balances for the United States in 2008. As you can see, net exports were –$708 billion, a deficit. The private sector saved $2,362 billion and invested $2,136 billion, so it had a surplus of $226 billion. The government sector's revenue from net taxes was $1,950 billion, and its expenditure was $2,883 billion, so the government sector balance was –$934 billion, a deficit.

Part (c) of Table 33.2 shows the relationship among the three balances. From the national income accounts, we know that real GDP, $Y$, is the sum of consumption expenditure, $C$; investment, $I$; government expenditure on goods and services, $G$; and net exports, $X - M$. Real GDP also equals the sum of consumption expenditure, $C$, saving, $S$, and net taxes, $NT$. Rearranging these equations tells us that net exports equals $(S - I)$, the private sector balance, plus $(NT - G)$, the government sector balance. That is,

$$\text{Net exports} = (S - I) + (NT - G).$$

Should we be concerned that the United States is a net borrower? The answer is probably not. Our international borrowing finances the purchase of new capital goods. In 2006, businesses spent $2,136 billion on new buildings, plant, and equipment. Government spent $496 billion on defense equipment and public structures. All these purchases added to the nation's capital, and much of it increased productivity. Governments also purchased education and health care services, which increased human capital.

Our international borrowing is financing private and public investment, not consumption.

## EYE on the GLOBAL ECONOMY

### Current Account Balances Around the World

The U.S. current account deficit in 2008 is the major international payments deficit. No other country has a deficit remotely similar to that of the United States.

For every deficit, there must be a corresponding surplus. The figure shows that the U.S. deficit is reflected in a large number of surpluses spread around the world. No single country has a surplus to match the U.S. deficit.

But China and the oil-exporting countries of the Middle East have surpluses that in total equal the U.S. deficit.

Japan, other advanced economies, and the newly industrialized Asian economies also have surpluses.

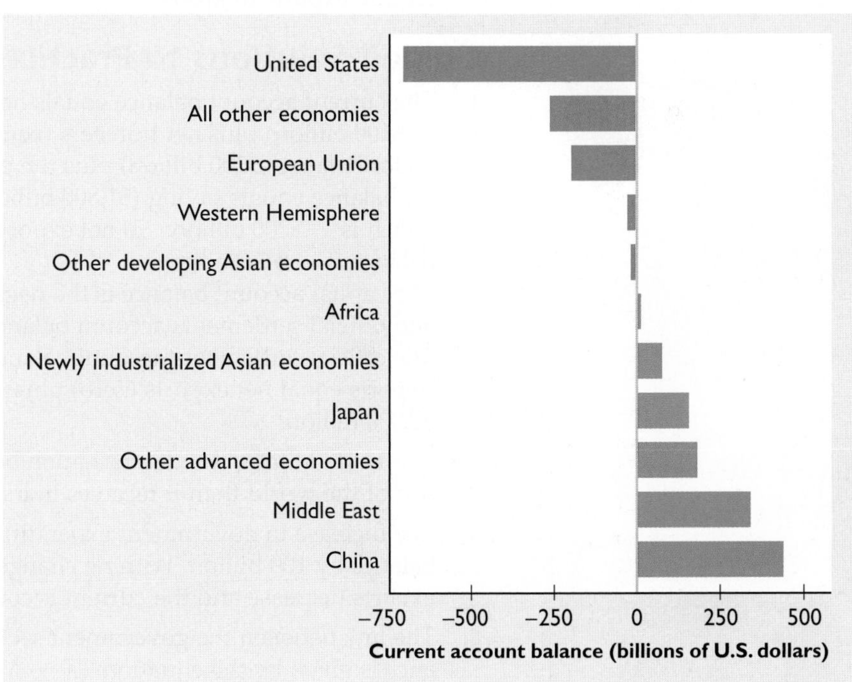


SOURCE OF DATA: International Monetary Fund, *World Economic Outlook*, April 2009.

Work these problems in Study Plan 33.1 to get instant feedback.

# CHECKPOINT 33.1

**Describe a country's balance of payments accounts and explain what determines the amount of international borrowing and lending.**

## Practice Problems

Use the following information about the United States to work Problems **1** to **3**.

Imports of goods and services: $2,000 billion; interest paid to the rest of the world: $500 billion; interest received from the rest of the world: $400 billion; decrease in U.S. official reserves: $10 billion; government sector balance: $200 billion; saving: $1,800 billion; investment: $2,000 billion; net transfers: zero.

1. Calculate the current account balance, the capital account balance, the official settlements account balance, and exports of goods and services.
2. Is the United States a debtor or a creditor nation?
3. If government expenditure on goods and services increases by $100 billion, how does the current account balance change?
4. **Something has got to give**
   As the recovery takes hold, the U.S. government must reduce its expenditure to trim its huge budget deficit. To keep aggregate demand growing, consumption, investment, or exports must grow. U.S. consumers are burdened with debt, U.S. firms have unused capital, so exports must grow.
   Source: *USA Today*, September 3, 2009
   Explain why a cut in government expenditure to trim the budget deficit will require exports to grow.

## Guided Solutions to Practice Problems

1. The current account balance equals net exports plus net interest from abroad (−$100 billion) plus net transfers (zero). Net exports equal the government sector balance ($200 billion) plus the private sector balance. The private sector balance equals saving ($1,800 billion) minus investment ($2,000 billion), which is −$200 billion. So net exports are zero, and the current account balance is −$100 billion.
   The capital account balance is the negative of the sum of the current account and official settlements account balances, which is $90 billion.
   The official settlements account balance is a *surplus* of $10 billion.
   Exports equal net exports (zero) plus imports ($2,000 billion), which equals $2,000 billion.
2. The United States is a debtor nation because it pays more in interest to the rest of the world than it receives in interest from the rest of the world.
3. The increase in government expenditure decreases the government sector balance by 100 billion. With no change in the private sector balance, net exports decrease and the current account deficit increases by $100 billion.
4. The link between the government sector balance and the private sector balance is given by the equation: $(X - M) = (S - I) + (NT - G)$. Rewrite the equation as $(G - NT) = (S - I) - (X - M)$. A cut in $G$ will decrease the left side of the equation. If consumption does not increase, then $S$ will increase. To make the right side of the equation decrease, $X$ must increase.

## 33.2 THE EXCHANGE RATE

When we buy foreign goods or invest in another country, we pay using that country's currency. When foreigners buy U.S.-made goods or invest in the United States, they pay in U.S. dollars. We get foreign currency, and foreigners get U.S. dollars in the foreign exchange market. The **foreign exchange market** is the market in which the currency of one country is exchanged for the currency of another. The foreign exchange market is not a place like a downtown flea market or produce market. It is made up of thousands of people: importers and exporters, banks, and specialist traders of foreign exchange, called foreign exchange brokers. The foreign exchange market opens on Monday morning in Hong Kong, which is still Sunday evening in New York. As the day advances, markets open in Singapore, Tokyo, Bahrain, Frankfurt, London, New York, Chicago, and San Francisco. As the U.S. West Coast markets close, Hong Kong is only an hour away from opening for the next business day. Dealers around the world are in continual contact, and on a typical day in 2009, more than $3 trillion changed hands.

**Foreign exchange market**
The market in which the currency of one country is exchanged for the currency of another.

The price at which one currency exchanges for another is called a **foreign exchange rate**. For example, in October 2009, one U.S. dollar bought 68 euro cents. The exchange rate was 68 euro cents per dollar. We can also express the exchange rate in terms of dollars (or cents) per euro, which in October 2009 was $1.48 per euro.

**Foreign exchange rate**
The price at which one currency exchanges for another.

**Currency appreciation** is the rise in the value of one currency in terms of another currency. For example, when the dollar rose from 86 euro cents in 1999 to 1.17 euros in 2001, the dollar appreciated by 36 percent.

**Currency appreciation**
The rise in the value of one currency in terms of another currency.

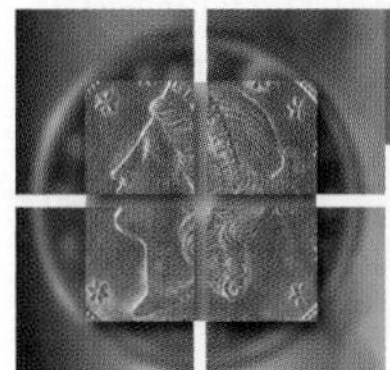

## EYE on the PAST

### The Dollar and the Euro Since 1999

From 1999 to 2001, the value of the dollar rose against the euro—the dollar *appreciated*. From 2002 to 2009, the value of the dollar fell against the euro—the dollar *depreciated*.

The rate of the dollar's depreciation was rapid during 2003, but it slowed during 2004 and for a few months the dollar appreciated again.

The dollar's slide resumed in 2006 and aside from another brief appreciation in 2008, the dollar kept on falling against the euro. The overall fall was from a high of 1.17 euros to a low of 0.68 euros.

SOURCE OF DATA: PACIFIC FX Service, University of British Columbia.

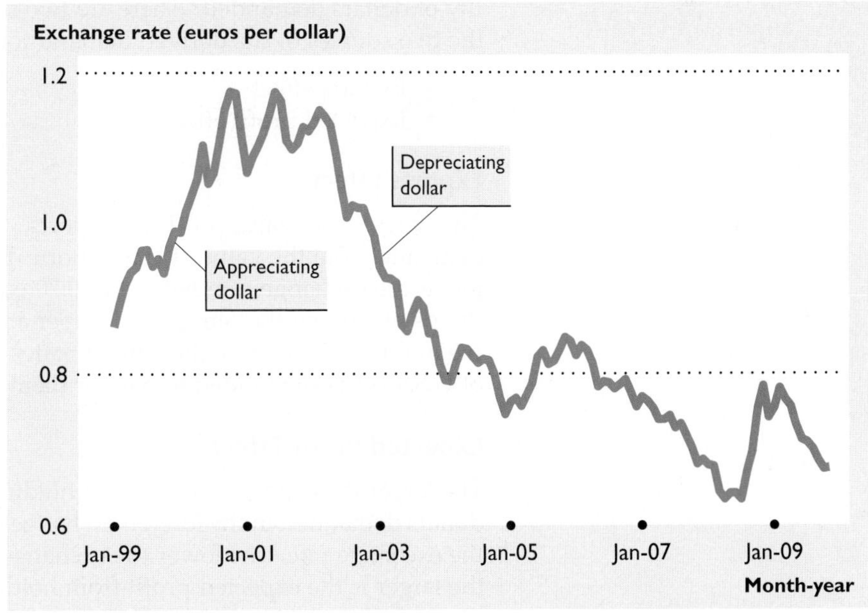

**Currency depreciation**
The fall in the value of one currency in terms of another currency.

**Currency depreciation** is the fall in the value of one currency in terms of another currency. For example, when the dollar fell from 1.17 euros in 2001 to 0.68 euros in 2009, the dollar depreciated by 42 percent. Why does the U.S. dollar fluctuate in value? Why does it sometimes depreciate and sometimes appreciate?

The exchange rate is a price. And like all prices, demand and supply determine the exchange rate. So to understand the forces that determine the exchange rate, we need to study demand and supply in the foreign exchange market. We'll begin by looking at the demand side of the market.

## Demand in the Foreign Exchange Market

The quantity of U.S. dollars demanded in the foreign exchange market is the amount that traders plan to buy during a given time period at a given exchange rate. This quantity depends on many factors, but the main ones are

- The exchange rate
- Interest rates in the United States and other countries
- The expected future exchange rate

Let's look first at the relationship between the quantity of dollars demanded in the foreign exchange market and the exchange rate.

## The Law of Demand for Foreign Exchange

People do not buy dollars because they enjoy them. The demand for dollars is a *derived demand.* People demand dollars so that they can buy U.S.-made goods and services (U.S. exports). They also demand dollars so that they can buy U.S. assets such as bank accounts, bonds, stocks, businesses, and real estate. Nevertheless, the law of demand applies to dollars just as it does to anything else that people value.

Other things remaining the same, the higher the exchange rate, the smaller is the quantity of dollars demanded. For example, if the price of the U.S. dollar rises from 0.70 euros to 0.80 euros but nothing else changes, the quantity of U.S. dollars that people plan to buy decreases. Why does the exchange rate influence the quantity of dollars demanded? There are two separate reasons, and they are related to the two sources of the derived demand for dollars. They are

- Exports effect
- Expected profit effect

### Exports Effect

The larger the value of U.S. exports, the larger is the quantity of dollars demanded. But the value of U.S. exports depends on the exchange rate. For example, if the exchange rate falls from 0.70 euros to 0.60 euros per U.S. dollar, other things remaining the same, the cheaper are U.S.-made goods and services to people in Europe, the more the United States exports, and the greater is the quantity of U.S. dollars demanded to pay for them.

### Expected Profit Effect

The larger the expected profit from holding dollars, the greater is the quantity of dollars demanded in the foreign exchange market. But expected profit depends on the exchange rate. The lower the exchange rate, other things remaining the same, the larger is the expected profit from holding dollars and the greater is the quantity of dollars demanded on the foreign exchange market.

**FIGURE 33.1**

The Demand for Dollars

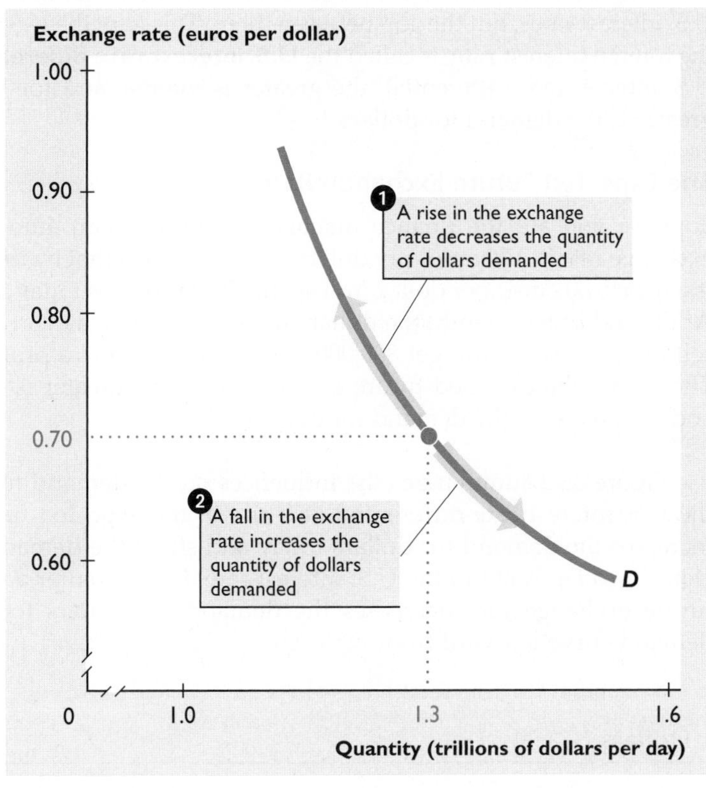


Other things remaining the same, the quantity of dollars that people plan to buy depends on the exchange rate.

1. If the exchange rate rises, the quantity of dollars demanded decreases and there is a movement up along the demand curve for dollars.
2. If the exchange rate falls, the quantity of dollars demanded increases and there is a movement down along the demand curve for dollars.

To understand this effect, suppose that you think the dollar will be worth 0.80 euros by the end of the month. If a dollar costs 0.75 euros today, you buy dollars. But a person who thinks that the dollar will be worth 0.75 euros at the end of the month does not buy dollars. Now suppose that the exchange rate falls to 0.65 euros per dollar. More people think that they can profit from buying dollars, so the quantity of dollars demanded today increases.

Figure 33.1 shows the demand curve for U.S. dollars in the foreign exchange market. For the two reasons we've just reviewed, when the foreign exchange rate rises, other things remaining the same, the quantity of dollars demanded decreases and there is a movement up along the demand curve, as shown by the arrow. When the exchange rate falls, other things remaining the same, the quantity of dollars demanded increases and there is a movement down along the demand curve, as shown by the arrow.

## Changes in the Demand for Dollars

A change in any other influence on the quantity of U.S. dollars that people plan to buy in the foreign exchange market brings a change in the demand for dollars. These other influences are

- Interest rates in the United States and other countries
- The expected future exchange rate

### Interest Rates in the United States and Other Countries

**U.S. interest rate differential**
The U.S. interest rate minus the foreign interest rate.

If you can borrow in another country and lend in the United States at a higher interest rate, you will make a profit. What matters is not the level of foreign and U.S. interest rates, but the gap between them. This gap, the U.S. interest rate minus the foreign interest rate, is called the **U.S. interest rate differential**. The larger the U.S. interest rate differential, the greater is the demand for U.S. assets and the greater is the demand for dollars.

### The Expected Future Exchange Rate

Suppose you are the finance manager of the German auto maker BMW. The exchange rate is 0.70 euros per dollar, and you expect that by the end of the month, it will be 0.80 euros per dollar. You spend 700,000 euros today and buy $1,000,000. At the end of the month, the dollar equals 0.80 euros, as you predicted, and you sell the $1,000,000. You get 800,000 euros. You've made a profit of 100,000 euros. The higher the expected future exchange rate, the greater is the expected profit and the greater is the demand for dollars.

Figure 33.2 summarizes the influences on the demand for dollars. A rise in the U.S. interest rate differential or a rise in the expected future exchange rate increases the demand for dollars today and shifts the demand curve rightward from $D_0$ to $D_1$. A fall in the U.S. interest rate differential or a fall in the expected future exchange rate decreases the demand for dollars today and shifts the demand curve leftward from $D_0$ to $D_2$.

**FIGURE 33.2**

Changes in the Demand for Dollars

myeconlab Animation

1 The demand for dollars increases if:

- The U.S. interest rate differential increases.
- The expected future exchange rate rises.

2 The demand for dollars decreases if:

- The U.S. interest rate differential decreases.
- The expected future exchange rate falls.

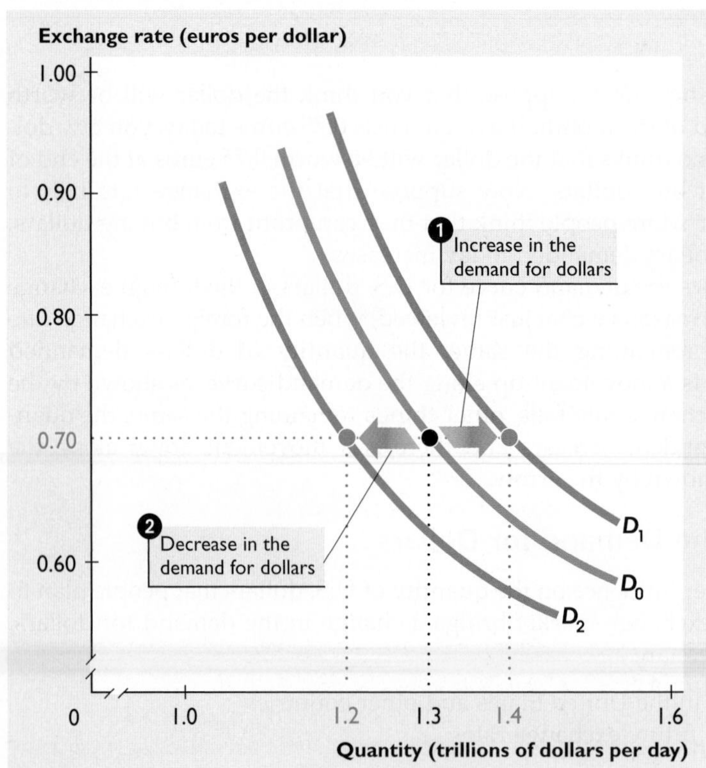

## Supply in the Foreign Exchange Market

The quantity of U.S. dollars supplied in the foreign exchange market is the amount that traders plan to sell during a given time period at a given exchange rate. This quantity depends on many factors, but the main ones are

- The exchange rate
- Interest rates in the United States and other countries
- The expected future exchange rate

Does this list of factors seem familiar? It should: It is the same list as that for demand. The demand side and the supply side of the foreign exchange market are influenced by all the same factors. But the ways in which these three factors influence supply are the opposite of the ways in which they influence demand.

Let's look first at the relationship between the quantity of dollars supplied in the foreign exchange market and the exchange rate.

## The Law of Supply of Foreign Exchange

Traders supply U.S. dollars in the foreign exchange market when people and businesses buy other currencies. They buy other currencies so that they can buy foreign-made goods and services (U.S. imports). Traders also supply dollars and buy foreign currencies so that people and businesses can buy foreign assets such as bank accounts, bonds, stocks, businesses, and real estate. The law of supply applies to dollars just as it does to anything else that people plan to sell.

Other things remaining the same, the higher the exchange rate, the greater is the quantity of dollars supplied in the foreign exchange market. For example, if the price of the U.S. dollar rises from 0.70 euros to 0.80 euros but nothing else changes, the quantity of U.S. dollars that people plan to sell in the foreign exchange market increases. Why does the exchange rate influence the quantity of dollars supplied?

There are two reasons, and they parallel the two reasons on the demand side of the market. They are

- Imports effect
- Expected profit effect

### Imports Effect

The larger the value of U.S. imports, the larger is the quantity of foreign currency demanded to pay for these imports. And when people buy foreign currency, they supply dollars. So the larger the value of U.S. imports, the greater is the quantity of dollars supplied on the foreign exchange market. But the value of U.S. imports depends on the exchange rate. The higher the exchange rate, other things remaining the same, the cheaper are foreign-made goods and services to Americans. So the more the United States imports, the greater is the quantity of U.S. dollars supplied on the foreign exchange market to pay for these imports.

### Expected Profit Effect

The larger the expected profit from holding a foreign currency, the greater is the quantity of that currency demanded and the greater is the quantity of dollars supplied in the foreign exchange market. But the expected profit from holding a foreign currency depends on the exchange rate. The higher the exchange rate, other things remaining the same, the larger is the expected profit from selling dollars and the greater is the quantity of dollars supplied on the foreign exchange market.

**FIGURE 33.3**

The Supply of Dollars

myeconlab Animation

Other things remaining the same, the quantity of dollars that people plan to sell depends on the exchange rate.

1 If the exchange rate rises, the quantity of dollars supplied increases and there is a movement up along the supply curve of dollars.

2 If the exchange rate falls, the quantity of dollars supplied decreases and there is a movement down along the supply curve of dollars.

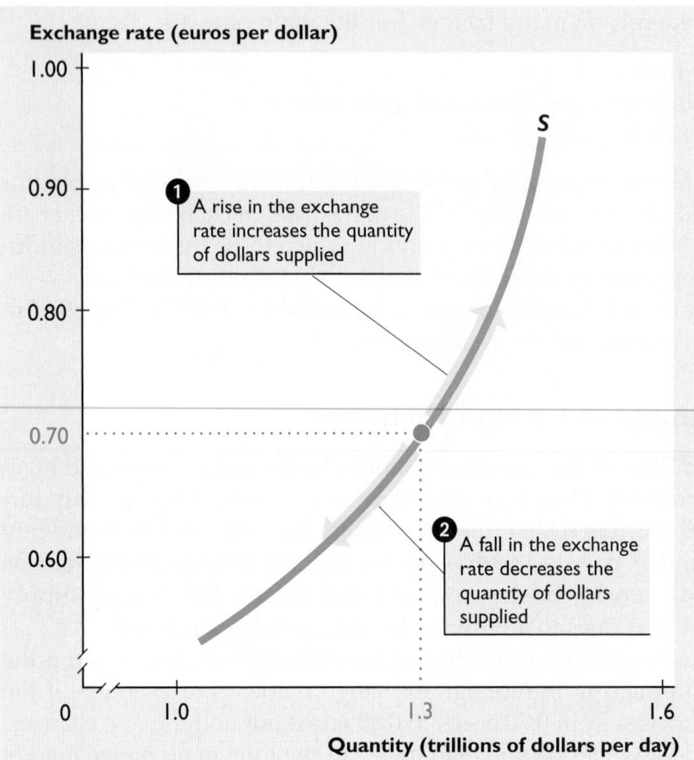


For the two reasons we've just reviewed, other things remaining the same, when the foreign exchange rate rises, the quantity of dollars supplied increases, and when the foreign exchange rate falls, the quantity of dollars supplied decreases. Figure 33.3 shows the supply curve of U.S. dollars in the foreign exchange market. In this figure, when the foreign exchange rate rises, other things remaining the same, there is an increase in the quantity of dollars supplied and a movement up along the supply curve, as shown by the arrow. When the exchange rate falls, other things remaining the same, there is a decrease in the quantity of dollars supplied and a movement down along the supply curve, as shown by the arrow.

## Changes in the Supply of Dollars

A change in any other influence on the quantity of U.S. dollars that people plan to sell in the foreign exchange market brings a change in the supply of dollars, and the supply curve of dollars shifts. Supply either increases or decreases. These other influences on supply parallel the other influences on demand but have exactly the opposite effects. These influences are

- Interest rates in the United States and other countries
- The expected future exchange rate

### Interest Rates in the United States and Other Countries

The larger the U.S. interest rate differential, the smaller is the demand for foreign assets and the smaller is the supply of dollars on the foreign exchange market.

### The Expected Future Exchange Rate

Other things remaining the same, the higher the expected future exchange rate, the smaller is the supply of dollars. To see why, suppose that the dollar is trading at 0.70 euros per dollar today and you think that by the end of the month, the dollar will trade at 0.80 euros per dollar. You were planning on selling dollars today, but you decide to hold off and wait until the end of the month. If you supply dollars today, you get only 0.70 euros per dollar. But at the end of the month, if the dollar is worth 0.80 euros as you predict, you'll get 0.80 euros for each dollar you supply. You'll make a profit of 0.10 euros per dollar. So the higher the expected future exchange rate, other things remaining the same, the smaller is the expected profit from selling U.S. dollars and the smaller is the supply of dollars today.

Figure 33.4 summarizes the influences on the supply of dollars. A rise in the U.S. interest rate differential or the expected future exchange rate decreases the supply of dollars today and shifts the supply curve leftward from $S_0$ to $S_1$. A fall in the U.S. interest rate differential or the expected future exchange rate increases the supply of dollars today and shifts the supply curve rightward from $S_0$ to $S_2$.

**FIGURE 33.4**

Changes in the Supply of Dollars

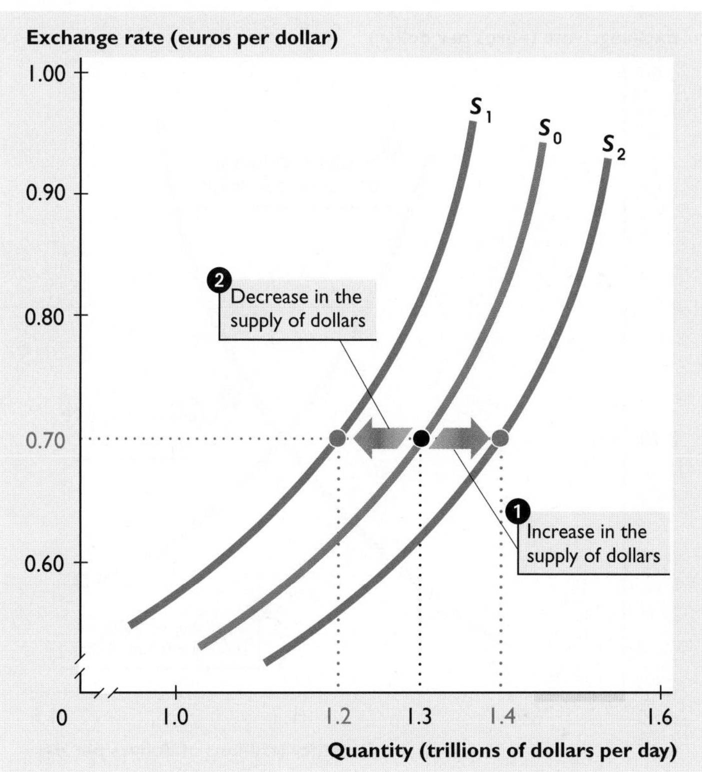


1. The supply of dollars increases if:
   - The U.S. interest rate differential decreases.
   - The expected future exchange rate falls.
2. The supply of dollars decreases if:
   - The U.S. interest rate differential increases.
   - The expected future exchange rate rises.

## Market Equilibrium

Demand and supply in the foreign exchange market determine the exchange rate. Just as in all the other markets you've studied, the price (the exchange rate) acts as a regulator. If the exchange rate is too high, there is a surplus—the quantity supplied exceeds the quantity demanded. If the exchange rate is too low, there is a shortage—the quantity supplied is less than the quantity demanded. At the equilibrium exchange rate, there is neither a shortage nor a surplus. The quantity supplied equals the quantity demanded.

Figure 33.5 illustrates market equilibrium. The demand for dollars is *D*, and the supply of dollars is *S*. The equilibrium exchange rate is 0.70 euros per dollar. At this exchange rate, the quantity demanded equals the quantity supplied and is $1.3 trillion a day. If the exchange rate is above 0.70 euros, for example, 0.80 euros per dollar, there is a surplus of dollars and the exchange rate falls. If the exchange rate is below 0.70 euros, for example, 0.60 euros per dollar, there is a shortage of dollars and the exchange rate rises.

The foreign exchange market is constantly pulled to its equilibrium by the forces of supply and demand. Foreign exchange dealers are constantly looking for the best price they can get. If they are selling, they want the highest price available. If they are buying, they want the lowest price available. Information flows from dealer to dealer through the worldwide computer network, and the price adjusts second by second to keep buying plans and selling plans in balance. That is, price adjusts second by second to keep the market at its equilibrium.

**FIGURE 33.5**

Equilibrium Exchange Rate

myeconlab Animation

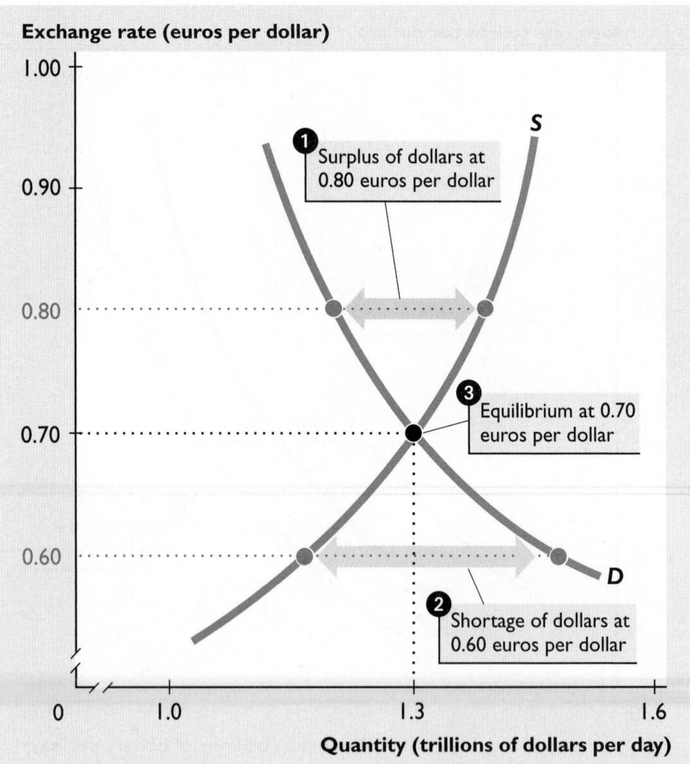


The demand curve for dollars is *D*, and the supply curve is *S*.

1. If the exchange rate is 0.80 euros per dollar, there is a surplus of dollars and the exchange rate falls.
2. If the exchange rate is 0.60 euros per dollar, there is a shortage of dollars and the exchange rate rises.
3. If the exchange rate is 0.70 euros per dollar, there is neither a shortage nor a surplus of dollars and the exchange rate remains constant. The market is in equilibrium.

# EYE on the DOLLAR

## Why Has Our Dollar Been Sinking?

Our dollar has been on a falling trend since the early 2000s but it hasn't always been sinking. Let's start by looking at a rising dollar.

### A Rising Dollar: 1999–2001

Between 1999 and 2001, the dollar appreciated against the euro. It rose from 0.86 euros to 1.17 euros per dollar. Figure 1 explains why this happened.

In 1999, the demand and supply curves were those labeled $D_{99}$ and $S_{99}$. The equilibrium exchange rate was 0.86 euros per dollar—where the quantity of dollars supplied equaled the quantity of dollars demanded.

During the next two years, the U.S. economy expanded faster than the European economy. Interest rates in Europe were 2 percentage points lower than in the United States, and the euro was expected to depreciate and the dollar was expected to appreciate.

With a positive U.S. interest rate differential and an expected dollar appreciation, the demand for dollars increased and the supply of dollars decreased. The demand curve shifted from $D_{99}$ to $D_{01}$ and the supply curve shifted from $S_{99}$ to $S_{01}$. These two reinforcing shifts made the exchange rate rise to 1.17 euros per dollar.

### A Falling Dollar: 2001–2009

Between 2001 and 2009, the dollar fell from 1.17 euros to 0.68 euros per dollar. Figure 2 explains this fall.

In 2001, the demand and supply curves were those labeled $D_{01}$ and $S_{01}$. The exchange rate was 1.17 euros per dollar. During the next few years, U.S. economic growth slipped below the European growth rate, European inflation fell, interest rates in Europe exceeded those in the United States, and the U.S. current account deficit continued to increase.

Under these conditions, currency traders expected the exchange rate to fall. The demand for dollars decreased and the supply of dollars increased. The demand curve shifted leftward to $D_{09}$ and the supply curve shifted rightward to $S_{09}$. The exchange rate fell to 0.68 euros per dollar.

Will the dollar keep falling? No one knows, but while U.S. interest rates remain low and the current account deficit remains high, a falling dollar is not unlikely.

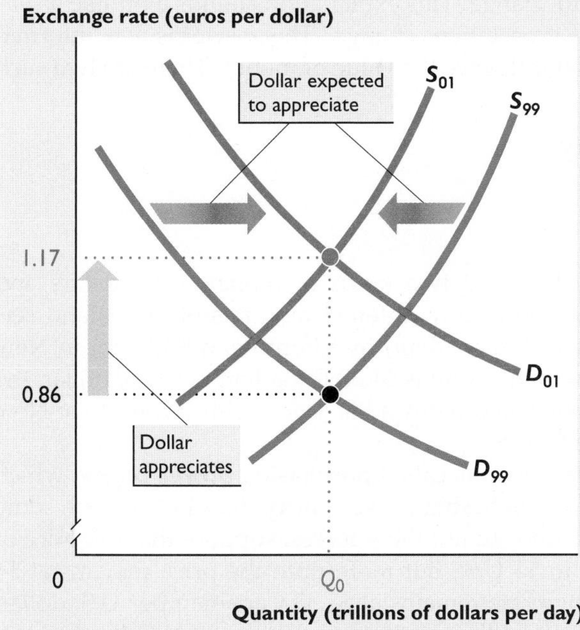


Figure 1 1999 to 2001

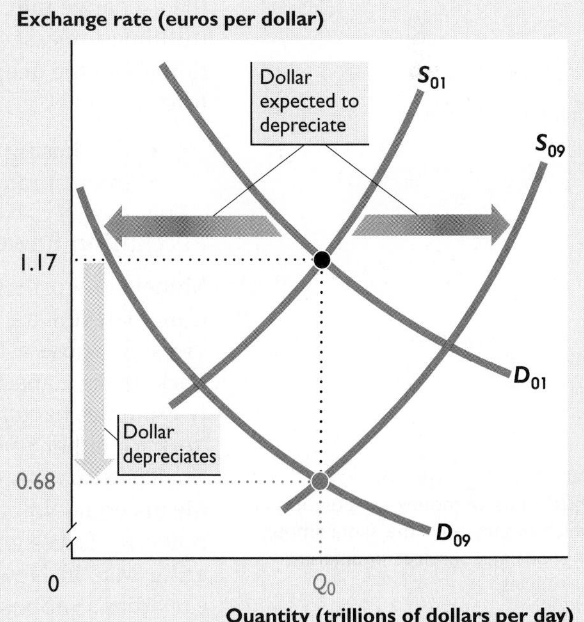


Figure 2 2001 to 2009

### Why Exchange Rates Are Volatile

You've seen that sometimes the dollar depreciates and at other times it appreciates. The exchange rates of other currencies are similarly volatile. The Japanese yen, Canadian dollar, and Mexican peso along with most currencies swing between appreciation and depreciation. Yet the quantity of dollars (and other currencies) traded on the foreign exchange market each day barely changes. Why?

A large part of the answer is that everyone in the foreign exchange market is potentially either a buyer or a seller—a demander or a supplier. Each has a price above which he or she will sell and below which he or she will buy.

This fact about the participants in the foreign exchange market means that supply and demand are not independent. The same shocks to the market that change the demand for a currency also change its supply. Demand and supply change in *opposite directions*, and result is large price changes and small quantity changes.

The two key influences that change both demand and supply in the foreign exchange market are the interest rate differential and the expected future exchange rate.

A rise in the U.S. interest rate differential *increases* the *demand* for U.S. dollars on the foreign exchange market and *decreases* the *supply*. A rise in the expected future exchange rate also increases the demand for U.S. dollars and decreases the supply.

These common influences that change demand and supply in *opposite directions* bring changes in the exchange rate and little change in the quantities of currencies traded. They can bring cumulative movements in the exchange rate or frequent changes of direction—volatility.

## Exchange Rate Expectations

The changes in the exchange rate that we've just considered occur in part because the exchange rate is expected to change. This explanation sounds a bit like a self-fulfilling forecast. What makes expectations change? The answer is new information about the deeper forces that influence the value of money. There are two such forces:

- Purchasing power parity
- Interest rate parity

### Purchasing Power Parity

Money is worth what it will buy. But two kinds of money, U.S. dollars and Canadian dollars, for example, might buy different amounts of goods and services. Suppose a Big Mac costs $4 (Canadian) in Toronto and $3 (U.S.) in New York. If the Canadian dollar exchange rate is $1.33 Canadian per U.S. dollar, the two monies have the same value. You can buy a Big Mac in either Toronto or New York for either $4 Canadian or $3 U.S.

**Purchasing power parity**
Equal value of money—a situation in which money buys the same amount of goods and services in different currencies.

The situation we've just described is called **purchasing power parity**, which means equal value of money. If purchasing power parity does not prevail, some powerful forces go to work. To understand these forces, suppose that the price of a Big Mac in New York rises to $4 U.S., but in Toronto the price remains at $4 Canadian. Suppose the exchange rate remains at $1.33 Canadian per U.S. dollar. In this case, a Big Mac in Toronto still costs $4 Canadian or $3 U.S. But in New

York, it costs $4 U.S. or $5.32 Canadian. Money buys more in Canada than in the United States. Money is not of equal value in both countries.

If all (or most) prices have increased in the United States and not increased in Canada, then people will generally expect that the U.S. dollar exchange rate is going to fall. The demand for U.S. dollars decreases, and the supply of U.S. dollars increases. The U.S. dollar exchange rate falls, as expected. If the U.S. dollar falls to $1.00 Canadian and there are no further price changes, purchasing power parity is restored. A Big Mac now costs $4 in either U.S. dollars or Canadian dollars in both New York and Toronto.

If prices increase in Canada and other countries but remain constant in the United States, then people will generally expect that the value of the U.S. dollar on the foreign exchange market is too low and that the U.S. dollar exchange rate will rise. The demand for U.S. dollars increases, and the supply of U.S. dollars decreases. The U.S. dollar exchange rate rises, as expected.

Ultimately, the value of money is determined by prices. So the deeper forces that influence the exchange rate have tentacles that spread throughout the economy. If prices in the United States rise faster than those in other countries, the exchange rate falls. And if prices in the United States rise more slowly than those in other countries, the exchange rate rises.

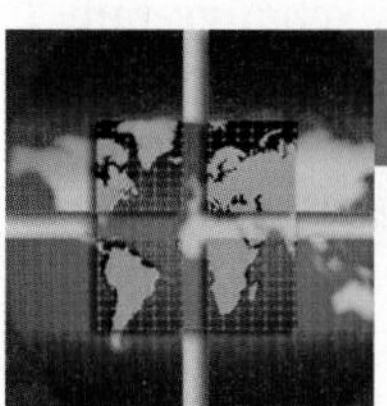

## EYE on the GLOBAL ECONOMY

### Purchasing Power Parity

Purchasing power parity (PPP) is a long-run phenomenon. In the short run, deviations from PPP can be large.

The figure shows the range of deviations from PPP in October 2009. At that time, the Danish krone was overvalued by more than 70 percent and the Swiss franc by 60 percent. An overvalued currency is one that, according to PPP, will depreciate at some point in the future.

The most undervalued currencies in October 2009 were the Mexican peso and Russian ruble. An undervalued currency is one that, according to PPP, will appreciate at some time in the future.

PPP theory predicts that a currency might depreciate or appreciate but not *when* it will depreciate or appreciate.

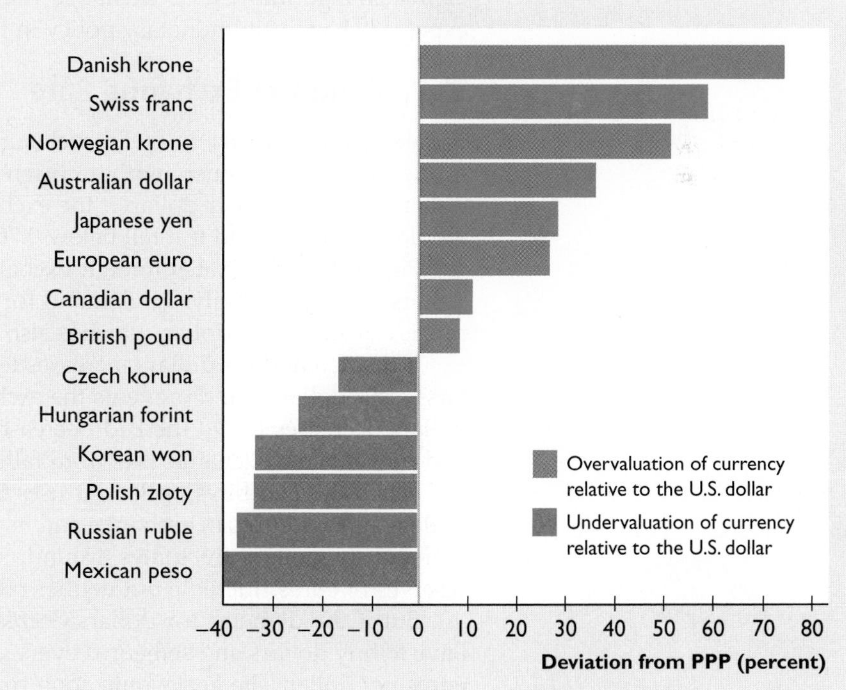


SOURCE OF DATA: PACIFIC FX Service, University of British Columbia, November 6, 2009.

### Interest Rate Parity

Suppose a Canadian dollar bank deposit in a Toronto bank earns 5 percent a year and a U.S. dollar bank deposit in a New York bank earns 3 percent a year. Why does anyone deposit money in New York? Why doesn't all the money flow to Toronto? The answer is: Because of exchange rate expectations. Suppose people expect the Canadian dollar to depreciate by 2 percent a year. This 2 percent depreciation must be subtracted from the 5 percent interest to obtain the net return of 3 percent a year that an American can earn by depositing funds in a Toronto bank. The two returns are equal. This situation is one of **interest rate parity**—equal interest rates when exchange rate changes are taken into account.

**Interest rate parity**
Equal interest rates—a situation in which the interest rate in one currency equals the interest rate in another currency when exchange rate changes are taken into account.

Interest rate parity always prevails. Funds move to get the highest return available. If interest rate parity did not hold because the Canadian dollar had too high a value on the foreign exchange market, the expected return in Toronto would be lower than in New York. In seconds, traders would sell the Canadian dollar, its exchange rate would fall, and the expected return from lending in Toronto would rise to equal that in New York.

## Monetary Policy and the Exchange Rate

Monetary policy influences the interest rate (see Chapter 27, pp. 698–701), so monetary policy also influences the interest rate differential and the exchange rate. If the Fed increases the U.S. interest rate and other central banks keep interest rates in other countries unchanged, the value of the U.S. dollar rises on the foreign exchange market. If other central banks increase their interest rates and the Fed keeps the U.S. interest rate unchanged, the value of the U.S. dollar falls on the foreign exchange market. So exchange rates fluctuate in response to changes and expected changes in monetary policy in the United States and around the world.

## Pegging the Exchange Rate

Some central banks try to avoid exchange rate fluctuations by pegging the value of their currency against another currency. Suppose the Fed wanted to keep the dollar at 0.70 euros per dollar. If the exchange rate rose above 0.70 euros, the Fed would sell dollars and if it fell below 0.70 euros, the Fed would buy dollars.

Figure 33.6 illustrates foreign exchange market intervention. The supply of dollars is $S$, and initially, the demand for dollars is $D_0$. The equilibrium exchange rate is 0.70 euros per dollar, which is also the Fed's target—the horizontal red line.

If the demand for dollars increases to $D_1$, the Fed increases the supply of dollars—sells dollars—and prevents the exchange rate from rising. If the demand for dollars decreases to $D_2$, the Fed decreases the supply of dollars—buys dollars—and prevents the exchange rate from falling.

When the Fed buys dollars, it uses its reserves of euros; when the Fed sells dollars, it takes euros in exchange and its reserves of euros increase. As long as the demand for dollars fluctuates around, so on average remains at, $D_0$, the Fed's reserves of euros fluctuate but neither run dry nor persistently increase.

But if the demand for dollars decreased permanently to $D_2$, the Fed would have to buy dollars and sell euros every day to maintain the exchange rate at 0.70 euros per dollar. The Fed would soon run out of euros, and when it did, the dollar would sink. If the demand for dollars increased permanently to $D_1$, the Fed would have to sell dollars and buy euros every day. The Fed would be piling up unwanted euros and at some point would let the dollar rise.

**FIGURE 33.6**

Foreign Exchange Market Intervention

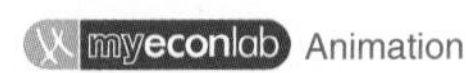


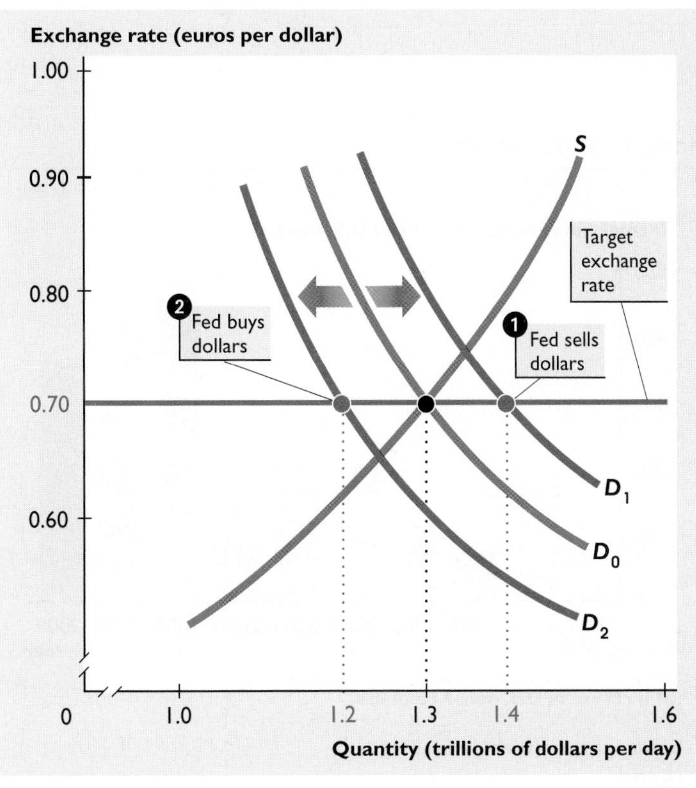


Initially, the demand for dollars is $D_0$, the supply of dollars is $S$, and the exchange rate is 0.70 euros per dollar. The Fed can intervene in the foreign exchange market to keep the exchange rate close to its target rate (0.70 euros per dollar in this example).

1. If demand increases from $D_0$ to $D_1$, the Fed sells dollars to increase the supply of dollars and maintain the exchange rate.

2. If demand decreases from $D_0$ to $D_2$, the Fed buys dollars to decrease the supply of dollars and maintain the exchange rate.

Persistent intervention on one side of the market cannot be sustained.

## The People's Bank of China in the Foreign Exchange Market

Although the Fed could peg the value of the dollar, it chooses not to do so. But China's central bank, the People's Bank of China, does intervene to peg the value of its currency—the yuan. *Eye on the Global Economy* on page 871 shows the result of this intervention.

During much of the period that the yuan has been pegged to the U.S. dollar, China has piled up U.S. dollar reserves. Figure 33.7(a) shows the numbers. During 2007 to 2009, China's reserves increased by more than $1 trillion.

Figure 33.7(b), which shows the market for U.S. dollars priced in terms of the yuan, explains why China's reserves increased. The demand curve $D$ and supply curve $S$ intersect at 5 yuan per dollar. If the People's Bank of China took no actions in the foreign exchange market, this exchange rate would be the equilibrium rate. (This particular value is only an example. No one knows what the yuan-dollar exchange rate would be with no intervention.)

By intervening in the market and buying U.S. dollars, the People's Bank can peg the yuan at 6.80 yuan per dollar. But to do so, it must keep holding the dollars that it buys. In Figure 33.7(b), the People's Bank buys $250 billion a year.

Only by allowing the yuan to appreciate can China stop accumulating dollars. That is what the People's Bank decided to do in July 2005. But China continues to intervene in the foreign exchange market to manage the rate of appreciation of the yuan. Eventually, when China's foreign exchange market becomes more accustomed to a floating yuan, it is likely that the People's Bank will lessen its intervention and the value of the yuan will be determined by market forces.

## FIGURE 33.7

### China's Foreign Exchange Market Intervention

myeconlab Animation

China has been piling up reserves of U.S. dollars since 2000. In 2007 through 2009, the build-up of reserves was very large. Part (a) shows the numbers.

Part (b) shows the market for the U.S. dollar in terms of the Chinese yuan. Note that a higher exchange rate (yuan per dollar) means a lower value of the yuan and a higher value of the dollar. The yuan appreciates when the number of yuan per dollar decreases.

1. With demand curve *D* and supply curve *S*, the equilibrium exchange rate is 5 yuan per dollar. (The actual equilibrium value is not known, and the value assumed is only an example.)
2. The People's Bank of China has a target exchange rate of 6.80 yuan per dollar. At this exchange rate, the yuan is *undervalued.*
3. To keep the exchange rate pegged at its target level, the People's Bank of China must buy U.S. dollars in exchange for yuan, and China's reserves of dollars pile up.

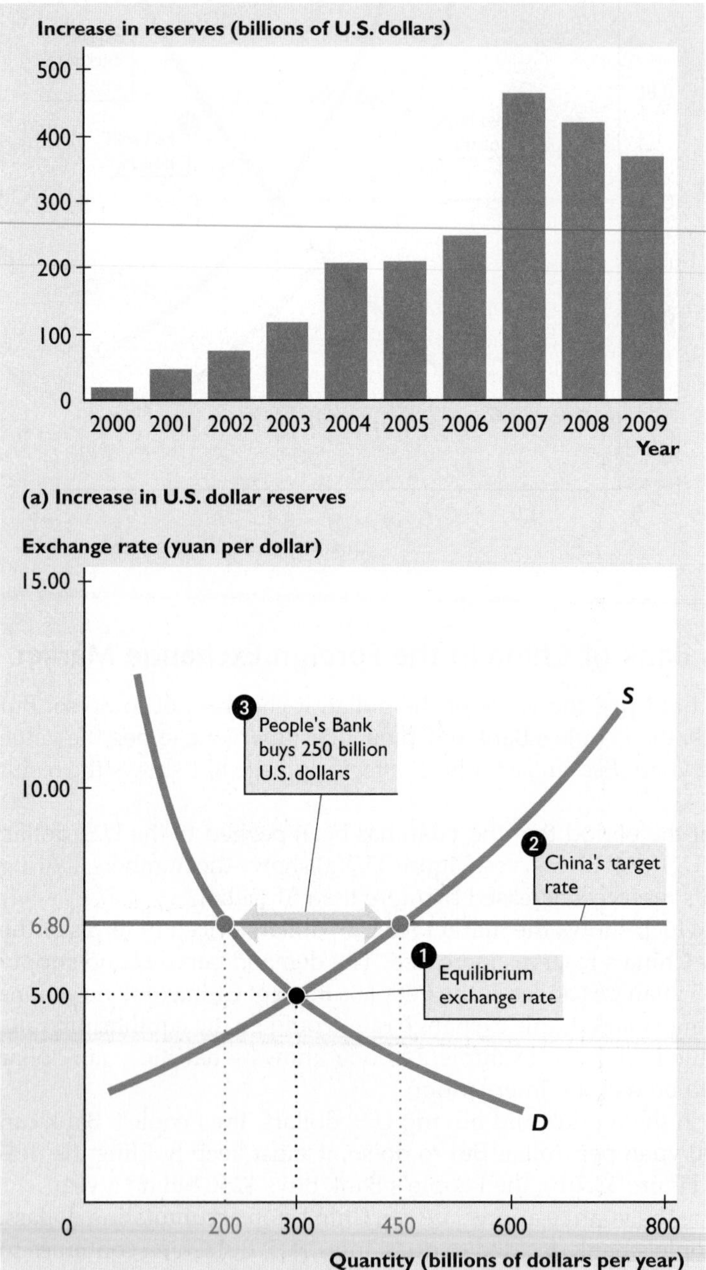


SOURCE OF DATA: The People's Bank of China.

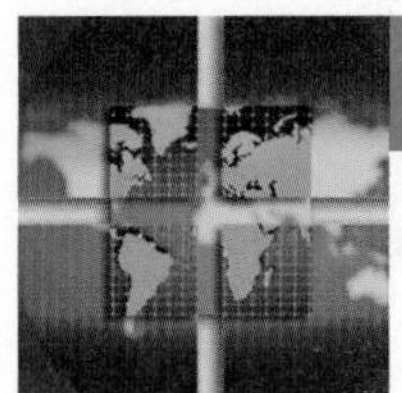

# EYE on the GLOBAL ECONOMY

## The Fixed Yuan

The Chinese central bank, the People's Bank of China, has pegged the value of the yuan in terms of the U.S. dollar for more than 10 years.

The figure shows the value of the yuan (yuan per U.S. dollar) from the early 1990s to 2009.

The yuan was devalued in January 1994. It appreciated a bit during 1994 and 1995. But it was then pegged at 8.28 yuan per U.S. dollar, a value that the People's Bank of China maintained for more than 10 years. In July 2005, the yuan began a managed float—a managed appreciation of the yuan. Then, in July 2008, the exchange rate was again pegged, this time at 6.8 yuan per dollar.

SOURCE OF DATA: PACIFIC FX Service, University of British Columbia.

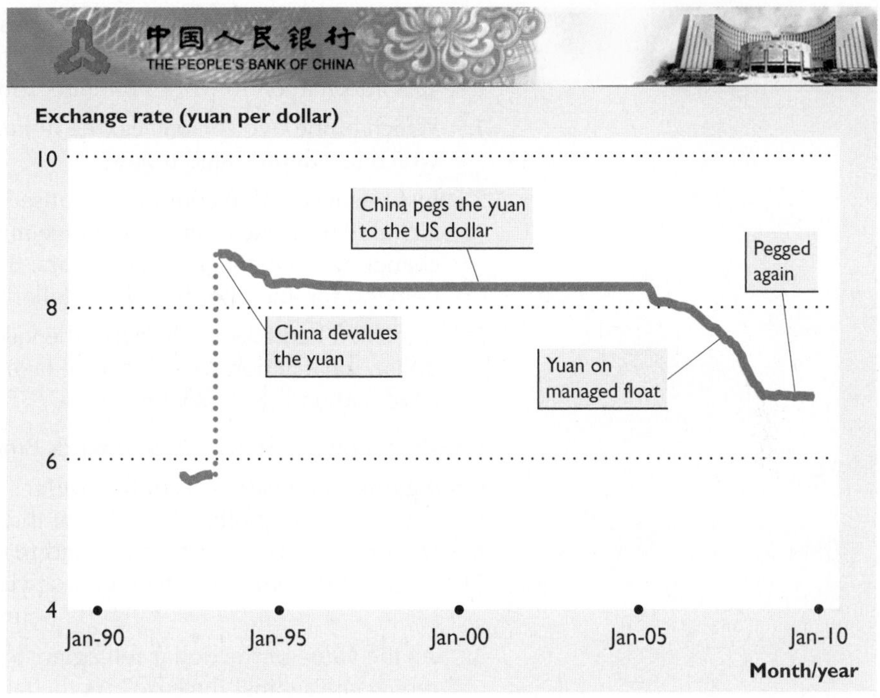

# EYE on YOUR LIFE

## Your Foreign Exchange Transactions

If you plan to go to Europe for a vacation next summer, you will need some euros. What is the best way to get euros?

You could just take your ATM/debit card or credit card and use an ATM in Europe. You'll get euros from the cash machine, and your bank account in the United States will get charged for the cash you obtain.

When you get euros, the number of euros you request is multiplied by the exchange rate to determine how many dollars to take from your bank account.

You have just made a transaction in the foreign exchange market. You have exchanged dollars for euros.

The exchange rate that you paid was probably costly. Your bank took a commission for helping you get euros. Some banks charge as much as 5 percent. Check in advance. It might be better to buy euros from your bank before you leave on your trip.

Another question has possibly occurred to you: How many euros will your budget buy next summer? Should you get the euros now at a price that is certain or would it be better to wait until closer to your travel date and take a chance on the value of the dollar then?

No one can answer this question. But you can buy euros today at a fixed price for delivery at a later date. (This transaction is made in a market called the forward exchange market.) Again, though, you'll end up paying a big commission for the service.

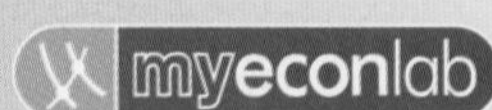

Work these problems in Study Plan 33.2 to get instant feedback.

## CHECKPOINT 33.2

**Explain how the exchange rate is determined and why it fluctuates.**

### Practice Problems

Suppose that yesterday, the U.S. dollar was trading on the foreign exchange market at 100 yen per dollar. Today, the U.S. dollar is trading at 105 yen per dollar. Use this information to work Problems **1** to **3**.

1. Which of the two currencies (the dollar or the yen) has appreciated and which has depreciated today?
2. List the events that could have caused today's change in the value of the U.S. dollar on the foreign exchange market. Did these events on your list change the demand for U.S. dollars, the supply of U.S. dollars, or both the demand for and supply of U.S. dollars?
3. If the Fed had tried to stabilize the value of the U.S. dollar at 100 yen per dollar, what action would it have taken? What effect would the Fed's actions have had on U.S. official reserves?

Use the following information to work Problems **4** and **5**.

**Gold gains as investors shun the dollar**

In the past seven months, the value of the dollar has slid by 15 percent against major currencies as investors migrated to other markets. Today, the dollar fell to $1.47 against the euro and the Japanese yen fell from 89 to 88.83 yen per dollar.

Source: *The New York Times*, October 6, 2009

4. As the value of the dollar fell against the euro, did the dollar appreciate or depreciate against the euro? As the Japanese yen strengthened against the dollar, did the dollar appreciate or depreciate against the yen?
5. What actions in the foreign exchange market lowered the dollar?

### Guided Solutions to Practice Problems

1. Because the price of the U.S. dollar is a larger number of yen, the U.S. dollar has appreciated. The yen has depreciated because it buys fewer dollars.
2. The main events might be an increase in the U.S. interest rate, a decrease in the Japanese interest rate, or a rise in the expected future exchange rate of the U.S. dollar.

   The events listed change both the demand for and supply of U.S. dollars. The events increase the demand for and decrease the supply of U.S. dollars.
3. To stabilize the value of the U.S. dollar, the Fed would have sold U.S. dollars to increase the supply of U.S. dollars in the foreign exchange market.

   When the Fed sells U.S. dollars, it buys foreign currency. U.S. official reserves would have increased.
4. Because the euro buys fewer dollars, the euro has appreciated and the dollar has depreciated. Because the dollar buys fewer yen, the dollar depreciated against the yen.
5. As investors increased their demand for gold, the demand for U.S. dollars decreased. As some holders of U.S. dollars wanted to switch to gold, the supply of dollars increased. The result was a depreciation of the U.S. dollar.

# CHAPTER SUMMARY

## Key Points

1 **Describe a country's balance of payments accounts and explain what determines the amount of international borrowing and lending.**

- Foreign currency is used to finance international trade and the purchase of foreign assets.
- A country's balance of payments accounts record its international transactions.
- Historically, the United States has been a net lender to the rest of the world, but in 1983 that situation changed and the United States became a net borrower, and in 1989 the United States became a debtor nation.
- Net exports are equal to the private sector balance plus the government sector balance.

2 **Explain how the exchange rate is determined and why it fluctuates.**

- Foreign currency is obtained in exchange for domestic currency in the foreign exchange market.
- The exchange rate is determined by demand and supply in the foreign exchange market.
- The lower the exchange rate, the greater is the quantity of dollars demanded. A change in the exchange rate brings a movement along the demand curve for dollars.
- Changes in the expected future exchange rate and the U.S. interest rate differential change the demand for dollars and shift the demand curve.
- The lower the exchange rate, the smaller is the quantity of dollars supplied. A change in the exchange rate brings a movement along the supply curve of dollars.
- Changes in the expected future exchange rate and the U.S. interest rate differential change the supply of dollars and shift the supply curve.
- Fluctuations in the exchange rate occur because fluctuations in the demand for and supply of dollars are not independent.
- A central bank can intervene in the foreign exchange market to smooth fluctuations in the exchange rate.

## Key Terms

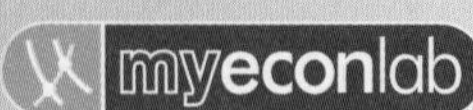

Work these problems in Chapter 33 Study Plan to get instant feedback.

## CHAPTER CHECKPOINT

### Study Plan Problems and Applications

Table 1 gives some data that describe the economy of Antarctica in 2050:

**TABLE 1**

| Item | (billions of Antarctica dollars) |
|---|---|
| Imports of goods and services | 150 |
| Exports of goods and services | 50 |
| Net interest | −10 |
| Net transfers | 35 |
| Foreign investment in Antarctica | 125 |
| Antarctica's investment abroad | 55 |

Use Table 1 to answer Problems **1** and **2**.

1. Calculate Antarctica's current account balance, capital account balance, and the increase in Antarctica's official reserves.
2. Is Antarctica a debtor nation or a creditor nation? Are its international assets increasing or decreasing? Is Antarctica borrowing to finance investment or consumption? Explain.
3. The U.S. dollar depreciates. Explain which of the following events could have caused the depreciation and why.
   - The Fed intervened in the foreign exchange market. Did the Fed buy or sell U.S. dollars?
   - People began to expect that the U.S. dollar would depreciate.
   - The U.S. interest rate differential increased.
   - Foreign investment in the United States increased.

Suppose that the inflation rate is lower in Japan than it is in the United States, and that the difference in the inflation rates persists for some years. Use this information to answer Problems **4** to **6**.

4. Will the U.S. dollar appreciate or depreciate against the yen and will purchasing power parity be violated? Why or why not?
5. Will U.S. interest rates be higher or lower than Japanese interest rates and will interest rate parity hold? Why or why not?
6. Explain how the expected future exchange rate will change.
7. **Aussie dollar hit by interest rate talk**
   The Australian dollar fell against the U.S. dollar to its lowest value in the past two weeks. CPI inflation was reported to be generally as expected, but not strong enough to justify expectations for an aggressive interest rate rise by Australia's central bank next week.
   
   Source: Reuters, October 28, 2009
   
   Explain why the expected rise of the Australian interest rate with no change in the U.S. interest rate lowered the current value of the Australian dollar against the U.S. dollar.

## Instructor Assignable Problems and Applications

Your instructor can assign these problems as homework, a quiz, or a test in **MyEconLab**.

1. If the European Central Bank starts to raise its policy interest rate before the Fed starts to raise the federal funds rate target, what do you predict will happen to the dollar/euro exchange rate? Illustrate your answer with an appropriate graphical analysis.
2. Table 2 gives some data that describe the economy of Atlantis in 2020:

**TABLE 2**

| Item | (billions of Atlantis dollars) |
|---|---|
| Government expenditure | 200 |
| Saving | 100 |
| Increase in official reserves of Atlantis | 5 |
| Net foreign investment in Atlantis | 50 |
| Net taxes | 150 |
| Investment | 125 |

Calculate the current account balance, the capital account balance, the government budget balance, and the private sector balance.

3. The U.S. dollar appreciates, and U.S. official reserves increase. Explain which of the following events might have caused these changes to occur and why.
   - The Fed intervened in the foreign exchange market and sold U.S. dollars.
   - The Fed conducted an open market operation and sold bonds.
   - People began to expect that the U.S. dollar would appreciate.
   - The U.S. interest rate differential narrowed.
4. Which of the following events might have caused the euro to appreciate and why?
   - The European Central Bank sold euros in the foreign exchange market.
   - The Fed intervened in the foreign exchange market and bought U.S. dollars.
   - The EU interest rate differential increased.
   - Profits increased in Europe, and U.S. investment in Europe surged.

Use the following information to work Problems **5** and **6**.

**Brazil's overvalued real**

This year the Brazilian real appreciated 33 percent against the dollar and has pushed up the price of a Big Mac in Sao Paulo to $US4.60, higher than the New York price of $US3.99. Brazil's interest rate is 8.75 percent a year compared to the U.S. interest rate at near zero, and foreign funds flowing into Brazil surged.

Source: *Bloomberg News*, October 27, 2009

5. Does purchasing power parity (PPP) hold between Brazil and the United States? If not, does PPP predict that the real will appreciate further or depreciate against the U.S. dollar?
6. Does interest rate parity hold between Brazil and the United States? If interest rate parity does hold, what is the expected rate of appreciation or depreciation of the Brazilian real against the U.S. dollar? If the Fed raised the interest rate while the Brazilian interest remained at 8.75 percent a year, how would the expected appreciation or depreciation of the real change?

Use the following information to work Problems **7** and **8**.

Suppose that the euro keeps appreciating against the U.S. dollar. The Fed decides to stop the euro from appreciating (stop the U.S. dollar from depreciating) and intervenes in the foreign exchange market.

**7.** What actions might the Fed take in the foreign exchange market? Could these actions persist in the long run? Would the Fed's actions prevent interest rate parity from being achieved? Why or why not?

**8.** Are there any other actions that the Fed could take to raise the foreign exchange value of the dollar? Explain your answer.

**9.** Many people think that a current account deficit is a sign that a nation is not able to compete in international markets. Explain why this view is incorrect and describe the factors that create a current account deficit.

Use the following information to work Problems **10** to **12**.

For most of the 1990s, Argentina pegged the value of its currency, the peso, to the U.S. dollar: 1 peso equaled 1 U.S. dollar. Then, at the end of 2001, the peso was allowed to find its own value on the foreign exchange market and it fell dramatically.

**10.** Why might it be difficult for Argentina to peg the value of its currency to the U.S. dollar?

**11.** Why, nonetheless, might it be a good idea for Argentina to peg the value of its currency to the U.S. dollar? What are the potential benefits to Argentina?

**12.** On balance, do you think a country such as Argentina should peg its currency to the U.S. dollar?

Use the following information to work Problems **13** and **14**.

Suppose that the U.K. pound is trading at 1.82 U.S. dollars per U.K. pound and at this exchange rate purchasing power parity holds. The U.S. interest rate is 2 percent a year and the U.K. interest rate is 4 percent a year.

**13.** Calculate the U.S. interest rate differential. What is the U.K. pound expected to be worth in terms of U.S. dollars one year from now?

**14.** Which country more likely has the lower inflation rate? How can you tell?

**15.** You can purchase a laptop in Mexico City for 12,960 Mexican pesos. If the exchange rate is 10.8 Mexican pesos per U.S. dollar and if purchasing power parity prevails, at what price can you buy an identical computer in Dallas, Texas?

# Glossary

**Ability-to-pay principle** The proposition that people should pay taxes according to how easily they can bear the burden. (p. 208)

**Above full-employment equilibrium** When equilibrium real GDP exceeds potential GDP. (p. 735)

**Absolute advantage** When one person is more productive than another person in several or even all activities. (p. 76)

**Aggregate demand** The relationship between the quantity of real GDP demanded and the price level when all other influences on expenditure plans remain the same. (p. 728)

**Aggregate planned expenditure** Planned consumption expenditure plus planned investment plus planned government expenditure plus planned exports minus planned imports. (p. 748)

**Aggregate supply** The relationship between the quantity of real GDP supplied and the price level when all other influences on production plans remain the same. (p. 722)

**Allocative efficiency** A situation in which the quantities of goods and services produced are those that people value most highly—it is not possible to produce more of a good or service without giving up some of another good that people value more highly. (p. 143)

**Antitrust law** A law that regulates oligopolies and prohibits them from becoming monopolies or behaving like monopolies. (p. 449)

**Automatic fiscal policy** A fiscal policy action that is triggered by the state of the economy. (p. 805)

**Automatic stabilizers** Features of fiscal policy that stabilize real GDP without explicit action by the government. (p. 805)

**Average cost pricing rule** A rule that sets price equal to average total cost to enable a regulated firm to avoid economic loss. (p. 398)

**Average fixed cost** Total fixed cost per unit of output. (p. 333)

**Average product** Total product divided by the quantity of a factor of production. The average product of labor is total product divided by the quantity of labor employed. (p. 328)

**Average tax rate** The percentage of income that is paid in tax. (p. 199)

**Average total cost** Total cost per unit of output, which equals average fixed cost plus average variable cost. (p. 333)

**Average variable cost** Total variable cost per unit of output. (p. 333)

**Balance of payments accounts** The accounts in which a nation records its international trading, borrowing, and lending. (p. 850)

**Balanced budget** The budget balance when revenues equal outlays. (p. 797)

**Balanced budget multiplier** The effect on aggregate demand of a *simultaneous* change in government expenditure and taxes that leaves the budget balanced unchanged. (p. 802)

**Banking system** The Federal Reserve and the banks and other institutions that accept deposits and provide the services that enable people and businesses to make and receive payments. (p. 670)

**Barrier to entry** Any constraint that protects a firm from competitors. (p. 376)

**Barter** The direct exchange of goods and services for other goods and services, which requires a double coincidence of wants. (p. 665)

**Below full-employment equilibrium** When potential GDP exceeds equilibrium real GDP. (p. 735)

**Benefit** The benefit of something is the gain or pleasure that it brings. (p. 11)

**Benefits principle** The proposition that people should pay taxes equal to the benefits they receive from public goods and services. (p. 208)

**Big tradeoff** A tradeoff between efficiency and fairness that recognizes the cost of making income transfers. (p. 161)

**Black market** An illegal market that operates alongside a government-regulated market. (p. 171)

**Bond** A promise to pay specified sums of money on specified dates. (p. 640)

**Budget deficit** The negative budget balance when outlays exceed revenues. (p. 797)

**Budget line** A line that describes the limits to consumption possibilities and that depends on a consumer's budget and the prices of goods and services. (p. 292)

**Budget surplus** The positive budget balance when revenues exceed outlays. (p. 797)

**Business cycle** A periodic but irregular up-and-down movement of total production and other measures of economic activity. (p. 524)

**Capital** Tools, instruments, machines, buildings, and other items that have been produced in the past and that businesses now use to produce goods and services. (pp. 37, 638)

**Capital account** Record of foreign investment in the United States minus U.S. investment abroad. (p. 850)

**Capital goods** Goods that are bought by businesses to increase their productive resources. (p. 34)

**Capture theory** The theory that regulation serves the self-interest of the producer and results in maximum profit, underproduction, and deadweight loss. (p. 396)

**Cartel** A group of firms acting together to limit output, raise price, and increase economic profit. (p. 432)

**Central bank** A public authority that provides banking services to banks and goverment and regulates financial institutions and markets. (p. 675)

***Ceteris paribus*** Other things remaining the same (often abbreviated as *cet. par.*). (p. 15)

**Chained-dollar real GDP** The measure of real GDP calculated by the Bureau of Economic Analysis. (p. 535)

**Change in demand** A change in the quantity that people plan to buy when any influence on buying plans other than the price of the good changes. (p. 88)

**Change in the quantity demanded** A change in the quantity of a good that people plan to buy that results from a change in the price of the good with all other influences on buying plans remaining the same. (p. 90)

**Change in the quantity supplied** A change in the quantity of a good that suppliers plan to sell that results from a change in the price of the good with all other influences on selling plans remaining the same. (p. 97)

**Change in supply** A change in the quantity that suppliers plan to sell when any influence on selling plans other than the price of the good changes. (p. 95)

**Circular flow model** A model of the economy that shows the circular flow of expenditures and incomes that result from decision makers' choices and the way those choices interact to determine what, how, and for whom goods and services are produced. (p. 48)

**Classical growth theory** The theory that the clash between an exploding population and limited resources will eventually bring economic growth to an end. (p. 621)

**Classical macroeconomics** The view that the market economy works well, that aggregate fluctuations are a natural consequence of an expanding economy, and that government intervention cannot improve the efficiency of the market economy. (p. 588)

**Coase theorem** The proposition that if property rights exist, only a small number of parties are involved, and transactions costs are low, then private transactions are efficient and the outcome is not affected by who is assigned the property right. (p. 274)

**Command system** A system that allocates resources by the order of someone in authority. (p. 141)

**Commercial bank** A firm that is chartered by the Comptroller of the Currency in the U.S. Treasury (or by a state agency) to accept deposits and make loans. (p. 670)

**Common resource** A resource that can be used only once, but no one can be prevented from using what is available. (p. 245)

**Comparative advantage** The ability of a person to perform an activity or produce a good or service at a lower opportunity cost than anyone else. (p. 75)

**Complement** A good that is consumed with another good. (p. 88)

**Complement in production** A good that is produced along with another good. (p. 95)

**Constant returns to scale** A condition in which, when a firm increases its plant size and labor employed by the same percentage, its output increases by that same percentage and its average total cost remains constant. (p. 340)

**Consumer Price Index** A measure of the average of the prices paid by urban consumers for a fixed market basket of consumption goods and services. (p. 564)

**Consumer surplus** The marginal benefit from a good or service minus the price paid for it, summed over the quantity consumed. (p. 149)

**Consumption expenditure** The expenditure by households on consumption goods and services. (p. 511)

**Consumption function** The relationship between consumption expenditure and disposable income, other things remaining the same. (p. 748)

**Consumption goods and services** Goods and services that are bought by individuals and used to provide personal enjoyment and contribute to a person's quality of life. (p. 34)

**Contractionary fiscal policy** A decrease in government expenditure on goods and services, a decrease in transfer payments, or an increase in taxes designed to decrease aggregate demand. (p. 804)

**Core inflation rate** The annual percentage increase in the PCE price index excluding the prices of food and energy. (p. 573)

**Correlation** The tendency for the values of two variables to move together in a predictable and related way. (p. 16)

**Cost of living index** A measure of the change in the amount of money that people need to spend to achieve a given standard of living. (p. 570)

**Creditor nation** A country that during its entire history has invested more in the rest of the world than other countries have invested in it. (p. 852)

**Cross elasticity of demand** A measure of the responsiveness of the demand for a good to a change in the price of a substitute or complement when other things remain the same. (p. 131)

**Cross-section graph** A graph that shows the values of an economic variable for different groups in a population at a point in time. (p. 24)

**Crowding-out effect** The tendency for a government budget deficit to raise the real interest rate and decrease investment. (p. 656)

**Currency** Notes (dollar bills) and coins. (p. 666)

**Currency appreciation** The rise in the value of one currency in terms of another currency. (p. 857)

**Currency depreciation** The fall in the value of one currency in terms of another currency. (p. 858)

**Current account** Record of receipts from the sale of goods and services to other countries (exports), minus payments for goods and services bought from other countries (imports), plus the net amount of interest and transfers received from and paid to other countries. (p. 850)

**Cyclical unemployment** The fluctuating unemployment over the business cycle that increases during a recession and decreases during an expansion. (p. 554)

**Deadweight loss** The decrease in total surplus that results from an inefficient underproduction or overproduction. (p. 157)

**Debtor nation** A country that during its entire history has borrowed more from the rest of the world than it has lent to the rest of the world. (p. 852)

**Decreasing marginal returns** When the marginal product of an additional worker is less than the marginal product of the previous worker. (p. 326)

**Deflation** A situation in which the price level is *falling* and the inflation rate is *negative*. (p. 567)

**Demand** The relationship between the quantity demanded and the price of a good when all other influences on buying plans remain the same. (p. 85)

**Demand curve** A graph of the relationship between the quantity demanded of a good and its price when all the other influences on buying plans remain the same. (p. 86)

**Demand for labor** The relationship between the quantity of labor demanded and the real wage rate when all other influences on firms' hiring plans remain the same. (p. 593)

**Demand for loanable funds** The relationship between the quantity of loanable funds demanded and the real interest rate when all other influences on borrowing plans remain the same. (p. 645)

**Demand for money** The relationship between the quantity of money demanded and the nominal interest rate, when all other influences on the amount of money that people wish to hold remain the same. (p. 696)

**Demand schedule** A list of the quantities demanded at each different price when all the other influences on buying plans remain the same. (p. 86)

**Depreciation** The decrease in the value of capital that results from its use and from obsolescence. (p. 518)

**Deregulation** The process of removing regulation of prices, quantities, entry, and other aspects of economic activity in a firm or an industry. (p. 396)

**Derived demand** The demand for a factor of production, which is derived from the demand for the goods and services that it is used to produce. (p. 461)

**Diminishing marginal rate of substitution** The general tendency for the marginal rate of substitution to decrease as the consumer moves down along the indifference curve, increasing consumption of the good measured on the $x$-axis and decreasing consumption of the good measured on the $y$-axis. (p. 314)

**Diminishing marginal utility** The general tendency for marginal utility to decrease as the quantity of a good consumed increases. (p. 298)

**Diminishing returns** The tendency for each additional hour of labor employed to produce a successively smaller additional amount of real GDP. (p. 592)

**Direct relationship** A relationship between two variables that move in the same direction. (p. 26)

**Discount rate** The interest rate at which the Fed stands ready to lend reserves to commercial banks. (p. 677)

**Discouraged worker** A marginally attached worker who has not made specific efforts to find a job within the past four weeks because previous unsuccessful attempts to find a job were discouraging. (p. 542)

**Discretionary fiscal policy** A fiscal policy action that is initiated by an act of Congress. (p. 805)

**Discretionary monetary policy** Monetary policy that is based on expert assessment of the current economic situation. (p. 840)

**Diseconomies of scale** A condition in which, when a firm increases its plant size and labor employed by the same percentage, its output increases by a smaller percentage and its average total cost increases. (p. 340)

**Disposable income** Market income plus cash benefits paid by the government minus taxes. (p. 500)

**Disposable personal income** Income received by households minus personal income taxes paid. (p. 519)

**Duopoly** A market with only two firms. (p. 432)

**Dumping** When a foreign firm sells its exports at a lower price than its cost of production. (p. 234)

**Earnings sharing regulation** A regulation that requires firms to make refunds to customers when profits rise above a target level. (p. 401)

**Economic depreciation** An opportunity cost of a firm using capital that it owns—measured as the change in the *market value* of capital over a given period. (p. 321)

**Economic freedom** A condition in which people are able to make personal choices, their private property is protected by the rule of law, and they are free to buy and sell in markets. (p. 628)

**Economic growth** The sustained expansion of production possibilities. (p. 73)

**Economic growth rate** The annual percentage change of real GDP. (p. 612)

**Economic profit** A firm's total revenue minus total cost. (p. 321)

**Economics** The social science that studies the choices that individuals, businesses, government, and entire societies make as they cope with *scarcity*, the *incentives* that influence those choices, and the arrangements that coordinate them. (p. 3)

**Economies of scale** A condition in which, when a firm increases its plant size and labor employed by the same percentage, its output increases by a larger percentage and its average total cost decreases. (p. 339)

**Efficiency wage** A real wage rate that is set above the full-employment equilibrium wage rate to induce greater work effort. (p. 603)

**Efficient scale** The quantity at which average total cost is a minimum. (p. 417)

**Elastic demand** When the percentage change in the quantity demanded exceeds the percentage change in price. (p. 116)

**Elastic supply** When the percentage change in the quantity supplied exceeds the percentage change in price. (p. 126)

**Entrepreneurship** The human resource that organizes labor, land, and capital to produce goods and services. (p. 38)

**Equation of exchange** An equation that states that the quantity of money multiplied by the velocity of circulation equals the price level multiplied by real GDP. (p. 707)

**Equilibrium expenditure** The level of aggregate expenditure that occurs when aggregate *planned* expenditure equals real GDP. (p. 756)

**Equilibrium price** The price at which the quantity demanded equals the quantity supplied. (p. 99)

**Equilibrium quantity** The quantity bought and sold at the equilibrium price. (p. 99)

**Excess burden** The amount by which the burden of a tax exceeds the tax revenue received by the government—the deadweight loss from a tax. (p. 194)

**Excess capacity** The amount by which the efficient scale exceeds the quantity that the firm produces. (p. 417)

**Excess demand** A situation in which the quantity demanded exceeds the quantity supplied. (p. 99)

**Excess reserves** A bank's actual reserves minus its desired reserves. (p. 680)

**Excess supply** A situation in which the quantity supplied exceeds the quantity demanded. (p. 99)

**Excludable** A good, service, or resource is excludable if it is possible to prevent someone from enjoying its benefits. (p. 244)

**Expected inflation rate** The inflation rate that people forecast and use to set the money wage rate and other money prices. (p. 781)

**Explicit cost** A cost paid in money. (p. 321)

**Export goods and services** Goods and services that are produced in one country and sold in other countries. (p. 34)

**Exports** The goods and services that firms in one country sell to households and firms in other countries. (pp. 54, 216)

**Exports of goods and services** Items that firms in the United States produce and sell to the rest of the world. (p. 512)

**Externality** A cost or a benefit that arises from production and that falls on someone other than the producer; or a cost or benefit that arises from consumption and that falls on someone other than the consumer. (p. 246)

**Factor markets** Markets in which the services of factors of production are bought and sold. (pp. 48, 460)

**Factor price** The price of the services of the factors of production. The wage rate is the price of labor, the interest rate is the price of capital, and rent is the price of land. (p. 460)

**Factors of production** The productive resources that are used to produce goods and services—land, labor, capital, and entrepreneurship. (p. 36)

**Federal budget** An annual statement of the revenues, outlays, and surplus or deficit of the government of the United States. (p. 796)

**Federal funds rate** The interest rate at which banks can borrow and lend reserves (interbank loans) in the federal funds market. (pp. 672, 824)

**Federal Open Market Committee** The Fed's main policy-making committee. (p. 676)

**Federal Reserve System (The Fed)** The central bank of the United States. (p. 675)

**Fiat money** Objects that are money because the law decrees or orders them to be money. (p. 666)

**Final good or service** A good or service that is produced for its final user and not as a component of another good or service. (p. 510)

**Financial institution** A firm that operates on both sides of the market for financial capital: It borrows in one market and lends in another. (p. 641)

**Financial stability** A situation in which financial markets and institutions function normally to allocate capital resources and risk. (p. 823)

**Firms** The institutions that organize the production of goods and services. (p. 48)

**Fiscal policy** Changing taxes, transfer payments, and government expenditure on goods and services. (p. 731) The use of the federal budget to achieve the macroeconomic objectives of high and sustained economic growth and full employment. (p. 796)

**Fiscal stimulus** An increase in government outlays or a decrease in tax revenues designed to boost real GDP and create or save jobs. (p. 801)

**Fiscal year** A year that begins on October 1 and ends on September 30. Fiscal 2011 begins on October 1, 2010. (p. 796)

**Foreign exchange market** The market in which the currency of one country is exchanged for the currency of another. (p. 857)

**Foreign exchange rate** The price at which one currency exchanges for another. (p. 857)

**Four-firm concentration ratio** The percentage of the total revenue in an industry accounted for by the four largest firms in the industry. (p. 410)

**Free rider** A person who enjoys the benefits of a good or service without paying for it. (p. 249)

**Frictional unemployment** The unemployment that arises from normal labor turnover—from people entering and leaving the labor force, from quitting jobs to find better ones, and from the ongoing creation and destruction of jobs. (p. 553)

**Full employment** When there is no cyclical unemployment or, equivalently, when all the unemployment is frictional, structural, or seasonal. (p. 555)

**Full-employment equilibrium** When equilibrium real GDP equals potential GDP. (p. 735)

**Full-time workers** People who usually work 35 hours or more a week. (p. 543)

**Functional distribution of income** The distribution of income among the factors of production. (p. 39)

**Game theory** The tool that economists use to analyze *strategic* *behavior*—behavior that recognizes mutual interdependence and takes account of the expected behavior of others. (p. 441)

**GDP price index** An average of the current prices of all the goods and services included in GDP expressed as a percentage of base-year prices. (p. 573)

**Gold standard** A monetary policy rule that fixes the dollar price of gold. (p. 843)

**Goods and services** The objects (goods) and the actions (services) that people value and produce to satisfy human wants. (p. 3)

**Goods markets** Markets in which goods and services are bought and sold. (p. 48)

**Government goods and services** Goods and services that are bought by governments. (p. 34)

**Government expenditure multiplier** The effect of a change in government expenditure on goods and services on aggregate demand. (p. 802)

**Government expenditure on goods and services** The expenditure by all levels of government on goods and services. (p. 512)

**Government sector balance** Net taxes minus government expenditure on goods and services. (p. 854)

**Great Depression** A period of high unemployment, low incomes, and extreme economic hardship that lasted from 1929 to 1939. (p. 545)

**Gross domestic product (GDP)** The market value of all the final goods and services produced within a country within a given time period. (p. 510)

**Gross investment** The total amount spent on new capital goods. (p. 638)

**Gross national product (GNP)** The market value of all the final goods and services produced anywhere in the world in a given time period by the factors of production supplied by the residents of the country. (p. 519)

**Herfindahl-Hirschman Index** The square of the percentage market share of each firm summed over the 50 largest firms (or summed over all the firms if there are fewer than 50) in a market. (p. 411)

**Horizontal equity** The requirement that taxpayers with the same ability to pay should pay the same taxes. (p. 208)

**Households** Individuals or groups of people living together. (p. 48)

**Household production** The production of goods and services in the home. (p. 527)

**Human capital** The knowledge and skill that people obtain from education, on-the-job training, and work experience. (p. 37)

**Hyperinflation** Inflation at a rate that exceeds 50 percent a *month* (which translates to 12,875 percent a year). (p. 710)

**Implicit cost** An opportunity cost incurred by a firm when it uses a factor of production for which it does not make a direct money payment. (p. 321)

**Import quota** A quantitative restriction on the import of a good that limits the maximum quantity of a good that may be imported in a given period. (p. 229)

**Imports** The goods and services that households and firms in one country buy from firms in other countries. (pp. 54, 216)

**Imports of goods and services** Items that households, firms, and governments in the United States buy from the rest of the world. (p. 512)

**Incentive** A reward or a penalty—a "carrot" or a "stick"—that encourages or discourages an action. (p. 13)

**Income elasticity of demand** A measure of the responsiveness of the demand for a good to a change in income when other things remain the same. (p. 132)

**Increasing marginal returns** When the marginal product of an additional worker exceeds the marginal product of the previous worker. (p. 326)

**Indifference curve** A line that shows combinations of goods among which a consumer is *indifferent*. (p. 313)

**Individual transferable quota (ITQ)** A production limit that is assigned to an individual, who is free to transfer the quota to someone else. (p. 285)

**Induced taxes** Taxes that vary with real GDP. (p. 805)

**Inelastic demand** When the percentage change in the quantity demanded is less than the percentage change in price. (p. 116)

**Inelastic supply** When the percentage change in the quantity supplied is less than the percentage change in price. (p. 126)

**Infant-industry argument** The argument that it is necessary to protect a new industry to enable it to grow into a mature industry that can compete in world markets. (p. 233)

**Inferior good** A good for which demand decreases when income increases and demand increases when income decreases. (p. 89)

**Inflationary gap** A gap that exists when real GDP exceeds potential GDP and that brings a rising price level. (p. 736)

**Inflation rate** The percentage change in the price level from one year to the next. (p. 567)

**Inflation targeting** A monetary policy strategy in which the central bank makes a public commitment to achieving an explicit inflation target and to explaining how its policy actions will achieve that target. (p. 840)

**Instrument rule** A decision rule for monetary policy that sets the policy instrument by a formula based on the current state of the economy. (p. 826)

**Interest** Income paid for the use of capital. (p. 39)

**Interest rate parity** Equal interest rates—a situation in which the interest rate in one currency equals the interest rate in another currency when exchange rate changes are taken into account. (p. 868)

**Intermediate good or service** A good or service that is used as a component of a final good or service. (p. 510)

**Inverse relationship** A relationship between two variables that move in opposite directions. (p. 27)

**Investment** The purchase of new *capital goods*—tools, instruments, machines, buildings, and additions to inventories. (p. 511)

**Job** A contract between a firm and a household to provide labor services. (p. 460)

**Job rationing** A situation that arises when the real wage rate is above the full-employment equilibrium level. (p. 602)

**Job search** The activity of looking for an acceptable vacant job. (p. 601)

**Keynesian macroeconomics** The view that the market economy is inherently unstable and needs active government intervention to achieve full employment and sustained economic growth. (p. 588)

***k*-percent rule** A monetary policy rule that makes the quantity of money grow at *k* percent per year, where *k* equals the growth rate of potential GDP. (p. 841)

**Labor** The work time and work effort that people devote to producing goods and services. (p. 37)

**Labor force** The number of people employed plus the number unemployed. (p. 540)

**Labor force participation rate** The percentage of the working-age population who are members of the labor force. (p. 542)

**Labor productivity** The quantity of real GDP produced by one hour of labor. (p. 616)

**Labor union** An organized group of workers that aims to increase wages and influence other job conditions of its members. (p. 470)

**Land** The "gifts of nature," or *natural resources*, that we use to produce goods and services. (p. 36)

**Law of decreasing returns** As a firm uses more of a variable input, with a given quantity of fixed inputs, the marginal product of the variable input eventually decreases. (p. 328)

**Law of demand** Other things remaining the same, if the price of a good rises, the quantity demanded of that good decreases; and if the price of a good falls, the quantity demanded of that good increases. (p. 85)

**Law of market forces** When there is a surplus, the price falls; when there is a shortage, the price rises. (p. 99)

**Law of supply** Other things remaining the same, if the price of a good rises, the quantity supplied of that good increases; and if the price of a good falls, the quantity supplied of that good decreases. (p. 92)

**Legal monopoly** A market in which competition and entry are restricted by the granting of a public franchise, government license, patent, or copyright. (p. 377)

**Linear relationship** A relationship that graphs as a straight line. (p. 26)

**Long run** The time frame in which the quantities of *all* resources can be varied. (p. 324)

**Long-run average cost curve** A curve that shows the lowest average cost at which it is possible to produce each output when the firm has had sufficient time to change both its plant size and labor employed. (p. 340)

**Long-run Phillips curve** The vertical line that shows the relationship between inflation and unemployment when the economy is at full employment. (p. 780)

**Lorenz curve** A curve that graphs the cumulative percentage of income (or wealth) against the cumulative percentage of households. (p. 485)

**Loss** Income earned by an entrepreneur for running a business when that income is negative. (p. 39)

**M1** Currency, traveler's checks, and checkable deposits owned by individuals and businesses. (p. 666)

**M2** M1 plus savings deposits and small time deposits, money market funds, and other deposits. (p. 666)

**Macroeconomic equilibrium** When the quantity of real GDP demanded equals the quantity of real GDP supplied at the point of intersection of the *AD* curve and the *AS* curve. (p. 734)

**Macroeconomics** The study of the aggregate (or total) effects on the national economy and the global economy of the choices that individuals, businesses, and governments make. (p. 14)

**Malthusian theory** Another name for classical growth theory—named for Thomas Robert Malthus. (p. 621)

**Margin** A choice on the margin is a choice that is made by comparing *all* the relevant alternatives systematically and incrementally. (p. 12)

**Marginal benefit** The benefit that arises from a one-unit increase in an activity. The marginal benefit of something is measured by what you *are willing to* give up to get *one additional* unit of it. (p. 12)

**Marginal cost** The opportunity cost that arises from a one-unit increase in an activity. The marginal cost of something is what you *must* give up to get one additional unit of it. (p. 12) The marginal cost of producing a good is the change in total cost that results from a one-unit increase in output. (p. 332)

**Marginal cost pricing rule** A rule that sets price equal to marginal cost to achieve an efficient output. (p. 396)

**Marginal external benefit** The benefit from an additional unit of a good or service that people other than the consumer of the good or service enjoy. (p. 257)

**Marginal external cost** The cost of producing an additional unit of a good or service that falls on people other than the producer. (p. 270)

**Marginally attached worker** A person who does not have a job, is available and willing to work, has not made specific efforts to find a job within the previous four weeks, but has looked for work sometime in the recent past. (p. 542)

**Marginal private benefit** The benefit from an additional unit of a good or service that the consumer of that good or service receives. (p. 257)

**Marginal private cost** The cost of producing an additional unit of a good or service that is borne by the producer of that good or service. (p. 270)

**Marginal product** The change in total product that results from a one-unit increase in the quantity of labor employed. (p. 326)

**Marginal propensity to consume** The fraction of a change in disposable income that is spent on consumption—the change in consumption expenditure divided by the change in disposable income that brought it about. (p. 750)

**Marginal propensity to import** The fraction of an increase in real GDP that is spent on imports—the change in imports divided by the change in real GDP. (p. 752)

**Marginal rate of substitution** The rate at which a person will give up good *y* (the good measured on the *y*-axis) to get more of good *x* (the good measured on the *x*-axis) and at the same time remain on the same indifference curve. (p. 314)

**Marginal revenue** The change in total revenue that results from a one-unit increase in the quantity sold. (p. 349)

**Marginal social benefit** The marginal benefit enjoyed by society—by the consumer of a good or service and by everyone else who benefits from it. It is the sum of marginal private benefit and marginal external benefit. (p. 257)

**Marginal social cost** The marginal cost incurred by the entire society—by the producer and by everyone else on whom the cost falls. It is the sum of marginal private cost and marginal external cost. (p. 270)

**Marginal tax rate** The percentage of an additional dollar of income that is paid in tax. (p. 199) The fraction of a change in real GDP that is paid in income taxes—the change in tax payments divided by the change in real GDP. (p. 762)

**Marginal utility** The change in total utility that results from a one-unit increase in the quantity of a good consumed. (p. 298)

**Marginal utility per dollar** The marginal utility from a good relative to the price paid for the good. (p. 300)

**Market** Any arrangement that brings buyers and sellers together and enables them to get information and do business with each other. (p. 48)

**Market demand** The sum of the demands of all the buyers in a market. (p. 87)

**Market equilibrium** When the quantity demanded equals the quantity supplied—buyers' and sellers' plans are in balance. (p. 99)

**Market for loanable funds** The aggregate of all the individual financial markets. (p. 644)

**Market income** A household's wages, interest, rent, and profit earned in factor markets before paying income taxes. (p. 484)

**Market supply** The sum of the supplies of all the sellers in the market. (p. 94)

**Markup** The amount by which price exceeds marginal cost. (p. 417)

**Means of payment** A method of settling a debt. (p. 664)

**Median voter theory** The theory that governments pursue policies that make the median voter as well off as possible. (p. 502)

**Medium of exchange** An object that is generally accepted in return for goods and services. (p. 665)

**Microeconomics** The study of the choices that individuals and businesses make and the way these choices interact and are influenced by governments. (p. 14)

**Minimum wage law** A government regulation that makes hiring labor services for less than a specified wage illegal. (pp. 177, 603)

**Mixed good** A private good, the production or consumption of which creates an externality. (p. 246)

**Monetarist macroeconomics** The view that the market economy works well, that aggregate fluctuations are the natural consequence of an expanding economy, but that fluctuations in the quantity of money also bring the business cycle. (p. 589)

**Monetary base** The sum of coins, Federal Reserve notes, and banks' reserves at the Fed. (p. 677)

**Monetary policy** Changing the quantity of money and the interest rate. (p. 731)

**Monetary policy instrument** A variable that the Fed can directly control or closely target and that influences the economy in desirable ways. (p. 824)

**Money** Any commodity or token that is generally accepted as a means of payment. (p. 664)

**Money income** Market income plus cash payments to households by the government. (p. 484)

**Money multiplier** The number by which a change in the monetary base is multiplied to find the resulting change in the quantity of money. (p. 685)

**Monopolistic competition** A market in which a large number of firms compete by making similar but slightly different products. (p. 348)

**Monopoly** A market in which one firm sells a good or service that has no close substitutes and a barrier blocks the entry of new firms. (pp. 348, 376)

**Multiplier** The amount by which a change in any component of autonomous expenditure is magnified or multiplied to determine the change that it generates in equilibrium expenditure and real GDP. (p. 760)

**Nash equilibrium** An equilibrium in which each player takes the best possible action given the action of the other player. (p. 442)

**National debt** The amount of government debt outstanding—the debt that has arisen from past budget deficits. (pp. 52, 797)

**Natural monopoly** A monopoly that arises because one firm can meet the entire market demand at a lower average total cost than two or more firms could. (p. 376)

**Natural rate hypothesis** The proposition that when the inflation rate changes, the unemployment rate changes *temporarily* and eventually returns to the natural unemployment rate. (p. 782)

**Natural unemployment rate** The unemployment rate when the economy is at full employment. (p. 555)

**Needs-tested spending** Spending on programs that entitle suitably qualified people and businesses to receive transfer payments that vary with need and with the state of the economy. (p. 805)

**Negative income tax** A tax and redistribution scheme that provides every household with a guaranteed minimum annual income and taxes all earned income at a fixed rate. (p. 503)

**Negative relationship** A relationship between two variables that move in opposite directions. (p. 27)

**Neoclassical growth theory** The theory that real GDP per person will increase as long as technology keeps advancing. (p. 623)

**Net borrower** A country that is borrowing more from the rest of the world than it is lending to the rest of the world. (p. 852)

**Net domestic product at factor cost** The sum of wages, interest, rent, and profit. (p. 517)

**Net exports of goods and services** The value of exports of goods and services minus the value of imports of goods and services. (p. 512)

**Net investment** The change in the quantity of capital—equals gross investment minus depreciation. (p. 638)

**Net lender** A country that is lending more to the rest of the world than it is borrowing from the rest of the world. (p. 852)

**Net taxes** Taxes paid minus cash benefits received from governments. (p. 512)

**Net worth** The total market value of what a financial institution has lent minus the market value of what it has borrowed. (p. 642)

**New growth theory** The theory that our unlimited wants will lead us to ever greater productivity and perpetual economic growth. (p. 623)

**Nominal GDP** The value of the final goods and services produced in a given year expressed in terms of the prices of that same year. (p. 520)

**Nominal interest rate** The dollar amount of interest expressed as a percentage of the amount loaned. (p. 580)

**Nominal wage rate** The average hourly wage rate measured in *current* dollars. (p. 578)

**Nonexcludable** A good, service, or resource is nonexcludable if it is impossible (or extremely costly) to prevent someone from enjoying its benefits. (p. 244)

**Nonrenewable natural resources** Natural resources that can be used only once and that cannot be replaced once they have been used. (p. 460)

**Nonrival** A good, service, or resource is nonrival if its use by one person does not decrease the quantity available to someone else. (p. 244)

**Normal good** A good for which demand increases when income increases and demand decreases when income decreases. (p. 89)

**Normal profit** The return to entrepreneurship. Normal profit is part of a firm's opportunity cost because it is the cost of not running another firm. (p. 321)

**Official settlements account** Record of the change in U.S. official reserves. (p. 850)

**Okun's Law** For each percentage point that the unemployment rate is above the natural unemployment rate, real GDP is 2 percentage points below potential GDP. (p. 775)

**Oligopoly** A market in which a small number of independent firms compete. (p. 348)

**Open market operation** The purchase or sale of government securities—U.S. Treasury bills and bonds—by the New York Fed in the open market. (p. 677)

**Opportunity cost** The opportunity cost of something is the best thing you *must* give up to get it. (p. 11)

**Output gap** Real GDP minus potential GDP expressed as a percentage of potential GDP. (p. 556)

**Part time for economic reasons** People who work 1 to 34 hours per week but are looking for full-time work and cannot find it because of unfavorable business conditions. (p. 543)

**Part-time workers** People who usually work less than 35 hours a week. (p. 543)

**Payoff matrix** A table that shows the payoffs for each player for every possible combination of actions by the players. (p. 442)

**PCE price index** An average of the current prices of the goods and services included in the consumption expenditure component of GDP expressed as a percentage of base-year prices. (p. 573)

**Perfect competition** A market in which there are many firms, each selling an identical product; many buyers; no barriers to the entry of new firms into the industry; no advantage to established firms; and buyers and sellers are well informed about prices. (p. 348)

**Perfect price discrimination** Price discrimination that extracts the entire consumer surplus by charging the highest price that consumers are willing to pay for each unit. (p. 392)

**Perfectly elastic demand** When the quantity demanded changes by a very large percentage in response to an almost zero percentage change in price. (p. 116)

**Perfectly elastic supply** When the quantity supplied changes by a very large percentage in response to an almost zero percentage change in price. (p. 126)

**Perfectly inelastic demand** When the percentage change in the quantity demanded is zero for any percentage change in the price. (p. 116)

**Perfectly inelastic supply** When the percentage change in the quantity supplied is zero for any percentage change in the price. (p. 126)

**Personal distribution of income** The distribution of income among households. (p. 39)

**Physical capital** The tools, instruments, machines, buildings, and other items that have been produced in the past and that are used to produce goods and services. (p. 638)

**Positive relationship** A relationship between two variables that move in the same direction. (p. 26)

**Potential GDP** The value of real GDP when all the economy's factors of production—labor, capital, land, and entrepreneurial ability—are fully employed. (pp. 523, 556, 591)

**Poverty** A state in which a household's income is too low to be able to buy the quantities of food, shelter, and clothing that are deemed necessary. (p. 489)

**Predatory pricing** Setting a low price to drive competitors out of business with the intention of setting a monopoly price when the competition has gone. (p. 451)

**Price cap** A government regulation that places an upper limit on the price at which a particular good, service, or factor of production may be traded. (p. 170)

**Price cap regulation** A rule that specifies the highest price that a firm is permitted to set—a price ceiling. (p. 400)

**Price ceiling** A government regulation that places an *upper* limit on the price at which a particular good, service, of factor of production may be traded. (p. 170)

**Price-discriminating monopoly** A monopoly that sells different units of a good or service for different prices not related to cost differences. (p. 378)

**Price elasticity of demand** A measure of the responsiveness of the quantity demanded of a good to a change in its price when all other influences on buyers' plans remain the same. (p. 114)

**Price elasticity of supply** A measure of the responsiveness of the quantity supplied of a good to a change in its price when all other influences on sellers' plans remain the same. (p. 126)

**Price floor** A government regulation that places a *lower* limit on the price at which a particular good, service, or factor of production may be traded. (p. 176)

**Price gouging** The practice of selling an essential item for a much higher price than normal, and usually occurs following a natural disaster. (p. 162)

**Price support** A price floor in an agricultural market maintained by a government guarantee to buy any surplus output at that price. (p. 183)

**Price taker** A firm that cannot influence the price of the good or service that it produces. (p. 349)

**Principle of minimum differentiation** The tendency for competitors to make themselves identical to appeal to the maximum number of clients or voters. (p. 254)

**Prisoners' dilemma** A game between two prisoners that shows why it is hard to cooperate, even when it would be beneficial to both players to do so. (p. 441)

**Private good** A good or service that can be consumed by only one person at a time and only by the person who has bought it or owns it. (p. 244)

**Private sector balance** Saving minus investment. (p. 854)

**Producer surplus** The price of a good minus the marginal cost of producing it, summed over the quantity produced. (p. 152)

**Product differentiation** Making a product that is slightly different from the products of competing firms. (p. 408)

**Production efficiency** A situation in which the economy is getting all that it can from its resources and cannot produce more of one good or service without producing less of something else. (p. 64)

**Production function** A relationship that shows the maximum quantity of real GDP that can be produced as the quantity of labor employed changes and all other influences on production remain the same. (p. 592)

**Production possibilities frontier** The boundary between the combinations of goods and services that can be produced and the combinations that cannot be produced, given the available factors of production and the state of technology. (p. 62)

**Profit** Income earned by an entrepreneur for running a business. (p. 39)

**Progressive tax** A tax whose average rate increases as income increases. (p. 199)

**Property rights** Social arrangements that govern the protection of private property—legally established titles to the ownership, use, and disposal of factors of production and goods and services that are enforceable in the courts. (pp. 273, 628)

**Proportional tax** A tax whose average rate is constant at all income levels. (p. 199)

**Public good** A good or service that can be consumed simultaneously by everyone and from which no one can be excluded. (p. 245)

**Public provision** The production of a good or service by a public authority that receives most of its revenue from the government. (p. 259)

**Purchasing power parity** Equal value of money—a situation in which money buys the same amount of goods and services in different currencies. (p. 866)

**Quantity demanded** The amount of any good, service, or resource that people are willing and able to buy during a specified period at a specified price. (p. 85)

**Quantity of labor demanded** The total labor hours that all the firms in the economy plan to hire during a given time period at a given real wage rate. (p. 593)

**Quantity of labor supplied** The number of labor hours that all the households in the economy plan to work during a given time period at a given real wage rate. (p. 595)

**Quantity of money demanded** The amount of money that households and firms choose to hold. (p. 695)

**Quantity supplied** The amount of any good, service, or resource that people are willing and able to sell during a specified period at a specified price. (p. 92)

**Quantity theory of money** The proposition that when real GDP equals potential GDP, an increase in the quantity of money brings an equal percentage increase in the price level. (p. 706)

**Rate of return regulation** A regulation that sets the price at a level that enables a firm to earn a specified target rate of return on its capital. (p. 400)

**Rational choice** A choice that uses the available resources to best achieve the objective of the person making the choice. (p. 10)

**Rational expectation** The inflation forecast resulting from use of all the relevant data and economic science. (p. 787)

**Rational ignorance** The decision not to acquire information because the marginal cost of doing so exceeds the marginal benefit. (p. 254)

**Real GDP** The value of the final goods and services produced in a given year expressed in terms of the prices in a *base year*. (p. 520)

**Real GDP per person** Real GDP divided by the population. (pp. 523, 612)

**Real interest rate** The goods and services forgone in interest expressed as a percentage of the amount loaned and calculated as the nominal interest rate minus the inflation rate. (p. 580)

**Real wage rate** The average hourly wage rate measured in the dollars of a given reference base year. (p. 578)

**Recession** A period during which real GDP decreases for at least two successive quarters; or defined by the NBER as "a period of significant decline in total output, income, employment, and trade, usually lasting from six months to a year, and marked by contractions in many sectors of the economy." (p. 524)

**Recessionary gap** A gap that exists when potential GDP exceeds real GDP and that brings a falling price level. (p. 736)

**Reference base period** A period for which the CPI is defined to equal 100. Currently, the reference base period is 1982–1984. (p. 564)

**Regressive tax** A tax whose average rate decreases as income increases. (p. 199)

**Regulation** Rules administered by a government agency to influence prices, quantities, entry, and other aspects of economic activity in a firm or an industry. (p. 396)

**Relative price** The price of one good in terms of another good—an opportunity cost. It equals the price of one good divided by the price of another good. (p. 296)

**Rent** Income paid for the use of land (p. 39)

**Rent ceiling** A regulation that makes it illegal to charge more than a specified rent for housing. (p. 170)

**Rent seeking** Lobbying and other political activity that aims to capture the gains from trade. The act of obtaining special treatment by the government to create economic profit or divert consumer surplus or producer surplus away from others. (pp. 237, 387)

**Required reserve ratio** The minimum percentage of deposits that the Fed requires banks and other financial institutions to hold in reserves. (p. 671)

**Resale price maintenance** An agreement between a manufacturer and a distributor on the price at which a product will be resold. (p. 449)

**Reserves** The currency in the bank's vaults plus the balance on its reserve account at a Federal Reserve Bank. (p. 671)

**Rival** A good, service, or resource is rival if its use by one person decreases the quantity available to someone else. (p. 244)

**Rule of 70** The number of years it takes for the level of any variable to double is approximately 70 divided by the annual percentage growth rate of the variable. (p. 613)

**Saving** The amount of income that is not paid in net taxes or spent on consumption goods and services. (p. 512)

**Scarcity** The condition that arises because wants exceed the ability of resources to satisfy them. (p. 2)

**Scatter diagram** A graph of the value of one variable against the value of another variable. (p. 24)

**Search activity** The time spent looking for someone with whom to do business. (p. 172)

**Seasonal unemployment** The unemployment that arises because of seasonal patterns. (p. 554)

**Self-interest** The choices that are best for the individual who makes them. (p. 4)

**Shortage** A situation in which the quantity demanded exceeds the quantity supplied. (p. 99)

**Short run** The time frame in which the quantities of some resources are fixed. In the short run, a firm can usually change the quantity of labor it uses but not its technology and quantity of capital. (p. 324)

**Short-run Phillips curve** A curve that shows the relationship between the inflation rate and the unemployment rate when the natural unemployment rate and the expected inflation rate remain constant. (p. 774)

**Shutdown point** The point at which price equals minimum average variable cost and the quantity produced is that at which average variable cost is at a minimum. (p. 353)

**Signal** An action taken by an informed person (or firm) to send a message to less-informed people. (p. 424)

**Single-price monopoly** A monopoly that must sell each unit of its output for the same price to all its customers. (p. 378)

**Slope** The change in the value of the variable measured on the $y$-axis divided by the change in the value of the variable measured on the $x$-axis. (p. 29)

**Social interest** The choices that are best for society as a whole. (p. 4)

**Social interest theory** The theory that regulation achieves an efficient allocation of resources. (p. 396)

**Stagflation** A combination of recession (falling real GDP) and inflation (rising price level). (p. 738)

**Standard of living** The level of consumption of goods and services that people enjoy, *on average*; it is measured by average income per person. (p. 523)

**Statistical discrepancy** The discrepancy between the expenditure approach and the income approach estimates of GDP, calculated as the GDP expenditure total minus GDP income total. (p. 518)

**Stock** A certificate of ownership and claim to the profits that a firm makes. (p. 640)

**Store of value** Any commodity or token that can be held and exchanged later for goods and services. (p. 665)

**Strategies** All the possible actions of each player in a game. (p. 442)

**Structural unemployment** The unemployment that arises when changes in technology or international competition change the skills needed to perform jobs or change the locations of jobs. (p. 553)

**Subsidy** A payment by the government to a producer to cover part of the cost of production. (pp. 183, 231, 260)

**Substitute** A good that can be consumed in place of another good. (p. 88)

**Substitute in production** A good that can be produced in place of another good. (p. 95)

**Sunk cost** A previously incurred and irreversible cost. (p. 11)

**Supply** The relationship between the quantity supplied and the price of a good when all other influences on selling plans remain the same. (p. 92)

**Supply curve** A graph of the relationship between the quantity supplied of a good and its price when all the other influences on selling plans remain the same. (p. 93)

**Supply of labor** The relationship between the quantity of labor supplied and the real wage rate when all other influences on work plans remain the same. (p. 595)

**Supply of loanable funds** The relationship between the quantity of loanable funds supplied and the real interest rate when all other influences on lending plans remain the same. (p. 647)

**Supply of money** The relationship between the quantity of money supplied and the nominal interest rate. (p. 698)

**Supply schedule** A list of the quantities supplied at each different price when all the other influences on selling plans remain the same. (p. 93)

**Supply-side effects** The effects of fiscal policy on potential GDP and the economic growth rate. (p. 808)

**Surplus** A situation in which the quantity supplied exceeds the quantity demanded. (p. 99)

**Tariff** A tax imposed on a good when it is imported. (p. 225)

**Targeting rule** A decision rule for monetary policy that sets the policy instrument at a level that makes the central bank's forecast of the ultimate policy goals equal to their targets. (p. 826)

**Taxable income** Total income minus a personal exemption and a standard deduction (or other allowable deductions). (p. 198)

**Tax incidence** The division of the burden of a tax between the buyer and the seller. (p. 192)

**Tax multiplier** The effect of a change in taxes on aggregate demand. (p. 802)

**Tax wedge** The gap created by a tax between what a buyer pays and what a seller receives. In the labor market, it is the gap between the before-tax wage rate and the after-tax wage rate. (p. 809)

**Time-series graph** A graph that measures time on the $x$-axis and the variable or variables in which we are interested on the $y$-axis. (p. 24)

**Total cost** The cost of all the factors of production used by a firm. (p. 331)

**Total fixed cost** The cost of the firm's fixed factors of production—the cost of land, capital, and entrepreneurship. (p. 331)

**Total product** The total quantity of a good produced in a given period. (p. 325)

**Total revenue** The amount spent on a good and received by the seller and equals the price of the good multiplied by the quantity of the good sold. (p. 122)

**Total revenue test** A method of estimating the price elasticity of demand by observing the change in total revenue that results from a price change (with all other influences on the quantity sold remaining unchanged). (p. 123)

**Total surplus** The sum of consumer surplus and producer surplus. (p. 155)

**Total utility** The total benefit that a person gets from the consumption of a good or service. Total utility generally increases as the quantity consumed of a good increases. (p. 298)

**Total variable cost** The cost of the firm's variable factor of production—the cost of labor. (p. 331)

**Tragedy of the commons** The absence of incentives to prevent the overuse and depletion of a commonly owned resource. (p. 280)

**Tradeoff** An exchange—giving up one thing to get something else. (p. 65)

**Transactions costs** The opportunity costs of making trades in a market or conducting a transaction. (pp. 159, 274)

**Transfer payments** Social Security benefits, Medicare and Medicaid benefits, unemployment benefits, and other cash transfers. (p. 798)

**Transfer payments multiplier** The effect of a change in transfer payments on aggregate demand. (p. 802)

**Trend** A general tendency for the value of a variable to rise or fall over time. (p. 24)

**Tying arrangement** An agreement to sell one product only if the buyer agrees to buy another, different product. (p. 451)

**Underground production** The production of goods and services hidden from the view of government. (p. 527)

**Unemployment rate** The percentage of the people in the labor force who are unemployed. (p. 541)

**Union wage** A wage rate that results from collective bargaining between a labor union and a firm. (p. 603)

**Unit elastic demand** When the percentage change in the quantity demanded equals the percentage change in price. (p. 116)

**Unit elastic supply** When the percentage change in the quantity supplied equals the percentage change in price. (p. 126)

**Unit of account** An agreed-upon measure for stating the prices of goods and services. (p. 665)

**U.S. interest rate differential** The U.S. interest rate minus the foreign interest rate. (p. 860)

**U.S. official reserves** The government's holdings of foreign currency. (p. 850)

**Utility** The benefit or satisfaction that a person gets from the consumption of a good or service. (p. 298)

**Utility-maximizing rule** The rule that leads to the greatest total utility from all the goods and services consumed. The rule is: 1. Allocate the entire available budget. 2. Make the marginal utility per dollar equal for all goods. (p. 300)

**Value of marginal product** The value to a firm of hiring one more unit of a factor of production, which equals the price of a unit of output multiplied by the marginal product of the factor of production. (p. 461)

**Velocity of circulation** The average number of times in a year that each dollar of money gets used to buy final goods and services. (p. 706)

**Vertical equity** The requirement that taxpayers with a greater ability to pay bear a greater share of the taxes. (p. 209)

**Voucher** A token that the government provides to households, which they can use to buy specified goods or services. (p. 261)

**Wages** Income paid for the services of labor. (p. 39)

**Wealth** The value of all the things that people own. (p. 638)

**Working-age population** The total number of people aged 16 years and over who are not in jail, hospital, or some other form of institutional care or in the U.S. Armed Forces. (p. 540)

# Index

Key terms and pages on which they are defined appear in **boldface**.

# Credits

(continuation from page ii)

Chapter 1: p. 1: David Shankbone/Wikimedia Commons; p. 3 top: Owen Franken/Stone Allstock/Getty Images; p. 3 bottom: George Rose/Getty Images; p. 4: Photodisc/Getty Images; p. 5 top: Feverpitch/Shutterstock.; p. 5 bottom: Library of Congress; p. 6 top: Courtesy REA Agency; p. 6 bottom: Getty Images; p. 7 top: Getty Images/Digital Vision; p. 7 center: Lakov Kalinin/Shutterstock; p. 7 bottom: Getty Images/Digital Vision; p. 8 top: Getty Images/Digital Vision; p. 8 bottom: Wally McNamee/CORBIS; p. 11 left: Scott T. Baxter/Getty Images, Inc.-Photodisc; p. 11 right: Getty Images, Inc.; p. 13 left: Yuri Arcurs/Shutterstock; p. 13 right: John Eder/Image Bank/Getty Images; p. 14: Jim Young/Reuters Limited; p. 15: Getty Images/Digital Vision; p. 17: CORBIS-NY.

Chapter 2: p. 33 TONY AVELAR/AFP/Getty Images; p. 35 top: Getty Images/Digital Vision; p. 35 top center: Monkey Business Images/Shutterstock; p. 35 bottom center: Photodisc/Getty Images; p. 35 bottom: Joe Sohm/VisionsofAmerica/Getty Images/Digital Vision; p. 38 top left: EyeWire Collection/Getty Images-Photodisc-Royalty Free; p. 38 top right: Jean Schweitzer/Shutterstock; p. 38 bottom left: Photodisc/Getty Images; p. 38 bottom right: Getty Images/Digital Vision; p. 44: Tatiana Markow/Sygma/Corbis-NY; p. 45 top: Bruce Connolly/CORBIS All Rights Reserved; p. 45 bottom: Earl & Nazima Kowall/CORBIS All Rights Reserved.

Chapter 3: p. 61: Greg Randles/Shutterstock; p. 75 top: Courtesy Sara Piaseczynski; p. 75 bottom: Jack Hollingsworth/Corbis Royalty Free.

Chapter 4: p. 83: Getty Images; p. 84 left: Steven Rubin/The Image Works; p. 84 center: Howard Grey/Getty Images/Digital Vision; p. 84 right: Prentice Hall School Division; p. 106: Yuri Arcurs/Shutterstock; p. 107: Shutterstock.

Chapter 5: page 113: Getty Images; p. 121 left: ©Darama/CORBIS All Rights Reserved; p. 121 right: ©Bennett Dean/Eye Ubiquitous/CORBIS All Rights Reserved; p. 124 top: Wayne Eastep/Srone Allstock/Getty Images; p. 124 center: Buddy Mays/CORBIS All Rights Reserved; p. 124 bottom: CORBIS-NY; p. 128: Scott David Patterson/Shutterstock.

Chapter 6: p. 139: Getty Images; p. 140: Noel Hendrickson/Getty Images; p. 141 top: Jordan Tan/Shutterstock; p. 141 top center: Frontpage/Shutterstock; p. 141 bottom center: Simon Bruty/Sports Illustrated/Getty Images; p. 141 bottom: Anya Ponti/Shutterstock; p. 142 top: iofoto/Shutterstock; p. 142 top center: Yxm 2008/Shutterstock; p. 142 bottom center: Sandra Cunningham/Shutterstock; p. 142 bottom: Natalia Bratslavsky/Shutterstock; p. 156: goldenangel/Shutterstock.

Chapter 7: p. 169: SAUL LOEB/AFP/Getty Images; p. 174: Stephen B. Goodwin/Shutterstock; p. 179: Stephen Coburn/Shutterstock.

Chapter 8: p. 191: Scott J. Ferrell/Congressional Quarterly/Getty Images, Inc.; p. 202: Getty Images; p. 209: Carlush/Shutterstock.

Chapter 9: p. 215: Getty Images; p. 217 top: John Froschauer/AP Wide World Photos; p. 217 bottom: Anna Sheveleva/Shutterstock; p. 221 top left: Chris O'Meara/AP Wide World Photos; p. 221 top right: Amy Waldman/The New York Times; p. 221 bottom left: Sokolovsky/Shutterstock; p. 221 bottom right: Lucian Coman/Shutterstock.

Chapter 10: p. 243 Anderson Ross/Getty Images; 246 top: Corbis Royalty Free; p. 246 top center: Zsolt Nyulaszi/Shutterstock; p. 246 bottom center: Peter Turnley/CORBIS All Rights Reserved; p. 246 bottom: Oksana Perkins/Shutterstock; p. 249 left: Corbis Royalty Free; p. 249 top right: Prisma Bildagentur AG/Alamy; p. 249 bottom left: Fat Chance Productions/CORBIS All Rights Reserved; p. 249 bottom right: Mike Brake/Shutterstock.

Chapter 11: p. 269: Armin Rose/Shutterstock; p. 275:

Vishnevskiy Vasily/Shutterstock; p. 281: ©Tom Stewart/CORBIS All Rights Reserved; p. 283: Christie's Images Ltd. 1990.

Chapter 12: p. 291 AFP/Getty Images; p. 294: magicinfoto/Shutterstock; p. 299 left: ©Bettmann/CORBIS All Rights Reserved; p. 299 right: Hulton Archive/Getty Images; p. 302: Diego Cervo/Shutterstock; p. 316: Jose Luis Peleaz Inc.

Chapter 13: p. 319: Getty Images; p. 339: ARTEKI/Shutterstock.

Chapter 14: p. 347: Evaristo Sa/Agence France Presse/Getty Images; p. 349 top: Orientaly/Shutterstock; p. 349 bottom: ©Jonathan Blair/CORBIS All Rights Reserved; p. 363: David Askham/Alamy; p. 364 Getty Images Inc.

Chapter 15: p. 375: Getty Images; p. 376: zulufoto/Shutterstock; p. 390: Michael Ledray/Shutterstock; p. 394: All material herein © 1998-2009 priceline.com Incorporated, all rights reserved. PRICELINE, PRICELINE.COM, NAME YOUR OWN PRICE and NO ONE DEALS LIKE WE DO are registered service marks and the NEGOTIATOR, NOFEE, and PRICEDROP PROTECTION are service marks of priceline.com Incorporated; p. 401: Getty Images, Inc.

Chapter 16: p. 407: AHMAD AL-RUBAYE/Agence France Presse/Getty Images; p. 408: Losevsky Pavel/Shutterstock; p. 420: Getty Images; p.424: Courtesy of Nike, Inc.

Chapter 17: p. 431: Andrey Burmakin/Shutterstock; p. 435: Beth Anderson; p. 436: Alastair Miller/Bloomberg News/Landov LLC; p. 439: Ronald Zak/AP Wide World Photos.

Chapter 18: p. 459 Getty Images; p. 466 top: Beth Anderson; p. 466 bottom: forestpath/Shutterstock.

Chapter 19: p. 483 Carl DeSouza/AFP/Getty Images.

Chapter 20: p. 509: Andy Sacks/Stone/Getty Images; p. 516: Jeff Christensen/Reuters/Corbis.

Chapter 21: p. 539: Robyn Beck/AFP/Getty Images; p. 540: Sokolovsky/Shutterstock; p. 543: Courtesy of U.S. Census Bureau; p. 551: Sokolovsky/Shutterstock; P. 553 top: Dmitry Yashkin/Shutterstock; p. 553 bottom: ©Jim Sugar Photography/CORBIS All Rights Reserved.

Chapter 22: p. 563: Emmanuel Faure/Stone/Getty Images; p. 570: AVAVA/Shutterstock; p. 571 top: Fedor Selivanov/Shutterstock; p. 571 center: Monkey Business Images/Shutterstock; p. 571 bottom: Ioana Drutu/Shutterstock; p. 576 top: Brendan Howard/Shutterstock; p. 576 bottom: Kirsten Sims.

Chapter 23: p. 587 top: Richard Passmore/Stone/Getty Images; p. 587 bottom: Jerome Tisne/Photographer's Choice/Getty Images; p. 605: PhotoDisc/Getty Images.

Chapter 24: p. 611: MAYSKYPHOTO/Shutterstock; p. 618 top: Minnesota Historical Society/Corbis; p. 618 bottom: TONGRO IMAGE STOCK/BRAND X/Corbis Royalty Free.

Chapter 25: p. 637: Frances Roberts/Alamy; p. 652 top: Frontpage/Shutterstock; p. 652 bottom: Frontpage/Shutterstock.

Chapter 26: p. 663: Alex Wong/Getty Images; p. 671: Scala/Art Resource, NY; p. 675: Win McNamee/Getty Images, Inc.; p. 681: Reuters/HO/Landov.

Chapter 27: p. 693: Getty Images; p. 710: Bettmann/CORBIS.

Chapter 28: p. 721 top: Susan Yates/Alamy; p. 721 bottom: ©Bob Krist/CORBIS All Rights Reserved.

Chapter 29: p. 747 top: Purestock/Getty Royalty Free; p. 747 bottom: iStockphoto; p. 758 top: ©Bibliotheque Nationale, Paris, France/Giraudon—Bridgeman Art Library; p. 758 bottom: ©Bettmann/CORBIS.

Chapter 30: p. 773: Jim Young/Reuters; p. 777: Courtesy of MIT Museum.

Chapter 31: p. 795: Scott J. Ferrell/Congressional Quarterly/Getty Images, Inc; p. 803: Gabriel Bouys/AFP/Getty Images.

Chapter 32: p. 821: Leon Neal/AFP/Getty Images; p. 842 left: Staff/AFP/Getty Images; p. 842 right: Courtesy of Anna J. Schwartz.

Chapter 33: p. 842: Rob Walls/Alamy.

**Figures and Tables**

Chapter 5: Some Price Elasticities of Demand, p. 121, Sources of Data: Ahsan Mansur and John Whalley, "Numerical Specification of Applied General Equilibrium Models: Estimation, Calibration, and Data," in *Applied General Equilibrium Analysis,* eds. Herbert E. Scarf and John B. Shoven (New York: Cambridge University Press, 1984), and Henri Theil, Ching-Fan Chung, and James L. Seale, Jr., Advances in Econometrics, Supplement I, 1989, International Evidence on Consumption Patterns (Greenwich, Conn.: JAI Press Inc., 1989). Reprinted with permission; Income Elasticities of Demand, p. 133, Sources of Data: Ahsan Mansur and John Whalley, "Numerical Specification of Applied General Equilibrium Models: Estimation, Calibration, and Data," in *Applied General Equilibrium Analysis,* eds. Herbert E. Scarf and John B. Shoven (New York: Cambridge University Press, 1984), and Henri Theil, Ching-Fan Chung, and James L. Seale, Jr., Advances in Econometrics, Supplement I, 1989, International Evidence on Consumption Patterns (Greenwich, Conn.: JAI Press Inc., 1989). Reprinted with permission.

## The Pearson Series in Economics

**Abel/Bernanke/Croushore**
*Macroeconomics**

**Bade/Parkin**
*Foundations of Economics**

**Bierman/Fernandez**
*Game Theory with Economic Applications*

**Blanchard**
*Macroeconomics*

**Blau/Ferber/Winkler**
*The Economics of Women, Men and Work*

**Boardman/Greenberg/Vining/Weimer**
*Cost-Benefit Analysis*

**Boyer**
*Principles of Transportation Economics*

**Branson**
*Macroeconomic Theory and Policy*

**Brock/Adams**
*The Structure of American Industry*

**Bruce**
*Public Finance and the American Economy*

**Carlton/Perloff**
*Modern Industrial Organization*

**Case/Fair/Oster**
*Principles of Economics**

**Caves/Frankel/Jones**
*World Trade and Payments: An Introduction*

**Chapman**
*Environmental Economics: Theory, Application, and Policy*

**Cooter/Ulen**
*Law & Economics*

**Downs**
*An Economic Theory of Democracy*

**Ehrenberg/Smith**
*Modern Labor Economics*

**Ekelund/Ressler/Tollison**
*Economics**

**Farnham**
*Economics for Managers*

**Folland/Goodman/Stano**
*The Economics of Health and Health Care*

**Fort**
*Sports Economics*

**Froyen**
*Macroeconomics*

**Fusfeld**
*The Age of the Economist*

**Gerber**
*International Economics*

**Gordon**
*Macroeconomics*

**Greene**
*Econometric Analysis*

**Gregory**
*Essentials of Economics*

**Gregory/Stuart**
*Russian and Soviet Economic Performance and Structure*

**Hartwick/Olewiler**
*The Economics of Natural Resource Use*

**Heilbroner/ Milberg**
*The Making of the Economic Society*

**Heyne/ Boettke / Prychitko**
*The Economic Way of Thinking*

**Hoffman/Averett**
*Women and the Economy: Family, Work, and Pay*

**Holt**
*Markets, Games and Strategic Behavior*

**Hubbard**
*Money, the Financial System, and the Economy*

**Hubbard/OBrien**
*Economics**

**Hughes/Cain**
*American Economic History*

**Husted/Melvin**
*International Economics*

**Jehle/Reny**
*Advanced Microeconomic Theory*

**Johnson-Lans**
*A Health Economics Primer*

**Keat/Young**
*Managerial Economics*

**Klein**
*Mathematical Methods for Economics*

**Krugman/Obstfeld**
*International Economics: Theory & Policy**

**Laidler**
*The Demand for Money*

*denotes  titles

Log onto www.myeconlab.com to learn more

**Leeds/von Allmen**
*The Economics of Sports*

**Leeds/von Allmen/Schiming**
*Economics**

**Lipsey/Ragan/Storer**
*Economics**

**Lynn**
*Economic Development: Theory and Practice for a Divided World*

**Melvin**
*International Money and Finance*

**Miller**
*Economics Today**

*Understanding Modern Economics*

**Miller/Benjamin**
*The Economics of Macro Issues*

**Miller/Benjamin/North**
*The Economics of Public Issues*

**Mills/Hamilton**
*Urban Economics*

**Mishkin**
*The Economics of Money, Banking, and Financial Markets**

*The Economics of Money, Banking, and Financial Markets, Business School Edition**

**Murray**
*Econometrics: A Modern Introduction*

**Nafziger**
*The Economics of Developing Countries*

**O'Sullivan/Sheffrin/Perez**
*Economics: Principles, Applications and Tools**

**Parkin**
*Economics**

**Perloff**
*Microeconomics**

*Microeconomics: Theory and Applications with Calculus*

**Perman/Common/McGilvray/Ma**
*Natural Resources and Environmental Economics*

**Phelps**
*Health Economics*

**Pindyck/Rubinfeld**
*Microeconomics**

**Riddell/Shackelford/Stamos/Schneider**
*Economics: A Tool for Critically Understanding Society*

**Ritter/Silber/Udell**
*Principles of Money, Banking & Financial Markets**

**Roberts**
*The Choice: A Fable of Free Trade and Protection*

**Rohlf**
*Introduction to Economic Reasoning*

**Ruffin/Gregory**
*Principles of Economics*

**Sargent**
*Rational Expectations and Inflation*

**Sawyer/Sprinkle**
*International Economics*

**Scherer**
*Industry Structure, Strategy, and Public Policy*

**Schiller**
*The Economics of Poverty and Discrimination*

**Sherman**
*Market Regulation*

**Silberberg**
*Principles of Microeconomics*

**Stock/Watson**
*Introduction to Econometrics*

*Introduction to Econometrics, Brief Edition*

**Studenmund**
*Using Econometrics: A Practical Guide*

**Tietenberg/Lewis**
*Environmental and Natural Resource Economics*

*Environmental Economics and Policy*

**Todaro/Smith**
*Economic Development*

**Waldman**
*Microeconomics*

**Waldman/Jensen**
*Industrial Organization: Theory and Practice*

**Weil**
*Economic Growth*

**Williamson**
*Macroeconomics*

# Macroeconomic Data

These macroeconomic data series show some of the trends in GDP and its components, the price level, and other variables that provide information about changes in the standard of living and the cost of living—the central questions of macroeconomics. You will find these data in a spreadsheet that you can download from your MyEconLab Web site.

| | NATIONAL INCOME AND PRODUCT ACCOUNTS | 1963 | 1964 | 1965 | 1966 | 1967 | 1968 | 1969 | 1970 | 1971 | 1972 |
|---|---|---|---|---|---|---|---|---|---|---|---|
| | **EXPENDITURES APPROACH** | | | | | | | | | | |
| the sum of | 1 Personal consumption expenditures | 383 | 412 | 444 | 481 | 508 | 558 | 605 | 648 | 702 | 770 |
| | 2 Gross private domestic investment | 94 | 102 | 118 | 131 | 129 | 141 | 156 | 152 | 178 | 208 |
| | 3 Government expenditures | 136 | 143 | 151 | 172 | 193 | 209 | 221 | 234 | 246 | 263 |
| | 4 Exports | 31 | 35 | 37 | 41 | 44 | 48 | 52 | 60 | 63 | 71 |
| less | 5 Imports | 26 | 28 | 32 | 37 | 40 | 47 | 51 | 56 | 62 | 74 |
| equals | 6 Gross domestic product | 618 | 664 | 719 | 788 | 832 | 910 | 984 | 1,038 | 1,127 | 1,238 |
| | **INCOMES APPROACH** | | | | | | | | | | |
| | 7 Compensation of employees | 345 | 371 | 400 | 443 | 475 | 524 | 578 | 617 | 659 | 725 |
| plus | 8 Net operating surplus | 159 | 171 | 190 | 203 | 206 | 219 | 226 | 219 | 243 | 275 |
| equals | 9 Net domestic product at factor cost | 504 | 542 | 589 | 646 | 681 | 743 | 803 | 837 | 902 | 1,001 |
| plus | 10 Indirect taxes less subsidies | 51 | 55 | 58 | 59 | 64 | 72 | 79 | 87 | 96 | 101 |
| | 11 Depreciation (capital consumption) | 63 | 66 | 71 | 77 | 83 | 90 | 99 | 108 | 118 | 127 |
| | 12 GDP (income approach) | 619 | 663 | 718 | 782 | 828 | 906 | 982 | 1,031 | 1,116 | 1,229 |
| | 13 Statistical discrepancy | –1 | 1 | 2 | 6 | 5 | 4 | 3 | 7 | 11 | 9 |
| equals | 14 GDP (expenditure approach) | 618 | 664 | 719 | 788 | 832 | 910 | 985 | 1,038 | 1,127 | 1,238 |
| | 15 Real GDP (billions of 2005 dollars) | 3,207 | 3,392 | 3,610 | 3,845 | 3,943 | 4,133 | 4,262 | 4,270 | 4,413 | 4,648 |
| | 16 Real GDP growth rate (percent per year) | 4.4 | 5.8 | 6.4 | 6.5 | 2.5 | 4.8 | 3.1 | 0.2 | 3.4 | 5.3 |
| | **OTHER DATA** | | | | | | | | | | |
| | 17 Population (millions) | 189.3 | 191.9 | 194.3 | 196.6 | 198.8 | 200.7 | 202.7 | 205.1 | 207.7 | 209.9 |
| | 18 Labor force (millions) | 71.8 | 73.1 | 74.5 | 75.8 | 77.3 | 78.7 | 80.7 | 82.8 | 84.4 | 87.0 |
| | 19 Employment (millions) | 67.8 | 69.3 | 71.1 | 72.9 | 74.4 | 75.9 | 77.9 | 78.7 | 79.4 | 82.2 |
| | 20 Unemployment (millions) | 4.1 | 3.8 | 3.4 | 2.9 | 3.0 | 2.8 | 2.8 | 4.1 | 5.0 | 4.9 |
| | 21 Labor force participation rate (percent of working-age population) | 58.7 | 58.7 | 58.9 | 59.2 | 59.6 | 59.6 | 60.1 | 60.4 | 60.2 | 60.4 |
| | 22 Unemployment rate (percent of labor force) | 5.7 | 5.2 | 4.5 | 3.8 | 3.8 | 3.6 | 3.5 | 4.9 | 5.9 | 5.6 |
| | 23 Real GDP per person (2005 dollars per year) | 16,940 | 17,675 | 18,576 | 19,559 | 19,836 | 20,590 | 21,021 | 20,820 | 21,249 | 22,140 |
| | 24 Growth rate of real GDP per person (percent per year) | 2.9 | 4.3 | 5.1 | 5.3 | 1.4 | 3.8 | 2.1 | –1.0 | 2.1 | 4.2 |
| | 25 Quantity of money (M2, billions of dollars) | 393.2 | 424.7 | 459.2 | 480.2 | 524.8 | 566.8 | 587.9 | 626.5 | 710.3 | 802.3 |
| | 26 GDP deflator (2005 = 100) | 19.3 | 19.6 | 19.9 | 20.5 | 21.1 | 22.0 | 23.1 | 24.3 | 25.5 | 26.6 |
| | 27 GDP deflator inflation rate (percent per year) | 1.1 | 1.5 | 1.8 | 2.8 | 3.1 | 4.3 | 5.0 | 5.3 | 5.0 | 4.3 |
| | 28 Consumer price index (1982–1984 = 100) | 30.6 | 31.0 | 31.5 | 32.4 | 33.4 | 34.8 | 36.7 | 38.8 | 40.5 | 41.8 |
| | 29 CPI inflation rate (percent per year) | 1.3 | 1.3 | 1.6 | 2.9 | 3.1 | 4.2 | 5.5 | 5.7 | 4.4 | 3.2 |
| | 30 Current account balance (billions of dollars) | 4.4 | 6.8 | 5.4 | 3.0 | 2.6 | 0.6 | 0.4 | 2.3 | –1.4 | –5.8 |

| 1973 | 1974 | 1975 | 1976 | 1977 | 1978 | 1979 | 1980 | 1981 | 1982 | 1983 | 1984 | 1985 |
|---|---|---|---|---|---|---|---|---|---|---|---|---|
| 852 | 933 | 1,034 | 1,151 | 1,278 | 1,428 | 1,591 | 1,756 | 1,940 | 2,076 | 2,289 | 2,501 | 2,718 |
| 245 | 249 | 230 | 292 | 361 | 438 | 493 | 479 | 572 | 517 | 564 | 736 | 736 |
| 282 | 318 | 358 | 383 | 414 | 454 | 501 | 566 | 628 | 680 | 733 | 797 | 879 |
| 95 | 127 | 139 | 150 | 159 | 187 | 230 | 281 | 305 | 283 | 277 | 302 | 302 |
| 91 | 128 | 123 | 151 | 182 | 212 | 253 | 294 | 318 | 303 | 329 | 405 | 417 |
| 1,382 | 1,500 | 1,638 | 1,825 | 2,030 | 2,294 | 2,562 | 2,788 | 3,127 | 3,253 | 3,535 | 3,931 | 4,218 |
| 811 | 890 | 949 | 1,059 | 1,181 | 1,336 | 1,498 | 1,648 | 1,820 | 1,920 | 2,036 | 2,246 | 2,412 |
| 310 | 314 | 351 | 392 | 444 | 509 | 546 | 561 | 653 | 669 | 756 | 911 | 971 |
| 1,121 | 1,204 | 1,300 | 1,452 | 1,625 | 1,844 | 2,045 | 2,208 | 2,473 | 2,589 | 2,792 | 3,156 | 3,383 |
| 112 | 122 | 131 | 141 | 153 | 162 | 172 | 191 | 224 | 226 | 242 | 269 | 287 |
| 141 | 164 | 190 | 208 | 232 | 261 | 299 | 344 | 393 | 434 | 451 | 474 | 505 |
| 1,374 | 1,490 | 1,621 | 1,801 | 2,009 | 2,268 | 2,515 | 2,743 | 3,090 | 3,248 | 3,485 | 3,899 | 4,175 |
| 8 | 10 | 16 | 24 | 21 | 26 | 47 | 45 | 37 | 5 | 50 | 32 | 42 |
| 1,382 | 1,500 | 1,638 | 1,825 | 2,030 | 2,294 | 2,562 | 2,788 | 3,127 | 3,253 | 3,535 | 3,931 | 4,217 |
| 4,917 | 4,890 | 4,880 | 5,141 | 5,378 | 5,678 | 5,855 | 5,839 | 5,987 | 5,871 | 6,136 | 6,577 | 6,849 |
| 5.8 | −0.6 | −0.2 | 5.4 | 4.6 | 5.6 | 3.1 | −0.3 | 2.5 | −1.9 | 4.5 | 7.2 | 4.1 |
| 211.9 | 213.9 | 216.0 | 218.1 | 220.3 | 222.6 | 225.1 | 227.7 | 230.0 | 232.2 | 234.3 | 236.4 | 238.5 |
| 89.4 | 91.9 | 93.8 | 96.2 | 99.0 | 102.3 | 105.0 | 106.9 | 108.7 | 110.2 | 111.6 | 113.5 | 115.5 |
| 85.1 | 86.8 | 85.8 | 88.8 | 92.0 | 96.0 | 98.8 | 99.3 | 100.4 | 99.5 | 100.8 | 105.0 | 107.2 |
| 4.4 | 5.2 | 7.9 | 7.4 | 7.0 | 6.2 | 6.1 | 7.6 | 8.3 | 10.7 | 10.7 | 8.5 | 8.3 |
| 60.8 | 61.3 | 61.2 | 61.6 | 62.3 | 63.2 | 63.7 | 63.8 | 63.9 | 64.0 | 64.0 | 64.4 | 64.8 |
| 4.9 | 5.6 | 8.5 | 7.7 | 7.1 | 6.1 | 5.8 | 7.1 | 7.6 | 9.7 | 9.6 | 7.5 | 7.2 |
| 23,200 | 22,861 | 22,592 | 23,575 | 24,412 | 25,503 | 26,010 | 25,640 | 26,030 | 25,282 | 26,186 | 27,823 | 28,718 |
| 4.8 | −1.5 | −1.2 | 4.3 | 3.6 | 4.5 | 2.0 | −1.4 | 1.5 | −2.9 | 3.6 | 6.3 | 3.2 |
| 855.5 | 902.1 | 1,016.2 | 1,152.0 | 1,270.3 | 1,366.0 | 1,473.7 | 1,599.8 | 1,755.4 | 1,910.3 | 2126.5 | 2309.9 | 2,495.7 |
| 28.1 | 30.7 | 33.6 | 35.5 | 37.8 | 40.4 | 43.8 | 47.8 | 52.2 | 55.4 | 57.6 | 59.8 | 61.6 |
| 5.6 | 9.0 | 9.4 | 5.8 | 6.4 | 7.0 | 8.3 | 9.1 | 9.4 | 6.1 | 4.0 | 3.8 | 3.0 |
| 44.4 | 49.3 | 53.8 | 56.9 | 60.6 | 65.2 | 72.6 | 82.4 | 90.9 | 96.5 | 99.6 | 103.9 | 107.6 |
| 6.2 | 11.0 | 9.1 | 5.8 | 6.5 | 7.6 | 11.3 | 13.5 | 10.3 | 6.2 | 3.2 | 4.3 | 3.6 |
| 7.1 | 2.0 | 18.1 | 4.3 | −14.3 | −15.1 | −0.3 | 2.3 | 5.0 | −5.5 | −38.7 | −94.3 | −118.2 |